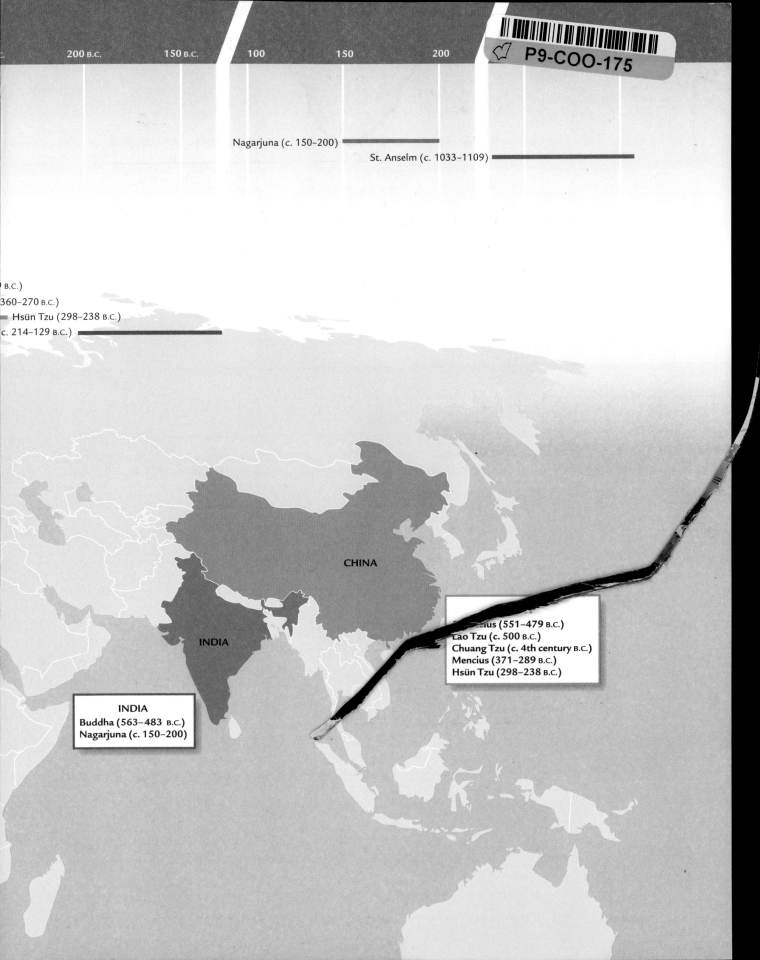

200 B.C.   150 B.C.   100   150   200   P9-COO-175

Nagarjuna (c. 150–200)

St. Anselm (c. 1033–1109)

B.C.)
360–270 B.C.)
Hsün Tzu (298–238 B.C.)
c. 214–129 B.C.)

CHINA

INDIA

Confucius (551–479 B.C.)
Lao Tzu (c. 500 B.C.)
Chuang Tzu (c. 4th century B.C.)
Mencius (371–289 B.C.)
Hsün Tzu (298–238 B.C.)

INDIA
Buddha (563–483 B.C.)
Nagarjuna (c. 150–200)

THE PHILOSOPHICAL JOURNEY

An Interactive Approach

Fifth Edition

William F. Lawhead
University of Mississippi

The McGraw·Hill Companies

Connect
Learn
Succeed™

THE PHILOSOPHICAL JOURNEY, AN INTERACTIVE APPROACH, FIFTH EDITION

Published by McGraw-Hill, a business unit of The McGraw-Hill Companies, Inc., 1221 Avenue of the Americas, New York, NY 10020. Copyright © 2011 by The McGraw-Hill Companies, Inc. All rights reserved. Previous editions © 2009, 2006, 2003, and 2000. No part of this publication may be reproduced or distributed in any form or by any means, or stored in a database or retrieval system, without the prior written consent of The McGraw-Hill Companies, Inc., including, but not limited to, in any network or other electronic storage or transmission, or broadcast for distance learning.

Some ancillaries, including electronic and print components, may not be available to customers outside the United States.

This book is printed on acid-free paper.

1 2 3 4 5 6 7 8 9 0 DOW/DOW 1 0 9 8 7 6 5 4 3 2 1 0

ISBN 978-0-07-353587-6
MHID 0-07-353587-7

Vice President & Editor-in-Chief: Michael Ryan
Vice President EDP/Central Publishing Services: Kimberly Meriwether David
Publisher: Beth Mejia
Sponsoring Editor: Mark Georgiev
Executive Marketing Manager: Pamela S. Cooper
Developmental Editor: Meghan Campbell
Project Manager: Melissa M. Leick
Design Coordinator: Margarite Reynolds
Cover Designer: Carole Lawson
Photo Research Coordinator: Sonia Brown
Cover Credit: Jack Hollingsworth/Getty Images
Buyer: Nicole Baumgartner
Media Project Manager: Sridevi Palani
Compositor: Lachina Publishing Services
Typeface: 10/12 Adobe Garamond
Printer: R. R. Donnelley

All credits appearing on page or at the end of the book are considered to be an extension of the copyright page.

Library of Congress Cataloging-in-Publication Data

Lawhead, William F.
    The philosophical journey : an interactive approach / William F. Lawhead.
    — 5th ed.
        p. cm.
    Includes index.
    ISBN-13: 978-0-07-353587-6
    ISBN-10: 0-07-353587-7
    1. Philosophy—Introductions. I. Title.
BD21.L36 2010
    100—dc22

                                                                    2010043103

www.mhhe.com

Preface

Socrates once complained in the *Protagoras* that eloquent orators and books are alike in that they provide massive amounts of information, "but if one asks any of them an additional question . . . they cannot either answer or ask a question on their own account." As I wrote this book, my challenge was to see to what degree I could provide a counterexample to Socrates' claim. Of course, Socrates is correct: There is no substitute for live philosophical conversations and debates. However, as you get acquainted with this book, you will find that it does ask you questions and provokes you to ask questions in turn. Instead of simply presenting information for you to passively absorb, its many exercises require your active involvement, and some will even provide the opportunity for you to dialogue with your friends about the philosophical issues discussed. For this reason, I chose the title *The Philosophical Journey: An Interactive Approach.*

Rather than being like a slide show of landscapes you have never visited, this book is a guided, exploratory journey in which you will have to scout the terrain yourself. I hope that the journey will be fun, but there is also much to be done en route. This philosophy text is as interactive as is possible within the medium of paper and ink. Students taking courses in philosophy are often asked, "What can you do with philosophy?" After taking this philosophical journey I have planned for you, I hope that you will realize that the really important question is, "What can philosophy do with you?" You will certainly not agree with everything you will read in these pages, but do anticipate the fact that engaging with these ideas will not leave you unchanged.

ORGANIZATION

This book presents philosophy by introducing the major philosophical topics, questions, positions, and philosophers. The different chapters are independent enough that they could be read in a different order if one so desired. However, you should start with the overview (section 1.0) in chapter 1, which will prepare you for the journey. The remaining five chapters then lead into each of the major areas of philosophy. The first section of each chapter, as well as each subtopic, has the following features:

- *Scouting the Territory*—a scenario that raises engaging, philosophical questions.
- *Charting the Terrain*—a more precise presentation of the topic and its significance.
- *Choosing a Path*—a presentation of the opposing alternatives to help you clarify your own thinking on the issue.
- *Conceptual Tools*—an occasional feature that introduces important distinctions, definitions, or terminology as helpful tools for understanding the topic.
- *What Do I Think?*—a questionnaire that will help you identify your current stand on the issue. An answer key will show you how philosophers label your own position and which answers are incompatible.

The opening section of each topic will be followed by sections that present and analyze the different alternatives that can be taken on the issue. Each of these sections has the following format:

- *Leading Questions*—a series of questions asked from the standpoint of the position in question that will get you thinking about the philosophy and its merits.
- *Surveying the Case for . . .* —a presentation of the position under consideration and the arguments supporting it.
- *A Reading from . . .* —several brief readings that will provide you with practice in analyzing philosophical passages and arguments. As always, you will be provided with guidelines for getting the most out of the passage.
- *Looking through X's Lens*—an exercise in which you will be asked to draw out the implications of the philosopher's position and apply the theory to novel situations.
- *Examining the Strengths and Weaknesses of X*—a series of considerations and questions that will guide you in forming your own response to the position.

Throughout the book will be a number of exercises that require you to interact philosophically with the issues. These include:

- *Philosophy in the Marketplace*—a question, survey, or scenario that will allow you to apply the Socratic method of doing philosophy through structured conversations with friends outside of class.
- *Thought Experiments*—exercises that will give you the opportunity to make your own philosophical discoveries and to compare your conclusions with those of the great philosophers as well as those of your classmates.
- *Stop and Think boxes*—a brief pause in your reading to form some tentative conclusions about an issue.
- *Spotlight on . . .* —additional information that helps illuminate the topic.

(For a more detailed explanation of these unique features of *The Philosophical Journey*, turn to pages 11–15.)

Both students and teachers will find that these features provide a great deal to think about and talk about. In my attempts to make philosophy an activity and not just a course, I began developing this approach to introducing philosophy more than 15 years ago. The activities I have experimented with that have made it into the book have been the ones that my students most enjoyed and that have made my task as a teacher easier. I hope that both the students and teachers using this book will find this to be true for them as well.

TEACHING AND LEARNING PACKAGE

Instructor's Manual

Written by myself, this manual begins with an overall introduction to *The Philosophical Journey* and a general discussion of how to use the sundry pedagogical features to advantage in the classroom. This discussion is followed by a chapter-by-chapter, section-by-section series of lecture and discussion tips, including how to use some of the specific "Thought Experiments" and other interactive activities in the text. Finally, the manual contains a series of objective and essay test questions tailored to each chapter and section. Carefully crafted as a true teaching tool, the various elements of this instructor's manual provide an excellent resource for both first-time and experienced philosophy teachers.

The Philosophical Journey Online Learning Center

Your students can continue their journey into philosophy online at *www.mhhe.com/lawhead5e*. This Online Learning Center has the following features:

- *Chapter Overviews.*
- *Topic Links* help students research philosophers and concepts from each chapter.
- A *Contemporary Connections* section attempts to relate philosophical concepts from each chapter to modern dilemmas and current events.
- An *Explorations* section invites students to investigate philosophical questions on their own on the Web.
- *Multiple Choice, True/False,* and *Fill-in-the-Blank Questions* help students assess their comprehension of chapter material.

ABOUT THE FIFTH EDITION

I am gratified by the responses to the first four editions of *The Philosophical Journey* that I have received from professors using the book, from students who have been introduced to philosophy through it, and from interested readers who read it for personal enrichment. This fifth edition continues to have the distinctive, interactive features that so many have enjoyed in the first four editions and that have been highlighted in the previous sections of this preface.

I am happy to say that section 4.6 on Asian religions has been added back to the book by popular request. It provides an opportunity to contrast and compare Western perspectives with some of their leading Asian counterparts. In section 2.3 empiricism is introduced with a new discussion of "Empiricism in the Ancient World," featuring Aristotle. Hence, Aristotle now is spotlighted in epistemology along with his coverage in ethics, political philosophy, and in a number of other passages. To accomodate the new material, the contemporary applications material has been trimmed out of chapters 3, 5, and 6 in an effort to keep the book manageable. However, the two most popular of the contemporary issues discussions, section 2.8 on scientific knowledge and section 4.7 on the relation between religion and science, have been retained. Throughout the book several of the readings have been trimmed and passages have been rewritten for the sake of greater clarity.

ACKNOWLEDGMENTS

From the first rough outline to the final chapter revisions I have had the help of numerous reviewers who read this text with an eye to its suitability for the classroom as well as its philosophical clarity and accuracy. I appreciate the comments of the following reviewers on the first three editions: Judy Barad, Indiana State University; Chris Blakey, College of the Canyons; David Carlson, Madison Area Technical College; Anne DeWindt, Wayne County Community College; Reinaldo Elugardo, University of Oklahoma; Louise Excell, Dixie State College; Kevin Galvin, East Los Angeles College; Eric Gampel, California State University at Chico; Garth Gillan, Southern Illinois University; Robert A. Hill, Pikes Peak Community College; Achim Kodderman, State University of New York College; Pat Matthews, Florida State University; Brian L. Merrill, Brigham Young University–Idaho; Mark A. Michael, Austin Peay State University; Benjamin A. Petty, Southern Methodist University; Michael Punches, Oklahoma City Community College; John F. Sallstrem, Georgia

College; Nancy Shaffer, University of Nebraska–Omaha; Kathleen Wider, University of Michigan, Dearborn; Gene Witmer, University of Florida; Jay Wood, Wheaton College.

The comments of the reviewers for the fifth edition helped me to make numerous improvements to the book. These reviewers are: Michael J. Booker, Jefferson College; Michael Boring, University of Colorado, Denver; Michael J. Cundall, Jr., Arkansas State University; Hye-Kyung Kim, University of Wisconsin, Green Bay; Joseph Michael Pergola, Lewis-Clark State College; Robert Reuter, Saint Joseph's College; Alan Schwerin, Monmouth University.

I am particularly grateful to both my current and former colleagues for sharing their expertise with me. Michael Lynch answered numerous questions on epistemology, Robert Westmoreland on ethics and political philosophy, and Neil Manson on contemporary design arguments. I have also had helpful conversations on philosophy of mind with Robert Barnard, on Greek philosophy with Steven Skultety, and on religion with Laurie Cozad, Willa Johnson, and Mary Thurkill. My former student, Richard Howe, suggested helpful improvements to chapter 4. My thanks to Ken Sufka for his course on brain science and many hours of stimulating conversations and debates. I am particularly grateful to my dean, Glenn Hopkins, who provided summer support for this and other projects. Finally, I want to thank all my Mississippi Governor's School students who interacted with me during the summers of 1987 to 2005 and who were the first to test out many of the exercises in this book.

I have been fortunate to work with one of the best editorial teams in the business. Ken King, my first editor, immediately grasped my vision for this book and energetically made it a reality. Jon-David Hague worked on the second and third editions, and Mark Georgiev helped me bring out both the fourth and this edition. I also appreciate the skillful work of Meghan Campbell, managing editor, and Anne Prucha, the project manager.

Whether you are a student or a teacher, I hope that you will enjoy interacting with my book as much as I enjoyed writing it. I would be glad to hear about your experiences with the book and its exercises as well as any suggestions you have for future improvements. You may write to me at Department of Philosophy and Religion, University of Mississippi, University, MS, 38677 or e-mail me at wlawhead@olemiss.edu.

William F. Lawhead

Contents

CHAPTER 3

The Search For Ultimate Reality   201

CHAPTER 4

The Search For God   319

CHAPTER 5

The Search For Ethical Values 415

To my grandchildren
Lauren, Will, Lillie, Layton, Lainie, and Bess—
May your lives be filled with the two dimensions
of philosophy: love and wisdom

Winslow Homer, *Adirondack Guide*, 1894

CHAPTER 1

INTRODUCTION TO THE PHILOSOPHICAL JOURNEY

Where Are We Going and How Will We Get There?

On completion of this chapter, you should be able to

1. Explain several approaches to what philosophy is all about.
2. Identify various areas of thought traditionally investigated by philosophers.
3. Discuss how philosophy is a journey.
4. Relate the story of Socrates' life and death.
5. Explain the Socratic method.
6. Discuss three central theses about living well held by Socrates.
7. Interpret various levels of meaning in Plato's Allegory of the Cave.
8. Apply six criteria for evaluating philosophical claims and theories.
9. Define an argument in the philosophical sense.
10. Distinguish the three kinds of arguments: deductive, inductive, inference to the best explanation.

In a 19th-century work, the Danish philosopher and literary genius Søren Kierkegaard depicted one of his fictional characters sitting in a café worrying about the fact that he has no mission or purpose in life.* He despairs over the fact that many in his age have served humanity and have achieved fame and admiration by making life easier and easier for people. He mentions the convenience and ease that have been brought by the invention of railways, buses, steamboats, the telegraph, and easily accessible encyclopedias. With a sense of failure he asks himself, "And what are you doing?" It seems clear to him that he could not compete with other people in making life easier. Searching for his mission in life, he finally comes up with this idea:

> Suddenly this thought flashed through my mind: "You must do something, but inasmuch as with your limited capacities it will be impossible to make anything easier than it has become, you must, with the same humanitarian enthusiasm as the others, undertake to make something harder." This notion pleased me immensely, and at the same time it flattered me to think that I, like the rest of them, would be loved and esteemed by the whole community. For when all combine in every way to make everything easier, there remains only one possible danger, namely, that the ease becomes so great that it becomes altogether too great; then there is only one want left, though it is not yet a felt want, when people will want difficulty. Out of love for mankind, and out of despair at my embarrassing situation, seeing that I had accomplished nothing and was unable to make anything easier than it had already been made, and moved by a genuine interest in those who make everything easy, I conceived it as my task to create difficulties everywhere.[1]

STOP AND THINK

Why would someone want to make life more difficult? In what ways could a philosopher such as Kierkegaard make life more difficult for his readers? Even more important, why would we want to read an author who took this as his mission in life?

PHILOSOPHY AND AEROBICS

You might get some perspective on the questions in the box if you notice that those things that are cheap and come easiest in life are usually those things that are worth little in the long run. A quarter will get you a gum ball from a machine. A gum ball is cheap and easy to obtain, but its only value is a few minutes of pleasure. On the other hand, the mother's labor pains bring forth new life, the musician's long hours of practice produce musical perfection, the athlete's pain and determination are rewarded with self-mastery and athletic records, and the writer's creative struggles in the face of dozens of rejection slips may produce a great novel. In each case, something of value was gained, but only as the result of great difficulty and persistent effort.

---

*Although it is not always safe to assume that the words of Kierkegaard's fictional characters reflect his own sentiments, in this case they repeat what Kierkegaard says many times over about himself.

Perhaps Kierkegaard's point is that only by facing the really difficult issues in life will we gain something that is truly valuable. His mission was to coax us, to irritate us, and to provoke us into making the effort necessary to overcome our reticence to face one of life's most difficult but rewarding tasks: honest, personal reflection. For Kierkegaard, this activity was the heart and soul of philosophy. Like many other strenuous but valuable activities, becoming a philosopher can involve intellectual labor pains, practice, determination, and creative struggling. But philosophy obviously does not produce the tangible rewards of the sort enjoyed by the mother, musician, athlete, or novelist. What, then, is the reward of doing philosophy? According to Kierkegaard, what philosophy can give us is *self-understanding*. Self-understanding involves knowing who I really am apart from the masks I present to others, the social roles I fulfill, or the labels and descriptions imposed on me by my society and my peers. It also involves understanding my beliefs and values and being aware of why I act the way I do, including knowing whether my actions result from my own authentic choices or from taken-for-granted, unexamined assumptions or the influences of my culture.

At first glance, it would seem that self-understanding is something that everyone would desire. But Kierkegaard thought that it was not only the most important goal in life, but the most difficult one. Furthermore, he claimed that it is something that we are often tempted to avoid. It is much easier to be complacent, to be self-satisfied, and to stick with beliefs that are comfortable and familiar than to be painfully and fully honest with ourselves and to subject our deepest convictions to examination. Fitness centers promote the saying, "No pain, no gain." The same is true with our struggles to become fully realized and actualized persons. In fact, philosophy could be viewed as "aerobics for the human mind." In Kierkegaard's day, everyone was claiming to provide the answers to everyone else's problems. Kierkegaard, however, thought that his greatest contribution to society would be to provide the problems to everyone's answers. Only in this way, he thought, would we be goaded into searching for those answers that are worthy of our belief. Kierkegaard has provided us with our first definition of philosophy: *Philosophy is the search for self-understanding.*

PHILOSOPHY AND LOVE

The term *philosophy* literally means "the love of wisdom." It is said that the first one to call himself a philosopher was Pythagoras, a Greek who lived somewhere between 570 and 495 B.C. and spent most of his life in southern Italy. He is, of course, best known for his famous mathematical theorem. When once asked if he was wise, he replied that no one could be wise but a god, but that he was a lover of wisdom. To love something does not mean to possess it but to focus our life on it. Whereas Pythagoras introduced the term *philosopher,* it was Socrates who made it famous. He said that the philosopher was one who had a passion for wisdom and who was intoxicated by this love. This description makes quite a contrast with the image of the philosopher as being cold and analytical—sort of a walking and talking computer. On the contrary, the cognitive and the emotional are combined in philosophy, for we do not rationally deliberate about those issues in life that are deeply trivial. When I pick up my copy of the daily campus newspaper, for example, I don't stand there and reason about which copy to grab. On the other hand, those issues that are most important to us are such things as our religious commitments (or lack of them), our moral values, our political commitments, our career, or (perhaps) who we will share our lives with. Unlike the trivial task of choosing a newspaper, such issues as our deepest loves, convictions, and commitments demand our deepest thought and most thorough rational reflection. Philosophy, in part, is the search for that kind of wisdom that will inform the beliefs and values that enter into these crucial decisions. Thanks to Pythagoras and Socrates, we now have a second definition: *Philosophy is the love and pursuit of wisdom.*

PHILOSOPHY AND PEANUT BUTTER

Everyone knows that philosophy deals with questions, with very basic questions such as, "Is there a God?" "Does life have meaning?" "Do I have freedom or am I determined by forces beyond my control?" "How do I decide what is morally right?" What makes these questions *philosophical* questions? One answer is that philosophical questions deal with our most basic concepts such as God, meaning, freedom, moral rightness. To get a better grasp on the nature of philosophical questions, try the following thought experiment.[2]

THOUGHT EXPERIMENT

1. Consider the following two questions.
   Where can I find the peanut butter?
   Where can I find happiness?

In what ways are these two questions similar? In what ways are they different? Which question is the easiest to answer? Which question is the most important one?

2. Look at what is represented on the cover of this book and answer this question: Is this a flimdoggal?

Are you having difficulty answering the question? Why?

3. Suppose that someone slipped you a drug that made it impossible for you to answer the following questions: Is this a hat or an ice cream sundae? Is this belief true or false? Is this real or an illusion? Is this action morally good or evil? Now ask yourself: What would be some practical problems created by these confusions?

The questions about where to find the peanut butter or happiness seem very similar, yet there is a world of difference between them. We have a tendency to suppose that the "real" issues are ones that are concrete and have verifiable and certain answers. If we believe that tendency, then we never ask any questions more profound than, "Where is the peanut butter?" The answer is concrete ("On the top shelf behind the mustard"), and we can be sure when we have found the answer ("Yep, this tastes like peanut butter"). On the other hand, we have many conflicting opinions about where to find happiness (religion, sensual pleasure, wealth, fame, a meaningful career, service to others, and on and on). We may think we have found happiness, but we can spend the rest of our lives trying to make sure that what we found is really it. Clearly, happiness is much more abstract and elusive than peanut butter. But maybe the goals in life that are the most abstract and elusive are the ones that are the most important to pursue.

Obviously, you could not decide if the cover of this book represented a flimdoggal because you did not know what such a thing is. What you would need in order to answer the question are the criteria for determining whether something is a flimdoggal, or a precise definition of the word *flimdoggal*. We have the same problem with words such as *God, meaning, freedom,* or *moral goodness.* However, because these words are so familiar (unlike *flimdoggal*), we often assume that we understand the corresponding concepts. Yet the concepts that philosophy analyzes are those that we dare not leave unclarified. If you could not distinguish a hat from an ice cream sundae, it could lead to some embarrassing moments as you tried to put a sundae on your head. But most of your life would be unaffected. On the other hand, if you were confused about the concepts of "true," "false," "real," "illusion," "good," or "evil," your life would be deeply impaired.

George Orwell, in his novel *1984,* depicts a totalitarian society that controls its citizens' minds by controlling their language. The society's official language of "Newspeak" does not have a word for freedom. Without the word *freedom,* people do not have the concept of freedom; without the concept they cannot think about freedom; and if they cannot think about freedom they cannot aspire toward it. The citizens feel a vague sense of discomfort with their society, but the government has robbed them of the ability to speak and think about the causes of this dissatisfaction. This novel illustrates why the meanings of words are so very important to philosophy. Sometimes philosophy is accused of simply being "arguments about words." It is true that some verbal disputes are fruitless, but not all. Words give us a grasp of our fundamental concepts, which govern our thinking, and our thinking in turn guides the way we deal with reality, the actions we perform, and the decisions we make. This discussion gives us our third definition of philosophy: *Philosophy is the asking of questions about the meaning of our most basic concepts.*

PHILOSOPHY AND COLDS

The topic of examining our lives and examining our beliefs introduces an important point about philosophy. In one sense, everyone is a philosopher. Everyone has some beliefs (no matter how tentative) about the existence of God, about how to determine if a statement is true or false, and about what is morally right and wrong (among other things). Whether you realize it or not, philosophical conclusions are woven into the conduct of your daily life. As you go through this book, you will find that many of your beliefs have been shared by some of the great philosophers in history. You will also find philosophical labels for many of your beliefs as well as arguments supporting them or arguments opposing them. With respect to philosophy, you are not like a spectator sitting in the stands, watching the professionals engage in a game of tennis. Instead, you are down on the court, already a participant in the activity of philosophy.

Whereas in a certain sense everyone is a philosopher, in another sense philosophy as a way of looking at things has to be learned and practiced. The problem is that too often we acquire our ideas, beliefs, and values the way we catch a cold. Like the cold virus, these ideas, beliefs, and values are floating around in our environment and we breathe them in without realizing it. The cold belonged to someone else, and now it is our cold. The beliefs and values were those of our culture, but now they are our own. It could be that they are true beliefs and excellent values, but how are we to know if we have internalized them unthinkingly? In examining our own and other people's fundamental beliefs, we must ask: Are these beliefs justified? What reasons do we have to suppose that they are true? What evidence counts against them? Thus, while everyone has philosophical beliefs, the philosophical journey takes us one step further. This acknowledgment gives us the fourth aspect of philosophy: *Philosophy is the search for fundamental beliefs that are rationally justified.*

If we summarize the discussion thus far, we have a multidimensional, working definition of philosophy. As you read through this book, note how each philosopher or philosophy addresses these four points. Philosophy is the

1. Search for self-understanding.
2. Love and pursuit of wisdom.
3. Asking of questions about the meaning of our basic concepts.
4. Search for fundamental beliefs that are rationally justified.

WHAT DO PHILOSOPHERS STUDY?

Many people have no idea what philosophy is all about. The term *philosophy* often conjures up the image of a vague, fuzzy realm of irreducibly subjective opinions. A common question is, "What do philosophers study?" No one seems to have this problem with other disciplines. For example (to put it glibly), biologists study frogs, geologists study rocks, historians study wars, and astronomers study stars. But what part of the universe or human experience do philosophers examine? The short answer, as one philosopher put it, is that "philosophy's center is everywhere and its circumference nowhere."³ But someone could raise the objection that this definition makes it seem as though philosophy covers the same territory that the other disciplines do. The answer to this objection is that philosophy is unique in comparison to other areas of study *not* because it thinks about different things, but because it thinks about things differently. This feature of philosophy can be made clear by comparing the sorts of questions asked by different disciplines with the sorts of questions asked by the philosopher in six different areas: logic, epistemology, metaphysics, philosophy of religion, ethics, and political philosophy.

Logic

The psychologist studies *how* people think and the *causes* of people's beliefs, whether their thinking is rational or irrational. But the philosopher studies how we *ought* to think if we are to be rational and seeks to clarify the good *reasons* for holding a belief. The study of the principles for distinguishing correct from incorrect reasoning is the area of philosophy known as logic, which is discussed at the end of this chapter under the heading "1.3: Argument and Evidence: How Do I Decide What to Believe?"

Epistemology

The historian seeks to increase our knowledge of the Civil War by gathering facts and determining which accounts of the events are the most true. The philosopher asks, What is knowledge? What is a fact? What is truth? How could we know that something is true or not? Is there objective truth, or are all opinions relative? Fundamental questions about the nature and source of knowledge, the concept of truth, and the objectivity or relativity of our beliefs are the concern of the theory of knowledge, or epistemology, which you encounter in chapter 2, "The Search for Knowledge."

Metaphysics

The physicist studies the ultimate constituents of physical reality such as atoms, quarks, or neutrinos. On the other hand, the philosopher asks, Is physical reality all that there is? The neurobiologist studies the activity of the brain, but the philosopher asks, Are all mental events really brain events, or is the mind something separate from the brain? The psychologist attempts to find causal correlations between criminal behavior and the individual's genetic inheritance or social influences. The philosopher, on the other hand, asks, Is all behavior (good or bad) causally determined, or do we have some degree of genuine freedom that cannot be scientifically explained? Is there necessarily a conflict between the scientific attempt to explain and predict behavior and our belief in human freedom? Metaphysics is the area of philosophy concerned with fundamental questions about the nature of reality. In chapter 3, "The Search for Ultimate Reality," you encounter different models of what reality is like as well as questions concerning *human* reality such as, What is the relationship between the mind and the body? and, Are we free or are our lives predetermined?

Philosophy of Religion

The astronomer studies the laws that govern the heavenly bodies such as the stars. However, the philosopher asks these questions: Is the existence and nature of the universe self-explanatory, or does it need an explanation or a divine creator that lies outside it? How do we account for the order in the world that makes science possible? Is the evidence of design sufficient to prove a designer?

The meteorologist asks, What causes hurricanes? and the medical researcher asks, What causes childhood leukemia? On the other hand, the philosopher asks, Is there any rational way to believe in a good, all-powerful God who permits the undeserved destruction by hurricanes or the suffering of innocent children? Or is the evidence of undeserved suffering an argument against such a God?

The sociologist studies the religious beliefs of various groups and the social needs that these beliefs fulfill without making any judgments about the truth or rationality of these beliefs. However, the philosopher asks, Is faith opposed to reason, compatible with reason, or supported by reason, or is faith something that necessarily goes beyond reason? These sorts of questions about the existence of God, the problem of evil, and the relationship of faith and reason constitute the area of philosophy known as philosophy of religion and it is discussed in chapter 4, "The Search for God."

Ethics

The anthropologist studies the moral codes of various societies and describes both their similarities and differences, but does not decide which ones are best. On the other hand, the philosopher asks, Are there any objectively correct ethical values, or are they all relative? Which ethical principles (if any) are the correct ones? How do we decide what is right or wrong? These questions are the concern of ethics, which is the topic of chapter 5, "The Search for Ethical Values."

Political Philosophy

The political scientist studies various forms of government, but the philosopher asks, What makes a government legitimate? What is justice? What is the proper extent of individual freedom? What are the limits of governmental authority? Is disobeying the law ever morally justified? These questions fall under the heading of political philosophy and are discussed in chapter 6, "The Search for the Just Society."

The Philosophical Foundations of Other Disciplines

In addition to these six topics that will be covered in this book, other areas in philosophy raise philosophical questions about specific disciplines. These additional areas of philosophy include philosophy of art (aesthetics), philosophy of education, philosophy of history, philosophy of language, philosophy of law, philosophy of mathematics, philosophy of psychology, philosophy of science, and so on.

WHAT IS THE PRACTICAL VALUE OF PHILOSOPHY?

Philosophers (and philosophy students) are frequently asked the question, What is the practical value of philosophy? This question seems to be easier to answer with respect to other disciplines. The study of computer science certainly leads to endless practical applications, not to mention career possibilities. Biological research can produce new cures for the diseases that plague us. Engineers learn how to build better bridges and produce marvelous inventions. Psychologists help us deal with test anxiety and other maladies. But what does philosophy do? A contemporary of Socrates, the satirical playwright Aristophanes, wrote a play titled *The Clouds* in which the actor representing Socrates delivered his speeches while suspended from the clouds in a basket. For many people, this image typifies the philosopher—someone who does not have his or her feet on the ground. Philosophy is often thought to be an optional enterprise, a detached, erudite hobby for the intellectually elite or the socially disabled. Someone once defined the philosopher as "a person who describes the impossible and proves the obvious."

In order to answer the question, What is the practical value of philosophy? we need to first clarify the concepts and question the assumptions contained in the question. What does it mean for something to be "practical"? A good answer might be that something is practical if it is an efficient and effective means for achieving a goal. If your goal is to learn your French vocabulary words for a test, a practical (efficient and effective) way to do this is to write the words on note cards that you can review throughout the day. But when we ask, "Is philosophy practical?" what goal do we have in mind? To answer this question we need to know what goals, ends, or values are really important in life in order to measure whether philosophy is or is not a practical means for achieving them. By now you may realize that to think about these issues is to think philosophically. Ironically, to ask whether philosophy is a useful activity you must have made some previous philosophical assumptions about what is important in life. In other words, unlike any other discipline, a person cannot criticize philosophy without having first engaged in philosophy!

More concrete points can be made about the value of studying philosophy. The American Philosophical Association has identified four important skills that we acquire in studying philosophy: (1) general problem solving, (2) communication skills, (3) persuasive powers, and (4) writing skills. Obviously, these skills are important in any discipline as well as any high-level career. In fact, studies have repeatedly shown that philosophy majors tend to do better than average on admissions tests for law school, medical school, and graduate programs in business administration, to name a few examples. Furthermore, in an economy that is based on the communication and analysis of information, the skills of analytical reasoning, critical reading, effective writing, and conceptual analysis are essential. Consequently, *The New York Times Career Planner* reports: "Philosophy is one fundamental area of study that has found a new role in the high-tech world."[4]

Although the analytical and logical side of philosophy is important, philosophy should not be thought of as a dull, impersonal, logic-chopping enterprise. The history of philosophy is the story of men and women with soaring imaginations who were able to think creatively and free our minds from the well-worn ruts left by our mundane, taken-for-granted assumptions. Philosophers have given us new conceptual lenses for looking at the world, asked questions that no one else thought to ask, discovered creative answers to age-old questions, and woven new patterns out of the threads of human experience. Philosophy can give you practical skills that can be applied to a wide range of tasks in school and in

Survey 10 friends who have not taken a philosophy class and ask them, What is philosophy? After you have collected all the responses, evaluate them on your own by considering the following questions:

• Are there any common themes throughout the 10 answers?
• How do the answers compare to the description of philosophy in this chapter?
• Are any features about philosophy missing in the responses?
• Which answers do you think are best? Why?
• Which answers do you think are least satisfactory? Why?

PHILOSOPHY
in the
MARKETPLACE

your career, but the most important benefit in studying philosophy is the changes it can make in your growth as a person. Hence, the question about the practical value of philosophy should not be framed as, "What can I do with philosophy?"—the question should be, "What can philosophy do with me?"

PHILOSOPHY AS A JOURNEY

Just so you will be forewarned, what you are holding in your hands is not merely a book *about* philosophy but a guidebook to a philosophical journey in which you will be *participating*. In each chapter you will have not only things to read but also things to do. I have chosen this approach because philosophy is not just a set of ideas; it is an activity. For this reason, the title of the book is *The Philosophical Journey*. I hope that you will find the philosophical journey to be fun, but it will also be a working expedition with many tasks to be accomplished. This book is for explorers who will be actively involved in making discoveries, not just passive viewers of a travelogue. Hence, each chapter provides sections that will engage you in intellectual versions of scouting the territory, charting terrain, choosing paths, surveying arguments, viewing perspectives, and critically examining what you have found. But you will not have to make these explorations unassisted, for this book is a field manual. It will point out significant landmarks, provide maps to the territory, caution you about crucial crossroads and pitfalls, and introduce you to some experienced trailblazers: the philosophers who have preceded you on this journey.

When I set out on my first canoe trip, I was not very good at it. Initially, my paddle thrashed around in the water and my efforts were rewarded more by sore muscles than by progress down the river. But in a short time I got the hang of canoeing and my paddle strokes became more productive. Soon my boat was gliding smoothly through the water, and I learned to anticipate obstacles or difficult stretches of water and to maneuver successfully around them. Learning to read, write, and think about philosophy is no different than learning any other skill. By the time you reach the end of this book, you should be better at it than when you began. However, the "philosophy as a journey" metaphor does have one limitation. Usually we take a journey to get to a specific destination (the campsite downriver, Grandma's house, back to school). The philosophical journey is different because it is never finished. There are always new ideas to explore, new problems to solve, and old territory to explore in fresh ways. In this way philosophy is more like the journey we take in a lifelong friendship than a short canoe trip.

GUIDEPOSTS FOR YOUR JOURNEY

To help you on your journey, here are some of the guideposts and activities to look for in each chapter. Do not skip over them, or the discussion following them will not be as meaningful. Each chapter is titled "The Search for . . ." and covers one of five main topics in philosophy. Specifically, these topics are the theory of knowledge, or epistemology (chapter 2); theories about reality, or metaphysics (chapter 3); philosophy of religion (chapter 4); ethics (chapter 5); and political philosophy (chapter 6). Some chapters contain subtopics that focus on a specific issue under the main heading. Each discussion on a main topic or subtopic is titled "Overview" and begins with an event that scouts the territory.

SCOUTING THE TERRITORY

The event in this section may be a story, a scenario, or a newspaper account that challenges you with philosophical puzzles concerning the topic. It usually does not consist of an explicit philosophical discussion but shows how philosophical issues make themselves felt in every area of life.

CHARTING THE TERRAIN—WHAT ARE THE ISSUES?

The next section consists of a more precise presentation of the philosophical problem and its significance. It makes you aware of the philosophical questions you need to answer as you make your way through the material.

CONCEPTUAL TOOLS

Some chapters will include a section that explains essential terms or makes important distinctions. These tools will help clarify the issues and establish the framework for the discussion that follows.

CHOOSING A PATH—WHAT ARE MY OPTIONS?

This section contains a brief description of the opposing alternatives on the issue. Typically, the section contains a chart that shows how the various positions line up on different aspects of the main issue. Besides giving you an initial comparison of the available viewpoints, the section helps you to clarify your own thinking on the issue.

WHAT DO I THINK?

Finally, the initial section on a philosophical topic or subtopic includes a brief questionnaire to enable you to see where you currently stand on the issue. (I say "currently" because it is perfectly permissible to change your mind as you study the different options in more detail.) The questions you are asked do not presuppose any prior knowledge of philosophy and are not factual in nature, so your honest opinion is all that is expected.

KEY TO THE QUESTIONNAIRE

After the questionnaire, the answers are analyzed in this key section. This key does not tell you which answers are right or wrong. Instead, it provides you with the philosophical labels for your own opinions. Do not worry if these labels are unfamiliar; they will be explained in time. Just keep your own position in mind, because in the remaining sections of the chapter, you will find that your own views have been defended or criticized by some of the great philosophers. As you read the remainder of each chapter, keep the following thoughts in mind: The issues being discussed are issues on which you have opinions. Some of the philosophers will agree with you and will be providing resources for your own thought. Do you find these resources helpful? Why? Other philosophers will be stepping on your toes. They will be issuing challenges to your thinking. How will you respond? They are trying to get you to buy their ideas. Are you buying? They will be trying to lock you into their position with their arguments. Can you evade the force of their arguments? If not, does your position need to be refined, modified, better supported, or abandoned?

LEADING QUESTIONS

Following the overview of each particular philosophical issue is a section on each position. Each philosophical alternative is introduced with the leading-questions exercise. This exercise consists of brief questions that are leading questions in two senses: They lead into the discussion of a particular philosophical position, and they are biased in favor of the position to be examined. The purpose of the questions is to make you initially sympathetic to the position that is being explained as well as to motivate you to be critical of how the questions are formulated. Hence, in answering the questions, look for the hidden assumptions they contain.

SURVEYING THE CASE FOR . . .

This section is the most substantial section concerning a particular position. It discusses and explains the position in question, and the arguments for that position are set out. As always, do not take these arguments at face value but examine them carefully to see if they provide good reasons for accepting the position.

A READING FROM . . .

Most of the sections on a particular point of view include brief readings from a philosopher that give you some practice in analyzing philosophical arguments. Questions are provided to suggest what to look for in the passage and to assist you in analyzing it. These passages have been selected because they are important to your understanding of the philosophical ideas. Do not skip over them, or you will miss some important material. Just as you cannot learn how to ski by reading about skiing but never getting out on the slopes, so you cannot develop philosophically without engaging with philosophical writings.

LOOKING THROUGH X'S LENS

Each philosophy is like a lens through which we can view human experience and the world at large. Each philosopher is claiming that his or her philosophy gives you the best picture of life. Accordingly, in this section you are asked: "If you were a follower of philosopher X, how would you view the following issues?" This exercise enables you to "try on" the philosopher's point of view in order to understand the position, see its implications, and discover its practical impact.

EXAMINING THE STRENGTHS
AND WEAKNESSES OF X

This section concludes the discussion of each philosophy. Philosophy is more than just a parade of opinions. Your philosophical journey will just be aimless meandering unless you absorb all the information and arguments available to you and make up your mind as to which viewpoints make the most sense. Probably no philosophy is 100 percent right or 100 percent wrong. So, you are asked to assess both the strengths and weaknesses of the position under discussion. Instead of telling you what to think about the position, the book provides questions that suggest both positive and negative points; it will be up to you to draw your own conclusions as to whether the strengths of the position outweigh its weaknesses.

BOXED EXERCISES

Scattered throughout each chapter are a number of other, boxed exercises that ask you to pause and think about a particular issue. Here are some examples of what you will be asked to do.

PHILOSOPHY *in the* MARKETPLACE

From time to time, you are asked to survey your friends who are not taking this course concerning their opinions on a particular issue. The survey questions do not assume that your friends know anything about the technical details of philosophy. Socrates thought that the best way to search for the truth was in dialogue with others. Accordingly, he spent his time in the marketplace, questioning his fellow Athenians about their views. These surveys give you the opportunity to try out the Socratic method of doing philosophy outside of class. My own students have reported that this exercise often provoked an evening-long discussion of the issue with their friends. Perhaps the answers you get on these surveys will raise issues that you will want to share with your professor and your classmates.

THOUGHT EXPERIMENT

Just as chemists perform experiments with test tubes to study the effects of certain chemicals and to see if their theories hold up, philosophers perform thought experiments to analyze the implications of certain ideas. The thought experiments in this book engage you in some of the following activities: analyzing concepts to find their essential components; finding out which concepts go together and which ones do not; discovering the implications of ideas; seeing if certain theories or commonsense beliefs hold up under testing; discovering alternative hypotheses to solve a conceptual puzzle; finding out which assumptions need to be modified and which need to be abandoned; testing the findings of other researchers (famous philosophers).

STOP AND THINK

This stop-and-think exercise asks you to pause in your reading and think about what has just been said. You are asked one or more questions that help focus your thinking on a particular point.

This box shines a brief light on background information, intriguing quotes, or other information that relates to the topic.

SPOTLIGHT
on

Finally, at the end of each of the chapters is a checklist to help you review the material in that chapter. It lists the names of the major philosophers covered in the chapter, mentions the key concepts, and includes suggestions for further reading.

As you can see, the philosophical journey is something more than simply learning facts, names, and dates. It is also more than simply clinging to personal opinions or passing them back and forth the way kids trade baseball cards. The philosophical journey involves the challenging work of reflecting on, evaluating, and seeking the justification for your own and other people's fundamental beliefs. But making this journey and sticking to it will bring you one of life's richest rewards, which is nothing less than *self-understanding.* To help you on your journey, this book attempts to achieve what Immanuel Kant, the 18th-century German philosopher, took as his goal as a teacher: "You will not learn from me philosophy, but how to philosophize, not thoughts to repeat, but how to think."[5]

1.1 SOCRATES AND THE SEARCH FOR WISDOM

The prisoner was housed in the state prison, only a stone's throw to the southwest of the agora, the bustling marketplace in Athens.* It seemed like just yesterday he had been walking in that very marketplace, discussing philosophy and questioning people on their views about all possible topics of human concern: knowledge, moral goodness, psychology, politics, art, and religion. But a month ago a jury made up of 500 citizens of Athens had voted to condemn him to death on the two charges of corrupting the minds of the youth and teaching about gods other than the official gods of Athens. Under normal circumstances the prisoner would have been executed soon after the trial, but an annual religious festival delayed his death by a month.

On the morning of his death, a group of friends arrived at his jail cell just as his wife and small baby were leaving to get some rest after spending the night with him. The group consisted of more than 10 of his local friends as well as 5 others who came from out of town. The prisoner was massaging his leg, which had just been released from its chains. He looked as he always had, as though this day was just another day in his life. The morning light streaming through the window reflected off his bald head and highlighted his curly, gray beard. His mantle, as always, hung awkwardly on his 70-year-old, short, and stocky

SOCRATES
(470–399 B.C.)

---

*This account is loosely based on the *Phaedo,* Plato's dialogue about Socrates' last hours.

Jacques Louis David's 1787 painting *The Death of Socrates.*

frame. People were always amused that one whose mind was so precise and orderly had such a humorous and unimposing physical appearance. But the solemnity of the occasion prevented any amusement on this day. The room was charged with emotion, and some friends were even weeping shamelessly. However, the condemned prisoner was extraordinarily calm and even cheerful as he waited for his death.

The year was 399 B.C., and the man facing execution for his ideas was Socrates, who had taught the wisdom of philosophy to many Athenians, including his best-known student, Plato. In the hours remaining in his life, Socrates revealed to his followers the secret of his calm composure. The philosopher is a person, he said, whose soul has been liberated by wisdom. Such a person has learned to know and therefore participate in ultimate Truth, Beauty, and Goodness. Since these concepts are eternal and are unchanged by the changes of the physical aspects that illustrate them, our ability to know these eternal truths indicates something eternal within us. Because the soul within us is eternal and intangible, Socrates argued, and because it alone is the real person, then no harm that occurs to the body can ever affect it. Socrates argued long and patiently throughout the day about his and everyone's immortality. Whereas his followers dreaded the impending loss of their friend, Socrates looked forward to being freed from the injustice of the state and reveled in the hope of entering into a realm of perfect justice where his teachings would be vindicated.

As sunset approached, Socrates' children were brought to see him one final time. The oldest was a young man, the middle one was a boy, and the youngest was still a baby. After they left, the prison warden, who had grown quite fond of Socrates and had visited him every day, came into the cell to say good-bye. He thanked Socrates for the conversations they had enjoyed together; then he burst into tears. By now Socrates was ready to leave, and he asked to receive the drink of poison hemlock that was to be the means of execution. He drank the cup in one breath; soon his legs began to feel heavy, and he lay down on his back. The prison guard monitored Socrates' body as the coldness and numbness started moving up from his limbs to his heart. Socrates' last words to his friends were instructions to make a sacrifice to Asclepius, the god of healing. At first the friends thought that strange, for one gave thanks to Asclepius after recovering from an illness and being returned to health. But then they remembered what Socrates had taught them and they knew that he believed he was soon to find wholeness and to be healed of the spiritual infirmities and limitations of this earthly life. About Socrates' death, his disciple Phaedo is reported to have said, "Such was the end . . . of our friend, whom I may truly call the most wise and just and best of all men I have ever known."[6]

Most accounts of a great figure's life begin with his or her birth. But in Socrates' case, his death tells us the most about his character and his life. Several questions arise out of this account of Socrates' death.

- Why was a philosopher considered so dangerous that he had to be put to death?
- Why was Socrates so committed to his philosophical ideas that he was willing to die for them?

The answers to these questions should become more evident the more you learn about this great philosopher. For now, it may be helpful to consider what you can learn about yourself from Socrates' example.

STOP AND THINK

Socrates lived and died in another land and in another time, but his life and death can provoke us to ask a number of questions about our own lives. To get an appreciation of Socrates' situation, ask yourself the following questions:

- What would make an idea dangerous?
- What ideas (if any) do I find to be uncomfortable, troubling, or even dangerous? Why?
- Can I think of any ideas in the past that society thought were dangerous but that turned out to be true?
- Can I think of any ideas that I once thought were dangerous but that I now accept?
- What ideas are worth living for?
- What ideas would I be willing to die for?

SOCRATES' LIFE AND MISSION

Now that we have learned about Socrates' death, what do we know about his life? Socrates was born in 470 B.C. in Athens. Unlike most of Socrates' students, who came from some of Athens' finest families, Socrates came from humble economic circumstances. His father was a sculptor and his mother a midwife. There are interesting similarities between Socrates' method of doing philosophy and the occupations of his parents, which he observed as a young boy. A sculptor takes a raw hunk of marble and chisels away at it, removing all the extraneous material until a finished, polished statue emerges. Similarly, in his conversations with the citizens of Athens, Socrates would take the raw, unrefined ideas of his contemporaries and hammer away at their opinions, removing what was unclear or erroneous, until he gradually achieved a closer approximation to the truth. Thinking, no doubt, of his mother, Socrates referred to himself as the "midwife of ideas." He claimed not to be able to teach anybody anything, but instead he asked artful questions that sought to bring to birth the truth that lay hidden within every human soul.

The most definitive information about Socrates' life comes from the account of his trial recorded by Plato in the *Apology*. (The term *apology* here does not mean expressing regret but refers to a formal defense such as one might introduce into a court of law.) In the following passage, Socrates tells the court how he got into so much trouble in the first place. The account begins with an event that was the turning point in Socrates' life.

FROM PLATO

Apology [7]

O men of Athens, I must beg you not to interrupt me, even if I seem to say something extravagant. For the word which I will speak is not mine. I will refer you to a witness who is worthy of credit, and will tell you about my wisdom—whether I have any, and of what sort—and that witness shall be the god of Delphi. You must have known Chaerephon; he was early a friend of mine, and also a friend of yours, for he shared in the exile of the people, and returned with you. Well, Chaerephon, as you know, was very impetuous in all his doings, and he went to Delphi and boldly asked the oracle to tell him whether—as I was saying, I must beg you not to interrupt—he asked the oracle to tell him whether there was anyone wiser than I was, and the Pythian prophetess answered that there was no man wiser. Chaerephon is dead himself, but his brother, who is in court, will confirm the truth of this story. Why do I mention this? Because I am going to explain to you why I have such an evil name. When I heard the answer, I said to myself, "What can the god mean and what is the interpretation of this riddle? I know that I have no wisdom, great or small. What can he mean when he says that I am the wisest of men? And yet he is a god and cannot lie; that would be against his nature." After a long consideration, I at last thought of a method of trying the question. I reflected that if I could only find a man wiser than myself, then I might go to the god with a refutation in my hand. I should say to him, "Here is a man who is wiser than I am; but you said that I was the wisest."

- In the passage you just read, what did the god say about Socrates through the voice of the prophetess?
- How does Socrates propose to disprove the god's statement?
- In the next passage, what advantage does Socrates say he has over the politicians of his day?

Accordingly I went to one who had the reputation of wisdom, and observed to him—his name I need not mention; he was a politician whom I selected for examination—and the result was as follows: When I began to talk with him, I could not help thinking that he was not really wise, although he was thought wise by many, and wiser still by himself; and I went and tried to explain to him that he thought himself wise, but was not really wise; and the consequence was that he hated me, and his hatred was shared by several who were present and heard me. So I left him, saying to myself, as I went away: "Well, although I do not suppose that either of us knows anything really beautiful and good, I am better off than he is—for he knows nothing, and thinks that he knows. I neither know nor think that I know. In this latter particular, then, I seem to have an advantage over him." Then I went to another, who had still higher philosophical pretensions, and my conclusion was exactly the same. I made another enemy of him, and of many others besides him.

After this I went to one man after another, being aware of the hatred which I provoked, and I lamented and feared this: but necessity was laid upon me. The word of the god, I thought, ought to be considered first. And I said to myself, "I must go to all who appear to know, and find out the meaning of the oracle." And I swear to you, Athenians, by the dog I swear!—for I must tell you the truth—the result of my mission was just this: I found that the men most in repute were all but the most foolish; and that some inferior men were really wiser and better.

I will tell you the tale of my wanderings and of the "Herculean" labors, as I may call them, which I endured only to find at last the oracle irrefutable. When I left the politicians, I went to the poets; tragic, dithyrambic, and all sorts. And there, I said to myself, you will be detected; now you will find out that you are more ignorant than they are. Accordingly, I took them some of the most elaborate passages in their own writings, and asked what was the meaning of them—thinking that they would teach me something. Will you believe me? I am almost ashamed to speak of this, but still I must say that there is hardly a person present who would not have talked better about their poetry than they did themselves. That showed me in an instant that not by wisdom do poets write poetry, but by a sort of genius and inspiration; they are like diviners or soothsayers who also say many fine things, but do not understand the meaning of them. And the poets appeared to me to be much in the same case; and I further observed that upon the strength of their poetry they believed themselves to be the wisest of men in other things in which they were not wise. So I departed, conceiving myself to be superior to them for the same reason that I was superior to the politicians.

At last I went to the artisans, for I was conscious that I knew nothing at all, as I may say, and I was sure that they knew many fine things; and in this I was not mistaken, for they did know many things of which I was ignorant, and in this they certainly were wiser than I was. But I observed that even the good artisans fell into the same error as the poets; because they were good workmen they thought that they also knew all sorts of high matters, and this defect in them overshadowed their wisdom. Therefore I asked myself on behalf of the oracle, whether I would like to be as I was, neither having their knowledge nor their ignorance, or like them in both. I answered to myself and the oracle that I was better off as I was. This investigation has led to my having many enemies of the worst and most dangerous kind, and has given occasion also to many falsehoods. I am called wise, for my hearers always imagine that I myself possess the wisdom which I find wanting in others.

Socrates is still convinced that he is ignorant and has nothing to teach, but now he knows why the god said he was wiser than anyone else in Athens.

- In what way is he wise?

In the next passage, Socrates anticipates that the court may let him go free on the condition that he cease to do philosophy and stop asking his annoying questions.

- What is his response to this potential offer of a plea bargain?
- What does he say is the mistake that the citizens of Athens are making?
- What does Socrates see as his mission?

Men of Athens, I honor and love you; but I shall obey the god rather than you, and while I have life and strength I shall never cease from the practice and teaching of philosophy, exhorting anyone whom I meet after my manner, and convincing him, saying: O my friend, why do you who are a citizen of the great and mighty and wise city of Athens, care so much about laying up the greatest amount of money and honor and reputation, and so little about wisdom and truth and the greatest improvement of the soul, which you never regard or heed at all? Are you not ashamed of this? And if the person with whom I am arguing says: Yes, but I do care; I do not depart or let him go at once; I interrogate and examine and cross-examine him, and if I think that he has no virtue, but only says that he has, I reproach him with undervaluing the greater, and overvaluing the less. And this I should say to everyone whom I meet, young and old, citizen and alien, but especially to the citizens, inasmuch as they are my brethren. For this is the command of the god, as I would have you know; and I believe that to this day no greater good has ever happened in the state than my service to the god.

I do nothing but go about persuading you all, old and young alike, not to take thought for your persons and your properties, but first and chiefly to care about the greatest improvement of the soul. I tell you that virtue is not given by money, but that from virtue come money and every other good of man, public as well as private. This is my teaching, and if this is the doctrine which corrupts the youth, my influence is ruinous indeed. But if anyone says that this is not my teaching, he is speaking an untruth. Wherefore, O men of Athens, I say to you, do as Anytus bids or not as Anytus bids, and either acquit me or not; but whatever you do, know that I shall never alter my ways, not even if I have to die many times.

STOP AND THINK

- Socrates has accused his fellow citizens of not keeping their priorities straight. If Socrates were to cross-examine you, what examples might he find in your life of placing great value on that which is trivial and undervaluing that which is of utmost importance?
- Socrates was a man who had a sense of mission in life—a mission that he would not forsake even to save his life. You, no doubt, are planning to get an education and to pursue a career that will give you an income. Apart from simply earning income, do you have a sense of mission in life?
- If so, how would you describe your mission?
- Is it important to have a sense of mission about your life? Why?

- In the next passage, why do you think that Socrates says that a bad person cannot harm a good person? Do you agree with this statement? Why?
- Why does Socrates think that his accusers (Meletus and Anytus) are harming themselves by prosecuting him?

Men of Athens, do not interrupt, but hear me; there was an agreement between us that you should hear me out. And I think that what I am going to say will do you good: for I have something more to say, at which you may be inclined to cry out; but I beg that you will not do this. I would have you know that, if you kill such a one as I am, you will injure yourselves more than you will injure me. Meletus and Anytus will not injure me: they cannot; for it is not in the nature of things that a bad man should injure one better than himself. I do not deny that he may, perhaps, kill him, or drive him into exile, or deprive him of civil rights; and he may imagine, and others may imagine, that he is doing him a great injury: but in that I do not agree with him; for the evil of doing as Anytus is doing—of unjustly taking away another man's life—is far greater.

- In the next passage, Socrates says to the jury that he is arguing not for his sake but for theirs. Why does he think that it is the citizens of Athens who are really being judged by the outcome of this trial and not him?
- Socrates goes on to compare himself to a gadfly (a large horsefly). Why does he describe himself in this way?
- What evidence does he give that his intentions were to unselfishly serve the people of Athens?

And now, Athenians, I am not going to argue for my own sake, as you may think, but for yours, that you may not sin against the god, or lightly reject his favor by condemning me. For if you kill me you will not easily find another like me, who, if I may use such a ludicrous figure of speech, am a sort of gadfly, given to the state by the god; and the state is like a great and noble steed who is tardy in his motions owing to his very size, and requires to be stirred into life. I am that gadfly which the god has given the state and all day long and in all places am always fastening upon you, arousing and persuading and reproaching you. And as you will not easily find another like me, I would advise you to spare me. I dare say that you may feel irritated at being suddenly awakened when you are caught napping; and you may think that if you were to strike me dead, as Anytus advises, which you easily might, then you would sleep on for the remainder of your lives, unless the god in his care of you gives you another gadfly. And that I am given to you by God is proved by this: If I had been like other men, I should not have neglected all my own concerns, or patiently seen the neglect of them during all these years, and have been doing yours, coming to you individually, like a father or elder brother, exhorting you to regard virtue; this I say, would not be like human nature. And had I gained anything, or if my exhortations had been paid, there would have been some sense in that; but now, as you will perceive, not even the impudence of my accusers dares to say that I have ever exacted or sought pay of anyone. They have no witness of that. And I have a witness of the truth of what I say; my poverty is a sufficient witness.

STOP AND THINK

Ask yourself the following questions:

- Who have been the gadflies in my life?
- Who were the people who challenged me and made me uncomfortable, but in doing so, made me a better person?
- In what way did they perform this role for me?

The list may include persons that you know, such as family, friends, or teachers; persons you have read about; and books, movies, or songs that have changed you.

In a trial such as Socrates', the defendant was expected to weep and beg for mercy from the court. He was also expected to bring his children, relatives, and friends into the courtroom to plead on his behalf. However, Socrates refused to resort to these emotional strategies, for he wanted to do as he always had done, to argue forcefully for the truth. If he was to be judged, he wanted to be judged on the basis of his life and ideas.

When the verdict was announced, 280 of the jury had declared him guilty and 220 voted for acquittal; the prosecutor recommended the death penalty. The custom in the Athenian court was for the defendant to now propose his own penalty and try to convince the jury to accept a lesser punishment. If Socrates had proposed that he be sent into exile, never to return to Athens, he might have satisfied his accusers. But Socrates would not play their game. He argued that he had been sent by his personal god to serve the citizens of Athens with his probing questions and he had done nothing but provide a great benefit to the city. Therefore, he proposed that he should receive what he really deserved and that was the honor reserved for the winners in the Olympics and the military heroes—a lifetime of free meals at the banquet table of the state's heroes. What was perceived as extraordinary arrogance turned the crowd against him, and the vote for the death penalty won by an even larger majority than before: 360 to 140.

After this crushing verdict, Socrates continued to philosophize in his final speech to the jury. The real danger in life is not death, he said, but living an evil life. We should not be willing to do or say anything to avoid death, thinking that by corrupting our souls we have gained any advantage.

The difficulty, my friends, is not in avoiding death, but in avoiding unrighteousness; for that runs faster than death. I am old and move slowly, and the slower runner has overtaken me, and my accusers are keen and quick, and the faster runner, who is unrighteousness, has overtaken them. And now I depart hence condemned by you to suffer the penalty of death, and they, too, go their ways condemned by the truth to suffer the penalty of wickedness and wrong. I must abide by my award—let them abide by theirs. I suppose that these things may be regarded as fated—and I think that they are as they should be. . . .

Wherefore, O judges, be of good cheer about death, and know this truth—that no evil can happen to a good man, either in life or after death. He and his are not neglected by the gods; nor has my own approaching end happened by mere chance. But I see clearly that to die and be released was better for me; and therefore my inner spiritual voice gave no sign. For which reason also, I am not angry with my accusers, or my condemners. They have done me no harm, although neither of them meant to do me any good; and for this I may gently blame them. . . .

The hour of departure has arrived, and we go our different ways—I to die, and you to live. Which is better only the god knows.

Socrates lived and died a philosopher—a lover of wisdom. Wisdom was, he thought, the most important goal we could pursue. Without it, we would be cursed with the most dire poverty a person could endure. The survey in "Philosophy in the Marketplace" asks you to think about and have others think about what it means to be wise.

SOCRATES' METHOD

If wisdom is the most important goal in life to Socrates, how did he go about pursuing it? Socrates' method of doing philosophy was to ask questions. That method was so effective that it has become one of the classic techniques of education; it is known as the Socratic method, or Socratic questioning. Plato referred to the method as *dialectic,* which comes from a Greek word for conversation. Typically, Socrates' philosophical conversations go

Ask at least five people from different backgrounds the following questions:

1. Name at least three commonly known persons (living or dead) whom you consider to be wise.
2. Why do you consider these persons to be wise?

Note: The stipulation to choose commonly known people is meant to rule out relatives and others whom most people would not know. A subject who answers with only religious leaders (e.g., Buddha, Solomon, or Jesus) should be asked also for some other examples in order to guarantee variety.

Review the answers: Are any categories of people notable by their absence? (e.g., were any women mentioned? artists? scientists?) Are any categories of people notable by their frequency? (e.g., are most of the people mentioned political figures? religious figures?) Were any philosophers mentioned? Do you find any other patterns in the answers? What can we learn about people's notions of wisdom from this survey? Do you agree with these conceptions of wisdom? Why?

PHILOSOPHY
in the
MARKETPLACE

through seven stages as he and his partner continually move toward a greater understanding of the truth:

1. Socrates unpacks the philosophical issues in an everyday conversation. (The genius of Socrates was his ability to find the philosophical issues lurking in even the most mundane of topics.)
2. Socrates isolates a key philosophical term that needs analysis.
3. Socrates professes ignorance and requests the help of his companion.
4. Socrates' companion proposes a definition of the key term.
5. Socrates analyzes the definition by asking questions that expose its weaknesses.
6. The subject produces another definition, one that improves on the earlier one. (This new definition leads back to step 5, and on close examination the new definition is once again found to fail. Steps 5 and 6 are repeated several times.)
7. The subject is made to face his own ignorance. (Finally, the subject realizes he is ignorant and is now ready to begin the search for true wisdom. Often, however, the subject finds some excuse to end the conversation or someone else makes an attempt at a new definition.)

Socrates' hope in utilizing this method was that in weeding out incorrect understandings, he and his conversational partner would be moving toward a clearer picture of the true answer. Because Socrates believed that the truth about the ultimate issues in life lay deeply hidden within us, this process of unpacking the truth within was like that of a midwife helping a mother in labor bring forth her child.

One of Socrates' most skillful techniques for showing the weakness of someone's position was his use of the *reductio ad absurdum* form of argument. This term means "reducing to an absurdity." Socrates would begin by assuming that his opponent's position is true and then show that it logically implies either an absurdity or a conclusion that contradicts other conclusions held by the opponent. Deducing a false statement from a proposition proves that the original assumption was false.

You can view the Socratic method in action by working through a passage from Plato's dialogue the *Republic*. (Because Socrates did philosophy by engaging in conversations and not by writing, everything we know about him comes from the writings of Plato and other contemporaries. Plato's earlier dialogues, such as the *Apology*, are thought to represent the historical Socrates. The *Republic* was written in Plato's middle period. The ideas, while expressed through the voice of Socrates, are thought to be Plato's own elaboration on and expansion of his teacher's thought.) The story begins with Socrates and his friends meeting in town on the occasion of a religious festival. They end up at the home of Polemarchus and meet his father, Cephalus, a retired and wealthy businessman. Cephalus talks about the joys of growing old and the virtue of having lived a fulfilled life. Socrates is keenly interested in what he has to say and begins to ask him about what has filled his life with peace and happiness. At this point in the story, we begin at the first step of Socrates' philosophical dialectic.

Unpacking the Philosophical Issues

Cephalus replies that the secret of his peace and happiness is a life lived on the basis of justice and piety. Socrates then begins to ask Cephalus about his concept of justice, which takes the two men to the next step of the dialectic.

Isolating a Key Philosophical Term

The result is that Socrates examines Cephalus's and the others' notions of justice and finds that none of their definitions is satisfactory. At that point, Thrasymachus, a rather smug and outspoken teacher, cannot contain himself any more and jumps into the conversation. He insists that Socrates stop playing games with them and offer his own definition of justice. As usual, Socrates claims that he is not knowledgeable on this issue and begs Thrasymachus to enlighten him with his wisdom. Thus, Socrates begins his conversation with Thrasymachus at the third step of his dialectic.

Professing Ignorance and Requesting Help

The following passage begins with Thrasymachus's cynical reply.

FROM PLATO

Republic[8]

Behold, he said, the wisdom of Socrates; he refuses to teach himself, and goes about learning of others, to whom he never even says thank you.

That I learn of others, I replied, is quite true; but that I am ungrateful I wholly deny. Money I have none, and therefore I pay in praise, which is all I have: and how ready I am to praise any one who appears to me to speak well you will very soon find out when you answer; for I expect that you will answer well.

Having flattered Thrasymachus's rather enormous ego, Socrates moves the conversation to the fourth step of his dialectic.

Proposing a Definition

- In the next passage, identify Thrasymachus's definition of justice.
- What arguments could be made in favor of this definition of justice?
- What are some of the implications of this definition?
- Does Thrasymachus offer a satisfactory notion of justice? Why?

Listen, then, he said; I proclaim that justice is nothing else than the interest of the stronger. And now why do you not applaud me? But of course you won't.

Let me first understand you, I replied. Justice, as you say, is the interest of the stronger. What, Thrasymachus, is the meaning of this? . . .

Well, he said, have you never heard that forms of government differ; there are tyrannies, and there are democracies, and there are aristocracies?

Yes, I know.

And the government is the ruling power in each state?

Certainly.

And the different forms of government make laws democratic, aristocratic, tyrannical, with a view to their several interests; and these laws, which are made by them for their own interests, are the justice which they deliver to their subjects, and he who transgresses them they punish as a breaker of the law, and unjust. And that is what I mean when I say that in all states there is the same principle of justice, which is the interest of the government; and as the government must be supposed to have power, the only reasonable conclusion is, that everywhere there is one principle of justice, which is the interest of the stronger.

With Thrasymachus's definition on the table, Socrates now moves to the next step of his philosophical method.

Analyzing the Definition by Asking Questions

In the following passage, notice how Socrates uses a reductio ad absurdum argument to show that Thrasymachus's position leads to a contradictory conclusion. Socrates' love of irony is evident at the end of this passage as he refers to Thrasymachus as the "wisest of men" just as he demolishes Thrasymachus's position.

- What is the contradictory conclusion that Socrates infers from the definition?
- How do you think Thrasymachus could modify his definition to avoid this absurd conclusion?
- Set out the steps of Socrates' argument in this passage.

Now I understand you, I said; and whether you are right or not I will try to discover. . . . Now we are both agreed that justice is interest of some sort, but you go on to say "of the stronger"; about this addition I am not so sure, and must therefore consider further.

Proceed.

I will; and first tell me, Do you admit that it is just for subjects to obey their rulers?

I do.

But are the rulers of states absolutely infallible, or are they sometimes liable to err?

To be sure, he replied, they are liable to err.

Then in making their laws they may sometimes make them rightly, and sometimes not?

True.

When they make them rightly, they make them agreeably to their interest; when they are mistaken, contrary to their interest; you admit that?

Yes.

And the laws which they make must be obeyed by their subjects,—and that is what you call justice?

Doubtless.

Then justice, according to your argument, is not only obedience to the interest of the stronger but the reverse?

What is that you are saying? he asked.

I am only repeating what you are saying, I believe. But let us consider: Have we not admitted that the rulers may be mistaken about their own interest in what they command, and also that to obey them is justice? Has not that been admitted?

Yes.

Then you must also have acknowledged justice not to be for the interest of the stronger, when the rulers unintentionally command things to be done which are to their own injury. For if, as you say, justice is the obedience which the subject renders to their commands, in that case, O wisest of men, is there any escape from the conclusion that the weaker are commanded to do, not what is for the interest of the stronger, but what is for the injury of the stronger? . . .

To summarize Socrates' argument thus far, he has begun with Thrasymachus's definition: (*a*) To be just is to do what is in the interest of the stronger person. However, Socrates has gotten him to admit that those in power can sometimes be mistaken as to what is in their own best interest. If so, then the rulers can foolishly pass laws that will not serve their interests. (Such is often the case in tyrannical governments where the laws become so oppressive they drive people to revolution.) However, because Thrasymachus has said that it is just for subjects to obey their powerful rulers, it follows that there will be occasions when the subjects will be required to obey laws that are not in the interest of the stronger person. In other words, we now have the conclusion (*b*): To be just is to do what is *not* in the interest of the stronger person. So, Thrasymachus has been led to assert both statements (A) and (B), but these statements contradict each other. If one's position leads to a contradiction, then the position cannot be true.

At this point, two members of the group, Polemarchus and Cleitophon, argue over whether Socrates has trapped Thrasymachus. To resolve their debate, Socrates asks Thrasymachus to clarify his position. This response gives Thrasymachus the chance to add an important qualification to his definition to avoid the contradiction Socrates has exposed. We are now at the sixth step of Socrates' dialectical method.

Producing an Improved Definition

- How does Thrasymachus modify the notion of ruler from that of his original definition?

Tell me, Thrasymachus, I said, did you mean by justice what the stronger thought to be his interest, whether it really is so or not?

Certainly not, he said. Do you suppose that I call he who is mistaken the stronger at the time when he is mistaken?

Yes, I said, my impression was that you did so, when you admitted that the ruler was not infallible but might be sometimes mistaken.

You argue like a quibbler, Socrates. Do you mean, for example, that he who is mistaken about the sick is a physician in that he is mistaken? or that he who errs in arithmetic or grammar is an arithmetician or grammarian at the time when he is making the mistake, in respect of the mistake? True, we say that the physician or arithmetician or grammarian has made a mistake, but this is only a way of speaking; for the fact is that neither the grammarian nor any other person of skill ever makes a mistake in so far as he is what his name implies; they none of them err unless their skill fails them, and then they cease to be skilled artists. No artist or sage or ruler errs at the time when he is what his name implies; though he is commonly said to err, and I adopted the common mode of speaking. But to be perfectly accurate, since you are such a lover of accuracy, we should say that the ruler, in so far as he is the ruler, is unerring, and, being unerring, always commands that which is for his own interest; and the subject is required to execute his commands; and therefore, as I said at first and now repeat, justice is the interest of the stronger.

In the previous passage, Socrates goaded Thrasymachus into thinking about the ideals that are embodied in any profession. Thus Socrates gets him to admit that a physician who harms a patient is not really fulfilling the ideals of medicine, but is only acting as a would-be physician. In this way Socrates tricks Thrasymachus into saying that someone is a true ruler, strictly speaking, only when he or she is faithfully practicing the skill of ruling. By using analogies from the arts of medicine, horsemanship, and piloting, Socrates gets his companion to admit that true rulers are those who look after the interests of their subjects and do not merely serve their own, selfish interests. The next passage begins with the voice of Socrates as he repeats the cycle of his dialectic on the new, revised definition of justice.

Reanalyzing the Definition by Asking More Questions

- Follow the steps of Socrates' argument by analogy as he gets Thrasymachus to reverse his original position.

Is the physician, taken in that strict sense of which you are speaking, a healer of the sick or a maker of money? And remember that I am now speaking of the true physician.
A healer of the sick, he replied. . . .
Now, I said, doesn't every art have some interest which it serves?
Certainly.
And does not every art exist to consider and provide for these interests?
Yes, that is the aim of art.
And the interest of any art is to be as perfect as possible—this and nothing else?
What do you mean?
I mean what I may illustrate negatively by the example of the body. Suppose you were to ask me whether the body is self-sufficing or has wants, I should reply: Certainly the body has wants; for the body may be ill and require to be cured, and has therefore interests to which the art of medicine ministers; and this is the origin and intention of medicine, as you will acknowledge. Am I not right?
Quite right, he replied. . . .
Then medicine does not consider the interest of medicine, but the interest of the body?
True, he said.
Nor does the art of horsemanship consider the interests of the art of horsemanship, but the interests of the horse; neither do any other arts care for themselves, for they have no needs; they care only for that which is the subject of their art?
True, he said.
But surely, Thrasymachus, the arts are the superiors and rulers of their own subjects?

To this he assented with a good deal of reluctance.

Then, I said, no science or art considers or commands the interest of the stronger or superior, but only the interest of the subject and weaker?

He made an attempt to contest this proposition also, but finally acquiesced.

Then, I continued, no physician, in so far as he is a physician, considers his own good in what he prescribes, but the good of his patient; for the true physician is also a ruler having the human body as a subject, and is not a mere money-maker; that has been admitted?

Yes.

And the pilot likewise, in the strict sense of the term, is a ruler of sailors and not a mere sailor?

That has been admitted.

And such a pilot and ruler will provide and prescribe for the interest of the sailor who is under him, and not for his own or the ruler's interest?

He gave a reluctant "Yes."

Then, I said, Thrasymachus, there is no one in any rule who, in so far as he is a ruler, considers or enjoins what is for his own interest, but always what is for the interest of his subject or suitable to his art; to that he looks, and that alone he considers in everything which he says and does.

When we had got to this point in the argument . . . every one saw that the definition of justice had been completely upset.

At this point, the first round of Socrates' intellectual bout with Thrasymachus comes to an end. With Thrasymachus's initial definition of justice defeated, we reach the seventh step of Socrates' dialectic.

Facing Ignorance

Thrasymachus is bloodied, but not defeated. He tacitly admits Socrates' point that justice is serving the interests of one's subjects. But now he takes a totally new approach and says that *injustice* is the only lifestyle that is profitable and is the one that the smart person would choose. So, instead of continuing to tout his perverse definition of justice (which Socrates has unraveled), Thrasymachus now makes injustice the ideal. Socrates' refutation of this thesis takes up most of the remainder of the *Republic,* and it leads him into a large-scale discussion of human nature, knowledge, reality, morality, and politics.

SOCRATES' TEACHINGS

As you may suspect, Socrates had some opinions about the practical value of philosophy. His trial illustrated the fact that his main philosophical concern was with ethics. Although he also philosophized about such topics as the nature of knowledge, the nature of reality, human nature, religion, and political philosophy, Socrates was interested in those topics primarily for the light they could shed on the question, How should we live if we are to be successful and fulfilled human beings? Socrates' teachings on this issue can be summarized in three theses. After listing them, I discuss each one in turn.

1. The unexamined life is not worth living.
2. The most important task in life is caring for the soul (the real person).
3. A good person cannot be harmed by others.

The Unexamined Life Is Not Worth Living

As was evident from his remarks at his trial, Socrates was concerned that his contemporaries were like dozing cattle who, at the end of their life, would sleepily look around, not knowing who they were, why they were that way, or what their life had been all about. In contrast, Socrates chose as his motto the inscription on the temple at Delphi: "Know thyself." The examined life and examined beliefs lead to lives that are responsible and fully awake. To use a metaphorical cliché, everyone in Socrates' society was so busy "keeping the ball rolling," they had never asked what the ball was, or why it was so important to keep it rolling, or where it was going. For Socrates, what is important was not so much what we do, for our activities and careers can change. What is important is who we are and who we are trying to become. Socrates' thesis is that making oneself as good as possible is the true goal in life and the key to genuine success.

The Most Important Task in Life Is Caring for the Soul

According to Socrates, the soul is not some ghostly shadow accompanying us, as Homer and the Greek poets assumed. Instead, the soul is the real person. It is our core personality or character and is the source of all our thoughts, values, and decisions. The state of a person's soul makes him or her either foolish or wise. Like the body, the soul (or the inner person) can be healthy or diseased, and for Socrates, ignorance is the most deadly disease of the soul. Of course, this ignorance is not the kind of ignorance that could be cured by memorizing an encyclopedia. Instead, the unhealthy soul is one that is ignorant of the true priorities in life. Although Socrates seemed to have believed in life after death, this belief was not his motive for being concerned about the moral health of his soul. As Gregory Vlastos says,

> The soul is as worth caring for if it were to last just twenty-four more hours, as if it were to outlast eternity. If you have just one more day to live, and can expect nothing but a blank after that, Socrates feels that you would still have all the reason you need for improving your soul; you have yourself to live with that one day, so why live with a worse self, if you could live with a better one instead?[9]

In Socrates' day there was an influential group of philosophers known as the **Sophists.** The Sophists were traveling educators who would offer practical courses for the payment of a fee. One of their main teachings was **skepticism,** the belief that we cannot have knowledge. Hence, to the Sophists, "moral goodness" and "truth" are just sounds that we make with our mouths; they do not refer to anything. One opinion is just as good as another, they taught. If we cannot know what is true or right, then the only goal in life is to achieve success by whatever means possible. Accordingly, the Sophists taught their students how to argue and how to influence people with their opinions. (Thrasymachus in the previous reading was a leading Sophist.)

Socrates was upset that although the Sophists were offering people a map of how to get through life, it was the wrong map. The Sophists claimed to teach people how to achieve success; however, they and their students assumed that success meant achieving wealth, fame, or power. To creatively superimpose the status symbols of our day onto theirs, Socrates' contemporaries thought that success meant driving a BMW chariot, wearing a Calvin Klein tunic, being a high-priced lawyer charging 100 drachmas an hour, or getting your picture on the front page of the *Athens Times*. But Socrates claimed that his contemporaries had not really examined what it meant to be a success in life. They were busy trying to be successful businesspersons, politicians, lawyers, physicians, athletes, or artists,

Sophists traveling educators during Socrates' day who would offer practical courses for a fee and who taught the doctrine of skepticism

skepticism the belief that we cannot have knowledge

PHILOSOPHY
in the
MARKETPLACE

Socrates is probably one of the best known philosophers in history. See how much people know about him by asking 5 to 10 people who have not had a philosophy class the following questions.

- Who was Socrates?
- What is the Socratic method of teaching?
- What were some of Socrates' teachings?
- Why was he put to death by the people of Athens?

It might be uncharitable to criticize your friends' answers unless they ask you what you think. Nevertheless, after you have collected various answers, rank them according to which ones you think are the most accurate and the least accurate. Based on your survey, how much does the general public know about Socrates?

but they never considered that realizing their potential as persons was the most important occupation they had in life.

A Good Person Cannot Be Harmed by Others

This statement follows from the rest of Socrates' teachings. If the real me, the most important part of who I am, is not my possessions nor the outward, physical part of me, then no one can corrupt me or damage me from outside. An evil person can cause great pain or even kill me, but what makes me the person I am cannot be affected or harmed by any outward force. More precisely, I cannot be harmed by others unless, of course, I allow my values, my beliefs, my emotions, and my direction in life to be influenced unthinkingly by those around me. To paraphrase Socrates' view, we can choose to be like driftwood, floating on the surface of life, passively turning this way or that as each wave or gust of wind influences our motion. In this case, we are allowing ourselves to be vulnerable to the effects and harm produced by others. On the other hand, we can choose to be like the captain of a sailboat who sets his or her own direction with the rudder and the sails. If we set our sights on wisdom, then our values, like the keel of the boat, will keep us on the course we set. We have to respond to the winds in society that are blowing about us, but we are in control and we make the winds serve our purpose rather than being at their mercy. Hence, the Socratic vision of the life of philosophical wisdom is one in which self-examination leading to self-knowledge gives us the wisdom to care for the best part of ourselves and liberates us from the control and harm of everything outside, making us inner-directed and fulfilled persons.

1.2 PLATO'S ALLEGORY OF THE CAVE

We can follow out some of Socrates' themes by exploring the ideas of Plato (c. 428–348 B.C.), Socrates' most famous disciple. (Further biographical information on Plato can be found in section 2.2.) If we are to search for wisdom and to know how to live our lives, Plato believed, we must have a correct understanding of knowledge and reality. Plato's view of reality, as well as his view of knowledge and personal enlightenment, is represented in his famous Allegory of the Cave, which has become a classic story in Western literature. In this allegory, Plato suggests the possibility that reality may be entirely different than our

This diagram of Plato's Allegory of the Cave represents chained prisoners whose only reality is the shadow world projected on the wall in front of them. They are unaware that behind them is the higher degree of reality of the fire and the statues that are casting the shadows. Still further up is the steep and rugged passage out of the cave to the upper world. A prisoner who follows this path will encounter the world of real objects and the sun. Plato used this story as a rough analogy to the modes of awareness and levels of reality discussed in his philosophy.

taken-for-granted assumptions suppose it to be. In telling this story, Plato uses the figure of his teacher Socrates to present his ideas. As you read the allegory, answer the following questions.

- Can you imagine the scene in the cave Socrates describes? Sketch a picture of all the elements in the cave.
- Glaucon says the people in the story are "strange prisoners." Socrates then gives the stunning reply that they are "like ourselves." Why do you suppose Socrates compares us to these prisoners?
- What do the shadows stand for?
- What are the "shadows" in our society? In your life?
- According to this story, what is enlightenment?
- In what sense does the freed prisoner *not* understand the shadows as well as his

friends do when he returns to the cave? In what sense does he understand the shadows *better* than his friends do?

- In what ways are the events in the enlightened prisoner's life like the events in the historical Socrates' life?
- Summarize what philosophical points you think Plato is making in this allegory.

FROM PLATO

Republic[10]

SOCRATES: And now, let me show in a parable how far our nature is enlightened or unenlightened. Imagine human beings living in an underground den, which has a mouth open towards the light. Here they have been from their childhood, and have their legs and necks chained so that they can not move, and can only see before them, being prevented by the chains from turning their heads around. Above and behind them a fire is blazing at a distance, and between the fire and the prisoners there is a raised walk; and you will see, if you look, a low wall built along the walkway, like the screen which marionette players have in front of them, over which they show the puppets.

GLAUCON: I see.

SOCRATES: And do you see men passing along the wall carrying all sorts of vessels, and statues and figures of animals made of wood and stone and various materials, which appear over the wall? Some of them are talking, others silent.

GLAUCON: You have shown me a strange image, and they are strange prisoners.

SOCRATES: Like ourselves; and they see only their own shadow, or the shadows of one another, which the fire throws on the opposite wall of the cave.

GLAUCON: True; how could they see anything but the shadows if they were never allowed to move their heads?

SOCRATES: And of the objects which are being carried in like manner they would only see the shadows?

GLAUCON: Yes.

SOCRATES: And if they were able to converse with one another, would they not suppose that they were naming what was actually before them?

GLAUCON: Very true.

SOCRATES: And suppose further that the prison had an echo which came from the cave wall, would they not be sure to believe when one of the passers-by spoke that the voice which they heard came from the passing shadow?

GLAUCON: No question.

SOCRATES: To them, the truth would be literally nothing but the shadows of the images.

GLAUCON: That is certain.

SOCRATES: And now look again, and see what will naturally follow if the prisoners are released and disabused of their error. At first, when any of them is liberated and compelled suddenly to stand up and turn his neck round and walk and look towards the light, he will suffer sharp pains. The glare will distress him, and he will be unable to see the realities of which in his former state he had seen the shadows; and then conceive some one saying to him, that what he saw before was an illusion, but that now, when he is approaching nearer to reality and his eye is turned towards more real existence, he has a clearer vision. What will be his reply? And you may further imagine that his instructor is pointing to the objects as they pass and requiring him to name them—will he not be perplexed? Will he not believe that the shadows which he formerly saw are truer than the objects which are now shown to him?

GLAUCON: Far truer.

SOCRATES: And if he is compelled to look straight at the light, will he not have a pain in his eyes which will make him turn away to take refuge in the shadows which he can see, and which he will conceive to be clearer than the things which are now being shown to him?

GLAUCON: True.

SOCRATES: And suppose once more, that he is reluctantly dragged up a steep and rugged ascent, and held fast until he is forced into the presence of the sun itself, is he not likely to be pained and irritated? When he approaches the light his eyes will be dazzled, and he will not be able to see anything at all of what are now called realities.

GLAUCON: Not all in a moment.

SOCRATES: He will need to grow accustomed to the sight of the upper world. And first he will see the shadows best, next the reflections of men and other objects in the water, and then the objects themselves; then he will gaze upon the light of the moon and the stars and the spangled heaven; and he will see the sky and the stars by night better than the sun or the light of the sun by day.

GLAUCON: Certainly.

SOCRATES: Last of all he will be able to see the sun, and not mere reflections of it in the water, but he will see the sun in its own proper place, and not in another; and he will contemplate the sun as it is.

GLAUCON: Certainly.

SOCRATES: He will then proceed to argue that this is what gives the season and the years, and is the guardian of all that is in the visible world, and in a certain way the cause of all things which he and his fellows have been accustomed to behold?

GLAUCON: Clearly, he would first see the sun and then reason about it.

SOCRATES: And when he remembered his old dwelling, and the wisdom of the den and his fellow-prisoners, do you not suppose that he would be happy about his change, and pity them?

GLAUCON: Certainly, he would.

SOCRATES: And if they were in the habit of conferring honors among themselves on those who were quickest to observe the passing shadows and to remark which of them went before, and which followed after, and which were together; and who were therefore best able to draw conclusions as to the future, do you think that he would care for such honors and glories, or envy the possessors of them? Would he not say with Homer, "Better to be the poor servant of a poor master" and to endure anything, rather than think as they do and live after their manner?

GLAUCON: Yes, I think that he would rather suffer anything than entertain these false notions and live in this miserable manner.

SOCRATES: Imagine once more, such a one coming suddenly out of the sun to be replaced in his old situation; would he not be certain to have his eyes full of darkness?

GLAUCON: To be sure.

SOCRATES: And if there were a contest, and he had to compete in measuring the shadows with the prisoners who had never moved out of the den, while his sight was still weak, and before his eyes had become steady (and the time which would be needed to acquire this new habit of sight might be very considerable), would he not be ridiculous? Men would say of him that up he went and down he came without his eyes; and that it was better not even to think of ascending; and if any one tried to loose another and lead him up to the light, let them only catch the offender, and they would put him to death.

GLAUCON: No question.

SOCRATES: This allegory is connected to the previous argument about the ascent of knowledge. The prison-house-cave is the world of sight; the light of the fire is the sun; and the journey upwards is the ascent of the soul into the intellectual world. My view is that in the world of knowledge the idea of the Good appears last of all, and is seen only with great effort; and when seen, is also inferred to be the universal author of all things beautiful and right, parent of light and of the lord of light in this visible world [the sun], and the immediate source of reason and truth in the higher world [the world of Forms]; and that this is the power upon which he who would act rationally either in public or private life must have his eye fixed.

GLAUCON: I agree, as far as I am able to understand you.

SOCRATES: Moreover, you must not wonder that those who attain to this wonderful vision are unwilling to descend to human affairs; for their souls are ever hastening into the upper world where they desire to dwell; which desire of theirs is very natural, if our allegory is to be trusted.

GLAUCON: Yes, very natural.

SOCRATES: And is there anything surprising in one who passes from divine contemplations to the evil state of man, appearing in a ridiculous manner; if, while his eyes are blinking and before he has become accustomed to the surrounding darkness, he is compelled to fight in courts of law, or in other places, about the images or the shadows of images of justice, and is endeavouring to meet the conceptions of those who have never yet seen absolute justice?

GLAUCON: Anything but surprising.

SOCRATES: Any one who has common sense will remember that the confusions of the eyes are two kinds, and arise from two causes, either from coming out of the light or from going into the light, which is true of the mind's eye, quite as much as of the bodily eye; and he who remembers this when he sees any one whose vision is perplexed and weak, will not be too ready to laugh; he will first ask whether that soul of man has come out of the brighter light, and is unable to see because unaccustomed to the dark, or having turned from darkness to the day is dazzled by excess of light. And he will count the one happy in his condition and state of being, and he will pity the other; or, if he have a mind to laugh at the soul which comes from below into the light, there will be more reason in this than in the laugh which greets him who returns from above out of the light into the den.

GLAUCON: That is a very just distinction.

SOCRATES: But then, if I am right, certain professors of education must be wrong when they say that they can put a knowledge into the soul which was not there before, like sight into blind eyes.

GLAUCON: They undoubtedly say this.

SOCRATES: Whereas, our argument shows that the power and capacity of learning exists in the soul already. Just as the eye was unable to turn from darkness to light without the whole body, so too the instrument of knowledge can only by the movement of the whole soul be turned from the world of becoming into that of unchanging reality, and learn by degrees to endure the sight of reality, and of the brightest and best of reality, or in other words, of the Good.

GLAUCON: Very true.

SOCRATES: And must there not be some art which will turn the soul about in the easiest and quickest manner? It is not the art of implanting the faculty of sight in the soul, for that exists already, but to ensure that, instead of looking in the wrong direction, away from the truth, it is turned the way it ought to be.

GLAUCON: Yes, such an art may be presumed.

Plato on Knowledge, Reality, and Value

What is the point of Plato's story? Is his purpose to point out that we should stay out of dank, dark caves and prefer the healthier environment of fresh air and sunshine? Obviously not, for Plato's story is an allegory in which the events in the narrative symbolize a deeper meaning. There are many levels at which the story can be interpreted. However, Plato's main point is that the relationship between the shadows and the upper, sunlit world is similar to the relationship between two levels of knowledge and two levels of reality.

With respect to knowledge, Plato believed that the world revealed to us in sense experience is like the land of shadows; it is an imperfect representation of higher truths that are revealed to us through reason. Similarly, with respect to reality, the shadows that the prisoners see are lesser realities that are representative of, or derived from, the wooden figures behind them, which themselves are replicas of the real objects in the upper world. These replicas symbolize Plato's view that levels of reality transcend the world of our sense experience. Accordingly, the physical world (like the shadows) has some degree of reality, but it is transcended by and must be understood in terms of the nonphysical world. It is because we can rise above the realm of particular, physical things and understand the higher nonphysical realities that we can understand anything at all.

To use one of Plato's favorite examples, consider the question, What is justice? Justice doesn't have any shape, weight, or color. Unlike a rock, it is not something that we encounter in sense experience but it is something that we can reason about and can use to judge the moral quality of human actions. If justice is not a physical thing and cannot be known with the five senses, can it, nevertheless, still be something real? There may be a number of ways to approach this question, but the two answers Plato considered are (*a*) what we call *justice* is merely what different individuals think it is according to their subjective opinion or (*b*) the word *justice* refers to something objective and real, but something that we can only know with our minds, not with our physical senses.

STOP AND THINK

Which of the above two answers seems most correct to you? Can you think of any other answers concerning the nature of justice? From these considerations, what can you conclude about the nature of moral properties such as justice?

Plato's answer is that alternative (*b*) is the only reasonable answer. If justice is not a nonphysical reality, then *justice* is merely a mark on this paper or a sound we make with our mouths that expresses our respective, subjective opinions. If there is no objective standard against which to measure our opinions, then one opinion can be no more true than another opinion. To shine a Platonic light on our own time, how can we say that sexual discrimination is wrong or the policies of Nazi Germany were unjust if *justice* refers to nothing more than what different individuals think it is? If justice is all a matter of subjective opinion, then why are our opinions any better than those of the sexists or the Nazis? Plato would reply that if the nature of justice is more than subjective opinion, then it must be something that we can know. For anything to be the object of knowledge it must be something real. Therefore, justice must be something real but nonphysical.

Plato's Allegory and the Questions of Philosophy

Whether or not you are inclined to be sympathetic toward Plato's philosophical views, his Allegory of the Cave can be used to illustrate the major philosophical questions we will discuss in the rest of this book. First, with respect to logic and critical thinking, Plato has not provided arguments for his conclusions at this point, but has illustrated his philosophical vision by means of an artful story. Nevertheless, he does offer us helpful reminders to assist us in thinking critically. The prisoners in the cave had never experienced anything but the shadows, so they assumed that the shadows were the whole of reality. When the liberated prisoner spoke of another level of reality, full of colors and depth, they considered him a fool, for his account went against their society's taken-for-granted belief system. This part of the allegory illustrates the importance of questioning our basic assumptions. It also cautions us to be wary of commonplace knowledge and reminds us that the majority can often be wrong. The great figures in history (philosophers such as Socrates, or scientists, artists, and social reformers) often found themselves in conflict with the basic assumptions of their culture. Likewise, we can be like the prisoners, naively accepting everything we hear, or we can try to be like the lone prisoner who learned to question the assumptions of his contemporaries.

Second, with respect to epistemology, Plato's story reminds us that the truth is not always what is obvious nor what is directly before our eyes. Compiling more and more data about the shadows would not have brought the prisoners closer to the truth. What was needed was a whole new perspective on the shadows. Furthermore, the allegory illustrates the fact that there can be a difference between human opinion and true knowledge. The prisoners genuinely and sincerely believed that their conclusions about reality were correct. However, the sincerity of our opinions, even widely held opinions, is no guarantee of their truth.

Third, Plato introduces the distinction between appearance and reality, which is an important theme in metaphysics. The majority of prisoners in the cave disagreed with their friend as to what is ultimately real. The enlightened prisoner came to see that the shadows were only a derivative, lower level of reality compared to the realities he experienced outside the cave. However, the majority claimed that the shadows were real and what their friend had experienced were confusing appearances. My discussion on metaphysics in chapter 3 includes debates over what is ultimately real and what is illusion.

Fourth, with respect to philosophy of religion, Plato's account suggests the possibility that a higher, nonphysical reality transcends the physical world, the way the higher realm in the allegory transcended the world of the cave. Such is the claim of most religious views. However, other philosophers will argue that there is no evidence of a higher level of reality beyond the natural world that science studies. The debate over the existence of a transcendent reality such as God will be the focus of our discussion of religion.

Fifth, Plato's story contains ethical concerns as well. Initially, the liberated prisoner was enjoying his newfound discovery of the higher, richer world outside the cave. Nevertheless, he felt an ethical obligation to go back into the cave and rescue his friends from their ignorance. The following questions can be asked here: Did the prisoner have a moral obligation to return to the cave, or would he have been justified in pursuing his own interests? What are ethical obligations? What is their basis? How should I balance my own pursuit of happiness with concern for the happiness of others?

Finally, although Plato does not discuss political philosophy at this point in the reading, he later raises the following political issues. Should society be based on the will of the majority when the majority is so often wrong? Or should political power be given to those who are most deserving (those who are the most enlightened)? Should the interests of the individual be subordinated to the best interests of society? Plato's allegory contains conflicting conceptions of what is true, real, and good. Is it possible and desirable to have a pluralistic society in which there are alternative conceptions of how we should live? Or should the state, through the majority, try to make everyone conform to one vision of how our lives should be lived? How do we separate the sphere in which individuals have the freedom to do as they choose and the sphere in which society has legitimate interests in regulating an individual's actions?

1.3 ARGUMENT AND EVIDENCE: HOW DO I DECIDE WHAT TO BELIEVE?

In section 1.0 I said that philosophy is the search for fundamental beliefs that are justified. When you read what a philosopher has written, avoid the bottom-line syndrome. This problem involves simply agreeing or disagreeing with the author's conclusion without paying attention to whether the philosopher has provided good reasons for believing the conclusion. Responding in this way defeats a major goal of philosophy—the goal of seeing whether our beliefs or those of others are justified. For example, someone who believes in God (a theist) would agree with the conclusion of Thomas Aquinas's arguments (i.e., "There is a God"). But some theists do not think that Aquinas's arguments are strong. It is important to realize that in demonstrating that an argument is weak, we have not shown that its conclusion is false. We have merely shown that the reasons the author has given for the conclusion do not guarantee its truth. Nevertheless, if the only arguments that can be found to support a conclusion are weak, we really have no reason to suppose that the conclusion is true. Remember, evaluating philosophies is not like tasting foods. ("I like this. I don't like that.") Instead, it is an attempt to find objective reasons why we should or should not believe that a claim is true. In this section, I briefly cover some techniques for evaluating philosophical claims and arguments.

EVALUATING PHILOSOPHICAL CLAIMS AND THEORIES

In order to evaluate and choose between competing philosophical claims and theories, philosophers have agreed on a number of criteria, or tests. We will consider the six most common ones. I have formulated each criterion so that it contains a keyword that begins with the letter *c* in order to make the points easy to remember. The criteria are

(1) conceptual *clarity,* (2) *consistency,* (3) rational *coherence,* (4) *comprehensiveness,* (5) *compatibility* with well-established facts and theories, and (6) having the support of *compelling* arguments. We will briefly look at each one in turn.

Clarity

Conceptual clarity is the first test that a philosophy must pass. If the terms or concepts in which the philosophy is expressed are not clear, then we don't know precisely what claim is being put forth. Suppose someone says, "The only thing in life that has value is pleasure." We need to ask, What does the author mean by "pleasure"? Is the term referring only to physical sensations, or do intellectual pleasures count? If it makes me feel good to sacrifice my own needs for those of others, am I really pursuing pleasure?

Consistency

Consistency is the second test that a philosophy must pass. A philosophy cannot contain any contradictions. One way a philosophy flunks this test is through **logical inconsistency,** which consists in making two assertions that could not both be true under any possible circumstances. The most obvious case of this inconsistency would be any claim of the form, "A is true and not-A is true." For example, if I claim that God determines everything that happens in the world at the same time that I claim that humans have free will, I appear to have an inconsistency. The first claim implies that God determines what choices we make, but this claim seems to conflict with the claim that we freely make our own choices. The terms *determines* and *free will* would have to be defined differently than they normally are to avoid the inconsistency. A second kind of inconsistency is more subtle. It is called **self-referential inconsistency,** and it occurs if an assertion implies that it itself cannot be true, or cannot be known to be true, or should not be believed. My statement that "All opinions are false" implies that the opinion I just expressed is false. Similarly, my claim that "Only statements that can be scientifically proven should be believed" is a statement that cannot be scientifically proven.

logical inconsistency two assertions that could not both be true under any possible circumstances

self-referential inconsistency an assertion that implies that it itself cannot be true, cannot be known to be true, or should not be believed

Coherence

Rational coherence is a criterion that considers how well the various parts of a philosophy "hang together." The elements of a philosophy may not be explicitly contradictory, but they can still fail to fit together very well. A philosopher who believes that God acts in the world but who fails to explain how that belief fits together with the belief that nature runs according to universal physical laws has articulated a philosophy that lacks coherence. Similarly, philosopher René Descartes argued that humans are made up of a physical body and a nonextended, nonphysical mind. Although he believed that the two interacted, he failed to make clear how such different types of substances could causally influence one another. This gap in his theory earned him low points on the coherence criterion in the minds of many critics.

Comprehensiveness

We evaluate a philosophy positively if it makes sense out of a wide range of phenomena; we evaluate it negatively if it ignores significant areas of human experience or raises more questions than it answers. A philosophy that illuminates humanity's scientific, moral,

Relativity (1953) by M. C. Escher. In this "impossible" picture, the artist presents a scene composed of many incompatible planes. This could be viewed as a visual analogy of a philosophy which violates the criteria of consistency and rational coherence. This violation occurs when the elements of a philosopher's theory either contradict each other or do not fit together in a coherent way.

aesthetic, and religious experience is better than one that explains only science but ignores the rest of human experience. To take a more specific example, a philosopher who claims that all knowledge is based on sensory data but who fails to explain how we can have mathematical knowledge or moral knowledge falls short on this criterion. Similarly, a philosopher who claims that all morality is derived from the Ten Commandments but who fails to explain how some cultures have developed similar moral principles even if they never heard of these commandments fails in terms of comprehensiveness.

Compatibility

Compatibility with well-established facts and theories is important because a good theory (in philosophy or science) is one that increases our understanding by unifying our knowledge. Hence, a theory that flies in the face of the rest of our understanding of the world may require us to lose more than we gain. For example, a philosophical theory about the mind should fit with the well-established findings of biology and psychology. There are, however, exceptions to this rule. Throughout history, well-argued theories in philosophy and science have sometimes required us to violate common sense and abandon centuries-old beliefs, resulting in new knowledge. Nevertheless, we should do so only when the new theory is better than its competitors and promises to replace our current beliefs with an increase in understanding.

Compelling Arguments

The final criterion for evaluating philosophical claims and positions is that they must have the support of compelling arguments. Philosophy is more than an intellectual cafeteria where we pick and choose what we like. Philosophers are making claims about what is true, what is real, and what is morally good. The claims that different philosophers make often conflict with each other. Hence, they cannot all be true. As you read through the chapters of this book, you will have to decide which of the many conflicting claims are worthy of your belief. Even if a philosophy can pass on the first five criteria, you do not have sufficient grounds for accepting it. You must look at what reasons the philosopher has provided or what further reasons you yourself can find for being convinced of the truth of the position you are considering. An argument attempts to show that from certain true (or plausible) statements, the claim under consideration either necessarily follows or is highly probable. The next section covers the basics of the nature of arguments to get you thinking about this issue. I cover this topic in more detail in the appendix in the back of the book, where I survey various argument forms and discuss which ones are logically compelling and which ones are not.

THE NATURE OF ARGUMENTS

argument a set of statements in which one or more of the statements attempt to provide reasons or evidence for the truth of another statement

premise a statement in an argument that serves to provide evidence for the truth of a claim

conclusion the statement in an argument that the premises are claimed to support or imply

premise indicators terms that usually indicate that a premise will follow

conclusion indicators terms that usually indicate that a conclusion will follow

Philosophers attempt to establish the truth of their claims by means of arguments. But the word *argument* has two different meanings in everyday discourse. Suppose that two students were discussing whether there is a God, and they began shouting at each other, saying, "Yes there is," "No there isn't," "Yes there is," "No there isn't." If the exchange began to be quite heated, we might say that they were having an argument. In this context, *argument* would mean "a contentious dispute." However, this definition is not what philosophers mean by argument. In philosophy, an **argument** is a set of statements in which one or more of the statements attempt to provide reasons or evidence for the truth of another statement. A **premise** is a statement in an argument that serves to provide evidence for the truth of a claim. A **conclusion** is the statement in an argument that the premises are claimed to support or imply.

An important step in analyzing an argument is deciding which statements are the premises and which is the conclusion. Often the conclusion is the last statement in a passage. However, an author may place the conclusion first or even in the middle. Using common sense and grasping the author's intentions are the best ways to figure out the elements of a particular argument. Key terms are often used to indicate which statements are premises and which are conclusions. **Premise indicators** are terms that usually indicate that a premise will follow. Typical examples of premise indicators are *since, because, for, given that.* **Conclusion indicators** are terms that usually indicate that a conclusion will follow. Typical examples of conclusion indicators are *therefore, so, hence, thus, consequently.*

When it comes to determining whether an argument is acceptable, we can get some tips from the field of architecture. In the late Middle Ages, cathedral architects were obsessed with the goal of designing each successive cathedral to reach higher into the skies than the previous ones. The crowning glory of the architects' craft was thought to be the Beauvais Cathedral in France, whose ceiling rose to a height of 157 feet. This competition to break architectural records came to a sudden halt in 1284, however, when the main structural arches of Beauvais collapsed, unable to bear the weight that had been imposed on them.

Recently, I visited a college campus in which the focal point was a six-story administrative building. The outside walls were made from a newly invented composite material containing concrete and stone that had been formed into huge panels. Unfortunately, the new material did not hold up and large chunks of the stone slabs began falling off the building. After hundreds of thousands of dollars were spent in vain attempts to fix the problem, the building finally had to be torn down.

STOP AND THINK

So what does architecture and building construction have to do with philosophy? Think of the ways in which constructing a building and constructing a philosophical position or argument are similar. Consider what is necessary for a building to be solid and well designed. Compare that with what is necessary for an argument to be solid and well designed. Think about the ways that the buildings mentioned in the text failed and the ways in which a philosophical argument can fail. Can you think of any further analogies or connections between buildings and philosophy?

The two examples of the failed buildings are not alike. In the case of the Beauvais Cathedral there was nothing wrong with the materials used; they were the solid blocks of stone used in all cathedrals. The problem was a structural one. The arches of the building were not designed to support the weight of the ceiling. Similarly, a philosophical argument can fail because of structural defects. These defects occur when the form of the argument is such that the premises do not provide adequate support for the conclusion. In the case of the contemporary college building, the architect's design of the skeletal structure of the building was okay but the materials that were attached to it were faulty. The concrete slabs cracked, fell apart, and disintegrated. Similarly, an argument can be defective if the premises are known to be false or are, at least, implausible.

Here is an example of an argument in which the form is structurally flawed even though the premises are true (nothing is wrong with the materials composing the argument):

1. If Ronald Reagan was a U.S. president, then he was famous.
2. Ronald Reagan was famous.
3. Therefore, Ronald Reagan was a U.S. president.

I think that your logical intuitions will tell you that even though both premises are true and the conclusion is true, the conclusion does not logically follow from the premises. This lack of logic can be shown by the fact that in 1960 both premises were true but the conclusion was false, because Ronald Reagan was famous for being a movie star and not a president. Hence, even though the conclusion happens to be true, it does not logically follow from the premises.

In the next example, the form of the argument is a good one, but the premises are false (the materials that fill out the form are faulty):

1. If President George Washington was a horse, then he had five legs.
2. President George Washington was a horse.
3. Therefore, President George Washington had five legs.

In this case, *if* the premises were true, the conclusion would have to be true. In other words, the conclusion logically follows from the premises. The problem, of course, is that this argument starts from false premises.

These examples provide us with two basic questions to ask about an argument: (1) If the premises were true, would they provide adequate logical support for the conclusion? and (2) Are the premises true (or at least plausible)? The answer to the first question concerns **logic,** the study of methods for evaluating arguments and reasoning. Any standard textbook in logic will provide many techniques for determining how strongly the premises support the conclusion, but in this chapter I can only provide a few guidelines. A rather simple way to approach the question is to ask yourself, How easy would it be to imagine that all the premises were true at the same time the conclusion was false? If there are many ways to imagine that the premises were true and the conclusion false, this finding may indicate that the truth of the premises does not provide strong support for the truth of the conclusion. No single technique exists for answering the second question. Basically, you have to decide what sort of claim is being made in each premise and then decide what sort of evidence or sources of information would help in checking the truth of each premise.

Several different kinds of arguments can be distinguished by the different ways that their premises support their conclusion. A **deductive argument** is one in which the author claims that the conclusion necessarily follows from the premises. Proofs in geometry and in other areas of mathematics would be one kind of deductive argument. If the author does not claim that the conclusion necessarily follows from the premises but claims merely that the premises make the conclusion highly probable, we say that it is an **inductive argument.** Most of science is based on inductive arguments. For example, before a pharmaceutical drug is released on the market, it is tested extensively. From these tests on a sample group of patients, it may be concluded that the drug is safe for use. Of course, there is no guarantee that some dangerous side effects have not been discovered yet. However, adequate testing provides a strong inductive argument that the drug is safe.

A deductive argument that lives up to its author's claim that the conclusion follows necessarily from the premises is said to be valid. In other words, a **valid argument** is an argument in which it is impossible for the premises to be true and the conclusion false. Another way of putting this is to say that in a valid argument, *if* the premises are true, the conclusion *must* be true. Notice that the definition does not say that a valid argument will always have true premises. Furthermore, a true conclusion does not indicate that the argument is valid. The truth of the conclusion must logically follow from the premises. An argument whose author claims that it provides this sort of support for its conclusion but fails to do so is **invalid.** Finally, a valid argument with true premises is a **sound argument.** In this case, the truth of the conclusion would be absolutely certain.

An inductive argument that lives up to its author's claim that the premises make the conclusion highly probable is a **strong argument.** A strong argument that actually does have true premises is a **cogent argument.** A cogent argument does not absolutely guarantee the conclusion (as does a sound argument), but it does give us good reasons for believing the conclusion.

A good argument (whether it is a valid deductive argument or a strong inductive argument) establishes a "price" for rejecting the conclusion. In other words, if you believe the premises then you should believe the conclusion because it either logically follows from the premises or the premises show that it is most probably true. Hence, if you reject the conclusion of a logical argument, you can do so only by rejecting one or more of the premises. But in a good argument, it would be implausible to reject the premises.

logic the study of methods for evaluating arguments and reasoning

deductive argument an argument in which it is claimed that the conclusion necessarily follows from the premises

inductive argument an argument in which it is claimed that the premises make the conclusion highly probable

valid argument an argument in which it is impossible for the premises to be true and the conclusion false

invalid argument an argument in which the truth of the conclusion fails to logically follow from the premises

sound argument a valid argument with true premises

strong argument an inductive argument in which true premises would make the conclusion highly probable

cogent argument a strong argument that has true premises

Another type of reasoning commonly used in philosophy (as well as science) is an **inference to the best explanation.** (This sort of reasoning is sometimes called abduction.) Unlike deductive and inductive arguments, an inference to the best explanation does not try to directly prove the truth of a theory; it tries to show that the theory is superior to all its competitors and that it is therefore the one most likely to be true. This way of showing that a particular theory is the best one makes use of the five criteria discussed thus far. An inference to the best explanation has the following form:

1. There is a collection of data that needs an explanation.
2. A theory is proposed that offers an explanation of the data.
3. This theory offers the best explanation of all known alternatives.
4. Therefore, until a better explanation is proposed, it is rational to believe this theory.

inference to the best explanation a form of reasoning that tries to show that a particular theory is superior to all its competitors and that it is therefore the one most likely to be true; sometimes called abduction

This method of reasoning can best be illustrated by an example from science. In the 1930s, scientists were puzzled by a type of event, known as beta decay, in which an atom disintegrates into its parts. The problem was that a measurable sum of energy seemed to disappear into thin air in the process, thus violating the law of conservation of energy, a sacred principle in physics. Wolfgang Pauli, a 21-year-old physicist, proposed that the missing energy could be accounted for by supposing that an unobserved particle was included with the other particles that were flung off from the atom. The problem was that to balance the numbers in the equations, this unknown particle had to have no electric charge, its mass had to be nearly zero or equal to zero, and besides being extremely small, it had to travel near the speed of light. In short, the mystery particle (which came to be called the neutrino) had to be completely incapable of being observed.

Physicists were reluctant to accept the existence of the neutrino because of the criterion of compatibility. It was incompatible with the long and firmly held belief that all entities accepted by science had to be observed. On the other hand, this theory not only was compatible with the conservation of energy but saved this more fundamental principle from being abandoned. Furthermore, in terms of the other criteria, the neutrino theory was clear and consistent, it brought coherence by preserving the closely knit fabric of physics, and it scored high on comprehensiveness because it eventually explained other events besides beta decay. Almost 30 years later, physicists designed a very elaborate and expensive experiment whose results suggested that they could detect the effects of a neutrino interacting with another particle. However, no matter how useful the neutrino postulate is and how many events it explains, we will never directly observe one. The only reason scientists believe in it is because it makes sense out of so many other events that we believe and can observe.

The evidence and explanations that are offered in science (as in the case of the neutrino) can provide very helpful models for understanding the explanations of philosophical theories. First, scientists cannot always directly observe the entities or events postulated by their theories (neutrinos, quarks, black holes, the big bang). Similarly, in philosophy we cannot directly observe with our senses the presence or absence of God, free will, moral values, or justice. Second, inferences to the best explanation in science and philosophy are evaluated using the six criteria that we have discussed in this chapter and can be used to justify belief in either neutrinos or in the claims made by philosophers. For example, various philosophers attempt to justify claims such as the following: There is a God, mental events are really brain events, humans have free will, the morality of an action is determined by the consequences. Even though the defense of such claims cannot take the form of a confirming observation, philosophers can try to show that these theories make the best sense of what we do know and observe.

AN EXAMPLE OF ARGUMENT ANALYSIS

To make this discussion of arguments more concrete, let's analyze an actual philosophical argument. We will examine an argument for ethical egoism. (Ethical egoism will be discussed in more detail in section 5.2.) Ethical egoists claim that it is not wrong to be selfish. In fact, they think that it is the only reasonable and moral way to live. Putting it more formally, ethical egoism is the claim that (a) if a person has a moral obligation to perform an action, it is an action that will maximize that person's own self-interest and (b) if an action will maximize a person's own self-interest then that person has a moral obligation to perform that action. Here is an argument that is sometimes used to defend part (a) of the ethical egoist's position.

1. If a person has a moral obligation to perform an action, he or she must be able to do it,
2. If a person is able to do an action, that action will follow the laws of human motivation.
3. So, if a person has a moral obligation to perform an action, that action will follow the laws of human motivation.
4. If an action follows the laws of human motivation, it is an action that the person does to maximize his or her own self-interest.
5. Therefore, if a person has a moral obligation to perform an action, it is an action that will maximize that person's own self-interest.

First, let's analyze the form of the argument. In other words, if the premises were true, how strongly would they support the conclusion? Premises 1 and 2 logically imply statement 3. Together they constitute a valid argument form called hypothetical syllogism (discussed in the appendix). Statements 3 and 4 logically imply statement 5. They also form a valid argument, for they have the form of a hypothetical syllogism. Now we know the argument is valid. But are the premises true? Premise 1 is a principle that most people accept. I cannot be morally obligated to do something that it is impossible for me to do. Premise 2 states that for it to be possible for me to perform an action, it must be psychologically possible for me to do it (the action must follow the laws of human motivation). For example, normal people cannot desire to maliciously harm someone whom they genuinely love. That response would violate human nature. So far, the premises we have examined seem plausible. Statement 3 logically follows from the first two premises and becomes a premise that helps support statement 5, the final conclusion.

The really controversial premise is number 4. It states that any action we choose to perform is motivated by self-interest. Is that true? Statement 4 is a theory about human motivation known as psychological egoism (also discussed in section 5.2). We can use some of our other criteria to evaluate the plausibility of this premise. How does it stand with respect to *comprehensiveness?* Does it ignore any areas of human experience? It seems to ignore the feelings of benevolence that people often have toward others. For the same reason, statement 4 has problems with respect to the criterion of *compatibility* with well-established facts. Examples of altruistic behavior (actions that serve the needs of others and not one's own self-interest) seem to be abundant. Of course, the psychological egoist could respond that when people serve the needs of others (e.g., build a home for the poor or offer a friend the last piece of pie), they are really serving their own interests. Maybe they are behaving unselfishly to feel good about themselves or they are trying to avoid the pain of guilt. But by collapsing the distinction between selfish behavior and unselfish behavior and saying that all behavior is selfish, aren't the psychological egoists muddying the meaning of these terms? In other words, it seems as though they are violating the principle of *conceptual clarity.*

Finally, apart from this argument, ethical egoists run into the problem of *self-referential inconsistency*. If I am an ethical egoist, I think that my only obligation is to serve my interests. But I am also promoting the philosophy that you should serve only your own interests. However, sometimes your interests will conflict with my interests. This would be the case, for example, if we are both competing for the same elected office. How can I embrace a philosophy that says I should seek only to promote my interests at the same time I am trying to convince you that you have an obligation to do what will be contrary to my interests?

You should be clear that what I have accomplished is to show that this particular argument fails to support ethical egoism. I have done this by showing that there are problems with the claim in premise 4 about human motivation (psychological egoism). An ethical egoist could respond by trying to defend premise 4 against my objections. However, there are other arguments in support of ethical egoism that do not make use of this premise. Hence, those who want to show that ethical egoism is implausible have to show that every argument that is offered in its support is likewise inadequate. Another strategy is to develop an argument that directly refutes ethical egoism. As you go through each position and argument in this book, try to follow the procedure in this example. Think of ways in which each position and argument could be criticized and then think of possible replies to the criticisms.

THE GOAL OF PHILOSOPHY

In conclusion, philosophy is not simply the sharing of personal opinions. It is the attempt to find reasons for accepting, rejecting, or modifying our own opinions and those of others. The goal of philosophical reflection is not simply to have emotionally satisfying beliefs, but the goal is to have beliefs that are true. In other words, we want beliefs that will provide us with the best possible understanding of ourselves and of our world so that we can live our lives effectively. The way in which we arrive at this understanding is through constructing and analyzing arguments for and against the various alternatives. Consequently, the philosophy which has the best arguments in its support is the one that deserves to be embraced. Although philosophical questions are difficult to answer and the proposed answers are likely to always be controversial, there are resources for coming to your own informed conclusions about them. The six criteria for evaluating philosophical claims and theories provided in this section will give you some tools for making your own assessment of which ideas are most likely to be true.

While this book ends on the last page and a philosophy course ends on the last day of the semester, thinking philosophically and responsibly is a lifelong task. The good news is that, as with any skill, the more you practice reading, thinking, writing, and discussing philosophy the better you will become at being a philosopher. That is why this book gives you so many opportunities to interact with the ideas and to do what philosophers do. As you jump into the remaining chapters of this book, keep one thing in mind: philosophy is hard, but the labor involved in a personal philosophical journey is always rewarded by the realization that you have taken charge of your life and are navigating your own course.

REVIEW FOR CHAPTER 1

Philosophers

1.0 Overview of the Journey
Søren Kierkegaard
Pythagoras
Socrates

1.1 Socrates and the Search for Wisdom
Thrasymachus
Sophists

Concepts

1.0 Overview of the Journey
philosophy

wisdom

self-understanding

understanding the meaning of our basic concepts

rational justification of belief

logic

epistemology

metaphysics

philosophy of religion

ethics

political philosophy

1.1 Socrates and the Search for Wisdom

Socrates as the midwife of ideas

Socrates' wisdom

Socrates as a gadfly

the Socratic method

reductio ad absurdum argument

"the unexamined life is not worth living"

"know thyself"

Socrates' view of the soul

skepticism

"a good person cannot be harmed by others"

1.2 Plato's Allegory of the Cave

the plight of the prisoners

the significance of the shadows

what the freed prisoner discovered

Plato's view of enlightenment

1.3 Argument and Evidence: How Do I Decide What to Believe?

six criteria for evaluating claims and theories

conceptual clarity

consistency

logical inconsistency

self-referential inconsistency

rational coherence

comprehensiveness

compatibility with well-established facts and theories

support of compelling arguments

argument (in philosophy)

premises

conclusion

premise indicators

conclusion indicators

deductive argument

inductive argument

valid and invalid

sound argument

strong argument

cogent argument

inference to the best explanation

SUGGESTIONS FOR FURTHER READING

General Works on Philosophy

Audi, Robert. *The Cambridge Dictionary of Philosophy.* Cambridge: Cambridge University Press, 1995. A very helpful summary of the central topics in philosophy.

Blackburn, Simon. *The Oxford Dictionary of Philosophy.* Oxford: Oxford University Press, 1996. A concise and readable reference work.

Copleston, F. C. *History of Philosophy.* 9 vols. New York: Doubleday, Image, 1946–1974. A comprehensive coverage of the history of philosophy. This series is a classic.

Craig, Edward, ed. *Routledge Encyclopedia of Philosophy.* 10 vols. London and New York: Routledge, 1998. The latest and most complete reference work on all philosophical topics.

Edwards, Paul, ed. *Encyclopedia of Philosophy.* 8 vols. New York: Macmillan, 1967. A good place to start to research a philosopher or topic. For current information, see Donald M. Borcher, ed., *The Encyclopedia of Philosophy Supplement* (New York: Simon & Schuster Macmillan, 1996).

Gaarder, Jostein. *Sophie's World: A Novel about the History of Philosophy.* Translated by Paulette Møller. New York: Berkley Books, 1994. Popular novel about a young girl who finds a piece of paper on which two questions are written: Who are you? and Where did the world come from? Her search for the answers takes her on a journey through the world of philosophy.

Kolak, Daniel. *The Mayfield Anthology of Western Philosophy.* Mountain View, Calif.: Mayfield, 1998. One hundred thirteen of the most important selections by 52 of the major philosophers of all time.

Lawhead, William F. *The Voyage of Discovery: A Historical Introduction to Philosophy.* 3d ed. Belmont, Calif.: Wadsworth, 2007. A chronological survey of philosophy by the author of this text.

Nagel, Thomas. *What Does It All Mean? A Very Short Introduction to Philosophy.* Oxford: Oxford University Press, 1987. A very readable, short introduction to philosophy.

Palmer, Donald. *Does the Center Hold? An Introduction to Western Philosophy.* 3d ed. New York: McGraw-Hill, 1996. An amusing but informative coverage of the major philosophical topics, complete with the author's own philosophical cartoons.

———. *Looking at Philosophy: The Unbearable Heaviness of Philosophy Made Lighter.* 4th ed. New York:

McGraw-Hill, 2006. A breezy, historical survey of the major philosophers with more than 350 of the author's cartoons.

Pojman, Louis. *Classics of Philosophy.* Oxford: Oxford University Press, 1998. More than 75 works (many of them complete) by the major philosophers.

Waithe, Mary Ellen, ed. *A History of Women Philosophers.* 4 vols. Dordrecht: Martinus Nijhoff/Kluwer Press, 1987, 1989, 1991, 1995. Covers women philosophers from ancient times to the 20th century.

Woodhouse, Mark. *A Preface to Philosophy.* 5th ed. Belmont, Calif.: Wadsworth, 1994. A practical handbook on reading, writing, and thinking about philosophy.

Socrates

Guthrie, W. K. C. *Socrates.* Cambridge: Cambridge University Press, 1971. A very clear introduction to the life and teachings of Socrates.

Lawhead, William. "The Sophists and Socrates." Chap. 3 in *The Voyage of Discovery: A Historical Introduction to Philosophy,* 3d ed. Belmont, Calif.: Wadsworth, 2007. An overview of Socrates and the Sophists.

Plato. *Apology, Euthyphro, Crito, Protagoras, Gorgias, Republic,* and *Phaedo.* Dialogues that provide Plato's depiction of the style and teachings of Socrates. They are available in numerous inexpensive paperback translations.

Stone, I. F. *The Trial of Socrates.* New York: Doubleday, Anchor Books, 1988. A national bestseller that provides useful information about Socrates and the Athenian culture. Stone tends to be more critical than most concerning Socrates' defense.

Vlastos, Gregory. *Socrates: Ironist and Moral Philosopher.* Ithaca, N.Y.: Cornell University Press, 1991. A readable book by a leading Socrates scholar.

Arguments and Critical Reasoning

Engle, S. Morris. *With Good Reason: An Introduction to Informal Fallacies.* 5th ed. New York: St. Martin's Press, 1994. A very good coverage of the informal fallacies.

Hurley, Patrick. *A Concise Introduction to Logic.* 6th ed. Belmont, Calif.: Wadsworth, 1997. One of the best traditional introductions to logic.

Layman, C. Stephen. *The Power of Logic.* 3d ed. New York: McGraw-Hill, 2005. Another very good introduction to logic.

Moore, Brooke, and Richard Parker. *Critical Thinking.* 8th ed. New York: McGraw-Hill, 2007. A very readable and entertaining introduction to logic and critical thinking.

Teays, Wanda. *Second Thoughts: Critical Thinking for a Diverse Society.* 3d ed. New York: McGraw-Hill, 2006. An introduction to critical thinking with an emphasis on current social issues and the media.

Tidman, Paul, and Howard Kahane. *Logic and Philosophy: A Modern Introduction.* 8th ed. Belmont, Calif.: Wadsworth, 1999. A readable but slightly more advanced coverage of basic logic.

NOTES

1. Søren Kierkegaard, *Concluding Unscientific Postscript,* trans. David F. Swenson and Walter Lowrie (Princeton: Princeton University Press, 1941), pp. 165–66.

2. I am grateful to David Schlafer, my former colleague, for some of the examples used in this thought experiment.

3. Maurice Merleau-Ponty, "Everywhere and Nowhere," in *Signs,* trans. Richard C. McCleary (Evanston, Ill.: Northwestern University Press, 1964), p. 128.

4. E. Fowler, *The New York Times Career Planner* (New York: Random House, 1987).

5. Quoted by T. K. Abbott in "Memoir of Kant," in *Kant's Critique of Practical Reason and Other Works on the Theory of Ethics,* trans. T. K. Abbott (London: Longmans, 1st ed. 1879; 6th ed., 1909; photo reprint, 1954), p. xxxiii (page citation is to the 1954 reprint).

6. Plato, *Phaedo* 118, in *The Dialogues of Plato,* 3d ed., rev., 5 vols., trans. Benjamin Jowett (New York: Oxford University Press, 1892).

7. Plato, *Apology* 20e–23a, 29d–31c, 39a–b, 41c–d, 42, in *The Dialogues of Plato.* Minor changes have been made to the punctuation and a few words have been changed for greater readability in this classic 19th-century translation.

8. Plato, *Republic* 338b–343a, in *The Dialogues of Plato.* Minor changes have been made in the translation.

9. Gregory Vlastos, "Introduction: The Paradox of Socrates," in *The Philosophy of Socrates,* ed. Gregory Vlastos (Garden City, N.Y.: Anchor Books, Doubleday, 1971), pp. 5–6.

10. Plato, *The Republic,* Bk. 7, §§14–18, in *The Dialogues of Plato,* vol. 1, trans. Benjamin Jowett (Oxford: Oxford University Press, 1920; reprinted, New York: Random House, 1937), pp. 773–77. Some changes have been made to the punctuation and wording to make the text more readable to a modern reader.

Michael Pole, *Tree and Root System*, 2002

CHAPTER 2

THE SEARCH FOR KNOWLEDGE

 CHAPTER OBJECTIVES

On completion of this chapter, you should be able to

1. Explain what epistemology is.
2. Identify the major arguments for skepticism.
3. Identify three anchor points of rationalism and indicate how these are illustrated in the thought of Socrates, Plato, and Descartes.
4. Identify three anchor points of empiricism and relate these to the views of Locke, Berkeley, and Hume.
5. Show how Kant's constructivist epistemology steers a middle course between rationalism and empiricism.
6. Discuss and critique several varieties of epistemic relativism, especially Nietzsche's radical perspectivism.
7. Explain how pragmatism introduces a significantly new perspective into traditional epistemology.
8. Describe some common criticisms of traditional epistemology made by feminists.
9. Describe the current issues in the philosophy of science.

SCOUTING THE TERRITORY: *What Can I Know?*

In a science fiction story, philosopher Jonathan Harrison tells of a famous neurologist, Dr. Smythson, who was pushing forward the frontiers of science in the year A.D. 2167.[1] Smythson was presented with the case of a newly born infant whose brain was normal but whose body was afflicted with so many problems that it was on the verge of ceasing to function. In a desperate attempt to preserve the child before his body shut down completely, the scientist separated the brain and its accompanying sensory nerves from the rest of the body. He then kept the brain alive by attaching it to a machine that replaced the abandoned body's support system.

So that his patient (now a conscious brain attached to a machine) could continue his cognitive development, Dr. Smythson used an electrical hallucination machine to stimulate the sensory nerves, which caused the brain to experience sights, sounds, smells, tastes, and tactile sensations. Hence, through this computer-controlled, electrical stimulation of the brain, Smythson created a virtual reality for the patient (now named Ludwig) that was indistinguishable from the experiences of reality you and I enjoy. By means of another electrical contraption, the doctor was able to read Ludwig's brain waves and monitor the patient's cognitive and emotional life. Eventually, by learning from his simulated world produced by the simulated bodily sensations (which Ludwig assumed was the real world and a real, physical body), Ludwig's intellectual development was equivalent to that of a well-educated and experienced adult.

To further enrich Ludwig's intellect, Dr. Smythson stimulated Ludwig's optic nerve with the contents of great works in philosophy. Ludwig studied the works of the skeptics who argued that, because we can only know the immediate contents of our own, internal, conscious experience, we cannot know whether there is a world external to our experience. Ludwig was shaken by this argument and worried about the possibility that his life was a dream from which he might someday awake and discover that all the objects and people he had previously experienced had been illusions. Upon thinking the argument through, however, he found it impossible to doubt that this solid, hard chair he now sat on was not real. (At this point the doctor was giving Ludwig's brain the same sorts of sensations you and I have when sitting on a chair.) Furthermore, Ludwig concluded that his two hands were certainly real, material objects (as the machine fed him simulated experiences comparable to that of holding up one's hands).

During this time period, Ludwig also read about researchers who discovered that the brain could be electrically stimulated such that the patient experienced artificial sensations that appeared to be coming from the body's contact with the external world. However, Ludwig rejected the skeptical possibility that one's entire experience of the world could be of this sort. At this point, although Ludwig considered these skeptical possibilities to be only fictional or hypothetical scenarios (not realizing that they described his actual lot in life), Dr. Smythson ceased allowing Ludwig to experience books that left him preoccupied with worries about illusion and reality.

The important point about this rather bizarre story is that it is logically possible that an incident like this could happen, even though at this point in our scientific research it is not yet medically possible to give someone the experience of an illusory world (although we do have the ability to stimulate the brain and produce a limited set of artificially created sensations). The theoretical possibility of someone being a brain in a vat and experiencing a virtual reality serves to raise the question of how we know that our experiences give us knowledge about the external world. However, we do not have to rely on the unusual scenario of this story to consider the possibility that all our knowledge could be mistaken. Stop and reflect on the difficulties you have had in determining what is true or false, reality or illusion within your experience.

 STOP AND THINK

Think about a time when you were absolutely convinced that something was true, only to find out later that you were wrong. If this situation has happened to you, how do you know that *anytime* you are certain of something, you are not similarly mistaken in thinking it is true when it is not?

Poor Ludwig was convinced that he was directly experiencing the external world when, in fact, he was simply a brain who was having illusory but seemingly real experiences of books, chairs, hands, sunsets, and so on. The problem is that, like Ludwig, you cannot jump outside your experience to compare its contents with the world outside. Everything you know about what exists outside your experience is mediated by means of your experiences. Because you have frequently found that your experiences can be wrong, how can you be sure they are ever right? The following thought experiment will explore the notions of knowledge, certainty, and justification.

THOUGHT EXPERIMENT: *Knowledge, Certainty, Justification*

1. Place a quarter on the table. Look at it from above. It will look like a circular patch of silver. Now look at it from an angle. You will see an elliptical silver image in your visual field. If you look at its edge straight on, it will appear to be a silver line. Now look at it from across the room. The item in your visual field will be a very small silver speck. Presumably, the quarter is not constantly changing its shape and size. But the image present to your eyes is changing its shape and size. It follows that what you see cannot be the quarter itself but merely a changing image of the quarter. Can we say therefore that the real quarter has a constant shape and size that is causing the changing images in your experience? But how can we make such a statement, because we can never jump outside our experience to see the real quarter? How do we know that there is any relationship between what appears within experience and what lies outside of it?

2. Write down five statements that you believe are true. (Try to vary the subject matter of these items.) In terms of the relative degree of certainty you have about these statements compared to one another, rank these statements from the most certain to the least certain. Which three of these statements have the highest degree of certainty for you? Why these three? For the remaining two statements, try to imagine conditions or new information that would raise doubts about their truth. How plausible are these possible doubts? Among the three statements that

(continued . . .)

(. . . continued)

have the highest degree of certainty, which one would you be least likely to doubt? Why? Try to formulate some general principles or criteria that you use in deciding whether the truth of a statement is more or less certain.

3. Is it important that we be able to justify our beliefs? What would be the problem with having beliefs that we believe are true but that we could not justify? Is it important to provide evidence for our beliefs to ourselves or only to others? Are there any problems with attempting to justify all our beliefs?

CHARTING THE TERRAIN OF KNOWLEDGE: *What Are the Issues?*

The questions raised in this thought experiment concern the nature and possibility of knowledge and truth as well as the justification of our beliefs. The area of philosophy that deals with questions concerning knowledge and that considers various theories of knowledge is called **epistemology.** The Greek word *episteme* means "knowledge" and *logos* means "rational discourse." Hence, epistemology is the philosophy of knowledge.

epistemology the area of philosophy that deals with questions concerning knowledge and that considers various theories of knowledge.

There are several kinds of knowledge. Think about the different kinds of knowledge that are expressed in these three statements: (1) "I know the president of this university as a personal friend," (2) "I know how to play the piano," or (3) "I know that Chicago is in Illinois." The third statement is an example of *propositional knowledge,* or "knowing that."

Here, the object of knowledge is the truth of some proposition or statement of fact. This sort of knowledge does not require direct acquaintance with what is being discussed, nor does it directly involve acquiring a skill. Although some epistemologists have concerned themselves with the first two kinds of knowledge, most theories of knowledge focus on propositional knowledge. Hence, our primary interest here concerns knowledge that can be stated in propositions.

Having limited our discussion to a particular kind of knowledge—propositional knowledge—we may now ask, What are the *necessary* and *sufficient* conditions for having this sort of knowledge? Perhaps the following thought experiment will help guide your intuitions on this matter.

THOUGHT EXPERIMENT: *Necessary and Sufficient Conditions for Knowledge*

Consider the following scenarios. In each case decide why it would or would not be correct to say that "Ernest *knows* that Brenda's birthday is today."

1. (a) Ernest believes that his friend Brenda's birthday is today.
   (b) Brenda's birthday really is next week.

2. (a) Ernest has no opinion about the date of Brenda's birthday.
   (b) Brenda's birthday is today.

(continued . . .)

(. . . continued)

3. (a) Ernest randomly throws a dart at the calendar while shouting "Brenda," and the dart lands on today's date.
   (b) Based on this chance result, Ernest decides that today is Brenda's birthday.
   (c) As a matter of fact, today is Brenda's birthday.

4. (a) Ernest glances at Brenda's driver's license and notices that today is her birthday.
   (b) Ernest has no reason to believe that the date on Brenda's license is inaccurate.
   (c) Based on these considerations, Ernest believes that today is Brenda's birthday.
   (d) It is true that today is Brenda's birthday.

THE DEFINITION OF KNOWLEDGE

What did you decide about the four scenarios in the thought experiment? Going as far back as Plato, philosophers have traditionally defined knowledge as *true justified belief.* If we accept this analysis, here is what we would have to say about the four scenarios. In case 1, Ernest could not be said to have knowledge because his belief is false. There is no such thing as false knowledge. However, we can have a false belief and mistakenly think we have knowledge. That is why, when we find out our mistake, we say, "I thought I knew the answer to the question, but I guess I didn't." In case 2, Ernest obviously does not have knowledge concerning Brenda's birthday because he has no beliefs about it whatsoever.

Case 3 is different from the first two because Ernest believes today is Brenda's birthday and his belief happens to be true. Nevertheless, it would be reasonable to say that he doesn't really *know* this fact because his belief, though true, is not justified. Beliefs that are based on a lucky guess or a happenstance throw of a dart seem to fall short of what is required to have knowledge. This conclusion lacks some sort of reasons or justification that would support his belief. The method Ernest used to form his belief in case 3 could just as easily have led him to a false belief. Case 4 has all the necessary and sufficient conditions for knowledge. Ernest has a true, justified belief concerning Brenda's birth date. As we will see in later sections, philosophers disagree about what counts as justification. Is absolute certainty required for justification? Is the impossibility of error? Or is a justified belief merely a highly probable belief that is beyond any reasonable doubts? In recent years, some philosophers have questioned this definition of knowledge. Nevertheless, while quibbling over the details, most philosophers throughout history have agreed that knowledge is true justified belief. Because the notion of *certainty* has played such a large role in epistemology, the following "Stop and Think" box will ask you to assess its importance.

STOP AND THINK

How important is it to be absolutely certain of your fundamental beliefs? Is there a difference between having a psychological feeling of confidence in your beliefs and having objective certainty? Is it even possible to achieve absolute certainty about any of your beliefs? If you think certainty is possible, what sorts of beliefs can provide you with such certainty? Is the basis of this certainty something that could be convincing to someone other than you? Is a high degree of probability an adequate substitute for absolute certainty? Why?

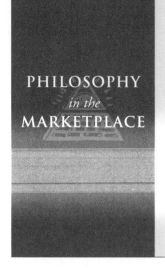

PHILOSOPHY
in the
MARKETPLACE

Ask five or more people the following question: Why do people believe what they do?[2] They can answer in terms of both their own, personal belief system or, more generally, what they think are the causes or reasons for most people's beliefs.

Write down their answers and later organize them under the following headings:

- Sociological reasons: One's beliefs are based on the influence of one's family, friends, or society.
- Psychological reasons: One's beliefs satisfy internal needs (for hope, meaning, purpose, identity, pleasure, and so on).
- Religious reasons: One's beliefs are based on a religious tradition, authority, revelation, or experience.
- Philosophical reasons: One's beliefs are based on logic, evidence, scientific facts, reasoning, sense experience, and so on.
- Other

Now evaluate each specific reason by asking, If this basis for belief is the only reason I could give myself for believing what I believe, would I be justified in continuing to hold this belief? Compare and discuss with several friends the answers you have gathered and your evaluations of them.

The Issue of Reason and Experience

One of the most important issues in a theory of knowledge is the relationship between reason and experience. Philosophers use a number of specialized terms to talk about this issue. The following terms will be useful in our discussions of some of the philosophical positions in this chapter.

A priori knowledge is knowledge that is justified independently of (or prior to) experience. What kinds of knowledge could be justified without any appeal to experience? Certainly, we can know the truth of definitions and logical truths apart from experience. Hence, definitions and logically necessary truths are examples of a priori knowledge. For example, "All unicorns are one-horned creatures" is true by definition. Similarly, the following statement is a sure bet: "Either my university's football team will win their next game or they won't." Even if they tie or the game is canceled, this would fulfill the "they won't win" part of the prediction. Hence, this statement expresses a logically necessary truth about the football team. These two statements are cases of a priori knowledge. Notice that in the particular examples of a priori knowledge I have chosen, they do not give us any real, factual information about the world. Even though the statement about unicorns is true, it does not tell us whether there are any unicorns in the world. Similarly, the football prediction does not tell us the actual outcome of the game. Experience of the world is required to know these things.

The second kind of knowledge is **a posteriori knowledge,** or knowledge that is based on (or posterior to) experience. Similarly, the adjective **empirical** refers to anything that is based on experience. Any claims based on experience purport to add new information to the subject. Hence, "Water freezes at 32 degrees Fahrenheit" and "Tadpoles become frogs" would be examples of a posteriori knowledge. We know the freezing point of water and the life cycle of tadpoles through experience. Thus far, most philosophers would agree on these points.

The difficult question now arises: Is there any a priori knowledge that does give us knowledge about the real world? What would that be like? It would be knowledge expressible in a statement such that (*a*) its truth is not determined solely by the meaning of its

---

a priori knowledge knowledge justified independently of, or prior to, experience

a posteriori knowledge knowledge based on, or posterior to, experience

empirical based on experience

terms and (*b*) it does provide information about the way the world is. Furthermore, since it is a priori, it would be knowledge that we could justify through reason, independently of experience. The question, then, is whether or not reason alone can tell us about the ultimate nature of reality. The philosophers discussed in this chapter will take different positions on this question.

Three Epistemological Questions

The previous "Philosophy in the Marketplace" survey probably demonstrated that even among nonphilosophers there is a wide range of opinions concerning how to justify our beliefs. As you read the rest of this chapter, try to see if some of your friends' answers match up with the views of any of the philosophers discussed. These different philosophies are attempts to answer basic questions about knowledge. Although an enormous number of philosophical problems concern knowledge, I am going to focus on three of the major problems. The philosophies I discuss in the remaining sections of this chapter are various attempts to answer the following three epistemological questions. (As you read these questions, you might consider whether you would answer each one with a yes or a no at this point in your understanding.)

1. Is it possible to have knowledge at all?
2. Does reason provide us with knowledge of the world independently of experience?
3. Does our knowledge represent reality as it really is?

CHOOSING A PATH: *What Are My Options Concerning Knowledge?*

Skepticism is the claim that we do *not* have knowledge. Most skeptics accept the traditional view that knowledge is true, justified belief, but go on from there to argue that it is impossible to have justified beliefs or that no one has provided any reasons to think that our beliefs are capable of being justified. Hence, the skeptics give a negative answer to the first epistemological question. Because skeptics think that knowledge is unattainable, they consider the remaining two questions to be irrelevant. The philosophers represented by the remaining positions think we *can* obtain knowledge, and hence, in contrast to the skeptic, they answer the first question in the affirmative. The disagreements among the nonskeptics concern the source and nature of knowledge.

skepticism the claim that we do not have knowledge

Rationalism claims that reason or the intellect is the primary source of our fundamental knowledge about reality. Nonrationalists agree that we can use reason to draw conclusions from the information provided by sense experience. However, what distinguishes the rationalists is that they claim that reason can give us knowledge *apart* from experience. For example, the rationalists point out that we can arrive at mathematical truths about circles or triangles without having to measure, experiment with, or experience circular or triangular objects. We do so by constructing rational, deductive proofs that lead to absolutely indubitable conclusions that are always universally true of the world outside our minds (a priori knowledge about the world). Obviously, the rationalists think the second question should be answered affirmatively.

rationalism the claim that reason or the intellect is the primary source of our fundamental knowledge about reality

Empiricism is the claim that sense experience is the sole source of our knowledge about the world. Empiricists insist that when we start life, the original equipment of our intellect is a tabula rasa, or blank tablet. Only through experience does that empty mind become filled with content. Various empiricists give different explanations of the nature of logical and mathematical truths. They are all agreed, however, that these truths are not already latent in the mind before we discover them and that there is no genuine a priori knowledge about the nature of reality. The empiricists would respond "No!" to the second

empiricism the claim that sense experience is the sole source of our knowledge about the world

epistemological question. With respect to question 3, both the rationalists and the empiricists think that our knowledge does represent reality as it really is.

Constructivism is used in this discussion to refer to the claim that knowledge is *neither* already in the mind *nor* passively received from experience, but that the mind *constructs* knowledge out of the materials of experience. Immanuel Kant, an 18th-century German philosopher, introduced this view. He was influenced by both the rationalists and the empiricists and attempted to reach a compromise between them. While Kant did not agree with the rationalists on everything, he did believe we can have a priori knowledge of the world as we experience it. Although Kant did not use this label, I call his position *constructivism* to capture his distinctive account of knowledge. One troubling consequence of his view was that because the mind imposes its own order on experience, we can never know reality as it is in itself. We can only know reality as it appears to us after it has been filtered and processed by our minds. Hence, Kant answers question 3 negatively. Nevertheless, because Kant thought our minds all have the same cognitive structure, he thought we are able to arrive at universal and objective knowledge *within* the boundaries of the human situation.

Epistemological relativism is the claim that there is no universal, objective knowledge of reality because all knowledge is relative to either the individual or his or her culture. In other words, the relativist believes that there is no one, true story about reality, but that there are many stories. Since we can no more jump outside our respective ways of viewing the world than we can our own skins, there is no way to say that a particular claim about reality is the only true one. It may seem that the relativist is denying knowledge the way the skeptic does. However, the relativists would insist that we *do* have knowledge but would deny that this knowledge is universal and objective. Knowledge is always knowledge *for* someone and is shaped by each knower's psychological, philosophical, historical, or cultural circumstances. Hence, while answering question 1 affirmatively, the relativist would respond with a no to the remaining two questions. There are many varieties of relativism as it has been defined here: Existentialism, pragmatism, and some forms of feminism are discussed in later sections to illustrate this epistemological outlook.

Table 2.1 presents the three epistemological questions just discussed and lists the answers provided by the five different positions.

The next exercise asks you to register your agreement or disagreement with 10 statements. In some cases, you may not be sure what you think; nevertheless, choose the response that you think seems to be the most correct.

constructivism the claim that knowledge is neither already in the mind nor passively received from experience but that the mind constructs knowledge out of the materials of experience.

epistemological relativism the claim that there is no universal, objective knowledge of reality because all knowledge is relative to either the individual or his or her culture

TABLE 2.1	*Three Epistemological Questions and Five Positions on Them*		
	Is Knowledge Possible?	Does Reason Provide Us with Knowledge of the World Independently of Experience?	Does Our Knowledge Represent Reality as It Really Is?
Skepticism	No	—	—
Rationalism	Yes	Yes	Yes
Empiricism	Yes	No	Yes
Constructivism (Kant)	Yes	Yes	No
Relativism	Yes	No	No

WHAT DO I THINK? *Questionnaire on Knowledge, Doubt, Reason, and Experience*

		Agree	Disagree
1.	It is impossible to ever truly know anything, for all we can ever have are merely opinions and beliefs.		
2.	It is possible to have objective knowledge of what reality is like in itself.		
3.	When my reason convinces me that something must be true, but my experience tells me the opposite, I trust my experience.		
4.	When we come into the world at birth, the mind is like a blank tablet. In other words, all the contents of the mind, anything that we can think about or know to be true, must have come to us originally through experience.		
5.	Our knowledge about reality can never be absolutely certain. However, if a belief is true and we have sufficient evidence of its probability, we have knowledge.		
6.	When my experience convinces me that something is the case, but my reason tells me it is illogical, I trust my reason.		
7.	At least *some* of the following ideas are directly known by the mind and are not learned from experience: (a) the laws of logic (b) the basic principles of mathematics (c) "every event has a cause" (d) the concept of perfection (e) the idea of God (f) moral concepts and principles (such as "It is wrong to torture an innocent person")		
8.	Through reason, it is possible to have knowledge about reality that is absolutely certain.		
9.	We can have universal and objective knowledge of how reality consistently *appears* to the human mind, but we can not know what reality is like *in itself*.		
10.	There is no absolute truth, for when I say that something is "true," I am saying nothing more than "it is true for me" or that "the majority of the people in my society agree that it is true."		

KEY TO THE QUESTIONNAIRE ON KNOWLEDGE

Statement 1 is an expression of skepticism. Strictly speaking, the skeptic would disagree with all the other statements, and all the other positions would disagree with this statement.

Statement 2 expresses epistemological objectivism. Some empiricists and all traditional rationalists would agree with this statement.

Statement 3 represents empiricism. It conflicts with statement 6.

Statement 4 represents empiricism. It conflicts with statement 7.

Statement 5 represents empiricism. It conflicts with statement 8.

Statement 6 represents rationalism. It conflicts with statement 3.

Statement 7 represents rationalism. It conflicts with statement 4.

Statement 8 represents rationalism. It conflicts with statement 5.

Statement 9 represents Kantian constructivism. This position would disagree with statements 1, 2, and 10. With qualifications, the Kantian constructivist could agree with some of the statements of empiricism and rationalism.

Statement 10 represents epistemological relativism. The subjectivist (or subjective relativist) says "true" equals "true for me," because according to this position, the individual is the measure of truth. The cultural relativist (or conventionalist) believes that "*x* is true" equals "the majority of one's culture or society agrees that *x* is true." Generally, the relativist disagrees with skepticism, rationalism, and Kantian constructivism. However, some forms of empiricism would be consistent with relativism.

Which position seems closest to your own? How consistent were your answers? In other words, did you agree with two statements that conflict with each other?

2.1 SKEPTICISM

LEADING QUESTIONS: *Skepticism*

1. How do we know that our sense experience ever reveals reality to us? We think that the water in our drinking glass is real because we can touch it (unlike the illusory water we see on the road). But maybe what we think we experience in the drinking glass is simply a deeper and more persistent illusion. After all, the illusory water on the road *looks* like real water even though it isn't. Similarly, maybe the water in the glass *feels* and *tastes* like real water even though it isn't. Perhaps everything we think is water is really like the illusory water on the road. While the latter fools only our eyes, maybe all the other kinds of illusory water are capable of fooling all five senses.

2. Take some ordinary, simple belief that you have. It might be something like "There is a book in front of me right now." Consider what reasons you have for thinking this belief to be true. Now, consider why you think each of those reasons is true. Continue this process as far as you can until you arrive at your most fundamental beliefs. Now, what reasons do you have for these fundamental beliefs? Does the process of finding reasons for our beliefs ever come to an end? Does it end with some beliefs we simply hold onto tenaciously without any reason? Or is there another alternative?

3. Right now, as you read this sentence, you believe that you are awake and not dreaming. But isn't it usually the case that when we are dreaming, we also think that we are awake

and actually experiencing the events in the dream? In our waking experience we believe that we are awake. But when we dream, we also believe we are awake. So how do we tell the difference? How do you know that right now you are not dreaming that you are reading about dreaming while you are really sleeping soundly in your own bed?

SURVEYING THE CASE FOR SKEPTICISM

Skepticism is the claim that we do not have knowledge. It makes sense to begin our discussion of epistemology with skepticism, for if the skeptic is right, there is no point in examining all the other approaches to knowledge. *Universal* skeptics claim that we have no knowledge whatsoever. They think that every knowledge claim is unjustified and subject to doubt. On the other hand, *limited* skeptics allow that we may have some knowledge, but they focus their skeptical doubts on particular types of knowledge claims. For example, one type of limited skeptic might agree that we can have mathematical or scientific knowledge, but might doubt that we know the truth or falsity concerning other types of claims such as moral judgments or religious claims. On the other hand, another limited skeptic might claim that mystical experience provides us with the truth about reality, but that science does not give us anything more than conjectures, guesses, and likely stories. The following thought experiment explores the degree to which you and your friends are or are not skeptical about three major domains of knowledge.

THOUGHT EXPERIMENT: *Skepticism and Knowledge*

For each of the following statements, check the box corresponding to one of the following three responses:

- I tend to either agree or disagree with this statement. (I do have knowledge.)
- At this point, I am not sure if this statement is true or false, but I think it is possible to find the answer. (Knowledge is possible, but I do not know the answer.)
- I do not believe it is ever possible to find the answer. (Knowledge is impossible.)

(While taking the survey, ignore the numbers in the boxes; they will be used later to analyze your responses.)

	I do have knowledge	Knowledge is possible, but I do not know the answer	Knowledge is impossible
1. There is a God.	1	2	3
2. There are no such events as supernatural miracles.	1	2	3
3. There is life after death.	1	2	3
4. One particular religion is the true one.	1	2	3

(continued . . .)

(. . . *continued*)

		1	2	3
5.	Science gives us our best information about reality.	1	2	3
6.	Science can tell us about the origins of the universe.	1	2	3
7.	Science can tell us about the origins of human life.	1	2	3
8.	Scientists will one day be able to explain all human behavior.	1	2	3
9.	Some actions are objectively right or wrong.	1	2	3
10.	The conventions of one's society determine what is right or wrong.	1	2	3
11.	Pleasure is the only thing in life that has value.	1	2	3
12.	Sometimes it could be one's moral duty to lie.	1	2	3

The responses to each statement have the point value that is indicated. In other words, every answer in the first column is worth one point. Each answer in the second column is worth two points, and each answer in the third column is three points.

Add up your scores for statements 1 through 4. This total is your religion score. If your religion score is 4–6, you are very confident that knowledge is possible concerning religious questions and are not a skeptic. If your score is 7–9, you tend to believe that there are answers to religious questions, but you are uncertain about the answers or have a moderate degree of skepticism. If your score is 10–12, you are very skeptical about the possibility of having knowledge concerning religious issues. Notice that *both* the religious believer and the atheist would be nonskeptics. The atheist would say that the statement "There is a God" is false. Hence, contrary to the skeptic, the atheist believes we can know the truth about this issue.

Add up your scores for statements 5 through 8. This total is your science score. If your science score is 4–6, you are nonskeptical about scientific knowledge. If your score is 7–9, you have some confidence in scientific knowledge along with a degree of skepticism on some issues. If your score is 10–12, you are very skeptical of the possibility of scientific knowledge.

Add up your scores for statements 9 through 12. This total is your score on moral knowledge. If your moral knowledge score is 4–6, you believe moral knowledge is possible and are not a skeptic. If your score is 7–9, you believe moral knowledge is possible, but have reservations about some issues. If your score is 10–12, you think we can have little or no knowledge about the truth or falsity of moral claims.

Try the previous thought experiment on five friends whose answers are likely to differ from yours. In each case, note any differences of the degree of skepticism between the various respondents. Discuss the reasons for your differences.

PHILOSOPHY
in the
MARKETPLACE

Those people who embrace skepticism must be able to give reasons for that skepticism. On the other hand, those people who reject skepticism must wrestle with the skeptic's arguments and show where those arguments go wrong. Remember that the traditional view of knowledge involves three conditions: truth, justification, and belief. If these conditions are essential for having knowledge, the skeptic, in order to show that we do not have knowledge, has to show that one of these conditions is missing. The most obvious target of the skeptic's attacks on knowledge claims is condition 2, which states that our beliefs must be justified in order for them to count as knowledge.

Before reading further, look at the highway picture for an example of a classic experiment in perception. Did you get the right answer, or were your eyes fooled? One way that skeptics attack knowledge claims is to point to all the ways in which we have been deceived by illusions. Our experience with perceptual illusions shows that in the past we have been mistaken about what we thought we knew. These mistakes lead, the skeptic claims, to the conclusion that we can never be certain about our beliefs, from which it follows that our beliefs are not justified.

Another, similar strategy of the skeptic is to point to the possibility that our apprehension of reality could be systematically flawed in some way. The story of Ludwig, the brain in the vat who experienced a false virtual reality, would be an example of this strategy. Another strategy is to suppose that there is an inherent flaw in human psychology such that our beliefs never correspond to reality. I call these possible scenarios **universal belief falsifiers.** The characteristics of a universal belief falsifier are (1) it is a theoretically possible state of affairs, (2) we have no way of knowing if this state of affairs is actual or not, and (3) if this state of affairs is actual, we would never be able to distinguish beliefs that are true from beliefs that seem to be true but are actually false. Note that the skeptic does not need to prove that these possibilities are actual. For example, the skeptic does not have to establish that we really are brains in a vat, but merely that this condition is possible. Furthermore, the skeptic need not claim that all our beliefs are false. The skeptic's point is simply that we have no fail-safe method for determining when our beliefs are true or false. Given this circumstance, the skeptic will argue that we cannot distinguish the situation of having evidence that leads to true beliefs from the situation of having the same sort of evidence plus a universal belief falsifier, which leads to false beliefs.

Obviously, the skeptic believes that nothing is beyond doubt. For any one of our beliefs, we can imagine a set of circumstances in which it would be false. For example, I believe I was born in Rahway, New Jersey. However, my birth certificate could be inaccurate. Furthermore, for whatever reasons, my parents may have wished to keep the truth from me. I will never know for sure. I also believe that there is overwhelming evidence that Adolf Hitler committed suicide at the close of World War II. However, it could be true (as conspiracy theorists maintain) that his death was faked and that he lived a long life in South America after the war. The theme of the skeptic is that certainty is necessary for there to be knowledge, and if doubt is possible, then we do not have certainty.

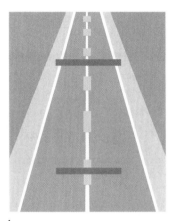

In this picture of a highway, which one of the two horizontal bars is the longer one? Use a ruler to check your judgment.

universal belief falsifiers strategies used by skeptics to attack knowledge claims by showing that there are possible states of affairs that would prevent us from ever distinguishing true beliefs from false ones

We now have the considerations in place that the skeptic uses to make his or her case. There are many varieties of skeptical arguments, each one exploiting some possible flaw in either human cognition or the alleged evidence we use to justify our beliefs. Instead of presenting various specific arguments, we can consider a "generic skeptical argument."

Generic Skeptical Argument

1. We can find reasons for doubting any one of our beliefs.
2. It follows that we can doubt all our beliefs.
3. If we can doubt all our beliefs, then we cannot be certain of any of them.
4. If we do not have certainty about any of our beliefs, then we do not have knowledge.
5. Therefore, we do not have knowledge.

> **STOP AND THINK**
>
> - What do you think of the generic skeptical argument? Is there any premise or inference you would question?
> - Do you agree with the claim that if we do not have absolute certainty, we do not have knowledge?

EARLY GREEK SKEPTICS

Skepticism arose in ancient Greek philosophy after several centuries of philosophical speculation that yielded little agreement about what reality was like. Some philosophers concluded that this massive amount of disagreement meant that no one had knowledge and that we possessed only a diversity of unfounded opinions. One of the earliest and most cantankerous of the skeptics was Cratylus, who was a fifth-century Athenian and a younger contemporary of Socrates. Cratylus believed that little could be known because everything was changing, including oneself. This belief led him to become skeptical about even the possibility of communication. Since the world, the speaker, the listener, and the words were in a constant state of flux, there was no possibility of stable meanings. Cratylus is said to have been true to his own skepticism by refusing to discuss anything. When someone attempted to assert an opinion, Cratylus merely wagged his finger, indicating that nothing could be known or communicated.

Pyrrho of Elis (360–270 B.C.), a philosopher in ancient Greece, inspired a skeptical movement that bore his name (Pyrrhonian skepticism). Pyrrho was skeptical concerning sense experience. He argued that for experience to be a source of knowledge, our sense data must agree with reality. But it is impossible to jump outside our experience to see how it compares with the external world. So, we can never know whether our experience is giving us accurate information about reality. Furthermore, rational argument cannot give us knowledge either, Pyrrho said, because for every argument supporting one side of an issue, another argument can be constructed to prove the opposing case. Hence, the two arguments cancel each other out and they are equally ineffective in leading us to the truth. The followers of Pyrrho stressed that we can make claims only about how things appear to us. You can say, "The honey *appears* to me to be sweet" but not, "The honey *is* sweet." The best approach, according to these skeptics, was to suspend judgment whenever possible and make no assumptions at all. They believed that skeptical detachment would lead to serenity. "Don't worry about what you cannot know," they advised.

Although Plato spent his life attempting to refute skepticism, an influential group of skeptics arose within the Academy, the school that Plato originally founded. The most clever of these was Carneades (who lived about 214–129 B.C.). Carneades represented Athens as an ambassador to Rome along with two other philosophers. The Romans were most interested in his public lectures because those lectures were their first exposure to philosophy. On the first day Carneades argued in favor of justice and eloquently commended its practice to the Romans. The next day, he argued the opposite position, using equally brilliant rhetoric to downgrade justice. This two-faced arguing was a favorite method of the Greek skeptics for undermining the belief that we can know anything to be true. Later skeptics, following Pyrrho, formalized lists of arguments supporting Pyrrho's philosophy. Some skeptics distilled these arguments down into two simple theses. First, nothing is self-evident, for any axiom we start with can be doubted. Second, nothing can be proven, for either we will have an infinite regress of reasons that support our previous reasons or we will end up assuming what we are trying to prove.

RENÉ DESCARTES (1596–1650)

Descartes's Life

Some of the best-known arguments for skepticism were produced by the French philosopher René Descartes. Descartes lived in exciting times. He was born almost 100 years after Columbus sailed to the Americas and half a century after Copernicus published the controversial thesis that the earth revolves around the sun. About the time that Descartes was born, Shakespeare was writing *Hamlet*. Descartes came from a wealthy, respected family in France. His inherited family fortune gave him the freedom to travel and write without having to provide for his own support. It also enabled him to receive one of the best educations available to a young man in France at that time.

In spite of the reputation of his college, Descartes felt a sense of disappointment and even bitterness about his education. He said about the philosophy he was taught that "it has been cultivated for many centuries by the most excellent minds and yet there is still no point in it which is not disputed and hence doubtful."[3] Feeling unsettled and restless, he decided to remedy the limitations of his formal education by traveling and studying "the great book of the world." On November 10, 1619, the harsh German winter confined him to a lonely stove-heated room where he spent the day in intense philosophical thought. There, Descartes says, he "discovered the foundations of a wonderful new science." The following night, his excitement over this discovery culminated in three vivid dreams during which he felt "the Spirit of Truth descending to take possession" of him. This experience convinced him that his mission in life was to develop a new philosophy, based on mathematical reasoning, that would provide absolute certainty and serve as the foundation of all the other sciences.

Descartes spent most of his life in Holland, where the liberal atmosphere provided a safe refuge for intellectuals working on controversial ideas. In 1633 he finished *The World,* a book on physics that contained the controversial thesis that the sun, not the earth, was the center of our universe. He was set to publish it when he learned that Galileo had been formally condemned by the Inquisition in Rome for promoting the same idea. Descartes prudently hid his manuscript with a friend, and it was published only after his death.

RENÉ DESCARTES
(1596–1650)

However, he did go on to publish numerous other works on philosophy, mathematics, and science, and he became world famous. In spite of his tensions with the theologians of his day, Descartes remained a sincere Catholic and always hoped that his works would be of service to theology.

Among Descartes's many correspondents was Queen Christina of Sweden, who was not only a monarch but a person with keen philosophical abilities. She read some of Descartes's manuscripts and sent him critiques of his arguments. In 1649, she invited him to come to Sweden to be her tutor. He wrote to a friend that he was reluctant to go to the land of "bears, rocks and ice." Nevertheless, he did not feel that he could turn down her request, and so he accepted the position. The new position turned out to be disastrous. Descartes had suffered from frail health all his life, and the frigid weather and the five o'clock in the morning tutoring sessions wore him down until he contracted pneumonia and died on February 11, 1650.

The Quest for Certainty

Descartes's lifelong passion was to find certainty. He felt as though his education had given him a collection of ideas based on little else but tradition; many of these ideas had been proven false by his own research. In despair he wrote, "I found myself beset by so many doubts and errors that I came to think I had gained nothing from my attempts to become educated but increasing recognition of my ignorance."[4] While his quest for certainty was a matter of great personal concern, Descartes also thought the quest was essential before science could make any real progress. Looking at the philosophical presuppositions of the sciences of his day, Descartes concluded that "nothing solid could have been built upon such shaky foundations."[5]

STOP AND THINK

Think of a time in your life when you lacked certainty about something that was important to you.

- How did this uncertainty make you feel?
- What attempts did you make to resolve your uncertainty?
- Were they successful?

Although Descartes did not end up a skeptic, he initially used skeptical doubt as a test to decide which beliefs were absolutely certain. Hence, his strategy for finding certainty could be called *methodological skepticism.* Descartes's method was to bathe every one of his beliefs in an acid bath of doubt to see if any survived. Descartes employed a very rigorous standard here. If he could think of any possibility that a belief of his could be mistaken, no matter how improbable this basis of doubt was, then he would suspend judgment concerning that belief. He realized that most of his beliefs would dissolve when subjected to such intense scrutiny, but if even one belief survived the skeptical attack, then he could be absolutely certain about that belief. Before we trace Descartes's journey through skeptical doubt, see if you can anticipate the path he will take by working through the next thought experiment.

🧪 **THOUGHT EXPERIMENT:** *Skeptical Doubt*

Use your imagination to see if you can find a way to doubt the truth of each of the following statements. In other words, try to conceive of a set of circumstances (no matter how improbable) that would cause your belief in the truth of each statement to be mistaken.

1. Lemons are yellow.
2. The moon is much farther away from me than the tops of the trees are.
3. I am (fill in your age) years old.
4. American astronauts have walked on the moon.
5. I am now reading a book.
6. This room is filled with light.
7. $2 + 3 = 5$
8. This page has four edges.
9. I am now doubting.
10. I exist.

Were you able to find possible grounds for doubting any of these statements? Were you able to doubt all of them? Compare your answers with Descartes's in the following readings.

Descartes carried out his project of philosophical demolition and reconstruction in a work called *Meditations on First Philosophy.* This work consisted of six meditations that traced his journey from skeptical doubt to absolute certainty. He opens his book with the resolution to critically examine all his opinions.

📖 FROM RENÉ DESCARTES

Meditations on First Philosophy[6]

Some years ago I was struck by the large number of falsehoods that I had accepted as true in my childhood, and by the highly doubtful nature of the whole edifice that I had subsequently based on them. I realized that it was necessary, once in the course of my life, to demolish everything completely and start again right from the foundations if I wanted to establish anything at all in the sciences that was stable and likely to last. But the task looked an enormous one, and I began to wait until I should reach a mature enough age to ensure that no subsequent time of life would be more suitable for tackling such inquiries. This led me to put the project off for so long that I would now be to blame if by pondering over it any further I wasted the time still left for carrying it out. So today I have expressly rid my mind of all worries and arranged for myself a clear stretch of free time. I am here quite alone, and at last I will devote myself sincerely and without reservation to the general demolition of my opinions.

🧠 **STOP AND THINK**

What do you think of Descartes's radical program for revising his belief system? The following questions will help you formulate your response.

(continued . . .)

(. . . continued)

- What are some beliefs that you once held that you abandoned in recent years?
- What factors caused you to reject those beliefs?
- What are the psychological (and other) advantages of simply hanging on tenaciously to your beliefs and not raising any questions about them?
- Do you agree or disagree with Descartes that it is better to examine and question your beliefs? Why?

When Descartes finds that he can doubt a belief, he does not mean that he has reasons to believe it is false, merely that it is *possible* for it to be false. If he discovers the possibility of falsity, he will neither continue to embrace the belief nor disbelieve it; instead, he will suspend judgment concerning it.

- In the next passage, Descartes realizes that it would be impossible to examine all his beliefs one by one. What alternative strategy does he employ?

But to accomplish this, it will not be necessary for me to show that all my opinions are false, which is something I could perhaps never manage. Reason now leads me to think that I should hold back my assent from opinions which are not completely certain and indubitable just as carefully as I do from those which are patently false. So, for the purpose of rejecting all my opinions, it will be enough if I find in each of them at least some reason for doubt. And to do this I will not need to run through them all individually, which would be an endless task. Once the foundations of a building are undermined, anything built on them collapses of its own accord; so I will go straight for the basic principles on which all my former beliefs rested.

As the first step of his methodological skepticism, Descartes examines his *general sense experiences* (such as statements 1 and 2 in the previous thought experiment). Our senses are imperfect instruments and can be led astray by optical illusions or other causes of mistaken judgments. Hence, they cannot provide an indubitable base on which to build our knowledge. However, having said this, are there any sense experiences that are so vivid that they can provide us with certainty?

Whatever I have up till now accepted as most true I have acquired either from the senses or through the senses. But from time to time I have found that the senses deceive, and it is prudent never to trust completely those who have deceived us even once.

Yet although the senses occasionally deceive us with respect to objects which are very small or in the distance, there are many other beliefs about which doubt is quite impossible, even though they are derived from the senses—for example, that I am here, sitting by the fire, wearing a winter dressing-gown, holding this piece of paper in my hands, and so on. Again, how could it be denied that these hands or this whole body are mine? Unless perhaps I were to liken myself to madmen, whose brains are so damaged by the persistent vapours of melancholia that they firmly maintain they are kings when they are paupers, or say they are dressed in purple when they are naked, or that their heads are made of earthenware, or that they are pumpkins, or made of glass. But such people are insane, and I would be thought equally mad if I took anything from them as a model for myself.

STOP AND THINK

Think of some times when your senses deceived you. What was it like to find out you were led into error? Do you agree with Descartes that a past deception makes it prudent never to completely trust your senses again?

You may find yourself agreeing with Descartes that although you have been deceived by your senses on some occasions, other sense experiences seem so real that you would think only a lunatic would doubt them. For example, it would be hard to doubt your belief that you are now surrounded by various real, physical objects (such as books, chairs, a floor). However, in the next passage, Descartes finds it possible to doubt even these sorts of beliefs.

• Can you guess Descartes's reason for doubting these sorts of *vivid sense experiences?*

A brilliant piece of reasoning! As if I were not a man who sleeps at night, and regularly has all the same experiences while asleep as madmen do when awake—indeed sometimes even more improbable ones. How often, asleep at night, am I convinced of just such familiar events—that I am here in my dressing-gown, sitting by the fire—when in fact I am lying undressed in bed! Yet at the moment my eyes are certainly wide awake when I look at this piece of paper; I shake my head and it is not asleep; as I stretch out and feel my hand I do so deliberately, and I know what I am doing. All this would not happen with such distinctness to someone asleep. Indeed! As if I did not remember other occasions when I have been tricked by exactly similar thoughts while asleep! As I think about this more carefully, I see plainly that there are never any sure signs by means of which being awake can be distinguished from being asleep. The result is that I begin to feel dazed, and this very feeling only reinforces the notion that I may be asleep.

At this point, Descartes's doubts become deeper and more severe. By thinking of his experiences in dreams he came up with a way to doubt the contents of his current experience. When Descartes wrote the previous passage, he was not claiming that he actually was dreaming, but merely that dreams can be so real that he had no way of knowing if he was dreaming or awake.

Even though dreams can confuse us about where we are and what we are doing, the *simple truths of arithmetic and geometry* seem to elude these doubts (statements 7 and 8 in the previous thought experiment).

Arithmetic, geometry and other subjects of this kind, which deal only with the simplest and most general things, regardless of whether they really exist in nature or not, contain something certain and indubitable. For whether I am awake or asleep, two and three added together are five, and a square has no more than four sides. It seems impossible that such transparent truths should incur any suspicion of being false.

So, has Descartes finally found his bedrock of certainty? Unfortunately, he has not, for he finds a reason to doubt even mathematical truths. At the end of *Meditation I,* Descartes stretches his imagination to come up with a universal belief falsifier that would make it possible to be mistaken even about seemingly obvious truths.

I will suppose therefore that . . . some malicious demon of the utmost power and cunning has employed all his energies in order to deceive me. I shall think that the sky, the

The Human Condition I (1934) by René Magritte. In a series of paintings, the Belgian artist Magritte depicted the epistemological problem of the relationship between the mind and reality that philosophers such as Descartes tried to solve. In this work, our view of the outside world is obscured by the canvas in front of the window. However, the images on the painted canvas (symbolizing the mind and its contents) seem to represent what is in the outside world. Or do they? How can we know if we can't see what is beyond the canvas? According to Magritte, this painting represents how we see the world: "we see it as being outside ourselves even though it is only a mental representation of it that we experience inside ourselves."

air, the earth, colours, shapes, sounds and all external things are merely the delusions of dreams which he has devised to ensnare my judgement. I shall consider myself as not having hands or eyes, or flesh, or blood or senses, but as falsely believing that I have all these things.

Once again, Descartes did not necessarily believe that such an evil demon exists but merely that its existence is logically possible. If the demon is possible, then it is possible that $2 + 3 = 17\frac{1}{2}$ (contrary to what we and Descartes believe), and it is possible that we and Descartes do not have bodies but that our minds are deluded into thinking we do. For example, the trilogy of *Matrix* films is based on the notion that evil but intelligent machines have trapped humans in a dream world that is indistinguishable from reality. The story of Ludwig discussed at the beginning of the previous section presents a similar scenario of a virtual reality. We could also imagine we are being victimized by a malicious psychologist who has injected us with a hallucinatory drug or that we are under the spell of a very skillful hypnotist. Hence, the deceiver hypothesis seems to be conceivable.

The End of Doubt

Descartes had hoped to use this method of doubt to distinguish beliefs that were certain from those that could be doubted. But now he seems to be overwhelmed by a flood of doubt from which he cannot recover. Ironically, at this point Descartes finds a lifeboat of certainty within his sea of doubt.

- Can you anticipate how Descartes will find certainty at this point?

FROM RENÉ DESCARTES

Meditations on First Philosophy[7]

So serious are the doubts into which I have been thrown as a result of yesterday's meditation that I can neither put them out of my mind nor see any way of resolving them. It feels as if I have fallen unexpectedly into a deep whirlpool which tumbles me around so that I can neither stand on the bottom nor swim up to the top. Nevertheless I will make an effort and once more attempt the same path which I started on yesterday. Anything which admits of the slightest doubt I will set aside just as if I had found it to be wholly false; and I will proceed in this way until I recognize something certain, or, if nothing else, until I at least recognize for certain that there is no certainty. Archimedes used to demand just one firm and immovable point in order to shift the entire earth; so I too can hope for great things if I manage to find just one thing, however slight, that is certain and unshakeable.

I will suppose then, that everything I see is spurious. I will believe that my memory tells me lies, and that none of the things that it reports ever happened. I have no senses. Body, shape, extension, movement and place are chimeras. So what remains true? Perhaps just the one fact that nothing is certain. . . .

I have convinced myself that there is absolutely nothing in the world, no sky, no earth, no minds, no bodies. Does it now follow that I too do not exist? No: if I convinced myself of something then I certainly existed. But there is a deceiver of supreme power and cunning who is deliberately and constantly deceiving me. In that case I too undoubtedly exist, if he is deceiving me; and let him deceive me as much as he can, he will never bring it about that I am nothing so long as I think that I am something. So after considering everything very thoroughly, I must finally conclude that this proposition, *I am, I exist,* is necessarily true whenever it is put forward by me or conceived in my mind.

Descartes's great discovery is that if he tries to doubt that he is doubting, then he is necessarily confirming the fact that he is doubting. Even the evil deceiver could not make him mistaken about this. Furthermore, if doubting or deception is occurring, *someone* has to do the doubting and be the victim of deception. None of this doubting could take place unless Descartes existed. Hence, Descartes's method of doubt led him to the bedrock certainty of the belief that "*I am, I exist.*" In other writings, Descartes expressed this certitude as *cogito ergo sum,* or "I think, therefore I am."

Obviously, if the only thing he was certain about was his own existence, Descartes had not gotten very far beyond total skepticism. In a later section on rationalism, however, we will see how Descartes attempts to build on this foundation to recover many of his former beliefs, but this time to acquire them in the form of genuine knowledge (true justified beliefs). My purpose for discussing Descartes here is to focus on the skeptical arguments that served as the first step in his project of reconstructing his belief system.

Descartes began his quest for knowledge with the assumption that if he had rational certainty concerning his beliefs, he necessarily had knowledge, and if he did not have certainty, he did not have knowledge. The skeptics who came after Descartes agreed with this assumption. However, as we will see in the next section, Descartes argues that there are a number of things of which we can be certain and, hence, we do have knowledge. On the other hand, the skeptics doubt whether Descartes or anyone can achieve such certainty. Lacking any grounds for certainty, the skeptics claim we cannot have knowledge about the real world. Thus, the skeptics think that Descartes's arguments for skepticism are stronger than his proposed answers. Such a philosopher was David Hume, whom we will encounter later when we examine empiricism.

LOOKING THROUGH THE SKEPTIC'S LENS

1. Human history is replete with wars being waged and people being killed in the name of dogmatic convictions that were allegedly "known" to be true. According to the skeptics, how would their view lead to a more tolerant society?

2. Is it possible to live our lives without certainty? If genuine knowledge is unattainable, should we just do nothing but curl up and die? Most skeptics would reply that skepticism is simply a reminder of the limitations of reason; it leaves us with a more modest view of ourselves and our powers. Accordingly, the early Greek skeptics prefaced all claims with the qualification, "It appears to me that . . ." Hence, in spite of their doubts, the skeptics still go about, living their practical lives. Is this practice objectionably inconsistent, or can one be a thoroughgoing skeptic and still be practical and enjoy life?

3. Even though the skeptics claim we cannot have genuine knowledge, could they still claim that some beliefs are more worthy of being embraced than others?

EXAMINING THE STRENGTHS AND WEAKNESSES OF SKEPTICISM

Positive Evaluation

1. Weeding a garden is not sufficient to make flowers grow, but it does do something valuable. In what way could the skeptics be viewed as providing a "philosophical weeding service" by undercutting beliefs that are naively taken for granted?

2. The skeptics are unsettling because they force us to reexamine our most fundamental beliefs. Is it better to live in naive innocence, never questioning anything, or is it sometimes worthwhile to have your beliefs challenged?

Negative Evaluation

1. The skeptics make the following claim: "Knowledge is impossible." But isn't this claim itself a knowledge claim that they declare is true? Is the skeptic being inconsistent?

2. The skeptics use the argument from illusion to show that we cannot trust our senses. But could we ever know that there are illusions or that sometimes our senses are deceived unless there were occasions when our senses weren't deceived?

3. Some skeptics would have us believe that it is possible that all our beliefs are false. But would the human race have survived if there was never a correspondence between some of our beliefs and the way reality is constituted? We believe that fire burns, water quenches thirst, vegetables nourish us, and eating sand doesn't. If we didn't have some sort of built-in mechanism orienting us toward true beliefs, how could we be as successful as we are in dealing with reality?

4. Is skepticism liveable? Try yelling to someone who claims to be a skeptic, "Watch out for that falling tree limb!" Why is it that a skeptic will always look up? Think of other ways in which skeptics might demonstrate that they *do* believe they can find out what is true or false about the world.

5. Is Descartes's demand for absolute certainty unreasonable? Can't we have justified beliefs based on inferences to the best explanation, probability, or practical certainty? Does certainty have to be either 100 percent or 0 percent?

2.2 RATIONALISM

LEADING QUESTIONS: *Rationalism*

1. Why don't mathematicians need laboratories to discover mathematical truths about numbers the way chemists need laboratories to discover chemical truths? How do mathematicians make their discoveries?

2. You know that the following statement is true: "All triangles have angles that add up to 180 degrees." What sort of method do we use to prove that this statement is true? Do we cut out hundreds of paper triangles and measure their angles? Why is it that we do not have to take a survey of numerous triangles to know the truth of this statement? Why do we believe that this property will necessarily be true of every possible triangle even though we can never examine every triangle?

3. Touch your nose. Now touch your ear. Now touch your rights. Why can't you touch or see your rights? Is it because your eyes aren't good enough? Is it because rights do not really exist? Most people believe that every person has basic rights and that entire cultures can be mistaken about what these rights are (think about Nazi Germany). If the judgments we make about human rights are not, in some sense, objective, then your rights are simply what your society decides they are. But if this conclusion is true, how could we ever accuse a society of violating human rights? On the other hand, if we do have basic, intrinsic rights, then they cannot be discovered in sensory experience. Rights have no shape, taste, sound, odor, or color. Is there any other alternative but to say that the truths about human rights are discovered through some sort of rational intuition?

4. You can think about dogs because you have the idea or concept of a dog. But where did your idea of a dog come from? Obviously, you can think about dogs because you have seen dogs. On the other hand, you can think about unicorns even though (presumably) they do not exist. The reason is that your idea of a unicorn is composed out of the parts of things you *have* experienced, such as horses and horned creatures. Now, what about your idea of perfection? Have you ever found anything in your experience that was absolutely perfect? If everything we experience falls short of perfection in some way, then it seems we could not have derived the idea of perfection from the data of our five senses. How, then, did we ever arrive at the idea of perfection?

SURVEYING THE CASE FOR RATIONALISM

"Seeing is believing"—or so we say. After all, what else but experience could be the basis of our knowledge about reality? Not only is observation the key ingredient in science, but eyewitness testimony is one of the most powerful kinds of evidence in a court of law. It seems that sense experience is the final court of appeal when it comes to deciding what is true and what reality is like. But let's take a second look at this assumption. Do we always base our beliefs on sense experience? I once went to a theater to see the famous illusionist David Copperfield. Throughout the show, objects appeared from nowhere or disappeared before our eyes, people magically changed places, and an assistant was sawed in half and restored. For two full hours the laws of physics took a holiday within the theater.

Those of us in the audience were amazed at what we experienced and had no explanations for it. Nevertheless, we still rejected the testimony of our eyes by thinking, "These things could not have happened. Our senses have been tricked by the magician's skill." Why were we so skeptical when we had witnessed such extraordinary phenomena with our own eyes? The answer is that our reason tells us that "something cannot come from nothing" and "material objects do not vanish into thin air." We will distrust our senses before we will abandon these beliefs. Hence, our reason seems to have veto power over our sense experience. We often trust our reason even in the face of apparently solid, experiential evidence. The rationalists raise this trust in reason into a full-fledged theory of knowledge.

Rationalism is a very influential theory about the source and nature of knowledge. This position may be summarized in terms of the three anchor points of rationalism. These three points are responses to the second question of epistemology, Does reason provide us with knowledge of the world independently of experience? As you read through the three points, complete the following tasks. (1) In each case, make sure you understand the point being made and think about how you would explain it in your own words to a friend. (2) Decide whether you agree or disagree with the position. (3) Make sure you can explain the basis for your opinions. (4) Compare your degree of agreement with rationalism with the answers you originally gave on the "What Do I Think?" questionnaire on the problem of knowledge in section 2.0.

THE THREE ANCHOR POINTS OF RATIONALISM

Reason Is the Primary or Most Superior Source of Knowledge about Reality

According to the rationalist, it is through reason that we truly understand the fundamental truths about reality. For example, most rationalists would say the truths in the following lists are some very basic truths about the world that will never change. Although our experience certainly does illustrate most of these beliefs, our experiences always consist of particular, concrete events. Hence, no experiences of seeing, feeling, hearing, tasting, or touching specific objects can tell us that these statements will always be true for every future event we encounter. The rationalist claims that the following statements represent a priori truths about the world. They are a priori because they can be known apart from experience, yet they tell us what the world is like.

Logical Truths

A and not-A cannot both be true at the same time (where A represents some proposition or claim). This truth is called the law of noncontradiction. (For example, the statement "John is married and John is not married" is necessarily false.)
If the statement X is true and the statement "If X, then Y" is true, then it necessarily follows that the statement Y is true.

Mathematical Truths

The area of a triangle will always be one-half the length of the base times its height.
If X is larger than Y and Y is larger than Z, then X is larger than Z.

Metaphysical Truths

Every event has a cause.
An object with contradictory properties cannot exist. (No matter how long we search, we will never find a round square.)

Ethical Principles

Some basic moral obligations are not optional.
It is morally wrong to maliciously torture someone for the fun of it.

Sense Experience Is an Unreliable and Inadequate Route to Knowledge

Rationalists typically emphasize the fact that sense experience is relative, changing, and often illusory. An object will look one way in artificial light and will look different in sunlight. Our eyes seem to see water on the road on a hot day, but the image is merely an optical illusion. The rationalist claims that we need our reason to sort out what is appearance from what is reality. Although it is obvious that a rationalist could not get through life without some reliance on sense experience, the rationalist denies that sense experience is the only source of knowledge about reality. Furthermore, experience can tell us only about particular things in the world. However, it cannot give us universal, foundational truths about reality. Sensory experience can tell me about the properties of *this* ball, but it cannot tell me about the properties of spheres in general. Experience can tell me that when I combine *these* two oranges with *those* two oranges, they add up to four oranges. However, only reason can tell me that two plus two will always equal four and that this result will be true not only for these oranges, or all oranges, but for *anything* whatsoever.

The Fundamental Truths about the World Can Be Known A Priori: They Are Either Innate or Self-Evident to Our Minds

Innate ideas are ideas that are inborn. They are ideas or principles that the mind already contains prior to experience. The notion of innate ideas is commonly found in rationalistic philosophies, but it is rejected by the empiricists. The theory of innate ideas views the mind like a computer that comes from the factory with numerous programs already loaded on

innate ideas ideas that are inborn; ideas or principles that the mind already contains prior to experience

its disk, waiting to be activated. Hence, rationalists say that such ideas as the laws of logic, the concept of justice, or the idea of God are already contained deep within the mind and only need to be brought to the level of conscious awareness. Innate ideas should not be confused with instinct. Instinct is a noncognitive set of mechanical behaviors, such as blinking the eyes when an object approaches them.

The theory of innate ideas is one account of how we can have a priori knowledge. Other rationalists believe that if the mind does not already contain these ideas, they are, at least, either self-evident or natural to the mind and the mind has a natural predisposition to recognize them. For example, Gottfried Leibniz (1646–1716), a German rationalist, compared the mind to a block of marble that contains veins or natural splitting points that allow only one sort of shape to be formed within it. Thus, the mind, like the marble, has an innate structure that results in "inclinations, dispositions, habits, or natural capacities" to think in certain ways. In contrast to this view, John Locke (a British empiricist) said: "There is nothing in the intellect that was not first in the senses." In response, Leibniz tagged the following rationalistic qualification at the end of Locke's formula, "except for the intellect itself."

Obviously, in saying that the mind contains rational ideas or dispositions, the rationalists do not believe a baby is thinking about the theorems of geometry. Instead, they claim that when a person achieves a certain level of cognitive development, he or she will be capable of realizing the self-evident truth of certain ideas. Leibniz pointed out that there is a difference between the mind *containing* rational principles and *being aware* of them. Rationalists give different accounts of how the mind acquired innate ideas in the first place. Socrates and Plato believed that our souls preexisted our current life and received knowledge from a previous form of existence. Theistic rationalists, such as Descartes, tend to believe that God implanted these ideas within us. Others simply claim that these principles or ideas naturally accompany rational minds such as ours.

THE RATIONALISTS' ANSWERS TO THE THREE EPISTEMOLOGICAL QUESTIONS

Section 2.0 contained three questions concerning knowledge: (1) Is knowledge possible? (2) Does reason provide us with knowledge of the world independently of experience? and (3) Does our knowledge represent reality as it really is? While differing on the details, all the rationalists give the same answers to these three questions. First, they all believe that knowledge is possible. Generally, we are able to discern that some opinions are better than others. For example, in the discipline of mathematics some answers are true and some are false. We could not know this fact if obtaining knowledge was impossible. Second, the rationalists agree that only through reason can we find an adequate basis for knowledge. For example, in mathematics and logic we are able through reason alone to arrive at truths that are absolutely certain and necessarily true. Third, rationalists agree that beliefs that are based on reason do represent reality as it truly is. In the following sections, I examine three classical rationalists to see how they illustrate the three anchor points of rationalism and answer the three epistemological questions.

SOCRATES (C. 470–399 B.C.)

In chapter 1, I introduced Socrates, one of the most interesting philosophical characters in history. He walked the streets of Athens in a disheveled toga, questioning everyone he met on topics ranging from philosophy to poetry. Although Socrates' conversations were typically full of banter and wit, underlying them was a serious commitment to some of the most fundamental axioms of rationalism. Specifically, Socrates believed in innate ideas, for he claimed that true knowledge and wisdom lay buried within the soul. Accordingly, he took it as his mission in life to serve as the midwife of ideas, helping others bring those insights into the light of day. For this reason, he denied that he could teach people anything, for a midwife does not give anyone a baby but merely assists in its birth.

In his dialogue *Meno,* Plato portrays Socrates and his friend Meno examining a dilemma involved in the search for truth. Meno expresses the difficulty this way:

> But how will you look for something when you don't in the least know what it is? How on earth are you going to set up something you don't know as the object of your search? To put it another way, even if you come right up against it, how will you know that what you have found is the thing you didn't know?[8]

Socrates' answer is that we can have knowledge deep within us (innate ideas) but not be aware of it. Hence, gaining knowledge is more like remembering something we had forgotten than it is acquiring new and unfamiliar information. Of course, Socrates does not think that facts about concrete particular things are innate, but only general truths about foundational issues in mathematics, epistemology, metaphysics, and ethics. To illustrate his view, Socrates helps a nearby uneducated boy discover the geometrical relationship between the sides of a square and its area. Without ever giving the boy any answers, Socrates asks him a series of insight-provoking questions until the young boy eventually arrives at the answer himself. According to Socrates' version of rationalism, the knowledge was written on the boy's soul in a previous life and lay there sleeping until Socrates awakened it. The following thought experiment provides some insights on why Socrates believes we have innate knowledge.

THOUGHT EXPERIMENT: *Innate Knowledge*

Try to give precise and adequate definitions of the terms *justice, love,* and *truth.* Ask some of your friends for their definitions. Compare and critique each other's definitions. It is hard to define such terms, isn't it? We use such terms in our daily discourse, but when put on the spot to define them, we feel as though our formulations fall short of what we are trying to describe. You might say, "I can't define *love,* but I know what it is." If I said that *love* is "using another person for your own advantage," you would reject that definition. Similarly, if I said *justice* is "treating those who have power better than those who are weak," you would not consider my definition an adequate statement of what justice is. So, the questions are, How can we (1) use these terms in our conversations, (2) recognize justice, love, and truth when we encounter them, and (3) reject some definitions of these terms as being inadequate if we can't state clearly what the words mean?

Socrates' answer would be that terms such as *justice, love,* and *truth* are different from terms such as *chiliarch,* which only a specialist in Greek military history might know. Socrates would say that the concept of love is written on the soul, but apart from philosophical inquiry we cannot know it explicitly. However, we must have some tacit understanding of love to recognize what is and what is not an example of love and to know which definitions of the term approximate the truth and which are inadequate. Hence, knowledge of these fundamental ideas must be innate and already contained within the human soul.

Socrates' answers to the three epistemological questions should be clear. (1) We are able to distinguish true opinions from false ones, so we must know the standards for making this distinction. (2) These standards could not be derived from experience so they must be unpacked through a rational investigation of the reservoir of all truth—the soul. (3) Since our rational knowledge provides us with information that enables us to deal successfully with the world and our own lives, it must be giving us an accurate picture of reality.

PLATO (c. 428–348 b.c.)

Plato's Life

PLATO
(c. 428–348 b.c.)

Plato came from an aristocratic Athenian family who groomed him to become a leading statesman in his society. To this end, he received the best education available in Athens. However, while still a young man, Plato's life took a completely different course as the result of meeting Socrates and becoming his student. When Socrates ran into trouble with the authorities and was put to death in 399, Plato and several other disciples of Socrates fled Athens to escape persecution. Plato roamed the world for several years, seeking wisdom. As his own philosophical thought developed, he began to write his famous series of dialogues as a tribute to Socrates and as an attempt to work out the implications of Socrates' teachings. Eventually, he returned to Athens and started a school of philosophical studies, which could be considered the first university in the Western world. His school was called the Academy because it was located in a grove outside the city wall that was dedicated to the hero Academus. The school was still operating 900 years later, but was closed in a.d. 529 by Christian rulers who had no tolerance for this stronghold of pagan thought. Nevertheless, the spirit of inquiry that Plato initiated lives on in education today in our contemporary use of the terms *academy* and *academics*.

It is difficult to neatly separate Socrates' and Plato's thought. Socrates never wrote anything and most of what we know of Socrates comes from Plato's dialogues in which he uses the character of his teacher to present his own ideas. A common interpretation is that Plato's earlier writings give us a more or less faithful representation of the historical Socrates. However, as Plato matured philosophically, the philosophical theories in his dialogues begin to expand and blossom. Hence, it is thought that in the later writings, Plato used the voice of Socrates to present distinctively Platonic doctrines. Nevertheless, although Plato gave us one of the most engaging, original, and influential versions of rationalism, his philosophy was always permeated by the spirit of his beloved teacher.

Plato on the Possibility of Knowledge

Plato began his theory of knowledge with an examination of the popular theory that sense experience is the basis of our knowledge (the position we now call empiricism). Because the Sophists of Plato's day based their opinions on sense experience, they were led into relativism and even skepticism. For example, the room can feel too hot to you and too cold to your friend. From examples like this, the Sophists argued that there is no objective truth, for everything is a matter of subjective opinion. However, according to Plato, since the physical world is constantly changing, sense perception gives us only relative and temporary information about changing, particular things. Being a typical rationalist, Plato thought that ultimate knowledge must be objective, unchanging, and universal. Furthermore, he argued that there is a difference between true opinions and knowledge, for our beliefs must be rationally justified to qualify as knowledge. Finally, Plato believed that the object of knowledge must be something that really exists. If sense experience were our only source of information, then Plato would agree with the Sophists that genuine knowledge is not possible. However, he agreed with Socrates that because we can recognize that some opinions are false, we must be capable of having knowledge. Therefore, reason must be able to provide us the knowledge we seek. Before we discuss Plato's version of rationalism, try the following thought experiment, which touches on some Platonic themes.

THOUGHT EXPERIMENT: *Reason and Knowledge*

1. Where are the multiplication tables? You may be tempted to say that they are in your head and written in books. In one sense, you would be right. But if there were no persons to think about multiplying numbers and all books containing these tables were destroyed, would the laws of mathematics still be true? Would they still, in some sense, exist? We can write down $2 \times 2 = 4$. However, the truths of mathematics are not literally identical to the ink on the page. Instead, the marks we make are simply ways we represent these truths. In what sense do mathematical truths come to us through reason and not through the eyes?

2. Compare the quantity and quality of justice in America's institutions, laws, and practices today with the degree of justice in the era of slavery. List several contemporary nations that exhibit a high degree of justice. List examples of nations that offer very little justice. If we are comparing two people in terms of how closely they resemble Elvis Presley, we know what sort of procedure to use. We hold up a photograph of Elvis and see who matches it the best. But how do you compare two nations in terms of their degree of justice? We can't see justice with our eyes, nor can we measure it with our scientific instruments. There are no "justice scopes" or "justice meters." What is *justice* that we can use it as a standard of comparison? How is it possible for us to know about it?

Plato and the Role of Reason

Do mathematical truths, such as those in the multiplication tables, exist within the mind or do they exist outside the mind? Plato would say both. If mathematical truths exist only in the mind, then why does physical reality conform to these truths? If mathematical truths are only mind-dependent ideas, then why can't we make the truths about triangles be anything we decide them to be? The world of *Alice's Adventures in Wonderland* was created in the mind of Lewis Carroll. He could have made the world's properties be anything he decided. But obviously, we can't make up such rules for the properties of numbers. We don't create these truths; we *discover* them. Thus, Plato would argue, these truths are objective and independent of our minds. But if they are independent of our minds, then they must refer to something that exists in reality. Although the number seven, for example, has objective properties that we discover, these properties are not physical. We do not learn the truths about numbers by seeing, tasting, hearing, smelling, or touching them. From this concept, Plato concludes that the world of mathematics consists of a set of objective, mind-independent truths and a domain of nonphysical reality that we know only through reason.

What about justice? What color is it? How tall is it? How much does it weigh? Clearly, these questions can apply to physical things, but it is meaningless to describe justice in terms of observable properties. Furthermore, no society is perfectly just. Hence, we have never seen an example of perfect justice in human history, only frail, human attempts to approximate it. Because reason can contemplate Justice Itself,* we can evaluate the deficient, limited degrees of justice found in particular societies. Particular nations come and go and the degree of justice they manifest can rise or fall. But the objects of genuine knowledge such as true Justice or true Circularity are eternal and unchanging standards and objects of knowledge.

In the following passage, Plato uses the character of Socrates to talk about perfect Justice, Beauty, Goodness, and Equality. He points out that we have never seen these standards in our experience of the physical world. For example, no matter how carefully we draw a circle on paper, the points on the drawn circle are not perfectly equal in distance from the center, but in true circles they are. Find out in this reading how Plato answers these questions through the voice of Socrates:

- Are the "equal" things we find in our experience (e.g., two sticks) the same as absolute equality?
- How is it that we can think about the perfect standards of Justice, Beauty, Goodness, and Equality if they are never found in our experience?
- Find the words that complete this sentence: "What we call learning will be ————, and surely we should be right in calling this ————." What does Socrates mean by this statement?
- According to Socrates, are absolute Equality, Goodness, and the rest simply ideas in our minds, or are they realities that exist independently of us?
- How does Socrates use his discussion of what we can know as an argument for the soul's existence in a previous form of life?

FROM PLATO

Phaedo[9]

Well, but there is another thing, Simmias: Is there or is there not an absolute justice? Assuredly there is.
And an absolute beauty and absolute good?
Of course.
But did you ever behold any of them with your eyes?
Certainly not. . . .
And shall we proceed a step further, and affirm that there is such a thing as equality, not of wood with wood, or of stone with stone, but that, over and above this, there is equality in the abstract? Shall we affirm this?
Affirm, yes, and swear to it, replied Simmias, with all the confidence in life.
And do we know the nature of this abstract essence?
To be sure, he said. . . .
And must we not allow that when I or anyone look at any object, and perceive that the object aims at being some other thing, but falls short of, and cannot attain to it—he who makes this observation must have had previous knowledge of that to which, as he says, the other, although similar, was inferior?
Certainly.
And has not this been our case in the matter of equals and of absolute equality?
Precisely.

---

*Following common practice, I capitalize *Universal* terms such as *Justice Itself, Beauty, Equality,* and the like, to indicate that Plato gives a special meaning to these terms.

Then we must have known absolute equality previously to the time when we first saw the material equals, and reflected that all these apparent equals aim at this absolute equality, but fall short of it?

That is true. . . .

Then before we began to see or hear or perceive in any way, we must have had a knowledge of absolute equality, or we could not have referred to that the equals which are derived from the senses—for to that they all aspire, and of that they fall short?

That, Socrates, is certainly to be inferred from the previous statements.

And did we not see and hear and acquire our other senses as soon as we were born?

Certainly.

Then we must have acquired the knowledge of the ideal equal at some time previous to this?

Yes.

That is to say, before we were born, I suppose?

True.

And if we acquired this knowledge before we were born, and were born having it, then we also knew before we were born and at the instant of birth not only equal or the greater or the less, but all other ideas; for we are not speaking only of equality absolute, but of beauty, goodness, justice, holiness, and all which we stamp with the name of essence in the dialectical process, when we ask and answer questions. Of all this we may certainly affirm that we acquired the knowledge before birth?

That is true. . . .

But if the knowledge which we acquired before birth was lost by us at birth, and afterwards by the use of the senses we recovered that which we previously knew, will not that which we call learning be a process of recovering our knowledge, and may not this be rightly termed recollection by us?

Very true. . . .

Then may we not say, Simmias, that if, as we are always repeating, there is an absolute beauty, and goodness, and essence in general, and to this, which is now discovered to be a previous condition of our being, we refer all our sensations, and with this compare them—assuming this to have a prior existence, then our souls must have had a prior existence, but if not, there would be no force in the argument? There can be no doubt that if these absolute ideas existed before we were born, then our souls must have existed before we were born, and if not the ideas, then not the souls.

Yes, Socrates; I am convinced that there is precisely the same necessity for the existence of the soul before birth, and of the essence of which you are speaking: and the argument arrives at a result which happily agrees with my own notion. For there is nothing which to my mind is so evident as that beauty, goodness, and other notions of which you were just now speaking have a most real and absolute existence; and I am satisfied with the proof.

In the passage you just read, Plato builds on the views of his teacher, Socrates, and argues that knowledge of perfect things, such as perfect Justice or absolute Equality, must be innate, for what we find in experience are only imperfect copies of these ideals. How can we know that something approximates, but falls short of, perfect Justice or Equality unless we are already familiar with true Justice or Equality? To use an analogy, you can recognize that someone is imitating Elvis only if you had some previous exposure to the real thing. Plato believed that the knowledge of these perfect ideals was written on the soul in a previous form of existence. Though it is there within us, we do not apprehend this knowledge clearly, because it is as though we have forgotten it. Hence, coming to know, for Plato, is a process of recollection in which we realize at the level of full, conscious awareness what we already possessed in a hazy, tacit manner. Have you ever had the experience of coming to know something for the first time although you felt as though you were unpacking and making explicit something you already understood albeit in a vague and implicit way? Think of some examples in your own experience that are similar to those in the next thought experiment.

THOUGHT EXPERIMENT: *Knowledge and Awareness*

Is it possible to know something and not know it? Certainly, we have all had the experience of trying to remember something, and after a great deal of effort, we recover the memory. For this reason, Plato uses the term *recollection* to speak of the process of discovery, which is really a process of *recovery*. Sometimes, this "bringing to birth" of understanding is facilitated by someone who serves as the midwife of our own ideas. How many of the following scenarios have been true in your experience?

- You are struggling to find the solution to a mathematical problem. Suddenly, you have a flash of insight and the solution emerges. The answer was not the result of new information you acquired. Instead, what you already knew came together in a new way.
- You are reading a novel in which a character describes the human situation in a particularly insightful way. You find that these words describe what you have always felt, but until now, you did not have the words to appropriate your own understanding.
- You feel vaguely uneasy about a course of action you are considering. You discuss it with a friend. She does not give advice but merely serves as a sounding board to your own reflections. In the course of this dialogue, your own thinking becomes clarified and your uneasiness is explained. You realize that you had known all along that the action would be wrong, but now you understand why it would be wrong.

Not all rationalists would agree that everything that was discovered in these examples would be cases of innate knowledge, although Socrates, for one, would say that problem solving, discovering the meaning of life, and ethical insights all arise out of innate understanding. Nevertheless, these cases illustrate how you might understand something but not be fully aware of what you know until it comes to the level of explicit awareness.

Plato on Universals and the Knowledge of Reality

Thus far, Plato has argued that there are some things that we could not know about (Justice, Goodness, Equality) if experience was our only source of knowledge. The soul must have somehow acquired knowledge independently of the senses. But what, exactly, are the objects of this special sort of knowledge? In answering this question, Plato builds on the distinction he has made between the here-and-now realm of sense experience and the unchanging realm of rational knowledge. He says that in the world of sense experience we find that particulars fall into a number of stable, universal categories. Without these categories, we could not identify anything or talk about particulars at all. For example, Tom, André, Maria, and Lakatria are all distinct individuals, yet we can use the universal term *human being* to refer to each of them. In spite of their differences, something about them is the same. Corresponding to each common name (such as "human," "dog," "justice") is a Universal that consists of the essential, common properties of anything within that category. Circular objects (coins, rings, wreathes, planetary orbits) all have the Universal of Circularity in common. Particular objects that are beautiful (roses, seashells, persons, sunsets, paintings) all share the Universal of Beauty. Particulars come into being, change, and pass away but Universals reside in an eternal, unchanging world. The rose grows from a bud, becomes a beautiful flower, and then turns brown and ugly and fades away. Yet the Universal of Beauty (or Beauty Itself) remains eternally the same. Plato believes that Universals are more than concepts, they are actually the constituents of reality. Hence, in answer to the third epistemological question, Plato believes that knowledge of Universals provides us with knowledge of the fundamental features of reality, which are nonphysical, eternal, and unchanging. Plato also refers to these Universals as "Forms." The following thought experiment will help you appreciate Plato's emphasis on Universals and universal truth.

THOUGHT EXPERIMENT: *Universals and Universal Truth*

Are Universals the basis for all knowledge?

- Have a friend write down a description of you. Have this person make it complete enough that someone who knew you would be likely to recognize that it was a description of you.
- Now, you do the same for your friend.
- Pick out several words in each description and think of someone else they would describe.

Did you find that in trying to describe someone, you had to resort to using universal concepts? Did you also find that every word that was used in the descriptions is a term that also describes other people? How does this exercise illustrate Plato's point that we always think and speak in terms of universals? Do you agree with Plato that universal concepts are the necessary means to make intelligible what we encounter in experience? *Is knowing universal truth more important than being individualistic?*

- What is the answer to 3 + 5 = ?
- Is it wrong to torture people for the fun of it?

Why is it that any rational person would answer these questions by saying "8" and "Yes, torture is wrong"? If someone insisted that the answer to the first question was "11," would we give him or her high marks for uniqueness, individuality, and originality? If someone said, "Torturing people is fun," would we admire this person's independent thinking? Or would we consider him or her irrational? If someone sincerely proclaimed that "squares are round" and that "triangles have both 3 and 10 sides," wouldn't we consider this person out of touch with reality? Persons who are insane typically think, speak, and act in ways that are unique, individual, idiosyncratic, and, hence, irrational. On the other hand, it seems that the more you and I are rational, the more our thinking will be alike. How do these questions illustrate Plato's point that our ability to understand reality correctly depends on our ability to rise above our individuality and think in ways that are objective and universal?

STOP AND THINK

Go back over the three anchor points of rationalism. Explain how Plato's thought illustrates each of these points.

Plato's philosophy had an extraordinary influence on Western thought. With some degree of exaggeration, perhaps, the philosopher-historian Alfred North Whitehead has said that "the safest general characterization of the European philosophical tradition is that it consists of a series of footnotes to Plato."[10] The rationalism Plato developed was given a new twist when René Descartes gave birth to modern philosophy in the 17th century.

RENÉ DESCARTES

Recall from the section on skepticism that Descartes was a 17th-century mathematician, scientist, and philosopher. He is considered the founder of modern rationalism because of his arguments that reason could unlock all the secrets of reality. Descartes began his philosophical journey with the attempt to doubt every one of his beliefs to see if he could find any that were certain beyond any possible doubt. Consequently, he discovered that the one thing he could not doubt was his own existence.

But this bedrock of certainty did not carry him very far. As Descartes said, "I am, then, in the strict sense only a thing that thinks; that is, I am a mind, or intelligence, or intellect, or reason."[11] In other words, the only thing he was certain about was the existence of his mind or consciousness. But wasn't he directly acquainted with the existence of his own body? Descartes did not think so. In our dreams we have the experience of running, eating, swimming, and engaging in all sorts of bodily activities. But the experiences we have of our bodies in dreams are illusory. Hence, at this point, Descartes could not be sure that the "body-like" experiences he was currently having really did correspond to a physical body.

Descartes on the Possibility of Knowledge

Although Descartes was certain he could not be deceived about his own existence, the possibility of a Great Deceiver cast a shadow over all his other beliefs. Unless he could find something external to his mind that would guarantee that the contents of his mind represented reality, there was little hope for having any knowledge other than that of his own existence. Descartes sought this guarantee in an all-powerful, good God. Hence, Descartes says, "As soon as the opportunity arises I must examine whether there is a God, and, if there is, whether he can be a deceiver. For if I do not know this, it seems that I can never be quite certain about anything else."[12] If Descartes could prove that such a God exists, then he could know that knowledge is possible. But notice how limited are the materials Descartes has at his disposal for proving God's existence. He cannot employ an empirical argument based on the nature of the external world, for that is an issue that is still in doubt. So, he must construct a rationalistic argument that reasons only from the contents of his own mind.

The Phantom Limb

Is it crazy for Descartes to worry about whether he has a body? Descartes was familiar with a phenomenon known as the "phantom limb." Someone who has had a leg amputated often feels itching in the missing foot. By habit, the person will reach down to scratch it, only to be reminded that the foot is no longer there! Apparently, the severed nerves in the stump send pain messages to the brain, which the brain mistakenly interprets as coming from the missing foot. If a person can experience a foot that no longer exists, it seemed logical to Descartes that he could not rule out the possibility that his mind was experiencing a "phantom body."

SPOTLIGHT

on

Descartes on the Role of Reason

In the following passage from *Meditation III,* Descartes says the "natural light of reason" shows him that (1) something cannot arise from nothing and (2) there must be at least as much reality in the cause as there is in the effect.

• What examples does he use to illustrate each of these principles?
• How does he apply these two principles to the existence of his own ideas?

FROM RENÉ DESCARTES

Meditations on First Philosophy [13]

Now it is manifest by the natural light that there must be at least as much <reality>* in the efficient and total cause as in the effect of that cause. For where, I ask, could the effect get its reality from, if not from the cause? And how could the cause give it to the effect unless it possessed it? It follows from this both that something cannot arise from nothing, and also that what is more perfect—that is, contains in itself more reality—cannot arise from what is less perfect. . . . A stone, for example, which previously did not exist, cannot begin to exist unless it is produced by something which contains . . . everything to be found in the stone; similarly, heat cannot be produced in an object which was not previously hot, except by something of at least the same order <degree or kind> of perfection as heat, and so on. But it is also true that the *idea* of heat, or of a stone, cannot exist in me unless it is put there by some cause which contains at least as much reality as I conceive to be in the heat or in the stone. . . . For if we suppose that an idea contains something which was not in its cause, it must have got this from nothing; yet the mode of being by which a thing exists objectively <or representatively> in the intellect by way of an idea, imperfect though it may be, is certainly not nothing, and so it cannot come from nothing. . . .

. . . So it is clear to me, by the natural light, that the ideas in me are like <pictures, or> images which can easily fall short of the perfection of the things from which they are taken, but which cannot contain anything greater or more perfect.

The longer and more carefully I examine all these points, the more clearly and distinctly I recognize their truth. But what is my conclusion to be? If the objective reality of any of my ideas turns out to be so great that I am sure the same reality does not reside in me . . . and hence that I myself cannot be its cause, it will necessarily follow that I am not alone in the world, but that some other thing which is the cause of this idea also exists.

---

* The terms in angle brackets are clarifications that Descartes added to the French version of his Latin text.

In examining the origins of his own ideas, Descartes concludes that his ideas of physical objects, animals, and other persons could be constructed from the ideas he has of himself, by creatively modifying the materials of his own experience. However, he does not think that he could have invented the idea of an infinite and perfect God. Why not? His reason for this conclusion goes back to the principle that "there must be at least as much <reality> in the . . . cause as in the effect." Pay attention to his discussion of whether the ideas of "infinite" and "perfect" could be derived from his ideas of "finite" and "imperfect" or whether the opposite must necessarily be the case.

So there remains only the idea of God; and I must consider whether there is anything in the idea which could not have originated in myself. By the word 'God' I understand a substance that is infinite, <eternal, immutable,> independent, supremely intelligent, supremely powerful, and which created both myself and everything else (if anything else there be) that exists. All these attributes are such that, the more carefully I concentrate on them, the less possible it seems that they could have originated from me alone. So from what has been said it must be concluded that God necessarily exists.

It is true that I have the idea of substance in me in virtue of the fact that I am a substance; but this would not account for my having the idea of an infinite substance, when I am finite, unless this idea proceeded from some substance which really was infinite.

And I must not think that, just as my conceptions of rest and darkness are arrived at by negating movement and light, so my perception of the infinite is arrived at not by means of a true idea but merely by negating the finite. On the contrary, I clearly understand that there is more reality in an infinite substance than in a finite one, and hence that my perception of the infinite, that is God, is in some way prior to my perception of the finite, that is myself. For how could I understand that I doubted or desired—that is, lacked something—and that I was not wholly perfect, unless there were in me some idea of a more perfect being which enabled me to recognize my own defects by comparison?

Nor can it be said that this idea of God is perhaps materially false and so could have come from nothing . . . On the contrary, it is utterly clear and distinct, and contains in itself more objective reality than any other idea; hence there is no idea which is in itself truer or less liable to be suspected of falsehood. This idea of a supremely perfect and infinite being is, I say, true in the highest degree; for although perhaps one may imagine that such a being does not exist, it cannot be supposed that the idea of such a being represents something unreal . . . The idea is, moreover, utterly clear and distinct; for whatever I clearly and distinctly perceive as being real and true, and implying any perfection, is wholly contained in it. It does not matter that I do not grasp the infinite, or that there are countless additional attributes of God which I cannot in any way grasp, and perhaps cannot even reach in my thought; for it is in the nature of the infinite not to be grasped by a finite being like myself. It is enough that I understand the infinite, and that I judge that all the attributes which I clearly perceive and know to imply some perfection—and perhaps countless others of which I am ignorant—are present in God either formally or eminently. This is enough to make the idea that I have of God the truest and most clear and distinct of all my ideas.

Descartes's argument here is that the ideas of "infinite" and "perfect" could not have come from himself or his experience, because neither he nor anything in his experience is infinite and perfect. Hence, they must have come from a being who has these qualities, namely, God. Ordinarily, the fact that I have certain ideas in my mind does not tell me there is an external reality that corresponds to them. However, Descartes argues that the idea of perfection is unique. If I could not have produced it myself, Descartes says, then "it will necessarily follow that I am not alone in the world, but that some other thing which is the cause of this idea also exists." In a passage in the beginning of *Meditation III* (that was not quoted), Descartes had concluded that the reason that he could be certain about his own existence was that this idea was absolutely clear and distinct. From then on, as illustrated in his discussion of God, if any idea is clear and distinct, he is confident that it also is true.

Descartes has argued that only if there is an infinite and perfect being (God) could Descartes have acquired the ideas of "infinite" and "perfect." The remaining question is how God gave him the idea of God. Here, Descartes illustrates the basic principle of rationalism, which is that an idea must be innate or already in the mind if it cannot be based on anything we have experienced.

Altogether then, it must be concluded that the mere fact that I exist and have within me an idea of a most perfect being, that is, God, provides a very clear proof that God indeed exists.

It only remains for me to examine how I received this idea from God. For I did not acquire it from the senses; it has never come to me unexpectedly, as usually happens with the ideas of things perceivable by the senses, when these things present themselves to the external sense organs—or seem to do so. And it was not invented by me either; for I am plainly unable either to take away anything from it or to add anything to it. The only remaining alternative is that it is innate in me, just as the idea of myself is innate in me.

And indeed it is no surprise that God, in creating me, should have placed this idea in me to be, as it were, the mark of the craftsman stamped on his work.

The argument that Descartes has given us in the previous passages can be summarized in this way:

1. Something cannot be derived from nothing. (In other words, all effects, including ideas, are caused by something.)
2. There must be at least as much reality in the cause as there is in the effect.
3. I have an idea of God (as an infinite and perfect being).
4. The idea of God in my mind is an effect that was caused by something.
5. I am finite and imperfect, and thus I could not be the cause of the idea of an infinite and perfect God.
6. Only an infinite and perfect being could be the cause of such an idea.
7. Therefore, God (an infinite and perfect being) exists.

STOP AND THINK

Originally, Descartes found it possible to doubt something as obvious as 2 + 3 = 5. But now he embraces the more complex and controversial metaphysical principle that "there must be at least as much <reality> in the efficient and total cause as in the effect," claiming that the "light of nature" makes this principle evident to us. How certain are you of this principle? Why do you have this degree of certainty about it? Do you agree or disagree with Descartes that it is impossible to doubt this principle? Why?

Does Descartes have a problem here? Has he relaxed his standards and failed to carry through his rigorous method of doubt by assuming his principles concerning causality? Is he slipping assumptions into his argument without warrant? What do you think?

Descartes on the Representation of Reality

Having satisfied himself that a perfect God exists, Descartes also knows that this God would not deceive him, for such an action would make God morally imperfect. In *Meditation IV*

Descartes considers what progress this knowledge offers him in the area of epistemology. Since God is not malicious or deceptive and has created our cognitive faculties, Descartes is confident that when he uses his reason properly, it cannot fail to lead him to the truth about reality. Any error he falls into is a result of carelessness in reasoning or in allowing his beliefs to go beyond what he can clearly and distinctly know. Having found a rational ground for trusting his sense experience, Descartes is now confident that he can have knowledge of the existence and nature of his body and the external world.

 STOP AND THINK

Go back over the three anchor points of rationalism. Explain how Descartes's thought illustrates each of these points.

LOOKING THROUGH THE RATIONALIST'S LENS

1. In spite of the differences between cultures, many moral principles seem almost universal. For example, the Golden Rule in Christianity states, "Do unto others as you would have them do unto you." In ancient Hebrew thought we find, "Love thy neighbor as thyself." Similarly, in the ancient Chinese writings, Confucius says, "Never do to others what you would not like them to do to you." How would the rationalist explain the fact that many moral principles are universal throughout all cultures?

2. In the American Declaration of Independence, Thomas Jefferson wrote, "We hold these truths to be self-evident, that all men are created equal, that they are endowed by their Creator with certain unalienable rights, that among these are life, liberty, and the pursuit of happiness." Since "rights" are not something that we can observe with the five senses, how would the rationalist explain our common conviction that people have rights?

3. Most of us are convinced of the truth of this statement: "Every event must have a cause." Even if we are unable to determine the cause of some event, we are convinced that one exists. What is the basis of our certainty about this statement? Just because our experience tells us that *most* events we have examined have had causes, is this observation a sufficient basis for concluding that *all* events will have causes? Since our experience of the world is limited, why are we convinced of the necessity of universal causality? What would a rationalist say about our certainty concerning this metaphysical principle?

4. In our world, grass is green. But we can imagine that the world had turned out differently so that grass was red. Typically, science fiction writers conceive of worlds very different from our own. However, are there any statements that are true about the world that would necessarily have to be true in any conceivable world? Are there any truths about the world that we cannot imagine could have been false? What would a rationalist say?

EXAMINING THE STRENGTHS AND WEAKNESSES OF RATIONALISM

Positive Evaluation

1. Do the rationalists have a trump card in their observation that from a very few intuitively known mathematical axioms, reason can derive a body of theorems that (amaz-

ingly) hold true in our exploration of the physical world? How do we account for this correlation between what the mind rationally proves and what we observe in experience?

2. Are the rationalists correct in claiming that without reason, experience would be a kaleidoscope of sights, sounds, tastes, odors, and textures without any intelligibility?

3. How do we know the laws of logic are correct? How could we ever prove the laws of logic, since all proofs assume them? Does the impossibility of proving the laws of logic indicate that we must know certain truths innately before we can gain any knowledge at all?

Negative Evaluation

1. The rationalists claim that the fundamental truths about reality are innate or self-evident to reason. Yet, the rationalists disagree among themselves and give contradictory accounts of the nature of reality, God, the self, and the principles of ethics. For example, Descartes thought that reason points to the existence of the traditional, biblical God. On the other hand, Spinoza, another rationalist, thinks that pantheism is the only rational view. Pantheism is the position that everything, including physical nature and ourselves, is part of God's being. Does this disagreement undermine the rationalists' claim that reason can give us universal and necessary truths on these issues? How might a rationalist attempt to explain this disagreement?

2. Some ancient and medieval rationalists claimed that the notion of a vacuum was rationally absurd and, hence, that it was impossible for one to exist. As the result of experiments, scientists eventually discovered that vacuums are possible, and we can create nearly perfect vacuums with our technology. Does this discovery cast doubt on the rationalists' claims that reason alone can tell us about reality?

3. Descartes and other rationalists argued that the idea of perfection must be innate because we never discover perfection in our experience. Can you use your imagination to think about the qualities of the perfect baseball player, chess player, lover, rose, and other such ideals? Obviously, we have never experienced a perfect baseball player or any representatives of the other ideals listed. Yet, it seems absurd to suppose that the idea of the perfect baseball player is innate within our minds. Does this exercise suggest (contrary to the rationalists) that we can construct the notion of perfection from the elements of our finite and imperfect experiences?

2.3 EMPIRICISM

LEADING QUESTIONS: *Empiricism*

1. What does rattlesnake meat taste like? What is the taste of squid, turtle, or ostrich meat? How do seaweed cakes or a chrysanthemum salad taste? Is there any way to answer these questions if you have never had the experience of tasting the food in question? To what degree do these examples suggest that experience is the source of all our knowledge about the world?

2. Suppose you were created just a minute ago. (You can imagine that either God or Dr. Frankenstein brought you into existence.) Imagine that you have all the mental capacity of a normal adult, but since you are newly created, you have not yet had much experience with the world. In looking at a bright dazzling fire, would you have any way of

knowing that it produces excruciating pain when you touch it? Without any previous experience, could you look at an ice cube and know that it would be cold?

3. Think about different things that exist in our world, such as a particular object, a group of things, or a person. For example, you could think about the Eiffel Tower, apples, or Abraham Lincoln. In each case, can you imagine the world without this entity? Since the nonexistence of these items is logically possible, how do you know that they exist? Could we know that something either did or did not exist apart from experience? By merely sitting at our desk and reasoning about the world, would we ever know what it contains? Isn't it experience and not reason that tells us about reality?

SURVEYING THE CASE FOR EMPIRICISM

The empiricists' theory of knowledge, like the rationalist's theory of knowledge, can be formulated in terms of three anchor points. Think about the reasons for your agreement or disagreement with each point. Contrast these three points with the corresponding ones for rationalism to see how the positions differ. After reading this section, consider your responses to the "What Do I Think?" questionnaire on the problem of knowledge in section 2.0. Are there any answers you would now change?

THE THREE ANCHOR POINTS OF EMPIRICISM

The Only Source of Genuine Knowledge Is Sense Experience

The empiricists compare the mind to a blank tablet upon which experience makes its marks. Without experience, they claim, we would lack not only knowledge of the specific features of the world, but also the ability even to conceive of qualities such as colors, odors, textures, sounds, and tastes. For example, if you had no taste buds, you could not even conceive what "bitter" might mean. If you had no eyes, the notion of "color" would be without content.

In saying that experience is our source of knowledge, the empiricist believes we have to be content with conclusions that are probable rather than absolutely certain, because most reasoning that is based on sense experience takes the form of inductive arguments.* Sense experience may be incapable of providing the absolute certainty that rationalists demand, but it is all we have to go on, the empiricists say. Why not, therefore, be content with knowledge that is probable and that leads us to successful engagements with the external world? John Locke, the 17th-century British empiricist, compared the scope of human knowledge to a light. We may wish the full light of the sun (absolute certainty) by which to see, but we must be content with what light we have. Hence, "the candle that is set up in us shines bright enough for all our purposes. The discoveries we can make with this ought to satisfy us."[14]

Reason Is an Unreliable and Inadequate Route to Knowledge Unless It Is Grounded in the Solid Bedrock of Sense Experience

The empiricists accuse the rationalists of taking fanciful flights of speculation without any empirical data to anchor them to reality. According to the empiricists, every idea, concept, or term must be tested by tracing it back to an original experience from which it was derived. For example, Hume says that "impressions" (sensory data) are what give our terms (or words) meaning:

---

*See section 1.3 for a discussion of inductive arguments.

When we entertain, therefore, any suspicion that a philosophical term is employed without any meaning or idea (as is but too frequent), we need but enquire, from what impression is that supposed idea derived? And if it be impossible to assign any, this will serve to confirm our suspicion. By bringing ideas into so clear a light we may reasonably hope to remove all dispute, which may arise, concerning their nature and reality.[15]

So the empiricists insist that both the meaning of our terms as well as the credibility of our beliefs must be subjected to a reality-based empirical test. Apart from experience, all we can do is compare one idea to another. However, it is possible to have a completely coherent, but false, system of ideas. For example, the universe described in George Lucas's "Star Wars" films is a coherent story woven around a series of allegedly historical events. But as coherent as the story may be, it does not describe anything real.

Because reason is not a sufficient guide to truth, the empiricists claim, it is not surprising that the various rationalists offer different and conflicting accounts of the nature of reality, God, and ethics. For example, within the rationalist tradition, Descartes thought that we had free will, but Spinoza said it is rationally necessary that everything is determined. Both Descartes and Leibniz provided rational arguments for the benevolence of God, but Spinoza argued that God was wholly without passions and could not have emotional feelings concerning us.

In spite of their critique of the rationalists' emphasis on reason, even the empiricists recognize the importance of reason in making our experience intelligible. They believe that the primary role that reason plays in the acquisition of knowledge is to organize the data of experience and draw conclusions from it. Nevertheless, contrary to the rationalists, empiricists claim that reason without experience is like a potter without clay or a computer without data. The mind needs something to reason *about* and where would it get this but from experience?

There Is No Evidence of Innate Ideas within the Mind That Are Known Apart from Experience

The empiricists offer a number of arguments to undermine the hypothesis that there are innate ideas latent within the mind. First, they point out that not everyone possesses these so-called self-evident truths. When we come into the world as infants, empiricists argue, the mind is a blank tablet, and experience must teach us what we need to know. Second, as was mentioned previously, the empiricists point out that the rationalists disagree among themselves concerning what ideas are rational and "innate."

Finally, even if we discover truths that seem to be universally known and that always hold true, these truths can be explained without positing innate ideas. Empiricists would say that such universal truths are either (1) expressions of the relations of our ideas or (2) generalizations from experience. In no case are there a priori truths that both tell us about the world and are known apart from experience.

The empiricists who stress alternative 1 claim that the rationalists' certitudes *do* consist of truths that can be known apart from experience, but for that reason, those truths do not tell us about the world. According to this view, the mathematical, logical, or metaphysical statements that the rationalist appeals to are based on definitions or linguistic conventions. For example, you can know a priori that "everything that has a shape has a size," because both properties are included in our definition of a spatial object. Hence, the rationalists' absolutely certain, necessary, and "innate" truths are no more mysterious and no more innate than the statement "all bachelors are single."

The empiricists who emphasize alternative 2 claim that the rationalists' universal truths are really highly probable generalizations from experience. For example, consider the claim "every event has a cause." Rather than being an a priori truth, the statement really expresses the empirical claim that, in general, whenever something happened, experience has shown us that it had a cause. We then use that experience as a basis for concluding that this statement is likely to be true in every case. Some empiricists would deny that we can ever know that statement to be true. Instead, they interpret "Every event has a cause" as a methodological principle such as "It is useful always to look for causes of events."

THE EMPIRICISTS' ANSWERS TO THE THREE EPISTEMOLOGICAL QUESTIONS

Remember once again that our three questions concerning knowledge were (1) Is knowledge possible? (2) Does reason provide us with knowledge of the world independently of experience? and (3) Does our knowledge represent reality as it really is? As we will see, although all the empiricists start from the same three anchor points of empiricism just discussed, they come to different interpretations of these three questions about knowledge. This discrepancy illustrates the point that philosophy involves not just taking a position on fundamental questions but also working out the implications of that position. The four empiricists we examine—Aristotle, John Locke, George Berkeley, and David Hume— provide us with four different accounts of the implications of empiricism. We examine each philosopher's answers to the three epistemological questions under the headings of (1) the possibility of knowledge, (2) the role of reason, and (3) the representation of reality.

EMPIRICISM IN THE ANCIENT WORLD: ARISTOTLE

Epistemology began in the ancient world when philosophers made the crucial turn from asking "What is reality like?" (metaphysics) to asking "How can I *know* what reality is like?" (epistemology). Some of their answers foreshadowed the position we now call empiricism. For example, Aristotle (384–322 B.C.) was a Greek philosopher who made experience the beginning point of knowledge and took issue with the rationalism of his teacher Plato.

Aristotle was born in Macedonia and grew up there. Following a long family tradition, Aristotle's father was a physician to the king. It is not unlikely that the scientific, empirical flavor of Aristotle's philosophy, his attention to detail, and his skills at classifying and analyzing the features of nature were inspired by his father's profession. Around age 18, Aristotle became a student in Plato's Academy in Athens. He studied and taught there with Plato for 20 years until the death of his teacher around 348 B.C. After that he spent several years traveling around the Greek islands, doing research in marine biology. In 342 B.C. he was summoned to the Macedonian court by King Philip. The philosopher was asked to become a tutor to 13-year-old Alexander, the royal heir, who would eventually be known as Alexander the Great. In 335 B.C. Aristotle returned to Athens and founded his own school and research institute, which became a rival to Plato's Academy. It was named the Lyceum because it was near the temple of the god Apollo Lyceus. For the next 12 years he directed the scientific research there and wrote most of his major works. The research in the Lyceum ranged over a wide variety of fields, including natural science and history. The Lyceum contained an extensive library, a museum, and both live and preserved collections of plants and animals.

Aristotle on the Possibility of Knowledge

In answer to question 1: Is knowledge possible? Aristotle would be quick to answer "Yes, obviously!" Aristotle raised several arguments against the skeptics who claimed that knowledge is impossible. For example, Aristotle said we can know the laws of logic. (Aristotle was the first one to set out the basic laws of logic.) One logical principle is the **law of noncontradiction.** This law states that it is impossible for something to be A and not-A at the same time. For example, it is meaningless to say, "This animal is a mammal and it is not a mammal." Since it is impossible to make meaningful assertions without abiding by the laws of logic, the skeptic is either resigned to silence or must acknowledge that we can know logical truths. Besides being a great philosopher, Aristotle was also an accomplished scientist. He performed a number of biological experiments and the school he founded contained an impressive museum. His scientific research demonstrated that with careful observation and a methodical collecting of facts, we can acquire knowledge about the world.

Aristotle not only says that knowledge is possible, but that the pursuit of knowledge is intrinsic to our humanity. He starts out his major work *Metaphysics* by saying, "All human beings by nature desire to know." He reveals his empirical orientation by claiming that the evidence we desire to know is found in "the delight we take in our senses; for even apart from their usefulness they are loved for themselves." Hence, our immersion in sense experience plays an important role in our acquisition of knowledge as well as our enjoyment of life. If we employ the correct method, Aristotle thinks, we will rise from the level of merely raw sense data to the more refined level of theoretical or scientific knowledge.

Aristotle and the Role of Reason

Question 2 asked: Does reason alone provide us with knowledge of the world? Consistent with the stance of empiricism, Aristotle says no. In his book *On the Soul*, Book 3, Chapter 4 (which could be considered the first textbook on psychology), Aristotle says that prior to experience the mind is like a blank tablet (in Latin, *tabula rasa*). There is nothing there until experience makes its mark on the tablet of the mind. The metaphor of the mind as a blank tablet is a compelling image that would be taken up by John Locke 2000 years later and would become the iconic image of empiricism thereafter. Obviously, if the mind is like the blank tablet apart from experience, this rules out the possibility of there being any innate knowledge, contrary to what Socrates, Plato, and all the other rationalists claimed. Hence if Aristotle had been Descartes's contemporary, he would have rejected the latter's claim that the ideas of infinity, perfection, and God are latent within the mind. Aristotle, as with the later empiricists, thought that it was absurd to suppose that we possess detailed and certain knowledge from birth but are unaware of it.

For Plato, Aristotle's teacher, we can understand particular things in the physical world only by relating them to the world of ultimate reality, which consists of Universals or the ideal Forms. For example, think about a hand-drawn circle. Plato would say that it falls short of being a real circle, because it's not perfect. Furthermore, it is made out of ink and the circumference has width, whereas a real circle is not made out of ink, nor does the circumference have width. We can understand the drawing only because we can compare it to the Form of Circularity, that ideal, perfect circle that can be known only within the mind. Similarly, Plato discusses political philosophy by reasoning about the Form of Perfect Justice with reference to which all imperfect human societies are compared.

Aristotle's approach is quite different. He believes that all knowledge begins with our experience of particular things. For example, instead of addressing political philosophy by starting with the concept of the perfect society, as Plato does, Aristotle surveyed some 158 constitutions of actually existing states to see what works best in which circumstances. Contrary to Plato, Aristotle would state that justice (or any other universal quality) cannot be understood in isolation from its concrete exemplifications. Aristotle's break with his teacher was dramatic. He once said that while Plato is dear, a philosopher is bound to honor truth above friendship.

While Aristotle thinks that our knowledge begins with concrete experience, he argues that in order to acquire knowledge we need more than sensations and more than an acquaintance with individual facts. The dog experiences the smells, the textures, and the tastes of things in its experience (such as its stash of bones) but does not have genuine knowledge. Science goes beyond knowledge of particular facts to arrive at general conclusions about the world.

How do we make this leap beyond particular facts? Aristotle says we arrive at general knowledge through a twofold process of induction and intuition. Through induction we become acquainted with the universal and necessary features within the changing world of particulars. He says that sense experience leaves its traces within memory. Numerous sense perceptions of the same sort strengthen each other in memory, and knowledge of the similar and universal qualities begin to emerge. Aristotle gives us this pictorial image of the process: "It is like the rout in battle stopped by first one man making a stand and then another, until the original formation had been restored." In other words, from an early age we are besieged with a booming, buzzing barrage of sensations. Initially, our minds are as confused as an army being overwhelmed in battle. Some of these sensations remain in memory, however, and the similar ones reinforce each other. An intelligible order begins to reveal itself as each universal takes its stand in the mind. Like soldiers holding their ground and then advancing to conquer new territory, the universals expand our understanding to greater and greater levels of generality. For example, we experience Tom, Dick, Susan, and Jane. We perceive their unique qualities, and we also experience their similarities. The mind can then extract the universal "human" from its particular examples. Through a similar process, we form the concepts of "dog," "lizard," "deer," and so forth. From this "stand" the mind advances to the universal of "animal" and eventually to the most fundamental universals that are found in all existing things, such as substance, quality, relation, and place.

While this process of making inductive generalizations from particulars accounts for most of our knowledge, some knowledge cannot be obtained in this way. This is knowledge of what Aristotle calls "first principles." These include the most fundamental principles of each of the sciences as well as mathematical and logical truths. Here is where intuition comes in. Aristotle is convinced that the world consists of a rational order. Experience alone cannot demonstrate this order to us but can acquaint us with it. However, only through a sort of intellectual intuition do we really "see" the universal and necessary truths that are the foundation of all genuine knowledge. For example, adding two apples and two apples, then two oranges and two oranges, may trigger the intellectual insight $2 + 2 = 4$. This universal and necessary mathematical truth is not based on the changing world of apples and oranges. However, the concrete experiences provoked the intellectual intuition. For Aristotle then, intuition is an additional step beyond the process of induction. Through intuition, the mind has the power to recognize, or come to know for the first time, universal truths that are lurking within experience.

Aristotle on the Representation of Reality

Our third epistemological question was: Does our knowledge represent reality as it really is? Once again, Aristotle says yes. To see why, imagine that you have a series of round holes in a board and you are trying to fit square pegs into them. You won't be able to do it because the shape of the objects (the square pegs) is not the same as the shape of the receptacles (the round holes). Similarly, Aristotle thinks that because language, thought, and reality seem to "fit together" they must share the same structure. First, thought and reality must be related. How could our minds ever come to know nature if there was not some sort of affinity between them? When we reason from one proposition to another proposition, we are not simply going from one mental item to another. Instead, we are going from one piece of information about the world to other facts that are true of the world. Second, language and reality must share the same structure. How could we even begin to speak about the world unless there is also an affinity between language and reality? Finally, language must have the same structure as thought, for how else could we put our thoughts into words?

Let us look more closely at the relationship between language and reality. Aristotle's Greek language (and our English language) has a subject-predicate structure. We say things like "Socrates is bald." In this case, the word "Socrates" is the subject and the words "is bald" make up the predicate. There is a strict logical relationship between words that refer to things and words that refer to properties. For example, we cannot say "bald is Socrates." Words referring to properties require a grammatical subject. Similarly, reality is divided up into individual, concrete things such as Socrates, the chair on which I am sitting, and the book you are holding. These individual things are called "substances" and are the fundamental units of reality. Aristotle says that substances "are the entities which underlie everything else, and . . . everything else is either predicated of them or present in them."

To sum up Aristotle's empiricism, all knowledge is based on sense experience. Apart from experience, the mind is like a blank tablet. From repeated sense experience we are able to form generalizations that reveal to us the nature of things and how the world works. However, the most fundamental principles (the first principles of each science, mathematical truths, and the laws of logic) are known through a unique sort of experience that is an intellectual intuition. Furthermore, Aristotle's empiricism is related to a particular view of reality. Knowledge is always based of the fundamental realities called substances. Substances are the concrete objects found in everyday experience. While Aristotle, like Plato, believes we can have knowledge of universal qualities ("human," "justice," "beauty"), he insists these universals are always embedded in the concrete objects that exemplify them and do not exist apart from them.

JOHN LOCKE (1632–1704)

Locke's Life

Although the roots of empiricism go back to ancient Greece, it was the English philosopher John Locke who laid the foundations of modern empiricism. A man of many talents and diverse interests, Locke studied theology, natural science, philosophy, and medicine at Oxford University. For about 17 years, he served as the personal physician and advisor to Lord Ashley (later to become the Earl of Shaftesbury). Locke was active in political affairs, and in addition to holding a number of public offices, he helped draft a constitution for the American Carolinas in 1669.

It is commonly held that the Age of Enlightenment was ushered in with the publication of Locke's seminal work *An Essay Concerning Human Understanding* in 1690. With the possible exception of the Bible, no book was more influential in the 18th century than Locke's *Essay*. According to his own account, the idea for the work began when Locke and five or six friends were engaged in a vigorous debate over matters concerning morality and religion. Locke soon realized that these very difficult matters could never be resolved until Locke and his friends first made an assessment of the capabilities and limits of our human understanding. As Locke put it, "If we can find out how far the understanding can extend its view; how far it has faculties to attain certainty; and in what cases it can only judge and guess, we may learn to content ourselves with what is attainable by us in this state."[16]

JOHN LOCKE
(1632–1704)

Locke on the Possibility of Knowledge

Locke thought that it was obvious that experience gives us knowledge that enables us to deal successfully with the world external to our minds. Therefore, Locke gives an affirmative answer to question 1: Is knowledge possible? Knowledge, however, is not something lying out there in the grass; it is located in our minds. So to understand knowledge we have to analyze the contents of our minds and see what they tell us about the world.

According to Locke, the building blocks of all knowledge are what he calls *ideas*. It is important to understand the unique meaning Locke gives to this term because it differs from the meaning it has for us today. He says that an idea is anything that is "the immediate object of perception, thought, or understanding."[17] He offers us a random collection of examples to illustrate what he means by ideas. Ideas are the sorts of things that are expressed by the words "whiteness, hardness, sweetness, thinking, motion, man, elephant, army, drunkenness and others."[18]

Like a chemist analyzing a compound down into its simplest elements, Locke tries to find the basic units composing our knowledge. The most fundamental and original atoms of thought are *simple ideas*. The mind cannot invent a brand-new simple idea or know an idea that it has not experienced. For example, a dictionary will define *yellow* as the color of a ripe lemon. The dictionary can refer you only to the elements of your experience to make the idea clear.

Simple ideas come in two varieties. The first kind consists of *ideas of sensation*, which are the ideas we have of such qualities as yellow, white, heat, cold, soft, hard, bitter, and sweet. The second category of simple ideas is *ideas of reflection*, which are gained from our experience of our own mental operations. This concept is what we today would refer to as knowledge from introspection. Hence, we have ideas of perception, thinking, doubting, believing, reasoning, knowing, and willing, as well as of the emotions and other psychological states. Because we can observe the mind at work, we can think about thinking (or any other psychological activity or state).

Like the camera film that receives and records the light that enters through its lens, so the human mind passively receives simple ideas through experience. However, these ideas are single sounds, colors, and other isolated bits of sensation. Where do we get the ideas of unified objects such as books and elephants? Locke believed that although the mind cannot originate simple ideas, it can process them into more *complex ideas*. Complex ideas are combinations of simple ideas that can be treated as unified objects and given their own names. Locke classifies complex ideas according to the three activities of the mind that produce them: compounding, relating, and abstracting. The first sort of complex ideas are formed by *compounding*, or uniting together two or more simple ideas. We can combine several ideas of the same type. For example, we can compound our limited experiences of space to form the idea of immense space spoken of by astronomers. We can also combine several different ideas. The idea we have of an apple is the combination of the simpler ideas of red, round, sweet, and so on.

By *relating* one idea with another, we can come up with complex ideas concerning relationships. For example, the idea of taller could come about only by relating and comparing our ideas of two things. Husband and wife, father and son, bigger and smaller, cause and effect are examples of ideas that are not experienced alone but are derived from observing relations.

Finally, *abstracting* from a series of particular experiences provides us with general ideas. Locke says that we can form the general idea of book by abstracting all the qualities particular books have in common and ignoring their individual distinctions. For example, individual books come in specific colors and sizes, but all books-in-general are rectangular objects containing pages with writing or pictures on them. When we refer to dogs, humans, buildings, or any other groups of things, we are abstracting the common properties found in our experiences of particular individuals.

Locke and the Role of Reason

Concerning the second question, Does reason alone provide us with knowledge of the world? Locke says no. Locke attacked the notion of innate ideas with the arguments discussed under the third anchor point of empiricism earlier in this section. To Locke, the notion that we could have innate knowledge that we were not aware of was "rubbish" because "no proposition can be said to be in the mind which it never yet knew, which it was never yet conscious of."[19] In contrast to the rationalists' theory that the mind naturally contains certain ideas, Locke proposes this model:

> Let us then suppose the mind to be, as we say, white paper, void of all characters, without any ideas; how comes it to be furnished? Whence comes it by that vast store, which the busy and boundless fancy of man has painted on it with an almost endless variety? Whence has it all the materials of reason and knowledge? To this I answer, in one word, from experience. In that all our knowledge is founded, and from that it ultimately derives itself.[20]

In other words, without experience the mind would have no content. However, once we have some experiences, then reason can process these materials by compounding, relating, and abstracting our ideas to produce more complex ideas. So reason alone cannot give us knowledge apart from experience.

A major dispute between the rationalists and empiricists concerns the origin of our ideas. They would both agree that our idea of "banana" had to come from experiencing bananas. However, what about our idea of perfection? This issue is comparable to the question, Which came first, the chicken or the egg? The rationalists think the idea of perfection is innate within the mind and from this fundamental idea we derive the idea of imperfection. You will recall that one of Descartes's arguments for God was based on the notion that the idea of perfection had to be planted in the mind by a perfect being, since it could not have come from experience. However, Locke says that we first arrive at the concept of imperfection from the things we experience and then imaginatively remove these imperfections until we form the concept of perfection. For example, I am aware that my knowledge of computers is limited. But my understanding is continually growing as my ignorance is replaced with knowledge. Accordingly, I can imagine a being whose knowledge does not have any of the gaps that mine has, and this image would be the concept of perfect knowledge. Hence, from within our experience we can reason about things that we don't experience. Try this Lockean way of arriving at concepts yourself in the following thought experiment.

THOUGHT EXPERIMENT: *The Origin of Ideas*

How would Locke give an empirical account of the origin of the following ideas by compounding, relating, and abstracting from the ideas formed through experience?

1. Infinity
2. God*
3. Moral goodness or evil

*Note that the issue here is not how could we know that God *exists,* but the prior question of how can we entertain the idea of "God" at all and give it *meaning?*

The empiricists think that our idea of infinity, similar to our idea of perfection, can begin with our idea of the finite (drawn from our own, limited experience), from which we derive the idea of infinity. We achieve this concept, Locke says, by imaginatively repeating and compounding our experiences of limited space, duration, and number, continuing this thought process without end. However, he cautions that we can have the idea of the infinity of space (imagining a body moving through space without end), but we cannot actually contain an infinite quantity in our finite minds. Our idea of infinity is more like a pointer to an unlimited quantity rather than the infinite quantity itself. To know the latter in all its fullness would require an infinite mind.

Similarly, we can derive the idea of God by imagining ourselves repeating and endlessly compounding our finite experiences of existence, duration, knowledge, power, wisdom, and all other positive qualities until we arrive at our complex idea of God. When it actually comes to demonstrating that such a being exists, Locke resorts to the traditional empirical evidence presented in the cosmological argument and the argument from design (see chapter 4 on the philosophy of religion).

Finally, Locke thinks that ethics can be put on an empirical foundation. Because we have no direct sensations that correspond to the concepts of good and evil, we must find some other sensations from which these notions may be derived. As is typical of empiricist moral theories, Locke's theory begins with our experiences of pain and pleasure. He says we call "good" whatever tends to cause us pleasure and "evil" anything that tends to produce pain. In this way, experience can teach us that certain types of behavior are morally good (such as keeping promises and preventing harm), because they lead to the most satisfying results. Locke contends that, in spite of all the cultural differences, the moral codes of most cultures have a great number of similarities. This commonality is because morality consists of the wisdom derived from the collective experience of the human race. Experience teaches us that a society based on treachery and deceit will not be a very pleasant place to live, nor is it likely to survive very long. Even though he thought experience can teach us what we need to know about morality, Locke tried to make this view consistent with his Christian beliefs. He believed that God made human experience such that living in conformity with divine law will produce the most satisfying experiences in the long run, both for the individual and for society.

Locke was so convinced of the truth of empiricism that he boldly issued a challenge to his readers to try to prove him wrong. Stated in his own words, the challenge is:

> Let any one examine his own thoughts, and thoroughly search into his understanding; and then let him tell me, whether all the original ideas he has there, are any other than of the objects of his senses, or of the operations of his mind. . . . And how great a mass of knowledge soever he imagines to be lodged there, he will, upon taking a strict view, see that he has not any idea in his mind but what one of these two have imprinted.[21]

PHILOSOPHY
in the
MARKETPLACE

Explain John Locke's challenge to several friends. Ask them to come up with ideas that cannot be traced to our experiences. Now you play the role of John Locke and try to give an empirical account of how these ideas or concepts could be derived from experience using the mental operations of compounding, relating, or abstracting. Finally, see if you can stump Locke yourself by finding an idea that defies his empirical analysis.

Locke on the Representation of Reality

The third epistemological question was, Does our knowledge represent reality as it really is? Locke believes it does, but he says we must get clear on what parts of our experience objectively represent reality and what parts only reflect our own subjectivity. His view of objective properties and subjective properties can be made clear by the following thought experiment.

THOUGHT EXPERIMENT: *Objective and Subjective Properties*

1. Have you found that the perceived color of a piece of clothing changes when you view it by the light of a lightbulb, a neon light, semidarkness, or sunlight? For example, have you ever thought that you were putting on matching socks only to find when you stepped outside that one was black and one was blue?
2. Why doesn't the shape, size, or motion of an object appear to change in different lights?
3. Have you ever disagreed with a friend as to whether the room is too hot or the iced tea too sweet? Why doesn't it make any sense to say one of you is right and the other is mistaken?
4. Hold a cut, raw onion under your nose as you bite into an apple. Does the normal taste of the apple appear to be different under these circumstances?

These thought experiments illustrate the fact that some properties, such as size, shape, or motion, are constant, whereas other properties, such as color, temperature, or taste, can change from one circumstance to another and are perceived differently by different people. Locke explains this difference by distinguishing between the two kinds of properties that an object may have. Properties that are objective, that are independent of us, and that are part of the makeup of the object itself are called **primary qualities.** The primary qualities of an object are its properties of solidity, extension, shape, motion or rest, and number. In other words, they are the properties that can be mathematically expressed and scientifically studied. Properties that are subjectively perceived, that are the effects the object has on our sense organs, and whose appearances are different from the object that produces them are **secondary qualities.** Secondary qualities are properties of color, sound, taste, smell, and texture. Locke sets out this theory in the following passage.

- In paragraph 12, how does Locke say that external bodies produce ideas of their primary qualities in us?
- In paragraphs 13 through 15, how does he distinguish primary qualities from secondary ones?

FROM JOHN LOCKE

An Essay Concerning Human Understanding[22]

How Bodies Produce Ideas in Us. . . .

12. *By motions, external and in our organism.*—If then external objects be not united to our minds when they produce ideas therein; and yet we perceive these *original* qualities in such of them as singly fall under our senses, it is evident that some motion must be thence continued by our nerves, or animal spirits, by some parts of our bodies, to the brains or the seat of sensation, there to produce in our minds the particular ideas we have of them. And since the extension, figure, number, and motion of bodies of an observable bigness, may

primary qualities the properties of an object that can be mathematically expressed and scientifically studied, that is, the properties of solidity, extension, shape, motion or rest, and number

secondary qualities the properties of an object that are subjectively perceived, that are the effects the object has on our sense organs, and whose appearances are different from the object that produces them, that is, the properties of color, sound, taste, smell, and texture

be perceived at a distance by the sight, it is evident some singly imperceptible bodies must come from them to the eyes, and thereby convey to the brain some motion; which produces these ideas which we have of them in us.

13. *How secondary qualities produce their ideas.*—After the same manner, that the ideas of these original qualities are produced in us, we may conceive that the ideas of *secondary* qualities are also produced, viz. by the operation of insensible particles on our senses. . . . Let us suppose at present that the different motions and figures, bulk and number, of such particles, affecting the several organs of our senses, produce in us those different sensations which we have from the colours and smells of bodies; e.g. that a violet, by the impulse of such insensible particles of matter, of peculiar figures and bulks, and in different degrees and modifications of their motions, causes the ideas of the blue colour, and sweet scent of that flower to be produced in our minds. It being no more impossible to conceive that God should annex such ideas to such motions, with which they have no similitude, than that he should annex the idea of pain to the motion of a piece of steel dividing our flesh, with which that idea hath no resemblance.

14. *They depend on the primary qualities.*—What I have said concerning colours and smells may be understood also of tastes and sounds, and other . . . sensible qualities; which, whatever reality we by mistake attribute to them, are in truth nothing in the objects themselves, but powers to produce various sensations in us; and depend on those primary qualities, viz. bulk, figure, texture, and motion of parts as I have said.

15. *Ideas of primary qualities are resemblances; of secondary, not.* From whence I think it easy to draw this observation,—that the ideas of primary qualities of bodies are resemblances of them, and their patterns do really exist in the bodies themselves, but the ideas produced in us by these secondary qualities have no resemblance of them at all. There is nothing like our ideas, existing in the bodies themselves. They are, in the bodies we denominate from them, only a power to produce those sensations in us: and what is sweet, blue, or warm in idea, is but the certain bulk, figure, and motion of the insensible parts, in the bodies themselves, which we call so.

- In paragraphs 16 and 17, how does Locke use fire and snow to illustrate the distinction between the two kinds of qualities?

16. *Examples.*—Flame is denominated hot and light; snow, white and cold; and manna, white and sweet, from the ideas they produce in us. Which qualities are commonly thought to be the same in those bodies that those ideas are in us, the one the perfect resemblance of the other, as they are in a mirror, and it would by most men be judged very extravagant if one should say otherwise. And yet he that will consider that the same fire that, at one distance produces in us the sensation of warmth, does, at a nearer approach, produce in us the far different sensation of pain, ought to bethink himself what reason he has to say— that this idea of warmth, which was produced in him by the fire, *is actually in the fire;* and his idea of pain, which the same fire produced in him the same way, is not in the fire. Why are whiteness and coldness in snow, and pain not, when it produces the one and the other idea in us; and can do neither, but by the bulk, figure, number, and motion of its solid parts?

17. *The ideas of the primary alone really exist.*—The particular bulk, number, figure, and motion of the parts of fire or snow are really in them,—whether any one's senses perceive them or no: and therefore they may be called *real* qualities, because they really exist in those bodies. But light, heat, whiteness, or coldness, are no more really in them than sickness or pain is in manna. Take away the sensation of them; let not the eyes see light or colours, nor the ears hear sounds; let the palate not taste, nor the nose smell, and all colours, tastes,

odours, and sounds, *as they are such particular ideas,* vanish and cease, and are reduced to their causes, i.e. bulk, figure, and motion of parts.

To return to the third epistemological question, our experience of primary qualities gives us knowledge of reality as it really is, but our experience of secondary qualities registers how the objective world affects our particular sense organs. Hence, we find it easy to agree on the size, number, position, and shape of a glass of iced tea because these are its objective, or primary, qualities. However, we might disagree on whether the tea is too sweet. This disagreement is because sweetness is a secondary quality that is not really in the tea but reflects the subjective ways that the tea affects different taste buds. One result of Locke's view of secondary qualities is that it strips the external world of all those features that artists represent and poets describe. What we have left is the world that science studies, a world of quantifiable, material properties. As we will see, George Berkeley criticizes Locke's distinction and argues that Locke's view leads to some surprising results.

STOP AND THINK

Go back over the three anchor points of empiricism. Explain how Locke's thought illustrates each of these points.

GEORGE BERKELEY (1685–1753)

Berkeley's Life

George Berkeley, Ireland's most famous philosopher, received his education at Trinity College in Dublin. There he was exposed to the philosophies of Descartes and Locke as well as the work of Newton and other leading scientists. In 1710 he was ordained as a priest in the Anglican Church and later became one of its bishops. He traveled to America in an attempt to set up a college for the sons of English planters and the native American Indians. Though his project failed for lack of funding, he had a decisive effect on American education. He provided Yale University with the finest library in America at that time and also donated books to Harvard University. Kings College (later to become Columbia University) was founded with his advice. In a poem, he praised the fresh, new spirit of America and predicted that American civilization would expand all the way to the western coast. As a result, the state of California established a university in a city named after Berkeley.

GEORGE BERKELEY
(1685–1753)

Berkeley on the Possibility of Knowledge and the Role of Reason

With Locke, Berkeley gave affirmative answers to the first two basic questions of epistemology. First, he believed that we do have knowledge. Second, he believed that it was only through experience and not reason that we have any knowledge of reality. However, it will soon be clear that Berkeley differed radically with Locke concerning what sort of reality is revealed to us within experience.

Berkeley began his philosophy where Locke began—with an analysis of experience. Following Locke, he refers to the concrete contents of our experience as ideas. Ideas are such things as the redness of a rose, the coldness of ice, the smell of freshly mown grass, the taste

---

*Their being is to be perceived.

of honey, and the sound of a flute. We also have ideas of our own psychological states and operations because we experience our own willing, doubting, and loving. Thus, ideas are images, feelings, or sense data that are directly present to the mind either in vivid sensory or psychological experiences or in the less vivid presentations of either memory or imagination. Hence, when Berkeley says we have the idea of an apple, he is not referring to an abstract concept but to the experience or memory of the combined ideas (experiences) of roundness, redness, hardness, and sweetness.

Berkeley's Theory of Experience

While agreeing with Locke on these points, Berkeley believed Locke had not been a consistent enough empiricist, and so Berkeley resolved to carry the theory of empiricism to its logical conclusions. In doing so, Berkeley ended up with the rather astonishing position that because (1) all we know is what we find in experience, it follows that (2) we can never know or even make sense of a material world that allegedly lies outside our own, private experiences. Read those last two claims over again to get clear on how Berkeley argues from (1) Locke's empiricism to (2) the denial of a world of independently existing matter. Berkeley's philosophy is commonly referred to as *subjective idealism,* although he himself called it *immaterialism.* **Idealism** is a position that maintains that ultimate reality is mental or spiritual in nature. Berkeley's position is known as subjective idealism because he believes reality is made up of many individual minds rather than one cosmic mind. According to Berkeley, reality is nonphysical and everything that exists falls into one of two categories: (1) minds (or spirits) and (2) the ideas they perceive. Hence, Berkeley claims that all the objects we encounter in experience (books, apples, rocks) fall into category 2 and are nothing more than mind-dependent collections of ideas. Berkeley expressed this belief by saying *Esse est percipi,* or "To be is to be perceived." For Berkeley, the only reasonable position possible is that

> all the choir of heaven and furniture of the earth, in a word, all those bodies which compose the mighty frame of the world, have not any subsistence without a mind—that their *being* is to be perceived or known.[23]

Berkeley's goal was made clear in the complete title of his 1710 work: *A Treatise concerning the Principles of Human Knowledge wherein the chief causes of error and difficulty in the Sciences, with the grounds of Scepticism, Atheism and Irreligion, are inquired into.* Even though Berkeley knew that Newton and Locke were Christians, he complained that their science and philosophy paved the way for atheism and skepticism. If nature is made up of particles of matter in motion, following deterministic laws, as Newton claimed, then there is no need to appeal to God to explain events. Similarly, if we can only know our own ideas (experiences), but reality exists apart from them, as Locke claimed, then we can never be sure that our ideas accurately represent reality, leaving us hopelessly mired in skepticism. In contrast, Berkeley argued that our experiences of objects in our environment necessarily come from God and not from matter, thus eliminating atheism. Furthermore, by arguing that there is no external, material reality beyond our ideas, then we are always in direct contact with reality (the contents of our experience) and skepticism has been refuted.

In the opening paragraphs of his *Principles,* Berkeley introduces his claim that empiricism entails that all the objects of experience are mind-dependent.

- According to Berkeley, what do we mean when we say something "exists"?
- Why is it a contradiction to suppose that houses, mountains, and rivers exist apart from our perception of them?

idealism the position that maintains that ultimate reality is mental or spiritual in nature

A Treatise Concerning the Principles of Human Knowledge[24]

1. It is evident to any one who takes a survey of the *objects* of human knowledge, that they are either ideas actually imprinted on the senses, or else such as are perceived by attending to the passions and operations of the mind, or lastly, ideas formed by help of memory and imagination—either compounding, dividing, or barely representing those originally perceived in the aforesaid ways. By sight I have the ideas of light and colors, with their several degrees and variations. By touch I perceive hard and soft, heat and cold, motion and resistance, and of all these more and less either as to quantity or degree. Smelling furnishes me with odors, the palate with tastes, and hearing conveys sounds to the mind in all their variety of tone and composition. And as several of these are observed to accompany each other, they come to be marked by one name, and so to be reputed as one thing. Thus, for example a certain color, taste, smell, figure and consistence having been observed to go together, are accounted one distinct thing signified by the name "*apple*"; other collections of ideas constitute a stone, a tree, a book, and the like sensible things—which as they are pleasing or disagreeable excite the passions of love, hatred, joy, grief, and so forth.

2. But, besides all that endless variety of ideas or objects of knowledge, there is likewise something which knows or perceives them and exercises divers operations, as willing, imagining, remembering, about them. This perceiving, active being is what I call *mind, spirit, soul,* or *myself.* By which words I do not denote any one of my ideas, but a thing entirely distinct from them, wherein they exist or, which is the same thing, whereby they are perceived—for the existence of an idea consists in being perceived.

3. That neither our thoughts, nor passions, nor ideas formed by the imagination, exist without the mind is what everybody will allow. And it seems no less evident that the various sensations or ideas imprinted on the sense, however blended or combined together (that is, whatever objects they compose), cannot exist otherwise than in a mind perceiving them.—I think an intuitive knowledge may be obtained of this by any one that shall attend to what is meant by the term *exists,* when applied to sensible things. The table I write on I say exists, that is, I see and feel it; and if I were out of my study I should say it existed—meaning thereby that if I was in my study I might perceive it, or that some other spirit actually does perceive it. There was an odor, that is, it was smelled, there was a sound, that is, it was heard; a color or figure, and it was perceived by sight or touch. This is all that I can understand by these and the like expressions. For as to what is said of the absolute existence of unthinking things without any relation to their being perceived, that seems perfectly unintelligible. Their *esse* is *percipi,** nor is it possible they should have any existence out of the minds or thinking things which perceive them.

4. It is indeed an opinion strangely prevailing amongst men, that houses, mountains, rivers, and in a word, all sensible objects have an existence, natural or real, distinct from their being perceived by the understanding. But, with how great an assurance and acquiescence soever this principle may be entertained in the world, yet whoever shall find in his heart to call it in question may, if I mistake not, perceive it to involve a manifest contradiction. For, what are the forementioned objects but the things we perceive by sense? and what do we perceive besides our own ideas or sensations? And is it not plainly repugnant that any one of these, or any combination of them, should exist unperceived?

Berkeley's argument in the preceding paragraph could be formulated in the following manner:

The Argument from the Mental Dependency of Ideas

1. Sensory objects (houses, mountains, rivers, and so on) are things present to us in sense experience.
2. What is presented to us in sense experience consists solely of our ideas (or sensations).
3. Ideas exist solely in our minds.
4. Therefore, sensible objects exist solely in our minds.

THOUGHT EXPERIMENT: *Mind-Dependent Ideas*

Does the Argument from the Mental Dependency of Ideas seem plausible to you? If not, why not? Let's explore Berkeley's line of reasoning further. Pick up a pencil. What are you experiencing? You are probably having visual sensations of a particular color, visual and tactile sensations of an extended length with round or hexagonal sides, and tactile sensations of hardness. Press the point of the pencil into your palm and now you will have the experience of pain associated with the pencil. But where is your pain? Obviously, it is not located out in the external world. Pain is an idea (in Berkeley's sense of the word) or an item within your experience. Yet this mind-dependent idea is part of your experience of the pencil. But Berkeley would say that all the other properties of the pencil have the same status. The sensations of color, shape, and extension in your experience are just that—items within your experience. In describing the properties of the pencil, you did not refer to anything external to your experience. How could you? If you met Bishop Berkeley, how would you respond to this argument?

SPOTLIGHT
on

An Attempt to Refute Berkeley

Samuel Johnson, the famous English writer and contemporary of Berkeley's, tried to demonstrate the foolishness of Berkeley's denial of matter by kicking a stone into the air and saying, "I refute him thus!" But what did Johnson show? He showed that he was feeling the experience of hardness and experiencing a round, gray image flying through his visual field. However, as the pain in his toe might have suggested to him, these sensations were internal to his experience and did not provide evidence of a material stone external to his perceptions, a stone to which his perceptions supposedly corresponded.

Berkeley on the Ideas of Matter

By means of multiple, ingenious arguments, Berkeley hammered away at the notion of matter, arguing that it is unintelligible and empty of content. According to him, *matter* is either (1) a misleading term for the collection of sensory experiences we have, such as texture and hardness (in which case it is internal to the mind) or (2) something external to the mind that is without shape, color, odor, taste, or texture. A mind-independent object could not have these qualities because these kinds of sensations are experienced within the mind. But if the objects did not have any such qualities, then it would be a kind of nothingness that we can never experience, know, or imagine.

Berkeley on the Representation of Reality

The third epistemological question was, Does our knowledge represent reality as it really is? On this issue Berkeley and Locke part company. According to Locke, we do not directly experience external objects, but their primary qualities (such as shape and size) produce ideas in us that accurately represent these real properties of the objects. This view is known as **representative realism.** Thus, what appears to us within experience is a trustworthy copy of the objective features of reality. However, Berkeley thought that this view was a dangerous one because it raised the question of how we can know that experience really is telling us what the world outside of our experience is like. Berkeley's position is that we can only know what reality is like if our ideas (the contents of our experience) are the only reality there is to be known. Since there is no world external to our experience, then Locke's distinction between primary qualities (objective) and secondary qualities (subjective) cannot be made. All the qualities of objects are qualities within experience and are equally objective.

In the next set of passages, Berkeley attacks Locke's representative realism (paragraph 8), eliminates the distinction between primary and secondary qualities (paragraphs 9 and 10), and argues that it is impossible to know an external world of matter (paragraph 18).

- What two sorts of reasons does Berkeley give to show that it is impossible for the ideas in our mind to resemble external objects (paragraph 8)?
- Why can we not make a distinction between mind-dependent secondary qualities and external primary qualities (paragraphs 9 and 10)?
- Why can neither sense experience nor reason tell us about matter (paragraph 18)?

8. But, say you, though the ideas themselves do not exist without the mind, yet there may be things like them, whereof they are copies or resemblances, which things exist without the mind in an unthinking substance. I answer, an idea can be like nothing but an idea; a color or figure can be like nothing but another color or figure. If we look but ever so little into our thoughts, we shall find it impossible for us to conceive a likeness except only between our ideas. Again, I ask whether those supposed originals or external things, of which our ideas are the pictures or representations, be themselves perceivable or no? If they are, then they are ideas and we have gained our point; but if you say they are not, I appeal to any one whether it be sense to assert a color is like something which is invisible; hard or soft, like something which is intangible; and so of the rest.

9. Some there are who make a distinction betwixt *primary* and *secondary* qualities. By the former they mean extension, figure, motion, rest, solidity or impenetrability, and number; by the latter they denote all other sensible qualities, as colors, sounds, tastes, and so forth. The ideas we have of these they acknowledge not to be the resemblances of anything existing without the mind, or unperceived, but they will have our ideas of the primary qualities to be patterns or images of things which exist without the mind, in an unthinking substance which they call "matter." By "matter," therefore, we are to understand an inert, senseless substance, in which extension, figure, and motion do actually subsist. But it is evident from what we have already shown that extension, figure, and motion are only ideas existing in the mind, and that an idea can be like nothing but another idea, and that consequently neither they nor their archetypes can exist in an unperceiving substance. Hence, it is plain that the very notion of what is called *matter* or *corporeal substance* involves a contradiction in it.

10. They who assert that figure, motion, and the rest of the primary or original qualities do exist without the mind in unthinking substances, do at the same time acknowledge that colors, sounds, heat, cold, and suchlike secondary qualities, do not—which they tell us are sensations existing in the mind alone, that depend on and are occasioned by the different size,

representative realism the view that we do not directly experience external objects, but their primary qualities (such as shape and size) produce ideas in us that accurately represent these real properties of the objects

texture, and motion of the minute particles of matter. This they take for an undoubted truth which they can demonstrate beyond all exception. Now, if it be certain that those original qualities are inseparably united with the other sensible qualities, and not, even in thought, capable of being abstracted from them, it plainly follows that they exist only in the mind. But I desire any one to reflect and try whether he can, by any abstraction of thought, conceive the extension and motion of a body without all other sensible qualities. For my own part, I see evidently that it is not in my power to frame an idea of a body extended and moved, but I must withal give it some color or other sensible quality which is acknowledged to exist only in the mind. In short, extension, figure, and motion, abstracted from all other qualities, are inconceivable. Where therefore the other sensible qualities are, there must these be also, to wit, in the mind and nowhere else. . . .

18. But, though it were possible that solid, figured, movable substances may exist without the mind, corresponding to the ideas we have of bodies, yet how is it possible for us to know this? Either we must know it by sense or by reason. As for our senses, by them we have the knowledge only of our sensations, ideas, or those things that are immediately perceived by sense, call them what you will; but they do not inform us that things exist without the mind, or unperceived, like to those which are perceived. This the materialists themselves acknowledge. It remains therefore that if we have any knowledge at all of external things, it must be by reason, inferring their existence from what is immediately perceived by sense. But what reason can induce us to believe the existence of bodies without the mind, from what we perceive, since the very patrons of matter themselves do not pretend there is any necessary connection betwixt them and our ideas? I say it is granted on all hands (and what happens in dreams, frenzies, and the like, puts it beyond dispute) that it is possible we might be affected with all the ideas we have now, though there were no bodies existing without resembling them. Hence, it is evident the supposition of external bodies is not necessary for producing our ideas; since it is granted they are produced sometimes, and might possibly be produced always in the same order, we see them in at present, without their concurrence.

According to Locke, primary qualities such as shape and extension are objective qualities existing in external objects, whereas secondary qualities such as color are subjective qualities. The difficulty is that because we can't get outside our minds to compare our ideas or experiences with the external world, how can we make this distinction between ideas that do and do not correspond to what is out there? For example, how do you know an apple is round? You know this because the experience of an apple is always the experience of a round, red patch in your visual field. Its roundness and its redness always go together in our experience. Hence, Berkeley argues, our experience of the primary qualities is always inseparable from our experience of the secondary qualities. Since the latter are subjective and mind-dependent (as Locke admits), it follows that the primary qualities are also.

Notice that in paragraph 18 Berkeley attempts to undermine skepticism. He agrees with the skeptic that we can never know if our experiences and ideas correspond with a reality outside our minds. But for that very reason Berkeley questions whether the notion of an externally existing matter is even intelligible, since the notion could never have any content. Instead, he postulates that reality is nothing more than our experiences (ideas) and everything that exists is exactly as it appears to us. If so, then skepticism is defeated, because we are always directly acquainted with the only reality there is.

The Cause of Our Ideas

There remains one, last question: What is the cause of our ideas if it is not an externally existing material world? Obviously, you produce some of your own ideas (your daydreams, for example), but you are not the cause of the sensations of the color, weight, and texture of the book that you are currently experiencing. So, what causes your ideas of the book? In the following passage, find Berkeley's answer to this question and the following ones.

- What is the cause of our sensations, if not matter? When Berkeley refers to "some other will or spirit," who is the "Author" of our ideas; who is he referring to?
- How do we distinguish between the ideas we produce in our imagination and the ideas that are "real things"?
- Without a world of matter, what are scientists discovering when they observe the "laws of nature"?

29. But, whatever power I may have over my own thoughts, I find the ideas actually perceivd by Sense have not a like dependence on my will. When in broad daylight I open my eyes, it is not in my power to choose whether I shall see or no, or to determine what particular objects shall present themselves to my view; and so likewise as to the hearing and other senses; the ideas imprinted on them are not creatures of my will. There is therefore some *other* will or spirit that produces them.

30. The ideas of sense are more strong, lively, and distinct than those of the imagination; they have likewise a steadiness, order, and coherence, and are not excited at random, as those which are the effects of human wills often are, but in a regular train or series, the admirable connection whereof sufficiently testifies the wisdom and benevolence of its Author. Now the set rules or established methods wherein the mind we depend on excites in us the ideas of sense, are called the *laws of nature;* and these we learn by experience, which teaches us that such and such ideas are attended with such and such other ideas in the ordinary course of things.

31. This gives us a sort of foresight which enables us to regulate our actions for the benefit of life. And without this we should be eternally at a loss; we could not know how to act anything that might procure us the least pleasure or remove the least pain of sense. That food nourishes, sleep refreshes, and fire warms us; that to sow in the seed-time is the way to reap in the harvest; and in general that to obtain such or such ends, such or such means are conducive—all this we know, not by discovering any necessary connection between our ideas, but only by the observation of the settled laws of nature, without which we should be all in uncertainty and confusion, and a grown man no more know how to manage himself in the affairs of life than an infant just born. . . .

33. The ideas imprinted on the senses by the Author of Nature are called *real things;* and those excited in the imagination being less regular, vivid, and constant, are more properly termed *ideas,* or *images of things,* which they copy and represent. But then our sensations, be they never so vivid and distinct, are nevertheless ideas, that is, they exist in the mind, or are perceived by it, as truly as the ideas of its own framing. The ideas of sense are allowed to have more reality in them, that is, to be more strong, orderly, and coherent than the creatures of the mind; but this is no argument that they exist without the mind. They are also less dependent on the spirit, or thinking substance which perceives them, in that they are excited by the will of another and more powerful spirit; yet still they are *ideas;* and certainly no idea, whether faint or strong, can exist otherwise than in a mind perceiving it.

According to Berkeley, only a mind can produce ideas. If our minds did not produce the ideas or experiences we encounter, then God's mind must have created them within us. God directly gives us the world of our experience without the intermediate step of external physical matter. Furthermore, God continuously maintains the world in existence, for even if we are not experiencing a particular object, it still exists within God's mind. Descartes worried that a malicious demon might be inserting experiences within his mind that were radically different from the reality that existed outside his mind. Berkeley, however, believed that a benevolent God was producing experiences within our minds and that these experiences are the only reality. Notice that Berkeley is not claiming that, say, the book you are reading does not exist or that it is not real. He is merely analyzing what he thinks it means to say something "exists." Since all our knowledge is derived from experience, then the contents of our experiences are all that can be meaningfully said to exist. This concept is what Berkeley means when he says, "To be is to be perceived."

Berkeley's immaterialism has also eliminated the problem of how the mind relates to the body (a problem I discuss in chapter 3). According to Berkeley, what we call our body is simply a collection of sensations experienced by the mind. Likewise, space is simply a series of visual and tactile sensations. When our visual image of a car looks unusually small, we say "it is far away." When our visual image begins to grow larger, we say "it is coming closer." Berkeley's notion that space (and time) are relative was a precursor to the views of modern physicists such as Albert Einstein.[25]

Knowing that we might consider his position wild and fantastic, Berkeley reassures us that in arguing for immaterialism,

> I do not argue against the existence of any one thing that we can apprehend either by sense or reflection. That the things I see with my eyes and touch with my hands do exist, really exist, I make not the least question. The only thing whose existence we deny is that which philosophers call matter or corporeal substance.[26]

We can still enjoy the coolness of water and the warmth of a fire. The only difference is that we will realize that these experiences are in the form of mental events provided us by God. According to Berkeley, you can reject the theory of an external, mind-independent, physical world and still have a world of real objects within your experience. Furthermore, science is still possible as long as we view it as the recording of regularities within our experiences and the predicting of future experiences based on this view.

STOP AND THINK

Go back over the three anchor points of empiricism. Explain how Berkeley's thought illustrates each of these points.

DAVID HUME (1711–1776)

Hume's Life

David Hume was born in Edinburgh, Scotland, into a Calvinist family of modest means. He attended Edinburgh University where he studied the standard subjects of classics, mathematics, science, and philosophy. He went on to publish a number of important works on human nature, the theory of knowledge, religion, and morality. However, his skeptical and religious opinions were too controversial for the people of that time and he was never able to obtain an academic position. He was first rejected for a position in ethics at Edinburgh University in 1745. (To rectify their oversight, the philosophy department there is now housed in a building named after him.) Twelve years later, he was also rejected for an academic position at the University of Glasgow.

His scandalous reputation was further enhanced by his *Natural History of Religion*, released in 1757. It was a less-than-sympathetic account of the origins of the religious

DAVID HUME
(1711–1776)

impulse in human experience. Learning from his previous experiences and having a desire "to live quietly and keep remote from all clamour," when Hume finished his *Dialogues Concerning Natural Religion,* he requested that it not be published until after his death. It has since become a classic in the philosophy of religion.

Although his philosophy was filled with the hard edges of skepticism, Hume was actually a kind and gentle soul in his personal relationships. His friends loved to call him "St. David," and, as a result, the street on which he lived is still called St. David Street today.

Hume's Empiricism

Hume was an empiricist, for he believed that all information about the world comes through experience. The contents of consciousness are what he calls *perceptions.* Perceptions include our original experiences, which he labels *impressions.* There are two kinds of impressions. First, there are sense data (such as visual data, sounds, odors, tastes, and tactile data). Second, we also have impressions of the "internal" world composed of the contents of our psychological experiences. Hence, Hume defines impressions as "all our more lively perceptions, when we hear, or see, or feel, or love, or hate, or desire, or will."[27] Perceptions also include what he calls *ideas,* or the contents of our memories and imagination. (Whereas Locke and Berkeley referred to all the contents of our minds as "ideas," Hume limits the word to refer to mental contents derived from our original experiences or impressions.) Obviously, our impressions are more vivid and trustworthy than the copies of them we find in our ideas. For an idea to have any meaning or legitimacy, it must be traced back to our original impressions or combinations of impressions.

Having argued that all our information about the world arises from experience, Hume adds the corollary that none of our knowledge about the world arises from reason. Reason can tell us only about the relationship between our own ideas. In other words, reason can map the connections between the ideas in our minds, but it cannot establish connections between those ideas and the external world.

- In the following passage, what does Hume say are the two kinds of objects of reasoning?
- Which kind of reasoning is the most certain?
- Why can this certainty not tell us anything about the external world?

FROM DAVID HUME

An Enquiry Concerning Human Understanding[28]

All the objects of human reason or enquiry may naturally be divided into two kinds, to wit, Relations of Ideas, and Matters of Fact. Of the first kind are the sciences of Geometry, Algebra, and Arithmetic; and in short, every affirmation which is either intuitively or demonstratively certain. That the square of the hypothenuse is equal to the square of the two sides, is a proposition which expresses a relation between these figures. That three times five is equal to the half of thirty, expresses a relation between these numbers. Propositions of this kind are discoverable by the mere operation of thought, without dependence on what is anywhere existent in the universe. Though there never were a circle or triangle in nature, the truths demonstrated by Euclid would for ever retain their certainty and evidence.

Matters of fact, which are the second objects of human reason, are not ascertained in the same manner; nor is our evidence of their truth, however great, of a like nature with the foregoing. The contrary of every matter of fact is still possible; because it can never imply a contradiction, and is conceived by the mind with the same facility and distinctness, as if ever so conformable to reality. That the sun will not rise tomorrow is no less intelligible a proposition, and implies no more contradiction than the affirmation, that it will rise. We should in vain, therefore, attempt to demonstrate its falsehood. Were it demonstratively false, it would imply a contradiction, and could never be distinctly conceived by the mind.

In this passage, Hume points to a huge gulf between reason and the world. He agrees with the rationalists that the logical relations between our ideas are absolutely certain and necessary. If we start with Euclid's definitions and axioms, for example, then the Pythagorean theorem absolutely follows. But this conclusion only establishes a certain relationship between two sets of ideas. It does not demonstrate that the Pythagorean theorem will be true in the physical world. We can only know this truth from observation. The fact that this theorem has always worked every time we have built a house does not guarantee that it will work tomorrow. We can deny any matter of fact (such as "the sun will always rise in the morning") without falling into a logical contradiction. The fact that we feel confident about certain facts about the world is merely the result of our expectations, which are based on past experience. This dichotomy between relations of ideas (which are logically necessary, but tell us nothing about the world) and matters of fact (which tell us about the world, but which are not certain) is often called "Hume's fork."

From this starting point, Hume drives empiricism to a radical extreme. He thinks that Locke and Berkeley have been inconsistent in working out the implications of empiricism. Hume's basic argument is: If all we know are the contents of experience, how can we know anything about what lies outside our experience? Hence, instead of empiricism leading us out of skepticism, Hume argues that it leads us to skeptical doubt.

> ## STOP AND THINK
>
> Think about the similarities and differences between (1) this book and (2) all your sense experiences of this book. Can you do it? Apparently not, because you can never leap outside your experience of the book to compare it with the book itself. How, then, do you know that your experiences of the book really do correspond to the object outside your experience?

Hume on Causality

principle of induction the assumption that the future will be like the past

uniformity of nature the thesis that the laws of nature that have been true thus far will continue to be true tomorrow

In a series of devastating arguments, Hume examines what we can know about the world. However, from the limited fund of our sense experience, Hume contends, we can learn nothing about what lies outside the subjective contents found within our experiences. According to Hume, most of our judgments about the world are based on our understanding of causes and effects. But our ability to infer causal connections between events assumes the principle of induction. The **principle of induction** could be summarized as the assumption that "the future will be like the past." This principle requires belief in the **uniformity of nature,** or the thesis that the laws of nature that have been true thus far will continue to be true tomorrow. But how do we know that the uniformity of nature is true? As you will see, Hume argues that just because we have discovered certain things to hold true in the past does not make it logically necessary that they will be true in the future.

An Enquiry Concerning Human Understanding[29]

All reasonings concerning matters of fact seem to be founded on the relation of *Cause and Effect*. . . . A man finding a watch or any other machine in a desert island, would conclude that there had once been men in that island. All our reasonings concerning fact are of the same nature. And here it is constantly supposed that there is a connexion between the present fact and that which is inferred from it. Were there nothing to bind them together, the inference would be entirely precarious. The hearing of an articulate voice and rational discourse in the dark assures us of the presence of some person: Why? because these are the effects of the human make and fabric, and closely connected with it. If we anatomize all the other reasonings of this nature, we shall find that they are founded on the relation of cause and effect, and that this relation is either near or remote, direct or collateral. Heat and light are collateral effects of fire, and the one effect may justly be inferred from the other.

The assumption that some events cause other events is central to our daily life as well as to modern science. If you suddenly feel a piercing pain in your foot, you will look around to find its cause. If you find that you stepped on a tack, you will understand why you felt the pain. The question now is, "How do we arrive at our knowledge of the relation be-tween particular causes and effects?" In the next passage, find the answers to the following questions.

- What judgment do we make when we find that particular objects are "constantly conjoined" in experience?
- What would someone like the biblical Adam originally know about the world?
- If you had no experience with the physical world, what are some possible guesses you might make concerning the effect of two billiard balls colliding?
- Why does Hume say "every effect is a distinct event from its cause"? What are the implications of this statement?

Note: throughout this and subsequent passages, the term *a priori* means "prior to experience."

If we would satisfy ourselves, therefore, concerning the nature of that evidence, which assures us of matters of fact, we must enquire how we arrive at the knowledge of cause and effect.

I shall venture to affirm, as a general proposition, which admits of no exception, that the knowledge of this relation . . . arises entirely from experience, when we find that any particular objects are constantly conjoined with each other. Let an object be presented to a man of ever so strong natural reason and abilities; if that object be entirely new to him, he will not be able, by the most accurate examination of its sensible qualities, to discover any of its causes or effects. Adam, though his rational faculties be supposed, at the very first, entirely perfect, could not have inferred from the fluidity and transparency of water that it would suffocate him, or from the light and warmth of fire that it would consume him. No object ever discovers, by the qualities which appear to the senses, either the causes which produced it, or the effects which will arise from it; nor can our reason, unassisted by experience, ever draw any inference concerning real existence and matter of fact. . . .

We fancy, that were we brought on a sudden into this world, we could at first have inferred that one billiard-ball would communicate motion to another upon impulse; and that we needed not to have waited for the event, in order to pronounce with certainty concerning it. Such is the influence of custom, that, where it is strongest, it not only covers our natural ignorance, but even conceals itself, and seems not to take place, merely because it is found in the highest degree.

But to convince us that all the laws of nature, and all the operations of bodies without exception, are known only by experience, the following reflections may, perhaps, suffice. Were any object presented to us, and were we required to pronounce concerning the effect, which will result from it, without consulting past observation; after what manner, I beseech you, must the mind proceed in this operation? It must invent or imagine some event, which it ascribes to the object as its effect; and it is plain that this invention must be entirely arbitrary. The mind can never possibly find the effect in the supposed cause, by the most accurate scrutiny and examination. For the effect is totally different from the cause, and consequently can never be discovered in it. Motion in the second billiard-ball is a quite distinct event from motion in the first; nor is there anything in the one to suggest the smallest hint of the other. A stone or piece of metal raised into the air, and left without any support, immediately falls: but to consider the matter *a priori,* is there anything we discover in this situation which can beget the idea of a downward, rather than an upward, or any other motion, in the stone or metal?

And as the first imagination or invention of a particular effect, in all natural operations, is arbitrary, where we consult not experience; so must we also esteem the supposed tie or connexion between the cause and effect, which binds them together, and renders it impossible that any other effect could result from the operation of that cause. When I see, for instance, a billiard-ball moving in a straight line towards another; even suppose motion in the second ball should by accident be suggested to me, as the result of their contact or impulse; may I not conceive, that a hundred different events might as well follow from that cause? May not both these balls remain at absolute rest? May not the first ball return in a straight line, or leap off from the second in any line or direction? All these suppositions are consistent and conceivable. Why then should we give the preference to one, which is no more consistent or conceivable than the rest? All our reasonings *a priori* will never be able to show us any foundation for this preference.

In a word, then, every effect is a distinct event from its cause. It could not, therefore, be discovered in the cause, and the first invention or conception of it, *a priori,* must be entirely arbitrary. And even after it is suggested, the conjunction of it with the cause must appear equally arbitrary; since there are always many other effects, which, to reason, must seem fully as consistent and natural. In vain, therefore, should we pretend to determine any single event, or infer any cause or effect, without the assistance of observation and experience.

Hume has argued that causes and effects are distinct events and the only reason we connect a particular cause with a particular effect is because the two have been "constantly conjoined" in our experience. In our past experience, for example, whenever a flame touched gunpowder, an explosion resulted. We expect that this result will be true in the future because we trust the principle of induction and believe that "the future will be like the past." But what grounds do we have for supposing this belief to be true? As you read the next passage, keep the following questions in mind.

- According to Hume, what do we always presume? Note: "sensible qualities" refers to the properties of an object that we experience (such as the red color of an apple) and "secret powers" refers to the capacity within an object to have causal effects.
- Why does Hume think that past experience cannot give us knowledge of the future?

- What two propositions are completely different, according to Hume? Do you agree?

FROM DAVID HUME

An Enquiry Concerning Human Understanding[30]

We always presume, when we see like sensible qualities, that they have like secret powers, and expect that effects, similar to those which we have experienced, will follow from them. . . . It is allowed on all hands that there is no known connexion between the sensible qualities and the secret powers; and consequently, that the mind is not led to form such a conclusion concerning their constant and regular conjunction, by anything which it knows of their nature. As to past *experience,* it can be allowed to give *direct* and *certain* information of those precise objects only, and that precise period of time, which fell under its cognizance: but why this experience should be extended to future times, and to other objects, which for aught we know, may be only in appearance similar; this is the main question on which I would insist. The bread, which I formerly ate, nourished me; that is, a body of such sensible qualities was, at that time, endued with such secret powers: but does it follow, that other bread must also nourish me at another time, and that like sensible qualities must always be attended with like secret powers? The consequence seems nowise necessary. At least, it must be acknowledged that there is here a consequence drawn by the mind; that there is a certain step taken; a process of thought, and an inference, which wants to be explained. These two propositions are far from being the same: *I have found that such an object has always been attended with such an effect, and I foresee, that other objects, which are, in appearance, similar, will be attended with similar effects.* I shall allow, if you please, that the one proposition may justly be inferred from the other: I know, in fact, that it always is inferred. But if you insist that the inference is made by a chain of reasoning, I desire you to produce that reasoning. The connexion between these propositions is not intuitive.

How do you know that if you touch a flame right now, you will experience pain? How do you know that if you taste sugar, it will be sweet? The answer is probably found in the two propositions Hume mentions in the previous passage. You probably are reasoning in this way: (1) *In the past, I have found that fire causes pain and sugar is sweet;* therefore, (2) *when I encounter similar examples of fire or sugar, their effects will be similar to the past cases.* Statement (1) is certainly true, but does it provide irrefutable evidence for statement (2)? To get from statement (1) to statement (2) you need the following intermediate step: (1a) *The future always will be like the past.* But how do you know statement (1a) is true? Is it possible to prove the truth of this statement?

- Why can't we simply argue in the following way: "We know that the future will be like the past because our past experience shows that events always follow this rule"?
- In what way is appealing to past experience to justify the principle of induction really arguing in a circle?

For all inferences from experience suppose, as their foundation, that the future will resemble the past, and that similar powers will be conjoined with similar sensible qualities. If there be any suspicion that the course of nature may change, and that the past may be no rule for the future, all experience becomes useless, and can give rise to no inference or conclusion. It is impossible, therefore, that any arguments from experience can prove this resemblance of the past to the future; since all these arguments are founded on the supposition of that resemblance. Let the course of things be allowed hitherto ever so regular; that alone, without some new argument or inference, proves not that, for the future, it will continue so. In vain do you pretend to have learned the nature of bodies from your past experience. Their secret nature, and consequently all their effects and influence, may change, without any change in their sensible qualities. This happens sometimes, and with regard to some objects: Why may it not happen always, and with regard to all objects? What logic, what process or argument secures you against this supposition?

Hume on Knowledge about the External World

Hume's skepticism even extends to doubts about the existence of the external world. Since Hume's empiricism dictates that all judgments about the world must be grounded in sense impressions, it follows that our belief in the external world must be based on experience. Certainly, we *seem* to have experiences of such objects as chairs, books, and trees that have a continuous and independent existence outside us. But can we really know that such experiences are connected to an external world?

- In the following passage, why does Hume say we cannot know that there is an external world?

FROM DAVID HUME

An Enquiry Concerning Human Understanding[31]

By what argument can it be proved, that the perceptions of the mind must be caused by external objects, . . . and could not arise either from the energy of the mind itself, . . . or from some other cause still more unknown to us? . . .

It is a question of fact, whether the perceptions of the senses be produced by external objects, resembling them. How shall this question be determined? By experience, surely, as all other questions of a like nature. But here experience is and must be entirely silent. The mind has never anything present to it but the perceptions, and cannot possibly reach any experience of their connexion with objects. The supposition of such a connexion is, therefore, without any foundation in reasoning.

The problem that Hume raises is that impressions are always data that are *internal* to our subjective experience, and, hence, we have no data about what is *external* to our experience. We tend to believe in a world that continues to exist apart from our experience because of the repeated experiences of similar impressions throughout time. For example, you believe that this book is the same one that you held yesterday because it looks the same as the previous one and you found it exactly where you left it. But all we can say, based strictly on experience, is that the impressions you are having now are similar to the impressions you had yesterday. To this data, the mind adds the ungrounded hypothesis that even when you were not having impressions of this book, the same entity existed continuously between yesterday and today.

We might be tempted to argue that only by postulating an external world can we explain how our impressions are caused. But as we discussed previously, Hume says that causality is only a relation that *we* impute to two kinds of events that have repeatedly occurred together *within* experience. Hence, we cannot make causal judgments about what lies *out-*

---

* See section 4.2 for Hume's skeptical arguments concerning the existence of God.

side experience. It is important to note that Hume does not actually deny that the external world exists. He agrees that it is a natural and almost unavoidable belief that we have. His point is that our fundamental beliefs are based on psychological habits that carry us far beyond what logic and experience could ever prove to us.

THOUGHT EXPERIMENT: *Humean Doubt*

Descartes thought that his mind, or his essential self, could not be doubted because he was directly acquainted with it. Do you think this belief is true? Let's try a Humean experiment. Introspect on your own, conscious experience right now. What do you find? You will probably find visual images, sensations, ideas, moods, and feelings. For example, you may find you are experiencing the whiteness of this page, the texture and weight of your clothes, the temperature of your room, and the thoughts that are going through your head as well as tiredness, curiosity, perplexity, and other psychological phenomena. Now, describe what is left when you subtract this passing flow of sensations and psychological states. When you ignore the momentary contents of your experience and mental life, do you find a continuous self or mind underlying them? Apart from these temporary psychological states, can the permanent self be an item within experience, or do you just assume that there is a self behind it all?

Hume on the Self

At this point, Hume has ended up where Descartes initially did in doubting everything external to his mind and its experiences. Does Hume then conclude, with Descartes, that at least he can be certain that he is a continuously existing self? No he doesn't, for even here he finds that our beliefs and assumptions have no foundation, but that they flow through the sieve of his skeptical arguments, leaving nothing behind but doubts. We often hear the popular phrase "I am trying to find myself." But can the self ever be found? What would the self look like if we found it? Answer the following questions as you read Hume's analysis of the self.

- Why can't there be any impression (experience) of the self?
- What does Hume find when he introspects on what he calls "myself"?
- What metaphor does he use to describe the mind?
- How can this metaphor mislead us?

FROM DAVID HUME

A Treatise of Human Nature [32]

There are some philosophers who imagine we are every moment intimately conscious of what we call our SELF; that we feel its existence and its continuance in existence; and are certain, beyond the evidence of a demonstration, both of its perfect identity and simplicity. . . .

Unluckily all these positive assertions are contrary to that very experience which is pleaded for them, nor have we any idea of *self.* . . . For from what impression could this idea be derived? . . . If any impression gives rise to the idea of self, that impression must continue invariably the same, through the whole course of our lives; since self is supposed to exist after that manner. But there is no impression constant and invariable. Pain and pleasure, grief and joy, passions and sensations succeed each other, and never all exist at the same time. It cannot, therefore, be from any of these impressions, or from any other, that the idea of self is derived; and consequently there is no such idea. . . .

For my part, when I enter most intimately into what I call myself, I always stumble on some particular perception or other, of heat or cold, light or shade, love or hatred, pain or pleasure. I never can catch myself at any time without a perception, and never can observe anything but the perception. . . .

The mind is a kind of theater, where several perceptions successively make their appearance, pass, re-pass, glide away, and mingle in an infinite variety of postures and situations. . . . The comparison of the theater must not mislead us. They are the successive perceptions only, that constitute the mind.

In other words, in our experience we find only a flow of psychological contents, but we do not find any mental container (the mind) that persists apart from them. In summary, Hume's skeptical conclusion concerning the self is based on the following argument. If all we can know are sensory impressions or our internal psychological states, then we can never experience the self. First, we cannot experience a self, because it is not something that has a color, shape, sound, odor, taste, or texture. Second, we cannot experience a continuously existing, substantial self, because our psychological states are only momentary phenomena.

Although Hume originally thought that philosophy could provide us with the foundations of all knowledge, his empiricism ended him up in skepticism concerning, among other things, the uniformity of nature, causality, the external world, the self, and God.* Given the extent and severity of his skepticism, how did Hume go on living? Hume's answer was simple and can be distilled into two propositions: (1) Reason cannot demonstrate even our most fundamental beliefs; (2) but there is no need to rationally demonstrate our fundamental beliefs for them to be practically useful. For Hume, skepticism is a theoretical position that reminds us to be less dogmatic and more modest and reserved about our beliefs, realizing that they are never completely justified. What saves us from the harsh implications of skepticism and returns us to life is the combination of nature, our gut-level instincts, the powerful demands of practical necessity, and even the distractions of our nonphilosophical life.

Most fortunately it happens, that since reason is incapable of dispelling these clouds, nature herself suffices to that purpose, and cures me of the philosophical melancholy and delirium. . . . I dine, I play a game of backgammon, I converse, and am merry with my friends; and when after three or four hours' amusement, I wou'd return to these speculations, they appear so cold, and strain'd, and ridiculous, that I cannot find in my heart to enter into them any farther.[33]

Hume on the Three Questions about Knowledge

Our first epistemological question was: Is it possible to have knowledge? Although Hume initially took the stance of empiricism, his position became infused with skeptical doubts. He arrived at his skeptical conclusions by developing the radical implications of empiricism in directions that Locke and Berkeley were not willing to go. Locke believed we could know that there were physical substances in the external world and mental substances (minds). Furthermore, Locke believed that through experience we could know the real properties of objects (the primary qualities such as size, shape, motion, etc.). Although Berkeley argued that the notion of an external, material world was unintelligible, he did believe in the existence of our minds and God. However, Hume pointed out that if all we can know are the sensory contents of experience, how can we have knowledge of an external world, our own minds, or God?

Hume believes he is more consistent than Locke or Berkeley, for he stays strictly within the bounds of experience. All we are left with, according to Hume, is the flow of sensory data. It is ironic that Locke, Berkeley, and Hume started out trying to avoid the ethereal speculation of the rationalists by grounding knowledge in the rock-solid foundation of experience. Instead, Hume showed that a rigorous empiricism merely leaves us with a stream of consciousness and does not allow us to draw any inferences about what lies beyond that limited domain. Hence, all that we can know are the subjective contents of our individual minds. But this conclusion means that it is impossible to distinguish between the way things appear to us and the way things really are. (Thus we lack a necessary condition for having knowledge, according to Hume.) So, Hume's answer to our first question is that we cannot have knowledge concerning any mind-independent reality. But for Hume, this answer is not the final word. Where reason fails us, nature saves the day. Although our knowledge is severely limited, we have natural instincts to believe in the external world and in causality. Our good fortune is the fact that when we act on these natural instincts and psychological habits, they seem to be practically effective. The problem, according to Hume, is the lack of a philosophical argument to explain why this is so.

Our second question was: Does reason alone tell us about reality? Hume's answer is that not only can experience not tell us about reality, but reason cannot either. Reason can tell us about the relationship of our ideas (logical truths, mathematical truths, and definitions), but it gives us no information about the world. For example, logic and the meaning of our terms tells us that "All unicorns have one horn." However, logic cannot tell us whether unicorns exist.

The third question about knowledge was, Does our knowledge represent reality as it really is? By now, Hume's answer should be clear. According to Hume's analysis, the only certainty we can have concerns the relationship of our own ideas. But since these judgments concern only the realm of ideas, they do not tell us about the external world. If so, then the attempt of the rationalists to *reason* about the ultimate nature of reality is doomed to failure. It also follows that any knowledge about reality must be based on a posteriori judgments. But Hume maintains that these judgments are never certain and merely give us information about what has been true in past experience. As the result of Hume's analysis, many empiricists concluded that insofar as metaphysics is understood to be the attempt to know what reality is really like, then it is an impossible goal. Accordingly, the empiricists who followed Hume concluded that the task of philosophy was much more limited than had been previously supposed. Philosophers, they said, could either analyze the logical relations between our concepts or draw generalizations from everyday experience and the findings of scientists. Beyond those analyses, however, little else could be known.

Hume drew some very brutal conclusions from his epistemology, as illustrated in one of his most famous passages.

> When we run over libraries, persuaded of these principles, what havoc must we make? If we take in our hand any volume; of divinity or school metaphysics, for instance; let us ask, Does it contain any abstract reasoning concerning quantity or number? No. Does it contain any experimental reasoning concerning matter of fact and existence? No. Commit it then to the flames: for it can contain nothing but sophistry and illusion.[34]

THOUGHT EXPERIMENT: *Hume's Two Tests for the Worth of Ideas*

Hume has given us two questions for evaluating the worth of any book that makes assertions or puts forth truth claims. These questions may be paraphrased as (1) Does it contain mathematical reasoning? and (2) Does it contain reasoning about what can be experienced through the senses?

(continued . . .)

(. . . continued)

- Based on these criteria, find concrete examples of books that Hume would want to burn.
- Do you agree with Hume that they "contain nothing but sophistry and illusion"?
- If you think that Hume's criteria are inadequate, what other criteria would you propose for evaluating books and the truth claims they contain?

STOP AND THINK

Go back over the three anchor points of empiricism. Explain how Hume's thought illustrates each of these points.

THOUGHT EXPERIMENT: *Metaphors for the Mind*

The mind is notoriously difficult to conceptualize and discuss. Typically, therefore, much of our mental terminology is replete with concrete metaphors drawn from the physical world. Locke's metaphor of the mind as a "blank white paper" that is written on by experience is an example. The following list consists of metaphors related to the education of young minds. In each case, try to decide if the metaphor best fits with a rationalist's or an empiricist's view of knowledge. First decide on the correct answer yourself, and then check your answers with those in the endnote.[35]

1. The teacher is a midwife of ideas who helps the students bring to birth the ideas latent within their minds.
2. The mind is like a rubber band that encompasses the information that it acquires from the world. Hence, the job of the teacher is to stretch the students' minds so that they can accommodate ever larger amounts of data.
3. The students' minds contain the seeds of understanding. The teacher is merely a gardener who prepares the soil and provides it with nourishment, so that the seeds can grow and produce fruit.
4. The teacher is a lamplighter who illuminates the students' minds so that the truth within will shine forth.
5. The mind is like a copy machine that reproduces images of the data it has scanned from the external world.
6. The teacher is a tour guide who leads the students into new and unfamiliar terrain.
7. The teacher is an archeologist who helps the students discover the treasures buried in the depths of their own minds.
8. The mind is like a window that provides access to the outside world. Ignorance, prejudice, and dogmatism are like a haze or obstacles that the teacher must remove in order for the light of truth to shine through the window of the intellect.
9. The mind is like a computer. Its capabilities are only as good as the data it receives.
10. The mind is like a computer. Without some built-in internal content such as logic circuits and an operating system, it is incapable of processing external data.

THE DEBATE BETWEEN THE RATIONALISTS
AND EMPIRICISTS TODAY

It would be incorrect to suppose that the issues that the rationalists and empiricists debated are dusty relics of philosophy that remained behind in the 17th and 18th centuries. Current research in psychology and cognitive science has shed new light on this controversy. However, recent scientific studies have not resolved the issues but have continued to fuel the philosophical debate. On the one hand are linguists, cognitive scientists, and philosophers who believe that we could not acquire the knowledge we have unless the mind already contained a certain amount of innate content or structure. This contemporary version of rationalism is sometimes called *nativism*. For example, Noam Chomsky, professor of linguistics at the Massachusetts Institute of Technology, argues that children's linguistic experience is too limited to explain the complex linguistic skills they develop. He theorizes that children are born with innate grammatical structures that are common to all languages. These innate rules form the necessary framework for acquiring the specific features of their native tongue. Similarly, in his influential work, *The Language of Thought,* philosopher Jerry Fodor argues that a universal language of thought underlies all empirically acquired languages:

> You can't learn a language unless you already know one . . . the language of thought is known (e.g., is the medium for the computations underlying cognitive processes) but not learned. That is, it is innate.[36]

Going beyond the domain of linguistic knowledge, Harvard cognitive scientist Steven Pinker marshals experimental data to argue that an infant seems to have a great amount of basic information about how the world works, information that the infant could not have acquired from experience. Citing research with infants and agreeing with classic rationalists such as Leibniz, Pinker argues that research with infants shows that such categories as space, time, number, and causation are part of our standard cognitive equipment in much the same way that we all come into the world with a pancreas. Pinker particularly brings science to bear on the philosophical issues in his 2002 book, *The Blank Slate: The Modern Denial of Human Nature.* The title refers to John Locke's claim that, apart from experience, the mind is a blank slate that lacks content (a claim that Pinker attempts to refute).[37] (Pinker updates the classical arguments by hypothesizing that our brains become "hardwired" with these innate structures through our evolutionary history.)

Another leading figure in the nativist movement is Harvard psychologist Elizabeth Spelke. She studies 3- to 4-month-old infants by presenting them with normal or predictable events, such as one ball imparting motion to another ball. She also presents to them "magical" or impossible events such as one ball suddenly stopping its motion and a second ball starting to roll without any contact between them. Through precise measurements of the babies' eye movements, she finds that the babies register surprise at the magical events but not at events that exhibit normal behavior. These studies with infants have led Spelke to the conclusion that we come into the world with "core knowledge systems" that serve as building blocks for future knowledge acquisition.[38]

Contemporary empiricists, however, are not cowed by these arguments. In addition to scientific objections to the design of these experiments, the critics pose a number of philosophical objections to the innateness thesis. First, they argue that many of the claims of the nativists are either vague or empty. Empiricists agree that we have native physical and cognitive capacities to learn language and to acquire knowledge about the world. However, possession of these capacities does not establish that the mind has innate content. Most of us also have a native capacity to ride a bicycle or to learn how to do geometry. The point is, all the nativist experiments that I have described in this section focus on practices that we have to learn to do through trial and error, experience, and education.

Second, contemporary empiricists argue, as did John Locke, that it makes no sense to say that our minds contain, much less follow, innate and universal rules of grammar (as linguistic nativists claim). How can children follow such rules in acquiring language if they are unaware of them? Even linguists who hold to the nativist theory have been unable to satisfactorily formulate these allegedly universal rules of grammar. Concepts or rules that are buried that deeply in unconscious brain processes hardly seem capable of explaining our behavior.

Third, empiricists reject Jerry Fodor's "the only game in town" argument. This phrase refers to Fodor's thesis that the theory of innate mental content is the only theory that can adequately explain our mental life. In response to all the nativists' arguments and scientific experiments, critics offer empiricist explanations as to how children use experience to acquire language and their understanding of the world. Empiricism, these critics claim, offers a simpler explanation of our knowledge, behavior, and mental life without the mysterious apparatus of innate knowledge. As Geoffrey Sampson glibly puts it:

> I see no more reason to ascribe an innate language propensity to infants than to postulate an innate driving propensity in order to explain why modern British teenagers are keen to learn to drive—there are such obvious social factors which explain the keenness without needing a nativist postulate.[39]

And so the debate goes on. Perhaps our increasingly sophisticated experiments in developmental psychology and increasingly sophisticated philosophical arguments will one day tip the scale in favor of one or the other of the warring camps or show us a way to reach a compromise between them.

SUMMARY OF RATIONALISM AND EMPIRICISM

The rationalists claimed that we can have knowledge independent of experience. While rejecting this thesis the empiricists countered with the alternative thesis that all genuine knowledge is based on experience. However, from this basic premise Locke developed a (more or less) commonsense philosophy, whereas Berkeley argued for the radical conclusion that it is meaningless to posit a material world that exists external to our minds. Finally, Hume argued that empiricism implies that we can know virtually nothing at all except for the logical relationships between our own ideas and the flow of sensations within experience. Immanuel Kant, an 18th-century German philosopher, faced this great divide between the rationalists and the empiricists and concluded that each position had insights to offer but that each was plagued with difficulties. As we see in the next section, Kant attempted to construct an alternative view that incorporated elements of both rationalism and empiricism while leaving their problems behind.

LOOKING THROUGH THE EMPIRICIST'S LENS

1. Many cultures that are otherwise diverse have similar moral codes that command honoring parents, caring for children, speaking the truth, and administering impartial justice in the courts. The rationalist might say that the universality of these moral principles is evidence that they are innate within every human mind. However, how might an empiricist argue that these moral principles and others like them are really based on our common, human experience?

2. Because an empiricist believes that all our knowledge is derived from experience, how would an empiricist's approach to the education of young children differ from that of a rationalist?

3. Review what John Locke said about complex ideas. Randomly choose one page each out of several books (e.g., a novel, a science text, a political work, a religious work). Examine every idea or concept discussed in these pages. How might an empiricist attempt to explain these ideas as complexes built up from the simple ideas that originate in our experience?

EXAMINING THE STRENGTHS AND WEAKNESSES OF EMPIRICISM

Positive Evaluation

1. In ancient Greece and throughout the Middle Ages, the views of most philosophers and scientists were influenced by rationalistic assumptions. They reasoned that it was logically necessary for an object that was in motion to be continuously acted on by some force that kept it in motion. They also reasoned that the heavenly bodies must move in perfectly circular orbits, since the circle is the most perfect of all the geometrical figures. Scientists eventually discovered that these conclusions were false. Empiricism stresses that we can know about the world only through observation and not by reasoning about the way the world must be. In what way do you think empiricism might have been conducive to the rise of modern science and a more adequate understanding of the world?

2. One virtue of basing our beliefs on experience, empiricists claim, is that experience is a self-correcting process. If our conclusions are mistaken, further experience can reveal our mistakes to us. For example, since the swans in Britain and Europe were at one time exclusively white, people in these countries concluded that whiteness was an essential property of swans. Later, as world travel increased, they discovered black and brown swans in New Zealand and had to revise their conception of swans. Do you think that the self-correcting nature of experience is a distinct advantage of empiricism?

Negative Evaluation

1. Empiricists such as Hume assert the following claim: "There are no logically necessary truths about the world." Because of this assertion, empiricists think that only experience and not reason can tell us what reality is like. But is this assertion based on logic? If so, isn't this assertion itself a claim to have logically necessary knowledge about the nature of the world? If this claim is not a logically necessary truth, then how could experience ever reveal its truth to us? If Hume's knowledge claim cannot be explained in terms of his own theory of knowledge, is something wrong with his claim? If so, are the rationalists then right that reason can give us knowledge about the world?

2. John Locke believed that our experiences tell us about the nature of reality. But how could we ever know if Locke's belief is true, since we cannot jump outside our experience to compare it with reality?

3. In his attempt to make Locke's empiricism more rigorous, Berkeley was led to deny the existence of an external material world. Similarly, Hume's thoroughgoing empiricism led to skepticism about almost everything we believe. Are these conclusions the inevitable result of

empiricism? By confining our knowledge to what may be obtained within our experience, do we end up with a great deal of knowledge about ourselves but very little about the reality outside our experience? How can an empiricist avoid these extreme results?

4. Because we do not experience such things as human rights, moral duties, moral good and evil, and justice with the five senses, is it possible to have a viable empirical theory of ethics? Locke says that experience can provide us with the data for inferring what is morally right or wrong. But does it? Or does experience simply tell us the effects of behavior without providing a basis for determining whether these results are morally good or evil? Hume says morality is based on our emotions. Hence, does the empiricist leave us with nothing more than facts about human psychology, but nothing that would make possible a genuine ethical theory concerning right and wrong, good and evil?

5. Hume's rigorous empiricism led to skepticism concerning a continuously existing self. He bases his argument on the fact that we do not find anything enduring within experience, only fleeting, fragmentary sensations. But could we even know this fact if there was no such thing as a continuous self? If we know we are experiencing a succession of loose and separate impressions, as Hume claims, don't we as experiencers have to be something more than a series of loose and separate states ourselves? According to Hume's theory, the self is nothing more than "a bundle or collection of different perceptions, which . . . are in a perpetual flux and movement." But if this theory were true, wouldn't each moment of time seem as though it was our first conscious experience, and wouldn't we lack awareness of what preceded it?

2.4 KANTIAN CONSTRUCTIVISM

 LEADING QUESTIONS: *Constructivism*

1. The rationalists argue that experience alone cannot give us knowledge, for our knowledge requires the rational principles found in the mind. The empiricists argue that reason cannot give us knowledge, for we require the contributions of experience. Is it possible that each philosophy is partially correct and partially wrong? Is it possible that some sort of combined position will be more adequate? Why not opt for a rational-empiricism or an empirical-rationalism that views knowledge as the combined product of both reason and experience?

2. How do you know that every event must have a cause? You have experienced particular events and their causes in the past, but what grounds do you have for saying *every* event in the future will have a cause? This universal claim does not seem to be based on a posteriori knowledge of individual events. On the other hand, the statement does not seem to be a logical truth, for there is no *logical* contradiction in saying that something happened without a cause. Why then, are we so certain that the statement "Every event must have a cause" is true?

3. Look at some object from different angles (a coin, coffee cup, a book). Look at its top, bottom, edge, front, and back. What you literally see is a series of different visual impressions, each with a different shape and perhaps other aspects that change as the object is rotated. Now, suppose that you were unable to relate these different impressions together to see them as multiple aspects of the *same* object. What would your world be like if you simply experienced a succession of phenomena without being able to synthesize them into the experience of meaningful objects? The fact that you *do* see these multiple experiences as representing aspects of one object means that you interpret these experiences by means of the categories of unity, plurality, identity, object, properties, and so on. These categories cannot be derived from experience, because it is in terms of these categories that your successive experiences are made to be coherent and meaningful. Where, then, do these categories come from?

4. Try to imagine an apple that grew to be blue instead of red. Try to imagine a tree that is like every other living tree except that it is as transparent as glass. Try to imagine that diamonds were soft and rubbery instead of hard. Such natural anomalies are unlikely, but it is possible to imagine dramatic changes in nature that would produce such objects. Now try to imagine an apple or a tree or a diamond that does not exist in space or time. It is fairly clear that you could not experience such objects apart from experiencing them as having spatial and temporal qualities. Why can we imagine objects lacking their normal color and solidity, but we cannot imagine them lacking spatial and temporal dimensions? Most properties of objects (such as their color or density), we learn from experience and we can imagine them being different than they are. On the other hand, space and time seem to be necessary preconditions for any experience at all. Spatiality and temporality do not seem to be optional qualities of the objects that appear within experience. Why?

SURVEYING THE CASE FOR KANTIAN CONSTRUCTIVISM

IMMANUEL KANT (1724–1804)

Kant's Life

Immanuel Kant was born in Königsberg in what was then known as East Prussia (now Kaliningrad, Russia), and he lived there all his life. He was raised in Pietism, a Protestant sect that emphasized faith and religious feelings over reason and theological doctrines. Although Kant later took the position that knowledge is necessarily confined within the bounds of reason, he was always sensitive to the longings of the heart that aspire to transcend these limits. Being one of the most brilliant intellectuals of his day, he spent his life as a professor at the local university where he lectured on everything from philosophy to geography.

By most standards Kant's life was rather rigid and orderly, as is described for us in the charming portrait by the poet Heinrich Heine:

IMMANUEL KANT
(1724–1804)

> I do not believe that the great clock of the cathedral there did its daily work more dispassionately and regularly than its compatriot Immanuel Kant. Rising, coffee drinking, writing, reading college lectures, eating, walking, all had their fixed time, and the neighbors knew that it was exactly half past three when Immanuel Kant in his grey coat, with his bamboo cane in his hand, left his house door and went to the Lime tree avenue, which is still called, in memory of him, the Philosopher's Walk.[40]

However, while Kant's daily life was routine and mundane, the same could not be said of his ideas. Although his political ideas were relatively conservative, his theory of knowledge (epistemology) was revolutionary. It began with a devastating critique of the dominant philosophical traditions (rationalism and empiricism) and ended by radically revising how we think about knowledge. As a result, we now categorize all philosophy as either pre-Kantian or post-Kantian.

Kant's Agenda

Kant began his epistemology with the conviction that we *do* have knowledge. He thought it was undeniable that the disciplines of arithmetic, Euclidian geometry, and Newtonian physics provide us with information about our world. He also believed that these disciplines involve universal and necessary principles such that no future discoveries will ever shake our conviction of their truth. For example, it seems to be the case that necessarily anything we experience will conform to the following rules:

- The shortest distance between two points will always be a straight line.
- All events will have a cause.

The problem is that principles such as these give us universal and certain knowledge about the world, and yet, as Hume pointed out, no collection of particular experiences could ever provide an absolutely necessary basis for such universal claims about all possible experience. For example, you may have observed a cause for every time your car does not start (no gas, a loose wire, a dead battery). But the most that these experiences can tell you is that on these particular occasions, these particular events had a cause. Though you may have observed that every event you have experienced has had a cause, this observation doesn't provide a basis for knowing with certainty that every future event you will experience will have a cause. In other words, a finite collection of examples cannot prove a necessary truth. Nevertheless, as Kant observed, we do think that it is necessarily true that "all events will have a cause."

The question then for Kant was, How is such universal and necessary knowledge possible? He thought that the rationalists and the empiricists each provided us with one-half of the answer and that a compromise between them was required. In other words, Kant concluded that both reason and experience play a role in constructing our knowledge. Accordingly, Kant's epistemology could justifiably be called "rational-empiricism" or "empirical-rationalism." He himself called it "critical philosophy" because he wanted to critique reason, which means that he wanted to sort out the legitimate claims of reason from groundless ones.

Hume maintained that the only way we could have knowledge that is universal, necessary, and certain is if it is knowledge of the relations of ideas. Hence, we can know that it is necessarily true that "all gray elephants are elephants." The problem is that such knowledge doesn't tell us about the world because from the truth of that statement alone we could not know that there are any elephants or, if there are any, that they are gray. Knowledge that does give us information, the empiricists said, had to be a posteriori knowledge. An example of such knowledge would be "Lemon juice is acidic." Kant called this sort of knowledge **synthetic a posteriori knowledge** because it synthesizes, or brings together, the concepts of "lemon juice" and "acidic." The two concepts are not logically related the way that "bachelor" and "unmarried" are, because we can imagine lemon juice being nonacidic. Hence only through experience (a posteriori knowledge) could we know that statement to be true. Unlike Hume and the empiricists, the rationalists thought that we also could have **synthetic a priori knowledge.** This knowledge would not be derived from experience, would be universal and necessary, but would also give us information about the world. With the rationalists, Kant thought that statements such as "All events have a cause" provided us with synthetic a priori knowledge. However, Kant also believed with the empiricists that all knowledge began with experience. Hence, he accused the rationalists of attempting to fly above experience to know what reality is like beyond our experience. But he agreed with Hume that this stepping out of experience cannot be done. So the problem Kant faced was, How, within the bounds of experience, is synthetic a priori knowledge possible?

Kant once said that he did not fear being refuted but he did fear not being understood. His fears were well-founded, for both his ideas and his writing style are difficult. But if you can grasp the gist of what he was saying, you will be rewarded by having understood one of the most influential and revolutionary theses in the history of thought. As the first step

synthetic a posteriori knowledge knowledge that is based on experience and that adds new information to the subject

synthetic a priori knowledge knowledge that is acquired through reason, independently of experience, that is universal and necessary, and that provides information about the way the world is

in his reconstruction of epistemology, Kant begins his major work, the *Critique of Pure Reason,* with a discussion of the sources of our knowledge.

- The first sentence of each of the first two paragraphs begins with a statement of the relationship between knowledge and experience. What are the two points that Kant makes?
- Which of these two points sounds like empiricism? Which one sounds like rationalism?

FROM IMMANUEL KANT

Critique of Pure Reason [41]

There can be no doubt that all our knowledge begins with experience. For how should our faculty of knowledge be awakened into action did not objects affecting our senses partly of themselves produce representations, partly arouse the activity of our understanding to compare these representations, and, by combining or separating them, work up the raw material of the sensible impressions into that knowledge of objects which is entitled experience? In the order of time, therefore, we have no knowledge antecedent to experience, and with experience all our knowledge begins.

But though all our knowledge begins with experience, it does not follow that it all arises out of experience. For it may well be that even our empirical knowledge is made up of what we receive through impressions and of what our own faculty of knowledge (sensible impressions serving merely as the occasion) supplies from itself. If our faculty of knowledge makes any such addition, it may be that we are not in a position to distinguish it from the raw material, until with long practice of attention we have become skilled in separating it.

This, then, is a question which at least calls for closer examination, and does not allow of any off-hand answer:—whether there is any knowledge that is thus independent of experience and even of all impressions of the senses. Such knowledge is entitled *a priori,* and distinguished from the *empirical,* which has its sources *a posteriori,* that is, in experience.

- Read the second paragraph again. Kant says that our empirical knowledge (our knowledge about the world) is made up of elements from two sources. What are they? Note: "faculty of knowledge" refers to the mind.
- Note that in the third paragraph he suggests (in effect) that there can be genuine knowledge (synthetic knowledge) that is a priori.

A few pages later, Kant criticizes the rationalists (such as Plato) for supposing that reason can operate without the materials of experience. What metaphor does he use to make this point?

The light dove, cleaving the air in her free flight, and feeling its resistance, might imagine that its flight would be still easier in empty space. It was thus that Plato left the world of the senses, as setting too narrow limits to the understanding, and ventured out beyond it on the wings of the ideas, in the empty space of the pure understanding. He did not observe that with all his efforts he made no advance—meeting no resistance that might, as it were, serve as a support upon which he could take a stand, to which he could apply his powers, and so set his understanding in motion.

In what you just read, Kant says, "All our knowledge begins with experience." On this issue there is no question that Kant cast his lot with the empiricists. But he was well aware that if the only source of knowledge was experience, then Humean skepticism is the logical outcome. To avoid this outcome Kant adds: "But though all our knowledge begins with experience, it does not follow that it all arises out of experience," thus indicating that some of the rationalists' assumptions were still needed. However, he cautions that reason operating apart from experience is like the dove flapping its wings in empty space. In both cases, reason and the dove's wings need something (experience or air) to work with or against to be effective.

In this brief passage, we can see Kant attempting to negotiate a tricky tightrope between the positions of rationalism and empiricism by standing firm on their insights without falling into the problems that each position had produced. He agreed with the empiricists that our knowledge could not soar beyond the limits of experience, that the contents of experience provided the materials for all knowledge. Hence, any metaphysical conclusions about what reality is like *beyond the limits of experience* had to be ruled out as ungrounded. This conclusion meant that a nonphysical self, the infinity of the universe, or God could not be objects of human knowledge. Notice that he did not say that such things could not exist but merely that we could not have knowledge of them. Although he agreed with Hume that knowledge claims about such metaphysical topics were illusions, Kant still was convinced that these concepts played an important role in human life. The problem was how to understand their appropriate role. Furthermore, while confining knowledge to the bounds of experience, Kant resisted Hume's conclusion that all we have left is a series of fragmented, discrete sensations. If this conclusion were true, then the sort of absolutely certain and universal laws that are essential to science could never be found. The problem Kant faced was how to have the rationalists' certain and necessary knowledge (a priori knowledge) without doing the impossible—leaping outside human experience to a Godlike view of reality. On the other hand, Kant wanted to start where Hume started (in experience), without ending up where Hume ended up (in skepticism).

Kant's Revolution

Kant received an insight concerning the nature of knowledge from the example of Copernicus's great innovation. Copernicus rejected the theory that the sun revolves around the earth because he thought it did not give us a well-ordered picture of the data. Accordingly, he proposed that we switch the center of focus and see if it would make more sense to suppose that the earth revolves around the sun. Similarly, Kant proposed a "Copernican revolution" in epistemology. The empiricists thought that the mind is passive when confronting the world and that the mind simply records the impressions provided by the senses. In this picture, *knowledge conforms to its objects*. But can we know that it does? To know this, you would have to leap outside your mind and compare the contents of your experience with the contents of reality. In order to stay within experience while avoiding Hume's skepticism, Kant (like Copernicus) reversed this commonsense picture. He asks us to consider the possibility that *objects conform to our knowledge*.[42] In other words, Kant suggests that the only way the fluctuating, fragmented assortment of sense data can provide us with the experience of *objects* is if the mind imposes a certain rational structure on it.

The rationalists argued that science is possible because there is a correspondence between the mind and the world. Kant agreed, but he changed the character of this correspondence. He says the "world" that science studies is not something beyond experience but is a world of experience that the mind has actively filtered, digested, shaped, and organized according to the mind's own structure. Hence, Hume was correct in saying that a series of particular observations cannot give us certainty and universal laws. What Hume did not realize, according to Kant, was that we can find certainty and universal knowledge within experience if the mind organizes experience in a necessary and universal way. In this sense, the mind does not conform to an external world, but the contents found in experience do conform to the structure of the mind. The mind *constructs* its objects out of the raw materials provided by the senses. For this reason, I have labeled Kant's position on knowledge *constructivism*.

It is important to get clear on what Kant is and is not saying here. He is not saying that the mind brings reality into existence out of nothing. But he is saying that the way in which reality *appears* to us (the only reality that we can know) depends on the contribution of both the senses and the intellect. The mind imposes its own form on the sense data, and through this activity we have objects to be known. The only world we can know is the world of our experience which is (partially) constructed by the mind. This world consists of things-as-they-appear-to-us, which Kant refers to as the **phenomena** (or the phenomenal realm). Outside our experience are the things-in-themselves known as the **noumena** (or the noumenal realm). Since we can't jump outside our experience to see reality as it actually is, we cannot assign any positive content to the notion of the noumena. The concept is merely a limiting concept or a way of pointing to what lies beyond any possible experience.

Obviously, in our discussion of Kant, it will be impossible for us to leap outside experience to compare our view of the world as structured by the mind with the way reality is in itself. However, throughout this chapter I use analogies from within experience to illustrate the way that our experience is both a product of what is out there and a product of the distinctive way in which we organize, process, and shape what appears. Keep in mind that in these examples we will be comparing one kind of datum *within* experience (appearance 1) with another kind of datum (appearance 2) as a rough analogy of the relationship between the objects of human experience (phenomena) and the reality that lies *outside* experience (noumena).

phenomena in Kant's theory, the things-as-they-appear-to-us that exist in the world of our experience, which is partially constructed by the mind

noumena in Kant's theory, the things-in-themselves that exist outside our experience

---

🧪 THOUGHT EXPERIMENT: *The Objects of Experience*

1. If you require glasses to read, take them off and look at the words on this page. If you don't need glasses, you can still achieve the same effect by moving the page close to your nose until the words are hopelessly blurred. Do the same with a small, colored picture that has many complex details. The effect is that no longer are you presented with meaningful objects, whether these objects are the words on this page or the details in the picture. Instead, your visual field consists of indistinguishable shapes and splotches of gray or patches of color. However, under optimal conditions (you are wearing your glasses or the book is a normal distance from your eyes) you will see words or pictures of objects. In much the same way, Kant says, we do not simply see the world as a swirl of shapes and colors, for the mind functions like the lenses to provide us with an array of representations that present themselves as objects within experience.

2. Suppose I made the prediction that when I turn on the television in the morning to watch the *Today* show, the weatherman Al Roker will be wearing a tie colored in various shades of gray.[43] Furthermore, suppose that I claim this knowledge about the real world is known a priori, independently of my past experience of seeing what sorts of ties he wears. Whether the tie is striped, polka dot, paisley, or whatever, I know ahead of time it will be shades of gray. How can I make this prediction? The answer will be provided in the discussion to follow.

Kant's project involved the search for the universal and necessary conditions of any possible experience. If we find that certain conditions are necessary for us to have any experience at all, then these conditions would provide us with synthetic a priori knowledge of what must be true of the world-as-we-experience-it. In the eyeglasses example, the objects that appear within the person's visual experience are a product of both the sensory data and the way in which the lenses process this input. The eyeglasses do not create reality, but they do influence how that reality will appear.

We could extend the analogy and suppose that the glasses are red-tinted and that they cause everything to appear triangular in shape. Imagine further that there is no way to remove the lenses and see the world without them. Under these conditions, you still could not know the contents of a room apart from experiencing it. However, if you understood the nature of the glasses, you would understand the universal conditions of any possible experience you could have. While the specific contents of your experiences would vary, you would know prior to experience that whatever appeared, it would be a red-tinted and triangular object. Furthermore, if everyone viewed the world through the same kind of lenses, we could have objective and universal knowledge (prior to specific experiences) of the general character of any possible human experience. However, since the glasses cannot be removed, what we could not know is what the world was like outside our ways of experiencing it. This analogy illustrates the point Kant was making when he said that the objects within experience conform to the order that the mind imposes on sensation.

In the case of the television weatherman, I could know a priori that his tie would be gray if I knew that I would be watching him on a black-and-white television set. Imagine that we all had the same kind of television set and that our only knowledge of the world was what we saw on it. Our television sets then would have two effects: (1) they would make it possible for us to have experiences of such things as the weatherman's tie, and (2) they would allow us to see the world only in a certain way. In an analogous way, Kant says that the mind makes it possible for us to have meaningful experiences, but it also causes us to experience the world in certain ways. The tie as it really is in the studio corresponds to the noumenal realm, and the tie as it appears on our television sets corresponds to the phenomenal realm. Only a being (perhaps God) who did not have the limitations of our cognitive apparatus could know what reality is like in itself. But once we know the way that our minds necessarily condition experience, we can have universal and necessary knowledge of what reality-as-experienced will be like.

Our Experience of Space and Time

Exactly how does Kant think the mind structures our experience of reality? Kant says that the mind imposes a spatial and temporal form on experience. Space and time are not mysterious "things" that appear within experience; instead, they are fundamental frames of reference within which objects appear to us. As an example of spatial perception, look at the objects about you in your room. Perhaps you are seeing books, a coffee cup, and a CD player. However, the books are not literally in your mind. Instead, you have certain images that are appearing in your experience. But no matter what the specific contents of your experience may be, these images are always located within a spatial framework. The fact that objects have a spatial appearance is one way in which the mind structures experience, according to Kant. But aren't objects in the external world literally in space? The only way you could know that they are would be to jump outside your experience to experience reality-in-itself. Hence, it is meaningless to talk about space apart from the spatial perspective found within experience.

The same sort of mental activity provides a temporal dimension to your experience. Time is not an entity existing in itself out there in the world. Instead, it is a framework within which objects are presented to us. Imagine someone striking a bell three times. If you had instant amnesia after hearing each note, you would not experience *three* strikes of the bell. Hence, in addition to receiving each bit of sense data, the mind must remember each one, relate them together within a temporal sequence, and synthesize them as three successive experiences of the same thing.

THOUGHT EXPERIMENT: *Space and Time*

Kant offers us two thought experiments to show that space and time are necessary features of our experience.[44]

1. One by one, imaginatively subtract all the objects from the world until nothing is left but empty space without objects. This image seems to be conceivable. Now try to imagine a world in which there are objects but no space. For example, think what it would be like to experience a box that didn't have three dimensions. It can't be done. Why not? The reason is that spatial qualities are different from the qualities and objects of sensation. The mind arranges sensations through the form of space, but space is not itself a sensation. We don't experience space but we experience objects that are spatially structured in a particular way.

2. Try to imagine time without any objects enduring through it. In other words, imagine yourself viewing an empty universe in which there are no objects, but as you are viewing this void, time is still ticking on. If Kant is correct, you could imagine one temporal moment after another that is empty of events. Now try to imagine yourself experiencing objects (trees, a sunset, moving clouds) but without any temporal succession. If Kant is correct, this image is impossible. The reason, he says, is that time is a universal condition for the very possibility of there being objects of experience at all. The form of temporality structures every possible experience of objects. Yet time is not itself a "thing" because it is not something with sensory properties.

Kant's theory of space and time seems rather fantastic. The spatial and temporal nature of our experience is so familiar we have a hard time imagining that these qualities could be only forms of our human experience. To make Kant's view even more plausible, imagine how the world appears to a fly, with its multifaceted eyes. Its experience of space is one in which every object appears hundreds of times. The fly's world is spatially structured in a very different way from ours. So *our* experience of space is not the only possible one. Similarly, to make it plausible that both our spatial and temporal experiences are uniquely human, Kant suggests that some other sort of being (perhaps God) might experience reality without our spatial limitations and might be able to know the past, present, and future in one, simultaneous experience.[45] So once again, maybe *our* spatially and temporally formed experience is not the only way that reality could be known. Even though we can suppose that reality could be experienced in radically different ways by God, our experience will always have a particular kind of spatial and temporal dimension.

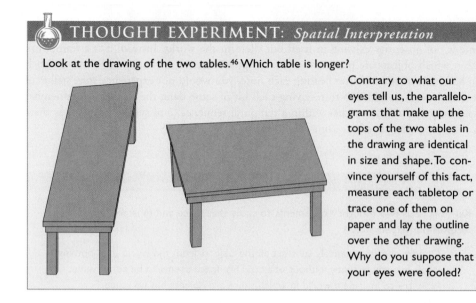

THOUGHT EXPERIMENT: *Spatial Interpretation*

Look at the drawing of the two tables.[46] Which table is longer?

Contrary to what our eyes tell us, the parallelograms that make up the tops of the two tables in the drawing are identical in size and shape. To convince yourself of this fact, measure each tabletop or trace one of them on paper and lay the outline over the other drawing. Why do you suppose that your eyes were fooled?

When you looked at the drawings of the tables in the thought experiment, you perceived them as three-dimensional objects. Accordingly, your mind imposed a spatial perspective on the picture that gave the appearance that the left table is receding away from you, while the long axis of the right table appears to be closer to your position in space. Once you imposed a depth interpretation on the collection of lines, your mind formed the judgment that the left table must be longer. In much the same way, when we look about our room, our visual field consists of rectangular, circular, or triangular shapes (among others). These shapes appear to us within a spatially structured field of vision. Of course, unlike the shapes in the drawing, we can move about the room. But the movement only gives us a series of tactile sensations that we have learned to correlate with our visual images. In the final analysis, Kant says, the experience of space and time is something that universally and necessarily characterizes our experienced world. But always remember that we are talking about *our experience of the world* and not what it is like outside our experience.

The Categories of the Understanding

To understand what comes next, it is important to know that Kant refers to the raw data of sense perception as *intuitions*. This term should not be confused with our use of the word to refer to a special gift of insight or a gut feeling. Instead, *intuition* in Kant's sense means "the object of the mind's direct awareness." For example, to experience the redness of a rose is to have a sensory intuition. Kant believes that two powers of the mind are at work in experience; he calls these powers *sensibility* and *understanding*. Sensibility is a passive power; it is the ability of the mind to receive sensory intuitions. The understanding is an active power that enables us to organize the intuitions we receive into meaningful objects by applying concepts to our experience.

Thus far Kant has been talking about our passive reception (sensibility) of perceptual data (intuitions) and the way in which the mind gives a spatial and temporal form to this data. However, if our experience consisted only of spatially and temporally organized intuitions, we would not have knowledge. Instead, we would experience a confusing barrage of unrelated colors and sounds within space and time (perhaps not unlike a newborn baby's experience). Hence, a further set of organizing principles is needed. These principles are provided by the understanding and are called the *categories of the understanding*. The understanding provides us with concepts (categories) that enable us to form intuitions into meaningful objects that can be the basis of thought. To use an analogy, imagine a cylindrical cookie press into which you place dough and squeeze it out the other end through a star-shaped hole. Just as the cookie is the product of a certain content (the dough) being processed by a shape (the cookie press), so knowledge is the product of our sensibility providing us with spatial and temporal intuitions and the understanding using its conceptual categories to organize these intuitions. For Kant, a concept is not a kind of image, for it has no content in itself (any more than the star-shaped hole in the cookie press has content). Instead, a concept is a rule for organizing our intuitions into objects of experience. In the next passage, think of intuitions as the dough and think of sensibility as that part of our cognitive apparatus that allows us to receive intuitions (the cookie press that holds the dough). Furthermore, think of the understanding as the source of our concepts and think of our concepts as the star-shaped hole (or round hole, or tree-shaped hole) in the cookie press that organizes and shapes the raw materials.

FROM IMMANUEL KANT

Critique of Pure Reason [47]

There are two stems of human knowledge, namely, *sensibility* and *understanding,* which perhaps spring from a common, but to us unknown root. Through the former, objects are given to us; through the latter, they are thought. . . . To neither of these powers may a preference be given over the other. Without sensibility no object would be given to us, without understanding no object would be thought. Thoughts without content are empty, intuitions without concepts are blind. It is, therefore, just as necessary to make our concepts sensible, that is, to add the object to them in intuition, as to make our intuitions intelligible, that is, to bring them under concepts. These two powers or capacities cannot exchange their functions. The understanding can intuit nothing, the senses can think nothing. Only through their union can knowledge arise.

- What does Kant mean when he says "thoughts without content are empty, intuitions without concepts are blind"? Rephrase this quote in your own words and try to explain it to a friend.

THOUGHT EXPERIMENT: *Perceptual Objects*

1. Consider the following collection of multishaded squares. Can you cause your eyes to form them into a pattern representing a well-known face? (Hint: hold the image at some distance from your eyes and squint your eyes, causing the individual squares to blur and merge.)

Figure 1

(continued . . .)

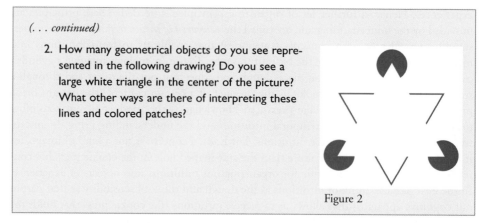

(. . . continued)

2. How many geometrical objects do you see represented in the following drawing? Do you see a large white triangle in the center of the picture? What other ways are there of interpreting these lines and colored patches?

Figure 2

Most people see Figure 1 as representing the face of Abraham Lincoln. But at first glance, the figure appears to be a chaotic collection of shaded patches. To see them as representing an object, the mind must form them into a single, unified pattern. Obviously, to recognize the figure as a picture of Lincoln you would have had to have seen a picture of Lincoln previously. Seeing the picture *as* Lincoln is a matter of past experience, but seeing the patches *as* an object is a matter of the mind's innate capacity for organizing your sensations. In other words, more is going on in perception than just light hitting the retina. The mind must take that data and impose a unity on it.

It is normal to view Figure 2 as containing three circles that are overlaid with two triangles. However, notice that what is actually presented to the eyes are three partial circles with a missing pie-shaped slice, and three open-ended angles (a total of six figures). Your mind takes this data and interprets the three curved shapes as complete circles that are partially obscured by a white borderless triangle laid over them. Similarly, your mind takes the three open angles and views them as the corners of a large triangle with a black border that is also partially obscured by the large white triangle. Notice that the white borderless triangle *literally is not in the picture.* The mind takes the empty, white space between the other shapes and creates the image of a triangle. This figure is a striking example of the mind creating its own objects out of the data presented to it.

These optical experiments do not exactly represent Kant's Copernican revolution, but they do show how what we experience is a composite of both sense data and the work of the mind. In these examples, the mind did not produce the data; it was imposed on you from without in the form of light rays from the picture hitting your retina. But this data appeared to you as a collection of shapes because your mind formed the data into meaningful objects. This aspect of our experience leads to an important feature of Kant's account of knowledge. Some concepts, such as "Lincoln," "dog," or "apple," obviously do not reside in the mind but are based on what we learn from experience. Kant calls these concepts *empirical concepts.* But before you could recognize that something is an apple, you first would have to recognize it as a unified object containing certain properties. Hence, your distinct sensations of redness, roundness, sweetness, and crunchiness are collected together and viewed as composing a single substance. Without the category of substance you would have just a chaos of sensations (intuitions). But substance is not something we experience as we do the sensations making up our experience of the apple. For this reason, Kant says that *substance is a pure concept.* It is one of the categories of the understanding that we do not derive from our sensations but that we bring to experience to organize it in terms of unified objects. Other categories include causality, unity, plurality, possibility, necessity.

Port St. Tropez (1899) by Paul Signac. This painting is an example of the technique of pointillism, which emerged during the period of postimpressionism. Instead of creating colors by mixing them on their palette, the pointillists applied dabs of pure color to the canvas, causing the mind of the viewer to blend the colors and organize the individual points into meaningful patterns of forms and objects. Similarly, according to Kant, all experience is a matter of the mind imposing its structure on the world by organizing bare sense data into meaningful objects.

Kant identifies 12 categories in all that serve as the framework within which all our judgments about the world are made.

It will be helpful to contrast Kant's account of experience with that of Hume. According to Hume, we are passive spectators of a world of continuously changing sensations (colors, shapes, sounds, smells, and textures). Within experience, Hume said, we find

> perceptions which succeed each other with an inconceivable rapidity and are in a perpetual flux and movement. . . . The mind is a kind of theatre, where several perceptions successively make their appearance; pass, re-pass, glide away, and mingle in an infinite variety of postures and situations.[48]

However, these sensations are not exactly what we experience, according to Kant. We do not experience mere patches of colors or unrelated sounds and other bits of sensation. Instead, we experience a world of meaningful objects. Things in experience could only appear that way if the mind was taking the fragmented "pings" of sensation and arranging them together into distinct objects that appear in space and have identity through time.

Since we can never turn off the mind's structuring of the sense data, we can never have a pure, unmediated experience of the world. However, we may come close through experiences such as the alarm clock going off in the morning. For a moment, we are bombarded with sensations (the raucous sound of the alarm and daylight streaming through the window). These nearly raw, unconceptualized experiences intrude on us as a "buzzing, blooming confusion" (as psychologist-philosopher William James once described the experience of a baby). Eventually, we begin to make sense of the experience when the following stream of thoughts occurs: "This uncomfortable sensation is a sound—this sound is a buzzer—caused by the alarm—which means morning—which means I have to get going." Even before this level of mental processing begins, however, the mind has already structured the experience in terms of the *forms* of (*a*) time and (*b*) space and the *categories* of (*c*) substance and (*d*) causality. For example, your first awareness of the alarm clock takes this form: "(*a*) There is an enduring stimulus (time), (*b*) external to me (space), (*c*) it is some object (substance), (*d*) but what is causing it? (causality)." Hence, even the most raw level of experience will be structured by the mind, and only because the mind brings order to experience are sensations able to become knowledge.

What Is Reality Like?

The good news of Kant's epistemology is that we can have objective, universal, and necessary knowledge of the world. The reason we can have this knowledge is that the world we know is always the world of experience, and the world of experience, no matter how much its content may vary, will always have a certain structure. Because of this structure, synthetic a priori judgments are possible. Just as I can know that the weatherman's tie will be gray, so I can know that "every event has a cause." In the first case, the judgment about the tie is an empirical one based on my knowledge of my receiving instrument. (Of course, this example is merely an analogy of what goes on in all experience.) In the second case (the one Kant is concerned with), the judgment about causality is a necessary one based on the nature of the human mind. What is crucial for Kant is that every human mind will structure experience in the same universal and necessary way. The bad news of Kant's position is that we can never know reality in itself because we can never jump outside our minds and see what reality is like before our minds have done their job of processing and filtering it. Think again about the representation of the weatherman on the black and white television. If our eyes were like that television set and unable to represent colors to us, then our entire world of experience would be in shades of black, white, and gray. We could never know about the colors in the real world. For Kant, that analogy is very similar to our actual lot in life. The only world we know is the world that appears to us in experience (phenomena). But because experience is structured by the mind, we can never know reality in itself (noumena).

Self, Cosmos, and God

If we accept Kant's account of how the mind and experience work together, then it is clear that the categories of the mind cannot give us knowledge of anything that transcends experience, any more than the cookie press by itself can give us cookies. The categories are merely empty forms of thought that must be filled with sensory content to produce knowledge. As 20th-century philosopher Norman Melchert says about the categories,

> Compare them to mathematical functions, such as x^2. Until some number is given as *x,* we have no object. If a content for *x* is supplied, say 2 or 3, then an object is speci-

fied, in these cases the numbers 4 or 9. The categories of substance, cause, and the rest are similar. They are merely operators, the function of which is to unite "in one consciousness the manifold given in intuition."[49]

The implications of Kant's epistemology are enormous. It means that we cannot know such things as the self, the world-as-a-whole, or God, for these things are outside the bounds of any possible experience. Kant refers to the attempt to reason about these topics "transcendent illusions." First, with respect to the self, we can, of course, know our own moods, feelings, thoughts, and the other contents of our internal experience. But as Hume pointed out, these items are simply fleeting experiences and do not give us the experience of a substantial, enduring self. The problem is that we want to use the concept of substance to think of that real self that underlies all these experiences. But because "substance" can only apply to the world of human experience, we can't use it to refer to a mysterious reality that underlies experience.

The second metaphysical illusion is the assumption that we can reason about the cosmos (or the world-as-a-totality). The problem is that all we can know are bits and pieces of world experience, but the totality is never experienced. Thus, to think of the world as a whole, we would have to take a Godlike perspective outside space and time. To make clear what happens when reason tries to fly beyond experience (remember the example of the dove), Kant gives a series of arguments that lead to conflicting conclusions (called "antinomies"). For example, he first argues that the world is finite in space and time and then turns around and argues that it is infinite. He argues that some events are free and then that all events are determined. Kant says that because rational arguments can establish contradictory conclusions on these topics, reason has gone beyond its proper bounds.

Finally, if our knowledge is limited to only what we can experience, then we are prevented from reasoning about God. He says that attempts to demonstrate God's existence are "altogether fruitless and by their nature null and void."[50] For example, we cannot reason about the cause of the world, for causality is only a way of relating the items within our experience. But if the limits of reason prevent us from proving God's existence, they also prevent us from disproving it as well. So in Kant's epistemology the theist and the atheist are in the same boat. In the final analysis, the notions of self, cosmos, and God are illusory if we think we can have knowledge of their objects, but Kant considers them important and irresistible notions. Though the ideas lack empirical content, they do serve the useful function of regulating our thought. They provide us with an ideal toward which we will always strive: knowledge that is a complete, unified, and systematic whole. Perhaps we can think of these notions like the converging lines in a painting that lead to an infinite point beyond the horizon. Like the perspective indicators in the painting, the concepts of self, cosmos, and God provide a meaningful framework for that which we actually do experience. With respect to God, Kant suggested that though we cannot have rational knowledge of this topic, we might still find the idea indispensable to make sense of morality. Hence, in the preface to his *Critique*, Kant says, "I have therefore found it necessary to deny *knowledge*, in order to make room for *faith*."[51]

To summarize, Kant believed that (1) we can *never know* reality as it is in itself, because (2) our minds *structure* our experience of reality. Furthermore, (3) there is a *single* set of forms and categories by which this structuring is done, which is *universal* to every human knower, and (4) this process is fundamentally *rational*. In the remaining sections of this chapter, we see that many of the philosophers after Kant accepted (1) and (2), but they discarded (3) and sometimes (4), leading to a wide range of post-Kantian philosophies that took a radically different direction from the one that he had charted.

LOOKING THROUGH KANT'S LENS

1. Look about you and briefly take note of the objects in your current experience (books, tables, chairs, a coffee cup). As you are viewing your surroundings, try to imagine that you had lost the ability to organize your sensations into a collection of objects and could only experience a fragmented, unrelated, and unintelligible flow of sensations (patches of colors and shapes). What would this experience be like? Does this exercise suggest that the mind plays a very important role in the construction of our experience of the world?

2. Try an experiment to imagine what your experienced world would be like without the form of spatiality imposed on it. Watch a car (or a person) as it comes from the distance toward you. Focus on what is actually appearing within your experience while trying to suspend any spatial interpretations you make about it. Think of the experience as a very small, carlike image that is growing in size within your visual field. If we did not organize our sensations spatially, this growing image is all we would see. We would have small images growing into large images instead of the experience of a car of constant size that appears in the distance and then moves closer to us.

3. Kant says that because all we can know is the world of experience (phenomena), science cannot tell us about any reality in the noumenal realm outside our physical sensations. Science tells us about the world only as it is perceived, measured, manipulated, experimented upon, and so on. Even though the world apart from our scientific interpretations is (strictly speaking) unknowable, we can formulate laws, explanations, and predictions within the realm of human experience. Given the fact that science cannot tell us about reality itself, why does Kant think that scientific knowledge is adequate? Given these limitations of science, why does Kant think that science could never be a threat to religious faith?

EXAMINING THE STRENGTHS AND WEAKNESSES OF KANTIAN CONSTRUCTIVISM

Positive Evaluation

1. Does Kant's recognition of the contributions of both reason and sensation in forming our knowledge make his epistemology more adequate than that of either the rationalists or the empiricists?

2. Try to imagine that you had a cognitive defect such that you could not think of the world in terms of causes and effects, yet your experience remained the same as it is now. Under these circumstances, flipping a switch followed by the light going on would be no different than coughing while at an intersection followed by the traffic light turning green. However, the fact is that we do connect flipping the switch and the light because the sequence is a regular and ordered one, but we do not connect coughing and the green light, because this sequence is not regular and does not follow any particular order. This scenario illustrates Kant's point that causality is not an item of experience (like the sensation of light), but is a way in which we inevitably organize our experiences into those sequences that are regular and those that are not. Could you imagine what life would be like if the mind did not have this feature?

Negative Evaluation

1. Kant says that the mind shapes and forms the reality we experience. But in order for this shaping and forming to take place, must there not be some measure of affinity between the categories of the mind and the nature of reality in itself? If the mind can interact with reality at all, isn't it unlikely that their respective structures are totally different? If there is this inevitable correspondence between the way in which the mind works and the way in which reality works, then is Kant wrong in claiming that we can never know what reality is like outside the mind?

2. Biology tells us that species that adapt to external conditions survive and those that do not adapt do not survive. Has the human species done so well in surviving because our cognitive abilities have developed in response to the external environment? If so, then isn't it true that our minds must conform to reality rather than our experience of reality conforming to the structure of the mind? Does this conclusion mean that Kant's Copernican revolution is mistaken?

3. Anthropologists have discovered that people in different cultures perceive spatial and temporal relationships differently. Does this discovery undermine Kant's theory that space and time are a priori and universal ways of shaping experience that are built into every human mind?

4. According to Kant, because our knowledge is confined within the boundaries of human experience, we can know nothing about reality as it is in itself (the noumenal realm). How, then, does he even know that the noumenal realm exists? To be consistent, shouldn't he suspend judgment and remain silent about a reality external to our experience?

2.5 EPISTEMOLOGICAL RELATIVISM

LEADING QUESTIONS: *Epistemological Relativism*

1. What are facts? We speak of facts as being hard, cold, objective, and stubborn. We are asked for the plain, observable, unvarnished facts. We are told to face the facts, to collect them, or to check them out. These comments might lead us to think that facts are physical things out there in the world, independent of us. But are facts items in the world alongside trees, rocks, and grass? We can trip over a rock, but can we trip over a fact? The moon looks round but what does a fact look like? We can photograph a sunset but can we photograph facts? We can weigh apples but can we weigh facts? You can say how many objects are in your room but how many facts are in your room? Is there space enough for all of them? If these questions have convinced you that facts are not out in the world, then where are they? Could we say that facts are somehow embedded in our language or belief systems? If so, then is a fact a function of who we are, how we see the world, and how we think or speak about it? What would be the implications of this "fact"?

2. We believe that the material objects of our everyday lives are incapable of vanishing into thin air by magic. If we can't find our keys, we believe that they are *somewhere;* they did not just cease to exist. But imagine a culture in which the people do believe that material objects sometimes disappear into nothingness (without being crushed, melted, burned up, or destroyed in other ways according to *our* laws of physics).[52] So, when you lose your keys in this culture and never find them again, these people would assume that the keys had just dematerialized without a trace. According to *their* laws of physics, nature

sometimes behaves this way. We have all had the experience of pulling a load of laundry out of the dryer and finding that one sock is missing. Sometimes, no matter how hard we search (in the laundry bag, in the washer, inside other clothing), we never find the missing sock. "So there you have it," the people from this culture say, "irrefutable evidence that occasionally things can simply vanish." How would you convince these people that they are wrong and that our laws of physics are right?

3. What do you see when you look at this diagram? You probably said that the picture was that of a cube or a box. In some cultures that do not have our conventions for drawing perspective, the people can only see the figure as a two-dimensional pattern, much like a plaid pattern. Their cultural conventions prevent their eyes from interpreting the drawing as representing a three-dimensional object. (Now see if *you* can visualize the figure as a flat pattern and not as a box.) Is it possible that our entire perspective on the world is like this exercise? Is it possible that your perceptual, conceptual, moral, aesthetic, and scientific ways of interpreting the world are merely how you see it and are no more objectively true or correct than other ways of interpreting it?

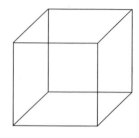

SURVEYING THE CASE FOR RELATIVISM

From Kant to Relativism

The philosophers whose views of knowledge and truth we have studied, such as Socrates, Plato, Descartes, Locke, and Berkeley, disagreed over the nature of knowledge and the best method for obtaining it. But they were all in agreement that if we obtain knowledge, we will have arrived at objective, universal truths about the world. In other words, they all agreed that there is one true story about the world.

The positions of all the philosophers just mentioned are various versions of objectivism. **Objectivism** (in epistemology) is the claim that there is one set of universal truths or facts about the world and that these truths are independent of us. Sometimes objectivism is called *absolutism*. However, because some people associate absolutism with a kind of nasty, dogmatic, authoritarian, and intolerant attitude, I have chosen to use *objectivism* instead. I would maintain that you can hold to objectivism (the belief that there are universal, mind-independent truths) without claiming that you necessarily have all the truth; thus, you can still be open-minded, willing to modify your beliefs, and tolerant and respectful of the views of others. We talk about "searching for the truth," but that search makes sense only if there is something to be found (unlike the search for the mythical pot of gold at the end of the rainbow).

Immanuel Kant was an objectivist, although he added a new twist to the position. His Copernican revolution in knowledge advanced the thesis that our knowledge of reality is not direct and unmediated, for our experience is always structured by the categories of the mind. From this thesis it follows that we can never know reality-in-itself. Still, Kant believed that the way in which our minds structure experience is the same for everyone. So Kant concluded that within the realm of human experience (what other realm could we know?), universal and objective knowledge was not only a possibility but an accomplished fact.

Now suppose Kant's revolution was correct (the mind structures our experience of reality). But suppose that he was wrong in maintaining there is one universal way in which all

objectivism the claim that there is one set of universal truths or facts about the world and that these truths are independent of us

human minds are structured or only one way in which it is possible to make sense out of the world. It would then follow that different people would experience the world in different ways. There would be no one set of truths about the world, and no particular set of opinions would be more true than another. I may think that my position is more "true" and a more "accurate" account of reality than yours, but I am always viewing your position and reality itself through my particular mental lens. We cannot jump outside our minds to compare our mental concepts with reality itself.

If you have followed this journey from Kant's objectivism (with its singular set of rational, mental categories) to the proposal that there are multiple ways of structuring experience, then you are beginning to understand what relativism is all about. *Epistemological relativism* is the claim that there can be no universal, objective knowledge of reality because all knowledge is relative to the conceptual system of either the individual or one's culture. In other words, epistemological relativism is the belief that the world has not one true story, but many stories.

This position is variously called conceptual, cognitive, or epistemological relativism, because it asserts the relativity of all concepts, beliefs, and knowledge claims. In chapter 5 we examine ethical relativism, which holds to the same sort of claim about ethical principles, judgments, and statements. The epistemological relativist says that *all* claims are relative, so this statement would necessarily include ethical claims. Hence, if you accept the first position, you would have to adopt the second as well. However, the reverse is not true, for you could believe that ethical beliefs are relative while holding that other sorts of beliefs (scientific beliefs, for example) are objective.

STOP AND THINK

Many popular phrases express the sentiments of relativism: "That may be true for you, but it's not true for me." "Beauty is in the eye of the beholder." "When in Rome, do as the Romans do." "We all have our own opinion about the matter, and who's to say whose belief is right?" "Different strokes for different folks." "It all depends on your point of view." "I believe this because that's just where I'm coming from."

- Can you think of other common ways of expressing relativism?
- Find examples in everyday conversations of expressions that suggest relativism.

Degrees of Relativism

To further focus the issue it is worth noting that there are several trivial forms of relativism that even an objectivist could accept. "For you, oysters taste delicious, but for me, they taste awful." Hardly anyone would deny that taste in foods is a relative matter that depends on individual preferences. One person's claim that oysters are delicious and my claim that they taste awful could be equally true because we are really not making a claim about the objective properties of oysters at all, but about our personal tastes. Hence, claims about the tastes of foods always imply that the phrase "to me" is implicitly tagged on to the end of the claim. Similarly, if I am standing on the front steps of the library, then for me, the library is "here." If you are across the street, then for you, the library is "there." Obviously, the terms *here* and *there*, as well as *left* and *right*, are always relative to the location of the speaker. But these "relative" statements really contain objective claims because the relative terms could be replaced by more objective spatial locators (such as the coordinates on a map).

Finally, a third kind of statement could be consistent with either objectivism or relativism, depending on how it is interpreted: "That's true for you but it is not true for me." This statement is ambiguous because it could have two different meanings. On the following interpretation the statement is trivially true: "If someone believes X, *then for that person* X is *thought* to be true." Of course! From the standpoint of medieval science it was "true" that the sun revolved around the earth. Similarly, according to some cultures it is "true" that the birth of twins will bring an evil curse to the society, so they must be destroyed. But this way of interpreting the original statement assumes that the statement is merely making a claim about the speaker's belief state, which still allows us to go on to ask if the belief in question really is true. (For the medievals it was true that the sun revolved around the earth, but does it *really*? Is there *really* a causal relationship between the birth of twins and bad fortune as these people think there is?) However, under another interpretation the original statement could be a full-fledged statement of relativism. Hence, the claim that "That's true for you but it is not true for me" could mean: "There is no objective truth about the matter, there are only different opinions, and one opinion is just as true as another."

THOUGHT EXPERIMENT: *Objective and Relative Truth*

The following is a list of different issues. You might have a certain opinion on the issue, but your opinion is not relevant for the purposes of this exercise. What is relevant is whether you think the issue is one for which there is an objectively true answer and objectively false answers. To say that a claim is "objective" means that the truth or falsity of the claim is independent of whether any individual or culture believes it to be true or false. In this sense, you can judge that a claim or an issue is objective even though you are not sure what the true answer might be. If you think a particular issue is an objective one, put a mark in the "objective" column by that claim. However, if you do not think that the issue has either an objectively true or false answer, that it is solely a matter of opinion, then decide whether the truth or falsity of the answer is a matter of individual opinion (check "individually relative") or is a matter that is relative to one's culture (check "culturally relative").

Issue: Whether or Not . . .	Objective	Individually Relative	Culturally Relative
1. Asparagus is delicious.			
2. Picasso's paintings have artistic merit.			
3. Johann Sebastian Bach is the greatest composer who ever lived.			
4. The Bible gives us the truest account of the purpose of life.			

(continued . . .)

5.	Abortion is morally wrong, no matter what the circumstances.			
6.	The institution of slavery in the United States was morally bad.			
7.	Democracy is the best form of government.			
8.	The earth is more than a billion years old.			
9.	The color of your eyes is determined by your genes.			
10.	The earth has been visited by space aliens.			

How you answered the questions indicates the degree to which you are a relativist. Statement 1 has to do with tastes in foods. Most people would say that this issue is relative to individual opinion. Statements 2 and 3 have to do with aesthetic judgments. You could be a relativist on these sorts of issues but an objectivist on others. If you think statement 4 is either true or false, you are an objectivist on religious issues. On the other hand, a religious relativist would say that this claim, like all religious claims, is purely a matter of personal choice, for there is no one, correct answer. Statements 5 and 6 deal with ethical claims. You could be a relativist on some ethical issues while believing that other ethical claims are objectively true no matter what an individual or culture believes. Statement 7 is a normative political judgment. Some objectivists would say it is true and others that it is false. A relativist would say that it depends solely on the preferences of the individual or a society. Statements 8, 9, and 10 are *claims* about empirical facts. To say that these statements are claims does not mean that they are true. You may think that the evidence shows that the earth is either older or younger than is claimed here. Furthermore, most (but not all) people think that the claim about aliens in statement 10 is false. The issue here is whether there is some set of objective facts that makes the claim true or false independent of our beliefs about it. Someone who thinks these last three issues are simply a matter of personal or cultural opinion is probably as thoroughgoing a relativist as one can be. How many issues did you label as either individually or culturally relative? Were there any issues that you said were objective ones? How do you distinguish between issues that are objective and those in which there is no higher truth other than personal or cultural opinion?

Skepticism versus Relativism

On these and similar issues, it is important to distinguish between the positions of skepticism and relativism. Although the skeptic and relativist both reject the possibility of arriving at objectively true answers to philosophical questions, they do so for different reasons.

Is there a difference between truth and falsehood? Or does it just depend on how you look at it?

The skeptic may accept the possibility that a philosophical question has one true answer, but simply claim that it is impossible for us to know the truth about the matter. In section 4.2, for example, we will see that David Hume took the objectivist stance that either there is an all-powerful, personal God who created the universe or there is not. He simply insisted that we had no way of knowing which alternative is true. On the other hand, the relativist says that there is no one true answer to any philosophical question. Truth claims are always relative to the beliefs of the individual or society. Hence, the relativist insists that any time you make a truth claim about God, the nature of reality, ethics, politics, and so on, your claim could be true only with respect to your point of view or that of your society. To put it simply, the relativist claims that all truth is relative in the same way that tastes in food are relative. For the relativists, we are always immersed within our particular historical age, particular culture, or personal perspective and can no more rise above these circumstances than we could jump out of our skins or lift ourselves up by our own bootstraps.

But does the relativist believe that there is no reality outside our belief systems? Well, yes and no. *Reality*, like *fact, rationality,* and *truth,* is a word and a concept. As such, it is always rooted in a particular conceptual and linguistic scheme. To ask if our belief system conforms to reality is like trying to use a pair of pliers to grab itself. We use our particular notion of reality to get a grip on our experience, but we can't use it to get a grip on our conceptual scheme because it is a part of what constitutes that scheme. To switch metaphors, I view the world through my eyeglasses, but I cannot take my glasses off and examine them without using some other glasses through which to see them. But how can I tell if this second pair of glasses is adequate unless I examine them through some other lenses? According to the relativists, we always and necessarily view the world through some sort of conceptual lenses, but there is no neutral instrument by means of which we can examine and evaluate our own or anyone else's conceptual lenses.

STOP AND THINK

Imagine that you were to make a list of all your beliefs. Now imagine that you made a second list of everything that was true. Would the lists be any different? Surely not. If you believe something, you do so because you think it is true, and if you consider something to be true, then you believe it. Is the relativist therefore correct in claiming that truth is always a function of our web of beliefs? Can we ever break out of our belief system to compare it with what lies outside it?

So here we are—stuck within the human situation and unable to lift ourselves up by our own bootstraps to see the world from a Godlike perspective. So what do we do? According to contemporary philosopher Richard Rorty, we keep talking. He says that the point of philosophy is "to keep the conversation going rather than to find objective truth."[53] Different personal, historical, and cultural viewpoints about philosophical, religious, and ethical issues (to name just a few) are like the images created by the turns of a kaleidoscope. Thousands of patterns are possible, each view is different and is fascinating in itself, some may work better for *us* than others, but no particular image is the "right" one or the most "accurate" one or the only one that everyone is compelled to view. To say that a belief is "true" is simply to claim that we find it good for *us* to believe it, according to Rorty.

Here are a few examples of how the same situation can be viewed differently, described differently, and evaluated differently, depending on your particular perspective.

- In American history books, the American Revolution is presented as one of the great turning points in world history. However, one of my professors once said that when he was a schoolboy in England, his history book covered the American Revolution in only a footnote, referring to it simply as "the revolt of the colonies."
- History books refer to 1492 as the year that "Columbus discovered America." However, that expression irritates Native Americans. How could Columbus "discover" America if it had never been hidden because their ancestors were already here? Instead, Native Americans view Columbus's "discovery" as "the invasion of our homelands by the Europeans."
- Sydney J. Harris, a newspaper columnist, loved to point out how the same facts could be described by different people in different ways. Some of my favorites are:

  - My children are permitted to engage in "self-expression," but your children are "spoiled."
  - I turn down invitations because I "enjoy privacy," but you turn down invitations because you are "antisocial."
  - I won't change my mind because I have "firm principles," but you won't change your mind because you are "fanatical."

Can you think of other examples in which the same facts are described in different ways?

Varieties of Relativism

You may have noticed that implicit in our discussion thus far has been the distinction between different kinds of relativism. When someone claims that all knowledge or truth is relative, the question that arises is, Relative to what? One answer is that beliefs are relative to each person's individual perspective. This assertion of individual relativism is commonly called **subjectivism.** The Greek Sophist Protagoras is said to have claimed:

> Each one of us is a measure of what is and of what is not; but there is all the difference in the world between one man and another just in the very fact that what is and appears to one is different from what is and appears to the other.[54]

Similarly, the 19th-century existentialist Friedrich Nietzsche repeatedly preached subjectivism in passages such as this one:

> Gradually it has become clear to me what every great philosophy so far has been: namely, the personal confession of its author and a kind of involuntary and unconscious memoir.[55]

When a young man came to the contemporary French philosopher Jean-Paul Sartre seeking ethical advice, the only advice Sartre would give him was "You are free, therefore choose—that is to say, invent."[56] If all truth claims are subjective and relative to an individual's perspective, then what could any assertion be except a "personal confession"? Hence, the subjectivist thinks that the qualifier "true for me" is implicit in all assertions.

subjectivism the claim that beliefs are relative to each person's individual perspective

cultural relativism the claim that all beliefs are relative to a particular culture

On the other hand, we could claim that all beliefs are relative to a particular culture. For obvious reasons, this claim is called **cultural relativism.** For example, the anthropologist Ruth Benedict claimed that rather than viewing Western culture as superior to those of "primitive" cultures, we should see it as merely one way people in society adjust to one another. As she puts it, "Modern civilization, from this point of view, becomes not a necessary pinnacle of human achievement but one entry in a long series of possible adjustments."[57] Is it wrong for women to wear blue jeans? It all depends. In American culture it is an everyday occurrence, whereas in other parts of the world it is deeply offensive and immoral. Can science tell us all that there is to know about reality? Many people in our society believe it can. But for Plato and for some people in our own time, science can provide us with only a partial view of reality at best, or at worst, it can give us knowledge of appearances only. It all depends on your particular conception of reality. But how can we compare or evaluate different conceptions of reality, the cultural relativist says, when any evidence or data or standards of rationality that could be used to evaluate our own or another's position will always be defined, accepted, rejected, or applied in terms of our particular conception of reality? Such an action is like filling out a job application and listing yourself as a reference.

Contemporary philosopher Willard V. O. Quine (1908–2000) has given us an interesting presentation of this perspective. (W. V. O. Quine spent most of his professional career at Harvard University. His writings on epistemology and metaphysics have been very influential within contemporary philosophy.) Quine describes each person's view of the world as a partially stable and partially fluctuating "web of belief." The "facts" cannot prove or disprove a conceptual scheme, because what we accept or reject as a fact and how we interpret it will always be decided in terms of the whole fabric of our web of belief. However, in the face of a particularly "recalcitrant experience," we may decide to modify or even jettison deep features of our belief system, for no foundational beliefs are incapable of being revised. Nevertheless, it is always *we* who are deciding what to do with the evidence rather than the evidence dictating our response. At the most fundamental level, Quine seems to be saying that large-scale, conflicting belief systems present alternatives that we embrace or reject based on our preferences, cultural traditions, and practical needs. Quine says, for example, that 20th-century people's belief in physical objects and the accompanying natural laws we associate with them are used to explain physical events. In contrast, the ancient Greek poet Homer told stories of the gods and their activities to explain what happened in the world. Quine prefers his web of belief over Homer's, but he recognizes that in the final analysis both sets of beliefs are merely different cultural and conceptual frameworks.

> For my part I do, qua lay physicist, believe in physical objects and not in Homer's gods; and I consider it a scientific error to believe otherwise. But in point of epistemological footing the physical objects and the gods differ only in degree and not in kind. Both sorts of entities enter our conception only as cultural posits.[58]

Is there no way to argue the superiority of contemporary physics over Greek mythology? The problem is that, from the standpoint of cultural relativism, what we define as "mythology" are merely those belief systems that differ significantly from our own. Quine says that he prefers his "myth" (the conceptual scheme of science) because it is the one that is most effective in making predictions and organizing our experiences.

> The myth of physical objects is epistemologically superior to most in that it has proved more efficacious than other myths as a device for working a manageable structure into the flux of experience.[59]

However, once Quine has headed down the road of cultural relativism, the fact that science is a tool that can accomplish this end does not prove that it is more rational a scheme than Homer's. It merely reflects Quine's choice as to what he will count as "rational."

STOP AND THINK

What are facts? For several days, keep your ears and eyes open and write down in a journal how the word *fact(s)* is used by you or by others in conversations, speeches, or in print. Analyze your entries. What view of facts is being assumed in each case? Do any of these assumptions run into the problems pointed out by the relativists?

Another form of relativism is **historical relativism.** There are significant differences between the way that we look at the world and the way that the ancient Greeks, the medievals, and people during the Renaissance viewed the world in their respective eras. The German philosopher Georg W. F. Hegel (1770–1831) was most influential in promoting the view that each historical age had different conceptual frameworks. He believed that each phase of history contained a "spirit of the age" that produced the cultural and intellectual life of the people. Hence, he claimed that ideas are not eternal truths but are reflections of their time and that the truth of any idea has to be evaluated in terms of its own historical setting.

> As far as the individual is concerned, each individual is in any case a *child of his time;* thus philosophy, too, is *its own time comprehended in thoughts.* It is just as foolish to imagine that any philosophy can transcend its contemporary world as that an individual can overleap his own time.[60]

Ironically, however, Hegel did not believe that relativism was the last word. He believed that there was a rational pattern to the evolution of ideas, such that each historical era provided a partial and incomplete perspective on the one, absolute truth. Furthermore, according to the Hegelian story, each new moment in history was bringing us closer to this universal truth. Hence, Hegel's picture was that of objectivism on the installment plan. Although he was an objectivist, Hegel (like Kant) provided fuel for relativism, for many thinkers adopted his historical relativism but discarded his view that objective truth would ultimately emerge from this changing kaleidoscope of historical perspectives.

historical relativism the claim that each historical age had different conceptual frameworks such that there are no universal truths but only truths that are correct for a particular age

Epistemological Subjectivism: Friedrich Nietzsche

One of the best-known defenders of subjectivism was the German philosopher Friedrich Nietzsche (1844–1900). Nietzsche was one of the forerunners of the 20th-century movement of existentialism, a philosophy that emphasizes subjective choosing over objective reasoning. There are both religious and atheistic existentialists. The 19th-century philosopher Søren Kierkegaard was an example of religious existentialism. (We introduced Kierkegaard in section 1.0 and discuss him and existentialism again in chapter 7.) Nietzsche, however, was a proponent of atheistic existentialism. Nietzsche was religiously devout in his younger years (we even have examples of his religious poetry), but he gradually drifted away from his earlier piety, and by the time he was in his 20s he was a spirited spokesman for antireligious thought. Nietzsche was a brilliant student and distinguished himself at the universities of Bonn and Leipzig where he studied classics and philology (the analysis of ancient texts). Plagued throughout his life by illness, he abandoned an academic

FRIEDRICH NIETZSCHE
(1844–1900)

career and devoted himself to his writings. Despite his problems, he wrote 18 books and a lengthy unfinished manuscript during the years 1872 to 1888. The ideas he left behind are disturbing and difficult, as was his life. In his final years, his physical and mental health collapsed from what appears to be a neurological disorder. Now considered a visionary who predicted some of the cultural crises that would plague the 20th century, he handed the torch over to the new century when he died on August 25, 1900.

Radical Perspectivism

Nietzsche's theory of knowledge can be stated quite simply: *we don't have any objective knowledge at all*. He is a paradigm case of a subjective relativist. The only reality we can know, he says, is the reality that is subjectively constructed by each individual. Ironically, Nietzsche seemed to have arrived at this position because he rejected the correspondence theory of truth, one of the most common starting points for an objectivist epistemology. The **correspondence theory of truth** states that (1) reality has a determinant, objective character and (2) a belief or statement is true or false to the degree to which it corresponds to or represents the objective features of reality. The cruel catch, according to Nietzsche, is that we can never have that sort of relationship to reality. By setting a high standard for truth and noting that we can never reach this ideal, Nietzsche concluded that we can never have objective truth. Like a goldfish who is confined to its bowl, looking out at the world from within it, each of us thinks, speaks, and lives within our own, subjective perspective. But what about facts? Aren't they out there, independent of us, and don't they function as an objective standard for the truth or falsity of our beliefs? "Not at all!" says Nietzsche:

> No, facts is precisely what there is not, only interpretations. We cannot establish any fact "in itself": perhaps it is folly to want to do such a thing.[61]

There cannot be any uninterpreted "facts" or "truths," for everything we encounter is seen from one perspective or another. Nietzsche calls this approach his theory of **perspectivism.** If Nietzsche is correct, then to suppose that there is an impersonal, objective, and perspective-free outlook on reality is like supposing that we could take a picture of the Lincoln Monument in which the perspective was neither from the north, east, south, west, or any direction whatsoever. Although there is obviously no *visual* perspective-free perception, most objectivists claim that a *conceptual* perspective-free standpoint is possible. Some have called this standpoint the "view-from-nowhere" assumption. But Nietzsche believes there is no such standpoint, for every judgment is made from someone's concrete, personal perspective.*

To understand Nietzsche's approach to truth, it is helpful to remember that he was a philologist.[62] In studying ancient texts, such as a Greek play, we never have the original manuscripts. What we have are copies of copies of copies that were passed down through the centuries and were put together from multiple, partial, and sometimes inconsistent versions of the original. During this process it was inevitable that errors and mistakes crept into the copies that were then passed on as part of the manuscript. Because of these errors, it was necessary for each ancient scribe copying the text or a present-day scholar reading the text to interpret and reconstruct it to make the best possible sense out of it. But in reconstructing the text, the copyist's or the scholar's outlook, personal judgment, and biases in interpretations became part of the text itself.

In much the same way, Nietzsche thought, each of us interprets the "text" of the world. In perceiving and thinking about the world, we are not like mirrors that passively

---

*Feminist epistemologists agree with Nietzsche on this point. See section 2.7.

correspondence theory of truth a theory that states that (1) reality has a determinant, objective character, and (2) a belief or statement is true or false to the degree to which it corresponds to or represents the objective features of reality

perspectivism the theory that there cannot be any uninterpreted "facts" or "truths," because everything we encounter is seen from one perspective or another

Read the following message inside the triangle, and then look up from your book and repeat what you saw.

People typically fail to read this message accurately because they bring to the text their expectations, their assumptions, their past experience, and their background knowledge. That misinterpretation is Nietzsche's point. We "see" what our conceptual frameworks or perspectives allow us to see or what they direct us to see. Did you say that the message was "Paris in the spring"? If so, your reading of the message was incorrect. Put your finger on each word of the message as you read it. If you are like me, the first time you repeated the message you got it wrong. If something as simple as this message can be reconstructed and interpreted according to our own framework of assumptions, what makes us think we operate any differently with the whole of reality? Try this same experiment with five friends and see how they do.

PARIS
IN THE
THE SPRING

PHILOSOPHY
in the
MARKETPLACE

record what is out there. Instead, we are reconstructing and interpreting the data to create a vision of the world that not only makes sense to us but that conforms to our subjective needs. The notion that we play an active role in constructing our knowledge is taken from Kant's insight. However, Kant believed there was a *single* way of structuring experience that was carried out by the categories of the human mind that were *universal to everyone* and that were fundamentally *rational.* For Nietzsche, however, there are *multiple* ways of structuring experience that are *relative to each individual,* and that are driven by our fundamentally *nonrational* nature, including our passions and our subjective interests, needs, and motives.

Romantic Primitivism

According to Nietzsche, if most people suddenly realized that what they considered to be most real and true was just a subjective perspective, they could not bear this shattering of their illusions. For this reason, Nietzsche thought that our perspectives arose from a very deep stratum within human consciousness that we are inclined to suppress and deny. (Nietzsche's analysis of the unconscious drives within us both foreshadowed and influenced the thought of Sigmund Freud, the founder of psychoanalysis.) I have called this aspect of Nietzsche's thought "romantic primitivism," for like the artists and poets within the romantic movement, Nietzsche believed that our primary interaction with the world is in terms of feelings rather than ideas. It is a "primitivism" because he believed that these emotional responses operated at the level of primitive, animal instincts. Nietzsche said that all judgments arise out of our "instincts, likes, dislikes, experiences, and lack of experiences"[63] and knowledge is "actually nothing but a *certain behavior of the instincts toward one another.*"[64] Think about how radically this epistemology differs from those of both the rationalists and empiricists, who believed that knowledge was produced by an intellectual consideration of rational and empirical truths.

Rather than reason being the primary instrument of knowledge, Nietzsche believed it is just a mask we use to disguise a primitive drive that controls our cognitive life. This drive is what he calls the *will to power.* It manifests itself as the desire to overcome, to dominate one's environment, to make one's personal mark on the world, to create, or to express oneself.

"Truth" is therefore not something there, that might be found or discovered—but something that must be created and that gives a name to a process, or rather to a will to overcome that has in itself no end—introducing truth, as a *processus in infinitum,* an active determining—not a becoming-conscious of something that is in itself firm and determined. It is a word for the "will to power."[65]

STOP AND THINK

Can you think of a time when you tried to rationalize a belief, decision, or action of yours? That is, you tried to find rational reasons for what you did when you really knew that it was based on emotional or other nonrational factors. To what degree is Nietzsche's analysis of human psychology illustrated by your own personal experience?

Nietzsche's view on knowledge is expressed in the following sections of one of his best-known books.

- In section 3, what does Nietzsche say secretly guides the thinking of the philosopher?
- What stands behind all logic?
- In section 4, what is said to be more important than the truth or falsity of a judgment?

FROM FRIEDRICH NIETZSCHE

Beyond Good and Evil[66]

3

After having looked long enough between the philosopher's lines and fingers, I say to myself: by far the greater part of conscious thinking must still be included among instinctive activities, and that goes even for philosophical thinking. We have to relearn here, as one has had to relearn about heredity and what is "innate." As the act of birth deserves no consideration in the whole process and procedure of heredity, so "being conscious" is not in any decisive sense the *opposite* of what is instinctive: most of the conscious thinking of a philosopher is secretly guided and forced into certain channels by his instincts.

Behind all logic and its seeming sovereignty of movement, too, there stand valuations or, more clearly, physiological demands for the preservation of a certain type of life. For example, that the definite should be worth more than the indefinite, and mere appearance worth less than "truth"—such estimates might be, in spite of their regulative importance for us, nevertheless mere foreground estimates, a certain kind of *niaiserie** which may be necessary for the preservation of just such beings as we are. Supposing, that is, that not just man is the "measure of things"—

4

The falseness of a judgment is for us not necessarily an objection to a judgment; in this respect our new language may sound strangest. The question is to what extent it is life-

---

*Folly, stupidity, silliness: one of Nietzsche's favorite French words. [Translator's note.]

promoting, life-preserving, species-preserving, perhaps even species-cultivating. And we are fundamentally inclined to claim that the falsest judgments (which include the synthetic judgments *a priori*) are the most indispensable for us; that without accepting the fictions of logic, without measuring reality against the purely invented world of the unconditional and self-identical, without a constant falsification of the world by means of numbers, man could not live—that renouncing false judgments would mean renouncing life and a denial of life. To recognize untruth as a condition of life—that certainly means resisting accustomed value feelings in a dangerous way; and a philosophy that risks this would by that token alone place itself beyond good and evil.

- In the next paragraph (section 5), why does Nietzsche accuse philosophers of being dishonest?
- Nietzsche refers to philosophers as "advocates" (i.e., lawyers). What is the significance of comparing them to lawyers? Is he praising them or criticizing them?
- As you read sections 5 and 6, make a list of all the ways Nietzsche characterizes the real source of philosophers' ideas.

5

What provokes one to look at all philosophers half suspiciously, half mockingly, is not that one discovers again and again how innocent they are—how often and how easily they make mistakes and go astray; in short, their childishness and childlikeness—but that they are not honest enough in their work, although they all make a lot of virtuous noise when the problem of truthfulness is touched even remotely. They all pose as if they had discovered and reached their real opinions through the self-development of a cold, pure, divinely unconcerned dialectic (as opposed to the mystics of every rank, who are more honest and doltish—and talk of "inspiration"); while at bottom it is an assumption, indeed a kind of "inspiration"—most often a desire of the heart that has been filtered and made abstract—that they defend with reasons they have sought after the fact. They are all advocates who resent that name, and for the most part even wily spokesmen for their prejudices which they baptize "truths"—and *very* far from having the courage of the conscience that admits this, precisely this, to itself; very far from having the good taste of the courage which also lets this be known, whether to warn an enemy or friend, or, from exuberance, to mock itself. . . .

6

Gradually it has become clear to me what every great philosophy so far has been: namely, the personal confession of its author and a kind of involuntary and unconscious memoir; also that the moral (or immoral) intentions in every philosophy constituted the real germ of life from which the whole plant had grown.

Indeed, if one would explain how the abstrusest metaphysical claims of a philosopher really came about, it is always well (and wise) to ask first: at what morality does all this (does *he*) aim? Accordingly, I do not believe that a "drive to knowledge" is the father of philosophy; but rather that another drive has, here as elsewhere, employed understanding (and misunderstanding) as a mere instrument. But anyone who considers the basic drives of man to see to what extent they may have been at play just here as *inspiring* spirits (or demons and kobolds) will find that all of them have done philosophy at some time—and that every single one of them would like only too well to represent just *itself* as the ultimate purpose of existence and the legitimate *master* of all the other drives. For every drive wants to be master—and it attempts to philosophize in *that spirit.*

To be sure: among scholars who are really scientific men, things may be different—"better," if you like—there you may really find something like a drive for knowledge, some small, independent clockwork that, once well wound, works on vigorously *without* any essential participation from all the other drives of scholar. The real "interests" of the scholar therefore lie usually somewhere else—say, in his family, or in making money, or in politics. Indeed, it is almost a matter of total indifference whether his little machine is placed at this or that spot in science, whether the "promising" young worker turns himself into a philologist or an expert on fungi or a chemist: it does not *characterize* him that he becomes this or that. In the philosopher, conversely, there is nothing whatever that is impersonal; and above all, his morality bears decided and decisive witness to *who he is*—that is, in what order of rank the innermost drives of his nature stand in relation to each other.

Nietzsche believed that a new kind of philosopher would arise. These new thinkers would transcend the dogmas of the past and would have the courage to realize that their thought did not arise out of impersonal reason, but that it was an expression of their own subjectivity.

- In the remaining sections, how does Nietzsche describe these new philosophers?
- In section 43, why does he say that there cannot be a "common good"?

42

A new species of philosophers is coming up: I venture to baptize them with a name that is not free of danger. As I unriddle them, insofar as they allow themselves to be unriddled—for it belongs to their nature to *want* to remain riddles at some point—these philosophers of the future may have a right—it might also be a wrong—to be called *attempters*.* This name itself is in the end a mere attempt and, if you will, a temptation.

43

Are these coming philosophers new friends of "truth"? That is probable enough, for all philosophers so far have loved their truths. But they will certainly not be dogmatists. It must offend their pride, also their taste, if their truth is supposed to be a truth for everyman—which has so far been the secret wish and hidden meaning of all dogmatic aspirations. "My judgment is my judgment": no one else is easily entitled to it—that is what such a philosopher of the future may perhaps say of himself.

One must shed the bad taste of wanting to agree with many. "Good" is no longer good when one's neighbor mouths it. And how should there be a "common good"! The term contradicts itself: whatever can be common always has little value. In the end it must be as it is and always has been: great things remain for the great, abysses for the profound, nuances and shudders for the refined, and, in brief, all that is rare for the rare.

44

Need I still say expressly after all this that they, too, will be free, *very* free spirits, these philosophers of the future—though just as certainly they will not be merely free spirits but something more, higher, greater, and thoroughly different that does not want to be misunderstood and mistaken for something else.

---

*The translator, Walter Kaufmann, points out that the German word *Versucher* can mean attempters, tempters, or experimenters. Nietzsche is making a triple play on words here.

Nietzsche and the Death of Absolutes

Nietzsche believed that if there is no objective truth, no standard apart from us by which our ideas may be measured, then it logically follows that there is no God. For if God existed, he would be an absolute standard of truth and value. But if Nietzsche is right, if our minds swim in a sea of personal interpretations, then belief in God is simply a symptom of the human craving for absolutes. God provides a safe harbor for those who are afraid to venture out into the open seas of thought with no craft other than their own judgments and opinions. Nietzsche believed that there was a growing realization that "God is dead," meaning that this ideology was no longer a live, cultural force in Western culture.

> The greatest recent event—that "God is dead," that the belief in the Christian god has become unbelievable—is already beginning to cast its first shadows over Europe.[67]

However, in spite of this cultural revolution, Nietzsche recognized that there would still be those who felt the need for God along with the need for absolute truth and for a rational, metaphysical knowledge of the "true world." Nietzsche thought that humanity falls into two categories. The first category consists of those who need absolutes and security, who have no confidence in their own abilities, and who wear the masks of objectivity to hide the awesome responsibilities of their own subjectivity. He calls these people "sheep," "little gray people," "shallow ponds," "the herd," "the psychologically weak," "the vulgar," "the lower types," and "slaves." The second category consists of the new philosophers, people who are self-affirming, who need no philosophical or spiritual crutches, and who celebrate both the limits and the glories of their humanity. Nietzsche calls them "the psychologically strong," "the noble," "the higher types," the "masters."

This dualistic personality theory amplifies Nietzsche's theme that philosophy is a personal confession and that all thought is a reflection of the type of person we are (psychologically weak or strong). Although you think that you have been judging Nietzsche's ideas, he wants you to know that his ideas have been judging you all along. Like Kierkegaard, Nietzsche meant his writings to force you to face yourself, along with your fears, convictions, and sacred idols. If you find his ideas challenging, intoxicating, and life-enhancing or if you find them terrifying, offensive, and abhorrent, he will have been successful in evoking this form of self-revelation, and he would have cared little about what you thought of him.

Nietzsche and Relativism

Because Nietzsche is clearly a relativist, how does he handle the Standard Criticism against relativists?* The critic would ask Nietzsche, "Why should I accept your theory of knowledge if, by your own account, all beliefs are nothing more than personal perspectives or interpretations?" Nietzsche loved to turn the tables on those who opposed him, so instead of evading the criticism, he enthusiastically embraced it. His reply to the people who criticized his relativism was, "Supposing that this also is only interpretation—and you will be eager to make this objection?—well, so much the better."[68] In other words, Nietzsche is willing to admit that his view is only one perspective among many in the hopes that you will recognize that your view is merely a subjective perspective as well. As his fictional character Zarathustra says, "This is my way; where is yours?"[69] We cannot compare our conflicting perspectives to reality in order to decide which is correct because all we have is

---

*See pp. 149–150 for the Standard Criticism of relativism.

reality-as-interpreted from some personal standpoint: Nietzsche's perspective, yours, mine, or someone else's. For this reason the world of thought is like the world of nature, where the survival of the fittest is the reigning principle. Philosophy is a struggle of egos as each person exercises his or her will to power.

If there is no objective truth, if all human judgments are nothing more than interpretations, then Nietzsche concludes that we should live our lives with a spirit of "experimentalism." An interesting theory should not be thought of as a photograph of reality, but should be treated as an invitation to view life in a new way. Thus, the proper response to an idea is not to ask, "Is it true?" but to exclaim, "Let us try it!"[70] A great thinker is one who "sees his own actions as experiments and questions."[71] By "experiment" Nietzsche means testing an outlook by dwelling within it and seeing whether it enhances or diminishes your life. In the final analysis, the superior ideas for Nietzsche are those that are the most life-enhancing, the most useful, or even the most interesting. Accordingly, he considered the search for variety more important than the quest for certainty.

> Deeply mistrustful of the dogmas of epistemology, I loved to look now out of this window, now out of that; I guarded against settling down with any of these dogmas, considered them harmful.[72]

> That the value of the world lies in our interpretation . . . that every elevation of man brings with it the overcoming of narrower interpretations; that every strengthening and increase of power opens up new perspectives and means believing in new horizons—this idea permeates my writings.[73]

🧪 THOUGHT EXPERIMENT: *Culture and Perception*

Before reading further, look at the figure here and answer the following questions:

1. Is this picture of a family or a group of strangers?
2. How many adults are in the picture?
3. Is this picture an indoor scene or an outdoor scene?
4. Are the people happy or sad?

After you have answered the questions yourself, present the picture and the questions to a number of friends. If you have friends who are international students, it would be particularly interesting to see how their answers compare with yours. Actually, the only important question is the third one. The rest were rather obvious and served merely to take the spotlight off the third question.

Did you say this picture was an indoor scene? If so, what were the clues that led you to this answer? If you are like me, you assumed that the rectangular figure "behind"

Simple reading material for adults: its preparation and use, Paris, UNESCO, 1963; p. 64 © UNESCO 1963. Used by permission of UNESCO.

(continued . . .)

the woman to the left of center is a window revealing some foliage outside. Furthermore, the Y-shaped figure rising up to the top of the picture looks like the corner of a room bathed in shadows. However, subjects from East Africa, when asked what they saw, described a family group in which a young woman is carrying a four-gallon tin on her head (a common sight in that region). Since North Americans do not have the convention (nor the skill) of balancing and transporting large objects on their head, they assume that the rectangular drawing is not a solid object but a window in the wall behind the woman. This simple example shows how our culture influences what we see and the judgments that we make.

The Standard Criticism of Relativism

Throughout his writings, Plato attacked the relativists of his day, a group of philosophers known as the Sophists. As I mentioned previously, the Sophist Protagoras said that "man is the measure of all things." By this statement, Protagoras was claiming that individual or social opinion is the only standard we have and all opinions are equally true. In response, Plato gives this exchange between Socrates and the mathematician Theodorus:

SOCRATES: Protagoras, for his part, admitting as he does that everybody's opinion is true, must acknowledge the truth of his opponents' belief about his own belief, where they think he is wrong.

THEODORUS: Certainly.

SOCRATES: That is to say, he would acknowledge his own belief to be false, if he admits that the belief of those who think him wrong is true?

THEODORUS: Necessarily.[74]

Through the voice of Socrates, Plato is arguing that relativists do not really believe that all opinions are equally true. Relativists believe they are correct and their opponents are *wrong* in their opinions about knowledge. The relativist seems to be making two claims: (1) "There is no objective truth," and (2) "Statement (1) is objectively true." With these statements, Plato claims, relativists have contradicted themselves.*

Plato's argument against the relativism of Protagoras is one version of what I will call the "Standard Criticism" of relativism, which could be formulated in this way:

1. The relativist makes the following claim R: "There are no universal, objective truths about the world."
2. But statement R is a claim about the world.
3. If statement R is considered to be an objective truth, then it contradicts itself.
4. If statement R is considered to be a relative truth, then the relativist is simply reporting on how he or she personally views the world and is really not making a claim about how things really are.
5. Since points 3 and 4 are the only alternatives, then either way the relativist's claim undermines itself.

---

*In the discussion of logic in the appendix, I set out a reconstructed version of this argument and labeled it a reductio ad absurdum argument; that is, this argument is a technique of refuting an opponent by first assuming his or her position and showing that it leads to an absurdity or a contradiction.

Try this exercise to get some distance from your own conceptual scheme. Those of us who are members of 21st-century Western scientific cultures believe that electrons exist and that they explain a great deal of what happens in the world we experience. But imagine that you have not been raised to think this way. (Perhaps you are a Yaqui Indian sorcerer.) With this approach in mind, interview students majoring in the sciences (particularly chemistry or physics) about electrons. If you are bold enough, you might even interview professors in these disciplines. Ask them this simple question: Why do you believe that electrons exist?

Whatever their answer may be, follow up with other questions as to why the subject thinks the reasons and explanations he or she has provided are true. After all, we cannot literally see electrons. Their existence is either assumed or deduced from other assumptions that we make about how the whole of reality is put together as well as how to interpret our scientific instruments. Keep pressing them with the questions and see if they reach a point at which they can only say something like, "That's just the way it is!" (Try to avoid irritating them.)

I have found that many of my colleagues who have Ph.D.s in chemistry are taken aback by this line of questioning. The existence of electrons is such an unquestioned and significant part of the framework in which we think, that people see little need to examine the grounds for this belief. Sometimes scientists respond that by postulating the existence of electrons they are able to make predictions and carry on successful experiments. In other words, the belief in electrons "works" as a guide to action. (You may want to keep their reasons in mind when you read section 2.6 on pragmatism and see the degree to which their responses are similar to William James's pragmatic theory of truth.) Finally, after interviewing the experts, ask the same question of several non-science majors to see what sorts of justifications they provide. To complete this exercise, answer the following questions yourself.

- Do you agree or disagree with the following statement: "In the final analysis, belief in electrons depends on accepting the large-scale conceptual framework of the modern scientific worldview." Why did you answer as you did?
- Could you ever convince someone that electrons exist if that person does not accept this conceptual framework?
- Do these considerations lend support to the conceptual relativist, or is it possible to justify the view that there is one true story about the world and electrons are a significant part of it?

Because this sort of criticism is at least as old as Plato, relativists are well aware that this argument is a major challenge that they must face. Different relativists respond to the criticism in different ways.

PREVIEW OF COMING ATTRACTIONS

After concluding our discussion of relativism, I devote the remaining sections of this chapter to examining two philosophical positions on knowledge that all fall under the heading of "Rethinking the Western Tradition." These two philosophies are pragmatism and feminism. Unlike the Asian philosophies of religion that will be discussed in section 4.6, which challenged the assumptions of Western thought from outside its boundaries, the next two positions arose as movements within the Western philosophical tradition. Nevertheless, the two movements each engage in a radical critique of their own family tree. Western philosophy has always been characterized by disagreements, controversies, and divisions, such as theism versus atheism or rationalism versus empiricism. But pragmatism and feminism contend that the majority of the debates throughout this tradition have always been staged on the platform of objectivism. Hence, these two views of knowledge, one of which arose in the late 19th century (pragmatism) and the other in the 20th century (feminism), take as their initial defining point their rejection of the majority's commitment to unqualified objectivism throughout Western philosophy. The various proponents of these two philosophies represent a mixture of attitudes toward relativism, but they all agree that there are no context-free truths, that experience of the world is, at best, always mediated through our personal lenses, and that our theories of knowledge and reality must focus on the knower as well as on that which is known. The degree to which these theses commit these philosophers to a full-blown relativism will have to be judged in each individual case.

LOOKING THROUGH THE RELATIVIST'S LENS

1. If we all became convinced that relativism is true, what would be lost by giving up the belief in objective truth? After all, most objectivists agree that human knowledge is fallible and that our best knowledge is always imperfect. Even the Bible's Apostle Paul, a paragon of objectivism, said that "it is as though we see through a dark glass" and "the knowledge I now have is imperfect."[75] Even though most people would agree that we have not finally resolved the question of "what is the absolutely correct set of objective truths?" we seem to have beliefs that work for us (and our culture) and that enable us to get through life satisfactorily. Why do we need to suppose there is only one way to live or to view the world? On the other hand, if we all suddenly became convinced that there is one set of objective truths, accepting that fact alone would not cause us to change most of the beliefs that we currently have. Each of us would be convinced that the beliefs we held were the best account of the one true story of the world. So, in practical terms, what difference does objectivism make?

2. Some relativists, such as Protagoras, claim that both (1) all beliefs are relative and (2) all beliefs are of equal value. Could a relativist hold to statement (1) but reject statement (2)? Couldn't a relativist reject some beliefs or entire systems of beliefs because they are contradictory or because they fail according to their own criteria or even because they bear very little correspondence to the world? Couldn't a relativist reject some beliefs as absurd while still claiming that there remain many incompatible beliefs that are equal in the degree to which they correspond to the world? Isn't this distinction between plausible and implausible relative beliefs consistent with relativism?

EXAMINING THE STRENGTHS AND WEAKNESSES OF RELATIVISM

Positive Evaluation

1. Since the beginning of civilization to our own day, human history has been one long string of differing opinions and debates over fundamental issues in philosophy, morals, religion, politics, and so forth, with each participant in the debate claiming that his or her position is the true one and the others are wrong. Even in science, physicists and astronomers have differing opinions over which physical theory is the correct one on many issues.

Just when scientists would reach a consensus, a new generation of scientists would come along and overthrow it. If there is one true story about the world, why is it so hard to figure out what it is? Doesn't the relativist have a simple and logical answer to that question?

2. Wouldn't a healthy dose of relativism be an antidote to all the dogmatism and intolerance in the world? Wouldn't it make people more humble and willing to consider alternative points of view? Would we have had all the wars, persecutions, and tyrannies in human history if people did not believe that they held the absolute truth?

Negative Evaluation

1. Does the fact that people disagree over fundamental issues necessarily prove that there is no objective truth? If you asked five people to give their opinion of the length of this line down to the nearest sixteenth of an inch, isn't it likely that you would get five different opinions? Do these differing opinions mean that there is no truth about the matter?

―――――――――――――――――――――――――

When opinions differ (as in the case of the line), there are several possibilities: (1) one opinion is correct and the others are wrong; (2) all the opinions are wrong but some are closer to the truth than others. But the relativist supposes that the only possibilities are (3) all opinions are of equal value or, at least, (4) there is no objective truth about which these opinions differ. Why should we suppose that (3) and (4) are the only alternatives? As in the case of the line, the fact that people's opinions differ does not mean that there is not one, correct truth about the matter.

2. Consider the following statements. Don't these sorts of statements make up a great deal of our everyday conversation, as well as underlie some of the most important themes in human life?

(1) I was mistaken in underestimating Susan's character.
(2) Our culture is wrong in neglecting the rights of this particular group.
(3) Nazi Germany was mistaken in supposing the Aryan race is superior to all others.
(4) The medievals were mistaken in believing that the moon has a perfectly smooth surface.

The problem is that every one of these meaningful statements seems meaningless from the perspective of relativism. Statement (1): If subjectivism is correct, can I ever say that my previous beliefs were incorrect? Mustn't I simply say that I have now chosen to change my beliefs? What would ever make me think my belief was mistaken if I am unable to apprehend a reality that is independent of my opinions about it? Statement (2): If cultural relativism is correct, can we ever say that our culture is morally wrong or factually mistaken if our standard of truth is relative to our particular culture? Statement (3): If we were all relativists, then prior to World War II, shouldn't America simply have said that we and the Nazis should "agree to disagree" and leave it at that? If relativism is correct, then how can we ever assert that the Nazis were wrong? Aren't we condemned to the rather bland statement that "the Aryan race is superior within the Nazi's conceptual framework, while all races are equal within the equalitarian framework"? Statement (4): In what sense were the medievals wrong if their belief fit comfortably with their entire conceptual framework?

2.6 RETHINKING THE WESTERN TRADITION: PRAGMATISM

LEADING QUESTIONS: *Pragmatism*

1. Suppose you have a friend who claims she has a certain belief. (It could be a belief concerning religion, ethics, politics, science, or any other topic.) But suppose that all her actions seem contrary to that belief. Would her actions be evidence that she did not really hold the belief she thought she did? Could we say that genuinely held beliefs will always make some sort of actual or potential difference in our actions?

2. We can say of a tool that it works, is efficient, gets the job done, is useful, lives up to our expectations, is better than the competition's, and serves our needs. To what extent could the same descriptions apply to an idea or a belief? Are some beliefs better than others because they are more useful when applied within our everyday lives? If this way of evaluating beliefs makes sense, what does this approach tell us about the nature of ideas and their role in our lives?

3. Have you ever rejected a belief for the sole reason that it didn't work when you used it to guide your actions?

SURVEYING THE CASE FOR PRAGMATISM

If philosophies came in colors, pragmatism would be painted red, white, and blue. It is the only major philosophical movement that was American-grown. The foremost pioneers of pragmatic thought were the Americans Charles Sanders Peirce, William James, and John Dewey, all of whom lived in the latter part of the 19th century and the early 20th century. The key terms in pragmatism radiate the spirit of American culture. For example, pragmatism is concerned with action and practical consequences, it judges ideas by how successful they are in getting their job done, and it urges us to calculate the "cash-value" of our ideas (to use William James's phrase). Unlike some philosophies that never escaped the confines of the academic ivory tower, pragmatism achieved an admirable degree of popular fame. For example, politicians and businesspeople love to speak of themselves as pragmatists. However, like so many philosophies that have become popularized, the philosophy in its original form is much more sophisticated than its popular adaptations are.

Pragmatism is a philosophy that stresses the intimate relation between thought and action by defining the meaning of our conceptions in terms of the practical effects we associate with them and the truth of our beliefs in terms of how successfully they guide our actions. For the pragmatist every belief is like a scientific hypothesis and every action based on that belief is like an experiment that either confirms or refutes the viability of that belief. It is no accident that two of the original pragmatists were scientists before they moved into the field of philosophy (Peirce and James). However, their concern with science was not with this or that particular result but with science as a method of inquiry. The pragmatists believed that this method of finding knowledge applied not simply to performing experiments in the laboratory, but also to making a moral decision, working out the meaning of life, educating our children, and setting public policy.

The popular notion is that pragmatic is opposed to theoretical, but the pragmatists oppose this false dichotomy. They stress that the best theories will make a practical difference in concrete life and that nothing can be practical if it is not undergirded by sound theory. Rather than viewing philosophy as an obscure, elitist enterprise that searches for

pragmatism a philosophy that stresses the intimate relation between thought and action by defining the meaning of our conceptions in terms of the practical effects we associate with them and the truth of our beliefs in terms of how successfully they guide our actions

eternal truths that lay far beyond the horizon of human experience, the pragmatists seek to bring philosophy out of the clouds and down to earth. Pragmatic philosophy, they believe, could be a creative instrument of change, addressing the problems of the contemporary culture in which we all live and bringing clarity and coherence to the science, art, religion, politics, and morality of a particular time. Before discussing the main themes of pragmatism, it will be helpful to learn a little bit about its founders and the key differences in their versions of pragmatism.

Charles Sanders Peirce (1839–1914)

C. S. Peirce was trained as a scientist, having received a master's degree in chemistry from Harvard. After working at the Harvard astronomical observatory for 3 years, he spent the next 30 years of his career doing scientific work for the U.S. Coast and Geodetic Survey. During this time he also lectured intermittently at Harvard and at Johns Hopkins University, although his nonconformist personality prevented him from ever securing a permanent academic position. Peirce wrote volumes of essays during his life, but his works, with the exception of a few articles, never saw the light of day until they were published long after his death. Although he was relatively unknown during his lifetime, he is now recognized as one of the most significant philosophers in the early 20th century.

CHARLES SANDERS PEIRCE
(1839–1914)

William James (1842–1910)

James was born in New York into a well-to-do family for whom intellectual and cultural debates were part of the dinner-table conversation. His brother Henry James was the well-known novelist. After spending years traveling the world and studying science, medicine, and painting abroad and in the United States, William James earned his medical degree from Harvard in 1869. He pioneered the then infant discipline of scientific psychology and in 1890 published *Principles of Psychology,* one of the first textbooks in the field. Eventually he made philosophy his full-time occupation and taught in Harvard's philosophy department. James not only achieved fame in the academic community but was in demand as a popular lecturer. He took Peirce's somewhat technical and obscure philosophy and made *pragmatism* a household word. Although the two men were friends and James continually helped Peirce with his financial problems, the original founder of pragmatism was never happy with James's popular version of the philosophy. Finally, Peirce gave up on the term and let James use it as he wished, announcing that his own philosophy should henceforth be known as "pragmaticism," saying that this label "is ugly enough to be safe from kidnappers."[76]

WILLIAM JAMES
(1842–1910)

John Dewey (1859–1952)

Dewey earned his doctorate at Johns Hopkins University (where Peirce was one of his professors). After teaching at the University of Michigan for a decade, he went to the University of Chicago as the head of the department of philosophy, psychology, and education. At Chicago he developed his ideas into a theory of progressive education and created an experimental elementary school to serve as a laboratory for testing his educational theories. Then, from 1904 to his retirement in 1929, he taught at Columbia University. Because of the broad scope of his philosophy and his educational ideas, Dewey was perhaps the most widely influential of the pragmatists. His theory of education became quite famous and transformed American school systems. Furthermore, he

JOHN DEWEY
(1859–1952)

lectured in Japan, China, Turkey, Mexico, and the Soviet Union, and his works have been translated into every major language.

The Varieties of Pragmatism

Although Peirce, James, and Dewey agreed on the basic principles of pragmatism, they differed in their application of this philosophy. Peirce was primarily interested in developing a theory of inquiry and meaning that would apply to our scientific conceptions. Although James shared with Peirce a background in the sciences, James was primarily concerned with the issues of psychology, morality, religion, and practical living. When Peirce spoke of the "practical consequences" and "usefulness" of our beliefs, he was speaking primarily of the sort of public, empirical observations that would lend themselves to scientific analysis. Unlike Peirce, James believed the consequences of a belief included the personal and practical impact it has in the life of an individual.

Dewey made pragmatism a comprehensive philosophy with implications for our understanding of nature, knowledge, education, values, art, social issues, religion, and just about every area of human concern. Of all the pragmatists, he was most concerned with the social applications of knowledge. Dewey believed that the scientific method, broadly conceived, could lead our society to creative solutions to our educational and social problems. In his mind, there was no dichotomy between science and human values. Science can succeed, he said, only in the context of free communication, free action, and mutual dialogue that includes as many points of view as possible. Hence, his pragmatism and his faith in science led him to vigorously defend the American ideal of democracy.

STOP AND THINK

Before examining the pragmatists' way of thinking about knowledge, take a minute to consider how you would answer the following two questions:

- What does it mean for a belief to be true?
- Why is it important to have true beliefs?

When you are finished reading the material by and about the pragmatists, I will ask you to answer these two questions again as a pragmatist might answer them.

The Role of Belief and the Nature of Ideas

The pragmatists criticized what they called "the spectator theory of knowledge." According to this outlook, the mind is like a passive mirror that reflects an external reality. Or to use another metaphor, the traditional view held that the mind was a container that holds ideas. But according to the pragmatists, this approach divorces meaning, truth, and knowledge from our practical engagement with the world. Dewey once said that the model of knowledge should not be that of a spectator viewing a painting but that of the artist producing the painting. Accordingly, epistemology should focus less on "knowledge" (a noun) and more on "knowing" (a verb). Because the world is changing, our society is changing, and our experience is continually changing, knowing the world is an ongoing, active process rather than the accumulation of static, finished results. For the pragmatists, cognition is a way of dealing with the dilemmas, perplexities, and problems that arise in experience and finding creative solutions that will enable us to act in effective ways. The word *pragmatism* can be traced back to a Greek word that means "action," "deed," or "practice." Accordingly, the pragmatists viewed ideas and beliefs as guides to action. As contemporary philosopher Abraham Kaplan says,

> Every actual case of knowing is one in which we are involved with what we know. We must do something with the object of knowledge for it to become known: manipulate it, take it apart, experiment on it.[77]

Besides rejecting the spectator view of knowledge, the pragmatists similarly criticized the *correspondence theory of truth*. This theory was the view that a statement or belief is true to the degree that it corresponds to reality. The problem is that a statement or belief is not a photograph of the external world, so in what sense does that statement or belief "correspond" to it? A statement has no magical powers to relate itself to reality. Similarly, if a belief is thought of as simply a piece of mental furniture it doesn't really relate to the world either. For the pragmatists the issue is not so much how a statement or belief relates to the world but how *we* can use that statement or belief in *our* relationship to our world. As Peirce says, "Our beliefs guide our desires and shape our actions."[78] Similarly, James said that "the true is the name of whatever proves itself to be good in the way of belief."[79] For example, if I believe that "the dog is dangerous," "the glass is fragile," or "sugar is soluble," these beliefs will lead to certain expectations of future experience that will guide me in the fulfillment of my aims, and if they are satisfactory beliefs, they will enable me to act in effective ways. Dewey called his version of pragmatism "instrumentalism," because he viewed ideas and beliefs as instruments for dealing with the situations we face in life. A saw is an effective instrument for cutting wood, but it is not much use for driving nails. Likewise, in evaluating our beliefs we have to ask, "How will this belief put me in a more successful relationship with my experience than will its alternatives?" Aristotle's physics answered many questions the ancient Greeks asked about nature, but it was abandoned in favor of Galileo's physics, because the latter could answer more questions more satisfactorily. In other words, Galileo's physics proved to be a more effective conceptual instrument in its own time.

If my actions always met with successful results, if my experience never raised any questions or posed any problems, I could rest comfortably in the beliefs I have, for they are doing their job. Peirce believed that inquiry and reasoning begin when my ideas prove inadequate to experience or when doubts are raised, which leads me to realize that I need to rethink my relationship to the environment. Similarly, Dewey said that inquiry is a transitional process between two stages: "a perplexed, troubled, or confused situation at the beginning and a cleared-up, unified, resolved situation at the close."[80] For example, every morning I turn the key in my ignition, believing that my car will start. But if the car does not start, then I must reassess the data, form hypotheses ("Perhaps the battery is low"), test my idea through overt action ("Do my lights still go on?"), and keep working at it until I find a set of ideas that unifies my experience, resolves the perplexity, and enables me to continue on with my tasks. Although this example is obvious and simplistic, the pragmatists claimed that *all* human inquiry proceeds in just this way. Hence, all thinking is problem solving, and there is no absolute division between the pattern of inquiry in the sciences, common sense, politics, morality, and religion. In every case, thinking involves a problem, hypotheses, plans of action, observations, facts, testing, and confirmation.

The intimate relationship between belief and action in the world is the basis of the pragmatists' rejection of skepticism. When Descartes went through his skeptical phase, he wondered whether the beliefs in his mind really corresponded with the external world.*

---

*See the discussion of Descartes's struggle with skepticism in section 2.1.

What gave him away, the pragmatists would say, is that as he was pondering skepticism, he still got up to stoke the stove when he was cold. Obviously, in spite of his theoretical skepticism (Peirce called it "paper doubt"), Descartes's actions showed that he had beliefs about the world that were successful in guiding his actions. There is no dichotomy between the knower and the world, the pragmatists say, because our ideas are always formed in interaction with the world, and if any of our ideas are mistaken, our experience will reveal those mistakes to us. Thought is not the process of moving from one idea to another and then wondering if any of those ideas have anything to do with reality. Instead, thought begins by being immersed in the world, and it is a process of moving from the present set of world experiences to future experiences.

A corollary of the pragmatists' view of inquiry as problem solving is the view that we have no guarantee that any particular belief will ever be immune from the need to be revised. An idea that leads us to successful action today may fail us when we face tomorrow's challenges. The position that all our knowledge is tentative and subject to revision is known as *fallibilism*. Peirce once made the paradoxical claim that the only infallible statement is that all statements are fallible. For the pragmatists, the quest for knowledge is not the search for eternal, necessary, foundational beliefs that are absolutely certain. Instead, they said, what we have are (1) provisional beliefs that work in practice thus far, joined with (2) a method of arriving at better beliefs.

⚗ THOUGHT EXPERIMENT: *Clarifying Meaning*

William James tells the story of coming across a group of people in a heated debate. One of their members was chasing a squirrel around a tree. However, no matter how quickly he moved, the squirrel would move around to the other side of the tree, always keeping the tree between himself and the man. Some of the members argued that the man had gone round the squirrel because he had completely circled the tree and the squirrel was on the tree. The other group argued that the man had not gone round the squirrel because he had never faced the squirrel's backside.

- Is there any practical difference between the two sides of the dispute?
- Because the consequences of each group's belief are the same, how would pragmatism clear up the controversy?
- Have you ever been in an argument that could have been resolved if the members of the opposing sides had bothered to clarify the meaning of their terms?

The Pragmatic Theory of Truth

A key feature of pragmatism is the pragmatic theory of truth. James said that true beliefs have the characteristic that they pay or have practical cash value. He defined truth in terms of what works or what gives satisfaction, or in terms of the practical consequences of our beliefs. It is important to notice that an advocate of the correspondence theory of truth could agree that the workability of a belief, or its tendency to lead to successful action, is an *indicator* that the belief provides an accurate picture of reality without agreeing that this factor *defines* what we mean by "truth."

However, James was not content to argue for this pragmatic test of truth. Instead, he put forth a radically new, pragmatic definition of what it means for a belief to be true. According to his definition, truth means "*that ideas (which themselves are but parts of our experience) become true just in so far as they help us to get into satisfactory relation with other parts of our experience.*"[81] In section 4.4 on pragmatic justifications for religious belief, we will read James's argument that faith could be pragmatically justified even if it could not be rationally demonstrated to be true. The religious application of his pragmatic theory of truth is captured in the following passage:

> [Pragmatism's] only test of probable truth is what works best and combines with the collectivity of experience's demands, nothing being omitted. If theological ideas should do this, if the notion of God, in particular, should prove to do it, how could pragmatism possibly deny God's existence? [Pragmatism] could see no meaning in treating as "not true" a notion that was pragmatically so successful.[82]

However, James thought that this pragmatic approach to truth applied to every issue in life and not just the religious sphere.

We can gain a window into James's approach to philosophy by examining an experi-ence he had at the beginning of his career that changed the course of his life. As a result of years of studying science and medicine, James became morbidly depressed by the thought that human beings might be nothing more than determined mechanisms doomed to live in a closed universe where nothing escapes the domination of physical laws. If determinism is true, James believed, then his life had no meaning, for all his choices would then be as inevitable and purposeless as the blind motion of atoms. On the other hand, if he was genuinely free, then the future was open and his choices made a difference both to the course of his life and to the world on which he acted. The problem was that he did not think that there could be any definitive scientific or philosophical proof of either belief. If reason could not tell him what to believe on a certain issue, James thought, it made sense to choose the belief that would maximize his life and produce the most value when put into action. For this reason, James resolved that if he was to go on living and find any sort of meaning in life at all, he would have to commit himself to the thesis that free will is not an illusion and base his actions on that conviction. Accordingly, in an 1870 diary entry, writ-ten when he was 28 and one year out of medical school, James resolved:

> My first act of free will shall be to believe in free will. . . . I will go a step further with my will, not only act with it, but believe as well; believe in my individual reality and creative power. . . . Life shall be built in doing and suffering and creating.[83]

This personal example illustrates James's version of the pragmatic method for forming our beliefs. As he has said, truth is a function of "what works best and combines with the col-lectivity of experience's demands." In some cases this definition will mean that an idea can be directly verified in terms of experimental, scientific data. For example, if I believe that an object is made out of iron, then it should be attracted to a magnet. However, the thesis of free will or the thesis of determinism do not produce any sorts of simple predictions concerning future experiences. Nevertheless, according to James, it is better to believe in free will because it will allow us to believe that our choices make a difference to the world and it will make our moral struggles meaningful, whereas determinism will not. Hence, in this very personal sense, the consequences of believing in free will lead to better results. James articulates this very broad pragmatic criteria for resolving philosophical issues in the following way:

> Of two competing views of the universe which in all other respects are equal, but of which the first denies some vital human need while the second satisfies it, the second will be favored by sane men for the simple reason that it makes the world seem more rational.[84]

Many critics accused James of saying that we should believe whatever it is comfortable to believe. James, however, always insisted that a belief would have pragmatic value only if it could be integrated with the rest of our beliefs or experiences and if it would successfully guide us in the long run. Hence, based on these considerations there are many *comfortable* beliefs that we should not entertain (e.g., "I don't need to study") because they would lead to conflicts with experience, would not be good guides to action, and would thereby be impractical. Similarly, there are many *uncomfortable* beliefs that I may have to embrace (e.g., "I have diabetes"), simply because they will provide the best guide to action over time.

When Dewey spoke about truth, he often fell back on Peirce's and James's notions of truth as "successfully guiding action," "satisfying the needs and conditions evoked by a problem," "working in action," and so on.[85] However, Dewey avoided using the word *truth* as much as possible, for it carried with it too much traditional, philosophical baggage. Typically, truth has been viewed as a static property of a proposition and has been viewed in terms of the correspondence theory. Because these views are ones that Dewey wanted to discard, he rarely used the word *truth* in his own philosophical writings.*

Instead of using the tainted word *truth,* Dewey typically explained the idea of knowledge in terms of the notion of "warranted assertibility."[86] This phrase means that those propositions that it is best for us to believe (or assert) are those that have arisen out of a process of inquiry, that have most successfully fit with our experience, and that seem best suited to guide us in our future engagements with the world. Of course, because the world and our experience are constantly changing, what we are warranted in asserting at this point may change as our growing experiences create new conditions that our beliefs must fulfill. This notion captures Dewey's conviction that there is no final end of inquiry at which our ideas will be perfectly adequate and beyond the need of further revision.

Pragmatism and Relativism

The different pragmatists take various positions on the issue of relativism. Peirce was clearly an antirelativist. According to his epistemology, two completely different beliefs could not be equally true, for in the long run experience would always favor one over the other. As Peirce put it:

> There are real things, whose characters are entirely independent of our opinions about them; those realities affect our senses according to regular laws, and . . . by taking advantage of the laws of perception, we can ascertain by reasoning how things really and truly are.[87]

Although Peirce emphasized the fact that our beliefs were always tentative and continually needed to be revised, he was confident that the self-correcting nature of the scientific method would guarantee that human inquiry was continually converging on truth and reality.

> The opinion which is fated to be ultimately agreed to by all who investigate is what we mean by the truth, and the object represented in this opinion is the real. That is the way I would explain reality.[88]

By defining truth with reference to community opinion, Peirce is not saying that truth is all a matter of convention. Instead, he is expressing his conviction that if the process of

---

*In an entire book devoted to the nature of inquiry *(Logic: The Theory of Inquiry),* Dewey mentions the word *truth* only once, in a footnote.

inquiry is carried on long enough, the difference between truth and error eventually will manifest itself in the court of human experience and we will discover how things really and truly are.

James was unclear on the issue of relativism. He was frequently criticized for preaching a thoroughgoing relativistic philosophy, but in response to these criticisms he reaffirmed his belief in a reality that existed independently of us. Nevertheless, the relativist within James comes out in passages such as this one:

> There is nothing improbable in the supposition that an analysis of the world may yield a number of formulae, all consistent with the facts. . . . Why may there not be different points of view for surveying it, within each of which all data harmonize, and which the observer may therefore either choose between, or simply cumulate upon another?[89]

Perhaps the most generous interpretation of James's views is that he was a pluralist about truth. This interpretation means that James believed that there were different kinds of truths, and consequently, the practical consequences of belief or disbelief would differ depending on the subject matter; that is, on some issues he was an objectivist whereas on other issues he was a relativist. For example, James says that "the future movements of the stars or the facts of past history are determined now once for all, whether I like them or not."[90] Here he is speaking like an objectivist by claiming that some facts are independent of our beliefs about them. On other issues, however, where science and logic alone do not resolve the issue for us, James was a relativist. Is there a purpose to the universe or is it purposeless? Because science cannot give us a definitive answer, James thought that each person should answer the question based on his or her own experience with life. On these sorts of issues, he says, "it is almost certain that personal temperament will here make itself felt, and that although all men will insist on being spoken to by the universe in some way, few will insist on being spoken to in just the same way."[91] Suppose we believe, he says, that a particular theory solves the problem we face more satisfactorily than another. "But that means more satisfactorily to ourselves, and individuals will emphasize their points of satisfaction differently. To a certain degree, therefore, everything here is plastic."[92]

Dewey believed, with the relativists, that there were no free-floating absolute truths that were completely independent of us and our concrete situation. However, he did not think that what we should believe was completely a matter of individual, subjective choice. All experience begins within a biological and cultural matrix and what we should believe will depend on our concrete situation and our goals. There are no truths or values that are valid for all time, but only beliefs or values that are optimal for a particular society in a particular context. For this reason, his position could be called contextualism. For example, Newton's physics worked for solving the scientific problems people faced in previous centuries, but in the 20th century, it proved inadequate to address the problems that arose at the level of subatomic events and in new discoveries in astronomy. Hence, some of the fundamental ideas of physics had to be revised. According to Dewey, inquiry is a continual process of adjusting means to ends. But as new ends arise within a changing world, we need new means, new ideas, and new theories. According to Dewey's instrumentalism, theories are instruments just like the slide rule. Just as slide rules are no longer used, so theories are not so much refuted as they are abandoned when we require new and more adequate instruments to meet our needs.

Are the pragmatists inconsistent in claiming that truth is not objective or fixed while apparently claiming that pragmatism is true? Perhaps to avoid this criticism, Dewey said that his or any philosophy had to be evaluated pragmatically:

There is . . . a first rate test of the value of any philosophy which is offered to us: Does it end in conclusions which, when they are referred back to ordinary life-experiences and their predicaments, render them more significant, more luminous to us, and make our dealings with them more fruitful?[93]

Obviously, Dewey thinks that pragmatism meets this test. Therefore, Dewey is saying, even though truth is not absolute, objective, and fixed, pragmatism should be adopted because it is a pragmatically useful way to approach experience.

The core of pragmatism's conception of truth was eloquently expressed in the following famous passage by James.

- As you read through this passage, write down all the ways in which James uses the words *practical, instruments,* and *useful,* and refers to the way that ideas have *cash-value, lead us, work,* and *pay.* What do these words tell you about his view of ideas and truth?
- In the first section, how does James describe the intellectualist position?
- What questions does the pragmatist ask of an idea?
- How does James define *true ideas?*

FROM WILLIAM JAMES

Pragmatism's Conception of Truth[94]

I fully expect to see the pragmatist view of truth run through the classic stages of a theory's career. First, you know, a new theory is attacked as absurd; then it is admitted to be true, but obvious and insignificant; finally it is seen to be so important that its adversaries claim that they themselves discovered it. Our doctrine of truth is at present in the first of these three stages, with symptoms of the second stage having begun in certain quarters. . . .

Truth, as any dictionary will tell you, is a property of certain of our ideas. It means their "agreement," as falsity means their disagreement, with "reality." Pragmatists and intellectualists* both accept this definition as a matter of course. They begin to quarrel only after the question is raised as to what may precisely be meant by the term "agreement," and what by the term "reality," when reality is taken as something for our ideas to agree with.

. . . The great assumption of the intellectualists is that truth means essentially an inert static relation. When you've got your true idea of anything, there's an end of the matter. You're in possession; you *know;* you have fulfilled your thinking destiny. You are where you ought to be mentally; you have obeyed your categorical imperative; and nothing more need follow on that climax of your rational destiny. Epistemologically you are in stable equilibrium.

Pragmatism, on the other hand, asks its usual question. "Grant an idea or belief to be true," it says, "what concrete difference will its being true make in any one's actual life? How will the truth be realized? What experiences will be different from those which would be obtained if the belief were false? What, in short, is the truth's cash-value in experiential terms?"

The moment pragmatism asks this question, it sees the answer: *True ideas are those that we can assimilate, validate, corroborate and verify. False ideas are those that we cannot.*

---

*When James speaks of "intellectualists," he is referring to rationalists.

That is the practical difference it makes to us to have true ideas; that, therefore, is the meaning of truth, for it is all that truth is known-as.

This thesis is what I have to defend. The truth of an idea is not a stagnant property inherent in it. Truth *happens* to an idea. It *becomes* true, is *made* true by events. Its verity is in fact an event, a process: the process namely of its verifying itself, its verification. Its validity is the process of its *validation*.

But what do the words verification and validation themselves pragmatically mean? They again signify certain practical consequences of the verified and validated idea. It is hard to find any one phrase that characterizes these consequences better than the ordinary agreement-formula—just such consequences being what we have in mind whenever we say that our ideas "agree" with reality. They lead us, namely, through the acts and other ideas which they instigate, into or up to, or towards, other parts of experience with which we feel all the while—such feeling being among our potentialities—that the original ideas remain in agreement. The connexions and transitions come to us from point to point as being progressive, harmonious, satisfactory. This function of agreeable leading is what we mean by an idea's verification. Such an account is vague and it sounds at first quite trivial, but it has results which it will take the rest of my hour to explain.

- In the next section, what does James say is the value of "extra" ideas (ideas that have no immediate use)?

Let me begin by reminding you of the fact that the possession of true thoughts means everywhere the possession of invaluable instruments of action; and that our duty to gain truth, so far from being a blank command from out of the blue, or a "stunt" self-imposed by our intellect, can account for itself by excellent practical reasons.

The importance to human life of having true beliefs about matters of fact is a thing too notorious. We live in a world of realities that can be infinitely useful or infinitely harmful. Ideas that tell us which of them to expect count as the true ideas in all this primary sphere of verification, and the pursuit of such ideas is a primary human duty. The possession of truth, so far from being here an end in itself, is only a preliminary means towards other vital satisfactions. If I am lost in the woods and starved, and find what looks like a cow-path, it is of the utmost importance that I should think of a human habitation at the end of it, for if I do so and follow it, I save myself. The true thought is useful here because the house which is its object is useful. The practical value of true ideas is thus primarily derived from the practical importance of their objects to us. Their objects are, indeed, not important at all times. I may on another occasion have no use for the house; and then my idea of it, however verifiable, will be practically irrelevant, and had better remain latent. Yet since almost any object may some day become temporarily important, the advantage of having a general stock of extra truths, of ideas that shall be true of merely possible situations, is obvious. We store such extra truths away in our memories, and with the overflow we fill our books of reference. Whenever such an extra truth becomes practically relevant to one of our emergencies, it passes from cold-storage to do work in the world and our belief in it grows active. You can say of it then either that "it is useful because it is true" or that "it is true because it is useful." Both these phrases mean exactly the same thing, namely that here is an idea that gets fulfilled and can be verified. True is the name for whatever idea starts the verification-process, useful is the name for its completed function in experience. True ideas would never have been singled out as such, would never have acquired a class-name, least of all a name suggesting value, unless they had been useful from the outset in this way.

From this simple cue pragmatism gets her general notion of truth as something essentially bound up with the way in which one moment in our experience may lead us towards other moments which it will be worth while to have been led to. Primarily, and on the common-sense level, the truth of a state of mind means this function of *a leading that is worth while*. When a moment in our experience, of any kind whatever, inspires us with a thought that is true, that means that sooner or later we dip by that thought's guidance into the particulars of experience again and make advantageous connexion with them.

> ### STOP AND THINK
>
> Notice in the passage you just read that when a belief grows active for us, according to James, you can say of it that (1) "it is useful because it is true" or that (2) "it is true because it is useful" and that "both these phrases mean exactly the same thing." But are they the same? Why?

Plato, Locke, Descartes, or any other traditional philosopher would agree that true ideas are useful, but they would vehemently deny that being useful is what makes an idea true. For example, the medievals held beliefs about the motions of the planets that were false. Yet, these false ideas endured for centuries because they still led astronomers to make successful predictions. (They were useful but false ideas.) However, James would reply that within the context of their times, for the tasks that they faced, these ideas had cash-value, they worked, they functioned as instruments of action. Hence, he might say that these ideas were true for the medievals, whereas they are false for us since they no longer function to fulfill our current needs or fit within the bounds of our greatly expanded experience.

• In the next passage, what does James mean by saying an idea "agrees" with reality?

To "agree" in the widest sense with a reality *can only mean to be guided either straight up to it or into its surroundings, or to be put into such working touch with it as to handle either it or something connected with it better than if we disagreed.* Better either intellectually or practically! And often agreement will only mean the negative fact that nothing contradictory from the quarter of that reality comes to interfere with the way in which our ideas guide us elsewhere. To copy a reality is, indeed, one very important way of agreeing with it, but it is far from being essential. The essential thing is the process of being guided. Any idea that helps us to *deal,* whether practically or intellectually, with either the reality or its belongings, that doesn't entangle our progress in frustrations, that *fits,* in fact, and adapts our life to the reality's whole setting, will agree sufficiently to meet the requirement. It will hold true of that reality.

Notice that in the next paragraph, James introduces what is now called the pragmatic or instrumentalist view of science. Because we cannot see subatomic particles (such as atoms or electrons) nor can we fully imagine them, and because the descriptions of them frequently fly in the face of common sense and our ordinary experience, James denies that scientists are giving us a literal description of what is present in experience. Instead, scientists are viewing reality *as if* it behaved this way and are constructing theoretical entities and formulas that work in making predictions. To use a rough analogy, statistics tell us that the average American family has 2.4 children. Obviously, no real family has this many children. However, the theoretical construct of the average family is a useful one and enables policy makers to predict the housing needs in the nation.

- In the next passage, what do our theories mediate between, according to James?
- If two theories are equally compatible with all our other truths, how do we decide between them?
- Does making this choice necessarily mean that the chosen theory is a "copy" of reality?
- If not, then what is its value?
- In what ways is the pursuit of truth similar to the pursuit of health and other goals in life?

Such is the large loose way in which the pragmatist interprets the word agreement. He treats it altogether practically. He lets it cover any process of conduction from a present idea to a future terminus, provided only it run prosperously. It is only thus that "scientific" ideas, flying as they do beyond common sense, can be said to agree with their realities. It is, as I have already said, *as if* reality were made of ether, atoms or electrons, but we mustn't think so literally. The term "energy" doesn't even pretend to stand for anything "objective." It is only a way of measuring the surface of phenomena so as to string their changes on a simple formula.

Yet in the choice of these man-made formulas we cannot be capricious with impunity any more than we can be capricious on the common-sense practical level. We must find a theory that will *work;* and that means something extremely difficult; for our theory must mediate between all previous truths and certain new experiences. It must derange common sense and previous belief as little as possible, and it must lead to some sensible terminus or other that can be verified exactly. To "work" means both these things; and the squeeze is so tight that there is little loose play for any hypothesis. Our theories are wedged and controlled as nothing else is. Yet sometimes alternative theoretic formulas are equally compatible with all the truths we know, and then we choose between them for subjective reasons. We choose the kind of theory to which we are already partial; we follow "elegance" or "economy." Clerk-Maxwell somewhere says it would be "poor scientific taste" to choose the more complicated of two equally well-evidenced conceptions; and you will all agree with him. Truth in science is what gives us the maximum possible sum of satisfactions, taste included; but consistency both with previous truth and with novel fact is always the most imperious claimant. . . .

Our account of truth is an account of truths in the plural, of processes of leading, . . . and having only this quality in common, that they *pay.* They pay by guiding us into or towards some part of a system that dips at numerous points into sense-percepts, which we may copy mentally or not, but with which at any rate we are now in the kind of commerce vaguely designated as verification. Truth for us is simply a collective name for verification-processes, just as health, wealth, strength, etc., are names for other processes connected with life, and also pursued because it pays to pursue them. Truth is *made,* just as health, wealth and strength are made, in the course of experience.

- In the next paragraph, what does James mean when he says that what is true is "the expedient"? How does this theory differ from the correspondence theory of truth?

"The true," to put it very briefly, is only the expedient in the way of our thinking, just as "the right" is only the expedient in the way of our behaving. Expedient in almost any fashion; and expedient in the long run and on the whole of course; for what meets expediently all the experience in sight won't necessarily meet all further experiences equally satisfactorily. Experience, as we know, has ways of *boiling over,* and making us correct our present formulas. . . .

. . . In the realm of truth-processes facts come independently and determine our beliefs provisionally. But these beliefs make us act, and as fast as they do so, they bring into sight or into existence new facts which redetermine the beliefs accordingly. So the whole coil and ball of truth, as it rolls up, is the product of a double influence. Truths emerge from facts; but they dip forward into facts again and add to them; which facts again create or reveal new truth (the word is indifferent) and so on indefinitely. The "facts" themselves meanwhile are not *true*. They simply are. Truth is the function of the beliefs that start and terminate among them.

STOP AND THINK

In the final paragraph of the previous reading, James says it makes no difference whether we say the facts "create" or "reveal" new truths. What is the significance of blurring this distinction? (Think about the difference between creating a message in the sand and revealing one that is already there but that we didn't notice previously.) Why would Descartes and Locke (unlike James) insist that the methods of science and philosophy reveal truths but do not create them?

If to reveal truths is the same as creating them, as James says, then they must not already be there until we make them. To illustrate James's point, the sculptor Michelangelo could "see" a statue in the block of marble. Of course, it wasn't *really* there until he carved and formed the marble. Still, he had to decide which forms would fit with the veins of the marble and which forms the marble would not support. In the same way, James is suggesting that our theories and beliefs must fit the facts, but that they are not already latent in the facts or dictated by them. We create those truths for our present situation that are "expedient" and that we can weave into our past and future experiences most effectively.

LOOKING THROUGH THE PRAGMATIST'S LENS

1. The pragmatists claim that ideas are instruments for engaging with the world of our experience and that a true belief is one that will lead to successful actions in the long run. How would they use these notions to respond to the skeptic's claim that we can never know if our beliefs are true or false?

2. The pragmatists test the adequacy of a claim in terms of its practical consequences. How would they use the pragmatic method to show why we should believe the following ideas?

- The Pythagorean theorem.
- Unjustified killing is wrong.
- Democracy is a better political system than is a monarchy.
- There is no social problem so severe that solutions to it cannot be found.

3. At the beginning of this section on the pragmatists, you were asked two questions about truth. Now imagine that you are a pragmatist and answer these same questions from that point of view.

- What does it mean for a belief to be true?
- Why is it important to have true beliefs?

In what ways (if any) do the pragmatist's answers differ from your original ones? Do you feel inclined to change your original answers? Why?

EXAMINING THE STRENGTHS AND WEAKNESSES OF PRAGMATISM

Positive Evaluation

1. The pragmatists remind us of the tentative and probable nature of all human knowledge. Individually and as a culture, our ideas are continually undergoing revision as experiences and new problems arise for which our current ideas are inadequate. Pragmatists have pointed out that the certitudes and dogmas of previous ages frequently turn out to be myths and superstitions in the light of new experiences and knowledge. In what ways is this observation a valuable insight?

2. The pragmatists have pointed to the intimate relationship between belief and action. Our actions demonstrate what we truly believe as opposed to what we think we believe or say we believe. Furthermore, all actions that are not simply blind physiological reactions are based on our beliefs about the world and our expectations about future experiences. Aren't the pragmatists on to something here in tying together belief and action?

3. The pragmatists emphasize the practical consequences of ideas, they view each belief as a tentative hypothesis to be embraced if it works or abandoned if it doesn't, and they stress that our beliefs enable us to move from one set of experiences to future experiences. In what ways is the pragmatic approach to truth similar to the scientific method? To what degree do these similarities help support pragmatism as a viable theory of truth?

Negative Evaluation

1. The pragmatists have said that an idea or belief is true or not depending on whether it works or leads to satisfactory results. But doesn't this definition of truth suggest the following problems?

- We can never say that an idea is true or false because we can never know all its long-range consequences.
- The same idea can be both true and false, since its consequences may be satisfactory for some people and unsatisfactory for others.

2. Isn't the pragmatic notion of truth paradoxical? For an idea to have pragmatic value for me, for it to work, isn't it necessary that I think in terms of the correspondence theory of truth? For example, suppose that my belief in life after death has value for me in James's sense. It fills my life with hope, it gives me confidence in the face of death, and it keeps me from despairing over the thought that after 70 years or so I will cease to exist. But is it possible for this belief to have this pragmatic value for me unless I suppose that this belief corresponds to what will happen after my death? Could it have pragmatic truth for me or could I even believe it if I thought its *only* value was the benefits I received from believing it?

3. Based on pragmatic considerations, James chose to believe in free will. This belief brought meaning to his life and gave him confidence that his actions mattered and could change the course of the future. But is this result enough to warrant a belief? Couldn't it be the case that his belief led to success but that his desire to believe in free will was inevitably determined by his personality and upbringing, and that everything he did and thought was actually determined?* Doesn't it seem that it is possible for this belief to be pragmatically successful and to have cash-value and yet for it to be a false picture of reality? Do these conclusions throw us back to correspondence with reality as the defining feature of truth?

4. Critics claim that James failed to distinguish between the psychological factors that lead a person to hold to a particular belief and the rational factors that would make that belief justified. Do you think this criticism is a strong one?

2.7 RETHINKING THE WESTERN TRADITION: FEMINIST EPISTEMOLOGY

LEADING QUESTIONS: *Feminist Epistemology*

1. A man is walking past a large hospital when he sees a physician in a white coat and a little girl coming toward him. As they come closer, he realizes the physician is an old friend whom he has not seen since their college days. They greet each other warmly and the friend says, "Since we last saw each other in college, I went on to medical school and I am now a surgeon at this hospital. I also married someone whom you don't know and have never met, and this is our daughter, Nancy." The man says to the little girl, "Nancy, you not only have your mother's name, but you also have her brown eyes." How did he know?

2. The words *man, he,* and *his* can obviously be used to refer to males. However, the English language has had the tradition of also using these words in a gender-neutral way to refer to the human race as a whole or to any human being. But can *man* ever have a completely gender-neutral use? For example, in the sentence, "If an individual wishes to protect his family, then he should have adequate insurance," the words "he" and "his" are presumed to refer to *any* individual, whether male or female. If so, then we should see nothing strange about this sentence: "If an individual wishes to protect his husband, wife, or children, then he should carry adequate insurance." But we find the phrase "his husband" peculiar because "his" is not really gender-neutral. On the other hand, the sentence, "If one wishes to have an abortion, then one should be free to do so" does not sound strange because "one" is genuinely free of any gender bias. But to say, "If a person wishes to have an abortion, then he should be free to do so" sounds odd because "he," unlike "one," is not gender-neutral.[95] In these examples, are the uses of the terms *man* or *he* really as generic and gender-neutral as has been claimed?

3. If you are a female, what things do you think males just don't understand? Why do you suppose this is? If you are a male, what things do you think females just don't understand? Why do you suppose this is? Are there situations that evoke distinctively male and female ways of looking at things? If so, how should this fact be taken into account when constructing a theory of knowledge?

---

*See the discussion on freedom and determinism in the next chapter, sections 3.5 to 3.8.

PHILOSOPHY
in the
MARKETPLACE

Answer the following questions yourself and then pose them to at least five females and five males.

- Do men and women think in different ways? How so? Give some examples.
- Do you believe that it is possible to get a man to think like a woman or, at least, to appreciate the female perspective on a given issue, and vice versa? Why?

SURVEYING THE CASE FOR FEMINIST EPISTEMOLOGY

The Background of Feminist Theory

Feminism is another contemporary movement that questions some of the underlying assumptions of the Western tradition in philosophy and seeks to develop a new model for doing philosophy. Like any living movement that is breaking new ground, feminists have many different and conflicting visions of what the character and agenda of their movement should be. However, although there is not an official creed or set of doctrines that all feminists agree upon, their thinking revolves around some common themes. **Feminism** is a movement within philosophy and other disciplines that (1) emphasizes the role of gender in shaping how we think and how society is structured, (2) focuses on the historical and social forces that have excluded women from full participation in the intellectual and political realms, and (3) strives to produce a society that recognizes women and men as both different and equal.[96] These three themes illustrate that feminism includes both a theoretical understanding of the way things are and an attempt to use this knowledge to transform the status quo.

A quick glance at standard works on the history of philosophy will reveal the notable absence of women prior to the 20th century, which is one example of the way in which women's voices have been excluded from our intellectual traditions. Actually, there were a number of women philosophers in every historical period starting with ancient Greece.[97] The reason that women intellectuals have had a hard time getting their voices heard is illustrated by the views about women held by notable philosophers. While the history of disparaging remarks that male philosophers have made about women is a long story, one of the earliest and most influential accounts was given by the Greek philosopher Aristotle. He believed that the normal outcome of mating was that of a male fetus, but if there was some *deficiency* in the process, a female would be formed. For this reason, he referred to females as "mutilated males" and said that the female character is "a sort of natural deficiency." Furthermore, he believed that the female contributed the material portion of the embryo while the male contributed the "principle of soul" or the capacity for reason.[98] Aristotle's biology of the sexes was repeated throughout the Middle Ages and beyond.[99]

There have been some notable exceptions to this disparagement and exclusion of women. For example, Plato in his *Republic* argued that it is inevitable that any given society would produce some women whose intellect and abilities would be superior to those of the average person. In his ideal society, these gifted women would take their place with men of like abilities to receive specialized training to make them the intellectual and political leaders of the nation. Similarly, John Stuart Mill, the 19th-century English philosopher, wrote a work on *The Subjection of Women* in which he argued that his society was cutting itself off from the benefits of utilizing the contributions of gifted women. Mill himself was

feminism a movement within philosophy and other disciplines that (1) emphasizes the role of gender in shaping how we think and how society is structured, (2) focuses on the historical and social forces that have excluded women from full participation in the intellectual and political realms, and (3) strives to produce a society that recognizes women and men as both different and equal

Try out the story of the surgeon and the little girl on a diverse collection of friends and acquaintances. Make sure half the respondents are females and half are males. How did they do? On the whole, were the females better than the males in finding the solution?

PHILOSOPHY
in the
MARKETPLACE

married to a brilliant woman, Harriet Taylor, who collaborated with him on many of his philosophical writings. For the most part, however, Aristotle's attitude prevailed in the philosophical tradition. He claimed that only the free adult male is qualified to rule society, because only he is invested by nature with full rational capacity. Hence, Aristotle says, "the courage of a man is shown in commanding, of a woman in obeying" and "silence is a woman's glory."[100]

The "Leading Questions" that opened this section indicate how deeply gender biases are rooted in our thinking. Were you able to figure out the answer to question 1? In responding to this story, many people (both male and female) are puzzled as to how the man could know the name and appearance of the girl's mother if he had never met her. Some suppose that the man knew the birth mother of the girl even though he did not know her adoptive mother (the current wife of the surgeon). Like so many issues in philosophy, the solution is found by questioning your underlying assumptions. Nothing in the story indicates that the surgeon is a man. However, when people think of a surgeon, they tend to imagine a man. Obviously, the simplest way to account for the facts of the story is to suppose that the college friend and surgeon is Nancy's mother.

Question 2 shows some problems with using male terms (such as *man*) to refer generically to both men and women. Yet in spite of these problems, this use is a traditional and common practice. For example, the glossary of one author's book has this entry: "Man (*as used throughout this book*) A human being, or the human creature regarded abstractly and without regard to gender; hence, the human race, or humanity."[101] But if it is possible to use *man* in this way, then there should not be anything odd about this sentence: "Man, like all mammals, is an animal that breast-feeds his young."[102] The pragmatist John Dewey published *Problems of Men* in 1946.[103] We might suppose from the title that the book discusses typical male problems such as baldness and diseases of the prostate. However, the book is really a discussion of the philosophical problems that *humanity* has faced through the ages. Feminists point out that these examples show the tendency to treat men and men's psychology and experiences as the standard while viewing women's experiences as unimportant, exceptional, subsidiary, or deviant.

Varieties of Feminism

Historically, the feminist movement can be divided into two eras. The period prior to about 1945 sometimes is known as first-wave feminism. The resurgence of the movement in the latter half of the 20th century often is referred to as second-wave feminism. Apart from these historical divisions, however, there are two varieties of feminists. The first group consists of (what are variously called) equity or liberal feminists. The equity feminists believe that basic social structures and intellectual traditions of Western culture should be retained. Their cause is that of allowing women to have full intellectual and political participation in society. The terms *freedom* and *opportunity* describe the focus of their concern. The second group of feminists are called gender or radical feminists. Gender feminists do not simply want to be included within the status quo because they are challenging and attempting to change the fundamental structures, assumptions, methods, and discourse of society, claiming that those aspects of society reflect male-dominated distortions. To put it glibly, equity feminists want their piece of the pie, while gender feminists radically critique the pie itself.

Whereas all enlightened persons, whether male or female, are in favor of the full intellectual and political equality of women, the second form of feminism (gender feminism) provokes a swirl of controversy in philosophy. (For the record, it would be a mistake to suppose that all female philosophers are feminists in this second sense and that all male philosophers are nonfeminists.)[104] A distinction is frequently made between the terms *sex* and *gender*. *Sex* is a biological category that refers to the obvious physical differences between males and females. *Gender* is a concept that is much more subtle and difficult to define because it includes social and psychological factors. *Gender* includes (but is not limited to) the notions of masculine-feminine, social roles, sexuality, and the apparent psychological differences between men and women.

Within gender feminism, some feminists are *essentialists,* claiming that there is a distinct and essential female nature. Essentialists differ as to whether this essential female nature is the product of women's biology or of relatively stable cultural factors that create the unique and common features of women's experiences. Feminists who are *nonessentialists* or *nominalists* deny that gender characteristics are fixed in any way at all. Furthermore, they tend to view descriptions of "women's nature" as social constructs that prevent women from changing and redefining themselves. Simone de Beauvoir was one of France's most celebrated 20th-century writers and an influential voice in the feminist movement. De Beauvoir expressed the nonessentialist position in her famous quote, "One is not born, but rather becomes, a woman."[105] Her point was that gender characteristics are not biologically determined, but they can be either socially imposed or subjectively chosen.

Ann Garry and Marilyn Pearsall provide a good introduction to feminist philosophy in the following passage. (Ann Garry is professor of philosophy at California State University, Los Angeles. Her publications are in feminist philosophy, philosophy of mind, and applied ethics. Marilyn Pearsall has taught philosophy and women's studies at a number of universities. She has edited several works on feminist studies.) In reading this selection, answer the following questions:

- What disagreements do feminists have with traditional philosophy?
- What do feminists hope to accomplish with respect to the discipline of philosophy?
- What do the authors say is "one of the hardest questions" that feminist philosophers face?

ANN GARRY
(1943–   )

FROM ANN GARRY AND MARILYN PEARSALL

Women, Knowledge, and Reality[106]

Feminist philosophy has two sources—the feminist movement and traditional academic philosophy. The feminist movement has opened our eyes to the deep and varied ways in which the ideals and institutions of our culture oppress women. In addition to providing a devastating critique of male-dominated society, feminists have affirmed the positive value of women's experience. Academic feminist philosophers build upon and contribute to the insights and work of the women's movement. Feminist philosophers examine and criticize the assumptions and presuppositions of the ideals and institutions of our culture. We write about a wide range of topics, from the most overtly political issues such as job discrimination, rape, and the use of sexist language, to the subtle underlying metaphysical and epistemological assumptions of our culture and our philosophical traditions.

Feminist philosophy, especially in its academic forms, also has its roots in traditional philosophy. Although traditional philosophy has been shaped by men who have taken their experiences, their values, and their views of the world as the standard for all human beings, it is in the philosophical traditions of these men that academic feminist philosophers were educated. Even today the philosophical methods we are taught to practice and the subject matter we are taught to consider appropriate for philosophy are by and large not feminist; they are the traditional male methods, fields, and topics of philosophy.

As feminist philosophers incorporated insights from our political practice into our academic work, we became aware that the androcentric* character of traditional philosophy made it limited, biased, and liable to oppressive use. This is true of theories not only in social and political philosophy and ethics, but also in metaphysics and theory of knowledge, the fields some consider the core of the western philosophical tradition. Although there is too much diversity in philosophy to permit easy generalization, we can say that feminist philosophers call attention to the themes pervading the various strands of western male thought that have led to distortion and bias in philosophy itself and have lent themselves readily to the oppression of women and other subordinate groups. . . .

There is more to feminist philosophy than the continuing critique and analysis of what has gone wrong. Feminist philosophers are trying in many diverse ways to reconstruct philosophy. We want to redefine the methods and subject matter of philosophy in ways that value women's experiences and enable women to move from the position of object to positions of subject, of knower, and of agent. We want to redeem philosophy, to "get philosophy right," recognizing the difficulty in even thinking about what standards, if any, there are for doing it "right."

In trying to reconstruct philosophy, one of the hardest questions is what can be salvaged from traditional philosophy and what should be rejected. While it would be foolish to disregard valuable insights of male philosophers, one cannot determine quickly what, if anything, is free from androcentric assumptions. This is an ongoing process that requires feminist philosophers to build upon each other's contributions, for what appears to be gender neutral one year may look obviously androcentric the next. Feminist philosophers realize that reconstructing or "revisioning" philosophy is a very large, open-ended project.

In the remaining portion of the passage, Garry and Pearsall give a brief answer to the question, "What can one expect to find when reading feminist philosophy?" Without attempting to set out rigid boundaries, they present some of the central themes found throughout feminist philosophical writings.

To start with, feminist philosophers are saying in a multiplicity of ways that gender matters—even in very abstract theories in which one might not suspect that it would. Because gender matters, we are prone to resist easy moves to speak in a "neutral," nongendered voice. We are also likely to focus on the ways in which values underlie and permeate theories; again, this is not just in fields one might expect, such as political philosophy, but also in the most fundamental questions of metaphysics and theory of knowledge.

Feminist philosophers also strive to connect theories to everyday experience. We ask fundamental philosophical questions about life, meaning, value, and being. Yet we try to ensure that our answers are not merely about some abstract "meaning of life," but are informed by the meaning of real lives and experiences. We place high value on differing experiences of diverse women, whether diverse in class, race, ethnicity, sexual orientation, age, or able-bodiedness. We try to be especially attentive to the ways in which the

---

*Male-centered.

oppressions associated with these categories, e.g., racism or class oppression, intersect with sexism. The diversity among women has led to interesting controversies about the possibility of speaking in a "woman's voice" or a "feminist voice."

In addition, feminist philosophers often seek to integrate what is valuable to their work from different disciplines, from several traditions within a discipline, or from different fields of study within a discipline. For example, a feminist philosopher writing about the self might draw on anthropologists and poets as well as philosophers from more than one tradition; she might also call attention to the ways in which questions of value cannot be separated from metaphysical theories of the self. She might find that traditional styles of writing philosophy are too limiting; her style might be more personal or otherwise different from those of traditional philosophers.

Copyright © 1989 by Unwin Hyman, Inc. Reproduced by permission of Taylor & Francis Books UK.

STOP AND THINK

From what you have just read, what do you think feminists will say about the role of gender and values in philosophizing about knowledge? What will be their notion of experience and the role it plays in epistemology?

ISSUES AND THEMES IN FEMINIST EPISTEMOLOGY

Although there are many divisions and disagreements within feminism, some similar threads of thought run throughout all feminist theory. A common theme throughout feminist epistemology is the critique of four, traditional, interrelated assumptions:

1. *The Generic Humanity Assumption:* There is one universal human nature. Epistemology, therefore, is the attempt to describe the cognitive structures common to all individuals.
2. *The View from Nowhere Assumption:* The particular identity of a knower (including gender, race, class, and historical circumstances) is irrelevant to the production and assessment of that person's knowledge claims.
3. *The Pure, Impersonal Reason Assumption:* (This view of rationality results from the view from nowhere assumption.) The ideal of rationality is that of pure objectivity, untainted by subjectivity or the emotions and interests of the knower.
4. *The Robinson Crusoe Assumption:** The acquisition of knowledge is primarily a project of isolated individuals, and this knowledge is independent of any social context and free of political implications.

The Generic Humanity Assumption

Feminists claim that the picture of one, universal, human nature has been created by taking men's experiences and psychology as the paradigm. Other points of view and models of humanity, particularly those that incorporate women's experiences, have been excluded

---

*Robinson Crusoe was the lead character in Daniel Defoe's 18th-century novel by that name. Crusoe was a sailor who was shipwrecked on an isolated tropical island. This metaphor is my own and is not common in the literature, but it summarizes a common theme in feminist theory.

from consideration or marginalized for being too subjective or unconventional. This exclusion is comparable to ducks claiming that there is only one standard for all well-formed water birds and describing this universal standard in such a way that it just happens to fit the description of a typical duck. To carry this analogy further, imagine that in applying this standard of excellence, the ducks proclaim that swans are imperfect, deformed ducks because of their very unducklike curved neck. Obviously, the problem is not that swans are deficient ducks but that the ducks have taken one particular standard for water birds and made this the norm while excluding all others from the realm of acceptability.

Feminists claim that this tendency to make male perspectives the norm infects most traditional theories of knowledge. Feminist philosopher Lorraine Code makes this charge, for example, against a contemporary work on rationality by a male philosopher.[107] She notes that "Richard Foley appeals repeatedly to the epistemic judgments of people who are 'like the rest of us.'" The problem is, Code says, "nowhere does he address the question of who 'we' are." She suggests that the standard knowers referred to by "we" in the coded language of epistemology are tacitly assumed to be people just like the author: "an adult (but not *old*), white, reasonably affluent (latterly middle-class) educated man of status, property, and publicly acceptable accomplishments."[108] By contrast, knowers who do not fit this description (women) and whose perspectives, experiences, approaches to knowledge, and standards of rationality do not fit the preferred model are considered to be outsiders, and their viewpoints are dismissed as irredeemably subjective, irregular, or irrational.

LORRAINE CODE
(1937–)

The View from Nowhere Assumption

Traditional epistemology has supposed that the ideal knower will look at reality free of any particular perspective or historical background and will carry out the project of knowing without any individual interests, engagements, or concerns. But such a knower would be a disembodied computer with no personal history or would have attained a disinterested, godlike perspective. For human knowers, however, such stances are both undesirable and impossible. Our personal history and concrete standpoint influence what we can know. For example, if I look out at the world from the top story of a building (or from the top level of the social hierarchy), while you view it from the basement (or from the lowest social, political, or economic level), what we see and how we see it will differ. Although she does not support this approach, philosopher Harriet Baber summarizes the feminist complaint against this perspective-free, view from nowhere epistemology in the following way:

> Advocates of feminist epistemology . . . reject [this approach] specifically on the grounds that the norms it embodies are male norms and hence that their acceptance sets standards which women find it difficult, or impossible, to meet. In particular they hold that the traditional epistemic ideal of an objective, detached observer, conducting his investigations in isolation from any historical or social context, is alien to women's engaged, concrete, contextual way of knowing.[109]

As Baber suggests, some feminists believe that the view from nowhere assumption is alien to women's ways of knowing the world and so excludes them from the category of being fully adequate knowers. However, most feminists think that the assumption is incoherent and that all knowers (feminist or nonfeminist, female or male) always approach the world from within some particular context, whether this context is defined by conceptual scheme, language, culture, gender, or whatever. According to this more expanded critique, the "view from nowhere" assumption is not just alien to women's approaches, but is an incorrect description of human knowledge in general.

The notion that the "typical knower" is a standardized, impersonal, faceless, nameless, featureless abstraction has been institutionalized in the practice of science. Science students are taught to depersonalize their reports with such statements as "the test tube was heated and a white precipitate was formed," as though no human agents or observers in the laboratory were conducting the experiment. We are familiar with locutions such as "the facts show that" or "science says" or "the data indicate that," as though the facts, science, and data have a voice of their own and speak their own interpretations to us. However, knowledge does not drop down from the heavens but is humanly created. Hence, when feminists talk about "knowledge," they also focus on "knowledge production" and ask, Who is making the knowledge claim? or What is his or her standpoint? For example, feminist philosopher Sandra Harding titled her book *Whose Science? Whose Knowledge?* to remind us that there is always a subjective person and point of view behind every knowledge claim.[110]

The claim that there is a point of view behind every knowledge claim is not unique to feminists. Particularly in the current century, this claim is made by a number of philosophers who otherwise would not be labeled as feminists. However, feminists are noted for stressing the role that gender plays in the point of view that a person brings to the knowing situation. Is gender important in the process of knowledge production? It would seem that gender is as incidental to what we can know as are physical attributes such as height, weight, or hair color. But according to feminists, gender plays too important a role in society not to take it into account in examining how knowledge arises. As Code says, "In cultures in which sex differences figure prominently in virtually every mode of human interaction, being female or male is far more fundamental to the construction of subjectivity than are such attributes as size or hair color."[111] Accordingly, Code argues for an epistemology that takes subjectivity into account (including gender) without sliding into an "anything goes" subjectivism:

> Knowledge is at once subjective and objective: subjective because it is marked, as product, by the processes of its construction by specifically located subjects; objective in that the constructive process is constrained by a reality that is recalcitrant to inattentive or whimsical structurings.[112]

The Pure, Impersonal Reason Assumption

The view from nowhere assumption leads to a certain kind of value-laden dichotomy when it comes to discussing rationality. The rational thinker is presumed to be one who has attained the objective, impersonal perspective idealized in the view from nowhere assumption. On the other hand, those for whom personal, subjective perspectives are considered important (feminists) are thereby considered to be less than adequately rational. I have called this description of rationality the pure, impersonal reason assumption.

Feminist epistemologists frequently refer to the bipolar thinking by means of which traditional epistemologists posit strict dichotomies such as reason vs. emotion, objective vs. subjective, mind vs. body, logic vs. intuition, or intellect vs. imagination. They have two criticisms of this approach. First, the paired concepts in each case are not mutually exclusive dichotomies as has been supposed.[113] For example, feminists claim that knowledge has both subjective and objective components and that we don't have to choose between one or the other.* Second, when epistemologists assert or assume these dichotomies, they place high priority on the first member of the pair, assuming that it describes the ideal knower, while they devalue the second member of the pair. Furthermore, the preferred alternative

---

*This point is the fallacy of the false dichotomy, which is discussed in the appendix to the text.

(such as objectivity) is taken to describe the male approach and the second (subjectivity) is assumed to be a stereotypically female trait. Feminists claim, however, that the psychological assumptions and value choices inherent in this approach are rarely questioned. Feminist writer Adrienne Rich summarized the problem, for example, by claiming that "objectivity" is nothing other than male "subjectivity."[114]

In an essay titled "The Man of Reason," Genevieve Lloyd, an influential feminist philosopher, discusses this traditional, one-sided ideal of rationality.[115] She demonstrates from the history of philosophy that reason has been so narrowly defined and women have been stereotyped in such a way that the ideal of "the man of reason" necessarily excludes women. Hence, men's areas of responsibility were intellect, reason, logic, and the life of the mind. Women were said to complement men with their gifts of a rich emotional life, imagination, intuition, and sensuousness. But the whole picture could be distilled down to the following two equations: male equals rational and female equals nonrational. According to Lloyd, "If women's minds are less rational than men's, it is because the limits of reason have been set in a way that excludes qualities that are then assigned to women."[116] However, Lloyd's solution is not to accept the traditional dichotomies and then embrace the "softer" half of each pair (such as intellect vs. emotion), elevating it to the position of prominence. She says that this approach was the mistake of the 19th-century romantics who rejected analytical reason in favor of the emotions. Instead, she rejects the classical dichotomies altogether and calls for a broader notion of reason that will include both men and women in its scope. Speaking about the "Man of Reason" ideal, she says, "What is needed for the Man of Reason is realization of his limitations as a *human* ideal, in the hope that men and women alike might come to enjoy a more human life, free of the sexual stereotypes that have evolved in his shadow."[117]

Not all feminists question these traditional dichotomies, however. Some have accepted the stereotypical distinctions between men and women, but have called for a reversal of priorities and valuations, claiming that women's ways of knowing are superior to those of men. Although she does not necessarily agree with this approach, Code lists the "feminine" traits that are said to give women an epistemological advantage:

> Features of women's experiences commonly cited are a concern with the concrete, everyday world; a connection with objects of experience rather than an objective distance from them; a marked affective tone; a respect for the environment; and a readiness to listen perceptively and responsibly to a variety of "voices" in the environment, both animate and inanimate, manifested in a tolerance of diversity.[118]

These traits seem to overlap the attributes commonly thought to characterize a good mother. Accordingly, in her book *Maternal Thinking,* Sara Ruddick, a well-known feminist ethical theorist, celebrates the values traditionally associated with mothering and femininity and generates a model of knowledge from such maternal traits as caring, intimacy, responsibility, and trust. She builds her case on the premise that "distinctive ways of knowing and criteria of truth arise out of practices."[119] For example, scientific thinking as a method of knowing reality developed within the laboratory but can be practiced in other areas of life as well, even by those who are not professional scientists. Similarly, Ruddick claims, maternal thinking can characterize a person's approach to every dimension of life (not just child care) and can be practiced by males and childless women as well.

To cite one final example, feminist philosopher Alison Jaggar believes both that women have a richer emotional life than men and that this fact makes them better knowers.[120] Taking her cue from recent work in the philosophy of science, Jaggar argues that all observation is selective and involves our values, motivations, interests, and emotions. These "subjective" factors direct our cognitive pursuits, shape what we know, and help determine its significance.* Furthermore, she argues that the emotions of marginalized people (such as women) make them epistemologically privileged with respect to some issues. Because they are "outsiders" to the mainstream of intellectual life and political power, women can have a much more discerning perspective on the prevailing cognitive and social structures, whereas such structures remain invisible to men.

Although some feminists applaud this attempt to highlight the positive features of women's distinctive ways of knowing, others are concerned that this form of essentialism will reinforce the stereotypes that have been used in the past to marginalize women. These concerns are expressed by Code:

> There is a persistent tension in feminist thought between a laudable wish to celebrate "feminine" values as tools for the creation of a better social order and a fear of endorsing those same values as instruments of women's continued oppression.[121]

Similar tensions have arisen as feminists have come to terms with scientific modes of knowing. A group of researchers has pointed out that a central issue among feminists is "the equation of the masculine with objectivity, science, and the scientific method in its emphasis on manipulation, control, and distance from the objects of study."[122] In reaction against this scientific mode of knowing, some feminists have opted for extreme subjectivism and an antiscience stance. However, Evelyn Fox Keller, who has published numerous articles in biology and the history and philosophy of science, has cautioned feminists to avoid the temptation "to abandon their claim for representation in scientific culture and, in its place, to invite a return to a purely 'female' subjectivity, leaving rationality and objectivity in the male domain, dismissed as a product of a purely male consciousness."[123]

The Robinson Crusoe Assumption

Like the fictional Robinson Crusoe, who was isolated on his little island, some philosophers have supposed that the search for knowledge is an individual project that is free from social or political entanglements. The best example of this assumption is Descartes, who thought he could suspend all his former beliefs as he searched for the grounds of certainty within the confines of his own mind. Descartes was able to maintain his self-image of being a completely independent and autonomous thinker because the 17th-century philosophical and cultural assumptions that permeated every step of his thinking remained completely invisible to him. In contrast, Code stresses that "knowledge production is a social practice of embodied, gendered, historically, racially, and culturally located knowers whose products bear the marks of their makers and whose stories need, therefore, to be told."[124]

For philosopher Helen Longino, knowledge always arises within a social context: "The development of knowledge is a necessarily social rather than individual activity, and it is the social character of scientific knowledge that both protects it from and renders it vulnerable to social and political interests and values."[125] To paraphrase poet John Donne, "No knower is an island." Our knowledge is initially transmitted to us by our culture, and our further search for knowledge is carried out within a community that informs our endeavors and to which we are responsible. In contrast, Descartes thought he could divorce himself from his community and begin the search for knowledge anew as an isolated individual. For Descartes, knowledge is purely an individual possession, and any facts about commu-

---

*Jaggar suggests, for example, that anthropologist Jane Goodall's important scientific contributions to our understanding of chimpanzee behavior were made possible only by her love and empathy for these animals.

nal knowledge are reducible to the knowledge held by individuals. Longino, however, claims that knowledge is first and foremost the product of communities, and individual knowers acquire that knowledge insofar as they are members of a community and accept its norms and background beliefs.

If it is the community of knowers that not only transmits knowledge but brings it to birth, then the more diverse that group of knowers is, the more likely it is that their multiple perspectives will prevent the quest for knowledge from following well-established ruts in the road while ignoring other possible alternatives. Because women have traditionally been "outsiders" with respect to the mainstream intellectual traditions, they tend to be more open to diverse and nontraditional points of view. Furthermore, feminists claim, women are in a better position to understand and critique the prevailing, taken-for-granted assumptions of these traditions.

If the good news in Longino's account is that the social nature of knowledge allows it to be refined by ongoing social criticism, the bad news is that the social character of knowledge production makes it possible for the process to be skewed by the values, ideology, and background assumptions of the dominant powers within society. For example, feminists observe that the appeal to "impersonal, objective thought" often disguises underlying personal interests and power structures. In criticizing the traditional ideal of reason, Lloyd says that besides making women second-class citizens in intellectual matters, the traditional, narrow definition of rationality has had negative political consequences for women. "Exclusion from reason has meant exclusion from power."[126] Similarly, in criticizing a recent work on rationality, Code asserts, "Critics must ask for whom this epistemology exists; whose interests it serves; and whose it neglects or suppresses in the process."[127]

Knowledge production cannot be divorced from power structures, for ideas will get a hearing, will be encouraged, will flourish, and will receive funding, institutional support, and legitimacy when they correspond to the prevailing social structure. On the other hand, those ideas that do not comply with the dominant discourse will be marginalized or dismissed. Hence, to the second-wave feminist movement, women's struggles for equality cannot be confined to just courts of law or legislatures. To change society, second-wave feminists say, we must change the ideas on which society is built.

FEMINIST EPISTEMOLOGY AND THE PROBLEM OF RELATIVISM

Does the feminist perspective in the theory of knowledge imply a problematic form of relativism? This issue has divided feminist thinkers. The tensions this topic provokes are suggested by Code: "Feminist epistemologists often find themselves working within an uneasy relationship to vexed questions about relativism: within an uneasiness generated out of the very act of identifying oneself as a *feminist* epistemologist."[128] Code tries to defend a version of relativism while avoiding the slippery slope that leads to an "anything goes" total relativism. Accordingly, she argues for a *mitigated relativism* (preferring this term to *mitigated objectivism,* which some philosophers have suggested she should use). As Code expresses it, "From the claim that no single scheme has absolute explanatory power, it does not follow that all schemes are equally valid. Knowledge is qualitatively variable: some knowledge is *better* than other knowledge. Relativists are in a good position to take such qualitative variations into account and to analyze their implications."[129]

Although all feminists emphasize the point that there is no view from nowhere and that knowledge is always to some degree relative to the particular circumstances and needs of a particular knower or community of knowers, many feminists are nevertheless decidedly opposed to any form of strong relativism. Their motivation is very clear. If they were to claim that "one opinion is as true as another opinion," they would be vulnerable to the Standard Criticism of relativism;* that is, they would be committed to saying that their observations, claims, and theories are *just* their opinion, merely a personal confession or a subjective preference (like tastes in foods) that have no more validity than opposing opinions. But there is a more specific reason why some feminist epistemologists wish to avoid slipping into relativism. If all opinions are of equal value, if reality does not dictate the superiority of some opinions over others, then the opinions of the Nazis, racists, and sexists have just as much value as those of the feminists.

Because of these unacceptable consequences of relativism, some feminists disassociate themselves from the position altogether. For example, Harding says, "One might be tempted to relativist defenses of feminist claims. . . . However, this temptation should be resisted. . . . Feminist inquirers are never saying that sexist and anti-sexist claims are equally plausible."[130] Similarly, feminist philosopher Jane Duran insists that "one can be contextually sensitive (aware of and responsive to relativistic concerns) without being a relativist."[131]

LOOKING THROUGH THE LENS OF FEMINIST EPISTEMOLOGY

1. From what you have just read, how would the adoption of a feminist perspective transform your understanding of the history of philosophy, theory of knowledge, metaphysics, ethics, political theory and practice, religion, and business? If women had not been excluded from social and intellectual life throughout history, how would our culture be different today?

2. Imagine that you had been born a member of the opposite sex. What are some possible advantages this act might give you as a knower, as a member of society, or in other ways? What disadvantages would you face that you currently do not have? To what degree are these advantages or disadvantages the result of how society has been structured in the past? To what degree are they the result of natural differences between males and females? Still imagining that you are a member of the opposite sex, what changes would you want to make in society?

3. A number of issues that divide feminists have been mentioned in this section. The following pairs of opposing claims have *all* been defended by feminists: (1a) There is an essential female nature; (1b) other than strictly biological facts, any content associated with *woman* or *female* is a social construct and has no fixed meaning; (2a) traits typically associated with females (caring, emotional, intuitive) are male stereotypes and tools of oppression; (2b) such female characteristics are real and enable women to have insights not available to men; (3a) objectivity is a myth, and feminists should embrace relativism and subjective ways of approaching the world; (3b) without a strong commitment to the possibility of objective knowledge, feminists' knowledge claims would be inconsequential. Imagine that you are attempting to develop your own, coherent version of feminism. Consistent with this project, argue for one or the other position on each of these controversial issues.

4. Most feminists have developed their philosophy out of the experience of being oppressed or excluded and marginalized from the mainstream of intellectual and social life. What if feminists achieved their political goals? What if women and women's perspectives achieved full intellectual, social, and political equality (or even dominance) in our society?

---

*See the discussion of the Standard Criticism of relativism in section 2.5.

Under these conditions, would there be any continuing need for a distinctively *feminist* philosophy? If so, would these changed conditions require a change in the direction and agenda of feminist thought? Or is feminist philosophy merely a stopgap measure necessitated by the current biases in society? Taking a position sympathetic to feminism, argue for one or the other of these conclusions.

5. What are some similarities between feminist epistemology and relativism? What are the similarities between feminist epistemology and pragmatism?

EXAMINING THE STRENGTHS AND WEAKNESSES OF FEMINIST EPISTEMOLOGY

Positive Evaluation

1. Traditional empiricists saw experience primarily in terms of isolated units of sensation (colors, sounds, tastes, odors, textures). However, feminists have a broader conception of experience that enables them to analyze experiences such as love, harassment, empowerment, self-awareness, or the subjective experience of being a woman or a man. Which approach to experience do you think provides the best basis for doing philosophy?

2. Because feminists emphasize the role of subjectivity, values, and vested interests in the production of knowledge, their complaint is not so much that male philosophers' approaches to knowledge have been developed out of their own experiences, values, and interests but that the presence of these biases has been denied. Instead of denying our subjectivity, isn't it better to honestly come to terms with our own subjectivity as knowers so that it can be examined, critiqued, evaluated, and possibly modified?

3. Feminist philosophers have spotlighted the social influences on knowledge, even with respect to science. They have also pointed out that theories and knowledge claims have political implications. In what ways are these concerns important to address?

4. It is obvious that women have been excluded from or marginalized within the domain of intellectual discourse. Now that women are making their voices heard within all the disciplines, what do you think are the sorts of insights they have to offer or changes they will make to the ways in which we think?

Negative Evaluation

1. Feminist thought emphasizes the concrete social-political-historical standpoint of a knower. But how many perspectives need to be taken into account? Recently, feminists have noted that their writings primarily represent the perspectives of white, middle-class, American, British, or European academic theorists and have ignored the different perspectives of women of color, working-class women, and African, Asian, Middle Eastern, and Latin American women. Because the experiences and perspective of a knower in relationship to a particular concrete community are central in feminist thought, doesn't this point imply that there will be as many perspectives as there are communities of knowers? Is there any common ground between the experiences of a white, single, agnostic, American woman academic living in a secular, liberal-democratic society and those of a black, married, Catholic, third-world, working woman living in a rigidly traditional and oppressive society? In the final analysis, are we left with a spectrum of irresolvable, multiple perspectives? If so, by what right do feminists suppose that they have the authority to speak for *all*

women, much less to propose theories that apply to all knowers? In other words, does feminist theory reduce to the sociology of a series of unique, specific communities?[132]

2. Many feminists claim that there are multiple and equally plausible interpretations of reality and that whether a theory or point of view is accepted as rational is a function of the prevailing social-political power structures. If so, does this claim diminish the importance of the pursuit of truth and, instead, place the priority on achieving social dominance and political power? In rejecting the self-interested perspective of male-dominated epistemology that is said to be driven by a social agenda, are feminists merely proposing an alternative, equally self-interested perspective that is a product of their own social agenda?[133]

3. Is there a problem with the term *feminist epistemology?* Feminists want to develop an epistemology that includes women's experiences and perspectives. But does the qualifier "feminist" imply that this theory is not a theory of knowledge per se but an account of knowledge as viewed specifically from a female standpoint or from the standpoint of those who embrace a certain ideology? Does this implication tend to segregate women philosophers' contributions to epistemology and give their insights the same limited status as women's sports, women's restrooms, and women's health care issues?[134] How can feminist philosophy serve to "remap the epistemological terrain," as feminists claim, if it is merely a circumscribed region within that geography? Or should feminists follow the lead of Harding and strive for "hypotheses that are free of gender loyalties"?[135] If this goal was accomplished, would feminists then have to drop the qualifier *feminist* from their theories?

2.8 APPLYING EPISTEMOLOGY: WHAT IS THE NATURE OF SCIENTIFIC KNOWLEDGE?,

 One of the most important realms of knowledge is scientific knowledge. Because of the centuries of success science has had in unlocking the secrets of nature, many people consider science to be the paradigm of the search for knowledge. Hence, an examination of science will serve as a useful laboratory for testing some of the epistemological views we have studied in this chapter.

Both rationalism and empiricism played an important role in the rise of modern science. In terms of rationalism, Copernicus, Descartes, and Galileo made important scientific contributions in following out their conviction that nature was based on rational, mathematical principles. In holding this conviction they were inspired by the ancient Greek rationalists. Although they relied on observations, they were willing to trust elegant mathematical theories, even though their scientific theories seemed to be contradicted by naive commonsense experience. For example, our naive experience seems to tell us that the earth is large and immobile and that it is the sun that is in motion. (Galileo once said his theory did violence to the senses.) Expressing his rationalistic inclinations, Galileo stated that nature was like a book written in a mathematical language and if we understand that language we can translate the book of nature. Similarly, the great 20th-century physicist, Albert Einstein, was a rationalist who believed there was a logically necessary mathematical order to the universe. His discoveries were made entirely by calculating a new mathematical framework for making sense out of empirical data that had been around for 50 years. He once said that his laboratory was his pencil.

While such rationalistic assumptions played an important role in the early period of science, it was empiricism that had the most dramatic effect. The English philosopher Francis Bacon (1561–1626) is noted for laying the foundation for modern inductive logic and for attempting to systematize the scientific method. His goal was to escape the speculative theories of the medievals and, instead of assuming that nature must fit our a priori assumptions, he urged scientists to look and see what nature is like. Accordingly, he proposed a program for systematically recording observations. Bacon described the scientific method as a "machine" into which is poured the scientist's observations of the facts of nature. He believed that through an almost mechanical process, the laws of science would pour forth.

Bacon's commonsense, standard view of science lasted well into the 20th century. The commonsense view of science, inaugurated by Bacon, asserts the following claims.

1. Objective observations of the facts of nature are made, untainted by any hypotheses or theories.
2. The observations are analyzed and generalizations are formed.
3. From these generalizations, scientific laws and theories are formulated.
4. Experimental testing of these theories will definitively prove them to be either true or false.

SEEING IS BELIEVING?

Let's begin to examine this view of science by looking at the first claim concerning observation. The commonsense view assumes that the eye is like a camera that is completely neutral and passive as it takes in stimuli from the external world. From Francis Bacon on, it has been thought that scientists must proceed by making observations, establishing the facts, and then, and only then, may they think about developing theories. However, there is much evidence that this is an oversimplified picture.

In the discussion of Kant in this chapter (section 2.4), there was a thought experiment in which the image of a large, white triangle seemed to be displayed. However, the "triangle" appears only because the mind imaginatively organizes the lines and colored patches in this way. Similarly, in section 2.5 on epistemological relativism, there is the message that people tend to incorrectly see as "Paris in the spring." Likewise, in this section there is the diagram of a box and also the drawing of an African family that people in different cultures see differently. The point is that seeing is not just a matter of light hitting the retina. "Seeing" is always "seeing as." In most cases, we don't just take in data from the world with our eyes and then think of a likely interpretation as a second step. Instead, we immediately see things *as* this or that sort of thing. People in modern Western cultures may see an arrangement of lines on paper as representing a three-dimensional box. However, people in cultures where the convention of perspective has not been introduced into their art will see those same lines as a two-dimensional pattern, similar to a plaid. How we see things is affected by our past experiences, including the knowledge, training, conceptual frameworks, and expectations that we bring to observation.

Take, for example, the Greek philosopher Aristotle, whose views on science reigned for over a thousand years until the time of Galileo. Aristotle believed that the "natural" state of earthbound objects was that of rest. It is obvious why he thought this. In our experience, an object such as a rock or a wagon will go into motion only if some external force acts on it. Likewise, if the motion of such objects is not continuously sustained by a force, they will eventually come to rest. So, for Aristotle, rest was natural and motion is what had to be explained. However, Galileo's physics and his law of inertia employed entirely different principles. He said that if an object is in motion, it will stay in motion unless some force (gravity, a brake, friction, etc.) causes it to stop. So, for Galileo, motion was self-sustaining and it was rest that had to be explained. When Aristotle saw a pendulum, he saw an object that had been thrust into motion and that was *striving to come to rest,* but that was struggling against the string that prevented its natural downward fall. In contrast, Galileo saw an object that was *striving to continue moving* in a straight line through space forever, but that was constrained by the string and the force of gravity, which were interfering with its natural tendency to stay in motion. What one scientist saw as normal and unmysterious, the other considered to be a phenomenon that needed explanation, and vice versa. In a sense, what each person saw was a function of his conceptual framework and assumptions.

Contrary to the commonsense, Baconian view of science, many philosophers of science assert that "all data are theory-laden." In other words, theories are not something that results from our observations; rather, a theory must guide our observations and experiments in order to know what facts are relevant to our investigation. This point has been made effectively in a fable by philosopher Karl Popper.

> Suppose that someone wished to give his whole life to science. Suppose that he therefore sat down, pencil in hand, and for the next twenty, thirty, forty years recorded in notebook after notebook everything that he could observe. He may be supposed to leave out nothing: today's humidity, the racing results, the level of cosmic radiation and the stock-market prices and the look of Mars, all would be there. He would have compiled the most careful record of nature that has ever been made; and, dying in the calm certainty of a life well spent, he would of course leave his notebooks to the Royal Society. Would the Royal Society thank him for the treasure of a lifetime of observation? It would not. . . . It would refuse to open them at all, because it would know without looking that the notebooks contain only a jumble of disorderly and meaningless items.[136]

An actual event in the history of science makes this point even better. In 1888, Heinrich Hertz produced and detected radio waves for the first time. Philosopher A. F. Chalmers ridicules the theory-neutral view of observation with these remarks:

> If [Hertz] is to be totally unbiased when making his observations, then he will be obliged to record not only the readings on various meters, the presence or absence of sparks at various critical locations in the electrical circuits, the dimensions of the circuit, etc. but also the colour of the meters, the dimensions of the laboratory, the state of the weather, the size of his shoes and a whole host of "clearly irrelevant" details.[137]

Chalmers goes on to point out that one of these seemingly irrelevant details was not irrelevant. It was the dimensions of Hertz's laboratory. Radio waves were being reflected off the walls back to the instruments, which interfered with Hertz's measurements. A bigger room was needed. Only from the standpoint of a theoretical perspective can one know which details and which observations will be relevant to one's experimental goals.

INDUCTION: DERIVING THEORIES FROM OBSERVATIONS

I have briefly suggested that there are a number of complexities involved in making observations. What we see is a product of both what the world presents to us and those conceptions and outlooks we bring to it. (If you read the section on Kantian constructivism, you will notice Kant's influence here.) Now we need to examine the way in which scientific laws are derived from observations. The commonsense view formulated by Francis Bacon suggests that scientific laws are simply "read off" from the observations that have been collected. This view is now called (pejoratively) "naive inductivism." There are a number of logical problems with this view of science.

The first problem with induction was raised by David Hume (see section 2.3). Hume pointed out that most of the conclusions we draw from experience, particularly causal judgments, are based on the principle of induction. Roughly, the principle of induction is the assumption that the future will be like the past. More specifically, it is the conviction that future observations will conform to the pattern of present observations or that a limited number of observations can tell us what generally will be the case.

Suppose we heat different metals and discover that every one of them expands when heated. Does this provide good logical grounds for concluding that "all metals expand when heated"? Can we go from what has been true in some cases to what will be true in all cases of the same kind? The problem with this type of inductive reasoning can be illustrated by the following argument, which is based on a number of observations labeled 1 through n.

(a) Swan S_1 is white.
(b) Swan S_2 is white.
(c) Swan S_n is white.
Conclusion: All swans are white.

This seemed to be a pretty convincing argument to British and European biologists prior to the 1600s, since all the swans in England and Europe were white. Later that century, however, a Dutch explorer traveled to Australia and found that swans there were black. Hence, no matter how many observations we gather that seem to support a particular conclusion, there is no guarantee that future observations will yield the same results. This is illustrated by Bertrand Russell's story of the inductivist turkey.

> The turkey found that, on his first morning at the turkey farm, that he was fed at 9 a.m. Being a good inductivist turkey he did not jump to conclusions. He waited until he collected a large number of observations that he was fed at 9 a.m., and made these observations under a wide range of circumstances, on Wednesdays and Thursdays, on warm days and cold days, on rainy days and dry days. Each day, he added another observation statement to his list. Finally, his inductivist conscience was satisfied and he carried out an inductive inference to conclude, "I am always fed at 9 a.m." Alas, this conclusion was shown to be false in no uncertain manner when, on Christmas eve, instead of being fed, he had his throat cut.[138]

This fable illustrates that an inductive inference with true premises can lead to a false conclusion. More seriously, throughout history many scientific theories have proven successful and fruitfully guided scientific research for many centuries before the problems with the theories begin to emerge. For example, Isaac Newton published his famous theory in 1687 and it reigned for 200 years until inconsistencies began to be revealed in the late 19th century.

It is tempting to suppose that we can rely on the principle of induction because it has always worked in the past. However, this is the logical fallacy of begging the question (as discussed in the appendix at the end of the book). To argue that "inductive reasoning has always worked in the past, so it will always work" is like saying "all swans that have been observed in the past have been white, so all swans we observe in the future will be white."

FALSIFICATION

These and other problems with induction have led many philosophers of science to the conclusion that a scientific theory can never be proven to be true with absolute certainty. Take the statement "All metals expand when heated." The word *all* does not refer just to heated metals that have been observed, but to all heated metals that ever were, that ever will be, whether or not they have been observed or will be observed in the future. In other words, it is impossible to verify such a statement with a finite set of observations. But this hypothesis can be proven false if we discover a metal that is heated but does not expand. All that it takes to falsify a theory is one observation.

Accordingly, philosopher of science Karl Popper argued that science progresses by means of conjectures and refutations. In other words, scientists propose speculative theories that are consistent with the fund of observations, but which are tentative guesses (conjectures). They then subject their theories to rigorous testing by making predictions derived from the theories and performing experiments (attempts at refutation). Those theories that lead to failed experiments are rejected. However, theories that endure rigorous testing are our best scientific accounts. In this way, we can definitely say that a theory is false. But we can never say that a theory is true. All we can say is that it has withstood our best attempts to falsify it and that it is better than all the other theories we have considered.

The more bold and comprehensive a theory is, the more it is capable of being subject to testing and possible falsification. Suppose I am an economist who has a theory that will predict what happens in the stock market. Consider these three statements:

(a) Tomorrow something will happen.
(b) Tomorrow XYZ stock will rise in price.
(c) Tomorrow XYZ stock will rise 30% in price.

Statement (a) is not very interesting, because no matter what happens it cannot turn out to be false. Statement (b) is better. It can be falsified and, therefore, makes a significant claim. Still, it is not a bold claim, for the stock will rise, or drop, or remain the same. Statement (c) is even better, because it makes a specific prediction and there are many ways that it can turn out to be false. However, if it is not falsified, and the theory continues to make predictions that turn out to be true, we would have much more interest in the theory. According to Popper, the hallmarks of an important scientific theory are that (1) it makes very specific and wide-ranging predictions about the world (it is very vulnerable to falsification) and (2) throughout extensive testing, it resists all our attempts to falsify it.

PROBLEMS WITH FALSIFICATION

In spite of the many strengths of the falsificationist's account of science, it has been subjected to a number of criticisms. First, falsifying a theory is not as simple as it seems at first. Suppose we have two witnesses to an accident. One says, "Harold came into the intersection first," and the other says, "Harold did not come into the intersection first." Clearly, one of the witnesses' statements is false. But which one? Similarly, if a theory is contradicted by an experimental observation, either something is wrong with the theory or something is wrong with the observation. But which is it? For example, Galileo's telescope showed that the moon had craters and that Jupiter had several moons. For various reasons, his contemporaries believed that the moon was a perfect sphere and that only the earth had a moon. Hence, the question was, "Have the current scientific views been refuted or are Galileo's observations in error?" Even though Galileo's account was correct, it was easy to dismiss Galileo's observations at that time. When his telescope was trained on earthly objects such as a tower, where we know what they look like, the telescope produced distortions in the image.

Second, the statement "All swans are white" can be falsified by the single observation "This swan is black." But scientific theories are not so simple, for all theories are a complex set of statements and all observations are complex situations. Every theory contains a series of auxiliary assumptions, and every experiment assumes that certain initial conditions are the case. The falsificationist assumes that every experiment begins with the following sort of premise:

If theory T is true, then observational prediction O will be true.

It follows that if O is not true, then theory T has been falsified. (This is a valid argument form known as "modus tollens" discussed in the appendix.) But if every theory and experimental situation contains additional assumptions, then we get this much more complex picture:

If theory T and assumption 1 and assumption 2 and assumption 3 . . . (and so on) are all true, then observational prediction O will be true.

What if O is false? Has T been refuted? Well maybe not, for any one of the auxiliary assumptions could be the problem. By modifying the assumptions, the theory can be saved from falsification.

This process can be illustrated from the history of science. Tycho Brahé (1546–1601), a Danish astronomer, thought he had refuted the Copernican theory that the earth revolves around the sun. He reasoned that if the earth moves, the angle at which we observe a fixed star should change throughout the course of a year. However, no change in the observation of the star could be detected. The problem was not that the Copernican theory was false, but that one of Brahé's auxiliary assumptions was false. Brahé assumed the stars were a lot closer than they are. It was not until the 1800s that scientists developed instruments powerful enough to detect the change in the observed angle of the stars.

A third problem with the falsificationist's account of science is that it does not fit the history of science. There are many cases similar to the previous one in which a theory's predictions turned out to be false. If a theory were abandoned every time it led to a false prediction, then many theories that are accepted today never would have survived. Instead, a prediction that does not turn out as it should is an occasion for scientists to do some problem solving, to reexamine their auxiliary assumptions, and to modify the theory. Of course, theories do get rejected. If a theory is so full of problems that it seems hopeless to retain it, the theory will be abandoned. But with respect to a very powerful and, up to that point, a very useful theory, scientists will reject it only if they have a more promising competitor to replace it with.

HISTORICAL RELATIVISM

The problems with the standard view of science and the inadequacies of the falsificationist's remedy were dramatically set forth by philosopher and historian of science Thomas Kuhn in his groundbreaking work, *The Structure of Scientific Revolutions*.[139] He rejected the traditional view that science advances through the accumulation of new discoveries that are added to the established fund of knowledge. Instead, Kuhn argued, science is "a series of peaceful interludes punctuated by intellectually violent revolutions." When a scientific revolution occurs, "one conceptual world view is replaced by another."

Kuhn coined the term "normal science" to refer to the longer-lasting, more tranquil periods in science. During these phases, scientific work is guided by a single paradigm. Although Kuhn described it in many different ways, a **paradigm** is basically a consensus within the community of scientists concerning what fundamental laws and theoretical assumptions are to be embraced, what problems need solving, how they should be conceptualized, and what phenomena are relevant to their solution. Paradigms are the more

paradigm a consensus within the community of scientists concerning what fundamental laws and theoretical assumptions are to be embraced, what problems need solving, how they should be conceptualized, and what phenomena are relevant to their solution

implicit, vaguer, and larger framework within which theories are produced. In what follows, I will discuss the three main features of Kuhn's account of paradigms as set out by physicist, philosopher, and theologian Ian Barbour.[140]

1. *All data are paradigm-dependent.* Previously, we questioned the simple slogan "Seeing is believing." Similarly, Kuhn uses many examples from the history of science to show that what scientists "see" is directed and influenced by what theories they embrace and their theories are products of the larger framework of what paradigm they adopt. Aristotle's and Galileo's differing views of a pendulum, discussed earlier, are examples of this.

2. *Paradigms are resistant to falsification.* Occasionally, scientists will encounter experimental results that do not conform to their paradigm. Initially, such maverick data will be labeled as "anomalies" or merely pieces of the puzzle that need more work to fit them into the picture. Hence, the notion that they might be falsifications of the prevailing theory is resisted. As discussed previously, a theory can be spared from falsification by modifying the peripheral auxiliary assumptions while preserving the core of the theory. However, as anomalies increase, the normal science of the period will enter into a crisis. Eventually, someone will propose a new paradigm, which, if successful in gaining a following, will overthrow the established one, and a scientific revolution will occur. According to Kuhn, notable examples of scientific revolutions are when Galileo's science replaced Aristotelian science and Einstein's relativity theory replaced Newtonian science.

3. *There are no rules for paradigm choice.* This is by far the most controversial feature of Kuhn's account of science. If all observations are theory-laden, then there are no theory-neutral observations that can be appealed to in order to decide the winner between two competing theories. Each theory will give an interpretation of the empirical data that makes it consistent with the particular theory's claims. Accordingly, Kuhn claims that there is no purely rational, objective path from the old paradigm to the new one because what counts as rationality and acceptable standards of scientific evidence will be defined in terms of a particular paradigm. Hence, according to Kuhn's story of the history of science, a scientific revolution (like a political one) is more the result of sociological factors than anything based on impartial evidence. He even goes so far as to describe the change in outlook as a "conversion." This has led critics to charge that Kuhn has denied the objectivity of science and its goal of producing a true account of reality. Many think that Kuhn's position comes very close to a kind of historical, epistemological relativism discussed in section 2.5, even though he had tried to evade this label in his later writings. This is the view that what is true or false, rational or not, and even what is good science or lame science is relative to a particular historical community of scientists and their prevailing paradigm.

A number of feminist philosophers have explored the implications of a feminist outlook for understanding the epistemology of science, and many of them build on the work of Kuhn. Feminists agree with Kuhn in rejecting the view that knowledge is based on pure, impersonal reason. (See section 2.7 for the feminists' criticism of this notion.) Furthermore, Kuhn's emphasis on the sociological factors in history that have caused the acceptance or decline of theories reinforces the feminists' emphasis on the social context of knowledge. Accordingly, feminist critics argue that both the content and the practice of science have been influenced by gender-related preferences in the choice of problems, models, and concepts that scientists examine.[141]

In response to the previous three claims made by Kuhn, Ian Barbour summarizes his own position in three statements. In each case the first half of the sentence acknowledges Kuhn's point that there are historically and culturally relative factors that influence the conduct of science. However, the second half of each sentence emphasizes Barbour's contention that there still remain objective, empirical, and rational constraints on science.

1. All data are paradigm-dependent, but there are data on which adherents of rival paradigms can agree.
2. Paradigms are resistant to falsification by data, but data does cumulatively affect the acceptability of a paradigm.
3. There are no rules for paradigm choice, but there are shared criteria for judgment in evaluating paradigms.[142]

REALISM VS. ANTI-REALISM

Scientific theories are full of statements about unobservable entities and processes. For example, scientists talk about DNA molecules, electrons, neutrinos, electromagnetic waves, black holes, and the big bang. Part of the appeal of science is that it tells us what is really going on behind the appearances. The natural supposition is that if a theory explains our observations and enables us to make successful predictions, then it is true. Furthermore, it is natural to assume that the entities that play a role in a well-supported theory actually exist. This position is known as scientific realism. **Scientific realism** is the traditional view that science is capable of giving us true accounts of the world and that the entities that play a role in our best scientific theories actually exist independent of our conceptual frameworks. The sorts of unobservable entities mentioned above are known as theoretical entities. But the realist would say that such theoretical entities actually exist because they can be detected with our instruments, can be manipulated, can be studied in terms of their causal effects, and can be the basis of successful experimental predictions. For these reasons, it is claimed, they are postulated as essential items in well-confirmed scientific theories.

However, some philosophers of science have questioned this outlook and have argued in favor of anti-realism. **Scientific anti-realism** is the claim that scientific theories do not give us a literally true account of the world. Instead, scientific theories are said to provide us with fruitful models, calculating devices, useful fictions, and ways to systematize our experience. I should note that there are many varieties of anti-realism and its advocates do not agree on all points. However, my discussion will be a synthesis of their main themes.

According to the anti-realist, theories are merely instruments for providing order to our observations and suggesting new observations. For this reason, some versions of anti-realism are labeled "instrumentalism." Henri Poincaré (1854–1912), a French physicist, mathematician, and philosopher, compared scientific theories to library catalogues. It makes no sense to call a catalogue true or false, and it makes no sense to say that it mirrors reality. Likewise, theories are said to be neither true nor false. Rather, scientific theories are useful or not for various tasks. This phrase makes it obvious that this brand of anti-realism is heavily indebted to pragmatism. (See section 2.6 where pragmatism was discussed.)

There are a number of arguments that have been put forth in defense of anti-realism. First, throughout the history of science, there have been many theories that were successful in explaining the phenomenon and in making successful predictions, but that were eventually abandoned. Hence, the fact that a theory is productive and experimentally successful in its day is not sufficient evidence that it gives us the true story about the world. For example, in 1704 Isaac Newton postulated that light is made up of small material particles. This explained why light travels in straight lines and can bounce off of surfaces. His theory led to successful scientific research for over 100 years. However, by the late 19th century, Newton's particles of light were no longer considered to exist. Instead, light was thought to be like waves moving through the medium of "aether," which was a kind of gas that was thought to permeate all of space. But the aether theory ran into problems and fell out of favor. In the 20th century, Albert Einstein revived the particle theory and the notion of photons became a part of physics. Eventually, physicists realized that light behaves both like

scientific realism the traditional view that science is capable of giving us true accounts of the world and that the entities that play a role in our best scientific theories actually exist independent of our conceptual frameworks

scientific anti-realism the claim that scientific theories do not give us a literally true account of the world, but that they provide us with fruitful models, calculating devices, useful fictions, and ways to systematize our experience

particles and like waves and learned to live with a wave-particle duality. This dual model has led to successful experimental predictions. However, the fact that it attributes seemingly incompatible properties to light adds fuel to the anti-realist's engine. Furthermore, the anti-realist argues that throughout all the changes in scientific theories and the postulation and abandonment of various theoretical entities, the observational and experimental results they led to are frequently retained and absorbed into the new theories.

The question naturally arises, "How can scientific theories be such useful guides if they do not tell us what the world is really like?" The anti-realist replies that a theoretical entity can be useful even though it does not refer to anything real. For example, we often hear statistics such as "The average American family has 2.4 children." Obviously, there is no such entity as the average American family, for there is no family that has 2.4 children. However, the construct of "the average American family" is a useful one for economists and social planners. Similarly, anti-realists claim, objects like electrons, genes, and DNA molecules are theoretical constructs that serve a scientific purpose without necessarily being real. Finally, anti-realists argue that the pragmatic usefulness of a scientific model does not dictate that it is giving us the one, true story about the world. Feminist philosopher of science and anti-realist Lynn Hankinson Nelson says,

> It is commensurate with our collective experience, as well as developments in philosophy of science, that there are indefinitely many theories that would enable us to successfully explain and predict experience, that no single system would be better than all others and, hence, that we have no reason to think there is one unique and full account to be discovered.[143]

The realists have a number of responses to the anti-realist's account. First, scientific realists argue that the progressive nature of science indicates that scientists are increasingly approximating a true picture of reality. A good scientific theory can predict novel and surprising results. If experiments confirm these results, then scientists' confidence in the theory increases. Likewise, theories are abandoned when they fail to be fruitful. Realists point out that it is hard to claim that scientists today do not have a better grasp of nature than they did 200 years ago. Both realism and anti-realism are theories about the nature of science. Obviously, neither one can be experimentally verified. However, they can make use of the method of "inference to the best explanation" as do scientists themselves. (See the discussion of this procedure in section 1.3.) Hence, realists claim that their theory gives the best account of the explanatory successes of science. Hilary Putnam suggests this when he states, "The positive argument for realism is that it is the only philosophy that doesn't make the success of science a miracle." A similar argument, known as the "convergence argument," points out that when many kinds of completely different experiments all seem to converge on some theory T, then either T is approximating the truth or it is sheer dumb luck that it is subject to so many kinds of experimental confirmations.

Second, realists note the fact that most scientists embrace realism, whether explicitly or implicitly. In fact, it has been argued that in the history of science the stance of realism actually led to scientific progress. Copernicus's theory that the earth revolved around the sun had a number of scientific objections that counted against it. Copernicus's friend, Osiander, glossed over these difficulties by taking an anti-realist stance. (This anti-realist interpretation of Copernicus also made his theory more palatable to the church authorities who were opposed to it.) In the foreword to Copernicus's major work, Osiander stated, "For the hypotheses [proposed by Copernicus] need not be true nor even probable; if they provide a calculus consistent with observation that alone is sufficient."[144] However, philosopher A. F. Chalmers points out that in contrast to this view, Copernicus and Galileo were both realists and, hence, were forced to address the empirical deficiencies in their theories and attempt to revise their theories instead of accepting the anti-realist gloss. In the case of Galileo, this led to major discoveries. Speaking for the realists, Chalmers says, "The moral that the realist wishes to draw from this is that anti-realism is unproductive because difficult questions, which demand a solution from a realist perspective, are swept under the carpet by anti-realists."[145]

In this section we have examined some of the issues and views with respect to scientific knowledge. This point and counterpoint debate between the different philosophies of science has consumed many pages in the past few decades. Only a few general conclusions can be safely drawn at this point. First, the scientific method still remains one of the most respected ways of acquiring knowledge. Second, making observations, framing theories, performing experiments, and confirming or falsifying theories are much more complicated processes than they appear to be at first. Third, even science is not immune from the need for philosophical clarification. We began this section by saying that an examination of science will serve as a useful laboratory for testing epistemological positions, as though science is philosophically neutral and well-defined enough that it can judge philosophical positions. Ironically, however, it now seems that the epistemological position you adopt will serve to define the nature of science and judge its possibilities.

REVIEW FOR CHAPTER 2

Philosophers

2.1 Skepticism
  Cratylus
  Pyrrho of Elis
  Carneades
  René Descartes
2.2 Rationalism
  Gottfried Leibniz
  Socrates
  Plato
  René Descartes
2.3 Empiricism
  Aristotle
  John Locke
  George Berkeley
  David Hume
2.4 Kantian Constructivism
  Immanuel Kant
  David Hume
2.5 Epistemological Relativism
  Immanuel Kant
  Willard V. O. Quine
  Georg W. F. Hegel
  Friedrich Nietzsche
  Plato
  Protagoras
2.6 Pragmatism
  C. S. Peirce

William James
John Dewey
2.7 Feminism
  Aristotle
  Plato
  John Stuart Mill
  Ann Garry and Marilyn Pearsall
  Lorraine Code
  Harriet Baber
  Sandra Harding
  Genevieve Lloyd
  Sara Ruddick
  Alison Jaggar
  Helen Longino
2.8 Scientific Knowledge
  Francis Bacon
  Aristotle
  Galileo
  Karl Popper
  Thomas Kuhn

Concepts

2.0 Overview of the Problem of Knowledge
  epistemology
  knowledge by acquaintance
  competence knowledge
  propositional knowledge
  true justified belief
  a priori knowledge
  a posteriori knowledge

empirical
the three epistemological questions
skepticism
rationalism
empiricism
constructivism
epistemological relativism
2.1 Skepticism
skepticism
universal skeptics
limited skeptics
universal belief falsifier
the generic skeptical argument
Descartes's evil demon
Descartes's bedrock certainty
perceptions (Hume)
impressions (Hume)
ideas (Hume)
principle of induction
uniformity of nature
a priori
Hume's skeptical arguments concerning causality,
the external world, the self
2.2 Rationalism
three anchor points of rationalism
innate ideas
Plato's reasons for rejecting sense experience
Universals
Plato's argument for Universals
phantom limb
Descartes's argument for God
2.3 Empiricism
three anchor points of empiricism
Aristotle's answers to the three questions
empiricists' arguments against innate ideas
ideas (Locke and Berkeley)
ideas of sensation
ideas of reflection
simple and complex ideas
compounding, relating, abstracting ideas (Locke)
Locke on primary and secondary qualities
Berkeley's immaterialism
argument from the mental dependency of ideas
representative realism
Berkeley on primary and secondary qualities
Berkeley on the cause of our ideas
Hume's view of the possibility of knowledge
Hume's view of reason
Hume's view of the representation of knowledge
Hume's two tests for the worth of ideas
2.4 Kantian Constructivism

critical philosophy
synthetic a posteriori knowledge
synthetic a priori knowledge
Kant's revolution
constructivism
phenomena
noumena
intuitions
sensibility
understanding
categories of the understanding
empirical concepts
pure concepts
Kant's view of our concepts of self, cosmos,
and God
2.5 Epistemological Relativism
objectivism
epistemological relativism
subjectivism
cultural relativism
historical relativism
Standard Criticism of relativism
2.6 Pragmatism
pragmatism
spectator theory of knowledge
correspondence theory of truth
pragmatic theory of truth
2.7 Feminism
feminism
first-wave feminism
second-wave feminism
equity feminists
gender feminists
sex vs. gender
essentialists vs. nonessentialists
generic humanity assumption
view from nowhere assumption
pure, impersonal reason assumption
Robinson Crusoe assumption
2.8 Scientific Knowledge
Bacon's commonsense view of science
problems with observation
naive inductivism
the principle of induction
problems with induction
falsification
problems with falsification
three features of Kuhn's historical relativism
paradigm
Barbour's response to Kuhn
scientific realism vs. scientific anti-realism

SUGGESTIONS FOR FURTHER READING

General Epistemology

Baergen, Ralph. *Contemporary Epistemology*. Fort Worth, Texas: Harcourt Brace College Publishers, 1995. A readable book that covers both the basic and advanced issues in epistemology.

Pojman, Louis. *What Can We Know? An Introduction to the Theory of Knowledge*. Belmont, Calif.: Wadsworth, 1994. A good overview of the topic.

Skepticism

Klein, Peter. *Certainty: A Refutation of Skepticism*. Minneapolis: University of Minnesota Press, 1981. A critical examination of skepticism.

Stroud, Barry. *The Significance of Philosophical Skepticism*. Oxford: Oxford University Press, 1984. A sympathetic analysis of skepticism.

Unger, Peter. *Ignorance: A Case for Skepticism*. Oxford: Clarendon Press, 1975. A challenging defense of radical skepticism.

Rationalism

Cottingham, John. *The Rationalists*. Vol. 4 of *A History of Western Philosophy*. Oxford: Oxford University Press, 1989. A readable and helpful discussion of Descartes and the early modern rationalists.

Descartes, René. *The Philosophical Writings of Descartes*. 2 vols. Translated by John Cottingham, Robert Stoothoff, and Dugald Murdoch. Cambridge: Cambridge University Press, 1985. One of the best translations of Descartes's works, including his *Meditations*.

Pinker, Steven. *The Blank Slate: The Modern Denial of Human Nature*. New York: Penguin Putnam, 2002. An accessible anti-empiricist discussion of contemporary theories and issues concerning human nature.

Pinker, Steven. *How the Mind Works*. New York: W. W. Norton, 1997. A wide-ranging discussion of the nature of the mind by a nativist.

Pinker, Steven. *The Language Instinct: How the Mind Creates Language*. New York: HarperCollins, 1994. A popular discussion of the nature of language, but one that favors nativism.

Empiricism

Aristotle. *The Basic Works of Aristotle*. ed. Richard McKeon. New York: Random House, 1941. Aristotle does not have a separate work on epistemology, but the topic is woven in with the other themes he addresses, particularly metaphysics.

Berkeley, George, David Hume, and John Locke. *The Empiricists*. New York: Anchor-Doubleday, 1961. An inexpensive collection of the major works of these three philosophers.

Cowie, Fiona. *What's Within? Nativism Reconsidered*. Oxford: Oxford University Press, 1999. Somewhat advanced and technical, but one of the most thorough critiques of some of the theses and arguments of nativism.

Woolhouse, R. S. *The Empiricists*. Vol. 5 of *A History of Western Philosophy*. Oxford: Oxford University Press, 1988. A good survey of the thought of Locke, Berkeley, Hume, and other early empiricists.

Kantian Constructivism

Jones, W. T. *Kant and the Nineteenth Century*. 2d. ed., rev. Vol. 4 of *History of Western Philosophy*. New York: Harcourt Brace Jovanovich, 1975. A good overview of Kant's philosophy, situating it in his century and developing his influences on later philosophy. It also includes short selections from Kant's writings.

Kant, Immanuel. *Prolegomena to Any Future Metaphysics*. Translated by James W. Ellington. Indianapolis, Ind.: Hackett Publishing, 1977. Kant is notoriously difficult to read, but this short introduction to his epistemology is a good place to begin.

Scruton, Roger. *Kant*. Oxford: Oxford University Press, 1983. A short introduction to Kant for beginners.

Epistemological Relativism

Gifford, N. L. *When in Rome: An Introduction to Relativism and Knowledge*. Albany: State University of New York Press, 1983. A helpful overview of relativism and the problem of knowledge.

Kaufmann, Walter, ed. *The Portable Nietzsche*. New York: Viking Press, 1968. A good collection of readings drawn from Nietzsche's major works.

Pragmatism

Thayer, H. S. *Meaning and Action: A Critical History of Pragmatism*. 2d ed. Indianapolis, Ind.: Hackett, 1981. One of the most comprehensive surveys of pragmatism.

Thayer, H. S. *Pragmatism: The Classic Writings*. Indianapolis, Ind.: Hackett, 1982. A good group of selections drawn from the writings of the leading figures in the movement.

Feminist Epistemology

Garry, Ann, and Marilyn Pearsall, eds. *Women, Knowledge, and Reality: Explorations in Feminist Philosophy.* Boston: Unwin Hyman, 1989. Contains some of the classic articles in feminist philosophy.

Tanesini, Alessandra. *An Introduction to Feminist Epistemologies.* Oxford: Blackwell, 1999. A very readable, well-organized introduction to the topic.

Tong, Rosemarie. *Feminist Thought: A More Comprehensive Introduction.* 2d ed. Boulder, Colo.: Westview, 1998. A helpful overview of the origins and development of feminist philosophy.

Scientific Knowledge

Chalmers, A. F. *What Is This Thing Called Science?* 3d ed. Indianapolis: Hackett, 1999. A very helpful and entertaining introduction to the philosophy of science.

Kuhn, Thomas. *The Structure of Scientific Revolutions.* 2d ed., enlarged. Chicago: University of Chicago Press, 1970. A classic work that itself caused a revolution in our understanding of science and that has had an impact on many disciplines.

Parsons, Keith. *Copernican Questions: A Concise Invitation to the Philosophy of Science.* New York: McGraw-Hill, 2006. A thorough survey of many of the issues discussed in this section.

Schick, Theodore. *Readings in the Philosophy of Science: From Positivism to Postmodernism.* New York: McGraw-Hill, 2006. An anthology of primary source readings covering a wide range of issues on this topic.

NOTES

1. Jonathan Harrison, "A Philosopher's Nightmare or the Ghost Not Laid," *Proceedings of the Aristotelian Society* 67 (1966–1967), pp. 179–88.
2. This exercise was taken from James W. Sire, *Why Should Anyone Believe Anything at All?* (Downers Grove, Ill.: InterVarsity Press, 1994).
3. René Descartes, *Discourse on the Method,* in *The Philosophical Writings of Descartes,* vol. 1, trans. John Cottingham, Robert Stoothoff, and Dugald Murdoch (Cambridge: Cambridge University Press, 1985), 1.8, pp. 114–15. The page references are to the part number and page number in the classic French edition, followed by the page number in this edition.
4. Ibid., 1.4, p. 113.
5. Ibid., 1.4, p. 115.
6. René Descartes, *Meditations on First Philosophy,* revised ed., trans. John Cottingham (Cambridge: Cambridge University Press, 1996), 1.17–23, pp. 12–15. The page references are to the meditation number and page number in the classic French edition, followed by the page number in this edition.
7. Ibid., 2.24–25, pp. 16–17.
8. Plato, *Meno,* trans. W. K. C. Guthrie, in *Collected Dialogues of Plato,* ed. Edith Hamilton and Huntington Cairns (New York: Bollingen Foundation, Pantheon Books, 1961), 80d. To allow the reader to find the selections from Plato in other editions, the references are made to the standard section numbers of Plato's manuscripts.
9. Plato, *Phaedo,* 65d, 74–75, 76e–77a, trans. Benjamin Jowett (1892).
10. Alfred North Whitehead, *Process and Reality: An Essay in Cosmology* (New York: Harper Torchbooks, Harper & Brothers, 1957), p. 63.
11. Descartes, *Meditations on First Philosophy,* 2.27, p. 18.
12. Ibid., 3.36, p. 25.
13. Ibid., 3.40–51, pp. 28–35.
14. John Locke, "Introduction," sec. 5, in *Essay Concerning Human Understanding,* vol. 1. Because there are so many editions of the empiricists' works, all references to them here are made in terms of the authors' original division numbers. A number of versions are available on the Internet and may be found by submitting the philosopher's name to any of the standard search engines. Some of these sites provide their own search tool, which enables you to find all the passages in which the philosopher uses a particular word.
15. David Hume, *An Enquiry Concerning Human Understanding,* ed. L. A. Selby-Bigge (Oxford: Clarendon Press, 1894), sec. 2.
16. Locke, "Introduction," sec. 4.
17. Locke, *Essay,* bk. 2, chap. 8, sec. 8.
18. Ibid., bk. 2, chap. 1, sec. 1.
19. Ibid., bk. 1, chap. 1, sec. 5.
20. Ibid., bk. 2, chap. 1, sec. 2.
21. Ibid., bk. 2, chap. 1, sec. 5.
22. Ibid., bk. 2, chap. 8, sec. 12–17.
23. George Berkeley, *Treatise Concerning the Principles of Human Knowledge,* pt. 1, sec. 6.
24. Ibid., pt. 1, sec. 1–4, 8–10, 18, 29–31, 33.

25. See Karl Popper, "A Note on Berkeley as Precursor of Mach and Einstein," in *Conjectures and Refutations* (New York: Harper and Row, 1965), pp. 166–74.

26. Berkeley, *Treatise,* pt. 1, sec. 35.

27. Hume, *An Enquiry Concerning Human Understanding,* sec. 2.

28. Ibid., sec. 4, pt. 1.

29. Ibid., sec. 4, pt. 1.

30. Ibid., sec. 4, pt. 2.

31. Ibid., sec. 12, pt. 1.

32. David Hume, *A Treatise of Human Nature,* ed. L. A. Selby-Bigge (Oxford: Clarendon Press, 1896), bk. 1, pt. 4, sec. 6.

33. Ibid., bk. 1, pt. 4, sec. 7.

34. Hume, *An Enquiry Concerning Human Understanding,* sec. 12, pt. 3.

35. R = Rationalism and E = Empiricism; 1-R, 2-E, 3-R, 4-R, 5-E, 6-E, 7-R, 8-E, 9-E, 10-R.

36. Jerry Fodor, *The Language of Thought* (New York: Crowell, 1975), p. 65.

37. Steven Pinker, *The Blank Slate: The Modern Denial of Human Nature* (New York: Penguin Putnam, 2002). See also Pinker's other books in the suggested readings at the end of this chapter.

38. Elizabeth Spelke's research is cited and summarized in Steven Pinker's books listed in the suggested readings.

39. Geoffrey Sampson, *Educating Eve: The "Language Instinct" Debate* (London: Cassell, 1997), p. 26.

40. Heinrich Heine, *Germany, Works,* vol. 5, pp. 136–37, quoted in *The Age of Ideology: The Nineteenth Century Philosophers,* ed. Henry D. Aiken (New York: New American Library, 1956), pp. 27–28.

41. Immanuel Kant, *Critique of Pure Reason,* trans. Norman Kemp Smith (New York: St. Martin's Press, 1965), B1–B2, pp. 42–43, 47. Kant published two editions of this work, the first in 1781 (referred to as A) and the second in 1787 (referred to as B). The references to this work are given in terms of the pagination of the original editions, which are indicated in the margins of most English translations, and then in the page numbers of the Kemp Smith edition.

42. Kant, *Critique of Pure Reason,* Bxvi, p. 22.

43. This example was taken from Merold Westphal, "A User-Friendly Copernican Revolution," in *In the Socratic Tradition: Essays on Teaching Philosophy,* ed. Tziporah Kasachkoff (Lanham, Md.: Rowman & Littlefield, 1998), p. 188.

44. Kant, *Critique of Pure Reason,* A24/B39, p. 68; A31/B46, pp. 74–75.

45. Ibid., B71–72, pp. 89–90.

46. From Roger N. Shepard, *Mind Sights* (New York: W. H. Freeman, 1990), p. 48.

47. Kant, *Critique of Pure Reason,* A15/B29, pp. 61–62; A51/B75, p. 93.

48. Hume, *A Treatise of Human Nature,* bk. 1, pt. 4, sec. 6.

49. Norman Melchert, *The Great Conversation,* 3d ed. (Mountain View, Calif.: Mayfield, 1999), p. 447.

50. Kant, *Critique of Pure Reason,* A636/B664, p. 528.

51. Ibid., Bxxx, p. 29.

52. This example was inspired by Norman Malcolm, "The Groundlessness of Belief," in *Reason and Religion,* ed. Stuart C. Brown (Ithaca, N.Y.: Cornell University Press, 1977), pp. 143–44.

53. Richard Rorty, *Philosophy and the Mirror of Nature* (Princeton, N.J.: Princeton University Press, 1979), p. 377.

54. Plato, *Theaetetus* 166d, trans. F. M. Cornford, in *Collected Dialogues of Plato,* p. 872.

55. Friedrich Nietzsche, *Beyond Good and Evil,* sec. 6, trans. Walter Kaufmann (New York: Random House, Vintage Books, 1966), p. 13.

56. Jean-Paul Sartre, "Existentialism Is a Humanism," trans. Philip Pairet, in *Existentialism from Dostoevsky to Sartre,* rev. and exp., ed. Walter Kaufmann (New York: Meridian, 1975), p. 356.

57. Ruth Benedict, "Anthropology and the Abnormal," in *The Journal of General Psychology* 10 (1934), p. 59.

58. Willard Van Orman Quine, "Two Dogmas of Empiricism," in *From a Logical Point of View,* 2d ed., rev. (New York: Harper & Row, 1961), p. 44.

59. Ibid.

60. G. W. F. Hegel, *Elements of the Philosophy of Right,* ed. Allen W. Wood, trans. H. B. Nisbet (Cambridge: Cambridge University Press, 1991), preface, pp. 21–22.

61. Friedrich Nietzsche, *The Will to Power,* trans. Walter Kaufmann and R. J. Hollingdale (New York: Vintage Books, 1967), sec. 481, p. 267.

62. For this insight on Nietzsche, I am indebted to W. T. Jones's book *A History of Western Philosophy,* 2d ed., rev., vol. 4, *Kant and the Nineteenth Century* (New York: Harcourt Brace Jovanovich, 1975), pp. 236–37.

63. Friedrich Nietzsche, *The Gay Science,* trans. Walter Kaufmann (New York: Vintage Books, 1974), sec. 335, pp. 263–64.

64. Ibid., sec. 333, p. 261.
65. Nietzsche, *The Will to Power*, sec. 552, p. 298.
66. Friedrich Nietzsche, *Beyond Good and Evil: Prelude to a Philosophy of the Future*, trans. Walter Kaufmann (New York: Vintage Books, 1966), pp. 11–14, 52–53.
67. Nietzsche, *The Gay Science*, sec. 343, p. 279.
68. Nietzsche, *Beyond Good and Evil*, sec. 22, pp. 30–31.
69. Friedrich Nietzsche, *Thus Spoke Zarathustra*, pt. 3, "On the Spirit of Gravity," sec. 2, in *The Portable Nietzsche*, trans. and ed. Walter Kaufmann (New York: Viking Press, 1968), p. 307.
70. Nietzsche, *The Gay Science*, sec. 51, p. 115.
71. Ibid., sec. 41, p. 108.
72. Nietzsche, *The Will to Power*, sec. 410, p. 221.
73. Ibid., sec. 616, p. 330.
74. Plato, *Theaetetus* 171a,b, trans. F. M. Cornford, in *Collected Dialogues of Plato*, pp. 876–77.
75. 1 Corinthians 13:12.
76. C. S. Peirce, *The Collected Papers of Charles Sanders Peirce*, vols. 1–6, ed. Charles Hartshorne and Paul Weiss (Cambridge, Mass.: Harvard University Press, 1931–1935), 5.276–77. References to Peirce's works are in terms of the volume number of this collection followed by the section number.
77. Abraham Kaplan, *The New World of Philosophy* (New York: Vintage Books, 1961), p. 28.
78. Peirce, "The Fixation of Belief," in *Collected Papers*, 5.371.
79. William James, "What Pragmatism Means," Lecture II in *Pragmatism: A New Name for Some Old Ways of Thinking* (New York: Longmans, Green, 1907), reprinted in William James, *Essays in Pragmatism*, ed. Albury Castell (New York: Collier Macmillan, Hafner Press, 1948), p. 155.
80. John Dewey, *How We Think* (Boston: Heath, 1933), p. 106.
81. James, "What Pragmatism Means," in *Essays in Pragmatism*, p. 147.
82. Ibid., pp. 157–58.
83. *The Letters of William James*, vol. 1, ed. Henry James (Boston: Atlantic Monthly Press, 1920), pp. 147–48.
84. William James, *Meaning and Truth: A Sequel to "Pragmatism"* (New York: McKay, 1909; reprint, Westport, Conn.: Greenwood Press, 1968), preface.
85. John Dewey, *Reconstruction in Philosophy*, enl. ed. (Boston: Beacon Press, 1948), pp. 156–57.
86. John Dewey, *Logic: the Theory of Inquiry* (New York: Holt, Rinehart, & Winston, 1938), p. 9.
87. Peirce, "The Fixation of Belief," in *Collected Papers*, 5.384.
88. Peirce, "How to Make Our Ideas Clear," in *Collected Papers*, 5.407.
89. James, "The Sentiment of Rationality," in *Essays in Pragmatism*, p. 12.
90. Ibid., p. 27.
91. Ibid., p. 21.
92. James, "What Pragmatism Means," in *Essays in Pragmatism*, p. 149.
93. John Dewey, *Experience and Nature*, 2d ed. (La Salle, Ill.: Open Court, 1929), pp. 9–10.
94. William James, "Pragmatism's Conception of Truth," Lecture IV in *Pragmatism: A New Name for Some Old Ways of Thinking*, reprinted in James, *Essays in Pragmatism*, pp. 159–62, 166–68, 170–71.
95. These examples were taken from Brooke Noel Moore and Richard Parker, *Critical Thinking*, 4th ed. (Mountain View, Calif.: Mayfield, 1995), p. 59.
96. In addition to the many books and anthologies that are now available on feminist philosophy, *Hypatia: A Journal of Feminist Philosophy* provides many examples of the current discussions in this field. (Hypatia was a 5th-century female leader of the Neoplatonist philosophical movement who was condemned to death as a heretic and died a brutal death at the hands of Christian fanatics.)
97. For a comprehensive survey of women in the history of philosophy, see *A History of Women Philosophers*, ed. Mary Ellen Waithe, 4 vols. (Dordrecht, Netherlands: Kluwer Academic, 1987–1994). This series covers women philosophers from ancient Greece through the 20th century.
98. Aristotle, *Generation of Animals*, 767b, 20–24; 737a, 27–8; 775a, 15; 730b, 1–30; 737a, 29.
99. For further examples of some male philosophers' conceptions of women, see Mary Briody Mahowald, ed., *Philosophy of Woman: Classical to Current Concepts* (Indianapolis, Ind.: Hackett, 1978).
100. Aristotle, *Politics*, 1260a, 23–30.
101. Samuel Enoch Stumpf, *Philosophy: History and Problems*, 5th ed. (New York: McGraw-Hill, 1994), p. 937.
102. See Casey Miller and Kate Swift, *Words and Women* (Garden City, N.Y.: Anchor Press/Doubleday, 1976), pp. 25–26.
103. John Dewey, *Problems of Men* (New York: Philosophical Library, 1946).
104. To get a glimpse of this disparity, see *The Monist 77*, no. 4 (October 1994), which is devoted to the topic

"Feminist Epistemology: For and Against." Some of the articles and references include female philosophers who are critical of feminist thought as well as male philosophers who are sympathetic to it.

105. Simone de Beauvoir, *The Second Sex*, trans. H. M. Parshley (New York: Knopf, 1975), p. 267.

106. Ann Garry and Marilyn Pearsall, eds., introduction to *Women, Knowledge, and Reality: Explorations in Feminist Philosophy* (Boston: Unwin Hyman, 1989), pp. xi–xiv.

107. Richard Foley, *The Theory of Epistemic Rationality* (Cambridge, Mass.: Harvard University Press, 1987).

108. Lorraine Code, *What Can She Know? Feminist Theory and the Construction of Knowledge* (Ithaca, N.Y.: Cornell University Press, 1991), p. 8, fn. 7.

109. Harriet Baber, "The Market for Feminist Epistemology," in *The Monist 77,* no. 4 (October 1994), p. 403.

110. Sandra Harding, *Whose Science? Whose Knowledge? Thinking from Women's Lives* (Ithaca, N.Y.: Cornell University Press, 1991).

111. Code, *What Can She Know?* pp. 11–12.

112. Ibid., p. 255.

113. This objection is also a key theme in the writings of postmodernist philosophers. See, for example, Jacques Derrida, *Margins of Philosophy,* trans. Alan Bass (Chicago: University of Chicago Press, 1982).

114. Adrienne Rich, *On Lies, Secrets, and Silence: Selected Prose: 1966–78* (New York: W. W. Norton, 1979), p. 207.

115. Genevieve Lloyd, "The Man of Reason," in *Women, Knowledge, and Reality: Explorations in Feminist Philosophy,* ed. Ann Garry and Marilyn Pearsall (Boston: Unwin Hyman, 1989), pp. 111–28. See also Lloyd's book *The Man of Reason: "Male" and "Female" in Western Philosophy* (Minneapolis: University of Minnesota Press, 1984).

116. Lloyd, "The Man of Reason," p. 124.

117. Ibid., p. 127.

118. Code, *What Can She Know?* p. 13.

119. Sara Ruddick, *Maternal Thinking: Toward a Politics of Peace* (Boston: Beacon, 1989), p. 13.

120. Alison M. Jaggar, "Love and Knowledge: Emotion in Feminist Epistemology," in Garry and Pearsall, *Women, Knowledge, and Reality,* pp. 129–55.

121. Lorraine Code, *What Can She Know?* p. 17.

122. Mary Field Belenky, Blythe McVicker Clinchy, Nancy Rule Goldberger, and Jill Mattuck Tarule, eds., *Ways of Knowing: The Development of Self, Voice, and Mind* (New York: Basic Books, 1986), p. 72.

123. Evelyn Fox Keller, "Feminism and Science," in *Signs: Journal of Women in Culture and Society 7,* no. 3 (1982), p. 593.

124. Lorraine Code, "Voice and Voicelessness: A Modest Proposal?" in *Philosophy in a Feminist Voice: Critiques and Reconstructions,* ed. Janet A. Kourany (Princeton, N.J.: Princeton University Press, 1998), p. 223.

125. Helen Longino, *Science as Social Knowledge: Values and Objectivity in Scientific Inquiry* (Princeton, N.J.: Princeton University Press, 1990), p. 12.

126. Lloyd, "The Man of Reason," p. 127.

127. Lorraine Code, "Taking Subjectivity into Account," in *Feminist Epistemologies,* ed. Linda Alcoff and Elizabeth Potter (New York: Routledge, 1993), p. 23.

128. Lorraine Code, *Rhetorical Spaces: Essays on Gendered Locations* (New York: Routledge, 1995), p. 185.

129. Code, *What Can She Know?* p. 3.

130. Sandra Harding, "Feminist Justificatory Strategies," in Garry and Pearsall, *Women, Knowledge, and Reality,* p. 196.

131. Jane Duran, *Toward a Feminist Epistemology* (Savage, Md.: Rowan & Littlefield, 1991), p. 197.

132. These worries are expressed in several feminist writings, such as the following: "How can feminist theory base itself upon the uniqueness of the female experience without rectifying thereby one single definition of femaleness as the paradigmatic one—without succumbing, that is, to an essentialist discourse on gender?" See Seyla Benhabib and Drucill Cornell, "Introduction: Beyond the Politics of Gender," in *Feminism as Critique: Essays on the Politics of Gender in Late-Capitalist Societies,* ed. Seyla Benhabib and Drucill Cornell (Minneapolis: University of Minnesota Press, 1987), p. 13.

133. One feminist writer complains about feminist theories that imply that "there is no truth, and that knowledge based on the female subject is as valid as knowledge based on an androcentric [male-centered] subject. . . . Only power can determine which epistemology will prevail." See Marnia Lazreg, "Women's Experience and Feminist Epistemology: A Critical Neo-Rationalist Approach," in *Knowing the Difference: Feminist Perspectives in Epistemology,* ed. Kathleen Lennon and Margaret Whitford (London: Routledge, 1994), p. 56.

134. Lazreg cautions against the "intellectual ghetto-ization" of feminist epistemology. See Lazreg, "Women's Experience and Feminist Epistemology." Similarly, Baber worries that the growing industry of feminist scholarship will lead to "academic pink-collar ghettos." See Harriet Baber, "The Market for Feminist Epistemology," *The Monist 77*, no. 4 (October 1994), p. 419.

135. Sandra Harding, *The Science Question in Feminism* (Ithaca, N.Y.: Cornell University Press, 1986), p. 138.

136. Quoted in J. Bronowski, *Science and Human Values* (New York: Harper & Row, 1965), p. 14.

137. A. F. Chalmers, *What Is This Thing Called Science?* (St. Lucia, Queensland: University of Queensland Press, 1976), p. 30.

138. Ibid., p. 13.

139. Thomas Kuhn, *The Structure of Scientific Revolutions,* 2d ed., enlarged (Chicago: University of Chicago Press, 1970).

140. Ian G. Barbour, *Religion and Science: Historical and Contemporary Issues* (New York: HarperCollins, 1997), pp. 125–26.

141. See the essays in *Sex and Scientific Inquiry,* ed. Sandra Harding and Jean F. O'Barr (Chicago: University of Chicago Press, 1987).

142. Ibid., p. 127.

143. Lynn Hankinson Nelson, "Epistemological Communities" in *The Gender of Science,* ed. Janet A. Kourany (Upper Saddle River, N.J.: 2002), p. 325.

144. Chalmers, *What Is This Thing Called Science?* p. 236.

145. Ibid.

Vincent van Gogh, *The Starry Night*, 1889

CHAPTER 3

THE SEARCH FOR ULTIMATE REALITY

 ## CHAPTER OBJECTIVES

On completion of this chapter, you should be able to

1. Provide an overview of various general metaphysical positions and their relations, including dualism, monism, materialism, and idealism.
2. State the mind-body problem.
3. Describe Cartesian mind-body dualism, locate its strengths and weaknesses, and evaluate Descartes's arguments for it.
4. Distinguish between the identity theory and eliminativist versions of physicalism.
5. Explain the nature of functionalism, the Turing Test, and Searle's Chinese room objection to strong AI.
6. Explain the hard determinist's position in the free will debate and assess its strengths and weaknesses.
7. Discuss the nature, strengths, and weaknesses of the libertarian's stance in the free will debate.
8. Describe and evaluate compatibilism as a solution to the free will debate.
9. Discuss the relationship between science and metaphysics.

SCOUTING THE TERRITORY: *What Is Reality?*

Go outside and look at the night sky this evening. You will see an overwhelming number of stars. It would seem to be completely obvious that these stars exist at the same time that you are viewing them. To confirm the testimony of your eyes, you could take a picture of these stars and they will leave their image on the film. However, astronomers tell us that many of these stars no longer exist! The reason is that light takes an enormous amount of time to travel from the distant stars to the earth. (For example, the center of the band of stars that make up the Milky Way is 25,000 light-years away from the earth. A light-year is the distance that light can travel in a year, which is about 5.88 trillion miles.) During this time, as the light from these stars is traveling through space, some of the stars may burn out or be destroyed by an explosion. Hence, a star can exist in our current experience because we are experiencing its light, while it does not currently exist at the point from which its light originated. Think about that statement for a minute. On the one hand, such a star obviously does not exist, because its material substance has been destroyed. On the other hand, the star obviously does exist because it affects our experience and has causal effects on our instruments and photographic equipment. In our part of the universe, the star is as real and capable of scientific observation and measurement as the chair on which you are sitting. So, are these stars real or not? Can we experience the reality of something in our spatial-temporal corner of the universe at the same time that it does not exist in other locations? Of course, to decide if some specific thing is real or not requires us to examine a more fundamental question: What is reality?

Exploring questions about the nature of reality is our next stop on the philosophical journey. The awe-inspiring experience of contemplating the night sky can give us a sense of continuity with the ages. As you gaze up at the moon or the Big Dipper constellation, consider the fact that thousands of years before you were born, the ancients were looking at the same breath-taking display. Furthermore, we not only see the same heavens that the ancients saw, but we also ask some of the same questions about the universe such as, What is the cosmos like and what is my place in it? As you take your own philosophical journey, keep in mind that many explorers before you have traveled the same terrain and in their writings have left you "maps" of what they found. Their findings can guide you in your journey, but you must not follow them uncritically. These guides can make you notice features of the territory that you might have missed, but their maps also may contain errors and lead you into dead ends and even dangerous territory. You must decide when the accounts of other explorers are helpful and when they need to be revised.

metaphysics the area of philosophy concerned with fundamental questions about the nature of reality

Philosophical questions about the nature of reality fall under the heading of **metaphysics**. The term *metaphysics* was originally coined by a scholar in the first century B.C. who was editing the manuscripts of the Greek philosopher Aristotle (384–322 B.C.). One of Aristotle's studies of nature was titled *Physics,* and it was followed by an unnamed work about the more general principles of reality. The editor assigned the title of *Metaphysics* to this later work. (The term literally means "that which comes after physics.") Even though *metaphysics* originally referred to the order of Aristotle's manuscripts, it has come to designate that area of philosophy that deals with the nature of reality. The original meaning is still appropriate, however, because the philosophical domain of metaphysics is "after" physics in the sense that it concerns those questions that remain after we have dealt with the factual questions that can be answered by the natural sciences.

CHARTING THE TERRAIN OF METAPHYSICS:
What Are the Issues?

The philosophical area of metaphysics contains some of the most difficult, profound, and abstract theories produced by the human mind. But in spite of their complexity, metaphysical questions actually arise out of some very basic human concerns. From day one, as tiny infants, we are faced with the task of coming to terms with reality and drawing conclusions about it without any previous knowledge to guide us. Similarly, at the dawn of Western philosophy in ancient Greece (around 600 B.C.), the early philosophers began to examine the nature of reality for themselves and began to think critically about the traditional stories and folk tales that had served to explain the universe prior to the development of philosophy and science. I would like to suggest a similarity between the cognitive development of a little child and the intellectual development of humanity. There used to be a theory in biology concerning the physical development of a human fetus. That theory was expressed in the slogan "ontogeny recapitulates phylogeny," which means that the stages of development of the individual organism within the womb repeat the stages of development of the human species as a whole. Whether or not this concept is useful in biology, I think that something like this idea has a measure of truth when applied to the history of thought.

What Is the Nature of Ultimate Reality?

The cognitive development of the baby illustrates in many ways the intellectual growth of the human race throughout history. For example, within the changing kaleidoscope of his experience, the baby must sort out what sensations represent objects that persist independently of him (such as a rattle) and what are simply transitory sensations (such as an itch). Some researchers believe that around age five or six months, a baby begins to develop a firm sense of object permanence.

Just as the baby must learn to sort out what is permanent in the world from what is changing, so the early Greeks were concerned with the *problem of permanence and change.* On the one hand, everything seems to be changing. The tides come and go, the seasons rotate, the planets shift their positions, there are floods and there are droughts. Yet, some constants seem to remain throughout these changes. What is permanent throughout the changes in the world? What can we count on? Where can we find a source of stability in the cosmos? Does some fundamental, physical element persist throughout all the changes? Or does some nonmaterial eternal principle control the form that physical transformations take?

For our next example, think about a toddler noticing her image in a mirror for the first time. She is intrigued by the little child she sees. She waves to her and the other child waves back. She jumps and the other girl jumps. Once again, the child eventually makes a breakthrough discovery. The thought occurs to her: "The other child is me!"—"But how can that be?" she thinks, "I am here and she is there!" This child is encountering another metaphysical problem: how to distinguish between appearance and reality.

The *problem of appearance and reality* is encountered in the toddler's experience with the world, and it was also one of the first problems that arose in humanity's intellectual infancy. A stick looks straight when we hold it, yet it seems bent when stuck in water. Fire appears to be more powerful than water when it causes water to evaporate, but water appears to be more powerful than fire when it extinguishes the flame. The moon looks small when it is high in the sky, but large when it is on the horizon. These experiences led the ancient Greeks to ask: In all our experiences, what things are just appearances and what things are real?

The Treachery of Images (1929) by René Magritte. In this famous picture, Magritte raises the problem of appearance and reality. When asked, "What is this?" we are inclined to say, "Obviously, it is a pipe." But the French phrase in the picture reminds us that "This is not a pipe." It is not really a pipe, for you cannot pick it up and put in your mouth and smoke it. It is merely an image. But in more subtle ways, is it possible that we can confuse images and appearances with reality itself? The problem of metaphysics is to sort out what is genuinely real from how things seem. For example, is the mind separate from the body, or does it only appear to be? Do we genuinely have free will, or do we only appear to?

Why is understanding reality important? From the very beginnings of critical, systematic inquiry in ancient times, philosophers and scientists thought that taking the time and effort to understand the nature of reality was vitally important even if there was never a practical payoff for having this knowledge. Plato, however, thought that an understanding of reality also had momentous practical consequences. He believed reality is that which we dare not misunderstand if we are to be truly fulfilled persons. To use a modern analogy of his view, if we live our lives on the basis of a false view of reality, we would be like travelers trying to find their way around New York City by following a map of Chicago. A wise person, Plato said, would always choose truth (no matter how uncomfortable it may be) over the short-term happiness of illusions. Do you think Plato is right? Isn't it often the case that our illusions and false beliefs can bring comfort while reality can be cruel and distressing? In the accompanying "Philosophy in the Marketplace" box is a test that you can give to yourself and a few friends to see to what degree a correct understanding of reality is important to you and your friends.

What Is the Nature of Human Reality?

Although many metaphysical issues concern the nature of reality "out there," a major part of metaphysics focuses on that part of reality that we know from both the inside and the outside—ourselves. Some philosophers have supposed that by examining our own nature we may get a clue as to the nature of the larger cosmos in which we live. Accordingly, in

PHILOSOPHY
in the
MARKETPLACE

Present several friends with the following survey and answer the questions yourself.

- Think of four or five beliefs you have that are very important to you and your conception of the world. (You do not need to share these beliefs if you don't want to.) Possible examples are:

1. There is a God.
2. There is life after death.
3. The scientific account of the world is essentially correct.
4. The universe conforms to the laws of logic.
5. I am a reasonably smart person.
6. There is some ultimate meaning or purpose to human life.
7. The significant other in my life is faithful to me.

- Now, suppose you begin to worry about the possibility that one or more of your beliefs are false. Yet you also realize that it is possible you might continue on in blissful ignorance all your life without ever finding out the truth. To solve this problem, scientists have developed a "reality meter" for testing beliefs. By pushing its button, you will be told which of your beliefs conform to reality and which are nothing but illusions. Think of your list again. Let's assume you are comfortable believing these things to be true, and if you found out otherwise, you would be deeply troubled. Would you decide to continue holding these beliefs because they give you a sense of peace, or would you activate the reality meter in spite of the chance that your new and more accurate knowledge of reality would be disillusioning? What would you do and why?

addition to questions about the nature of reality in general, I explore several related problems concerning the type of reality that characterizes persons.

Let's return to the case of the toddler studying her own reflection. Her fascinating encounter with the mirror teaches her that she can experience herself both as a subject and as an object. As a subject, she is immersed within the world as a subjective center of consciousness. But she can also stand back and view herself as an object to study and understand. One of the mysteries little children eventually begin to wrestle with is the relationship between me and my experiences on the one hand, and that which is not me on the other.

Similarly, in the beginnings of philosophy in the Western world, the ancient Greek philosophers at first asked questions only about the cosmos out there. Gradually, like the infant, they became more self-aware. As they contemplated the stars, it occurred to them that if they take one step back (conceptually), another question arises: Who or what is the self that is contemplating the stars? Eventually, metaphysical questions about reality in general were supplemented with metaphysical questions about human nature. The two major metaphysical questions about the nature of persons concern (1) the mind-body problem and (2) freedom and determinism.

The Mind-Body Problem

Think once again about your experience of viewing the stars. Physical events are going on as light impinges on your retina, which sends signals through your optical nerve to the brain. But mental events are also going on, such as the thought, "The night sky is so beautiful!" How are we to understand these two dimensions? You are a part of the world as one object among many. You have spatial location, you can move, fall down, and be hit by a falling apple just like any other object. But you also have a sense of being separate from the world. You experience yourself as an island of consciousness that is not out there among the other objects. Within the world of your conscious, subjective experiences, for example, you encounter inner realities such as pain or joy, which seem to be different from the objects in the outer world such as rocks and flowers. You may have the sense that you know the contents of your experience by somehow "looking" inside, but how is the inside related to the outside? What sort of reality (if any) do the words *consciousness* or *mind* refer to, and how is it related to the reality of bodies, brains, and chemical elements? Is it possible that everything that happens to you and within you (including your thoughts) can be explained by physical laws? Perhaps there is no inner nonphysical world at all. Maybe what *appears* to be the inner world of your mind and your thoughts is *really* a series of events that happen in nature just like the beating of your heart. On the other hand, would such a physical explanation leave out something that needs to be explained? Such questions are metaphysical questions and fall under the heading of the *mind-body problem;* they are addressed in greater detail in section 3.1, and positions on the problem are discussed in sections 3.2, 3.3, and 3.4.

Freedom and Determinism

As you look at the stars, you have no control over how the light affects your retina. That effect is simply something that happens to you. But what about your other responses? Are they also simply something that happens to you? You may think any number of things as you view the stars: "Isn't that romantic?" or, "I wish I knew more about astronomy." Are these thoughts and responses freely chosen or are they the inevitable outcome of your personality or your culture? Are you just as determined as the stars or the planets you are studying? Perhaps your response to the stars depends on whether you tend to be primarily a romantic person or an intellectual person. Either way, did you choose your personality, or was it determined by your genes or your environmental influences? If all your behavior and choices are determined either by your genes, social conditioning, or (perhaps) by God's will, then can you ever be held morally responsible for what you do? These metaphysical questions fall under the heading of *freedom and determinism;* they are discussed in further detail in section 3.5, and positions on the problem are discussed in sections 3.6, 3.7, and 3.8.

This introduction has been a brief overview of three metaphysical problems: (1) the nature of ultimate reality, (2) the mind-body problem, and (3) freedom and determinism. These three problems concerning the nature of reality do not cover all the issues in metaphysics, but if you work your way through these three crucial issues, you will have gone a large way toward deciding what sort of universe you live in and your place within it. In the remaining sections of this chapter, I focus on the last two problems (mind-body, freedom-determinism). Issues concerning the nature of reality will not receive separate treatment, because they reveal themselves in the debates over the other two problems.

In chapter 4, I treat the existence of God under the topic of philosophy of religion. But obviously this topic could just as easily fall under metaphysics, because the question about the existence of God is a question about the ultimate nature of reality. The stance you take on any one of these four issues (God, reality, mind, and freedom) does not necessarily lock you into a specific answer on the other three questions. Nevertheless, some combinations of positions from each of these issues fit together better than others. For example, some people believe that reality is permeated by intelligence and purpose. Others believe that reality is basically made up of matter and that everything that happens is the result of either mechanistic causes or chance. Obviously, a person who believes in God would tend to favor the first view over the second. Some philosophers, however, have said that the world is like God's body, so that he is at least partly material in nature just as we are. Furthermore, some philosophers have suggested that God could have made the world to function like a machine while allowing some events to be random rather than preplanned. So don't think that there is necessarily only one way to work out the connections between the various aspects of metaphysics. Try your hand at figuring out some of the possible connections.

THOUGHT EXPERIMENT: *The Implications of Theism and Atheism*

- If you believed in God, which of the following positions on the nature of reality, mind, and freedom would fit best with this belief? Are several alternatives equally compatible with theism? Which positions would be the hardest to reconcile with the claim that there is a God? Are any alternatives absolutely contradictory to the notion that there is a God?
- If you did not believe in God, which positions on the nature of reality, mind, and freedom would fit best with this belief? Are several alternatives equally compatible with atheism? Which positions would be the hardest to reconcile with the claim that there is no God? Are any alternatives absolutely contradictory to the notion that there is no God?

1. Everything that happens in the world happens to fulfill some purpose.
2. Many events simply happen and do not have a purpose.
3. Humans are completely physical beings.
4. Humans have a nonphysical mind.
5. Everything that happens in the world (including human actions) is determined and inevitable.
6. Some events are not determined.

CHOOSING A PATH: WHAT ARE MY OPTIONS CONCERNING METAPHYSICS?

As I mentioned previously, this chapter consists of two subtopics (mind-body, freedom-determinism). Hence, I save the discussion of the options on these questions for the appropriate sections. For now, I briefly set out some of the options concerning the nature of ultimate reality that show up in all discussions of specific topics in metaphysics. To paint the picture of metaphysics in broad brush strokes, I divide philosophers into two main groups: (1) those who claim there is only one kind of reality and (2) those who claim there are two kinds of realities. The first position is **metaphysical monism** and the second is **metaphysical dualism.**

There are basically two kinds of monism. The first kind is **metaphysical materialism,** which claims that reality is totally physical in nature. Obviously, the materialist would say that if the word *mind* has any meaning at all, it has to be explained in terms of the body (for example, the brain and its states). The materialist does not accept the existence of a nonphysical mind. When I discuss the mind-body problem, I use a special term—*physicalism*—to refer to materialism as applied to the mind-body problem. (The reasons for using this term will be explained later.)

metaphysical monism a metaphysical position that claims that there is only one kind of reality

metaphysical dualism a metaphysical position that claims that there are two kinds of realities

metaphysical materialism a type of monism that claims that reality is totally physical in nature

idealism a type of monism that claims that reality is entirely mental or spiritual in nature

The second type of monism is **idealism.** The idealist believes that reality is entirely mental or spiritual in nature. The term *idealist* in everyday conversation refers to someone who is optimistic, is a visionary, and has a pie-in-the-sky outlook. In this sense, even a materialist could have a very idealistic personality. In metaphysics, however, *idealism* does not refer to a personal stance toward life but to a claim about the ultimate nature of reality.

Metaphysical idealism is a feature of the ancient Hindu tradition. A dominant theme in many versions of Hinduism is that our individual minds are really partial manifestations of God's mind and that all of reality is an expression of the divine mind, much as the world of Hamlet poured forth from Shakespeare's mind. In our discussion of empiricism in section 2.3, we looked at how George Berkeley derived his subjective idealism from empiricism. He argued that since we can never experience an external, material reality that is independent of our minds, the very idea of matter is meaningless. Immanuel Kant (see section 2.4) sought to distinguish his view from Berkeley's. However, Kant ended up with his own version of idealism (called *transcendental idealism*), because he believed that space and time were forms that the mind imposed on experience and that all the objects of experience were constructed by the mind. So idealism has been a persistent position throughout the span of human history. Because idealism is discussed in other chapters (especially the reading from Berkeley), I do not address it in a separate section in this chapter.

Both forms of monism have the advantage of simplicity; that is, both forms claim that reality can be explained in terms of a single principle or category (whether it is physical or mental). Accordingly, they both argue that a dualism that posits both mind and matter as equally real will never be able to explain how these two very different types of reality could ever fit together into one unified universe. Both forms agree that trying to relate an independent physical reality and the mental are like trying to plug an American-made hair dryer into a European electrical system. The two just can't work together. This criticism of dualism, which both materialists and idealists share, will be discussed in section 3.2.

The major alternative to monism is dualism. The dualist maintains that one part of reality is physical and another part is nonphysical. Typically, minds and/or God are the leading candidates for this other half of reality. Dualism is obviously a compromise position, because the dualist (along with the materialist) can accept physical reality and the physicists' explanation of it while insisting that there is more to the big picture than the physical dimension alone. On the other hand, the dualist (with the idealist) claims that the mind is fully real and cannot be explained in terms of the physical. Although dualism has a more complicated, bi-level view of reality than does either of the monisms, dualists would maintain that they better capture the complexity of reality as we experience it. In section 3.2 we examine René Descartes's arguments for dualism.

The three positions discussed so far are summarized in table 3.1.

TABLE 3.1 *Three Metaphysical Positions and Their Responses to Central Metaphysical Questions*

	Can There Be More More Than One Type of Reality?	Is Matter a Fundamental Type of Reality?	Is Mind a Fundamental Type of Reality?
Materialism	No	Yes	No
Idealism	No	No	Yes
Dualism	Yes	Yes	Yes

CONCEPTUAL TOOLS: *The Basics of Metaphysics*

Simplifying Complexity

One of Lewis Carroll's short stories tells of a country in which its geographers prided themselves on how far they had advanced the science of mapmaking. Their ultimate project was to create a map that was so accurate that 1 inch on the map would represent 1 inch of their country. The humor of the story is that instead of being the perfect map that the geographers envisioned, it would be totally useless, for it would be as complex and large as the territory it was representing. Similarly, a theory of reality that consisted simply of a list of all the objects and events encountered in the world would not be very useful. The goal of understanding the world is achieved by following three principles: (1) simplify, (2) simplify, and (3) simplify. In the face of the overwhelming multiplicity of things, qualities, and events in our experience, we continually seek to understand them in terms of as few categories and principles as possible.

Let's return to our child metaphor again. Before long, a young child comes to understand that in spite of the differences between knives, pencils, needles, and thornbushes, they all have the property of being pointed and sharp and that sharp, pointed things have the property of causing pain. Consequently, when she encounters an unfamiliar sharp, pointed object in the future, she will be able to relate it to what she already understands. Having developed this elementary classification of reality, she has simplified her world in a way that will enable her to deal with it more effectively. Furthermore, once she begins to acquire language, she will have the powerful tools of linguistic and conceptual categories to divide up reality. Hence, although metaphysics carried out at a sophisticated philosophical level can be abstract, intimidating, abstruse, and seemingly disengaged from practical life, it is actually the unavoidable outgrowth of our lifelong project of coming to terms with reality.

The principle motivating this quest to simplify our understanding of reality has come to be called **Ockham's razor** (named after William of Ockham, the 14th-century thinker who formulated it). This principle states that we should "shave" off all unnecessary entities and explanatory principles in our theories. The great physicist Isaac Newton, for example, showed that events as diverse as the falling of an apple, the motion of the tides, and the orbits of the planets could be explained with a few basic physical laws instead of a complicated series of numerous principles that explained each type of phenomenon. With these mathematically formulated laws he brought an elegant simplicity to our understanding of nature.

> **Ockham's razor** the principle that we should eliminate (shave off) all unnecessary entities and explanatory principles in our theories

Science and Metaphysics

Speaking of Newton, the thought may have occurred to you, "Isn't it the job of scientists to tell us about reality? What contribution can metaphysics possibly make?" Two quick answers will have to suffice. First, the question, Is there more to reality than that portion that science can discover? is not a scientific question. To ask it we must stand outside of science and philosophically discern its limits and range of competence. If it is possible that reality consists of more than the physical world (e.g., nonphysical minds, God, values), then through philosophical reasoning and not through science alone can we learn whether this dimension exists and what it is like. Second, metaphysics integrates our scientific understanding of the world with our nonscientific concerns. For example, how does our scientific view of the world cohere with the belief that persons have freedom and moral responsibility? The problem is that if we don't understand the distinction between scientific questions and metaphysical questions, we find it too easy to slide from rather well-established scientific theories to controversial philosophical conclusions, not realizing that we have sneaked philosophical assumptions into our science.

In spite of these differences, there are some broad methodological similarities between science and metaphysics. As I pointed out in section 1.3, both science and philosophy evaluate theories on the basis of the six criteria: conceptual clarity, consistency, rational coherence, comprehensiveness, compatibility with well-established facts and theories, and having the support of compelling arguments. Furthermore, both science and metaphysics go beyond what is observed and try to construct large-scale theories that will explain and make sense out of what is observed. Consequently, both science and metaphysics cannot directly verify their theories but must make use of the method of *inference to the best explanation* (see section 1.3).

The Bottom-Line Issue in Metaphysics

ontology the area of metaphysics that asks what is most fundamentally real

Ontology is that area of metaphysics that asks the question, What is most fundamentally real? We briefly examine this question here. Although you will face many other sorts of metaphysical issues, such as the mind-body problem or freedom and determinism, the stance you take on ontology will set the tone for all your other metaphysical inquiries. How do we define *fundamental reality?* If you read between the lines of most metaphysicians' writings, you will find that they use at least two principles for characterizing what is fundamentally real.[1] (1) *Fundamental reality is that upon which everything else depends.* For some people, this reality may be a spiritual reality, such as God. While all theists say that God is the one ultimate reality on which everything depends, some theists say that God has created other, semi-independent realities such as minds, souls, or the physical world. Once God has created these other realities, they say, these things have their own form of existence and cannot be reduced to anything more basic. For other thinkers, fundamental reality may be physical particles, forces, or energy. (2) *Fundamental reality is that which cannot be created or destroyed.* If we found out that what we accept to be fundamentally real could be brought into being or destroyed by something else, then it would be dependent, which would violate the first criterion because there would be something even more fundamental than it. For the theist, God cannot be created or destroyed. On the other hand, if the physical world is ultimate, then it had no beginning. Someone who took this position might say that a table can be created or destroyed but the particles or energy composing it were never created nor can they be destroyed. Given these two principles, and ignoring all the myriads of fascinating details for the moment, every metaphysical theory attempts to lump things into the following three broad categories: things that are not real; realities that can be reduced to more fundamental realities; and things that are fundamentally real.

Things That Are Not Real

Most adults would say, for example, that even though Santa Claus is a pleasant story, he is not real. On the other hand, children for whom Christmas is a part of their family tradition think that Santa Claus is the explanation for the presents under the Christmas tree. As an adult, your metaphysical picture is much simpler. Instead of believing in a world that contains the *three* entities of parents, presents, and Santa, you now believe that the situation only requires the *two* entities of parents and presents and that the former is the cause of the latter. Similarly, for example, some philosophers believe that there are two kinds of events: those that result from deterministic causes and those that result from human free will. Others (analogous to the case of Santa) claim that free will does not exist and that everything, including human actions, can be understood in terms of deterministic causes. This approach could be called the *eliminativist strategy* for simplifying and ordering reality.

Realities That Can Be Reduced to More Fundamental Realities

We frequently talk about "the weather." Do these conversations mean that weather is something that exists? Obviously, weather is not a fiction the way the tooth fairy is. *The weather* is just a term that we use to refer to more basic realities such as temperature, high and low pressure fronts, humidity, precipitation, and so on. Every time we refer to the weather, we are referring to these more basic entities and processes. This is where the issue of appearance and reality comes in. Suppose you are driving along the road on a hot day. You see a puddle of water on the road up ahead, but when you drive closer, it disappears. What you saw appeared to be water, but it really wasn't water. It wasn't nonexistent, for you really did see something. The water vision can be explained in terms of heat waves that duplicate some of the visual appearances of water. Similarly, metaphysicians continually apply the this-is-really-that approach. Some say that "minds are really brain-events"; others claim that "what appears to be a physical object is really a collection of mental events." This approach could be called the *reductionist strategy* in metaphysics.

Things That Are Fundamentally Real

This category is the bottom-line aspect of metaphysics. The question posed here is, What is ultimately real in terms of which everything else can be explained? As you read about each philosopher in this chapter, ask yourself, What does this philosopher believe is the most ultimate reality?

To conclude this overview of metaphysics, I will ask you to develop a sense of your own metaphysical views by ordering a rather common list of items with respect to their reality.

WHAT DO I THINK? *Questionnaire on What Is Most Real*

Rank each of the following items on a scale of 0 to 10 according to its degree of reality. Items that you think don't exist should be given a 0, and items that are most real should be given a 10. Anything in between is a lesser or derivative kind of reality.

Rank		Rank	
	1. Your body.		9. A rose.
	2. Your mind.		10. Beauty.
	3. Einstein's brain.		11. A friend.
	4. Einstein's ideas.		12. Love.
	5. Electrons.		13. The U.S. Supreme Court building.
	6. God.		14. Justice
	7. Your car.		15. A tooth.
	8. Your car appearing in a dream.		16. The tooth fairy.

What sorts of items received a 0? Do they have anything in common? What sorts of items received a 10? Do they have anything in common? What principle(s) did you use to decide if an item was more than 0 but less than 10? Do you think there can be degrees of reality, or is everything either a 0 or 10?

There is no key for your answers because there are too many ways to approach these issues. Instead, keep in mind your rankings as well as your answers to the follow-up questions so that you can compare your position with those we discuss next. We turn now to one of the most difficult issues in philosophy, the mind-body problem.

3.1 OVERVIEW: THE MIND-BODY PROBLEM

SCOUTING THE TERRITORY:
What Is the Mind? What Is the Body?

What is your mind, and what is its relationship to your body? The ancient Greeks wrestled with this mystery and could not resolve it to everyone's satisfaction. The difficulty of the problem is indicated by the fact that it is still with us today, with many competing, alternative solutions being offered and the proponents of each position claiming that theirs is the absolutely correct one. The following story gives one perspective on the controversy.

FROM HUGH ELLIOT

Tantalus[2]

Suppose there existed a Tantalus* who was condemned for evermore to strike with a hammer upon an anvil. Suppose that Tantalus, his hammer, and his anvil were concealed from the observer's view by a screen or otherwise, and that a light, carefully arranged, threw the shadow of the hammer and anvil upon a wall where it could easily be seen. Suppose an observer, whose mind was *tabula rasa* [a blank tablet] were set to watch the shadow. Every time the shadow of the hammer descended upon the shadow of the anvil, the sound of the percussion is heard. The sound is only heard when the two shadows meet. The hammer's shadow occasionally beats fast, occasionally slow: the succession of sounds exactly corresponds. Perhaps the hammer raps out a tune on the anvil; every note heard follows upon a blow visible in the shadows. The two series correspond invariably and absolutely; what is the inevitable effect upon the observer's mind? He knows nothing of the true cause of sound behind the screen: his whole experience is an experience of shadows and sounds. He cannot escape the conclusion that the cause of each sound is the blow which the shadow of the hammer strikes upon the shadow of the anvil.

The observer is in the position of an introspective philosopher. Introspection teaches us nothing about nerve currents or cerebral activity: it speaks in terms of mind and sensation alone. To the introspective philosopher, it is plain that some mental or psychical process is the condition of action. He thinks, he feels, he wills, and then he acts. Therefore the thinking and feeling and willing are the cause of the acting. Introspection *can* get no farther. But now the physiologist intervenes. He skillfully dissects away the screen and behold! there is a real hammer and a real anvil, of which nothing but the shadow was formerly believed to exist. He proves that states of consciousness are shadows accompanying cerebral functioning; he shows that the cause of action lies in the cerebral functioning and not in the shadows which accompany it.

Elliot's point in telling this story is to suggest that we naively think that the cause of all our thoughts, feelings, and activities is a nonphysical mind. However, the mind and its

---

*Tantalus was a figure in Greek mythology who was punished by having to carry out an eternal task.

activities are compared to the shadow images that are really the products of the physical hammer and anvil that lie behind the screen. Eliot believes that the real you is your brain, which is the seat and cause of all your cognitive functioning. What you find in introspection is merely an appearance or an illusion.

However, the metaphor of shadows reminds us of Plato's Allegory of the Cave, discussed in section 1.2. So we could take our cue from Plato and interpret Elliot's story differently than he did. Plato would say that the shadows, or the appearances, in Elliot's story refer to the physical world known by the senses. The real world, according to Plato, represented by the hammer and the anvil behind the screen, is the nonphysical world in which the soul or the mind resides. In introspection, we discover the real world of our minds and their ideas. Because science can only examine physical data, it cannot penetrate the screen of physical events to discover the mental reality behind it.

So we now have two major perspectives. Each one gives a different account of the true cause of our thinking, feeling, and willing. Is the brain the source of all our activities, and what we call *the mind* merely a faulty interpretation of the neurochemical events taking place behind the scenes, as Elliot suggests? Or is it that "behind the screen" of our physical embodiment is a nonphysical mind that is the seat of consciousness through which we control all that we think and do? The nature of the mind and its relationship to the body is one of the most perplexing problems in philosophy. Some philosophers think that recent research on the brain has solved the problem, while others think that it has only made the problem more complex. In the next few sections, I examine the different dimensions of the mind-body problem and the alternative solutions that have been proposed.

THOUGHT EXPERIMENT: *Physical and Mental Properties*

Complete the following six tasks (A1 to B3):

A1. Add to this list five more specific kinds of physical objects: quarters, oxygen atoms, tomatoes, dictionaries, ball bearings, . . .

A2. Add to this list five more specific items that describe properties of various physical objects: green, weighs 10 lb., wet, 30 ft. tall, square, . . .

A3. Add to this list five more types of physical locations, positions, or motions that could describe a friend: across the room, sitting, running, jumping, shouting, waving, . . .

B1. Add to this list five more kinds of mental contents: hopes, ideas, dreams, pains, doubts, . . .

B2. Add to this list five more items that could be used to describe different people's minds: intelligent, imaginative, pessimistic, clever, devious, . . .

B3. Add to this list five more items that describe a mental activity: thinking, guessing, hoping, wondering, doubting, . . .

- Compare the list of properties in A2 with those in B2. Write down some of the general ways in which they differ.
- Compare the list of activities in A3 with those in B3. Write down some of the general ways in which they differ.
- Apply some of the adjectives in A2 to the items in B1 and add a location or some activity in A3 to this description, for example, "A green hope that is sit-

(continued . . .)

(. . . continued)

ting in the car."
- Apply some of the adjectives in B2 and B3 to the items in A1, for example, "intelligent, thinking quarters."

Why is it that we end up with nonsense when we combine items from lists A and B? Of course, these descriptions *could* make sense if we were speaking metaphorically (we could take *sharp* as it applies to knives and speak of a "sharp" mind). However, our concern here is only with literal descriptions. Thus, it seems to make no sense to say that your idea of God is two inches long, weighs one-eighth of a gram, is located precisely three inches away from your idea of justice, and is the color red. Neither could we say that your mind was triangular in shape. Similarly, it makes no sense to say that a beaker of chemicals is doubting or believing. Why?

This exercise illustrates the fact that we have two ways of speaking: words that describe *physical* bodies, properties, and events, and words that describe *mental* contents, properties, and events. Do these two completely different ways of *speaking* suggest that there are two completely different kinds of *reality* (bodies and minds)? If so, what are some other reasons to think that bodies and minds are different sorts of things? On the other hand, if you think the body and the mind are not separate realities, then why is the language of physical events so different from that of mental events?

In addition to the different properties of minds and bodies, there is another issue. This issue has to do with the relation between the mind and the body and arises from the fact that the mind and the body seem to causally affect one another. To explore this issue, follow the instructions in A4 and B4 of the next thought experiment.

THOUGHT EXPERIMENT: *Mental and Physical Causation*

A4. Complete sentences 3 and 4, and in sentence 5, add one or more specific examples of your own about how your mind affects your body:

1. I worry (mental event) and lose my appetite (physical event).
2. I think I am driving too fast, so I press the brake.
3. I desire to have another piece of pizza, and my hand . . .
4. I decide to vote for a particular candidate, and I . . .
5.

B4. Complete sentences 3 and 4, and in sentence 5, add one or more specific examples of your own about how your body affects your mind:

1. I drink too much coffee (physical event), causing me to become irritable (mental event).
2. I stub my toe, and I experience pain.
3. I didn't get any sleep last night, and in class, my mind . . .
4. Someone special hugs me, and I feel . . .
5.

This exercise suggests that not only do we commonly think of the mind and body as two different things, but we think of them as interacting. Some mental events seem to cause physical events, and some physical events seem to cause mental events. Even though we ordinarily speak this way, philosophers make it their task to examine our taken-for-granted assumptions. In the final analysis, we might conclude that there are good philosophical reasons for our ordinary ways of speaking. On the other hand, we may find that these common assumptions need to be clarified, revised, or even abandoned.

CHARTING THE TERRAIN OF THE MIND-BODY PROBLEM: *What Are the Issues?*

The previous exercises support three commonsense beliefs that characterize our traditional concept of the mind and the body:

1. The body is a physical thing.
2. The mind is a nonphysical thing.
3. The mind and body interact and causally affect one another.

Having listed these beliefs, we still face one nagging problem: Exactly how does a nonphysical thing (the mind) interact with a physical thing (the body)? Physical things interact by pushing, pulling, merging, energizing, attracting, magnetizing, and so forth. However, all these sorts of interactions involve physical forces that can be explained by the laws of physics. Most people, if asked, would tend to agree with the statement, "The motion of a physical body is completely subject to physical laws." However, if the mind is not a physical thing, then it cannot affect a body through gravitational, electrical, magnetic, or mechanical force. How, then, can there be any causal relationship between the mind and body? To explain this interaction by referring to the brain is of very little help, because the brain is simply another sort of physical body. The difficulty in understanding how a nonphysical thing such as the mind can have any causal interaction with a physical body suggests a fourth proposition:

4. Nonphysical things cannot causally interact with physical things.

We now seem to have four, equally plausible propositions, but they cannot all be true. You can believe any combination of three of them, but when you add the remaining proposition, you end up in a contradiction. It seems that we are forced to decide which one of the four preceding propositions we are going to reject. Unfortunately, there is a price to pay for rejecting any of them, and that price is the necessity of rejecting the commonsense reasons that led us to think that particular belief was plausible in the first place. As we will see, each of the positions on the mind-body problem avoids the difficulty by rejecting one of the four propositions. In the "Philosophy in the Marketplace" survey, you and your friends will be asked how you avoid the difficulty by indicating which of the four statements you reject.

mind-body dualism
the claim that the mind and the body (which includes the brain) are separate entities

CHOOSING A PATH: *What Are My Options Concerning the Mind and the Body?*

A number of positions have been taken on the mind-body problem, but two of them stand out as being the most significant alternatives. These positions are mind-body dualism and physicalism. **Mind-body dualism** is the claim that the mind and the body (which includes

Answer the following questions yourself, and ask them of five of your friends.

- At this point in your thinking, which three of the following statements do you believe the most strongly? Or, in other words, which one of the four statements do you think is the least plausible?
- What are your reasons for your three affirmative choices and your one negative choice?

1. The body is a physical thing.
2. The mind is a nonphysical thing.
3. The mind and body interact and causally affect one another.
4. Nonphysical things cannot causally interact with physical things.

the brain) are separate entities. The body is a physical thing, whereas the mind is a nonphysical (immaterial or spiritual) thing. (For the sake of brevity, whenever I discuss dualism with respect to the mind and body in the remainder of this chapter, I will refer to mind-body dualism as simply *dualism*.) **Physicalism** is the claim that the self is identical to, or the product of, the activities of the body or the brain and that there is no nonphysical aspect of a person.

physicalism the theory that human beings can be explained completely and adequately in terms of their physical or material components

interactionism a type of dualism that claims that the mind and body, though different, causally interact with one another

The most common version of dualism is called **interactionism.** Interactionism adds to the dualistic thesis the claim that the mind and body, though different, causally interact with one another. This version of dualism was defended by the 17th-century French philosopher Descartes and represents the commonsense view of the issue that we explored earlier. Note that many religious views commonly identify the real person with his or her soul, which is said to be a nonphysical or spiritual entity. In discussing dualism, we will assume that the terms *soul* and *mind* may be used interchangeably, because they both refer to the nonphysical component within us that constitutes the real person.

To get a clearer picture of these two philosophies, let's see how each position would explain an everyday event like answering the phone. Dualistic interactionism can be represented by the following diagram. The symbol BS stands for a brain state or event, and the symbol MS stands for a mental state or event.

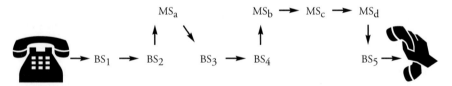

Dualistic Interactionism. The phone rings, causing electrical signals to be sent to the brain (BS_1). These electrical signals cause other brain states (BS_2), which produce the sensation of sound in the mind (MS_a). This mental event causes more brain activity (BS_3, BS_4), which causes the mental event of recognizing that the phone is ringing (MS_b). This mental event, or thought, causes the desire to pick up the phone (MS_c). This mental desire leads to the mental act of willing to pick up the phone (MS_d). This mental act sets in motion further brain activity (BS_5), which causes your hand to pick up the phone.

Keeping the original labels of the brain states the same, let's transform the mental states into brain states. We now have the physicalist's diagram of the same event.

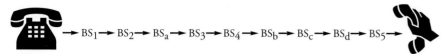

$\rightarrow BS_1 \rightarrow BS_2 \rightarrow BS_a \rightarrow BS_3 \rightarrow BS_4 \rightarrow BS_b \rightarrow BS_c \rightarrow BS_d \rightarrow BS_5 \rightarrow$

Physicalism. The phone rings, causing electrical signals to be sent to the brain (BS_1). These electrical signals cause other brain states (BS_2), which produce the sensation of sound (BS_a). This sensation causes more brain activity (BS_3, BS_4), which produces the recognition that the phone is ringing (BS_b). This recognition causes you to want to pick up the phone (BS_c), which causes you to decide to pick up the phone (BS_d), which causes more brain activity (BS_5), which causes your hand to pick up the phone. Some brain states are unconscious (BS_1 to BS_5), while some brain states operate at a very high level that we call consciousness (BS_a to BS_d). Nevertheless, whether conscious or not, the physicalist claims that all events are neurochemical events in the brain.

Even though interactionism and physicalism are the most common positions throughout the history of philosophy, there are other options worth mentioning. The overview of metaphysics at the beginning of this chapter discussed idealism. Idealism is like the photographic negative of physicalism. Whereas the physicalist says that human beings are nothing but matter, the idealist says that human beings (and all of reality) are nothing but mental substances. The idealist solves the mind-body problem by believing that the mind and the body are not really two different, irreducible kinds of reality. Instead, the idealist claims, the physical world and the body are just a collection of mental experiences or are aspects of a larger mental reality. The idealist's view of the mind has been presented previously in discussing the views of George Berkeley in section 2.3.

There are also different varieties of physicalism. The two most common versions are **identity theory** (or **reductionism**) and **eliminativism.** Even though identity theorists deny that there is a separate, nonphysical mind, they think it is meaningful to talk about the mind because they claim that all talk about the mind can be translated into talk about brain states. On the other hand, the eliminativist thinks that our mental vocabulary should be eliminated altogether in favor of a physiological vocabulary. Hence, for the eliminativists, to talk about whether the mind is or is not physical or whether it does or does not interact with the body is like asking, "Are leprechauns in favor of nuclear disarmament?" or "Do ghosts enjoy modern art?" Once you have decided that leprechauns and ghosts do not exist, these questions are meaningless. Similarly, the eliminativists want to discard all language that refers to mental events because they believe there are no such things.

The various positions that we have discussed are summarized in table 3.2 in terms of their answers to five questions.

Notice that table 3.2 contains five questions and four positions. Each one of the positions avoids the mind-body problem by answering *No* to one of the questions. Both varieties of physicalists refrain from answering the fifth question because they do not think there is any nonphysical mental reality at all. The eliminativists also refrain from answering questions 3 and 4 because they deny that the term *mind* refers to anything.

One more position, called **functionalism,** is discussed in a later section. Functionalism could not be placed on the chart because its advocates question the way that the mind-body issue has been divided up in the chart. They reject the dualist's claim that the mind is a separate substance. Yet they reject the identity theorist's claim that mental events are identical to brain events. They also reject the eliminativist's claim that there are no mental events. Instead, functionalists argue that the realm of the mental is characterized by particular patterns of input-processing-output. Hence, functionalists claim that the brain is like the physical hardware of the computer and the mind is like the computer program that

identity theory a type of physicalism that denies the existence of a separate, nonphysical mind but retains language that refers to the mind; also called reductionism

reductionism see identity theory

eliminativism a type of physicalism that denies the existence of a separate, nonphysical mind and discards all language that refers to mental events

functionalism a philosophy that claims that the mind is characterized by particular patterns of input-processing-output

TABLE 3.2 *Positions on the Mind-Body Problem*

	Is the Body a Physical Thing?	Do We Have a Mind?	Is the Mind a Nonphysical Thing?	Do the Mind and Body Interact?	Is It Impossible for a Nonphysical Thing to Interact with a Physical Thing?
Dualism: Interactionism	Yes	Yes	Yes	Yes	No
Idealism	No	Yes	Yes	Yes	Yes
Physicalism: Identity Theory (Reductionism)	Yes	Yes	No	Yes	—
Physicalism: Eliminativism	Yes	No	—	—	—

is run on the hardware but is logically distinct from it. In sections 3.2, 3.3, and 3.4, we take a closer look at dualism, physicalism, and functionalism, respectively.

WHAT DO I THINK? *Questionnaire on Mind-Body*

Before reading any further, complete this survey. Express your opinion by putting an X in the appropriate box to the right of each statement. If you agree with the statement, mark "Agree" and if you disagree, mark "Disagree." Do not write anything in the boxes that are shaded. You may not feel strongly one way or another and wish to say "undecided." However, you must mark whichever answer seems *most* likely to you at this point. This questionnaire is only a survey of your opinions, so there are no right or wrong answers for the purposes of this exercise.

	A1	B	A2
1. The physical world is the only kind of reality there is.	Agree	Disagree	
2. The mind is something nonphysical yet real.		Agree	Disagree
3. The *mind* is nothing more than a word that refers to the sum of those cognitive activities produced by the brain.	Agree	Disagree	
4. The mind and the brain interact even though they are different entities.		Agree	Disagree
5. When I make a decision, the immediate cause of this event is the physical events occurring in my brain.	Agree	Disagree	
6. The act of making a mental decision is *not* a physical event, *nor* does it have a physical cause.		Agree	Disagree
7. A physical event can be caused only by another physical event.	Agree	Disagree	

(continued . . .)

	A1	B	A2
8. An act of my will is *not* a physical event, but it can cause my body to perform some physical action.		Agree	Disagree
9. Even if we cannot accomplish this as yet, everything that a person does or thinks or feels is capable of a scientific explanation.	Agree	Disagree	
10. The mind and its activities will never be completely explained by the science of the brain.		Agree	Disagree
	A1	**B**	**A2**

KEY TO THE MIND-BODY QUESTIONNAIRE

Add up all the answers you checked in column A1. (This column has only "Agree" answers.) Place this total in the box marked A1 at the bottom of the column. Next, add up all the answers you checked in column A2. (This column has only "Disagree" answers.) Place this total in the box marked A2 at the bottom of the column. Add together the scores in boxes A1 and A2 and place the total in the shaded box here. Finally, add together all the answers (both "Agree" and "Disagree") that you checked in column B. Transfer this total to the unshaded box below.

A1 + A2 = [shaded box]   B = [unshaded box]

The shaded box (A1 + A2) represents the position of physicalism. The unshaded box (B) represents the position of dualism. Whichever box contains the larger number is the position closest to your own. As I have mentioned, other positions can be taken on the mind-body problem (such as functionalism) that disagree with the dichotomies assumed by this questionnaire. Nevertheless, if you had to choose between dualism and physicalism, this questionnaire does indicate which position you would favor.

3.2 DUALISM

LEADING QUESTIONS: *Dualism*

1. In the movie *All of Me,* the mind of the character played by Lily Tomlin took over the body of the character played by Steve Martin. Of course, the premise of one person inhabiting another's body provided a great deal of slapstick comedy material. In spite of the improbability of such an event, is it still conceivable? Can you imagine remaining the person you are while inhabiting a different body?

2. Can you imagine yourself witnessing your own funeral? Is it conceivable that you could see your body in the casket, with your grieving friends silently viewing it, while you were a bodiless spirit or a center of consciousness watching this event from a remote

position? Whether or not you believe in personal immortality, is it possible to at least imagine this scenario?

3. Most of us spend a great deal of time communicating with computers. Our computers send us messages such as, "You used an invalid filename." Through artificial intelligence research, computers have developed extraordinary abilities. They now can play very challenging games with chess masters. No matter how technologically advanced computers become, however, will they ever have minds? When you play chess, you are conscious and aware of what is going on. However, can we imagine that the collection of circuits and software in a computer will someday produce consciousness? In the final analysis, isn't the computer a calculating machine that lacks anything approaching the internal subjective experience you have?

4. You can frequently know what is going on in someone's mind. For example, a person's facial expression can reveal that he or she is experiencing puzzlement, joy, anger, fear, or boredom. But in spite of these ways in which our bodies and behavior give clues of our mental life, isn't a large portion of what is going on in your mind private and known by you alone? Isn't there a rather clear boundary between your private mental contents and that part of you that is public?

The assumptions underlying these questions represent some very traditional and common intuitions about the mind and the body. Even though our mind and our body seem to be joined together throughout our lives, most people can imagine the possibility of the two existing separately. But even though we think we can imagine this possibility, is it really coherent? Furthermore, even if it is coherent, are there any reasons to suppose that the mind actually is separate from the body? The dualist wants to convince you that the answer to both of these questions is yes.

SURVEYING THE CASE FOR DUALISM

The 17th-century philosopher René Descartes is not merely a representative of mind-body dualism; he is its most famous advocate. Hence, we can get a very good look at dualism by surveying Descartes's views.

In the section on skepticism (section 2.1), we examined Descartes's attempts to find certainty by doubting every one of his beliefs to see if any withstood critical examination. The one belief he could not doubt was "I exist." However, the certainty of his own existence applied only to his existence as a mind, a mental substance distinct from his body. Descartes believed he was directly and immediately acquainted with his mind or his consciousness, but his belief that he had a physical body that existed in the external world was simply something he inferred from his physical sensations. The problem is that in dreams and hallucinations we can experience bodily sensations that are illusions and that do not reflect what is really in the external world. As I pointed out in the discussion of rationalism, however, when Descartes developed his rationalistic proof for the existence of God, this problem was solved. Because he found the existence of a perfect God rationally irrefutable, he was confident that this God would not allow him to be massively deceived about the existence of his own body and the external world.

Based on these considerations, Descartes concluded not only that he was not just a mind but also that his mind was associated with a body. The picture that emerges is that human beings are made up of two different kinds of reality that are somehow linked together. On the one hand, we have bodies and are a part of the physical world. According to Descartes, the body is a machine made out of flesh and bone. Your joints and tendons act like pivots, pulleys, and ropes. Your heart is a pump and your lungs are bellows. Because the body is a physical thing, it is subject to the laws of physics and is located in space and time. According to Descartes, animals are also machines, and their behavior is sheerly a product of mechanical laws. Humans, however, are unique in that in addition to their bodies, they also possess minds. According to Descartes, your mind (which is identical to your soul and your consciousness) is the "real" you. If you lose an arm or a leg, your bodily mechanism is impaired but you are still as complete a person as before. Descartes's position can be called mind-body dualism, or *psychophysical dualism*. Since Descartes has given the classic statement of this position, it is also commonly referred to as *Cartesian dualism* in his honor.

DESCARTES'S ARGUMENTS FOR MIND-BODY DUALISM

Descartes's Basic Premise

Descartes offers several arguments to convince us that the mind and body are two separate realities. Although he argues for his dualism in a number of different ways, implicit within all his arguments is the same basic premise, often labeled the *Principle of the Nonidentity of Discernibles:* If two things do not have exactly identical properties, then they are not identical.

On the face of it, this principle seems to be fairly clear and obvious. For two things to really be the same thing, they must have the same properties. If there are discernible differences between them, then they must be different things. For example, the 19th-century figure Samuel Clemens and the popular American writer Mark Twain are the same individual. Hence, anything that is true of the person designated by "Samuel Clemens" will be true of the person referred to by "Mark Twain" and vice versa. On the other hand, according to this strict definition of identity, so-called identical twins are different persons who have some very basic similarities. If nothing else, they differ (or are discernible) because they occupy different portions of space.

Let's examine a practical application of this principle. Suppose Ziggy is accused of breaking down the locked cafeteria door with an axe and stealing a banana cream pie. The crime lab analyzes the blows to the door and determines that the thief had to be left-handed and more than six feet tall. Furthermore, the police discover blond hairs on the discarded axe that obviously belong to the trespasser. However, Ziggy is right-handed, five feet tall, and has black hair. Because the properties of Ziggy differ from the properties of the thief, the two cannot be the same person. Therefore, Ziggy is innocent.

 THOUGHT EXPERIMENT: *Applying Descartes's Principle*

Apply the method of reasoning we just learned to the mind-body problem.

- List typical properties of minds that differ from the properties of bodies.
- Does it seem as though these differences are sufficient to establish that the mind and the body are different things?
- In the discussion that follows, see how your list compares with Descartes's.

Descartes has a standard form of argument that he frequently uses to show that the mind and body are different. This form of argument makes use of the Principle of the Nonidentity of Discernibles, because he examines the properties both of minds and of bodies to show that minds and bodies are different sorts of realities. These arguments for dualism have this generic form:

1. The body has property A.
2. The mind has property non-A.
3. If two things do not have exactly identical properties, then they cannot be identical.
4. Therefore, the mind and the body are not identical. They are two completely different entities.

The Argument from Doubt

One of Descartes's central arguments is based on what can and cannot be doubted. In his *Discourse on the Method* he recounts his journey out of skepticism when he realized he could not doubt his own existence, even though he could doubt the existence of the external world, including his own body.

FROM RENÉ DESCARTES

Discourse on the Method[3]

Next I examined attentively what I was. I saw that while I could pretend that I had no body and that there was no world and no place for me to be in, I could not for all that pretend that I did not exist. I saw on the contrary that from the mere fact that I thought of doubting the truth of other things, it followed quite evidently and certainly that I existed. . . . From this I knew I was a substance whose whole essence or nature is simply to think, and which does not require any place, or depend on any material thing, in order to exist. Accordingly this "I"—that is, the soul by which I am what I am—is entirely distinct from the body, and indeed is easier to know than the body, and would not fail to be whatever it is, even if the body did not exist.

Descartes's argument could be expressed like this:

The Argument from Doubt

1. I can doubt my body exists.
2. I cannot doubt my mind exists.
3. If two things do not have exactly identical properties, then they cannot be identical.
4. Therefore, the mind and the body are not identical.

Premises 1 and 2 identify two different properties of the body and the mind that Descartes discovered when he employed his method of doubt. He found he could be absolutely certain of his mind, but because of the possibility of illusion (dreams and hallucinations), he could be mistaken and hence uncertain about the existence of his body. Descartes offered this argument as a logical proof that the mind and the body could not be the same thing.

This argument has problems, however. The property of being subject to doubt is not the same sort of property as being 6 feet tall or being bald. The fact that I can doubt something is as much a psychological property of me as it is of the object of my doubt. To see the difficulties with this argument, consider the following argument that has essentially the same form:

1. I am in doubt as to whether the 16th president of the United States ever had a beard.
2. I am not in doubt that Abraham Lincoln had a beard.
3. If two things do not have exactly identical properties, then they cannot be identical.
4. Therefore, the 16th president of the United States and Abraham Lincoln are not identical.

Everyone knows that Lincoln had a beard, but some people are not sure about whether the 16th president did. The problem is that some people do not realize that Abraham Lincoln was the 16th president of the United States. Hence, it is possible that Descartes is more certain about his mind than he is of his body simply because he does not understand the nature of each fully enough to see that they are identical.

The Argument from Divisibility

The following argument makes use of the same argument form as before but avoids the difficulty of dealing with our psychological attitudes. See if you can extract the outline of the argument from this passage.

FROM RENÉ DESCARTES

Meditations on First Philosophy [4]

The first observation I make at this point is that there is a great difference between the mind and the body, inasmuch as the body is by its very nature always divisible, while the mind is utterly indivisible. For when I consider the mind, or myself in so far as I am merely a thinking thing, I am unable to distinguish any parts within myself; I understand myself to be something quite single and complete. Although the whole mind seems to be united to the whole body, I recognize that if a foot or arm or any other part of the body is cut off, nothing has thereby been taken away from the mind. As for the faculties of willing, of understanding, of sensory perception and so on, these cannot be termed parts of the mind, since it is one and the same mind that wills, and understands and has sensory perceptions. By contrast, there is no corporeal or extended thing that I can think of which in my thought I cannot easily divide into parts; and this very fact makes me understand that it is divisible. This one argument would be enough to show me that the mind is completely different from the body, even if I did not already know as much from other considerations.

Using the same generic argument form as before, we could summarize the previous passage in this way:

The Argument from Divisibility

1. The body is divisible.
2. The mind is indivisible.
3. If two things do not have exactly identical properties, then they cannot be identical.
4. Therefore, the mind and the body are not identical.

In this argument, Descartes's first premise is based on the notion that all material objects are spatially extended and anything spatially extended is divisible. Hence, because the body is a material object, it can always be divided in two and divided and divided again (as in an autopsy).

It seems easy enough to grant Descartes the truth of the first premise, but what about the second premise? Certainly if we assume that the mind is a spiritual substance, then because a spiritual thing lacks extension, it cannot be divided (or at least divided in the way a body is). But the notion that the mind is a spiritual entity is what Descartes is trying to prove, so simply assuming this point seems to beg the question. Without making this assumption, can we simply look at our mental experience and discover that, whatever the mind might be, it is not the sort of thing that has parts or can be divided? Or is Descartes's second premise questionable? Is it possible for the mind to have divisions or distinguishable parts in some sense?

STOP AND THINK

Have you ever felt as though you were of "two minds" about something? Have you ever felt conflicts or tensions within your mind? Have you ever experienced conflicts between memories, beliefs, or feelings? Do these sorts of divisions within the mind count against Descartes's premise 2? What would he say?

Some would argue, contrary to Descartes, that our mental life seems to be divided. For example, we can feel both love and anger at the same time toward someone. Or we frequently find that our moral principles pull us in one direction and our feelings in another. The annals of psychiatry are full of cases of multiple personalities, or cases in which someone knows some discomforting fact in one part of the psyche while another part of the person's mind works overtime to deny it. One type of brain surgery, known as cerebral commissurotomy, is commonly used to treat epilepsy. The surgeon severs the bundle of nerves (the corpus callosum) that connects the two hemispheres of the brain. Patients with these split brains experience a fragmentation within their experience. The part of the brain that processes visual data cannot communicate with the part that processes things linguistically. These considerations seem to indicate that whatever it is that makes up the mind, it is something that has components. This conclusion at least makes plausible the suggestion that different parts of our brain produce different facets of our mental life and, hence, results in diluting the sharp distinction Descartes is trying to draw here between the mind and the body.

The Argument from Consciousness

Yet another argument can be found in Descartes's writings, one that is based on the fact that his mind is a thinking thing while his body is not. By *thinking* Descartes does not simply mean *reasoning*. Descartes uses the word *thinking* to refer to the entire range of conscious states such as knowing, doubting, wishing, willing, imagining, sensing, and so on. Hence, his point is that his mind is unlike anything in the natural world, because he is conscious. By way of contrast, Descartes says that "when I examine the nature of the body, I find nothing at all in it which savours of thought."[5] The argument from consciousness (or thinking) is found in passages such as the following one.

Meditations on First Philosophy[6]

Thus, simply by knowing that I exist and seeing at the same time that absolutely nothing else belongs to my nature or essence except that I am a thinking thing, I can infer correctly that my essence consists solely in the fact that I am a thinking thing. It is true that I may have (or to anticipate, that I certainly have) a body that is very closely joined to me. But nevertheless, on the one hand I have a clear and distinct idea of myself, in so far as I am simply a thinking, non-extended thing; and on the other hand I have a distinct idea of body, in so far as this is simply an extended, non-thinking thing. And accordingly, it is certain that I [that is, my soul, by which I am what I am], am really distinct from my body, and can exist without it.

The outline of the argument from consciousness follows the outlines of previous arguments, except that Descartes includes the premise that "material objects cannot have the property of consciousness." Because the body is a material object, it cannot be conscious, but we know from our own immediate experience that our mind is conscious. From these premises, Descartes arrives again at his dualist conclusion.

STOP AND THINK

Do you think the argument from consciousness supports the theory that the mind is different from the body? Why? How might a physicalist respond to this alleged difference between the mind and the body?

Descartes's Compromise

Descartes's theory of dualism has sometimes been called the Cartesian compromise. Descartes was an enthusiastic champion of the new, mechanistic science. He was also a sincere Catholic. One of his concerns, therefore, was to reconcile the scientific and religious views of the world. By dividing reality up into completely separate territories, he was able to accomplish this goal. One part of reality is made up of physical substances that can be studied by science and explained by mechanistic principles. This part of the universe is a giant, clocklike mechanism. All events in this realm are determined by the laws that physicists discover. Hence, we make observations, formulate physical laws, and make accurate predictions about physical events. In so far as we are bodies, science can explain our physical motions. The other part of reality consists of mental or spiritual substances. Our minds are free to think and will as we wish because mental substances are not governed by mechanical laws. In this way, persons (unlike their bodies) have genuine free will. If you jump into a swimming pool, for example, the falling of your body is governed by the laws of nature. Your decision to make that jump, however, is freely chosen and cannot be explained by physics.

In the physical realm, science is the dominant authority and gives us the truth. We do not consult the Church or the Bible to see how fast the heart pumps its blood; science informs us about such facts. But according to the Cartesian compromise, science cannot tell us about the eternal destiny of our souls, it can tell us only about our bodies. Hence, in the spiritual realm, says Descartes, religion still retains its authority and truth.

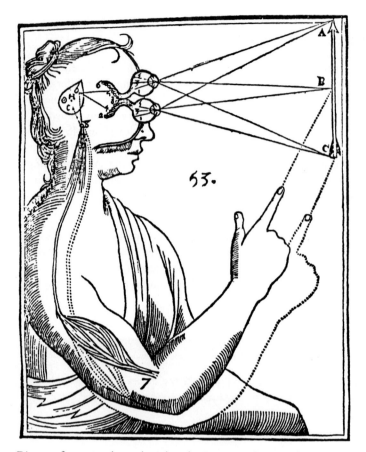

Diagram from a work on physiology by Descartes showing the pineal gland, optical system, and nerve bundles. Descartes believed this gland to be the locus of the soul (mind) and its point of contact, or interaction, with the body.

Descartes had one remaining problem. Although the mind and body are separate, he was convinced that they interact. Accordingly, Descartes's specific version of dualism is called *interactionism.* It seems easy to understand how mental entities interact (one idea leads to the thought of another idea), and it seems easy to understand how physical entities interact (a billiard ball collides with another one, setting it in motion). The problem is, however, how can a spiritual substance (the mind) causally interact with a physical substance (the body)?

Descartes was well aware of this problem; nevertheless, his attempts to answer this question were the least satisfactory part of his philosophy. In his day, scientists were aware of the existence of the pineal gland, but they did not know what the gland did. So, Descartes had an organ (the pineal gland) whose function was unknown. He had a function (mind-body interaction) whose location was unknown. He concluded that he could solve both these problems with one hypothesis: The pineal gland is where the mind and body interact. Descartes thought that the pineal gland was affected by "vital spirits," and through this intermediary, the soul could alter the motions in the brain, which then could affect the body and vice versa.[7] Obviously, explaining mind-body interaction by referring to the pineal gland does not solve the problem, because this gland is merely another material object that is part of the body. If the "vital spirits" that mediate the causal interaction are some sort of physical force like magnetism, then we still do not know how the physical can affect the mental and vice versa. The same problem exists if "vital spirits" are mental in nature.

LOOKING THROUGH THE DUALIST'S LENS

1. How does the dualist's view of the mind and body imply that scientific, physical explanations of persons are incomplete?

2. How does dualism allow for deterministic explanations of nature while preserving human freedom?

3. How does dualism allow for a compromise between science and religion?

4. How does dualism serve to explain immortality?

5. If you were a disciple of Descartes, how would you improve on his explanation of the interaction of the mind and body?

6. Artificial intelligence programs are now able to play superior chess and do many other tasks that duplicate what human intelligence can accomplish. What would be Descartes's view of artificial intelligence programs? Would he agree that computers can think? Why?

EXAMINING THE STRENGTHS AND WEAKNESSES OF DUALISM

Positive Evaluation

1. Descartes's view allows him to accept the scientific account of the physical world while retaining traditional notions of the mind and human freedom. How important is this advantage?

2. Descartes's view claims that the properties of matter could never produce something as mysterious and marvelous as consciousness or self-awareness, because these qualities could come only from a type of reality that is nonmaterial. Do you think Descartes's theory explains consciousness better than any physicalist theory ever could?

Negative Evaluation

1. Descartes had a major problem explaining how a nonspatial mind can influence a spatially located brain. Do you think Descartes's account of where and how mind-body interaction takes place is satisfactory? If not, can you even conceive of another explanation that does not fall into the same problems?

2. If the mind is the seat of our mental life and consciousness whereas the body is simply a machine made out of flesh, as Descartes thought, why does physical damage to the brain have such a dramatic effect on a person's mental life?

3. What happens to your mind when you are knocked unconscious or are given anesthesia? Both situations cause a disruption to the brain's normal functioning. But if the mind is separate from the body, we would expect that in these situations we would continue to experience mental awareness even though the connections between the mind, the brain, and the body were temporarily impaired. If the real you is your mind, and your mind

is identical to your conscious mental life, as Descartes maintains, then where does your mind (and you) go when you are unconscious?

 ## LEADING QUESTIONS: *Physicalism*

1. Why is it not a good idea to have an all-night party before a big test? Why do the labels on cough and allergy medicines caution against driving or operating machinery while taking the medicine? Why do most people have trouble concentrating in class after they have had a big meal? What effects do multiple cups of coffee tend to have on a person's mental state or temperament? Why do these sorts of changes in our bodies affect not only our physical performance but our mental performance as well?

2. Why do animals such as frogs or rabbits have relatively small brains, whereas high-level mammals such as dogs, apes, and humans have larger and more complex brains? Why is there a correlation between the size and complexity of the brain and the level of intelligent behavior exhibited by a species?

3. You think to yourself, "I am thirsty." You then decide to get a drink. Obediently, your hand reaches out to grab a glass of ice water. How did your thoughts produce this motion in the physical world? What sort of links in the causal chain run from your thoughts to your body's muscles?

4. We know that our nervous system automatically governs such functions as our digestion and heartbeat apart from our conscious control of them. However, we like to think that our mental life is under our conscious control. But how do we explain the fact that images, thoughts, or unpleasant memories spontaneously intrude into our consciousness? Why is it that thinking about one idea often will cause another idea to spring up unexpectedly within our mind? How can the contents of our minds be affected by causes that we do not voluntarily control?

SURVEYING THE CASE FOR PHYSICALISM

Both the problems with dualism and our increasing knowledge of how the brain functions have led some philosophers to the proposal that the mind is not a special kind of non-physical entity that somehow interacts with the body. One of the leading alternatives to mind-body dualism is physicalism, the theory that human beings can be explained completely and adequately in terms of their physical or material components. Accordingly, the physicalist claims that when we talk about the mind or mental processes, we are really talking about something physical (such as brain activity) or else we are talking about something that doesn't exist at all. There are many varieties of physicalistic theories of the person. The psychological theory of behaviorism, for example, is a form of physicalism (behaviorism is discussed under the topic of freedom and determinism). Some versions of functionalism are also examples of physicalism (see section 3.4). The two versions of physicalism I discuss in this section are identity theory (or reductionism) and eliminative materialism.

Most physicalists claim that *all* elements of reality (not just human beings) are 100 percent physical and capable of being explained by science. This claim implies that there are no spiritual or supernatural realities (such as God), and such physicalists would embrace metaphysical materialism. However, because a few theists are physicalists *only* with regard

Discuss the following questions with at least five acquaintances.

1. What is the mind?
2. Is the mind identical to the brain and its activities? Why?
3. If the answer to question 2 was yes, then answer question 5(a).
4. If the answer to question 2 was no, then answer question 5(b).
5. (a) If the mind is really identical to the brain's activities, how can you control or be responsible for your thoughts, values, and choices, since they are simply the outcome of impersonal, determined, neurochemical processes?
   (b) If the mind and brain are different, how is it possible for them to causally interact?

PHILOSOPHY *in the* MARKETPLACE

to the mind-body problem, I will use the term *physicalism* in a narrow sense to refer only to a certain position within the philosophy of mind. Basically, the physicalist's case rests on two pillars. The first pillar is the problems with dualism, which the physicalist believes are unsolvable. The second pillar is based on all the progress that has been made in brain science. Next I present each of these pillars in turn.

The Problems with Dualism

Many arguments have been raised against Cartesian dualism. However, the following four considerations are among those arguments that are raised most frequently.

Where Does Interaction Take Place?

The most common form of dualism is dualistic interactionism, which is the twofold claim that (1) the mind and body are separate entities and (2) they are capable of causal interaction. This position was defended by Descartes and is a position that retains a great deal of commonsense appeal to the average person. Because dualistic interactionism is the most popular version of dualism, it's the version I discuss here. Although dualistic interactionism is a very common position, it has a number of problems. Its critics have raised the question of where this interaction takes place. Every brain event has a physical location, but a nonphysical mental event could not. Yet, if the mind is to interact with the body (presumably through the brain), it would seem that this interaction would have to take place in some spatial location. Descartes suggested that the pineal gland is this location. However, we now have no reason to believe that the pineal gland plays any role with respect to consciousness, and there are no other plausible candidates to take its place. So dualists have a major gap in their story of the person.

How Does Interaction Occur?

Every physical event involves the employment of force. Physicists understand force as the product of mass and acceleration. But if nonphysical mental events have neither mass nor motion, how can they exert the force necessary to cause changes in the physical world? Mental events cannot push or pull physical objects. Neither can they electrically stimulate them nor exert gravitational or magnetic force on them. In other words, mental events cannot employ the sort of causality that produces changes in the physical world. Furthermore, since mental events are nonphysical, it would seem that they cannot be affected by the sorts of causal forces that operate within the body. Therefore, it seems impossible for minds to affect bodies and vice versa.

What about the Conservation of Energy?

A fundamental principle that is essential to science is the principle that the amount of energy in a closed physical system remains constant. To set a billiard ball in motion requires us to expend some energy. This energy is transformed into the ball's motion as well as the heat that is produced by friction. Because energy is a physical property, it cannot be found in a nonmaterial mind. But if your body is set in motion by a mental event, then new energy has entered the world and the principle of the conservation of energy is violated. Similarly, if motion in your body is translated into a nonmaterial mental event, then energy has been lost from the physical world.

What about the Success of Brain Science?

A standard principle in forming scientific theories is the principle of simplicity (see the discussion of Ockham's razor in section 3.0). The physicalist claims that if we can account for all "mental" phenomena in terms of brain events, then the notion of a nonmaterial mind becomes extraneous. Once research on the brain is complete, we will not be plagued by the mysteries of the mind-body problem because this problematic dualism will no longer exist. The physicalist claims that we already know enough about the brain and how it affects cognition to be confident that brain events tell the whole story about us.

THOUGHT EXPERIMENT: *The Case of the Missing Socks*

While doing our laundry, we all have had the experience of pulling our clothes out of the dryer, only to discover that one sock is missing. Often, we will search everywhere and not be able to find the missing sock. After a time we may even build up a whole collection of single socks that lack a partner. Imagine that someone proposed the theory that a species of invisible, alien beings called "sockgrabbers" is inhabiting laundry rooms. The sockgrabbers steal our socks, eat them, and through some mysterious process convert them into energy that sustains their form of life.

- Would you find this theory plausible? Why?
- The sockgrabber believer can argue that we have irrefutable evidence that something is taking the socks, because they frequently disappear without a trace. How might you argue, against the believer, that it is irrational to believe in sockgrabbers?
- How might Ockham's razor be used to question the plausibility of the sockgrabber theory?

Obviously most of us would reject the sockgrabber theory. It just does not fit with everything we know about the world. This theory answers one question (Where did the socks go?) but leaves too many other, unanswerable questions in its wake. Besides, there is a much simpler account. We frequently lose things (e.g., keys, reading glasses, library cards), and sometimes we find them again and sometimes we do not. However, even when we cannot find an item, we have no reason to suppose that it just vanished or was eaten by some sort of invisible creature. Even if we think we put only complete pairs of socks in the wash, we could be mistaken. Hence, this commonsense theory allows us to account for the data in question in a way that is consistent with the rest of our knowledge about the world. The chief virtue of this approach is that we do not need to postulate additional, unobservable entities such as sockgrabbers who have mysterious properties unlike anything else in reality. The point of the story is obvious. The physicalist believes that explaining the activities of the person by referring to an immaterial mind is analogous to explaining the missing socks by referring to invisible, alien sockgrabbers. In both cases, there is a simpler, scientific, and physicalistic explanation.

The Positive Case for Physicalism

The second pillar of physicalism is the positive case based on brain research. For example, scientists have studied people who have suffered damage to various portions of the brain and have found that different kinds of brain damage produce regular and specific breakdowns in a person's psychological functioning. Also, studying the activities of normal brains with our sophisticated medical instruments shows that when a person is performing a certain task (imagining a scene, speaking, calculating a sum), characteristic changes take place in the brain.

There seems to be a very clear correlation between what we normally think of as mental events and changes in brain states. The constant correlation between mental events and brain events plus the principle of Ockham's razor makes physicalism seem very attractive. Physicalism, it is claimed, is simply the result of an inference to the best explanation.

What about the dualist's argument that the properties of the mind and body are irreducibly different? The physicalist would say that their respective properties *appear* to be different but that nevertheless the properties and activities of the mind can be explained by the properties and activities of the body (the brain). Consider a compact disc (CD) recording. If we examine the surface of the CD, we will observe nothing that has the characteristics of sound. The sounds produced by a CD player have such properties as being melodious, dissonant, lively, haunting, and so forth. Obviously, these properties are not part of the physical description of the disc's surface. However, we realize that every sound produced by the CD is caused by the physical makeup of the disc as it is acted upon by the CD player. Hence, even though our mental activities seem to be different from physical processes, maybe they are nothing more than the events happening in our brains, just as the sounds we hear are nothing more than physical events produced by the CD player.

This concept is not so mysterious, for we commonly find that the same entity can take on different forms and have different properties. For example, H_2O can take on the form of a gas (steam), a solid (ice), or a liquid (water). Yet, for all the differences in their physical properties, these forms are all essentially the same substance. Furthermore, a complex combination of entities can produce properties that are not found in the parts. Hence, emergent properties can be produced that originally were not there. Hydrogen and oxygen by themselves will fuel a fire, but when chemically combined to form water, the product will quench a fire. Similarly, the tail of the firefly contains two chemicals that produce light when they interact even though light is not a property of either chemical by itself. Hence, the properties of the whole are not always the properties of the parts. Each individual neuron of the brain, by itself, is neither conscious nor intelligent. But, physicalists suggest, the cumulative effect of neuronal interaction is the sort of phenomena we know as consciousness and intelligence. Consciousness may be nothing more than a by-product of low-level physical processes, much as a rainbow is the result of the interaction of light and raindrops.

A Brain Injury

On the morning of September 13, 1848, Phineas P. Gage, a 25-year-old railroad man, survived one of the most bizarre and brutal accidents ever recorded in medical history. Before the accident, this construction foreman for the Rutland and Burlington Railroad was known to his friends and coworkers as an easygoing, friendly, and intelligent person. However, the event that forever changed his life occurred when he was packing a load of explosives down a narrow hole that had been drilled into a huge rock. As he was tamping the gunpowder with an iron rod, the friction created a spark, which caused the charge to explode with a tremendous force. The $3\frac{1}{2}$-foot-long iron rod, weighing 13 pounds, was propelled like a rocket, hitting Gage in the head. It entered his cheek just below his left eye, tore through a portion of his brain, and ripped through his skull, eventually landing 50 feet away.

His coworkers loaded him into an oxcart and took him to a hotel, where two doctors did their best to clean the massive wound. From the time he was injured and throughout the doctors' attempts to stop the bleeding, Gage never lost consciousness. Over the next couple of weeks he bled severely, became quite confused, and lost the sight in his left eye. However, Phineas Gage lived for 13 more years, which most physicians consider to be a medical marvel. The skull of Phineas Gage and the metal rod that injured him are currently on display at the Warren Anatomical Museum in Boston.

Although Gage survived physically, his former personality did not. The Phineas Gage who was a likeable, gentle, intelligent man became someone who was a mean, undependable, slow-witted dolt. Although most of his brain continued to function more or less normally, the portion of the brain that controls the personality had been irreparably changed. The affable person his friends once knew was gone, and an ill-tempered and stupid brute remained. Given these changes, was Gage still Gage? To what extent do you think *your* personality is a product of the state of your brain?

Identity Theory

Physicalists disagree over the details of their theory. The *identity theory* (or *reductionism*) treats mental events as real but claims that they are *identical* to brain events. Hence, when we talk about beliefs, pains, desires, we can *reduce* these terms to talk about brain states. For example, a brain scientist could translate the statement "Phoebe is feeling pain in her hand" to "A particular C-fiber is signaling neurons in the S1 region of the cortex, approximately 30 millimeters up from the lateral fissure." Or if I say, "Raul believes that Scott is up to no good," I am really saying, "There is a certain configuration in Raul's cortex that causes various verbalizations such as 'Scott is slime' in certain situations and that causes certain other kinds of negative behavioral or physiological responses in Raul." Hence, the identity theory claims a one-to-one identity between a particular mental state and a particular brain state.

We can continue to use our mentalistic language as long as we keep in mind the real object of our talk. To use an analogy, we still talk of the sun "rising" and "setting." We now realize, however, that we are really talking about the rotation of the earth. The identity theorist cautions that nouns such as *mind, belief, desire, motive,* or *pain* tempt us to suppose that these terms refer to certain kinds of nonphysical entities. However, when we speak of *the dance,* we are not referring to some entity apart from the motions of various people's bodies. It would be silly for someone to say, "I hear the music and see the couples moving

SPOTLIGHT

on

The Physicalist's View of the Person

R. Buckminster Fuller (1895–1983) was an engineer, architect, essayist, poet, inventor, and all-around visionary. Educated at Harvard and the United States Naval Academy, Fuller had a long career in industry and lectured at Yale, Harvard, and a host of other universities. He designed the geodesic dome and invented the Dymaxion three-wheeled automobile in the 1930s. His books include *No More Secondhand God, Education Automation, Ideas and Integrities, The Unfinished Epic Poem of Industrialization,* and *An Operating Manual for Spaceship Earth.* The excerpt that follows is from *Nine Chains to the Moon* (1938).

In reading this tongue-in-cheek description of a human, try to figure out what part of you is being described in each phrase. (Please ignore the outdated convention of referring collectively to human beings as "man.") Do you think this sort of description is adequate? Does it leave anything out?

What's a Man?—R. Buckminster Fuller[8]

"What is that, mother?"

"It's a man, darling."

"What's a man?"

Man?

A self-balancing, 28-jointed adapter-base biped; an electrochemical reduction-plant, integral with segregated stowages of special energy extracts in storage batteries, for subsequent actuation of thousands of hydraulic and pneumatic pumps, with motors attached; 62,000 miles of capillaries; millions of warning signal, railroad and conveyor systems; crushers and cranes (of which the arms are magnificent 23-jointed affairs with self-surfacing and lubricating systems, and a universally distributed telephone system needing no service for 70 years if well managed); the whole, extraordinarily complex mechanism guided with exquisite precision from a turret in which are located telescopic and microscopic self-registering and recording range finders, a spectroscope, *et cetera,* the turret control being closely allied with an air conditioning intake-and-exhaust, and a main fuel intake.

Within the few cubic inches housing the turret mechanisms, there is room, also, for two sound-wave and sound-direction-finder recording diaphragms, a filing and instant reference system, and an expertly devised analytical laboratory large enough not only to contain minute records of every last and continual event of up to 70 years' experience, or more, but to extend, by computation and abstract fabrication, this experience with relative accuracy into all corners of the observed universe. There is, also, a forecasting and tactical plotting department for the reduction of future possibilities and probabilities to generally successful specific choice.

about, but where is *the dance?" The dance* simply is the music and the motions of the couples. Hence, when we speak of *beliefs, desires,* and *thoughts,* we are not referring to anything apart from different states or activities in the brain.

According to the identity theory, the relationship between the mind and the body is analogous to the relationship between Superman and Clark Kent, or between Lewis Carroll (the author of *Alice's Adventures in Wonderland*) and the Reverend Charles Dodgson, or between Samuel Clemens and the writer Mark Twain. In each case, the two entities are identical. Hence, every mental state you have, such as the sensation of red, a pleasant memory, a stabbing pain, your belief that "Mars is a planet," your desire for a good job, a feeling of guilt, your decision to rent the movie *Gone with the Wind,* and so on, is numerically identical to some physical state, event, or process in your brain.

There are a number of advantages to the identity theory. As with all versions of physicalism, with identity theory the mind is no longer viewed as a mysterious, immaterial substance. Everything that we need to know about the mind can be discovered through empirical brain research. Furthermore, the causal interaction between the mind and the body is no longer a problem. Mental events simply are physical events and have physical causes and consequences. Your decision to rent a movie is a brain event that is caused by your previous brain states and, perhaps, by some outside stimuli. What you experience as a decision is a brain event that sets into motion other brain events and a complex set of physiological reactions that result in you hopping in the car to drive to the video store.

The chief advantage of the identity theory over the other forms of physicalism is that we can retain our ordinary ways of speaking while still claiming that neurological research will ultimately give us the final story on all mental events. In other words, we can still talk about beliefs, desires, hopes, and fears as causing other mental states as well as causing behavior as long as we keep in mind that these terms are just traditional, laypersons' ways of talking about brain processes.

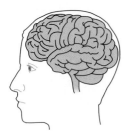

Are your mental states of believing, loving, and choosing identical to brain states?

ELIMINATIVISM

The other form of physicalism is *eliminativism.* The eliminativist believes that our mentalistic talk is so deeply flawed that it must be abandoned, because there is no hope of correlating our talk about beliefs and desires with our talk about brain states, as the identity theorist does. The eliminativist labels traditional psychological theories as **folk psychology.** Before the rise of modern science, people relied on folk science or bizarre theories about what causes events in the world. For example, the ancient Greeks explained the falling of a stone by saying the stone *desired* to return to its mother, the earth. Similarly, fate was thought to be a real force in the world that caused events to happen. References to desires in stones or to the activity of fate cannot be translated into the terminology of modern physics. Because rocks do not have desires and fate is not a causal force, the Greeks were not talking about anything at all. Hence, we abandoned these folk theories and now talk in terms of an entirely different characterization of physical and historical events. Similarly, the eliminativist believes that as our brain research advances, we will abandon our traditional mentalistic terminology and explanations just as we have abandoned the mythological folk science of the Greeks. The eliminativist claims we literally do not have beliefs or desires, nor are there really such states or activities as believing or desiring going on within us. Instead, we merely have certain kinds of brain states and processes. Because the theories of dualism, identity theory, and functionalism all talk about mental states and activities, they would all be considered examples of folk psychology, according to the eliminativist.

folk psychology
pejorative term used by eliminativists to characterize traditional psychological theories

---

THOUGHT EXPERIMENT: *Are There Mental Events?*

Are there such things as mental events? For example, are there such things as beliefs? In what sorts of situations is it correct to explain behavior by referring to what the

(continued . . .)

(. . . continued)

subject *believed*? In the following cases, check *yes* or *no* to indicate whether you think it is meaningful to literally attribute a belief to the subject in question.

1.	Harry smelled smoke and called the fire department because he *believed* his house was on fire.	Yes	No
2.	When Pavlov's dogs heard the bell ring, they began to salivate because they *believed* food was coming.	Yes	No
3.	The robin poked at the ground because it *believed* a worm was beneath the surface.	Yes	No
4.	The amoeba oozed around the particle because it *believed* it was food.	Yes	No
5.	Someone held a flame under the thermostat and, even though the room was 50 degrees, the mechanism turned the air conditioner on because it *believed* the room was too warm.	Yes	No

Were there any situations in which you thought it did make sense to speak of the behavior as caused by a belief? Were there any situations in which you thought it did not make sense to speak of a belief as playing a causal role in the action? What was the basis of your yes and no answers?

Most dualists would say that beliefs can be present only to conscious, intelligent minds such as Harry's. Identity theorists claim that beliefs are really particular kinds of brain states, so only creatures with a brain, such as Harry (and perhaps the dog), can have beliefs. Some artificial intelligence researchers and functionalists would say that everything from Harry down to the thermostat has beliefs. These theorists view mental activities as patterned processes by means of which inputs are transformed into outputs. Hence, both brains and intelligent machines are capable of exhibiting the same sorts of patterns. The eliminativist, on the other hand, would agree with the dualist that it makes no sense to attribute mental qualities like "believing" to a thermostat, for it is simply a mechanism that is following the laws of physics. However, for the same reason, the eliminativist says that we do not need the category of "belief" to explain Harry's actions. His behavior is the product of the neurochemical events taking place in his brain.

The following selection is by philosopher Jeffrey Olen. After spending several years writing for newspapers, magazines, radio, and children's television, he says he became interested in philosophy almost by accident and ended up completing a Ph.D. at Temple University. He has taught at the University of Wisconsin–Stevens Point, Temple University, the University of Colorado at Colorado Springs, and Regis University in Colorado Springs. Before jumping into his essay, three points need to be made. First, Olen uses the term *materialism* to refer to the anti-dualistic view of the mind that I have been calling *physicalism*. In the context of this selection, the two terms are synonymous. Second, Olen's account primarily discusses identity theory, although the criticisms of dualism would be embraced by the eliminativist version of physicalism as well. Third, Olen is not necessarily an adherent of materialism (physicalism), because he tends to embrace functionalism. Nevertheless, he has given us a lucid account of the reasons behind the materialist's, or physicalist's, position.

Der Mensch als Industriepalast (1926) by Fritz Kahn. In this whimsical painting, whose title is translated as *Man as an Industrial Palace,* the artist depicts the human body (along with its various organs and the brain) as one vast, complicated machine. The brain in the picture is composed of a number of subsystems, including different monitors, various decision-makers, data processing operations, and a system of electrical connections for sending commands to the rest of the body. Although the analogy between our brains and the one depicted in this artwork is crude, it is not too far off the mark. Current brain science has revealed that our brain is likewise a network of subsystems that interact through electrochemical processes. But is this picture complete? Are you just a machine made out of meat? Where is the mind or the soul within this machine? Is the structure of the machine adequate to explain everything that you are and do? The answer that the physicalist would provide is that, indeed, the marvelous and complicated mechanism of the brain can explain thought and consciousness without resorting to the addition of a mysterious, nonphysical mind.

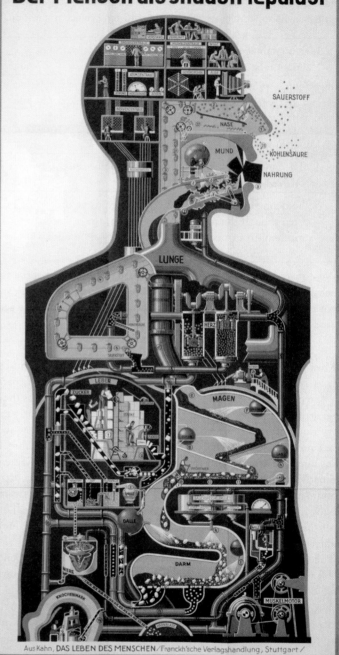

FROM JEFFREY OLEN

Persons and Their World[9]

We describe human beings in many different ways. Some of these descriptions are not significantly different from our descriptions of the rest of the world. Since we all have bodies, we can be given purely physical descriptions. We can be described as having a certain weight, size, shape, and so forth. But there are other ways of describing human beings that do not seem to apply to the rest of the world. We love, contemplate, write and read poetry, for example, and are held morally responsible for our actions. Thus, we seem on the one hand to be part of nature, and on the other hand to be somehow separate from it. We make this separation not only between ourselves and inanimate objects, but between ourselves and other animals as well. A beaver's dam is generally considered to be part of nature. Hoover Dam is not. Through their activity, other animals contribute to nature. Through our activity, we alter it.

Why do we distinguish ourselves from beavers—or any other animals—in this way? In part, because our products are products of the *human mind.* Even if we allow that animals can think and feel, the human mind is taken to be different. Because of its sophistication, because of its ability to set itself apart from nature through contemplation, planning, and choice, we do not think of its operations as being controlled by natural laws. Human actions are not blind. They are governed by *reason.*

So we are subject to mental descriptions and physical descriptions, have mental qualities and physical qualities, minds and bodies. But what is a mind? What are these mental qualities? How are they related to the physical world? Are we *really* set apart from nature? . . .

At this point, many philosophers have made the following argument. Human beings obviously think, feel, decide, and so forth. Since it is the mind that is responsible for such things, we obviously have minds. If there are minds, they must have some effects. It is reasonable to suppose that they have the effects we ordinarily believe them to have. That is, it is reasonable to believe that they cause us to behave in certain ways. But it is the brain that causes us to behave the way we do. Therefore, the mind must be the brain. That is, the mind is a physical object.

To say that the mind is physical is to adopt a *materialist* theory of mind. Materialists, unlike dualists, believe that human beings are purely physical beings, and that any mental state must be some state of the physical body. Materialism has none of the problems of interactionism. . . . Unlike interactionism, it does not make the mind's effects on behavior at all mysterious, nor does it violate the law of conservation of energy. . . .

MIND-BRAIN IDENTITY

One form of materialism is the view that mental states are *identical* with *brain states.* To have a certain kind of mental state is the same thing as having a certain type of brain state. To think a certain sort of thought is to have a certain sort of thing happen in the brain. To feel pain is to have another sort of thing happen in the brain. To wish for good weather is to have another sort of thing happen in the brain. This theory is called the *mind-brain identity theory.* Although it has been accepted by many contemporary philosophers, it is most closely associated with the Australians D. M. Armstrong and J. J. C. Smart.

Once we reject interactionism . . . it seems natural to accept the identity theory. But before we embrace it, we should remember why we were inclined to accept dualism in the first place. There were two reasons. First, there was the privacy of mental objects.

Only I can see the dogs and cats in my dreams. Only I can know what I'm thinking. Second, we said that mental objects cannot have the qualities that physical objects have. Thoughts and wishes and fears cannot have weight or size or shape or definite spatial location. But according to the identity theory, a mental state is identical with a brain state. In that case, how can a mental state be private? How can we deny that it has shape or size?

The identity theorist's response to these questions is a tricky one. It goes like this: Nobody else can see the dogs and cats in my dreams because there are no dogs and cats in my dreams. They simply do not exist. Neither do thoughts and wishes and fears. That is why they cannot have size or shape: because they do not exist.

At first glance, this answer seems as preposterous as the claim that decisions do not affect behavior. If there are no such things as thoughts and wishes and mental images, then what can mental states possibly be? If thoughts are not identical with brain states, what are the mental states that are identical with brain states?

The identity theorist's response is this: Mental states are not *objects,* like tables or chairs. They are *events,* like the kicking of a football. *Thinking* is a mental state. So are *wishing* and *hoping* and *dreaming.* These are all mental events, things that we do. But there are no such objects as *thoughts, wishes, hopes,* or *images.*

What is the difference between an event and an object? An event is a happening, an occurrence. It is what objects do, what happens to objects. Take, for example, the event of kicking a football. If I kick a football, there are only two objects involved—me and the ball. There is also the event of my kicking the ball, but that event is *not* a third object. True, we sometimes talk as though there were such objects as kicks. We say that someone made a good kick, or that a kick saved a game, or that a field-goal kicker made five kicks during a game. But that is just a manner of speaking. There are no such objects as kicks.

Similarly, there are no such objects as handshakes. If I shake a friend's hand, the only objects involved are my hand and my friend's hand. We can talk as though there were a third thing. We can say, for example, that I gave my friend a firm handshake, but that is not at all like giving someone a firm container. To give a firm handshake is to shake hands firmly. That is, there is only the event of shaking hands, but no such object as a handshake. Shaking hands is something we do.

So it is with mental states, the identity theorist says. We can think that today is Monday. That is something that we do. It is an event. Even though we can talk about our thought that today is Monday, that does not mean that there is an object in our mind that is the thought that today is Monday. It is merely a manner of speaking, like talking about a firm handshake or a good kick. Similarly, we can dream that a dog is chasing a cat. That is also something we do. It is also an event. Even though we can talk about dream dogs and dream cats, that does not mean that there are mental dogs and cats running around in our minds. It is merely a manner of speaking.

So of course a scientist cannot poke around in our brains and find the sentence that today is Monday, or a little dog chasing a little cat. But the scientist can observe the thinking process or the dreaming process. These processes or events do exist, and they are as public as any other event. Since the thoughts, dogs, and cats do not exist, they cannot be seen.

Thus, the alleged privacy of the mind is an illusion. Mental objects are not private. They simply do not exist. Only mental events exist, and they are identical with brain processes.

Moreover, we can now see why mental states cannot have certain qualities, such as weight. Thoughts are weightless for the same reason that handshakes and kicks are. Only objects can have weight. Events cannot. Thus, the major objection to materialism can be answered. But, apart from the difficulties we found with dualism, is there any reason to think the identity theory true?

IDENTITY AND CORRESPONDENCE

Many philosophers have felt that the identity theory can be proved by the scientist. To show how, let us look at how another identity theory was proved.

As some of you may have learned in high-school science, temperature is the same thing as mean kinetic molecular energy (the average energy of a substance's molecules due to their motion). How did the scientist learn this?

Scientists found that whenever a bowl of water has a certain temperature, it also has a certain mean kinetic molecular energy (MKE), and that whenever it has a certain MKE, it also has a certain temperature. That is, a *one-to-one correspondence* was discovered between temperature and MKE. Once this correspondence was discovered, it was possible to replace the laws of temperature with certain laws about the motion of molecules. Why should this be so? Why should temperature and MKE correspond so perfectly? Why should the laws of temperature be replaceable by laws of the motion of molecules? The simplest answer is that temperature is *identical* with MKE. And that is the answer that scientists accept.

Suppose that the same kind of correspondence can be found between mental states and brain states? Suppose that whenever I have a certain sensation, it can be shown that exactly the same type of brain state occurs. Let's say that whenever I feel a particular sort of pain, there is a particular sort of firing in my brain. Wouldn't the simplest explanation of this correspondence be that the pain is *identical* with the firing? Wouldn't this explanation be preferable to saying that the sensation is some useless by-product of the brain state? Why suppose that there is some mysterious private entity that does nothing at all?

Let us illustrate this way of thinking by imagining a story that parallels what we have said so far.

Some people who have never seen a watch find one alongside a road. They pick it up and examine it, noticing that the second hand makes a regular sweep around the watch's face. After some discussion, they conclude that the watch is run by a gremlin inside. They remove the back of the watch but cannot find the gremlin. After further discussion, they decide that it must be invisible. They also decide that it makes the hands go by running along the gears inside the watch. They replace the watch's back and take it home.

The next day the watch stops. Someone suggests that the gremlin is dead. Someone else suggests that it's probably sleeping. They shake the watch to awaken the gremlin, but the watch remains stopped. Someone finally turns the stem. The second hand begins to move. The person who said that the gremlin was asleep smiles triumphantly. The winding has awakened it.

After some months, someone claims that the watch can work without a gremlin. He takes apart the watch and explains the movements inside to the others. The others claim that he is leaving out what really makes the watch run. Of course, the winding contributes to the turning of the gears. But only because it wakes up the gremlin, which then resumes its running. Finally, a number of people begin to agree. The gremlin is not needed to run the watch. But because they are so used to believing in gremlins, they do not say that there is no such gremlin inside. Instead, they say that it is there, but only as a resident. It does not contribute to the watch's working.

THE FAR SIDE® BY GARY LARSON

© 1982 FarWorks, Inc. All Rights Reserved/Dist. by Creators Syndicate

The Far Side® by Gary Larson © 1982 FarWorks, Inc. All Rights Reserved. The Far Side® and the Larson® signature are registered trademarks of FarWorks, Inc. Used with permission.

What do the words *jitters, heebie jeebies, creeps,* and *willies* refer to? If you say, "He gives me the creeps," why is it absurd for me to ask, "How many creeps did he give you?" What is the source of humor in this The Far Side® cartoon? Why would the eliminativist claim that the dualist is making the same sort of mistake?

But the man who figured out that the watch worked without the intervention of a gremlin is dissatisfied. If we do not need the gremlin to explain how the watch works, why continue to believe that it exists? Isn't it simpler to say that it does not?

Think of the watch as the human body, and the gremlin as some nonphysical substance called the mind. In the beginning, the people that discovered the watch were interactionists. When it was claimed that the watch worked without the intervention of the gremlin, some people agreed but some did not. . . . But once it was accepted that the gremlin served no purpose, it was no longer reasonable to assume that it was still there. Of course, no one could prove for certain that it did not exist, but it seemed foolish to believe otherwise.

The identity theorist claims that it is equally unreasonable to accept mind-body dualism. A nonphysical mind is just as suspect as the gremlin. The only difference between the two cases is this: whereas there is no gremlin at all, there is a mind. The mistake is in thinking that it is anything over and above the brain.

THOUGHT EXPERIMENT: *Dualism, Identity Theory, and Physicalism*

To review, the Cartesian dualist believes that the mind and body are *separate* entities, although mental events can *cause* physical events and vice versa. The identity theorist believes that mental events and brain events are really *identical* even though they may be described differently. The eliminativist believes that all talk about mental events assumes a prescientific folk psychology that should be *eliminated* in favor of the latest scientific theories about the brain.

To test your understanding of the three theories discussed thus far, consider the relationship between each of the following pairs of events. In each row, decide whether the relationship between the two events (A and B) is *analogous* to the relationship between the mind and body as described by dualism (D), identity theory (IT), or eliminativism (E). After making your choices, check them with the answers in the footnote.*

Event A	Event B	Positions		
1. The sun came up in the morning.	1. The rooster crowed.	D	IT	E
2. A haunting melody is emanating from the violin.	2. The friction of the bow on the strings is producing sound waves.	D	IT	E
3. The presents were left under the tree by Santa Claus.	3. The presents were left under the tree by your parents.	D	IT	E
4. The people in the town were stricken with boils caused by a witch's curse.	4. The drinking water was contaminated by a virus, which caused a plague to spread throughout the town.	D	IT	E
5. Lightning bolts flashed across the sky.	5. There was a sudden discharge of electrons between the clouds.	D	IT	E
6. Someone flipped the light switch.	6. The ceiling light went on.	D	IT	E

*1 = D, 2 = IT, 3 = E, 4 = E, 5 = IT, 6 = D

LOOKING THROUGH THE PHYSICALIST'S LENS

1. Refer back to Fuller's description of a human being. If the physicalist is correct, this sort of description of persons is more accurate than our traditional ways of talking. For example, if we say that "Jeff is attracted to Anya," we are really saying that "Jeff's neurological response to the visual, auditory, olfactory, and tactile data he receives from Anya produces brain states that cause verbalizations such as 'Let's go out Friday night.' Furthermore, when he is in spatio-temporal proximity to Anya, his heart rate will increase and there will be an increase in hormonal activity." Using similar techniques, could we form

adequate translations of each one of the following sentences about the mind into a purely physicalistic language?

    a. Shakespeare had a very creative mind.
    b. Mother Teresa was very compassionate.
    c. Nikki believes that gambling is immoral.

2. Injuries to the brain of Phineas Gage caused his personality to change for the worse. Does it not, then, seem plausible that we could use chemicals and other means to change a person's personality for the better? What if we could create saintly persons by adjusting the chemicals in their brains? Is this action plausible? How would such an ability change our concept of persons? How would it change our concept of moral responsibility?

3. Refer back to the Far Side cartoon. This cartoon is based on comments such as "He gives me the heebie jeebies" or "She makes me have the willies" or "I get the jitters whenever I speak in public." From these phrases, the cartoon foolishly and humorously implies that the heebie jeebies, willies, or jitters are literally *things* that we can give, have, or get. What would be a more logical way of describing what we mean when we make these assertions? That you do not think the heebie jeebies are things indicates that you are a reductionist or eliminativist with respect to these entities. How is this example relevant to the physicalist's stance toward mentalistic language?

EXAMINING THE STRENGTHS AND WEAKNESSES OF PHYSICALISM

Positive Evaluation

1. For some time now, brain researchers have been able to attach wires to a person's head and study the brain's electrical impulses by projecting their images onto the screen of a monitor. For example, when a person is asked to mentally choose a playing card, researchers can determine precisely when the choice has been made by watching the patterns of the brain waves on the screen. To what degree does this research support the physicalist's claims over those of the dualist?

2. From all that we know today, doesn't it seem undeniable that the brain is an essential part of all our mental activities? To what degree does this connection support the physicalist's claim that all the advances in the brain sciences indicate that nothing is left for a nonphysical mind to explain?

3. The thesis of physicalism provides a unified account of all human phenomena by integrating our explanations of mental processes with our explanation of physical processes. Hence, while dualism fragments the person into two separate parts and has to explain how the parts interact, the physicalist does not have this problem. How important is this more unified account in evaluating the plausibility of physicalism?

4. Can you think of any feature or activity of the mind that could not, in principle, be given a physicalistic explanation?

Negative Evaluation

1. The biologist J. B. S. Haldane said, "It seems to me immensely unlikely that mind is a mere by-product of matter. For if my mental processes are determined wholly by the motions of atoms in my brain, I have no reason to suppose that my beliefs are true. . . .

And hence I have no reason for supposing my brain to be composed of atoms."[10] In your own words, restate the argument against physicalism that Haldane is making here. Do you agree or disagree with his point?

2. Let us suppose that there is a brain scientist who is completely color-blind.[11] She experiences only black, white, and gray. Theoretically, she could have *complete* scientific knowledge of your brain states while you were experiencing a sunset. However, she still would not know what it was like to experience color. In this case, would it be legitimate to say that a scientific knowledge of the brain gives us only a partial account of the sorts of things that the mind experiences? Are there aspects of our mental life that can be known only by a conscious subject through his or her subjective experiences and that cannot be known through third-person, scientific, objective descriptions of the brain? Does this example show that your mental experiences cannot be completely reduced or understood in terms of brain states? How would a physicalist respond?

3. The philosopher, mathematician, and scientist Gottfried Wilhelm Leibniz (1643–1716) used this thought experiment to show that even if a machine's output produced what seemed like thoughts or perception, we would never find conscious perception within this physical system.

> Supposing that there were a machine whose structure produced thought, sensation, and perception, we could conceive of it as increased in size with the same proportions until one was able to enter into its interior, as he would into a mill. Now, on going into it he would find only pieces working upon one another, but never would he find anything to explain Perception.[12]

If he were writing today, Leibniz might say that even if a computer can defeat a human chess master, we will find only electronic chips and wires within this mechanism; we will not find conscious awareness within it. In what way is Leibniz's argument a criticism of physicalism? How strong is this criticism?

4. One of the physicalist's arguments is that mental events (making a decision, feeling a pain, recognizing a symbol) always seem to be correlated with measurable brain events. However, does the fact that two things always occur together necessarily imply that they are identical? For example, every mammal with a heart is also a creature with kidneys. The two conditions always occur together in nature. Obviously, however, having a heart is not identical to having a kidney. How might a dualist use this fact as an analogy to explain the relation between mental events and changes in the brain?

3.4 FUNCTIONALISM AND ARTIFICIAL INTELLIGENCE

LEADING QUESTIONS: *Functionalism and Artificial Intelligence*

1. Artificial light really *is* light. It exposes camera film in the same way that natural light does. Hence, the fact that it is "artificial" does not mean that it is fake or simulated light. It simply means that it was created by human technology and not nature. So, if scientists create artificial intelligence in computers that can duplicate the cognitive activities of humans, wouldn't it make sense to consider their artificial intelligence to be real intelligence?

2. How do we know that a person is intelligent? Don't we know by the way the person behaves and responds to situations and, in particular, by how well he or she does on intelligence tests? Because some computers in research laboratories today can successfully perform many of the tasks on intelligence tests, shouldn't we say that such computers are intelligent and can think? If not, are we being inconsistent in not judging a computer's intelligence by the standards we use to judge human beings?

3. Suppose that even the most advanced computers will never have emotions. Does that deficiency mean that they could not have minds? Some science fiction films depict alien beings who clearly have minds but not the sort of emotional life that we have. Is it necessary to have emotions to have a mind?

4. Computers today do not have consciousness or self-awareness. How important is consciousness to cognition? How many of our cognitive activities are carried out in full consciousness? We tie our shoes, drive a car, or find our way to class without consciously thinking about what we are doing. Nevertheless, we take in data, process it, make judgments, make adjustments in our bodily motions, and perform tasks without conscious attention to these activities. Could someone (or something) have a mind and not have self-awareness? When we are asleep, do we still have minds?

5. Suppose we encounter extraterrestrial beings who have brains very different from our own. Suppose their brains consisted of some strange, organic compound made up of a substance called PQR instead of proteins. But suppose that these beings experienced pain similarly to the way that we do and that they clearly had beliefs, desires, and attitudes. In other words, suppose that their psychological life was the same as ours. Would it make sense to say they had minds even though their brain matter was different? Now suppose that their brains were not made out of organic stuff but were complex metallic mechanisms. If their psychological makeup was still the same, would we say they had minds?

6. Descartes and the dualists believe that minds must be nonphysical things. But suppose our bodies contained an immaterial substance that had the cognitive capabilities of an oyster. Would we want to call this substance a mind? In the final analysis, isn't a mind identified not by what it is made out of (physical or spiritual substance) but by how it functions?

Although some contemporary thinkers look to brain science to answer our questions about the mind, others look to computer science or artificial intelligence. Whatever you conclude about artificial intelligence, looking more closely at it will help you clarify what constitutes a mind. I continue our exploration of philosophy of mind by examining the answers provided by two related movements that arose in the latter half of the 20th century. These two movements are a philosophy of mind known as *functionalism* and a theory about cognition known as *strong artificial intelligence*. To provide some historical background, it will be useful to look at a controversy that occurred in the 19th century.

THE AMAZING CHESS-PLAYING MACHINE

In 1836, the poet Edgar Allan Poe wrote an essay entitled "Maelzel's Chess-Player" in *The Southern Literary Messenger*. The subject of the essay was an alleged chess-playing machine invented by a Wolfgang von Kempelen that was being exhibited by J. N. Maelzel (the inventor of the musician's metronome). The chess-playing device consisted of a cabinet that contained a system of densely packed machinery: metal wheels, rods, levers, and so on. The top of the cabinet contained a chessboard presided over by a mechanical human figure

Kasparov (left) in the first game. Deep Blue (center) is telling the moves to its assistant.

whose left arm was moved by the machinery within the cabinet. During exhibitions, the arm would move the chess pieces and the machine would play a respectable game of chess with a human opponent. In his essay, Poe argued that the machine was a fraud and suggested that a small man concealed within the cabinet was making the moves. (In fact, Poe's suspicions were correct.) His most interesting point, however, was the thesis that *in principle* no machine could play the game of chess. Poe argued that machines can make mathematical calculations but cannot play chess because there is an unbridgeable gulf between these two activities. In Poe's own words:

> Arithmetical or algebraical calculations are, from their very nature, fixed and determinate. Certain *data* being given, certain results necessarily and inevitably follow. These results have dependence upon nothing, and are influenced by nothing but the *data* originally given. And the question to be solved proceeds, or should proceed, to its final determination, by a succession of unerring steps liable to no change, and subject to no modification. . . . But the case is widely different with the Chess-Player. With him there is no determinate progression. No one move in chess necessarily follows upon any one other. From no particular disposition of the men at one period of a game can we predicate their disposition at a different period.[13]

The gist of his argument is quite simple. Almost at every point in a chess game, a number of moves are possible (usually about 30). The moves made by an expert do not follow by logical necessity, as in a mathematical series. Hence, because the sequence of moves is not determined, a *choice* must be made. This choice (Poe assumed) made it impossible for a machine to play chess. His conclusion concerning Maelzel's chess-playing "machine" was that "it is quite certain that the operations of the Automaton are regulated by *mind* and by nothing else."[14] Hence, Poe thought that there were some absolute limits on the possibilities of artificial intelligence (hereafter referred to as AI).

Poe would have been surprised and deeply troubled if he knew that on May 11, 1997, an IBM computer named Deep Blue defeated Garry Kasparov, the world chess champion, in a six-game chess match. A year earlier, Deep Blue had defeated Kasparov in their very first encounter, even though the human player went on to either win or tie the remaining games. Speaking about one of Deep Blue's moves, Kasparov said, "It was a wonderful and extremely human move. . . . I had played a lot of computers but I had never experienced anything like this. I could feel—I could *smell*—a new kind of intelligence across the table."[15]

STOP AND THINK

In the light of recent developments in AI, we could take one of three possible positions concerning Poe's argument:

1. Poe was right. You need a mind to play chess and, therefore, many of today's computers have minds.
2. Poe was wrong. You don't need a mind to play chess.
3. Computers don't *really* play chess, but only simulate it.[16]

Which of these three positions do you favor at this point? Why?

SURVEYING THE CASE FOR FUNCTIONALISM

Before we get into the controversies surrounding computer intelligence, it will be helpful to look at a recent theory within the philosophy of mind known as functionalism. Consider the following questions. What is a belief? What distinguishes the mental state of "believing that X is true" from that of "doubting that X is true"? Compare these questions with another one. What distinguishes a chess pawn from a queen? In answering this question, you might be tempted to refer to the characteristic shape of each piece. But on further reflection it is clear that this answer is not correct. You can buy chess sets in which the pieces have many different, unconventional shapes. Some chess sets are made up of American civil war figures. Other chess sets use very modernistic, abstract shapes. In fact, you do not even need a board or chess pieces to play chess; many people play the game by mail. The squares on the board and the individual pieces are represented by numbers and letters. What makes it a movement of a *pawn* in chess is not the chemical composition of the piece or its shape, but the distinctive pattern of its movement as well as its powers and relations to the other pieces. Chess moves have to be made with *something,* but this something can be many types of things (pieces of wood, symbols on paper, or even human beings). This sort of property is what philosophers call **multiple realizability.** The same chess move can be realized (embodied, instantiated) in multiple ways and in different media. This concept is important in understanding the philosophy of functionalism.

multiple realizability the property by which something can be realized (embodied, instantiated) in multiple ways and in different media

Functionalism consists of both a negative critique and a positive theory. The negative part describes what mental states are not. They are *not* what the identity theory and behaviorism say they are. The identity theory says that mental events or states (believing, doubting, willing, feeling pain, and so on) are identical to a particular brain state. However, the functionalist argues that what is essential to a mind is not a certain sort of material (the wet, gray, fleshy-stuff of the brain). Instead, the functionalist claims, minds are constituted by a certain pattern or relation between the parts of a system, independent of the material that embodies the system. In other words, mental events have the property of multiple realizability. Even if it turns out that our brains are what produce *our* psychological properties, there could be other ways that psychological states could occur. Hence, minds have the property of multiple realizability. (Think of the analogy with chess.)

Traditional chess pieces.

We could formulate a similar functionalist critique of dualism. Let's agree with the dualist that reality is made up of physical substances and immaterial substances. However, we could imagine that the latter was simply a hunk of dumb, inert, immaterial stuff. Certainly, this stuff would not constitute a mind. To be a mind, this immaterial substance would have to embody a series of functional states that bore the sorts of causal relations to each other and to inputs and outputs that we would identify as psychological states (beliefs, hopes, fears, desires, and so on).

Strictly speaking, functionalism is neutral on the issue of dualism versus physicalism. There is no official position on what a system must be made out of to have mental states. However, the fact is that most functionalists are physicalists. They would say that it happens to be the case that our functional mental states are identified with brain states. However, Jerry Fodor, a leading functionalist, suggests that functional mental states could be embodied in all kinds of media.

> Could calculating machines have pains, Martians have expectations and disembodied spirits have thoughts? The modern functionalist approach to psychology raises the logical possibility that they could.[17]

Hence, the functionalist would say that we could imagine alien beings (Martians) that have a completely different biochemistry from ours but the same sort of psychological makeup. This belief is why we find plausibility in science fiction stories that contain aliens like ET or loveable robots like R2D2 and C3PO. Fodor also suggests (perhaps tongue in cheek) that if it is possible to imagine intelligent, immaterial spirits (such as angels), then functionalism would apply to their psychological constitution as well.

Functionalism also differs from behaviorism. The behaviorist claims we can do psychology simply by studying the way certain external stimuli are correlated with external behavior. Nay, nay, says the functionalist. We must also understand the internal, psychological processing that is going on. Functionalists claim that mentalistic terms (*belief, desire, love*) do not alone refer to behavior or dispositions to behavior. Unlike the behaviorist, the functionalist says that mental states can function as the inner causes of behavior. Furthermore, the functionalist claims that behavior cannot be explained without understanding the internal processes that produce it. Hence, contrary to behaviorism, functionalism believes

A chess game played with live, human figures.

that internal states such as beliefs, desires, and wishes play a causal role within the organism. These states may be realized in brain states, but they also could be realized in other ways.

The positive side of functionalism is the theory that mental states are defined in terms of their causal role (how they function). What does it mean to desire something? According to the functionalist, desiring (as with any type of mental state) has certain causal relations to (1) sensory inputs, (2) other mental states, and (3) actions or responses. For example, if I desire a drink of water and if I see (1) a glass of liquid that causes me to have the belief that "this liquid is water," then this desire plus this belief will produce (2) a volitional state that results in (3) the action of my picking up the glass and drinking the water. Note that the functionalist differs from the behaviorist in claiming that relations between mental states have to be taken into account to explain the behavior.

Let's use another analogy: an antique, mechanical adding machine and an electronic calculator are very different in terms of their physical operations, but functionally they are equivalent. Each machine takes (1) inputs representing numbers and arithmetic operations, which activate (2) internal procedures for processing the inputs according to the laws of mathematics, and each machine has (3) a number-display system to represent the results. Similarly, by defining mental states in terms of their functional roles and not in terms of the substance in which they are found, the functionalist can claim that creatures that lack our biochemistry can still have the same cognitive life that we have, whether these creatures be extraterrestrial aliens or computers.

In the following reading, Jerry Fodor sets out some of the advantages of functionalism.

FROM JERRY FODOR

The Mind-Body Problem[18]

In the past 15 years a philosophy of mind called functionalism that is neither dualist nor materialist has emerged from philosophical reflection on developments in artificial intelligence, computational theory, linguistics, cybernetics and psychology. All these fields, which are collectively known as the cognitive sciences, have in common a certain level of abstraction and a concern with systems that process information. Functionalism, which seeks to provide a philosophical account of this level of abstractions, recognizes the possibility that systems as diverse as human beings, calculating machines and disembodied spirits could all have mental states. In the functionalist view the psychology of a system depends not on the stuff it is made of (living cells, metal or spiritual energy) but on how the stuff is put together.

Fodor goes on to discuss two alternative theories. The first is identity theory, which identifies mental states with brain states. The second theory is logical behaviorism, which attempts to translate all mental terms into talk about behavior or behavioral dispositions. He states that in the 1970s, these theories were the only viable alternatives to dualism, yet each theory had its problems.

- According to Fodor, how does functionalism combine the best points of both theories?
- What is the comparison the functionalist makes with computer science?

All of this emerged 10 or 15 years ago as a nasty dilemma for the materialist program in the philosophy of mind. On the one hand the identity theorist (and not the logical behaviorist) had got right the causal character of the interactions of mind and body. On the other the logical behaviorist (and not the identity theorist) had got right the relational character of mental properties. Functionalism has apparently been able to resolve the dilemma. By stressing the distinction computer science draws between hardware and software the functionalist can make sense of both the causal and the relational character of the mental.

According to the functionalist, the hardware of the computer (the wires, chips, and so on) are like the brain or whatever substance underlies the mental states. The software is a set of logical relationships that direct the processing of inputs, the changing states of the system, and the outputs. Software is analogous to the mind. Hence, differently designed computer systems can run functionally similar software (e.g., a chess game). In both systems, the logical relationships will be the same (the software will allow the pawns to move only one square at a time), even though what is happening at the hardware level may be completely different. Similarly, the mind is a pattern of relationships that could be embodied in different kinds of substances.

- In the final passage, find where Fodor describes a headache in terms of its causal relations to (1) inputs, (2) other mental states, and (3) responses.
- How does Fodor distinguish functionalism from both logical behaviorism and eliminativism?

The intuition underlying functionalism is that what determines the psychological type to which a mental particular belongs is the causal role of the particular in the mental life of the organism. . . . A headache, for example, is identified with the type of mental state that among other things causes a disposition for taking aspirin in people who believe aspirin relieves a headache, causes a desire to rid oneself of the pain one is feeling, often causes someone who speaks English to say such things as "I have a headache" and is brought on by overwork, eyestrain and tension. . . .

Functionalism construes the concept of causal role in such a way that a mental state can be defined by its causal relations to other mental states. In this respect functionalism is completely different from logical behaviorism. Another major difference is that functionalism is not a reductionist thesis. It does not foresee, even in principle, the elimination of mentalistic concepts from the explanatory apparatus of psychological theories.

SURVEYING THE CASE FOR ARTIFICIAL INTELLIGENCE

Functionalists tend to find important analogies between human psychology and computers. In computer jargon we make a distinction between hardware and software. Hardware is the actual physical computer, including its chips and circuits. The software is the program giving the computer its instructions. Hence, the same hardware could run a word processor, an action game, a music synthesizer, or an artificial intelligence program that plays world-class chess. Similarly, two computers with different hardware designs (a Macintosh and an IBM) could run exactly the same program. Using the computer analogy, the identity theorist would explain our mental states by examining the hardware of the brain. On the other hand, the functionalist would say the makeup of the brain is irrelevant. What constitutes a mind is the software, or the patterns of activity that characterize different mental states, including the causal role of these states in the life of the organism. Hence, the transition from functionalism to artificial intelligence is easy. If computers could be programmed to have cognitive states functionally equivalent to those states in human psychology that we identify as thinking, believing, wanting, remembering, willing, and so on, and if their ability to process information is comparable to ours, it would seem to follow that such computers would be intelligent and would have minds.

THOUGHT EXPERIMENT: *Minds versus Computers*

Look through this list of activities and put a check in column A if the activity requires a mind. Put a check in column B if the activity can be performed by today's computers. Put a check in column C if you think it is at least possible that computers will be able to do this activity someday. Obviously, if you already put a check in column B for a particular activity, you should not also put a check in C.

Activity	A Requires a Mind	B Today's Computers Can Do It	C It Is Possible That Future Computers Will Be Able to Do It
1. Add up a sum of numbers.			
2. Play chess.			
3. Learn from experience.			
4. Understand language.			
5. Read a story and paraphrase it.			
6. Read a story and draw inferences from it.			

(continued . . .)

(. . . continued)

		(A)	(B)	(C)
7.	Make decisions.			
8.	Write poetry.			
9.	Have emotions.			
10.	Have consciousness.			
Totals:		**(A)**	**(B)**	**(C)**
			(B) + (C)	

First, add together the number of checks you placed in column A and enter the total at the bottom of that column. *For the remaining two columns, consider only those rows in which you placed a check in column A.* Now, for all those rows (*and only those rows*), add together the number of the checks you placed in column B and enter that total at the bottom. Do the same for column C. Finally, add together the totals for columns B and C.

In tabulating your responses to the thought experiment, the degree to which the combined totals of columns B and C are equal to or almost equal to the total for column A is the degree to which you agree with a position known as strong artificial intelligence. The strong AI thesis states that it is possible for computers to literally have the same sorts of mental states and powers that humans have. The degree to which the combined totals of columns B and C are closer to zero indicates your disagreement with the position of strong AI. I now discuss the position of strong AI.

Does the Turing Test Measure Intelligence?

To answer the question, "Can computers think?" we need a criterion of what constitutes thinking. How do we measure human intelligence? We do so through IQ tests, which consist of a series of cognitive problems. Let us suppose that a computer could do about as well on a standard IQ test as an average person. This result would be a score of 100. If this score is a measure of human intelligence, why shouldn't we acknowledge that computers are intelligent if they perform just as well?

In our everyday life, of course, we do not give intelligence tests to one another. Nevertheless, we can recognize that other people have normal intelligence. How? One way is to talk to them. If they give reasonable answers in the context of a conversation, we are inclined to say that they have normal intelligence. In 1637, Descartes claimed that being able to use language flexibly was a skill that definitively separated humans from machines. He imagined that a very sophisticated robot could be designed to utter words and even say "ouch" if you touched it in a particular place. However, in the following passage, Descartes insisted that a machine would never have the versatility of human rationality.

> But it is not conceivable that such a machine should produce different arrangements of words so as to give an appropriately meaningful answer to whatever is said in its presence, as the dullest of men can do.[19]

In 1950 the British mathematician Alan Turing proposed a test to determine whether a computer can think or not.[20] Turing is considered to be the founding father of modern

This illustration is a depiction of the Turing Test being used to decide if a computer program has duplicated human intelligence. The man in the middle is alternatively carrying on a conversation with a live human being (on the right) and with a computer running an artificial intelligence program (on the left). Alan Turing claimed that if the interrogator could not tell whether he was communicating with a human or a computer, this would prove that the computer was capable of thought.

Turing Test test produced by Alan Turing to determine whether a computer can think or not

ALAN TURING
(1912–1954)

computer science. Although he never built a computer himself, he laid the theoretical and mathematical foundations that were essential for designing our modern computers. Here is a contemporary version of his proposal, which has since become immortalized as the **Turing Test** (Turing himself called it "the imitation game"). Let us suppose that you and several other judges are seated in a room in front of a computer terminal. Your terminal is communicating with a terminal in another room. You communicate interactively with the unseen person in the other room by typing in questions on your keyboard and reading the other person's responses on your monitor. The key feature of the test is that in some of the sessions you are not communicating with a flesh-and-blood person but with an artificial intelligence program running on a computer. Turing's claim was that if the computer program could fool a panel of judges into thinking they were communicating with a human being a significant percentage of the time, this deception would be proof that the computer program was capable of thought. Hence, Turing replaced the abstract and rather vague question, "Can computers think?" with an operational test of intelligence—"Can computers pass the Turing Test?" The theory behind this test can be summed up by the cliché, "If it looks like a duck, walks like a duck, and quacks like a duck—it is a duck!" In other words, if a computer's responses fulfill the criteria we use to judge that a human is intelligent, then we are committed to saying that the computer is intelligent.

The Turing Test

In 1990, the computer scientist Dr. Hugh Loebner established a $100,000 prize for anyone who could write a computer program that passes the Turing Test. The contest runs once a year at different university campuses and is administered by the Cambridge Center for Behavioral Studies in Massachusetts. Thus far, no one has claimed the grand prize, and until that happens, an award of $20,000 is given each year to a contestant for designing the "most human computer."

SPOTLIGHT

on

STOP AND THINK

- What questions would you ask to determine whether you were communicating with a computer?
- Why do you think a computer could not (could never) give humanlike answers to these questions?

Descartes was convinced that machines could never be intelligent because they do not have immaterial minds and because he thought having such a mind is necessary to be a thinking being. Based on the technology of his day, he assumed that machines were mechanically rigid and inflexible in the sorts of operations they could perform. He also believed that understanding language requires a mind that possesses the ability to process an infinite variety of sentences. Hence, Descartes argued that understanding language was a criterion that could be used to distinguish machine responses from genuine intelligence. Descartes's argument could be summarized in this fashion:

1. Machines have the sort of intelligence we have if and only if they can understand language.
2. Machines cannot understand language.
3. Therefore, machines cannot have the sort of intelligence we have.

Alan Turing agreed with Descartes's first premise but was optimistic about the abilities of future machines. Consequently, his argument was:

1. Machines have the sort of intelligence we have if and only if they can understand language.
2. Machines can understand language.
3. Therefore, machines can have the sort of intelligence we have.

Although Turing realized that the machines of his day could not pass the Turing Test, he believed that someday machines would be technologically capable. In fact, he claimed that by the year 2000 (50 years from the time he was writing), machines would be fooling human interrogators a significant percentage of the time.

I believe that at the end of the century the use of words and general educated opinion will have altered so much that one will be able to speak of machines thinking without expecting to be contradicted.[21]

strong AI thesis the claim that an appropriately programmed computer really is a mind and can be said to literally understand, believe, and have other cognitive states

weak AI thesis the claim that artificial intelligence research may help us explore various theoretical models of human mental processes while acknowledging that computers only simulate mental activities

MARVIN MINSKY
(1927–   )

Some philosophers have expanded Turing's thesis into the claim that the ability to pass the Turing Test is a logically sufficient condition for having a mind. In other words, an appropriately programmed computer really *is* a mind and can be said to *literally* understand, believe, and have other cognitive states. This thesis is known as the **strong AI thesis.** The **weak AI thesis** is the relatively innocuous claim that artificial intelligence research may help us explore various theoretical models of human mental processes while acknowledging that computers only simulate mental activities. There is a clear connection between functionalism and strong AI. Functionalism claims that a mind is anything that has the functional capabilities to behave in ways characteristic of human minds. The materials composing the system (wet gray matter or electrical circuits) are irrelevant to its status as a mind. Hence, if a computer running an artificial intelligence program has the same psychological constitution as human beings, then it has a mind.

STOP AND THINK

Is the Turing Test an effective way to test for intelligence? If a computer passes the Turing Test, can we be sure that this computer thinks or has a mind? Why?

Marvin Minsky and Strong AI

One of the leading defenders of strong AI is Marvin Minsky. For most of his professional career, Minsky has been involved in groundbreaking artificial intelligence research at the Massachusetts Institute of Technology. In the following passage, he predicts that someday computers will not only equal human intelligence, but will surpass it and that machines will achieve self-consciousness.

FROM MARVIN MINSKY
Why People Think Computers Can't[22]

When people ask if a machine can be self-conscious, they always seem to expect the answer to be no. I propose to shock the reader by explaining why machines may be capable, in principle, of possessing even more and better consciousness than people have. . . .

When and if we choose to build more artfully conceived intelligent machines, we should have many new options that were not available during the brain's evolution, for the biological constraints of vertebrate evolution must have dictated many details of the interconnections of our brains. In the new machines, we will be able to provide whatever paths we wish. Though the new machines still cannot possibly keep track in real time of everything they do, we surely should be able (at least in principle) to make those new, synthetic minds vastly more self-conscious than we are, in the sense of being more profound and having insightful knowledge about their own nature and function. Thus, in the end, those new creatures should have more interesting and richer inner lives than do people. . . .

There is absolutely no known technical reason to doubt that we could build truly intelligent machines. It may take a very long time, though, to learn enough about commonsense reasoning to make machines with manlike versatility. We already know some ways of making useful, specialized, expert systems. We don't yet know that many ways of making these systems learn enough to improve themselves in interesting ways. However, there are already some ideas about this topic on the scientific horizon. . . .

In years to come, we will learn more ways of making machines behave sensibly. . . . We will learn more about new kinds of knowledge and processes and how to use them to make still more new knowledge. We will come to think of learning and thinking and understanding not as mysterious, single, special processes, but as entire worlds of ways to represent and transform ideas. In turn, those new ideas will suggest new machine architectures, and they in turn will further change our ideas about ideas. No one can now tell where all these new ideas will lead. One thing is certain, though: there must be something wrong with any reasoned claim today to know any fundamental differences between men and possible machines. And there is a simple reason why such arguments must be erroneous: we simply do not know enough yet about the real workings of either men or possible machines.

STOP AND THINK

In the passage just quoted, Marvin Minsky suggests the following claims. For each one, set down the reasons why you either agree with the claim or disagree with it.

1. Someday, computers will be able to have greater self-understanding than we do.
2. Learning, thinking, and understanding are not "mysterious" but are basically complex "ways to represent and transform ideas."
3. It is possible that in the future there will be no basic differences between human minds and those of machines.

John Searle's Chinese Room

Whether artificial intelligence programs will ever be able to pass the Turing Test is primarily a technological question. The really interesting philosophical question is, Assuming that a computer could pass the Turing Test, would this result be a sufficient condition for saying that the computer has a mind? The contemporary philosopher John Searle attempted to refute the strong AI thesis held by Marvin Minsky and others by offering his famous 1980 Chinese room thought experiment.[23]

Try this simplified version of the Chinese room thought experiment yourself. We shall begin by assuming you have no knowledge of the Chinese language. Now, imagine that you are in a room with a rather large rule book giving directions (in English) on how to respond to Chinese sentences with appropriate Chinese replies. The instruction manual does not contain stock sentences, for there is no way to predict what sentences it will need to process. Furthermore, it does not explain the meaning of the symbols to you. Instead, the manual contains formal rules for syntactically analyzing one set of Chinese symbols and constructing another set of Chinese symbols that a native speaker would recognize as an appropriate response. Chinese speakers slip messages under the door written in Chinese. These papers contain various marks made up of straight and curved lines, none of which you understand. You look these figures up in the book. Next, following the instructions, you write out another set of symbols and pass this message back to the Chinese speakers outside. Unknown to you, their messages are questions and, thanks to the rule book, your responses are articulate answers to these questions written in Chinese.

THOUGHT EXPERIMENT: *Searle's Chinese Room*

To imagine what this process would be like, we can use typographical symbols to mimic the Chinese rule book. Let us suppose that you are given the following set of symbols:

& ! ¶ @ %

You look up the symbols in the book and find that the following rules are relevant:

#357 When you encounter the symbols & !, replace them with the symbols £ ¥.

#938 When you encounter the symbol @, replace it with ℞ and leave everything following it the same.

Following these rules, figure out what your response should be. This task should be easy enough, but the answer is in the footnote.*

response:

Unknown to you, the message means "Are you enjoying my questions?" and your response means "I am enjoying your questions."

Let us suppose that you are so successful at conversing in written Chinese by means of the rule book that those on the outside agree that they have been communicating with a competent speaker of the Chinese language.

- What would be the implications of this result?
- Would this experiment support or count against the strong AI thesis?

———————————

*According to the rules, your response should be: £ ¥ ¶ ℞ %.

You can see that Searle is trying to construct something like a Turing Test for understanding Chinese. At this point, Searle appeals to our intuitions. You have passed the Turing Test by fooling the people on the outside that you are fluent in Chinese. However, in spite of this success, you still do not understand a single word of Chinese. Clearly, something different is going on when you are manipulating Chinese symbols than when you are receiving and responding to messages in English, which you do understand.

STOP AND THINK

How would you describe the difference between manipulating Chinese symbols according to formal rules and responding to English messages?

intentionality a feature of certain mental states (such as beliefs) by which they are directed at or are about objects or states of affairs in the world

Searle claims that this formal manipulation of symbols is comparable to what goes on in a computer's AI program. His point is that no matter how effective a computer program may be in simulating conversation, it will never produce real understanding. Hence, a computer program can simulate intelligence, but it cannot duplicate it. Contrary to the strong AI thesis, Searle claims a computer program is nothing like a mind because *its* states are different from *our* cognitive states. To put it more technically, the computer lacks intentionality. **Intentionality** is a feature of certain mental states (such as beliefs) by which they are directed at or are about objects or states of affairs in the world. Intentionality is defined in terms of content and not formal relationships. For example, if you believe that a particular object is an apple, not only are you in a certain psychological state, but your state is one that is directed at a particular object in the world.

Let's apply Searle's concern about intentionality to the case of the Chinese rule book. Suppose the rule book tells you that the response to symbol #### is the symbol &&&&. But for you, these symbols lack any meaning. In other words, they do not refer to anything external to themselves (intentionality is lacking). On the other hand, the symbol "dog" is more than a set of marks for you. It produces a mental state that refers to a certain type of furry creature. If you ask a computer running an AI program, "Can dogs fly?" it may not have the answer programmed into it. But from the information in its database that "dogs do not have wings" and "most things that fly have wings," it might be able to infer the answer and generate the sentence, "Dogs do not fly." The point is that in producing this answer, the computer is manipulating and generating symbols just as you were in the Chinese room. Therefore, the computer's states do not have intentionality. The symbol "dog" in its memory is related to other symbols but it does not refer to the real world. Only a mind with intentionality, such as yours, is capable of using that symbol to refer to something else. It follows from Searle's position that, at best, passing the Turing Test may be *evidence* that the producer of the apparently intelligible responses has a mind, but this feat alone does not *constitute* having a mind.

Searle used this thought experiment to argue against behaviorism and functionalism. It is interesting to note that Searle himself is a physicalist. He believes that our mental states are caused by the unique causal powers of our brain. His point is that a computer program that merely manipulates symbols could never have the causal powers to produce understanding. Hence, Searle claims the behaviorist and the functionalist are wrong because they ignore the unique causal powers of the physical brain in their philosophy of mind. However, dualists have used his example to argue not only against behaviorism and functionalism but also against physicalism. We will see later in this section why dualists think Searle's conclusions point in this direction.

Some people think that Searle misses the point. He contends that computers can simulate cognitive processes but they cannot duplicate them. In another article, Searle points out that

> We can do a computer simulation of the flow of money in the British economy, or the pattern of power distribution in the Labour party. We can do computer simulation of rain storms in the home counties, or warehouse fires in East London. Now, in each of these cases, nobody supposes that the computer simulation is actually the real thing; no one supposes that a computer simulation of a storm will leave us all wet, or a computer simulation of a fire is likely to burn the house down. Why on earth would anyone in his right mind suppose a computer simulation of mental processes actually had mental processes?[24]

Searle's argument is a pretty good one, isn't it? Well, not everyone thinks it is. Daniel Dennett, a philosopher of mind at Tufts University, replies to Searle's argument in this way:

> But now suppose we made a computer simulation of a mathematician, and suppose it worked well. Would we complain that what we had hoped for was *proofs,* but alas, all we got instead was mere *representations* of proofs? But representations of proofs *are* proofs, aren't they?[25]

In other words, in some cases (a rainstorm) the simulation or representation of something is quite different from the real thing. In other cases, the representation of something (a mathematical proof) is equivalent to the real thing. The word *artificial* is ambiguous because it can serve two purposes. We might use it to make this contrast: artificial versus genuine. In this sense, artificial flowers or artificial diamonds are not real flowers or diamonds, but only simulate the genuine articles. On the other hand, we can use *artificial* to make a different sort of contrast: artificial versus natural. Artificial light is not natural because it is produced by human technology. But in contrast to artificial flowers, artificial light is real light. So maybe intelligence can be artificial in that it is created by computer programs rather than nature at the same time that it can be real intelligence.

The Chess-Playing Machine Revisited

At this point, it will be useful to examine the three responses to Edgar Allan Poe's critique of the chess-playing machine mentioned in the "Stop and Think" box at the beginning of this section. As we go through these points, consider whether you have changed your mind about the original issue. The first response was:

1. Poe was right. You need a mind to play chess and, therefore, many of today's computers have minds.

This response correlates to the theory of strong AI. If computers can perform those tasks that we associate with human intelligence, then computers have minds.

The second response was:

2. Poe was wrong. You don't need a mind to play chess.

This response is one way that a critic of strong AI would deal with the fact that computers now play chess. This response points to an interesting tendency. Critics of strong AI use arguments of this form:

1. If something has a mind, it can do X.
2. Computers cannot do X.
3. Therefore, computers do not have minds.

In Poe's case, X was the ability to play chess. Other examples of X might be the ability to understand language, the ability to learn, the ability to write original poetry, the ability to make intelligent decisions, or the ability to solve problems. There are two difficulties here. The first is that many people cannot learn to play chess or write poetry. Nevertheless, we still consider them to have minds. We should not necessarily expect computers to do things that many humans cannot do. Another difficulty is that every time a computer program is developed that does X, then the ante is raised, so to speak. Poe assumed that machines could never play chess. We now know that computers can play chess. So, critics of strong AI now reject the chess-playing version of premise 1. But if we keep changing our criteria for what constitutes having mental abilities merely to avoid attributing these abilities to computers, then we really are not playing fair.

The third response was:

3. Computers don't *really* play chess, but only simulate it.

This response is similar to Searle's response concerning the ability of computers to understand language. We have already discussed Searle's and Dennett's disagreement over what constitutes a simulated performance and a genuine performance. Other versions of this response insist that conscious awareness is necessary for actions to be genuinely intelligent or for something to have a mind. These sorts of arguments run like this:

Present the thought experiment titled "Minds versus Computers" (pp. 248–249) to five friends. If possible, also discuss it with faculty or others who are knowledgeable in a field related to cognitive science (psychology, computer science, or artificial intelligence). How did your friends' answers compare with your own? Were there any differences between the answers of laypersons and those of the professionals?

1. If something has a mind, it has subjective, conscious experiences.
2. Even computers that pass the Turing Test do not have subjective, conscious experiences.
3. Therefore, even computers that pass the Turing Test do not have minds.

Many theorists would say that this point is the one that Searle should have made from his thought experiment. Although the person manipulating Chinese symbols according to rules has consciousness, he or she does not have an understanding of what those symbols mean. Even less does a computer have understanding, for it lacks both intentionality and consciousness. The missing ingredient seems to be some sort of subject-related understanding and awareness. This subjective awareness does not fit well with identity theory or with the computational model of the mind.

Here is where the dualist rejoins the battle. The dualist would agree with the functionalist that the unique nature of mental events is not explained by the specific physical makeup of our brains. The dualist would agree with Searle and the antifunctionalists that abstract, formal relationships cannot constitute minds. The existence of consciousness and subjective points of view are brute facts about our world, and it could be argued that, as yet, there are no plausible explanations of how they arise out of physical systems. The problem with this argument is that it is hard to put your finger on consciousness and describe it. One philosopher has said: If you have it you know what it is, and if you don't have it there is no use trying to explain it to you. But how large a role does conscious awareness play in our activities? Is consciousness simply a surface-level phenomenon that floats on all the cognitive processing that occurs below it? If it is, then is it less important than the dualist thinks it is?

STOP AND THINK

Think about all the ways in which cognitive processing (e.g., problem solving, decision making, driving a car) occurs at the subconscious level. To what degree is conscious awareness present or absent in activities that are considered to be intelligent?

LOOKING THROUGH THE LENS OF FUNCTIONALISM AND STRONG AI

1. To treat severe cases of epilepsy, physicians will remove half the patient's brain. They have found that, in time, the person can resume a normal life because the remaining half of the brain takes over most of the cognitive and motor skills once performed by the missing half. How does this research support the functionalist's claim that our mental states are not identical with any particular physical embodiment, but that they are a collection of

psychological patterns and causal relations that could be realized in different sorts of physical media?

2. In the movies *ET* and *Star Wars* (numerous other science fiction films would also be relevant), we have creatures, such as aliens (ET) or robots (R2D2, C3PO), whose physical makeup is quite different from ours. Yet these creatures have beliefs, desires, and feelings just like ours, and they embody a psychology similar to ours. In the context of the story, if the robots R2D2 or C3PO were opened up, we would find nothing but wires. Still, we can imagine ourselves relating to them just as we would any other companion. We would feel sorry for them if they became damaged. Do our emotional reactions to these characters indicate that we would have a disposition to treat such advanced but different beings as psychologically like us? Does this indication lend some plausibility to functionalism?

3. Most functionalists do not address the question of life after death, but could a functionalist still believe in immortality? Hint: My ideas are embodied in the physical ink and paper of this book. If the only copy of this book were destroyed, could the ideas in this book be "resurrected" in some other medium for future generations of students to ponder? Benjamin Franklin's tombstone expresses a somewhat functionalist notion of life after death:

> This body of B. Franklin in Christ Church cemetery,
> Printer, Like the Cover of an old Book,
> Its Contents torn out,
> And stript of its Lettering and Gilding,
> Lies here, Food for Worms.
> But the work shall not be lost;
> For it will, as he believed,
> Appear once more in a new and more elegant Edition,
> Corrected and Improved by its Author.

4. People frequently object to the strong AI thesis by claiming that computers are not really intelligent but are merely doing what they have been programmed to do. But in what sense is this statement true of you? If you play chess, you follow the rules that you have been taught just as a computer does. When a computer learns to play chess, it is not only programmed with the rules, but it receives feedback and correction when it makes a strategic mistake. Subsequently, it makes decisions based on probable outcomes learned from experience. Is education, then, simply a sophisticated form of programming? If so, do computers learn and make decisions differently than humans do? What would an advocate of strong AI say?

5. Skeptics concerning artificial intelligence frequently say that computers will never reach the level of having minds because they will never be able to have emotions. Are emotions necessary in order to have a mind? Don't our emotions sometimes interfere with our ability to think? Without emotions, can computers, therefore, be better thinkers than we are? But maybe computers or robots will be able to have emotions some day. When a bully harasses us, we may feel the emotion of fear or anger. But what is fear? Fear is based on the judgment that something is dangerous to our well-being. It is also the disposition to respond by running or taking other actions. Isn't it possible to create a computer to have causal responses functionally identical to fear? In the movie *Star Wars,* the robots C3PO and R2D2 exhibited emotions. Hence, could the advocate of strong AI reasonably say that

either emotions are not necessary to have a mind or that emotional response patterns could be part of a computer's program?

6. Because the advocate of strong AI believes that computers will eventually have all the capabilities that will enable them to have minds like ours and because a computer behaves in the way it has been programmed to behave, does it necessarily follow that an advocate of strong AI is committed to the position that we, like computers, are "programmed" or determined in our behavior?

EXAMINING THE STRENGTHS AND WEAKNESSES OF FUNCTIONALISM AND STRONG AI

Positive Evaluation

1. Throughout the history of AI research, critics have continually said that computers will never really be intelligent, because they cannot do X (play chess, understand language, make decisions). However, every time a computer accomplishes one of these cognitive tasks, the critics still are not convinced. Are the critics raising the standard every time computers achieve it? What criteria would you use to decide whether computers really were intelligent? Are there any reasons to suppose that future computers will not be able to fulfill these criteria?

2. You can do many things without consciously attending to exactly how you do them. For example, you can judge if a tree is close or far away, decide if a poem is good or is drivel, determine if a person is angry or happy, decide if it is likely that the football team will win its next game. Because you can do these things, doesn't it make sense that you are unconsciously following some procedure to do them? Why can't the procedures we use to carry out our cognitive tasks be formulated and taught to computers?

Negative Evaluation

1. One of the most important features that we normally associate with minds is consciousness. Both the functionalists and strong AI advocates talk about the relations between inputs, the various states of cognitive processing, and outputs, but consciousness is never discussed. Can the functionalist's theory account for the fact that our minds exhibit conscious awareness? If functionalists cannot account for this awareness, can their theory of the mind and its cognitive activities still be complete? Is it possible that something we would recognize as consciousness could emerge from a very sophisticated computer? If a computer does not have consciousness, can it meaningfully be said to think? Do negative answers to all these questions refute functionalism and strong AI?

2. Give a functionalist's account of the mental state of pain in terms of the inputs that cause it, the relations it has to other mental states, and the behavior it produces. Furthermore, imagine a computer realizing all these functional states. Does this account contain anywhere the subjective feeling of being in pain that we associate with the mental state of pain? If not, does this absence count against the functionalist's theory that a particular mental state is simply a pattern of causal relations between inputs, other mental states, and actions? Does this absence count against the strong AI claim that computers can have minds?

SCOUTING THE TERRITORY: *Freedom and Determinism*

On February 9, 1979, identical twins Jim Lewis and Jim Springer met for the first time. Separated at birth, the twins had lived completely apart for 39 years. During this time, there had been no contact between the two brothers or between the two sets of adoptive parents. In the midst of their euphoria over their rediscovery of each other, the twin brothers became aware of a series of eerie similarities in their lives and behavior:

Both had been named James by their adoptive parents.
Both had been married twice.
Both of their first wives were named Linda.
Both of them married women named Betty the second time.
Both of them gave nearly the same name to the oldest son:
James Alan and James Allan.
Both of them chain-smoked the same brand of cigarettes.
Both of them drank the same brand of beer.
Both had served as sheriff's deputies.

As they shared further details of their separate lives, they discovered further facets of their lifestyles that had developed along parallel tracks. Both of them had owned dogs named Toy, pursued a hobby of making miniature furniture in garage workshops, drove Chevys, vacationed on the same beach on the Florida Gulf Coast, and lived in the only house on their block.

Identical twins that have been reared apart are an ideal living laboratory for behavioral scientists. This case and thousands like it are helping scientists get a handle on one of humanity's oldest mysteries: To what degree is human behavior influenced by heredity or environment, genes or life experiences, nature or nurture? If identical twins are raised in separate and different environments, any similarities in their behavior provide support for the thesis that much of our behavior is a product of our genes. On the other hand, the differences between such twins would have to be a result of differences in their environment or life's experiences.

A month after the twin Jims met, Dr. Thomas Bouchard of the University of Minnesota paid them to spend a week at his research center. When he gave them a test that measured personality variables, the twins' scores were so close that they appeared to be the test scores of the same person taking the test twice. Brain-wave tests produced graphs that looked like the skyline of the same city. Measurements of their intelligence, mental abilities, gestures, voice tones, likes, and dislikes were remarkably similar as well. Similar studies of identical twins raised in different environments have shown a high correlation between twins' beliefs and attitudes, including their social, political, moral, and religious views.[26]

What are we to make of these studies? Obviously you did not choose many of the features that make you the person you are: the color of your eyes, hair, and skin; your sex; or your height. It would seem to be equally obvious that many facts about you are the result of decisions that you freely made: your favorite music, your spouse, your job, the name of your dog, and your ethical beliefs. Throughout your life you feel as though it is up to you to examine the alternatives, to deliberate, and to make a choice. Surely the twins in these studies felt as though they were freely making these sorts of decisions. Yet it appears as though they were being forced down parallel tracks by causes of which they were not aware.

In the context of this chapter, we say that a person's action or choice is *determined* when it is the inevitable result of prior causes operating on the person. These causes could be the result of psychological or physiological forces.

The studies just described focus on the possible influence of people's genes on their behavior. However, it must not be overlooked that there are always many differences between identical twins. In one study, identical twins who had been separated seemed to have developed different interests because of differences in their upbringing. One twin became a concert pianist; the other had no interest in playing the piano. However, even if our genes do not account for the whole story of our lives, we still have to contend with the claim that who we are is determined by our upbringing and life experiences.

Although the verdict on these issues is not yet in and behavioral scientists are still debating the data, many theorists claim that we are a lot more determined in the decisions we make than we would like to think. In other words, these theorists claim that our decisions are not the spontaneous result of free will, but are the necessary outcome of psychological or physiological causes operating on us, just as our blood pressure is determined by biological causes. But then what happens to our sense of self? Are we completely determined? What reasons do we have for thinking we are not determined? If we are determined, what are the implications for moral responsibility? These questions are some of the most puzzling but unavoidable ones in philosophy today. The following thought experiment explores the notions of choices and their causes as well as the concepts of action and responsibility.

THOUGHT EXPERIMENT: *Actions and Responsibility*

1. List three different things you did simply because they were what you wanted to do (e.g., going to a particular movie, reading a novel, taking a nonrequired course).
   a. _____
   b. _____
   c. _____
   Why do you like the activities on your list? Did you choose to like the things that you like to do? YES NO (Circle one)
   a. If your answer is YES: What caused you to like the things that you like to do?
   b. If your answer is NO: How did you come to like the things that you like to do?

2. Suppose a friend of yours swings his or her arm and knocks over an object that has a great deal of sentimental value to you, shattering it into a million pieces.
   a. Under what circumstances would you say this person clearly was morally responsible for the action?
   b. List as many circumstances as you can in which the person definitely caused the item to be broken but in which you would *not* consider him or her to be morally responsible for this event in the fullest sense of the word.
   c. List circumstances (if any) in which you would not be sure whether the person was morally responsible for breaking the item. (Your uncertainty should not be based on any lack of knowledge concerning the relevant facts.)

CHARTING THE TERRAIN OF FREEDOM AND DETERMINISM: *What Are the Issues?*

The previous thought experiment touched on the first issue that concerns us here; that issue is the question of how to account for the origin of our actions. Think about the last movie you watched or novel you read. Why did you watch *that* movie or read *that* novel? Presumably, your action was the result of an act of your will, based on a choice, that reflected what you wanted to do at that moment. But this presumption raises the question, How do your acts of will, choices, and wants come about? Are they psychological events that simply pop into being without any cause? Is this sudden appearance what you mean when you say that you freely made a decision? If so, why does one mental choice rather than another happen to pop into your head? Another possibility is that your choices and wants are themselves brought about by other events, such as your previous psychological states and other causes operating on you. But this possibility only pushes the question back further, and we must again figure out whether our choices are uncaused events or the result of a series of linked causes extending back into the past. As we shall see, each of these alternatives has its problems.

The other issue raised in the thought experiment concerns moral responsibility. When are we morally responsible for our behavior, and what sorts of circumstances would diminish our responsibility? If our actions are ultimately the result of causes over which we have no control, can we ever be morally responsible?

W. Somerset Maugham's novel *Of Human Bondage* contains a conversation in which the character Philip says,

> "Before I do anything I feel that I have a choice, and that influences what I do; but afterward, when the thing is done, I believe that it was inevitable from all eternity."—"What do you deduce from that?" asked Hayward.—"Why merely the futility of regret. It's no good crying over spilt milk, because all the forces of the universe were bent on spilling it."[27]

Philip's comments represent one perspective on the issues I have just introduced. The first issue concerns freedom. We feel free, but are we genuinely free? If I *feel* nauseated, then it follows that I *am* genuinely nauseated. But does freedom work this way? If we *feel* as though we *are* free, does it necessarily follow that we *are* free? Isn't it possible to be mistaken about whether we are free? Philip says that when we do something, such as spilling milk, "all the forces of the universe were bent on spilling it." Is his conclusion true? Are our actions simply the product of the forces of nature acting on or within us? Is it possible that there is a scientific explanation (genetic, physiological, psychological) for everything we do? Why? How do actions that are the outcome of natural causes affect our sense of autonomy, dignity, and freedom? Another issue arises in Philip's comments. If we are determined to act the way we do, is it meaningless to feel regret over our actions? Can we judge another person to be morally responsible or capable of either blame or praise if his or her actions were inevitable? After you complete the next "Stop and Think" exercise, the "Philosophy in the Marketplace" survey will allow you to discuss these issues with your friends.

STOP AND THINK

Imagine yourself talking to Philip on the phone. Explain to him why you agree or disagree with the following two claims he made:

1. All our actions are "inevitable from all eternity."
2. If all our actions are determined, it is foolish to feel regret for our actions.

Do the following exercise yourself, and present it to at least five friends. Consider each one of the following scenarios as a separate case; that is, the facts in one case do not carry over to the other cases. In each situation, decide whether Dave was morally responsible or worthy of blame for killing Todd. In other words, answer the following two questions:

a. In which of these cases should Dave be sentenced as a criminal who committed murder?

b. In which of these cases should we say that even though Dave tragically caused the death of Todd, Dave was not fully morally responsible for this event?

1. Dave had an undiagnosed brain tumor that one day suddenly caused muscle spasms in his arm and hand. This unexpected spasm caused Dave to involuntarily pull the trigger of his gun and fatally wound Todd while the two were in the woods hunting.

2. Dave was suffering from shell shock and mental instability after serving in a brutal war overseas. Waking up from a blackout, he hallucinated that he was still in the war and that his good friend Todd was the enemy. Thinking that he was acting in self-defense, Dave shot and killed Todd.

3. Dave is normally a quiet, gentle person, but he was hypnotized by an evil psychiatrist and ordered to kill Todd. While in a deep, hypnotic trance, Dave carried out the order.

4. Dave was showing off his handgun to his neighbor Todd. Because Dave did not realize that the gun was loaded, he was handling it carelessly. It accidentally went off and killed Todd.

5. One night in a bar, Dave had way too much to drink. He got into a vicious argument with Todd, who was also drunk and verbally abusive. In a state of alcoholic rage, Dave went to his car and came back with a gun and shot Todd. Dave woke up the next morning in jail with no memory of what happened the night before.

6. Dave's father was a violent and brutal drug dealer who finally took off forever when Dave was 8 years old. Thereafter, Dave's mother had an unending succession of abusive, live-in boyfriends. Dave never experienced love but only physical and psychological abuse. He carried the emotional pain and anger deep within his twisted personality like a ticking time bomb. Finally, at age 22, Dave's bomb exploded. Dave was provoked into a meaningless, heated argument with Todd (a total stranger who reminded him of his abusive father). In a fit of uncontrollable rage, Dave pulled out a gun and shot Todd.

7. Dave was having an affair with Todd's wife and wanted her husband out of the way. After weeks of planning and stalking Todd, Dave shot and killed him as Todd left his gym.

PHILOSOPHY *in the* MARKETPLACE

CONCEPTUAL TOOLS: *Thinking about Freedom*

Before I set out the alternatives, I need to clarify the word *freedom* because everyone has a different notion of what it means to be free. Basically, two kinds of freedom are relevant to our discussion of philosophy. Different authors have given these two freedoms different labels, but what is important is the distinction being made and not the terminology.

We have **circumstantial freedom** when we have the ability and the opportunity to perform whatever action we choose. Circumstantial freedom is a negative condition, because it means we are free *from* external forces, obstacles, and natural limitations that

circumstantial freedom the ability and the opportunity to perform whatever action we choose, that is, freedom from external forces, obstacles, and natural limitations that restrict or compel our actions

metaphysical freedom the power of the self to choose among genuine alternatives; free will

restrict or compel our actions. In this sense, you would not be free to go to the movies if you were tied up or if someone was holding a gun to your head (external forces). Similarly, you are not free to jump 50 feet in the air (a natural limitation).

Notice that the fact that you have circumstantial freedom says nothing about how your choices originate. Bees constructing a honeycomb have circumstantial freedom even though their activity is driven by blind instinct. Similarly, all philosophers would agree that your pursuit of a particular career is circumstantially free (assuming no one is holding a gun to your head). However, your freedom in this sense does not rule out the possibility that your career choice is the inevitable outcome of your genetic inheritance, personality, biochemistry, social conditioning, or other determining causes.

All philosophers would agree that it is possible for us to have the circumstantial freedom to act as we desire. The controversy is whether we have the second kind of freedom. I have called this second kind of freedom **metaphysical freedom** because whether we have this kind of freedom depends on what sort of universe we live in and on what is fundamentally true about human nature. As we will see, some philosophers deny that we have this freedom. Metaphysical freedom is identical to what we ordinarily mean when we talk about free will, a concept that refers to the power of the self to choose among genuine alternatives. Metaphysical freedom does not relate to external circumstances but to our internal condition. Here, the self is the creative, originating cause of a decision or action. If we have this freedom, then we could have made different choices in the past than the ones we did.

It follows that if we have metaphysical freedom (free will), then the given circumstances and our psychological makeup prior to a decision are *not* sufficient to make a particular choice necessary or inevitable. External circumstance and our personality may exert some influence over our decisions, but in the final analysis, which of several alternatives we act on is decided by our free, spontaneous choice. Naturally, our ability to exercise our metaphysical freedom on a particular occasion could be limited by our lack of circumstantial freedom. Nevertheless, metaphysical freedom allows the self the capacity to make free and undetermined choices within the bounds of its external limitations. Because all philosophers agree that normally we have a certain amount of circumstantial freedom, the main controversy is whether we have metaphysical freedom.

CHOOSING A PATH: *What Are My Options Concerning Human Freedom?*

We can formulate the issue of freedom and determinism in terms of three statements and different combinations of responses to these statements. The three statements are:

1. We are determined.
2. If we are determined, then we lack the freedom necessary to be morally responsible.
3. We do have the freedom necessary to be morally responsible.

These statements create an inconsistent triad, which means it is impossible for all three statements to be true. You can accept any two of these statements, but to do so requires that you reject the third statement.

STOP AND THINK

Try picking different pairs of the three statements and convince yourself that each pair implies the falsehood of the remaining statement.

You can take one of three positions on the issue of freedom and determinism: hard determinism, libertarianism, and compatibilism. Each position is defined by which two statements are accepted and which one is rejected. We will briefly examine each of these statements and the terminology associated with them. Then we will see how these statements serve to define the three philosophical alternatives.

Statement 1: We Are Determined

Those philosophers who agree with this statement do so because they believe that all events are the necessary result of previous causes. This position is known as **determinism.** If determinism were true and if it were possible to have complete knowledge of the universe at the present moment, then we could predict not only the state of the universe in the next minute but also everything that will happen in the future. The French astronomer Pierre-Simone Laplace (1749–1827) expressed this idea by imagining the perspective of a super-intelligent being:

> We ought then to consider the present state of the universe as the effect of its previous state and as the cause of that which is to follow. An intelligence that, at a given instant, could comprehend all the forces by which nature is animated and the respective situation of the beings that make it up, if moreover it were vast enough to submit these data to analysis, would encompass in the same formula the movements of the greatest bodies of the universe and those of the lightest atoms. For such an intelligence nothing would be uncertain, and the future, like the past, would be open to its eyes.[28]

Because our choices, beliefs, desires, and actions are themselves events, the determinist claims that they, too, are the necessary result of previous causes. Determinists disagree as to which type of cause is most important in producing our behavior, whether it be our genetic inheritance, biochemistry, behavioral conditioning, or even God's will. Nevertheless, they all agree that everything that happens in nature and in human behavior is the inevitable outcome of the causal order. Determinists acknowledge that we can have circumstantial freedom but deny that we have metaphysical freedom. In our subsequent discussion of determinism, you will see that there are two forms of determinism (hard determinism and compatibilism), but both of them begin by affirming statement 1.

It is important to understand the significance of the determinist's claim. If you are a determinist, you would have to agree that the following statement by John Stuart Mill, a 19th-century British philosopher, applies to you.

> Correctly conceived, the doctrine called Philosophical Necessity is simply this: that, given the motives which are present to an individual's mind, and given likewise the character and disposition of the individual, the manner in which he will act might be unerringly inferred: that if we knew the person thoroughly, and knew all the inducements which are acting upon him, we could foretell his conduct with as much certainty as we can predict any physical event.[29]

On the other hand, in his short novel *Notes from Underground,* Fyodor Dostoyevsky has his character express the conviction that determinism would strip us of our humanity and that we would end up being no more than parts in the machine of nature, much like an organ stop (part of the mechanism of a pipe organ).

determinism the claim that all events are the necessary result of previous causes

Two Men Holding Arrows by Tomek Olbinski. In this playful picture, the artist depicts a man holding a dull gray arrow pointing in one direction, while inside it is another man holding a cloud-like arrow pointing in the other direction. The libertarian might say that the gray arrow represents the causal influences on us that incline us to act in a deterministic manner. Still, within us is the element of free will (depicted by the man with the cloud-filled arrow) that allows us to transcend our causal influences and to make free choices contrary to the deterministic tendencies that operate on us. The determinist might interpret the gray arrow as representing not merely tendencies but as the sum of inescapable causes (personality, behavioral conditioning, genes, biochemistry) that make us what we are and determine what we do. As such, they will motivate the man to move in the direction in which they point. The determinist also might interpret the interior man as clinging to his feelings of freedom (represented by the clouds), but might add that these feelings are illusory. After all, even if the interior man thinks he aspires to go to the left, his strongest motives are located in the larger arrow (the deterministic causes), which will inevitably carry him to the right. Thus, determinism reigns supreme over our illusory feelings of freedom. Which interpretation do you think best depicts the human situation?

Indeed, if there really is some day discovered a formula for all our desires and caprices—that is, an explanation of what they depend upon, by what laws they arise, how they develop, what they are aiming at in one case and in another and so on, that is a real mathematical formula—then, most likely, man will at once cease to feel desire, indeed, he will be certain to. For who would want to choose by rule? Besides, he will at once be transformed from a human being into an organ-stop or something of the sort; for what is a man without desire, without free will and without choice, if not a stop in an organ?[30]

Statement 2: If We Are Determined, Then We Lack the Freedom Necessary to Be Morally Responsible

This statement expresses the thesis of **incompatibilism,** for it claims that determinism is incompatible with the sort of freedom required to be morally responsible for our behavior. What does it mean to be morally responsible for an action? It means that we deserve praise or rebuke, credit or blame, reward or punishment for that action. The issue is not whether rewards or punishments are effective in causally determining a person's behavior. Instead, for the incompatibilists, moral responsibility is a question of whether we *deserve* reward or punishment. We can deserve these consequences, they say, only if we had genuine alternatives such that we could have chosen to act otherwise than we did. In other words, the incompatibilist claim is that having moral responsibility requires that we have metaphysical freedom.

incompatibilism the claim that determinism is incompatible with the sort of freedom required to be morally responsible for our behavior

Statement 3: We Do Have the Freedom Necessary to Be Morally Responsible

All three positions that we will discuss agree that some sort of freedom is a necessary condition for moral responsibility. Philosophers express this belief by saying, "Ought implies can." Accordingly, all three positions would agree that if you lack circumstantial freedom in a situation (a gun is held to your head, you are drugged, or you are tied up), then you cannot be responsible for what you do or don't do when suffering from these constraints. However, they disagree over which of the following two options is correct: (1) Circumstantial freedom is a sufficient condition for a person to be morally responsible or (2) circumstantial freedom is merely a minimal, necessary condition for responsibility and a person must also have metaphysical freedom to be held morally accountable for his or her behavior.

Three Positions on Freedom, Determinism, and Responsibility

The position of **hard determinism** claims that all our choices are determined and that we do not have moral responsibility for our actions. Accordingly, the hard determinist agrees with statement 1 (we are determined) and agrees with statement 2 (if we are determined, then we lack the freedom necessary to be morally responsible) and therefore rejects statement 3 (we do have the freedom necessary to be morally responsible). By accepting statement 2, the hard determinist is affirming incompatibilism. Hard determinists reject statement 3 because they claim that moral responsibility requires metaphysical freedom (free will), but that is something we lack. In a speech to prisoners in jail, Clarence Darrow,

hard determinism the dual claims that (1) having metaphysical freedom is a necessary condition for people to be morally responsible for their choices in any meaningful sense of the word and (2) we do not have the metaphysical freedom required for moral responsibility

the famous defense attorney, forthrightly expressed the hard determinist's denial of moral responsibility.

> I do not believe there is any sort of distinction between the real moral conditions of the people in and out of jail. One is just as good as the other. The people here can no more help being here than the people outside can avoid being outside. I do not believe that people are in jail because they deserve to be. They are in jail simply because they cannot avoid it on account of circumstances which are entirely beyond their control and for which they are in no way responsible.[31]

Darrow's position was that if we want to prevent people from becoming criminals, we must eliminate the social conditions that make people criminals.

Libertarianism is the position that rejects determinism and asserts that we *do* have metaphysical freedom. (The libertarianism we are concerned with here is a metaphysical position and is entirely different from the political philosophy of the same name.) The libertarian rejects statement 1 (we are determined), accepts statement 2 (if we are determined, then we lack the freedom necessary to be morally responsible), and accepts statement 3 (we do have the freedom necessary to be morally responsible). In contrast to the determinist, the libertarian claims that at least some human choices are free and exempt from causal necessity. Free choices are grounded in the free will of the person and hence are not the inevitable result of previous causes. Accordingly, the libertarian claims that it is often impossible (even in principle) to predict every detail of a person's behavior. Libertarians and hard determinists agree that being determined is incompatible with moral responsibility (incompatibilism), for without metaphysical freedom our character and choices are the inevitable product of forces beyond our control. Since libertarians believe we do have metaphysical freedom and thus are not determined, they believe we have the capacity to be morally responsible. On the other hand, since hard determinists deny that we have metaphysical freedom by claiming we are determined, they also deny that we have the capacity to be morally responsible. In response to Darrow's speech to the prisoners, the libertarian would assert that criminals are accountable for their actions because they are free and are not completely determined by their circumstances.

It may seem that this discussion has covered all the options. However, there is another variety of determinism known as compatibilism. **Compatibilism** is the claim that we are both determined *and* that we have moral responsibility. In other words, compatibilists accept statement 1 (we are determined), reject statement 2 (if we are determined, then we lack the freedom necessary to be morally responsible), and accept statement 3 (we do have the freedom necessary to be morally responsible). Since compatibilists are determinists, what sort of freedom do they think we have? According to the compatibilist, an action is free to the degree that it is not the product of external compulsion. If the immediate cause of your action is your own psychological states, including your will, choices, values, or desires, then it is a free or voluntary action for which you can be held responsible. At the same time, the compatibilist insists that your personality, motives, and values are completely determined by previous causes. In other words, the compatibilist denies that we have metaphysical freedom. However, contrary to the hard determinist and the libertarian, the compatibilist believes that circumstantial freedom is the only kind of freedom necessary for us to be responsible for our choices and actions. In response to Darrow's speech, the compatibilist would say that criminals, as well as law-abiding citizens, are morally responsible for their actions if their actions were the outcome of who they are and what they believe, value, or desire. At the same time, the compatibilist would insist that everyone's wants, desires, and motives are causally determined.

libertarianism the thesis that we *do* have metaphysical freedom; a rejection of determinism

compatibilism the thesis that we are both determined *and* have the sort of freedom necessary to be morally responsible for our actions; sometimes called soft determinism

TABLE 3.3 *Three Positions on Freedom and Determinism*			
	1	2	3
Philosophical Positions	We Are Determined	If We Are Determined, Then We Lack the Freedom Necessary to Be Morally Responsible	We Are Morally Responsible
Hard Determinist	Agrees	Agrees	Disagrees
Libertarian	Disagrees	Agrees	Agrees
Compatibilist	Agrees	Disagrees	Agrees

The discussion of the three positions on freedom and determinism is summarized in table 3.3.

 **STOP AND THINK**

Go back over the seven scenarios concerning Dave's shooting of Todd. In each case, decide what the hard determinist, libertarian, and compatibilist would say about Dave's responsibility for his actions. Note: In a few of the scenarios, it might be debatable which answer would be consistent with the position in question.

WHAT DO I THINK? *Questionnaire on Freedom and Determinism*

For each statement, mark whether you agree or disagree. Note that each numbered statement has two answers that are the same. If the response you choose for a particular statement has two identical answers, be sure to check them both. In other words, if you agree with statement 1, you should check agree twice.

1. Everything that happens in the world is a necessary result of previous causes.	Agree	Disagree	Agree
2. If it would be possible for scientists to know my past, my biochemical makeup, and all the causes acting on and within me, then my behavior would be perfectly predictable.	Agree	Disagree	Agree
3. When I feel that a decision is completely spontaneous and uncaused, that simply means that I am ignorant of all the causes that necessarily generated that decision.	Agree	Disagree	Agree
4. Some choices I make are not the necessary result of previous causes.	Disagree	Agree	Disagree

(continued . . .)

(. . . continued)

	H	L	C
5. Sometimes I regret a decision I made. In these cases I believe that, at the time I made the particular decision, I genuinely could have made a different choice.	Disagree	Agree	Disagree
6. Although physiological, sociological, and psychological conditions *influence* my choices, they do not totally *determine* them.	Disagree	Agree	Disagree
7. For an action to be free, it cannot be completely determined by previous causes.	Agree	Agree	Disagree
8. Even if I am 100 percent determined to behave the way I do, my actions are free if they result from my own choices, values, and desires.	Disagree	Disagree	Agree
9. If everything I think, decide, or do is completely determined by physiological or psychological causes that control me, then it is impossible for me to be morally responsible for any of my actions.	Agree	Agree	Disagree
10. Even if my choices are completely determined by previous causes, I am morally responsible for a particular action as long as the immediate cause of that action was my own choice and not some form of external coercion.	Disagree	Disagree	Agree
Add up the number of checks in each column (H, L, C) and put the total in the box for that column.			
	H	L	C

![key icon] **KEY TO THE QUESTIONNAIRE ON FREEDOM AND DETERMINISM**

The H column contains the answers for *hard determinism.* The L column represents *libertarianism.* The C column represents *compatibilism.* Whichever column had the most checks is the position closest to your own.

Statements 1 through 6 Deal with the Issue of Determinism

Statements 1, 2, 3: If you answered "Agree" to any of these statements, you should have answered the same for all three. If you answered "Agree" to these statements, you are a determinist.

Statements 4, 5, 6: If you answered "Agree" to any of these statements, you should have answered the same for all three. If you answered "Agree" to these statements, you are a libertarian. Your answer to statements 1, 2, and 3 should be the opposite of the answers for 4, 5, and 6.

Statements 7 and 8 Deal with the Issue of Freedom

Statement 7: If you answered "Agree," you are an incompatibilist, which means you are either a hard determinist or a libertarian. If you answered "Disagree," you are a compatibilist.

Statement 8: If you answered "Agree," you are a compatibilist. If you answered "Disagree," you are an incompatibilist and either a hard determinist or a libertarian. Your answer here should be the opposite of that for statement 7.

Statements 9 and 10 Deal with the Issue of Moral Responsibility

Statement 9: If you answered "Agree," you are an incompatibilist and either a hard determinist or a libertarian. If you answered "Disagree," you are a compatibilist.

Statement 10: If you answered "Agree," you are a compatibilist. If you answered "Disagree," you are an incompatibilist and either a hard determinist or a libertarian. Your answer here should be the opposite of that for statement 9.

- Which position did your answers favor?
- How consistent were your answers?

3.6 HARD DETERMINISM

LEADING QUESTIONS: *Hard Determinism*

1. Suppose you have laid down your hard-earned cash to purchase the car of your dreams. As you take it out for a drive, however, you find that the windshield wipers spontaneously go on and off for no apparent reason, as does the radio and the horn. Frustrated and irate, you drive the car back to the dealer. After the car has been in the shop for an hour, the dealer comes out and says to you, "It's really strange. There is no cause for the behavior of your car. These events are just happening on their own." Would you accept this explanation? Why?

2. Think about your unique personality traits. Are you an extrovert or an introvert? Are you an assertive or passive person? Are you very emotional, or are you naturally calm, stable, and unmoveable? Are you decisive or indecisive? Did you choose these personality traits? Could you decide to be an emotional person on Mondays, Wednesdays, and Fridays and an even-tempered, rocklike person on Tuesdays, Thursdays, Saturdays? Why? If you did not choose your personality, then where did it come from or what caused it?

3. How does your personality affect your behavior and choices? If you did not choose your personality, then are you morally responsible for actions that result from it?

THE DEBATE OVER DETERMINISM

The 20th-century psychologist B. F. Skinner wrote the novel *Walden Two* to present his ideas about human behavior. It contains the following dialogue between a behavioral scientist (Frazier) and a philosopher (Castle). Frazier (who represents Skinner) maintains that everything we do is determined by prior conditioning. Castle opposes him by maintaining that we have free will. As you read the dialogue, decide which character comes closest to representing your viewpoint.

"My answer [to the question of freedom] is simple enough," said Frazier. "I deny that freedom exists at all. I must deny it—or my program [of developing a science of behavior] would be absurd. You can't have a science about a subject matter which hops capriciously about. Perhaps we can never *prove* that man isn't free; it's an assumption. But the increasing success of a science of behavior makes it more and more plausible."

"On the contrary, a simple personal experience makes it untenable," said Castle. "The experience of freedom. I *know* that I'm free. . . ."

"The 'feeling of freedom' should deceive no one," said Frazier. "Give me a concrete case."

"Well right now," Castle said. He picked up a book of matches. "I'm free to hold or drop these matches."

"You will, of course, do one or the other," said Frazier. "Linguistically or logically there seem to be two possibilities, but I submit that there's only one in fact. The determining forces may be subtle but they are inexorable. I suggest that as an orderly person you will probably hold—ah! you drop them! Well, you see, that's all part of your behavior with respect to me. You couldn't resist the temptation to prove me wrong. It was all lawful. You had no choice. The deciding factor entered rather late, and naturally you couldn't foresee the result when you first held them up. There was no strong likelihood that you would act in either direction, and so you said you were free."

"That's entirely too glib," said Castle. "It's easy to argue lawfulness after the fact. But let's see you predict what I will do in advance. Then I'll agree there's law."

"I didn't say that behavior is always predictable, any more than the weather is always predictable. There are often too many factors to be taken into account. We can't measure them all accurately, and we couldn't perform the mathematical operations needed to make a prediction if we had the measurements."

- Do you think Frazier is correct in claiming that science requires us to deny human freedom?
- Why does Castle believe he is free?
- Do you think Castle has a good reason for believing in freedom?
- How does Frazier reconcile the fact that our behavior is not always predictable with his belief in determinism?
- Do you tend to agree with Frazier or Castle? Why?

SURVEYING THE CASE FOR HARD DETERMINISM

One afternoon, I walked into the student union at my university and found that a large crowd had gathered to watch a professional hypnotist demonstrating his skills. The main attraction was three male students with glazed-over eyes seated on chairs. They had obviously been placed in a hypnotic trance and were responding to everything the hypnotist said. He told them that they were on a spaceship hurtling through space, which caused them to press back against their chairs and grimace as he described the effects of acceleration on them. Next, he told them that they were making a rather rough landing on a planet, and the three students rocked and jerked as the hypnotist's fictional scenario became reality within their minds. Finally, he told them the planet was very cold and they needed to fight the onset of hypothermia. To the delight of the spectators, these three strangers began to huddle together and embrace each other while shivering from the "frigid" air. It is certain that they would not have behaved this way if they had not been in a hypnotic trance and under the control of the hypnotist.

We have all read similar accounts of how a person's ability to make free decisions has been diminished by hypnosis or brainwashing or by the effects of drugs, disease, or some form of mental incapacity. When someone's behavior is being caused by factors over which he or she has no control, it seems fairly clear that such an individual would lack the capacity to exercise free will. But are these cases exceptions to the general rule? Do we normally have free will except under these extreme conditions? The determinist would say that hypnotism, brainwashing, or abnormal medical conditions are simply unusual ways by which our behavior or mental states may be caused. According to the determinist, our behavior, even under conditions that we may consider "normal," is still the inevitable result of causes that are acting on and within us.

As was stated in the previous section, all versions of determinism (hard determinism and compatibilism) agree with statement 1, "We are determined." However, the hard determinist (and not the compatibilist) agrees with statement 2, "If we are determined, then we lack the freedom necessary to be morally responsible." Finally, the hard determinist rejects statement 3 and claims instead that "we are *not* morally responsible for actions." In what follows, I will discuss the two pillars of determinism or two ways of arguing for the truth of statement 1. The first pillar consists of a series of arguments against the claim that we have free will (in the sense of metaphysical freedom). In other words, this pillar will consist of problems with libertarianism. The second pillar consists of positive arguments for determinism. The hard determinist and the compatibilist both accept these arguments against metaphysical freedom (libertarianism) and in support of determinism. Finally, I will discuss the issue of moral responsibility and why the hard determinist claims we don't have it (the issue at the heart of statements 2 and 3). This issue separates the hard determinist and the compatibilist, for the compatibilist believes we are capable of moral responsibility.

THE PROBLEMS WITH LIBERTARIANISM

Libertarianism Is in Conflict with the Scientific View of the World

Throughout history, science has progressed by replacing explanations of events based on voluntary, spontaneous acts of free will with explanations in terms of deterministic laws. For example, the ancient Greeks believed that a stone fell to the ground because it *desired* to be reunited with its mother the earth. Other natural events such as solar eclipses, plagues, bountiful crops, or thunderstorms were thought to be caused by the arbitrary will of the gods. Our ability to understand the world took a great leap forward when people came to realize that the causes of these events have nothing to do with stones or gods desiring or willing anything. Instead, we came to view such events as rooted in a deterministic system of natural laws. Applying this system to our own day, the determinist would point out that we are gaining a better understanding of human behavior by looking for the causal laws that explain it. As the psychologist B. F. Skinner said, "A scientific analysis of behavior must, I believe, assume that a person's behavior is controlled by his genetic and environmental histories rather than by the person himself as an initiating, creative agent."[33]

Libertarianism Requires the Problematic Notion of Uncaused Events

According to the determinist, the belief that human actions are a product of free will implies that some events (acts of the will) simply happen without any cause to produce them or explain them. For example, if you decide to join a political party, what caused your decision? Why did you decide to join *that* party while your neighbor decided to join an opposing party? You might explain your choice in terms of your values, beliefs, or ideals, but where did these values, beliefs, and ideals come from? At some point, the determinist claims, the belief in free will requires us to suppose that some psychological events simply happen and happen in a certain way, but without any cause that can explain them. While some determinists still find it appropriate to explain human actions in terms of wants, desires, or motives that activate the will, they still would insist that these psychological states must have a causal history that explains them.

Libertarianism Fails to Explain the Fact That We Can Influence Other People's Behavior

A common presupposition of all human interaction, says the determinist, is that it is possible to causally affect one another's behavior. If human actions and volitions were not the result of causes acting on them, it would be useless to reward or punish people. In a world that has no deterministic causes, the way people behaved would be completely unpredictable and capricious. However, it is obvious that we can, to a large degree, predict and influence how people will behave. This ability implies causal connections between the causes that precede an act of the will and the behavior that results. The degree to which we can understand a person's psychological state and the causes operating on it is the degree to which we can predict what that person will do. The degree to which we can control the causes acting on a person is the degree to which we can influence what that person will do. The activities of parenting, educating, rewarding, and punishing all assume determinism.

THOUGHT EXPERIMENT: *Behavior Modification and Prediction*

- List several occasions in the recent past when you successfully influenced or modified the behavior of another person. (It can be a trivial example.) What means did you use? How is it possible to affect another person's behavior?
- List several occasions when you predicted a friend's behavior or anticipated his or her response to a situation. How is it possible to know ahead of time what another person will do?

THE POSITIVE CASE FOR DETERMINISM

The determinist claims that human actions are just as much the product of causal necessity as is any other event in nature. The basic argument of the determinist could be formulated in the following way:

1. Every event, without exception, is causally determined by prior events.
2. Human thoughts, choices, and actions are events.
3. Therefore, human thoughts, choices, and actions are, without exception, causally determined by prior events.

Premise 1 is a statement of the thesis of universal causation. The only way to avoid determinism is to reject the thesis of universal causation. But is it plausible to reject this thesis? We all believe that changes in the weather, the behavior of our car, the interaction of chemicals, and every other kind of event in the physical world are the necessary result of previous causes. However, libertarians like to think that human behavior is an exception to the rest of nature, because they believe that our choices (including those of the determinists) are freely arrived at and not determined by prior events. The determinist would reply that the defenders of free will are being inconsistent. Why should we think that what we do is somehow immune from the sort of causal necessity that operates in the rest of the world?

STOP AND THINK

Libertarians claim that natural events are part of a deterministic, causal system at the same time that they insist human actions are the result of an undetermined free will. Is there a problem with making this distinction between the way natural events are caused and the way human actions are brought about?

It is important to be clear about the fact that the determinist is claiming that every event is 100 percent determined by prior causes. Most defenders of free will would acknowledge that we have certain psychological tendencies (one person tends to like crowds and another prefers solitude) and would agree that we are influenced by the way we were raised. However, the recognition that we all have certain behavioral tendencies and we all have influences on our behavior falls short of the thesis that everything you think, feel, choose, and do is 100 percent determined by the causes acting on you. The issue of universal causation offers only two extremes and no middle ground. Either *all* human behavior is determined by previous causes (determinism), or *some* human behavior is not determined by previous causes (libertarianism).

It is also important to realize that this issue is not one of personal preference. You miss the point if you say, "It's fine for the determinists if they like to think that their actions are controlled by previous causes, but as for me, I prefer to think my behavior is free." We are not talking about attitudes toward life here but about the nature of reality. Either the determinist is right about the way reality works and the libertarian is wrong, or vice versa. The truth about this issue has nothing to do with what view of human nature you find subjectively pleasing to believe.

Typically, determinists believe that all of reality is physical in nature and that all events are controlled by natural laws. However, some thinkers are **theological determinists** who believe that God is the ultimate cause of everything that happens in the world, including human actions. According to this form of determinism, you make the choices that you do because God made you the sort of person that you are. Hence, all your actions were predetermined by God before the creation of the world.

theological determinist one who believes that God is the ultimate cause of everything that happens in the world, including human actions

THOUGHT EXPERIMENT: *Does Theism Imply Determinism?*

How would you respond to the following argument?

Theism (belief in God) logically implies determinism, for the following reasons. Assuming that there is a God, when he created the world he knew ahead of time that you would be born and that you would make all the choices you did in the past and will make in the future. If he did not want you to do the things you have done, then he would have

(continued . . .)

(. . . continued)

created a world in which you were never born or he would have created a world in which you turned out to be a different sort of person than the one he actually created. Furthermore, he could have made you a person that made other choices. Hence, you and your choices are a product of God's creation in the same way that Hamlet and his choices are a product of Shakespeare's creation.

One of the advantages of determinism is that if it is true, a science of human behavior is possible. Such behavioral sciences as psychology, sociology, and economics attempt to formulate laws that allow us to predict and explain human behavior. Although these sciences are still incomplete, it would be hard to argue that we have learned nothing about human behavior from the research done in these disciplines. The question is, Will it ever be possible to have a complete science of human behavior or at least one that is complete enough to explain the causes of human thoughts, emotions, and actions the way the biologist, chemist, physicist, and astronomer explain the causes of events in nature?

Typically, we think of human behavior as the result of psychological factors such as our beliefs, desires, attitudes, emotions, motives, intentions, values, and personality. Because these factors are considered to be "internal," we feel as though we are not causally determined by external forces (unlike the motion of a billiard ball). But where did your personality come from? Did you decide what it would be? How did you come to have the moral values that you have? If you say that you simply chose them, what caused you to choose one set of values over another set? You have not finished explaining your action by saying, "I *wanted* to do it." The question still remains, "What caused you to want the things that you do?" It seems likely that our psychological makeup did not spring up spontaneously from nowhere. The determinist would insist that your choice of a particular course of action and your possession of certain values and desires are facts about the world that need explaining just as much as the fact that you were born with a certain hair color or that you have the flu.

That much of your behavior originates from within (unlike the billiard ball) is consistent with the determinist's claims. Everything we choose to do is a result of our psychological state and the surrounding circumstances or external stimuli at a particular time. Consequently, the picture the determinist paints concerning the cause of an action looks like this:

Your psychological state is the immediate, determining cause of your behavior in a given situation, but your psychological state was itself the product of a multitude of previous causes.

Response to Objections

A number of objections are typically raised against determinism. I will examine four of them and present the determinist's response. In each case, consider whether you think the determinist gives an adequate reply.

Pose the following questions to five acquaintances, and record their answers *and* the reasons for their answers. When you are finished gathering responses, decide which person gave you the strongest reasons for his or her position.

- Will science ultimately be able to explain you completely and adequately? The "you" that is to be explained includes your personality, values, choices, and actions. Why?

1. *When I make a choice, I have the undeniable feeling that the choice is free.* Many of us resist the notion that there are causes of our behavior. We like to think of ourselves as free. Indeed, we typically have the feeling that we are acting freely. But feeling we are free and actually being free are two different matters. The determinist would say that we feel we are free because we are ignorant of all the external and internal forces (physical and psychological) acting on us.

2. *When I make a choice, I could always have chosen differently.* We have the sense that there is nothing inevitable about the choices we make because we can imagine ourselves acting differently than we did in the past. Let us suppose, for example, that a young woman has to decide between a scholarship offering her a free education at Middleline University (an adequate but quite ordinary state school) and an opportunity to go, without a scholarship and at great expense, to Highstatus University, a very prestigious school. Suppose she chooses Highstatus U. but insists she could have gone to the other school if she had chosen to do so. Doesn't it seem as though she made a free choice and was not compelled to decide as she did?

How does the determinist respond to the "I could have done otherwise" argument? The determinist would claim that whenever you say, "I could have done otherwise," you simply mean, "I would have done otherwise if I had wanted to, which is to say, if those psychological states that determined my action had been different." In our example, the woman's desire to go to the prestigious school was stronger than her desire to save money. She could have chosen otherwise only if her psychological makeup at the time had been different. Given her psychological state and the external circumstances, her choice was inevitable. Notice that we often think about "what could have been" even when we know an event was determined by previous causes. Suppose you are driving along a mountain road and a huge boulder comes crashing down, hitting the highway behind you where you were a half second ago. You say, "I could have been killed." But what you mean is that if the causes acting on the boulder had been different, the results would have been tragically different. You do not mean that the boulder could have freely behaved differently from the way it did, given all the causes acting upon it. So when you say, "I could have done otherwise," you're saying that if your psychological state had been different or if the external circumstances had been different, you would have acted differently. But given your psychological state and the external conditions, your behavior was just as inevitable as that of the boulder.

THOUGHT EXPERIMENT: *Decisions*

Think about some decision you made that had a lot of significance for you (call it decision A). Now, relive your making of that decision in your imagination, but imagine

(continued . . .)

(. . . continued)

yourself making a different decision (call it decision B). Do you find that you also need to imagine yourself having different beliefs, attitudes, motives, or desires in order to produce a different decision? If so, is the determinist correct in saying that our decisions are a product of our psychological states? If you can imagine yourself making a different decision without a change in your psychological state, then why did your original psychological state produce decision A when it could have equally produced decision B? Is there some component of your decision making that is random and uncaused? Does it make sense to say that purely random behavior is any more free than determined behavior?

3. *The fact that sometimes I have to deliberate to make a decision proves that I am not determined.* Another reason we feel free is that we frequently have to deliberate at length when we have trouble making up our minds. In such situations, we feel as though the decision is not already "programmed" within us, but that the outcome is entirely up to what we freely decide. If our behavior is determined, why is it sometimes so hard to make a decision?

In this situation, according to the determinist, we are caught between two conflicting causes, each one pulling us in a different direction. For example, we want to earn money for the summer, but we also want to travel with friends. Each choice has positive and negative aspects (more money means less fun, more fun in traveling means less money). Our difficulty in deciding is a sign that the causal determinants acting on us are almost equal. If we do make a decision, it is because the marginally stronger desire won out over the weaker one. The fact that we have these conflicting desires is, itself, the result of our causal history.

4. *It is impossible to predict another person's behavior.* While agreeing that a person's behavior may not be perfectly *predictable in practice,* the determinist would say that all human behavior is *predictable in principle.* We may never be 100 percent accurate in predicting an individual's behavior because a human's psychological makeup is so complex that we cannot know someone's total psychological state in detail. To use an analogy, we cannot predict the weather perfectly. However, we do know enough about its causes to make some fairly good probability judgments. The reason that our predictions are not perfect is that the variables that affect the weather's behavior are too complex and numerous to make an accurate prediction possible.

Even though the behavior of the weather is not predictable in detail, we do not suppose that this unpredictability is because the forces of nature have free will to do as they please. We recognize that the weather's behavior conforms perfectly to the forces of causal necessity such that if we had perfect knowledge of all the variables, we would be able to predict every detail of this weekend's weather. Similarly, the determinist claims, *if* we knew *all* the causes operating on you at a particular time, then your behavior would be as predictable as the rolling of a billiard ball. However, we do know enough about human psychology to know in general how people will behave. In fact, isn't it true that the more you get to know a person, the more you can anticipate how he or she will react to a particular situation?

THE DENIAL OF MORAL RESPONSIBILITY

Thus far, we have discussed the two pillars of hard determinism: the problems with libertarianism and the positive case for determinism. These pillars are shared with compatibilism, the other form of determinism. It is the denial of moral responsibility that sets the hard determinist apart from the compatibilist. We are morally responsible for an action when we can be justly praised or blamed for it and are capable of deserving either reward or punishment. The muscle spasm that causes your arm to jerk could not be helped; you could not be blamed for this behavior because it was just something that happened to you. The question is, "If we are completely determined, can we be responsible for any of our behavior?" Under these circumstances, is it meaningful to say that some actions are voluntary? The hard determinist claims that determinism is incompatible with moral responsibility, whereas the compatibilist believes the two can be reconciled.

To begin thinking about this issue, consider the following passage from Samuel Butler's utopian satire *Erewhon,* in which a judge is passing sentence on a prisoner. The judge considers the possible defense that the prisoner was not responsible for his crime because he was a victim of an unfortunate childhood and past events that caused him to be the sort of person who violated the laws of the state.

- Do you agree that it is possible that this criminal's upbringing could prevent him from being morally responsible for his crimes?
- On the contrary, do you agree with the judge that a criminal's causal history is irrelevant and that it is just to punish him for any crimes he committed?

 FROM SAMUEL BUTLER

Erewhon[34]

"Prisoner at the bar, you have been accused of [a] great crime . . . and after an impartial trial before a jury of your countrymen, you have been found guilty. Against the justice of the verdict I can say nothing: the evidence against you was conclusive, and it only remains for me to pass such a sentence upon you as will satisfy the ends of the law. That sentence must be a very severe one. It pains me much to see one who is yet so young, and whose prospects in life were otherwise so excellent brought to this distressing condition by a constitution which I can only regard as radically vicious; but yours is no case for compassion: this is not your first offense: you have led a career of crime and have only profited by the leniency shown you upon past occasions to offend yet more seriously against the laws and institutions of your country. . . .

"It is all very well for you to say that you came of unhealthy parents, and had a severe accident in your childhood which permanently undermined your constitution; excuses such as these are the ordinary refuge of the criminal; but they cannot for one moment be listened to by the ear of justice. I am not here to enter upon curious metaphysical questions as to the origin of this or that—questions to which there would be no end were their introduction once tolerated. . . . There is no question of how you came to be wicked, but only this—namely, are you wicked or not? This has been decided in the affirmative, neither can I hesitate for a single moment to say that it has been decided justly. You are a bad and dangerous person, and stand branded in the eyes of your fellow countrymen with one of the most heinous known offences."

No doubt, many citizens would agree with these sentiments. On the evening news, we hear of crafty defense attorneys arguing that their client was not responsible for committing a crime because he or she was under psychological distress or had a deprived childhood or was temporarily insane. Are these defenses nothing more than feeble attempts to excuse criminals for making immoral and illegal choices? In response to these courtroom tactics, we might be provoked to say, "Who cares about the defendant's upbringing, past experiences, or psychological problems? Did he commit the crime or didn't he? If he did, then to jail with him!" However, Butler has played a joke on us. The "crime" in the previous passage is pulmonary consumption. The judge points out that the defendant had been arrested for previous offenses such as aggravated bronchitis and did not learn a lesson. The point of the satire, however, is that it is foolish to hold a sick person responsible for conditions over which he or she had no control. Butler believed that our criminal system is just as unreasonable as the one in Erewhon. If every event in the universe has a cause, then both the criminal's and the saint's behavior is the outcome of causal processes that they were powerless to prevent. If Butler is correct, then the criminal, like the person with a lung disease, should not be punished but should be treated and his condition modified so that he will no longer be harmful to society.

STOP AND THINK

- Now that you know the prisoner's "crime" in the story, do you think he should be punished?
- Do you agree with the hard determinist that our psychological condition (which produces our choices) is just as much a product of causes we cannot control as is our physical condition?

Remember that both the hard determinist and the defender of free will (the libertarian) are incompatibilists because they agree with the statement that if we are determined, then we lack the freedom necessary to be morally responsible. They would also both agree with the statement that if we are not determined, then we do have the freedom necessary to be morally responsible. For both the hard determinist and the libertarian, metaphysical freedom is a necessary condition for moral responsibility. Even if we have circumstantial freedom when we act (e.g., no one is holding a gun to our head), if our will is not free of determining causes, then we can no more be held responsible for our actions than we can for the genes we have inherited. Of course, the hard determinist and the libertarian differ over the first clause of each statement, so they differ in their conclusions concerning our capacity to be morally responsible. Although the hard determinists recognize that we do make choices, they believe these choices result from our personality, values, interests, desires, or motives, which are ultimately the products of deterministic causes. For this reason, moral responsibility, according to the hard determinist, is not a human possibility.

A good example of the hard determinists' denial of moral responsibility can be found in the courtroom strategies of Clarence Darrow (1857–1938), one of America's most famous criminal attorneys. In a celebrated case, Darrow defended two teenagers for murdering a 14-year-old boy. The confessed killers were Nathan Leopold Jr. (age 19) and Richard Loeb (age 18). Both came from wealthy Chicago families and were brilliant students; Leopold had already graduated from the University of Chicago and Loeb from the University of Michigan. The murder was the result of an intellectual "experiment" in which they attempted to commit the perfect crime. When they were captured, an outraged public demanded the death penalty. However, Clarence Darrow argued that the two boys were the helpless victims of their heredity and environment. Hence, they were no more responsible for their crime, he said, than they were for the color of their eyes. After Darrow had spoken for 12 hours presenting his final arguments, the silence of the courtroom was broken only by the judge's weeping. The jury was moved by his arguments and chose life sentences for the boys over the death penalty. The following passage is an excerpt from Darrow's summation. Find the phrases that indicate that Darrow was not only a determinist, but a hard determinist as well.

The Leopold and Loeb Trial[35]

This weary old world goes on, begetting, with birth and with living and with death; and all of it is blind from the beginning to the end. I do not know what it was that made these boys do this mad act, but I do know there is a reason for it. I know that they did not beget themselves. I know that any one of an infinite number of causes reaching back to the beginning might be working out in these boy's minds, whom you are asked to hang in malice and in hatred and injustice. . . .

Nature is strong and she is pitiless. She works in her own mysterious way, and we are her victims. We have not much to do with it ourselves. Nature takes this job in hand, and we play our parts. In the words of Omar Khayyam, we are only:

> But helpless pieces in the game He plays
> Upon this checkerboard of nights and days;
> Hither and thither moves and checks, and slays,
> And one by one back in the closet lays.

What had this boy to do with it? He was not his own father; he was not his own mother; he was not his own grandparents. All of this was handed to him. He did not surround himself with governesses and wealth. He did not make himself. And yet he is to be compelled to pay. . . .

I know that one of two things happened to Richard Loeb: that this terrible crime was inherent in his organism, and came from some ancestor; or that it came through his education and his training after he was born. . . .

To believe that any boy is responsible for himself or his early training is an absurdity that no lawyer or judge should be guilty of today. Somewhere this came to the boy. If his failing came from his heredity, I do not know where or how. None of us are bred perfect and pure; and the color of our hair, the color of our eyes, our stature, the weight and fineness of our brain, and everything about us could, with full knowledge, be traced with absolute certainty to somewhere. . . .

If it did not come that way, then I know that if he was normal, if he had been understood, if he had been trained as he should have been it would not have happened. . . .

Every effort to protect society is an effort toward training the youth to keep the path. Every bit of training in the world proves it, and it likewise proves that it sometimes fails. I know that if this boy had been understood and properly trained—properly for him— and the training that he got might have been the very best for someone; but if it had been the proper training for him he would not be in this courtroom today with the noose above his head. If there is responsibility anywhere, it is back of him; somewhere in the infinite number of his ancestors, or in his surroundings, or in both. And I submit, Your Honor, that under every principle of natural justice, under every principle of conscience, of right, and of law, he should not be made responsible for the acts of someone else.

What are the practical consequences of such a view? Should we release all the criminals from jail, since they were not morally responsible for their crimes any more than they were for their eye color? Darrow's position was that we should cure the ills in society that cause criminal behavior. Most hard determinists claim that the criminal is someone with a psychological problem who should be treated the way we treat someone who has a physical disease. We confine someone with an infectious disease to prevent harm to others even though the patient may not have done anything to contract the disease. Furthermore, we would try to cure the patient so that he or she no longer carries the infection.

As Butler's satirical piece suggests, the fact that you are a law-abiding citizen and others are criminals is the result of differences between your background and those of criminals, just as there are differences between a person who came from a healthy home and one who came from a disease-ridden home. How many social psychopaths came from normal, loving homes? Hence, the hard determinist would say that to protect society, it is reasonable to confine criminals if they cannot help but commit crimes. The unpleasant consequences of crime will be determining causes that will help prevent future crimes. While removed from society, the criminal can receive therapy or behavior modification that will change the psychological state that resulted in the criminal act in the first place. What the hard determinist would not agree to is punishment for punishment's sake or punishment that assumes the criminal had the freedom to do otherwise than he or she did.

THOUGHT EXPERIMENT: *Determinism and Differences in Behavior*

Critics of determinism frequently point to cases in which two people, even two siblings, grew up under the same adverse circumstances, but one became a criminal and the other a respectable citizen. How would the determinist respond to the fact that the (apparently) same social conditions produce radically different behaviors?

We can use the following illustration to see how the determinist would tackle this objection. Take two identical pieces of paper and hold them in front of you side by side. Now release them at the same time. The papers will twist and turn in different ways as they drift to the ground and will land in different positions.

- Since the initial conditions seemed the same but the results were different, does it follow that the papers must have freely chosen how they would fall?
- Isn't it reasonable to assume that a difference in two effects must be traced to a difference in their causes?
- According to the determinist, what would be the application of this analogy to human behavior?

BENEDICT (BARUCH) SPINOZA (1632–1677)

Spinoza's Life

Spinoza was a 17th-century philosopher who is noted for his vigorous denial of human freedom. Spinoza's parents were Portuguese Jews who fled to Holland to escape religious persecution. As a young man, Spinoza showed great promise and was raised to be a rabbi. However, at age 20, he began to study philosophy and encountered what were then considered to be the "radical" ideas of the French philosopher Descartes. As Spinoza's own philosophy began to develop, it expanded beyond the boundaries of orthodox Jewish teachings. Finally, when he was nearly 24 years old, the Ecclesiastical Council condemned him as a heretic and forbade any member of the Jewish community from even speaking with him. Spinoza spent the rest of his life writing philosophy while supporting himself by grinding lenses for scientific instruments.

Spinoza's Determinism

Spinoza's position on the nature of reality is called **pantheism,** for he believed that God constituted the whole of reality. It follows from this belief that everything in nature, including individual persons, are modes or aspects of God's being. Spinoza was also a thoroughgoing determinist, for he believed that all things existed and happened by necessity. Even God does not act from freedom of the will, because his actions flow from the necessities built into his own nature. Furthermore, God's nature could not be other than it is, for either this would mean that God was caused by something outside himself and, thereby, he would not be supreme, or it would mean that God's nature was the cause of his own nature, which would be absurd since the effect would be identical to the cause. Hence, for Spinoza, "all things follow from the eternal decree of God, according to that same necessity by which it follows from the essence of a triangle that its three angles are equal to two right angles."[36] Spinoza thought that we could find peace of mind if we realized that all things are as they necessarily must be. He claimed this philosophical viewpoint would free us from the tyranny of our emotions, because it is useless to be agitated by the emotions of fear, anger, regret, hope, or joy when the details of our lives are as necessary as the properties of a triangle.

The implications of Spinoza's position for freedom of the will are clear. Free will is an illusion based on inadequate knowledge of the divine nature and of how the whole scheme of things logically proceeds from that nature. Spinoza suggested that if a stone traveling through the air were conscious, it would feel as though it were free and were choosing to move and land where it does.[37] To see the force of Spinoza's point, I have constructed the following imaginary dialogue between Spinoza and the stone.

> **pantheism** the belief that God constitutes the whole of reality and that everything in nature, including individual persons, are modes or aspects of God's being

A Dialogue with a Virtuous Stone

SPINOZA: Mr. Stone, I am going to let go of you and we will see what happens. (Spinoza lets go of the stone, and, naturally, it falls to the ground.)

SPINOZA: Mr. Stone, when I let go of you just then, you fell downward. Why is that?

STONE: I fell downward because I chose to. I could have flown upward if I had wanted to do so.

SPINOZA: In that case, show me how you can fly upward when I release you this time. (Spinoza lets go of the stone, and, once again, it falls downward.)

SPINOZA: What's wrong? Why didn't you fly upward?

STONE: I could have chosen to fly upward, but I didn't. Flying up is an immoral, disgusting thing to do. It would be obscene. No self-respecting stone would do anything other than go down. I've been taught to know the difference between right and wrong, you see.

SPINOZA: In other words, you were completely free to fall down and completely free to fly upward. However, you will always choose the former alternative because of your personal values and morals.

STONE: That is exactly right. Everything I do is based on my own free choices. Other things such as planets and cannonballs may be determined to behave a certain way, but stones have free will.

SPINOZA: I see.

STOP AND THINK

Think about a decision you made recently in which you had to choose between what was morally right and wrong. On what did you base your decision? Did you have the freedom to make a choice different from the one you actually made? What inclined your will one way rather than another? Is it possible that you are like Spinoza's stone, thinking that your decision was completely free when it was actually determined by psychological forces acting on you? Why?

According to Spinoza, we are like that stone in all relevant respects. First, we think that we are an exception to the rest of nature. "Whereas causal laws control what happens in the world outside of me," we say, "my uncaused free will allows me to choose what I will do." But are we as foolish as the stone in thinking we are the grand exception to all of nature? Second, Spinoza says people are like the stone in that they

> are deceived because they think themselves free, and the sole reason for thinking so is that they are conscious of their own actions, and ignorant of the causes by which those actions are determined.[38]

In other words, if we correctly understood reality, we would realize that events (including human choices) do not spring into being out of a vacuum. Everything that happens is a product of preceding causes. Put the same stone in the same set of circumstances and its behavior would be the same in each case. According to the determinist, if we could keep constant the exact psychological state you were in when you made a particular choice (whom to date, what school to attend, what subject to major in) and if we could put you back into the exact same set of circumstances, your behavior would always be the same. Obviously, you sometimes change your mind or choose differently from the way you did in the past. However, the hard determinist would say that it takes a difference to make a difference. If your choices change from what they were in the past, it is because of something different about your psychological state or something different about the circumstances.

LOOKING THROUGH THE HARD DETERMINIST'S LENS

1. Every society is based on the assumption that what we do can affect people's behavior. Parents raise their children a certain way, the schools try to produce informed, responsible citizens, and the laws try to prevent people from committing crimes. Granted, we sometimes fail in these tasks. But when our methods of changing behavior fail, we seek causal explanations for these failures. We say that our children were influenced too much by television, our educational methods need changing, or a particular criminal was too warped by an antisocial background for the laws to have any deterrent effect. If behavior is not caused, then why do we even try to produce certain behaviors in people? How do our parenting practices and our educational and criminal systems support the determinist's claim that there are causal factors behind every behavior?

2. How would a determinist explain each of the following items?
   a. your choice of friends
   b. the career choices you have made or are considering
   c. your moral values

d. why some people, such as Mother Teresa, turn out to be humanitarians and others, such as Adolf Hitler, become tyrants

3. If hard determinism is true, people are not morally responsible for their actions. If our society accepted this claim, what changes would be made to our public policy? How would these changes affect our treatment of criminals?

EXAMINING THE STRENGTHS AND WEAKNESSES OF HARD DETERMINISM

Positive Evaluation

1. Does it seem that determinism captures some of the basic intuitions we assume in our daily life? For example, we do assume that the more we understand a person's personality, the better we are able to anticipate or predict his or her behavior. We assume that we are able to causally influence other people's behavior. We assume that a person who does something (risks her life, commits a heinous crime, shows mercy to his enemy, turns down a job offer) can offer an explanation for what he or she did. Don't these facts lend support to determinism?

2. Since science has opened up our understanding of nature by formulating the laws that explain events, isn't it likely that a science of behavior will likewise enable us to understand the causes that determine human actions?

3. Isn't it a strength of determinism that it eliminates the need to postulate the existence of events such as acts of the will for which there is no cause or explanation?

4. Doesn't it make sense to say with the hard determinist that we cannot blame or praise people for events they could not control? If our actions and choices are the result of a long series of causes, just as our eye color, our physical condition, and our personalities are, can we really be held responsible for them?

Negative Evaluation

1. Have the determinists made an illegitimate jump from the observation that "*some* behavior is conditioned and predictable" to the much stronger claim that "*all* behavior is conditioned and predictable"?

2. Does it make sense to develop and defend a theory that says that all human activities, including that of developing theories and defending them, are ultimately the product of external causes over which we have no control and for which we are not responsible? Does determinism imply that our philosophical beliefs are as much the outcome of a series of causes as is the production of an egg within a chicken? Does it follow from this implication that you are conditioned to be either a determinist or a libertarian and there is nothing you can do about it? If so, is this conclusion a problem? Is there any room in such a theory for notions such as rational or logical or even true? If not, is the lack of such notions a problem for this theory?

3. If hard determinism is true, there is no such thing as moral responsibility. According to this position, some people have been conditioned to behave in socially acceptable ways and others have been determined to act antisocially. What do you think are the implications of doing away with the notion of moral responsibility? Do you think this is even possible?

LEADING QUESTIONS: *Libertarianism*

1. Think about a time when you had difficulty making up your mind. Perhaps you did not feel strongly drawn to either of two alternatives, but you finally just decided on one of them. Or maybe you were strongly inclined toward two completely opposite alternatives and, after a great deal of struggle and deliberation, you resolutely made your choice. Doesn't the fact that your choice required deliberation indicate that it was not already "programmed" in you but that the decision was, at that moment, entirely up to you?

2. Think of something you did that was entirely spontaneous and out of character. Perhaps your friends were surprised to see you behave in such an unpredictable way. Doesn't this action indicate that sometimes we simply initiate our behavior on the spot without it being the inevitable and predictable outcome of antecedent causes?

3. As you matured and became your own person, didn't you find that you had to choose which of your parents' values and beliefs you would continue to embrace and which ones you wanted to modify or reject? Because we can sometimes choose which influences we will allow to guide our lives and which ones we won't, doesn't this choice indicate that we have some measure of freedom over our lives and are not just conditioned to behave in a certain fashion?

SURVEYING THE CASE FOR LIBERTARIANISM

It will be recalled that the libertarian claims that (1) we are not determined and (2) we do have freedom of the will (metaphysical freedom) and (3) we have the capacity to be morally responsible for our actions. I will first set out the case for libertarianism in terms of two pillars. The first pillar consists of some of the problems of determinism (according to libertarians). The second pillar consists of the positive arguments for libertarianism. Finally, I examine two views of freedom corresponding to two varieties of libertarianism: agency theory and radical existential freedom.

THE PROBLEMS WITH DETERMINISM

The Determinist Makes an Unwarranted Generalization from a Limited Amount of Evidence

The determinist may be able to show that our genetic makeup, our biochemical condition, or our past experiences have an influence on our behavior and choices. But there is a difference between being *influenced* by previous causes and being totally *determined* by them. Influences may create certain tendencies, but their outcome is neither inevitable nor perfectly predictable. The presence of a determining cause, however, necessarily produces the effect and makes it perfectly predictable. For example, if you had a religious upbringing as a child, it would not be surprising if this religious background had an influence on your present values and beliefs. However, since many people break with their parents' belief system, it seems clear that our upbringing can influence us but not determine us. Furthermore, the most that the determinist can claim, based on experiments and case studies, is that "*some* behavior is determined." But it is a big leap from that statement to the conclusion that "*all* behavior is determined." Determinism, therefore, can never be decisively proven. Before considering the next criticism, think through the following thought experiment.

THOUGHT EXPERIMENT: *Reasons and Causes*

In which of the following cases would you say that Maria is rational in believing that "candidate Dale Miller is the best choice for mayor"?

1. Maria has analyzed Miller's platform and believes that his ideas are better than those of any other candidate.
2. Maria has a strange brain tumor that causes her to like Miller, but without that tumor, she would support Miller's opponent.
3. A Freudian psychiatrist analyzes Maria and finds that Miller's physical appearance subconsciously reminds her of her father, whom she adored. So she supports Miller, thinking she likes him because of his policies when she is really working out her childhood relationship with her father.

- Is there a difference between behavior that is caused and behavior that is based on reasons? How could this difference be characterized?
- When we find that someone's thoughts or choices are based on causes over which the person has no control, doesn't this discovery diminish the degree to which we take this person seriously?
- What is our reaction when we find that our *own* thoughts or choices are based on causes that control us and not our own reasons ("I was tired," "I felt pressured," "I was irritable from too much coffee")? Doesn't this discovery diminish the degree to which we feel that those thoughts and choices are our own?

Determinism Undermines the Notion of Rationality

The previous thought experiment suggested two ways that you may arrive at a belief. It can be the result of *causes* within or without you over which you have no control, or it can be the product of *reasons* that you have freely chosen to guide your behavior. We tend not to take seriously beliefs that are the result of impersonal, irrational causes. However, the determinist would have to say that the brain tumor or the Freudian dynamics that caused Maria's behavior are not exceptions to the normal course of events, because all behavior is deterministically caused. According to this viewpoint, the psychological factors that produce your deliberations, thoughts, and behavior are ultimately the result of external causes over which you have no control. But if your thoughts are the result of impersonal, irrational causes, can they really be considered rational?

The British astronomer Arthur Eddington expressed this argument in the following way:

> If the mathematical argument in my mind is compelled to reach the conclusion which a deterministic system of physical law has preordained that my hands shall write down, then reasoning must be explained away as a process quite other than that which I feel it to be. But my whole respect for reasoning is based on the hypothesis that it is what I feel it to be.[39]

Determinism Confuses the Methodological Assumptions of Science with Metaphysical Conclusions

According to the deterministic psychologist B. F. Skinner, "A scientific analysis of behavior must, I believe, assume that a person's behavior is controlled by his genetic and environmental histories rather than by the person himself as an initiating, creative agent."[40] But two objections may be raised against Skinner's account of behavioral science. First, this methodological assumption is not necessary. Can't a behavioral scientist study the tendencies or probabilistic regularities within human behavior without assuming that behavior is 100 percent determined or inevitable down to the last detail? Second, this methodological assumption may be useful without being a true description of reality. The methodological principle "it is helpful to think of humans *as though* they are mechanisms ruled by causes" may be helpful in guiding us to seek out the regularities in human behavior. However, that assumption in no way guarantees that such causal regularities are present in all behavior. To borrow an analogy from the 20th-century British philosopher Bertrand Russell (one that was used for other purposes), the prospector bases his activity on the principle "always look for gold," but that principle does not imply that there will always be gold to be found. Likewise, it is fruitful for the behavioral scientist to follow the rule "always look for causes," but that rule doesn't mean that all human behavior is caused.

THE POSITIVE ARGUMENTS FOR LIBERTARIANISM

Having examined the problems libertarians find in determinism, we now look at the positive arguments that libertarians provide for their own position. Although there are several arguments for libertarianism, the following three are the most common.

The Argument from Introspection

What is your right hand doing at this present moment? Holding this book? Taking notes with a pen? Scratching your head? Before you read further, I want you to do something different with your hand. Did you do it? Did you feel as though that action was the inevitable result of previous causes acting on you? Of course, you were responding to my directive, but you really didn't have to do anything. You could have chosen to ignore my little object lesson. Hence, what you did (or didn't do) was a matter of your own decision. Now do something different (e.g., stand up, stick your foot out). Once again, did you feel as though that action was caused or inevitable? Didn't you have the sense that you could have acted differently than you did?

   According to the libertarian, this ordinary sort of experience that our actions are freely chosen and that we could have acted otherwise than we did provides forceful counterexamples to the determinist's claim that our actions are determined and inevitable. The determinist claims, however, that in those situations in which we face multiple alternatives and feel as though we are freely choosing among them, there is always one motivating cause within our current psychological state that compels us because it is the strongest one. For example, you may be torn between wanting to see a movie or going to a concert. If you decide to see the movie, the determinist would say, it is because your psychological state was such that the desire to see the movie was the stronger determining cause acting on you at that time. Therefore, the determinist claims that "persons always act upon their strongest desire." But in a specific case, how can we identify our "strongest desire" except by identifying it (after the fact) with the desire upon which we acted? Now it looks as though the determinist's claim is "persons always act upon the desire upon which they act." This claim, of course, is an empty truth and does nothing to advance the determinist's case.

Contrary to what the determinist claims, the libertarian would argue that sometimes we can choose or overrule our desires. The alcoholic would certainly say that the desire to drink is a compelling one. But through treatment and sheer will power, the alcoholic can learn to control that desire and even extinguish it. Part of the process of moral development is learning to control some desires and encourage others. The fact that this process takes time and effort suggests that we are not "programmed" to behave in one specific way.

By way of rebuttal, the determinist would be quick to point out that our feeling of freedom could be an illusion and that our introspective accounts are sometimes mistaken. However, our own actions are the only type of event in the world that we know both from the inside and the outside. Hence, the libertarian argues, we should give a high priority to the prima facie evidence of our own experience on this issue. According to his biographer, the famous 18th-century English writer Samuel Johnson once said, "All theory is against freedom of the will; all experience for it."

The Argument from Deliberation

Frequently our choices and actions are preceded by a period of deliberation during which we weigh the evidence, consider the pros and cons of our alternatives, calculate the probable consequences of an action, and evaluate all these data in terms of our values and desires. In this situation, the libertarian claims, we experience the fact that the decision is not already latent in the causes acting on us; instead, we have a distinct sense that we are actively deciding what the decision will be. Contrary to the determinist's account, when we deliberate we are not simply like a metal ball suspended between two opposing magnetic fields. Rather than passively awaiting the outcome of the war between our conflicting motives, goals, or desires, we often find ourselves actively choosing which one will prevail.

The Argument from Moral Responsibility

If someone devotes his or her spare time to building houses for the poor, we might say that person's actions are morally good, commendable, admirable, laudable, and praiseworthy. On the other hand, if someone emotionally hurts people by pretending to love them only to get something from them, we might say that person's behavior is morally bad, shabby, despicable, contemptible, and blameworthy. But could we make these judgments about a person if his or her actions were the inevitable outcome of deterministic causes? It seems that being justified in making moral judgments about persons and praising or blaming them requires that their actions be freely chosen. If the determinist is correct in saying that all our behavior is the result of causes over which we have no control, then a tyrant such as Hitler and a great humanitarian such as Mother Teresa are morally equal, since both of them simply behaved as they were caused to behave. Looked at in this way, Mother Teresa should no more be praised for her actions or Hitler condemned for his than Mother Teresa should be applauded for having low blood pressure and Hitler denounced for having high blood pressure. In the final analysis, determinism implies that our eye color, blood pressure, and moral character are all products of causes that operate upon us and whose outcomes we did not choose. But doesn't this philosophy wreak havoc with morality, one of the most significant features of our humanity?

STOP AND THINK

What do you think would happen if you cheated, defamed, lied, or broke an important promise to a hard determinist? Do you think he or she would dismiss your behavior as unfortunate but excusable (since everyone's behavior is allegedly determined), or would you imagine that the determinist would think ill of you, responding no differently than a libertarian would? To what degree is this scenario relevant or irrelevant to the assessment of determinism?

The libertarian claims that if determinism is true, then our moral judgments and ethical struggles are absurd. As the scientist Arthur Eddington aptly expressed it:

> What significance is there in my mental struggle to-night whether I shall or shall not give up smoking, if the laws which govern the matter of the physical universe already pre-ordain for the morrow a configuration of matter consisting of pipe, tobacco, and smoke connected with my lips?[41]

The hard determinist would respond that just because a theory conflicts with our sensibilities does not mean that it is false. Maybe we have to "bite the bullet" and abandon our notion of moral responsibility. However, the libertarian would respond that there are more reasons to believe in moral responsibility than there are for believing in universal, deterministic causality. To quote Arthur Eddington once again:

> To me it seems that responsibility is one of the fundamental facts of our nature. If I can be deluded over such a matter of immediate knowledge—the very nature of the being that I myself am—it is hard to see where any trustworthy beginning of knowledge is to be found.[42]

If the libertarian is correct about these issues, then at least *some* behavior is freely chosen, initiated, and performed by persons based on their rational deliberations and value choices. In the final analysis, the libertarian does not need to claim that the issue is one of a simple dichotomy between being totally free or totally unfree. Maybe realizing our potential to be free is like realizing our potential to be a good tennis player. It is all a matter of degree. On the one hand, we can allow ourselves to be like objects, buffeted about by the forces acting on us (personality dispositions, peer pressure, cultural influences), or, on the other hand, we can strive to rise above those influences and take charge of who we are and what we do.

In the following passage, the contemporary sociologist Peter Berger tries to account for the fact that we are often causally conditioned (like puppets). But he also contends that through greater self-knowledge, we can become liberated from the causal influences acting on us and experience true, libertarian freedom.

> We see the puppets dancing on their miniature stage, moving up and down as the strings pull them around, following the prescribed course of their various little parts. We learn to understand the logic of this theater and we find ourselves in its motions. We locate ourselves in society and thus recognize our own position as we hang from its subtle strings. For a moment we see ourselves as puppets indeed. But then we grasp a decisive difference between the puppet theater and our own drama. Unlike the puppets, we have the possi-

bility of stopping in our movements, looking up and perceiving the machinery by which we have been moved. In this act lies the first step towards freedom.[43]

AGENCY THEORY

There are several varieties of libertarianism, based on different conceptions of freedom. Some philosophers, such as Roderick Chisholm and Richard Taylor, have argued for libertarianism by developing a position known as **agency theory.** They reject the following dichotomy: "An event is either (1) the necessary outcome of previous causes or (2) an uncaused, random event that simply happens." This version of libertarianism rejects both determinism and indeterminism. While agency theorists may agree that both kinds of events occur in the world (e.g., the motion of billiard balls and subatomic events), these philosophers insist on a third category of events as well, events that are brought about by agents. Another way of explaining this theory is to say that there are two kinds of causes operating in the world. On the one hand, there is **event-causation,** which occurs when a prior event necessarily causes a subsequent event. Examples of event-causation would be a solar eclipse, an earthquake, the rise in my blood pressure after drinking coffee, the boiling of water, or an acorn falling to the earth. On the other hand is **agent-causation.** Any event that is brought about through the free action of an agent (person, self) is the result of agent-causation. Examples of agent-causation would be voting, choosing to see a particular movie, making a promise, phoning a friend.

The notion of agent-causation seems to capture what we ordinarily mean when we say that our actions are free. We have a sense that *we* make choices and initiate actions, that we have the power to act or not act in certain ways, and that we decide which action to take. This view implies that the universe is such that not all events are caused by the sort of causes studied by the physicists. It also implies that agents or persons are unique entities who do not follow the laws that govern electrons, rocks, sunflowers, or frogs. I do not freely choose to will my heart to beat because this automatic event is caused by the sorts of causes that scientists study. However, according to the agency theory, I do freely choose to support a political candidate, to stick to my diet, or to read a novel.

It is important to note that the libertarian does not need to make the claim that *all* human actions are free and undetermined. A libertarian merely asserts that *some* human actions are free and undetermined. In other words, the libertarian could recognize that under unusual circumstances (brainwashing, hypnotism, states of psychological or physical stress) a person's behavior might not be free. If such circumstances were not under the agent's control, the libertarian would say that person was not morally responsible for what he or she did. However, the libertarian claims that for the most part, while our decisions may be *influenced* by a number of factors, they are not causally *determined* by previous conditions (prior psychological states or external factors).

In the following reading contemporary American philosopher Richard Taylor argues for free will on the basis of agency theory. He admits that this theory may seem strange initially, for it posits a kind of causality seen nowhere else in nature. Nevertheless, he thinks it does the best job of accounting for human experience.

- According to Taylor, what two conditions are necessary for an action to be free?
- Why do you think Taylor distinguishes between the "reason for an action" and the "cause of an action"?
- Why does Taylor not consider his pulse to be *his* action?

agency theory a version of libertarianism that rejects both determinism and indeterminism; this theory claims that events are brought about by agents

event-causation occurs when a prior event necessarily causes a subsequent event

agent-causation occurs when an event is brought about through the free action of an agent (person, self)

Metaphysics [44]

The only conception of action that accords with our data is one according to which people—and perhaps some other things too—are sometimes, but of course not always, self-determining beings; that is, beings that are sometimes the causes of their own behavior. In the case of an action that is free, it must be such that it is caused by the agent who performs it, but such that no antecedent conditions were sufficient for his performing just that action. In the case of an action that is both free and rational, it must be such that the agent who performed it did so for some reason, but this reason cannot have been the cause of it.

Now, this conception fits what people take themselves to be; namely, beings who act, or who are agents, rather than things that are merely acted upon, and whose behavior is simply the causal consequence of conditions that they have not wrought. When I believe that I have done something, I do believe that it was I who caused it to be done, I who made something happen, and not merely something within me, such as one of my own subjective states, which is not identical with myself. If I believe that something not identical with myself was the cause of my behavior—some event wholly external to myself, for instance, or even one internal to myself, such as a nerve impulse, volition, or whatnot—then I cannot regard that behavior as being an act of mine, unless I further believe that I was the cause of that external or internal event. My pulse, for example, is caused and regulated by certain conditions existing within me, and not by myself. I do not, accordingly, regard this activity of my body as my action, and would be no more tempted to do so if I became suddenly conscious within myself of those conditions or impulses that produce it. This is behavior with which I have nothing to do, behavior that is not within my immediate control, behavior that is not only not free activity, but not even the activity of an agent to begin with; it is nothing but a mechanical reflex. Had I never learned that my very life depends on this pulse beat, I would regard it with complete indifference, as something foreign to me, like the oscillations of a clock pendulum that I idly contemplate.

- In the next passage, what two notions are said to be completely different from the ones we apply to the rest of nature?
- Why does Taylor hesitate to use the word *cause* when referring to the origin of human actions?

Now this conception of activity, and of an agent who is the cause of it, involves two rather strange metaphysical notions that are never applied elsewhere in nature. The first is that of a *self* or *person*—for example, a man—who is not merely a collection of things or events, but a self-moving being. For on this view it is a person, and not merely some part of him or something within him, that is the cause of his own activity. . . .

Second, this conception of activity involves an extraordinary conception of causation according to which an agent, which is a substance and not an event, can nevertheless be the cause of an event. Indeed, if he is a free agent then he can, on this conception, cause an event to occur—namely, some act of his own—without anything else causing him to do so. . . .

This conception of the causation of events by things that are not events is, in fact, so different from the usual philosophical conception of a cause that it should not even bear the same name, for "being a cause" ordinarily just means "being an antecedent sufficient condition or set of conditions." Instead, then, of speaking of agents as *causing* their own acts, it would perhaps be better to use another word entirely and say, for instance, that they *originate* them, *initiate* them, or simply that they *perform* them.

- Taylor says that, at first, his notion of the nature of persons may seem "dubious." Why then does he think it is superior to the accounts of indeterminism and determinism? Do you agree or disagree?

Now this is, on the face of it, a dubious conception of what a person is. Yet it is consistent with our data, reflecting the presuppositions of deliberation, and appears to be the only conception that is consistent with them, as determinism and simple indeterminism are not. The theory of agency avoids the absurdities of simple indeterminism by conceding that behavior is caused, while at the same time avoiding the difficulties of determinism by denying that every chain of causes and effects is infinite. Some such causal chains, on this view, have beginnings, and they begin with agents themselves. Moreover, if we are to suppose that it is sometimes up to me what I do, and understand this in a sense which is not consistent with determinism, we must suppose that I am an agent or a being who initiates his own actions, sometimes under conditions which do not determine what action I shall perform. Deliberation becomes, on this view, something that is not only possible but quite rational, for it does make sense to deliberate about activity that is truly my own and depends in its outcome upon me as its author, and not merely upon something more or less esoteric that is supposed to be intimately associated with me, such as my thoughts, volitions, choices, or whatnot.

© 1992. Reproduced in print and electronically by permission of Pearson Education, Inc., Upper Saddle River, New Jersey.

THOUGHT EXPERIMENT: *Behavior and Choices*

Consider the following list of four kinds of actions or behaviors. For each category, list several actions you have performed that would fit in that category. You may find that you will have no items to list under one or more of the categories.

1. Behaviors that clearly were not a matter of choice in that they did not result from an act of your will. In other words, what you did was the inevitable outcome of causes over which you had no control. (An example might be blinking your eyes when a bright light flashed.)
2. Actions that did result from an act of your will but that you felt you were forced to do because your options were limited or because you were operating under some sort of coercion.
3. Actions in which causal factors had an influence on what you did but did not determine your action completely and inevitably, because you felt as though you did choose among genuine alternatives.
4. Actions that were truly your own and that you freely chose to perform without any causal influences affecting the outcome of your own act of willing.

- Did you leave any categories empty? If so, why?
- What criteria did you use to decide if an action was or was not free of causal influences?
- For which of the actions you listed would you accept moral responsibility for what you did? In other words, which actions would justly merit your praise or blame? What criteria do you use to decide the degree to which you are morally

(continued . . .)

(. . . continued)

responsible for what you do? Or do you agree with the hard determinist that there is no such thing as moral responsibility?
- If you listed examples under category 3 or 4, what made you choose to do what you did and not something else? In what sense was this factor *not* a determining cause that made your action inevitable?

RADICAL EXISTENTIAL FREEDOM

JEAN-PAUL SARTRE
(1905–1980)

The most extreme version of libertarianism has been proposed by the famous French existentialist philosopher and novelist Jean-Paul Sartre (1905–1980). Sartre was born in Paris and lived most of his life there. After receiving an education at one of France's most prestigious universities, he began his career by teaching philosophy. However, his rise to fame as a writer began in 1938 when he published *Nausea,* his first novel and a best-seller. Four years later Sartre resigned his professorship and for the rest of his life was able to live on his literary income alone. When World War II broke out, Sartre was called into military service but was captured and confined to a Nazi prison camp for approximately a year. While there, he wrote and produced plays for his fellow prisoners. He was allowed to return to Paris because of poor health, but he immediately became active in the underground movement of the French Resistance, writing for a number of anti-Nazi newspapers. In 1943, he published his philosophical masterpiece, *Being and Nothingness: A Phenomenological Essay on Ontology.* It has been called "the principal text of modern existentialism." In recognition of his many novels and plays, Sartre was awarded the Nobel prize for literature in 1964, but he refused to accept the honor and the substantial cash prize because he did not want to become a tool of the establishment. On April 15, 1980, Sartre died of heart failure. As the hearse bearing his body drove to the cemetery, a crowd of about 50,000 people, most of them students, accompanied it through the streets of Paris.

Sartre claims that we are always free, even in situations in which most other libertarians would acknowledge that we are not. As Sartre expresses it, "Man can not be sometimes slave and sometimes free; he is wholly and forever free or he is not free at all."[45] Sartre was an atheist, and he based his radical view of freedom on the claim that each of us is thrust into existence without anyone or anything determining what we are or what our purpose shall be. This view means that for humans, "their existence comes before their essence." Sartre explains this phrase in one of his most famous essays.

> What is meant here by saying that existence precedes essence? It means that, first of all, man exists, turns up, appears on the scene and, only afterwards, defines himself. If man, as the existentialist conceives him, is indefinable, it is because at first he is nothing. Only afterward will he be something, and he himself will have made what he will be. Thus, there is no human nature, because there is no God to conceive it. Not only is man what he conceives himself to be, but he is also only what he wills himself to be after this thrust toward existence.[46]

Sartre expresses his radical view of freedom by saying that freedom is not something that we *have* but something which we *are*. In his memorable phrase, he says we are "condemned to be free." But can this radical view of freedom be reconciled with the facts of our experience? I did not choose many of the features of my past or my present. I was born an American, I am a male, I grew up near Chicago. These facts are some of the givens of my situation that I was not free to choose and yet they seem to set limits on the course of my life. Sartre calls these features a person's **facticity.** Yet for Sartre, facts by themselves do not have any meaning, for it is only by our choices that we invest facts with meaning. I was born an American. My birth is part of my facticity because it cannot be changed. But what significance do I attach to that fact? Do I swell up with nationalistic pride and wave the flag, or do I burn it in shame for America's past and present sins? I am a male. But what does that fact mean? Does it mean that I am a tough, macho man who expresses his manhood by dominating women, hunting, spitting, and drinking beer while watching football? Or do I choose to be a sensitive male, one who is not afraid to eat quiche, cry, and be moved by great art? Of course these images are stereotypes, but they illustrate the point that in spite of our facticity, freedom prevails in the end, for we continually decide how the facts of our situation fit into our present self-conception and projects. Likewise, the women's movement in the latter part of the 20th century was (and still is) an attempt to define and give meaning to the facticity of being a female. Simone de Beauvoir, a famous French writer and Sartre's lifelong companion, expressed this struggle by saying, "One is not born, but rather becomes, a woman."[47] Briefly, her view was that what it means to be a woman is not biologically determined; a female either allows socially defined roles to be imposed on her or she freely chooses what her identity as a woman shall be.

In addition to our facticity, there is what Sartre calls our **transcendence.** Transcendence is the root of our freedom, for it refers to the fact that we define ourselves by our possibilities and by all the ways in which each of us is continually creating our own future in terms of our choices, our plans, our dreams, and our ambitions. Because of our transcendence, what we have been or done in the past does not dictate our future. Sartre acknowledges that it seems as though my past actions weigh on me and determine who I am, but only because of the way they enter into my present engagements. For example, he says that my marriage vows limit my possibilities and dictate my conduct, but only because each day I continue to embrace them and define myself as a committed husband. I could view my vows as a stupid mistake, as something that is now void and inoperative, as having no more hold over me, and as something to be set aside as part of the dead past.[48] Hence, each moment of our existence we are creating our present selves out of the possibilities that define our transcendence. If there is continuity in our lives (such as a long-lasting relationship), it is only because we have continually reaffirmed past choices. Even to refuse to choose and to stoically let things happen is itself a choice.

Sartre goes so far as to say that even our emotions or passions are not forces that control us; instead, they are ways that we apprehend the world and act in it. For example, a man may be unable to solve a problem and responds in anger by tearing up the paper it is written on. In doing so, he relieves himself of the burdens of his failure by eliminating the situation that caused them.[49] In another example, Sartre cites the case of a patient who is on the verge of revealing her deepest secrets to a psychiatrist, but her sobbing prevents her from continuing. Described in this way, her emotions appear to be a mechanistic cause that inhibits her freedom. However, Sartre argues that she sobs in order to be free of the obligation of continuing her confession.[50] Again, he points out that if I am threatened (say, in war), I may flee my responsibilities and run because of my fear of dying. But the emotion of fear enters into my behavior only because I have chosen living as the supreme value. Another person may stand by his or her post in the face of danger because of a commitment to duty and honor. We do not have passion on the one hand and moral fortitude on the other as causes of the two reactions. Instead, both are manifestations of fundamental, free choices.

When we deny our freedom and our responsibility for who we are, Sartre says we are in **bad faith.** Recognizing the radical nature of our freedom leads to anguish because we are burdened with the responsibility of having to make choices and being unable to fall back

facticity Sartre's term for those features of our past or present that we were not free to choose and yet they seem to set limits on the course of our lives

transcendence Sartre's term for the root of our freedom, for our ability to define ourselves by our possibilities and all the ways in which each of us is continually creating our own future in terms of our choices, our plans, our dreams, and our ambitions

bad faith Sartre's term for when we deny our freedom and our responsibility for who we are

Garfield ® by Jim Davis

In what sense is Garfield guilty of bad faith? (GARFIELD © 1983 Paws, Inc. Used by permission of Universal Uclick. All rights reserved.)

on any excuses. Hence, we are continually tempted to think we can escape our freedom, and by doing so, we fall into bad faith. Bad faith can be an attempt to deny my facticity. For example, I can refuse to acknowledge that I have repeatedly committed cowardly actions and, instead, think of myself as having the heart and soul of a hero in spite of the fact that I have never acted heroically.[51] On the other hand, bad faith can result when I deny my transcendence and refuse to acknowledge that I am continually faced with possibilities and choices. For example, I can say, "I am a coward" and view this fact as an unalterable feature of my identity. In this way I can seek to escape the burden of being responsible for my actions and suppose that they are determined by my nature just as iron filings are necessarily drawn to a magnet.

STOP AND THINK

Have there been times in your life when you have been guilty of bad faith and have tried to escape the burden of being responsible for your life? Were these incidents cases of denying your facticity? (You rationalized your behavior or wouldn't face what you had done.) Or were some of these cases a matter of denying your transcendence? (You made yourself think you didn't have any other possibilities, or you said, "I am a [coward, loser, lazy person, fool in love, emotional person, shy person, victim of my circumstances, or whatever]" and used that definition of yourself as an excuse for what you did, as though it determined your actions for all time.)

Before we conclude our discussion of Sartre's radical view of freedom, two points are worth noting. First, I said earlier that Sartre tied human freedom to his claim that there is no God who defines human nature. However, a number of religious existentialists reject his atheism while agreeing with most of his analysis of the dynamics of freedom, responsibility, and bad faith.* Second, Sartre embodies a very radical kind of libertarianism. He believed that we are either 100 percent determined or 100 percent free. However, most libertarians have no problems acknowledging that there are some extreme situations in which our freedom is diminished or even negated. They simply insist that the majority of our everyday actions are not determined.

---

*Although he lived before Sartre, Søren Kierkegaard would be an example of a religious existentialist who had a lot in common with Sartre. See discussions of Kierkegaard's thought in sections 1.0 and 4.4 and chap. 7.

Being and Nothingness

In the following passage from his major work, Sartre expresses his view of radical freedom. He claims that even if I am thrown into a situation I did not create, a war, for example, I am always free in terms of how I choose to respond to it. To be free, for Sartre, is not to float high above all concrete situations. To be free is to choose and to act, which cannot be done unless there is a set of circumstances in which to choose and act. So the facts of my life are not limits or obstacles to my freedom, but they are the arena within which my freedom may be exercised. I may have not chosen a war in which I find myself, but it is still *my* war for I must now define myself in terms of it. I can accept it wholeheartedly, or I can escape it through suicide or desertion. If these latter alternatives seem too drastic, it is because *I perceive them* as drastic and choose to prefer the war over them. (Sartre's service in the French underground during World War II had a definite impact on his philosophical writings about freedom, choices, responsibility, and anguish.)

FROM JEAN-PAUL SARTRE

Being and Nothingness [52]

Thus there are no *accidents* in life; a community event which suddenly bursts forth and involves me in it does not come from the outside. If I am mobilized in a war, this war is *my* war; it is in my image and I deserve it. I deserve it first because I could always get out of it by suicide or by desertion; these ultimate possibles are those which must always be present for us when there is a question of envisaging a situation. For lack of getting out of it, I have *chosen* it. This can be due to inertia, to cowardice in the face of public opinion, or because I prefer certain other values to the value of the refusal to join in the war (the good opinion of my relatives, the honor of my family, *etc.*). Any way you look at it, it is a matter of a choice. This choice will be repeated later on again and again without a break until the end of the war. Therefore we must agree with the statement by J. Romains, "In war there are no innocent victims." If therefore I have preferred war to death or to dishonor, everything takes place as if I bore the entire responsibility for war. Of course others have declared it, and one might [be] tempted perhaps to consider me as a simple accomplice. But this notion of complicity has only a juridical sense, and it does not hold here. For it depended on me that for me and by me this war should not exist, and I have decided that it does exist. There was no compulsion here, for the compulsion could have got no hold on a freedom. I did not have any excuse; for as we have said repeatedly in this book, the peculiar character of human-reality is that it is without excuse. Therefore it remains for me only to lay claim to this war.

Sartre goes on to point out that it is useless to imagine what my life would have been like if I had lived in another time in which there was no war, for that would not have been me. Who I am is this present person facing this present war. I must integrate it into the self that I am in the process of creating and take responsibility for what I make of myself and what I make of this war. As Sartre says, "I must be without remorse or regrets as I am without excuse; for from the instant of my upsurge into being, I carry the weight of the world by myself alone without anything or any person being able to lighten it." [53] As he says in the next passage, this weight of responsibility includes my own existence.

Yet this responsibility is of a very particular type. Someone will say, "I did not ask to be born." This is a naive way of throwing greater emphasis on our facticity. I am responsible for everything, in fact, except for my very responsibility, for I am not the foundation of my being. Therefore everything takes place as if I were compelled to be responsible. I am *abandoned* in the world, not in the sense that I might remain abandoned and passive in a hostile universe like a board floating on the water, but rather in the sense that I find myself suddenly alone and without help, engaged in a world for which I bear the whole responsibility without being able, whatever I do, to tear myself away from this responsibility for an instant. For I am responsible for my very desire of fleeing responsibilities. To make myself passive in the world, to refuse to act upon things and upon Others is still to choose myself, and suicide is one mode among others of being-in-the-world.

Sartre points out that my being born is not simply a brute fact (nothing is); it is part of my facticity that I invest with meaning as I choose who I am and the stance I take toward my life. In the next section he goes on to list possible ways of viewing my birth, all of which are ways in which I embrace the fact of my existence and "choose" my birth.

I am ashamed of being born or I am astonished at it or I rejoice over it, or in attempting to get rid of my life I affirm that I live and I assume this life as bad. Thus in a certain sense I *choose* being born. This choice itself is integrally affected with facticity since I am not able not to choose, but this facticity in turn will appear only in so far as I surpass it toward my ends. Thus facticity is everywhere but inapprehensible; I never encounter anything except my responsibility. That is why I cannot ask, "*Why* was I born?" or curse the day of my birth or declare that I did not ask to be born, for these various attitudes toward my birth—*i.e.,* toward the *fact* that I realize a presence in the world—are absolutely nothing else but ways of assuming this birth in full responsibility and of making it *mine.* Here again I encounter only myself and my projects so that finally my abandonment—*i.e.,* my facticity—consists simply in the fact that I am condemned to be wholly responsible for myself.

In this way, Sartre says that every event presents itself as an opportunity, but an opportunity that we can make use of or neglect. Although we are initially thrown into a world not of our own making, we are, nevertheless, faced with the responsibility (and anguish) of making choices and bearing our absolute freedom without making excuses. However, he points out that "most of the time we flee anguish in bad faith."

 ## LOOKING THROUGH THE LIBERTARIAN'S LENS

1. If you were a libertarian judge or social planner, how would your view of the treatment of criminals differ from that of a determinist?

2. If you were a libertarian educator, how might your method of teaching differ from that of a determinist?

3. How might a libertarian psychologist's methods of dealing with a client's emotional problems differ from those of a determinist?

4. What religious conceptions of God, human nature, and moral evil would be consistent with the libertarian's view of human freedom? What religious conceptions would be incompatible with libertarianism? For example, some theologians say that God controls *everything* that happens in the world, which implies that God controls every human action. What would a libertarian say?

5. If you were a libertarian, what criteria would you use to decide if a person was morally responsible for his or her actions? In answering this question, you might reconsider the cases concerning Dave and Todd in section 3.5.

6. All day tomorrow, imagine that you are a libertarian. How does being a libertarian affect your view of your own and others' actions? The next day, imagine that you are a hard determinist. What difference does being a hard determinist make to your attitudes and reactions? Thinking over the events of these two days, consider the different accounts the libertarian and the hard determinist would give of the same event.

7. Consider an action you performed or a choice you made in which you felt as though you had no alternatives and the choice was one you were forced to make. How would Sartre explain that you were really free?

EXAMINING THE STRENGTHS AND WEAKNESSES OF LIBERTARIANISM

Positive Evaluation

1. Doesn't libertarianism do the best job of explaining what we experience internally when we deliberate, choose, and act? You can observe another person from the outside and entertain the following theory: "She is like a machine, because her internal psychological states, including her present thoughts, are the result of causes that she did not control." But can you meaningfully make the same claim about yourself and think that it is true?

2. Apart from the libertarian notion of agent-causation, can we ever say that anyone's beliefs have been arrived at rationally? If determinism is true, then the determinist's conclusions are ultimately the product of impersonal causes acting on him or her. Likewise, the libertarian's conclusions are ultimately the product of impersonal causes acting on him or her. We simply believe what we have been determined to believe and have no power to change that. Doesn't libertarianism offer a better perspective than this one on human cognition?

3. The philosopher William James (1842–1910) said that

> I cannot understand the willingness to act, no matter how we feel, without the belief that acts are really good and bad. I cannot understand the belief that an act is bad, without regret at its happening. I cannot understand regret without the admission of real, genuine possibilities in the world.[54]

In what way are James's comments an argument for free will and against determinism?

Negative Evaluation

1. According to the libertarian, we experience our own freedom when we make choices. But in our dreams, we have the feeling that we are making choices even though we know that dreams are the product of the physiological and psychological causes that produce them. Hence, we can feel as though we are free even though causes are producing our behavior.

2. According to some thinkers, the scientific view of the world is based on the conviction that events follow fixed laws and that there is a cause for everything being the way that it is. If this statement is a correct account of science, does libertarianism then fly in the face

of modern science? If so, because nothing can compete with modern science in unveiling the nature of reality, don't these facts negate libertarianism?

3. According to libertarianism, every free act is based on a volition or an act of the will. But in a given case, why did a particular volition come about at the precise time that it did and why was it directed toward this or that outcome? (Why did you decide to listen to music at this precise time and not three minutes earlier or later? Why did you decide to listen to this particular CD and not the others that were available?) Isn't the libertarian forced to admit that either our volitions pop into our heads uncaused (in which case, they are unexplained, indeterministic events that *happen* to us) or they are the result of previous acts of the will? In the latter case, we are caught in an infinite regress. For example, your decision to listen to music was based on your decision to relax, which was based on your decision to take a break from studying, which was based on your decision to do *x,* and so on. Doesn't it seem that libertarianism leads to the notion that our free actions are based on an absurd and impossible infinite series of willings?

4. Isn't it the case that the better you get to know a person, the more his or her actions are predictable? Doesn't this finding indicate that the more knowledge we have of people's past, their personality, and the present circumstances that are affecting them, the more we understand the causes that are operating on them to produce their behavior? Aren't we convinced that a person's past experiences are a key to understanding why he or she became a saint or a serial killer? If so, doesn't this argument undermine libertarianism?

3.8 COMPATIBILISM

 LEADING QUESTIONS: *Compatibilism*

1. The hard determinist claims that all human actions are caused or determined by previous events and concludes from this claim both that we never act freely and that we are never morally responsible for our actions. But if you shoved a hard determinist, wouldn't it make a difference to him or her whether you did it voluntarily (because you meant to do it) or involuntarily (because you were shoved by someone yourself)? Isn't it impossible to deal with human interactions without the category of moral responsibility? No matter what our theory about human behavior, don't we all make a distinction between voluntary and involuntary behavior?

2. Even though the libertarians believe that we can act freely, don't they try to cause others to behave in a certain ways? Like most people, libertarians use praise and blame, reward and punishment to affect other people's behavior. How can we change someone else's behavior if there are no causal forces affecting what people do?

3. In each of the following scenarios, what is the difference between the (a) version and the (b) version? (1a) John broke the vase because he was shoved into it. (1b) John broke the vase because he was angry at its owner. (2a) Nikki cried out because she stepped on a tack. (2b) Nikki cried out because she wanted to get people's attention. In each set of cases, the external behavior is the same (breaking the vase, crying out). In each set of cases, there is a cause for the behavior (a shove, anger, pain, or need for attention). Is it important to distinguish whether the cause was external or whether it came from the agent's own, psychological state? If so, why is this distinction important?

Both the hard determinist and the libertarian claim that the concepts of determinism and freedom are inconsistent notions. In their view, the terms *free* and *determined* are like the terms *round* and *square.* In neither case can both pairs of terms be true of something at the same time. In other words, both the hard determinist and the libertarian agree that (1) if we are determined, then we are not free, and (2) if we are free, then we are not determined. They also agree that mere circumstantial freedom is not a sufficient condition for moral responsibility. To be responsible for your actions, you must also have metaphysical freedom (free will). Hence, they both accept the doctrine of *incompatibilism:* If we are determined, we lack the freedom necessary to be morally responsible.

But are these two positions the only options? If we were to reject their common assumption of incompatibilism, then we would be able to reconcile determinism and moral responsibility. Those philosophers who do just that embrace the position known as compatibilism. As I stated in section 3.5, *compatibilism* is the claim that we are determined *and* have the sort of freedom necessary to be morally responsible for our actions. Whereas hard determinism and libertarianism take an "either-or" stance on the issue of freedom and determinism, the compatibilist takes a "both-and" position. By doing so, the compatibilist claims to avoid the severe implications of hard determinism, such as the elimination of our traditional notions of moral responsibility and human freedom. In the same stroke, the compatibilist hopes to sweep away the alleged difficulties associated with libertarianism.

Sometimes compatibilism is called **soft determinism.** However, do not interpret this label to mean that the compatibilist is "soft" on determinism. The compatibilist agrees with the hard determinist that the thesis of universal causation applies to all human actions. In other words, the compatibilist believes human actions are 100 percent determined just as much as the hard determinist does. The difference between the two positions is that the compatibilist believes that the implications of determinism are not as hard and severe as the hard determinist believes (hence the label *soft* determinism). Because the two types of determinism share many areas of agreement, I do not have to spend as much time presenting the arguments for compatibilism. All the arguments presented for the determinism half of hard determinism would apply to compatibilism as well. What we do need to explore is why compatibilists reject the thesis of incompatibilism and how they hope to reconcile determinism and freedom. To put the issue in the form of a question, "Can the compatibilists reconcile what seems irreconcilable?" In other words, can they "eat their cake and have it too"? Only a careful examination of the case for compatibilism will tell.

soft determinism see compatibilism

SURVEYING THE CASE FOR COMPATIBILISM (SOFT DETERMINISM)

Question: How will the compatibilists try to convince us that being determined is consistent with being free? Answer: They argue for their position by arguing for a particular conception of freedom. They claim that free actions are those that are done voluntarily. To say that an action is voluntary, according to the compatibilist, does not mean that the action lacks inevitable determining causes operating upon the person. Instead, a voluntary action is said to be one in which the determining causes reside within the agent as opposed to being external to him or her. *External* causes are such things as physical forces or physical conditions. On the other hand, *internal* causes are the agent's own personality, values, motives, beliefs, desires, and other psychological states. Of course, the compatibilist would say that these internal factors do not appear out of nowhere, for they have their origin in the agent's causal history. The major difference between compatibilism and the other two positions is that the compatibilist does not believe that a lack of causal determination is necessary to have moral responsibility. Basically, the compatibilist says that you are acting freely if you have circumstantial freedom. You are free and responsible as long as your actions are not forced by external conditions but are controlled mainly by your own psychological states.

In question 3 of the "Leading Questions," John and Nikki were not acting freely when he was shoved into the vase and she involuntarily cried out in pain. But they were acting freely or voluntarily when he broke the vase to get even and she cried out to get attention. In the latter two cases, they were both acting on the basis of their own, internal desires and motives. The person you have come to be is a product of many kinds of causes (genetic, cultural, past experience, and so on). Hence, you did not make yourself but were made by these causes. But when I want to know if you should be blamed or praised for your actions, I need to know only if these actions came from your own beliefs, values, desires, motives, or choices. I do not need to know the rather complicated story of how you came to be the sort of person you are.

Are you starting to think of questions you would like to ask the compatibilist? One question that may come to mind is, "How could I have been free in performing an action unless I had genuine alternatives? In other words, if I performed action X freely, then it must have been the case that I could have done otherwise." In response the compatibilist would say you were caused to choose action X by your own psychological states, but you *could have* chosen to do action Y *if* your psychological state had been significantly different at the time. This point is illustrated by the following thought experiment.

THOUGHT EXPERIMENT: *The Context of Choices*

To understand the compatibilist's combination of determinism and freedom, let's consider the case of Vernon. His physician has warned him that he is overweight and needs to reduce his calorie intake. On his way home from work, Vernon passes a bakery and purchases a pound of fudge candy, which he immediately consumes. What caused him to take this action? We can imagine that the following circumstances and psychological factors played major roles in Vernon's decision.

1. Vernon tends to lack self-discipline.
2. He tends to choose immediate gratification over long-term goals.
3. He is not concerned about his weight or how he looks.
4. Because he feels good, he is not too concerned about his physician's warning.
5. He craves fudge candy.
6. He has just received three rejections of the novel he is seeking to publish.
7. The disappointment causes him to feel sorry for himself.
8. When he eats fudge he feels happy.
9. He was too busy to stop for lunch and is very hungry.
10. The fudge candy is prominently displayed in the store window.

- Given all these conditions, was it inevitable that Vernon would eat the fudge?
- Was Vernon acting freely when he ate the fudge?
- Can Vernon be held responsible for making a bad choice; that is, can he be blamed, criticized, and scolded for not taking care of himself?

The compatibilist, being a determinist, would say that given the psychological and physical conditions preceding this action, it was inevitable that Vernon acted as he did. If we could roll back time a dozen times to the exact instant Vernon made his choice with all the same conditions, he would always choose to eat the fudge. It would be inconceivable, the compatibilist would say, that under those same exact conditions the decision could have been different. What could have caused the outcome to be different except some difference in the conditions preceding it? To think otherwise is to suppose that Vernon's action was uncaused, inexplicable, and mysterious. If his action was not caused, then it was the result of some psychological coin flip in his head. But even coin flips and their outcome have causes, even though the results may be unpredictable. Vernon's action was obviously caused, for it had to be the result of the strongest desire that he had at the time.

Vernon could have chosen to do otherwise than he did only if a difference in the external or internal conditions had caused his strongest desire to be different. Suppose, for example, he received only two rejection slips and was still waiting to hear from the third editor or he was feeling in poor health that day or he had eaten lunch previously or the fudge was not displayed in the window. Any one of these factors may have swung the decision the other way. The same is true if his psychological state had been different at the time. For example, suppose he had an ounce more of self-discipline or he was worried about his weight or he tended to react stoically to rejection instead of getting depressed.

At the same time, the compatibilist would say (unlike the hard determinist) that Vernon was acting freely and was responsible for his behavior, even though it was inevitable. Vernon did what he wanted to do and his action was based on his own personality, desires, wants, motives, and volition. His action was voluntary, because he was not forced to behave the way he did by any external compulsion. The external factors played a role, but only because he responded to them on the basis of his own psychological needs and desires. What more could we want in the way of freedom?

STOP AND THINK

Can you think of an action that you performed that was the inevitable result of who you are, the strongest desire that you had at that time, and other psychological conditions, and yet the action was one that you considered to be free and voluntary and for which you could be held responsible?

You now reply, "But don't we sometimes behave one way in a certain set of circumstances and then later behave another way in exactly the same set of circumstances? Doesn't this behavior show that we are not determined?" The answer is that the two sets of circumstances are never exactly the same. Furthermore, *you* are never exactly the same from one minute to the next. Perhaps you find it boring to always make the same choices or perhaps the outcome of the first choice was not completely satisfactory so you decided to choose differently the second time. Choosing to act a certain way not only has effects on your external environment, but it has internal effects as well. For this reason, your preferences and desires and, consequently, your choices can vary from moment to moment.

Again you ask, "Granted that my actions are the product of my desires, values, and motives, don't I sometimes choose to change my desires, values, and motives?" Yes, but what caused this change in your psychological state? Why did you decide to change at this point in time and not earlier or later? Furthermore, what caused you to change in exactly this particular way? The motive to change some features of your personality had to grow from a seed that already existed in your personality. This seed produced the desire to change your psychological makeup only when it was activated by some cause (e.g., an experience, something you read, or your own reflections on your life). For example, some people's personalities are such that they are very set in their ways and choose not to change, whereas other people are more flexible. So it would seem that any desire to change your personality is actually rooted in an even deeper desire in your personality (such as the desire to always be growing and improving). Such a change is your free choice, but it is a choice that comes from the person you are and how your personality is put together. In the final analysis, of course, you did not originally create or choose your personality. So determinism reigns supreme. Yet, the compatibilist insists, no matter how your personality was formed and by what causal mechanisms, your personality is *you,* and as long as your decisions are made by you, freedom also reigns supreme.

Compatibilism: W. T. Stace

A very forceful defense of compatibilism was given by W. T. Stace (1886–1967). (Walter T. Stace was born in Britain and received his education at Trinity College in Dublin. In 1932 he came to the United States to teach at Princeton University.) Stace agrees with the hard determinist that every human action is determined by previous causes. However, he agrees with the libertarian that without free will there can be no morality. To be morally responsible for an action requires that you freely chose to perform the action on the basis of your own motives, desires, and values. You cannot be either blamed or praised for an action if you were compelled to do it. But how can we consistently combine determinism with free will? Don't they exclude one another? Stace claims that the problem is merely a verbal one, that it is based on an incorrect definition of free will.

To provide a clear-cut case of how a wrong definition can lead to a false conclusion about reality, Stace imagines that someone defines "man" as a type of five-legged animal and, on the basis of this definition, denies the existence of men. The true story, of course, is not that men do not exist, but that "man" has been incorrectly defined. Similarly, Stace thinks that "free will" has been incorrectly defined, which is why it seems incompatible with determinism and why both hard determinists and libertarians think determinism is inconsistent with moral responsibility. In the following reading, Stace explains why a better understanding of the notion of freedom will resolve all the difficulties and controversies.

- What is the incorrect definition of free will, according to Stace?
- What has this incorrect definition led to?

FROM WALTER T. STACE

Religion and the Modern Mind[55]

Throughout the modern period, until quite recently, it was assumed, both by the philosophers who denied free will and by those who defended it, that *determinism is inconsistent with free will.* If a man's actions were wholly determined by chains of causes stretching back into the remote past, so that they could be predicted beforehand by a mind which knew all the causes, it was assumed that they could not in that case be free. This implies that a certain definition of actions done from free will was assumed, namely that they are actions not wholly determined by causes or predictable beforehand. Let us shorten this by saying that free will was defined as meaning indeterminism. This is the incorrect definition which has led to the denial of free will. As soon as we see what the true definition is we shall find that the question whether the world is deterministic, as Newtonian science implied, or in a measure indeterministic, as current physics teaches, is wholly irrelevant to the problem.

To clarify the correct understanding of *free will,* Stace provides several imaginary dialogues that illustrate how the phrase is used in ordinary conversation. In each of these cases, ask yourself whether the action was voluntary or involuntary.

JONES: I once went without food for a week.

SMITH: Did you do that of your own free will?

JONES: No. I did it because I was lost in a desert and could find no food.

But suppose that the man who had fasted was Mahatma Gandhi. The conversation might then have gone:

GANDHI: I once fasted for a week.

SMITH: Did you do that of your own free will?

GANDHI: Yes. I did it because I wanted to compel the British Government to give India its independence.

Take another case. Suppose that I had stolen some bread, but that I was as truthful as George Washington. Then, if I were charged with the crime in court, some exchange of the following sort might take place:

JUDGE: Did you steal the bread of your own free will?

STACE: Yes. I stole it because I was hungry.

Or in different circumstances the conversation might run:

JUDGE: Did you steal of your own free will?

STACE: No. I stole because my employer threatened to beat me if I did not.

At a recent murder trial in Trenton some of the accused had signed confessions, but afterwards asserted that they had done so under police duress. The following exchange might have occurred:

JUDGE: Did you sign the confession of your own free will?

PRISONER: No. I signed it because the police beat me up.

- In the next conversation, what does the philosopher (a hard determinist) say is irrelevant to the case?
- Why are the philosopher's comments absurd?

Now suppose that a philosopher had been a member of the jury. We could imagine this conversation taking place in the jury room.

FOREMAN OF THE JURY: The prisoner says he signed the confession because he was beaten, and not of his own free will.

PHILOSOPHER: This is quite irrelevant to the case. There is no such thing as free will.

FOREMAN: Do you mean to say that it makes no difference whether he signed because his conscience made him want to tell the truth or because he was beaten?

PHILOSOPHER: None at all. Whether he was caused to sign by a beating or by some desire of his own—the desire to tell the truth, for example—in either case his signing was causally determined, and therefore in neither case did he act of his own free will. Since there is no such thing as free will, the question whether he signed of his own free will ought not to be discussed by us.

The foreman and the rest of the jury would rightly conclude that the philosopher must be making some mistake. What sort of a mistake could it be? There is only one possible answer. The philosopher must be using the phrase "free will" in some peculiar way of his own which is not the way in which men usually use it when they wish to determine a question of moral responsibility. That is, he must be using an incorrect definition of it as implying action not determined by causes.

Suppose a man left his office at noon, and were questioned about it. Then we might hear this:

JONES: Did you go out of your own free will?

SMITH: Yes. I went out to get my lunch.

But we might hear:

JONES: Did you leave your office of your own free will?

SMITH: No. I was forcibly removed by the police.

We have now collected a number of cases of actions which, in the ordinary usage of the English language, would be called cases in which people have acted of their own free will. We should also say in all these cases that they *chose* to act as they did. We should also say that they could have acted otherwise, if they had chosen. For instance, Mahatma Gandhi was not compelled to fast; he chose to do so. He could have eaten if he had wanted to. When Smith went out to get his lunch, he chose to do so. He could have stayed and done some work, if he had wanted to. We have also collected a number of cases of the opposite kind. They are cases in which men were not able to exercise their free will. They had no choice. They were compelled to do as they did. The man in the desert did not fast of his own free will. He had no choice in the matter. He was compelled to fast because there was nothing for him to eat. And so with the other cases. It ought to be quite easy, by an inspection of these cases, to tell what we ordinarily mean when we say that a man did or did not exercise free will. We ought therefore to be able to extract from them the proper definition of the term. Let us put the cases in a table:

Free Acts	*Unfree Acts*
Gandhi fasting because he wanted to free India.	The man fasting in the desert because there was no food.
Stealing bread because one is hungry.	Stealing because one's employer threatened to beat one.
Signing a confession because one wanted to tell the truth.	Signing because the police beat one.
Leaving the office because one wanted one's lunch.	Leaving because forcibly removed.

It is obvious that to find the correct definition of free acts we must discover what characteristic is common to all the acts in the left-hand column, and is, at the same time, absent from all the acts in the right-hand column. This characteristic which all free acts have, and which no unfree acts have, will be the defining characteristic of free will.

Is being uncaused, or not being determined by causes, the characteristic of which we are in search? It cannot be, because although it is true that all the acts in the right-hand column have causes, such as the beating by the police or the absence of food in the desert, so also do the acts in the left-hand column. Mr. Gandhi's fasting was caused by his desire to free India, the man leaving the office by his hunger, and so on. Moreover there is no reason to doubt that these causes of the free acts were in turn caused by prior conditions, and that these were again the results of causes, and so on back indefinitely into the past. Any physiologist can tell us the causes of hunger. What caused Mr. Gandhi's tremendously powerful desire to free India is no doubt more difficult to discover. But it must have had causes. Some of them may have lain in peculiarities of his glands or brain, others in his past experiences, others in his heredity, others in his education. Defenders of free will have usually tended to deny such facts. But to do so is plainly a case of special pleading, which is unsupported by any scrap of evidence. The only reasonable view is that all human actions, both those which are freely done and those which are not, are either wholly determined by causes, or at least as much determined as other events in nature. It may be true, as the physicists tell us, that nature is not as deterministic as was once thought. But whatever degree of determinism prevails in the world, human actions appear to be as much determined as anything else. And if this is so, it cannot be the case that what distinguishes actions freely chosen from those which are not free is that the latter are determined by causes while the former are not. Therefore, being uncaused or being undetermined by causes, must be an incorrect definition of free will.

- If the presence or absence of determining causes is not what distinguishes voluntary from involuntary actions, what does make them different?

What, then, is the difference between acts which are freely done and those which are not? What is the characteristic which is present to all the acts in the left-hand column and absent from all those in the right-hand column? Is it not obvious that, although both sets of actions have causes, the causes of those in the left-hand column are *of a different kind* from the causes of those in the right-hand column? The free acts are all caused by desires, or motives, or by some sort of internal psychological states of the agent's mind. The unfree acts, on the other hand, are all caused by physical forces or physical conditions outside the agent. Police arrest means physical force exerted from the outside; the absence of food in the desert is a physical condition of the outside world. We may therefore frame the following rough definitions. *Acts freely done are those whose immediate causes are psychological states in the agent. Acts not freely done are those whose immediate causes are states of affairs external to the agent.*

It is plain that if we define free will in this way, then free will certainly exists, and the philosopher's denial of its existence is seen to be what it is—nonsense. For it is obvious that all those actions of men which we should ordinarily attribute to the exercise of their free will, or of which we should say that they freely chose to do them, are in fact actions which have been caused by their own desire, wishes, thoughts, emotions, impulses, or other psychological states.

- In the next passage, why does Stace assert that determinism is consistent with the notions of moral responsibility, blame, and punishment?

But that determinism is incompatible with moral responsibility is as much a delusion as that it is incompatible with free will. You do not excuse a man for doing a wrong act because, knowing his character, you felt certain beforehand that he would do it. Nor do you deprive a man of a reward or prize because, knowing his goodness or his capabilities, you felt certain beforehand that he would win it. . . .

Suppose that your child develops a habit of telling lies. You give him a mild beating. Why? Because you believe that his personality is such that the usual motives for telling the truth do not cause him to do so. You therefore supply the missing cause, or motive, in the shape of pain and the fear of future pain if he repeats his untrustful behavior. And you hope that a few treatments of this kind will condition him to the habit of truth-telling, so that he will come to tell the truth without the infliction of pain. You assume that his actions are determined by causes, but that the usual causes of truth-telling do not in him produce their usual effects. You therefore supply him with an artificially injected motive, pain and fear, which you think will in the future cause him to speak truthfully.

The principle is exactly the same where you hope, by punishing one man, to deter others from wrong actions. You believe that the fear of punishment will cause those who might otherwise do evil to do well.

We act on the same principle with non-human, and even with inanimate, things, if they do not behave in the way we think they ought to behave. The rose bushes in the garden produce only small and poor blooms, whereas we want large and rich ones. We supply a cause which will produce large blooms, namely fertilizer. Our automobile does not go properly. We supply a cause which will make it go better, namely oil in the works. The punishment for the man, the fertilizer for the plant, and the oil for the car, are all justified by the same principle and in the same way. The only difference is that different kinds of things require different kinds of causes to make them do what they should. Pain may be the appropriate remedy to apply, in certain cases, to human beings, and oil to the machine. It is, of course, of no use to inject motor oil into the boy or to beat the machine.

- In his final argument, why does Stace claim that moral responsibility, praise or blame, reward or punishment are not only consistent with determinism, but require it?

Thus, we see that moral responsibility is not only consistent with determinism, but requires it. The assumption on which punishment is based is that human behavior is causally determined. If pain could not be a cause of truth-telling, there would be no justification at all for punishing lies. If human actions and volitions were uncaused, it would be useless either to punish or reward, or indeed to do anything else to correct people's bad behavior. For nothing that you could do would in any way influence them. Thus, moral responsibility would entirely disappear. If there were no determinism of human beings at all, their actions would be completely unpredictable and capricious, and therefore irresponsible. And this is in itself a strong argument against the common view of philosophers that free will means being undetermined by causes.

LOOKING THROUGH THE COMPATIBILIST'S LENS

1. Think about a choice that you believe you made freely, and then answer the following questions. What indicates to you that this decision genuinely was your own choice (a free choice) and not one that you were coerced into making? Can you ever know completely all the causal factors that made you the person that you are? Can you ever know completely all the causal factors that made you choose as you did? Is it necessary to know the answers to the last two questions in order to answer the first question?

2. To what degree do you think your actions are predictable by your friends or family? To what degree are your friends' actions predictable? How can an action be predictable with a certain degree of probability unless it is determined to that degree? Can an action be predictable, yet still be said to be free? What would a compatibilist say? What do you say?

EXAMINING THE STRENGTHS AND WEAKNESSES OF COMPATIBILISM

Positive Evaluation

1. By rejecting the claim that some events (psychological states) are uncaused, is the compatibilist's position more consistent with the most well-founded principles of physics and the behavioral sciences than that of the libertarian?

2. In building a theory around the notions that some actions are voluntary and some are involuntary, that some are free and some are not, is the compatibilist more consistent with the way we ordinarily speak than is the hard determinist?

3. Does compatibilism provide an effective way of preserving moral responsibility while also explaining why praise, blame, reward, punishment, laws, education, and experience in general can shape, modify, and change people's behavior?

Negative Evaluation

1. Suppose you found out that since the age of eight, you have been the subject of a scientific experiment. Scientists found that from a distance, they could bombard your brain with ultrasonic rays that would cause you to have the particular values, likes, dislikes, and beliefs that you now have. Your tastes in foods, your choice of a career, your musical preferences, your personality traits, your moral and political beliefs, and your attitude toward religion were all part of a master plan that was programmed into you. Furthermore, not only your desires but your positive or negative evaluations of those desires have been inserted into you. Would this discovery change how you viewed your life? Why? Even though your choices have been based on your own psychological dispositions, is it meaningful to say they were free, because your psychological states were programmed by scientists? Do these considerations pose a problem for the compatibilist claim that we have free will even if we are determined?

2. What do you think of the following critique of compatibilism?

If determinism is true, then our acts are the consequences of the laws of nature and events in the remote past. But it is not up to us what went on before we were born, and neither is it up to us what the laws of nature are. Therefore, the consequences of these things (including our present acts) are not up to us.[56]

REVIEW FOR CHAPTER 3

Philosophers

3.0 Overview of Metaphysics
    Aristotle
3.1 Overview: The Mind-Body Problem
    Hugh Elliot
    René Descartes
3.2 Dualism
    René Descartes
3.3 Physicalism
    Jeffrey Olen
3.4 Functionalism and Artificial Intelligence
    Jerry Fodor
    René Descartes
    Alan Turing
    Marvin Minsky

    John Searle
    Daniel Dennett
3.5 Overview: Freedom and Determinism
    John Stuart Mill
    Fyodor Dostoyevsky
    Clarence Darrow
3.6 Hard Determinism
    B. F. Skinner
    Samuel Butler
    Clarence Darrow
    Benedict Spinoza
3.7 Libertarianism
    Arthur Eddington
    Peter Berger
    Richard Taylor
    Jean-Paul Sartre
3.8 Compatibilism
    W. T. Stace

Concepts

3.0 Overview of Metaphysics
  metaphysics
  the problem of permanence and change
  the problem of appearance and reality
  the mind-body problem
  the problem of freedom and determinism
  Ockham's razor
  ontology
  two characteristics of fundamental reality
  three categories for classifying things
  the eliminativist strategy
  the reductionist strategy
3.1 Overview: The Mind-Body Problem
  four commonsense propositions about the mind
    and body
  dualism
  physicalism
  interactionism
  Cartesian dualism
  idealism
  identity theory (reductionism)
  eliminativism
  functionalism
3.2 Dualism
  mind-body dualism (psychophysical dualism)
  Cartesian dualism
  Principle of the Nonidentity of Discernibles
  Descartes's argument from doubt
  Descartes's argument from divisibility
  Descartes's argument from consciousness
  Descartes's compromise
  interactionism
3.3 Physicalism
  physicalism
  four problems of dualism
  identity theory (reductionism)
  eliminativism
  folk psychology
3.4 Functionalism and Artificial Intelligence
  functionalism
  multiple realizability
  the Turing Test
  the strong artificial intelligence thesis
  the weak artificial intelligence thesis
  John Searle's Chinese room
  intentionality
3.5 Overview: Freedom and Determinism
  circumstantial freedom

  metaphysical freedom
  determinism
  incompatibilism
  hard determinism
  libertarianism
  compatibilism
3.6 Hard Determinism
  three objections to libertarianism
  the basic argument of the determinist
  theological determinism
  four responses to the determinist's objections
  the determinist's replies to the four responses
  the determinist's view of moral responsibility
  pantheism
3.7 Libertarianism
  three objections to determinism
  the argument from introspection
  the argument from deliberation
  the argument from moral responsibility
  agency theory
  event-causation
  agent-causation
  radical existential freedom
  facticity
  transcendence
  bad faith
3.8 Compatibilism
  compatibilism
  the compatibilist's concept of free actions

SUGGESTIONS FOR FURTHER READING

General Metaphysics

Taylor, Richard. *Metaphysics.* 4th ed. Englewood Cliffs, N.J.: Prentice Hall, 1992. An easy introduction to the topic, including chapters on the mind-body problem and freedom-determinism.

van Inwagen, Peter. *Metaphysics.* Boulder, Colo.: Westview Press, 1993. An engaging, contemporary introduction to metaphysics.

The Mind-Body Problem

Beakley, Brian, and Peter Ludlow, eds. *The Philosophy of Mind: Classical Problems and Contemporary Issues.* Cambridge, Mass.: MIT Press, 1992. A good anthology, covering a range of positions.

Carruthers, Peter. *Introducing Persons: Theories and Arguments in the Philosophy of Mind.* Albany: State University of New York Press, 1986. A fairly accessible discussion of the various theories and issues.

Churchland, Paul. *Matter and Consciousness.* Cambridge, Mass.: MIT Press, 1990. An accessible and important introduction to the issues from a physicalist perspective.

Dennett, Daniel. *The Intentional Stance.* Cambridge, Mass.: MIT Press, 1989. An entertaining but somewhat advanced discussion of the contemporary debate.

Flanagan, Owen. *The Science of the Mind.* 2d ed. Cambridge, Mass.: MIT Press, 1991. A discussion of the leading positions.

Gregory, R. L. *The Oxford Companion to the Mind.* Oxford: Oxford University Press, 1987. An important resource.

Guttenplan, Samuel. *A Companion to the Philosophy of Mind.* Oxford: Blackwell, 1994. A useful reference guide to the subject.

Kim, Jaegwon. *Philosophy of Mind.* Boulder, Colo.: Westview Press, 1996. A somewhat advanced overview of the various topics and theories.

Lycan, William, ed. *Mind and Cognition.* Oxford: Blackwell, 1991. Another good anthology.

Rosenthal, David, ed. *The Nature of Mind.* Oxford: Oxford University Press, 1991. A well-known anthology.

Dualism

Descartes, René. *Meditations on First Philosophy,* Meditations II and VI. Many translations are available. The classic statement of dualism.

Nagel, Thomas. *The View from Nowhere.* Oxford: Oxford University Press, 1986. While Nagel is not a radical dualist like Descartes, he does maintain that the mental cannot be reduced to the physical.

Robinson, Howard, ed. *Objections to Physicalism.* Oxford: Oxford University Press, 1997. A collection of articles criticizing the physicalist solution to the mind-body problem.

Swinburne, Richard. *The Evolution of the Soul.* Rev. ed. Oxford: Oxford University Press, 1997. Swinburne is a contemporary dualist who attempts to reconcile this position with the findings of recent science.

Physicalism

Brown, Warren S., Nancey Murphy, and H. Newton Malony, eds. *Whatever Happened to the Soul? Scientific* and *Theological Portraits of Human Nature.* Minneapolis: Fortress Press, 1998. A series of essays by Christian theologians, scientists, and philosophers who attempt to develop a nonreductive physicalism that is consistent with a religious view of the nature of personhood.

Chalmers, David. *The Conscious Mind: In Search of a Fundamental Theory.* Oxford: Oxford University, 1996. A much-discussed and controversial critique of physicalism. Although Chalmers is not a Cartesian dualist, he does think that mental properties cannot be reduced to physical properties.

Churchland, Patricia. *Brain-Wise: Studies in Neurophilosophy.* Cambridge, Mass.: MIT Press, 2002. An attempt to show that brain science continues to shed light on philosophical questions about the mind, including notions such as the self, consciousness, knowledge, and freedom of the will.

Dennett, Daniel. *Consciousness Explained.* Boston: Little, Brown, 1991. An interesting attempt to explain consciousness from the standpoint of physicalism.

Levin, Michael E. *Metaphysics and the Mind-Body Problem.* Oxford: Clarendon Press, 1979. A vigorous defense of physicalism.

Shear, Jonathan, ed. *Explaining Consciousness: The Hard Problem.* Cambridge, Mass.: MIT Press, 1998. A series of responses, sympathetic and critical, to David Chalmers's thesis that consciousness is the hard problem that physicalism cannot solve.

Functionalism and Artificial Intelligence

Fodor, Jerry. "The Mind-Body Problem." *Scientific American,* January 1981, pp. 114–23. A popular presentation of the functionalist's solution to the mind-body problem.

Lieber, Justin. *Can Animals and Machines Be Persons?* Indianapolis: Hackett, 1985. An entertaining fictional dialogue dealing with the nature of the mind in the light of animal and machine intelligence.

Moody, Todd. *Philosophy and Artificial Intelligence.* Englewood Cliffs, N.J.: Prentice Hall, 1993. An introduction to the implications of artificial intelligence for philosophy of mind.

Searle, John. *Mind, Brains, and Science.* Cambridge, Mass.: Harvard University Press, 1984. An engaging analysis of the issues; includes a version of Searle's classic Chinese room refutation of functionalism.

Freedom and Determinism

Trustead, Jennifer. *Free Will and Responsibility.* Oxford: Oxford University Press, 1984. A readable introduction to the topic.

Watson, Gary, ed. *Free Will.* Oxford: Clarendon Press, 1982. A collection of important articles on the topic.

Hard Determinism

Honderich, Ted. *How Free Are You? The Determinism Problem.* Oxford: Oxford University Press, 1993. A readable argument against the belief in free will.

Skinner, B. F. *Walden Two.* New York: Macmillan, 1948. A highly entertaining novel depicting a utopian community based on the philosophy of hard determinism.

Libertarianism

Kane, Robert. *The Significance of Free Will.* Oxford: Oxford University Press, 1996. Considered to be one of the best recent defenses of libertarianism.

Compatibilism

Dennett, Daniel. *Elbow Room: The Varieties of Free Will Worth Wanting.* Cambridge, Mass.: MIT Press, 1984. An entertaining and well-argued defense of compatibilism.

van Inwagen, Peter. *An Essay on Free Will.* Oxford: Clarendon Press, 1982. A highly original study that is strongly critical of compatibilism.

Science and Religion

Barbour, Ian. *Religion and Science: Historical and Contemporary Issues.* New York: HarperCollins, 1997. Although his focus is on religion and science, Barbour does a very good job of tracing the relations between science and philosophy through the centuries and discusses the metaphysical implications of various scientific theories.

Burtt, Edwin A. *The Metaphysical Foundations of Modern Physical Science.* Atlantic Highlands, N.J.: Humanities Press, 1996. A good discussion of how metaphysics and science worked together in forming the ideas of scientists from Copernicus to Newton.

NOTES

1. Robert Solomon makes these points in *The Big Questions,* 4th ed. (Fort Worth, Texas: Harcourt Brace Jovanovich, 1994), p. 108.

2. Hugh Elliot, "Tantalus," in *Modern Science and the Illusions of Professor Bergson* (1912), quoted in Daniel Kolak and Raymond Martin, *The Experience of Philosophy,* 3d ed. (Belmont, Calif.: Wadsworth, 1996), p. 411.

3. René Descartes, *Discourse on the Method,* in *The Philosophical Writings of Descartes,* vol. 1, trans. John Cottingham, Robert Stoothoff, and Dugald Murdoch (Cambridge: Cambridge University Press, 1985), 4.32–33, p. 127. The references are to the part number and page number in the classic French edition, followed by the page number in this edition.

4. René Descartes, *Meditations on First Philosophy,* revised ed., trans. John Cottingham (Cambridge: Cambridge University Press, 1996), 6.85–86, p. 59. The references are to the meditation number and page number in the classic French edition, followed by the page number in this edition.

5. René Descartes, *Author's Replies to the Fourth Set of Objections,* in *The Philosophical Writings of Descartes,* vol. 2, trans. John Cottingham, Robert Stoothoff, and Dugald Murdoch (Cambridge: Cambridge University Press, 1984), p. 160.

6. Descartes, *Meditations on First Philosophy,* 6.78, p. 54.

7. René Descartes, *Passions of the Soul,* in *The Philosophical Writings of Descartes,* vol. 1, 1.31, p. 340.

8. R. Buckminster Fuller, "The Phantom Captain," in *Nine Chains to the Moon* (Carbondale: Southern Illinois University Press, 1938), pp. 18–19.

9. Jeffrey Olen, *Persons and Their World* (New York: Random House, 1983), pp. 213–14, 220–24.

10. J. B. S. Haldane, *Possible Worlds and Other Papers* (New York: Harper & Brothers, 1928), p. 220.

11. For an extended discussion of this argument, see Frank Jackson, "Epiphenomenal Qualia," *Philosophical Quarterly* 32 (1982): pp. 127–36; and "What Mary Didn't Know," *Journal of Philosophy* 83 (1986): pp. 291–95.

12. Gottfried Leibniz, *The Monadology,* sec. 17, in *Discourse on Metaphysics/Correspondence with Arnauld/Monadology,* trans. George Montgomery (La Salle, Ill.: Open Court Publishing Co., 1902; reprint ed., 1968), p. 254.

13. Edgar Allan Poe, "Maelzel's Chess-Playing Machine," *Southern Literary Messenger* (April 1836); reprinted in *The Portable Poe,* ed. Philip Van Doren Stern (New York: Penguin Books, 1977), pp. 511–12.

14. Poe, "Maelzel's Chess-Playing Machine," p. 513.

15. Garry Kasparov, "The Day That I Sensed a New Kind of Intelligence," *Time Magazine,* March 25, 1996, p. 55.

16. These three responses to Poe's articles were suggested by Todd C. Moody, *Philosophy and Artificial Intelligence* (Englewood Cliffs, N.J.: Prentice Hall, 1993), p. 9.

17. Jerry Fodor, "The Mind-Body Problem," *Scientific American,* January 1981, p. 114.

18. The three passages are from Fodor, "The Mind-Body Problem," pp. 114, 118, and 118, respectively.

19. Descartes, *Discourse on the Method,* 5.56–57, p. 140.

20. Alan Turing, "Computing Machinery and Intelligence," *Mind* 59, no. 236 (1950); reprinted in *The Mind's I,* ed. Douglas Hofstadter and Daniel Dennett (New York: Bantam Books, 1981), pp. 57–67.

21. Ibid., 57.

22. Marvin Minsky, "Why People Think Computers Can't," in *The Computer Culture,* ed. Denis P. Donnelly (Cranbury, N.J.: Associated University Presses, 1985), pp. 40–43.

23. John R. Searle, "Minds, Brains, and Programs" in *The Behavioral and Brain Sciences,* vol. 3, reprinted in Hofstadter and Dennett, *The Mind's I,* pp. 353–73.

24. John Searle, *Minds, Brains, and Science* (Cambridge, Mass.: Harvard University Press, 1984), pp. 37–38.

25. Hofstadter and Dennett, *The Mind's I,* p. 94.

26. For more information on the case of the two Jims, see Donald Dale Jackson, "Reunion of Identical Twins, Raised Apart, Reveals Some Astonishing Similarities," *Smithsonian* 11 (October 1980): pp. 48–56. For further studies of twins separated at birth, see Lawrence Wright, "Double Mystery," *The New Yorker,* August 7, 1995, pp. 44–62; and Lawrence Wright, *Twins: And What They Tell Us about Who We Are* (New York: John Wiley & Sons, 1997).

27. W. Somerset Maugham, *Of Human Bondage* (New York: Penguin Books, Signet Classic, 1991), pp. 357–58.

28. Pierre-Simone Laplace, *Philosophical Essay on Probabilities,* trans. Andrew I. Dale (New York: Springer-Verlag, 1995), p. 2.

29. John Stuart Mill, *A System of Logic,* bk. 6, chap. 2, sec. 2 in *Collected Works of John Stuart Mill,* vol. 8, ed. J. M. Robson (Toronto: University of Toronto Press, 1974), pp. 836–37.

30. Fyodor Dostoyevsky, *Notes from Underground,* trans. Constance Garnett, in Walter Kaufmann, *Existentialism from Dostoyevsky to Sartre,* rev. and exp. ed. (New York: Meridian, 1975), p. 72.

31. Clarence Darrow, "Address to the Prisoners in the Cook County Jail," in *Attorney for the Damned,* ed. Arthur Weinberg (New York: Simon and Schuster, 1957), pp. 3–4.

32. B. F. Skinner, *Walden Two* (New York: Macmillan, 1948), pp. 257–58.

33. B. F. Skinner, *About Behaviorism* (New York: Alfred Knopf, 1974), p. 189.

34. Samuel Butler, *Erewhon and Erewhon Revisited* (New York: Random House, The Modern Library, 1927), pp. 106–7.

35. *State of Illinois versus Leopold and Loeb.*

36. Benedict de Spinoza, *Ethics,* ed. James Gutmann, trans. William Hale White and Amelia Hutchinson Stirling (New York: Hafner, 1966), 2.49, Note. The first number in the reference refers to the book number of Spinoza's manuscript and the number following the decimal point indicates the proposition number.

37. Letter 58 (to G. H. Schuller) in Baruch Spinoza, *The Ethics and Selected Letters,* ed. Seymour Feldman, trans. Samuel Shirley (Indianapolis: Hackett, 1982), p. 250.

38. Spinoza, *Ethics,* 2.35, Note.

39. Arthur Eddington, *New Pathways in Science* (New York: Macmillan, 1935), pp. 90–91.

40. Skinner, *About Behaviorism,* p. 189.

41. Arthur Eddington, quoted in L. Susan Stebbing, *Philosophy and the Physicists* (New York: Dover Publications, 1958), p. 242.

42. Eddington, *New Pathways in Science,* p. 90.

43. Peter L. Berger, *Invitation to Sociology: A Humanistic Perspective* (Garden City, N.Y.: Doubleday, Anchor Books, 1963), p. 176.

44. Richard Taylor, *Metaphysics,* 4th ed. (Englewood Cliffs, N.J.: Prentice-Hall, 1992), pp. 51–53.

45. Jean-Paul Sartre, *Being and Nothingness,* trans. Hazel E. Barnes (New York: Simon & Schuster, Washington Square Press, 1956), p. 569.

46. Jean-Paul Sartre, "Existentialism," trans. Bernard Frechtman, in *Existentialism and Human Emotions* (New York: Philosophical Library, 1957), p. 15.

47. Simone de Beauvoir, *The Second Sex,* trans. H. M. Parshley (New York: Knopf, 1975), p. 267.

48. Sartre, *Being and Nothingness,* p. 640.

49. Jean-Paul Sartre, *The Emotions: Outline of a Theory,* trans. Bernard Frechtman (New York: Philosophical Library, 1948), p. 37.

50. Ibid., pp. 26–32.

51. Sartre, *Being and Nothingness,* p. 111.

52. Ibid., pp. 708–11.

53. Ibid., p. 710.

54. William James, "The Dilemma of Determinism," in *Essays in Pragmatism* (New York: Macmillan, Hafner Press, 1948), p. 59.

55. W. T. Stace, *Religion and the Modern Mind* (New York: Lippincott, 1952), pp. 249–58.

56. Peter van Inwagen, *An Essay on Free Will* (Oxford: Clarendon Press, 1983), p. 16.

William Blake, frontispiece from *Europe. A Prophecy*, 1794

CHAPTER 4

THE SEARCH
FOR GOD

 CHAPTER OBJECTIVES

Upon completion of this chapter you should be able to

1. Provide an overview of various evidentialist and nonevidentialist approaches to the issue of justifying religious belief.
2. Present the key steps of the first cause and contingency versions of the cosmological argument and state strengths and weaknesses of each.
3. Outline the argument from design (teleological argument) and discuss the merits of Hume's objections to it.
4. Discuss the various views on both the theory of evolution and cosmic fine-tuning as well as their implications for the argument from design.
5. Explain Anselm's version of the ontological argument together with the objections raised by Gaunilo and Kant.
6. Summarize Pascal's wager and various possible criticisms of it.
7. Contrast the positions of Clifford and James on the justifiability of belief in the face of insufficient evidence.
8. Discuss Kierkegaard's subjectivist justification of religious belief.
9. State the problem of evil and weigh the effectiveness of the greater goods defense (including Hick's soul-making variety), the free will defense, and the natural order defense.
10. Describe the four models of relating science and religion.

SCOUTING THE TERRITORY: *The Impact of Religion*

Love and anger, guilt and ecstasy, humor and solemnity, optimism and cynicism, peace and doubt, hope and despair—religion seems capable of evoking a response corresponding to every peak and valley on the spectrum of human emotional life. Why is this? In the following passage, philosopher and theologian Peter Kreeft attempts to assess the impact of the idea of God.

FROM PETER KREEFT

Does God Exist?¹

The idea of God is either a fact, like sand, or a fantasy, like Santa.

If it is a fantasy, a human invention, it is the greatest invention in all of human history. Measure it against all the other inventions, mental or physical. Put on one side of the scale the control of fire, the domestication of animals, and the cultivation of wheat; the wheel, the ship, and the rocket ship; baseball, the symphony orchestra, and anesthetics—and a million other similarly great and wonderful things. Then put on the other side of the scale a single idea: the idea of a being that is actual, absolute, perfect, eternal, one, and personal; all-knowing, all-loving, all-just, all-merciful, and all-powerful; undying, impervious, unbribeable, uncompromising, and unchangeable; a cosmic creator, designer, redeemer, and provider; cosmic artist, musician, scientist, and sage; the infinite abyss of pure Being who is yet a person, a self, an "I." It is disputable whether such a being is a fact or a fantasy, but it is indisputable that if it is a fantasy, it is by far the greatest fantasy in history. If it is humanity's invention, it is humanity's masterpiece.

The idea of God has guided or deluded more lives, changed more history, inspired more music and poetry and philosophy than anything else, real or imagined. It has made more of a difference to human life on this planet, both individually and collectively, than anything else ever has. To see this clearly for yourself, just try this thought experiment: suppose no one in history had ever conceived the idea of God. Now, rewrite history following that premise. The task daunts and staggers the imagination. From the earliest human remains—religious funeral artifacts—to the most recent wars in the Mideast, religion—belief in a God or gods—has been the mainspring of the whole watch that is human history.

STOP AND THINK

Try Kreeft's thought experiment by answering the following questions.

- How would human history be different if no one had ever conceived of God?
- How would the absence of religion have affected the following areas of human experience: art, literature, music, science, morality, politics, law, philosophy?
- What would have been better in human experience if there had been no religion?
- What would have been worse in human experience if there had been no religion?
- To what degree, if any, do such considerations count for or against the truth of religious claims?

CHARTING THE TERRAIN OF RELIGION:
What Are the Issues?

Many people have found the idea of God to be comforting, inspiring, and the source of hope. But the philosophy of religion is concerned not with the psychological benefits of believing in the idea of God, but rather with the question of whether the word *God* refers to anything in reality. As Kreeft put it, "God is either a fact, like sand, or a fantasy, like Santa." But once we start raising questions about the existence of God, a number of other questions arise. How can we decide whether God exists? Are there rational arguments that demonstrate that God exists or, at least, that his existence is probable? Is there evidence that counts against God's existence? Is it impossible or inappropriate to approach this question in an objective way? Should we fall back on faith or subjective considerations in making up our minds? What about the existence of suffering in the world? Isn't it pretty hard to square this fact with the belief in an all-powerful, loving God?

Most of our discussion surrounding these questions deals with the monotheistic conception of God found in such religions as Judaism, Islam, and Christianity. **Monotheism** claims that one God created the world and sustains it while transcending it. (Hereafter, I refer to this position as simply "theism.") But to limit philosophy of religion to these particular traditions assumes that a prior question has been raised and answered in favor of monotheism. This question is, "If God exists, what is the nature of this being?" To increase our range of options, we examine Hinduism, an Indian religion that has a completely different conception of God from that which predominates in Western thought. Finally, in asking whether the notion of God is essential to religion at all, we examine Buddhism, one of the world's great religions, yet one in which the notions of God and the supernatural are noticeably absent.

> **monotheism** the claim that one God created the world and sustains it while transcending it

CHOOSING A PATH: *What Are My Options Concerning Religious Belief?*

The claim that belief in God must be supported by objective evidence is known as **evidentialism.** Both religious believers and atheists can be evidentialists. The theistic evidentialist thinks that there is objective evidence for God. The atheistic evidentialist believes that we must have evidence in order for our belief in God to be rational, but goes on to argue that such evidence is lacking. Generally, all agnostics, that is, people who do not think there is sufficient evidence either for theism or atheism, are evidentialists.

> **evidentialism** the claim that belief in God must be supported by objective evidence

The theists who are evidentialists would, of course, agree that it is possible to demonstrate the existence of God through rational, objective arguments. They believe in the possibility and success of natural theology. **Natural theology** is the project of attempting to provide proofs for the existence of God based on reason and experience alone. In other words, the natural theologian does not appeal to supernatural revelation or faith of any sort to support his or her claims about God. The natural theologian does not necessarily reject revelation or faith, but he or she believes that it is possible to demonstrate God's existence, and perhaps the truth of other religious claims, solely through philosophical reasoning. The objective evidence that is used to support this belief is the subject of the sections that follow. The three main forms of objective arguments for God are the cosmological argument; the teleological, or design, argument; and the ontological argument.

> **natural theology** the project of attempting to provide proofs for the existence of God based on reason and experience alone

Atheism is the claim that God does not exist. Typically, atheists are evidentialists. However, while all atheists deny that God's existence may be proven, many atheists also would say that you cannot absolutely prove that God *doesn't* exist. They make this claim because

> **atheism** the claim that God does not exist

in most cases it is impossible to prove, beyond any possible doubt, a negative claim concerning the existence of something.

STOP AND THINK

- Can you absolutely prove that Santa Claus does not exist? How would you go about proving that there is no possibility that he exists?
- If you cannot prove his *non*existence, then you have the following two responses to choose from:
  1. I do not know whether Santa Claus does or does not exist.
  2. Because no plausible evidence suggests that Santa Claus exists, the rational person will believe that he does not exist.
- Which of these options do you think is more reasonable? Why?

Most rational adults believe that there is no Santa Claus even though they cannot provide *direct* evidence for this claim. It is very difficult to prove the *non*existence of something (such as leprechauns, unicorns, life in outer space, and so on). The fact that no credible person has ever seen a leprechaun does not rule out the possibility that one might be lurking out there in the woods somewhere. After all, we were once unaware of the existence of viruses because we did not have the instruments to detect them. Nevertheless, unless some hard, positive evidence turns up for the existence of leprechauns or Santa Claus, a rational person is justified in doubting their existence. The reason for this doubt is twofold: (1) The burden of proof is on those who make claims concerning the existence of extraordinary beings such as Santa Claus (as well as elves, space aliens, vampires, or unicorns) and (2) all the phenomena that we once needed the Santa hypothesis to explain (toys under the Christmas tree) can now be explained through other, more naturalistic hypotheses (indulgent parents). Although we cannot prove the nonexistence of such beings with the certainty of a mathematical proof, the lack of evidence of their existence and the reasonableness of alternative hypotheses make disbelief rational.

Similarly, the atheist argues that most of us (even the religious believer) live on the assumption that the events that happen around us are the result of natural causes. Those people who assert the existence of an extraordinary being such as God, a being who defies scientific explanation and who transcends the world of nature, have the burden of providing the evidence for their thesis. Furthermore, the atheist would say that, analogous to the Santa hypothesis, people once appealed to God or supernatural causes to explain things for which they had no other explanation (solar eclipses, disease, the origin of biological species, and so on). Hence, many atheists believe that they do not need to absolutely prove the truth of atheism. Instead they claim it is sufficient merely to show that the religious believer has failed to provide valid arguments establishing the existence of God. The task for the atheist, then, is to show that all the rational arguments of the natural theologian are invalid or inconclusive.

On the other hand, most atheists do think that there is positive evidence for the thesis that God does not exist. Although a number of different arguments are used,[2] the most common argument that atheists appeal to is based on the problem of evil. They claim that the existence of evil (such as the suffering of innocent people due to natural (disasters) is evidence that casts doubt on the God hypothesis. This problem is discussed in section 4.5.

Agnosticism is the position that not enough evidence exists for us to know whether there is or is not a God. This position is sometimes called *religious skepticism.* Agnostics are evidentialists, because they agree that objective evidence is necessary to believe in God's existence, but they believe that such evidence is unavailable. However, they also say that objective evidence is necessary to claim that God does *not* exist. Hence, unlike both the theist and the atheist, the agnostic does not think we can know anything concerning God's existence. Accordingly, the agnostic thinks we must suspend judgment on this issue. Some degree of uncertainty or doubt about God's existence does not make a person an agnostic. Many theists would claim that they personally lack full knowledge or indubitable certainty about God. Agnosticism (as it is being defined here) is the claim that it is *in principle* impossible for *anyone* to have knowledge that God exists. I do not devote a separate section to agnosticism, because the agnostic could be viewed as a person who agrees with the negative case of both the theist and the atheist. In other words, the agnostic agrees with the atheist that the believer's arguments are fallacious or inconclusive. In fact, many of the refutations of the arguments for God have actually been made by agnostics. However, the agnostic also agrees with the believer that the atheist's arguments against God's existence are also fallacious or inconclusive.

Those people who embrace **nonevidentialism** hold that it is not rationally required to have objective, rational evidence for our basic beliefs and stance toward life. The nonevidentialist claims that there is a basis for religious belief other than reason. Accordingly, the nonevidentialist says that we must and, in fact, do form our ultimate commitments on the basis of subjective, personal factors and not on rational arguments. Although there are people on both sides of the God issue who reject evidentialism, it is a position that appeals more to theists than to atheists. There are several varieties of theistic nonevidentialists. The first category consists of people who maintain that the rational, objective arguments for God are either ineffective or unnecessary while at the same time they offer subjective or pragmatic considerations to move an individual in the direction of faith. These thinkers believe that objective evidence cannot decide the God issue, but that there are practical or subjective reasons for believing in God. The considerations referred to here differ from the typical forms of objective evidence and argument used in natural theology because they make a direct appeal to the subjective concerns of the individual and his or her stance toward life. To illustrate this appeal, I provide readings from Blaise Pascal, the 17th-century mathematician and philosopher, and William James, the 20th-century pragmatist.

A second, more radical form of nonevidentialism is **fideism,** which claims that religious belief must be based on faith alone and cannot be justified by appeal to either objective or subjective reasons. The fideist believes that there is a tension between faith and reason such that we must choose between the two. If we know something on the basis of objective evidence, the fideist claims, then it makes no sense to say we believe it on faith. For example, if a woman hired a detective to maintain a 24-hour surveillance of her husband to see if he was cheating on her, it would be obvious that she did not have faith in him. Hence, for the fideist, faith is a kind of leap or a subjective commitment that goes far beyond what we can know on the basis of objective evidence. According to the fideist, God must be approached through faith, by following your heart, and not by searching for evidence in the sterile, dry valley of objective reason. If subjective and pragmatic considerations are seen as arguments or justifications for religious belief, then the extreme fideist would reject these considerations as well. Søren Kierkegaard, the 19th-century founder of religious existentialism, will illustrate this position.

Just for the record, a few atheists have been nonevidentialists. The most striking example is Friedrich Nietzsche, the 19th-century founder of the movement of atheistic existentialism, who was discussed in section 2.5. Nietzsche believed that there are no rational,

agnosticism the claim that there is not enough evidence for us to know whether God does or does not exist; sometimes called religious skepticism

nonevidentialism the claim that it is not rationally required to have objective, rational evidence for our basic beliefs and stance toward life

fideism the claim that religious belief must be based on faith alone and cannot be justified by appeal to either objective or subjective reasons

TABLE 4.1 *Spectrum of Viewpoints on the Existence of God*

	Theistic Evidentialism (Natural Theology)	Atheistic Evidentialism	Agnosticism	Nonevidential Theism (Pragmatism, Subjectivism)	Fideism
1. Objective evidence is required for religious belief.	Agree	Agree	Agree	Disagree	Disagree
2. Objective evidence is available.	Agree	Disagree	Disagree	Disagree	Disagree
3. Persuasive practical or subjective reasons for belief are available.	(May agree or disagree)	Disagree	Disagree	Agree	Disagree
4. Belief in God must be based on faith alone and not on reasons.	Disagree	Disagree	Disagree	Disagree	Agree
5. God exists.	Agree	Disagree	Undecided	Agree	Agree
6. God does not exist.	Disagree	Agree	Undecided	Disagree	Disagree
7. We cannot know if God does or does not exist.	Disagree	Disagree	Agree	Disagree	Depends on what you mean by "know"

objective grounds for choosing a worldview. All of a person's beliefs are based on his or her personal stance toward life. Timid people will subjectively choose the comfort of religion, he said, whereas emotionally strong, self-reliant people will subjectively choose atheism. He was fond of expressing his nonevidentialism in statements such as: "Gradually it has become clear to me what every great philosophy so far has been: namely, the personal confession of its author and a kind of involuntary and unconscious memoir."[3]

The spectrum of viewpoints we have discussed are summarized in table 4.1.

CONCEPTUAL TOOLS: *Arguments for the Existence of God*

All arguments fall into two main groups, and the arguments for the existence of God are no exception. First, there are a posteriori arguments. (*A posteriori* in Latin means "from what comes later"; in other words, it refers to what comes after experience.) These arguments depend on premises that can be known only on the basis of experience. For example, we may *observe* the order in the world and from that conclude that it exhibits a design that is the product of an intelligent, cosmic designer. Knowledge that is based on experience is sometimes called empirical knowledge. Second, there are a priori arguments. (*A priori* in Latin means "from what is prior," referring to what is prior to experience.) An a priori argument is based on reason alone and does not require empirical premises. Let's take an example from the realm of mathematics. In Euclidean geometry we begin with axioms that are considered to be self-evident; from these, we deduce a number of theorems. We learn the essential truths about triangles by reasoning about them a priori and not by observing or measuring dozens of triangles. In the sections to come, we look at two a posteriori arguments for the existence of God: the cosmological argument and the argument from design. We also look at one of the most famous a priori arguments in philosophy: the ontological argument for God. But first, take the following questionnaire to see where you stand on these issues.

WHAT DO I THINK? *Questionnaire on the Existence of God*

		Agree	Disagree
1.	For someone's belief in God to be rational, he or she must have objective evidence supporting this belief.		
2.	It is possible to demonstrate the existence of God through rational, objective arguments.		
3.	Objective evidence cannot decide the God issue, but there are practical or subjective reasons for believing in God.		
4.	Belief in God must be based on faith alone and cannot be justified either by objective or by subjective reasons.		
5.	God exists.		
6.	God does not exist.		
7.	We should refuse to believe either that God exists or that God does not exist.		

KEY TO THE QUESTIONNAIRE ON THE EXISTENCE OF GOD

Statement 1: If you agree with this statement, you are an evidentialist, either of the theistic, atheistic, or agnostic variety. If you disagree, you are a nonevidentialist.

Statement 2: If you agree, you are a theistic evidentialist or, in other words, a supporter of natural theology. If you disagree, you are an opponent of natural theology and are either a nonevidentialist theist or an atheist or agnostic.

Statement 3: If you agree, you are a nonevidentialist theist and are either a religious pragmatist or subjectivist.

Statement 4: If you agree, you are a fideist, a believer in one version of nonevidential theism.

Statement 5: If you agree, you are a theist.

Statement 6: If you agree, you are an atheist.

Statement 7: If you agree, you are an agnostic.

Notice that statements 5, 6, and 7 represent three conclusions concerning the existence of God. However, as I pointed out in chapter 1, an important issue in philosophy is not just *what* you believe, but the reasons *why* you and others have these beliefs. Hence, statements 1 through 4 concern what reasons are available or necessary to justify beliefs about God.

4.1 THE COSMOLOGICAL ARGUMENT FOR GOD

 LEADING QUESTIONS: *The Cosmological Argument*

1. A magician walks into the spotlight on stage and rolls up his sleeves. He convincingly shows you and the rest of the audience that both hands are empty. He then cups his hands together and out pops a live, fluttering, white dove. You are astonished and bewildered. Would this experience convince you that things like doves can simply pop into existence without a cause? Or would you insist that the magician is a masterful sleight-of-hand artist rather than accept what your eyes apparently saw? Why?

2. Walking downtown, you notice a light being reflected off the side mirror of a pickup truck. Curious about the source of this light, you notice that it is coming from the surface of a store window. The question now is, "What is the source of the light beam bouncing off the window?" You now notice that it is coming from light being reflected by the store window across the street. You still want to know: "What is the ultimate source of the mysterious light?" The following scenarios are three proposed answers to this question. Which one do you think is most plausible? Why?

- The light has no ultimate source; it is an infinite number of light beams and reflective surfaces. For every surface that is reflecting the light, there is another reflective surface that is bouncing light to it. Thus, every manifestation of the light has a source, and each one of these sources has another source that is sending it light. This series of causes and effects goes on infinitely.
- The light has no ultimate source; it does not have a cause. Light simply arose spontaneously within the system of reflective surfaces.
- The ultimate source of the light is the sun, which generates its own light and is the first cause of the light being progressively reflected from one surface to the next.

 ## SURVEYING THE CASE FOR THE COSMOLOGICAL ARGUMENT

These simple examples from show business and optics present some of the basic principles of the cosmological argument for God. Both cases dealt with the issues of causality and dependency and the notion that something cannot come from nothing. Doves and beams of light just do not pop into existence out of thin air. They both have a cause for appearing when and where they do. To put it another way, doves and beams of light depend on something outside themselves for their existence. Although there are many versions of the cosmological argument, they all begin with the fact that the universe is not self-explanatory and argue from there that the cosmos depends on a self-sufficient cause outside itself. Hence, the cosmological argument seeks to provide an answer to the question, Why is there something rather than nothing?

ST. THOMAS AQUINAS (1225–1274)

One of the foremost defenders of the cosmological argument was Thomas Aquinas. He was born into a noble family who resided in southern Italy about halfway between Rome and Naples. Aquinas was groomed by his family for a career of service in the Church. His parents' motives, however, were not as pious as they may seem; their dream was that Aquinas would rise to a position of ecclesiastical authority where he would be politically influential and even wealthy.

ST. THOMAS AQUINAS
(1225–1274)

Around age 14 Aquinas was sent to the University of Naples. It was an exciting place to be, for it abounded with new ideas; the recently discovered Aristotelian texts were beginning to have an impact on Christian thought. Aquinas came under the influence of the newly formed Dominican Order, which he joined sometime around 1244. His parents' plans seemed to be proceeding nicely, but they were not pleased, because the Dominicans did not aspire to be influential administrators but were humble and impoverished preachers and scholars. Nevertheless, Aquinas persuaded his family that the Dominicans were his calling and went on to earn the highest degree in theology.

Aquinas spent the remainder of his life lecturing and writing while residing alternately in Paris and Italy; he also made frequent journeys to conduct the business of his order and the Church. Aquinas died at age 49, on his way to attend the Council of Lyons to carry out a diplomatic mission.

He was an astoundingly prolific writer; his works fill some 25 volumes. He is said to have kept four secretaries busy at once, dictating different manuscripts in progress to them, which they would then transcribe. Although his philosophy is considered the official model for Catholic thought, Aquinas has influenced Protestant philosophers and other religious thinkers as well.

The First Cause Argument

One version of the cosmological argument is sometimes called the "First Cause argument." It argues that because the world contains things whose existence was caused, there necessarily had to be a First Cause of the entire series. Aquinas produced a famous version of this argument. Actually, he offered five arguments for the existence of God (or "the five ways," as he called them). The argument that is based on the notion of causation is his "second way."

FROM THOMAS AQUINAS

Summa Theologica[4]

The second way is from the nature of efficient cause.* In the world of sensible things we find there is an order of efficient causes. There is no case known (neither is it, indeed, possible) in which a thing is found to be the efficient cause of itself; for so it would be prior to itself, which is impossible. Now in efficient causes it is not possible to go on to infinity, because in all efficient causes following in order, the first is the cause of the

---

*When Aquinas uses the term *efficient cause,* he is speaking about one of the four kinds of causes described by Aristotle. Basically, "efficient cause" refers to the same thing that we refer to as simply a cause. The "first cause" is a cause beyond which there is no further cause. It is the original cause that brought about all the subsidiary causes and effects. When he refers to the "ultimate cause" he is referring to the very last cause in a series that actually brings about a certain effect. By "sensible things" he simply means physical things, or those things that can be perceived by the senses.

intermediate cause, and the intermediate is the cause of the ultimate cause, whether the intermediate cause be several, or one only. Now to take away the cause is to take away the effect. Therefore, if there be no first cause among efficient causes, there will be no ultimate, nor any intermediate, cause. But if in efficient causes it is possible to go to infinity, there will be no first efficient cause, neither will there be an ultimate effect, nor any intermediate efficient causes; all of which is plainly false. Therefore it is necessary to admit a first efficient cause, to which everyone gives the name of God.

The first cause argument that Aquinas uses could be formulated in this way:

1. The world contains things whose existence depends upon some cause.
2. Everything that exists is either uncaused or caused to exist by another.
3. There cannot be an infinite regress of causes.
4. So there must be an uncaused first cause.
5. An uncaused first cause is (in part) what we mean by God.
6. Therefore, God exists.

Almost no one would object to the first premise. Every moment of our lives we are confronted with examples of things whose existence is a result of some external cause. The second premise is a crucial one. It claims that something is either the sort of thing that requires no cause or its cause lies outside itself. Notice that the argument never says that "*everything* has a cause for its existence," for this premise would imply that God's existence had a cause.

At this point it is worth noting that Aquinas believed, with the Greek philosopher Aristotle, that it is logically possible that the world always existed. Aquinas believed that even if the world was eternal, it would be eternally dependent on something outside itself to sustain it in existence. Thus, when Aquinas talks about the cause of the world, he does not necessarily mean a first cause in time but instead a cause that is responsible for all other causes that are currently operating. Think about it this way. Right now your existence as a living, breathing human is dependent on there being oxygen in the atmosphere. But the existence of oxygen in your environment is dependent on there being plants and the earth's gravity. Likewise, these causes are at this present moment dependent on other conditions for their existence. These conditions are dependent on other conditions, and so forth. So right here and now, there is a hierarchical series of causes on which your existence depends. Aquinas's point is that this whole series that is operating here and now must be dependent on something that is not itself dependent on something else. For Aquinas, this situation would be true even if the world had always existed. As a matter of fact, Aquinas did believe that the universe had a beginning, but he based this belief on the Bible and not on philosophical arguments. There is, however, a version of the argument known as the *kalām* cosmological argument, defended by some medieval Islamic, Jewish, and Christian philosophers, that begins with the premise that the universe had a beginning in time.[5]

Critics have had the most problems with the third premise of Aquinas's argument. Why can't there be an infinite series of causes? Isn't the series of whole numbers an infinite series? One possible reply to this objection is that numbers are abstractions and not concretely existing things like mountains or galaxies. It makes sense for scientists to inquire into the origins of mountains or galaxies, but it does not make sense to ask how and when did the number seven begin to exist.

Nevertheless, some critics of the cosmological argument claim it is possible to conceive of an infinite series of physical causes. They argue, in fact, that since Aquinas believed that it makes sense to say there must be an uncaused first cause (God), why couldn't this uncaused cause of the universe simply be matter or energy instead?

STOP AND THINK

- Does it make sense to suppose that the series of causes producing a present event could go on infinitely, never ending in a first cause?
- Does it make sense to speak of an uncaused being, such as God?
- Which of these two ideas is the most implausible?

The Argument from Contingency

Later versions of the cosmological argument shifted the focus from the problem with a regress of causes to that of a regress of reasons or explanations for an event. These arguments are based on the **principle of sufficient reason.** This principle (which I abbreviate as PSR) states that everything that exists must have a reason that explains why it exists and why it has the properties it does. This reason could be that the being in question is uncaused; that is, it is self-sufficient and does not depend on anything outside itself. Or the being in question could be caused by something else that provides a sufficient explanation why it exists and exists just the way it does and not otherwise. In the next reading, Richard Taylor makes explicit use of this principle.

principle of sufficient reason the principle that everything that exists must have a reason that explains why it exists and why it has the properties that it does

STOP AND THINK

What is the basis for the truth of the principle of sufficient reason? The following four options are the most common ones. Which one do you think best explains PSR?

- It is a generalization from human experience. We have always found that everything has a cause or an explanation.
- It is a necessary truth, like the laws of logic. It is impossible to conceive of it as being false, for it is intuitively obvious.
- It is a presupposition of all inquiry. Without it, we could not make anything intelligible. It is involved in all our reasoning about the world.
- It is a questionable principle, and we have no reason to suppose that it is true.

This version of the cosmological argument begins with the fact that the world is a collection of things that are **contingent.** For something to be contingent means that it is possible for it to either exist or not exist. In other words, neither its existence nor its nonexistence is logically necessary. If we accept PSR, then we believe that there has to be a sufficient reason for the existence of anything. However, because a contingent being does not contain the reason for its existence within itself, then whether it exists or not must be explained by something outside it. Because the world consists of contingent things, the argument goes, so the world itself is contingent. Ultimately, everything could not be contingent, so there has to be a reason for the world's existence that is noncontingent, nondependent, self-sufficient, and uncaused. Sometimes the opposite of a contingent being is said to be a **necessary being.** A necessary being is one who contains the reason for its

contingent being a being whose existence depends on something outside itself, such that neither its existence nor its nonexistence is logically necessary

necessary being a being who contains the reason for its existence within its own nature

Interior of Sainte-Chapelle. This magnificent, 13th-century chapel in Paris can be used as a symbol of the intellectual project of Thomas Aquinas. The fundamental structures of Gothic cathedrals such as this one were based on the unyielding and universal laws of geometry and physics. At the same time, the rising arches of the earthly material of stone and the natural light streaming through the jewel-like stained glass served to provoke a sense of transcendence. In the same way, Aquinas attempted to create a philosophical structure with the tools of logic to point the intellect to God. For this reason, Aquinas's philosophical system, illustrated by the cosmological argument, has been called a "cathedral of reason."

existence within its own nature. In other words, it does not depend on anything for its existence and nothing can prevent it from existing. Obviously, God would be such a being. In his third way, Aquinas anticipates this argument, but he does not make use of PSR.

In the following passage, the American philosopher Richard Taylor (1919–2003) develops the argument from contingency. (Richard Taylor was a professor of philosophy at the University of Rochester.) Taylor argues that even if the world had no beginning, it would still need a cause.

- After reading this passage, try to figure out what Taylor's point will be concerning the mysterious, translucent ball.
- How does Taylor define and defend the PSR?

Metaphysics[6]

The Principle of Sufficient Reason

Suppose you were strolling in the woods and, in addition to the sticks, stones, and other accustomed litter of the forest floor, you one day came upon some quite unaccustomed object, something not quite like what you had ever seen before and would never expect to find in such a place. Suppose, for example, that it is a large ball, about your own height, perfectly smooth and translucent. . . .

. . . Now whatever else you might wonder about it, there is one thing you would hardly question; namely, that it did not appear there all by itself, that it owes its existence to something. You might not have the remotest idea whence and how it came to be there, but you would hardly doubt that there was an explanation. The idea that it might have come from nothing at all, that it might exist without there being any explanation of its existence, is one that few people would consider worthy of entertaining. . . .

The principle involved here has been called the principle of sufficient reason. Actually, it is a very general principle, and is best expressed by saying that, in the case of any positive truth, there is some sufficient reason for it, something which, in this sense, makes it true—in short, that there is some sort of explanation, known or unknown, for everything. . . .

The principle of sufficient reason can be illustrated in various ways, . . . and if one thinks about it, he is apt to find that he presupposes it in his thinking about reality, but it cannot be proved. It does not appear to be itself a necessary truth, and at the same time it would be most odd to say it is contingent. If one were to try proving it, he would sooner or later have to appeal to considerations that are less plausible than the principle itself. Indeed, it is hard to see how one could even make an argument for it, without already assuming it. For this reason, it might properly be called a presupposition of reason itself. . . . We shall, then, treat it here as a datum—not something that is provably true, but as something that people, whether they ever reflect upon it or not, seem more or less to presuppose. . . .

- In the next passage, how does Taylor apply PSR to the world?
- Why does he claim that if we apply PSR to individual things in the world (such as the ball), we must apply it to the world itself?

The Existence of a World

From the principle of sufficient reason it follows, of course, that there must be a reason, not only for the existence of everything in the world but for the world itself, meaning by "the world" simply everything that ever does exist, except God, in case there is a god. This principle does not imply that there must be some purpose or goal for everything, or for the totality of all things; for explanations need not, and in fact seldom are, teleological or purposeful. All the principle requires is that there be some sort of reason for everything. And it would certainly be odd to maintain that everything in the world owes its existence to something, that nothing in the world is either purely accidental, or such that it just bestows its own being upon itself, and then to deny this of the world itself. . . .

Consider again the strange ball that we imagine has been found in the forest. Now we can hardly doubt that there must be an explanation for the existence of such a thing, though we may have no notion what that explanation is. It is not, moreover, the fact of its having been found in the forest rather than elsewhere that renders an explanation necessary. It matters not in the least where it happens to be, for our question is not how it happens to be *there* but how it happens to exist at all. If we in our imagination annihilate the forest, leaving only this ball in an open field, our conviction that it is a contingent thing and owes its existence to something other than itself is not reduced in the least. If we now imagine the field to be annihilated, and in fact everything else as well to vanish into nothingness, leaving only this ball to constitute the entire physical universe, then we cannot for a moment suppose that its existence has thereby been explained, or the need of any explanation eliminated, or that its existence is suddenly rendered self-explanatory. If we now carry this thought one step further and suppose that no other reality ever has existed or ever will exist, that this ball forever constitutes the entire physical universe, then we must still insist on there being some reason independent of itself why it should exist rather than not. If there must be a reason for the existence of any particular thing, then the necessity of such a reason is not eliminated by the mere supposition that certain other things do *not* exist. And again, it matters not at all what the thing in question is, whether it be large and complex, such as the world we actually find ourselves in, or whether it be something small, simple and insignificant, such as a ball, a bacterium, or the merest grain of sand. We do not avoid the necessity of a reason for the existence of something merely by describing it in this way or that. And it would, in any event, seem plainly absurd to say that if the world were comprised entirely of a single ball about six feet in diameter, or of a single grain of sand, then it would be contingent and there would have to be some explanation other than itself why such a thing exists, but that, since the actual world is vastly more complex than this, there is no need for an explanation of its existence, independent of itself.

Beginningless Existence

It should now be noted that it is no answer to the question, why a thing exists, to state *how long* it has existed. A geologist does not suppose that he has explained why there should be rivers and mountains merely by pointing out that they are old. Similarly, if one were to ask, concerning the ball of which we have spoken, for some sufficient reason for its being, he would not receive any answer upon being told that it had been there since yesterday. Nor would it be any better answer to say that it had existed since before anyone could remember, or even that it had always existed; for the question was not one concerning its age but its existence. If, to be sure, one were to ask where a given thing came from, or how it came into being, then upon learning that it had always existed he would learn that it never really *came* into being at all; but he could still reasonably wonder why it should exist at all. If, accordingly, the world—that is, the totality of all things excepting God, in case there is a god—had really no beginning at all, but has always existed in some form or other, then there is clearly no answer to the question, where it came from and when; it did not, on this supposition, *come* from anything at all, at any time. But still, it can be asked why there is a world, why indeed there is a beginningless world, why there should have perhaps always been something rather than nothing. And, if the principle of sufficient reason is a good principle, there must be an answer to that question, an answer that is by no means supplied by giving the world an age, or even an infinite age.

- In the next passage, what is the analogy Taylor makes concerning the flame and the beams of light?
- Even if the world had *always* existed, why does this fact not eliminate the need for a God?

Creation

This brings out an important point with respect to the concept of creation that is often misunderstood, particularly by those whose thinking has been influenced by Christian ideas. People tend to think that creation—for example, the creation of the world by God—*means* creation *in time,* from which it of course logically follows that if the world had no beginning in time, then it cannot be the creation of God. This, however, is erroneous, for creation means essentially *dependence,* even in Christian theology. If one thing is the creation of another, then it depends for its existence on that other, and this is perfectly consistent with saying that both are eternal, that neither ever came into being, and hence, that neither was ever created at any point of time. Perhaps an analogy will help convey this point. Consider, then, a flame that is casting beams of light. Now there seems to be a clear sense in which the beams of light are dependent for their existence upon the flame, which is their source, while the flame, on the other hand, is not similarly depen-dent for its existence upon them. The beams of light arise from the flame, but the flame does not arise from them. In this sense, they are the creation of the flame; they derive their existence from it. And none of this has any reference to time; the relationship of dependence in such a case would not be altered in the slightest if we supposed that the flame, and with it the beams of light, had always existed, that neither had ever *come* into being.

Now if the world is the creation of God, its relationship to God should be thought of in this fashion; namely, that the world depends for its existence upon God, and could not exist independently of God. If God is eternal, as those who believe in God generally assume, then the world may (though it need not) be eternal too, without that altering in the least its dependence upon God for its existence, and hence without altering its being the creation of God. The supposition of God's eternality, on the other hand, does not by itself imply that the world is eternal too; for there is not the least reason why something of finite duration might not depend for its existence upon something of infinite duration—though the reverse is, of course, impossible.

- How do the previous considerations provide reasons for the existence of God?
- Is it implausible to suppose that the world depends on nothing but itself?

God

If we think of God as "the creator of heaven and earth," and if we consider heaven and earth to include everything that exists except God, then we appear to have, in the foregoing considerations, fairly strong reasons for asserting that God, as so conceived, exists. Now of course most people have much more in mind than this when they think of God, for religions have ascribed to God ever so many attributes that are not at all implied by describing him merely as the creator of the world; but that is not relevant here. Most religious persons do, in any case, think of God as being at least the creator, as that being upon which everything ultimately depends, no matter what else they may say about him in addition. It is, in fact, the first item in the creeds of Christianity that God is the "creator of heaven and earth." And, it seems, there are good metaphysical reasons, as distinguished from the persuasions of faith, for thinking that such a creative being exists.

If, as seems clearly implied by the principle of sufficient reason, there must be a reason for the existence of heaven and earth—i.e., for the world—then that reason must be found either in the world itself, or outside it, in something that is literally supranatural, or outside heaven and earth. Now if we suppose that the world—i.e., the totality of all things except God—contains within itself the reason for its existence, we are supposing that it exists by its very nature, that is, that it is a necessary being. In that case there would, of course, be no reason for saying that it must depend upon God or anything else for its existence; for if it exists by its very nature, then it depends upon nothing but itself, much as the sun depends upon nothing but itself for its heat. This, however, is implausible, for we find nothing about the world or anything in it to suggest that it exists by its own nature, and we do find, on the contrary, ever so many things to suggest that it does not. For in the first place, anything which exists by its very nature must necessarily be eternal and indestructible. It would be a self-contradiction to say of anything that it exists by its own nature, or is a necessarily existing thing, and at the same time to say that it comes into being or passes away, or that it ever could come into being or pass away. Nothing about the world seems at all like this, for concerning anything in the world, we can perfectly easily think of it as being annihilated, or as never having existed in the first place, without there being the slightest hint of any absurdity in such a supposition. . . .

. . . Ultimately, then, it would seem that the world, or the totality of contingent or perishable things, in case it exists at all, must depend upon something that is necessary and imperishable, and which accordingly exists, not in dependence upon something else, but by its own nature.

© 1992. Reproduced in print and electronically by permission of Pearson Education, Inc., Upper Saddle River, New Jersey.

A common criticism of the argument from contingency is that the notion of a necessary being is unclear. Necessity, critics claim, is a property that applies only to propositions. For example, "all bachelors are unmarried" is a necessary proposition in the sense that it is impossible for it to be false. But what would it mean for the *existence* of something to be "necessary"? Anything that we can imagine existing, they say, we can also imagine not existing. It certainly seems logically possible to imagine God as not existing, so what sense can we make of the notion that God's existence is necessary? In a later part of his essay, Taylor responds to this objection by saying that the existence of a square circle is impossible (its nonexistence is necessary). Hence, if there are things whose nonexistence is necessary, why can't there be something whose existence is necessary? If there are things whose existence is dependent, why can't there be something whose existence is nondependent?

STOP AND THINK

Do you think Taylor's response is plausible? Or is the notion of a necessarily existing being an odd concept that has been manufactured simply to make the argument from contingency work? Can we imagine the possibility that God does not exist? If so, then does it make sense to say that his existence is necessary? Which view of necessary existence makes the most sense?

Another criticism of the argument from contingency makes the accusation that it commits the fallacy of composition (discussed in the appendix to this text). Critics claim that the argument reasons in this way:

1. Every contingent being requires a sufficient reason for its existence.
2. Therefore, the collection of contingent beings known as the universe requires a sufficient reason for its existence.

However, the existence of any member of the collection could be explained by some other member of the collection without the whole collection itself requiring an explanation.

Once you have explained the existence of every house on your street by referring to some builder or another who constructed each one, you don't need an additional explanation for the collection of houses. The agnostic Bertrand Russell attempted to show the fallacy in the previous argument by constructing an obviously fallacious argument that uses the same reasoning.

1. Every human being has a mother.
2. Therefore, the entire collection of human beings has a mother.

Of course, as I mentioned previously, when the critics of the cosmological argument maintain that there is not an uncaused first cause of the universe, they must either assume that it is meaningful to conceive of an infinite series of contingent causes going back into an infinite past or that the universe popped into being out of nothing. Although it is difficult to imagine an infinite series of past events, the critics point out that the limits of our imagination may not be the final word. Many of the scientific discoveries of the 20th century would have defied the imagination of previous generations. In making up your own mind as to whether the cosmological argument is plausible, consider the pros and cons that have been discussed.

LOOKING THROUGH THE LENS OF THE COSMOLOGICAL ARGUMENT

1. Why is there something rather than nothing? The answer provided by the cosmological argument is clear. However, think about all the other possible answers. Three possibilities are: (1) The universe is just there and that is all we can say. We can't ask about its cause. (2) The universe came into being out of nothing. (3) Every event had a cause that preceded it in the past, and this series goes back in time forever. Can you think of any other alternatives? How would a defender of the cosmological argument respond to each of these alternative answers?

2. Since the universe appears to be expanding, scientists have now concluded that the existence of the universe is the result of a singular event, called the big bang, that happened 10 to 20 billion years ago. They believe that from an infinitesimal point, a cataclysmic explosion occurred that produced all the energy, matter, space, and time in the universe as we know it. Hence, this well-accepted scientific theory suggests that the universe has not always existed, but that it had its origins in a singular event. In what ways does the big bang theory lend support to the cosmological argument?

EXAMINING THE STRENGTHS AND WEAKNESSES OF THE COSMOLOGICAL ARGUMENT

Positive Evaluation

1. Science is the search for the causes of all the events in our world. But while each particular event can be explained by referring to some particular set of causes that preceded it, what is the cause of this whole series of causes and effects itself? Doesn't the cosmological argument attempt to carry forward and complete the scientific activity of seeking for causes by asking about the ultimate cause of everything?

2. It seems possible to imagine an infinite and unending future by imagining that each event will be followed by yet one more event. But can we conceive of an infinite past? If the universe had no beginning and always existed, then an infinite series of events would have occurred in the past. But that infinite series of events would have taken an infinite

amount of time to complete, and we would never have reached our present point in time. Can't we avoid the paradox of an infinite past by arguing that the past is finite and that there was a point at which it all began? Doesn't this argument suggest that the universe depends on an uncaused cause?

Negative Evaluation

1. Critics have argued that the cosmological argument begins with the claim that the universe could not exist without a cause and then concludes that an uncaused being (God) is the explanation. But as the 19th-century philosopher Arthur Schopenhauer said, the law of universal causation "is not so accommodating as to let itself be used like a hired cab, which we dismiss when we have reached our destination." Is the proponent of the cosmological argument being inconsistent here? Why is the notion of God as an uncaused cause accepted when the notion of an uncaused universe is rejected?

2. Does the cosmological argument commit the *fallacy of composition* (see the appendix)? The argument claims that in addition to each event having an immediate cause, the entire series of cause and effects (the universe) must itself have a cause. But consider this analogous argument: "Each person in this class has a mother, therefore, the entire class itself must have had a mother." Obviously, what is true of each member of the class (each had a mother) is not true of the class as a whole. Similarly, just because every individual event in the universe has a cause, does it follow that the universe as a whole must have had a cause?

3. The cosmological argument for God concludes that there is a first cause that explains why the universe exists. But even if we accept this argument, does it prove the existence of the God of religion, a being who is infinite, intelligent, benevolent, and purposeful? Couldn't the cause of the universe be a finite, random, and impersonal cause? Does the cosmological argument give us any grounds for supposing that the first cause is singular? Couldn't a number of causes have worked together to form the universe? Isn't it too great a leap from the need for the universe to have a cause to the conclusion that this cause is a monotheistic God?

4.2 THE DESIGN ARGUMENT FOR GOD

 LEADING QUESTIONS: *The Argument from Design*

1. Suppose that scientists received an unusual sequence of radio signals that originated somewhere in outer space. Furthermore, suppose that the signals could be interpreted as representing numbers and that the numbers were an ordered sequence of prime numbers (1, 3, 5, 7, 11, 13, 17, . . .). Would these signals be evidence that there is intelligent life in outer space?

2. Suppose you were walking along a beach and came across numerous sticks that had apparently been washed up by the tide. However, suppose that amidst the random clutter of sticks, some of them were arranged in this way: I LOVE PAM. How probable is it that this arrangement came about by chance? How probable is it that the arrangement was the result of intelligent planning?

3. Suppose you are playing poker with a character known as Slick. He gives the deck a thorough shuffle and deals the cards. He wins the first round because he has four aces in

his hand. You know that the odds of drawing four aces from a shuffled deck are 1 in 54,145. You play again and again and again. No matter how many hands are dealt and who the dealer is, Slick always wins by having the four aces. It is logically possible that Slick is very, very lucky and that he was randomly dealt the aces each time. Nevertheless, how likely is it that you would suspect that Slick's winning hands were the result of planning and trickery and not chance?

SURVEYING THE CASE FOR THE DESIGN ARGUMENT

All the leading questions are examples of apparent design. I call it "apparent" design because it is not impossible that the results came about through blind chance. However, in each case, we would find it highly unlikely that sheer randomness is the explanation. The most likely explanation is that the results were the product of intelligent, purposeful design. It is probable that the series of prime numbers were generated by a being who knows mathematics, the message in the sand was written by a lover, and the winning poker hands were the result of Slick's deceptive card manipulation. The issue of chance versus design is the central theme in this section's argument for God.

One of the most popular arguments for God's existence is based on the evidence of design in the world. For obvious reasons, this argument is called "the argument from design," but philosophers usually call it the **teleological argument** for the existence of God. The name comes from the Greek word *telos,* which means "end" or "goal." The argument is called the teleological argument because it points to the fact that many things and processes in the universe seem as though they were designed to fulfill purposeful ends or goals. Like the cosmological argument, the teleological argument is an a posteriori argument, because it reasons from certain observed features of the world. The data that it uses constitute evidence of apparent design in the world. Its main thesis is "evidence of design implies a designer." Any argument for God based on the evidence of design must address two issues. First, how do we distinguish the mere appearance of design from genuine design? Second, can the order in nature be explained by any hypothesis other than that of an intelligent, purposeful cause that is above nature but operates on it?

teleological argument the argument for God's existence based on the evidence of design in the world

---

THOUGHT EXPERIMENT: *Chance versus Design*

Sometimes we find objects in nature that were obviously created by impersonal, natural causes (rock formations, dandelions, moss growing on trees). Other times, we find objects lying about that were obviously created by intelligent, purposeful causes (arrowheads, a coin, initials scratched onto a rock). At times, archeologists and explorers may not be sure whether the objects they found are products of nature or human craftsmanship. For example, archeologists might find a collection of rocks that appear to be placed in the pattern of an arrow, but that pattern could conceivably have appeared by coincidence. Similarly, explorers might dig up a metallic deposit that is normally found in the earth but that appears to be shaped in the form of some symbol. In both cases the question "design or chance?" is the issue.

- In ambiguous cases like these, what sorts of criteria would you use to decide whether something is the result of random, natural causes or purposeful design?

(continued . . .)

WILLIAM PALEY
(1743–1805)

(. . . continued)

- Have you ever made the mistake of thinking that something was humanly designed when it was really the product of chance, natural causes? How did you find out you were mistaken?
- To what degree does the problem of deciding whether something exhibits design or not affect the teleological argument?

WILLIAM PALEY (1743–1805)

One of the most famous and clearest versions of the teleological argument was given by William Paley, a British clergyman and philosopher. The following excerpt is from his book *Natural Theology, or Evidences of the Existence and Attributes of the Deity Collected from the Appearances of Nature* (1802).

FROM WILLIAM PALEY

Natural Theology[7]

In crossing a heath, suppose I pitched my foot against a *stone,* and were asked how the stone came to be there, I might possibly answer that for anything I knew to the contrary it had lain there for ever; nor would it, perhaps, be very easy to shew the absurdity of this answer. But suppose I had found a *watch* upon the ground, and it should be inquired how the watch happened to be in that place. I should hardly think of the answer which I had before given, that for any thing I knew the watch might have always been there. Yet why should not this answer serve for the watch as well as for the stone; why is it not as admissible in the second case as in the first? For this reason, and for no other, namely, that when we come to inspect the watch, we perceive—what we could not discover in the stone—that its several parts are framed and put together for a purpose, e.g., that they are so formed and adjusted as to produce motion, and that motion so regulated as to point out the hour of the day; that, if the different parts had been differently shaped from what they are, or placed after any other manner or in any other order than that in which they are placed, either no motion at all would have been carried on in the machine, or none that would have answered the use that is now served by it. . . . This mechanism being observed . . . the inference we think is inevitable, that the watch must have had a maker—that there must have existed, at some time and at some place or other, an artificer or artificers who formed it for the purpose which we find it actually to answer, who comprehended its construction and designed its use. . . .

. . . For every indication of contrivance, every manifestation of design, which existed in the watch, exists in the works of nature, with the difference on the side of nature of being greater and more, and that in a degree which exceeds all computation.

The teleological argument (or the design argument) has this general form:

1. The universe exhibits apparent design, that is, the ordering of complex means to the fulfillment of intelligible goals, ends, or purposes.
2. We have usually found a purposive, intelligent will to be the cause of such design or order.
3. Therefore, it is reasonable to conclude that the universe was caused by a purposive, intelligent will.

A Philosopher's Lesson (1766) by Joseph Wright. This painting depicts a scientist (called a "natural philosopher" in that day) using a mechanical model of the solar system in a lecture. Although the rise of modern science sometimes provoked tensions with religion, many philosophers and scientists argue that the intricate workings of the universe provide evidence of design. Such design, it is claimed, could be explained only as the product of divine intelligence.

There are several things to notice about the teleological argument. First, it is based on an analogy. It attempts to draw our attention to the alleged similarities between human creations (clocks, statues, computer programs, and so on) and the universe as a whole. Hence, the strength of the argument depends on how confident we are that meaningful similarities exist. The teleological argument's claim that the universe exhibits evidence of design is much less obvious than the cosmological argument's claim that contingent beings exist and depend on prior causes. Second, most versions of the argument take the form of probabilistic arguments or arguments to the best explanation. In other words, they do not show that it is absolutely necessary that the universe had a designer but that a designer is the most probable explanation. Finally, of all the theistic arguments, the teleological argument probably is the least abstract, the easiest to understand, and has the most popular appeal.

THOUGHT EXPERIMENT: *The Watch Analogy*

Make two lists, one describing the ways in which the universe is like a watch and another listing the ways in which it is not like a watch. Which list is longest or most significant?

DAVID HUME

Not everyone has been persuaded by the argument from design. David Hume, the Scottish skeptic, provided a formidable series of objections to this argument. Hume was introduced in the discussion of empiricism (section 2.3), and details of his life may be found there. Hume's critique of the design argument was presented in his *Dialogues Concerning Natural Religion,* published in 1779, three years after his death. Ironically, although these criticisms came out 23 years before William Paley wrote his book and even though Paley criticized Hume on other issues, he never directly responded to Hume's objections to the arguments for God. As the title of his book suggests, Hume's arguments are presented in the course of a conversation between three fictional characters. Cleanthes is a natural theologian who presents some of the standard arguments for God. Demea is an orthodox believer who alternates between faith and rational arguments to justify his beliefs. Finally, Philo the skeptic provides the refutations of the traditional religious arguments.

In the course of the dialogue, Cleanthes presents the following version of the argument from design:

1. In human creations (watches, houses, ships) we find the adaptation of means to ends that are the result of design, thought, wisdom, and intelligence.
2. In nature we find a similar adapting of means to ends, but on a much grander scale.
3. From similar effects we may infer similar causes.
4. So, it must be the case that the magnificent mechanism of the universe is the result of a very great, wise, intelligent designer.

In responding to this argument, Philo employs a twofold strategy. The arguments that compose the first strategy deny that there are relevant similarities between human machines and nature. The second strategy concedes this point but claims that the design argument does not give us anything like the Judeo-Christian God.

Philo's First Strategy

Philo claims that the analogy between human creations (such as machines or houses) and the universe is weak, for there are too many differences between them to know anything about the cause of the universe. Under this strategy (which I call A), Hume has at least three arguments (A1, A2, and A3). The following passage presents strategy A1 through the voice of Philo.

- See if you can formulate Philo's argument in your own words.
- Why can we infer that a house had a creator, but cannot infer that the universe did?

 FROM DAVID HUME

Dialogues Concerning Natural Religion[8]

That a stone will fall, that fire will burn, that the earth has solidity, we have observed a thousand and a thousand times; and when any new instance of this nature is presented, we draw without hesitation the accustomed inference. The exact similarity of the cases gives us a perfect assurance of a similar event; and a stronger evidence is never desired nor sought after. But wherever you depart, in the least, from the similarity of the cases, you diminish proportionably the evidence; and may at last bring it to a very weak *analogy,* which is confessedly liable to error and uncertainty. . . .

If we see a house, CLEANTHES, we conclude, with the greatest certainty, that it had an architect or builder; because this is precisely that species of effect which we have experienced to proceed from that species of cause. But surely you will not affirm, that the universe bears such a resemblance to a house, that we can with the same certainty infer a similar cause, or that the analogy is here entire and perfect. The dissimilitude is so striking, that the utmost you can here pretend to is a guess, a conjecture, a presumption concerning a similar cause; and how that pretension will be received in the world, I leave you to consider.

In the preceding argument (A1), Philo insists that in order to infer the nature of something, it must be similar to other things with which we are familiar. In an example not included in the previous quotation, he says that if we have observed the circulatory system in many humans, we may conclude that it will be the same in other humans that we have not examined. But if you knew only about the circulatory system in frogs or fishes or the movement of fluids within plant life, your ability to conclude anything about humans would become successively weaker in each case. Similarly, in the preceding passage, Philo argues that the differences between a house and the universe are so great, the fact that the first had an intelligent designer does not allow us to infer that the universe did also.

• In the following passage, what is Philo's point concerning the hair and the leaf?

But can you think, CLEANTHES, that your usual phlegm and philosophy have been preserved in so wide a step as you have taken, when you compared to the universe houses, ships, furniture, machines, and, from their similarity in some circumstances, inferred a similarity in their causes? Thought, design, intelligence, such as we discover in men and other animals, is no more than one of the springs and principles of the universe, as well as heat or cold, attraction or repulsion, and a hundred others, which fall under daily observation. It is an active cause, by which some particular parts of nature, we find, produce alterations on other parts. But can a conclusion, with any propriety, be transferred from parts to the whole? Does not the great disproportion bar all comparison and inference? From observing the growth of a hair, can we learn any thing concerning the generation of a man? Would the manner of a leaf's blowing, even though perfectly known, afford us any instruction concerning the vegetation of a tree?

In the preceding argument (A2), Philo asks that because (human) intelligence and design are only a fraction of the many kinds of causality that we observe operating in the world, why do we pick out intelligence as the factor that caused the whole system? He then argues that we cannot reason from the part to the whole. By observing a hair or a leaf, we could not learn how a human or a tree originates. Since we know only about limited portions of the universe, how can we conclude anything about how the whole universe was produced?

STOP AND THINK

On this last point, the theist might reply that scientists today frequently argue from the part to the whole. From a single hair, scientists can infer what species it came from. Furthermore, if it is a human hair, they can determine the owner's gender, race, and what diseases he or she had.

• Can you think of any other ways in which we reason from the part to the whole?
• In the light of these examples, what do you think of Philo's second argument (A2)?

- In the next passage, what does Philo say is a major difference between our knowledge of the causes of ships or cities and our attempts to reason about the origin of the world?

When two *species* of objects have always been observed to be conjoined together, I can *infer*, by custom, the existence of one wherever I *see* the existence of the other: And this I call an argument from experience. But how this argument can have place, where the objects, as in the present case, are single, individual, without parallel, or specific resemblance, may be difficult to explain. And will any man tell me with a serious countenance, that an orderly universe must arise from some thought and art like the human; because we have experience of it? To ascertain this reasoning, it were requisite that we had experience of the origin of worlds; and it is not sufficient, surely, that we have seen ships and cities arise from human art and contrivance.

In the passage you just read (argument A3), Philo claims that we have an insufficient database for causal reasoning about the cosmos. We can infer that x causes y when we have observed many repeated cases of events of type x followed by events of type y. For example, research on the causes of Alzheimer's disease would get nowhere if scientists had only one patient to examine. Similarly, we have only one example of a universe to study. So we have no information about what sorts of causes produce a universe.

PHILO'S SECOND STRATEGY

In Philo's second strategy (B), he concedes the premises of his opponent and assumes that we can reason from like effects to like causes in the case of machines and the universe. But then he turns Cleanthes' own argument against him. Philo argues that the teleological argument leaves us with an all-too-human deity.

- According to Philo, what are several consequences of comparing a machine and its human creator to the universe and its creator?

Now, CLEANTHES, said PHILO, with an air of alacrity and triumph, mark the consequences. *First,* by this method of reasoning, you renounce all claim to infinity in any of the attributes of the Deity. For, as the cause ought only to be proportioned to the effect, and the effect, so far as it falls under our cognisance, is not infinite; what pretensions have we, upon your suppositions, to ascribe that attribute to the Divine Being? You will still insist, that, by removing him so much from all similarity to human creatures, we give in to the most arbitrary hypothesis, and at the same time weaken all proofs of his existence.

Secondly, You have no reason, on your theory, for ascribing perfection to the Deity, even in his finite capacity, or for supposing him free from every error, mistake, or incoherence, in his undertakings. There are many inexplicable difficulties in the works of Nature, which, if we allow a perfect author to be proved *a priori,* are easily solved, and become only seeming difficulties, from the narrow capacity of man, who cannot trace infinite relations. But according to your method of reasoning, these difficulties become all real; and perhaps will be insisted on, as new instances of likeness to human art and contrivance. At least, you must acknowledge, that it is impossible for us to tell, from our limited views, whether this system contains any great faults, or deserves any considerable praise, if compared to other possible, and even real systems. Could a peasant, if the

Aeneid were read to him, pronounce that poem to be absolutely faultless, or even assign to it its proper rank among the productions of human wit, he, who had never seen any other production?

But were this world ever so perfect a production, it must still remain uncertain, whether all the excellences of the work can justly be ascribed to the workman. If we survey a ship, what an exalted idea must we form of the ingenuity of the carpenter who framed so complicated, useful, and beautiful a machine? And what surprise must we feel, when we find him a stupid mechanic, who imitated others, and copied an art, which, through a long succession of ages, after multiplied trials, mistakes, corrections, deliberations, and controversies, had been gradually improving? Many worlds might have been botched and bungled, throughout an eternity, ere this system was struck out; much labour lost, many fruitless trials made; and a slow, but continued improvement carried on during infinite ages in the art of world-making. In such subjects, who can determine, where the truth; nay, who can conjecture where the probability lies, amidst a great number of hypotheses which may be proposed, and a still greater which may be imagined?

Here Philo takes Cleanthes' own point that like effects prove like causes and argues that if the universe is to be compared to the creation of a human machine, then the following conclusions are more probable than that of the biblical God: (1) God is not infinite, for a finite effect (the universe) requires only a finite cause; (2) God is not perfect, for, from our limited perspective, we cannot tell if his creation is as good as possible (in fact, the presence of natural evil and suffering suggest that the world is very defective); (3) God is not perfectly intelligent, for human inventions came about through trial and error.

In the remainder of this part of the discussion, Philo suggests other ways in which the analogy between the creators of machines and the creator of the universe would imply that the cause of the universe has all the limitations we find in human inventors. He says, for example, that we may as well conclude that God did not work alone, for the most complex of human machines are produced by a crew of designers and workers. Furthermore, if the cause of the universe is similar to human creators, then it is mortal, comes in two genders, and is physical. Finally, Hume has Philo suggest that instead of comparing the universe to a machine, we could just as easily think of it as an animal or a vegetable that evolves through blind, organic, natural processes.

It is important to note that in putting forth these counterarguments to the teleological argument, Hume is not claiming that there is no God or that he is finite and stupid or that there is a plurality of gods. Hume is simply saying that the evidence does not give us any more reason for believing in the biblical God than it does for these other alternatives. The most we can conclude from nature, he says, is that "the cause or causes of order in the universe probably bear some remote analogy to human intelligence."[9] However, this conclusion is too ambiguous or obscure to give much comfort to the theist. In the final analysis, Hume is an agnostic or a religious skeptic. He believes that we have no evidence for thinking that God does or does not exist.

The debate over the design argument did not end with Hume's critique. In the past two centuries, and particularly in the past few decades, advances in science have given both the defenders and the critics of the argument new data to incorporate into their philosophical discussions. In section 4.6, we will use the contemporary debate over the design argument as a way of addressing the issue of the relationship between religion and science.

LOOKING THROUGH THE LENS OF THE ARGUMENT FROM DESIGN

1. Although science has sometimes been considered the enemy of religion, the fact remains that many of the great scientists since the beginnings of modern science to our day (e.g., Copernicus, Galileo, Kepler, Newton, Einstein) have also been persons of great religious faith. What connections might there be between the belief in a God of reason and order who created the universe and the belief that studying the world scientifically will be fruitful?

2. According to atheism, we are just complex collections of particles of matter who seek to create our little islands of meaning within an otherwise meaningless universe. According to theism, however, our search for meaning, purpose, and values fits into the grand scheme of things. The argument from design says that both the universe as a whole and the human beings in it are the products of an intelligent, purposeful, and benevolent divine architect. What implications does the argument from design have for how we should treat nature and one another? Does theism provide a better basis for explaining why we think of ourselves and our neighbors as having a special dignity and worth?

EXAMINING THE STRENGTHS AND WEAKNESSES OF THE ARGUMENT FROM DESIGN

Positive Evaluation

1. Theism provides an explanation for the delicate balance of complex variables that maintains the universe and makes the existence of life on our planet possible. On the other hand, the atheist must chalk this balance up to an enormous series of fortunate but random events that had no prevision of the ends they were achieving. But modern science was first developed by theists who believed that the world has a rational order, and science continues to require this belief. For this reason, the scientist and religious mystic Albert Einstein referred to the belief that the world is mathematically ordered as a "miracle creed." Although the argument from design is not absolutely conclusive, could it be argued that theism provides the best explanation for the order in the universe?

2. Many scientists today are searching for signs of intelligent life in outer space. For example, they are analyzing radio signals from space to see if the signals contain anything other than random noise. If, for example, scientists received a packet of signals that represented a significant portion of the prime number series, they would conclude that this signal could not have happened by chance but that it was the product of intelligence. How is this scientific search for intelligence, using design and purposive patterns as criteria, supportive of the approach taken by the argument from design for the existence of a divine intelligence?

Negative Evaluation

1. Progress in science has continually replaced explanations of events in terms of God's purposes with impersonal, natural explanations. For example, disease was once thought to be the result of God's punishment. But we now know that disease is the result of viruses

and other natural causes and that both believers and atheists alike are subject to the same diseases. Similarly, the harmonious functioning among the biological systems of our bodies was once thought to be the result of divine planning. But we now know that only those species whose systems function well will survive. Don't these examples suggest that all the so-called evidence of design in the world will eventually be seen as the result of random, impersonal processes?

2. If we add up all the evidence of design, purpose, and benevolence in the world and compare that with all the evidence of randomness, chance, and evil, don't they balance each other out? Don't we have a tendency to impose patterns of design on the phenomena, much as we do when we "see" meaningful faces or shapes in the clouds? When we roll two dice 100 times, it is likely that combinations adding up to 7 will occur more often than the combinations adding up to 2 or 12. However, this "pattern" is not the result of any design but is based on the law of probabilities. Is all the evidence of design in the world the result of our tendency to impose meaningful patterns on random processes? Do we have any reason to believe that the patterns in nature are purposeful and not the result of probability and chance? Isn't the claim that the world exhibits design really rather doubtful?

4.3 THE ONTOLOGICAL ARGUMENT FOR GOD

LEADING QUESTIONS: *The Ontological Argument*

1. Suppose I told you that in my pocket was a round square. Would you believe me? Why not? How could you know that a round square does not exist even though you have had no experience of the contents of my pocket? Do these questions suggest that reason can give us some information about existence?

2. The most common conception of God in Western thought is that he is a perfect being. It would be absurd to suppose that God had all the properties commonly attributed to him, except that he was absent-minded and forgetful. Forgetfulness is a deficiency that could not be part of the nature of a perfect God. Similarly, could we imagine that there is a God, but that he just happens to be hanging around the universe? Could God's existence be a fluke or something that was dependent on other conditions? Don't these questions suggest that the concept of God is the concept of a being whose existence is necessary and who does not depend on anything else for existence?

SURVEYING THE CASE FOR THE ONTOLOGICAL ARGUMENT

The preceding questions raise the following issues: Can reason alone tell us about what does or does not exist in reality? Is it possible to say that the concept of God is that of a perfect being at the same time we say that such a perfect being lacks existence? Does God necessarily exist? Is it meaningful to attribute necessary existence to anything? These issues are central to an argument for God's existence known as the ontological argument. The adjective *ontological* is derived from the Greek and literally means "having to do with the science of being." Thus, this argument attempts to derive God's existence from the very concept of God's being. Before looking at the argument itself, consider the following thought experiment borrowed from contemporary philosopher William Rowe.[10]

The following table consists of two lists. On the left are things that exist and on the right are things that do not exist.

Things That Exist	*Things That Do Not Exist*
1. The Empire State Building	1. The Fountain of Youth
2. Dogs	2. Unicorns
3. The Planet Mars	3. The Abominable Snowman
4. ?	4. Round Squares

Notice that the first three items on each list have this feature in common: It is logically possible that the world could have been such that they were on the other list. For example, dogs exist, but we can imagine that this world could have been one in which there were no dogs. Real, live unicorns do not exist, but there is no logical absurdity in imagining that they could have been on the left list if the world had turned out differently. These sorts of things, whose existence and nonexistence is possible, are known as *contingent* beings. When we discussed the cosmological argument I pointed out that contingent beings are sometimes identified as dependent beings. They can either exist or not exist; consequently, if they do exist it is because their existence is dependent on causes outside themselves.

The last item on the right list is unique. Round squares do not exist, but unlike the other items on this list, it is logically impossible for them to have been on the left list. It is logically impossible for round squares to exist. Think of some other things that belong on the right list but that are *logically* impossible to put on the left list.

The question is whether there could be an item on the left list that *logically could not* be on the right list. Such an item would be something that necessarily exists; it would be logically impossible for this item not to exist. We can summarize our results in this way. There are things that (1) exist, but whose nonexistence is logically possible (dogs), (2) do not exist, but whose existence is logically possible (unicorns), and (3) do not exist and whose existence is logically impossible (round squares). Now, why shouldn't there be a final category, (4) something that exists and whose *nonexistence* is *logically impossible*? What would be in this category? Some philosophers say that this category is precisely what we mean by God. Before going on, answer these remaining questions: Could there be something in category 4? Is the notion of a necessary being meaningful? Why or why not?

ST. ANSELM
(1033–1109)

ST. ANSELM (1033–1109)

These questions land us right in the heart of the ontological argument. The ontological argument for God's existence was first proposed by a medieval monk, St. Anselm, who went on to become the Archbishop of Canterbury. Anselm was convinced that his faith was so rational that logically compelling arguments could be constructed to demonstrate the rationality of faith to anyone but the most obstinate fool. Of course, Anselm was already a believer when he discovered his famous argument. In fact, the argument is presented in the form of a prayer. Nevertheless, he thought that reason could help him understand more fully what he originally believed on faith. As he put it, "I do not seek to understand that I may believe, but I believe in order to understand."[11]

- In the following passage, what does Anselm mean when he defines God as "a being than which nothing greater can be conceived"?
- What is the distinction Anselm makes between something "existing in the understanding alone" and "existing in reality"?
- Why can the greatest conceivable being not exist in the understanding alone?

FROM ST. ANSELM

Proslogium[12]

And so, Lord, do thou, who dost give understanding to faith, give me, so far as thou knowest it to be profitable, to understand that thou art as we believe; and that thou art that which we believe. And indeed, we believe that thou art a being than which nothing greater can be conceived. Or is there no such nature, since the fool hath said in his heart, there is no God? (Psalms 14:1). But at any rate, this very fool, when he hears of this being of which I speak—a being than which nothing greater can be conceived—understands what he hears, and what he understands is in his understanding; although he does not understand it to exist.

For, it is one thing for an object to be in the understanding, and another to understand that the object exists. When a painter first conceives of what he will afterwards paint, he has it in his understanding, but he does not yet understand it to be, because he has not yet painted it. But after he has made the painting, he both has it in his understanding and he understands that it exists, because he has made it.

Hence, even the fool is convinced that something exists in the understanding, at least, than which nothing greater can be conceived. For, when he hears of this, he understands it. And whatever is understood, exists in the understanding. And assuredly that, than which nothing greater can be conceived, cannot exist in the understanding alone. For, suppose it exists in the understanding alone: then it can be conceived to exist in reality; which is greater.

Therefore, if that, than which nothing greater can be conceived, exists in the understanding alone, the very being, than which nothing greater can be conceived, is one, than which a greater can be conceived. But obviously this is impossible. Hence, there is no doubt that there exists a being, than which nothing greater can be conceived, and it exists both in the understanding and in reality.

Anselm's version of the ontological argument could be formulated as follows:

1. I have, within my understanding, an idea of God.
2. This idea of God is the idea of the greatest possible being.
3. A being is greater if it exists in reality than if it exists only in the understanding.
4. If God exists in the understanding alone, then a greater being can be conceived, namely, one that also exists in reality.
5. But premise 4 is a contradiction, for it says I can conceive of a greater being than the greatest conceivable being.
6. So if I have an idea of the greatest conceivable being, such a being must exist both in my understanding and in reality.
7. Therefore, God exists in reality.

According to Anselm, to deny that God exists, it is necessary to have the idea of God in mind. Hence, God exists in the understanding (even for the atheist). Furthermore, Anselm claims that whatever we mean by "God," we must mean the most perfect, greatest possible being. But if I think of God (the greatest possible being) as existing only in my imagination, I have encountered a contradiction (premise 4). This form of argument, known as a *reductio ad absurdum,* assumes the opposite of what a person is trying to prove and goes on to show that it leads to an absurdity or contradiction. Anselm considers the atheistic possibility that God exists in the understanding alone, but argues that this possibility leads to a contradiction (the greatest conceivable being is not the greatest conceivable being). However, these premises all depend on the controversial premise 3. Does existing in reality make something better? Wouldn't it be better if cancer cells, the national debt, and automobile crashes existed in the imagination alone and not in reality? In what follows we see how premise 3 of Anselm's argument was turned against him by his critics.

Some of Anselm's critics claim that his argument proves too much. For example, Gaunilo, a monk who was a contemporary of Anselm, wrote a sarcastic reply titled "On Behalf of the Fool." Gaunilo was a fellow Christian, so he believed that God existed, but he did not think that Anselm's argument was a good one. To prove his claim, Gaunilo argued that the same form of argument could be used to demonstrate the necessary existence of a perfect island. To see Gaunilo's point, work through the following thought experiment.

THOUGHT EXPERIMENT: *The Perfect Island*

Go over the argument again and whenever it mentions God (or "a being than which nothing greater can be conceived"), plug in one of the following entities instead: a perfect island, the perfect boyfriend (or girlfriend), the perfect baseball player. This argument counters Anselm's reductio ad absurdum with another reductio ad absurdum. Surely there is something wrong, the critic charges, if an argument for God also allows us to prove the existence of a perfect island.

- Do you think Gaunilo's point is a fatal objection to Anselm's argument?
- Is there a significant difference between using the argument to prove God's existence and using it to prove the existence of a perfect island?
- How might Anselm reply to this objection?

Another objection made against the ontological argument states that *existence* is not a property that can be listed among the other properties that define God's perfection, such as wisdom, benevolence, power, and so on. This criticism was put forth by Immanuel Kant (1724–1804) among others. To see the force of this objection, try the two thought experiments in the next box.

THOUGHT EXPERIMENT: *The Property of Existence*

1. Imagine a gold ring circling one of your fingers. Now add to your image of the ring the year of your graduation etched into the metal. Think of the ring as also bearing the name of your school. Now add to this image a large, perfect diamond set into the ring. Now add to your image of the ring the property of existence. Has this last step changed your concept of the ring at all? While I was describing

(continued . . .)

(. . . continued)

the ring, you could add the various properties to your image or concept of the ring. In thinking about the ring, however, you were already thinking of it as though it existed. Hence, existence does not seem to be another property that could enhance the concept of the ring.

2. Suppose that the following two lists represent Julie's and Christin's conception of the "perfect" partner.

Julie's Perfect Partner	Christin's Perfect Partner
1. Intelligent	1. Intelligent
2. Sensitive	2. Sensitive
3. Sense of humor	3. Sense of humor
4. Good cook	4. Good cook
	5. Existence

Notice that the two lists are identical, with one exception. Unlike Julie, Christin has added the property of existence to the list. Are their lists really different? Has Christin really added anything in addition to Julie's concept of the perfect partner? Wouldn't it be true that anyone whose properties matched up with Christin's list would also match up with Julie's list? Does this experiment show that existence really isn't a property that can make the concept of something better?

LOOKING THROUGH THE LENS OF THE ONTOLOGICAL ARGUMENT

1. With respect to most things in the world, the *idea* of something tells us nothing about its existence. For example, to have the idea of a kangaroo does not tell you whether kangaroos exist in the world. But isn't the idea of God absolutely unique? Shouldn't we expect that the idea of God would have logically unique properties? This world just happens to be one in which strange creatures like kangaroos do exist and Santa Claus does not exist. But could this world be one in which God just happens to exist or not exist?

2. Some philosophers (such as David Hume) maintain that logic does not tell us about the world but only about the relations between our ideas. But what would be the point of having logically well-ordered ideas if our ideas told us nothing whatsoever about reality? According to the proponents of the ontological argument, does logic tell us anything about reality?

EXAMINING THE STRENGTHS AND WEAKNESSES OF THE ONTOLOGICAL ARGUMENT

Positive Evaluation

1. With respect to most things we can think about (e.g., giraffes and unicorns), it is possible that they exist and also possible that they do not exist; experience is the only way we have of telling us which is which. But there are some things whose nonexistence is logically necessary (round squares). Logic (and not experience) tells us that they cannot exist. Accordingly, couldn't there be something (God) whose existence is logically necessary

and whose nonexistence is logically impossible? If logic can tell us about reality in the case of round squares, why can't it tell us about the existence of God?

2. If we can imagine that something does not exist, it is because we can imagine conditions that prevented its existence. For example, unicorns do not exist because the biological conditions that would cause them to evolve never occurred. Snowflakes do not exist in the desert, because the high temperatures prevent them from forming. Can you imagine any conditions that would prevent a nondependent being such as God from existing? If the concept of God is the concept of a being who could not be caused to exist or prevented from existing, then isn't the concept of God necessarily that of an existing being? If so, then doesn't God necessarily exist?

Negative Evaluation

1. Isn't atheism a logically possible position? Can't we conceive of a logically possible universe in which there is no God? If so, doesn't our ability to imagine such a universe imply that God's existence is not logically necessary? Doesn't the fact that we can conceive of an atheistic universe undermine the ontological argument?

2. The concept of a unicorn contains the idea of a creature with one horn. Hence, if a unicorn exists, then it follows that a one-horned creature exists. But the "if" in the previous sentence indicates that it is not necessary that a one-horned creature exists. Similarly, couldn't we agree with the ontological argument that the idea of God contains the idea of a necessarily existing being? Hence, *if* God exists, then it follows that a necessarily existing being exists. But, like the "if" in the sentence describing the unicorn and its properties, doesn't the "if" in the previous sentence indicate that we cannot assume that a necessarily existing being is real? In other words, doesn't the ontological argument simply show the properties that are contained within the *idea* of God? But is this argument enough to show that God and his properties do exist?

4.4 PRAGMATIC AND SUBJECTIVE JUSTIFICATIONS OF RELIGIOUS BELIEF

 LEADING QUESTIONS: *The Pragmatic and Subjective Justifications for Belief*

1. Have you ever faced an unavoidable decision when you did not know which choice was the correct one? Lacking knowledge concerning the correct choice, what considerations entered into your making the decision?

2. Can you think of situations in which refusing to make a choice actually commits you to a choice by default? (For example, deciding whether to marry a person you have been dating for a long time, or deciding whether to accept a particular job.)

3. Is it possible to prove everything we believe? If so, how would we prove the premises of every single proof for all our beliefs? Are there other grounds for belief besides logically airtight proofs?

SURVEYING THE CASE FOR PRAGMATIC AND SUBJECTIVE JUSTIFICATIONS

Not all theists believe that it is necessary or even possible to prove the existence of God before a person chooses to believe in him. Theists who take this position could be broadly categorized as *nonevidentialist* theists. Ironically, these religious philosophers agree with Hume and other critics that the philosophical arguments for God fail. Nevertheless, non-evidential theists think that other considerations besides rational proofs could lead an individual on a personal journey to a belief in and relationship with God. I have characterized these considerations as pragmatic and subjective justifications for religious belief. In this section, we examine Blaise Pascal, William James, and Søren Kierkegaard as representatives of this approach. Although these different writers each have their unique approach to the issue of faith, reason, and belief in God, they tend to agree on the following three essential points.[13]

1. *Reason is insufficient to provide rational grounds for belief in God's existence.* These writers all believe that theoretical, philosophical, or rational arguments can neither prove nor disprove the existence of God. God is infinite, but human reason, knowledge, and experience are finite. Thus, it is a mathematical impossibility to start from within the human situation and reason ourselves to God. If we stopped here, the nonevidentialists would be no different from an agnostic such as Hume, and they would have to conclude with him that we must suspend judgment with regard to God. However, it is with the next point that nonevidentialists break with agnosticism.

2. *It is impossible to take a neutral standpoint with respect to God's existence.* We cannot be neutral when it comes to the question of God, say these authors. We will either live our lives as though there is a God, or by default, we will live our lives as though there is not a God. I can suspend judgment on whether there is life in outer space. If the evidence is not compelling one way or another, I can refuse to believe either option, for it will not make any difference to my daily life. However, I don't have the leisure to suspend judgment with respect to the religious option. To borrow an example from William James, it is as though we are lost in a snowstorm on a mountain. We can choose to stay put and hope that a rescue party will find us, but we risk being frozen to death while we wait. Or we can try to make our way down the mountain ourselves, risking the possibility that we will take the wrong path and fall down an icy precipice. The point is that we have to choose. To do nothing is to choose the first option. Either way, however, we must act without knowledge. These three authors claim this situation is what we face with religious belief.

3. *When reason cannot guide us in making an unavoidable decision, it is legitimate to appeal to subjective justifications in deciding what to believe.* Even though we lack knowledge and evidence, these philosophers believe they can offer some personal and practical considerations that will make the religious option the most appealing. However, they do not believe that we should use subjective considerations for every decision (Pascal was a mathematician and scientist, and James was trained as a medical doctor). When objective evidence and reasons are available, we should use them. These philosophers claim, however, that it is legitimate to listen to the heart when we are forced to choose and when the intellect cannot give us guidance in making this choice. For Pascal and James, the subjective grounds for religious belief took the form of practical arguments that would enable faith to go beyond the limits of reason and objective evidence. In Kierkegaard's case, however, his fideism presented the subjectivity of religious belief as a "leap of faith." It was a leap

BLAISE PASCAL
(1623–1662)

that not only transcended reason's limits (Pascal's and James's position) but also allowed the believer to embrace what seemed absurd or irrational from the standpoint of objective reason.[14]

BLAISE PASCAL (1623–1662)

The French thinker Blaise Pascal was a brilliant mathematician, physicist, inventor, and philosopher. As a child growing up in Paris, he demonstrated his remarkable intellectual gifts. He published his first mathematical discovery at the age of 16 and later provided the basis for the modern theory of probability. He later invented a calculating machine that was more powerful than any of that time. For this reason, the computer programming language PASCAL was named after him. Furthermore, his experiments with the barometer made important contributions to 17th-century science. A profound religious experience in 1654, however, changed his life and turned his interests to philosophy and theology.

Although Pascal knew well the power of reason and science, he was also convinced of their limits when it comes to the ultimate issues in human life, such as religion. Concerning these issues, he thought that only personal, subjective considerations could give us any guidance. Accordingly, he once said, "the heart has its reasons which reason does not know." In the following passage, Pascal appeals to the reasons of the heart by means of his famous "wager."

- Find Pascal's statements that illustrate the three themes of the subjective justification of faith discussed in the beginning of this section.
- According to Pascal, what considerations should lead a person to believe in God?

FROM BLAISE PASCAL

Thoughts [15]

"God is, or He is not." But to which side shall we incline? Reason can decide nothing here. There is an infinite chaos which separated us. A game is being played at the extremity of this infinite distance where heads or tails will turn up. What will you wager? According to reason, you can do neither the one thing nor the other; according to reason, you can defend neither of the propositions.

Do not, then, reprove for error those who have made a choice; for you know nothing about it. "No, but I blame them for having made, not this choice, but a choice; for again both he who chooses heads and he who chooses tails are equally at fault, they are both in the wrong. The true course is not to wager at all."

Yes; but you must wager. It is not optional. You are embarked. Which will you choose then? Let us see. Since you must choose, let us see which interests you least. You have two things to lose, the true and the good; and two things to stake, your reason and your will, your knowledge and your happiness; and your nature has two things to shun, error and misery. Your reason is no more shocked in choosing one rather than the other, since you must of necessity choose. This is one point settled. But your happiness? Let us weigh the gain and the loss in wagering that God is. Let us estimate these two chances. If you gain, you gain all; if you lose, you lose nothing. Wager, then, without hesitation that He is. "That is very fine. Yes, I must wager; but I may perhaps wager too much." Let us see. Since there is an equal risk of gain and of loss, if you had only to gain two lives, instead of one, you might still wager. But if there were three lives to gain, you would have to play (since you are under the necessity of playing), and you would be imprudent, when you are forced to play, not to chance your life to gain three at a game where there is an equal risk of loss and gain. But there is an eternity of life and happiness.

- In the final passage, Pascal addresses those readers who want to believe in God but find themselves in the grips of unbelief. What is his advice?

"Yes, but I have my hands tied and my mouth closed; I am forced to wager, and am not free. I am not released, and am so made that I cannot believe. What, then, would you have me do?"

True. But at least learn your inability to believe, since reason brings you to this, and yet you cannot believe. Endeavour, then, to convince yourself, not by increase of proofs of God, but by the abatement of your passions. You would like to attain faith and do not know the way; you would like to cure yourself of unbelief and ask the remedy for it. Learn of those who have been bound like you, and who now stake all their possessions. These are people who know the way which you would follow, and who are cured of an ill of which you would be cured. Follow the way by which they began; by acting as if they believed, taking the holy water, having masses said, etc. Even this will naturally make you believe, and deaden your acuteness. "But this is what I am afraid of." And why? What have you to lose?

With respect to the way reality is, Pascal seems to think that there are only two alternatives: either God does or does not exist. Similarly, with respect to my belief about the subject, I can believe that God either does or does not exist. These various alternatives lead to four possibilities, as indicated in table 4.2. Each alternative results in a certain amount of gain or loss. However, the outcomes are not balanced, for one alternative results in infinite gain and another in infinite loss.

What If I Believe in God? First, if I should choose to believe in God, there will be a cost, for I will have to sacrifice my own autonomy. In other words, I cannot live my life any way I want to but must fulfill those moral obligations that I believe God demands of me. Accordingly, belief in God also means I cannot live life in the fast lane. I must forgo many earthly pleasures that are inappropriate for a believer. If I believe in God but he does not

TABLE 4.2 *Pascal's Belief Alternatives*

		The Way Reality Is	
		God Exists	**God Does Not Exist**
My Belief	**I Believe in God**	Gain (*infinite*): an eternity of life and happiness	Gain (finite): I have lived a good life with a sense of purpose
		Loss (finite): sacrifice of autonomy and temporal pleasures	Loss (finite): sacrifice of autonomy and temporal pleasures
	I Do Not Believe in God	Gain (finite): achieve autonomy and temporal pleasures	Gain (finite): achieve autonomy and temporal pleasures
		Loss (*infinite*): no eternal life or happiness	Loss (finite): no sense of purpose or meaning

exist, my belief and personal sacrifices are in vain. But in the long run, perhaps the loss of temporal pleasures is a relatively minor inconvenience. Furthermore, even if my belief in God is mistaken, I have led a decent life with a sense of purpose. The major point that Pascal makes here is that if I believe in God and he really does exist, I will have gained eternal life and happiness—an infinite gain beyond all price. On the other hand, if God does not exist, my loss is minimal.

What If I Do Not Believe in God? Whether God exists or not, if I am not a believer I will obtain the finite gain of being able to live my life the way I want to (autonomy) and can pursue whatever earthly pleasures I choose without fear of eternal consequences. However, if God does exist and I have failed to believe in him, then I will suffer an infinite loss. I will be deprived of the eternal life and happiness that await me in God's heaven.

What Is the Purpose of Pascal's Wager? It is important to note that though Pascal was a devout believer, he himself did not become religious as a result of this wager. In fact, it was as the result of his personal religious experience one night that made him such a passionate religious writer. However, he is addressing those who (unlike him) are hardened, calloused unbelievers. The somewhat crass approach to religious decision making posed by the wager is an attempt to shake such people out of their complacency and make them consider the significance of the religious option. As the final passage in this reading illustrates, Pascal does not think that we can have faith as a result of a simple act of the will. But after considering the wager, we may be motivated to put ourselves in a position where the dawning of faith will take place.

STOP AND THINK

Have you ever made a decision when you did not know which choice was the correct one, but you decided on the basis of what the consequences of each choice would be if you were either right or wrong? Make a chart similar to table 4.2 that lists the alternatives you faced and the consequences of each outcome. Given the fact that you were acting without knowledge, was this basis a good way to make a decision? How did the decision turn out?

THOUGHT EXPERIMENT: *Pascal's Wager*

The following questions are based on some standard criticisms of Pascal's wager. In each case, consider the strength of the criticism that is implied and think how Pascal might reply to it.

1. Isn't it inappropriate to decide to believe in God using the same strategy we would use at the roulette wheel in a casino? Can we suppose that such a calculating, self-serving concern for the "payoff" of faith can really constitute genuine, religious faith? Aren't we expected to love God for himself and not for what we can get out of the deal? If you were Pascal, how would you reply?

2. Doesn't Pascal assume that you can simply force yourself to believe something? Suppose I told you that I would give you a million dollars if you believe the moon is made out of green cheese (and hooked you up to a lie detector to tell if you

(continued . . .)

(. . . continued)

really believed my statement). Could you will yourself to believe this statement in the face of all the evidence? Can we *choose* our beliefs the way we choose our clothes, or is belief something that *happens* to us? Can we simply will ourselves to believe in God for no other reason than that this belief seems to be the best bet?

3. Pascal assumes that God will punish those people who do not believe in him. But what if someone finds it difficult or even immoral to believe in something without any evidence? Is it possible that God might reward her for being intellectually honest, even if her faithfulness to the truth as she understands it prevents her from having religious belief? How does this possibility affect Pascal's argument?

4. Pascal seems to assume that the only options are to believe in the Christian God or to not believe in the Christian God. But don't we have more options than these? Look through an encyclopedia of religion that lists all the religions from animism to Zoroastrianism to see how many there are. Because Pascal does not think that there are any objective reasons for religious belief, don't we also have to consider all these other religious options? What would Pascal's wager look like if we included all these other religious options?

- Which of these four considerations do you think is the easiest for Pascal to respond to?
- Which one is the most threatening to his pragmatic justification of religious belief?

One of the leading critics of the attempt to base belief on anything other than rigorous evidence was British philosopher W. K. Clifford (1845–1879). Clifford argued that believing has ethical implications. We have no right to believe anything unless we have earned that right through a rational, critical investigation of the belief in question. In a famous essay called "The Ethics of Belief," Clifford illustrates his point by telling the story of a shipowner who sent a ship full of families off to sea. He knew that the ship was old and probably should be inspected. However, he put aside all his doubts and convinced himself that it was seaworthy, trusting in the providence of God to see the passengers safely to their destination. In spite of his sincere convictions, the ship went down in the middle of the ocean, killing all the passengers, while the shipowner collected his insurance money.

Clifford complains that in spite of the fact that the shipowner really did end up believing the ship was sound, he had no evidence for that belief and even some evidence against it. It would have made no difference if the ship, by good fortune, had completed the trip, for the man still had no right to hold a belief without evidence. Thus, when Pascal urges us to choose to believe in God without rational evidence, Clifford would say we are being asked to disregard our ethical duty to find a foundation for our beliefs. He summarizes his position by saying, "It is wrong always, everywhere, and for any one, to believe anything on insufficient evidence."

WILLIAM JAMES

In his classic essay "The Will to Believe" (1896), William James responded to Clifford's ethics of belief (we previously encountered James in the discussion of pragmatism in section 2.6). In this essay James defines an "option" as any choice we face between two contrasting beliefs.

Options may be (1) living or dead, (2) forced or avoidable, and (3) momentous or trivial. Asking you to believe in either the Greek god Zeus or the Norse god Thor would be a dead option if neither choice is a live one for you. On the other hand, facing a choice between being a Christian or an atheist might be a living option for you, depending on your circumstances and inclinations.

Next, if you faced a choice between believing that there is life in outer space or believing there is no life in outer space, you could avoid this option by suspending judgment about the issue and having no opinion. It is an avoidable option. James, however, believes that in morality and religion, we are faced with forced options. What you believe about God will affect your actions and your stance toward life. If you try to avoid thinking about the religious option, you will, by default, end up living your life as though there is no God. On this issue, you are forced to choose.

Finally, your option is either momentous or trivial. James says a trivial option is one in which the opportunity is not unique, the stake is insignificant, or the decision is reversible if it later turns out to be unwise. Following these criteria, which DVD you rent this weekend is a trivial matter. James agrees that when an option is avoidable, then it may be appropriate to follow Clifford's advice and withhold our belief until we get more evidence. When an option is trivial, we do not need to spend much time thinking about it at all. However, James argues that if we seriously consider the question of religious belief (it is a live option for us), then we will find that it is a forced, momentous decision. The problem is, however, that James does not think reason can give us sufficient evidence to make a decision one way or another on this issue. When we face a decision that meets these three criteria (a live, forced, momentous option) and when we cannot have objective, rational certainty, then we have the right to believe what is subjectively and pragmatically appealing.

FROM WILLIAM JAMES
The Will to Believe [16]

The thesis I defend is, briefly stated, this: *Our passional nature not only lawfully may, but must, decide an option between propositions, whenever it is a genuine option that cannot by its nature be decided on intellectual grounds; for to say, under such circumstances, "Do not decide, but leave the question open," is itself a passional decision,—just like deciding yes or no,—and is attended with the same risk of losing the truth.*

James goes on to point out that every knower is faced with two duties: "We must know the truth; and we must avoid error." But these duties are not two versions of the same commandment, for a person can follow one and not the other with different results. If a scientist is willing to risk error in seeking the truth, she may spend years attempting to prove a hypothesis she only hopes and suspects is true. The great scientific discoveries have been made by researchers who have been willing to boldly seek the truth even though they were not absolutely sure that they were on the right track. However, if a scientist's main rule is to avoid error, she will pursue only research that is absolutely certain to bring results and will avoid investing her time in any hypothesis that has the least chance of being wrong. Clifford, James says, thinks that avoiding error is the supreme principle in life and advises us to suspend judgment on matters about which we cannot be certain. But James replies that when our choices are forced and momentous, the risks of error may be inconsequential when the possibility of having really important knowledge with enormous benefits lies before us.

We see, first, that religion offers itself as a *momentous* option. We are supposed to gain, even now, by our belief, and to lose by our nonbelief, a certain vital good. Secondly, religion is a *forced* option, so far as that good goes. We cannot escape the issue by remaining sceptical and waiting for more light, because, although we do avoid error in that way *if religion be untrue,* we lose the good, *if it be true,* just as certainly as if we positively chose to disbelieve. . . . Scepticism, then, is not avoidance of option; it is option of a certain particular kind of risk. *Better risk loss of truth than chance of error,*—that is your faith-vetoer's exact position. He is actively playing his stake as much as the believer is; he is backing the field against the religious hypothesis, just as the believer is backing the religious hypothesis against the field. To preach scepticism to us as a duty until "sufficient evidence" for religion be found, is tantamount therefore to telling us, when in presence of the religious hypothesis, that to yield to our fear of its being error is wiser and better than to yield to our hope that it may be true. It is not intellect against all passions, then; it is only intellect with one passion laying down its law. And by what, forsooth, is the supreme wisdom of this passion warranted? . . .

. . . I, therefore, for one, cannot see my way to accepting the agnostic rules for truth-seeking, or willfully agree to keep my willing nature out of the game. I cannot do so for this plain reason, that *a rule of thinking which would absolutely prevent me from acknowledging certain kinds of truth if those kinds of truth were really there, would be an irrational rule.* That for me is the long and short of the formal logic of the situation, no matter what the kinds of truth might materially be.

STOP AND THINK

Which rule do you think would provide the best guide for life?

- Clifford's rule: Better risk the loss of truth than the chance of error by believing only what we know is true.
- James's rule: Better risk the chance of error than the loss of truth by believing what might maximize our good.

SØREN KIERKEGAARD (1813–1855)

I discussed Søren Kierkegaard in the opening pages of chapter 1, where I presented his idea of philosophy as the search for self-understanding. Although Kierkegaard's thought was permeated by his Christian perspective and his view that faith takes priority over reason, much of what he says can be expanded beyond the topic of religious commitment per se to cover the whole of our human engagement with the world. For this reason, Kierkegaard's existentialist outlook has influenced not only religious philosophers and theologians, but nonreligious writers as well.

Kierkegaard's Life

Born in Copenhagen, Denmark, Søren Kierkegaard was the youngest of seven children. One of the major influences in his life was his father, who was not only a highly successful merchant but also a devout and pious Lutheran. However, the father was tormented throughout his whole life by a morbid sense of guilt for all his moral failures, which included the seduction of the young housemaid soon after his first wife died. Consequently,

SØREN KIERKEGAARD
(1813–1855)

he gave his son a very oppressive religious upbringing in a vain attempt to spare the boy from similar miseries.

When Kierkegaard was 17, he enrolled in the University of Copenhagen and began studying theology to please his father. However, he soon found that he had little interest in theology and began studying philosophy and literature instead. Rebelling against what he considered a crazy religious upbringing, he spent most of his time drinking, partying, and making grand appearances at the theater to enhance his public image as a carefree, cultured, sophisticate. While outwardly he was known as the life of the party, inwardly he was in despair and suicidal. Just before his father's death in 1838, Kierkegaard reconciled with his father. The son realized that his father's harsh religious training was actually a loving attempt to spare him from the melancholy and guilt his father experienced. With this new understanding of his father's love, Kierkegaard returned to Christianity, returned to the study of theology, and became one of Christendom's most passionate writers.

The rest of Kierkegaard's life was singularly devoted to writing literary, philosophical, and theological works. Though they represented a wide variety of styles and specific topics, his writings were all directed to calling individuals to live authentic, passionate, and honest lives, repudiating the temptation to find meaning and identity in institutions or abstractions. In the course of preaching this message, he found himself in a lifelong, vicious battle with both the popular press and his own Danish State Church. He accused the press of undermining individuality and promoting mediocrity and inauthenticity by creating the abstraction of the faceless, anonymous "public." He accused the church of the same thing, saying that it had turned authentic Christianity into a comfortable, taken-for-granted, cultural institution. Nearly broke and in poor health, Kierkegaard died at the age of 42 on November 11, 1855.

Truth and Subjectivity

Is truth objective, or is it personal? Is it possible to have true ideas that make no difference to your life? Which is more difficult: to acquire correct knowledge or to make correct decisions? Here are Kierkegaard's answers:

> What I really lack is to be clear in my mind *what I am to do,* not what I am to know, except in so far as a certain understanding must precede every action. The thing is to understand myself, to see what God really wishes me to do; the thing is to find a truth which is *true for me,* to find *the idea for which I can live and die.*[17]

With these words (written in a journal when he was a university student), Kierkegaard declared his life's mission. These brief words contain two of the major themes in his philosophy: (1) Acting decisively and finding self-understanding, rather than acquiring theoretical knowledge, are the crucial tasks each of us faces in life; and (2) all the objective truth in the world will be useless if I do not subjectively appropriate it, if I do not make it something that is "true for me."

With Pascal and James, Kierkegaard believed that the philosophical arguments for God's existence were logically fallacious because they attempt to compile the *finite* materials of experience and reason to arrive at a God who is *infinite.* In other words, the numbers just don't add up. Theoretical arguments, he claimed, also distract us from our real need. The word *theory* comes from a Greek word whose root is related to the word *theater.* When we are in a theater, we are spectators viewing the action on stage from a distance. Similarly, Kierkegaard complained, many people go through life as detached spectators, theorizing about it but never really becoming engaged with it. To switch metaphors, a fideist such as

Kierkegaard believes that the person who presents rational arguments for God is like someone who comes upon a man dying of thirst and gives him a lecture on the chemical properties of water.

Kierkegaard also agreed with Pascal and James that it was impossible to maintain a neutral stance on the issue of religious belief. But Kierkegaard was much more of a fideist than the other two in that he believed that faith was a powerful source of belief rather than something that would tip a close balance between belief and unbelief. Indeed, he believed that faith not only could go beyond reason, but was often contrary to reason. When faith and reason are in conflict, he claimed, faith must always be given the priority. Hence, basing our beliefs on faith enables us to overcome any obstacles or objections that reason may put in our way.

Kierkegaard is often difficult to read, because he believed that the truth could be communicated only indirectly. Accordingly, he rarely presents his ideas in a straightforward fashion but instead presents them in such a way that they sneak up on you. He continually uses a number of literary devices such as pseudonyms, irony, humor, satire, parables, and thought experiments to make his points. Perhaps the best way to present his ideas on religious belief is to present a number of short selections from his writings on this topic. In the first set of quotations, Kierkegaard expresses his conviction that religious belief cannot be based on objective arguments. If we have rational arguments for a conclusion (the Pythagorean theorem, for example), then we *know* it, but we do not have *faith* in it. But belief in God must be freely chosen, not compelled by logic; it is a matter of subjective commitment, not objective truth. Accordingly, Kierkegaard sometimes refers to religious belief as a "leap of faith" to a higher plane of existence. Notice in the following passages the tension he posits between the approach of faith and that of theoretical reason.

FROM SØREN KIERKEGAARD

Selections

For if the God does not exist it would of course be impossible to prove it; and if he does exist it would be folly to attempt it.

There is no other road to faith; if one wished to escape risk, it is as if one wanted to know with certainty that he can swim before going into the water.

Belief is not a form of knowledge but a free act, an expression of the will. . . . The conclusion of belief is not so much a conclusion as a resolution, and it is for this reason that belief excludes doubt.[18]

An objective uncertainty held fast in an appropriation-process of the most passionate inwardness is the truth, the highest truth attainable for an existing individual. . . .

But the above definition of truth is an equivalent expression for faith. Without risk there is no faith. Faith is precisely the contradiction between the infinite passion of the individual's inwardness and the objective uncertainty. If I am capable of grasping God objectively, I do not believe, but precisely because I cannot do this I must believe. If I wish to preserve myself in faith I must constantly be intent upon holding fast the objective uncertainty, so as to remain out upon the deep, over seventy thousand fathoms of water, still preserving my faith.

Anything that is almost probable, or probable, or extremely and emphatically probable, is something he can almost know, or as good as know, or extremely and emphatically almost *know*—but it is impossible to believe.[19]

In the next passage, Kierkegaard continues the theme that Christianity is not something that can be approached objectively through the speculative, detached reason of the philosopher. Instead it must be embraced subjectively, for only if we have passion will we know the truth. At the end of the first paragraph he suggests that the truth can be found only if you are "in a specific condition." This condition is one of raw honesty and genuine spiritual thirst. The person who is complacent and self-satisfied will be closed to the truth and unable to find it. Kierkegaard liked to point out that you can sometimes achieve a result (for example, the solution to a puzzle) without having to struggle for it yourself (you look up the answer in the back of the book). For some goals in life, however, you can achieve the result (physical fitness, for example) only if you go through a certain process yourself (exercise). Kierkegaard believed that self-understanding (or, as he puts it, "becoming a self") is a result that *cannot* be obtained without going through a very difficult process of subjective inwardness ourselves. In the final paragraph of this section he expresses his belief that we can gain a true sense of our authentic self only when we stand before an infinite God who knows us as we are.

> The speculative philosopher . . . proposes to contemplate Christianity from the philosophical standpoint. . . . The philosopher contemplates Christianity for the sake of interpenetrating it with his speculative thought; aye, with his genuinely speculative thought. But suppose this whole proceeding were a chimera, a sheer impossibility; suppose that Christianity is subjectivity, an inner transformation, an actualization of inwardness, and that only two kinds of people can know anything about it: those who with an infinite passionate interest in an eternal happiness base this their happiness upon their believing relationship to Christianity, and those who with an opposite passion, but in passion, reject it—the happy and the unhappy lovers. Suppose that an objective indifference can therefore learn nothing at all. Only the like is understood by the like, and the old principle: [Whatever is known is known in the mode of the knower], must be so expanded as to make room for a mode of knowing in which the knower fails to know anything at all, or has all his knowledge reduced to an illusion. In the case of a kind of observation where it is requisite that the observer should be in a specific condition, it naturally follows that if he is not in this condition, he will observe nothing.[20]
>
> But this self acquires a new quality or qualification in the fact that it is the self directly in the sight of God. . . . And what an infinite reality this self acquires by being before God![21]

Kierkegaard stressed that there is a difference between knowing the truth as something out there external to me and living the truth as something that affects every aspect of my life. For example, a person could intellectually embrace a very elevated moral theory but be a scoundrel in actual practice. Such a person would objectively know the truth but would not be subjectively living in that truth. In contrast, a person could live a morally exemplary life but be incapable of articulating those moral principles in a propositional form. These points are brought out in the next selection from Kierkegaard's writings.

• In the following reading, note the kinds of contrasts Kierkegaard makes between objectivity and subjectivity.

When the question of truth is raised in an objective manner, reflection is directed objectively to the truth, as an object to which the knower is related. Reflection is not focussed upon the relationship, however, but upon the question of whether it is the truth to which the knower is related. If only the object to which he is related is the truth, the subject is accounted to be in the truth. When the question of the truth is raised subjectively, reflection is directed subjectively to the nature of the individual's relationship; if only the mode of this relationship is in the truth, the individual is in the truth even if he should happen to be thus related to what is not true. Let us take as an example the knowledge of God. Objectively, reflection is directed to the problem of whether the object is the true God; subjectively, reflection is directed to the question whether the individual is related to a something in *such a manner* that his relationship is in truth a God-relationship. On which side is the truth now to be found?[22]

Kierkegaard presents the previous points in a concrete way in one of his most famous parables. He depicts someone who has theologically correct ideas, but no passion. He contrasts this person with a man who has theologically incorrect ideas but is passionate about his relationship to God.

- In the following parable, who does Kierkegaard favor? Why?

If one who lives in the midst of Christendom goes up to the house of God, the house of the true God, with the true conception of God in his knowledge, and prays, but prays in a false spirit; and one who lives in an idolatrous community prays with the entire passion of the infinite, although his eyes rest upon the image of an idol: where is there most truth? The one prays in truth to God though he worships an idol; the other prays falsely to the true God, and hence worships in fact an idol.[23]

In a controversial and extreme statement of his fideism, Kierkegaard expresses the tension between reason and faith by saying that Christianity is *absurd* when viewed through the eyes of our rational understanding. Because reason has its limits, it cannot make sense of Christianity with its inadequate categories, so it must be transcended in a leap of faith. Does Kierkegaard really believe that Christianity is absurd? Perhaps not, for in the final quotation he suggests that from within the standpoint of faith, we gain a new sort of understanding that puts things into perspective.

For the absurd is the object of faith and the only object that can be believed. . . . Christianity has declared itself to be the eternal essential truth which has come into being in time. It has proclaimed itself as the *Paradox,* and it has required of the individual the inwardness of faith in relation to that which stamps itself as . . . an absurdity to the understanding.[24]

When the believer has faith, the absurd is not the absurd—faith transforms it.[25]

THOUGHT EXPERIMENT: *Objectivity and Subjectivity*

1. In other areas of life, we seem to place a high value on reason and objective evidence. For example, the scientific theory that has the best arguments and the most evidence is accepted over one that has little rational support. The politician who has the best arguments for her economic proposals is favored over the opponent who has no reasons for his position. Should things be any different with religious belief? Why?

2. Why would a God give us reason if, as Kierkegaard claims, it plays little to no role in forming our religious beliefs?

3. Kierkegaard believed that Christianity was a paradox and seemed absurd to our understanding. For example, he believed that God and Jesus were one and yet

(continued . . .)

(. . . continued)

that Jesus died and God the father did not. But how are we to distinguish a religious teaching like this that goes beyond our understanding from the sort of rational contradiction that even Kierkegaard would reject, such as "God is good and God is not good?" Once we go beyond or abandon reason, haven't we given up our ability to distinguish truth from nonsense?

LOOKING THROUGH THE LENS OF THE PRAGMATIC AND SUBJECTIVE JUSTIFICATIONS OF RELIGIOUS BELIEF

1. Isn't it possible for the decision to marry someone to be a reasonable decision? But isn't the decision to marry the love of your life a decision that is based on personal, subjective considerations and not universal, impersonal, logical arguments? Aren't many of the decisions that you make in life justified decisions at the same time that they are personal and subjective decisions? How does your conclusion about these questions apply to Pascal's and James's justifications of religious belief?

2. If the evidentialist is correct, then wouldn't it be true that the only persons who have a right to be religious believers are those who are capable of providing philosophical proofs for the existence of God? Isn't there something strange about limiting religious belief only to intellectuals? If there was a personal God, isn't it reasonable to suppose that the way to discover him would be through a personal, individual journey and not through an impersonal, rational argument? What would Kierkegaard say?

EXAMINING THE STRENGTHS AND WEAKNESSES OF THE PRAGMATIC AND SUBJECTIVE JUSTIFICATIONS OF RELIGIOUS BELIEF

Positive Evaluation

1. Can every decision in life be based on rational arguments? What about the decision to be rational? Can that decision be based on rational arguments without assuming what we are trying to prove? Can the decision to believe in the scientific method be justified by the scientific method without arguing in a circle? In both of these cases, aren't we making a subjective decision about what sorts of persons we will be and how we will live our lives? According to Pascal, James, and Kierkegaard, isn't the same process involved in deciding to be religious believers?

2. What if we conclude that the philosophical arguments for and against the existence of God are equally persuasive and cancel each other out? What do we do when reason leaves us indecisive? Don't Pascal, James, and Kierkegaard have a point when they say that the neutral standpoint is impossible? Don't we have to decide to live on the basis of belief in God or else live as practical atheists? If so, aren't we justified in choosing the religious option if that option seems to make the most sense out of life?

Interview 10 people who do not mind being asked questions about their personal religious beliefs. Try to find as broad a range of beliefs as possible; that is, don't ask 10 people who are likely to give the same answers, such as people who all attend the same church. Ask each person the following questions.

1. Do you believe in God?
2. What are your reasons?
3. What is your conception of the God you do or do not believe in?
4. What sort of data or experience (if any) might cause you to change your belief? Why?

After you have completed the survey and recorded the answers, go back over the answers and see how they can be catalogued according to some of the positions and arguments we have discussed. Did anyone give a reason for their belief in God that is similar to either the cosmological, teleological, or ontological arguments? Did anyone's answer seem similar to the pragmatic and subjective reasons for belief that were discussed? In their answers to questions 2 or 4, did anyone mention the problem of evil or undeserved suffering? What reasons were given (if any) for not believing in God? Were there any significant differences in the 10 answers to question 3? Evaluate the reasons that were provided for the answers. Which reasons do you think were the best ones? Which reasons were the weakest?

PHILOSOPHY
in the
MARKETPLACE

Negative Evaluation

1. Take the subjective justifications for religious belief but imagine that the same justifications are being used by the following true believers:

- Someone who asks you to have faith in the Nazi ideology.
- Someone who asks you to have faith in communism.
- A follower of a religious cult whose faith teaches that if you sell all your possessions and join their community, space aliens will take you on a ship to a world beyond the stars where you will live for all eternity in perfect bliss.

If Pascal's, James's, or Kierkegaard's subjective justifications are a sufficient basis for believing in religion, why shouldn't they provide legitimacy to these faiths as well?

2. Do Pascal, James, and Kierkegaard face a dilemma? Either they are claiming that theism is true based on the fact that it is the most rationally justified belief, or they are not. If they are not attempting to argue for the truth of theism, then they are simply offering us their own autobiographical journeys. If the latter is the case, then they are simply saying to us: "As for my own life, I have decided to be religious." But why should their choices make any claims on us? This problem particularly applies to Pascal and Kierkegaard because they were Christians (James's religious beliefs were more nonspecific). As such, they presumably believed that Christianity was true. But because not all beliefs are true, they must have some way of deciding that Christianity is true and other options are not. However, once they begin justifying the truth of their religious beliefs, they will be appealing to reason and abandoning their nonevidentialism. So, could it be argued that the claims of Pascal, James, and Kierkegaard in favor of religious belief are arbitrary and merely autobiographical? If not, then don't they have to attempt to provide a rational justification of their religious truth claims?

STOP AND THINK

Go back over the reasons for believing in God that have been presented in this and previous sections (the cosmological, teleological, and ontological arguments, and the pragmatic-subjective reasons). Which seems to be the strongest? What do you think is the major weakness (if any) of each argument?

4.5 THE PROBLEM OF EVIL: ATHEISTIC AND THEISTIC RESPONSES

LEADING QUESTIONS: *The Problem of Evil*

1. If you were a parent, wouldn't you do everything in your power to prevent your child from needless suffering? Since so many innocent children in the world suffer from painful diseases, how can there be a loving, powerful God?

2. If you had to make a choice between a world in which there is human freedom but also suffering innocent children and a world in which there is no human freedom but also no children who are suffering, which one would you choose? Why?

3. Was there ever a time when you experienced suffering (emotional or physical) that seemed meaningless, but you found out later that the suffering ultimately served some good purpose?

SURVEYING THE CASE FOR ATHEISM: *The Argument from Evil*

problem of evil the difficulty of reconciling the existence of suffering and other evils in the world with the existence of God

moral evil bad actions and their unfortunate results for which humans (or other moral agents) are morally responsible

natural evil the suffering to humans and animals resulting from natural causes such as genetic defects, diseases, earthquakes, and tornadoes

Most atheists or agnostics base their case on the lack of evidence for God's existence. However, atheists have at least one very powerful positive argument for their position: that there cannot be a loving, all-knowing, all-powerful God, because there is so much evil and suffering in the world. The difficulty of reconciling the existence of suffering and other evils in the world with the existence of God is called the **problem of evil.** Traditionally, philosophers have distinguished between two kinds of evil. **Moral evil** consists of the bad actions and their unfortunate results for which humans (or other moral agents) are morally responsible. Lying, theft, murder, and rape, for example, are moral evils committed by people who cause the evil results of distrust, loss of property, and physical or emotional harm. **Natural evil** consists of the suffering to humans and animals that results from natural causes such as genetic defects, diseases, earthquakes, and tornadoes. To avoid the atheist's charge of incoherence, the theist has the burden of explaining why God would allow either moral or natural evils to occur.

The problem of evil was given literary expression by the 20th-century French novelist Albert Camus. In his novel *The Plague,* Camus tells the story of the town of Oran, which slowly becomes ravaged by an epidemic of the bubonic plague. Quarantined from the outside world, the people of Oran find themselves trapped in a prison of death and agony as they and their loved ones die slow, painful deaths. Among other themes presented in the novel, the town becomes a symbol of the human situation, and the various responses of its citizens represent different attitudes toward life. The religious response is represented by the town's priest, Father Paneloux. The atheist or agnostic response is represented by Dr.

Bernard Rieux, a physician who works tirelessly to alleviate the victims' suffering. The reading selection begins with the narrator's account of the death throes of a small child who has been infected by the plague.

FROM ALBERT CAMUS

The Plague [26]

And just then the boy had a sudden spasm, as if something had bitten him in the stomach, and uttered a long, shrill wail. For moments that seemed endless he stayed in a queer, contorted position, his body racked by convulsive tremors; it was as if his frail frame were bending before the fierce breath of the plague, breaking under the reiterated gusts of fever. . . . When for the third time the fiery wave broke on him, lifting him a little, the child curled himself up and shrank away to the edge of the bed, as if in terror of the flames advancing on him, licking his limbs. . . . From between the inflamed eyelids big tears welled up and trickled down the sunken leaden-hued cheeks. When the spasm had passed, utterly exhausted, tensing his thin legs and arms, on which, within forty-eight hours, the flesh had wasted to the bone, the child lay flat, racked on the tumbled bed, in a grotesque parody of crucifixion. . . .

Paneloux gazed down at the small mouth, fouled with the sores of the plague and pouring out the angry death-cry that has sounded through the ages of mankind. He sank on his knees, and all present found it natural to hear him say in a voice hoarse but clearly audible across the nameless, never ending wail:

"My God, spare this child!"

But in spite of the priest's prayer, the child's wailing continues without ceasing. After a while, however, the poor boy's tragic suffering comes to an end. Dr. Rieux is with him as he dies.

And now the doctor grew aware that the child's wail, after weakening more and more, had fluttered out into silence. . . . For it was over. . . . His mouth still gaping, but silent now, the child was lying among the tumbled blankets, a small, shrunken form, with the tears still wet on his cheeks.

When the plague first broke out, Father Paneloux gave a confident, moralistic sermon in which he claimed that the sickness was God's judgment on the townspeople for their sins. After viewing the suffering of this innocent child, however, his attitude changes. No longer confident, he preaches a sermon in which he says we cannot understand the reason for this suffering but still must cling to our faith in God. The following passage contains his closing remarks.

"We should go forward, groping our way through the darkness, stumbling perhaps at times, and try to do what good lay in our power. As for the rest, we must hold fast, trusting in the divine goodness, even as to the deaths of little children, and not seeking personal respite. . . .

"My brothers"—the preacher's tone showed he was nearing the conclusion of his sermon—"the love of God is a hard love. It demands total self-surrender, disdain of our human personality. And yet it alone can reconcile us to suffering and the deaths of children, it alone can justify them, since we cannot understand them, and we can only make God's will ours."

A different response toward the suffering in the world is represented by Dr. Rieux. Throughout the novel, this physician risks his life nursing the victims of the plague.

Darwin and the Problem of Evil

Charles Darwin, the famous evolutionist, started out as a theist but gradually abandoned his religious beliefs and became an agnostic. Apparently, the problem of evil that Darwin encountered in his studies of nature moved him to abandon religion. The beginning of his doubts was evidenced in a letter to a friend in which he wrote: "I cannot see as plainly as others do, and as I should wish to do, evidence of design and beneficence on all sides of us. There seems to me too much misery in the world. I cannot persuade myself that a beneficent and omnipotent God would have designedly created the Ichneumonidae with the express intention of their feeding within the living bodies of Caterpillars, or that a cat should play with mice."[27]

However, unlike Paneloux, Dr. Rieux thinks that there is no way to reconcile the agony of innocent people with the existence of a good God. When a friend asks the doctor why he gives of himself so selflessly when he doesn't believe in God, the physician replies as follows:

> His face still in shadow, Rieux said that he's already answered: that if he believed in an all-powerful God he would cease curing the sick and leave that to Him. But no one in the world believed in a God of that sort; no, not even Paneloux, who believed that he believed in such a God. And this was proved by the fact that no one ever threw himself on Providence completely. Anyhow, in this respect Rieux believed himself to be on the right road—in fighting against creation as he found it.

After the boy dies, Paneloux tries to comfort the doctor, but Rieux shouts at him for trying to justify the suffering of innocent children such as this one. However, Rieux then apologizes, saying, "I'm sorry. But weariness is a kind of madness. And there are times when the only feeling I have is one of mad revolt." Paneloux goes on to explain how he copes with the suffering.

> "I understand," Paneloux said in a low voice. "That sort of thing is revolting because it passes our human understanding. But perhaps we should love what we cannot understand."
>
> Rieux straightened up slowly. He gazed at Paneloux, summoning to his gaze all the strength and fervor he could muster against his weariness. Then he shook his head.
>
> "No, Father. I've a very different idea of love. And until my dying day I shall refuse to love a scheme of things in which children are put to torture."

STOP AND THINK

How would you respond to the child's death? Would you agree with Father Paneloux or with Dr. Rieux? Or is there a third approach you would take?

A Formulation of the Argument from Evil

Why do innocent people such as the boy in Camus's story suffer from apparently meaningless pain? Why didn't God spare the child from a torturous death as the priest prayed for him to do? Why are there so many evils in nature, as Darwin suggests? Camus's story and

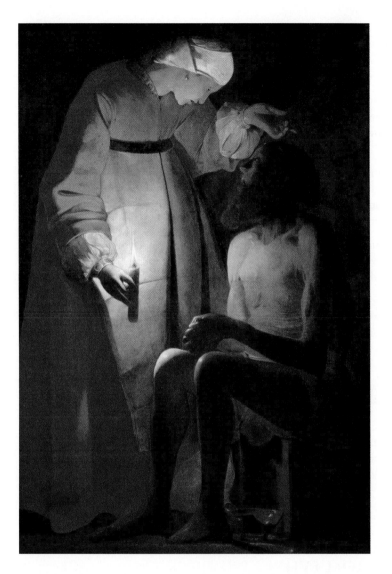

Job and His Wife (early 1630s) by George de La Tour. The moving but disturbing Biblical story of Job has served throughout the ages as a dramatic symbol of the problem of evil. In the story, God allowed Job to be stripped of his possessions as well as his family and to become afflicted with excruciating boils. Although his three friends theorize that Job's suffering must have been the result of his secret sins, Job had always been a faithful servant of God. In the end, Job simply comes to accept the sovereignty, providence, and goodness of God in the face of circumstances that Job is incapable of understanding. Still, the nagging question remains, "If there is (allegedly) a loving, all-powerful God that governs the world, why do bad things happen to good people?" This is the question that the atheist asks and that the theist has to answer.

Darwin's observations illustrate the mystery, the paradox, and the problem of evil. The problem of evil can be formulated in terms of four propositions, all of which are propositions that the traditional theist wants to affirm. However, it seems difficult to reconcile the following four statements:

1. God is perfectly good.
2. God is all-knowing (omniscient).
3. God is all-powerful (omnipotent).
4. Evil exists.

By themselves, these four propositions do not constitute a contradiction the way that the statements "Bob is a bachelor" and "Bob is a husband" contradict one another. Hence, to establish the conclusion that God does not exist, the atheist must add one more premise to complete the argument.

5. If God exists and is a being who is good, all-knowing, and all-powerful, then there would be no evil in the world.
6. Therefore, God does not exist.

This argument is valid and, hence, if you accept the premises, you must accept the conclusion. However, if you think the conclusion is false, then you must reject at least one of the five premises. Let's consider the premises of the argument to see what options are available to the theist.

STOP AND THINK

If you were a theist (it doesn't matter if you really are or not), which of the five premises would you reject in order to reject the conclusion that "God does not exist"? Why do you think that premise is the best one to reject? What are the implications of rejecting that premise? What else would you have to prove in order to show that this premise is false?

RELIGIOUS RESPONSES TO THE ARGUMENT FROM EVIL

General Theistic Strategies

Most theists would not want to reject premises 1, 2, or 3. Those premises all seem central to traditional, religious conceptions of God. If God was deficient in either goodness, knowledge, or power, it is claimed, he would be not a God but a "godling," a wimpy being unworthy of worship. However, if you reject any one of these premises, the problem is solved. For example, the ancient Greeks were polytheists, and many of their gods were not good ones but were vicious, vindictive, petty beings. Hence, because the Greeks rejected premise 1 (God's goodness), they did not have any problem understanding evil. The bad things that happen in our world result from blind fate or the actions of one or more mean-spirited gods, according to the typical Greek view.

Some philosophers reject or weaken premise 2 (God is all-knowing) by arguing that God's knowledge is limited.[28] It is limited, they say, because he cannot know the future in perfect detail, since the future has not yet happened and is, in part, the product of the choices of free agents such as ourselves. But this philosophy, by itself, does not solve the problem, for even if God could not anticipate every evil that would occur, it would seem that he could intervene and eliminate the evils once they make their presence known. For example, once the Nazis made clear their plans for world domination, why didn't God cause massive mechanical failures in their tanks and gas ovens, thus preventing the Holocaust?

Another nontraditional view rejects premise 3 (God is all-powerful). John Stuart Mill, William James, personal idealists such as Edgar S. Brightman, and process philosophers such as Alfred North Whitehead, Charles Hartshorne, John Cobb, and David Ray Griffin have explored this alternative. Similarly, the best-selling book *When Bad Things Happen to Good People* by Rabbi Harold Kushner argues that God has not yet completed creation and is continually working with us to make the world better.[29] If nature and human agents have any degree of autonomy and power at all, then God is limited in what he could do to eliminate evil.

In discussing God's power, it is important to note that even traditional Christian thinkers throughout the centuries have seldom maintained that the statement "God is all-powerful" is equivalent to "God can do anything." Certainly, the whole problem of evil is based on the notion that God cannot bring about totally unjustified, irredeemable evil, for this action would be contrary to his nature. Hence, God cannot do anything, for he cannot act contrary to his nature. However, this one qualification is hardly a limit on God's power. Furthermore, most traditional philosophers and theologians have said that God cannot do what is logically impossible. He cannot do the following sorts of things: create a round square, make one plus one equal three, make a stone heavier than he can lift, or cause himself not to exist. Since all these notions are nonsense, God's inability to bring them about is not a limit on his rational powers. If God could do what is *logically impossible,* then he could be both good and evil at the same time, and it would be impossible to think about God at all. The claim that God cannot do what is logically impossible is an important one because it plays a major role in some theistic responses to the problem of evil.

What about premise 4, the claim that "evil exists"? Some Asian religions claim that evil is an illusion. That conclusion would solve the problem, but many people believe that the real-life suffering of innocent children that Camus depicted in his novel just seems too real to consider it an illusion. Although he did not say that evil is an illusion, the early Christian writer St. Augustine (354–430) nevertheless claimed that evil lacks independent, substantial reality. Everything that God creates is good, he said, but what is good can become corrupted. Thus evil is something negative, for it is the absence of good. Hence, just as a shadow is not an independent reality in itself but is the absence of light, so what we perceive as evil are the ways in which the world falls short of God's goodness. Even if we view evil in this way, however, we can still ask why God allows these absences of his goodness to occur. For most theists, denying the reality of evil does not seem to be a good strategy for coping with the problem. Disease, the devastation of tornadoes and earthquakes, and other features of this world that produce pain and suffering seem to be gratuitous, brute evils that need some sort of explanation if theism is to be plausible.

Premise 5, the claim that a good and powerful God would prevent or eliminate evil, seems to be the point at which the traditional theist might want to launch his or her response. Perhaps God allows certain evils because in some way or other, these evils are necessary or are morally justified. Indeed, most theists who propose solutions to the problem of evil recognize that evils such as pain exist (they accept premise 4) but try to suggest ways in which these evils are justified or unavoidable, even for a good and powerful God (they reject premise 5). The attempt to do so is known as a **theodicy,** or a justification of God's permitting evil to occur in the world. Hence, many theodicists modify premise 5 to state, "If God exists and is a being who is good, all-knowing, and all-powerful, then there

theodicy the attempt to justify God's permitting evil to occur in the world

would be no *unjustified* evil in the world." They then go on to defend the claim that "there are no unjustified evils in the world." In this way theodicists attempt to show that the existence of evil or suffering does not count against the existence of God. The two most common responses of theists to the problem of evil are known as the "greater goods defense" and the "free will defense." I discuss each strategy in turn. But first, work through the following thought experiment.

THOUGHT EXPERIMENT: *Reasons for Evil*

To anticipate what is to come, consider the following situations:

1. Think of a time when you knowingly did something or entered into a situation that caused you (or someone you loved) to suffer. The suffering could be physical pain or emotional pain or some other kind of unpleasant experience. Your own or the other person's suffering was not something you desired in itself. Nevertheless, you allowed this suffering to happen because you knew that in the end, something good would come from it. In what way do you think that making this suffering or allowing it to occur was justified and unpreventable?

2. Suppose you are a parent who has a great deal of control over your children. Using the threat of punishment, you might be able to force them to behave in moral and responsible ways. For example, you could force them to clean their rooms, do their homework, and abstain from using profanity in their speech. But could you force them to *want* to do these things as a matter of their own free choice? Could you not only force them to *do* what is good but also force them to *desire* to do what is morally good, even when you are not around and no reward or punishment is involved? If you could not force them to desire what is good, how might you, nevertheless, influence them in this direction?

- How might these two thought experiments be relevant to the problem of evil?

The Greater Goods Defense

greater goods defense the claim that God allows some evil to exist because it is necessary to the achievement of a greater good

The claim that God allows some evil to exist because it is necessary to the achievement of a greater good is known as the **greater goods defense.** This argument assumes that (1) some evils are necessary to achieving certain good ends, (2) the good that is achieved outweighs the evil, and (3) the same or a greater amount of good could not have been attained by any means that did not involve the presence of these evils. A simple example illustrates this point. When my wife and I first took our new baby to the doctor for a checkup, the pediatrician gave our child a shot that immunized him against all sorts of dread childhood diseases. Our baby, of course, did not understand what was going on. He screamed in pain and looked up at his mother with eyes that said, "I trusted you and put my faith in you. But you betrayed that trust by carrying me into this torture chamber where an evil man stuck needles into my bottom!" Why did we allow our son to suffer this pain? We did not delight in his pain and it distressed us to hear his cries, but we knew the pain was the only way to achieve the greater good of health. Hence, the evil of the pain was justified according to the threefold criteria listed previously.

SPOTLIGHT

on

An Ancient Chinese Parable—What Is the Meaning of It All?

There was an old man whose only wealth was the one horse he owned. One day his horse escaped and took off into the mountains. His friends and neighbors came to comfort him saying, "Old man, what bad luck you have had." The man replied, "Bad luck? Good luck? Who can say?" A week later, the horse returned and brought with him a whole herd of wild, mountain horses. The man's wealth was suddenly increased beyond measure. His friends and neighbors came to rejoice with him saying, "Old man, what good luck you have had." The man replied, "Good luck? Bad luck? Who can say?" The next day, when the man's son was trying to break in the wild horses, one of the horses threw him, causing him to break his leg. His friends and neighbors came to bring comfort saying, "Old man, what bad luck you have had." The man replied, "Bad luck? Good luck? Who can say?" The next day, the army came to town to forcibly draft all the young men to go fight in a bloody war from which few of them would return. However, the army did not take the old man's son; he was allowed to stay home because he was crippled. The man's friends and neighbors came to rejoice with him saying, "Old man, what good luck you have had." The man replied, "Good luck? Bad luck? Who can say?"

- Just for fun, can you make up some more lines to the story?
- Can we ever know what the ultimate outcome of the events in our lives will be?
- How might this story relate to the problem of evil?
- Which one of the following two meanings do you derive from this story? Why?

1. The suffering we experience always has a purpose, even if we cannot know what it is at the time.
2. Life is ambiguous and purposeless. Good things happen and bad things happen because of chance events, but there is no meaning to those occurrences. We can never count on how things will turn out.

In this example, the trade-off between the pain and the good it achieved was very clear to the parents but not to the child. Similarly, if there is a God, it is conceivable that we are often like the baby who does not see the big picture and, therefore, does not understand that his pain is a necessary means to avoid an even greater evil (a deadly disease) and to achieve an ultimate good (health). Some theists use such considerations to respond to the problem of evil. They claim that there is an infinite gap between God's perspective and our own. Although we have sufficient reasons for believing in God, they say, we cannot explain or understand why evil exists. It will always be a mystery to be coped with on the basis of trust. Other theists have tried to set out some ways in which we can understand how God's permitting evil to occur may be morally justified, just as my wife and I were justified in allowing our baby to experience temporary pain. At the same time, such theists acknowledge that we can never explain the reason for each and every particular suffering that God allows.

In developing the greater goods defense, theists formulate the argument that certain moral goods such as courage, compassion, fortitude, forgiveness, and forbearance are human traits and are responses that enrich us as human beings, which would not be possible if there were no evil in the world. In alleviating, resisting, and overcoming evil, not only do we help those around us and make the world a better place, but we also make ourselves better persons in the process. But couldn't God simply give us fully developed moral characters without making us struggle against evil to achieve this goal? The answer to this question is effectively presented in Aldous Huxley's futuristic novel *Brave New World*. He depicts a society in which all crime, all suffering, and every negative feature of our society has been eliminated and in which its people are model citizens and supremely happy. But rather than being a utopian paradise, the world is dehumanizing because these results have been achieved through behavioral conditioning and a happiness drug called *soma*. The director of this "brave new world" explains the benefits of his society in this way:

> There's always *soma* to calm your anger, to reconcile you to your enemies, to make you patient and long-suffering. In the past you could only accomplish these things by making a great effort and after years of hard moral training. Now, you swallow two or three half-gramme tablets and there you are. Anybody can be virtuous now. You can carry at least half your morality about in a bottle. Christianity without tears—that's what *soma* is.[30]

THOUGHT EXPERIMENT: *Means versus Ends*

Suppose that you could take different drugs that would instantly transform you into a moral saint, an accomplished piano player, a successful athlete in a sport of your choice, a straight A student, or a great artist. Undoubtedly, such results would gain you public admiration, fame, wealth, and other goods. But would you feel as though you were worthy of this admiration? Would you feel good about how you obtained your achievements? Is it only the results that count in life, or are the processes and the means for achieving those results important too? If you swallow a pill that makes you virtuous, are you really virtuous? Or do moral achievements necessarily involve effort and struggle?

John Hick's Greater Goods Defense

If the notion of a "brave new world" pill that makes people instantly virtuous does not seem quite right, then you can appreciate the solution to the problem of evil proposed by the Christian theologian and philosopher John Hick (born in 1922). John Hick was educated at Edinburgh, Oxford, and Cambridge universities and was Danforth Professor of Religion at Claremont Graduate School until his retirement in 1994. He has published a number of highly regarded works in the philosophy of religion. Hick develops what he calls the "minority report" in the history of theology. This view is that when God initially created humanity, there was still some work to be done in making us a completed product. However, this remaining work could not be accomplished by God alone; we have to contribute to the process. Using the greater goods defense, Hick argues that even God himself could not achieve certain results without allowing us to struggle against evil and to endure suffering.

- In the following passage, what does Hick say was "easy for divine omnipotence"?
- What "cannot be performed by omnipotent power as such"?

FROM JOHN HICK

Evil and the God of Love[31]

Instead of regarding man as having been created by God in a finished state, as a finitely perfect being fulfilling the divine intention for our human level of existence, and then falling disastrously away from this, the minority report sees man as still in process of creation. . . .

And so man, created as a personal being in the image of God, is only the raw material for a further and more difficult stage of God's creative work. This is the leading of men as relatively free and autonomous persons, through their own dealings with life in the world in which He has placed them, towards that quality of personal existence that is the finite likeness of God. . . .

In the light of modern anthropological knowledge some form of two-stage conception of the creation of man has become an almost unavoidable Christian tenet. At the very least we must acknowledge as two distinguishable stages the fashioning of *homo sapiens* as a product of the long evolutionary process, and his sudden or gradual spiritualization as a child of God. But we may well extend the first stage to include the development of man as a rational and responsible person capable of personal relationship with the personal Infinite who has created him. This first stage of the creative process was, to our anthropomorphic imaginations, easy for divine omnipotence. By an exercise of creative power God caused the physical universe to exist, and in the course of countless ages to bring forth within it organic life, and finally to produce out of organic life personal life; and when man had thus emerged out of the evolution of the forms of organic life, a creature had been made who has the possibility of existing in conscious fellowship with God. But the second stage of the creative process is of a different kind altogether. It cannot be performed by omnipotent power as such. For personal life is essentially free and self-directing. It cannot be perfected by divine fiat, but only through the uncompelled responses and willing co-operation of human individuals in their actions and reactions in the world in which God has placed them. Men may eventually become the perfected persons whom the New Testament calls "children of God," but they cannot be created ready-made as this.

The value-judgement that is implicitly being invoked here is that one who has attained to goodness by meeting and eventually mastering temptations, and thus by rightly making responsible choices in concrete situations, is good in a richer and more valuable sense than would be one created *ab initio* [from the beginning] in a state either of innocence or of virtue. In the former case, which is that of the actual moral achievements of mankind, the individual's goodness has within it the strength of temptations overcome, a stability based upon an accumulation of right choices, and a positive and responsible character that comes from the investment of costly personal effort. I suggest, then, that it is an ethically reasonable judgement, even though in the nature of the case not one that is capable of demonstrative proof, that human goodness slowly built up through personal histories of moral effort has a value in the eyes of the Creator which justifies even the long travail of the soul-making process.

- In the following passage, what conception contrary to Christian thought does Hick say anti-theistic writers assume?
- Why is pleasure not the supreme value a parent tries to achieve for his or her children?
- In your own words, state what Hick means by "soul-making."
- According to Hick, what greater goods are achieved by God's allowing us to suffer?

If, then, God's aim in making the world is "the bringing of many sons to glory," that aim will naturally determine the kind of world that He has created. Antitheistic writers almost invariably assume a conception of the divine purpose which is contrary to the Christian conception. They assume that the purpose of a loving God must be to create a hedonistic paradise; and therefore to the extent that the world is other than this, it proves to them that God is either not loving enough or not powerful enough to create such a world. They think of God's relation to the earth on the model of a human being building a cage for a pet animal to dwell in. If he is humane he will naturally make his pet's quarters as pleasant and healthful as he can. Any respect in which the cage falls short of the veterinarian's ideal, and contains possibilities of accident or disease, is evidence of either limited benevolence or limited means, or both. Those who use the problem of evil as an argument against belief in God almost invariably think of the world in this kind of way. . . .

But if we are right in supposing that God's purpose for man is to lead him from human *Bios,* or the biological life of man, to that quality of *Zoe,* or the personal life of eternal worth, which we see in Christ, then the question that we have to ask is not, Is this the kind of world that an all-powerful and infinitely loving being would create as an environment for his human pets? or, Is the architecture of the world the most pleasant and convenient possible? The question that we have to ask is rather, Is this the kind of world that God might make as an environment in which moral beings may be fashioned, through their own free insights and responses, into "children of God"?

Such critics as Hume are confusing what heaven ought to be, as an environment for perfected finite beings, with what this world ought to be, as an environment for beings who are in process of becoming perfected. For if our general conception of God's purpose is correct the world is not intended to be a paradise, but rather the scene of a history in which human personality may be formed towards the pattern of Christ. Men are not to be thought of on the analogy of animal pets, whose life is to be made as agreeable as possible, but rather on the analogy of human children, who are to grow to adulthood in an environment whose primary and overriding purpose is not immediate pleasure but the realizing of the most valuable potentialities of human personality.

. . . How does the best parental love express itself in its influence upon the environment in which children are to grow up? I think it is clear that a parent who loves his children, and wants them to become the best human beings that they are capable of becoming, does not treat pleasure as the sole and supreme value. Certainly we seek pleasure for our children, and take great delight in obtaining it for them; but we do not desire for them unalloyed pleasure at the expense of their growth in such even greater values as moral integrity, unselfishness, compassion, courage, humour, reverence for the truth, and perhaps above all the capacity for love. We do not act on the premise that pleasure is the supreme end of life; and if the development of these other values sometimes clashes with the provision of pleasure, then we are willing to have our children miss a certain amount of this, rather than fail to come to possess and to be possessed by the finer and more precious qualities that are possible to the human personality. A child brought up on the principle that the only or the supreme value is pleasure would not be likely to become an ethically mature adult or an attractive or happy personality. And to most parents it seems more important to try to foster quality and strength of character in their children than to fill their lives at all times with the utmost possible degree of pleasure. If, then, there is any true analogy between God's purpose for his human creatures, and the purpose of loving and wise parents for their children, we have to recognize that the presence of pleasure and the absence of pain cannot be the supreme and overriding end for which the world exists. Rather, this world must be a place of soul-making. And its value is to be judged, not primarily by the quantity of pleasure and pain occurring in it at any particular moment, but by its fitness for its primary purpose, the purpose of soul-making.

Suppose you had to choose between two people to be your roommate. The first person grew up in a wealthy home. As a child, she (or he) always had everything she could possibly desire. Her parents gave her expensive toys, clothes, ponies, horses, and cars. They never said no to her. She never faced any disappointments, sorrows, or challenges. Life had always been easy for her. Because of her childhood, she grew up to be blasé, cocky, and carefree. The second person came from very difficult circumstances. As a child, she had to earn money to help her family get by. She suffered from poverty, illness, and the loss of loved ones. She survived and even prevailed because she developed the virtues of persistence, fortitude, patience, and hope. Through these experiences, she learned to have confidence in her own ability to overcome any difficulty and to be optimistic and joyful in the worst of circumstances. Furthermore, because of her own struggles, she became a person of great compassion, empathy, and understanding.

- Which person do you think would make the best roommate? Why?
- How does this scenario relate to John Hick's soul-making theodicy?

Criticisms of John Hick's Argument

John Hick's theodicy has been very influential, but it has also been subjected to a great deal of criticism. Edward H. Madden and Peter H. Hare, for example, accuse Hick of committing the "all or nothing" fallacy.[32] They concede that we may become better persons if we have to face obstacles and some suffering. But Hick assumes that God's choice is between all the torturous amount of suffering we have in the actual world and no suffering at all.

Everyone suffers on some occasions, but some people turn out to be decent, compassionate, morally sensitive individuals without enduring the gross amount of suffering that is inflicted on others. Hence, do we really need the amount of suffering that currently exists? As Madden and Hare state it, "Even if some undeserved and unnecessary suffering is necessary to make possible compassion, it is obvious that a minute percentage of the present unnecessary suffering would do the job adequately."

Furthermore, suffering, rather than contributing to the process of "soul-making," often brings about "soul-breaking," because people are crushed, defeated, demoralized, and dehumanized by great suffering. Accordingly, Madden and Hare argue: "One must remember that while unjust suffering may increase compassion, it also creates massive resentment. This resentment often causes individuals indiscriminately to lash out at the world. The benefits of compassion are probably more than offset by the damage done by resentment."

The Free Will Defense

Another way of dealing with the problem of evil is the **free will defense.** Its strategy is to claim that God could not create creatures (such as us) who have freedom of the will but who are incapable of doing evil. Remember that when religious philosophers say God is omnipotent, they usually mean that he has the power to do anything that is logically possible. Hence, it is not a limit on God's power to say that he cannot create free creatures who are programmed to do only what is good. Such creatures would be like well-behaved robots,

> **free will defense** the claim that God could not create creatures (such as us) who have freedom of the will but who are incapable of doing evil

and, hence, it would be a contradiction to suppose that they were free. Thus, God had a choice. He could create a world (A) in which there is no freedom of the will and, consequently, no moral evil, or create a world (B) with free agents and, consequently, allow for the possibility that people will use their freedom to do moral evil. Which world would be the best choice? We can imagine world A as one populated only with well-behaved robots. They would pick one another up after a fall, would never damage one another's logic circuits, and maybe would even sing praises to God with their voice synthesizers. However, these morally behaving beings would no more be able to choose to do good than a calculator can choose to give the correct sum. Hence, this world, though free of evil, would lack something that is of ultimate value both to God and ourselves, namely, human freedom.

Accordingly, the argument goes, God chose to create world B, a world in which creatures can make free choices. However, to possess freedom means that we have the ability to make good choices as well as bad choices. In creating free agents, according to this account, God took a risk. He necessarily could not guarantee that we would choose good over evil. Like a parent, he can try to influence and persuade us in the right direction, but he cannot force us to act one way as opposed to another. The result is that we live in a world in which people choose to act in ways that are courageous, compassionate, forgiving, merciful, and loving. But it is also a world in which people freely choose to act in ways that are immoral, malicious, despicable, hateful, and destructive. Hence, God does not will or cause evil to occur, but in order to allow free agents such as us to exist, he has to allow us the freedom to commit evil acts. God could prevent the inhumane evils and horrors of human history such as Hitler and Auschwitz only by excluding the great moments in humanity represented by Jesus, the Buddha, Socrates, Confucius, Michelangelo, Leonardo da Vinci, Johann Sebastian Bach, Abraham Lincoln, Mahatma Gandhi, Sojourner Truth, Helen Keller, Albert Einstein, Martin Luther King Jr., and Mother Teresa.[33]

At first glance, the free will defense might sound like a version of the greater goods defense, because it claims that the existence of freedom of the will is such a great good that the world would be impoverished without it. However, the two strategies differ, even though they are compatible. The greater goods defense claims that enduring evil is necessary for achieving certain goods of supreme value. On the other hand, the free will defense claims that the world is a better one if there is free will, but that the existence of free will necessarily makes possible the existence of evil. Hence, in this argument, evil is an unfortunate and unavoidable possibility created by something that is good rather than being an instrument for achieving a greater good. Another difference is that the greater goods defense can explain both natural evils and moral evils, because it claims that suffering can cause good results that could not be obtained without it whether this suffering has natural or human causes. The free will defense, however, is primarily an explanation of why God allows human moral evil to exist.

Critics have raised several problems with the free will defense. First, the defense assumes that it is impossible for creatures to be free at the same time that they are incapable of doing evil. This particular view of freedom is known as *libertarianism*, which claims that human freedom is incompatible with a guaranteed, predictable outcome. In chapter 3 we discussed this position as well as *compatibilism*, an opposing view that claims that if our actions are determined by our own nature and not by external constraints, then we are free. Hence, by applying the compatibilist's view of freedom to the free will defense, we are compelled to ask, Why couldn't God make us such that we would always freely choose the good? After all, God is said to be free, but his nature is such that he cannot do evil. Why couldn't these features exist in beings God has created? In many accounts of the afterlife, it is said that people will live an eternally blissful existence in heaven, will be free, and will no longer commit sins. Why couldn't God make this kind of life occur in the present world?

Ask 10 people the following question: Why do bad things happen to good people? In their answers, how many respondents mentioned God? How many used some version of the greater goods defense or the free will defense? What other explanation for undeserved suffering was given? Which answers do you think were the weakest? Which answers were the most plausible? Why?

A second response to the free will defense admits that a certain measure of freedom of the will would make this world better than if free will was totally lacking. But couldn't we get along with a little bit less free will if it meant less suffering in the world? For example, our society seeks to preserve human freedom at the expense of allowing certain sorts of evils to occur. Under ordinary circumstances, it is not a crime to ridicule someone's looks, which causes that person emotional pain. You have the moral freedom to choose whether you will say things to others that are hurtful or that are uplifting. However, should you choose to engage in serious harm such as assaulting a person and causing him or her physical injury, society does step in to prevent such an evil. Why couldn't God do the same with the human race as a whole? For example, he could stand back and give us the freedom to make good or bad moral choices with respect to lying, malicious gossip, slandering, theft, or other forms of wickedness. At the same time, he could intervene or make us such that we would be incapable of severe evils such as murder, rape, or child abuse. Thus, the criticism is that the value of having free agents in the world does not justify the amount of moral evil that results. A moderate amount of human freedom and a moderate amount of moral evil might make a better world.

The Natural Order Defense

The greater goods defense can handle both forms of evil (natural and moral), because it claims that suffering can produce a greater good whether the suffering is caused by humans or nature. However, the free will defense views evil as a result of the immoral choices that result from human freedom. This defense addresses such evils as slavery, murder, and war, but how can it explain the suffering caused by natural events such as disease, the destructive power of a hurricane, or an earthquake that destroys homes and lives? (Think of Albert Camus's depiction of the suffering caused by a precipitous plague.)

One way in which a free will defense can account for natural evils is to say that in order for there to be free choices, whether these choices are good or evil ones, there has to be a fixed, reliable order of natural causes and effects. For example, C. S. Lewis argues that for persons (he calls them "souls") to interact in a meaningful way and for humans to be free, the physical world must have a regular order that we all can recognize and share. C. S. Lewis (1898–1963) was a Fellow of Magdalen College at Oxford University when he wrote *The Problem of Pain*. Although he published many literary studies and works of fiction, he is best known for his popular defenses of Christianity.

FROM C. S. LEWIS
The Problem of Pain[34]

Society, then, implies a common field or "world" in which its members meet. . . . But if matter is to serve as a neutral field it must have a fixed nature of its own. . . .

Again, if matter has a fixed nature and obeys constant laws, not all states of matter will be equally agreeable to the wishes of a given soul, nor all equally beneficial for that particular aggregate of matter which he calls his body. If fire comforts that body at a certain distance, it will destroy it when the distance is reduced. . . .

Yet again, if the fixed nature of matter prevents it from being always, and in all its dispositions, equally agreeable even to a single soul, much less is it possible for the matter of the universe at any moment to be distributed so that it is equally convenient and pleasurable to each member of a society. If a man traveling in one direction is having a journey down hill, a man going in the opposite direction must be going up hill. If even a pebble lies where I want it to lie, it cannot, except by a coincidence, be where you want it to lie. And this is very far from being an evil: on the contrary, it furnishes occasion for all those acts of courtesy, respect, and unselfishness by which love and good humour and modesty express themselves. But it certainly leaves the way open to a great evil, that of competition and hostility. And if souls are free, they cannot be prevented from dealing with the problem by competition instead of by courtesy. And once they have advanced to actual hostility, they can then exploit the fixed nature of matter to hurt one another. The permanent nature of wood which enables us to use it as a beam also enables us to use it for hitting our neighbour on the head. The permanent nature of matter in general means that when human beings fight, the victory ordinarily goes to those who have superior weapons, skill, and numbers, even if their cause is unjust.

We can, perhaps, conceive of a world in which God corrected the results of this abuse of free will by His creatures at every moment: so that a wooden beam became soft as grass when it was used as a weapon, and the air refused to obey me if I attempted to set up in it the sound waves that carry lies or insults. But such a world would be one in which wrong actions were impossible, and in which, therefore, freedom of the will would be void; nay, if the principle were carried out to its logical conclusion, evil thoughts would be impossible, for the cerebral matter which we use in thinking would refuse its task when we attempted to frame them. All matter in the neighbourhood of a wicked man would be liable to undergo unpredictable alterations. . . . Fixed laws, consequences unfolding by causal necessity, the whole natural order, are at once the limits within which [our] common life is confined and also the sole condition under which any such life is possible. Try to exclude the possibility of suffering which the order of nature and the existence of free wills involve, and you find that you have excluded life itself.

© C.S. Lewis Pte. Ltd. 1962. Extract reprinted by permission.

LOOKING THROUGH THE ATHEIST'S LENS

1. Many religious people cannot understand how an atheist can live his or her life if there is no ultimate meaning or purpose to it. However, atheists reply that just because there is no ultimate meaning to human existence on a cosmic scale does not mean that we cannot find meaning in our daily lives, our friendships, our families, and our careers. Think about the things that happened to you this week or things that you did that were not religious in nature but that brought you happiness, were meaningful, or gave you a sense of accomplishment. Isn't it possible to live a happy, rewarding, and meaningful life on the basis of these experiences alone?

2. Many atheists throughout history have been compassionate, morally sensitive individuals, much like Dr. Bernard Rieux in Albert Camus's novel *The Plague*. Yet such people live morally exemplary lives without the guidance of sacred texts and divine commands. Does it follow from this observation that religion is not necessary for morality?

3. When we were children, we looked to our parents to take care of us, to tell us what to do, and to help us make decisions. However, as we became more mature and approached

adulthood, we had to learn how to live our own lives and make our own decisions. Is it true, as some atheists claim, that atheism calls us to live our lives as adults, whereas theism appeals to our immature tendencies to be dependent and to need guidance?

EXAMINING THE STRENGTHS AND WEAKNESSES OF ATHEISM

Positive Evaluation

1. The theist argues that the world needs a cause and finds the explanation in a God who is eternal and uncaused. Is this answer any better than the atheist's answer that the universe or matter and energy themselves are eternal and uncaused?

2. Before the rise of modern science, people thought that all natural events, such as disease and the motion of the planets, were the result of God's activity. However, science has continually shown that events in the world once thought to be mysterious can be explained as the product of natural causes. Do these findings suggest that in the scientific age God is no longer a necessary hypothesis?

3. In Camus's novel *The Plague,* Dr. Rieux said that he was "fighting against creation as he found it" and that "I shall refuse to love a scheme of things in which children are put to torture." Rieux's point is that if suffering is part of God's plan, then people are not supposed to fight against suffering. In other words, if suffering makes us better persons, then I am not doing you a favor if I try to alleviate your suffering; I should simply accept your suffering as part of God's scheme of things. However, most of us, like Dr. Rieux, feel compelled to fight against suffering. Are we then fighting against God's will? Do these considerations undermine the notion that suffering serves a divine purpose?

4. Religious philosophers have tried to show ways in which the presence of suffering could be compatible with the existence of an all-powerful, loving God. But does it seem that even the best responses to the problem of evil turn out to be less than conclusive? Don't these explanations wear thin when we confront the suffering of an innocent child? Can't we point to instances of suffering that do not have any conceivable good purpose and that seem to be beyond explanation and justification?

Negative Evaluation

1. Some atheists argue with the psychiatrist Sigmund Freud that religion is a psychological crutch that emotionally weak persons use to get through life. Certainly, religion fulfills the emotional needs of many people. But can this argument be turned against the atheist? List some reasons why someone might find the existence of God to be psychologically threatening and the belief in atheism to be an emotionally comfortable crutch.

2. Most religious and secular systems of ethics have some notion of the intrinsic worth, dignity, and equality of each person. But if we are just a random collection of atoms impersonally coughed up by nature, as the atheist believes, do we have any rational basis for believing in the intrinsic worth, dignity, and equality of all persons? Does the notion of the intrinsic worth of all persons fit better with the view that we are made by a loving God and that we bear God's image?

3. Daniel H. Osmond, professor of physiology and medicine at the University of Toronto, argues that modern science arose from the theistic belief in the divinely ordered rationality of the universe. From this historical point he goes on to explain: "To be sure,

many scientists today are able to do science without necessarily believing in a Purposeful Creator. But in order to do so, they must implicitly accept an ordered universe that can be known. . . . Purpose lies outside their domain of scientific discourse much as the roots of a tree lie outside the trunk. In each case the latter cannot stand without the former though the former is hidden from view."[35] Is it plausible, as Osmond maintains, that the "trunk" of science depends on the "hidden roots" of theistic belief? Does theism have the best explanation for the existence of this intricately ordered universe and of minds that are capable of theoretically examining this order?

4.6 RETHINKING THE WESTERN TRADITION: ASIAN RELIGIONS

 LEADING QUESTIONS: *Asian Religions*

1. The Judeo-Christian tradition claims that God created the world and that the world and God are distinctly different beings. But if this claim were true, wouldn't the world limit God, because it stands outside his being? To look at it another way, if God is everywhere, don't we have to view nature as included in the very being of God? If God is all-inclusive and nothing stands apart from God, then aren't we simply an aspect of God and isn't our distinct individuality an illusion?

2. How would you define religion? Is belief in a personal God essential for an outlook or way of life to be considered a religion at all? Or could you be religious and concerned about living a spiritual life without believing in a God that is to be worshiped?

3. What is the self? If you look inward, you will find nothing but a changing kaleidoscope of sensations, feelings, thoughts, and psychological states. Is the self something more than these changing phenomena? Does some permanent, unchanging "super-self," or soul, exist beneath this passing flow of psychological states? Or is there nothing there, nothing permanent beyond the stream of consciousness you experience?

Thus far our discussion of religion has revolved primarily around the Western concept of the Judeo-Christian God. Some philosophers have argued for the existence of such a God, whereas others have argued against his existence. We would be remiss, however, if we failed to examine the assumption that these arguments are the only options. Consequently, a brief look at the religious traditions of Asia provides us with some alternative views. To focus our discussion, I address only two of the many Asian traditions, namely, Hinduism and Buddhism. Although both religions arose in India and share a great deal in common, they also take differing positions on the points raised in the leading questions. I discuss each religion in turn, and to best contrast these religions with each other and with Western thought, I discuss each religion in terms of its historical origins and its views on faith and reason, God, the world, the self, the goal of life, human destiny, and the problem of evil.

STOP AND THINK

How much do you know about Hinduism and Buddhism at this point? Go back to the three leading questions on Asian religions and write down how you think a Hindu and a Buddhist would answer them. After you have read the following sections, review your answers and see how accurate they were.

SURVEYING THE CASE FOR HINDUISM

Historical Origins

Unlike religions such as Christianity, Islam, or Buddhism, Hinduism had no single founder. Its first expression came from a collection of ancient and anonymous sacred texts that came from even older hymns of worship. The earliest writings are the Vedas ("body of knowledge"). Some scholars estimate that the oldest one, the *Rig Veda,* may have been written approximately 1500 years B.C. This estimate would place it hundreds of years before Moses, allowing Hindus to claim that theirs is the oldest living religion. Devout Hindus still consider the Vedas to be divinely inspired knowledge, and the writings are still commonly believed to form the basis of all later scriptures. Another set of sacred writings make up the Upanishads, which are commentaries on the Vedas. The Upanishads are the most philosophical of ancient Hindu writings, for they present the world as a rational whole. The title *Upanishads* is composed of root words that mean *near, down,* and *to sit.* Hence, the name of this collection of writings suggests the picture of a pupil sitting down near a teacher to learn the truth that liberates. There are at least 108 of these writings, but only 10 to 13 are considered the principal ones. Some scholars believe that the earliest of the Upanishads was recorded around 1000 B.C., whereas others say the manuscripts evolved from 800 B.C. on. The authors of these books are anonymous, but the books are considered to be revelation produced by sages whose spiritual experience gave them special insight into divine matters.

Just as the expressions of Christianity range from the informal, emotional services of Pentecostal fundamentalists to the high rituals of the Greek Orthodox church, so the wide range of doctrines and practices found in Hinduism prevent it from being easily summarized. It is often said that anything that can be affirmed of Hinduism can be denied of it as well. For our purposes, I focus on the tradition of Advaita Vedanta pantheism, because it is one of the most philosophical forms of Hinduism and it makes the most effective contrast with Western religions. *Pantheism* is the view that God and the world are identical or are different manifestations of the same, one reality. This view is in contrast to the theistic view in which the world is dependent upon God while it remains a separate reality from the being of God.

Although many Westerners may not be familiar with the technical details of Hinduism, they have been exposed to some of its manifestations. The method of nonviolent resistance that Mohandas K. Gandhi used to bring social reform to India, for example, was inspired by the Hinduism of his youth. The Hare Krishna movement, which has drawn many American converts into its fold over the past four decades, is a form of Hinduism. Within the world of popular culture, the Beatles were influenced by the transcendental meditation of the Maharishi Mahesh Yogi, and in George Harrison's song "My Sweet Lord" the background singers sang praises to Hindu deities.[36] Likewise, the pantheism found in some versions of Hinduism has found Western expressions. The New Age movement and such entertainers as Shirley MacLaine and Tina Turner have been influenced by pantheistic thought.[37] Also, movies such as the *Star Wars* series have popularized pantheistic thought. In *The Empire Strikes Back,* for example, Yoda's teachings about the Force refer to a divine-like energy that permeates everything.

GANDHI
(1869–1948)

Faith and Reason in Hinduism

Like many of Hinduism's doctrines, the Hindu view of religious knowledge is complex and the position expressed depends on what passages are emphasized. Similar to the Biblical writings of Western religion, the ancient Hindu scriptures are very poetic and metaphorical. Both sets of scriptures were written to awaken people to their spiritual calling and were not intended to be philosophical treatises. Nevertheless, the Upanishads contain within them seeds of philosophical arguments that later writers were able to develop. For example, the cosmological argument is hinted at by the claim that God (Brahman) is "the Self-Existent" or the "Creator of the Universe." Similarly, the teleological, or design, argument is suggested by a number of passages. After a review of the physical and organic processes in the world, we are told that "All this is guided by intelligence, is based on intelligence. The world is guided by intelligence. The basis is intelligence. [Brahman] is intelligence."[38] Another scripture says that "if there were no elements of intelligence, there would be no elements of being."[39]

A number of other passages, however, are pessimistic about the possibility of proving a supreme, infinite God from the materials of our finite experience. Speaking of God, one scripture says, "He has no master in the world, no ruler, nor is there even a sign of Him [by which He can be inferred]."[40] Another argument against natural theology is based on the notion that the world being created at some point in time is merely a metaphorical expression, for the world has eternally existed with God. Both the cosmological and the teleological arguments assume that the world is the creation of God's will. But to will something is to desire it, and we desire things because we lack something. But how can a supreme, perfect being lack anything or desire anything? As one ancient commentary on the Upanishads puts it, "What desire is possible for Him who is the fulfilment of all desires?"[41]

Some Hindu writers such as Sarvepalli Radhakrishnan express the view, similar to the position of fideism found in Western thought, that God cannot be known by reason but only through faith or religious experience. Radhakrishnan (1888–1975) was born in south India and became one of the most frequently read Indian philosophers in the Western world. Besides holding teaching positions at various Indian universities, he served as a professor of Eastern religions and ethics at Oxford University. He was not only a great scholar but a statesman as well, for he was president of India from 1962 to 1967.

Radhakrishnan explicitly argues that truth has to be personally appropriated. As the following passage illustrates, Radhakrishnan believed that intuition, insight, and experience allowed us to know God with a directness and immediacy unavailable to reason:

> Everything is known to us only through experience. Even such an abstract science as mathematics is based on the experience of stated regularities. Philosophy of religion must base itself on religious experiences. The existence of God means the real or the possible experience of this Being. If the genuine standard of knowledge is experience, we must deny the character of knowledge to our ideas of God unless they are traced to the experience of God.[42]

The Hindu View of God

The Hindu term for the ultimate reality is *Brahman*. It is derived from a root that means "to be great" or "to expand." In other words, Brahman is that Being whose greatness or expansion is unlimited. Some of the titles used to refer to Brahman are the Absolute, Lord of All, Supreme Ruler, the Soul of the Whole Cosmos, Light, Truth, the Supreme Person, and the Adorable God. Brahman is said to be infinite, indivisible oneness, all knowing, all powerful, immortal, all pervading, and unchanging as well as being supreme love and goodness. With respect to us, Brahman is the fulfillment of all desires, the source of all blessings, the upholder of all things.

At first glance, these descriptions make Brahman sound very similar to the Judeo-Christian God depicted in the Bible. The problem is that Brahman has not only all these properties, but also none of these, because the ultimate reality is inexpressible and indefinable. To try to categorize the ultimate reality in terms of human language and concepts is like trying to capture the ocean in a bucket. Paradoxically, those believers who think they understand the divine reality do not, while those who truly understand it realize they don't. The indefinable nature of Brahman is captured in the following two passages.

FROM THE UPANISHADS

Not by speech, not by mind,
Not by sight can He be apprehended.
How can He be comprehended
Otherwise than by one's saying "He is"?[43]

It is conceived of by him by whom It is not conceived of.
He by whom It is conceived of, knows It not.
It is not understood by those who [say they] understand It.
It is understood by those who [say they] understand It not.[44]

The complexity of Hindu thought is illustrated by the fact that the first passage in this reading speaks of Brahman as personal ("He") and the second one uses the impersonal pronoun "It." Western minds are very dualistic. We want everything to either fall into a certain category or fall outside it. For example, Western thinkers would say that God, women, and men are personal beings, whereas gravity, rocks, and daisies are impersonal beings. In which category (personal or impersonal) does Hinduism place God? The answer is both. God is both personal and impersonal, for neither category alone adequately describes the Supreme Reality. Radhakrishnan explains the use of contradictory descriptions of God in this way:

We are like little children on the seashore trying to fill our shells with water from the sea. While we cannot exhaust the waters of the deep by means of our shells, every drop that we attempt to gather into our tiny shells is part of the authentic waters. Our intellectual representations differ simply because they bring out different facets of the one central reality.[45]

Accordingly, when describing Brahman we can only say what it is not. The Sanskrit expression *neti, neti* ("Not thus! Not so!") is repeatedly used to speak of this incomprehensible reality.[46] In Western theology this method of describing God is known as the "way of negation."

[Brahman] is not that which is conscious of the inner (subjective) world, nor that which is conscious of the outer (objective) world, nor that which is conscious of both, nor that which is a mass of consciousness. It is not simple consciousness nor is It unconsciousness. It is unperceived, unrelated, incomprehensible, uninferable, unthinkable, and indescribable. The essence of the Consciousness manifesting as the self. . . . It is all peace, all bliss, and non-dual.[47]

As opposed to the Western emphasis on the transcendence of God and the duality between God and creation, Vedanta Hinduism sees Brahman as not only immanent in, but identical to, the world. One scripture compares Brahman to a lump of salt dissolved in water. The salt is invisible to the eye, but to those who taste the water, the flavor of the salt is pervasive throughout it.[48] Many passages such as the following present nature as though it is God's body.

> The heavens are His head; the sun and moon, His eyes; the quarters [regions of space], His ears; the revealed Vedas, His speech; the wind, His breath; the universe, His heart. From His feet is produced the earth. He is, indeed, the Inner Self of all beings.[49]

> That immortal Brahman alone is before, that Brahman is behind, that Brahman is to the right and left. Brahman alone pervades everything above and below; this universe is that Supreme Brahman alone.[50]

THOUGHT EXPERIMENT: *The World and Brahman*

Consider the following Hindu argument.

1. Brahman (God) is perfect to the maximum degree.
2. If Brahman is perfect to the maximum degree, then it must be unlimited.
3. So Brahman is unlimited.
4. If the world was its own reality that existed separately from Brahman, then Brahman would be limited by it.
5. Therefore, the world does not exist as its own reality separate from Brahman.

Do you agree with the conclusion that the world is *not* a separate reality from God? If you do not agree, then because the argument is valid, you must reject one or more of the premises (1–4). Which premise, if any, would you reject or modify? Or do you accept the conclusion of the argument?

Anyone who has ever seen Indian art or heard the stories of their gods is familiar with the multiplicity of gods found in their popular religion. Vishnu, Siva, Kali, and Krishna are some of the most common ones. Scholars estimate that there are around 33 million gods in popular Hindu religion. Some scholars believe that primitive Indian polytheism was replaced by monotheism in the same way that the multitude of Greek gods were replaced by the one God in Western thought. But others point out that in the *Rig Veda,* the most ancient of the Indian scriptures, the creation of the world is presented as the product of one, supreme God referred to as "That One."[51] In the various Hindu scriptures, we are given a number of different stories. We are told that (1) the gods are many and each one controls a different aspect of reality; that (2) although there are many gods, Brahman is the greatest of them all; that (3) Brahman created the other gods; and that (4) all gods are really different manifestations of Brahman. The unity of all the plural deities in the one God is a persistent theme in many of the Upanishads. A typical expression of this latter interpretation is the following passage: "When they (the priests) speak of particular gods, saying: 'Sacrifice to him,' 'Sacrifice to that one,' [they are mistaken]; for these are all His manifestations: He Himself is all the gods."[52]

The notion that all the gods are merely different expressions of the same reality allows the Hindu to be very tolerant of other religions. The different gods, including the God of the Jewish faith and the God of Christianity, are like the sunlight breaking into many colors when passing through a prism. Each religion, like each color in the sunlight, gives us a partial aspect of the one reality.

The World in Hindu Thought

If all of reality is really the one, vast unified being of Brahman, why do we experience the world as a plurality of distinct things? The answer is in the doctrine of *maya*. This word is often translated as "illusion," but this translation can be misleading. Maya is how Brahman appears from our perspective, so the image is not completely unreal, as is, say, the illusory water in the desert seen by a thirsty, hallucinating traveler. Hindu writers tell the story of a man going through a forest at night who jumped back when he saw a snake on the ground in front of him. When he returned to that spot in the daytime, he realized it was only a rope. Likewise the world we experience is really there, but it is not seen for what it is. Hence, the world of our senses—the world of many, distinct, individual objects—is maya. To use another metaphor, the world we experience is like the reflection on the surface of a mirror. The reflection is really there, but we must not mistake it for reality itself. The person who views the world as a collection of many attributes or substances will live a life that is scattered and fragmented. "As rainwater falling on a mountain peak runs down the rocks in all directions, even so he who sees the attributes as different from Brahman verily runs after them in all directions."[53]

The Self in Hindu Thought

If Brahman is the only reality, then who or what are you? You are like a drop of water floating on the crest of a wave on the surface of the ocean. The drop may feel as though it is a distinct individual with its own identity and independent destiny. But that feeling is an illusion, because when the wave subsides, the drop will merge with that great body of water from which it came. Similarly, you are an aspect of and are enfolded within the undivided being of Brahman. But you may protest, "I experience myself as a distinct individual with my own unique feelings, bodily sensations, thoughts, and desires. How can this experience be an illusion?" Look at it in this way. Your feelings, sensations, thoughts, and desires are fleeting, ephemeral, transitory phenomena. One day you are depressed because things are not going your way and the whole world looks gloomy. The next day you get an A on your calculus test or you receive a letter from a close friend, and you are now buoyant and elated. But what is it that stays the same, what is it that is the real *you* throughout all the mood swings, changing psychological states, and passing thoughts? You not only experience tiredness, anger, doubt, joy, but you are also aware of and reflect on the feelings you are experiencing. It is almost as though what exists is the self that is having the experiences and a higher self that is observing the lower self and its experiences.

Hinduism says that the changing, temporal self, *jiva,* is the self that you experience most directly and immediately, but it is insubstantial, for it changes and dissipates with each passing moment. The real you, that which endures throughout all changes, is *atman.* Atman is that part of you that allows you to be an ongoing, continuous being through time; atman is that part of you that is eternal and indestructible.

STOP AND THINK

Have you ever been so caught up in the whirl of your daily life, rushing from one event to another or always trying to be what others expect you to be, that you felt as though you were losing contact with the deep, inner core of who you are? Or perhaps you have asked, "Who am I?" That question is easy enough to answer by giving your name

(continued . . .)

(. . . continued)

or by defining yourself in terms of your academic major, relationships, or affiliations. But this response is not really adequate, for these circumstances could have been different or they could change, and you would still be *you*. People sometimes say, "I am trying to *find* myself." But what is the self that it is capable of getting "lost"? Are you nothing more than your outward activities or your physical location and properties or just the changing flow of your inward psychological states, or is there something more to you—something that can't be pinned down, defined, or studied scientifically? If these questions make sense to you, then you are trying to sort out the jiva from the atman. You are trying to find that true self that stands behind all the outward appearances and activities.

Now comes the crucial turn. Hinduism teaches that the eternal soul of each individual (atman) is the same as the Soul (Atman) of the cosmos. Furthermore, this cosmic Soul—Atman (capitalized)—is one and the same as Brahman. In teaching about Brahman, the Hindu scriptures frequently add, "That art thou." The following passages stress the unity of each individual with God (Brahman) or the soul of the universe (Atman).

> Then Ushasta, the son of Chakra, questioned him. "Yājnavalkya," said he, "explain to me the Brahman that is immediately and directly perceived—the self that is within all."
> "This is your self that is within all."[54]

> For truly, everything here is Brahma; this self (atman) is Brahma.[55]

> These rivers, my dear, flow, the eastern toward the east, the western toward the west. They go just from the ocean to the ocean. They become the ocean itself. As there they know not "I am this one," "I am that one"—even so, indeed, my dear, all creatures here, though they have come forth from Being, know not "We have come forth from Being." . . . That which is the finest essence—this whole world has that as its soul. That is Reality. That is Atman (Soul). That art thou.[56]

Let's try an analogy to explain the Hindu view of the self. Imagine a street with 10 houses, and each house has a completely different stained glass window on its southern side. Each resident thinks that the source of the light streaming through his or her window is unique, for its colors and patterns are different than that of the neighbors' windows. But the fact is that the same sun is illuminating the interior of each person's house. The light only appears to be different in each case because it is being filtered through different panes of glass. Now suppose that the inhabitants had been imprisoned in their own houses all their lives with no windows other than the stained glass one through which to view the outside world. If the window only transmitted light but was too dark to show much else, the residents would have a diminished view of what the world was like outside their individual house. They even might think that the window itself was the source of light rather than being simply an opening through which they experienced a partial manifestation of something greater. Now suppose that the doors to the houses were unlocked and the residents were able to step outside into the brilliance and majesty of the fully visible sun itself. Can you imagine what a change of perspective that experience would cause? The sun, of course, is Brahman, and the individual windows are jiva. The experience of seeing the sun itself and basking in its undiluted light corresponds to what the Hindu scriptures call liberation.

If this view is correct, then the Western individualistic culture is based on an ideal that is at odds with the nature of reality. We and the rest of nature are all part of the one, majestic being of Brahman. We eat the fruit grown on trees and vegetables that come from the earth, so the being of those plants and the minerals in their soil now become part of our bodies. When we die, our bodies will return to the soil. Every time you inhale, the oxygen produced by plants and the air that others have breathed becomes a part of your physical system. Every time you breathe out, some of your physical being now becomes a part of nature. As these examples illustrate, the divisions between individual things in the world are artificial, for ultimately we are all bonded together in the one being of Brahman.

The Goal of Life in Hinduism

According to Hinduism, the goal in life is to overcome the illusion of duality and separateness and to realize our oneness with the Absolute Being. We are told that "if a man knows Atman here, he then attains the true goal of life"[57] and "he who knows the Supreme Brahman verily becomes Brahman."[58] Kabīr, a religious teacher, says that God is not a far-away, absent deity that we must hunt for, but is as close to us as water is to the fish.

> I laugh when I hear that the fish in the water is thirsty. You wander restlessly from forest to forest while the Reality is within your own dwelling. . . . The truth is here!
> . . . Until you have found God in your own soul, the world will seem meaningless to you.
> Your Lord is near; yet you are climbing the palm-tree to seek him.[59]

Hinduism offers many roads to the one goal of spiritual fulfillment. Since people are not all the same and since they start their spiritual journey at different points, there must be different ways available for achieving this goal. These various paths take the form of different kinds of *yoga*. This word is related to the English word *yoke*, which means both to unite and to place under discipline. Briefly, all forms of yoga involve disciplining the body and the mind to achieve physical and spiritual integration and to unite the person with the divine dimension within. One form is the way of wisdom, an approach that appeals to intellectuals. The way of wisdom leads a person to spiritual fulfillment through correct thinking and overcoming ignorance. A second yoga is the path of devotion, which is for those who relate to life with their emotions. Here a person seeks a relationship of intense love with the divine. A third path is for those people who are oriented toward action. It focuses on moral action in the world without concern for personal consequences. The fourth path is for people who are more experimental; it involves participation in physical, psychological, and spiritual exercises that lead to a serene, detached awareness. More or less nonreligious versions of this fourth form of yoga have become popular in the West as a form of mental and physical exercise.

Hinduism and Human Destiny

Although achieving oneness with the cosmic Soul is our ultimate destiny, it doesn't happen overnight; it takes time and effort. To understand this effort, we need to look at the best-known and least-understood concept in Indian philosophy—the doctrine of karma. **Karma** is the moral law of cause and effect that governs our actions in the world. In the physical realm, laws govern everything that happens and dictate that every cause has a definite effect. In the same way, the Hindu scriptures teach, a law of cause and effect governs the moral and the spiritual realm. Every action you perform will have its effect not

karma in Hinduism, the moral law of cause and effect that governs our actions in the world

only on the world around you but also on your own soul, depending on the moral quality of the action. Every action, thought, word, and desire shapes our future experiences. The doctrine of karma is sometimes thought to be a form of fatalism, as though we are in the grip of forces we cannot control. This approach is incorrect, however, because your own actions control your destiny such that whatever you sow, that is what you shall reap.

Although your karma may have immediate effects, it is impossible for all the consequences of your actions to be realized in your current life. Therefore, Indian thought affirms **reincarnation,** the doctrine that your soul came from a previous form of existence and that when you die you will be reborn into another life. Each successive rebirth reflects the moral development (or lack of it) in your previous life. Hence, karma affects not only your condition in this present life, but also in the next life, whether you find yourself to be a king, a slave, or a mosquito. "As a person puts on new garments, giving up old ones, the soul similarly accepts new material bodies, giving up the old and useless ones."[60]

reincarnation the doctrine that your soul came from a previous form of existence and that when you die you will be reborn into another life

STOP AND THINK

Westerners sometimes have trouble accepting the notion of reincarnation because it is largely foreign to our tradition. The question that we sometimes ask is, "How can I have been reincarnated from a previous life if I have no memory of my former mode of existence?" One answer that Hindu thinkers give is to point to your belief that you are continuous with and the same person as the little baby you once were even though you have no memories of that former state of your existence. Hence, we can accept continuity of the self even without conscious connection in our memories between our current experiences and the experiences of the baby. "As the embodied soul continuously passes, in his body, from boyhood to youth to old age, the soul similarly passes into another body at death. A sober person is not bewildered by such a change."[61]

- How would you reply to this argument?
- Is the analogy between the successive phases of your present life and the doctrine of reincarnation a good one?

The ultimate goal of our deepest longings (whether we realize it or not) is the final release of *moksha*. Moksha is best translated as "liberation" rather than "salvation." When we achieve moksha, we are released from all the finite and mortal conditions of life. There are many names for the goal: God-realization, oneness with the Absolute, supreme bliss, cosmic consciousness, or simply release or freedom. When we become spiritually perfected, we find release from the karma-driven cycle of birth, death, and rebirth.

Unenlightened souls who are still caught up in their own individuality return to earth to pursue their unfulfilled desires, but not so for the person who has transcended the individual self and its unquenchable desires:

But as to the man who does not desire—who is without desire, who is freed from desire, whose desire is satisfied, whose only object of desire is the Self—[his breath does not depart]. Being Brahman, he merges in Brahman.

Regarding this there is the following verse:
"When all the desires that dwell in his heart are got rid of, then does the mortal become immortal and attain Brahman in this very body."

Just as the slough of a snake lies, dead and cast away, on an ant-hill, even so lies this body. Then the self becomes disembodied and immortal Spirit, the Supreme Self . . . , Brahman, the Light.[62]

Because a person achieves this eternal state of bliss by overcoming the illusion of the individual self and by realizing that he or she is one with God, there is no sense of the individual, personal immortality found in Western thought. The liberated souls are compared to many rivers that have merged with the ocean and are no longer this or that river.[63] In a striking analogy, this unity with Brahman is compared to a romantic embrace (or sexual ecstasy) in which the lovers are absorbed in the pure pleasure of the moment and are not thinking about themselves or anything else.[64]

Hinduism and the Problem of Evil

If everything is an aspect of God, how does Hinduism account for the existence of evil in the world? One answer is that the law of karma implies that all suffering is just and is the outcome of choices that we have made in this life or a previous life. There are problems with this answer, however, just as there are with theistic solutions. This response implies that the innocent victim of suffering (say, someone who has a painful disease) is really to be blamed for his or her condition, which would suggest that we should not feel as compassionate for such a person as we normally do.

The karmic answer to the problem of evil has a number of problems with it, but the Hindu treatment of moral good and evil is equally radical. We are told that the distinction between good and evil, in the final analysis, is not fully real. As long as we have not yet achieved spiritual fulfillment, we are still required to wrestle with the issue of moral versus immoral choices. But in Brahman there is only total unity, and when we experience our identity with this oneness, all opposing dualities are dissolved. Hence, when a person achieves freedom from the dreamworld of this life, good and evil are no longer an issue. The enlightened person becomes untroubled, accepting reality as it is, and achieves detachment from everything, including all past, present, and future actions. This teaching is reiterated in many passages such as the following four scriptures.

> When a seer sees the brilliant
> Maker, Lord, Person, the Brahma-source,
> Then, being a knower, shaking off good and evil,
> Stainless, he attains supreme identity [with Him].[65]

Him [who knows this] these two do not overcome—neither the thought "Hence I did wrong," nor the thought "Hence I did right." Verily, he overcomes them both. What he has done and what he has not done do not affect him.[66]

Now, the Soul (Atman) is the bridge [or dam], the separation for keeping these worlds apart. Over that bridge [or dam] there cross neither day nor night, nor old age, nor death, nor sorrow, nor well-doing, nor evil-doing.[67]

Just as one driving a chariot looks down upon the two chariot-wheels, thus he looks down upon day and night, thus upon good deeds and evil deeds, and upon all the pairs of opposites. This one, devoid of good deeds, devoid of evil deeds, a knower of Brahma, unto very Brahma goes on.[68]

SURVEYING THE CASE FOR BUDDHISM

Historical Origins: The Buddha's Life

BUDDHA
(563–483 B.C.)

Contrary to popular opinion, Buddha is the title (but not a name) of Siddhartha Gautama (563–483 B.C.), the historical founder of Buddhism. The title "Buddha" means "the enlightened one." Siddhartha, the one who would become a Buddha, was born in northeastern India and was raised in the Hindu tradition. His father was a wealthy ruler who sought to provide his son with every luxury while sheltering him from the cruel world outside. When he was 16, while still living within the confines of his father's palace, Siddhartha married a young woman who bore him a son. However, when he was in his early 20s, he escaped from his carefully supervised environment and slipped out to visit a nearby city. There, according to legend, he encountered four life-changing sights. First, he saw a gaunt, trembling old man whose body manifested the degeneration of old age. Next, he saw a man suffering from a dread disease, lying by the roadside. Third, he passed a funeral procession with the corpse surrounded by grief-stricken relatives. Still stunned by his first encounters with the sufferings produced by old age, illness, and death, Siddhartha saw a monk experiencing the peace of deep meditation.

These experiences showed him the vanity of seeking fulfillment in the physical realm and started him on his quest for the solution to the human condition. One night, at age 29, he could no longer suppress his spiritual longings, and he silently said goodbye to his wife and son while they slept and fled into the forest to seek enlightenment. There he exchanged his fine garments with a ragged beggar, shaved his head, and renounced the carefree life of luxury he had enjoyed up until then. Siddhartha began his spiritual journey by spending seven years as a beggar-monk and sought enlightenment through Hindu asceticism (the practice of self-denial and extreme fasting). His self-imposed diet of a few seeds, herbs, rice, and fruit led to a physical collapse. Later he said of this stage in his life, "If I sought to feel my belly it was my backbone which I found in my grasp." One day, overcome by malnourishment, he fell unconscious. Shortly thereafter a girl from a nearby village revived him with a bowl of warm rice. This experience made him realize that ascetic practices do not lead to enlightenment but only to self-destruction.

After traveling until nightfall, Siddhartha sat down under a fig tree, resolving that he would not move from this spot until he had found the answers he sought. He sat there all night, passing through various stages of awareness, experiencing all his previous lives, and seeing the web of all beings who are interwoven into a ceaseless drama of birth, death, and rebirth until the mystery of human life became revealed to him. At this point, when Siddhartha was 35 years old, he became the Buddha, an "Enlightened One" or "One who is awake." Having found enlightenment, he spent most of the next half-century going about teaching his answer to the problems of life and proposing his "Middle Way," a balance between sensual indulgence and fanatical asceticism. He founded a religious order and was eventually joined by his wife and son. At the age of 80 he passed away in the arms of one of his disciples, saying, "Decay is inherent in all compound things. Work out your own salvation with diligence."

Because of the power of Siddhartha's personality and teachings, Buddhism spread very rapidly. After the Buddha's death, his followers split into several factions. Ultimately, two major traditions emerged, each with its own interpretation of the master's teachings. The Theravada school sees the Buddha as a holy man who attained enlightenment and pointed others to the way. They stick very closely to the original teachings of their master. The Mahayana Buddhists, however, see the Buddha as a savior. In addition to considering him divine and praying to him, they have expanded and added to the original doctrines. In this discussion of Buddhism, I present the Theravada interpretation because it closely follows the most ancient Buddhist scriptures.

Faith and Reason in Buddhism

The relationship between faith and reason has been a major concern throughout Western religious philosophy. What did the Buddha have to say about these topics? The answer is that he had little use for either faith or reason. With respect to reason, the Buddha was opposed to all speculating, theorizing, and debating. Early Buddhist thought contained nothing to compare to the philosophical arguments found in Western philosophy. Instead the Buddha continually pointed people to their own experience as a means of persuading them of the value of his insights.

- In the following passage, what does the Buddha say about our ability to study his "Way"?
- What is his attitude toward analytic thinking?

 FROM THE BUDDHA

Selected Teachings

We merely talk about "studying the Way" using the phrase simply as a term to arouse people's interest. In fact, the Way cannot be studied. If concepts based on [factual] study are retained, they only result in the Way being misunderstood. . . . If you will now and at all times, whether walking, standing, sitting, or lying, only concentrate on eliminating analytic thinking, at long last you will inevitably discover the truth.[69]

In a writing called "Questions Not Tending to Edification," the story is told that a man once approached the Buddha and wanted all his philosophical questions answered before he would practice the way that Buddha taught. Here is how the Buddha responded:

It is as if a man had been wounded by a poisoned arrow and when attended to by a physician were to say, "I will not allow you to remove this arrow until I have learned the caste, the age, the occupation, the birthplace, and the motivation of the person who wounded me." That man would die before having learned all this. In exactly the same way, anyone who should say, "I will not follow the teaching of the Blessed One until the Blessed One has explained all the multiform truths of the world"—that person would die before the Buddha had explained all this.[70]

Not only is the value of analytic reason diminished in Buddhist thought, but Buddhism also offers little that corresponds to the notion of faith. Rather than presenting himself or his teachings as the object of faith, the Buddha claimed that his own teachings were merely a means to an end that may be abandoned once the teachings have carried us to our destination. In a well-known parable Buddha tells the story of a man on a journey who comes upon a great river that restricts his progress. On his side of the river are many perils that he wants to escape, while on the other bank it is calm and peaceful. So he constructs a raft that he uses to carry himself across the river. Once the man has crossed to the safety of the other side, the Buddha asks, would anyone consider this man to be wise if he continued to carry his raft with him on his shoulders when he no longer needed it? The Buddha concludes the story by saying, "In this way I have taught you Dharma [the truth], like the parable of the raft, for getting across, not for retaining."[71]

The Question of God in Buddhism

What is remarkable about early Buddhist thought is the almost complete absence of any mention of the gods or the supernatural realm. Accordingly, some people say the Buddha's teaching was basically atheistic, whereas others say he was a religious skeptic (an agnostic). What is clear is that the Buddha's silence concerning theology pointed to the irrelevance of any God or gods to the human condition. Even when he does mention the gods of traditional Indian religion, they are always treated as rather minor, unimportant, and unknowable beings. As I mentioned previously, the earlier followers of Buddha and those who still practice Theravada Buddhism do not consider their founder to be a god but simply a man who showed the way to liberation through his teachings and his example. Although followers later added the edifice of institutional religion onto Buddhist teaching, the Buddha himself seemed to be opposed to the religious authorities, rituals, and traditions of his day. In many Buddhist shrines, the Buddha is represented solely by a footprint, symbolizing that he is no longer here but has left his mark and has showed us the direction in which we should go. This view of the Buddha is captured by the following well-known story.

It is said that soon after his enlightenment the Buddha passed a man on the road who was struck by the Buddha's extraordinary radiance and peaceful presence.
The man stopped and asked,
"My friend, what are you? Are you a celestial being or a god?"
"No," said the Buddha.
"Well, then, are you some kind of magician or wizard?"
Again the Buddha answered, "No."
"Are you a man?"
"No."
"Well, my friend, then what are you? The Buddha replied, "I am awake."[72]

The way to salvation or liberation is a journey that people must make for themselves, using their own resources and knowledge of the truth. They must not look for the external help of any god or even the Buddha himself. On his deathbed he said these last words to his followers.

Be ye lamps unto yourselves. Rely on yourselves, and do not rely on external help. Hold fast to the truth as a lamp. Seek salvation alone in the truth. Look not for assistance to any one besides yourselves. . . . Those who, either now or after I am dead, shall be a lamp unto themselves, relying upon themselves only and not relying upon any external help . . . it is they . . . who shall reach the very topmost height![73]

The Buddhist View of the World

A central concept in Buddhism is the transitory nature and perpetual perishing of every natural object. The Buddha once said,

Thus shall ye think of all this fleeting world:
A star at dawn, a bubble in a stream;
A flash of lightning in a summer cloud,
A flickering lamp, a phantom, and a dream.[74]

We view the world as made up of "things," but according to Buddhism the world is actually an interwoven series of processes. Our concepts and words are like photographs that freeze and fragment the world, whereas reality is more like an ongoing movie. The Buddha frequently used the metaphor of a wave to make this point. We watch the wave from the beach as it moves across the surface of the water. "It" starts in the distance and rapidly makes "its" way toward us. In speaking of it as "*the* wave," we delude ourselves into thinking it is one, continuous, singular object, whereas the shape and motion of the wave is actually made up of completely different particles of water from moment to moment. The point is that once we understand that everything is fleeting and perishable, we will not look to the physical world for our source of fulfillment.

The Self in Buddhist Philosophy

Everything in the world lacks permanence, and the same is true of the self. The Buddha's famous *anatta* ("no-self") doctrine states that there is no soul, self, or mind that is an enduring object that persists through time. Contemporary science tells us that your surface skin cells are discarded and replaced every 30 days. The rest of the cells in your body change every seven years. So when you see an old friend whom you haven't seen for some time, you are literally looking at completely different particles of matter. Thousands of years before this fact was known, the Buddha taught that there is nothing permanent in your physical makeup. Similarly there is nothing permanent in your psychological makeup, for you are a stream of consciousness that is constantly changing. This doctrine is remarkably similar to that of David Hume, the 18th-century Scottish philosopher introduced in section 2.3, who said, "What we call a *mind* is nothing but a heap or bundle of different perceptions, united together by certain relations."[75]

If there is no permanent soul or self, then who (or what) are you? The Buddha taught that you are made up of five transient streams or aggregates. These are material shape, the feelings, the perceptions, the dispositions (or impulses), and consciousness. In the following passage, you are compared to musical sounds or moving air. We use nouns to refer to them ("the melody" or "the wind"), but there is no enduring entity within or behind these transitory events.

When body and mind dissolve, they do not exist anywhere, any more than musical notes lay heaped up anywhere. When a lute is played upon, there is no previous store of sound; and when the music ceases it does not go anywhere in space. It came into existence on account of the structure and stem of the lute and the exertions of the performer; and as it came into existence so it passes away.

In exactly the same way, all the elements of being, both corporeal and non-corporeal, come into existence after having been non-existent; and having come into existence pass away.

There is no self residing in body and mind, but the cooperation of the conformations produces what people call a person. Paradoxical though it may seem: There is a path to walk on, there is walking being done, but there is no traveler. There are deeds being done, but there is no doer. There is blowing of the air, but there is no wind that does the blowing. The thought of self is an error and all existences are as hollow as the plantain tree and as empty as twirling water bubbles.[76]

In other words, a melody is simply a collection of the notes, but it does not exist apart from them. Similarly, the blowing of the air and the wind are not two things; there is nothing more to the wind but the blowing of the air. Likewise, you are simply the collection of all the processes and activities that are happening right now, but there is no self that exists apart from these processes. There is no enduring personal identity throughout all your activities, because apart from your activities that are happening at any given time, there is nothing left over to constitute the self. The Hindu believes that the individual self is an illusion because it is really a manifestation of Atman, the Soul of the cosmos, or God (Brahman). In contrast, the Buddhist believes that the individual self is an illusion because there is really nothing there beyond the passing flow of events.

Buddhism and the Problem of Evil

It is necessary to introduce the topic of evil earlier in the discussion of Buddhism than I did for Western religion or Hinduism because the problem of evil and the existence of suffering is the main theme of the Buddha's teachings. According to Buddhism, the cause of suffering is twofold. First, much of our suffering is the result of our own desires and our preoccupation with the illusion of the self. Second, suffering is simply a fact of life that we must face; no divine purpose is being achieved by suffering. We will look at each of these causes in turn.

The theme of suffering is addressed in the most fundamental creed of Buddhism, which is called the "Four Noble Truths." The first two diagnose the human condition and the last two point to the solution. These truths may be briefly stated in the following way: (1) We experience suffering in life. (2) Suffering is caused by selfish cravings and desires. (3) There is a way to end suffering. (4) The way to end suffering is through enlightened living. These Four Noble Truths were presented by the Buddha in his first sermon, which was delivered in a park at the edge of town soon after he received enlightenment. Here is how one translator renders the truths.

> And this is the Noble Truth of Sorrow. Birth is sorrow, age is sorrow, disease is sorrow, death is sorrow; contact with the unpleasant is sorrow, separation from the pleasant is sorrow, every wish unfulfilled is sorrow—in short, all the five components of individuality are sorrow.
>
> And this is the Noble Truth of the Arising of Sorrow. It arises from craving, which leads to rebirth, which brings delight and passion, and seeks pleasure now here, now there—the craving for sensual pleasure, the craving for continued life, the craving for power.
>
> And this is the Noble Truth of the Stopping of Sorrow. It is the complete stopping of that craving, so that no passion remains, leaving it, being emancipated from it, being released from it, giving no place to it.
>
> And this is the Noble Truth of the Way which leads to the Stopping of Sorrow. It is the Noble Eightfold Path—[having] Right Views, Right Resolve, Right Speech, Right Conduct, Right Livelihood, Right Effort, Right Mindfulness, and Right Concentration.[77]

Buddhism is sometimes accused of being pessimistic, for it seems to dwell on the negative features of life. On the contrary, the Buddha did not deny that life can have its moments of pleasure and happiness, but his point is that all pleasures are momentary events that come to an end and leave us with regret and a longing for more. As long as we pin our sense of well-being on that which is fated to slip through our hands, we will always be restless and empty. The word that was translated as "sorrow" in the last passage is *dukkha,* which can also mean "suffering," "pain," "evil," and "disease," as well as "impermanence," "emptiness," "imperfection," and "frustration." The word is sometimes used to refer to an axle of a wheel that is off-center. It can also refer to a bone that has slipped out of its socket.[78] Accordingly, the contemporary historian of religion Huston Smith rephrases the First Noble Truth in this way:

> Life as typically lived is out of joint. Something is awry. Its pivot is not true. This restricts movement (blocks creativity), and causes undue friction (interpersonal conflict).[79]

We are like a child who has reached into a jar of candy and gotten his hand stuck. He doesn't realize that the cause of his distress is that his hand is clenched into a fist around the candy, making it too large to slip out of the opening. If he would just let go, his hand would be freed. Similarly, the cause of suffering and the obstacle to enlightenment is our tendency to cling to such notions as "I," "me," "mine," and "self." We are filled with grasping desires, but we do not control our desires—they control us. They are like raging beasts inside us that drive us on in a never-ending, frantic quest to feed them. From our desires come frustration, resentment, greed, selfishness, self-conscious anxieties, inadequacy, fear, and all the negative attitudes and emotions that cause suffering. But if we desire nothing, if we learn contentment, we will never be frustrated. To eliminate desire and, hence, to eliminate suffering, we must stop saying "I want, I want" and stop thinking in terms of "me, me, me."

THOUGHT EXPERIMENT: *Desire and Freedom*

1. Think about yourself as a little child. Try to recall the things that caused this little child joy, sadness, fear, anxiety, envy, and yearning, things that you now realize were of little significance and that no longer have any emotional effect on you. What caused you to change? Is it because you are now more informed, mature, wiser, and have a broader understanding than you did as a child? Now consider the things that cause you joy, sadness, fear, anxiety, envy, and yearning *today*. Can you imagine that someday you might grow to see these things as having little significance as well? Is it possible that 40 years from now, you will consider all your current emotional crises to be somewhat trivial in the context of the big picture? Does this experiment suggest anything about the transitory and ephemeral nature of our desires?

2. Consider the following argument for the Buddhist perspective:
   (1) If there are things we desire, either we will get all that we want or we won't.
   (2) If we *do* get all that we want, we will suffer from both boredom, for there will be nothing more for which to strive, and anxiety, because of the fear that we will lose what we have.
   (3) If we do *not* get all that we want, we will suffer from frustration.
   (4) So, if we have desires, we will suffer.
   (5) Therefore, freedom from suffering comes only by being free from desire.
   Is this argument a good one? Why?

The other explanation for suffering (as the First Noble Truth explained) is that it is simply an inevitable fact of life. Because Buddhism does not have the Judeo-Christian notion of an all-powerful, loving God whose sovereign will controls every event in the world, it does not have to justify the presence of suffering. The Buddhist attitude toward suffering is illustrated by this ancient story.

Once a woman was stricken with grief over the death of her young boy. She came to the Buddha hoping that he could bring her son back to life. He instructed her to go to every house in the village and fetch some mustard seeds from every home in which no one had died. She came back empty-handed, for everyone she had met had been touched by the sorrow of death. Holding her son's body in her arms, she said, "Dear little son, I thought that you alone had been overtaken by this thing which men call death. But you are not the only one death has overtaken. This is a law common to all mankind." After laying her son's body to rest, she sought refuge in the way of the Buddha.[80]

The Goal of Life in Buddhism

Although the Buddha did not offer a magic pill to save us from the intrusion of illness, pain, old age, and death, he did teach a way of being immune from their hold over us. It consists of being free from our narrow concern with ourselves and our interests; eliminating our grasping nature and our desires, passions, wants, and cravings; achieving a sense of distance from the transitory features of the world; mastering ourselves and all that is negative and destructive within us; cultivating a peaceful, focused, and purified outlook and lifestyle; and concentrating on that which really matters.

Buddhism and Human Destiny

The Buddha retained the Hindu doctrine of karma—the law of cause and effect. He believed that harmful actions cause harmful results, much like a stone hitting the water causes ripples that continue on long after the stone has sunk. Likewise he believed in reincarnation, which he called the "Wheel of Rebirth." But now the obvious question is, "How can one be reborn if there is no permanent self to make the journey from one life to another?" To answer this question, the Buddha frequently used the example of a candle flame. Suppose a candle is burning down until its wick is almost all consumed and you then light another candle with it. As this second candle starts to go out, you light yet another candle from its flame. Is the flame in the third candle the same one you had at the beginning? Is the flame some sort of permanent substance that passes from candle to candle the way a water pitcher can be passed from one person to another? Obviously there is continuity in this process, because each candle is lit from the flame of the previous candle. However, the flame is not one continuous object lighting three successive candles. It is not even a continuous object from moment to moment when it is burning in one candle. In this way, the cycle of rebirth takes place without a continuous soul or self.

Even though the Buddha believed in karma and rebirth, he did not think that being reborn in another life is punishment imposed on us for past actions. Instead, rebirth is a sign that a person has not let go of the self sufficiently. If we have not yet attained liberation, we will get what we think we want, but what we think we want is not what we need. Clinging to our own desire for individuality, we will be trapped in its illusions and limitations.

nirvana in Buddhism, an unchanging, peaceful state of mind that allows us freedom from the illusion of individuality and the limitations of the self

To escape the prison of our desires and our illusions is to achieve **nirvana.** The word refers to the extinguishing of a flame from lack of fuel. Nirvana is not a place (like heaven) but is a state of mind. It is not to be found somewhere over the rainbow but in the here and now. A person who achieves nirvana enters an unchanging, peaceful state and achieves freedom from the illusion of individuality and the limitations of the self. Nirvana is like a deep, relaxing sleep, only better. However, in the final analysis, it cannot be described.

Nirvana grants all one can desire, brings joy, and sheds light. As a mountain peak is lofty and exalted, so is Nirvana. As a mountain peak is unshakable, so is Nirvana. As a mountain peak is inaccessible, so is Nirvana inaccessible to all the passions. As no seeds can grow on a mountain peak, so the seeds of all the passions cannot grow in Nirvana. And finally, as a mountain peak is free from all desire to please or displease, so is Nirvana.[81]

It might seem as though a person who had been liberated from the passions and who has achieved perfect contentment would be oblivious to the needs and suffering of those about him or her. But Buddhists follow the example of their master who, after achieving nirvana, did not choose to stay alone in his state of perfect bliss but turned back to care for those who were still suffering and in need of enlightenment. The Buddha continually taught that we must live a life of compassion, but we can have compassion without being a victim of passion. You can imagine a child who is injured and whose father is emotionally distraught. Because the parent is so overwhelmed and focused on his own emotional state, he is ineffective in tending to the needs of the child. However, a physician who is emotionally uninvolved can calmly dress the wound. The physician's detachment serves to make her compassion that much more effective.[82] Likewise, a life of detachment is compatible with a life of compassion and service to others.

THOUGHT EXPERIMENT: *Experiencing Nirvana*

You can use your own experience to get a glimpse of what the Buddha is saying. When have you been most miserable? It probably has been when you were totally absorbed in yourself. You were nurturing emotional hurts or feeling sorry for yourself. Perhaps you were in a situation in which you were painfully self-conscious, worrying about how you looked, how you were dressed, what people thought of you. On the other hand, you probably can remember times during which you experienced the joy of being totally absorbed with others or with some project. You "came out of yourself" because you were immersed within someone else's joy or with their suffering. You found happiness in your total involvement with others or with something larger than yourself because you were no longer focusing on yourself and your petty concerns. This experience of self-abandonment is but a glimpse of the experience of nirvana.

The Buddha's disciples frequently asked what happens when a person has achieved nirvana and then dies. Is this person reborn to a better life, or does he or she go to heaven? The Buddha refused to delve into speculative questions, considering them irrelevant. In the following passage the Buddha (Gotama) explains this irrelevancy to Vaccha, a wandering ascetic.

"But, Vaccha, if the fire in front of you were to become extinct, would you be aware that the fire in front of you had become extinct?"

"Gotama, if the fire in front of me were to become extinct, I should be aware that the fire in front of me had become extinct."

"But, Vaccha, if some one were to ask you, 'In which direction has that fire gone,— east, or west, or north, or south?' what would you say, O Vaccha?"

"The question would not fit the case, Gotama. For the fire which depended on fuel of grass and wood, when that fuel has all gone, and it can get no other, being thus without nutriment, is said to be extinct."

"In exactly the same way, Vaccha, all that form has been abandoned, uprooted, pulled out of the ground like a palmyra-tree, and become non-existent and not liable to spring up again in the future. The saint, O Vaccha, who has been released from what is styled form, is deep, immeasurable, unfathomable, like the mighty ocean. To say that he is reborn would not fit the case. To say that he is not reborn would not fit the case. To say that he is both reborn and not reborn would not fit the case. To say that he is neither reborn nor not reborn would not fit the case.[83]

The religious life . . . does not depend on the dogma that the world is eternal; nor does the religious life . . . depend on the dogma that the world is not eternal. Whether the dogma obtain . . . that the world is eternal, or that the world is not eternal, there still remain birth, old age, death, sorrow, lamentation, misery, grief, and despair, for the extinction of which in the present life I am prescribing.[84]

SUMMARY OF HINDU AND BUDDHIST THOUGHT

In Herman Hesse's moving novel about the life of Siddhartha Gautama and how he attained enlightenment, Hesse has captured the Asian sense of the unity of the cosmos, a unity in which all distinctions between the self and others, the self and nature, pleasure and sorrow, good and evil are dissolved. In the climactic passage of the story Siddhartha bends down and listens to the message of the river. The final message is the humming sound of "Om," a word that has no specific intellectual content, because it refers to anything and everything. Asian mystics use it both to refer to the ultimate meaning of the cosmos, its total unity, and perfection and to transport themselves to the highest level of awareness. The following passage could represent the experience sought by both the Hindu and the Buddhist.

 FROM HERMAN HESSE

Siddhartha[85]

Siddhartha tried to listen better. The picture of his father, his own picture, and the picture of his son all flowed into each other. Kamala's picture also appeared and flowed on, and the picture of Govinda and others emerged and passed on. They all became part of the river. It was the goal of all of them, yearning, desiring, suffering; and the river's voice was full of longing, full of smarting woe, full of insatiable desire. The river flowed on towards its goal. Siddhartha saw the river hasten, made up of himself and his relatives and all the people he had ever seen. All the waves and water hastened, suffering, towards goals, many goals, to the waterfall, to the sea, to the current, to the ocean and all goals were reached and each one was succeeded by another. The water changed to vapor and rose, became rain and came down again, became spring, brook and river, changed anew, flowed anew. But the yearning voice had altered. It still echoed sorrowfully, searchingly, but other voices accompanied it, voices of pleasure and sorrow, good and evil voices, laughing and lamenting voices, hundreds of voices, thousands of voices. . . .

. . . He could no longer distinguish the different voices—the merry voice from the weeping voice, the childish voice from the manly voice. They all belonged to each other: the lament of those who yearn, the laughter of the wise, the cry of indignation and the groan of the dying. They were all interwoven and interlocked, entwined in a thousand ways. And all the voices, all the goals, all the yearnings, all the sorrows, all the pleasures, all the good and evil, all of them together was the world. All of them together was the stream of events, the music of life. When Siddhartha listened attentively to this river, to this song of a thousand voices; when he did not listen to the sorrow or laughter, when he did not bind his soul to any one particular voice and absorb it in his Self, but heard them all, the whole, the unity; then the great song of a thousand voices consisted of one word: Om—perfection.

LOOKING THROUGH THE HINDU'S AND THE BUDDHIST'S LENS

1. Much of human history has been scarred by the conflict between competing religions. However, a common Hindu teaching is that the different religious traditions are like different paths up the same mountain. According to Radhakrishnan, we can overcome the conflict between religions "only if we accept something like the Hindu solution, which seeks the unity of religion not in a common creed but in a common quest." How would world history have been different if everybody had accepted the Hindu solution?

2. Most Hindu traditions teach that Brahman (God) is immanent within nature and that the world is his body. How would embracing this view affect our society's tendency to abuse our natural environment?

3. What examples can you find in literature, magazines, television, and everyday conversation of the emphasis that our society places on the self and individuality? What would the Buddhist say about this emphasis?

4. Advertisers and others in our society try to make you believe that your worth and the measure of your success in life is determined by the amount of wealth you have accumulated, the car you drive, the clothes you wear, the status of your profession, or the organizations to which you belong. What would the Hindu or Buddhist say about these sorts of values that are prevalent in our society? How would they define success?

5. Both Hinduism and Buddhism teach that we must view the material world the way we view a child's toy—as something trivial and of no lasting importance to us. If you were to follow the advice of these Asian religious philosophies, what would be the childish "toys" in your life that are keeping you from spiritual and ethical enlightenment?

6. Suppose that a friend's home caught on fire and your friend not only lost all his or her possessions and shelter but was also severely burned and scarred for life. How would the theist seek to comprehend such suffering? How would an atheist explain it? A Hindu? A Buddhist?

EXAMINING THE STRENGTHS AND WEAKNESSES OF HINDUISM AND BUDDHISM

Positive Evaluation

1. Hinduism presents a view of the universe that can offer both intellectual and spiritual satisfaction. Everything in the world is permeated by the divine. Ultimately there is no fragmentation or dichotomy between God and nature or the sacred and the secular, for the world is one with God's own nature. Wouldn't this outlook bring unity and harmony to our fragmented lives?

2. If everyone believed with the Hindus that every individual soul is really a manifestation of the divine soul, wouldn't it transform human relationships? Would hatred, war, and racism be possible in the light of that belief?

3. How would your personality, times of diminished self-esteem, or self-doubt be transformed if you believed as Hindus do that below the surface of your personality you are really identical with the soul of God?

4. To what degree would you find release from emotional suffering if you adopted the Buddhist perspective of floating on the surface of life's waves instead of letting them engulf you? If you viewed your daily hurts, frustrations, and sorrows as though they were as temporal and ephemeral as yesterday's shadows, wouldn't this view make a significant difference to your life?

Negative Evaluation

1. Hindu thought claims that Brahman (God) transcends language, reason, and the laws of logic. For this reason, Hindus describe Brahman in contradictory terms (personal and impersonal, other than the world and identical with it). And yet in making this claim, don't they assume that our logic and conceptual categories are applicable to Brahman? For example, Hindus use the law of excluded middle in assuming that reason either is or is not applicable to Brahman.* They also use the law of contradiction in assuming that Brahman cannot be both limited and not limited.**

2. Hindu pantheism claims that the individual self is really one with the universe, while the Buddhist no-self doctrine claims that the self is an illusion. But how is it that within this unified, undifferentiated universe, aspects of this universe arose that suffer from the illusion of an individual self? To the degree that my beliefs are false, I genuinely am something apart from the rest of the fabric of reality. How can I be one with the universe, as these Asian philosophies claim, at the same time that my beliefs alienate me from the way the universe is?

3. Certainly the Buddhist is correct to point out that we would be happier and more content if we let go of some of our self-obsessive cravings and desires. But throughout history there have been creative geniuses who were driven by the thirst to achieve success or to accomplish some sort of personal goal. Many of these people have had enormous egos at the same time they made enormous contributions to humanity. From these personal desires and strivings, for example, have come great inventions or advances in medicine and science that have reduced human suffering, enriched our lives, and advanced civilization. Wouldn't the world and the quality of human life have been poorer if these history-changing people had done nothing but led contemplative lives and abandoned their strivings and thirst to achieve their individual goals? Is desire the problem in human life (as Buddhism claims) or only wrongly directed desires?

4. Buddhism teaches that we should neutralize our emotions and live a life of detachment from everything that is passing. In the 1960s, folk singer Paul Simon wrote a song in which his fictional character sang, "I am a rock, I am an island. And a rock feels no pain; and an island never cries."[86] Although a rock (a person who strives for detachment) is invulnerable to pain, he or she also is closed to the possibility of love and could never have a deep friendship, be an effective parent, or become emotionally involved in the fight for a just cause. Aren't there times when directed passion is appropriate and justified (for example, when a person is fighting social injustice)?

In contemporary discussions, an important issue for philosophy of religion is the relationship between a religious view of the world and the scientific outlook. I will begin our discussion of this issue by considering four basic models of the relationship between science and religion.

First is the *adversarial* model. According to this view, science and religion attempt to answer the same questions about reality but give conflicting answers. Hence, their relationship is characterized as one of extreme tension, or even that of two warring enemies. One version of this model advocates that religion should be abandoned in favor of science. For example, in an opinion piece titled "Scientists, Face It! Science and Religion Are Incompatible," Cornell historian of science William Provine relates that someone wrote to him, asking "Is there an intellectually honest Christian evolutionist position? Or do we simply have to check our brains at the church house door?" Provine's reply was straightforward: "The answer is, you indeed have to check your brains."[87]

The opposing version of this model claims that scientific theories should be abandoned when they appear to conflict with the revealed truths of religion. For example, although the 17th-century physicist Isaac Newton was also a Christian theologian, many leading religious thinkers in his day believed that his mechanistic explanations in physics eliminated any role for God in the world. For that reason, they argued, Newtonian science should be rejected. In a recent book, British journalist Bryan Appleyard writes, "our science as it is now, is absolutely *not* compatible with religion" and later goes on to assert that science is "spiritually corrosive, burning away ancient authorities and traditions."[88] Note that most religious adversarialists do not reject all science but only those particular scientific claims (such as those of the evolutionists) that are deemed to conflict with religious doctrines.

The remaining three models attempt to argue for the compatibility of science and religion but use different strategies to accomplish this. The second of our four models could be called *territorialism*. Its advocates claim that science and religion cannot conflict because they deal with different realms (or territories) of reality. Science tells us about the physical world, and religion tells us about spiritual realities. Thus, instead of being enemies, science and religion are considered to be good neighbors. Each tends to its own property while having polite conversations over the fence that divides them. The paradigmatic model of the territorialist was the French philosopher René Descartes.* In Descartes's dualistic model, reality is divided into two parts: physical reality (planets, rocks, our own bodies), which science can explain completely; and nonphysical reality, consisting of God and our minds (or souls). Science can adequately deal with the world of physical, deterministic, mechanistic causes. However, religion (undergirded by philosophy) tells about the world of nonphysical realities.

The third model is a position that I will call *perspectivalism*. Unlike the adversarialists, perspectivalists think it is inconceivable that any well-accepted scientific theory could ever conflict with religion. What distinguishes perspectivalists from the territorialists is that the perspectivalists do not believe that science and religion *describe different realities*. Instead, they say, science and religion *describe reality in different ways*. Hence, science and religion deal with the same reality but ask different questions about it, for different purposes, each giving different but complementary answers concerning the world in which we live. For example, imagine a tragic graveside scene. In anguish, a loved one of the deceased asks, "Why did she die?" A scientist replies, "The victim contracted botulism from eating contaminated food. The toxin blocked the release of the neurotransmitter acetylcholine and caused muscle paralysis that resulted in respiratory failure." This scientific account may be correct, but it does not provide the sort of answer the bereaved was seeking. The question "Why did she die?" was concerned with the mystery and tragedy of death in human experience and the problem of evil. Any possible religious or philosophical answer to that question would not conflict with the scientific answer.

In this view, science answers "how" questions and religion answers "why" questions. Science seeks causes and religion seeks meaning. Science is characterized by objective detachment and religion by subjective involvement. At times, Galileo shrewdly embraced this model in his attempts to counter the religious attacks on his science. As Galileo put it, religion has been given to us to "teach us how to go to heaven, not how the heavens go." Perspectivalism continues to be a popular view of many theologians and religiously oriented scientists today.

Finally, the fourth position is that of the *harmonizers*. Some people see the relationship between science and religion as that of a blissful marriage. The harmonizers attempt to show that the findings of science and the revealed truths of religion are perfectly consistent and even that science proves, points to, or at least makes plausible the claims of religion.

From the 19th century up to our day, the debate over the design argument for God has been given new life as scientific data concerning the origins of life and the origins of the cosmos have provided new ammunition for all four of these models. Accordingly, in the next two sections I will use the contemporary debate over the design argument as a case study of how religion and science do or do not relate together.

EVOLUTION AND DESIGN: ENEMIES OR PARTNERS?

Evolution and the Adversarial Model

In the 19th century, the design argument ran against one of its most difficult problems in the scientific work of Charles Darwin (1809–1882). Until then the hypothesis of intelligent design seemed to be the best explanation available for the order manifested within biological systems. For example, though there are countless varieties of teeth in nature, each creature has the type of teeth necessary to chew the sort of food its stomach requires. Canines have sharp teeth for ripping meat, and meat is the type of food that their stomachs can process. On the other hand, a canine's teeth would not work for horses, who must eat grass to sustain themselves. Many theistic scientists prior to Darwin argued that this harmony between each animal's teeth and its dietary needs could not be the product of chance, but had to be the result of an intelligent, benevolent, and purposeful design.[89]

With the 1859 publication of Darwin's theory of evolution in *Origin of Species,* however, the teleological argument seemed to lose some of its persuasive force. Darwin's findings can be briefly summarized as follows: (1) *Random variations* occur in animals and plants that are inherited by their offspring. (2) Since more offspring are produced than the environment can sustain, there is a *struggle for survival.* (3) Those individuals in which the variations are advantageous will be more likely to survive than the others, resulting in the *survival of the fittest.* Consequently, those individuals will tend to live longer, produce more offspring, and pass on their advantageous biological traits. (4) Over a long period of time the process of *natural selection* produces populations of organisms that are highly developed and well-suited for survival. The pre-Darwinian defenders of the teleological argument assumed that divine design preceded the creation of each species and that it explained why there is so much harmony, efficiency, and order in the biological realm. Darwin's theory of natural selection, however, presented the reverse picture. In this alternative view, nature produces random changes with no purpose in mind and the appearance of design is the end result of blind, natural selection. A forceful presentation of the Darwinian objection to divine purpose is made in biologist Richard Dawkins's best-selling book *The Blind Watchmaker,* which has the subtitle *Why the Evidence of Evolution Reveals a Universe without Design.* His reply to Paley's argument is, "All appearance to the contrary, the only watchmaker in nature is the blind forces of physics."[90]

Some religious proponents of the adversarial position also see evolutionary and religious explanations as irreconcilable enemies who are competing for the same explanatory territory. However, unlike their atheistic counterparts, the religious adversarialists argue that molecular biology, cell biology, and biochemistry are on their side. In other words, they claim that the complexity of biological organisms could not have developed from random processes but had to be the result of intelligent design. In contemporary discussions, this view has been dubbed the "intelligent design theory" (or ID theory for short). ID theorists do not necessarily deny that some evolutionary mechanisms are at work in nature. Their main contention is that without the intervention of an intelligent designer, the mechanisms proposed by evolutionary theories cannot explain the biological phenomena.

A leading defender of ID is biologist Michael Behe, who argues that we can see evidence of design in systems that manifest irreducible complexity. Behe defines irreducible complexity as

A single system composed of several well-matched, interacting parts that contribute to the basic function, wherein the removal of any one of the parts causes the system to effectively cease functioning.[91]

Hence, such complexes function only when they are up and running as completed systems. They could not have evolved in a piecemeal, gradual way through random modifications of previous parts, because the parts would be nonfunctional apart from their integrated role in the complex. With these systems, it is all-or-nothing. One of the examples of irreducible complexity that Behe discusses is the bacterial flagellum. This mechanism functions like a biological outboard motor that enables certain kinds of bacteria to swim. The flagellum contains the biological equivalents of a motor, drive shaft, and propellor. Behe claims that in the scientific literature "no one has ever proposed a serious, detailed model for how the flagellum might have arisen in a Darwinian manner."[92]

Similarly, mathematician William Dembski, a leading ID theorist, has developed a mathematical "explanatory filter" to distinguish when the best explanation is purposeful design as opposed to blind natural laws or brute chance. A key criterion for Dembski is "specified complexity." A nonbiological example of specified complexity would be a combination lock whose dial contains 100 numbers and which must be turned to a certain combination of five numbers for it to unlock. The probability of guessing the correct combination is one in ten billion. Accordingly, Dembski argues that the abundance of specified complexity in the biological realm is so large and its probability of occurring by chance is so low that the inference to intelligent design is warranted.[93]

Critics reply to the ID theory arguments by pointing out that in the past, evolutionists have encountered such seemingly unexplainable complexity but eventually discovered an evolutionary explanation. Furthermore, biologists can point to complex systems that have evolved through the modification of earlier systems that originally served a different purpose, thereby undermining Behe's all-or-nothing argument.[94]

Evolution as Compatible with Religion

Although Charles Darwin's theory of evolution is often thought to be in conflict with religion, Darwin himself was a theist when he first published *The Origin of Species by Means of Natural Selection* in 1859. (His only earned academic degree was in theology.) Even though he became an agnostic later in life, Darwin originally saw his scientific findings as confirming divine design. He said that the strongest argument for the existence of God was

> the extreme difficulty or rather impossibility of conceiving this immense and wonderful universe, including man with his capacity of looking far backward and far into futurity, as the result of blind chance or necessity. When thus reflecting I feel compelled to look to a First Cause having an intelligent mind in some degree analogous to that of man; and I deserve to be called a Theist.[95]

Hence, Darwin theorized that God supervised the overall scheme of nature while allowing chance to play a role in the details.[96]

Although Darwin later had doubts about even this very general notion of design, other scientists, theologians, and philosophers took up his thesis that evolution posed no threat to the teleological argument. F. R. Tennant (1866–1957), who represented all three of those professions, developed a "wider teleological argument" that allowed particular instances of design, such as the development of the human eye, to be explained by natural causes but argued that natural processes and laws were merely instruments used by God. Thus, the evidence of design was found in the system of laws that made evolution possible.[97] Similarly, many contemporary theologians, philosophers, and scientists find no intrinsic conflict between evolutionary explanations and divine design. For example, physicist and theologian Ian Barbour says that

> A patient God could have endowed matter with diverse potentialities and let it create more complex forms on its own. In this interpretation God respects the integrity of the world and lets it be itself, just as God respects human freedom and lets us be ourselves.[98]

Hence, modern versions of the argument reject Paley's analogy in which God, like a watchmaker, designs every detail of the system of nature at a single point in time. Instead, we have purposeful design on the "installment plan," which takes place over the long process of evolution, allows for some randomness in nature, and looks for design in the total system rather than in every detail.

The persons discussed in the last paragraph are all harmonizers. However, territorialists and perspectivalists offer their own, distinctive approach to making evolution compatible with religion. Territorialists take a dualistic approach, saying that evolution explains how biological humanity (our physical makeup) emerged. But then, they say, a supernatural event occurred, adding a spiritual nature to our biological body. For example, in 1996, Pope John Paul II stated that the Church has held for some time that "there was no opposition between evolution and the doctrine of the faith" as long as we add the qualification that "the spiritual soul is immediately created by God."[99] On the other hand, theologian Langdon Gilkey articulated the perspectivalist view on evolution in a book on the Christian doctrine of creation. He states that the purpose of the Biblical account of creation is not to answer the question "On what day were the crocodiles created?" Instead, Gilkey explains, the doctrine of creation provides "an answer to the religious question about the meaning and purpose of our finite life."[100]

COSMOLOGY AND DESIGN: CONFLICT OR CONGRUENCE?

Some versions of the contemporary debate over the design argument do not focus on the details of biology but look to the big picture; that is, they ask why the nature of the universe is such that it enabled life to occur in the first place. This approach looks to cosmology to answer this question. Cosmology is a science that studies the origin and structure of the universe, making use of the resources of both astronomy and physics. The discovery, in the early part of the 20th century, that the universe is expanding eventually led to the well-accepted calculation that it all began some 10 to 20 billion years ago in an intense explosion known as the "big bang."* A second later, space was filled with subatomic particles such as protons, neutrons, and electrons. After millions of years, as the universe expanded and cooled, atoms began to form and, eventually, stars, galaxies, and planets. In the latter half of the 20th century, these startling discoveries in cosmology stirred up the pot for both scientists and philosophers. Here is how philosopher Neil Manson describes it:

> A series of breakthroughs in physics and observational astronomy led to the development of the Big Bang model and the discovery that the Universe is highly structured, with precisely defined parameters such as age, mass, entropy (degree of disorder), curvature, temperature, density, and rate of expansion.

Furthermore, Manson says, precise measurements of the values of these parameters

> led to the discovery of numerous "anthropic coincidences" and supported the claim that the Universe is fine-tuned for life—that is, that the values of its parameters are such that, if they differed even slightly, life of any sort could not possibly have arisen in the Universe.[101]

A term that is frequently tossed about in these debates is the *anthropic principle*. The problem is that the term is used in many ways by thinkers on both sides of the design debate. The safest way of understanding the term is to say that it refers to a set of facts (which almost everyone on either side of the debate accepts). These facts add up to the generalization (referred to in the passage by Manson) that the "Universe is fine-tuned for life" in the sense that a slight variance in the numbers would have made it impossible for life as we know it to arise. Although scientists, for the most part, agree with this conclusion, there is wide disagreement about its explanation and philosophical implications.

What are these examples of fine-tuning? They are too numerous (and too technical) to list here, but I can offer a few examples. A number of parameters concerning the age, size, density, and rate of expansion of the universe could not have been different and still have produced life. For example, world-renowned physicist Stephen Hawking writes that "If the rate of expansion one second after the Big Bang had been smaller by even one part in a hundred thousand million million it would have recollapsed before it reached its present size."[102] On the other hand, if the rate of expansion had been greater by one part in a million, it would have expanded too rapidly for galaxies, stars, and planets to form.[103] In either case, life would be impossible.

Another critical, numerical constant concerns the formation of the basic elements. If the "strong nuclear force," which binds the nuclei of atoms together, were even slightly weaker, the

---

*The scientific hypothesis that the universe and time itself had a beginning has played a role in new versions of the cosmological argument. (See the mention of the *kalām* cosmological argument in section 4.1.) Here, however, we are interested in the implications of the big bang for the argument from design.

only thing in the universe would be hydrogen. On the other hand, if this fundamental force were stronger by a small percentage, virtually no hydrogen would exist in the universe. Without hydrogen, there would be no stable stars such as the sun, and there would be no water. Without the sun and without water, of course, life as we know it would not have emerged.[104]

Cosmology and the Harmonizers

From the standpoint of physics and astronomy, there is no reason why the universe could not have been ordered differently than it is. Yet it so happens that the precise conditions of our universe are those necessary to produce and sustain life. Can this situation be explained through a lucky combination of impersonal, random events, or is the best explanation that of a purposive intelligence guiding the whole show? The harmonizers, of course, think that these numbers point to a purposive design. Although he recognized that the significance of the numbers is subject to interpretation, the intricate structure of the universe led the renowned British mathematical physicist Paul Davies to conclude that

> It is hard to resist the impression that the present structure of the universe, apparently so sensitive to minor alterations in the numbers, has been rather carefully thought out . . . the seemingly miraculous concurrence of these numerical values remain the most compelling evidence for cosmic design.[105]

The famous astronomer Fred Hoyle is reported to have had his atheism shaken when he discovered the remarkable nuclear resonance structure of carbon and oxygen that is critical to the existence of life.[106] Hoyle compared the formation of life by the random shuffling of molecules to "a whirlwind passing through an aircraft factory and blowing scattered components into a functioning Boeing 747." This discovery led Hoyle to conclude that the order of the universe is not an accident but that "the universe is a put-up job."[107] Freeman Dyson, who served for 41 years as a professor of physics at the Institute for Advanced Study in Princeton, states, "The more I examine the universe and the details of its architecture, the more evidence I find that the universe in some sense must have known we were coming."[108] In contrast to the harmonizers, territorialists and perspectivalists have virtually nothing to say about this issue, because they believe that nothing we learn in astronomy or physics could have any significance for the human soul or the values by which we live.

Cosmology and the Anti-Religious Adversarial Position

These contemporary defenders of the design argument have been kept busy defending their arguments from the attacks of their critics. Because most critics accept the data on which these design arguments rest, they have attempted to question the inference from the scientific data to God in at least two ways. They either question the logic of the inference to design or attempt to provide alternative, nontheistic explanations of the universe's fine-tuning.

In questioning the logic of the design inference, some critics say the notion of probability makes no sense when talking about possible universes. We can say that an outcome is probable or improbable when dealing with a finite system (for example, when playing a slot machine or a poker game), but not with the infinite variety of possible universes. However, the fine-tuning argument supposes that the numerical values of a possible universe are limited or that some values are more probable than others. The problem is, critics claim, that neither of these assumptions can be supported by current physical theory.[109]

Another response to the fine-tuning argument is to propose that the big bang did not produce just *our* universe. Instead, it actually produced an enormously large or even an infinite number of universes that are in isolation from one another, each one being structured according to different parameters and having completely different physical laws. If it is possible that multiple universes exist, then it would not be unlikely that at least one of them would be capable of producing life. However, critics of this alternative complain that it is highly speculative, it is unsupported by independent evidence, and it is a last-ditch effort to avoid the design argument.

Both the formulations of the argument from design and assessments of its strength have changed over the centuries, because this argument is so dependent on the current state of our scientific knowledge. Hence, new scientific discoveries in the future will continue to shift the balance one way or another. In the meantime, each of us will have to decide whether our world is best explained through purposeful fine-tuning or through chance.

REVIEW FOR CHAPTER 4

Philosophers

4.0 Overview of Philosophy of Religion
Peter Kreeft
4.1 The Cosmological Argument for God
St. Thomas Aquinas
Richard Taylor
4.2 The Design Argument for God
William Paley
David Hume
4.3 The Ontological Argument for God
St. Anselm
Gaunilo
Immanuel Kant
4.4 Pragmatic and Subjective Justifications of Religious Belief
Blaise Pascal
W. K. Clifford
William James
Søren Kierkegaard
4.5 The Problem of Evil: Atheistic and Theistic Responses
Albert Camus
John Hick
C. S. Lewis
4.6 Rethinking the Western Tradition: Asian Religions
Buddha

Concepts

4.0 Overview of Philosophy of Religion
monotheism
evidentialism
natural theology
atheism
agnosticism (religious skepticism)
nonevidentialism
fideism
a posteriori arguments
empirical knowledge
a priori arguments
4.1 The Cosmological Argument for God
cosmological argument
first cause argument
principle of sufficient reason
argument from contingency
contingent being
necessary being
4.2 The Design Argument for God
argument from design (teleological argument)
David Hume's critique of the design argument
4.3 The Ontological Argument for God
ontological argument
reductio ad absurdum argument
Gaunilo's critique of the ontological argument
Immanuel Kant's objection to the ontological argument
4.4 Pragmatic and Subjective Justifications of Religious Belief
pragmatic and subjective justifications of belief
nonevidentialist theism
three essential points of the nonevidentialist theists
Pascal's wager
Clifford's ethics of belief
James's view of religious belief
Kierkegaard's view of religious belief

SUGGESTIONS FOR FURTHER READING

General Philosophy of Religion

Peterson, Michael, William Hasker, Bruce Reichenbach, and David Basinger. *Reason and Religious Belief.* 3d ed. New York: Oxford University Press, 2003. A clearly written examination of the issues from a theistic perspective.

Pojman, Louis, ed. *Philosophy of Religion: An Anthology.* 4th ed. Belmont, Calif.: Wadsworth, 2003. A balanced collection of readings on the topic. One of the best.

Rowe, William. *Philosophy of Religion: An Introduction.* 3d ed. Belmont, Calif.: Wadsworth, 2001. A clearly written but scholarly introduction to the main issues.

Wainwright, William J. *Philosophy of Religion.* 2d ed. Belmont, Calif.: Wadsworth, 1999. A readable and well-argued text from a theistic perspective.

The Classical Arguments for God, and Their Critics

Hick, John, ed. *The Existence of God.* New York: Macmillan, 1964. A good collection of articles about the standard theistic arguments.

Hume, David. *Dialogues Concerning Natural Religion,* 1779. Available in many different paperback editions. Contains not only the classical critique of the argument from design but Hume's skeptical attacks on the other theistic arguments as well.

Moreland, J. P., and Kai Nielsen. *Does God Exist? The Debate between Theists and Atheists.* Amherst, N.Y.: Prometheus Press, 1993. A lively debate on the existence of God and other religious issues by a theist and an atheist.

Swinburne, Richard. *The Existence of God.* Rev. ed. Oxford: Oxford University Press, Clarendon Press, 1991. A thoroughgoing, contemporary defense of theism.

Arguments for Atheism

Mackie, J. L. *The Miracle of Theism: Arguments for and against the Existence of God.* Oxford: Oxford University Press, 1982. A clear and lively discussion of theism by a leading atheistic philosopher. According to Mackie, the "miracle" is that anyone is a theist.

Martin, Michael. *Atheism: A Philosophical Justification.* Philadelphia: Temple University Press, 1990. Perhaps the most complete critique of theism and justification of atheism in print.

Smith, George H. *Atheism: The Case against God.* Amherst, N.Y.: Prometheus Press, 1980. A popular presentation of the case for atheism.

The Problem of Evil

Adams, Marilyn McCord, and Robert Merrihew Adams, eds. *The Problem of Evil.* Oxford: Oxford University Press, 1990. A collection of contemporary articles on the subject by a wide range of authors.

Howard-Snyder, Daniel, ed. *The Evidential Argument from Evil.* Bloomington, Ind.: Indiana University Press, 1996. A well-balanced collection of contemporary articles.

Lewis, C. S. *The Problem of Pain.* New York: Simon and Schuster, Touchstone Books, 1996. A popular theistic analysis of the problem of evil.

World Religions

Carmody, Denise L., and T.L. Brink. *Ways to the Center: An Introduction to World Religions.* 6th ed. Belmont,

Calif.: Wadsworth, 2005. A well-received introduction to world religion with coverage of Hinduism and Buddhism.

Molloy, Michael. *Experiencing the World's Religions: Tradition, Challenge, and Change.* 5th ed. New York, NY.: McGraw-Hill, 2009.

Science and Religion

Barbour, Ian. *Religion and Science: Historical and Contemporary Issues.* New York: HarperCollins, 1997. A thorough survey of the relationship between science and religion, covering the range of alternatives as well as theological implications of contemporary scientific issues.

Dawkins, Richard. *The Blind Watchmaker: Why the Evidence of Evolution Reveals a Universe without Design.* New York: W. W. Norton, 1996. The title says it all.

Dembski, William. *Intelligent Design: The Bridge between Science and Theology.* Downers Grove, Ill.: InterVarsity Press, 1999. An argument against evolution by one of the leading proponents of intelligent design theory.

Manson, Neil, ed. *God and Design: The Teleological Argument and Modern Science.* London: Routledge, 2003. A helpful series of essays—representing a spectrum of viewpoints—on the implications of evolutionary and cosmological theories for the design argument.

Ruse, Michael. *Can a Darwinian Be a Christian? The Relationship between Science and Religion.* Cambridge: Cambridge University Press, 2000. Ruse favors an affirmative answer to this question.

NOTES

1. Peter Kreeft, introduction to J. P. Moreland and Kai Nielsen, *Does God Exist? The Great Debate* (Nashville: Thomas Nelson, 1990), p. 11.

2. For some good summaries of atheistic arguments, see Michael Martin, *Atheism: A Philosophical Justification* (Philadelphia: Temple University Press, 1990); and George H. Smith, *Atheism: The Case against God* (Amherst, N.Y.: Prometheus Press, 1980).

3. Friedrich Nietzsche, *Beyond Good and Evil,* trans. Walter Kaufmann (New York: Random House, Vintage Books, 1966), sec. 6, p. 13.

4. Thomas Aquinas, *Summa Theologica,* in *Basic Writings of Saint Thomas Aquinas,* vol. 1, ed. Anton C. Pegis (New York: Random House, 1945), part I, question 2, article 3, p. 22.

5. For an extensive discussion of this argument, see William Lane Craig, *The Kalām Cosmological Argument* (New York: Barnes and Noble, 1979).

6. Richard Taylor, *Metaphysics,* 4th ed. (Englewood Cliffs, N.J.: Prentice Hall, 1992), pp. 100–105, 107.

7. William Paley, *Natural Theology: Selections* (Indianapolis: Bobbs-Merrill, Library of Liberal Arts, 1963), pp. 3–4, 13.

8. David Hume, *Hume's Dialogues Concerning Natural Religion,* ed. Norman Kemp Smith (London: Oxford University Press, 1935), Part II: pp. 178; 182–83, 185; Part IV: pp. 205–7.

9. Ibid., Part XII: p. 281.

10. This example can be found in William Rowe, *Philosophy of Religion: An Introduction* (Belmont, Calif.: Wadsworth, 1978), p. 32.

11. St. Anselm, *Proslogium,* chap. 1, in *Saint Anselm: Basic Writings,* trans. S. N. Deane (La Salle, Ill.: Open Court, 1962).

12. St. Anselm, *Proslogium,* chap. 2, in *St. Anselm: Basic Writings.*

13. The discussion of these three points is based on C. Stephen Evans, *Subjectivity and Religious Belief: An Historical, Critical Study* (Grand Rapids, Mich.: William B. Eerdmans, Christian University Press, 1978), chap. 1.

14. Contrary to the view that Kierkegaard was the sort of fideist who is opposed to reason, some commentators see him as providing subjective justifications for why we should take the leap of faith. See Marilyn Gaye Piety, "Kierkegaard on Rationality," *Faith and Philosophy* 10, no. 3 (July 1993); C. Stephen Evans, *Faith beyond Reason: A Kierkegaardian Account* (Grand Rapids, Mich.: William B. Eerdmans, 1998); and Merold Westphal, *Kierkegaard's Critique of Religion and Society* (Macon, Ga.: Mercer University Press, 1987).

15. Blaise Pascal, *Thoughts,* trans. William F. Trotter, The Harvard Classics, vol. 48 (New York: P. F. Collier, 1910), Sec. 233, pp. 84–87.

16. William James, "The Will to Believe," in *Essays in Pragmatism,* ed. Alburey Castell (New York: Macmillan, Hafner Press, 1948), pp. 95, 105–6, 107.

17. Søren Kierkegaard, *The Journals of Søren Kierkegaard,* August 1, 1835, trans. Alexander Dru, in *A Kierkegaard Anthology,* ed. Robert Bretall (New York: Modern Library, 1946), pp. 4–5.

18. Søren Kierkegaard, *Philosophical Fragments,* trans. David Swenson and Howard V. Hong (Princeton:

Princeton University Press, 1962), pp. 49, 103n, 103–4.

19. Søren Kierkegaard, *Concluding Unscientific Postscript,* trans. David Swenson and Walter Lowrie (Princeton: Princeton University Press, 1941), pp. 182, 189.

20. Ibid., p. 51.

21. Søren Kierkegaard, *The Sickness unto Death* in *Fear and Trembling and The Sickness unto Death,* trans. Walter Lowrie (Princeton: Princeton University Press, 1968), p. 210.

22. Søren Kierkegaard, *Concluding Unscientific Postscript,* p. 178.

23. Ibid., pp. 179–80.

24. Ibid., pp. 189, 191.

25. *Søren Kierkegaard's Journals and Papers,* vol. 1, trans. and ed. Howard and Edna Hong (Bloomington: Indiana University Press, 1967), no. 10, p. 7.

26. Albert Camus, *The Plague,* trans. Stuart Gilbert (New York: Random House, Vintage Books, 1972), pp. 199, 201, 211–12, 120, 202–3.

27. Charles Darwin, letter to Asa Gray (May 22, 1860), in *The Life and Letters of Charles Darwin,* vol. 2, p. 105.

28. A movement known as process philosophy limits God's knowledge of the future. See Charles Hartshorne, *Omnipotence and Other Theological Mistakes* (Albany: State University of New York Press, 1984).

29. Harold S. Kushner, *When Bad Things Happen to Good People* (New York: Schocken Books, 1981).

30. Aldous Huxley, *Brave New World* (New York: Harper and Row, 1946), p. 162.

31. John Hick, *Evil and the God of Love,* rev. ed. (New York: Harper and Row, 1966, 1977), pp. 253–59.

32. Edward H. Madden and Peter H. Hare, *Evil and the Concept of God* (Springfield, Ill.: Charles C. Thomas, 1968), pp. 83–90, 102–3. Reprinted in Louis Pojman, *Philosophy of Religion: An Anthology* (Belmont, Calif.: Wadsworth, 1994), pp. 181–85.

33. This way of expressing the point was borrowed and modified from a passage in David Ray Griffin, *God, Power, and Evil: A Process Theodicy* (Philadelphia: Westminster Press, 1976), p. 309.

34. C. S. Lewis, *The Problem of Pain* (New York: Macmillan, 1962), pp. 31–34.

35. Daniel H. Osmond, "A Physiologist Looks at Purpose and Meaning in Life," in Templeton, *Evidence of Purpose,* p. 148.

36. George Harrison, "My Sweet Lord," from the album *All Things Must Pass* (Apple Records, New York).

37. See Shirley MacLaine, *Out on a Limb* (New York: Bantam, 1983) and *Dancing in the Light* (New York: Bantam, 1985); and Nancy Griffin, "Tina," in *Life* (August 1985), pp. 23–28.

38. *Aitareya Upanishad* 5.3, in *The Thirteen Principal Upanishads,* trans. Robert Hume (London: Oxford University Press, 1921), p. 301. Because there are multiple translations of the Upanishads, references will be made in terms of the divisions of the original writings as well as the page numbers of the particular translation used.

39. *Kaushitaki Upanishad* 3.8, in Hume, *Thirteen Principal Upanishads,* p. 327.

40. *Svetasvatara Upanishad* 6.9, in *The Upanishads,* vol. 2, trans. Swami Nikhilananda (New York: Ramakrishna-Vivekananda Center, 1952), p. 135.

41. Acharya Gaudapada, *Karika* 1.9, in Nikhilananda, *The Upanishads,* vol. 2, p. 235.

42. Sarvepalli Radhakrishnan, *Recovery of Faith* (New York: Harper & Brothers, 1955), p. 104.

43. *Katha Upanishad* 6.12, in Hume, *Thirteen Principal Upanishads,* p. 360.

44. *Kena Upanishad* 11, in Hume, *Thirteen Principal Upanishads,* p. 337.

45. Sarvepalli Radhakrishnan, *The Hindu View of Life* (New York: Macmillan, 1927), p. 36.

46. See *Brihad-Aranyaka Upanishad* 2.3.6, in Hume, *Thirteen Principal Upanishads,* p. 97.

47. *Mandukya Upanishad* 7, in Nikhilananda, *The Upanishads,* vol. 2, p. 236.

48. *Brihad-Aranyaka Upanishad* 2.4.12, in Hume, *Thirteen Principal Upanishads,* p. 101.

49. *Mundaka Upanishad* 2.1.4, in *The Upanishads,* vol. 1, trans. Swami Nikhilananda (New York: Ramakrishna-Vivekananda Center, 1949), p. 282.

50. Ibid., 2.2.11, p. 294.

51. *Rig Veda* 10.129, in *Sources of Indian Tradition,* eds. William Theodore de Bary, Stephen Hay, Royal Weiler, and Andrew Yarrow (New York: Columbia University Press, 1958), p. 18.

52. *Brihadaranyaka Upanishad* 1.4.6, in *The Upanishads,* vol. 3, trans. Swami Nikhilananda (New York: Ramakrishna-Vivekananda Center, 1956), p. 117.

53. *Katha Upanishad* 2.1.14, in Nikhilananda, *The Upanishads,* vol. 1, p. 167.

54. *Brihadaranyaka Upanishad* 3.4.1, in Nikhilananda, *The Upanishads,* vol. 3, p. 214.

55. *Mandukya Upanishad* 2, in Hume, *Thirteen Principal Upanishads*, p. 391.

56. *Chandogya Upanishad* 6.10.1–3, in Hume, *Thirteen Principal Upanishads*, pp. 246–47.

57. *Kena Upanishad* 2.5, in Nikhilananda, *The Upanishads*, vol. 1, p. 240.

58. *Mundaka Upanishad* 3.2.9, in Nikhilananda, *The Upanishads*, vol. 1, p. 309.

59. Quoted in Radhakrishnan, *Recovery of Faith*, p. 112.

60. *Bhagavad-gita As It Is*, trans. A. C. Bhaktivedanta Swami Prabhupada (Sydney: The Bhaktivedanta Book Trust, 1986), 2:22, p. 104.

61. Ibid., 2:13, p. 91.

62. *Brihadaranyaka Upanishad* 4.4.6–7, in Nikhilananda, *The Upanishads*, vol. 3, pp. 293–95.

63. *Chandogya Upanishad* 6.10.1, in Hume, *Thirteen Principal Upanishads*, p. 246.

64. *Brihadaranyaka Upanishad* 4.3.21, in Nikhilananda, *The Upanishads*, vol. 3, p. 276.

65. *Mundaka Upanishad* 3.1.3, in Hume, *Thirteen Principal Upanishads*, p. 374.

66. *Brihad-Aranyaka Upanishad* 4.4.22, in Hume, *Thirteen Principal Upanishads*, p. 143.

67. *Chandogya Upanishad* 8.4.1, in Hume, *Thirteen Principal Upanishads*, p. 265.

68. *Kaushitaki Upanishad* 1.4, in Hume, *Thirteen Principal Upanishads*, p. 305.

69. E. A. Burtt, ed., *The Teachings of the Compassionate Buddha* (New York: Mentor, 1982), pp. 202–3.

70. Jack Kornfield, ed., *Teachings of the Buddha* (Boston: Shambhala, 1996), p. 26.

71. Ibid., p. 91.

72. Ibid., p. xiii.

73. Burtt, *Teachings of the Compassionate Buddha*, pp. 49–50.

74. Kornfield, *Teachings of the Buddha*, p. 141.

75. David Hume, *A Treatise of Human Nature*, ed. L. A. Selby-Bigge (Oxford: Clarendon Press, 1896), bk. 1, pt. 4, sec. 2.

76. Kornfield, *Teachings of the Buddha*, p. 18.

77. de Bary et al., *Sources of Indian Tradition*, p. 102.

78. Huston Smith, *The Illustrated World's Religions* (New York: HarperCollins, Harper San Francisco, 1994), p. 71.

79. Ibid.

80. Paraphrased from Burtt, *Teachings of the Compassionate Buddha*, pp. 43–46.

81. Kornfield, *Teachings of the Buddha*, p. 45.

82. This analogy is based on one from Abraham Kaplan, *The World of Philosophy* (New York: Random House, Vintage Books, 1961), p. 262.

83. Sarvepalli Radhakrishnan and Charles A. Moore, eds., *A Source Book in Indian Philosophy* (Princeton, N.J.: Princeton University Press, 1957), p. 291.

84. Burtt, *Teachings of the Compassionate Buddha*, p. 35.

85. Herman Hesse, *Siddhartha*, trans. Hilda Rosner (New York: Bantam Books, 1951), pp. 134–36.

86. Paul Simon, "I Am a Rock," © 1965 Paul Simon (BMI).

87. William Provine, "Scientists, Face It! Science and Religion Are Incompatible," *The Scientist* 2, no. 16 (September 5, 1988): 10.

88. Bryan Appleyard, *Understanding the Present: Science and the Soul of Modern Man* (New York: Doubleday, 1993), pp. 8–9.

89. See Richard S. Westfall, *Science and Religion in Seventeenth-Century England* (New Haven, Conn.: Yale University Press, 1958), especially chapter 3, "The Harmony of Existence."

90. Richard Dawkins, *The Blind Watchmaker: Why the Evidence of Evolution Reveals a Universe without Design* (New York: W. W. Norton, 1987), p. 5.

91. Michael Behe, *Darwin's Black Box* (New York: The Free Press, 1996), p. 39.

92. Michael Behe, "The Modern Intelligent Design Hypothesis," in *God and Design: The Teleological Argument and Modern Science,* ed. Neil Manson (London: Routledge, 2003), p. 280.

93. William Dembski, *No Free Lunch: Why Specified Complexity Cannot Be Purchased without Intelligence* (Lanham, Md.: Rowman and Littlefield, 2002) and *The Design Inference* (Cambridge: Cambridge University Press, 1998).

94. Kenneth R. Miller, *Finding Darwin's God* (New York: HarperCollins, 1999).

95. Charles Darwin, *The Life and Letters of Charles Darwin,* vol. 1, ed. Francis Darwin (New York: Basic Books, 1959), p. 282.

96. *The Life and Letters of Charles Darwin,* vol. 2, ed. Francis Darwin (New York: Basic Books, 1959), p. 105.

97. F. R. Tennant, *Philosophical Theology,* vol. 2, *The World, the Soul, and God* (Cambridge: Cambridge University Press, 1956), pp. 78–120.

98. Ian Barbour, *Religion and Science* (New York: HarperCollins, 1997), p. 246.

99. John Paul II, "Message to Pontifical Academy of Sciences on Evolution," reprinted in *The Scientist* 11, no. 10 (May 12, 1997), pp. 8–9.

100. Langdon Gilkey, *Maker of Heaven and Earth: The Christian Doctrine of Creation in the Light of Modern Knowledge* (Garden City, N.Y.: Doubleday, 1959), pp. 8, 39.

101. Introduction to Manson, *God and Design,* p. 4.

102. Stephen Hawking, *A Brief History of Time* (New York: Bantam, 1988), pp. 121–22.

103. John Leslie, "The Anthropic Principle, World Ensemble, Design," *American Philosophical Quarterly* 19, no. 2 (April 1982), p. 141.

104. Paul Davies, *God and the New Physics* (New York: Simon and Schuster, 1983), pp. 187–88.

105. Ibid., p. 189.

106. Reported by Hoyle's friend and Harvard astronomer Owen Gingerich in "Dare a Scientist Believe in Design?" in *Evidence of Purpose: Scientists Discover the Creator,* ed. John Marks Templeton (New York: Continuum, 1996), p. 24.

107. Hoyle's comments are reported by Paul Davies in *Are We Alone?* (New York: HarperCollins, Basic Books, 1995), pp. 27–28, 118.

108. Freeman Dyson, *Disturbing the Universe* (New York: Harper and Row, 1979), p. 250.

109. Neil Manson, "There Is No Adequate Definition of 'Fine-Tuned' for Life," *Inquiry* 43 (September), pp. 341–51.

Auguste Rodin, *Burghers of Calais,* 1884–86

CHAPTER 5

THE SEARCH FOR ETHICAL VALUES

 CHAPTER OBJECTIVES

Upon completion of this chapter you should be able to

1. Explain the divine command theory and some common objections to it.
2. Show evidence of having reflected on the question, Why be moral?
3. Assess both subjective ethical relativism and conventional ethical relativism and critically evaluate several influential arguments for the latter.
4. Distinguish between psychological and ethical egoism, clarify certain common misconceptions about ethical egoism, and weigh the strength of various arguments for ethical egoism.
5. Describe the difference between consequentialist (teleological) and deontological approaches to ethics.
6. Summarize utilitarianism, point out some differences between the approaches of Bentham and Mill, and present some strengths and weaknesses of utilitarianism.
7. Explain Kant's notion of the good will, the two criteria for the moral worth of an action, and Kant's two versions of the categorical imperative.
8. State the difference between an ethics of conduct and virtue ethics and describe Aristotle's conception of virtues, including his doctrine of the mean.
9. Identify objections feminists have raised to traditional ethical theory and explain the differences between the two approaches to feminist ethics.
10. Discuss the ethical issues involved in embryonic stem cell research and the application of deontological ethics and consequentialism to this issue.

SCOUTING THE TERRITORY: *Why Be Moral?*

Why should you worry about being a moral person? Is moral goodness something that you should pursue for its own sake, or is it desirable simply because of the consequences? To use an analogy, no one enjoys going to the dentist to get his or her teeth drilled and most people do not choose to go on a severely restrictive diet for its own sake. Instead, we take these actions only because of the results they bring—physical health. If going to the dentist or dieting did not pay in terms of better health, we would have little reason to do either one. Is morality like that? Is the only reason for being a morally good person the fact that the external consequences are desirable whereas the external consequences of being immoral are undesirable?

The question, "Why be moral?" was taken up in Plato's dialogue the *Republic.* In this work, Glaucon (Plato's brother) asks Socrates whether justice (or moral goodness) is something that a person ought to pursue not only for its consequences but for its own sake. In order to goad Socrates, Glaucon defends the position that most reasonable people (if they were truly honest) would agree that being a just and moral person is not desirable in itself but is only desirable for the social rewards that it brings and the unpleasant consequences it avoids. For example, people are moral because being so will help them get along with others, give them a good reputation, and generally enhance their success in society. Similarly, people avoid being immoral because this behavior will lose them friends, damage their social standing, or land them in jail. In other words, being moral is purely an unpleasant but self-serving pursuit motivated by the desirability of the external results, similar to getting your teeth filled or going on a diet.

To make his point as sharply as possible, Glaucon tells the story of a shepherd named Gyges who discovers a ring that will make him invisible when it is turned a certain way. This ring enables him to do whatever he wishes without worrying about society's sanctions. Glaucon uses this story as a thought experiment to demonstrate his thesis. He thinks that it will reveal to us the true nature of morality. Think about it. If you had the power to make yourself invisible, you would no longer have to worry about being arrested, punished, or even rebuked. Under the cloak of invisibility, you could commit any kind of crime and misdeed you wished, and the general public as well as your friends would be unaware of your evil behavior. According to Glaucon's assessment of human nature, there would be no reason to be moral under these circumstances. Based on your observable behavior, you would seem to be a model citizen. At the same time, you could act as you wished in terms of your private behavior. Hence, according to Glaucon, not only would there be no reason to be moral, there would be every reason to get away with all that you could. Only the fool would do otherwise, since only appearances and the social consequences of our actions matter.

What do you think? Do you agree with Glaucon that most people would act this way? As you read about the story of Gyges, ask yourself how you would behave if you had the magic ring. The reading begins when Gyges first discovers his extraordinary powers.

FROM PLATO

Republic [1]

Now the shepherds met together, according to custom, that they might send their monthly report about the flocks to the King. Having the ring on his finger, Gyges came into their assembly and as he was sitting among them he chanced to turn the setting of the ring inside his hand, when instantly he became invisible to the rest of the company and they began to speak of him as if he were no longer present. He was astonished at this, and again touching the ring he turned the setting outward and reappeared. He made several trials of the ring, and always with the same result—when he turned the setting inward he became invisible, when outward he reappeared. Whereupon he contrived to be chosen one of the messengers who were sent to the court; where as soon as he arrived he seduced the Queen, and with her help conspired against the King and slew him and took the kingdom. Suppose now that there were two such magic rings, and a just man put on one of them and an unjust man the other. No man can be imagined to be of such an iron nature that he would stand fast in justice. No man would keep his hands off what was not his own when he could safely take what he liked out of the market, or go into houses and lie with anyone at his pleasure, or kill or release from prison whom he would, and in all respects be like a god among men. Then the actions of the just would be as the actions of the unjust; they would both come at last to the same point. And this we may truly affirm to be a great proof that a man is just, not willingly or because he thinks that justice is any good to him individually, but of necessity, for wherever anyone thinks that he can safely be unjust, there he is unjust. For all men believe in their hearts that injustice is far more profitable to the individual than justice, and he who argues as I have been supposing, will say that they are right. If you could imagine anyone obtaining this power of becoming invisible, and never doing any wrong or touching what was another's, he would be thought by the lookers on to be a most wretched idiot, although they would praise him to one another's faces, and keep up appearances with one another from a fear that they too might suffer injustice.

To expand on this experiment, Glaucon then asks us to imagine two men. One is perfectly unjust, or evil, and the other has a perfectly just, or moral, character. However, the evil man (being very clever) manages to fool his society and he maintains a spotless reputation while committing the worst crimes and immoral actions imaginable. On the other hand, the society totally misunderstands the good man. Although he is perfectly just, his society wrongly inflicts him with an evil reputation and persecutes and torments him because of it. Under these circumstances, would there be any point in being moral? Glaucon entertains the cynical view that it is not really necessary to be a truly moral person. It is sufficient merely to *appear* to be moral to one's society *if one can get away with it*. When John F. Kennedy was considering entering into national politics, his family members debated among themselves whether he would be a successful congressman. His father, Joseph Kennedy, ended the discussion by saying, "You must remember—it's not what you are that counts, but what people think you are."[2] Perhaps the elder Kennedy was right—people's opinions of you are important to being a successful candidate. However, do people's opinions make you a *qualified* candidate? Even if putting forth the appearance of success is useful in politics or business, is appearance all that matters in ethics? Glaucon thinks it is. What do you think?

Some people say that we can fool society in this way, but we can't fool God. They say the true reason for being moral (both on the inside as well as in our behavior) is to be rewarded in the afterlife and avoid unpleasant consequences. But isn't this viewpoint just a variation on Glaucon's? In both cases, the motive for being a moral person is a matter of the carrot or the stick (reward versus punishment). It's only a matter of detail as to whether you think it is society or God that wields the carrot and the stick.

Perhaps this issue can be made clearer with another analogy. We can imagine a young man who is engaged to an enormously wealthy young woman. With great eloquence he insists that he loves her for herself and not for her money. But upon finding out that she gave away all her fortune to the poor, he breaks off the engagement, admitting that he no longer has any reason to marry her. It is one thing to love a person for his or her own sake and for how your lover causes you to become enriched and fulfilled as a person. This relationship has rewards, but they are internal and intimately related to the person you love. It is quite another thing to profess love for that person for sake of the external rewards that the relationship will bring, such as money, purely physical pleasure, or status. Similarly, there is a difference between desiring to be a moral person for its own sake (including internal rewards such as self-respect) and being moral because of the external rewards it brings in society (or the afterlife).

STOP AND THINK

If you were like Gyges and had the power to make yourself invisible so that no one would know what you did and there would be no negative consequences for immoral behavior, would this power cause any changes in how you behave? If you were convinced there was no afterlife in which your behavior would be either rewarded or punished, would this belief make any changes in your ethical decisions? Would you choose to be the immoral person who was mistakenly thought to be a saint by your society, or would you choose to be the genuinely moral person who was misunderstood and punished by your society? Under these circumstances would you agree or disagree with Glaucon that there would be no point in being just and moral? Why?

Although all the philosophical questions discussed in this book have far-reaching and practical consequences for how we live, none have such a direct and immediate impact on the persons we are and how we conduct our daily lives as does our thinking about morality. Although the topic of ethics is complex and has many dimensions, the questions raised by Plato's story of the ring cut to the heart of the issue. As you go through the various theories on ethics covered in this chapter, you should consider how the different philosophers would respond to Glaucon. At the end of this introductory section on ethics, we briefly consider Glaucon's questions once again. But before we do that, we need to look more closely at the nature of morality.

 ## CHARTING THE TERRAIN OF ETHICS: *What Are the Issues?*

What Is Ethics?

Ethics is quite a different philosophical field from those that we have studied thus far. In previous chapters we have pondered questions such as: "Does God exist?" "What is knowledge?" "How is the mind related to the body?" "Do we have free will?" In our studies of all the previous philosophical fields, we have been attempting to *describe* what *is* true about the world. In ethics, however, we are concerned with what we *ought* to do, what consequences *ought* to be achieved, and what sort of persons we *ought* to become. In other words, ethics is a *normative* inquiry and not a descriptive one. It seeks to establish and prescribe norms, standards, or principles for evaluating our actual practices. Some authors distinguish morality and ethics. They speak of *descriptive morality* as referring to the actual practices of a people and a culture and its beliefs about which behaviors are good or bad. In this sense, anthropologists study and describe various cultures' moral beliefs and practices without being concerned with whether those beliefs are genuinely good. On the other hand, *normative ethics* is used to designate the philosophical task of discerning which moral principles are rationally defensible and which actions are genuinely good or bad. *Ethical theories* are the end products of this type of philosophical inquiry. Using this distinction, we could say that it was *moral* in Nazi Germany to persecute the Jews (*descriptive morality*) at the same time that we say that from the standpoint of *normative ethics* this practice was abhorrently *immoral*. However, because this chapter is not concerned simply with the practices or beliefs of this or that culture but with the normative questions of which moral beliefs are rational and which actions are genuinely good, I use *morality, ethics,* and related terms interchangeably.

CONCEPTUAL TOOLS: *Philosophical Ethics and Religion*

Because ethics seeks to establish principles that prescribe what we ought or ought not to do, it has similarities to other domains of human existence that seek to guide behavior, such as religion. In fact, many people think that not only do religion and ethics overlap but that they are inseparable. It will be worthwhile, therefore, to pause on our journey to examine and distinguish philosophical ethics and religion.

It is a historical fact that religion is deeply bound up with morality. It would be hard, if not impossible, to find an established religious tradition that does not contain extensive ethical teachings. In fact, some of the great religions of the world, such as Buddhism and Confucianism, are primarily ethical outlooks on life rather than a series of doctrines about a deity. However, in spite of the historical influence of religion on our moral traditions, some authors claim that religion promotes an inferior brand of morality that inhibits mature moral development.[3] On the other hand, some would argue that religious considerations enhance morality in one or more of the following ways: Religion can inspire us to be moral, reinforce our willpower to be moral, give us hope that good will ultimately prevail over evil, provide us with moral guidance, and demonstrate that morality is deeply rooted in the nature of reality itself.[4] Notice that a person could agree that religion enriches personal morality in these ways but still believe that there could be a viable morality without religion. As interesting as these claims may be, it would take us too far afield to evaluate them. Instead, we need to take a brief look at a related but much stronger claim: "Morality necessarily depends on religion." The claim that religion is necessary for morality was eloquently stated by Leo Tolstoy:

> The attempts to found a morality apart from religion are like the attempts of children, who, wishing to transplant a flower that pleases them, pluck it from the roots that seem to them unpleasing and superfluous, and stick it rootless into the ground. Without religion there can be no real, sincere morality, just as without roots there can be no real flower.[5]

The **divine command theory** is the theory that the rightness or wrongness of an action is intrinsically related to the fact that God either commands it or forbids it. There are a number of versions of this theory, and it is defended by some (but not all) theologians and religious philosophers.[6] However, many philosophers (even religious ones) think that a sound ethical theory can be developed independently of religious assumptions, and furthermore, they argue that there are problems with divine command theories. The first problem is the lack of agreement as to which religious text or authority should guide our ethical deliberations: the Bible, for example, or the Koran, the Hindu *Upanishads,* Buddha's teachings, and so on. To successfully live together in the same society, we need to arrive at

divine command theory
the theory that the rightness or wrongness of an action is intrinsically related to the fact that God either commands it or forbids it

some common ethical norms. But how can we do this in our pluralistic society if there is no agreement as to which religious authority (if any) should be followed? Furthermore, how can people be held ethically accountable for their behavior if many have never been exposed to whatever religious tradition is supposed to be normative? The second problem is that even if we agree to live under the guidance of a particular religious tradition, we may disagree as to how to interpret its teachings. For example, Christians both defend and attack capital punishment on the basis of the same tradition and sacred texts. Similarly, although the Bible often condemns lying, it contains passages in which God is said to reward people for lying on his behalf and even commands individuals to lie.[7] Minimally, some sort of philosophical reflection is necessary to sort out all these discrepancies. Third, some ethical questions cannot be answered by traditional religious teachings apart from philosophical considerations. Is it morally acceptable to make cloned duplicates of humans? When numerous people need an organ transplant or a kidney dialysis machine but the medical supplies are scarce, what is the just way to allocate these resources? To what extent do journalists have an obligation to serve the public's right to know and to what extent do they have an obligation to protect an individual's privacy? Most religious traditions are clear on ethical topics such as adultery, murder, and stealing, but many ethical dilemmas in contemporary society are not addressed by these traditions.

A further problem is that the divine command theory makes it impossible or meaningless to declare that God and his will are good without some prior conception of moral goodness that is understood independently of God and his will. This point is illustrated by the following "Stop and Think" exercise.

STOP AND THINK

Consider the following claim of the divine command theory:

- Good is defined as *that which God wills*.

Now substitute this definition of good into the following claim:

- God's will is *good*.

Why is the resulting claim an empty one?

This exercise illustrates the fact that defining "good" in terms of God's will makes it impossible to say anything meaningful about the goodness of God or his will, for we end up with the empty statement "God's will is that which God wills." Thus, it seems that we need some sort of independent concept of "good."

In Plato's dialogue *Euthyphro,* Socrates raises the question, "Do the gods approve of certain actions because these actions are good, or are certain actions good because the gods approve of them?" We can phrase this question in terms of monotheism by asking, "Does God approve of certain actions because these actions are good, or are certain actions good because God approves of them?" The first alternative is Plato's answer and the second is that of the divine command theory. Let's look at the second alternative first: If "good" and "bad" are simply arbitrary labels that God attaches to actions based on his sovereign will, then it seems that God could have declared that hatred, adultery, stealing, and murder are morally good. Some philosophers have bitten the bullet and accepted this conclusion. (William of Ockham, a 14th-century Christian philosopher, seems to have defended this problematic conclusion.) On the other hand, most philosophers have found this conclusion abhorrent. The philosopher Gottfried Leibniz (1646–1716) explains why:

In saying, therefore, that things are not good according to any standard of goodness, but simply by the will of God, it seems to me that one destroys, without realizing it, all the love of God and all his glory; for why praise him for what he has done, if he would be equally praiseworthy in doing the contrary?[8]

In contrast, the first alternative's claim that "God approves of certain actions because they are good" suggests that God has a reason for approving certain actions—the reason being that they are good. But if so, then we should be able to evaluate the goodness (or badness) of the actions themselves and approve or disapprove of them for the same reason that God does, which implies that we can have a conception of ethics that is independent of God's will (although it might be consistent with it).

The final reason for questioning the necessity of religion for ethics is that many people are morally good persons but are not religious and were not raised in a religious background. Somehow these people are able to distinguish right and wrong, come to some of the same moral conclusions as religious people, and live morally commendable lives without appealing to a religious basis for their ethical stance.

These considerations suggest that whatever ethical guidance someone may find in a particular religious tradition, everyone needs to engage in philosophical reflection on ethics based on human experience and reason and not merely authority or tradition.*

Dimensions of Ethical Evaluation

One problem we face in seeking to reflect on ethics is that the factors relevant to making moral decisions are so numerous that it is difficult to know what role they should play in our moral judgments. Typically, ethical theories have something to say about actions, motives, consequences, and character, and subject these factors to moral evaluation. But after all is said and done, which of these factors is most important or has priority over the others? The following thought experiment will get you thinking about these priorities and will prepare you to examine the answers offered by the various ethical theories.

 THOUGHT EXPERIMENT: *Are All Cases of Truth Telling Equally Moral?*

The moral evaluation of actions is certainly an important issue in ethics. We frequently judge that a person did the right thing or did what was wrong. For example, we are told that it is good to tell the truth or, even more strongly, it is our moral obligation to tell the truth and not lie. The following three scenarios depict examples of telling the truth. Consider the ways in which they differ. In each case, think about how you would evaluate the action morally and why you made the judgments you did.

1. When Andre was asked, "Did you have a good reason for missing the required morning meeting?" he is tempted to lie, saying that he had a class scheduled at that time. Instead, however, he tells the truth: "No, I was too lazy to get out of bed." He tells the truth because it is his moral obligation to do so.

(continued . . .)

---

*Some philosophers have attempted to reformulate a divine command theory of ethics that avoids some of these objections. For two examples, see the "Suggestions for Further Reading" at the end of this chapter.

(. . . continued)

2. When Brandee was asked, "Did you have a good reason for missing the required morning meeting?" she is tempted to lie, saying that she had a class scheduled at that time. Instead, however, she tells the truth: "No, I was too lazy to get out of bed." She tells the truth because she knows her excuse can be checked out and her lie exposed.

3. Chris says to the dean, "Do you know what? Professor Fields came to class sober today." That statement is the absolute truth because the professor never took an alcoholic drink in his life. However, Chris knows that the dean will infer that Professor Fields sometimes does not come to class sober and hopes that this inference will ruin this lousy teacher's reputation.

All things being equal, most of us would say that telling the truth is the morally right thing to do, and in these three cases, each person told the truth. However, these three cases have significant differences. Andre tells the truth because it is his moral duty to do so, even though the consequences may be bad for him. In the same situation, Brandee tells the truth not because she wants to do the right thing for its own sake but because she thinks she won't be able to get away with a lie. If Brandee believed that she could tell a lie and never be discovered, do you think she would do it? Chris tells the literal truth, but with the motive of deceiving the dean and hurting the professor. Clearly, the motive of the person who performed the action plays a role in our moral judgments. The next three cases ask you to consider the person's motives in light of other factors that are present.

THOUGHT EXPERIMENT: *How Important Are Motives?*

Again, consider the ways in which each case is similar to or different from the others. Think about how you would evaluate each action morally and why you made the judgments you did.

1. Danielle's roommate Tasha asks her if she thinks the short story that Tasha has just written is any good. Danielle says that it is a wonderfully written story, which is a lie because she really thinks it is wretched. However, she doesn't want to hurt Tasha's feelings. Based on Danielle's encouragement, Tasha reads the story to a writing group and is thoroughly humiliated. She never trusts her roommate again.

2. Out of compassion, Esther gives $500 to a charity for starving children. Inspired by her example, many other students donate to the charity money that they would ordinarily spend partying. However, in order to obtain the money for the charity, Esther had to steal it from a rich stranger's purse. The stranger has so much money that she never realizes it is missing. As a result of Esther's generosity and example, many children are fed.

3. Fred shoves Reggie to the ground simply to be mean. Unintentionally, however, his doing so had the consequence of shoving Reggie out of the way of a falling brick that might have killed him.

In the first two cases, each person is acting from a good motive—the desire to help people. For Danielle, however, the consequences turned out badly. To what degree should this consequence affect our moral judgment of her actions? Even though Danielle thought the consequences of her lie would be for the best, could she really know what the consequences would be? Would it have been better if she had stuck with her duty of telling the truth and let the consequences take care of themselves? What if the consequences had been good? Suppose Danielle's lie had encouraged Tasha to write more and better stories? If both her motive and the consequences had been good, would her lie then be morally acceptable? Esther also had a good motive—she wanted to help children. Esther's situation had good consequences and no obviously bad consequences. Children were helped, students were inspired to be charitable, and the stranger never missed her money. Does it make a difference that Esther's generosity was the result of an act of theft? Can an action be morally wrong if the immediate consequences are good, if there are no bad consequences, and if it is done from a good motive? In Fred's case, the action (shoving someone out of harm's way) would be commendable if done by a quick-thinking, courageous person of good will. However, Fred's motive was to harm Reggie. So, do you think that motives are more important or less important than good consequences when you assess the morality of an action? The next thought experiment asks you to assess the role of consequences in making moral judgments.

 THOUGHT EXPERIMENT: *How Important Are Consequences?*

1. Gary has been charged with delivering a professor's painting to a museum. On his way there, he notices a small girl drowning in a river. Knowing that every second counts, he throws her the painting to use as a float until he can get to her. Unable to spare the time fooling with his clothes, he then jumps into the water wearing the good suit that he borrowed from his roommate. In spite of Gary's best efforts, the child drowns. He didn't save the child, but he ruined both the professor's painting and his friend's suit.
2. Hallie sacrifices her weekends to work on a project that builds homes for the poor. She figures that the publicity from this work will help her campaign for student body president and will look good on her résumé. The families that move into the homes she has helped construct are overjoyed with the fruits of her labor.

In these last two examples, the actions considered by themselves are morally good. Gary's motive was to fulfill his duty to save lives when possible, but his consequences turned out badly. Would this fact be relevant or irrelevant in our moral assessment of Gary's actions? Hallie performed a good action and, unlike poor Gary's failed efforts, the consequences were exceedingly good both for the families and for herself. But then there is the nagging problem of her motive. She was acting only for her own selfish gain and not for the people she helped. After considering all three of these thought experiments, what role do you think the goodness or badness of actions, motives, and consequences should play in ethics? All three factors may be important, but the ethical theories we examine in this chapter give priority to one or more of these factors over the others. In terms of your current understanding, how do you think the factors should be weighted?

THE QUESTION "WHY BE MORAL?" RECONSIDERED

Glaucon's Question

Before looking at various theories that concern how to decide what is right or wrong, we first need to ask why such a decision is an important issue at all. In the beginning of this chapter the question "What is the point of morality?" was raised by Glaucon, one of the characters in Plato's *Republic*. This question actually can be broken down into two questions: (1) "Why does society need morality?" and (2) "Why should I be moral?"

The first question is the easier one to answer. Thomas Hobbes, a 17th-century British philosopher, answered that question by imagining that everybody lived in a "state of nature" in which there was no government, no society, and no commonly agreed-upon morality.[9] In such a situation, everybody would be serving his or her own individual interests without regard for anyone else. Without laws or morality you would be free to club people over the head to steal their food. The problem is that someone stronger than you could then beat you up and steal your food. Hobbes says that human existence under these conditions would be "a war of all against all" and that everybody would find life to be "solitary, poor, nasty, brutish, and short." For this reason, Hobbes says, people would come together and agree to restrict their own behavior if others restrict their behavior and would form a government to enforce these agreements. In this way, both morality and law would emerge. The end result would be, as Glaucon described, that people would behave morally to avoid social and legal sanctions.

The problem is that this account explains only why I would want there to be moral laws that people around me feel compelled to follow. This situation is clearly in my self-interest. However, it does not answer the second question: "Why should I be moral?" If everyone else was behaving morally, but I only *appeared* to be moral, I would have the best of both worlds. I could cheat, lie, and steal to my own advantage while admonishing everyone else to be honest and truthful when dealing with me. If I could successfully pull this off (and some people seem to), why shouldn't I behave this way? The reply may be that it would be inconsistent or *unfair* to expect others to be honest with me when I chose to be dishonest. This answer won't do, however, for *fairness* is a moral principle and telling me I ought to be fair is telling me I ought to be moral, and that brings us back to the original question: "Why should I be moral?"

Morality and the Self

Perhaps, in the final analysis, it is impossible to convince someone to be moral if they do not already appreciate the importance of morality for its own sake. Someone could argue that you ought to act morally because of the consequences of behaving this way. The desired consequences of acting morally might be winning society's approval or avoiding God's punishment and earning his rewards. But, as was pointed out in the original discussion of Glaucon's story, this attitude does not represent a concern for morality. Its motive is nothing more than a calculating, self-seeking, prudent concern for one's own gain. If morality serves some other ends or interests outside the moral domain, then we might as well dispense with morality altogether and simply concern ourselves with the most efficient way to achieve those other, nonmoral goals. The moral point of view is something a person either has or does not have. People who have acquired the moral point of view by the way they were raised or through the events in their own personal development may fail in their moral endeavors and sometimes yield to temptation, but they will understand why

Have several friends read the following two situations and discuss their answers to the questions:

> Suppose someone whom you have known for years and who has done many things for you asks a favor of you that will take considerable time and trouble when you had planned on doing something else. You have no doubt that helping out the person is what you ought to do but you ask yourself all the same *why* you ought to do it. Or suppose you tell a blind news vendor that it's a five-dollar bill you are handing him, and he gives you four dollars and some coins in change, whereas actually you handed him only a one-dollar bill. Almost everyone would agree that such an act is wrong. But some people who agree may still ask, "Tell me why I shouldn't do it just the same."[10]

Which of your friends' answers do you think was best? Why? How do your friends' answers compare to the answers given in the text?

PHILOSOPHY
in the
MARKETPLACE

morality should be their goal. Morality is a commitment to a certain life plan, a decision to be a certain sort of person.

On the other hand, people who reject the moral point of view will see no point in worrying about whether an action is right or wrong. They may be satisfied with their form of life, may feel themselves more or less happy and fulfilled human beings, and may manage to get along in society, but their sense of fulfillment and their development as persons are limited. Such persons are like Dickens's character Scrooge, who is blind to the value of friendship and gloats that his life is better than ours because he doesn't have to buy anyone Christmas presents.[11] Or, the person who is blind to morality is like a little child who has not yet developed the capacity to have romantic feelings. To this child, the time and effort we spend in nurturing a romantic relationship is a silly waste when we could be having the supreme pleasure of playing video games. Or, compare the morally challenged person to the totally color-blind person who sees only shades of gray and wonders why we make such a fuss over sunsets. In these analogies, the persons think they are serving their own interests and believe that they know what life is about, but only because they have not experienced an important dimension of human experience (friendship, romantic passion, or colors) that has the potential to make life richer. If Scrooge, in particular, had lived his entire life without any meaningful human relationships, he would have been left a severely limited human being. But true friendships require us to respect others and to sometimes sacrifice our own self-interests for another, and with these actions we have entered into the moral point of view.

In saying that morality enables us to flourish as human beings, that it makes us more fulfilled and richer persons, aren't I really saying that morality pays, that it serves our self-interests? Haven't I now returned to Glaucon's cynical position? The answer is that there is a difference between short-term, superficial self-interest (Glaucon's concern) and long-term, deep self-interest. This difference can be explained by referring to the example of friendships once again. At the superficial level, a friendship can be costly in terms of the time, sacrifices, and emotional energy it requires. However, is there a value to close friends? Do friendships serve our self-interest? I think the answer is that friendships are for our good not because of what we get, but because of what we *become*. If we value friendships only for their superficial payoffs (money, sex, social status), we are like a person who has experienced puddles, but never the ocean. A deep friendship develops capacities within us that we would have never discovered in any other way. Morality is like that.

I practice my basketball shots, play my guitar, learn to program in a new computer language, and try to solve challenging intellectual problems, but not because these pursuits will win me fame or fortune. Instead, I want to be the best person I possibly can and develop what skills and capacities I have for their own sake. Making myself the best person I can be, whether athletically, musically, intellectually, or morally, is a matter of fulfilling my long-term, deep self-interests. Particularly with respect to morality, there is a paradox here. I can best fulfill myself by making my narrow self-interests secondary to my moral commitments. Self-fulfillment and happiness are usually not found by pursuing them directly. Instead, they are a by-product of pursuits that lead us beyond ourselves. But by being less concerned with what I get out of life, I open up new dimensions of what I can become as a person. As Socrates said, our most important possession is our soul, or our inner person. Our health, careers, fame, friends, and material possessions can come and go as the result of external circumstances, but nothing external can affect the persons that we are. In this area of our lives we are in control and can make ourselves as excellent or corrupt as possible. Why should we choose to live with a worse self when we can live with an excellent one instead? This focus on ethics as preserving the integrity of one's self was captured in Robert Bolt's play *A Man for All Seasons.* It tells the true story of Thomas More, a 16th-century government figure in England. At this time, King Henry VIII had divorced his wife to marry another woman and asserted his authority over that of the Church. He required all his officials to take an oath of allegiance to him, approving of what he had done, or be executed. However, such an oath would have violated More's ethical and religious convictions. More's wife and daughter visit him in prison, trying to convince him that an oath is just words and paying this lip service to the king would have no real ethical implications. To this, More replies:

> When a man takes an oath . . . he's holding his own self in his own hands. Like water. (*He cups his hands*) And if he opens his fingers *then*—he needn't hope to find himself again.[12]

More's words are a good description of what morality is all about. It is holding my own self in my hands and making sure that I don't lose it by grasping at other things.

CHOOSING A PATH: *What Are My Options Concerning Ethics?*

Ethical relativism is the position that there are no objective or universally valid moral principles, because all moral judgments are simply a matter of human opinion. In other words, there is no right or wrong apart from what people consider to be right or wrong. Obviously, all individuals have the responsibility of forming their own opinions about morality. It is equally obvious that it is more difficult to find the correct answer to ethical questions than it is to find the correct answer to arithmetic problems. But the ethical relativist goes further and claims that there are no objective considerations by means of which we can say that a particular moral judgment is mistaken or that some moral judgments are better than others. This position comes in two versions, depending upon whose opinion is considered to be the standard for morality.

Subjective ethical relativism is the doctrine that what is right or wrong is solely a matter of each individual's personal opinion. Just as some people like the color purple and some

ethical relativism the position that there are no objective or universally valid moral principles, because all moral judgments are simply a matter of human opinion

subjective ethical relativism the doctrine that what is right or wrong is solely a matter of each individual's personal opinion

detest it, and each person's judgment on this matter is simply a matter of his or her individual taste, so there is no standard other than each person's own opinion when it comes to right or wrong. This doctrine implies that it is impossible for an individual to be mistaken about what is right or wrong.

Conventional ethical relativism (conventionalism) refers to the claim that what is *really* right or wrong is relative to each particular society and is based on what that society *believes* is right or wrong. For example, whether it is moral for women to wear shorts is a question of whether you are talking about mainstream American society or the Iranian culture. Although it is not too controversial to acknowledge that standards of appropriate dress are culturally relative, the conventional ethical relativist makes the stronger claim that *all* moral issues are like this one. In other words, there are no universal objective moral standards that can be used to evaluate the ethical opinions and practices of a particular culture. This doctrine implies that it is impossible for a society to be mistaken about what is right or wrong.

Ethical objectivism is the view that there are universal and objectively valid moral principles that are relative neither to the individual nor to society. Because objectivism is a very general doctrine that covers a wide range of more specific ethical theories, various objectivists will differ as to what the correct moral principles are and how we can know them. Nevertheless, they all agree that in every concrete situation there are morally correct and morally wrong ways to act. Furthermore, they would agree that if a certain action in a given situation is morally right or wrong for a particular person, then it will be the same for anyone who is relevantly similar and facing relevantly similar circumstances. Ethical objectivism implies that it is possible for an individual or an entire society to sincerely believe that their actions are morally right at the same time that they are deeply mistaken about this assumption.

The next four theories all fall under the heading of ethical objectivism. Although these theories disagree about what ethical principles should be followed, they all agree that there are one or more nonarbitrary, nonsubjective, universal moral principles that determine whether an action is right or wrong.

Ethical egoism is the theory that people always have a moral obligation to do only what is in their own self-interest. According to this position, the locus of value is the individual and there can be no higher value for me than my own life and its well-being and no higher value for you than your own life. This theory is a version of ethical objectivism and should not be mistaken for subjective ethical relativism, for the egoist would say that my moral judgments can be wrong if I put another person's interests before my own. Of course, the egoist's principle will dictate different, and sometimes competing, courses of action. For example, it is in my best interests to promote the flourishing of the philosophy program at my university, whereas it is in a coach's interest to promote the flourishing of the football program. Nevertheless, the egoist would maintain that competing interests can lead to the best outcome. In business, for example, if each company tries to capture the market with the best product, society as a whole benefits. Similarly, in a court of law, each lawyer promotes the best interests of his or her client, and we presume that this procedure will help ensure that all aspects of the case will be revealed.

Utilitarianism is the theory that the right action is the one that produces the greatest amount of happiness for the greatest number of people. Accordingly, utilitarians claim that the morality of an action cannot be divorced from its consequences. The utilitarian would agree with the egoist that a person's own interests need to play a role in moral decisions. However, according to utilitarianism, a person's own interests have to balance against those of all others in calculating the morality of an action. This formula would allow the same

conventional ethical relativism the claim that what is really right or wrong is relative to each particular society; also called ethical conventionalism

ethical objectivism the view that there are universal and objectively valid moral principles that are relative neither to the individual nor to society

ethical egoism the theory that people ought always to do only what is in their own self-interest

utilitarianism the theory that the right action is the one that produces the greatest amount of happiness for the greatest number of people

Kantian ethics the theory that we have absolute moral duties that are determined by reason and that are not affected by the consequences

virtue ethics any theory that sees the primary focus of ethics to be the character of the person rather than that person's actions or duties

feminist ethics the attempt to correct male biases in traditional ethical theory by emphasizing relationships over abstract principles and compassion over analytical reason

type of action to be moral in one set of circumstances and immoral in a different situation if the consequences were different. Nevertheless, while the moral evaluation of an action may be relative to the circumstances, an unchanging, universal, ethical principle is still being followed.

Kantian ethics is a theory that states we have absolute moral duties that are determined by reason and that are not affected by the consequences. Obviously, its approach to morality is radically different from that of the utilitarians. For Kantian ethics, the rightness or wrongness of an action is intrinsic to the type of action it is. (When we examine this theory in more detail later in this chapter, we discuss how the Kantian determines what these duties are.) The Kantian, for example, would say that we have a moral obligation to tell the truth, even if it produces harm. On the other hand, lying is considered wrong, even if it produces a good outcome.

Virtue ethics refers to any theory that sees the primary focus of ethics to be the character of the person rather than that person's actions or duties. The previous theories are concerned primarily with rules or principles for deciding how to act. They do not ignore the issue of what makes a good person, but they define the goodness of persons in terms of either what actions they perform or what principles they employ. According to virtue ethics, however, these theories reverse the proper order. The good person is not one who performs good actions, but good actions are defined as those that a person with a good moral character would do. Whereas the previous theories ask, "What should I do?" virtue ethics asks, "What sort of person should I be?" Plato would fall under the heading of virtue ethics, because he gave very little specific guidance on how to make moral decisions. Instead, he talked at length on how to attain a morally sound character.

Feminist ethics is a new development in recent decades that questions some of the fundamental assumptions of traditional ethical theory. Feminist theory is still developing and full of multiple perspectives, so it is hard to summarize it in a brief statement. For example, some feminists agree with ethical relativism, whereas others are more aligned with some version of ethical objectivism. However, in spite of their differences, most feminists agree that there are distinctively male and female ways of viewing a situation and that these views will make a decided difference in our ethical perspective. Feminists complain that traditional ethical theories are one-sided because they typically represent the style, aims, concerns, questions, and theoretical assumptions of men. Some psychological studies, for example, seem to suggest that males tend toward a judicial model of ethical decision making in which abstract principles and reason predominate. Females, however, are more concerned with relationships and the emotional textures of a situation. These differences play out in completely different theoretical approaches to ethical issues. Whereas some feminists want to replace the male-biased approaches with new perspectives, others simply want to supplement the historically one-sided approaches with a more balanced perspective. Although feminist theorists bring a fresh new perspective to ethics, they often work within and use the resources of the other theories as much as they critique the limitations of those theories.

This spectrum of ethical theories is summarized in tables 5.1 and 5.2. These tables are followed by a questionnaire for you to take. Unfortunately, it is impossible to represent feminist ethics in these simplified schemes because writers who can be characterized as representing the feminist perspective on ethics can be found within each of the traditional categories. Feminist writers are distinguished not so much by how they answer the following questions, but by the way that they bring gender issues to bear on the traditional questions and theories in moral philosophy.

TABLE 5.1 *Three Questions Concerning Moral Relativity and the Answers of the Two Forms of Ethical Relativism*

	Are Moral Principles Relative to Human Opinion?	Are Moral Judgments Relative to Each Individual's Opinion?	Are Moral Judgments Relative to Each Society's Opinion?
Subjective Ethical Relativism	Yes	Yes	No
Conventional Ethical Relativism	Yes	No	Yes

Note that because both the subjective ethical relativist and the conventional ethical relativist deny that there are any moral principles that apply to all persons, they would answer no to the questions in table 5.2. On the other hand, because the advocates of each of the four positions in table 5.2 are all ethical objectivists, they would answer no to the three questions in table 5.1.

TABLE 5.2 *Five Questions Concerning the Nature of Morality and the Answers of Four Kinds of Ethical Objectivism*

	Are There Moral Principles or Truths That Are Objectively Valid?	Is Serving One's Own Self-Interest the Only Moral Duty?	Do the Consequences of an Action Make It Right or Wrong?	Are Actions Right or Wrong in Themselves, Independently of Their Consequences?	Is Morality More Concerned with the Character of a Virtuous Person Than with Rules of Conduct?
Ethical Egoism	Yes	Yes	Yes—but only the consequences for the individual performing the action	No	No
Utilitarianism	Yes	No	Yes	No	No
Kantian Ethics	Yes	No	No	Yes	Morality is concerned with both
Virtue Ethics	Yes	No	No	Only as they relate to certain character traits	Yes

WHAT DO I THINK? *Questionnaire on Ethics, Actions, Consequences, Motives, and Character*

	Agree	Disagree
1. Moral judgments are not true except as being an expression of personal opinion. Just as "Oysters are delicious" expresses the speaker's personal opinion, so *all* moral judgments, such as "Capital punishment is morally wrong" or "Physician-assisted suicide is morally permissible," are sheerly a matter of personal opinion.		
2. When we declare that an action is morally right or wrong, we simply mean that the majority of the people in our society consider it to be right or wrong.		
3. It is possible that an action (such as owning slaves) could be morally wrong even if the person who did it or all the members of that person's society sincerely believed that the action was morally permissible.		
4. The only moral duty that anyone ever has is to do those actions that will be good for him or her in some way.		
5. The only thing that counts in deciding if an action is morally good is whether it leads to the overall best possible consequences for the greatest number of people. Motives are irrelevant.		
6. Some actions (such as lying) are always morally wrong even if, in a particular case, the action would result in more happiness than unhappiness.		
7. What makes an action morally right or wrong depends entirely on whether it is what a morally virtuous person would do. Any application of moral rules is secondary and after the fact.		
8. Males and females approach ethical issues with different perspectives and different concerns.		
9. It is morally wrong for anyone, in any culture, at any time, under any circumstances, to torture an innocent child for no reason at all.		

KEY TO THE QUESTIONNAIRE ON ETHICS

Statement 1 is an expression of subjective ethical relativism. It conflicts with statements 3 and 9.

Statement 2 expresses conventional ethical relativism. It also conflicts with statements 3 and 9.

Statement 3 represents ethical objectivism, because it implies that right and wrong are independent of human opinion. It conflicts with statements 1 and 2.

Statement 4 is the defining principle of ethical egoism.

Statement 5 is a statement of utilitarianism.

Statement 6 expresses Kantian ethics.

Statement 7 represents virtue ethics.

Statement 8 represents one version of feminist ethics. Because feminist theory is so diverse, different versions of feminist ethics could be compatible with any of the other statements.

Statement 9 is an expression of ethical objectivism. It conflicts with statements 1 and 2.

5.1 ETHICAL RELATIVISM VERSUS OBJECTIVISM

LEADING QUESTIONS: *Ethical Relativism and Ethical Objectivism*

1. *Questions from the Ethical Relativist:* Why do people disagree over whether raw oysters taste good? Why do some people like tattoos and body piercing and others find these personal adornments distasteful? Why is it considered morally permissible to wear brief swimsuits in some cultures and immoral in others? Why do some people think abortion is morally permissible and others think it is absolutely wrong? Why do people disagree over the morality of capital punishment? Is there a reason why these disagreements and disputes never seem to be resolved? Could the answer be that *all* these cases are simply a matter of the preferences and viewpoints of particular individuals or society?

2. *Questions from the Ethical Relativist:* Who's to judge what is right or wrong? How can we say that the moral beliefs and practices of another individual or society are wrong simply because they differ from our own morality? Isn't it arrogant, presumptuous, and intolerant to do so? Isn't it better to live and let live, deciding for ourselves what we think is right or wrong and allowing others to do the same for themselves? Hasn't history shown that wars, persecutions, and inquisitions have resulted when people decide that they will be the moral authorities for the rest of humanity?

3. *Questions from the Ethical Objectivist:* Suppose that you have fallen into the hands of a group of scientists in another country. They want to perform medical experiments on you that will be extremely painful and will result in your death. They justify these experiments by saying that you will help them advance science and that the research leading to your death will result in life-saving drugs that will benefit thousands in their country and throughout the world. You protest that what they are about to do is morally wrong. However, they patiently explain that morality is relative and is only a matter of personal or social opinion. Because they think that using your body for their ends is right and killing for the sake of medical research is legal in their society, they explain that your moral outrage is simply a matter of your personal opinion. They ask, "Who are you to say that we are morally wrong? Each person has to judge rightness or wrongness for himself or herself." How would you attempt to convince them that what they are about to do is morally wrong? Doesn't this scenario show that it is implausible to suppose that morality is subjective? Isn't it absurd to claim that as long as the scientists sincerely believe they are doing the right thing, no one should question their actions?

4. *Questions from the Ethical Objectivist:* Philosopher James Rachels argues that certain moral rules are essential for any society to survive and that a healthy society will condone violations of these rules only under exceptional conditions. The three rules he lists are (1) infants should be cared for, (2) lying is wrong, and (3) murder is wrong. What would a society be like if it did not value these basic moral rules? In 1964, anthropologist Colin Turnbull discovered the Ik, an isolated tribe in northern Uganda who were facing severe conditions of starvation. Consequently, food was no longer shared, but fathers and mothers gathered it for themselves and kept it from their children. After age three, children had to fend for themselves. The desperate children learned to steal food by extracting it from the mouths of the elderly and those who were weaker. Honesty was thought foolish and clever lying was valued, whereas affection and trust were considered dysfunctional. According to Turnbull's account, the society was in a state of near-total cultural collapse because of the breakdown of its moral and social fabric. Isn't it implausible to suppose that moral rules such as those Rachels lists are sheerly relative and optional? Can morality be completely a matter of personal or social preference? Isn't there a universal core morality that is essential to human flourishing?

Leading questions 1 and 2 represent the viewpoint of ethical relativism. *Ethical relativism* is the theory that there are no objective or universally valid moral principles, because all moral judgments are simply a matter of human opinion. Ethical relativism is the theory in ethics that corresponds to epistemological relativism in the theory of knowledge (see section 2.5). If a person believes there is no objective truth in general (epistemological relativism), then he or she must believe that there are no ethical truths (ethical relativism). The reverse is not necessarily true, however, for a person could be a relativist in ethics but believe there are objective truths in other areas (such as science).

Ethical relativism comes in two versions depending on how the relativist answers the question, Are moral principles relative to the individual or to society? The first alternative is *subjective ethical relativism,* or *ethical subjectivism,* and the second version is *conventional ethical relativism,* or *ethical conventionalism.* Questions 3 and 4 represent the outlook of ethical objectivism. *Ethical objectivism* is the view that there are universal and objectively valid moral principles that are relative to neither the individual nor society. We first examine the two versions of ethical relativism and then survey the case for ethical objectivism.

SURVEYING THE CASE FOR ETHICAL RELATIVISM

As leading question 1 illustrates, ethical relativism seeks to account for all the disagreement in matters that touch on ethics or values. The reason for this disagreement, the relativist claims, is that there is no objective basis for deciding between conflicting moral outlooks. In contrast, other areas of human experience, such as mathematics, physics, and medicine, have clear-cut procedures for coming to agreement. Furthermore, in the sciences, at least, the objects studied (e.g., atoms or tumors) exist independently of our opinions of them, making it possible to test our theories against the brute facts. On the other hand, the subjects of ethical discourse, such as right, wrong, good, and bad, do not seem to be waiting out in the world for us to discover their properties. Hence, the ethical relativist concludes that right and wrong have no existence or properties apart from human opinions concerning them. As question 2 illustrates, relativists place a high value on tolerance because they believe there is no true story about ethics and they see ethical judgments primarily as preferences for a certain type of conduct, lifestyle, or society.

In examining ethical relativism we need to get clear on exactly what is claimed to be relative and in what ways or for what reasons it is relative. Consider the following claim:

A. What is morally right for me is not necessarily morally right for you.

The problem here is that this claim is ambiguous, and because some interpretations of it are certainly true, some people may think that ethical relativism is also true. The first interpretation is as follows:

A1. What I think is morally right is not necessarily what you think is morally right.

This statement does not establish ethical relativism, for no ethical objectivist would disagree with it. To use a nonmoral example, many thinkers in ancient Greece believed that the earth was a flat disk, while others, such as Aristotle, claimed that it was a sphere. The fact that there was a conflict of opinions and each person thought that his was correct does not imply that there is no correct opinion on this matter. Similarly, the fact that two people have differing moral opinions does not imply that there is not a correct answer. One person could be right and the other mistaken, or they both could be incorrect and the correct moral opinion might be a third option.

The next interpretation focuses on the fact that a single, objective moral principle can dictate different actions in different circumstances. The final interpretation says that the moral principles themselves are relative. Let's examine the claim that the circumstances can sometimes be relevant to the morality of a particular action.

A2. An action can be morally right for me and morally wrong for you.

Ordinarily, during the summer I water my lawn. However, for someone (call him Karim) who lives in a water-starved region where water is necessary to preserve life, watering the lawn would be immoral. Thus, the same action (watering the lawn) is morally permissible for me but morally wrong for someone else. I water my lawn because (among other reasons) I care for my neighbors (they don't want my ugly lawn lowering their property values). Similarly, Karim is showing care for his neighbors by not wasting precious water. So, even though an action is right for me and is wrong for Karim, we are adhering to the same moral standard (caring for others). So far, this interpretation is completely consistent with ethical objectivism, for a person can believe there is a single set of universal and objective moral standards at the same time he or she believes that those standards can command different actions in different concrete situations.

The third interpretation is the only one that expresses *moral relativism:*

A3. A moral principle can be correct for me but not necessarily correct for you.

Since this statement uses the normative term *correct,* it is not merely describing the fact that people have different moral beliefs, as statement A1 does. Instead, statement A3 is claiming that moral principles themselves are completely relative. It is this form of moral relativity that will be the focus of our discussion, because it is making a controversial and large-scale claim about the nature of morality itself. This claim could take the form either that what *an individual believes* is right or wrong *really* is right or wrong (subjectivism) or that what *a particular culture believes* is right or wrong *really* is right or wrong (conventionalism). Let's discuss each of these alternatives in turn.

Subjective Ethical Relativism (Subjectivism)

According to ethical subjectivism, when *anyone* (not just the subjectivist) makes a moral judgment such as, "It is morally right to tax the rich to support the poor," or, "Nudity on late night television should be permitted," or, "Abortion is wrong," he or she is simply reporting or expressing personal approval (or disapproval) of an action as well as his or her attitudes and feelings. As Ernest Hemingway wrote:

So far, about morals, I know only that what is moral is what you feel good after and what is immoral is what you feel bad after and judged by these moral standards, which I do not defend, the bullfight is very moral to me because I feel very fine while it is going on and have a feeling of life and death and mortality and immortality, and after it is over I feel very sad but very fine.[13]

This theory reduces ethics to the same plane as individual tastes in food. Although there may be some similarities among the people of a particular culture concerning what food dishes are delicacies and what are repulsive, in the final analysis it is simply a matter of individual taste. Similarly, ethical subjectivism claims that moral judgments are personal preferences rather than an attempt to decide what is true or false concerning moral issues.

One of the earliest expressions of subjective ethical relativism can be found in the Sophists who taught in Greece in the fifth century B.C. (See the discussion of Socrates' arguments against the Sophists in section 1.1.) The Sophists taught that *right* and *wrong* are simply words whose meanings were arbitrary and dependent on human opinion. This belief was expressed by Protagoras's famous slogan, "Man is the measure of all things." Some of the more cynical Sophists taught that you should follow the moral conventions of society when it is prudent to do so, but do what you think is right when you can get away with it.

In the 20th century, one of the most famous expressions of ethical subjectivism is found in the writings of the French existentialist Jean-Paul Sartre. (See the discussion of Sartre's existentialist view of human freedom in section 3.7.) Sartre quotes Dostoyevsky's statement, "If God did not exist, everything would be permitted." However, whereas Dostoyevsky was making this point to emphasize the necessity of there being a God, the atheist Sartre uses it to make clear the implications of atheism. For Sartre, because there is no God, there is no realm of values and moral rules apart from us that we can use to guide our behavior. Each of us must choose for ourselves the values that will guide our lives. Sartre stresses the enormous responsibility and even anxiety we must bear in facing this subjective choice. He tells of a young man who came to him for advice during World War II. The young man wanted to know whether the morally right action would be to stay home to care for his mother or abandon her to fight the Nazis. The advice Sartre gave to him was, "You are free, therefore choose—that is to say, invent. No rule of general morality can show you what you ought to do."[14] That comment is a classic statement of subjectivism. Morality is not discovered; it is chosen or invented by each individual, much like creating a work of art.

Subjective ethical relativism is a curious position, because it says that there are no moral principles other than those that each individual chooses for herself or himself. But if there are no moral standards other than the ones I invent for myself, then it seems impossible for me to ever do what was morally wrong. Of course, someone might be able to claim that I have failed to live according to my own moral principles. But that criticism is easy to fix, for I can simply claim that according to my beliefs, hypocrisy is morally permissible. Furthermore, it seems impossible for there ever to be a viable society of moral subjectivists, each doing his or her own thing. Minimally, a society needs some common standards of morality to which all its members are subject, to allow them to rise above the conflicts that are inevitable between individual whims, idiosyncrasies, preferences, and desires. Without a common morality, the human situation would be, in the words of the 18th-century philosopher Thomas Hobbes, "a war of all against all."[15] Because subjective ethical relativism is so problematic, ethical relativism would seem to rise or fall with its strongest version, which is conventionalism.

Where Do We Come From? What Are We? Where Are We Going? (1897) by Paul Gauguin. Gauguin, a French postimpressionist, abandoned a business career to pursue his art. His most famous works were done in Tahiti, where he moved to escape civilization in quest of a simpler, more innocent environment. In this classic painting he depicts a culture very different from that of European society. The standards of modesty, lifestyle, and ethical ideals of the native Tahitians differ radically from those of Gauguin's (and our) culture. Thus, his painting illustrates the point made in Ruth Benedict's essay that "morality differs in every society, and is a convenient term for socially approved habits."

Conventional Ethical Relativism (Conventionalism)

The theoretical problems with subjectivism as well as the practical problems of sustaining a society on that basis help make the case for the conventionalist version of ethical relativism. This theory is actually an ancient one, for morality has typically been embedded within cultural traditions throughout human history, whereas individualism of any sort was not very prevalent before the Renaissance.

Long ago the Greek historian Herodotus (485–430 B.C.) cleverly illustrated the way in which people's moral opinions are shaped by their society:

FROM HERODOTUS

The Histories [16]

If one were to offer men to choose out of all the customs in the world such as seemed to them the best, they would examine the whole number, and end by preferring their own; so convinced are they that their own usages far surpass those of all others. . . . That people have this feeling about their laws may be seen by very many proofs: among others, by the following. Darius, after he had got the kingdom, called into his presence certain Greeks who were at hand, and asked—"What he should pay them to eat the bodies of their fathers when they died?" To which they answered, that there was no sum that would tempt them to do such a thing. He then sent for certain Indians, of the race called Callatians, men who eat the dead bodies of their fathers, and asked them, while the Greeks stood by, and knew by the help of an interpreter all that was said—"What he should give them to burn the bodies of their fathers at their decease?" [The practice of the Greeks.] The Indians exclaimed aloud, and forbade him to use such language. Such is men's customary practice; and Pindar was right, in my judgment, when he said, "Custom is the king o'er all."

To apply this story to the conventional ethical relativist's account, let's imagine that there are two Greeks, Alcinus and Xerxes, and two Callatians, Bredor and Yerbon (A, X, B, and Y for short).[17] Suppose the facts are as follows:

Greek Society (Burning the Dead Is Moral)	Callatian Society (Burning the Dead Is Immoral)
A believes burning the dead is moral.	B believes burning the dead is immoral.
X believes burning the dead is immoral.	Y believes burning the dead is moral.

Which one of these individuals (A, B, X, Y) has correct moral beliefs? The subjectivist would say that all are equally correct since morality is a matter of individual opinion. However, a conventionalist would say that A and B have correct moral beliefs, even though their beliefs contradict each other, because A's morality and B's morality conform to that of their society. On the other hand, the conventionalist would say X and Y have incorrect moral beliefs because they are in conflict with the morality of their respective societies. The following thought experiment asks you to consider your own moral values and the degree to which they are or are not a result of your cultural background.

> ### THOUGHT EXPERIMENT: *How Did You Learn about Morality?*
>
> - How did you arrive at your ideas of morality? What factors played a role in your moral development (family, friends, role models, teachers, books, films)?
> - Imagine that you were born into a different family, in a different region of the world, and in a different culture. Do you think these circumstances would make a difference in your current notions of right or wrong?
> - In what ways do your moral judgments and values differ from those of your parents? What factors caused your opinions to differ from theirs?
> - To what degree do these reflections support or contradict the claims of conventional relativism?

RUTH BENEDICT (1887–1948)

RUTH BENEDICT
(1887–1948)

Conventionalism is typically defended by surveying the wide range of ethical beliefs and practices throughout the world. This defense is illustrated in the writings of Ruth Benedict, who used her anthropological studies to show us that much of our behavior arises from the prevailing standards of the culture in which we were raised. (Ruth Benedict was one of America's foremost anthropologists. She taught at Columbia University, and her book *Patterns of Culture* [1934] is considered a classic of comparative anthropology.) Benedict's conclusions were exceedingly controversial when she first introduced them, because they challenged the tendency of anthropologists to judge and evaluate various societies in terms of the "superior" values and "rational" outlook of Western culture. Instead, as the following selection illustrates, Benedict urged that in investigating any culture we should attempt to understand it in terms of the unique internal standards of those people without judging them to be either inferior or superior to our own.

- As you read through this selection, assess the degree to which Benedict's descriptions of other cultures either support or fail to support the thesis of ethical relativism.

- What would be some of the implications of Benedict's relativism? Are any implications good? Are any problematic?

FROM RUTH BENEDICT

Anthropology and the Abnormal[18]

The most spectacular illustrations of the extent to which normality may be culturally defined are those cultures where an abnormality of our culture is the cornerstone of their social structure. It is not possible to do justice to these possibilities in a short discussion. A recent study of an island of northwest Melanesia by Fortune describes a society built upon traits which we regard as beyond the border of paranoia. In this tribe the exogamic groups* look upon each other as prime manipulators of black magic, so that one marries always into an enemy group which remains for life one's deadly and unappeasable foes. They look upon a good garden crop as a confession of theft, for everyone is engaged in making magic to induce into his garden the productiveness of his neighbors'; therefore no secrecy in the island is so rigidly insisted upon as the secrecy of a man's harvesting of his yams. Their polite phrase at the acceptance of a gift is, "And if you now poison me, how shall I repay you this present?" Their preoccupation with poisoning is constant; no woman ever leaves her cooking pot for a moment untended. Even the great affinal economic exchanges that are characteristic of this Melanesian culture area are quite altered in Dobu since they are incompatible with this fear and distrust that pervades the culture. They go farther and people the whole world outside their own quarters with such malignant spirits that all-night feasts and ceremonials simply do not occur here. They have even rigorous religiously enforced customs that forbid the sharing of seed even in one family group. Anyone else's food is deadly poison to you, so that commonality of stores is out of the question. For some months before harvest the whole society is on the verge of starvation, but if one falls to the temptation and eats up one's seed yams, one is an outcast and a beachcomber for life. There is no coming back. It involves, as a matter of course, divorce and the breaking of all social ties.

Now in this society where no one may work with another and no one may share with another, Fortune describes the individual who was regarded by all his fellows as crazy. He was not one of those who periodically ran amok and, beside himself and frothing at the mouth, fell with a knife upon anyone he could reach. Such behavior they did not regard as putting anyone outside the pale. They did not even put the individuals who were known to be liable to these attacks under any kind of control. They merely fled when they saw the attack coming on and kept out of the way. "He would be all right tomorrow." But there was one man of sunny, kindly disposition who liked work and liked to be helpful. The compulsion was too strong for him to repress it in favor of the opposite tendencies of his culture. Men and women never spoke of him without laughing; he was silly and simple and definitely crazy. Nevertheless, to the ethnologist used to a culture that has, in Christianity, made his type the model of all virtue, he seemed a pleasant fellow. . . .

. . . Among the Kwakiutl it did not matter whether a relative had died in bed of disease, or by the hand of an enemy, in either case death was an affront to be wiped out by the death of another person. The fact that one had been caused to mourn was proof that one had been put upon. A chief's sister and her daughter had gone up to Victoria, and either because they drank bad whiskey or because their boat capsized they never came back. The chief called together his warriors, "Now I ask you, tribes, who shall wail? Shall I do it or shall another?" The spokesman answered, of course, "Not you, Chief. Let some

*By "exogamic groups" Benedict is referring to tribes who marry only persons from another tribe.

other of the tribes." Immediately they set up the war pole to announce their intention of wiping out the injury, and gathered a war party. They set out, and found seven men and two children asleep and killed them. "Then they felt good when they arrived at Sebaa in the evening."

The point which is of interest to us is that in our society those who on that occasion would feel good when they arrived at Sebaa that evening would be the definitely abnormal. There would be some, even in our society, but it is not a recognized and approved mood under the circumstances. On the Northwest Coast those are favored and fortunate to whom that mood under those circumstances is congenial, and those to whom it is repugnant are unlucky. This latter minority can register in their own culture only by doing violence to their congenial responses and acquiring others that are difficult for them. The person, for instance, who, like a Plains Indian whose wife has been taken from him, is too proud to fight, can deal with the Northwest Coast civilization only by ignoring its strongest bents. If he cannot achieve it, he is the deviant in that culture, their instance of abnormality.

This head-hunting that takes place on the Northwest Coast after a death is no matter of blood revenge or of organized vengeance. There is no effort to tie up the subsequent killing with any responsibility on the part of the victim for the death of the person who is being mourned. A chief whose son has died goes visiting wherever his fancy dictates, and he says to his host, "My prince has died today, and you go with him." Then he kills him. In this, according to their interpretation, he acts nobly because he has not been downed. He has thrust back in return. The whole procedure is meaningless without the fundamental paranoid reading of bereavement. Death, like all the other untoward accidents of existence, confounds man's pride and can only be handled in the category of insults.

Behavior honored upon the Northwest Coast is one which is recognized as abnormal in our civilization, and yet it is sufficiently close to the attitudes of our own culture to be intelligible to us and to have a definite vocabulary with which we may discuss it. The megalomaniac paranoid trend is a definite danger in our society. It is encouraged by some of our major preoccupations, and it confronts us with a choice of two possible attitudes. One is to brand it as abnormal and reprehensible, and is the attitude we have chosen in our civilization. The other is to make it an essential attribute of ideal man, and this is the solution in the culture of the Northwest Coast.

These illustrations, which it has been possible to indicate only in the briefest manner, force upon us the fact that normality is culturally defined. An adult shaped to the drives and standards of either of these cultures, if he were transported into our civilization, would fall into our categories of abnormality. He would be faced with the psychic dilemmas of the socially unavailable. In his own culture, however, he is the pillar of society, the end result of socially inculcated mores, and the problem of personal instability in his case simply does not arise. . . .

Every society, beginning with some slight inclination in one direction or another, carries its preference farther and farther, integrating itself more and more completely upon its chosen basis, and discarding those types of behavior that are uncongenial. Most of those organizations of personality that seem to us most uncontrovertibly abnormal have been used by different civilizations in the very foundations of their institutional life. Conversely the most valued traits of our normal individuals have been looked on in differently organized cultures as aberrant. Normality, in short, within a very wide range, is culturally defined. It is primarily a term for the socially elaborated segment of human behavior in any culture; and abnormality, a term for the segment that that particular civilization does not use. The very eyes with which we see the problem are conditioned by the long traditional habits of our own society.

It is a point that has been made more often in relation to ethics than in relation to psychiatry. We do not any longer make the mistake of deriving the morality of our locality and decade directly from the inevitable constitution of human nature. We do not elevate it to the dignity of a first principle. We recognize that morality differs in every society, and is a convenient term for socially approved habits. Mankind has always preferred to say "It is morally good" rather than "It is habitual," and the fact of this preference is matter enough for a critical science of ethics. But historically the two phrases are synonymous.

The concept of the normal is properly a variant of the concept of the good. It is that which society has approved. A normal action is one which falls well within the limits of expected behavior for a particular society. Its variability among different peoples is essentially a function of the variability of the behavior patterns that different societies have created for themselves, and can never be wholly divorced from a consideration of culturally institutionalized types of behavior.

- State in your own words Benedict's thesis concerning normality and abnormality.
- She says that the statement "It is morally good" is synonymous with what other phrase? Do you agree that these phrases are essentially the same? Why?
- How would you summarize Benedict's view of morality?
- Do you agree with her that the differences between cultures are sufficient to prove that there are no objective rights or wrongs? Why?

STOP AND THINK

In the suicidal plane attacks on New York and Washington, D.C., in 2001, we have a striking example of a clash of cultural values as well as political ideologies. The terrorists were acting on the basis of what they believed were the mandates of their religion. Although intentionally taking the lives of innocent persons in the name of religious convictions may conflict with our religious or cultural beliefs, this conflict clearly did not exist for the suicidal pilots. In their eyes, they were fighting evil and acting to promote what was good and God's will. How would an ethical relativist (like Benedict) deal with this situation? Would she have to say that it is presumptuous for us to judge the terrorists wrong, because we are only applying our cultural standards to judge their cultural standards (something she thinks we should not do)? What alternatives does the ethical relativist have in this sort of situation?

Although many people might agree with Benedict's descriptions of various cultures, the question remains whether such descriptions are sufficient to make the case for ethical relativism. Philosopher John Ladd defines ethical relativism (or the conventionalist version being discussed here) in the following way:

Ethical relativism is the doctrine that the moral rightness and wrongness of actions varies from society to society and that there are no absolute universal moral standards binding on all men at all times. Accordingly, it holds that whether or not it is right for an individual to act in a certain way depends on or is relative to the society to which he belongs.[19]

As Ladd points out, two logically independent theses are embedded within this definition. The first is the *diversity thesis*. This thesis states that moral beliefs, rules, and practices differ from society to society. The *dependency thesis* asserts that moral beliefs, rules, and practices are essentially dependent on the cultural patterns of the society in which they occur. Hence, if the Greeks in Herodotus's account had been raised in the Callatian society, they would have thought it right to eat the bodies of their dead fathers. Likewise, if the Callatians had been raised as Greeks, it would have been right for them to burn the bodies of their dead fathers.

Using Ladd's analysis, the argument of the ethical relativist could be formulated in the following way:

1. Whether an action is right or wrong is dependent on the moral beliefs and practices of a particular society. (Dependency thesis)
2. Moral beliefs and practices vary from society to society. (Diversity thesis)
3. Therefore, whether an action is right or wrong varies from society to society. (Conventional ethical relativism)

First, let's look at the dependency thesis. It is surely correct that morality is intimately intertwined with cultural traditions. But is this connection sufficient to prove that moral beliefs cannot be evaluated independently of these cultural traditions? To use a nonmoral example, it is part of our Western cultural tradition that most teenagers learn chemistry in school, but in other, nontechnological cultures teenagers might be trained in hunting and not chemistry. But should we conclude that the principles of chemistry have no validity apart from our particular culture? We recognize close to 100 chemical elements, but the ancient Greeks recognized only earth, air, fire, and water. Should we conclude that the issue of how many elements there really are is simply dependent on culture? Similarly, the abolition of slavery in our society was motivated by a more consistent reflection on the implications of our democratic ideals and the biblical roots of our culture. But should we conclude that slavery is wrong only for people in our culture?

Furthermore, remember that in our discussion of action relativism, we noted that two cultures can share the same moral principle (caring for one's neighbors) but that the *application* of this principle may be dependent on the specific conditions of the culture (watering the lawn or not). Hence, in a weak sense it is true that morality is dependent on culture, but there are few reasons to accept the strong dependency required to establish ethical relativism.

What about the diversity thesis? Benedict has documented the wide range of moral practices and attitudes throughout the world. But in spite of this diversity, some anthropologists have argued that there is also a common core of agreement. As anthropologist Clyde Kluckhohn has noted:

> Every culture has a concept of murder, distinguishing this from execution, killing in war, and other "justifiable homicides." The notions of incest and other regulations upon sexual behavior, the prohibitions upon untruth under defined circumstances, of restitution and reciprocity, of mutual obligations between parents and children—these and many other moral concepts are altogether universal.[20]

Furthermore, although it may seem at first that conflicting moral judgments are based on conflicting moral principles, the difference may actually be based on the nonmoral differences in factual beliefs. For example, in many tribal cultures it is customary to kill one's parents when they are no longer capable of providing for themselves. This practice is not only radically different from the way we are expected to treat our parents, but people in our culture would be inclined to judge it morally abhorrent. But do these tribes differ from us morally? Surprisingly, the answer is no, for the difference is to be found at the level of factual beliefs. These people kill their aged parents because they believe that the physical condition of your body at the time of death will be your condition in the afterlife throughout all eternity. Given this belief, it is important to die before you become an invalid. If your children will not perform this service for you, it is a great disgrace. Furthermore, for cultures who face a harsh environment, the struggle for existence dictates that they spend their energy and resources caring for the young and not their infirm senior members. These cultures have basically the same principles that we do: (1) Honor your parents, (2) provide for the young, and (3) serve the overall good of society. However, their application of these principles differs from ours because they have different nonmoral beliefs about death and because their physical conditions are different.

Finally, the diversity thesis does not imply ethical relativism, because it merely describes what people do but does not address the issue of what they ought to do. If we found out, for example, that the majority of parents sexually abuse their children, this discovery would not mean that their actions were right. But ethical relativism makes the claim that if the majority of people in a culture believe something is right, then that belief or action is morally right for them.

LOOKING THROUGH THE LENS OF ETHICAL RELATIVISM

1. There seem to be some features of human experience that are universal, such as mating, birth, child rearing, property, some form of social organization, some system of justice, suffering, and death. How does the relativist explain the fact that every society has some form of morality based on these and other common features of human life? How can the relativist defend the view that morality is completely relative to human opinion at the same time that these common facts seem to indicate some similarities in the moral rules of different societies?

2. If everyone in history had been conventional ethical relativists, what differences would we have seen in history and in the world today? What differences would be better? What would be worse?

3. In the 19th century, Christian missionaries often coerced tribal people in Africa to abandon their practice of polygamy. However, since the women tended to outnumber the men (due to the death of males in war and hunting), many women were left without any means of support. Consequently, some desperate women were forced to move to the cities to become prostitutes. What would the ethical relativist say about this attempt to change a society's moral practices?

4. The ethical objectivist can explain the fact that individuals or cultures change their moral views or practices (such as abandoning slavery) by saying that they come to discover better or truer ethical standards. However, if morality is based simply on individual or social opinion and there are no objective standards against which to measure that morality, as the relativist claims, then why would people be inclined to believe that their present morality is wrong? In other words, how might the relativist explain changes in people's moral outlook?

EXAMINING THE STRENGTHS AND WEAKNESSES OF ETHICAL RELATIVISM

Positive Evaluation

1. Ethical relativism can easily explain the diversity of moral opinions and the difficulty of arriving at a consensus on controversial moral issues. How strongly does this factor count in favor of the plausibility of the relativist's position?

2. The conventionalist's moral standard is that an action is morally right or wrong if it is considered such by society. Doesn't such a standard have these advantages: It gives us a clear procedure for resolving ethical disputes, it is democratic, and it creates social harmony? Doesn't this standard reflect the approach that we often take in ethics?

3. Ethical relativism encourages people to follow the principle "live and let live." It places a high value on tolerance and is a corrective to the evils of ethnocentrism (the attitude that your society is superior to all others). It reminds us that people shouldn't be condemned just because they do things differently than we do. Aren't these attitudes laudable?

4. Ethical relativism provides for a flexible morality. People don't have to adhere to one set of moral rules etched in granite for all time; instead, ethical relativism allows morality to change as people's needs and attitudes change, as society progresses, and as circumstances change. Just as the horse and buggy gave way to the automobile, shouldn't morality be a function of society's growing needs?

Negative Evaluation

1. At the time Ruth Benedict was writing her article (1934) the Nazis were beginning to take over Europe. (Benedict was silent about this cultural "practice" in her paper.) Someone has said that no one can watch the movie *Schindler's List* (which depicts the Nazis' atrocities) and remain an ethical relativist. Wouldn't an ethical relativist have to say that the rest of the world had no right to condemn the elitist, racist, and genocidal actions of the Nazis as long as the Nazis were being consistent with their own moral ideals? Doesn't ethical relativism imply that we can never criticize the accepted practices of another society, no matter how evil those practices are? Does this approach expose a problem with ethical relativism?

2. Can morality be simply a function of what the 51 percent majority in a society says it is? Let's say the majority of people believed that physician-assisted suicide was wrong last week, but this week the polls show that the majority opinion has changed. Do these polls mean that physician-assisted suicide was wrong last week but is morally right this week? Isn't this approach odd and problematic? We may be able to change people's *opinions* of the rightness or wrongness of a controversial practice through an effective advertising campaign, but do we want to say that the *morality* of a practice can be changed through a public relations campaign?

3. If conventionalism is correct, then how can we ever decide the rightness or wrongness of something that has no clear social consensus? For example, I cannot possibly decide the morality of a new medical controversy such as cloning genetically identical babies until I find out what the rest of society thinks. But, likewise, no one else in society can decide the morality of this new procedure without knowing what the majority thinks. In other words, when we face new moral problems that have no already-established social consensus, we could never decide for ourselves what is right, and, consequently, there could never be a majority opinion about what is right.

4. If morality depends on social consensus, how large does a group have to be to constitute a valid standard for morality? Does it require 1,000 people? How about 100 people or even 10 people? Although we may each be a citizen of a particular nation, we are also members of any number of subcultures within that nation, each of which has different cultural practices. If morality is relative to our culture, could I claim that it is right for me to murder people because I belong to the Mafia subculture in which this practice is acceptable?

Furthermore, one person can belong to several different subcultures that have conflicting moral codes. Suppose, for example, that Tanya is a black, feminist, Roman Catholic living in a society that tolerates discrimination against blacks and women and that also finds abortion and pornography acceptable. Racism, sexism, abortion, and pornography each could be both morally right and wrong for Tanya depending on which of her several subcultures she uses as her standard for moral evaluation. By reducing morality to human opinion, doesn't the relativist rob it of its action-guiding function altogether? Shouldn't human opinions be subject to moral norms and not the other way around?

SURVEYING THE CASE FOR ETHICAL OBJECTIVISM

Ethical objectivism is the position that certain moral principles are universal (they apply to all persons in all times) and objective (they are not based on the opinions of individuals or cultures). Hence, for this position, there are objectively right and wrong answers to ethical questions just as there are objectively true and false answers to questions in mathematics, medicine, or physics. Unlike ethical relativism, the ethical objectivist does not believe that morality is like tastes in food or social customs. Hence, the ethical objectivist claims that it is possible for individuals or entire cultures to be mistaken in their moral opinions and practices.

ethical objectivism the position that certain moral principles are universal (they apply to all persons in all times) and objective (they are not based on the opinions of individuals or cultures)

Objectivism and Absolutism

Ethical objectivism should be distinguished from ethical absolutism. **Absolutism** claims that not only are moral principles objective but also they cannot be overridden and there cannot be any exceptions to them. As we will see, Kantian ethics (section 5.4) is an example of ethical absolutism. Absolutism is a more narrow position than objectivism and could be considered a subcategory within it. Hence, all absolutists are objectivists, but the reverse is not true. The ethical absolutist, for example, would say that we have an obligation to tell the truth and not lie, and this duty cannot be violated for any reason. On the other hand, the ethical objectivist could say that a rule like "do not lie" is an objective moral principle but that this principle can be overridden when it conflicts with a more pressing obligation such as saving a life. Hence, if lying to a homicidal maniac would prevent him from killing someone, then our duty to preserve life overrides our duty to tell the truth. W. D. Ross (who is discussed in section 5.4) presents an example of the more moderate position of ethical objectivism. Although he did believe that there were universal, objective moral principles, he did not believe that any of them were absolute and without exceptions, for when two or more of these principles conflict, one would have to be subordinated to the other.

absolutism the claim that not only are moral principles objective but also they cannot be overridden and there cannot be any exceptions to them

Ethical relativism claims that "*all* moral principles are relative," whereas ethical objectivism claims that "*some* moral principles are *not* relative." These claims are contradictory, so one is true and one is false; there could be no compromise that embraces them both. Notice, however, that the objectivist could claim that *some* moral issues are relative as long as he or she also maintains that there is a core of moral principles that are universal and objective. In other words, the objectivist does not need to say that there is only one right answer to every single ethical question but merely has to claim that there can be wrong answers and that on *some* ethical issues there are moral principles that everyone ought to follow. For example, an objectivist might say that monogamy is best for some societies but polygamy is best for others, given their circumstances and conditions. At the same time, while recognizing some degree of acceptable diversity in social arrangements, the objectivist would say that treating family members with benevolence and care, doing no harm, and respecting each person's dignity and worth are universal, objective moral principles that cannot be violated. Furthermore, the specific actions that would constitute treating a family member benevolently might vary with social customs and conditions, even though the principle followed in each case would be the same. For example, the Greeks burned their dead because they thought this ritual was the proper way to honor the spirits of the dead, whereas the Callatians ate their dead for the same reason. Both were attempting to honor their family members, but did so through different specific actions.

Problems with Relativism

One of the attractions of ethical relativism is that it seems to place a high value on tolerance—something that most people think is an important principle. But just because a theory approves of something good does not imply that the theory is true. Furthermore, the objectivist would agree with the relativist that tolerance is good and intolerance is bad. However, the objectivist philosophers would say that only *they* have a right to make this claim, because tolerance is being offered as an objective moral standard that is universally binding. By claiming that all ethical opinions are of equal value, the relativist is in the uncomfortable position of having to tolerate intolerance. If tolerance is to be our sole guiding ideal, should we then consider the sincere ethical judgments of racists and Nazis to be morally acceptable?

STOP AND THINK

I once had a student who wrote a forceful essay in defense of ethical relativism. He claimed that right and wrong are relative to individual opinion and that no one had any basis for imposing his or her conception of morality on others. The student finished the essay by writing in large letters "Everyone OUGHT to be tolerant. It is always WRONG to be intolerant."

- How might an ethical objectivist argue that this student is being inconsistent?
- What if my personal morality was one that embraced the virtue of intolerance? What could this student say about that? Wouldn't an ethical relativist have to say that for me (or for some cultures) intolerance is morally right?

Another problem with relativism (both versions) is that it makes it impossible to criticize the behavior of other persons or cultures. Our campus once had an anthropologist speak in a public forum in defense of cultural relativism. To make his point, he described many cultures whose sexual behavior and other moral practices differ radically from what is acceptable in our society. He concluded by saying, "Who can say that they are wrong, simply because their morality differs from ours?" Knowing that his wife ran the local women's and children's domestic violence shelter, I asked him if he could consistently live with his ethical relativism. After all, there are many cultures and even subcultures in our society in which violence to women is tolerated. Even many of the women victims themselves, who have been raised in the values of that culture, accept violence as the way things should be. As I suspected, however, there were limits to the anthropologist's tolerance and relativism. He replied that a minimal moral rule must be the protecting of women and children, even though he realized that this acknowledgment undermined his own thesis of ethical relativism. When ethical relativists find that their own rights or the rights of those they love are being violated, they quickly begin to see the attractiveness of ethical objectivism.

A Common Core Morality

Although many examples of common moral principles could be cited, here is how different cultures have expressed two fundamental moral principles.[21]

The Law of General Beneficence

> "Utter not a word by which anyone could be wounded." (Hindu)
>
> "I have not brought misery upon my fellows." (Ancient Egyptian)
>
> "Speak kindness . . . show good will." (Babylonian)
>
> "Men were brought into existence for the sake of men that they might do one another good." (Roman)
>
> "Never do to others what you would not like them to do to you." (Ancient Chinese)
>
> "Love thy neighbour as thyself." (Ancient Jewish)
>
> "Do unto others what you would have them do unto you." (Christian)

The Law of Good Faith and Truthfulness

> "A sacrifice is obliterated by a lie and the merit of [charitable giving] by an act of fraud." (Hindu)
>
> "With his mouth was he full of *Yea*, in his heart full of *Nay?*" (Babylonian List of Sins)
>
> "I have not spoken falsehood." (Ancient Egyptian)
>
> "The Master said, Be of unwavering good faith." (Ancient Chinese)
>
> "Hateful to me as are the gates of Hades is that man who says one thing, and hides another in his heart." (Greek)
>
> "The foundation of justice is good faith." (Roman)
>
> "Anything is better than treachery." (Old Norse)
>
> "Thou shalt not bear false witness against thy neighbor." (Ancient Jewish)

SPOTLIGHT

on

Is There a Core Morality?

Many objectivists argue that a universal core of moral principles can be found throughout every flourishing culture. Of course, we can always find cultures such as the Ik and societies such as Nazi Germany that have moral principles that seem to deviate from the norm. (The Ik culture was briefly discussed in leading question 4 at the beginning of this section.) However, the fact that the Ik culture is not flourishing and that the Nazi society was grim and paranoid and resisted by some of its own people suggests that in both cases something was wrong with these societies' moral ideals. In spite of the wide range of moral practices throughout the world and history, some anthropologists have found a number of common moral principles.

The existence of a core of moral values or practices that seem to be universal among flourishing, healthy societies serves as counter evidence to the examples of diversity provided by Benedict and other relativists. As I mentioned previously, the ethical objectivist does not need to deny that there is some measure of moral disagreement or diversity among different cultures. Such moral disagreements could be a result of the fact that people can make mistakes about what is morally correct. Just as the medievals were mistaken in believing that the earth was the center of the universe, so people in earlier centuries mistakenly believed that slavery was morally permissible. On the other hand, differences in morality also could result from the fact that some moral issues permit differences of opinion. The standards of modesty in one culture may differ from the standards of another culture. However, the objectivist might admit that moral standards with regard to clothing and behavior may be culturally based. Minimally the objectivist merely has to maintain that there are some features of morality that are not optional nor simply a matter of cultural convention.

In the following essay James Rachels proposes that the arguments for ethical relativism, which he calls "cultural relativism," fail to make their case. (James Rachels was a professor of philosophy at the University of Alabama. He is well known for his books and articles on philosophy of religion and ethics.) Furthermore, he points out that there are many reasons why we should find ethical relativism implausible and ethical objectivism correct. In the original essay, he begins by mentioning the funeral practices of the Greeks and the Callatians, which we have already discussed. The following selection begins with his discussion of traditional Eskimo customs.

- How do Eskimo practices lend support to the thesis of cultural relativism?
- How does Rachels later show that their treatment of babies is consistent with objectivism?
- Why does Rachels think the diversity thesis is flawed? (He calls it the "cultural differences argument.")
- What are the three consequences of cultural relativism?
- Why does Rachels believe there must be some moral rules that are common to every culture?

FROM JAMES RACHELS

The Challenge of Cultural Relativism [22]

1. How Different Cultures Have Different Moral Codes

. . . Consider the Eskimos. They are a remote and inaccessible people. Numbering only about 25,000, they live in small, isolated settlements scattered mostly along the northern fringes of North America and Greenland. Until the beginning of this century, the outside world knew little about them. Then explorers began to bring back strange tales.

Eskimo customs turned out to be very different from our own. The men often had more than one wife, and they would share their wives with guests, lending them for the night as a sign of hospitality. Moreover, within a community, a dominant male might demand—and get—regular sexual access to other men's wives. The women, however, were free to break these arrangements simply by leaving their husbands and taking up with new partners—free, that is, so long as their former husbands chose not to make trouble. All in all, the Eskimo practice was a volatile scheme that bore little resemblance to what we call marriage.

But it was not only their marriage and sexual practices that were different. The Eskimos also seemed to have less regard for human life. Infanticide, for example, was common. Knud Rasmussen, one of the most famous early explorers, reported that he met one woman who had borne twenty children but had killed ten of them at birth. Female babies, he found, were especially liable to be destroyed, and this was permitted simply at the parents' discretion, with no social stigma attached to it. Old people also, when they became too feeble to contribute to the family, were left out in the snow to die. So there seemed to be, in this society, remarkably little respect for life.

To the general public, these were disturbing revelations. Our own way of living seems so natural and right that for many of us it is hard to conceive of others living so differently.

JAMES RACHELS
(1941–2003)

And when we do hear of such things, we tend immediately to categorize those other peoples as "backward" or "primitive." But to anthropologists and sociologists, there was nothing particularly surprising about the Eskimos. Since the time of Herodotus, enlightened observers have been accustomed to the idea that conceptions of right and wrong differ from culture to culture. If we assume that our ideas of right and wrong will be shared by all peoples at all times, we are merely naive.

2. Cultural Relativism

To many thinkers, this observation—"Different cultures have different moral codes"—has seemed to be the key to understanding morality. The idea of universal truth in ethics, they say, is a myth. The customs of different societies are all that exist. These customs cannot be said to be "correct" or "incorrect," for that implies we have an independent standard of right and wrong by which they may be judged. But there is no such independent standard; every standard is culture-bound. The great pioneering sociologist William Graham Sumner, writing in 1906, put the point like this:

> The "right" way is the way which the ancestors used and which has been handed down. The tradition is its own warrant. It is not held subject to verification by experience. The notion of right is in the folkways. It is not outside of them, of independent origin, and brought to test them. In the folkways, whatever is, is right. This is because they are traditional, and therefore contain in themselves the authority of the ancestral ghosts. When we come to the folkways we are at the end of our analysis.

This line of thought has probably persuaded more people to be skeptical about ethics than any other single thing. *Cultural Relativism,* as it has been called, challenges our ordinary belief in the objectivity and universality of moral truth. It says, in effect, that there is no such thing as universal truth in ethics; there are only the various cultural codes, and nothing more. Moreover, our own code has no special status; it is merely one among many.

As we shall see, this basic idea is really a compound of several different thoughts. It is important to separate the various elements of the theory because, on analysis, some parts of the theory turn out to be correct, whereas others seem to be mistaken. As a beginning, we may distinguish the following claims, all of which have been made by cultural relativists:

1. Different societies have different moral codes.
2. There is no objective standard that can be used to judge one societal code better than another.
3. The moral code of our own society has no special status; it is merely one among many.
4. There is no "universal truth" in ethics—that is, there are no moral truths that hold for all peoples at all times.
5. The moral code of a society determines what is right within that society; that is, if the moral code of a society says that a certain action is right, then that action is right, at least within that society.
6. It is mere arrogance for us to try to judge the conduct of other peoples. We should adopt an attitude of tolerance toward the practices of other cultures.

Although it may seem that these six propositions go naturally together, they are independent of one another, in the sense that some of them might be true even if others are false. In what follows, we will try to identify what is correct in Cultural Relativism, but we will also be concerned to expose what is mistaken about it.

3. The Cultural Differences Argument

Cultural Relativism is a theory about the nature of morality. At first blush it seems quite plausible. However, like all such theories, it may be evaluated by subjecting it to rational analysis; and when we analyze Cultural Relativism we find that it is not so plausible as it first appears to be.

The first thing we need to notice is that at the heart of Cultural Relativism there is a certain *form of argument*. The strategy used by cultural relativists is to argue from facts about the differences between cultural outlooks to a conclusion about the status of morality. Thus we are invited to accept this reasoning:

1. The Greeks believed it was wrong to eat the dead, whereas the Callatians believed it was right to eat the dead.
2. Therefore, eating the dead is neither objectively right nor objectively wrong. It is merely a matter of opinion, which varies from culture to culture.

Or, alternatively:

1. The Eskimos see nothing wrong with infanticide, whereas Americans believe infanticide is immoral.
2. Therefore, infanticide is neither objectively right nor objectively wrong. It is merely a matter of opinion, which varies from culture to culture.

Clearly, these arguments are variations of one fundamental idea. They are both special cases of a more general argument, which says:

1. Different cultures have different moral codes.
2. Therefore, there is no objective "truth" in morality. Right and wrong are only matters of opinion, and opinions vary from culture to culture.

We may call this the *Cultural Differences Argument*. To many people, it is very persuasive. But from a logical point of view, is it a *sound* argument?

It is not sound. The trouble is that the conclusion does not really follow from the premise—that is, even if the premise is true, the conclusion still might be false. The premise concerns what people *believe:* in some societies, people believe one thing; in other societies, people believe differently. The conclusion, however, concerns *what really is the case.* The trouble is that this sort of conclusion does not follow logically from this sort of premise.

Consider again the example of the Greeks and Callatians. The Greeks believed it was wrong to eat the dead; the Callatians believed it was right. Does it follow, *from the mere fact that they disagreed,* that there is no objective truth in the matter? No, it does not follow; for it *could* be that the practice was objectively right (or wrong) and that one or the other of them was simply mistaken.

To make the point clearer, consider a very different matter. In some societies, people believe the earth is flat. In other societies, such as our own, people believe the earth is (roughly) spherical. Does it follow, *from the mere fact that they disagree,* that there is no "objective truth" in geography? Of course not; we would never draw such a conclusion because we realize that, in their beliefs about the world, the members of some societies might simply be wrong. There is no reason to think that if the world is round everyone must know it. Similarly, there is no reason to think that if there is moral truth everyone must know it. The fundamental mistake in the Cultural Differences Argument is that it attempts to derive a substantive conclusion about a subject (morality) from the mere fact that people disagree about it.

It is important to understand the nature of the point that is being made here. We are *not* saying (not yet, anyway) that the conclusion of the argument is false. Insofar as anything being said here is concerned, it is still an open question whether the conclusion is true. We *are* making a purely logical point and saying that the conclusion does not *follow from* the premise. This is important, because in order to determine whether the conclusion is true, we need arguments in its support. Cultural Relativism proposes this argument, but unfortunately the argument turns out to be fallacious. So it proves nothing.

4. The Consequences of Taking Cultural Relativism Seriously

Even if the Cultural Differences Argument is invalid, Cultural Relativism might still be true. What would it be like if it were true?

In the passage quoted on p. 427, William Graham Sumner summarizes the essence of Cultural Relativism. He says that there is no measure of right and wrong other than the standards of one's society: "The notion of right is in the folkways. It is not outside of them, of independent origin, and brought to test them. In the folkways, whatever is, is right."

Suppose we took this seriously. What would be some of the consequences?

1. *We could no longer say that the customs of other societies are morally inferior to our own.* This, of course, is one of the main points stressed by Cultural Relativism. We would have to stop condemning other societies merely because they are "different." So long as we concentrate on certain examples, such as the funerary practices of the Greeks and Callatians, this may seem to be a sophisticated, enlightened attitude.

However, we would also be stopped from criticizing other, less benign practices. Suppose a society waged war on its neighbors for the purpose of taking slaves. Or suppose a society was violently anti-Semitic and its leaders set out to destroy the Jews. Cultural Relativism would preclude us from saying that either of these practices was wrong. We would not even be able to say that a society tolerant of Jews is *better* than the anti-Semitic society, for that would imply some sort of transcultural standard of comparison. The failure to condemn *these* practices does not seem "enlightened"; on the contrary, slavery and anti-Semitism seem wrong *wherever* they occur. Nevertheless, if we took Cultural Relativism seriously, we would have to admit that these social practices also are immune from criticism.

2. *We could decide whether actions are right or wrong just by consulting the standards of our society.* Cultural Relativism suggests a simple test for determining what is right and what is wrong: all one has to do is ask whether the action is in accordance with the code of one's society. Suppose a resident of South Africa is wondering whether his country's policy of *apartheid*—rigid racial segregation—is morally correct. All he has to do is ask whether this policy conforms to his society's moral code. If it does, there is nothing to worry about, at least from a moral point of view.

This implication of Cultural Relativism is disturbing because few of us think that our society's code is perfect—we can think of ways it might be improved. Yet Cultural Relativism would not only forbid us from criticizing the codes of *other* societies; it would stop us from criticizing our *own*. After all, if right and wrong are relative to culture, this must be true for our own culture just as much as for others.

3. *The idea of moral progress is called into doubt.* Usually, we think that at least some changes in our society have been for the better. (Some, of course, may have been changes for the worse.) Consider this example: Throughout most of Western history the place of women in society was very narrowly circumscribed. They could not own property; they could not vote or hold political office; with a few exceptions, they were not permitted to

have paying jobs; and generally they were under the almost absolute control of their husbands. Recently much of this has changed, and most people think of it as progress.

If Cultural Relativism is correct, can we legitimately think of this as progress? Progress means replacing a way of doing things with a *better* way. But by what standard do we judge the new ways as better? If the old ways were in accordance with the social standards of their time, then Cultural Relativism would say it is a mistake to judge them by the standards of a different time. Eighteenth-century society was, in effect, a different society from the one we have now. To say that we have made progress implies a judgment that present-day society is better, and that is just the sort of transcultural judgment that, according to Cultural Relativism, is impermissible.

Our idea of social *reform* will also have to be reconsidered. A reformer such as Martin Luther King, Jr., seeks to change his society for the better. Within the constraints imposed by Cultural Relativism, there is one way this might be done. If a society is not living up to its own ideals, the reformer may be regarded as acting for the best: the ideals of the society are the standard by which we judge his or her proposals as worthwhile. But the "reformer" may not challenge the ideals themselves, for those ideals are by definition correct. According to Cultural Relativism, then, the idea of social reform makes sense only in this very limited way.

These three consequences of Cultural Relativism have led many thinkers to reject it as implausible on its face. It does make sense, they say, to condemn some practices, such as slavery and anti-Semitism, wherever they occur. It makes sense to think that our own society has made some moral progress, while admitting that it is still imperfect and in need of reform. Because Cultural Relativism says that these judgments make no sense, the argument goes, it cannot be right.

5. Why There Is Less Disagreement Than It Seems

The original impetus for Cultural Relativism comes from the observation that cultures differ dramatically in their views of right and wrong. But just how much do they differ? It is true that there are differences. However, it is easy to overestimate the extent of those differences. Often, when we examine what *seems* to be a dramatic difference, we find that the cultures do not differ nearly as much as it appears.

Consider a culture in which people believe it is wrong to eat cows. This may even be a poor culture, in which there is not enough food; still, the cows are not to be touched. Such a society would *appear* to have values very different from our own. But does it? We have not yet asked why these people will not eat cows. Suppose it is because they believe that after death the souls of humans inhabit the bodies of animals, especially cows, so that a cow may be someone's grandmother. Now do we want to say that their values are different from ours? No; the difference lies elsewhere. The difference is in our belief systems, not in our values. We agree that we shouldn't eat Grandma; we simply disagree about whether the cow *is* (or could be) Grandma.

The general point is this. Many factors work together to produce the customs of a society. The society's values are only one of them. Other matters, such as the religious and factual beliefs held by its members and the physical circumstances in which they must live, are also important. We cannot conclude, then, merely because customs differ, that there is a disagreement about *values*. The difference in customs may be attributable to some other aspect of social life. Thus there may be less disagreement about values than there appears to be.

Consider the Eskimos again. They often kill perfectly normal infants, especially girls. We do not approve of this at all; a parent who did this in our society would be locked up. Thus there appears to be a great difference in the values of our two cultures. But suppose we ask *why* the Eskimos do this. The explanation is not that they have less affection for their children or less respect for human life. An Eskimo family will always protect its babies if conditions permit. But they live in a harsh environment, where food is often in short supply. A fundamental postulate of Eskimo thought is: "Life is hard, and the margin of safety small."A family may want to nourish its babies but be unable to do so.

As in many "primitive" societies, Eskimo mothers will nurse their infants over a much longer period of time than mothers in our culture. The child will take nourishment from its mother's breast for four years, perhaps even longer. So even in the best of times there are limits to the number of infants that one mother can sustain. Moreover, the Eskimos are a nomadic people—unable to farm, they must move about in search of food. Infants must be carried, and a mother can carry only one baby in her parka as she travels and goes about her outdoor work. Other family members can help, but this is not always possible.

Infant girls are more readily disposed of because, first, in this society the males are the primary food providers—they are the hunters, according to the traditional division of labor—and it is obviously important to maintain a sufficient number of food gatherers. But there is an important second reason as well. Because the hunters suffer a high casualty rate, the adult men who die prematurely far outnumber the women who die early. Thus if male and female infants survived in equal numbers, the female adult population would greatly outnumber the male adult population. Examining the available statistics, one writer concluded that "were it not for female infanticide . . . there would be approximately one-and-a-half times as many females in the average Eskimo local group as there are food-producing males."

So among the Eskimos, infanticide does not signal a fundamentally different attitude toward children. Instead, it is a recognition that drastic measures are sometimes needed to ensure the family's survival. Even then, however, killing the baby is not the first option considered. Adoption is common; childless couples are especially happy to take a more fertile couple's "surplus." Killing is only the last resort. I emphasize this in order to show that the raw data of the anthropologists can be misleading; it can make the differences in values between cultures appear greater than they are. The Eskimos' values are not all that different from our values. It is only that life forces upon them choices that we do not have to make.

6. How All Cultures Have Some Values in Common

It should not be surprising that, despite appearances, the Eskimos are protective of their children. How could it be otherwise? How could a group survive that did not value its young? This suggests a certain argument, one which shows that all cultural groups must be protective of their infants:

(1) Human infants are helpless and cannot survive if they are not given extensive care for a period of years.
(2) Therefore, if a group did not care for its young, the young would not survive, and the older members of the group would not be replaced. After a while the group would die out.
(3) Therefore, any cultural group that continues to exist must care for its young. Infants that are *not* cared for must be the exception rather than the rule.

Similar reasoning shows that other values must be more or less universal. Imagine what it would be like for a society to place no value at all on truth telling. When one person spoke to another, there would be no presumption at all that he was telling the truth—for he could just as easily be speaking falsely. Within that society, there would be no reason to pay attention to what anyone says. (I ask you what time it is, and you say "Four o'clock." But there is no presumption that you are speaking truly; you could just as easily have said the first thing that came into your head. So I have no reason to pay attention to your answer—in fact, there was no point in my asking you in the first place!) Communication would then be extremely difficult, if not impossible. And because complex societies cannot exist without regular communication among their members, society would become impossible. It follows that in any complex society there *must* be a presumption in favor of truthfulness. There may of course be exceptions to this rule: there may be situations in which it is thought to be permissible to lie. Nevertheless, these will be exceptions to a rule that is in force in the society.

Let me give one further example of the same type. Could a society exist in which there was no prohibition on murder? What would this be like? Suppose people were free to kill other people at will, and no one thought there was anything wrong with it. In such a "society," no one could feel secure. Everyone would have to be constantly on guard. People who wanted to survive would have to avoid other people as much as possible. This would inevitably result in individuals trying to become as self-sufficient as possible—after all, associating with others would be dangerous. Society on any large scale would collapse. Of course, people might band together in smaller groups with others that they *could* trust not to harm them. But notice what this means: they would be forming smaller societies that did acknowledge a rule against murder. The prohibition of murder, then, is a necessary feature of all societies.

There is a general theoretical point here, namely, that *there are some moral rules that all societies will have in common, because those rules are necessary for society to exist.* The rules against lying and murder are two examples. And in fact, we do find these rules in force in all viable cultures. Cultures may differ in what they regard as legitimate exceptions to the rules, but this disagreement exists against a background of agreement on the larger issues. Therefore, it is a mistake to overestimate the amount of difference between cultures. Not *every* moral rule can vary from society to society.

- Having examined the pros and cons, do you think ethical relativism or ethical objectivism is the stronger position? Explain.

LOOKING THROUGH THE LENS OF ETHICAL OBJECTIVISM

1. Contemporary philosopher Louis Pojman lists four purposes of morality: (1) to keep society from falling apart, (2) to ameliorate human suffering, (3) to promote human flourishing, (4) to resolve conflicts of interest in just ways.[23] Do you agree with his list? Are there any other purposes you would add or any you would subtract? If morality in general does serve some set of goals, how strong is the implication that there is an objective set of moral principles? What are some moral principles that would be necessary to achieve one or more of these four goals?

2. Does an objectivist have to be dogmatic? Can an objectivist be humble and tentative about his or her own grasp of morality? Is it possible for an objectivist to believe that there are universal, objective moral truths without claiming that his or her moral principles are necessarily the correct ones? In other words, can a person be an ethical objectivist without claiming moral infallibility?

3. Don't individuals and societies sometimes modify and change their morality? Don't we sometimes find that we mistakenly believed something was right but now believe it is

wrong, or find that in the past we thought something was wrong but now we realize it is right? In doing so, aren't we measuring our individual and social moral opinions against a moral standard that is independent of these opinions?

4. Relativists often appeal to the claim that (1) "everyone has a right to his or her own opinion." But does this claim imply that (2) "everyone's opinion is equally right"? What is the difference between the two claims? Could an objectivist be tolerant, respectful of the opinions of others, and believe in free speech by accepting claim 1 but still reject claim 2?

EXAMINING THE STRENGTHS AND WEAKNESSES OF ETHICAL OBJECTIVISM

Positive Evaluation

1. Is it possible to avoid having any objective moral principles at all? Is it possible to consistently live and defend relativism? Don't the relativists contradict themselves when they say, "You *should not* judge another person's or culture's morality"? Isn't this statement like saying, "You should never use the word *never*" or, "You should always avoid the word *always*"? If you break a promise to a relativist or cheat him of what he is due, do you think he would accept your defense that he should not rebuke you because morality is simply a matter of opinion?

2. As long as there are at least two persons in the world, there will always be conflicts. But one of the purposes of morality is to provide an objective, rational, and impartial way to resolve conflicts. Doesn't relativism leave us without any basis for rationally resolving moral conflicts? If every person or society is allowed to embrace whatever morality pleases them or is convenient, isn't morality then useless?

Negative Evaluation

1. It is notoriously difficult to find agreement concerning what actions are right or wrong. Taking the issue one step back, it is also difficult to find agreement concerning what principles should be used to determine the rightness or wrongness of an action. There are facts about planets and stars that serve to confirm or refute our theories about them. But rightness or wrongness do not seem to be observable features of nature against which our moral theories can be tested. Unlike scientific inquiry, there are no meters, telescopes, or microscopes for observing and measuring the moral qualities of actions. Don't these considerations support the relativist's claim that morality is a function of opinions, attitudes, emotions, or social traditions rather than objective truth?

2. Even though other societies have moral codes very different from ours, many of them seem to flourish and provide a basis for human happiness. Doesn't the existence of such societies suggest that there are no moral absolutes but that morality is a matter of what works for a particular society?

5.2 ETHICAL EGOISM

LEADING QUESTIONS: *Ethical Egoism*

1. Isn't it true that any action that you consider to be good is one that will achieve some goal that you find to be valuable? If you find a goal to be valuable, doesn't that mean that

it is a goal that you desire? Doesn't it follow that any action that you consider to be good will be one that satisfies some desire of yours? Can we then say that your ethics are based on the satisfaction of your own desires?

2. Suppose you had the choice of spending your life savings to save the life of the person you love versus spending it to save the lives of 10 strangers. Which would you choose? Would it be selfish to save the life of the one person who matters to you personally instead of saving the lives of 10 others? Would this choice be morally justified?

3. Is it always bad for people to be concerned only with serving their own interests? For example, you try to get the best score for yourself on a test. But if the test is graded on a curve, the better you do the worse others will do. Is there anything wrong with that? In business, each company is out to get the largest profits by capturing the market with the best product at the lowest price. But when companies seek to maximize their profits in this way, it often creates the best results for the consumers. Isn't this good? Similarly, in a court of law, each lawyer promotes the best interests of his or her client, and we presume that this procedure will help ensure that all aspects of the case will be revealed. Isn't this good? If caring for others is a moral ideal, then shouldn't you *not* try to excel beyond your fellow students? Shouldn't companies seek to help their competitors? Shouldn't a lawyer help the opposition strengthen its case? Of course, all these suggestions for being a caring person are absurd. Don't these examples illustrate that, contrary to common opinion, serving your own interests can be not only morally acceptable, but even positively good?

As these questions suggest, the proper role of self-interest in life and in an ethical theory is an important topic in ethics. Philosophers debate whether selfishness is bad and even whether unselfishness is possible. These issues arise in Somerset Maugham's novel *Of Human Bondage*. In a Paris bar, Philip Carey and Cronshaw (two characters in the novel) are having a conversation. Philip expresses the belief that people sometimes act unselfishly and implies that it is a person's moral obligation to do so. This remark provides the opportunity for Cronshaw to expound his ethical philosophy.

FROM W. SOMERSET MAUGHAM

Of Human Bondage [24]

"You will find as you grow older that the first thing needful to make the world a tolerable place to live in is to recognize the inevitable selfishness of humanity. You demand unselfishness from others, which is a preposterous claim that they should sacrifice their desires to yours. Why should they? When you are reconciled to the fact that each is for himself in the world you will ask less from your fellows. They will not disappoint you, and you will look upon them more charitably. Men seek but one thing in life—their pleasure. . . .

"Man performs actions because they are good for him, and when they are good for other people as well they are thought virtuous: if he finds pleasure in giving alms he is charitable; if he finds pleasure in helping others he is benevolent; if he finds pleasure in working for society he is public-spirited; but it is for your private pleasure that you give twopence to a beggar as much as it is for my private pleasure that I drink another whiskey and soda. I, less of a humbug than you, neither applaud myself for my pleasure nor demand your admiration."

Philip is horrified by his friend's egoistic philosophy and retorts, "But have you never known people to do things they didn't want to instead of things they did?" To this Cronshaw replies:

"No. You put your question foolishly. What you mean is that people accept an immediate pain rather than an immediate pleasure. The objection is as foolish as your manner of putting it. It is clear that men accept an immediate pain rather than an immediate pleasure, but only because they expect a greater pleasure in the future. Often the pleasure is illusory, but their error in calculation is no refutation of the rule. You are puzzled because you cannot get over the idea that pleasures are only of the senses; but, child, a man who dies for his country dies because he likes it as surely as a man eats pickled cabbage because he likes it. It is a law of creation. If it were possible for men to prefer pain to pleasure the human race would have long since become extinct."

- Do you agree with Cronshaw's philosophy? Why?
- What reasons could be given to support it? On what basis could it be argued that his philosophy is false?
- Given his philosophy, how does Cronshaw explain the fact that people sometimes help one another, do what is painful, and even sacrifice their lives?

In the first two sentences of this passage, Cronshaw actually makes two claims. The first asserts the "inevitable selfishness of humanity." This comment is a psychological claim about human motivation that is known as **psychological egoism.** We examine this position shortly. What is of interest for the moment is the second statement that it is "preposterous" to claim that people *should* sacrifice their desires for others. The position that Cronshaw is ridiculing here is known as **altruism,** which is the claim that we should be unselfishly concerned for the welfare of others and should act for the sake of other people's interests and needs. In contrast, Cronshaw is embracing **ethical egoism**, which is the position that people ought always to do only what is in their own self-interest. According to this position, all moral duties are ultimately duties to myself. Any supposed moral obligations I have toward others and society can only be justified if they enhance my own self-interest.

At first glance it may seem that the term *ethical egoism* is as contradictory as the term *married bachelor.* The term *egoism* is often associated with the qualities of being self-centered, selfish, egotistical, avaricious, and greedy. Egoism is condemned from the pulpit and denounced in newspaper editorials as the sanctuary of cynics, users, scoundrels, and manipulators. When baseball manager Leo Durocher said, "Nice guys finish last," there was no great rush to nominate him for the Nobel Peace Prize for humanitarian efforts. In the 1970s the media branded the youth of that time as the Me Generation because of their alleged disregard for any cause other than their own personal interests. Playing off the spirit of the times, a magazine called *Self* appeared on the scene. Best-selling books such as Robert Ringer's *Looking Out for #1* and David Seabury's *The Art of Selfishness* appealed to those seeking to rationalize the policy of "me first." The Sermon on the Mount says, "Blessed are the meek, for they will inherit the earth." However, to the egoist, the only thing the meek will inherit is the *dirt.* Given these popular conceptions of the position, isn't egoism antithetical to the very notion of ethics? Don't most ethical systems call us to rise above our own selfish interests to fulfill our duty or to serve the interests of others?

On the other hand, is self-love necessarily bad? After all, even the Bible commands that you should "love your neighbor as you love yourself." Even though it is calling for altruism, this ethical principle still makes self-love the paradigm for our attitude toward others. As I point out in the discussion to follow, ethical egoists maintain that their philosophy is

psychological egoism the theory that people always act so as to serve their own interests, or at least what they believe to be their interests

altruism the claim that we should be unselfishly concerned for the welfare of others and should act for the sake of other people's interests and needs

ethical egoism the position that people ought always to do only what is in their own self-interest

maligned only because it is misunderstood. They claim either that all human behavior is motivated by self-interest or that if it is not, rationality dictates that it should be.

SURVEYING THE CASE FOR ETHICAL EGOISM

Some Common Misconceptions about Egoism

Before examining the arguments for ethical egoism, it will be worthwhile to first weed out some inaccurate conceptions of the position. First, it is sometimes thought that egoism says, "Do whatever you want to do." If so, how would it be possible for anyone ever to do what was morally wrong if doing what we want is sufficient to be ethical? This formulation of egoism must be incorrect, because the person who acts from altruistic motives is doing what he or she wants to do, but the egoist would say that acting in this way is morally mistaken. Furthermore, what you want to do at the moment may not be what is best for you. For example, your immediate desire may be to party all night instead of studying for a test. In this case, however, serving your own immediate desire is not in your best self-interest. Thus, acting on the basis of your self-interest may be different from acting on the basis of your desires.

Rather than urging us to gratify our *subjective* desires, ethical egoism says we ought to be concerned with our *objective* self-interest. But even if I always seek to serve my best interests, there is a difference between what I believe is in my self-interest and what genuinely is. I may believe that investing in a certain stock is in my self-interest, but I may be mistaken about this investment. For the egoist, therefore, miscalculation, ignorance, stupidity, and weakness of the will are obstacles to the morally fulfilled life, as they are for any ethics that is concerned with the objective consequences of our actions. Many of the immediate objections to ethical egoism can be disarmed once we realize that the most plausible versions of egoism are concerned with the long-term consequences of our actions and call for rational, enlightened self-interest, based on the best available knowledge about a person's self and circumstances.

STOP AND THINK

Can you think of a time in which you did what you wanted to do, seeking to fulfill some desire that you had, but it did not serve your best self-interest?

Another misconception of ethical egoism is to believe that we are never obligated to act in a way that will benefit other people or even to believe that it is always wrong to do so. However, seeking to serve my own interests does not necessarily lead to narrow-minded, selfish actions. To be successful in life, I probably need to have a good reputation and be liked by people so that they will be inclined to help me out and promote my interests. For example, if I am a successful businessperson, I could spend all my wealth on expensive cars, yachts, and jewelry. But if I donate a substantial amount of money to the local college, I may feel a sense of personal satisfaction, I will receive good publicity, and this public admiration will be good for my business. Egoism is primarily concerned with ends and not means. Hence, making others happy could be a means that serves the ends of my own interests. You often cannot identify an ethical egoist by observing outward behavior alone; you must know something about the motive or moral theory that is the source of that person's behavior. Thus, a wise ethical egoist might find it rational to be pleasant toward others, help them out with their needs, give to charities, and so on. From the ethical egoist's perspective, however, the happiness we produce in others can only be incidental to what makes such actions morally right. The ethical egoist would have to say that altruistic actions are morally justified only if they ultimately serve our self-interest in the long run.

STOP AND THINK

Can you think of a time in which you acted in a way that benefited others but you were actually benefiting yourself in doing so?

Finally, it is a mistake to suppose that an advocate of ethical egoism is necessarily an *egotist*. Egotism is a personality trait and not an ethical theory. The egotist is someone who always wants to be the center of attention and who is a pushy, narcissistic, self-promoting person with an inflated ego. Such people tend to be irritating and obnoxious and are rarely successful in winning friends and influencing people. Paradoxically, the egotist is unlikely to be successful at living out the philosophy of egoism. Hence, an enlightened ethical egoist can be charming, amiable, modest, and considerate of others if exhibiting these traits is to his or her advantage in the long run.

The Varieties of Ethical Egoism

Several types of ethical egoism need to be distinguished before we can analyze the philosophy in detail. First, a person who embraces *personal ethical egoism* makes the following claim: "As for me, I believe I ought to always act in ways that will maximize my self interest, but I have no opinion about how you should act." This expression is of a personal policy, but it is not a theory about what makes an action morally right for anyone (other than the speaker). As such, it does not make an impersonal, objective claim about the nature of moral obligation that solicits our acceptance. Consequently, this claim is incapable of either defense or refutation. The only response to be made to this position is, "Thank you for sharing that with me."

On the other hand, if I were someone who advocates *individual ethical egoism* I would make the following claim: "The morally right act is the one that serves the interests of me (the author of this book)." According to this position, for you to be a moral person, whenever you act you should always ask, "How will this action benefit the author of my philosophy book?" Of course, this form of egoism is absurd and grotesque, and no one is likely to take it very seriously. If morality is dependent on how an action affects *me*, then before I was born there were no moral obligations and after I die morality would come to an end, because before and after I existed no action would produce any harm or benefit to me. Furthermore, this position is indefensible, for how could I make the case that I am so special that everyone ought to always serve my individual interests? Although some people may practice individual ethical egoism, it lacks the impartiality and universal appeal that is necessary to be a credible ethical theory.

The only version of ethical egoism that has any hope of persuading anyone is *universal ethical egoism*. Whereas the individual ethical egoist says, "Every person ought to do only what will further *my* interests," the universal ethical egoist says, "Every person ought to do only what will further *his or her own* interests." In other words, this position claims that when anyone acts (not just the speaker) the standard of right action is that person's own interests, whoever that person may be. Accordingly, this position has the impartiality and

Egoism and Benevolence

Friedrich Nietzsche, a powerful spokesman for egoism, thought that the emotion of pity is despicable. Weak people pathetically affirm their own superiority by pitying someone more wretched than they are. In the following passage, however, he says that the noble human being (the egoist) can help the less fortunate, but only because the superior types have an abundance of psychological wealth, not because they need to feel good about themselves.

> In the foreground there is the feeling of fullness, of power that seeks to overflow, the happiness of high tension, the consciousness of wealth that would give and bestow: the noble human being, too, helps the unfortunate, but not, or almost not, from pity, but prompted more by an urge begotten by excess of power.[25]

Similarly, Ayn Rand (a contemporary advocate of egoism) said that the egoist who values his own self can value the potential and humanity in others and even help a stranger in an emergency as long as he makes no significant sacrifice of his own interests.

> The moral purpose of a man's life is the achievement of his own happiness. This does not mean that he is indifferent to all men, that human life is of no value to him and that he has no reason to help others in an emergency. But it *does* mean that he does not subordinate his life to the welfare of others, that he does not sacrifice himself to their needs, that the relief of their suffering is not his primary concern, that any help he gives is an *exception,* not a rule, an act of generosity, not of moral duty, that it is *marginal and incidental*—as disasters are marginal and incidental in the course of human existence—and that *values,* not disasters, are the goal, the first concern and the motive power of his life.[26]

universal appeal that is necessary for a full-fledged ethical theory. To express this position figuratively, the supreme principle of morality is that "you should cultivate your garden and I should cultivate mine." Now that we have concluded that universal ethical egoism is the only version of egoism that should be taken seriously, our next task is to examine it further by considering some important issues raised by this position.

Selfishness, Self-Interest, and Others

In ordinary usage, there is a difference between the terms *selfish* and *self-interest* when applied to motives or behavior.[27] Examples of selfish behavior would be acting to benefit myself with no regard for the harm others may suffer from my actions, or acting unfairly to gain an advantage for myself while depriving others of what they are due. However, the fact that I am acting for the sake of my own self-interest does not *necessarily* mean I am being selfish in these ways. If I exercise regularly for the sake of my health, I am acting in my own self-interest, but I am not acting selfishly.

How do ethical egoists define *self-interest?* Some egoists define self-interest in terms of pleasure. However, we should not think that they are talking only about raw, physical pleasure. There are, for example, also intellectual pleasures, the pleasures of enjoying great art, and the pleasures of friendship. The position that claims that pleasure is the only thing that has value is known as **hedonism.** (I discuss hedonism more fully in section 5.3,

hedonism the position that pleasure is the only thing that has value

FRANK & ERNEST: © Thaves/Dist. by United Feature Syndicate, Inc.

"Utilitarianism.") However, other egoists think that pleasure is too narrow a notion to define self-interest; they speak more broadly in terms of happiness or self-realization. Hence, for the purposes of our discussion, we will consider "acting in our self-interest" in the broadest possible way as the rational pursuit of those ends that will contribute to our personal happiness, to the achievement of the good life for ourselves, or to the maximization of our own good and well-being.

You may be inclined to think that it is impossible for an ethical egoist to have friends or to love someone, because friendship and love often require a certain measure of self-sacrifice. In her book *The Virtue of Selfishness: A New Concept of Egoism,* Ayn Rand argues that a true sacrifice is "the surrender of a greater value for the sake of a lesser one or of a nonvalue." Obviously, this sacrifice is not something an ethical egoist would make. However, because Rand does not think that love necessarily involves sacrifice, she finds no incompatibility between being a rational, consistent egoist and a lover. She says that, contrary to the ethics of sacrifice, the egoist is a "trader." When the egoist's actions benefit someone else at some cost to himself, he is not making a sacrifice but an exchange: He is exchanging something that has lesser value to obtain some end that has more value for him. Hence, the soldier who is willing to die fighting for the cause of freedom does so because it is in his interest to risk death rather than live in a dictatorship. Similarly, Rand says that genuine love is not self-sacrificing because it involves valuing another person who exemplifies the values and qualities we cherish in ourselves.

> Love and friendship are profoundly personal, selfish values: love is an expression and assertion of self-esteem, a response to one's own values in the person of another. One gains a profoundly personal, selfish joy from the mere existence of the person one loves. It is one's own personal, selfish happiness that one seeks, earns and derives from love.[28]

STOP AND THINK

Do you agree with Rand's theory of love? Does it describe what most people think of as love? Does it describe what actually motivates people to fall in love? What could be said in favor of her view? How might someone criticize her account of love?

Rand goes on to give the example of a man who passionately loves his wife and spends a fortune to cure her of a serious disease. According to Rand, this example is a paradigm of egoistic (and thus moral) behavior because the wife's companionship is of greater value to the man than is his money. As she puts it, "It would be absurd to claim that he does it as

CALVIN AND HOBBES © 1991 Watterson. Used by permission of Universal Uclick. All rights reserved.

a 'sacrifice' for *her* sake, not his own, and that it makes no difference to *him,* personally and selfishly, whether she lives or dies."[29] In contrast, Rand claims that if it were possible to use that money to save the lives of 10 other women who meant nothing to him as opposed to saving his wife, the morality of altruism would obligate him to choose this unselfish alternative. Having clarified some of the main themes in ethical egoism, we now consider three arguments that are used to support it.

Argument 1: Psychological Egoism Implies Ethical Egoism

Recall the opening passage from *Of Human Bondage,* where Cronshaw expressed his belief in the "inevitable selfishness of humanity" and went on to say that "Man performs actions because they are good for him." I said that this comment was an expression of psychological egoism. *Psychological egoism* is the theory that, as a matter of fact, people always act so as to serve their own interests (or at least, what they believe to be their interests). In other words, rather than claiming that altruism is simply misguided, the psychological egoist claims that human nature makes it impossible. According to this view, all apparently altruistic or self-sacrificing behavior is really a disguised egoism that serves the interests of the agent. Notice that this theory is a *psychological* theory about people's motives, inclinations, or dispositions. As such, it is not an *ethical* theory, for it does not *prescribe* how we *ought* to act but only purports to *describe* how we *do* act. In other words, psychological egoism expresses a factual statement, whereas ethical egoism establishes an ethical standard. Even though the two positions are making different claims and even though one is a psychological theory and the other an ethical theory, the fact remains that psychological egoism is frequently used to support ethical egoism. As Cronshaw argued, because the laws of nature dictate that humans inevitably serve only their own interests, it is preposterous to suppose that they have a moral obligation to do anything else but that.

According to official figures, close to 3,000 people died in the terrorist attacks on New York on that dreadful day of September 11, 2001. Many more thousands survived, mainly through the efforts of brave rescue workers who pulled people out of the World Trade Center's burning towers. Among those who perished were some 300 New York firefighters and police officers who bravely entered the fiery towers in an attempt to rescue total strangers. As one survivor said of the rescuers, "They were going up as I was coming down." Does this example of sacrificial behavior provide a definitive rebuttal of psychological egoism? How would psychological egoists attempt to preserve their view of human motivation in the face of this counterexample? What is your assessment of the psychological egoist's possible reply?

The argument for ethical egoism that is currently being considered is based not only on the thesis of psychological egoism, but also on the principle that "ought" implies "can." In other words, I cannot have a moral obligation to do something if it is impossible to do it. For example, I cannot have an obligation to swim to save a drowning child if I am unable to swim.

The argument can be formulated in the following way:

1. I have a moral obligation to perform an action only if I am able to do it. (Ought implies can)
2. I am able to perform an action only if I do it to maximize my own self-interest. (Psychological egoism)

Therefore

3. I have a moral obligation to perform an action only if I do it to maximize my own self-interest.

Therefore

4. Ethical egoism is true.

The part of the argument that requires the closest scrutiny is premise 2, which assumes psychological egoism. First, it seems strange to conclude that I have an obligation to always act on the basis of my self-interest if (as premise 2 states) I am incapable of doing otherwise. It is like saying, "You have a moral obligation to blink when an object approaches your eye" or, "You have a moral obligation to grow hair on your head." Because under normal circumstances these results are inevitable, it seems superfluous to include them within the realm of morality. Morality has to do with choices that we are free to make or not make, not with what we will do no matter what. Notice that it is precisely for this reason that the hard determinist claims that we do not have moral responsibility (see the discussion of hard determinism in 3.5 and 3.6).

A second major problem with psychological egoism is the abundant counterexamples against it. People sometimes seem to have a clear-headed understanding of what is in their best self-interest but still act contrary to it. For example, many smokers know that their habit is causing their health to deteriorate but make no effort to change their behavior. Furthermore, it seems that if psychological egoism is true, then no one would ever act unselfishly, benevolently, or altruistically, but obviously people do act this way. A sister will donate one of her kidneys to a sibling who needs it, people will give money to a charity rather than spend it on themselves, and a soldier will sacrifice his life in war for the sake of his country.

In reply to the self-destructive behavior, the psychological egoist might say that smokers have an abstract understanding of the dangers of smoking but still believe that the stimulation and psychological benefits of nicotine are of such advantage to them that it is worth the risk. To say that we always act from the motive of maximizing our self-interest does not mean that we always correctly calculate what is best for us.

In addressing the benevolent behavior, the psychological egoist recognizes that people often act in a way that serves the interests of others but deny that they do it *for the sake of others.* In other words, even when your actions benefit someone else, you are not doing it from a benevolent motive (it is claimed), but you are doing it to serve your own interests (in some way). This point is illustrated by Robert Ringer's remarks on the great social reformer Mahatma Gandhi in *Looking Out for #1.*

> Can I honestly say that I believe Gandhi was acting selfishly when he "sacrificed" himself for the freedom of the Indian people? No, I can't say that I believe it. It would be more proper to say that I know it for a fact. . . . Whatever Gandhi did, out of rational or irrational choice, he did because he chose to do it. . . . Martyrs are selfish people—the same as you and me—but with insatiable egos.[30]

It is clear that psychological egoists must claim that there is an ulterior, self-centered motive behind every allegedly benevolent action. They must even dogmatically insist that when we sincerely believe we are acting for the sake of others, we are really self-deceived about our true, egoistic motives. This position is implausible, however, because it collapses important distinctions between radically different types of behavior. According to this position, both the college student who spends his weekends partying and the one who spends them donating her labor to build homes for the poor are really acting for themselves. If psychological egoism is true, then there is no difference between the sadist and the saint, or the coward and the hero. The problem is not simply that it is objectionable to view the sadist and the saint as similiar but that it is dubious to suppose that they are operating from the same motive.

An argument to support psychological egoism could be formulated in the following manner. In examining this argument, try to decide which of the premises is the weakest.

1. Whenever we act we are always trying to achieve some goal that we desire.
2. Whenever we achieve some goal that we desire, we obtain personal satisfaction.
3. So, whenever we act we are always trying to obtain personal satisfaction.
4. Obtaining personal satisfaction serves our self-interest.
5. Therefore, whenever we act we are always trying to serve our self-interest.

Bishop Butler (1692–1752), a clergyman and famous essayist on ethics, wrote a classic refutation of this argument. He pointed out that just because a person desires something does not mean that the person's own satisfaction is the object of that desire. For example, if I desire a cold drink, then it is true that my own physical pleasure is the ultimate object of that desire. But if I desire to delight my friend with an unexpected gift, the object of the desire is my friend's happiness. So the problem with the argument is that statement 3 does not follow from the first two statements. The argument equivocates between "we obtain personal satisfaction" and "we are trying to obtain personal satisfaction."* It is true that we usually feel a sense of satisfaction when we get what we desire, but the personal satisfaction

---

*See the fallacy of equivocation in the appendix to the text.

is often the consequence of getting what we desire, not its goal. I could not get a sense of satisfaction from making my friend happy if I did not have a prior concern for the welfare of my friend for her own sake.

These points touch on what is sometimes called the "paradox of hedonism." If we pursue pleasure (or more generally, happiness) as our all-consuming goal, we'll probably have a hard time finding it. As the following thought experiment illustrates, happiness usually comes to us as a by-product of pursuing other goals that we value.

THOUGHT EXPERIMENT: *The Pursuit of Pleasure*

Have you ever been in a state of mind in which you were desperate to have fun at all costs? You had a rough week, but it is now Friday night and you are at a party. The entire evening you keep saying, "I hope I have a good time! Am I having a good time yet? I'll be crushed if the evening ends and I didn't have a good time. I just HAVE to have a good time!" Every time you talk to someone or dance to the music, you are constantly measuring your pleasure quotient on some sort of internal scale. Each moment you are at the party, you are worried that there is someone else you should be talking to or something else you could do to maximize the pleasure of the moment. This pathetic drive for pleasure, of course, is likely to be counterproductive. If you had relaxed and taken things as they came, you might have met some new and interesting people, participated in good conversations, and enjoyed the music, all without worrying about whether each action would adequately maximize your self-interest. When we cease to be frantically obsessed with our own pleasure, we often look back on the day's events after they are over and suddenly notice that we had a good time and really enjoyed what we had been doing. While pleasure and happiness are important ingredients in life, they often are the indirect rewards for pursuing other things that have value, such as friendships, intellectual challenges, political causes, artistic endeavors, participation in sports, nature walks, and humanitarian projects.

- Can you think of actual events in your own life when the direct pursuit of pleasure failed, but the pursuit of other goals brought personal satisfaction as a result?

Contemporary philosopher Joel Feinberg exposes a fundamental problem with psychological egoism through the following dialogue:

"All men desire only satisfaction."

"Satisfaction of what?"

"Satisfaction of their desires."

"Their desires for what?"

"Their desires for satisfaction."

"Satisfaction of what?"

"Their desires."

"For what?"

"For satisfaction"—etc., ad infinitum.[31]

In the final analysis, the relationship between psychological and ethical egoism does not seem to be tight enough to claim that one logically implies the other. On the one hand, a person could be a psychological egoist without being an ethical egoist. The Christian philosopher Augustine (354–430), for example, was a psychological egoist because he believed that our natural inclination was always to serve our own selfish ends instead of serving God. However, he was not an ethical egoist because he added that our psychological nature was corrupted by sin and only through divine grace could we rise above our egoism and be empowered to do what we ought to do. On the other hand, a person could be an ethical egoist without being a psychological egoist. The contemporary writer Ayn Rand was an ethical egoist because she believed that "the moral purpose of a man's life is the achievement of his own happiness." But Rand was not a psychological egoist, because she believed that the majority of people are muddle-headed altruists who do not behave egoistically at all. This belief is illustrated by her claim that the practice of altruism is the source of society's ills: "For a view of the nature of altruism, its consequences and the enormity of the moral corruption it perpetrates, I shall refer you to . . . any of today's newspaper headlines."[32]

Argument 2: Ethical Egoism Leads to the Best Society

Ethical egoists sometimes argue that if we were all egoists, life would be a whole lot better for everyone. The economist Adam Smith (1723–1790) argued that in a competitive, free-enterprise economic system, people try to enhance their own wealth by producing the best product at a lower price than the competitors do. Although everyone is motivated by his or her own self-interest and is not consciously trying to serve the overall good, the "invisible hand" of marketplace dynamics creates the best situation for consumers. Even if we would grant that this economic system is the best, however, some critics question whether you can apply principles that work in business transactions to the ethics of personal relations. Nevertheless, the marketplace does provide examples of how serving self-interest can also serve the greater good.

Similarly, in the following passage Ayn Rand argues that we have two choices: (1) embrace "rational selfishness," which will cause society to flourish or (2) embrace altruism, which will lead to the destruction of all that is worthwhile in society.

> It is only on the basis of rational selfishness—on the basis of justice—that men can be fit to live together in a free, peaceful, prosperous, benevolent, *rational* society. . . .
>
> It is philosophy that sets men's goals and determines their course; it is only philosophy that can save them now. Today, the world is facing a choice: if civilization is to survive, it is the altruist morality that men have to reject.[33]

To be fair to Rand, she would argue that the good of society is an *effect* of everyone adopting rational selfishness, but it is not the *reason* for adopting it. Although Rand doesn't rest her case for egoism on its social benefits, she does claim there is a perfect harmony between selfishness and the social good.

The problem with the "good of society" argument is that it is paradoxical. Although the argument is used to defend ethical egoism, it actually undermines it. The argument seems to be saying that we should pursue our own self-interest, because doing so will lead to the greatest good for the greatest number. But if we are egoists, why should we be concerned with the greatest good of society? In essence, this second argument for ethical egoism actually claims that everyone pursuing his or her own interests is a means to the *end* of the general happiness of the many. As we see in the next section, the principle that we should maximize the greatest happiness for the greatest number of people is the fundamental ethical principle of utilitarianism. But utilitarianism is decidedly different from egoism, for it allows each individual's self-interest to count only as one vote to be tallied along with the interests of others. Furthermore, it hardly seems plausible to suppose that what is good for me or what is good for you will always neatly line up with what is good for society as a whole, as Rand and others suppose. On the contrary, it seems possible that an action that would maximize my self-interest could be harmful to the rest of humanity. For example, I could build a factory that would bring me enormous profits but would deplete the natural resources and cause pollution problems in the long run. If the cumulative, negative effects on the environment would not be felt in my lifetime, then they would not affect my self-interest.

Argument 3: Ethical Egoism Is the Ultimate Ethical Principle

The first argument for ethical egoism makes a questionable inference from an equally questionable psychological theory, and the second argument justifies egoism by appealing to nonegoistic ends. The third argument avoids these problems by claiming that if we are truly rational persons, we will realize that self-interest is a fundamental, irreducible value that is the source of all other values.

AYN RAND
(1905–1982)

This argument was forcefully articulated in the writings of Ayn Rand (1905–1982). Although Rand grew up in Russia, she rebelled against what she perceived as the excessive governmental tyranny and disintegration of free inquiry that followed the communist revolution. In 1926 she escaped to America and began her career as a Hollywood screen-writer. Throughout her life, she defended both ethical egoism and capitalism in her essays and literary works. Among her best-known novels are *We the Living* (1936), *The Fountain-head* (1943), and *Atlas Shrugged* (1959). Rand called her personal philosophy *Objectivism*. All ethical egoists are ethical objectivists, because they affirm that there are ethical principles that are universal. However, the reverse is not true, because most ethical objectivists do not embrace egoism. To avoid confusion concerning this terminology, when I use the term *objectivism* in this text, I am referring to the more general category, but when Rand uses the term, she is referring specifically to her version of ethical egoism. In the following passage, Rand argues that egoism is the ultimate ethical principle.

FROM AYN RAND
The Virtue of Selfishness [34]

An *ultimate* value is that final goal or end to which all lesser goals are the means—and it sets the standard by which all lesser goals are *evaluated*. An organism's life is its *standard of value*: that which furthers its life is the *good,* that which threatens it is the *evil.* . . .

The Objectivist ethics holds man's life as the *standard* of value—and *his own life* as the ethical *purpose* of every individual man. . . .

Value is that which one acts to gain and/or keep—*virtue* is the act by which one gains and/or keeps it. The three cardinal values of the Objectivist ethics—the three values which, together, are the means to and the realization of one's ultimate value, one's own life—are: Reason, Purpose, Self-Esteem, with their three corresponding virtues: Rationality, Productiveness, Pride. . . .

[Altruism is] the ethical theory which regards man as a sacrificial animal, which holds that man has no right to exist for his own sake, that service to others is the only justification of his existence, and that self-sacrifice is his highest moral duty, virtue and value.

Rand's argument could be formulated in the following way:

1. There can be no higher value than our own life, for without it, there could be no other values.

2. "Our own life" includes more than biological survival; it also includes our interests, projects, and the goods we earn and create for ourselves, for without these factors we would have no life worth living.
3. Rationality is the basic instrument for human survival, because we cannot live according to instinct as do animals.
4. Altruism, the opposite of egoism, is irrational, because it destroys the value of our life and thereby undermines the only basis for value in our life.
5. Only ethical egoism affirms the right of each of us to make our life the ultimate value and thereby makes it possible for us to pursue any values at all.
6. Therefore, ethical egoism is the only rationally defensible ethical theory.

Notice that Rand assumes a false dichotomy between pure ethical egoism and pure ethical altruism.* Because the form of altruism she describes is so extreme, however, egoism seems like the only rational choice. For example, an empty-headed altruist might embrace the foolish principle, "Never spend money on your own health care, but always use what money you have for the health of others." But if I followed this principle, I would always have to provide money for your health care and never spend it on mine. Furthermore, if you followed this principle, you would have to take the money I gave you and spend it on someone else. Finally, if everyone followed this principle, no one would be able to get any health care. But contrary to what Rand supposes, rejecting her ethical egoism does not require us to be extreme altruists. It is morally right for me to make sure my reasonable needs and those of my family are taken care of before I tend to the needs of others (rejection of pure altruism). This moral right, however, does not mean that I have no obligation whatsoever to sacrifice some of my trivial needs or desires when possible in order to help provide for the life, health, and basic well-being of my fellow human beings (rejection of pure egoism).

STOP AND THINK

Can you think of a situation in which you would be morally justified to serve your own interests even if it required sacrificing someone else's interests or even if it indirectly resulted in harm to someone else? Suppose, for example, that the only way you could save your own life would be if you allowed another innocent person to die. (Think of the Titanic, which did not have enough lifeboats for everyone.) Could a nonegoist justify this action? Why? Are there less extreme situations in which you would be morally justified to serve your own interests at the expense of someone else's interests? Could there be any situations in which serving your own interests at the expense of another's would not be justified?

Ethical Egoism and the Conflict of Interests

Some critics of ethical egoism argue that it is contradictory for me to seek to serve my own interests and not yours at the same time that I claim that others ought to seek their own interests and not mine. If I am an egoist, why would I advise you to seek any interests other

---

*See the discussion of the false dichotomy fallacy in the appendix at the end of the text.

than my own? However, this criticism may not be as problematic as it appears at first. For example, if I am a skilled runner who loves the excitement of competition, I will wish that I win the race at the same time that I wish for you to do your best to win the race. If I found out that my manager had bribed the other runners to allow me to win, I would be robbed of the thrill of victory. Hence, there is a difference between what I believe you ought to do and the actual outcome I desire. (I believe that if you are rational you should try to win the race, but I desire that you will be unsuccessful.)

A critic of egoism could reply to this example by saying that a race is a rather limited domain of human action and the ethical principles that work in an athletic competition may not be applicable to life in general. In the serious issues in life it seems that there can be irreconcilable conflicts of interest between people. Ethical egoism, unlike other theories, offers us no impartial way to resolve these conflicts. However, Rand argues that ethical egoism "holds that the *rational* interests of men do not clash—that there is no conflict of interests among men who do not desire the unearned, who do not make sacrifices nor accept them, who deal with one another as *traders,* giving value for value."[35] She describes a trader as "a man who earns what he gets and does not give or take the undeserved. . . . He deals with men by means of a free, voluntary, unforced, uncoerced exchange—an exchange which benefits both parties by their own independent judgment."[36] However, it is not clear that her hero, the trader, is a thoroughgoing egoist. It seems that he is a trader whose pursuit of self-interest is constrained by principles of impartiality and fairness. Rand's deviation from pure egoism becomes clear in the following example.

Suppose you and I are both pursuing the same job. If I am an ethical egoist and *if I knew I could get away with it,* don't I have the obligation to do whatever is necessary to ensure that I get the job? For example, I could spread malicious rumors about you, snatch your job application out of the mailbox, or secretly slip you a drug so that you are a babbling idiot during the interview. In other words, this ethical stance would lead to the same behavior championed by Glaucon at the beginning of this chapter. In discussing this example, however, Rand indicates that this behavior would be wrong, for it ignores the key considerations of reality, context, responsibility, and effort.[37] Here is a summary of her discussion. (1) *Reality:* The mere fact that I want the job does not mean that I am entitled to it or deserve it. (2) *Context:* For me to have a job there has to be a successful business to hire me, and a business can be successful only if it can and does choose the best candidate among a pool of competitors. (3) *Responsibility:* If I seek something I desire, I have to take responsibility for all the conditions that are required to fulfill that desire. (4) *Effort:* Rational people know that they have a right only to that which they have earned or deserve.

Rand certainly embraces a more attractive version of ethical egoism than a vicious egoism in which people are allowed to seek their own ends while robbing others of what they deserve. However, critics claim that the degree to which her egoism is attractive is the degree to which she subordinates self-interest to the principles of rational consistency, impartiality, fairness, and justice. When she starts to work out the practical implications of her ethical egoism, it begins to sound more like Kantian ethics than egoism.* Even though getting a particular job may be in my best interests, Rand says it would be irrational for me to pursue it or even desire it if you are better qualified. Critics, however, question whether this conclusion is consistent with her egoism. Rand may be correct that the world would be better if people were *generally* rewarded according to their merit, but that could be consistent with me wanting to make myself the exception to the rule. She could object that my exception would violate the ideals of impartiality and rational consistency. But being

---

*See the discussion of Kantian ethics in section 5.4 of this chapter.

guided by these ideals would require us to abandon the main thesis of egoism, because the principles of impartiality and rational consistency imply that we should not serve our individual interests with total disregard for the interests of others, particularly if there are no significant differences between ourselves and others or if the differences are not due to our own efforts. For example, many people have achieved much of what they have in life through their own effort and merit. But many of these same people have also had the good fortune to be born with good health, in a good family, and in a prosperous society. While it is right that they should receive the just rewards of their efforts, it is also irrational for them to suppose that they may smugly enjoy the fruits of the good fortune that they did not earn with no regard for the suffering of others, when the less fortunate may have done nothing to deserve their lot in life.

THOUGHT EXPERIMENT: *What Are the Implications of Ethical Egoism?*

Some critics say that ethical egoism is unacceptable because it would justify clearly immoral actions. For example, critics charge that the ethical egoist would have to say that it would be morally wrong for the plantation owners in the 1840s to have freed their slaves or even to have treated them as fellow human beings, since it would be against the plantation owners' self-interest. On the other hand, Rand claims that, according to rational ethical egoism, slavery and racial discrimination are wrong because there could be no such thing as a "right" to enslave other people or to violate their individual rights.[38]

- Who is correct (the critics or Rand) concerning what is logically implied by egoism?

LOOKING THROUGH THE EGOIST'S LENS

1. How might an ethical egoistic justify performing the following actions? (a) Refusing to cheat on a test, even if you could get away with it; (b) helping your neighbor move some furniture; (c) diminishing your profits by giving your most productive employees a raise; (d) saving the life of the person you love at great risk to yourself.

2. The psychological egoist claims that we are all selfish. However, Rand (who is an ethical egoist but not a psychological egoist) says that while we *should* be selfish, most people are altruists. She points out, for example, that the word *selfishness* is identified with evil in popular usage. Furthermore, she complains that the well-accepted government programs of appropriating everyone's tax dollars and using them for the common good in education, health, and welfare show that our society consists primarily of brainwashed altruists. Do you agree with Rand that very few people in our society are rational egoists? Or do you think that egoism is fairly prevalent?

3. As little children we are taught to behave ethically for selfish reasons. Mother says, "If you want your friend to share her toys with you, you must share your toys with her." Furthermore, we are rewarded or praised if we are good and punished or scolded if we are bad. Popular television evangelists preach that following their precepts will bring personal success, prosperity, and health. Does selfishness play more of a role in our ethical life than most people would like to admit?

EXAMINING THE STRENGTHS AND WEAKNESSES OF EGOISM

Positive Evaluation

1. Is self-love or serving your own interests over those of others necessarily wrong? Isn't it right for you to spend the money you earned on your tuition as opposed to distributing it among others? The American Declaration of Independence says we have unalienable rights that include life, liberty, and the pursuit of happiness. Aren't these rights egoistic concerns? The document doesn't guarantee the right of everybody to be happy, nor does it say that you have an obligation to secure other people's happiness. Instead, it says you have a right to pursue your own happiness.

2. I am the best judge of my own wants and needs and you are the best judge of yours. Each of us is also in the best position to pursue our own wants and needs effectively. On the other hand, when others try to do what they think is "best" for us, they often end up being intrusive and making a mess of things. Furthermore, when I consider others' needs more important than my own, am I not showing a lack of self-esteem? Doesn't altruism also show a lack of respect for others by treating them as helpless beggars who are dependent on me for their well-being? Isn't charity degrading to the recipients, treating them as too incompetent to look after their own interests? Isn't it a healthier ethics to place the highest value on my own self and interests and to give others the dignity and the right to pursue their interests? What do you think?

3. The Golden Rule says, "Do unto others as you would have them do unto you." Doesn't this rule imply that the reason to treat others decently is that it is to your advantage to do so, because they will be more inclined to treat you decently? Isn't the primary reason for being honest, keeping promises, and fulfilling the other demands of morality the fact that it will be in your best interests to act this way? Isn't egoism really the basis of our commonsense morality?

Negative Evaluation

1. Ethical egoists often present a choice between pure egoism (being concerned exclusively with our own interests) and pure altruism (being concerned exclusively with others' interests). Because a policy of always sacrificing our own interests is untenable, ethical egoism seems to win out by default. But isn't this argument a false dichotomy? Wouldn't a more defensible ethical theory attempt to balance our own interests with those of others?

2. Suppose you and I are only casual acquaintances who are stranded in a lifeboat in the ocean and are waiting for rescuers to find us. I have managed to bring along a quantity of food and water, but you have none. Suppose further that you are an ethical egoist. What moral advice should you give me? If you tell me that I only have an obligation to serve my own interests, then I should keep the food and water for myself and let you die. On the other hand, if you want to live, then you will tell me that I have a moral obligation to sacrifice some of my resources for your sake. But this statement would require you to renounce your ethical egoism. Does this scenario show that it is impossible to consistently live and promote ethical egoism? How might an ethical egoist respond?

3. Harvard philosopher John Rawls proposes the following thought experiment for deciding what would be the most rational and impartial principles for governing society.[39] Suppose that you had the ability to determine what sort of society you would live in and

what principles will guide it. Of course, if you are a brown-eyed, female athlete named Kisha, you might like a society that gives the most benefits to brown-eyed, female athletes named Kisha. Such a society, however, would hardly be a defensible social structure to choose, for it is not based on rational and impartial considerations. To guarantee that your choices will be rational and impartial, Rawls says you must choose behind the "veil of ignorance." You must choose your society without knowing your race, sex, natural abilities, religion, interests, social position, income, or physical and psychological makeup. Not knowing if you would be poor, disabled, or lacking in natural abilities, would you choose a society based on egoism in which all members look out for themselves? Or would you choose a society that offered some degree of altruistic concern for the least advantaged?

4. Most people consider racism and sexism to be unacceptable policies because they arbitrarily advocate treating some individuals differently without justification. In the following argument, contemporary philosopher James Rachels claims that ethical egoism is similarly an arbitrary and unacceptable doctrine:

1. Any moral doctrine that assigns greater importance to the interests of one group than to those of another is unacceptably arbitrary unless there is some difference between the members of the groups that justifies treating them differently.
2. Ethical Egoism would have each person assign greater importance to his or her own interests than to the interests of others. *But there is no general difference between oneself and others, to which each person can appeal, that justifies this difference in treatment.*
3. Therefore, Ethical Egoism is unacceptably arbitrary.[40]

Is Rachels's argument a decisive refutation? How might an ethical egoist respond?

5.3 UTILITARIANISM

 LEADING QUESTIONS: *Utilitarianism*

1. Suppose I told you that it is your moral obligation to submit to a procedure that would cause you pain. Your natural reply would be, "Why do I have a moral duty to endure pain?" But suppose I then explained that your body has a one-in-a-million biochemical property such that a painful medical procedure would cause your body to produce antibodies that could be used to save the lives of hundreds of little children who are stricken with a rare and fatal disease. Does my explanation of the consequences of this action clarify why I claimed that you had a moral duty to endure the painful procedure? Similarly, aren't all our moral obligations and duties meant to lead to actions that result in the best overall consequences? Would it make any sense to say that some of our moral duties have no good effects, but only cause human misery? Aren't the consequences of an action what determines its rightness or wrongness?

2. Most people would say that it would usually be morally wrong to act in a way that violated any of the following rules: (1) tell the truth, (2) keep your promises, (3) do not kill innocent persons. Can you think of situations in which you would be morally justified to break each of those rules if doing so would create an enormous amount of good for humanity but if adhering to the rule would create an enormous amount of human unhappiness and suffering? Are there any actions that we normally think are wrong that could not be justified in certain situations? Are moral rules anything more than "rules of thumb"?

The first leading question suggests that moral duties have a purpose. It supposes that the principle "Do your duty for duty's sake" makes no sense if fulfilling an alleged moral obligation neither avoids some harm nor results in some good. The second question suggests that common moral commands are rules of thumb that produce desirable results in most cases, but they can be overridden when the circumstances and consequences require it. For example, consider the following three situations, corresponding to each of the moral rules that were listed. (1) A homicidal maniac with an axe asks you where he can find your friend. By lying to him you will save your friend and facilitate the murderer's capture. (2) You promised to help someone review for a test, but you fail to keep the promise because you suddenly have to drive an injured person to the emergency room. (3) You are fighting a just war against an evil tyrant who has murdered thousands of innocent victims in a bordering country. If a chemical warfare factory is bombed, it will save the lives of thousands of innocent civilians, but you know that three innocent people living near the factory will perish. Regardless of whether you agree with the action taken in all these cases, you are forced to think hard about the question, Does the end justify the means? The philosophers we study in this section would reply, "If the end doesn't justify the means, there is nothing else that could!" To further test your intuitions on the relationship between moral duties and consequences, consider the following thought experiment.

THOUGHT EXPERIMENT: *The Promise*

You and a friend have been shipwrecked on a desert island. Only a limited amount of food remains and it is doubtful that it will keep both of you alive until you are rescued. Because your friend is injured, it is unlikely that he will survive. He tells you that you can have all the food, but makes you promise that you will see to it that his nephew gets the millions of dollars in treasure that your friend discovered. You promise him you will do exactly as he requested. A few days later your friend dies, happy in the knowledge that you will carry out his last wish. After you are rescued, you seek to fulfill your promise by looking up the man's nephew (his only living relative). However, you are dismayed to find out that the nephew is living an extravagant and wasteful life consisting of drug abuse and huge gambling losses. You realize that if you keep your promise, it would not take long for the nephew to squander the entire fortune on his self-destructive and dissipated lifestyle. You are fairly sure that your friend knew the life his nephew was leading. As you are considering what to do, you notice an advertisement for a famous children's hospital that does research on childhood diseases such as leukemia and rare forms of cancer. If you gave the money to the hospital, it could be used to alleviate the suffering of many little children as well as fund research to prevent future suffering. Since your friend is dead, you are the only one who knows about the money and the promise. What should you do with the money? Why would your choice be the right thing to do?

Compare your response in the thought experiment to the following three decisions and justifications. Which one comes closest to the answer you gave?

MIMI: I would keep the money for myself. Although my friend found the treasure, I helped him die a peaceful death, so it is morally right that I should have it. Why should I hand over any of the money to that worthless nephew? I don't even know him, and, furthermore, he would only waste the money, whereas I could use it to pay for worthwhile things such as my education. Any promises I made to my friend became null and void when he died. It's unfortunate that children are dying, but I don't know them either and have no obligations toward them. I can't save the world, but I do have an obligation to do what is best for me.

MILLARD: I would give the money to the children's hospital or some other worthy cause. This action is morally right because it would produce the best consequences for the greatest number of people. Of course, the nephew will be deprived of the money, but he didn't know it had been promised to him anyway. Besides, he probably would have used the money in self-destructive ways, so I would actually be doing him some good by saving him from self-inflicted harm. Since my friend is dead, it would have no impact on him whether I kept my promise or how I used the money. Of course, I would love to keep the money for myself, but the happiness it would cause me would pale in comparison to the amount of good it would do for the sick children. Besides, it wouldn't be right to break the promise simply for selfish reasons, but it would be justified to help alleviate human suffering. This course of action is the morally right one for it would apparently not harm anyone, but it would produce a tremendous amount of good.

KANDICE: I would keep my promise and give my friend's money to his nephew. I have no doubt that this is my moral obligation regardless of what the consequences may be. After all, can I really predict the consequences with any certainty? Maybe the nephew would be so moved by his uncle's generosity that it would turn his life around and a great deal of good would come from this transformation. If someone made a promise to me on my deathbed, I would expect that she would carry it out, no matter what she thought about my wishes. So, it would be inconsistent and unfair for me to do otherwise. I would love to give the money to the children's hospital, but it is not mine to give. At any rate, the consequences are a matter of sheer speculation, but I do know that I made a solemn promise to a friend on his deathbed and that is what defines my moral duty.

As you may have suspected, Mimi (me-me) is thinking like an ethical egoist. She thinks that her only moral obligation is to serve her own self-interest. Because we have already discussed this position in the previous section, it is the remaining two decisions that are our concern at present. Millard thinks that the consequences of an action determine whether it is right or wrong. Because the consequences of breaking the promise and giving the money to the hospital are far better than keeping the promise, the moral principle he follows dictates that the former action is his moral duty. Kandice thinks that the consequences should play no role in deciding what to do. She claims that the nature of the action itself (keeping a promise or breaking it) determines her moral obligations.

Millard's ethical reasoning identifies him as a consequentialist. **Consequentialism** refers to any ethical theory that judges the moral rightness or wrongness of an act according to the desirability or undesirability of the action's consequences. To put it glibly, the consequentialist believes that "all's well that ends well." This type of theory is also known as *teleological ethics* (from the Greek word *telos,* meaning end or purpose). Kandice, on the other hand, took a deontological approach in resolving this ethical dilemma. **Deontological ethics** (from the Greek word *deon,* meaning duty) judges the moral rightness or wrongness of an act in terms of the intrinsic moral value of the act itself. (Some philosophers call deontological theories *formalistic ethical theories* because they judge the act in terms of its form, that is, in terms of the kind of act it is.) Deontological ethics is a *nonconsequentialist* theory because it holds that our duty to perform an action (or to refrain from doing it) is based on the nature of the act itself and not on its consequences. Kandice was concerned

consequentialism any ethical theory that judges the moral rightness or wrongness of an act according to the desirability or undesirability of the action's consequences; also called teleological ethics

deontological ethics any ethical theory that judges the moral rightness or wrongness of an act in terms of the intrinsic moral value of the act itself

Let five or more friends read the story of the deathbed promise and then ask them the following questions. (You can present the story to one friend at a time or as a group discussion.)

- What do you think should be done with the money?
- Why do you think your choice is the right thing to do and is better than any other alternative?

Decide whether each person's answer is closest to Mimi's (egoism), Millard's (consequentialism), or Kandice's (deontological ethics, or nonconsequentialism). Discuss with your friends some of the issues raised by their response. Some of your respondents might attempt a compromise, such as giving some of the money to the nephew and some to the hospital (and maybe even some to themselves). Because this compromise neither keeps the promise (strictly speaking) and probably does not produce the best consequences possible, ask them why they think this solution is the right one.

PHILOSOPHY
in the
MARKETPLACE

only with the moral obligation of keeping her promise no matter what the consequences might be. In this section we examine the most common form of consequentialism, known as *utilitarianism.* In the next section, we will contrast utilitarianism with *Kantian ethics,* the most common deontological ethical theory.

Because consequentialism claims that ethics is concerned with the goodness or badness of the consequences of our actions, there are two questions that every consequentialist must answer: (1) What has intrinsic value, and (2) Who should receive this value? Something has **intrinsic value** if it is good or desirable in itself, whereas something has **instrumental value** if its desirability is in terms of other ends it achieves. For example, we might believe that health has intrinsic value, whereas getting a shot has instrumental value only because it helps us achieve health.

Technically speaking, consequentialists can disagree on what has intrinsic value. Consequentialists would agree that the good action is one that produces the best consequences, but they may disagree as to whether good consequences could be defined as those that promote God's will, or knowledge, or beauty, or so on. Most consequentialist theories, however, define intrinsic value in terms of pleasure or, more broadly, happiness. Consequentialists argue that everything else that is good (even health) has only instrumental value in helping to bring about happiness. If you ask me why I am doing something and I reply, "It makes me happy," it doesn't make any sense to go on to ask, "Why do you do things that make you happy?" Since happiness seems to have intrinsic value, the pursuit of it needs no other justification.

We have already encountered one variety of consequentialist ethics in our discussion of ethical egoism. The ethical egoist claims that acts that produce happiness or well-being have intrinsic value, but quickly adds that the proper recipient of those consequences is the person who performed the act. Utilitarianism is in agreement with the egoist on the role of consequences in ethics, but disagrees about the recipient of the value. For the utilitarian, the proper recipient of that which has value is the greatest number of people possible. If happiness has value, utilitarians argue, then that value ought to be maximized and distributed among as many people as possible.

Utilitarianism defines a morally right action as one that produces at least as much good (utility) for all people affected by the action as any alternative action that could be performed. This definition of utilitarianism is often referred to as the *principle of utility.* This

intrinsic value the property that something has if it is good or desirable in itself

instrumental value desirability of something in terms of other ends it achieves

definition does not specify what is good or has value, but as I just mentioned, utilitarians have typically identified value with happiness. Let's now examine utilitarianism as it has been formulated and defended by its two founders as well as by contemporary philosophers.

SURVEYING THE CASE FOR UTILITARIANISM

JEREMY BENTHAM (1748–1832)

JEREMY BENTHAM
(1748–1832)

Although the main themes of utilitarianism were developed in the 18th century by several Scottish philosophers (including David Hume), its first explicit and systematic formulation is credited to the British philosopher Jeremy Bentham. Bentham was the son of a London attorney who had ambitious plans for Jeremy to become famous in a career in law. After studying law at Oxford University and graduating at age 15, however, Bentham discovered that although he had no interest in practicing law, he was interested in changing it. Having lived through the American Revolution, the French Revolution, the Napoleonic wars, and the rise of parliamentary government in England, Bentham was convinced that the political instability of the times was due to the irrational and chaotic foundations of the current legal systems and social structures. Accordingly, Bentham's philosophy of utilitarianism was an attempt to provide a rational and scientific foundation for law and morality. The opening lines of one of his best-known books make clear what this foundation will be.

FROM JEREMY BENTHAM

An Introduction to the Principles of Morals and Legislation[41]

I. Nature has placed mankind under the governance of two sovereign masters, *pain* and *pleasure*. It is for them alone to point out what we ought to do, as well as to determine what we shall do. On the one hand the standard of right and wrong, on the other the chain of causes and effects, are fastened to their throne. They govern us in all we do, in all we say, in all we think: every effort we can make to throw off our subjection, will serve but to demonstrate and confirm it. In words a man may pretend to abjure their empire: but in reality he will remain subject to it all the while. The *principle of utility* recognises this subjection, and assumes it for the foundation of that system, the object of which is to rear the fabric of felicity by the hands of reason and of law. Systems which attempt to question it, deal in sounds instead of sense, in caprice instead of reason, in darkness instead of light.

psychological hedonism the claim that the only causes operating in human behavior are the desires to obtain pleasure and avoid pain

ethical hedonism the theory that the moral rightness or wrongness of an action is a function of the amount of pleasure or pain it produces

This passage contains the thesis of **psychological hedonism,** which is the claim that the only causes operating in human behavior are the desires to obtain pleasure and avoid pain. Basically, this thesis is a version of psychological egoism (discussed in the previous section) with the additional claim that when people pursue their self-interest they are really pursuing pleasure and avoiding pain. But Bentham says that our two "sovereign masters" of pain and pleasure not only "determine what we shall do," but they also "point out what we ought to do." Hence, from his psychological theory he attempts to derive an **ethical hedonism,** which is the theory that the moral rightness or wrongness of an action is a function of the amount of pleasure or pain it produces. Critics claim that the problems of psychological egoism discussed in the last section and the difficulties of deriving an ethical theory from it are duplicated and even magnified in Bentham's hedonistic version.

As I said before, utilitarianism is a version of consequentialism, or teleological ethics. Accordingly, in the next two paragraphs, Bentham sets out the principle of utility as the foundation of all ethics.

II. The principle of utility is the foundation of the present work: it will be proper therefore at the outset to give an explicit and determinate account of what is meant by it. By the principle of utility is meant that principle which approves or disapproves of every action whatsoever, according to the tendency which it appears to have to augment or diminish the happiness of the party whose interest is in question: or, what is the same thing in other words, to promote or to oppose that happiness. I say of every action whatsoever; and therefore not only of every action of a private individual, but of every measure of government.

III. By utility is meant that property in any object, whereby it tends to produce benefit, advantage, pleasure, good, or happiness, (all this in the present case comes to the same thing) or (what comes again to the same thing) to prevent the happening of mischief, pain, evil, or unhappiness to the party whose interest is considered: if that party be the community in general, then the happiness of the community: if a particular individual, then the happiness of that individual.

Because pleasure is the only thing that has value, an action that maximizes the greatest amount of pleasure possible is the best action. In other words, the fundamental rule of utilitarianism is, "Act always to promote the greatest happiness for the greatest number." But because there are so many different kinds of pleasures, the question now arises, "Which kind of pleasure is the best one to pursue?" Should we simply pursue bodily pleasures or should we, instead, pursue the "higher," more cultivated pleasures such as reading great books and enjoying significant art and music?

Bentham consistently points out that there is no sensible meaning to the notion of "higher" or "lower" pleasures. Pleasures can differ only in their quantity. Bentham expresses this point in a memorable quotation: "Prejudice apart, the game of pushpin is of equal value with the arts and sciences of music and poetry. If the game of pushpin furnish more pleasure, it is more valuable than either."[42] Pushpin was a rather trivial 18th-century children's game. If he were writing today, Bentham might say, "If they produce the same amount of pleasure, playing video games is as worthy a pleasure as reading poetry."

Bentham provides a method to scientifically quantify and calculate the value of different pleasures. This method is commonly referred to as Bentham's "hedonic calculus." When considering any action, we should evaluate the amount of pleasure or pain it will produce according to the following seven dimensions:

1. *Intensity:* How strong is the pleasure?
2. *Duration:* How long will the pleasure last?
3. *Certainty or Uncertainty:* How likely or unlikely is it that the pleasure will occur?
4. *Propinquity or Remoteness:* How soon will the pleasure occur?
5. *Fecundity:* How likely is it that the proposed action will produce more sensations of the same kind (either pleasure or pain)?
6. *Purity:* Will the sensations be followed by sensations of the opposite kind? (Will the pain be followed by pleasure, or the pleasure by pain?)
7. *Extent:* How many other people will be affected?

Let's look at how these criteria are applied. It is obvious that receiving $25 would not produce as much pleasure as receiving $30, so assuming that all factors are equal, you would prefer the action whose outcome was $30. However, if the $25 would be given to you now when you need it for school expenses, but the $30 would not be received for another 40 years, it might be rational to choose the action that leads to the lesser but more immediate pleasure. Here's another example. Going to a party tonight would produce a high amount of immediate pleasure, but if it caused you to flunk a medical school admissions test tomorrow, the pleasure would be an impure one because the long-range pain of not pursuing your career would outweigh the immediate pleasure. Thus, all of Bentham's factors have to be taken into account in calculating which action is best.

Even when we are faced with more complicated moral dilemmas, Bentham claims that the process of calculation is simple:

1. For each person affected by a proposed action, add up the total amount of units of pleasure (or desirable consequences) produced and subtract from that figure the amount of pain (or undesirable consequences) produced.
2. Merge the calculations for each individual into the sum total of pleasure and pain produced for the community.
3. Do this calculation for alternative courses of action.
4. The morally right action is the one that produces the greatest sum total of pleasure.

Thus, on Bentham's analysis, moral dilemmas are turned into problems of addition and subtraction in which decisions are made by looking at the final balance, much as we would look at an accountant's ledger of credits and debits. Although the process looks awkward and even bizarre, Bentham thinks that it formalizes what we actually do in practice, because we are constantly making assessments of the pluses and minuses of the consequences of any course of action.

STOP AND THINK

Can you think of an occasion in which you made a decision by informally following the sort of procedure and criteria Bentham recommends? How did the decision turn out? On reflection, do you think this method was the best way to decide what to do? Why?

Notice that so far we have not discussed what specifically has value. To be desired or valued by someone is all that it takes for something to have genuine value for that person. Obviously, what gives me pleasure may differ from what produces pleasure for you. Although the principle of utility provides an objective moral principle, it has no absolute standard of value, for values are claimed to be relative and subjective. Each one of us affected by an action has an equal vote in determining the worthiness of that action. Thus, ethics is not the search for some hidden, unobservable quality called "moral goodness." Ethical decisions are no more complicated or sublime than planning the menu for a dinner party in which you take into account your guests' likes and dislikes.

Bentham was basically a psychological hedonist, because he believed that we are fundamentally motivated by pleasure and pain. However, unlike the ethical egoist, Bentham argued that we must not be concerned only about our own interests, but that we should strive for the greatest amount of happiness in society. With the proper legislation and using his principle of utility, he thought we could create the best society for everyone.

THOUGHT EXPERIMENT: *The Happiness Machine*

To see whether you agree with Bentham that happiness or pleasure is the supreme goal in life, try the following thought experiment.[43]

(continued . . .)

(. . . continued)

Suppose that you had the opportunity to step into a "happiness machine" that would give you any experiences you desired. While in the machine, neurophysiologists would stimulate your brain so that, for example, you would think and feel you were winning an athletic event, writing a great novel, making a friend, or enjoying some physically and psychologically satisfying experience. To avoid boredom, the quality and types of happiness would be varied. Whatever types of experiences bring you happiness or pleasure in real life would be simulated in your brain. All the time that you are enjoying a life of uninterrupted happiness, you would be floating in a tank, with electrodes attached to your brain. Of course, while in the tank you won't have the feeling that you're there; you will feel as though the simulated experiences are actually happening. In addition to this psychological satisfaction, all the rest of your biological needs would be provided for, and your life span would not be any different than it would have been outside the happiness machine. You would be free to leave the machine at any time, although you know that everyone who ever entered the machine never chose to leave it.

- Isn't pleasure, contentment, satisfaction, and happiness what we all seek in life?
- If so, would there be any reason not to live your life plugged into the machine?
- Would you choose to be plugged into the machine, having a life of total contentment and pleasure from the experiences it simulates? Why?
- Would a consistent Benthamite be obligated to enter the machine?

If the unqualified pursuit of happiness or pleasure is the goal in life, then it seems that we all ought to climb into the happiness machine. However, many people think something is missing here. The artificial happiness induced by the machine is not something that we have achieved for ourselves, and it is inconsistent with our potential and dignity as human beings. In Bentham's day his philosophy was labeled the "pig philosophy," because he emphasized simply the quantity of pleasure and did not give sufficient priority to the type of pleasures that are worthy of human beings alone. For this reason, his disciple and godchild John Stuart Mill sought to develop a more refined version of utilitarianism.

JOHN STUART MILL (1806–1873)

John Stuart Mill was born in London, the eldest son of nine children. His father, James Mill, was a businessman as well as a philosopher, economist, historian, and disciple of Bentham. Educated at home, Mill began studying Greek and arithmetic at age three. By the time he was 13 years old, he was better educated than any university graduate of the time. Although he was one of history's greatest ethical and political thinkers, Mill made his living as an executive of a trading firm in London, writing philosophy on the side. His wife, Harriet Taylor, was a brilliant woman who had a deep influence on him and was his joint author in many of his most important works. While serving a term in Parliament, Mill unsuccessfully tried to amend the Reform Bill of 1867 to give women the vote. He also published *The Subjection of Women* in 1869, in which he argued for the political empowerment of women on utilitarian grounds. Mill died in Avignon, France, on May 8, 1873.

JOHN STUART MILL
(1806–1873)

In developing his moral philosophy, Mill accepted the main outlines of Bentham's hedonism, claiming that happiness (the experience of pleasure and the absence of pain) is the only thing that is desirable in itself. This theme is introduced in the following passage.

Utilitarianism [44]

The creed which accepts as the foundation of morals, "Utility," or the "Greatest Happiness Principle," holds that actions are right in proportion as they tend to promote happiness, wrong as they tend to produce the reverse of happiness. By happiness is intended pleasure, and the absence of pain; by unhappiness, pain, and the privation of pleasure. To give a clear view of the moral standard set up by the theory, much more requires to be said; in particular, what things it includes in the ideas of pain and pleasure; and to what extent this is left an open question. But these supplementary explanations do not affect the theory of life on which this theory of morality is grounded—namely, that pleasure, and freedom from pain, are the only things desirable as ends; and that all desirable things (which are as numerous in the utilitarian as in any other scheme) are desirable either for the pleasure inherent in themselves, or as means to the promotion of pleasure and the prevention of pain.

Higher Quality Pleasures

Thus far, Mill's position seems indistinguishable from Bentham's. However, as Mill develops his version of utilitarianism further, he differs from Bentham on several crucial issues. The first issue is the criteria for evaluating pleasure. Bentham maintained a *quantitative* hedonism. However, Mill adds a *qualitative* hedonism, for he insists that pleasures can differ in their quality and not just in their amount. He says that those pleasures that are the product of our intellectual and more refined capacities are higher and better than physical pleasures. But how does he make the case that some pleasures are higher? Look for Mill's answer in the following passage.

If I am asked, what I mean by difference of quality in pleasures, or what makes one pleasure more valuable than another, merely as a pleasure, except its being greater in amount, there is but one possible answer. Of two pleasures, if there be one to which all or almost all who have experience of both give a decided preference, irrespective of any feeling of moral obligation to prefer it, that is the more desirable pleasure. If one of the two is, by those who are competently acquainted with both, placed so far above the other that they prefer it, even though knowing it to be attended with a greater amount of discontent, and would not resign it for any quantity of the other pleasure which their nature is capable of, we are justified in ascribing to the preferred enjoyment a superiority in quality, so far outweighing quantity as to render it, in comparison, of small account.

Now it is an unquestionable fact that those who are equally acquainted with, and equally capable of appreciating and enjoying, both, do give a most marked preference to the manner of existence which employs their higher faculties. Few human creatures would consent to be changed into any of the lower animals, for a promise of the fullest allowance of a beast's pleasures; no intelligent human being would consent to be a fool, no instructed person would be an ignoramus, no person of feeling and conscience would be selfish and base, even though they should be persuaded that the fool, the dunce, or the rascal is better satisfied with his lot than they are with theirs. They would not resign what they possess more than he for the most complete satisfaction of all the desires which they have in common with him. If they ever fancy they would, it is only in cases of unhappiness so extreme, that to escape from it they would exchange their lot for almost any other, however undesirable in their own eyes. A being of higher faculties requires more to make him happy, is capable probably of more acute suffering, and certainly accessible to it at more points, than one of an inferior type; but in spite of these liabilities, he can never really wish to sink into what he feels to be a lower grade of existence. We may give what explanation we please of this unwillingness; we may attribute it to pride, a name which is given indiscriminately to some of the most and to some of the least estimable feelings of which mankind are capable: we may refer it to the love of liberty and personal independence, an appeal to which was with the Stoics one of the most effective means for the inculcation of it; to the love of power, or to the love of excitement, both of which do really enter into and contribute to it: but its most appropriate appellation is a sense of dignity, which all human beings possess in one form or other, and in some, though by no means in exact, proportion to their higher faculties, and which is so essential a part of the happiness of those in whom it is strong, that nothing which conflicts with it could be, otherwise than momentarily, an object of desire to them.

THOUGHT EXPERIMENT: *Is Physical Pleasure the Only Goal in Life?*

Take a look at some animal that is enjoying the good life (your family pet, for example). Think about the fact that this pet has food, shelter, and medical care provided for him as well as the companionship of his human friends (and possibly other animals as well). He doesn't have to worry about classes, the complications of personal relationships, his personal values, the mind-body problem, his checking account, a career, the economy, political tensions in the world, or the environment. Instead, he naps and plays when he wishes and takes life as it comes. While in the midst of the stress and crush of your daily life, you may think it would be nice to exchange places with him. But would you really? Would you choose to permanently give up the joys and pains of learning new things and growing as a person and facing new challenges in order to have a life of pure pleasure and contentment? Does this example support Mill's point that it is not pleasure as such, but those sorts of pleasures that are appropriate to human life, that are worth pursuing?

The next passage contains one of Mill's most memorable lines. He says that it is easier for a pig or a fool to be satisfied than for a Socrates, but that the life of Socrates is far superior. Do you agree with Mill on this point?

Whoever supposes that this preference takes place at a sacrifice of happiness—that the superior being, in anything like equal circumstances, is not happier than the inferior—confounds the two very different ideas, of happiness and content. It is indisputable that the being whose capacities of enjoyment are low, has the greatest chance of having them fully satisfied; and a highly endowed being will always feel that any happiness which he can look for, as the world is constituted, is imperfect. But he can learn to bear its imperfections, if they are at all bearable; and they will not make him envy the being who is indeed unconscious of the imperfections, but only because he feels not at all the good which those imperfections qualify. It is better to be a human being dissatisfied than a pig satisfied; better to be Socrates dissatisfied than a fool satisfied. And if the fool, or the pig, are of a different opinion, it is because they only know their own side of the question. The other party to the comparison knows both sides.

Mill criticizes Bentham for having too limited a view of human nature. Human beings, Mill insists, are more than pleasure-seeking organisms. In seeking pleasure they also seek to

Read the earlier thought experiment concerning the happiness machine and the first two questions accompanying it to five or more friends. What answers do they give, and what reasons do they provide? Do any of their answers sound similar to Mill's qualitative hedonism and his preference to be a dissatisfied human rather than a happy pig? Do any of your friends question the hedonistic assumption that pleasure or happiness is the only thing that has value? Or do some think the machine is a good idea? Discuss their answers with them.

develop their "higher faculties" and to become "well-developed human beings." Mill says that in Bentham's account,

> Man is never recognized by him as a being capable of pursuing spiritual perfection as an end; of desiring, for its own sake, the conformity of his own character to his standard of excellence, without hope of good or fear of evil from [any] other source than his own inward consciousness.[45]

However, in saying that we strive to realize our potential as human beings as an end in itself, Mill seems to have moved away from the utilitarian doctrine of psychological hedonism and has substituted for it an elevated view of human nature that emphasizes the need to fulfill our unique dignity and potential as human beings rather than to simply maximize our own or others' happiness. Otherwise, how can he say, "It is better to be a human being dissatisfied than a pig satisfied; better to be Socrates dissatisfied than a fool satisfied"?

Self-Interest or Altruism?

The second issue on which Mill disagreed with Bentham concerned the question of whether self-interest was the basis for all our actions. Bentham did recognize that we sometimes experience personal pleasure from making others happy, which he called the "pleasure of benevolence." He also noted that attending to other persons' interests is often the best way to promote our own interests. In the final analysis, however, Bentham tended toward an egoistical hedonism, because he thought that the most universal motive for action was always the individual's self-interest. On the other hand, Mill emphasized much more strongly that we naturally have social feelings for humanity and the desire for unity with our fellow-creatures. Although both Bentham and Mill believed in "the greatest happiness for the greatest number," Mill made a special effort to stress that in a utilitarian calculation, your own happiness cannot be given any more weight than the happiness of another person.

> The happiness which forms the utilitarian standard of what is right in conduct, is not the agent's own happiness, but that of all concerned. As between his own happiness and that of others, utilitarianism requires him to be as strictly impartial as a disinterested and benevolent spectator. In the golden rule of Jesus of Nazareth, we read the complete spirit of the ethics of utility. "To do as you would be done by," and "to love your neighbour as yourself," constitute the ideal perfection of utilitarian morality.[46]

UTILITARIANISM: *Objectivism or Relativism?*

Several features of utilitarianism are important to understand. The utilitarianism theory falls under the heading of *ethical objectivism*. The utilitarian believes that there is a universal, objective moral principle that everyone ought to follow—the principle of utility. Hence, as with all varieties of ethical objectivism, the utilitarian believes that it is possible

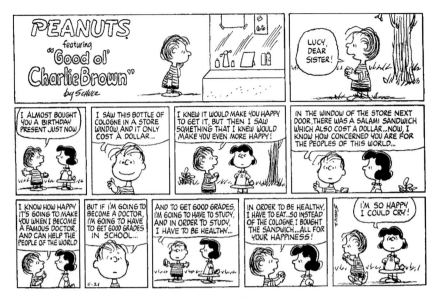

Peanuts: © 2010 Peanuts Worldwide LLC., dist. by UFS, Inc.

for a person to be mistaken about rightness or wrongness. The morally right action for you to perform in a particular situation (your moral duty) is not necessarily the action you think is right, nor is it necessarily identical to what you subjectively desire. The rightness or wrongness of an action is an objective matter of the goodness or badness of its consequences.

Sometimes people incorrectly think that utilitarianism is a form of relativism because the utilitarian does not hold that any given action is absolutely right or wrong in itself. However, far from being a relativist, the utilitarian holds that there is an objective moral principle that requires different actions in different situations. Let's look at a nonethical example. It is a universal medical principle that "everyone ought to eat nutritious meals." Although everyone ought to follow this principle, the specific eating habits and amounts of food that this principle dictates for a 100-pound accountant will be different from those for a 250-pound football player. Similarly, the utilitarian would say that everyone ought to follow the principle of utility in making moral choices, but following this principle may dictate different actions in different, specific circumstances, depending on the persons involved, the nature of the circumstances, and the consequences of the particular action. For example, telling a lie in a court of law could have very bad consequences for all concerned, whereas telling Aunt Tillie you love her meat loaf (a lie) might be charitable. For the utilitarian, all lies are not alike, because they do not all have the same consequences; therefore, lying in general cannot be morally evaluated apart from the concrete consequences of particular lies.

If consequences determine the rightness or wrongness of an action, then the morality of a particular type of action can change over time if the consequences change. At one time, for example, an unwanted pregnancy and the contracting of a sexually transmitted disease were possible consequences of sexual intercourse. However, improved contraceptive technology and more effective means to prevent and cure these diseases led to more ability to control the bad consequences of sexual intercourse. From a purely utilitarian standpoint, these changes would have an effect on the morality of promiscuous sexual intercourse. With the rise of diseases, such as AIDS, that have resisted all known cures, however, the consequences of promiscuous sexual behavior changed once again, and monogamous sexual relationships gained new popularity. Of course, if you are a careful utilitarian, the previously mentioned obvious consequences of sexual behavior are not the only ones that you need to consider. Other factors might be the emotional effects of your sexual behavior on yourself and others, including how the behavior negatively or positively affects your ability to sustain long-term relationships such as marriage; the affects this behavior will have on society; and so on. Nevertheless, for the utilitarian, the three factors determining the morality of sexual behavior (or any behavior) are consequences, consequences, and consequences.

THE CONSEQUENCES OF CONSEQUENTIALISM:
A Test Case

One of the frequent criticisms of utilitarianism is that it leads to morally problematic and even abhorrent conclusions. The questions posed in the following "Stop and Think" box will get you thinking about the plausibility, limits, and consequences of utilitarianism, or consequentialist ethics.

STOP AND THINK

Would it be morally permissible to bring about or to allow the death of one innocent person if it spared a vast number of people from some major harm? Why? If you answered the question affirmatively, then how great would the harm being prevented have to be in order to justify one person's death? Can you think of any examples in which our society sacrifices the lives of some individuals for the good of the many? How about war? How about the way our society sets medical research priorities and allocates money for health care? How about the level of safety standards that are required of products and in the workplace? Are there trade-offs made here between the costs and the risks? If automobile manufacturers made all cars so safe that everyone would survive a crash, would you be able to afford a car? Are utilitarian considerations at work in these situations, even when lives are at stake?

Although some people would agree that under the right circumstances it would be morally permissible to sacrifice one person to save the *lives* of many, most people would probably say that sacrificing one life for the *convenience* of the many would be morally reprehensible. This conclusion, however, has been questioned on consequentialist grounds by Alastair Norcross. (Alastair Norcross is an Associate Professor of Philosophy at Rice University. He has written numerous articles in defense of consequentialist ethical theory.) Norcross argues in the spirit of utilitarianism that for a consistent consequentialist there would have to be a point at which the total sum of minor pains or inconveniences of a very large number of persons would outweigh the bad consequences of the death of one person. Furthermore, he argues for the surprising conclusion that most of us agree with practices of our society in which that exact policy is pursued. (Remember that utilitarianism is one variety of consequentialist ethics, so everything Norcross says about the latter applies to the former.)

FROM ALASTAIR NORCROSS
Comparing Harms: Headaches and Human Lives [47]

Consequentialists are sometimes unsettled by the following kind of example: a vast number of people are experiencing fairly minor headaches, which will continue unabated for another hour, unless an innocent person is killed, in which case they will cease immediately.

There is no other way to avoid the headaches. Can we permissibly kill that innocent person in order to avoid the vast number of headaches? For a consequentialist, the answer to that question depends on the relative values of the world with the headaches but without the premature death, and the world without the headaches but with the premature death. If the latter world is at least as good as the former, it is permissible to kill the innocent. Furthermore, if the all-things-considered values of the worlds are comparable, and if a world with more headaches is, *ceteris paribus,** worse than a world with fewer, it is reasonable to suppose that a world with a vast (but finite) number of headaches could be worse than a world that differs from it only in lacking those headaches and containing one more premature death. In short, there is some finite number of headaches, such that it is permissible to kill an innocent person to avoid them. Call this claim *life for headaches*. Many people balk at *life for headaches*. In fact, many people think that there is no number of people such that it is permissible to kill one person to save that number the pain of a fairly minor headache. Deontologists might think this, because they endorse what Scheffler calls "agent-centered restrictions." Such restrictions forbid certain kinds of action, even when their results are at least as good as all alternatives. Thus, a deontologist might agree that the world without the headaches but with the premature death is better all things considered than the world with the headaches but without the premature death, and yet maintain that it is impermissible to kill the person in order to avoid the headaches. A consequentialist, however, who agrees with this ranking of the two worlds must also claim that it is permissible to kill the innocent person.

Norcross follows this introduction with a lengthy series of arguments to show that a consistent consequentialist cannot avoid the *life for headaches* conclusion. The consequentialist, of course, believes that the decision to choose one alternative over another is morally justified by calculating and comparing the total sum of good consequences and bad consequences for all affected by each proposed action, and choosing the alternative that produces the greatest amount of good (and least harm) for the greatest number of people. Therefore, Norcross argues, there is a point at which the cumulative amount of minor, individual headaches would produce a sum of pain such that the elimination of this quantity of pain would outweigh the bad consequence of sacrificing one individual.

Norcross acknowledges that his argument for *life for headaches* could appear to be a fairly weighty argument against consequentialist ethics. However, in the following passage he argues that *life for headaches* is not as unpalatable as it may seem at first. In fact, he claims, "most of us, consequentialists and nonconsequentialists alike, accept at least some other claims that do not differ significantly from *life for headaches*."

Thousands of people die in automobile accidents every year in the United States. It is highly probable that the number of deaths is positively correlated with the speed limits in force on highways, at least within a certain range. One of the effects of raising speed limits is that there are more accidents, resulting in more deaths and injuries. One of the effects of lowering speed limits is that there are fewer accidents. Higher vehicle safety standards also affect both the numbers of accidents and the severity of the injuries sustained when accidents do occur. Another effect of raising speed limits is that more gasoline is consumed, which raises the level of particulate pollution, which also leads to more deaths. Stricter standards for fuel efficiency also affect the amount of gasoline consumed. There are, then, many different measures that we, as a society, could take to lower the number of automobile-related deaths, only some of which we do take. There are also many measures we could take, that would raise the number of such deaths, some of which we do take. Furthermore, it is not obvious that we are wrong to fail to do all we

---

*Ceteris paribus means "other things being equal."

can to reduce the number of deaths. For the purposes of this discussion, I will focus on just one aspect of this failure, the failure to impose a national speed limit of 50 miles per hour in the US.

If there were a national speed limit of 50 mph, it is overwhelmingly likely that many lives would be saved each year, as compared with the current situation. One of the costs of the failure to impose such a speed limit is a significant number of deaths. The benefits of higher speed limits are increased convenience for many. Despite this, it is far from obvious that the failure to impose a 50 mph speed limit is wrong. In fact, most people believe what I will call *lives for convenience:*

Lives for convenience: We are not morally obligated to impose a national speed limit of 50 mph (or less).

If we reject *life for headaches* as obviously wrong, we must find a morally significant difference between it and *lives for convenience.*

Norcross's facts are well documented. When it was proposed that we raise the speed limits on U.S. highways, we could calculate with some degree of precision the increase in deaths this change would cause. This unfortunate result was thought to be justified because it would save the majority of people, who are not victims, the inconvenience of slower speeds and it would reduce the costs to transport goods. The actual results of raising the speed limits have supported the original predictions. Norcross says that if you think these findings show that the speed limits should be set at 50 mph, then you should support highway speed limits of 40 mph, or 30 mph, or lower, since each reduction in speed will save even more lives.

> ## STOP AND THINK
>
> Do you agree with Norcross's argument that *lives for convenience* is a justified trade-off? If not, would you lobby for 20 mph highway speed limits in order to save lives? Is there a relevant moral difference between the *lives for convenience* principle that the United States and other countries have adopted and Norcross's *life for headaches* principle? What would that difference be and how would you argue for it?

In the remainder of his article, Norcross argues that there is no relevant difference between our sacrificing lives so that the majority can drive faster and his headache example. The fact that the victims of highway deaths are randomly chosen whereas the victim in the headache example is a specific, known individual does not seem to be a relevant difference. In fact, randomly bringing about the deaths of thousands of people seems to be worse than specifically targeting one person. Norcross also argues that there is no relevant difference between bringing about a death that is intended and bringing about many deaths that are merely foreseen when they could be prevented by our actions.

In the following passage, Norcross responds to yet one more attempt to argue that the highway speeds are morally justified while the *life for headaches* death is not.

The victims of higher speed limits, even though they may have neither chosen nor benefited from those limits, have at least freely chosen to undertake the risk of being harmed. The dangers of driving, or being driven, are well known. Those who choose to travel by road, therefore, are at least partly responsible for any harm that befalls them. The same cannot be said of the prospective victim of *life for headaches.*

Once again, this is clearly not applicable to the victims of higher levels of particulate pollution. Nor does it seem to be true of all the victims of road accidents. Many children are killed on the roads. Many of these may have had no say over whether they were to travel that way. Perhaps we will say that their parents voluntarily assumed the risk on their behalf. But this seems to be an inadequate reply. Would our reaction to *life for headaches* be significantly different, if the prospective victim were a child, chosen at random from among those whose parents had agreed to the selection procedure? Besides, it is not clear how *free* is the choice to travel by road, even for well-informed adults. For many of the victims of road accidents, the alternatives may have been excessively burdensome, if not nonexistent. Many people do not have access to basic services, such as groceries and health-care providers, except by road.

Norcross's arguments are troubling. They show some of the hard conclusions that may have to be accepted by a consequentialist such as the utilitarian. They also show that, whether we like it or not, we all reason like utilitarians on some issues affecting life and death.

THE PROBLEM OF JUSTICE AND RIGHTS

Many critics object to utilitarianism precisely because it leads to the sort of problematic conclusions found in the headaches case. Critics charge that there is no room in utilitarianism for justice and individual rights, which are commonly thought to be nonnegotiable concerns in moral deliberations. Because all that counts for the utilitarian is the total sum of happiness or utility, why should it matter how this happiness is distributed or whether an individual's rights are violated? Bentham, for example, had no use for the notion of natural rights; because rights are not quantifiable, they are not scientifically observable, and no one can agree on what our rights are. Although Bentham favored the American Revolution, he lamented the fact that the American political philosophy was based on a notion— human rights—that was so vague and subject to objections. The issue of utility versus justice and rights, along with a suggestion as to how a utilitarian might deal with this problem, is the subject of the following thought experiment.

> ### 🧪 THOUGHT EXPERIMENT: *The Blacksmith and the Baker*
>
> An 18th-century Danish poet, Johan Herman Wessel, wrote the tale of "The Blacksmith and the Baker" in verse. The story concerns a rather mean blacksmith who killed a man in a barroom brawl while in a drunken rage. The blacksmith is about to be sentenced to death by a judge when four upstanding citizens speak on his behalf. Their argument is that the man is the only blacksmith in this small town and his services are desperately needed. It would accomplish nothing to execute him, but it would be detrimental to the welfare of the community to deprive people of his skills. The judge is sympathetic to their plea but responds that the law requires a life for a life. If he let a murder go unpunished, it would undermine respect for the law and be harmful to the fabric of the society. The citizens point out that the town has an old and scrawny baker who is on the last leg of his life. He is a somewhat disreputable and unpopular fellow, although he is innocent of any crime. Because the town has two bakers, he would not be missed. So, for the greatest good of the greatest number, the judge lets the blacksmith go while framing the baker and making him pay for the murder with his life. The old baker wept pitifully when they took him away.[48]
>
> *(continued . . .)*

(. . . continued)

- Does this story illustrate the problems that utilitarianism has with the principle of justice?
- Obviously, willfully condemning an innocent man to death is morally abhorrent. However, in good utilitarian fashion, keeping the blacksmith and sacrificing the baker seems to create the best consequences for the town. How would a utilitarian respond to the judge's decision? Can the utilitarian condemn the action by appealing to the *long-term* bad consequences a society would incur if it framed and executed innocent persons? Or does the problem remain that the principle of utility can always override a concern for justice?

Utilitarians in the 20th century have clarified or modified some of their principles and responded to the sorts of objections discussed. Likewise, nonutilitarians have continued to provide examples and arguments to expose what they consider to be problems in the theory. Whether you think utilitarianism is for better or worse, a few moments' reflection will make clear how much Bentham and Mill have influenced our contemporary thinking in the moral and political spheres.

LOOKING THROUGH THE UTILITARIAN'S LENS

1. Utilitarianism is not just a historical movement in 19th-century British philosophy; it is alive and well in contemporary society. Find examples of utilitarian justifications of ethical conclusions in newspaper stories, editorials, letters to the editor, political or legislative proposals, and everyday conversations. In each case, how could the author use utilitarian principles to respond to possible objections to his or her conclusions?

2. Take some current moral controversy and imagine two utilitarians arguing the opposing sides of the issue. There are, for example, utilitarian arguments both for and against abortion, based on differing assessments of the consequences for the individuals involved and for society in general of either prohibiting abortion or permitting it. Remember, many kinds of arguments can be made on both sides of an issue like abortion, but the utilitarian analysis of an issue should not appeal to any notion of intrinsic rights of the individuals involved, nor should it make use of any religious assumptions. Argue both sides of the issue as utilitarians would by assessing both the good achieved and the harms produced for all individuals affected by the action and by assessing the long-term effects on society. Now that you have considered the utilitarian pros and cons, which side of the moral controversy represents the most consistent expression of utilitarian ethical theory?

3. For each of the seven points of Bentham's hedonistic calculus, try to provide a concrete example of a pleasure that might be forbidden because it violates that principle.

4. Think of an issue on which a follower of Jeremy Bentham's ethics and a follower of John Stuart Mill's theory would differ concerning the morally correct action to take. Limiting your options to these two theories for the sake of the exercise, which position do you think provides the best ethical guidance?

5. Think of a concrete moral decision in which an ethical egoist such as Plato's Glaucon or Ayn Rand would differ with a utilitarian as to the morally right thing to do. How would the egoist and the utilitarian justify their decisions? Which position do you think provides the best ethical guidance?

6. Harriet Taylor and her husband and coauthor, John Stuart Mill, wrote a number of essays in the 19th century arguing that women should be accorded full social, political, and legal equality with men. However, because the notion of "natural rights" finds little room in utilitarian theory, their arguments were based on what would create the most social good. See if you can construct an argument for women's equality that is based on the utilitarian principle of maximizing the greatest good for society.

EXAMINING THE STRENGTHS AND WEAKNESSES OF UTILITARIANISM

Positive Evaluation

1. Utilitarians have an answer to the question, Why be moral? They argue both that it is in your best interests to be moral and that it fulfills the best impulses within human nature. The utilitarians link morality with our basic interests and inclinations instead of making natural enemies out of happiness and morality; does this link make their theory more convincing than other theories?

2. Utilitarianism claims to provide a clear-cut procedure for making ethical decisions instead of relying on vague intuitions or abstract principles. Furthermore, it allows us to use the findings of psychology and sociology to determine which policies will promote human happiness and the social good. To what degree do these considerations strengthen the utilitarian's case?

3. The utilitarian theory leads to impartiality, fairness, and greater social harmony because it requires us to balance our interests with those of others. In doing so, doesn't utilitarianism provide an effective antidote for the evils of discrimination based on race, gender, religion, and other unjust criteria?

4. Although people have many different and conflicting moral beliefs, everyone agrees that, all things being equal, pain is bad and pleasure is good. Given this basic fact, doesn't utilitarianism provide a common ground for a minimal, public morality? If so, isn't this finding an important consideration in its favor?

5. Because utilitarianism does not rigidly label actions as absolutely right or wrong, it allows for a great deal of flexibility and sensitivity to the particular circumstances surrounding an action. Furthermore, it allows our moral policies to be adjusted and to change with the changes in society and with the changing consequences of our actions over time. Don't these factors make utilitarianism a very practical theory?

6. Utilitarians argue that their view is commonsensical and widely practiced, for their theory underlies many of the decisions we make in everyday life and has produced many of the socially beneficial changes in the laws and policies of our society. Do you agree that these claims have merit? If so, don't they lend considerable support to utilitarianism?

Negative Evaluation

1. Most people would agree that Bentham's hedonistic utilitarianism is too vulgar. What conscientious person would affirm that living at the level of an animal and pursuing only the pleasures of the body is just as good as developing the life of the mind? On the other hand, although Mill's modified version is more appealing, how can he claim that one pleasure is "better" than another? Wouldn't we need to have some criterion other than pleasure to judge the value of competing pleasures? Yet, if pleasure is the only criterion of

value, is there any way to rank pleasures except in terms of their quantity? Doesn't this conclusion send us right back to Bentham's version?

2. The utilitarian principle can be broken down into two goals: (1) create the greatest amount of happiness, and (2) create happiness for the greatest number. In case 1, suppose you could create the greatest amount of happiness for a community of 10 people by making 4 people supremely happy while 6 people were miserable. In case 2, suppose you could make all 10 people moderately happy, with none experiencing any misery. However, the total amount of happiness would not be as great as in the first case. If the total amount of pleasure over pain is what counts, then case 1 is morally preferable. If creating happiness for the greatest number is what counts, then case 2 would be best. Does this example show an incoherence in the utilitarian principle? Would it be possible for the utilitarian to make adjustments to the theory to avoid this problem?

3. Wouldn't the utilitarian have to say that slavery would be morally justified if the benefits to the society outweighed the burdens of the slaves? Doesn't the greatest happiness principle imply that an unjust distribution of benefits and harms can be moral as long as the action results in a greater amount of total happiness than unhappiness when compared to any other alternative? Could the utilitarian argue that there would always be alternatives to slavery that would do a better job of maximizing utility? Do you think this reply is plausible?

4. Suppose that someone you love (a parent or a sibling) will die without a kidney transplant. You are willing to sacrifice one of your kidneys to save the life of this special person. However, you learn that a famous scientist, who is on the verge of finding a cure for cancer, also needs a donor kidney to live. Although the scientist is a stranger to you, your unique biochemistry will allow your kidney to be transplanted successfully into the body of someone who is not related to you. Your loved one holds a rather unimportant job and makes very little impact on society in general. However, no one can replace the work of the scientist and the benefits to society of her research. No kidney other than yours can be successfully transplanted in either case. Should you maximize the benefits to society by saving the scientist, or should you save the special person in your life? What would you do? Why? What would the utilitarian advise you to do? In responding to this scenario, most people would say that we have special obligations toward family members and friends that have priority over general obligations toward strangers. However, critics charge that utilitarian theory is unable to account for *special moral responsibilities,* because everyone who is affected by our choices should be counted equally in light of the total outcome for society in general. If you were a utilitarian, how would you respond? Would you defend the hard view that each of us has a moral obligation to society to give the kidney to the scientist and not to our loved one? Or would you argue that giving priority to the critical needs of those who are close to us would be best for society in the long run? Would this position permit moral obligations that conflicted with the utilitarian principle?

5.4 KANTIAN ETHICS

 LEADING QUESTIONS: *Kantian Ethics*

1. Suppose that Dr. Eunice Utilitarian is asked by a hospitalized patient how he is doing. Knowing that his health is rapidly deteriorating and fearful that the shock of hearing the truth will worsen his condition, the physician decides that she could achieve the best

consequences by lying to him and waiting to tell him the truth at a better time. However, can you think of some unintended bad consequences that might result from this benevolent lie? What if the physician lied by saying, "You're doing great," and the patient died without making out a will because he thought there was no urgency? Could the physician be held morally responsible for the bad consequences of the lie? On the other hand, what if she told the truth and it so depressed the patient that he gave up his will to live? Could she then be held responsible for the bad consequences of telling the truth? Could it be that the best policy in such a situation is to avoid the known evil (lying) and let the consequences happen as they will?

2. When my children were young I had the rule, "You must always fasten your seat belt when riding in a car." One day, my son pointed out that I seldom wore my seat belt while I drove. Was I being inconsistent by giving commands that I did not follow? Was it morally wrong for me to be inconsistent? What is the problem with saying, "Do as I say, not as I do"? Why do we think that people ought to "practice what they preach"? Why is the Golden Rule, "Do unto others as you would have them do unto you," often cited as one of the supreme rules of morality? What role does consistency play in being a moral person and in deciding what rules we should follow?

3. What if we could make 100 people extremely happy by unfairly causing an undeserving innocent person cruel and humiliating embarrassment? What if the one person's emotional pain was the only bad result? Would it be morally wrong to create happiness in this way? If so, how could you convince those in favor of the action that it was wrong? If the principle "maximize happiness" could be used to justify this action, what other general moral rule could we formulate that would make it impossible to justify any actions of this sort?

4. Generally, people think that such principles as "Tell the truth" and "Keep your promises" are good ones to follow. However, we all have been in situations in which it seems that an exception to these rules should be made. Once we begin allowing exceptions to moral rules, isn't it pretty easy to always rationalize and justify breaking these rules when it is expedient or convenient to do so? When we don't take these moral commands as absolutes and allow exceptions to them, aren't we really watering them down into insipid rules such as, "Always keep a promise unless you think it is better not to"? Doesn't such an insipid rule allow for so many loopholes that it is ineffective in guiding our actions? If you knew that someone was following this rule, how much confidence would you place in an important promise that she made? If *everyone* followed this rule, would there be any point in taking promises seriously?

These four leading questions draw attention to four leading themes in Immanuel Kant's deontological ethical theory: (1) the irrelevance of consequences in determining our obligations or the moral rightness and wrongness of actions, (2) the importance of consistency for living the moral life and choosing our moral rules, (3) the irreducible dignity and worth of every person, and (4) the necessity of having moral absolutes that are not qualified by any exceptions. We explore these themes in the remainder of this section.

SURVEYING THE CASE FOR KANTIAN ETHICS

IMMANUEL KANT

We encountered Kant's philosophy previously in our discussion of his theory of knowledge. (See section 2.4, "Kantian Constructivism," for brief biographical information on Kant.) If he had written nothing else but his theory of knowledge, he would still be considered one of history's most important thinkers. It is a testimony to his genius, however, that he also is a landmark in the field of ethics. Writing in the late 18th century, Kant obviously was not attempting to refute the 19th-century utilitarianism of Jeremy Bentham and John Stuart Mill. Nevertheless, because Kant was responding to the British empiricists who would later influence the utilitarians, his writings read like an argument directed against Bentham and Mill. For this reason, I have presented these thinkers in reverse chronological order. Rather than being a historical museum piece, Kant's moral philosophy remains one of the most influential theories today. Although many philosophers enthusiastically defend and apply his theory, and others harshly criticize it, no one who wants to think seriously about ethics can afford to ignore his ideas. Consequently, the Kantian approach to ethics still stands today as one of the leading resources of ethical insight as we face the troubling issues our contemporary culture is encountering in the areas of political, legal, medical, and business ethics.

Kant's View of Morality

We could take as the model of Kant's entire philosophy his statement that "two things fill the mind with ever new and increasing admiration and awe . . . *the starry heavens above me and the moral law within me.*"[49] The starry heavens stand for the world of sensory experience. Kant's epistemology attempted to set out the principles by which we are able to have knowledge of the world of physical nature. (This epistemology was discussed in section 2.4.) But human experience consists of more than sense data impinging upon us and the force of physical laws, because we also feel the pull of the moral law. For example, when you deeply desire to go out with friends, but this desire is vetoed by the realization that you promised a friend you would help her move, you are feeling the pull of duty.

When Kant talks about our moral experience, he looks inward to find the moral law and not outward to the consequences of our actions (such as happiness). In this one detail we get an indication that his ethical theory is going to be radically different from that of the utilitarians. Kant's moral theory emphasizes absolute duties, motives, the dignity and worth of persons, and a moral law that is absolute and unchanging. In this emphasis, he retains some of the elements of his own Christian roots. But when it comes to deciding what the moral law is, no mention is made of God and his commands. Kant says our ability to identify God with the highest good and to attribute goodness to the great religious figures in history requires that we already have a prior conception of moral perfection. Even a person who was not raised in a religious tradition possesses her innate capacities as a rational human being that both make her capable of knowing the moral law and require her to be subject to it. Thus, Kant did not abandon the moral precepts of his religious tradition, but neither did he base his ethics upon them. Instead, he thought that secular, rational ethics and the best in religious morality pointed in the same direction.

Kant's uncompromising rationalism led him to insist that the principles of morality cannot be derived from any empirical facts about human practices such as we find in anthropology or psychology. Kant believed that we cannot move from a description of what is being done to any notion of what we *ought* to do. A statistical survey of how people actually behave would not tell us how we ought to behave. Hence, if moral principles cannot be derived from experience, then the mind must bring its own, rational principles to the realm of moral experience. (Kant's claim that in morality the principles of reason structure the content of experience is analogous to his Copernican revolution in epistemology discussed in section 2.4.) Accordingly, in Kant's analysis, acting morally can be understood in terms of acting rationally, whereas acting immorally can be considered as one species of acting irrationally.

The Good Will

Kant's moral theory begins with the claim that the only thing in the world that has absolute, unqualified moral value is a *good will*. A person who has a good will is one who acts from no motive other than the motive of doing what is right. In other words, such a person acts out of respect for the moral law and for the sake of duty, and no other considerations enter into the decision. It is important to understand from the beginning that Kant does not think that you are acting morally simply if your intentions are good or your motives are pure. The good will means more than sincerely thinking you are performing the right action. You must also correctly discern what is your moral duty. But how do we know what our duties are? Kant will get to that, but for now he is concerned with the good will as the motivating force in all morality. In the first paragraph of the following passage Kant acknowledges that there are other qualities that we count as good and lists 12 of them under the headings of "talents of the mind," "qualities of temperament," and "gifts of fortune." (In the second paragraph he lists three additional qualities of temperament.) However, he argues that such qualities are not truly good in themselves, for without a good will, such "good" qualities actually can be bad. For example, if a hardened criminal is intelligent, cool-headed, courageous, powerful, and persevering, these positive qualities would only enhance the evil he could do.

- In the following passage, why does Kant say that happiness and uninterrupted prosperity would not be good without a good will? How does this opinion differ from what the utilitarians would say?
- The utilitarians stressed that morality has to do with the consequences of our actions. What does Kant think about this approach?

FROM IMMANUEL KANT
Foundations of the Metaphysics of Morals [50]

The Good Will

Nothing in the world—indeed nothing even beyond the world—can possibly be conceived which could be called good without qualification except a *good will*. Intelligence, wit, judgment, and the other talents of the mind, however they may be named, or courage, resoluteness, and perseverance as qualities of temperament, are doubtless in many respects good and desirable. But they can become extremely bad and harmful if the will, which is to make use of these gifts of nature and which in its special constitution is called character, is not good. It is the same with the gifts of fortune. Power, riches, honor, even health, general well-being, and the contentment with one's condition which is called happiness, make for pride and even arrogance if there is not a good will to correct their influence on the mind and on its principles of action so as to make it universally conformable to its end. It need hardly be mentioned that the sight of a being adorned with no feature of a pure and good will, yet enjoying uninterrupted prosperity, can never give pleasure to a rational impartial observer. Thus the good will seems to constitute the indispensable condition even of worthiness to be happy.

Some qualities seem to be conducive to this good will and can facilitate its action, but, in spite of that, they have no intrinsic unconditional worth. They rather presuppose a good will, which limits the high esteem which one otherwise rightly has for them and prevents their being held to be absolutely good. Moderation in emotions and passions, self-control, and calm deliberation not only are good in many respects but even seem to constitute a part of the inner worth of the person. But however unconditionally they were esteemed by the ancients, they are far from being good without qualification. For without the principle of a good will they can become extremely bad, and the coolness of a villain makes him not only far more dangerous but also more directly abominable in our eyes than he would have seemed without it.

The good will is not good because of what it effects or accomplishes or because of its adequacy to achieve some proposed end; it is good only because of its willing, i.e., it is good of itself. And, regarded for itself, it is to be esteemed incomparably higher than anything which could be brought about by it in favor of any inclination or even of the sum total of all inclinations. Even if it should happen that, by a particularly unfortunate fate or by the [stingy] provision of a stepmotherly nature, this will should be wholly lacking in power to accomplish its purpose, and if even the greatest effort should not avail it to achieve anything of its end, and if there remained only the good will (not as a mere wish but as the summoning of all the means in our power), it would sparkle like a jewel in its own right, as something that had its full worth in itself. Usefulness or fruitlessness can neither diminish nor augment this worth. Its usefulness would be only its setting, as it were, so as to enable us to handle it more conveniently in commerce or to attract the attention of those who are not yet connoisseurs, but not to recommend it to those who are experts or to determine its worth.

STOP AND THINK

Pick three of the personal qualities Kant lists in the first two paragraphs of the previous passage. Make up your own examples of how these qualities actually could be bad if the person possessing them lacked a good will.

If the notion of a good will is at the heart of morality, how do we identify such a will when we are trying to evaluate our own moral character or those of others? What is the relationship between the good will and the actual consequences of our actions as well as our intentions, motives, and feelings? Take a minute to explore these issues in the following thought experiment.

THOUGHT EXPERIMENT: *The Good Will*

Suppose that Gretchen sees a drowning boy, and being a good swimmer, she leaps into the water to save him. Now consider each of the following additions to this scenario, and in each case, ask if Gretchen possesses what Kant means by a good will.

1. Though the waters were dangerous, Gretchen overcame her fears because she felt a duty to attempt the rescue. Tragically, however, her efforts were in vain, for the child drowned.
2. Gretchen did her best to save the child because she knew his parents were wealthy and she figured she might be in for a substantial reward.
3. Because of the dangers, Gretchen knew no one would blame her if she decided not to risk the rescue. Nevertheless, she was moved by pity upon hearing the child's cries and she knew she would be racked with guilt feelings and could not live with herself if she didn't at least attempt a rescue.

The first two cases should have been easy. In the previous reading, Kant said that a good will would "sparkle like a jewel in its own right," and the external circumstances could neither add to nor subtract from its worth. Hence, even if Gretchen's actions did not achieve the good consequence of saving the child, the goodness of her will that motivated these actions still shines brightly. In the second case, it is obvious that she was not acting out of a sense of duty (the essential feature of a good will), but only for her own selfish gain.

What about the third case, where Gretchen is driven by pity and the desire to avoid guilt? Isn't pity a morally worthy emotion and doesn't guilt often motivate us to do the right thing? In this case Gretchen is acting on the basis of her feelings, or what Kant calls *inclination.* The problem with inclination, however, is that our feelings come and go but the demands of morality are a constant. What if Gretchen happened to be emotionally numb that day and felt neither the pull of pity nor the push of guilt acting on her? Lacking these feelings, wouldn't she still have a duty to act? Kant insists that emotions cannot be the motive force in morality because sometimes the moral person must do things that he or she does not really feel like doing. For this reason, Kant insists that morality must be based on rational principles and cannot be driven by any variable conditions such as feelings or inclinations.

In the next two selections, Kant elaborates on this theme by setting out several propositions that define the essential features of duty. (Note: In this passage and later ones Kant uses the term *maxim* to refer to a general rule that guides how we act.)

- In the next passage, Kant makes a distinction between (1) acting *in accordance with* duty and (2) acting *from* duty. Can you state the difference between them in your own words and by providing examples?
- Why does Kant say the merchant acted in accordance with duty but not from duty?
- Why is it normally not morally heroic to do what is necessary to sustain your own life? On the other hand, what does Kant say about the anguished man who is inclined to end his life but chooses to preserve it?

The First Proposition of Morality: To Have Moral Worth, an Action Must Be Done from a Sense of Duty

We have, then, to develop the concept of a will which is to be esteemed as good of itself without regard to anything else. It dwells already in the natural sound understanding and does not need so much to be taught as only to be brought to light. In the estimation of the total worth of our actions it always takes first place and is the condition of everything else. In order to show this, we shall take the concept of duty. It contains that of a good will, though with certain subjective restrictions and hindrances; but these are far from concealing it and making it unrecognizable, for they rather bring it out by contrast and make it shine forth all the brighter.

I here omit all actions which are recognized as opposed to duty, even though they may be useful in one respect or another, for with these the question does not arise at all as to whether they may be carried out *from* duty, since they conflict with it. I also pass over the actions which are really in accordance with duty and to which one has no direct inclination, rather executing them because impelled to do so by another inclination. For it is easily decided whether an action in accord with duty is performed from duty or for some selfish purpose. It is far more difficult to note this difference when the action is in accordance with duty and, in addition, the subject has a direct inclination to do it. For example, it is in fact in accordance with duty that a dealer should not overcharge an inexperienced customer, and wherever there is much business the prudent merchant does not do so, having a fixed price for everyone, so that a child may buy of him as cheaply as

PHILOSOPHY *in the* MARKETPLACE

Ask several friends to decide which of the following two people best illustrates what it means to be a genuinely moral person. Ask them to explain their decision.

- Heidi frequently makes personal sacrifices to help other people who are in need. Even though emotionally she tends to be cold and indifferent to the needs of others, she knows that it is her moral duty to help others when she can.
- Kendra frequently makes personal sacrifices to help other people who are in need. She has a cheerful, compassionate disposition, and it makes her feel alive to do something good for someone else. Because helping others is second nature to her, it never occurs to her to consider it a moral obligation.

any other. Thus the customer is honestly served. But this is far from sufficient to justify the belief that the merchant has behaved in this way from duty and principles of honesty. His own advantage required this behavior; but it cannot be assumed that over and above that he had a direct inclination to the purchaser and that, out of love, as it were, he gave none an advantage in price over another. Therefore the action was done neither from duty nor from direct inclination but only for a selfish purpose.

On the other hand, it is a duty to preserve one's life, and moreover everyone has a direct inclination to do so. But for that reason the often anxious care which most men take of it has no intrinsic worth, and the maxim of doing so has no moral import. They preserve their lives according to duty, but not from duty. But if adversities and hopeless sorrow completely take away the relish for life, if an unfortunate man, strong in soul, is indignant rather than despondent or dejected over his fate and wishes for death, and yet preserves his life without loving it and from neither inclination nor fear but from duty—then his maxim has a moral import.

As Kant's examples make clear, acting *in accordance with* duty simply means that our external behavior conforms with what we ought to do. The merchant, for example, dealt honestly with his customers (which was his duty), but it served his interests to do so, because having a reputation for honesty is good for business or because he was afraid of being arrested for unfair business practices. As the case of the merchant demonstrates, we can do the right thing for prudential or selfish reasons. The problem is that doing our duty because of the desirable consequences that would result implies that if the consequences were different, we would no longer have a reason to act in accordance with duty. In this case, whether we have a reason to act in accordance with duty depends more on external circumstances over which we have no control and less on our internal moral character.

On the other hand, acting *from* duty means that the motive for acting is simply the desire to perform the action because it is right. Then and only then does the action have moral worth, for it proceeds from a good will. Kant's theory is an example of *deontological ethics,* because the nature of the action itself and the person's motive are what determine the action's moral value. His theory is in contrast with *teleological ethics,* or *consequentialism,* such as the utilitarian theory, which claims that the goal or outcome of an action is what determines its moral value.

STOP AND THINK

Can you think of a time when you have done something *in accordance with* duty but not *from* duty? If duty did not motivate your behavior, what was your motive? If this motivation was not present, would you still have acted in accordance with duty?

In the next passage Kant focuses specifically on our emotions and inclinations. We have a duty to act kindly and benevolently whenever possible, and many people are moved to do so because they experience pleasure in making others happy. Surely (we might think) such people are morally praiseworthy. However, Kant argues that such responses fall short of what characterizes a good will. We do not choose our emotions and inclinations, and neither do we decide what constitutes our pleasurable experiences. That we happen to feel satisfied when we make others happy is a pleasurable experience over which we have no control. We are the passive recipients of such experiences, and for that reason, they cannot be the product of our rational choices. But ethics has to do with the choices we make and why we make them and cannot be based on our involuntary emotional reactions, our personality, or the whims of fortune.

In the following passage, which is continuous with the last one, Kant sheds further light on the first proposition of morality, that is, to have moral worth an action must be done from a sense of duty.

- Why does Kant say that the actions of the naturally sympathetic person lack moral worth?
- According to Kant, do we have duties to ourselves?
- What is Kant's interpretation of the biblical command to love our neighbor?

To be kind where one can is duty, and there are, moreover, many persons so sympathetically constituted that without any motive of vanity or selfishness they find an inner satisfaction in spreading joy, and rejoice in the contentment of others which they have made possible. But I say that, however dutiful and amiable it may be, that kind of action has no true moral worth. It is on a level with [actions arising from] other inclinations, such as the inclination to honor, which, if fortunately directed to what in fact accords with duty and is generally useful and thus honorable, deserve praise and encouragement but no esteem. For the maxim lacks the moral import of an action done not from inclination but from duty. But assume that the mind of that friend to mankind was clouded by a sorrow of his own which extinguished all sympathy with the lot of others and that he still had the power to benefit others in distress, but that their need left him untouched because he was preoccupied with his own need. And now suppose him to tear himself, unsolicited by inclination, out of this dead insensibility and to perform this action only from duty and without any inclination—then for the first time his action has genuine moral worth. Furthermore, if nature has put little sympathy in the heart of a man, and if he, though an honest man, is by temperament cold and indifferent to the sufferings of others, perhaps because he is provided with special gifts of patience and fortitude and expects or even requires that others should have the same—and such a man would certainly not be the meanest product of nature—would not he find in himself a source from which to give himself a far higher worth than he could have got by having a good-natured temperament? This is unquestionably true even though nature did not make him philanthropic, for it is just here that the worth of the character is brought out, which is morally and incomparably the highest of all: he is beneficent not from inclination but from duty.

To secure one's own happiness is at least indirectly a duty, for discontent with one's condition under pressure from many cares and amid unsatisfied wants could easily become a great temptation to transgress duties. But without any view to duty all men have the strongest and deepest inclination to happiness, because in this idea all inclinations are summed up. But the precept of happiness is often so formulated that it definitely thwarts some inclinations, and men can make no definite and certain concept of the sum of satisfaction of all inclinations which goes under the name of happiness. It is not to be wondered at, therefore, that a single inclination, definite as to what it promises and as to the time at which it can be satisfied, can outweigh a fluctuating idea, and that, for example, a man with the gout can choose to enjoy what he likes and to suffer what he may, because according to his calculations at least on this occasion he has not sacrificed the enjoyment of the present moment to a perhaps groundless expectation of a happiness supposed to lie in health. But even in this case, if the universal inclination to happiness did not determine his will, and if health were not at least for him a necessary factor in these calculations, there yet would remain, as in all other cases, a law that he ought to promote his happiness, not from inclination but from duty. Only from this law would his conduct have true moral worth.

It is in this way, undoubtedly, that we should understand those passages of Scripture which command us to love our neighbor and even our enemy, for love as an inclination cannot be commanded. But beneficence from duty, when no inclination impels it and even when it is opposed by a natural and unconquerable aversion, is practical love, not pathological love; it resides in the will and not in the propensities of feeling, in principles of action and not in tender sympathy; and it alone can be commanded.

Trans. Lewis White Beck, 2nd ed., © 1990. Reproduced in print and electronically by permission of Pearson Education, Inc.,Upper Saddle River, New Jersey.

STOP AND THINK

Do you think Kant is correct in favoring the person who is cold and indifferent but who dutifully performs an act of kindness instead of the person who is naturally sympathetic and who spontaneously and joyfully spreads happiness? Isn't it morally better for someone to be inclined to be sympathetic, benevolent, and faithful rather than grimly calculating and performing his or her moral duty? As you will see, this issue constitutes a major difference between Kant's ethics and virtue ethics (which is discussed in section 5.5).

In the next passage, Kant presents the second principle concerning moral duties. There are actually three principles, but to simplify the discussion we will not discuss the third one. (Remember that a maxim is the principle that you are following when you choose to perform a concrete action.)

The Second Proposition of Morality

The second proposition is: An action performed from duty does not have its moral worth in the purpose which is to be achieved through it but in the maxim by which it is determined. Its moral value, therefore, does not depend on the realization of the object of the action but merely on the principle of volition by which the action is done, without any regard to the objects of the faculty of desire. From the preceding discussion it is clear that the purposes we may have for our actions and their effects as ends and incentives of the will cannot give the actions any unconditional and moral worth. Wherein, then, can this worth lie, if it is not in the will in relation to its hoped-for effect? It can lie nowhere else than in the principle of the will, irrespective of the ends which can be realized by such action. . . .

Trans. Lewis White Beck, 2nd ed., © 1990. Reproduced in print and electronically by permission of Pearson Education, Inc.,Upper Saddle River, New Jersey.

Thus far, Kant has been stressing that an action has moral worth if it is done for the sake of the moral law. However, he has not yet answered the question, "How do we determine what is the moral law?" Without an answer to this question, the good will would be well-intentioned but morally blind. A moral law is a kind of command or imperative that directs us to do something or not do something. To understand the kinds of commands that are essential to ethics, Kant says it is important to make a distinction between two kinds of imperatives. The first is a **hypothetical imperative** and says, "If you want X, then do Y." This rule tells me what I ought to do, but the ought is contingent on my desiring the goal that follows the "if." For example, I may be told, "If you want a nice lawn, then you must fertilize your grass." Kant calls this type of hypothetical statement a technical imperative. It tells me what means I must use to achieve an end that I may desire. However, if I couldn't care less whether I have a nice lawn or not, then the command is of no concern to me. Hence, a genuinely moral *ought* cannot take the form of a hypothetical imperative, for this statement would make my moral duties dependent sheerly on what subjective goals I happen to have. A further problem with hypothetical imperatives is that they do not question whether an end is good but only provide guidance on how to attain it. For example, I may be told, "If you want to murder a rival colleague, you ought to use a strong poison." This point illustrates that some hypothetical imperatives are useful for obtaining immoral ends.

Some hypothetical imperatives fall under the heading of pragmatic imperatives, or counsels of prudence. These imperatives offer advice on how to enhance our own welfare and happiness. When we were children, we were given these sorts of rules by our parents, for example, "If you want people to believe you, then you ought always to tell the truth" or "If you want to be happy, you should seek other people's happiness." Although the goals contained in these commands may be worthy ones, these rules are not moral commands because they depend on subjective conditions that create our own happiness.

According to Kant, a genuinely moral command is not a hypothetical imperative. Instead, the moral law is presented to us as a **categorical imperative.** It tells me what I ought, should, or must do, but it does not depend on any prior conditions or subjective wants and wishes, and it contains no qualifications. A categorical imperative takes the form, "Do X!" It is not preceded by an *if* clause because it tells me what I am morally commanded to do under all conditions and at all times. However, if such a moral law does not come from some external lawgiver such as God, who issues such commands to me? The lawgiver, for Kant, is reason itself. A rational rule is one that is universal and consistent; it is universal in that it applies to all people, at all times, and in all circumstances, and it is consistent in that it does not lead to any contradictions.

Before applying the categorical imperative to morality, let's look at how rationality functions in several examples that do not directly involve ethics. In mathematics it is a rule that two plus two equals four. It does not matter who is doing the calculation or what the circumstances are, and it does not matter whether we like the consequences of applying the rule. The rule must be followed if we are to be rational. However, some rules are, by their very nature, irrational, because they could not be consistently followed by everyone or because they undermine the very activity to which the rule applies. Suppose your mother has a dinner table rule that says, "Before you serve yourself, make sure everyone else is served first." If *everyone* followed this rule, no one would ever be able to eat (thus defeating the whole purpose of the rule). Similarly, suppose a baseball player signs a contract that sets out all the conditions that bind both the employee and the employer. However, the last line of the contract reads, "If either of the parties wishes not to abide by the above conditions, they don't have to." At that point the contract ceases to be a contract. A contractual condition that undermines the very meaning of a contract is an irrational condition. In the same way, the criterion for the rules we use in ethics is that the rules must be rationallyconsistent.

With these examples to build on, we can now set out the categorical imperative that Kant regards as the supreme moral principle. Actually, Kant formulates several versions of the categorical imperative. The next passage gives us the first version.

hypothetical imperative a rule that tells us only what means to use to achieve a desired end

categorical imperative in Kant's theory, a moral law that tells us what we ought to do but does not depend on any prior conditions or subjective wants and wishes, and contains no qualifications

The Categorical Imperative I: Conformity to a Universal Law

There is, therefore, only one categorical imperative. It is: Act only according to that maxim by which you can at the same time will that it should become a universal law.

Now if all imperatives of duty can be derived from this one imperative as a principle, we can at least show what we understand by the concept of duty and what it means, even though it remains undecided whether that which is called duty is an empty concept or not.

The universality of law according to which effects are produced constitutes what is properly called nature in the most general sense (as to form), i.e., the existence of things so far as it is determined by universal laws. [By analogy], then, the universal imperative of duty can be expressed as follows: Act as though the maxim of your action were by your will to become a universal law of nature.

Trans. Lewis White Beck, 2nd ed., © 1990. Reproduced in print and electronically by permission of Pearson Education, Inc.,Upper Saddle River, New Jersey.

A maxim is a subjective rule on which an individual actually acts as opposed to an objective principle upon which one should act. A maxim has the form "Whenever I'm in circumstances C, I will do X in order to achieve Y." Notice, however, that Kant has not given us any specific maxims for guiding our behavior. Instead, he has given us a principle for deciding which maxims establish our actual moral obligations and which ones do not. Hence, the first formulation of the categorical imperative has given us a principle for choosing maxims that will establish our moral duties. This principle is known as the *principle of universalizability.* An action-guiding principle is *universalizable* if it is possible for everyone to act on it and if we could rationally wish ("will" in Kant's terminology) that everyone would act upon it.

Kant's universal law version of the categorical imperative could be stated in terms of a three-step test.

1. State the maxim on the basis of which you are planning to act.
2. Try to formulate your maxim in terms of a universal law.
3. See if you can consistently and rationally will that everyone follow this universalized maxim.

Let's apply this three-step test to one of Kant's own examples. Suppose you need to borrow some money but to do so you must promise to repay it even though you know full well that you will not be able to keep the promise. (1) State the maxim on which you are acting: "If I need to make a promise, I may do so even though I do not intend to keep it." (2) Universalize your maxim: "If anyone needs to make a promise, they may do so even if they do not intend to keep it." (3) Ask if you could rationally will that this rule would become a universal law that everyone followed. Surely, the answer is that you could not will for everyone to follow this law. If everyone adopted this rule, then promise making would be meaningless and there would not be any point in making or accepting promises. Your deceitful promise will be accepted *only* if others have respect for promises. Hence, you can apply your rule concerning promises only if no one else follows it.

Notice that Kant's point is *not* that a society in which people did not keep their promises would be very unpleasant. With this inference, the empirical consequences of the action become the criteria of whether the action is right or wrong. Kant's point is a more subtle, logical one. What he is saying is that a moral rule governing an activity (promise making) that would eliminate the activity in question would be a self-defeating rule (and thereby an inconsistent or irrational one).

Some Kantian scholars point out that the categorical imperative is primarily a test of which actions are permissible. If an action flunks the test (e.g., breaking promises), then it

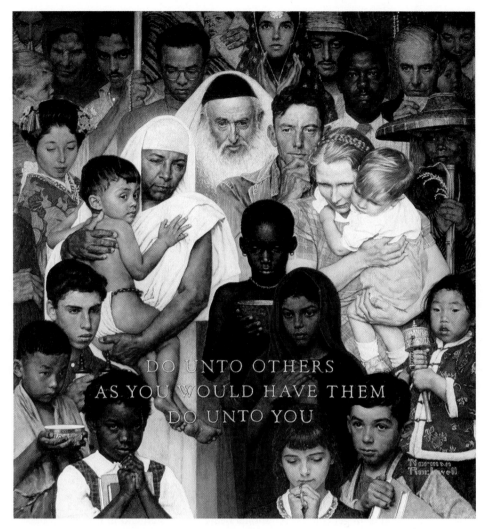

Golden Rule (1961) by Norman Rockwell. As suggested by Rockwell's painting, versions of this supreme principle of ethics can be found in the moral teachings of every tradition and every great civilization going back to antiquity. The moral objectivists would claim that this finding supports their view that a core of moral values seems to be universal among healthy societies. More specifically, the Golden Rule also mirrors some of the themes found in Kantian ethics, especially that of the principle of universalizability.

is impermissible or morally forbidden. However, the opposing rules "Always tie your left shoe first" and "Always tie your right shoe first" are both universalizable and so the actions they govern are both permissible but neither one by itself is morally obligatory. However, if a maxim cannot be followed universally ("Break your promises when it is convenient to do so") and the opposing action is universalizable ("Always keep your promises"), then the latter rule is a moral obligation.

Kant's criteria of universalizing our maxims capture some of our everyday moral intuitions. When you were young your mother probably censured your behavior at some time or other by saying, "What if everyone behaved the way you do?" The Golden Rule says, "Do unto others as you would have them do unto you." We say to people, "Don't make yourself an exception. Don't be a hypocrite." Hence, the professor who flunks students for plagiarizing their papers at the same time that he steals and publishes another person's research is making himself an exception to the rule that he expects his students and colleagues to follow.

THOUGHT EXPERIMENT: *Universalizing Principles*

See if you can apply Kant's criterion of universalizability found in his first version of the categorical imperative. All of the following principles could be consistently followed if they were only a particular individual's personal policy. But in each case, decide if it would be possible or rationally consistent to universalize the maxim. Remember, the issue is not simply whether you would like the results, but whether the principle would undermine itself if everyone followed it without exception.

1. Never say "I love you" to someone unless that person says it to you first.
2. Always pay your debts on time.
3. When running a business, always charge less for your product than the competitor.
4. Never help someone out unless you get something in return.
5. Share some of your wealth with those less fortunate.
6. Give all your money to those who have less than you do.
7. Cheat on your tests whenever possible.
8. Never cheat on a test.

Kant's first version of the categorical imperative approached ethics at the level of formal principles. His second formulation of the categorical imperative focuses more concretely on the persons with whom we interact.

The Categorical Imperative II: Persons as Ends in Themselves

Now, I say, man and, in general, every rational being exists as an end in himself and not merely as a means to be arbitrarily used by this or that will. In all his actions, whether they are directed to himself or to other rational beings, he must always be regarded at the same time as an end. All objects of inclinations have only a conditional worth, for if the inclinations and the needs founded on them did not exist, their object would be without worth. The inclinations themselves as the sources of needs, however, are so lacking in absolute worth that the universal wish of every rational being must be indeed to free himself completely from them. Therefore, the worth of any objects to be obtained by our actions is at all times conditional. Beings whose existence does not depend on our will but on nature, if they are not rational beings, have only a relative worth as means and are therefore called "things"; on the other hand, rational beings are designated "persons" because their nature indicates that they are ends in themselves, i.e., things which may not be used merely as means. Such a being is thus an object of respect and, so far, restricts all [arbitrary] choice. Such beings are not merely subjective ends whose existence as a result of our action has a worth for us, but are objective ends, i.e., beings whose existence in itself is an end. Such an end is one for which no other end can be substituted, to which these beings should serve merely as means. For, without them, nothing of absolute worth could be found, and if all worth is conditional and thus contingent, no supreme practical principle for reason could be found anywhere.

Thus if there is to be a supreme practical principle and a categorical imperative for the human will, it must be one that forms an objective principle of the will from the conception of that which is necessarily an end for everyone because it is an end in itself. Hence this objective principle can serve as a universal practical law. The ground of this principle is: rational nature exists as an end in itself. Man necessarily thinks of his own existence in this way; thus far it is a subjective principle of human actions. Also every other rational being thinks of his existence by means of the same rational ground which holds also for myself; thus it is at the same time an objective principle from which, as a supreme practical ground, it must be possible to derive all laws of the will. The practical imperative, therefore, is the following: Act so that you treat humanity, whether in your own person or in that of another, always as an end and never as a means only.

Trans. Lewis White Beck, 2nd ed., © 1990. Reproduced in print and electronically by permission of Pearson Education, Inc.,Upper Saddle River, New Jersey.

Kant did not think that these two versions of the categorical imperative were two distinct principles; he considered them two ways of making the same point. Many commentators, however, are not sure that they are the same. Nevertheless, on Kant's behalf, it could be argued that the second version is really expressing the criterion of universalizability of the first version by saying that we should always act toward others in ways that we would want everyone else to act toward us.

What does Kant mean when he says, "Act so that you treat humanity, whether in your own person or in that of another, always as an end and never as a means only"? This principle seems to be saying that each person has intrinsic worth and dignity and that we should not use people or treat them like things. Kant's argument for this principle could be paraphrased in the following manner. Mere things such as cars, jewels, works of art, or tools have value only if persons endow them with value. In other words, a Rembrandt painting will sell for a million dollars only because many people desire it. Accordingly, such things have only *conditional* value, because if people stop desiring them, they will be worthless. However, persons are not things. Since persons are the source of all conditional value, they cannot have conditional value themselves; they must have *absolute* or *intrinsic* value. No one can give you your worth as a person, nor can they take it away. An acquaintance may treat you like a thing whose only value is to serve his ends, but such a person is being inconsistent. He is acting as though he alone has absolute value while others are mere things to be used. Thus, he is following the maxim "I will treat others as things," but he could not consistently and rationally will others to follow this rule in return. Consequently, he is making himself an exception.

STOP AND THINK

Have you ever experienced a situation in which someone used you merely as a means to get something that person wanted? How did that experience make you feel? Why did you feel that way? Have you ever treated someone else merely as a means? What end were you trying to achieve? If you had followed Kant's categorical imperative, how would you have behaved differently?

Sometimes it may seem as though we cannot avoid using people as things to serve our own ends. When you buy stamps from the postal clerk, for example, you are using that person as a source of stamps. However, notice that Kant said we should treat persons always as an end and never as a means *only*. Hence, even in impersonal transactions in which we are mainly interested in a person for the services that he or she can perform for us, we should never act in a rude or manipulative manner, and we should always be mindful of the fact that it is a person with whom we are dealing.

An important feature of this formulation of the moral imperative is that Kant explicitly claims that we should treat ourselves with respect and not merely as a means to some end. Many ethical theorists (the utilitarians, for example) believe that ethics governs only our relations with others. Kantian ethics implies that we have moral duties to ourselves and not just to others. For this reason, Kant condemns suicide. If I decide to terminate my life in order to escape my pains and disappointments, I am treating myself as though I were a thing that is determined by external circumstances. Instead, I should respect the dignity and worth of my own personhood and treat it as having a value that transcends every other consideration. In the act of suicide, I am destroying a person (myself) and treating that person as a means in order to achieve some other end (freedom from burdens). In another application of this principle, Kant says that even if I were stranded alone on a desert island, I would have duties to myself. For example, I should do what I could to improve myself and make use of my talents instead of lapsing into idleness and indulgence.

Absolute Duties

Kant believes that if there is to be morality at all, then moral rules must hold for all people, at all times, in all circumstances, and with no exceptions. In one respect, the notion of absolute moral duties is a good one. Because one rule that the categorical imperative generates is that we ought not to kill an innocent person, Kant's absolutism would forbid society from killing you even if your murder created the best consequences for society. Thus, unlike utilitarianism, Kantian ethics would not allow exceptions to the principles of justice and individual rights. However, there are problems with moral absolutism. Consider the case of the inquiring stranger in the following thought experiment.

> ## THOUGHT EXPERIMENT: *The Case of the Inquiring Stranger*
>
> Suppose that a friend is fleeing from a murderous maniac and comes to your home begging you for help. Because he is your friend and is innocent of any wrongdoing, you hide him in your attic. Moments later, the murderer comes to your door and asks if your friend is in the house. (Let's suppose that your silence will tip him off that your friend is inside.)
>
> - Should you tell the truth or lie?
> - What moral principles and arguments would you use to justify this action?
> - What do you think Kant would say?

Even if we agree that lying (as a general rule) is wrong, most people would say that in *this* case lying to the inquiring stranger is morally justified. Surely it is more important to save an innocent life than to tell the truth. This story is not simply a far-fetched, hypothetical case; many real-world examples of this situation exist. In World War II, for example, Europeans hid innocent people from the Nazis and lied to protect these potential victims. Kant, discussing this example in his essay "On a Supposed Right to Lie from

Altruistic Motives," points out that in this case we are violating our moral duty to the truth because we think the consequences of doing so will be good. But can we ever know what the consequences will be? Suppose that you lie and say that your friend is not in your house but that you saw him running down the street. Unknown to you, your friend has slipped out the back door and is running down the street, where the murderer catches and kills him. Kant says that your lie would have been instrumental in causing the innocent person's death. On the other hand, Kant says that if you had told the truth, the murderer might have been apprehended by the neighbors while he searched your house. Kant's conclusion is: "Therefore, whoever tells a lie, however well intentioned he might be, must answer for the consequences, however unforeseeable they were, and pay the penalty for them. . . . To be truthful (honest) in all deliberations, therefore, is a sacred and absolutely commanding decree of reason, limited by no expediency."[51] Kant's point is that we can never be completely sure of the consequences of our actions, so they cannot play a role in determining our duty. Instead, we must stick with our known duties.

Several replies could be made to Kant's analysis. First, he is too pessimistic about our ability to always predict the consequences. Surely there are situations in which we could be reasonably sure about what will happen if we perform this or that action. Particularly when a life is at stake, we better do whatever seems to have the best chance of preserving that life. If you had acted on your duty to the truth, as Kant says you should do, and if your action had the indirect result of causing your friend's death, can you wash your hands so simply of the results of your choice?

A second problem is that Kant didn't seem to realize that qualifications and exceptions could be built into universal and absolute rules. For example, in the case of the inquiring stranger, why couldn't you follow the rule "Always tell the truth unless doing so would cause an innocent person's death"? This rule is universalizable, because everyone could follow it without contradiction, and we could wish that everyone did follow it. Or the rule could be "Always tell the truth to those who have a right to know the truth." This universal rule would require us to tell the truth to a friend, an employer, or a judge, but it might allow us to be less than truthful to a murderer, a Nazi, a malicious gossip, or an acquaintance inquiring about important issues of security and confidentiality.

Finally, Kant did not address the problem of what to do when duties conflict. This situation certainly occurred in the case with the inquiring stranger, because our duties of telling the truth and preserving lives were in conflict. Some philosophers have tried to keep Kant's important insights while modifying his position to deal with the problem of conflicts between duties. W. D. Ross, for example, distinguishes between two kinds of duties.[52] A **prima facie duty** is one that is morally binding *unless* it conflicts with a more important duty. (Prima facie literally means "at first glance.") An **actual duty** is one that we are morally obligated to perform in a particular situation after we have taken all the circumstances into account. Prima facie duties are always in effect, but any particular one can be superseded by a higher duty. This rule is analogous to the law of gravity, which is always in effect but can be superseded by the more powerful force of a rocket engine. Of course, even though we may be justified in violating one prima facie duty to fulfill another one, we still have an obligation to make amends to anyone who was harmed by our doing so.

Without claiming that this list is complete, Ross sets out seven prima facie duties: (1) *fidelity*—keeping our promises, telling the truth; (2) *reparation*—compensating others for wrongs we have done; (3) *gratitude*—showing appreciation for benefits others have bestowed on us; (4) *justice*—distributing goods with impartiality and equity; (5) *beneficence*—promoting other people's good, (6) *self-improvement*—trying to become a better person; and (7) *nonmaleficence*—refraining from harming others.

prima facie duty a duty that is morally binding unless it conflicts with a more important duty

actual duty a duty that we are morally obligated to perform in a particular situation after we have taken all the circumstances into account

Ross does not believe in any formula for ranking these duties in some sort of absolute hierarchy. To decide which of the prima facie duties is the actual duty we should act on in a given situation requires a morally sensitive and wise assessment of the circumstances. For example, my actual duty may be to stop and help a stranded motorist even though it may require me to break a promise (such as an appointment). If that promise impacts an international treaty on which world peace depends, however, then the actual duty of that promise may be more important than preventing a minor harm. Furthermore, Ross stresses the highly personal character of duty. For example, my general duty to help others is normally more pressing when it comes to my family members than it is for strangers. Although Ross does not provide us with a clear-cut procedure for determining which duty is our actual one in a given situation, he has captured Kant's concern for universally binding duties while giving us some means to resolve conflicts between them.

LOOKING THROUGH THE LENS OF KANTIAN ETHICS

1. Kant says that we should always treat persons as ends in themselves and never merely as a means. What implications would following this principle have for your social life, including your actual or potential romantic involvements?

2. According to classical utilitarianism, ethics has to do with how our actions affect others. If I were alone on a desert island I could do whatever pleases me; I would have no moral obligations. But Kant thinks that we have moral duties to ourselves, such as the duty to preserve our own life, to develop our natural talents, to improve ourselves, and so on. What do you think? Do you have moral duties to yourself, or is it morally permissible to do anything you want as long as it doesn't affect someone else?

3. In Victor Hugo's novel *Les Miserables* (made into a musical and a movie), the hero, Jean Valjean, is a former convict living under an illegal false identity. Not only is he the mayor of his town and a public benefactor, but he owns a successful business on which most of the townspeople depend for employment. He learns that some unfortunate beggar has been mistaken for him and will be sent away to prison. The real Jean Valjean decides it is his moral duty to reveal who he is, even though it may destroy all the good work he has done and cause him to be sent back to prison to serve a cruel and unjust life sentence.

- What would a Kantian say Jean Valjean should do? Why?
- What would a utilitarian say? Why?
- What do you think Jean Valjean should do? Give your reasons.

4. Peruse newspaper stories, editorials, letters to the editor, political or legislative proposals, and everyday conversations to find examples of ethical justifications that reflect the spirit of Kantian ethics.

EXAMINING THE STRENGTHS AND WEAKNESSES OF KANTIAN ETHICS

Positive Evaluation

1. Kant's ethics is admirable in emphasizing the importance of rationality, consistency, impartiality, and respect for persons in the way we live our lives. By stressing the fact that moral absolutes cannot be violated, he prevents any loopholes, self-serving exceptions, and personal biases in the determination of our duties. Consequently, he saves us from the

temptation to rationalize our behavior for the sake of convenience and expediency or from doing an end run around our moral obligations.

2. Can we ever be completely sure of the consequences of our actions? Haven't there been times when you thought you were doing the best thing, based on the anticipated consequences, but the results turned out badly? Don't such situations raise a problem with the philosophy of basing our moral decisions on the consequences? Contrary to utilitarianism and other forms of consequentialism, Kant argues that consequences should never play a role in determining our moral obligations. Based on rational, moral deliberations, we can be certain about our moral obligation to tell the truth, for example. However, we cannot know with equal certainty the good or bad consequences of either telling the truth or lying. Isn't this consideration important? Isn't it often the case that doing the right thing will sometimes make people unhappy? In such cases, don't we have to do our duty anyway?

3. Unlike utilitarianism, Kant's theory strictly prohibits some actions, such as murder, breaking promises, or violating a person's rights to serve some other end. In doing so, Kant's ethics avoids utilitarianism's problems in which (critics claim) the goodness of the overall consequences could justify some very reprehensible actions. Isn't Kant's theory a better moral theory than one in which "anything goes" as long as the overall consequences are good?

Negative Evaluation

1. Is the good will always good without qualification, as Kant supposes? Can't I be an inept, bungling do-gooder, always conscientiously trying to do my duty but creating human misery as a result? Take, for example, the oppressive, controlling mother of an adult child who assumes her duty is always to be "helpful" until the child finally screams in frustration, "Please, mother, I would rather do it myself!" As the old saying goes, "The road to hell is paved with good intentions." It seems clear that many Nazis saw themselves as fulfilling a moral mandate to "save" Europe from political and cultural decay. It could be argued that my single-minded focus on my duty coupled with a self-righteous or insensitive blindness to the consequences of my actions could be a form of moral fanaticism. Is moral fanaticism a potential problem for Kantian ethics?

2. Kant tends to make a very sharp dichotomy between doing our duty for duty's sake and doing it because of our inclinations. But shouldn't you be commended if you spontaneously and joyfully do your duty because you are filled with compassion, because it is second nature to you, and because being moral has become a habitual feature of your personality? Kant seems to think that doing our duty must be a matter of rational calculation in which our inclinations and emotions play no role. Isn't there something one-sided about this approach? Shouldn't morality be related to our emotions, our habitual or spontaneous behavior, what we love, what we disdain, and what we feel good about, and not just to our actions, rational deliberations, and rules of conduct?

3. Kant's commitment to absolute duties offers us no solution when our duties conflict. In the case of the inquiring stranger, you have a duty to tell the truth, but you also have a duty to preserve life. Kant's advice is to tell the truth and let the consequences happen as they may, because you cannot be completely certain of the consequences. Besides, he says, you will have done your duty, and it is the stranger who is responsible for the murder and not you. But aren't we responsible not only for what we do but also for what we knowingly allow to happen? If your telling the truth about the location of your friend allows the murderer to find his victim, don't you bear some responsibility for the death? Isn't the

preservation of life a higher and more weighty duty than telling the truth? Shouldn't reasonable exceptions to moral rules be allowed, especially when those rules make it impossible to fulfill a higher duty?

4. Is the principle of universalizability found in the first version of the categorical imperative subject to arbitrariness and subjectivity, contrary to what Kant thinks? Kant thinks that we have a moral duty to help others who are less fortunate, because if we were in their place we would want someone to help us. But the ethical egoist Ayn Rand claims that "everyone should tend to his or her own interests and not to the needs of others." She also claims that if she were in need, she would neither expect nor want you to sacrifice your interests for hers, because she finds that being dependent on others is demeaning. So it is possible for others to universalize moral rules that are contrary to those of Kant. Does this possibility suggest that in spite of Kant's belief that his ethics is based on pure rationality, a good deal of subjectivity has crept into it?

5.5 VIRTUE ETHICS

 LEADING QUESTIONS: *Virtue Ethics*

Contemporary philosopher Michael Stocker posed the following thought experiment to test our ethical intuitions.

> Suppose you are in a hospital, recovering from a long illness. You are very bored and restless and at loose ends when Smith comes in once again. You are now convinced more than ever that he is a fine fellow and a real friend—taking so much time to cheer you up, traveling all the way across town, and so on. You are so effusive with your praise and thanks that he protests that he always tries to do what he thinks is his duty, what he thinks is best. You at first think he is engaging in a polite form of self-deprecation, relieving the moral burden. But the more you two speak, the more clear it becomes that he was telling the literal truth: that it is not essentially because of you that he came to see you, not because you are friends, but because he thought it his duty, perhaps as a fellow Christian or Communist or whatever, or simply because he knows of no one more in need of cheering up and no one easier to cheer up.[53]

1. From a utilitarian point of view, Smith was acting morally because he maximized happiness by cheering you up. From a Kantian point of view, Smith was acting morally because he was acting in accordance with his duty and from a sense of duty. What, then, is the problem with his hospital visit?

2. What is the difference between someone helping you (a) for the sake of maximizing the total amount of happiness in the world, (b) for the sake of fulfilling his duties as a friend, (c) to help sustain the general practice of friendship, and (d) *out of* a personal sense of friendship for the sake of you as a person whom he cherishes? Why do the first three motives seem somewhat impersonal and abstract?

3. Utilitarianism says we should act for the sake of good consequences and Kantianism says we should act for the sake of our rational moral duty, but Stocker (the author of this thought experiment) objects that in either case we are failing to value the recipient of the action as a person for his or her own sake. Such theories "treat others externally, as essentially replaceable, as mere instruments or repositories of general and non-specific value" and

in doing so, these theories "preclude love, friendship, affection, fellow feeling, and community."[54] In what way does Stocker's story attempt to illustrate these points?

4. If Smith's benevolent actions, their consequences, and his sense of duty are blameless, what is it that Smith lacks?

Up until the last few decades, ethical theory has been dominated by the debate between the utilitarians and the Kantians or between those who stress the consequences of an action and those who are more concerned with whether the nature of the act itself fulfills or violates a moral duty. Nevertheless, in spite of their differences, both ethical theories are in agreement that the morality of *actions* is the primary focus of ethics. However, in ordinary life we assess the moral qualities not only of actions but of *persons* as well. We might say of a person that she is admirable, decent, good, honorable, moral, saintly, and, in short, has a virtuous moral character. On the other hand, we might judge that she is bad, base, corrupt, disreputable, immoral, reprehensible, and, in short, has a deplorable moral character. Some philosophers do not seem to connect morality with a person's actions. Instead, they claim, morality should be concerned with our likes and dislikes, desires, attitudes, dispositions to behave in certain ways, personal ideals and life goals, what sorts of things make us happy, and in general those personal qualities that define our stance toward life.

This position, found both in ancient and contemporary thought, is known as virtue ethics. *Virtue ethics* is an ethical theory that focuses on those character traits that make someone a good or admirable person rather than simply on the actions the person performs. According to the previously discussed theories the primary question in ethics is, "What should I do?" On the contrary, for virtue ethics the fundamental question in ethics is, "What sort of person should I be?" This point is made by Stocker's story about Smith's hospital visit, for even though Smith did the right thing and conscientiously fulfilled his moral duty according to utilitarian or Kantian theory, he lacked the virtue of compassion. Accordingly, something is lacking in his moral development as a person. Virtue ethics says that in ethics we should first be concerned with what it means to be a virtuous person, and then the dos and don'ts of concrete action will follow from this.

STOP AND THINK

What reasons can be given in support of each of the following statements?

1. Ethics should be based on the notion of what it means to be a good person.
2. Ethics should be based on the concept of what it means for an action to be morally right or obligatory.

After weighing the reasons given in support for each one, which statement do you think best describes what should be the main concern of an ethical theory?

SURVEYING THE CASE FOR VIRTUE ETHICS

WHAT IS VIRTUE?

One difficulty in understanding the word *virtue* is the fact that it has acquired a number of diverse associations over the centuries. In our day, to say someone is "virtuous" suggests that they are very pious or, perhaps, sexually pure. Sometimes it even has a negative connotation, for example, when it is applied sarcastically to someone who is obnoxiously sanctimonious. To understand virtue ethics, we have to go back to ancient Greece where the theory began. In Greek philosophy the concept of virtue was expressed with the word *aretē*. To have *aretē* means "to have the quality of excellence" or "to be doing what you do in an excellent way." This concept of virtue is still alive today in our English word *virtuosity*. A virtuoso violinist is one who can play the violin with admirable technical skill. For the Greeks *anything* could be said to have virtue if it was an excellent example of its kind. Thus, they said that the virtue of a knife is its ability to cut things. The virtue of a race horse is to run very fast. The shipbuilder, the wrestler, the physician, and the musician each have a particular kind of virtue related to their specific task, but philosophers such as Socrates were concerned with the question, "What does it mean to be a virtuous (excellent) human being?" In other words, being fully human is a task or skill in itself, which is more fundamental than all the specific skills we may acquire. That's why we refer to a vicious tyrant as being "inhuman." He is so lacking in the virtues that constitute an excellent character that he doesn't deserve the label "human." According to Socrates and virtue ethics, being moral boils down to being successful at the art of living. People who routinely, and without any qualms, lie, cheat, exploit people, and are insensitive to the sufferings of others lack the virtues of honesty, integrity, justice, and compassion, and have the corresponding vices. According to Socrates and Plato the character of such a person is malformed, deficient, and dysfunctional and is the moral equivalent of a bodily organ that is diseased.[55] Consequently, Socrates asserted that the most important goal for humans is not just living but "living well."[56] Contrary to contemporary advertisements that equate the good life with possessing popularity, fame, fortune, and premium beverages or cars, Socrates identified "living well" with possessing a certain quality of character, for he says that "living well and honorably and justly mean the same thing."[57]

A **virtue** can be defined as a trait of character that is to be admired and desired because it is a constituent of human excellence. Virtues are intrinsically valuable for their own sake, but they are also valued because they promote human flourishing both for the individual who possesses them and for society in general. Typical examples of moral virtues (but not a complete list) are generosity, compassion, honesty, fidelity, integrity, justice, conscientiousness, and courage. Although the boundaries are hard to draw, moral virtues should be distinguished from personality traits such as charm or shyness. We may find certain personality traits to be appealing or unappealing, but they are not the focus of our evaluation of a person's moral character. If character traits are the subject of moral evaluation, then everyone must at least have the potential to have them. If we do not possess them, we must be able to acquire them by training, practice, and through a personal program of self-improvement. Otherwise, judging someone negatively for lacking a certain virtue would be like criticizing that person for being born with defective eyesight.

> **virtue** a trait of character that is to be admired and desired because it is a constituent of human excellence

---

STOP AND THINK

As you look over your life, what character traits have you acquired or strengthened that made you a better human being than before? Was your acquisition of these traits facilitated by someone's influence, by your own attempts at self-improvement, or by a combination of factors? Suppose you could go to a trading post at which you could leave behind a trait, an attitude, or a desire that you think diminishes you as a human being and exchange it for one that is better. What would you leave behind, and what new characteristic would you acquire? What concrete changes would this trade make in your life? Why do you think this trade would improve you as a person?

Like most theories, virtue ethics is defended with a two-pronged approach. First, the assumptions and methods of competing theories are critiqued. Because the main alternatives to virtue ethics are utilitarianism and Kantian ethics, the virtue ethicist must demonstrate that those theories have irredeemable limitations and flaws. But simply showing that your opponents' theories have problems is not enough to show that yours should be adopted. Therefore, the second approach is to make a positive case for the theory being promoted in order to show its superiority to the alternatives. Following this two-pronged approach, I begin by discussing the virtue theorist's critique of utilitarianism and Kantian ethics.

THE PROBLEMS WITH THE UTILITARIAN VIEW

As you might suspect, the virtue ethicist charges that the utilitarian and Kantian theories are inadequate because they fail to give virtue the priority it deserves in our ethical lives. Although utilitarian and Kantian ethical theories are primarily concerned with right conduct, they do not neglect virtuous character traits entirely. In those theories, however, virtue has value mostly for its tendency to serve other ends. Thus, the two theories view virtue as having instrumental value rather than intrinsic value. First, consider the following thought experiment in the light of utilitarian theory.

THOUGHT EXPERIMENT: *Are Good Actions Enough?*

Suppose that someone (call her Millie) performed the following actions: (1) told the truth when pressured to do otherwise, (2) rescued a child in a dangerous situation, (3) donated time to a charity, and (4) spent her free time visiting Aunt Gertrude in the nursing home. Furthermore, let's add the stipulation that in each case Millie's actions maximized happiness more than any other alternative would.

- What judgment would the utilitarian make concerning the moral goodness of Millie's actions in each case?

Now suppose that in the previous cases Millie acted from the following motives: (1) she calculated that truth telling would earn her a reward in the afterlife, (2) she hoped that her courageous rescue would earn her fame, (3) she anticipated that her charitable work would be good for her political campaign, and (4) she hoped to inherit her aunt's fortune.

- With this additional information, what would *you* say about the moral goodness of Millie's actions?

It seems clear that the utilitarian would have to say that, in spite of her questionable motives, Millie performed the morally right action in each situation because the consequences resulted in maximizing happiness. Nothing in the utilitarian rules for right conduct talks about motives. However, if your moral intuitions are similar to mine, when we find out Millie's motives for these benevolent actions, we tend to think less of her as a person rather than admiring her. Are the utilitarians sheerly "happiness accountants" who only worry about how the figures add up? Are they totally unconcerned about people's motives and character? The answer is that utilitarian theory *does* take these factors into account. If people performed benevolent actions only to get into heaven, win fame, succeed in politics, or get an inheritance, then they would not be inclined to act morally when they believed there was no payoff. Hence, utilitarians think it is important to encourage certain character traits in people and instill them in their children, because a person who has a virtuous character is more likely to choose to do the morally right action (the action that maximizes the general good). In this theory, virtue has merely instrumental value, not intrinsic value.

THE PROBLEMS WITH THE KANTIAN VIEW

Kant seems to be more concerned with the person's character than the utilitarians are, because he says it is not enough to do the right thing (acting in accordance with duty). Instead, for an action to be genuinely moral it also must be performed from the right motive (acting for the sake of duty). For Kant, the only thing that is good without qualification is the good will, or the motive to do our duty. We could characterize this motive as the virtue of *conscientiousness*. But while Kant exalts this one virtue, he downplays the other virtues as playing a secondary role in morality or even as expressions of our inclinations and emotions. The following thought experiment illustrates the problem with Kant's narrow approach to moral virtue.

> **THOUGHT EXPERIMENT:** *Is Acting for the Sake of Duty Enough?*
>
> Consider the following two scenarios:
>
> 1. Kantian Karl finds that someone has left a purse behind in the classroom. Seeking to find the name of its owner, he discovers that it contains a substantial amount of money. He could use the money to pay the balance on his tuition bill and has a strong inclination to keep it. Being a good Kantian, however, he realizes that his rational, moral duty is to return the purse to its owner. He seriously considers keeping the money, convincing himself that he needs it more than its owner does, but his attempts to rationalize this course of action are repeatedly interrupted by the insistent demands of the moral law within him. Breaking out in a sweat as he oscillates between temptation and duty, he finally sets his chin and decides that he will do what duty demands. He returns the purse with the money intact to its rightful owner.
> 2. Virtuous Virginia finds that someone has left a wallet behind in the classroom. Seeking to find the name of its owner, she discovers that it contains a substantial amount of money. Virginia believes that achieving personal excellence is the most important goal in life, so all her life she has striven to improve herself intellectually, athletically, musically, and morally. She has a mature, fully developed moral character, so honesty is part of her very being. Consequently, it does not even occur to her to keep the money for herself. Without a second thought, she immediately takes action to return the wallet with the money to its rightful owner.
>
> Both Karl and Virginia performed the right action and did it for moral reasons. But suppose we now want to assess not just their actions, but their moral character. Which person, Karl or Virginia, has the most moral worth? How important is this consideration?

In the first scenario, Kantian Karl faithfully but grudgingly did his duty, but to do so he had to wrestle against his inclinations. In contrast, Virtuous Virginia did her duty because she had developed such moral habits that she was naturally inclined to do what is right. Kant tended to make such a rigid dichotomy between moral duty and desire that if an action (such as Virginia's) reflected our habitual way of behaving or followed from our personal nature, emotions, desires, and inclinations, that action had no moral worth. However, Aristotle said that

> the man who does not rejoice in noble actions is not even good; since no one would call a man just who did not enjoy acting justly, nor any man liberal [generous] who did not enjoy liberal actions [generosity]; and similarly in all other cases. . . . Hence we ought to have been brought up in a particular way from our very youth, as Plato says, so as both to delight in and be pained by the things that we ought; for this is the right education.[58]

Contrary to Kant, Aristotle thought that ethics was a matter of the emotions and not simply of reason alone. Following Aristotle, contemporary virtue ethicists claim that virtuous persons not only do their duty for its own sake but do it happily and spontaneously, and find their deepest desires and inclinations fulfilled in doing so.

In summary, utilitarianism and Kantianism, the two major ethical theories in modern philosophy, are theories based on rules or principles and focus single-mindedly on the ethics of conduct. The analogy between ethical theory and the law is obvious in these approaches. On the other hand, virtue ethics thinks this emphasis is misplaced and wants to return the focus of ethics to that of character and the emotions. If the legal metaphor underlies rule-based theories, then gardening is the metaphor of virtue ethics. The virtues are those conditions that are essential for humans to grow, blossom, and flourish. And we may elaborate the gardening metaphor by noticing that each one of us is both the gardener and the flower. Hence, for the virtue theorist, the question to ask about a proposed action is not, "What are the consequences?" or, "Could I universalize the principle on which I am acting?" Instead, the virtue theorist would ask, "What would this proposed action do to me in my project of becoming an admirable and worthy human being?"

THE POSITIVE CASE FOR VIRTUE ETHICS

The viewpoint offered by virtue ethics can be summarized by the following five themes. Although different theorists will emphasize some points over others, together these themes weave a pattern depicting an alternative picture of what ethics is all about.

1. Virtues Are Necessary Conditions for Human Flourishing and Well-Being One common theme in virtue ethics is that, given our physical and psychological nature, the moral virtues are necessary for us to flourish and to fare well in life. Socrates thought that asking for a reason to be moral was like asking, "Why should I want to flourish?" Obviously, the notion of "flourish" here does not mean that possessing the moral virtues will necessarily guarantee us friends, wealth, and a life of ease, because moral persons have often been rejected by their society, poor, and inflicted with great suffering. Whether or not we are graced with external rewards, we have a natural desire to be as excellent as possible in what we do. Few of us will win great fame or fortune for our athletic, musical, or intellectual skills. Yet we want to do as well as we can in these and other endeavors simply because striving for excellence, that is, maximizing our potential as human beings, is rewarding in itself and gives us a sense of personal accomplishment. Virtues, rather than having a causal relationship to flourishing, are said to have a constitutive relationship. A spark can *cause* an explosion, but getting the ball across your opponent's goal line does not cause your team to have a touchdown. Instead, it is what *constitutes* a touchdown. Similarly, possessing the virtues is, the argument goes, what constitutes human well-being.

Alasdair MacIntyre, one of the most influential voices in contemporary virtue ethics, describes the role that the virtues play in our individual and community endeavors:

> The virtues therefore are to be understood as those dispositions which will not only sustain practices, but which will also sustain us in the relevant kind of quest for the good, by enabling us to overcome the harms, dangers, temptations and distractions which we encounter, and which will furnish us with increasing self-knowledge and increasing knowledge of the good. The catalogue of the virtues will therefore include the virtues required to sustain the kind of households and the kind of political communities in which men and women can seek for the good together and the virtues necessary for philosophical inquiry about the character of the good.[59]

2. Moral Rules Are Inadequate Unless They Are Grounded in a Virtue-Based Ethics Although downplaying the role of moral rules in the study of ethics, the virtue ethicist does not deny their role in the moral life altogether. Nevertheless, the proponents of virtue ethics question the sufficiency of moral rules apart from a virtuous character. For example, I will not be inclined to follow moral rules nor will I be able to know how they are to be applied if I do not possess virtue. Philosopher Gregory Trianosky expresses the standpoint of virtue ethics in this way:

> It has sometimes been pointed out that rules or principles of right action must be applied, and conflicts between them adjudicated. But the rules themselves do not tell us how to apply them in specific situations, let alone how to apply them well, or indeed when to excuse people for failing to comply with them. For these tasks, it is claimed, an account of the virtues is required. . . .
>
> Next, it has been argued that much of right conduct cannot be codified in rules or principles. Moral situations are too complex; moral rules too general and simplistic. . . . Moreover, except when one can look to some morally exemplary or paradigmatic individual, the extent to which one decides well will depend largely on the extent to which one has already developed a virtuous character.[60]

3. Judgments about Character Are More Fundamental Than Judgments about the Rightness or Wrongness of Conduct This claim goes further than the last one, because some recent utilitarians and Kantians have attempted to supplement the ethics of duty with considerations of character. However, the claim of virtue ethics is that the notion of virtue is neither a supplement to moral rules nor dependent upon them because virtue is the primary moral category. As virtue ethicist Harold Alderman says:

> Rules and other notions of the good are, at best, either analytic clarifications of what we mean by virtuous character, maps which indicate how it might be acquired, or a sign that someone actually has it.[61]

Just as the utilitarian and the Kantian will often come to the same moral judgment even though they justify it on different grounds, so the virtue ethicist will usually agree with them concerning the right thing to do in a certain situation. However, the distinctive nature of virtue ethics reveals itself in the fact that, within this position, considerations of virtue can sometimes trump considerations of utility or duty. Philosopher Justine Oakley makes this point with the following example:

> Suppose I console a close friend of mine who is grieving over the irretrievable breakdown of his marriage, and that in consoling him, I stay with him longer than would be required by my duty to him as a friend. A virtue ethicist might regard my staying

longer to console him as right, even if my doing so meant cancelling an appointment with a business associate I'd promised to meet for lunch, and also meant that I thereby failed to maximise overall utility. What makes it right to console the friend here is that this is the sort of thing which someone with an appropriate conception of friendship will be disposed to do, rather than because this brings about the best overall consequences, or because this is our duty as a friend.[62]

4. Virtue Ethics Is More Comprehensive, Because It Deals with the Whole Person and Not Simply the Person Insofar as He or She Performs an Action Action and rule-based theories of ethics are too narrow, because they focus primarily on those moments in life when a person is contemplating an action and specifically only on that category of actions for which there are either good and bad consequences at stake or duties to be fulfilled or violated. Consequently, such theories promote a sort of "moral minimalism" in which the primary concern is, "How can I avoid being blameworthy for the way I acted?" Such theories divide human life into (1) moral situations and (2) nonmoral situations. Theories of conduct are concerned primarily with domain (1), in which we are faced with choices that are either obligatory or forbidden, whereas domain (2) is the realm of the permissible in which the demands of morality are indifferent to what we do. But should morality be quarantined to such a narrow slice of human life? Shouldn't morality be concerned with the whole of our lives and not just those situations in which we face possible wrongdoing? Does ethics offer any guidance to those aspects of life in which the demands of moral rules and duties are not pressing upon me? Does it have anything to say about my ideals, aspirations, desires, interests, emotional responses—all those factors that express the person I am and the person I hope to become, apart from how I behave? Does ethics concern my choices, trivial and momentous, such as what friends to cultivate, what career to pursue, what books to read, or what recreations to enjoy? For example, according to the rule-based ethics of either utilitarianism or Kantianism, the moral value of benevolence is primarily an issue in those situations in which I ought to help others and in which not doing so would be wrong. However, philosopher J. L. A. Garcia argues that this rule-based, action-oriented notion of benevolence is much too minimalistic.

> For a benevolent person will have some inclination to help others even when she is not directed (required) to do so by the moral rules, i.e. when it is supererogatory.* More important, a benevolent person will be inclined to want and hope that others prosper even when she realizes that she cannot by her actions help them and she will be inclined to be pleased with others' good fortune and displeased with their bad fortune when their fortune is, again, unrelated to her own action. In short, the virtue of benevolence cannot be simply a disposition to action, because it consists, not in action, but in various forms of mental response, which may or may not be expressed in action.[63]

If we go back to the story of Smith visiting you in the hospital, we can now see clearly why his benevolent actions were so disturbing. He was acting out of a sense of duty and with the intention to maximize utility, but what was lacking was a spirit of benevolence, a desire to help, a caring attitude, a disposition to feel pleasure in helping you, and happiness in seeing your spirits lifted.

In contrast to the ethics of conduct that dwells on how I perform transitory actions and the motives that direct me at those moments, virtue ethics is concerned with settled character traits that endure beyond those occasions. As the virtue ethicist David Solomon expresses it:

---

*Garcia is using *supererogatory* to refer to actions that are not obligatory but go beyond the demands of duty.

The moral life is not, on this view, best regarded as a set of episodic encounters with moral dilemmas or moral uncertainty (although anyone's moral life will certainly contain moments of this kind); it is rather a life-long pursuit of excellence of the person. The kind of guidance appropriate to such a pursuit will be quite different from that envisioned by many modern ethical theories. . . . The task of an [ethics of virtue] is not determinately to guide action; that task is left to the virtues. Virtue theories do not propose algorithms for solving practical difficulties; they propose something more like a fitness program to get one ready to run a race.[64]

Virtue ethics has been criticized for not providing us with definitive rules for making decisions, but Solomon's point is that it does something better: It gives us guidance in becoming the sorts of persons who can effectively make moral decisions.

5. *The Key to Morality Is Found in the Character of Moral Role Models* Although not all proponents of virtue ethics take this approach, many stress the importance of role models (also called paradigmatic individuals, ideal types, or moral exemplars) in ethical development and decision making. As little children, we acquire a good deal of our moral training by imitating people we admire, such as parents, relatives, teachers, historical figures, and even fictional characters. People such as Buddha, Confucius, Socrates, Jesus, Abraham Lincoln, Gandhi, or Mother Teresa (the list could go on) inspire us not only through their teachings but through the quality of their lives and personalities. Hence, for virtue ethics, the personalities encountered in biographies, history, literature, and even traditional children's stories such as those collected in William Bennett's *The Book of Virtues,* provide as much if not more moral insight than do all the principles of the philosophers. As Daniel Statman, a leading scholar of virtue ethics, says:

Becoming a good person is not a matter of learning or "applying" principles, but of imitating some models. We learn to be virtuous the same way we learn to dance, to cook, and to play football—by watching people who are competent in these areas, and trying to do the same. According to [virtue ethics], education through moral exemplars is more effective than education focused on principles and obligations, because it is far more concrete.[65]

As Statman suggests, we cannot learn to dance, cook, or play football by reading a book or listening to a lecture. Accomplished persons can tell us about these activities and even offer principles to keep in mind that will help us catch on, but in the final analysis we need to watch the actions of people who have mastered the art and to practice the activity until we become as much like these exemplars as possible. Accordingly, Rosalind Hursthouse defines *right action* as "what a virtuous agent would do in the circumstances."[66]

STOP AND THINK

What persons have been moral role models for you? Were they all persons you knew, or were some of them people you read about? Were any of them teachers? Were some of them historical figures? Were any of them fictional characters? Did your moral paradigms change as you grew older? Why? What did you learn from them about life and about being an excellent human being? How would you have been different if you had not been influenced by them? To what degree could you put into words or express as principles what you learned from them? To what extent could the insight they gave you not be verbally expressed? Have you ever felt as though you played this role for someone else—a younger sibling or a friend perhaps?

ARISTOTLE (384–322 B.C.)

Virtue ethics in the Western world can trace its roots back to Socrates, Plato, the Stoics, and early Christianity, but Aristotle has had the most influence on the development of this perspective. Aristotle was born in Macedonia, a kingdom north of Greece. Around age 18, he sought out the best education offered in his day and became a student in Plato's Academy in Athens. Aristotle studied and taught there with Plato for 20 years until the latter's death. Later in life, while gratefully acknowledging Plato's influence on him, Aristotle sharply criticized his teacher's ideas, explaining that although truth and friends are both dear, we ought to honor truth above our friends. After leaving Athens, Aristotle pursued various careers, including tutoring the young Macedonian prince who would later be known as Alexander the Great.

Eventually Aristotle returned to Athens and founded his own school and research institute, called the Lyceum. There he taught a wide range of subjects that included biology, physics, medicine, psychology, chemistry, mathematics, philosophy, rhetoric, political science, and literary criticism. When Alexander the Great died in 323 B.C., a wave of anti-Macedonian rage swept through Athens, and Aristotle feared that his associations with Alexander would put him in danger. Remembering the fate of Socrates but feeling no need to be a martyr, Aristotle fled the city, "lest the Athenians should sin twice against philosophy." He died the following year.

Although his scientific ideas were overthrown long ago, Aristotle's ethical theory continues to inform contemporary philosophy. Aristotle begins his discourse on ethics by observing that all human action aims at some end. But if human life is to be something other than a fragmented and meaningless pursuit of multiple goals, all intermediate goals must ultimately aim at some final good we desire for its own sake. Aristotle says that this goal is *happiness*. Happiness must be the final, unquestioned goal in life, for it makes no sense to ask, "Why are you spending your life pursuing happiness?" The Greek term he uses is *eudaimonia*. Happiness should not be confused with pleasure; its meaning is best thought of as "well-being" or "living well" or "having a life worth living." The problem is that *happiness* is a rather vague term, and different people have different conceptions of it. But if happiness is the supreme good in life, then Aristotle says it is best understood by getting clear on the end or function of human life.

When Aristotle refers to the function or end of human life, he is not necessarily referring to some sort of divine purpose. Rather, he is assuming that every type of thing in nature contains a certain essential nature that makes it what it is. Hence, human nature contains a characteristic activity that is essential to our self-fulfillment as human beings.

- How does Aristotle argue that humans must have a particular function or purpose?
- What function do we have that is uniquely human?

FROM ARISTOTLE

Nicomachean Ethics [67]

Book 1

The best way of arriving at such a definition [of happiness] will probably be to ascertain the function of man. For, as with a flute player, a sculptor, or any artist, or in fact anybody who has a special function or activity, his goodness and excellence seem to lie in his function, so it would seem to be with man, if indeed he has a special function. Can it be said that, while a carpenter and a cobbler have special functions and activities, man, unlike them, is naturally functionless? Or, as the eye, the hand, the foot, and similarly each part of the body has a special function, so may man be regarded as having a special function apart from all these? What, then, can this function be? It is not life; for life is

ARISTOTLE
(384–322 B.C.)

apparently something that man shares with plants; and we are looking for something peculiar to him. We must exclude therefore the life of nutrition and growth. There is next what may be called the life of sensation. But this too, apparently, is shared by man with horses, cattle, and all other animals. There remains what I may call the active life of the rational part of man's being. Now this rational part is twofold; one part is rational in the sense of being obedient to reason, and the other in the sense of possessing and exercising reason and intelligence. The active life too may be conceived of in two ways, either as a state of character, or as an activity; but we mean by it the life of activity, as this seems to be the truer form of the conception.

The function of man then is an activity of the soul in accordance with reason, or not apart from reason. Now, the function of a man of a certain kind, and of a man who is good of that kind—for example, of a harpist and a good harpist—are in our view the same in kind. This is true of all people of all kinds without exception, the superior excellence being only an addition to the function; for it is the function of a harpist to play the harp, and of a good harpist to play the harp well. This being so, if we define the function of man as a kind of life, and this life as an activity of the soul or a course of action in accordance with reason, and if the function of a good man is such activity of a good and noble kind, and if everything is well done when it is done in accordance with its proper excellence, it follows that the good of man is an activity of the soul in accordance with virtue, or, if there are more virtues than one, in accordance with the best and most complete virtue. But we must add the words "in a complete life." For as one swallow or one day does not make a spring, so one day or a short time does not make a man blessed or happy. . . .

Inasmuch as happiness is an activity of the soul in accordance with perfect virtue, we must now consider virtue, as this will perhaps be the best way of studying happiness. . . . Clearly it is human virtue we have to consider; for the good of which we are in search is, as we said, human good, and the happiness, human happiness. By human virtue or excellence we mean not that of the body, but that of the soul, and by happiness we mean an activity of the soul. . . .

Aristotle thinks that happiness is to be found by living according to our nature and fulfilling what it means to be human, which entails a life lived according to a certain plan or strategy that is furnished by reason. Although Aristotle thought that philosophical contemplation was the highest and most satisfying form of happiness, he did not think that we necessarily had to be cloistered intellectuals; he thought that involvement in politics and the life of our culture was necessary to be fully human. Instead, the rational life is one that can be lived continuously in the midst of our other engagements. When he speaks of the activity of the soul in accordance with reason or virtue, he is not talking about something specific that we do but about the manner in which we do all things in life.

Because we are rational beings as well as beings who feel, desire, and act, the road to happiness involves two dimensions. We must rationally judge what is the best way to live, and our appetites, feelings, and emotions must be disciplined to follow that judgment. As Aristotle indicates in the next passage, these two dimensions require two kinds of human excellence: *intellectual virtues* (related to that part of us that reasons) and *moral virtues* (related to that part of us that does not reason but that is capable of following reason). The moral virtues include such character traits as courage, generosity, truthfulness, justice, and so on. Although Aristotle's focus is on the moral virtues in this passage, the two kinds of virtues are mutually supportive. The good life cannot be had if either of these virtues is neglected.

- The intellectual virtues can be fostered by teaching, but how are the moral virtues acquired? In other words, how do we become just, courageous, or temperate (self-controlled)?

Book 2

Virtue then is twofold, partly intellectual and partly moral, and intellectual virtue is originated and fostered mainly by teaching; it demands therefore experience and time. Moral virtue on the other hand is the outcome of habit, and accordingly its name, *ethike,* is derived by a slight variation from *ethos,* habit. From this fact it is clear that moral virtue is not implanted in us by nature; for nothing that exists by nature can be transformed by habit.

Thus a stone, that naturally tends to fall downwards, cannot be habituated or trained to rise upwards, even if we tried to train it by throwing it up ten thousand times. Nor again can fire be trained to sink downwards, nor anything else that follows one natural law be habituated or trained to follow another. It is neither by nature then nor in defiance of nature that virtues grow in us. Nature gives us the capacity to receive them, and that capacity is perfected by habit.

Again, if we take the various natural powers which belong to us, we first possess the proper faculties and afterwards display the activities. It is obviously so with the senses. Not by seeing frequently or hearing frequently do we acquire the sense of seeing or hearing; on the contrary, because we have the senses we make use of them; we do not get them by making use of them. But the virtues we get by first practicing them, as we do in the arts. For it is by doing what we ought to do when we study the arts that we learn the arts themselves; we become builders by building and harpists by playing the harp. Similarly, it is by doing just acts that we become just, by doing temperate acts that we become temperate, by doing brave acts that we become brave. The experience of states confirms this statement, for it is by training in good habits that lawmakers make the citizens good. This is the object all lawmakers have at heart; if they do not succeed in it, they fail of their purpose; and it makes the distinction between a good constitution and a bad one.

Again, the causes and means by which any virtue is produced and destroyed are the same; and equally so in any part. For it is by playing the harp that both good and bad harpists are produced; and the case of builders and others is similar, for it is by building well that they become good builders and by building badly that they become bad builders. If it were not so, there would be no need of anybody to teach them; they would all be born good or bad in their several crafts. The case of the virtues is the same. It is by our actions in dealings between man and man that we become either just or unjust. It is by our actions in the face of danger and by our training ourselves to fear or to courage that we become either cowardly or courageous. It is much the same with our appetites and angry passions. People become temperate and gentle, others licentious and passionate, by behaving in one or the other way in particular circumstances. In a word, moral states are the results of activities like the states themselves. It is our duty therefore to keep a certain character in our activities, since our moral states depend on the differences in our activities. So the difference between one and another training in habits in our childhood is not a light matter, but important, or rather, all-important.

STOP AND THINK

How did you learn how to be generous, self-controlled, fair, or truthful? Do you agree with what Aristotle says about how the virtues are acquired? Is it possible to practice the art of being moral, much like we practice playing a musical instrument or a sport? What practical steps could you take to develop your moral qualities?

In the next passage, Aristotle continues the theme that we acquire the moral virtues by practicing them. When a child first learns to play the piano, the teacher must show the pupil what to do. By modeling the teacher's behavior, the child begins to acquire the skill. After a while, however, the mature musician does not need the teacher to place her fingers where they go. Instead, the skilled musician looks at the music and instantly responds because of the built-in habits she has acquired. In much the same way, Aristotle thinks that the moral virtues are habits that we acquire such that moral behavior becomes an ingrained, natural response.

- In the next passage, Aristotle says that a person is not temperate or just simply because he or she does temperate or just actions. What three conditions are necessary for an action to qualify as a genuinely moral action?
- Why does Aristotle think that having the correct philosophical theory is insufficient for being a moral person? (He may have been referring to Socrates here, who thought that knowing the good would cause a person to do the good.)

Acts in accordance with virtue are not justly or temperately performed simply because they are in themselves just or temperate. The doer at the time of performing them must satisfy certain conditions; in the first place, he must know what he is doing; secondly, he must deliberately choose to do it and do it for its own sake; and thirdly, he must do it as part of his own firm and immutable character. If it be a question of art, these conditions, except only the condition of knowledge, are not raised; but if it be a question of virtue, mere knowledge is of little or no avail; it is the other conditions, which are the results of frequently performing just and temperate acts, that are not slightly but all-important. Accordingly, deeds are called just and temperate when they are such as a just and temperate person would do; and a just and temperate person is not merely one who does these deeds but one who does them in the spirit of the just and the temperate.

It may fairly be said that a just man becomes just by doing what is just, and a temperate man becomes temperate by doing what is temperate, and if a man did not so act, he would not have much chance of becoming good. But most people, instead of acting, take refuge in theorizing; they imagine that they are philosophers and that philosophy will make them virtuous; in fact, they behave like people who listen attentively to their doctors but never do anything that their doctors tell them. But a healthy state of the soul will no more be produced by this kind of philosophizing than a healthy state of the body by this kind of medical treatment.

Aristotle's description of the morally good act is consistent with Kant's analysis. Both would agree that I am not acting justly unless I am acting deliberately and on the basis of knowledge (it cannot be an accident that I did the right thing). Furthermore, they would agree that I must perform the action for its own sake (and not for some reward, for example). Nevertheless, when Aristotle emphasizes that acting morally must be an ingrained habit and when he says in the next passage that morality is concerned with both "emotions and actions," Kant would worry that such actions would be based on my inclinations, involuntary passions, and temperament instead of on a rational calculation of my duty. It is on this point that virtue ethics differs most radically from Kantian ethics.

In the next passage, Aristotle discusses his famous *doctrine of the mean*. The "mean" referred to here is the intermediate position between two extremes or vices. The virtuous person is the one who has just the right amount of a certain quality or trait.

- In the first paragraph, Aristotle lists several qualities in which there can be an excess or a deficiency as well as the correct balance. For several of them, think of concrete situations in which we would say that a person had too much, too little, or just the right amount of the quality in question.

- Having said that virtue is a balance between the extremes, Aristotle offers in the last paragraph emotions or actions for which there is no correct balance. Why does he make these exceptions to his general rule?

Every art then does its work well, if it regards the mean and judges the works it produces by the mean. For this reason we often say of successful works of art that it is impossible to take anything from them or to add anything to them, which implies that excess or deficiency is fatal to excellence but that the mean state ensures it. Good artists too, as we say, have an eye to the mean in their works. Now virtue, like Nature herself, is more accurate and better than any art; virtue, therefore, will aim at the mean. I speak of moral virtue, since it is moral virtue which is concerned with emotions and actions, and it is in these we have excess and deficiency and the mean. Thus it is possible to go too far, or not far enough in fear, pride, desire, anger, pity, and pleasure and pain generally, and the excess and the deficiency are alike wrong; but to feel these emotions at the right times, for the right objects, towards the right persons, for the right motives, and in the right manner, is the mean or the best good, which signifies virtue. Similarly, there may be excess, deficiency, or the mean, in acts. Virtue is concerned with both emotions and actions, wherein excess is an error and deficiency a fault, while the mean is successful and praised, and success and praise are both characteristics of virtue.

It appears then that virtue is a kind of mean because it aims at the mean. . . .

Virtue then is a state of deliberate moral purpose, consisting in a mean relative to ourselves, the mean being determined by reason, or as a prudent man would determine it. It is a mean, firstly, as lying between two vices, the vice of excess on the one hand, the vice of deficiency on the other, and, secondly, because, whereas the vices either fall short of or go beyond what is right in emotion and action, virtue discovers and chooses the mean. Accordingly, virtue, if regarded in its essence or theoretical definition, is a mean, though, if regarded from the point of view of what is best and most excellent, it is an extreme.

But not every action or every emotion admits of a mean. There are some whose very name implies wickedness, as, for example, malice, shamelessness, and envy among the emotions, and adultery, theft, and murder among the actions. All these and others like them are marked as intrinsically wicked, not merely the excesses or deficiencies of them. It is never possible then to be right in them; they are always sinful. Right or wrong in such acts as adultery does not depend on our committing it with the right woman, at the right time, or in the right manner; on the contrary, it is wrong to do it at all.

Aristotle's view that the moral virtues constitute a balance between two extremes can be illustrated with the following chart made up of his own examples.

Activity	Vice (excess)	Virtue (mean)	Vice (deficit)
Confidence in Facing Danger	Rashness	Courage	Cowardice
Enjoying Pleasure	Self-indulgence	Temperance	Being puritanical
Giving of Money	Vulgarity	Generosity	Stinginess
Truth Telling about Oneself	Boastfulness	Self-honesty	Self-deprecation

In the previous passage Aristotle said that virtue entails finding the "mean relative to ourselves." Hence, the mean will not be the same for every individual under all circumstances. The genius of Aristotle's ethics is his recognition that universal and objective principles are always the same but prescribe different actions for different people and within different circumstances. For example, we may praise the courage of a young child who overcomes his terror of the water and sticks his face in the water. On the other hand, it would not be an act of courage for a professional lifeguard to do the same thing. Similarly, a widow who gives a dollar to charity when this amount is a substantial portion of her income is exhibiting the virtue of generosity. If she inherits a million dollars, however, then giving only a dollar would be exhibiting the vice of stinginess. When we are deciding what to do, how are we to know where to find the right balance point? Aristotle says that it is "determined by reason, or as a prudent man would determine it." Hence, finding the right balance for ourselves is a matter of experience and learning from the examples of those virtuous persons who have practical wisdom.

THE VIRTUES IN CONFUCIAN THOUGHT

CONFUCIUS
(551–479 B.C.)

Many ethical systems in non-Western traditions also focus more on the virtuous character than on rules of conduct. The sayings of Confucius are a good example of this focus. Although there are differences between the list of Aristotelian virtues and Confucian virtues, there are also significant overlaps. Interestingly, one of the works in Confucian literature is *The Doctrine of the Mean,* which parallels Aristotle's advice to seek a balance between the extremes. The following passage contains selected proverbs from the 20 sections of the sayings of Confucius. In this passage, Confucius describes the virtues of the superior person, a word that could also be translated as "noble person," "person of honor," or "wise person."

FROM CONFUCIUS

The Analects [68]

1.4 I daily examine myself on three points: In planning for others, have I failed to be conscientious? In my dealing with friends, have I failed to be sincere? In teaching, have I failed to practice what I have taught?

1.8 Give a prominent place to loyalty and sincerity.

1.16 Sorrow not because men do not know you; but sorrow that you know not men.

2.14 The superior man is not one-sided.

2.24 To see what is right and not to do it, that is cowardice.

4.16 The superior man seeks what is right; the inferior one, what is profitable.

4.24 The superior man is slow to promise, prompt to fulfill.

4.25 Virtue dwells not in solitude; she must have neighbors.

5.9 Rotten wood cannot be carved.

SPOTLIGHT

on

Confucius

An ancient version of virtue ethics is found in the thought of the great Chinese moral and spiritual leader Confucius. He was born in 551 B.C. during a time of social turmoil in China and died about 479 B.C. He was actually called K'ung Fu Tzu by his people, but he is known in the West by the Latin version of his name. During his life Confucius served his country as both a teacher and a government official, but he served people throughout the ages with the inspiration of his collected sayings. Having lived through unsettled times, he concluded that people would flourish only if there were excellent individuals who would create a harmonious society and a harmonious society that would create virtuous individuals. Although Confucianism is one of the world's great religions, Confucius did not consider himself anything more than a man, and he spoke very little about the gods but offered instead a moral system for guiding a person's life. Although Confucianism came under hard times after the Communist revolution, it has had considerable influence on Chinese culture and throughout East Asia.

5.15 There are the four essential qualities of the superior man; he is humble, he is deferential to superiors, he is generously kind, and he is always just.

6.18 Better than the one who knows what is right is he who loves what is right.

7.36 The superior man is always calm, the inferior (small-minded) man is constantly in a state of disturbance.

8.2 Without a sense of proportion, courtesy becomes oppressive; calmness becomes bashfulness; valor becomes disorderliness; and candor becomes rudeness.

7.36 The superior man makes the most of other people's good qualities, not the worst of their bad ones.

13.26 The superior man can be dignified without being proud; the inferior man can be proud without being dignified.

15.20 The superior man is exacting with himself; the inferior man is exacting with others.

16.10 The superior man must be mindful of nine things: to be clear in vision, quick to listen, genial in expression, respectful in manner, true in utterance, serious in duty, inquiring in doubt, self-controlled in anger, just and fair when the way to success is open before him.

A CONTEMPORARY APPLICATION OF VIRTUE ETHICS

Virtue ethics is often criticized for offering us a set of admirable ideals but failing to provide concrete guidance with respect to specific actions. What are needed, the critics say, are moral rules from which we can deduce the moral quality of an action. For many people, the moral wrongness of adultery, for example, follows from the fact that it violates a moral rule, whether that rule is from the Ten Commandments or Kant's categorical imperative or utilitarian rules about avoiding consequences that cause more harm than good. In the following passage, however, contemporary philosopher Janet Smith applies the perspective of virtue ethics to show how the moral quality of adultery can be assessed by considering whether this action is something a virtuous person would do. Her article actually deals with abortion, but in this passage she uses adultery to illustrate the perspective of virtue ethics.

Moral Character and Abortion [69]

The very importance of the attempt to live an ethical life lies in the fact that in acting the individual forms herself or himself either for the better or for the worse. . . . One of the foremost questions to be asked by the moral agent in the decision to do an action is: What kind of person will I become if I do this act?

Let us now consider how the choice to commit adultery might reveal and affect one's moral character. . . . If it is true . . . that adulterers can be said to have undesirable moral characteristics and/or that they are forming undesirable moral characters through their choice to commit adultery, this would be taken as an indication . . . that adultery is a morally bad action. . . .

For an analysis in accord with an ethics of virtue, answers to the following questions would be useful: What sort of people generally commit adultery? Are they, for instance, honest, temperate, kind, etc.? . . . Why do adulterers choose to have sex with people other than their spouses? Are their reasons selfish or unselfish ones? Do they seem to speak of their reasons for their choice honestly or do they seem to be rationalizing? What sort of lives have they been leading prior to the action that they choose; are they the sorts of lives that exhibit the characteristics we admire? . . .

Most may agree that some true generalizations could be made about adulterers that would lead us to think that in general adultery is not compatible with the moral virtues that we admire. The reaction of the American public to the extra-marital affairs of [clergyman] Jim Bakker and [politician] Gary Hart reveal well the widespread view that lying predictably accompanies the act of adultery and that adulterers are not to be trusted. Certainly, if someone told us that he or she wanted to be an honest, trustworthy, stable and kind individual with good family relationships, and wanted to know if an adulterous affair would conflict with this goal, we would have little hesitation in advising against adultery.

JANET SMITH
(1950–)

SUMMARY OF VIRTUE ETHICS

Although it is an ancient theory, the revival of virtue ethics in our day has opened new and interesting issues in contemporary philosophy. Rather than simply repeating the ideas of the Greeks, recent proponents of this position have taken advantage of contemporary insights drawn from the fields of psychology, anthropology, history, moral education, and literature. In turn, the theory of virtue ethics has also made contributions to these and other disciplines and has brought new perspectives to the fields of business ethics and medical ethics. Contemporary virtue ethics started out as a reaction against traditional moral philosophy, but its criticisms of utilitarianism and Kantianism have forced the philosophers in these traditions to take account of virtue and character more fully than Mill and Kant did. Thus, attempts have been made in recent decades to modify these traditional positions and to develop utilitarian and Kantian versions of an ethics of virtue. On the other hand, some philosophers accuse the virtue ethicists of attacking a strawman and claim that sufficient resources exist in traditional utilitarianism or Kantianism to accommodate all the legitimate concerns of virtue ethics.[70] (See the discussion of the strawman fallacy in the appendix at the end of the text.) Although virtue ethics started out as a radical alternative to the traditional systems, the discussions it has produced have resulted in a movement to synthesize the ethics of duty with the ethics of virtue. As Robert Louden, a sympathetic critic of virtue ethics, concludes, "It is important now to see the ethics of virtue and the ethics of rules as adding up, rather than as cancelling each other out."[71]

Read the following paragraph to 5 to 10 people from different backgrounds and ask them the questions that follow it:

A wide range of people were asked, "What persons are good examples of moral role models—persons whose lives and personalities have guided you in your attempts to be a better person?" Some of the answers given were parents, relatives, teachers, Moses, Buddha, Confucius, Socrates, Jesus, Muhammad, St. Francis, Abraham Lincoln, Gandhi, Martin Luther King Jr., and Mother Teresa.

- Besides these common answers, what other people would you add to the list?
- What was it about these persons that made them admirable?
- Why did they have a moral influence on you or others?

After gathering the responses, study the similarities and differences between the persons listed. How many males and how many females were on the list? What were their occupations? What historical period and culture did they live in? What challenges did they face? What can your friends' responses teach you about which sorts of moral role models have the most influence?

PHILOSOPHY
in the
MARKETPLACE

LOOKING THROUGH THE LENS OF VIRTUE ETHICS

1. Suppose you are a parent of a small child. It is easy to teach a list of dos and don'ts with the appropriate rewards and sanctions. But how do you instill character in your child? Can virtue be taught? How so? Besides direct teaching, what are other ways of facilitating the development of virtue in your child? What virtues would you want him or her to develop?

2. If you were a utilitarian, how would you explain to a friend that cheating on a test is wrong? How would you explain this action if you were Kant? How would you explain what is wrong with cheating if you were a virtue ethicist?

3. Have you ever made an ethical decision by imagining that you were in the shoes of a wise, virtuous person whom you admire and trying to discern how he or she would act? Whether you have or not, to what degree do you think this exercise would be a helpful way to make a decision?

4. In an influential article, philosopher Susan Wolf questions whether it is desirable to be a moral saint (a person who is as morally worthy as a human can be). She says she is glad that neither she nor any of her friends "is such a person."

> For the moral virtues . . . are apt to crowd out the non-moral virtues, as well as many of the interests and personal characteristics that we generally think contribute to a healthy, well-rounded, richly developed character.
>
> In other words, if the moral saint is devoting all his time to feeding the hungry or healing the sick or raising money for Oxfam [a charity], then necessarily he is not reading Victorian novels, playing the oboe, or improving his backhand. Although no one of the interests or tastes in the category containing these latter activities could be claimed to be a necessary element in a life well lived, a life in which *none* of these possible aspects of character is developed may seem to be a life strangely barren. . . .

A moral saint will have to be very, very nice. It is important that he not be offensive. The worry is that, as a result, he will have to be dull-witted or humourless or bland.[72]

Do you agree with Wolf's analysis? Is she correct in saying that the perfectly virtuous person lacks the "ability to enjoy the enjoyable in life"? What would an advocate of virtue ethics say about this analysis?

 ## EXAMINING THE STRENGTHS AND WEAKNESSES OF VIRTUE ETHICS

Positive Evaluation

1. Virtue ethics seems to capture some important concerns in our ordinary way of thinking about ethics. As philosopher Robert Solomon says, "The very idea that the good person is one who acts according to the right principles—be they categorical imperatives or the principle of utility—has always struck me as colossally out of tune with the manner in which ordinary people (and most philosophers) think about and judge themselves and their actions. As a matter of fact it makes my blood run cold."[73] Do you agree with Solomon's account of our ordinary ethical thinking? How strongly does this approach support virtue ethics?

2. One of the standard ways of criticizing an ethical theory such as egoism, utilitarianism, or Kantianism is to show that it would allow us to justify an action that is clearly morally wrong. Doesn't this argument show that moral theories are subject to our commonsense moral intuitions and not the other way around? Furthermore, it could be argued that our commonsense moral intuitions are typically tied to our conception of the sorts of actions that would be performed by the morally ideal person. Does this argument support the virtue ethicist's case that ethics starts with the notion of moral virtue and moral principles and theories follow from that?

3. The charge is sometimes made that virtue ethics is impractical because it does not provide us with rules for making moral decisions in complex situations. But in this respect is the theory any worse off than competing ethical theories? Even if we follow the rules of the utilitarian or the Kantian, are rules alone enough to guide us? Is acting in complex moral situations simply an exercise in logic in which the rules tell us what to do? Or does the application of moral rules require the sensitive judgment of a virtuous person? Daniel Statman points out that even for rule-based ethics, "the virtuous person is not the person who has excellent knowledge of some set of principles, meta-principles and meta-meta-principles, but the person who has right perception as to which rules should apply here and now. And this person must be, among other things, sensitive, compassionate and perceptive—the same features so praised in VE [virtue ethics]."[74] Does Statman's comment suggest that a virtuous character is more fundamental to ethics than rules are?

4. Defenders of virtue ethics say that it goes beyond the minimal morality of right and wrong conduct. Instead, its concern with conduct includes in its scope those traits that lead us beyond the demands of duty. Apart from actions it also emphasizes the good, the admirable, and the noble within us as well as those personal characteristics and emotional and mental responses that make us good persons. Do these considerations tip the balance in favor of virtue ethics?

Negative Evaluation

1. Virtue ethics has been criticized for assuming a classical and antiquated view of human nature. Many versions assume with Aristotle that there is an innate purpose to human life and that there is a single model of human excellence and flourishing. However, doesn't our pluralistic society exhibit a lack of agreement about the purpose of human life, the standards of excellence, and the definition of flourishing? In fact, don't many of us question whether there is one *ideal* that is applicable to all? Furthermore, isn't there a great deal of disagreement about the correct list of moral virtues? For example, Aristotle thought pride was a virtue, but for early Christianity and for Confucius, the good person is one who shuns pride and strives for humility. To what degree do these considerations undermine virtue ethics?

2. Can it be argued that the ethics of character depends on the ethics of conduct, the reverse of what the virtue ethicist claims? Could someone have the virtue of compassion if he never performed compassionate acts when appropriate? Virtue ethics defines right actions as those that a virtuous person would perform. But how can we define a virtuous person apart from saying she is a person who has a disposition to perform right actions? Hasn't this reasoning led us into a circle? For example, how can we judge that a person has the virtue of justice apart from the fact that she acts in accord with the duty of justice? Don't these considerations imply that the notions of right conduct and moral duties are more fundamental than the notion of virtuous character?

3. Virtue ethics has been accused of making moral goodness a matter of luck. For example, according to virtue ethics, it is not enough to *act* benevolently out of a sense of duty; to be a morally good person I must have benevolent *feelings* toward people. However, can I will myself to have certain feelings? If I have the virtue of benevolence it must have come in one of two ways. First, it can be a natural disposition that was given to me as a gift of nature, possibly as a result of my genetic inheritance. Or it can be inculcated within me by my social training. But these options leave out the person who lacks a benevolent nature because neither nature nor her poor home environment produced it in her. Either way, she is not at fault. Yet even if bad moral luck has cursed her with a cold and ungenerous personality, can't she (in good Kantian fashion) still dutifully act in morally good ways through an extraordinary act of will? Given these considerations, how important are moral character traits as opposed to dutiful, right actions?

4. Can virtue ethics be criticized for failing to provide us with specific action-guiding principles? Let's take as an example an ethical question that is in the news these days: Is it morally permissible to clone humans? In other words, should someone be allowed to create a cloned child who is the genetic replica of the DNA donor? Although this question has no clear-cut answer, at least utilitarians and Kantians have some definite principles in terms of which the issue can be debated. The utilitarian would assess the pluses and minuses of the likely social, psychological, and biological consequences for all who would be affected by the procedure. The Kantian would ask if the cloned child was being created merely as a means to the parent's egotistical ends, and so on. But if we ask, "What would a virtuous person say about cloning?" either no answer is forthcoming or the answer would be based on utilitarian or Kantian considerations. Similarly, isn't it hard to imagine what moral exemplars such as Buddha, Jesus, or Gandhi would do with cases in medical ethics that they never encountered? Does this problem imply that virtue ethics is not as helpful as the other theories are?

LEADING QUESTIONS: *Feminist Ethics*

1. The classic collection of children's stories known as Aesop's fables contains the following story of the porcupine and the moles:

> It was growing cold, and porcupine was looking for a home. He found a most desirable cave but saw it was occupied by a family of moles.
>
> "Would you mind if I shared your home for the winter?" the porcupine asked the moles.
>
> The generous moles consented and the porcupine moved in. But the cave was small and every time the moles moved around they were scratched by the porcupine's sharp quills. The moles endured this discomfort as long as they could. Then at last they gathered courage to approach their visitor. "Pray leave," they said, "and let us have our cave to ourselves once again."
>
> "Oh no!" said the porcupine. "This place suits me very well."

What is the problem here and what is the best way to solve it?

2. Think about a moral dilemma you have encountered in which you had to decide the right thing to do. Which of the following two sets of considerations (A or B) were the most important to you in solving the problem?

A. (1) using logic and reason to find a solution, (2) being aware of and concerned about the rights of those affected by my actions, (3) making sure I don't interfere with anyone's rights, (4) treating everyone equally, (5) following the principles of justice, impartiality, fairness, (6) making sure my actions can be defended in terms of rules that are universal and apply to all.

B. (1) bringing love, care, and compassion to the situation, (2) being aware of and concerned about people's needs, (3) looking for ways that I can help people, (4) trying to arrive at a solution that everyone could accept, (5) trying to connect with the people involved and working to create communication and cooperation, (6) being attentive to relationships and my responsibilities to other people.

SURVEYING THE CASE FOR FEMINIST ETHICS

In a study published in 1988, a number of adolescents were presented with the porcupine and moles dilemma you just read.[75] The majority of the males solved the problem in terms of the principles of rights and justice, saying, for example, "It is the moles' house, so the porcupine has to go." However, the majority of the females responded in terms of the principles of cooperation and care. For example, some of their solutions were "The moles and the porcupine must talk and share the house," "Wrap the porcupine in a towel," or "Both of them should try to get together and make the hole bigger." The researchers believe that their data support the recent and much-discussed theory that there are differences in the ways that males and females typically solve moral problems.

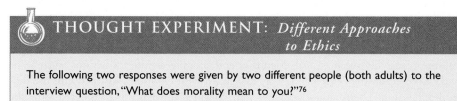

STOP AND THINK

Based on your experience, do you think there are differences in the ways in which males and females approach issues in morality? If so, what are some of these differences? If you do see differences in how men and women view ethics, what implications (if any) are there for ethical theory in the fact that differences exist?

In my discussion of feminist epistemology in section 2.7, I laid out the main themes of feminist thought and their disagreements with traditional theories of knowledge. Feminists are equally dissatisfied with traditional ethical theories. According to recent feminist philosophers, traditional moral theories tend to focus on the considerations listed under A in the second leading question while neglecting the moral orientation represented by B. Furthermore, the feminist philosophers point out that, for historical reasons, the traditional moral theories have been developed by males. These facts raise a number of questions such as, Are traditional moral theories such as Kantianism and utilitarianism one-sided? Do they reflect a male bias? Theorists in the recently developed movement of feminist ethics tend to answer these questions affirmatively. In this section we address the following questions: What is feminist ethics? What is the feminist critique of traditional ethical theories? How do feminists propose to reshape the foundations of morality?

Before the 1980s, there was no field called feminist ethics. Today, however, feminist perspectives in ethics are the source of fertile discussions not only in philosophy but also in the fields of psychology, education, medicine, theology, business, and law. It is much more difficult to summarize the feminist approach to ethics than it is to give a capsule summary of the Kantian or utilitarian theories, because feminist theory is a continually developing body of thought that is the work of many different thinkers representing a multiplicity of perspectives. Although feminists see themselves as engaged in a shared project, they have many different opinions as to how that project should be realized. For example, in her book *Feminist Thought: A More Comprehensive Introduction,* philosopher Rosemarie Tong lists nine varieties of feminist theory: liberal, radical, Marxist-socialist, psychoanalytic, gender feminism, existentialist, postmodern, multicultural-global, and ecofeminism. Under each of these categories, Tong also lists a number of subdivisions. Not only does each version of feminism have different emphases, but they often come to radically different conclusions on substantive issues. Nevertheless, for all their differences, most feminists are agreed that traditional ethical theories are inadequate and one-sided and need to be replaced or modified because they have ignored the insights of women's moral experiences.

THOUGHT EXPERIMENT: *Different Approaches to Ethics*

The following two responses were given by two different people (both adults) to the interview question, "What does morality mean to you?"[76]

(continued . . .)

(. . . continued)

Response A

I think it is recognizing the right of the individual, the rights of other individuals, not interfering with those rights. Act as fairly as you would have them treat you. I think it is basically to preserve the human being's right to existence. I think that is the most important. Secondly, the human being's right to do as he pleases, again without interfering with somebody else's rights.

Response B

We need to depend on each other, and hopefully it is not only a physical need but a need of fulfillment in ourselves, that a person's life is enriched by cooperating with other people and striving to live in harmony with everybody else, and to that end, there are right and wrong, there are things which promote that end and that move away from it, and in that way it is possible to choose in certain cases among different courses of action that obviously promote or harm that goal.

- Which response best characterizes your view of morality?
- Which response would you guess was made by a man?
- Which response would you guess was made by a woman?
- What clues in each response led you to answer the way you did?

The answers will be given later in this section when we examine Carol Gilligan's theory of moral development.

Gender Bias in Ethical Theory

Although there have been women philosophers going all the way back to ancient Greece, they were largely neglected throughout the history of philosophy. Consequently, feminists contend, the ethical theories that have shaped our understanding of morality were written by men and reflect a male point of view. For example, at the beginning of his work on ethics, Aristotle said that "the function of *man* is an activity of the soul in accordance with reason." The most charitable explanation of this wording would be that Aristotle was using *man* generically to include both males and females. If so, then any male bias in his work is limited to a rather insensitive choice of words rather than a deep-seated omission in the content of his theory. Unfortunately, when Aristotle referred to "man" in his works he really did mean *males*. According to him, males are the only creatures to have a true capacity for reasoning. Women, on the other hand, have other purposes (such as childbearing) and a different set of virtues. (See the earlier discussion of Aristotle's view of women in section 2.7.)

Other philosophers throughout history have followed Aristotle in making reason a uniquely male virtue and in focusing on the traditional male domains such as the state, law, war, and the marketplace in their ethical theories. Not only did the activities within these public spheres serve as metaphors of ethical transactions, but these arenas also were thought to be the places in which ethical dilemmas and morally significant actions were to be found. Women, on the other hand, were associated with emotions, instinct, and the biological dimension. Their natural activities were confined to what was considered to be the morally neutral private sphere in which the biological needs of food, shelter, and reproduction were met, while all that was distinctively human and of moral significance was carried out by men in the public sphere.

In the 20th century, for example, philosopher J. O. Urmson discussed moral "saints" who make sacrifices beyond the call of duty, but he added, "Let us be clear that we are not now considering cases of natural affection, such as the sacrifice made by a mother for her child; such cases may be said with some justice not to fall under the concept of morality."[77] However, in response to this distinction, feminist philosopher Virginia Held notes that "without feminist insistence on the relevance for morality of the experience in mothering, this context is largely ignored by moral theorists. And yet from a gender-neutral point of view, how can this vast and fundamental domain of human experience possibly be imagined to lie 'outside morality'?"[78]

If women bring unique perspectives and experiences to the activity of moral inquiry, what differences do these contributions make to their ethical theories? We might suppose at first that feminist ethics will be distinguished by simply a focus on ethical issues that are of particular concern to women, issues that may not have received adequate attention from ethical theories developed by men. Indeed, many of the writings of female philosophers in ethics emphasize issues such as discrimination against women, sexual harassment, sexual assault, pornography, abortion, reproductive technologies, changing conceptions of sexuality-marriage-family, and the implications of gender differences and stereotypes. But we would be wrong to suppose that feminist ethics simply supplements traditional ethics with discussions of "women's issues." Feminist ethicists think it would be counterproductive, among other reasons, to approach issues that concern women with ethical theories that grew out of male-biased social and philosophical soil. Instead, feminists see themselves as giving ethical theory a complete overhaul by recentering it and by bringing into prominence themes, concepts, and approaches that typically have been ignored. As ethical theorists Eve Browning Cole and Susan Coultrap-McQuin say:

> [Feminists] argue that traditional moral philosophy has been a largely male-directed enterprise and has reflected interests derived predominantly from men's experience. In other words, because men's experience has often involved market transactions, their moral theories concentrate on promise-keeping, property rights, contracts, and fairness.[79]

In contrast to the paradigm of the impersonal and often anonymous contractual relationships of the public sphere, feminist writers tend to model their ethics on the person-to-person relationships and concrete contexts entailed in friendships and families. Philosophers Eva Kittay and Diana Meyers have said that

> a morality of rights and abstract reason begins with a moral agent who is separate from others, and who independently elects moral principles to obey. In contrast, a morality of responsibility and care begins with a self who is enmeshed in a network of relations to others, and whose moral deliberation aims to maintain these relations.[80]

Hence, as opposed to the abstract principles of Kantian universalizability or utilitarian maximization of the general good, feminist ethics concentrates on such concepts as care, empathy, and personal understanding. According to feminist philosopher Alison Jaggar, feminists allege that Western ethics has preferred the

> supposedly masculine or male-associated values of independence, autonomy, intellect, will, wariness, hierarchy, domination, culture, transcendence, product, asceticism, war and death over the supposedly feminine or female-associated values of interdependence, community, connection, sharing, emotion, body, trust, absence of hierarchy, nature, immanence, process, joy, peace and life.[81]

Jaggar goes on to say that feminist ethics has sometimes been construed (by both some of its proponents as well as some of its critics) as a proposal to replace a male-biased approach with a female-biased approach. In other words, it has been associated with one or more of the following goals:

> putting women's interests first; focusing exclusively on so-called women's issues; accepting women (or feminists) as moral experts or authorities; substituting "female" (or feminine) for "male" (or masculine) values; or extrapolating directly from women's moral experience.[82]

Although not claiming that it would be impossible to find examples of this sort of feminist inversion of the male biases they critique, Jaggar says that most feminists would be "morally outraged" by the blatant partiality and immorality of such proposals. Similarly, while acknowledging that feminists seek to bring gender issues to the foreground in ethics, Rosemarie Tong denies that feminists are doing so in a way that replaces one wrong with another:

> *The fact that an approach to ethics is gendered does not necessarily mean it is sexist.* An approach to ethics becomes sexist only when it systematically excludes the interests, identities, issues, and values of one or the other of the two sexes, and feminist ethicists have no plans to do unto men what nonfeminist ethicists did unto women.[83]

TWO APPROACHES TO FEMINIST ETHICS

A distinction is frequently made between what is sometimes labeled *feminine* ethics and *feminist* ethics. Philosopher Betty A. Sichel distinguishes them in the following manner:

> "Feminine" at present refers to the search for women's unique voice and, most often, the advocacy of an ethics of care that includes nurturance, care, compassion, and networks of communication. "Feminist" refers to those theorists, whether liberal or radical or other orientation, who argue against patriarchal domination, for equal rights, a just and fair distribution of scarce resources, etc.[84]

Stating the distinction in slightly different terms, philosopher Susan Sherwin asserts that a feminine approach to ethics "consists of observations of how the traditional approaches to ethics fail to fit the moral expressions and intuitions of women," whereas a feminist approach to ethics "applies a specifically political perspective and offers suggestions for how ethics must be revised if it is to get at the patterns of dominance and oppression as they affect women."[85] However, while acknowledging the accuracy of this distinction, Tong finds these labels to be misleading because they imply that only the latter group of philosophers are genuinely feminist. Instead, she refers to the two approaches to ethics as "care-focused feminist ethics" and "power-focused feminist ethics."[86] Using Tong's labels, let's examine each approach in turn.

Care-Focused Feminist Ethics

One of the foundational works in feminist ethics, particularly of the care-based variety, was *In a Different Voice,* published in 1982 by Harvard psychologist Carol Gilligan. (Her theories were briefly discussed in section 2.7, "Rethinking the Western Tradition: Feminist Epistemology.") Gilligan responded to the work of Lawrence Kohlberg, one of the leading researchers in the area of moral development. Kohlberg traced six stages that people go

CAROL GILLIGAN
(1936–)

through in their moral development, starting as little children. These six stages are (1) the "carrot and stick" orientation, in which children are motivated by reward and punishment; (2) the "you scratch my back and I'll scratch yours" orientation, in which children do what satisfies their own needs and occasionally the needs of others; (3) the "good-boy/nice-girl" orientation, in which immature adolescents conform to society's standards to receive others' approval; (4) the "law and order" orientation, in which mature adolescents do their duty to show respect for authority and to maintain the given social order; (5) the "social contract/legalistic" orientation, in which people follow institutionalized rules that are perceived as rational, and they are concerned with the general good; and (6) the "universal ethical principles" orientation, a Kantian perspective in which self-imposed, internalized, universal principles such as justice, reciprocity, and respect for persons inform people's personal conscience.

Gilligan was puzzled by the fact that in Kohlberg's studies, women and girls rarely progressed past the "good-boy/nice-girl" status of stage (3), whereas men and boys routinely were measured at stages (5) and (6). Kohlberg presumed that his six stages represented progressively higher stages of moral development, which suggested that females were generally more deficient in their moral development than were males. However, Gilligan concluded that the problem was not with women's moral development but with the male bias built into Kohlberg's theory. As an alternative to this single hierarchy, Gilligan argued that there were two models in ethical reasoning. One model is an "ethics of justice" model in which rules, rights, and logic predominate, and the other is an "ethics of care" in which relationships, responsibilities, and emotions predominate. Gilligan does not think that either approach is superior; she sees them as complementary and equally important in our moral lives. In her original work and in later writings Gilligan emphasized that these two different "voices" are differentiated not by gender but by their themes. Nevertheless, most of her studies focus on the fact that males and females are socialized differently, with the result that males tend to gravitate toward the ethics of justice and females toward the ethics of care.

STOP AND THINK

How did you label the responses in the thought experiment titled "Different Approaches to Ethics"? Response A was made by a 25-year-old male. He identified morality with justice (fairness, rights, the Golden Rule) and stressed the individual's right to do as he pleases as long as it doesn't intrude on another person's rights. Response B was made by a 25-year-old female who emphasized that morality is concerned with cooperation and promoting harmonious relationships.

- How do these responses illustrate Gilligan's theory?
- How accurately do these responses represent men's and women's styles of approaching morality?
- Do you tend toward the "ethics of justice" approach or the "ethics of care" approach?

Do not be concerned with whether your approach to morality fits Gilligan's categories of "male" or "female" ethics. A number of researchers (some feminists included) question whether the evidence demonstrates that there are gender-specific modes of moral reasoning. Psychologist John Broughton, for example, cites dozens of studies that contradict Gilligan's results. Furthermore, he argues that Gilligan misinterpreted some of her own

Ask an equal number of females and males the following questions:

- Based on your experience, do you think there are differences between the ways females and males typically approach ethical issues and solve moral problems?
- If so, what are some of these differences?
- If there are differences, is one way better than the other, or are they equally satisfactory and complementary to one another?

What did you learn from your friends' responses? How many thought there were significant differences between males and females in ethics? Were those who found differences predominantly one gender or the other? As you read the rest of this section, see how your friends' answers compare with the various answers given by feminist writers.

interviews, because a number of male subjects exhibited a caring, relationship-based ethics whereas some of the female subjects had concerns about justice and rights.[87] Some philosophers argue that the differences between males and females in ethical styles are negligible when compared to the differences between subjects ranked in terms of cognitive skills, educational level, and social class.[88] Regardless of whether either of the two moral orientations can be associated with a certain gender, care-focused feminists typically argue that the two orientations do represent two distinctly different approaches and that the care-relationships approach has been neglected in ethical theory.

Maternal, Care-Focused Ethics

Gilligan thinks that although the ethics of justice and the ethics of care are different, they are complementary and both are needed in ethics. Contrary to Gilligan, however, some feminists argue that a care-based ethics is superior. Many of them go even further and take women's experiences of mothering to be the paradigm for understanding ethics, developing what has been called maternal ethics. However, Virginia Held does not limit the experience of mothering to women, because instead of speaking of "mother" she speaks of a "mothering person" (someone who can be either female or male) and suggests that the wording "the nurturing of children" may be preferable to "mothering."[89] Similarly, in her book *Maternal Thinking,* moral philosopher Sara Ruddick says that the maternal traits of caring, intimacy, responsibility, and trust can characterize your stance toward life and others, even if you are a childless woman or a man.[90] (Ruddick's model of maternal thinking was briefly discussed in section 2.7.)

In her often-quoted book *Caring: A Feminine Approach to Ethics and Moral Education,* ethical theorist Nel Noddings carries out the project of "reclaiming the feminine" by arguing that those qualities such as compassion, caring, and empathetic feelings that were often ignored or given marginal status in traditional ethical theory are actually the foundation stones of moral maturity. She says that we approach human relationships not on the basis of abstract rights, but in terms of concern for a particular individual's concrete needs. As opposed to an ethical orientation based on abstract principles, a parent who is caring for a child, for example, will consult her own "feelings, needs, impressions, and . . . sense of personal ideal" and will try to identify herself with the child as closely as possible to know what is in the child's best interest.[91]

From the experience of being cared for, we learn the goodness of the caring relationship, and, in turn, we learn how to care for others ourselves. Once we have developed the

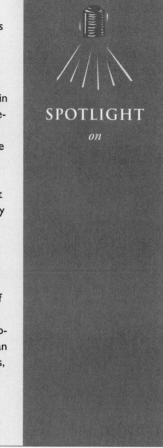

SPOTLIGHT

on

Male and Female Psychology

A study was done in which college students were asked to write stories about pictures they were shown. The pictures alternately depicted situations involving personal affiliation and impersonal achievement. According to Carol Gilligan, the research suggested that

> men and women perceive danger in different social situations and construe danger in different ways—men seeing danger more often in personal affiliation than in achievement and construing danger to arise from intimacy, women perceiving danger in impersonal achievement situations and construing danger to result from competitive success. The danger men describe in their stories of intimacy is a danger of entrapment or betrayal, being caught in a smothering relationship or humiliated by rejection and deceit. In contrast, the danger women portray in their tales of achievement is a danger of isolation, a fear that in standing out or being set apart by success, they will be left alone.[92]

For example, one of the pictures showed two trapeze artists performing high in the air—a man, hanging by his knees from the trapeze, was grasping the wrists of a woman in mid-air. Although the picture did not depict a safety net, researchers found that 22 percent of the women added nets in the stories they wrote, whereas only 6 percent of the men imagined the presence of a net. On the other hand, 40 percent of the men either mentioned the absence of a net in their stories or implied its absence by describing one or both of the acrobats as falling to their deaths. In analyzing the results, Gilligan says, "Thus, the women saw the scene on the trapeze as safe because, by providing nets, they had made it safe, protecting the lives of the acrobats in the event of a fall.... As women imagine the activities through which relationships are woven and connection sustained, the world of intimacy—which appears so mysterious and dangerous to men—comes instead to appear increasingly coherent and safe."[93]

spontaneous sentiment of *natural* caring, a more deliberative *ethical* caring becomes a moral possibility for us. However, contrary to Kant, who thought that the call of duty must give a deaf ear to our natural inclinations, Noddings believes that the "I must" of moral obligation is always related to the best of our natural inclinations. As Noddings writes, "An ethic built on caring strives to maintain the caring attitude and is thus dependent upon, and not superior to, natural caring."[94]

At this point, we might be inclined to ask, "Can the values, traits, and practices that are found in the intimate relationships of a family offer any ethical guidance as we go out into the larger world beyond the home?" Maternalistic, care-focused feminists think they can. For example, political theorist Kathy Ferguson urges women to use the "values that are structured into women's experience—caretaking, nurturance, empathy, connectedness" to create new models of society and institutions that are not based on the principle of domination.[95] In other words, although the experiences of caretaking and nurturing are more typically associated with women and especially mothers, these experiences can provide important ethical insights and serve as a paradigm for nonmothers as well. Furthermore, maternal, care-focused feminists claim that we can generalize from these concrete experiences to construct a comprehensive ethical theory that can be disseminated throughout the

Mother and Child (1893) by Mary Cassatt. This painting of a mother lovingly attending to the needs of her child illustrates the main themes of care-focused feminist ethics. The mother is not acting on the basis of abstract principles or a stern sense of moral duty (principles that feminists think characterize traditional ethics). Instead, she is expressing her spontaneous feelings of caring, compassion, intimacy, and empathy. Care-focused feminists claim that these values, which are so natural to women's experiences, can be used to construct more adequate ethical and political models. As Joan Tronto says, "care is not solely private or parochial; it can concern institutions, societies, even global levels of thinking."

public sphere as a politics of compassion. Hence, to the title of her book *Maternal Thinking*, Ruddick adds the subtitle *Toward a Politics of Peace*. These feminists have no doubts that the ethics of care will be better suited than alternative theories to address the problems associated with world hunger, poverty, war, the environment, exploitation in the workplace, health care, and education. In discussing the approach taken by maternal ethics, philosopher Jean Grimshaw asks whether, "given, for instance, the experience of women in pregnancy, childbirth, and the rearing of children, might there be, for example, some difference in the way they will view the 'waste' of those lives in war."[96] In summarizing this more expanded application of care-focused ethics, political theorist Joan Tronto says, "care is not solely private or parochial; it can concern institutions, societies, even global levels of thinking."[97]

PHILOSOPHY
in the
MARKETPLACE

Read the following ethical dilemma to an equal number of males and females, and ask them the questions that follow. If their answers are too brief or vague, you might want to ask follow-up questions to make sure you understand their reasoning. After collecting their answers, analyze them by referring to the two sets of moral considerations (A and B) in leading question 2 at the beginning of this section. Do the males and females tend to give different sorts of answers? Did the males tend to use the factors in list A? Did the females tend to use the factors in list B? What conclusions can you draw from your survey?

In Europe a woman was near death from a special kind of cancer. There was one drug that doctors thought might save her. It was a form of radium that a druggist in the same town had recently discovered. The drug was expensive to make, but the druggist was charging 10 times what the drug cost to make. He paid $200 for the radium and charged $2,000 for a small dose of the drug. The sick woman's husband, Heinz, went to everyone he knew to borrow the money, but he could only get together about $1,000, which is half of what it cost. He told the druggist that his wife was dying, and asked him to sell it cheaper or let him pay later. But the druggist said, "No, I discovered the drug and I'm going to make money from it." So Heinz got desperate and began to think about breaking into the man's store to steal the drug for his wife.[98]

- Should Heinz steal the drug?
- Why?

Power-Focused Feminist Ethics

The care-focused version of feminist ethics has had an enormous influence, both in terms of its critique of the limitations of traditional ethical theory as well as its positive program for recentering ethics. However, not all feminists believe that care-focused ethics is the way to go. Those who adhere to what Tong has called power-focused feminist ethics believe that ethical questions cannot be addressed in isolation from questions about the power structures in society and the patterns of dominance and oppression that exist. Tong notes that this approach emphasizes that nonfeminist philosophers subordinate women to men by "neglecting, downplaying, trivializing, or totally ignoring women's moral interests, issues, insights, and identities."[99] Jaggar says that although power-focused feminist ethicists share some of the aims of feminists in general, the former place a higher priority on the following goals: "First, to articulate moral critiques of actions and practices that perpetuate women's subordination; second, to prescribe morally justifiable ways of resisting such actions and practices; and, third, to envision morally desirable alternatives that will promote women's emancipation."[100]

Critics of Care-Focused Ethics

Ethicist Susan Mendus sums up the power-focused feminist critique of the ethics of care by citing three related problems:

The first is that its emphasis on difference implies a view of women which, historically, has been associated with policies of political exclusion. The second is that it implies an over-simple, and static, view of female identity, which misdescribes women's role in modern life, and the third is that it appeals to an inappropriate analogy between familial and political relationships.[101]

Concerning Mendus's first point on the political exclusion of women, some feminists see our current conceptions of mothering, the family, and the home as miniature versions of the more general oppression in society. Critics charge that when the care-focused feminists make these domains the paradigm for ethics, they are further solidifying women's secondary status. For example, some feminists have agreed with John Broughton, a male critic of Carol Gilligan, who states that Gilligan's theory tends to "perpetuate the status quo, to affirm the established division of labor, and to foreclose the possibility of radical transformation."[102] In other words, Broughton says, Gilligan "leaves women in almost the same position that Aristotle left them."[103] Similarly, in response to maternal ethics, political scientist Mary Dietz argues that love, intimacy, and caring cannot be the basis for political action or discourse. As she puts it, "Not the language of love and compassion, but only the language of freedom and equality, citizenship and justice, will challenge nondemocratic and oppressive political institutions."[104]

The second complaint is that care ethics provides an inappropriate description of female identity. Psychologist Zella Luria asks, "Do we truly gain by returning to a modern cult of true womanhood? Do we gain by the assertion that women think or reason in one voice and men in another?"[105] Similarly, in the title of her insightful article, philosopher Patricia Scaltsas asks the question, "Do Feminist Ethics Counter Feminist Aims?" In response to claims that empathy and care are distinctively female virtues, she says:

> Although the traditional role of women in society might have led to the development of certain virtues, the *confinement* of women to that role has had destructive results in their development as individuals in society. . . .
>
> . . . The danger is that these female values, ways of thinking, and experiences will degenerate into the traditional dichotomies between male and female capacities and characteristics which have been used to try to justify excluding women from educational, professional, and political opportunities and locking them into roles of irrational love-givers or love-giving simpletons.[106]

The problem, some feminists complain, is that women have been socialized to believe that their moral responsibilities require them to be sacrificially altruistic, and they think that if they fail to suppress their own identities, interests, and needs, they are being selfish. In response to this socialization, some feminists even recommend a healthy dose of egoistic self-interest as an antidote. Feminist philosopher Sara Hoagland suggests, for example, that feminists replace the questions, "Am I good?" or "Is this good?" with the question, "Does this contribute to my self-creation, freedom and liberation?"[107] Hoagland is concerned with the possibility that in following Noddings's ethics of care, "I get my ethical identity from always being other-directed," the result will be that "being moral" becomes another term for "being exploited."[108]

In response to such criticisms, feminist theorist Sheila Mullett distinguishes between "distortions of caring" and "undistorted caring."[109] She says that caring cannot be authentic if a person is economically, socially, or psychologically compelled to care. She acknowledges, therefore, that an ethics of caring can be fully realized only when women achieve sexual equality and freedom from conditions that support male domination and female

Two Feminist Interpretations of Relationships

Earlier we discussed Gilligan's analysis of an experiment in which men and women were told to write stories about a picture of two trapeze artists, a man holding the wrists of a woman. Gilligan found that significantly more women added safety nets in the story, which she assumed illustrated the fact that the women were more comfortable with relationships. The women saw the relationship between the man and the woman as safe, Gilligan said, because the women subjects had made it safe. Marilyn Friedman, however, says that in a male-dominated society, many women have found the current patterns of heterosexual relationships to be problematic and even oppressive. Hence, she sees a different theme in the results of the study: "Perhaps, on the contrary, women added nets as external safety devices precisely because they perceived the relationships as being, in themselves, *unsafe*."[110]

SPOTLIGHT
on

subordination. Until then, women must be cautious in caring and ask if it is serving their own self-realization and if it is taking place within the "framework of consciousness-raising practice and conversation."[111]

Finally, many feminists agree with Mendus that the ethics of care, based as it is on the model of family relationships, is inadequate for the realm of public and political morality. For example, Dietz argues that

> maternal virtues cannot be political in the required sense because . . . they are connected to and emerge out of an activity that is special, distinctive, unlike any other. We must conclude, then, that this activity is unlike the activity of citizenship; the two cannot be viewed as somehow encompassing the same attributes, abilities, and ways of knowing.[112]

The problem is that the mother-child relationship contains an inequality of power and control, whereas the ideal political sphere allows the citizens to interact as equals. Furthermore, at the personal level it is natural for me to be partial and give priority to the needs of those with whom I am intimately involved, but such partiality is inappropriate at the political level. As John Broughton says about Gilligan's care ethics,

> Gilligan does not seem to acknowledge the importance of respect or responsibility in the relationship of a government to its nation's citizens, of nation-states to each other, or of states, governments, and citizens to past or future generations. "Caring" is limited as the basis of an ethical orientation unless it can overcome the parochiality that its association with friends and family tends to convey.[113]

Philosopher Marilyn Friedman's writings on ethics, social philosophy, and feminist theory provide a good illustration of power-focused feminist ethics. In the following selection Friedman begins with some of the standard criticisms against care-based ethics. Although recognizing that the ethics of care has been neglected in traditional theories and that it is an important component in ethics, she still insists that caring cannot be the sole or even the major moral duty that overrides all others. Instead, she says, caring must find its place in a "liberatory" feminist ethic in which "enlightened care" includes the caring of the caregiver for herself and a concern for her own "personal flourishing" as well as a willingness to abandon caring when it serves as the cause of her oppression.

MARILYN FRIEDMAN
(1945–)

- See if you can summarize and list Friedman's objections to an ethics of care.

Liberating Care [114]

A Critical Overview of Care Ethics

Care ethics offers at least one very alluring feature: high moral esteem for the traditional caring work done by women. Yet, because of certain problems in care ethics, feminists wonder whether, on balance, this ethic hinders more than it helps women seeking to overcome their cultural subordination. Claudia Card and Joan Tronto, for example, observe that merely presenting care ethics as a distinctively female ethic is not enough to establish its moral adequacy or its moral superiority to other ethical perspectives. Barbara Houston worries that to celebrate feminine virtues and perspectives is to risk glorifying the oppressive conditions under which they arose.

Card and Tronto point out that relationships differ in their worth, that not every relationship is valuable, and that care ethics provides no basis for critical reflection on relationships. Card suggests that, having developed under conditions of oppression, the care perspective has been needed for adaptation to those oppressive conditions and may not embody genuine virtue. In the views of both Card and Houston, care ethics ignores the possibility that a history of oppression has inflicted moral damage on women. Of special concern to feminists is the moral damage that further entrenches women's subordination, for example, the morally hazardous forms of deference that are a frequent risk when women care for men.

Card and Sarah Hoagland, in addition, both point out that care ethics lacks a political or institutional focus. It ignores the institutionally structured differentials of power and authority among different persons, especially those that constitute the gender hierarchy. It is thereby incapable of conceptualizing the oppressive, institutionally patriarchal context in which care takes place and that may compromise the otherwise high moral value of care. In Jeffner Allen's view, the nonviolence of care is a liability to women under oppressive circumstances, for it disables women from resisting whatever abuse they experience in heterosexual relationships.

Hoagland and Tronto, furthermore, recognized that care ethics ignores moral responsibilities to distant strangers and those for whom we do not feel particularly caring; care ethics thereby threatens to devolve into a mere defense of conventional relationships. Care ethics also fails to represent diversity among women. Either it suffers from positive biases of race, class, ethnicity, and national culture, as Michele Moody-Adams charges, or, at the very least, it suffers by its simple failure to represent specific differences among women, such as the racial diversity discussed by Carol Stack. . . .

To sum up: resisting the varied forms of female subordination calls for more than simply elevating esteem for women's traditionally sanctioned forms of labor and attendant modes of consciousness. To elevate social esteem for care ethics is to combat women's subordination to the extent of resisting only one of its many manifestations. This approach, by itself, does not (yet) constitute a sufficiently rich or fully liberatory *feminist* ethic. Worse yet, care ethics appears to bolster some of the practices and conceptions that subordinate women.

To portray care ethics as a distinctively female ethic reinforces the stereotypic gender assumptions that women are especially suited for the domestic, nurturing realm, that men are unsuited for this realm, and that women are particularly unsuited for the traditionally masculine worlds of public work and activity. The apparent incapacity of care ethics to deal with the moral relationships of public life, relationships among strangers, or among persons who share no affective ties, contributes greatly to this impression. If care ethics is supposed to represent the preferred perspective of substantial numbers of women, and if its mutual integration with justice considerations is not widely convincing, then the promotion of care ethics as a female ethic cannot help but reinvigorate stereotypes of women's incapacity to handle the moral challenges of public life.

Furthermore, care ethics might also undermine women's resolve to resist, say, violence or reproductive control by others, by appearing to endorse the *overridingness* of the moral duties to care, nurture, and maintain relationship with anyone with whom one comes into intimate contact, regardless of the moral quality of the relationship. Gilligan's focus on what she sees as the inclusiveness of the caring attitude suggests this unqualified orientation simply to maintaining connections with others. A care ethic, in this respect, is vulnerable to Hoagland's objection that it morally nullifies some of the most effective strategies available to women for resistance to abuse, exploitation, and coercion, strategies such as withdrawal altogether from relationship.

In another passage (not quoted here), Friedman questioned the Gilligan thesis that caring is a distinctively female moral orientation. Nevertheless, she agrees that caring is an important dimension of the moral life, for men as well as women. In the next passage, Friedman attempts to preserve what was of value in the ethics of care by developing a notion of "enlightened care" within the context of an ethics of liberation. According to her view, the moral responsibility for caring ends when it endangers the caregiver's well-being. Furthermore, consistent with the power-focused version of feminist ethics, she suggests that caring must be viewed within the larger social context in which relationships are embedded, in which the dynamics of power, domination, and exploitation take on institutional dimensions, and in which the positive aspects of community may be developed.

Care for Women as Care Givers

A fully liberatory feminist ethic must legitimate a woman's care for herself and her pursuit of caring and nurturing from others. From the standpoint of care ethics, it is important to recognize that women, who are normally relied upon to provide the bulk of nurturant care for others, are vulnerable in various ways. The forms of care that women need are not vouchsafed in the course of our caring for others. Even though women's caring for others sustains networks of interpersonal relationships, the existence of these relationships does not guarantee women's safety or equality of social status with men. Caring remains a risky business for women.

The care that can make a moral difference to a woman's life is roughly twofold. On the one hand, there is the kind of care involved in resisting our own devaluation, denigration, harassment, marginalization, exclusion, exploitation, subordination, domination, or openly violent abuse. Systematic attempts to overcome such harms may take the form of petitioning or pressuring societal institutions either to alter their own structures toward greater gender equity or to intercede more effectively on behalf of women in so-called private affairs, as in woman-battering cases. But rescue is not always available, and some of the problems in question arise out of social institutions and practices that are culturally sanctioned and widely tolerated. To protect ourselves, we as women must often rely on our own self-assertive efforts against oppressive practices. Thus, one major form of care for oneself concentrates on the variously necessary ways of protecting oneself against harm by others.

The second major category of care for self that a fully liberatory feminist ethic should offer involves positive flourishing, self-development that goes beyond merely resisting subordination or oppression. To be fully liberatory for women, such an ethic must develop ideals for a variety of personal achievements and excellences (other than those that center around self-protection). Care ethics does, of course, glorify the virtue of caring for and nurturing others. But this is not the only sort of human excellence that women can attain. Thus, a fully liberatory feminist ethic, with an eye toward the lives of women as typical care givers, should idealize forms of personal flourishing in addition to excellent care giving.

The sort of care for oneself involved in flourishing is significantly different from the sort that concentrates on protecting oneself from harm. The familiar criticisms that the women's movement in the United States concentrates on the needs of middle-class, white women and ignores the needs of low-income women or women who are not white have much to do with this distinction. Many women in our culture lack access to the resources for forms of personal development that extend beyond self-protective and survival needs. To sue the Rotary Club for barring female applicants from membership is a different sort of feminist project from volunteering support services at a battered women's shelter. Yet each is, in its own way, a quest by women to care for themselves and for some other women, a quest to surmount some facet of subordination or oppression facing some women and to live as well as conditions permit. Both of these wide-ranging sorts of concerns, self-protection as well as personal flourishing, require moral anchorage in a notion of care for oneself.

On Noddings's formulation of care ethics, not much primary importance is attached to caring for oneself. As Hoagland observes, the responsibility to care for oneself is derivative in Noddings's system; it derives from the responsibility to maintain one's capacity to care for others, a goal that requires staying in good care-giving shape. Caring for oneself as such appears to have no intrinsic value. . . .

My emphasis on the importance of caring for oneself and of being cared for in return by those for whom one cares introduces into care ethics an emphasis on self that is lacking in Noddings's formulation and that appears only in undeveloped form in Gilligan's version. On the approach I am recommending, the self is still defined, at least in part, by her relationships. My approach, however, incorporates the recognition that the caregiving self is herself someone who needs care and that her needs as such make legitimate moral demands on those to whom she is close.

There is room in care ethics for a cautious strain of individualism, one that is consistent with a theoretical emphasis on interconnection and the social nature of persons. Responsibilities to care should not eclipse those features of the care giver that constitute her as an individual, nor should they obscure those dimensions of meaning in her life that are independent of her care-giving role. Subordination, exploitation, abuse, and oppression occur to individuals—individuals in relationships, to be sure, but individuals nevertheless. Care ethics requires a notion of individuality (together with an adequate conception of human groups) in order to illuminate who is subordinated, who is oppressed, and why and how this occurs on a daily piecemeal basis. . . .

More so than Noddings and Gilligan, then, I construe the needs, wants, hopes, fears, and so forth of the care-giving self as legitimately helping to set the moral agenda for her relationships with other adults. The caring self, in such relationships, should care for herself and should expect her loved ones to reciprocate the care that she provides for them to the extent that they are able to do so. Self-assertion is not inimical to caring but, rather, helps to ensure that caring is mutual and undefiled by subordination of the care-giver. . . .

However we respond to this assessment of caretaking practices, it seems that we can no longer take a wholly benign view of the role of caring in women's lives, especially in the context of heterosexual relationships. If my analysis is correct, then it, together with the other feminist criticisms of care ethics outlined at the beginning of this chapter, yields a complex portrait of care. On the one hand, care is essential for the survival and development of both individuals and their communities, and care giving is a noble endeavor as well as being often morally requisite. On the other hand, care is simultaneously a perilous project for women, requiring the sacrifice of other important values, its very nobility part of its sometimes dangerously seductive allure. An ethic of care, to be fully liberatory for women, must not fail to explore and reflect this deep complexity.

- How would you paraphrase and summarize Friedman's requirements for a "liberating care ethic"?

🧪 THOUGHT EXPERIMENT: *Feminist Epistemology and Ethics*

The discussion on feminist epistemology in section 2.7 is relevant to the feminist approach to ethics, because how we understand knowledge in general will affect our approach to moral knowledge. Remember that feminists critique four hidden assumptions in traditional views of knowledge: the "generic humanity" assumption, the "view from nowhere" assumption, the "pure, impersonal reason" assumption, and the "Robinson Crusoe" assumption. It would be helpful to your understanding of feminist ethics to review those four assumptions that feminists criticize. After rereading the material on those four assumptions, consider the following questions:

- What implications do those four assumptions have for ethical theory?
- Why would feminists claim that those four assumptions would lead to a one-sided view of ethics?

SUMMARY OF FEMINIST ETHICS

It should be clear by now that although feminists insist that women's "voices" need to be heard in the realm of ethics, they do not always speak with one voice. Some of the controversies we have examined and that are still being discussed within the feminist movement are as follows: Is there a male bias in traditional ethical theories, and is it of such proportions that a total reconstruction of moral theory is required? Is there a difference between males and females in their ethical orientations? If so, how should that difference be characterized? If there are such differences, are they rooted in our biological natures or our social conditioning? Are a justice-based ethics and a care-based ethics equally correct and complementary, or is one superior to the other? Do the insights gathered from women's experiences in nurturing provide a basis for a more satisfactory approach to ethics? Can these insights be appropriated by men? On the other hand, does a care-focused ethics reinforce sexual stereotypes and prevent women from critically examining their status in society? Should women be concerned simply with elaborating better ethical theories, or is their first priority to challenge the conditions in society that oppress them?

👤 STOP AND THINK

As you think about what you have read in this section, try to articulate for yourself what themes are common throughout all the versions of feminist ethics. Second, whether you are male or female, decide on your own answers to the questions raised in this summary.

LOOKING THROUGH THE LENS OF FEMINIST ETHICS

1. Annette Baier says that "the great moral theorists in our tradition not only are all men, they are mostly men who had minimal adult dealings with (and so were then minimally influenced by) women." For the most part, she says, they were "clerics, misogynists, and puritan bachelors," and thus it is not surprising that they focus their philosophical attention "so single-mindedly on cool, distanced relations between more or less free and equal adult strangers."[115] Granted that the great moral theorists were all men, but do you think that maleness affected their theories in the way that Baier claims? Think back over the readings throughout this chapter on ethics. If you had not known the gender of the different authors, would you have been able to tell if they were male or female?

2. If you were a mother (perhaps you are), do you think the experience of motherhood would affect the way you viewed ethics? How so?

3. From your own experience and from what you have read, do you think there are differences between the ways that men and women approach ethical issues? What would be the implications of differences that are rooted in our biological natures? What would be the implications of differences that are caused by our social conditioning?

4. What do you think are the contributions and limitations of an ethics of care when applied beyond personal relationships to ethical issues in society and public policy?

5. Take one of the theories within feminist ethics and imagine that this theory had been the dominant moral tradition throughout the history of our society. In this case, how would history and today's society be different? What differences would this theory have made in our institutions, politics, laws, and social arrangements? Which of these changes (if any) would have been better? Which (if any) would have been worse?

EXAMINING THE STRENGTHS AND WEAKNESSES OF FEMINIST ETHICS

Positive Evaluation

1. The feminist writers have focused attention on what they believe is a much too restrictive view of rationality. Too often, being rational is identified with being distant, cool, and abstract, and feelings are dismissed as mere sentimentality. But feminists have insisted that sympathy, compassion, and concern can provide rational grounds for moral action. Do you think this point strengthens the case for their theory?

2. Whether or not it's true that males and females have different ethical orientations, doesn't Carol Gilligan have a point when she says that the rational, justice-based approach that focuses on rules and rights and the empathetic, caring-based approach that focuses on relationships are both important and complementary? Don't we all tend to be unbalanced in one direction or the other, and wouldn't we be better persons if we learned to listen to "voices" that are different from our own?

3. It is certainly true that women's voices have been ignored or silenced in the past as well as in our contemporary world. Wouldn't our moral traditions and our political life have been better if our intellectual and political conversations had been more broadly based and more inclusive? Isn't it significant that many corporations and institutions are making voluntary

efforts (and not simply for legal reasons) to step up their efforts to include women in positions of leadership? Aren't they finding that women bring insights and perspectives that would be missing without their input?

4. Whether you are a male or a female, don't you sometimes find it helpful to seek out advice or at least a sympathetic ear from a woman friend? Don't you find this conversation particularly helpful when you are dealing with a sensitive relationship problem with someone you love or a family member? Do women tend to have a better understanding of relationships or, at least, a distinctive perspective on them? If so, why? What implications does this quality have for contributions that women can make and have made to ethical theory?

Negative Evaluation

1. The American Declaration of Independence talks eloquently about human equality, dignity, and innate rights at the same time that its signers owned slaves. The problem was not in the principles they embraced but in their failure to apply them consistently and impartially. Could the same be true with traditional ethical theory? Isn't it possible that all the problems feminists point to in society are the result not of the failures of our ethical traditions but of the inadequate ways they have been applied?

2. Many feminists emphasize the ethics of care, but are they the only ones who are showing concern? After all, the duty and virtue of beneficence is solidly based in Aristotelian, Kantian, utilitarian, and recent virtue ethics. For example, although some feminists complain that women have been conditioned to submerge their needs and interests to tend to the needs of the male ego, Kant reminds us that we should not treat ourselves merely as a means to some other end but that we should view ourselves as persons who have intrinsic worth and dignity. Furthermore, the utilitarians point out that our own desires and interests must be included in the balance when we are calculating what action will produce the most happiness. Some male philosophers in previous ages may have had demeaning attitudes toward women, but don't their ethical theories have the resources to address most of the feminists' concerns? Isn't it ironic that of all the ethical theorists presented in this chapter, it was a woman thinker, Ayn Rand, whose ethics was most antithetical to many of the central concerns of the feminists?

3. Many feminist ethicists criticize traditional ethics for emphasizing the abstract principles of rights and justice. But shouldn't these principles be fundamental, key concepts in any viable ethical theory? In her book on human rights, Patricia Williams reflects on the bill of sale for her great-great-grandmother, which describes her ancestor as an eleven-year-old female slave. Williams says that, given the progress our society has made in overcoming racial injustice in the last century, the word "rights" is "deliciously empowering to say."[116] Similarly, hasn't all the progress that women have made in this century, and particularly in the past few decades, been the result of social and legal changes that emanate from an ethical concern for rights and justice? Haven't many of these changes been facilitated by male theorists and politicians? Does a feminist ethic undermine feminist goals?

4. Although they criticize ethical theories based on abstract, universal principles, can feminist ethicists avoid them? For example, feminist ethics seems to be based on the universal principle that *everyone* should be caring, compassionate, and attentive to others' needs. If feminist insights can be shared and can serve as guidelines in our moral lives, aren't they capable of being formulated as universal principles, the very thing feminists disdain in Kantian ethics?

REVIEW FOR CHAPTER 5

Philosophers

5.0 Overview of Ethics
Plato
Gottfried Leibniz
Thomas Hobbes

5.1 Ethical Relativism versus Objectivism
Protagoras
Jean-Paul Sartre
Herodotus
Ruth Benedict
John Ladd
James Rachels

5.2 Ethical Egoism
Friedrich Nietzsche
Ayn Rand
Bishop Butler
Joel Feinberg
Adam Smith
John Rawls

5.3 Utilitarianism
Jeremy Bentham
John Stuart Mill
Alastair Norcross

5.4 Kantian Ethics
Immanuel Kant
W. D. Ross

5.5 Virtue Ethics
Michael Stocker
Alasdair MacIntyre
Aristotle
Confucius
Janet Smith

5.6 Rethinking the Western Tradition:
Feminist Ethics
Carol Gilligan
Virginia Held
Sara Ruddick
Nel Noddings
Marilyn Friedman

Concepts

5.0 Overview of Ethics
Glaucon's theory of ethics
descriptive morality versus normative
ethics
divine command theory
ethical relativism

subjective ethical relativism
conventional ethical relativism
ethical objectivism
ethical egoism
utilitarianism
Kantian ethics
virtue ethics
feminist ethics

5.1 Ethical Relativism versus Objectivism
ethical relativism
subjective ethical relativism
conventional ethical relativism
ethical objectivism
diversity thesis
dependency thesis
moral absolutism

5.2 Ethical Egoism
psychological egoism
altruism
ethical egoism
egoism versus egotism
personal ethical egoism
individual ethical egoism
universal ethical egoism
selfishness versus self-interest
hedonism

5.3 Utilitarianism
consequentialism
teleological ethics
deontological ethics
intrinsic value
instrumental value
utilitarianism
psychological hedonism
ethical hedonism
Bentham's hedonic calculus
quantitative hedonism
qualitative hedonism

5.4 Kantian Ethics
the good will
acting in accordance with duty versus
acting from duty
deontological ethics
teleological (or consequentialist) ethics
Kant's two propositions of morality
hypothetical imperative
categorical imperative
a universalizable principle
prima facie duty
actual duty

SUGGESTIONS FOR FURTHER READING

General Works on Ethics

Birsch, Douglas. *Ethical Insights: A Brief Introduction.* Mountain View, Calif.: Mayfield, 1999. An analysis and evaluation of the major theories along with their practical applications.

Boss, Judith. *Analyzing Moral Issues.* Mountain View, Calif.: Mayfield, 1999. An introduction to the major theories with applications to contemporary moral issues.

————. *Perspectives on Ethics.* Mountain View, Calif.: Mayfield, 1998. A collection of readings ranging from classical to contemporary.

Newberry, Paul. *Theories of Ethics.* Mountain View, Calif.: Mayfield, 1999. A historically organized anthology ranging from Socrates to the contemporary period.

Pojman, Louis. *Ethical Theory: Classical and Contemporary Readings.* 3d ed. Belmont, Calif.: Wadsworth, 1998. An excellent anthology.

————. *Ethics: Discovering Right and Wrong.* 3d ed. Belmont, Calif.: Wadsworth, 1999. A short and engaging introduction to the leading theories and issues.

Rosenstand, Nina. *The Moral of the Story: An Introduction to Questions of Ethics and Human Nature.* Mountain View, Calif.: Mayfield, 1994. An overview of classical and modern approaches to ethical theory that uses examples from fiction and film.

Divine Command Theories of Ethics

Adams, Robert. *The Virtue of Faith.* New York: Oxford University Press, 1987. Contains several chapters that attempt to reformulate the divine command theory so as to avoid the traditional objections.

Quinn, Philip. *Divine Commands and Moral Requirements.* Oxford: Clarendon Press, 1978. Another attempt to establish a metaphysical link between morality and God.

Westmoreland, Robert. "Two Recent Met physical Divine Command Theories of Ethics." *International Journal for Philosophy of Religion* 39, no. 1 (February 1996): pp. 15–31. A critical response to the divine command theories discussed by Adams and Quinn.

Ethical Relativism versus Objectivism

Ladd, John. *Ethical Relativism.* Belmont, Calif.: Wadsworth, 1973. A collection of basic readings on the topic.

Mackie, J. L. *Ethics: Inventing Right and Wrong.* London: Penguin Books, 1976. A defense of relativism.

Wong, David. *Moral Relativity.* Berkeley: University of California Press, 1985. Defends a sophisticated version of ethical relativism.

Egoism

Gauthier, David, ed. *Morality and Rational Self-Interest.* Englewood Cliffs, N.J.: Prentice Hall, 1970.

Rand, Ayn. *Atlas Shrugged.* New York: Signet, 1996. All of Rand's novels promote the virtues of egoism in fictional form. This one seemed to be her favorite and depicts her thesis of the problems of an altruistic society and the possibility and desirability of a society of pure egoists.

————. *The Virtue of Selfishness: A New Concept of Egoism.* New York: New American Library, 1989. A collection of articles written by Rand defending her version of ethical egoism.

Utilitarianism

Bentham, Jeremy. *Introduction to the Principles of Morals and Legislation.* Edited by W. Harrison. Oxford: Oxford University Press, 1948. Bentham's classic defense of his theory.

Brandt, Richard. *A Theory of the Good and Right.* Oxford: Clarendon Press, 1979. A contemporary classic that defends a sophisticated version of utilitarianism.

Mill, John Stuart. *Utilitarianism.* Indianapolis: Bobbs-Merrill, 1957. One of the founding documents of the utilitarian movement.

Quinton, Anthony. *Utilitarian Ethics.* London: Macmillan, 1973. A clear exposition of classical utilitarianism.

Scheffler, Samuel. *Consequentialism and Its Critics.* Oxford: Oxford University Press, 1988. An advanced discussion of the strengths and limitations of consequentialist theories.

———. *The Rejection of Consequentialism.* Rev. ed. Oxford: Oxford University Press, 1994. An important discussion of the limits of consequentialism.

Smart, J. J. C., and Bernard Williams, eds. *Utilitarianism and Beyond.* Cambridge, England: Cambridge University Press, 1982. Contains a number of important readings.

Kantian Ethics

Kant, Immanuel. *The Foundations of the Metaphysics of Morals.* Translated by Lewis White Beck. Indianapolis: Bobbs-Merrill, 1959.

Wolff, Robert. *The Autonomy of Reason: A Commentary on Kant's "Groundwork of the Metaphysics of Morals."* New York: Harper and Row, 1973. A helpful commentary on Kant's work.

Virtue Ethics

Crisp, Roger, and Michael Slote, eds. *Virtue Ethics.* Oxford: Oxford University Press, 1997. A collection of important recent essays on the topic.

French, Peter, Theodore Uehling Jr., and Howard Wettstein, eds. *Ethical Theory: Character and Virtue.* Midwest Studies in Philosophy, vol. 13. Notre Dame, Ind.: University of Notre Dame Press, 1988. Contains a good collection of previously unpublished essays.

Kruschwitz, Robert, and Robert Roberts, eds. *The Virtues: Contemporary Essays on Moral Character.* Belmont, Calif.: Wadsworth, 1987. A readable collection of essays with an extensive bibliography.

Statman, Daniel, ed. *Virtue Ethics: A Critical Reader.* Washington, D.C.: Georgetown University Press, 1997. Includes contributions by both defenders and critics of virtue ethics. The editor's introduction is one of the best surveys of this topic in print.

Feminist Ethics

Cole, Eve Browning, and Susan Coultrap McQuin, eds. *Explorations in Feminist Ethics: Theory and Practice.* Bloomington: Indiana University Press, 1992. A collection of articles representing the various viewpoints in the movement.

Frazer, Elizabeth, Jennifer Hornsby, and Sabina Lovibond, eds. *Ethics: A Feminist Reader.* Oxford: Blackwell, 1992. An anthology of both historical and contemporary articles.

Gatens, Moira, ed. *Feminist Ethics.* Aldershot, England: Dartmouth Publishing, 1998. A massive collection of articles, covering some of the main controversies in the movement.

Tong, Rosemarie. *Feminist Approaches to Bioethics.* Boulder, Colo.: Westview, 1997. Part 1 gives a helpful overview of the variety of theories in feminist ethics.

———. *Feminist Thought: A More Comprehensive Introduction.* Boulder, Colo.: Westview, 1998. A comprehensive overview of the movement, including a discussion of the leading feminist ethical theories.

NOTES

1. Plato, *Republic,* trans. Benjamin Jowett (New York: P. F. Collier, 1901), bk 2, lines 359e–360b. I have made minor changes to the wording and punctuation for greater readability.

2. Quoted in Peter Collier and David Horowitz, *The Kennedys: An American Drama* (New York: Summit Books, 1984), p. 150.

3. See Patrick H. Nowell-Smith, "Morality: Religious and Secular," in Louis Pojman, ed., *Philosophy of Religion: An Anthology,* 3d ed. (Belmont, Calif.: Wadsworth, 1998); and James Rachels, "God and Human Attitudes," in *Religious Studies, 7* (1971): pp. 325–38.

4. See George Mavrodes, "Religion and the Queerness of Morality," in Pojman, *Philosophy of Religion;* Louis Pojman, "Ethics: Religious and Secular," *The Modern Schoolman* 70 (November 1992): pp. 1–30; and Louis Pojman, "Is Contemporary Moral Theory Founded on a Misunderstanding?" *Journal of Social Philosophy* 22 (fall 1991): pp. 49–59.

5. "Religion and Morality," in *Leo Tolstoy: Selected Essays,* trans. Aylmer Maude (New York: Random House, 1964), p. 31.

6. For discussions and defenses of the divine command theory, see Paul Helm, ed., *The Divine Command Theory of Ethics* (Oxford: Oxford University Press, 1979); Gene Outka and J. P. Reeder, eds., *Religion and Morality: A Collection of Essays* (Garden City, N.Y.: Anchor Books, 1973); and Philip Quinn, *Divine Commands and Moral Requirements* (Oxford: Oxford University Press, 1978).

7. For Biblical approval of specific acts of lying, see Exodus 1:15–20 and Joshua 2:1–6 (in conjunction with Hebrews 11:31). For divinely commanded lying, see 1 Samuel 16:1–3.

8. Gottfried Leibniz, *Discourse on Metaphysics,* sec. 2, trans. George R. Montgomery (1902).

9. Thomas Hobbes, *Leviathan* (1651). All quotes are from chapter 13.

10. This exercise was given by John Hospers in *Human Conduct* (New York: Harcourt Brace Jovanovich, 1961), p. 174.

11. This apt analogy was taken from Louis Pojman, *Ethics: Discovering Right and Wrong* (Belmont, Calif.: Wadsworth, 1995), p. 229.

12. Robert Bolt, *A Man for All Seasons* (New York: Random House, 1962), p. 140.

13. Ernest Hemingway, *Death in the Afternoon* (New York: Scribner, 1932), p. 4.

14. Jean-Paul Sartre, "Existentialism Is a Humanism," in *Existentialism from Dostoyevsky to Sartre,* ed. Walter Kaufmann (New York: Meridian, 1989), p. 356.

15. Hobbes, *Leviathan,* chap. 13.

16. Translation adapted from George Rawlinson, trans., *The History of Herodotus* (New York: D. Appleton, 1859–1861), bk. 3, chap. 38.

17. This example was adapted from one by Emmett Barcalow, *Open Questions,* 2d ed. (Belmont, Calif.: Wadsworth, 1997), p. 289.

18. Ruth Benedict, "Anthropology and the Abnormal," *The Journal of General Psychology* 10 (1934): pp. 59–82.

19. John Ladd, *Ethical Relativism* (Belmont, Calif.: Wadsworth, 1973), p. 1.

20. Clyde Kluckhohn, "Ethical Relativity: Sic et Non," *Journal of Philosophy* 52 (1955): pp. 663–77.

21. These and other examples can be found in C. S. Lewis, *The Abolition of Man* (New York: Touchstone, 1975), pp. 93–95, 103–4.

22. James Rachels, "The Challenge of Cultural Relativism," in *The Elements of Moral Philosophy* (New York: Random House, 1986), pp. 13–22.

23. Pojman, *Ethics: Discovering Right and Wrong,* p. 16.

24. W. Somerset Maugham, *Of Human Bondage* (New York: Signet, 1991), pp. 229–30.

25. Friedrich Nietzsche, *Beyond Good and Evil,* trans. Walter Kaufmann (New York: Vintage Books, 1966), sec. 260.

26. Ayn Rand, "The Ethics of Emergencies," in *The Virtue of Selfishness: A New Concept of Egoism* (New York: Signet Books, 1964), p. 49.

27. For my discussion of this point I am indebted to Paul Taylor's discussion in his *Principles of Ethics: An Introduction* (Belmont, Calif.: Wadsworth, 1975),p. 42.

28. Rand, "The Ethics of Emergencies," p. 44.

29. Ibid., pp. 44–45.

30. Robert Ringer, *Looking Out for #1* (New York: Fawcett Crest, 1977), p. 50.

31. Joel Feinberg, "Psychological Egoism," in *Reason and Responsibility,* 7th ed., ed. Joel Feinberg (Belmont, Calif.: Wadsworth, 1989), p. 495.

32. Rand, *The Virtue of Selfishness,* pp. vii–viii.

33. Ibid., pp. 32, 35.

34. Rand, "The Objectivist Ethics," in *The Virtue of Selfishness,* pp. 17, 25, 34.

35. Ibid., p. 31.

36. Ibid.

37. Rand, "The 'Conflicts' of Men's Interests," in *The Virtue of Selfishness,* pp. 50–56.

38. Rand, "Racism," in *The Virtue of Selfishness,* pp. 126–34.

39. John Rawls, *A Theory of Justice* (Cambridge, Mass.: Harvard University Press, 1971), pp. 11–17.

40. James Rachels, *The Elements of Moral Philosophy* (New York: Random House, 1986), pp. 77–78.

41. Jeremy Bentham, *An Introduction to the Principles of Morals and Legislation* (1789), chap. 1.

42. Jeremy Bentham, *The Rationale of Reward,* in *The Works of Jeremy Bentham,* vol. 2, ed. John Bowring (Edinburgh: William Tait, 1843), p. 253.

43. This thought experiment is adapted from one proposed in Robert Nozick, *Anarchy, State, and Utopia* (New York: Basic Books, 1974), pp. 42–43.

44. John Stuart Mill, *Utilitarianism* (1863), chap. 2.

45. John Stuart Mill, "Bentham," in *Collected Works of John Stuart Mill,* ed. J. M. Robson, vol. 10, *Essays on Ethics, Religion, and Society* (Toronto: University of Toronto Press, 1969), p. 95.

46. John Stuart Mill, *Utilitarianism,* chap. 2.

47. Alastair Norcross, "Comparing Harms: Headaches and Human Lives," *Philosophy and Public Affairs* 26 (spring 1997): pp. 135–36, 159–60, 163.

48. Adapted from Nina Rosenstand, *The Moral of the Story: An Introduction to Questions of Ethics and Human Nature* (Mountain View, Calif.: Mayfield, 1994), p. 148.

49. Immanuel Kant, *Critique of Practical Reason,* trans. Lewis White Beck (Chicago: University of Chicago Press, 1949), pt. 2, conclusion.

50. Immanuel Kant, *Foundations of the Metaphysics of Morals,* trans. Lewis White Beck (Indianapolis: Bobbs-Merrill, Library of Liberal Arts, 1959), pp. 9–10, 13–17, 38–47. I have added my own section headings to Kant's text. Trans. Lewis White Beck, 2nd ed., © 1990. Reproduced in print and

electronically by permission of Pearson Education, Inc.,Upper Saddle River, New Jersey.

51. Immanuel Kant, "On a Supposed Right to Lie from Altruistic Motives," in *Critique of Practical Reason and Other Writings in Moral Philosophy,* trans. Lewis White Beck (Chicago: University of Chicago Press, 1949), p. 348.

52. William David Ross, *The Right and the Good* (Oxford: Oxford University Press, 1932).

53. Michael Stocker, "The Schizophrenia of Modern Moral Theories," *Journal of Philosophy* 73 (August 12, 1976): p. 462.

54. Ibid., pp. 460, 461.

55. Plato, *Gorgias* 479b.

56. Plato, *Crito* 48b.

57. Ibid.

58. Aristotle, *Nicomachean Ethics* 1099a, 1104b, in *The Basic Works of Aristotle,* trans. and ed. Richard McKeon (New York: Random House, 1941).

59. Alasdair MacIntyre, *After Virtue,* 2d ed. (Notre Dame, Ind.: University of Notre Dame Press, 1984), p. 219.

60. Gregory Velazco y Trianosky, "What Is Virtue Ethics All About?" in *Virtue Ethics: A Critical Reader,* ed. Daniel Statman (Washington, D.C.: Georgetown University Press, 1997), p. 52. The author's in-text citations have been omitted.

61. Harold Alderman, "By Virtue of a Virtue," in Statman, *Virtue Ethics,* p. 162.

62. Justine Oakley, "Varieties of Virtue Ethics," *Ratio* 9 (September 1996): p. 135.

63. J. L. A. Garcia, "The Primacy of the Virtuous," *Philosophia* 20 (July 1990): p. 70.

64. David Solomon, "Internal Objections to Virtue Ethics," in *Ethical Theory: Character and Virtue,* Midwest Studies in Philosophy, vol. 13 (Notre Dame, Ind.: University of Notre Dame Press, 1988), p. 437.

65. Daniel Statman, "Introduction to Virtue Ethics," in Statman, *Virtue Ethics,* p. 13.

66. Rosalind Hursthouse, "Virtue Theory and Abortion," in Statman, *Virtue Ethics,* p. 228.

67. *Aristotle's Nicomachean Ethics,* trans. James Weldon (New York: Macmillan, 1897).

68. Confucius, *The Analects,* trans. William Jennings, in *The Sacred Books of the East,* ed. Max Muller (Oxford: Clarendon Press, 1879–1910).

69. Janet Smith, "Moral Character and Abortion," in Joram Graf Haber, *Doing and Being* (New York: Macmillan, 1993), pp. 442–56.

70. See, for example, Mark Strasser, "The Virtues of Utilitarianism," *Philosophia* 20 (July 1990): pp. 209–26; Michael Slote, "Utilitarian Virtue," in *Ethical Theory: Character and Virtue,* Midwest Studies in Philosophy, vol. 13 (Notre Dame, Ind.: University of Notre Dame Press, 1988), pp. 384–97; and Robert Louden, "Kant's Virtue Ethics," in Statman, *Virtue Ethics,* pp. 286–99.

71. Robert Louden, "On Some Vices of Virtue Ethics," in Statman, *Virtue Ethics,* p. 191.

72. Susan Wolf, "Moral Saints," *Journal of Philosophy* 79 (August 1982): pp. 419–39.

73. Robert Solomon, "Beyond Reason, The Importance of Emotion in Philosophy," in *Revising Philosophy,* ed. James Ogilvy (Albany: State University of New York Press, 1992), p. 32.

74. Statman, "Introduction to Virtue Ethics," p. 23.

75. D. Kay Johnston, "Adolescents' Solutions to Dilemmas in Fables: Two Moral Orientations—Two Problem Solving Strategies," in *Mapping the Moral Domain: A Contribution of Women's Thinking to Psychological Theory and Education,* ed. Carol Gilligan, Janie Victoria Ward, and Jill McLean Taylor, with Betty Baridge (Cambridge, Mass.: Harvard University Press, 1988), pp. 49–71.

76. Lawrence Kohlberg, *Moral Education* (Cambridge, Mass.: Moral Education Research Foundation, Harvard University, 1973), quoted in Carol Gilligan, *In a Different Voice: Psychological Theory and Women's Development* (Cambridge, Mass.: Harvard University Press, 1982, 1993), pp. 19–20.

77. J. O. Urmson, "Saints and Heroes," in *Essays in Moral Philosophy,* ed. A. I. Melden (Seattle: University of Washington Press, 1958), p. 202.

78. Virginia Held, "Feminist Reconceptualizations in Ethics," in *Philosophy in a Feminist Voice: Critiques and Reconstructions,* ed. Janet Kourany (Princeton, N.J.: Princeton University Press, 1998), pp. 94–95.

79. Eve Browning Cole and Susan Coultrap-McQuin, "Toward a Feminist Conception of Moral Life," in *Explorations in Feminist Ethics: Theory and Practice,* ed. Eve Browning Cole and Susan Coultrap-McQuin (Bloomington, Ind.: Indiana University Press, 1992), p. 2.

80. Eva Feder Kittay and Diana T. Meyers, eds., *Women and Moral Theory* (Totowa, N.J.: Rowan and Littlefield, 1987), p. 10.

81. Alison Jaggar, "Feminist Ethics," in *Encyclopedia of Ethics,* ed. Lawrence Becker and Charlotte Becker (New York: Garland, 1992), p. 364.

82. Ibid.

83. Rosemarie Tong, *Feminist Approaches to Bioethics* (Boulder, Colo.: Westview Press, 1997), p. 52.

84. Betty A. Sichel, "Different Strains and Strands: Feminist Contributions to Ethical Theory," *Newsletter on Feminism* 90, no. 2 (Winter 1991): p. 90.

85. Susan Sherwin, *No Longer Patient: Feminist Ethics and Health Care* (Philadelphia: Temple University Press, 1992), pp. 42–43.

86. Tong, *Feminist Approaches to Bioethics,* p. 38.

87. John Broughton, "Women's Rationality and Men's Virtues: A Critique of Gender Dualism in Gilligan's Theory of Moral Development," *Social Research* 50, no. 3 (Autumn 1983): pp. 597–642.

88. See some of the critical responses to Gilligan's theory reprinted in *Caring Voices and Women's Moral Frames,* ed. Bill Puka (New York: Garland Publishing, 1994).

89. Virginia Held, "Non-contractual Society: A Feminist View," in *Science, Morality, and Feminist Theory,* ed. Marsha Hanen and Kai Nielsen (Calgary: The University of Calgary Press, 1987), pp. 116, 119.

90. Sara Ruddick, *Maternal Thinking: Toward a Politics of Peace* (Boston: Beacon Press, 1989).

91. Nel Noddings, *Caring: A Feminine Approach to Ethics and Moral Education* (Berkeley: University of California Press, 1984), p. 3.

92. Gilligan, *In a Different Voice,* p. 42.

93. Ibid., p. 43.

94. Noddings, *Caring: A Feminine Approach,* p. 80.

95. Kathy Ferguson, *The Feminist Case against Bureaucracy* (Philadelphia: Temple University Press, 1984), pp. 25, 119–203.

96. Jean Grimshaw, "The Idea of a Female Ethic," in *A Companion to Ethics,* ed. Peter Singer (Oxford: Blackwell, 1992).

97. Joan C. Tronto, "Care as a Basis for Radical Political Judgments," *Hypatia* 10, no. 2 (Spring 1995): p. 145.

98. Lawrence Kohlberg, *The Psychology of Moral Development: The Nature and Validity of Moral Stages,* Essays on Moral Development, vol. 2 (San Francisco: Harper and Row, 1984), p. 640.

99. Tong, *Feminist Approaches to Bioethics,* p. 49.

100. Jaggar, "Feminist Ethics," p. 361.

101. Susan Mendus, "Different Voices, Still Lives: Problems in the Ethics of Care," *Journal of Applied Philosophy* 10, no. 1 (1993): p. 21.

102. Broughton, "Women's Rationality and Men's Virtues," p. 626.

103. Ibid.

104. Mary G. Dietz, "Citizenship with a Feminist Face: The Problem with Maternal Thinking," *Political Theory* 13, no. 1 (February 1985): p. 34.

105. Zella Luria, "A Methodological Critique," in "On *In a Different Voice:* An Interdisciplinary Forum," *Signs* 11, no. 2 (Winter 1986): p. 320.

106. Patricia Ward Scaltsas, "Do Feminist Ethics Counter Feminist Aims?" in Cole and Coultrap-McQuin, *Explorations in Feminist Ethics,* pp. 19, 23.

107. Sara Lucia Hoagland, quoted in Tong, *Feminist Approaches to Bioethics,* p. 50.

108. Sara Lucia Hoagland, "Some Thoughts about *Caring,*" in *Feminist Ethics,* ed. Claudia Card (Lawrence: University Press of Kansas, 1991), p. 250.

109. Sheila Mullett, "Shifting Perspectives: A New Approach to Ethics," in *Feminist Perspectives,* ed. Lorraine Code, Sheila Mullett, and Christine Overall (Toronto: University of Toronto Press, 1989), p. 119.

110. Marilyn Friedman, "Liberating Care," in *What Are Friends For? Feminist Perspectives on Personal Relationships and Moral Theory* (Ithaca: Cornell University Press, 1993), p. 150.

111. Mullett, "Shifting Perspectives: A New Approach to Ethics," p. 114.

112. Dietz, "Citizenship with a Feminist Face," pp. 30–31.

113. Broughton, "Women's Rationality and Men's Virtues," p. 614.

114. Marilyn Friedman, "Liberating Care," pp. 142–83. I have deleted Friedman's extensive footnotes.

115. Annette Baier, "Trust and Anti-Trust," *Ethics* 96 (January 1986): pp. 247–48.

116. Patricia J. Williams, *The Alchemy of Race and Rights* (Cambridge, Mass.: Harvard University Press, 1991), p. 164.

The Code of Hammurabi, 1792–1750 BCE

CHAPTER 6

THE SEARCH FOR THE JUST SOCIETY

 CHAPTER OBJECTIVES

Upon completion of this chapter you should be able to

1. Present some of the strengths and weaknesses of anarchism.
2. Compare, contrast, and evaluate the social contract theories of Hobbes and Locke.
3. Critically evaluate various accounts of justice, including Plato's notion of a meritocracy, Aquinas's view of justice as conformity to natural law, Mill's utilitarian approach to justice, and Rawls's theory of "justice as fairness."
4. Contrast the attitudes toward the appropriate relation between the individual and the state expressed in the classical liberal perspective of Mill and in Marx's collectivist account.
5. Explain the nature of civil disobedience, offer several arguments for and against it, and discuss the positions on it taken by Socrates, Gandhi, and Martin Luther King Jr.
6. Discuss the ethical arguments for and against expanding the government's database of DNA information about its citizens.

SCOUTING THE TERRITORY: *Thinking about Government*

Why is there government? What is it that makes a government legitimate? What is its purpose? What are its limits? To answer these questions, the 17th-century English philosopher Thomas Hobbes wrote his classic book *Leviathan* in 1651. Using a thought experiment, he imagined what human life would be like if there were no government, a condition that he called the "state of nature." Hobbes surmised that without a government to maintain order and regulate human interactions, this condition would be "a war of all against all" as each person did whatever he or she could get away with doing. If there were no government, then the notions of *justice* and *injustice* would be merely words. In short, Hobbes concluded that human life without government would be "solitary, poor, nasty, brutish, and short." From there he developed a theory about how people would go about forming a government and what powers they would assign to it.

Most of us would agree with Hobbes that a government of some sort is a practical necessity. But do we need as much government as we currently have? Does the government need to poke its nose into our personal affairs as much as it does? Every time we look at a paycheck and see how much of our original income has been eaten up by the income and payroll taxes, we are reminded of the presence of the government in our lives. Many of us despair over what we perceive as the heavy hand of the government in collecting excessive taxes, imposing unnecessary regulations, creating huge bureaucracies, and squandering our hard-earned money on people and causes that we deem undeserving. Henry David Thoreau, the 19th-century American writer, expressed his antigovernment sentiments by saying, "that government governs best that governs least."

Is government as bad as Thoreau thought it was? Even though Thoreau thought his society had too much government, there was less government in his day than in our present society. However, with less government, people also had virtually no protection from harmful medicines and dangerous products sold by unscrupulous or negligent persons. The workplace had few health and safety standards. If you deposited money in a bank, you had no guarantee that you could get it back if the bank failed. In today's world, a college education would be beyond the reach of anybody but the most wealthy without government-supported financial aid and loans. Furthermore, even if a student is not receiving direct financial aid, his or her college education is made possible by tax-supported federal programs. The high costs of technology and other resources make it impossible for major universities, as well as most colleges, to fulfill their mission without the direct or indirect support of the local, state, and federal governments.

So, we are back to Thomas Hobbes's point that government seems to be a necessary part of human life. But even if we agree on that point, we are still left with a host of questions concerning the nature of government and what exact role it should play in human affairs. These issues make up the central core of political philosophy.

CHARTING THE TERRAIN OF POLITICAL PHILOSOPHY: *What Are the Issues?*

The first issue we discuss in this chapter is, "What is the justification of the government's authority?" The government may have the power and the force to rule its people, but not every ruler or use of force is legitimate. So, what conditions make it legitimate for the government to be in power? Obviously, this issue is a fundamental one, for if a government

Government Bureau (1956) by George Tooker. Too often, the government appears to us as it does in this painting. The government bureaucrats are depicted as forbidding, nameless, impersonal powers who control our lives. Furthermore, the individuals who are being processed by the government agents are likewise reduced to faceless, anonymous, downtrodden, empty people. (Notice that the images of the same man and woman are repeated throughout the lines of waiting people.) Nevertheless, in spite of the negative aspects of government, most people recognize that it is necessary to our well-being. Hence, philosophers have asked: What is the purpose of government? How is it justified? What makes a government just? What are the limits of the government's authority over our lives?

is not legitimate then all other issues about the proper role of government and our relationship to it do not arise.

The second issue we discuss concerns the theory of justice. We frequently evaluate a government in terms of efficiency. During political campaigns, candidates typically promise that if they are elected to office, they will make the government do its job more effectively. But is efficiency the only criterion for judging a government? After all, it has frequently been pointed out that when the fascist dictator Benito Mussolini took charge of Italy in the 1920s, he succeeded in making the trains run on time. Similarly, the communist dictator Joseph Stalin brought mechanization to Russian agriculture during the early part of the 20th century. Although these rulers brought efficiency to their respective societies, it is clear that they did not bring justice. Obviously, we want our government to be efficient, but we also want it to be just. This point raises several questions: "What is justice?" and "How can we determine whether a government is just or not?"

The third issue we examine concerns the relationship between the individual and the state, between freedom and control. We all cherish our individual freedoms. But too much individual freedom would lead to social chaos. Hence, some degree of government control is necessary. But too much government control would lead to an unacceptable level of tyranny. So where do we draw the line between individual freedom and government control? Is the government to be thought of as our servant, doing only those things we cannot do for ourselves? Or is the government to be thought of as our parent, looking out for our best interests? In other words, is the major responsibility of government to serve us by maximizing our individual liberties but allowing us to live our individual lives as we please? Or is the major responsibility of government to produce the best results for ourselves and society in general, even if this goal requires limiting our freedom?

The final issue we examine concerns the topic of civil disobedience. If we agree that government is something necessary and even good, then it would seem that obeying the government is necessary and good. To have laws that no one obeys is no better than having no laws at all. But are there situations in which it would be bad and even immoral to obey the government? Under what conditions would it be morally permissible to break the law? These two questions are the focus of the fourth section of this chapter on political philosophy.

 CHOOSING A PATH: *What Are My Options Concerning Political Philosophy?*

Two positions are discussed under the topic of the justification of government. The first is an extreme position, and the second is one of the most influential theories in the history of political thought. The extreme position is *anarchism.* The anarchist replies to the question, "What makes the authority of a government legitimate?" with the simple answer, "No government ever has legitimate authority." The second theory responds to the question, "What makes the authority of a government legitimate?" by saying, "A government is legitimate if it rules with the consent of its citizens." In modern history, this "consent of the governed" theory has been labeled the *social contract theory.*

The first position discussed in section 6.2 about the nature of justice is *justice as merit.* This position maintains that because all people do not contribute to society equally, they should not have political equality. The just society, it is argued, is one in which all people receive what they are due (especially political power) according to their merit. The next position is known as the *natural law theory.* It claims that a government is just if its laws and actions conform to a universal moral law and that this moral law exists independently of human preferences or society's decisions. The third position on justice that we examine is the *utilitarian theory.* Consistent with their ethical theory, the utilitarians claim that a just society is one that produces the greatest happiness for the greatest number of people. Finally, we survey the theory of *justice as fairness* developed by the contemporary American philosopher John Rawls. He believes that if we all were truly rational and fair, we would opt for a society in which everyone has the opportunity to succeed to the best of his or her abilities at the same time that it maintains a minimal level of social and economic equality. This theory entails maximizing political liberty while improving the condition of the most disadvantaged.

In section 6.3 on the individual and the state, we look at two positions that are located at opposing ends of the political spectrum. One position, *individualism,* believes that the best society is the one in which individual liberty is at a maximum and the government's intrusion in our lives is kept to what is minimally necessary. We examine John Stuart Mill's *classical liberalism* as an example of this position. The opposing position states that the best results will be achieved if the government plays a large role in regulating society and providing for people's needs. This position is sometimes called *collectivism* because it claims that the collective, the common good, or the state (the government) should have the final authority over individual preferences. I use Marxism as a representative of this theory.

TABLE 6.1 *Four Questions in Political Philosophy and Responses to Them*

What Is the Justification of Government?	Anarchism: government is not justified	Social contract theory: the consent of the governed		
What Is Justice?	Justice is merit: giving everybody what they deserve, based on their contribution or merit	Natural law theory: conformity to a universal moral law	Utilitarianism: whatever produces the greatest good for the greatest number	Justice is fairness: it includes maximizing political equality and maximizing the position of the least advantaged
Which Should Be Given Priority: Individual Liberty or the Good of the Community?	Individualism: individual liberty	Collectivism: the good of the community		
Is Civil Disobedience Ever Morally Permissible?	Socrates: no	Martin Luther King Jr.: yes	Mohandas Gandhi: yes	

Finally, we examine the pros and cons of civil disobedience. The first position maintains that civil disobedience is never morally justified, and Socrates is used to represent this position. The second position maintains that there are circumstances in which obeying the law would be immoral and disobeying the law would be morally permissible, perhaps even our moral duty. We examine the arguments of Martin Luther King Jr. and Mohandas Gandhi in support of this position. Obviously, the first position has the burden of proving why it is always wrong to disobey the government. The second position has to show why it is sometimes morally permissible to do so and to provide principles for deciding when our normal duty to obey the government may be suspended in the name of a higher moral obligation.

This chapter presents four questions in political philosophy and offers various responses to those four questions. Your answer to each question may impact your answers to the other questions, but I will let you think through their connections for yourself. Table 6.1 summarizes this overview by listing the questions and the answers that we discuss in the next four sections of this chapter.

WHAT DO I THINK? *Questionnaire on Political Philosophy*

	Agree	Disagree
1. It is never morally justified for someone to control another rational adult's life. Therefore, whatever *practical* needs the government serves, its exercise of power over us is not *morally* justified.		

	Agree	Disagree
2. It is morally justified for the government to exercise power over our lives if we have chosen to delegate that power to it.		
3. Those who have the most ability are the ones who should be the rulers of society and have the most political power. Hence, justice has nothing to do with democratic equality.		
4. The main criterion for determining if governments and their laws are just or not is how moral they are.		
5. The just society is simply one that maximizes the greatest happiness for the greatest number.		
6. The just society is one that maximizes political liberty while giving priority to those who are least advantaged.		
7. The best society is one that places the highest priority on maximizing individual liberty and minimizing government control.		
8. The best society is one that places the highest priority on giving government the power to make life better for everyone, even at the sacrifice of some individual freedom.		
9. Disobeying the law is never morally justified.		
10. There are circumstances in which disobeying the law might be our moral obligation, even if we go to jail for it.		

KEY TO THE QUESTIONNAIRE ON POLITICAL PHILOSOPHY

Statement 1 represents anarchism. It conflicts with statement 2.

Statement 2 represents the social contract theory. It conflicts with statement 1.

Statement 3 represents the theory of justice as merit. It conflicts with statements 4, 5, and 6.

Statement 4 represents the natural law theory. It conflicts with statements 3, 5, and 6.

Statement 5 represents the utilitarian theory of justice. It conflicts with statements 3, 4, and 6.

Statement 6 represents John Rawls's theory of justice as fairness. It conflicts with statements 3, 4, and 5.

Statement 7 represents the position of individualism concerning the degree of individual liberty versus government control. It conflicts with statement 8.

Statement 8 represents the position of Marxism. It conflicts with statement 7.

Statement 9 represents the position of opponents of civil disobedience. It conflicts with statement 10.

Statement 10 represents the position of supporters of civil disobedience. It conflicts with statement 9.

6.1 THE JUSTIFICATION OF GOVERNMENT

LEADING QUESTIONS: *The Justification of Government*

1. *Leading Questions of the Anarchist:* Suppose a stranger broke into your home while you were away and, instead of robbing you, washed and folded your laundry and vacuumed your carpets. Obviously, the stranger performed a service for you, but would this action justify the stranger breaking into your home without your permission? Similarly, the government provides a number of benefits for us, but do these actions morally justify the government in exercising its power over our individual lives?

2. *Leading Questions of the Anarchist:* The government obviously has the force to impose its will on us, but having force does not equal having morally justified authority. Doesn't the power of the government violate the basic principle that each person should have autonomy and control over his or her own life? Although the practical benefits of government are obvious, does it have any morally justified authority over us, or is its control simply based on its power?

3. *Leading Questions of the Social Contract Theorist:* When you accept a job, you sign a contract agreeing that you will do certain things for your employer, and your company agrees to provide you with a certain salary and benefits. If both parties are free to sign the contract or not, what could possibly be wrong with this arrangement? Isn't our relationship to the government like such a contract? We consent to allow the government to have a certain amount of authority over us for our benefit and the good of society. Isn't this arrangement an adequate justification of the government's authority?

4. *Leading Questions of the Social Contract Theorist:* As long as you live in a free society, you have the option of living in that society, obeying its laws, and receiving its services. If you don't like that arrangement, you can choose to live elsewhere. By living in your present society and accepting its benefits, haven't you consented to abide by the government's laws?

There is a distinction between having power and having the proper authority to use that power. As these leading questions suggest, this distinction is important when discussing the role of the government in our lives. The following thought experiment asks you to think about the issue of authority and the proper exercise of power.

THOUGHT EXPERIMENT: *Authority versus Power*

In each pair of the following scenarios, similar actions are being performed. In each case, how does situation (a) differ from situation (b)?

1. (a) You fill out your federal income tax form and find that you owe the government $1,000. You write out a check for this amount, knowing that if you do not pay the government what it demands of you, the penalties will be severe.

   (b) While you are walking home at night, a robber with a gun steps out of the shadows and demands all the money in your wallet. You hand your money over, knowing that the consequences of not doing so will be severe.

(continued . . .)

(. . . continued)

2. (a) In a criminal trial, a judge determines that the defendant is guilty of fraud and sentences her to several years in prison.

    (b) You decide that the saleswoman who sold you a defective car is guilty of fraud and so you forcibly lock her up in your basement for several years.

3. (a) During a time of international crisis, your best friend is drafted into the army to fight for the country's interests. He doesn't particularly want to go to war but is forced to do so by the government.

    (b) You are having a dispute with your neighbor concerning the damage that the neighbor's dog did to your garden. At gunpoint, you force your unwilling friend to attack your neighbor for you.

In one sense, each of the pairs of actions in the thought experiment is similar. In the first pair of cases, you are forced to give up your money. In the second set, a wrongdoer is being punished. In the third pair, someone is being forced to fight for a cause. Obviously, all the cases labeled (a) involve what are customarily considered to be the legitimate exercise of governmental power. In all the (b) cases, however, power is being used to force someone to do something, but there is no proper authority to use that power. What does it mean to have legitimate authority to control or regulate the behavior of others? How does legitimate authority differ from simply having power? How is the government different from the robber? Or is it? Is the government's ability to restrict our freedom in various ways simply due to the fact that it has the most guns?

In the context of politics, authority means not only having power but also having the right (the legitimate authority) to use that power in certain specified ways. But what is the basis of the alleged right of the government to restrict our freedom to act as we wish? On what basis is government justified—not this or that particular government but government in general?

Throughout most of human history as we know it, there has been some form of social organization, and whenever people have come together in groups, there has been some form of leadership that implicitly or explicitly had the character of a government. But as the previous thought experiment illustrated, the claim that a person or a group of people represents the government entails the claim that their use of power is legitimate. Without this latter claim, there is no distinction between a government and a mob with weapons.

Governmental authority has been justified in several ways. The most ancient view is the *divine right theory*, which states that the king, queen, pharaoh, emperor, or whoever received his or her authority to rule from God or the gods. All the great civilizations that followed this theory of government also had moral codes and standards of justice that the ruler was expected to follow if his or her rule was to be pleasing to the divine powers. In most cases, no one in the society had the power to question whether the ruler was living up to this code (with the possible exception of a priest or priestess). Hence, the code of justice generally served little purpose in tempering the power of the ruler, who had total control over defining or interpreting what was just. In the final analysis, most governments that claimed they ruled under divine authority either actually had the consent of their subjects as well or were based on sheer power, and the religious justifications served merely as a public relations story.

Another approach to government is the *justice theory*. According to this account, the legitimacy of the government hangs directly on the issue of whether it is serving the cause of justice (however that cause is defined). The ancient Greek philosophers Plato and Aristotle, for example, seemed to justify the authority of government on this basis. In section 6.2, we examine various theories of justice. The issue of justice, however, seems to address the question of whether a government that is already in place is acting rightly or wrongly; it doesn't answer the question of why the government is legitimate in the first place.

The remainder of this section focuses on two important theories about the legitimacy of government: *anarchism* and the *social contract theory*. We discuss each of these two theories in turn.

SURVEYING THE CASE FOR ANARCHISM

As we look at various governments throughout history and in the world today, most of us naturally make the judgment that some of those governments have been bad ones (Hitler's regime, for example). One political position, however, claims that *all* governments are bad in the sense that none of them have the authority or the right to exercise their power over people. **Anarchism** is the position that there is no conceivable justification for government. At times, when we feel alienated from our own government and struggle with the laws, taxes, and the burdens it imposes on us, we are tempted to think of the government as "them" instead of as "us." At those times, anarchism has a certain emotional appeal. But the defense of anarchism must be based on arguments rather than simply negative feelings about the government. Before examining the arguments for anarchism, let's consider the various forms it can take.

Naive anarchism is characterized by the belief that in the absence of governmental control, people would exist in harmony and peace. According to this view, government is an unnecessary evil that restricts human freedom and flourishing. A critical assumption of this view is that human nature is basically good and that it is society in its current form that corrupts us and leads to bad behavior. Advocates of this position sometimes suggest that society ought to be broken down into smaller, manageable communities, such as communes, in which people would live together and relate on a personal level, much like a large, happy family. The problem is, of course, that this position is based on an implausible and far too optimistic view of human nature. Evoking the model of the family is naive, because sometimes even family relationships need to be regulated by society's authorities and laws, such as when an inheritance is contested, when domestic violence is involved, or when a divorce requires decisions about child custody and property settlements. Naive anarchism fails in the face of the obvious need for society to restrict or regulate its members' actions for the benefit of all.

Another expression of anarchism, the one that is commonly associated with the term, takes the position that if government is unjustified, then it is an evil that should be overthrown—by violent means if necessary. In the past few decades in the United States, we have seen some of its own citizens blowing up government buildings as a form of protest against the government's authority. However, this version of anarchism cannot be taken seriously, for its advocates blindly follow their principles without regard for practical consequences. Usually, greater harm results from people acting on this position than from the evils they are seeking to eradicate. Furthermore, once the government is destroyed, what then? How will we manage to coexist? Like the naive anarchists, the militant anarchists have an unrealistic view of the possibilities of human life without laws.

The only version of anarchism worth considering, therefore, is theoretical anarchism. **Theoretical anarchism** agrees with the basic premise that government has no legitimate authority, but holds that even though the exercise of governmental power is theoretically unjustified, it may be necessary, as a matter of practical necessity, to tolerate its existence.

anarchism the position that there is no conceivable justification for government

theoretical anarchism the theory that government has no legitimate authority even though we may have to tolerate its existence as a matter of practical necessity

STOP AND THINK

Have you ever obeyed a law that you thought was not justified or right simply because the situation of having no laws at all would be worse than having some laws that are questionable? Have you ever followed a leader that you did not think deserved the position simply because following an undeserving leader is better than having no leader at all? If you have ever been in either of these situations, then your response is similar to that of the theoretical anarchist with respect to *all* laws, elected officials, and governments.

One of the most eloquent contemporary defenses of theoretical anarchism has been developed by Robert Paul Wolff. (Robert Paul Wolff is professor of Afro-American studies and philosophy at the University of Massachusetts, Amherst. He has written in the areas of Kantian philosophy, ethics, and social-political philosophy.) In this first passage, he sets out the difference between the power of the government (which is an obvious fact) and its alleged authority to exercise that power over its citizens (which is the point of contention).

- What does it mean for something to be a state, according to Wolff?
- How does Wolff distinguish the power of the state from its authority?

FROM ROBERT PAUL WOLFF

In Defense of Anarchism [1]

The Concept of Authority

Politics is the exercise of the power of the State, or the attempt to influence that exercise. Political philosophy is therefore, strictly speaking, the philosophy of the state. If we are to determine the content of political philosophy, and whether indeed it exists, we must begin with the concept of the state.

The state is a group of persons who have and exercise supreme authority within a given territory. Strictly, we should say that a state is a group of persons who have supreme authority within a given territory *or over a certain population*. A nomadic tribe may exhibit the authority structure of a state, so long as its subjects do not fall under the superior authority of a territorial state. The state may include all the persons who fall under its authority, as does the democratic state according to its theorists; it may also consist of a single individual to whom all the rest are subject. We may doubt whether the one-person state has ever actually existed, although Louis XIV evidently thought so when he announced, "L'etat c'est moi" [I am the State]. The distinctive characteristic of the state is supreme authority. . . .

Authority is the right to command, and correlatively, the right to be obeyed. It must be distinguished from power, which is the ability to compel compliance, either through the use or threat of force. When I turn over my wallet to a thief who is holding me at gunpoint, I do so because the fate with which he threatens me is worse than the loss of money which I am made to suffer. I grant that he has power over me, but I would hardly suppose that he has *authority*, that is, that he has a right to demand my money and that I have an obligation to give it to him. When the government presents me with a bill for taxes, on the other hand, I pay it (normally) even though I do not wish to and even if I think I can get away with not paying. It is after all, the duly constituted government, and hence it has a *right* to tax me. It has *authority* over me. Sometimes, of course, I cheat the government, but even so, I acknowledge its authority, for who would speak of "cheating" a thief?

To *claim* authority is to claim the right to be obeyed. To *have* authority is then—what? It may mean to have that right, or it may mean to have one's claim acknowledged and accepted by those at whom it is directed. The term "authority" is ambiguous, having both a descriptive and a normative sense. Even the descriptive sense refers to norms or obligations, of course, but it does so by *describing* what men believe they ought to do rather than by *asserting* that they ought to do it. . . .

What is meant by *supreme* authority? Some political philosophers have held that the true state has ultimate authority over all matters whatsoever that occur within its venue. Jean-Jacques Rousseau, for example, asserted that the social contract by which a just political community is formed "gives to the body absolute command over the members of which it is formed; and it is this power, when directed by the general will, that bears . . . the name of 'sovereignty.'" John Locke, on the other hand, held that the supreme authority of the just state extends only to those matters which it is proper for a state to control. The state is, to be sure, the highest authority, but its right to command is less than absolute. One of the questions which political philosophy must answer is whether there is any limit to the range of affairs over which a just state has authority.

In the next passage, Wolff bases his argument against government on the notion of *autonomy* (a concept he derived from Immanuel Kant even though Kant was not an anarchist). A condition for having autonomy is freedom of choice, but autonomy entails much more than that. Autonomy also involves *taking* responsibility for your actions in the sense of making your own choices, standing behind them, being accountable, and not delegating to anyone else the decisions that are yours to make. Autonomy also involves *being* responsible in making decisions, by basing them on good reasons and by reflecting on your motives and the consequences of your actions. According to Wolff, being an autonomous person is a moral obligation.

- In the following passage, how does Wolff reconcile the fact that we can learn about our moral obligations from others while still being autonomous?
- What is the difference between doing what someone tells you to do because that person tells you to do it, and doing what someone tells you to do because you can see that it is reasonable and conforms to your moral duty?

Concept of Autonomy

The fundamental assumption of moral philosophy is that men are responsible for their actions. From this assumption it follows necessarily, as Kant pointed out, that men are metaphysically free, which is to say that in some sense they are capable of choosing how they shall act. Being able to choose how he acts makes a man responsible, but merely choosing is not in itself to constitute *taking* responsibility for one's actions. Taking responsibility involves attempting to determine what one ought to do, and that, as philosophers since Aristotle have recognized, lays upon one the additional burdens of gaining knowledge, reflecting on motives, predicting outcomes, criticizing principles, and so forth.

The obligation to take responsibility for one's actions does not derive from man's freedom of will alone, for more is required in taking responsibility than freedom of choice. Only because man has the capacity to reason about his choices can he be said to stand under a continuing obligation to take responsibility for them. It is quite appropriate that moral philosophers should group together children and madmen as being not fully responsible for their actions, for as madmen are thought to lack freedom of choice, so children do not yet possess the power of reason in a developed form. It is even just that we should assign a greater degree of responsibility to children, for madmen, by virtue of their lack of free will, are completely without responsibility, while children, insofar as they possess reason in a partially developed form, can be held responsible to a corre-sponding degree.

Every man who possesses both free will and reason has an obligation to take responsibility for his actions, even though he may not be actively engaged in a continuing process of reflection, investigation, and deliberation about how he ought to act. A man will sometimes announce his willingness to take responsibility for the consequences of his actions, even though he has not deliberated about them, or does not intend to do so in the future. Such a declaration is, of course, an advance over the refusal to take responsibility; it at least acknowledges the existence of the obligation. But it does not relieve the man of the duty to engage in the reflective process which he has thus far shunned. . . .

The responsible man is not capricious or anarchic, for he does acknowledge himself bound by moral constraints. But he insists that he alone is the judge of those constraints. He may listen to the advice of others, but he makes it his own by determining for himself whether it is good advice. He may learn from others about his moral obligations, but only in the sense that a mathematician learns from other mathematicians—namely by hearing from them arguments whose validity he recognizes even though he did not think of them himself. He does not learn in the sense that one learns from an explorer, by accepting as true his account of things one cannot see for oneself.

Since the responsible man arrives at moral decisions which he expresses to himself in the form of imperatives, we may say that he gives laws to himself, or is self-legislating. In short, he is *autonomous*. As Kant argued, moral autonomy is a combination of freedom and responsibility; it is a submission to laws which one has made for oneself. The autonomous man, insofar as he is autonomous, is not subject to the will of another. He may do what another tells him, but not *because* he has been told to do it. He is therefore, in the political sense of the word, *free*.

In saying that we have a moral obligation to be autonomous and "self-legislating," Wolff sets up an inevitable conflict with any government that claims the authority to legislate our lives for us. Thus, he rejects the possibility of there being a *de jure* state, meaning a state that is legitimate and has the right to command our obedience.

- Although Wolff believes the state has no legitimate authority, why does he say that an autonomous person still may believe it necessary to comply with the laws of the government?
- How does Wolff's example of obeying the laws of a foreign country illustrate his attitude toward the laws of his own country?

The Conflict between Authority and Autonomy

The defining mark of the state is authority, the right to rule. The primary obligation of man is autonomy, the refusal to be ruled. It would seem, then, that there can be no resolution of the conflict between the autonomy of the individual and the putative authority of the state. Insofar as a man fulfills his obligation to make himself the author of his decisions, he will resist the state's claim to have authority over him. That is to say, he will deny that he has a duty to obey the laws of the state *simply because they are laws*. In that sense, it would seem that anarchism is the only political doctrine consistent with the virtue of autonomy.

Now, of course, an anarchist may grant the necessity of *complying* with the law under certain circumstances or for the time being. He may even doubt that there is any real prospect of eliminating the state as a human institution. But he will never view the commands of the state as *legitimate,* as having a binding moral force. In a sense, we might characterize the anarchist as a man without a country, for despite the ties which bind him to the land of his childhood, he stands in precisely the same moral relationship to "his" government as he does to the government of any other country in which he might happen to be staying for a time. When I take a vacation to Great Britain, I obey its laws, both because of prudential self-interest and because of the obvious moral considerations concerning the value of order, the general good consequences of preserving a system of property, and so forth. On my return to the United States, I have a sense of reentering *my* country, and if I think about the matter at all, I imagine myself to stand in a different and more intimate relation to American laws. They have been promulgated by *my* government, and I therefore have a special obligation to obey them. But the anarchist tells me that my feeling is purely sentimental and has no objective moral basis. All authority is equally illegitimate, although of course not therefore equally worthy or unworthy of support, and my obedience to American laws, if I am to be morally autonomous, must proceed from the same considerations which determine me abroad.

The dilemma which we have posed can be succinctly expressed in terms of the concept of a *de jure* state. If all men have a continuing obligation to achieve the highest degree of autonomy possible, then there would appear to be no state whose subjects have a moral obligation to obey its commands. Hence, the concept of a *de jure* legitimate state would appear to be vacuous, and philosophical anarchism would seem to be the only reasonable political belief for an enlightened man.

Copyright 1970 by Robert Paul Wolff. Reproduced with permission of the University of California Press.

STOP AND THINK

What do you think of Wolff's argument? Do you think he has effectively made the case for what we have called theoretical anarchism? Why?

LOOKING THROUGH THE ANARCHIST'S LENS

1. If you broke a legal contract with an anarchist, saying that the laws governing contracts have no legitimate authority over you, how might the anarchist respond? Would it be inconsistent for the anarchist to take you to court? In other words, could the anarchist use the law to his or her benefit without violating anarchist principles?

2. History is full of shameful events in which people blindly followed the laws of a corrupt government. In these cases, if the majority of people had been anarchists, would the consequences have been different?

3. Would it be inconsistent for an anarchist to vote in either local, state, or national elections? On the one hand, the anarchist would be following his or her legitimate self-interest in supporting political leaders who will do the best job. On the other hand, by voting in elections, the anarchist is tacitly approving of the system of governmental authority. What should the anarchist do?

EXAMINING THE STRENGTHS AND WEAKNESSES OF ANARCHISM

Positive Evaluation

1. Has the anarchist made a legitimate point in stressing the importance of taking responsibility for our own lives and refusing to blindly follow an authority?

2. What would the anarchist say about the slogan of the radical patriot, "My country, right or wrong"? Do you think the anarchist's response is better than that of unquestioning patriotism?

Negative Evaluation

1. Even though Wolff is an anarchist, he says he obeys the laws on the basis of "the obvious moral considerations concerning the value of order" and "the general good consequences of preserving a system of property." In making these statements, hasn't Wolff provided reasons why government should exist and why, under the best circumstances, it can legitimately exercise authority? Hasn't he undermined his argument for anarchism?

2. Contrary to Wolff, can't we believe in the legitimacy of our government and take his argument to be merely pointing out that some extreme circumstances offer morally legitimate grounds for a revolution or civil disobedience?

3. Unless he or she lives on a desert island that is not part of any national territory, the anarchist benefits from the security and convenience of living in a state in which the government provides or supports national defense, police, legal rights, highways, educational systems, medical care, and so forth. Is it inconsistent for the anarchist to enjoy these government programs while claiming that the government has no right to collect taxes or to provide these services?

SURVEYING THE CASE FOR SOCIAL CONTRACT THEORY

social contract theory the theory that the justification of a government and its exercise of power is based on an explicit or implicit agreement made between the individuals who live under that government or between the citizens and the government

In opposition to anarchism and all other theories of government, the **social contract theory** claims that the justification of a government and its exercise of power is based on an explicit or implicit agreement made between the individuals who live under that government or between the citizens and the government. In other words, the government has the authority to make laws, enforce penalties for violating those laws, and exercise control over the lives of its citizens only because each citizen has given the government that authority.

The social contract theory answers the question of why the government has the right to impose its laws upon its citizens: the citizens have formed a contract to create the government and have given it the right to exercise power over their lives for their mutual benefit. But this theory raises a problem. Because neither you nor I have had anything to do with the creation of our government, what does this theory have to say about our relationship to our government? The founders of the United States government, such as Thomas Jefferson, literally brought the government into existence, delegated powers to it in the Constitution, and signed their names to the contract. However, you and I have never entered into such an explicit agreement with the government. In response to this problem, the social contract theorist would maintain that by living in this country and being the recipients of its benefits, we have implicitly agreed to be a part of this governmental system.

The government has provided us with education, with roads, with protection by the military and the police, with laws that protect our lives, property, and rights. Hence, it is claimed, by accepting the benefits of the government, we have tacitly agreed to the original contract by which it was formed. (We will see in section 6.4 that Socrates uses this point in his argument against civil disobedience.)

If you were born in the United States, you are a citizen by virtue of your birth. However, when you become an adult, you can decide for yourself whether you want to be a party to the social contract. You are, of course, always free to leave. If you emigrate to another country, however, you must go through the process of changing your citizenship. In effect, you sign a new contract with a new government.

We can imagine a government that was forced on the people by a foreign power (as the outcome of a war, for example). We can furthermore imagine that this government, nevertheless, serves its people well. But if the people did not somehow bring this government into being, then no matter how moral the government is, it has no legitimacy according to the social contract theory. Notice that the social contract theory does not specify what form the government must take. It addresses only the issue of how the government gets its authority. The people could choose to have a monarchy, a democracy, a socialistic government, or whatever system they wanted to create. The British philosopher Thomas Hobbes (1588-1679), an early advocate of the social contract theory, thought that when the people create a government, they should give it absolute power so that it can govern effectively. Many social contract theorists, however, believe that the government must provide for regular elections to guarantee that it is ruling with the citizens' consent. The Universal Declaration of Human Rights adopted by the General Assembly of the United Nations expresses this point when it says that "the will of the people shall be expressed in periodic and genuine elections which shall be by universal and equal suffrage and shall be held by secret vote or by equivalent free voting procedures."

THOUGHT EXPERIMENT: *Forming Your Own Social Contract*

Imagine that you and a group of like-minded people have gathered together to form a new nation. What sort of social contract would you form? Using the U.S. Constitution as a model (or the constitution of some other nation, historical or contemporary), what changes would you make to it? What would the government be prohibited from doing? What would it be required to do? What sorts of freedoms would you have that you do not have under current laws? What laws would you make that we currently do not have? How extensive (or how minimal) would the new government's involvement be in the areas of education, public health, safety standards, standard of living, the arts, religion, morals, and the regulation of business? Do you think your new government would be better? Why?

John Locke's Social Contract Theory

We encountered the English philosopher John Locke in section 2.3, where we discussed his empiricist theory of knowledge. (A short account of his life can be found there.) Besides being interested in the theory of knowledge, Locke also wrote extensively on political philosophy. Locke's political philosophy consisted of many interwoven themes. First, Locke was a natural law theorist (natural law theory is discussed in section 6.2), which means, briefly, that he believed that the conduct of individuals and society was governed by a

right a justified claim to something, usually implying that other people have certain duties with respect to the possessor of the right

universal, objective, moral law, not a law based on human conventions. Locke believed that this moral law was instituted by God. Furthermore, he argued that this natural law guaranteed us basic, natural, inherent rights by virtue of the fact that we are human. A **right** is a justified claim to something, usually implying that other people have certain duties with respect to the possessor of the right. For example, if you have the right to free speech, then others (including the government) have an obligation not to interfere with your ability to express your opinions (as long as your doing so does not violate someone else's rights).

Some rights can be granted by law. For example, a 16-year-old may have the right to drive a car. However, rights granted by law can be taken away (the minimum driving age can be changed to 18). Locke insisted, however, that some rights are natural, human rights that cannot be taken away by the government. These rights are sometimes said to be *indefeasible* (cannot be made void) or *inalienable* (cannot be taken away). According to Locke, we possess these rights in the state of nature, before government came on the scene. Among these natural, moral rights are the preservation of our life, health, liberty, and possessions. In contrast, Thomas Hobbes, Locke's predecessor, said that in the state of nature we have the right to anything we want, *but only as long as we have the physical power to obtain what we want.* In other words, we have no moral claims over other people. For that reason, Hobbes said that without government, "nothing can be unjust." When we form a government, according to Hobbes, we renounce many of our rights and liberties. However, Locke believed that both prior to government and after we form a government, we possess God-given inherent rights.

Locke's view of rights has major implications for political theory. If we have natural, indefeasible, inalienable rights, then the government can never justifiably violate these rights. If it does so, then it is no longer a legitimate government. Locke's social contract theory has to be understood with his theory of natural rights as its background. We create the government with the social contract, but we do not surrender our rights to the government, nor does it create our rights. Instead, we bring the government into being in order to protect our natural rights.

In the following reading, Locke starts out as Hobbes did by describing the hypothetical "state of nature" in which people exist prior to forming a government. However, the philosophers disagreed concerning what the state of nature would be like. Hobbes believed that, without the iron will of an absolute government, such a condition would be "a war of all against all," in which human life is "solitary, poor, nasty, brutish, and short." However, Locke gives us a somewhat different picture of this situation.

- Can you detect the differences in Locke's vision of what the state of nature would be like in contrast to Hobbes's pessimistic assessment of human nature?
- Without any civil laws, what sort of law governs rational people in nature, according to Locke?

FROM JOHN LOCKE

An Essay Concerning the True Original, Extent and End of Civil Government [2]

The State of Nature

6. The state of Nature has a law of Nature to govern it, which obliges every one, and reason, which is that law, teaches all mankind who will but consult it, that being all equal and independent, no one ought to harm another in his life, health, liberty or possessions;

for men being all the workmanship of one omnipotent and infinitely wise Maker; all the servants of one sovereign Master, sent into the world by His order and about His business; they are His property, whose workmanship they are made to last during His, not one another's pleasure. And, being furnished with like faculties, sharing all in one community of Nature, there cannot be supposed any such subordination among us that may authorize us to destroy one another, as if we were made for one another's uses, as the inferior ranks of creatures are for ours. Everyone as he is bound to preserve himself, and not to quit his station willfully, so by the like reason, when his own preservation comes not in competition, ought he as much as he can to preserve the rest of mankind, and not unless it be to do justice on an offender, take away or impair the life, or what tends to the preservation of the life, the liberty, health, limb, or goods of another. . . .

19. And here we have the plain difference between the state of nature and the state of war, which however some men have confounded, are as far distant as a state of peace, good-will, mutual assistance and preservation, and a state of enmity, malice, violence and mutual destruction, are one from another.

Unlike Hobbes, Locke had an optimistic view of human nature and believed that most people were basically reasonable. Hence, rather than life being a vicious state of war, Locke thought that life in nature would be one of peace, goodwill, and mutual assistance. There would be a few troublemakers, of course, but the rest could assist one another to address any violations of each other's natural rights. Furthermore, Hobbes and many other political thinkers thought that there could not be any property without a government to define property rights. However, Locke argued that while natural resources (air, water, soil, and plants) belong to everybody, if you mix your labor with nature (gathering fruits, tilling the soil, planting seeds), then that part of nature becomes your rightful property and no government is necessary to decide this arrangement.

- In what way does the following passage make clear that Locke believes in the social contract theory of government?

The Origins of Political Society

95. Men being, as has been said, by nature all free, equal, and independent, no one can be put out of this estate and subjected to the political power of another without his own consent, which is done by agreeing with other men, to join and unite into a community for their comfortable, safe, and peaceable living, one amongst another, in a secure enjoyment of their properties, and a greater security against any that are not of it. This any number of men may do, because it injures not the freedom of the rest; they are left, as they were, in the liberty of the state of Nature. When any number of men have so consented to make one community or government, they are thereby presently incorporated, and make one body politic, wherein the majority have a right to act and conclude the rest.

96. For, when any number of men have, by the consent of every individual, made a community, they have thereby made that community one body, with a power to act as one body, which is only by the will and determination of the majority. . . .

97. And thus every man, by consenting with others to make one body politic under one government, puts himself under an obligation to every one of that society to submit to the determination of the majority, and to be concluded by it; or else this original compact, whereby he with others incorporates into one society, would signify nothing, and be no compact if he be left free and under no other ties than he was in before in the state of

Nature. For what appearance would there be of any compact? What new engagement if he were no farther tied by any decrees of the society than he himself thought fit and did actually consent to? This would be still as great a liberty as he himself had before his compact, or any one else in the state of Nature, who may submit himself and consent to any acts of it if he thinks fit. . . .

99. Whosoever, therefore, out of a state of Nature unite into a community, must be understood to give up all the power necessary to the ends for which they unite into society to the majority of the community, unless they expressly agreed in any number greater than the majority. And this is done by barely agreeing to unite into one political society, which is all the compact that is, or needs be, between the individuals that enter into or make up a commonwealth. And thus, that which begins and actually constitutes any political society is nothing but the consent of any number of freemen capable of majority, to unite and incorporate into such a society. And this is that, and that only, which did or could give beginning to any lawful government in the world.

If, as Locke claims, the state of nature is one of complete freedom, governed by reason, goodwill, and mutual assistance, why bother with government at all? Locke provides three reasons why people would want to contract together to form a government. People need: (1) an established and unbiased interpretation of the natural moral law embedded in nature, (2) an impartial judge to apply the established law to settle disputes and conflicts of interest, and (3) a power to support the rights of those who are victims of injustice and to enforce the law.

- Whereas Hobbes thought people would set up an absolute government as an act of desperation, what does Locke say about the motivation for government in the following passage?

The Motivation for Government

127. Thus mankind, notwithstanding all the privileges of the state of Nature, being but in an ill condition while they remain in it are quickly driven into society. Hence it comes to pass, that we seldom find any number of men live any time together in this state. The inconveniences that they are therein exposed to by the irregular and uncertain exercise of the power every man has of punishing the transgressions of others, make them take sanctuary under the established laws of government, and therein seek the preservation of their property. It is this that makes them so willingly give up every one his single

SPOTLIGHT
on

The Concept of the Separation of Powers

Notice that Locke suggests that in the government there should be a separation of powers (the legislative and executive branch). Later in the essay he adds a third branch, the federative power, which is similar to our secretary of state. Taking his lesson from the problems of the king having total, absolute power, Locke came up with the brilliant idea of dividing the government into parts, each of which could limit the power of the other branches. Influenced by Locke, Montesquieu (1689–1755) suggested that the third branch should be the judicial one. When the founders of the American republic divided the government into three branches, they were drawing on the ideas of both Locke and Montesquieu.

power of punishing to be exercised by such alone as shall be appointed to it amongst them, and by such rules as the community, or those authorised by them to that purpose, shall agree on. And in this we have the original right and rise of both the legislative and executive power as well as of the governments and societies themselves.

For Locke, life without government is an "ill condition" and full of "inconveniences." If government is a convenience, not a necessity, then we can dictate the terms of the bargain. Instead of *surrendering* our rights and power to the government as Hobbes proposed, we *delegate* it for the mutual preservation of our lives, property, and liberties. The government is our creation; therefore, it is our servant, not an absolute power over us. As Locke puts it, the actions of the government are "to be directed to no other end but the peace, safety, and public good of the people."[3] In this theory are the foundations of what has come to be called "classical liberalism," the notion that the government should have only as much power as is necessary to do for us what we cannot (or cannot conveniently and efficiently) do for ourselves.

John Locke was one of the most influential philosophers of his time. His concepts of the state of nature, the natural moral law, natural rights, the social contract, and the right of revolution were the intellectual currency of 18th-century political thought. When writing the American Declaration of Independence, Thomas Jefferson said that his ideas were not new but followed the thought of writers such as Locke. When the colonists shouted, "No taxation without representation!" they were virtually quoting Locke. Through Montesquieu and others, Locke also influenced French thought. Locke might not have sanctioned the American and French revolutions (because he was too much of a moderate), but it is certain that these movements grew from seeds he had planted. Notice that for Locke, the social contract theory has implicit within it a right of revolution. If the government has been imposed on people without their consent, or if it is not fulfilling its contract (by violating people's rights, for example), then the government is no longer legitimate, citizens no longer have any obligations to the government, and a revolution is morally and politically justified.

- How many echos from John Locke's political philosophy can you find in the opening lines of the American Declaration of Independence?

FROM THE DECLARATION OF INDEPENDENCE (JULY 4, 1776)

When in the Course of human events, it becomes necessary for one people to dissolve the political bands which have connected them with another, and to assume among the Powers of the earth, the separate and equal station to which the Laws of Nature and of Nature's God entitle them, a decent respect to the opinions of mankind requires that they should declare the causes which impel them to the separation.

We hold these truths to be self-evident, that all men are created equal, that they are endowed by their Creator with certain unalienable Rights, that among these are Life, Liberty, and the pursuit of Happiness. That to secure these rights, Governments are instituted among Men, deriving their just powers from the consent of the governed. That whenever any Form of Government becomes destructive of these ends, it is the Right of the People to alter or to abolish it, and to institute new Government, laying its foundation on such principles and organizing its powers in such form, as to them shall seem most likely to effect their Safety and Happiness.

LOOKING THROUGH THE LENS OF THE SOCIAL CONTRACT THEORY

1. Think about your own country and its constitution. If you were a social contract theorist, what events would have to occur in your nation to claim that the social contract had been broken? In other words, under what conditions would your government no longer be legitimate and would a political revolution be justified?

2. If all the governments throughout history had agreed with the principles of the social contract theory, how would history have been different?

EXAMINING THE STRENGTHS AND WEAKNESSES OF THE SOCIAL CONTRACT THEORY

Positive Evaluation

1. Doesn't this theory, by emphasizing that a government is legitimate if it rules with the consent of the governed, capture most people's intuitions about what makes a government good? Isn't it the case that the really bad governments in history and in our contemporary world are governments that have violated this principle?

2. The social contract theory says that the power of the government has been delegated to it in order to put an end to the chaos and injustice we would suffer if it were not there. Hence, isn't it a strength of this theory that it does not dictate a certain form of government but does provide a criterion for defining the scope and limits of the government? Don't we want a government that has no more and no less power than we decide it should have?

3. The social contract theory emphasizes that the government derives its power from its citizens, that our rights cannot be violated by the government, and that the government is our servant (rather than the other way around). Hence, doesn't this theory go a long way in preserving the rights of the citizens against the coercive power of the government?

Negative Evaluation

1. The social contract theory is based on the story of a hypothetical "state of nature" in which people lived without government and then formed a "social contract" to invent a government. However, even the defenders of the theory acknowledge that they cannot point to an actual historical situation in which such a formation occurred. Instead, all we find in history are situations in which one form of government arose from a previous form of government. If the main thrust of the social contract theory is based on a hypothetical, fictional thought experiment, does this basis undermine the value of the theory as a justification of actual governments?

2. Even if all governments were actually formed in the way that this theory suggests, would this fact lend any further plausibility to the theory? Do the origins of a government matter in deciding whether it is legitimate today? Couldn't a government have been imposed on its people hundreds of years ago in an illegitimate way, and couldn't its present-day citizens still consider it a legitimate government in its present form?

3. Historically, the United States was formed by a contract among white males. But native Americans, African slaves, and women played no role in this process. Furthermore, people in these groups were denied any participation in the political process for most of

this nation's history. According to the social contract theory, wouldn't this information suggest that for the people in these groups the government is not legitimate? Even if everyone has his or her political rights protected today, can we really say that the poor and the powerless have much influence over who gets elected? Furthermore, even if the poor and the powerless are beneficiaries of the government's services, doesn't their lack of political power cast doubts on the degree to which the government rules with the "consent of the governed"? Does this theory idealize how political power really comes about?

6.2 THE QUESTION OF JUSTICE

LEADING QUESTIONS: *The Nature of Justice*

1. *Questions from Plato:* If you needed a heart operation, would you want the decisions in the operating room to be made by an accomplished heart surgeon or by a democratic vote of your friends? Should teaching positions be open to anyone who wants them or only to those who are qualified to teach the subject matter? If you were the coach of a professional basketball team, would you attempt to choose the very best players or would you give everyone an equal chance? In all areas of society, we give people privileges, power, and opportunities based on their merit or qualifications and not on the basis of democratic equality. Likewise, when the issue is who should run our society, shouldn't the decision be based on merit and not democracy?

2. *Questions from Thomas Aquinas:* If justice is simply what the laws of a particular society declare it to be, then could we ever say that those laws were unjust? Doesn't there have to be some standard of justice that transcends human decisions and the will of the majority?

3. *Questions from John Stuart Mill:* Does it make sense to talk abstractly of the justice of a society or its laws apart from their consequences? Isn't a society just if it fulfills people's needs and produces the greatest amount of satisfaction that is possible? Do we need any concept of justice beyond that?

4. *Questions from John Rawls:* Isn't justice basically fairness? And aren't conditions fair when they are what we would choose if we were completely rational and objective and were freed from our personal biases?

These leading questions reflect the theories of justice of the four thinkers we examine in this section. When we think of justice, we typically think of the criminal justice system in which wrongdoers are tried, convicted, and punished for their crimes. Thus, when a criminal is found guilty and given an appropriate prison sentence, we say that justice has been done. Likewise, when an innocent person is declared not guilty, we consider this decision to be just. On the other hand, if a criminal is released on a technicality, we feel as though the system of justice has failed us. All these examples involve that form of justice known as *retributive justice,* or the proper allotment of punishment proportionate to the severity of a crime.

But retributive justice is only a small part of a much larger issue. Society does not merely distribute punishment. Society is organized to also distribute or regulate the attainment of positive benefits such as wealth, goods, privilege, and power. Retributive justice is concerned with giving a criminal the punishment that he or she is due. But society must also decide how people in general are to receive what they are due in terms of the burdens necessary to make society work (such as taxes) and in terms of benefits to be received (such as income, medical care, education, and political power). How should resources be distributed, given the fact that there is not enough for everyone to receive all that they would like or need? Should everyone receive an equal amount? Should those who have the most needs receive the most? Should those who make the greatest contribution to society receive the greatest share? All these issues fall under the heading of *distributive justice,* or the proper distribution of benefits and burdens among its citizens.

SURVEYING THE CASE FOR JUSTICE AS MERIT

Most accounts of justice assume that whatever it is, it involves giving everybody what they are due. But how do we determine what people are due? One answer is that the determination should be by merit. The foremost defender of this position is Plato. Plato was a thoroughly systematic philosopher, so his political theory has to be put in the context of his theory of knowledge and reality, which we encountered in sections 1.2, "Plato's Allegory of the Cave," and 2.2, "Rationalism." Plato believed that all of life (including the life of society) had to be based on a correct assessment of what reality is like. Our understanding of reality is like a map that guides us in every decision we make. If the map is wrong, we will never be able to achieve our goals. Hence, those people who deserve the most political power are those who are best able to discern the nature of reality. But ultimate reality, according to Plato, can be known only through reason. Because people are not equal in their rational capacities, they should not be equal in their ability to exercise political power. Plato's ideal society, in which political power is proportionate to merit, is known as a **meritocracy.**

meritocracy A society in which political power is proportionate to merit

From these brief remarks, it should be clear that Plato was not a great fan of democracy. In fact, he was one of history's harshest critics of this political philosophy. By the time Plato was born, the new invention of Athenian democracy had replaced the age-old system of monarchy. The Athenians were proud of their system of government in which all laws, trials, and other public decisions were voted on by an assembly of the adult male citizens. No doubt, Plato's negative assessment of democracy was influenced by the fact that it was by a popular vote of the Athenian citizens that his teacher, Socrates, was condemned to death. This event, which Plato considered to be an outrageous miscarriage of justice, led him to spend the rest of his life searching for the blueprint of the just society. For Plato, democracy was equivalent to mob rule. He described democracy as a thousand-headed beast in which each head is pulling in its own direction, seeking to satisfy its personal desires.

Plato's alternative is based on his theory that "the state is the individual written large." To express this concept in contemporary terms, Plato believed that psychology and political science follow the same principles. Those factors that constitute either a healthy or pathological individual will be the same factors that constitute a healthy or pathological society. In Plato's psychological theory, each individual is made up of three parts: the appetites (or desires), the spirited part (which includes the emotions), and reason. The healthy individual is one in whom these three parts play their appropriate role and work together in harmony. However, this concordance occurs only when the desires and the spirited part are governed by reason.

Similarly, Plato thought that there were three kinds of people in society: (1) those who are ruled by their appetites, (2) those who are ruled by their passions and motivated by ambition, loyalty, honor, and courage, and (3) those who are fully governed by reason. The first group are called the *producers.* Because their appetitive nature inclines them toward material acquisition and physical comfort, they are best suited to care for the production of goods and services in society. This group includes not only the laborers but also the merchants, physicians, businesspeople, and bankers. The second group are the *auxiliaries,* those whose courage and passion for ambition and honor makes them suited to be the protectors of society. This group corresponds to our police and military as well as to other federal agents and administrators who support the policies of the rulers. The final group are the *guardians,* whose intelligence qualifies them to establish the laws and policies of the state.

Plato believed that, in the same way that harmony is realized in a healthy individual, justice is realized in a society when each group plays its appropriate role and when the first two classes are ruled by the intellectual elite. Ironically, although the producers have the least political power, they are afforded the most freedom and economic gain. They can marry whom they wish, can own property, and can acquire personal wealth and luxuries as long as society does not become unbalanced with too much wealth and too much poverty. The rulers, on the other hand, cannot own property, for Plato wanted to guarantee that they would be motivated sheerly by the desire to serve society and not by the prospect of personal gain. However, they alone have political power and the ability to make political decisions and set the direction that society will take. The other two classes merely do their jobs and follow the direction of the rulers.

In the following passage, Plato presents his theory of justice through the voice of Socrates. Socrates is leading the discussion.

FROM PLATO

Republic[4]

Well then, tell me, I said, whether I am right or not: You remember the original principle which we were always laying down at the foundation of the State, that one man should practise one thing only, the thing to which his nature was best adapted—now justice is this principle or a part of it.

Yes, we often said that one man should do one thing only.

Further, we affirmed that justice was doing one's own business, and not being a busybody; we said so again and again, and many others have said the same to us.

Yes, we said so.

Then to do one's own business in a certain way may be assumed to be justice. Can you tell me whence I derive this inference?

I cannot, but I should like to be told.

Because I think that this is the only virtue which remains in the State when the other virtues of temperance and courage and wisdom are abstracted; and, that this is the ultimate cause and condition of the existence of all of them, and while remaining in them is also their preservative; and we were saying that if the three were discovered by us, justice would be the fourth or remaining one.

That follows of necessity.

If we are asked to determine which of these four qualities by its presence contributes most to the excellence of the State, whether the agreement of rulers and subjects, or the preservation in the soldiers of the opinion which the law ordains about the true nature of dangers, or wisdom and watchfulness in the rulers, or whether this other which I am mentioning, and which is found in children and women, slave and freeman, artisan, ruler, subject,—the quality, I mean, of every one doing his own work, and not being a busybody, would claim the palm—the question is not so easily answered.

Certainly, he replied, there would be a difficulty in saying which.

Then the power of each individual in the State to do his own work appears to compete with the other political virtues, wisdom, temperance, courage.

Yes, he said.

And the virtue which enters into this competition is justice?

Exactly.

Let us look at the question from another point of view: Are not the rulers in a State those to whom you would entrust the office of determining suits at law?

Certainly.

And are suits decided on any other ground but that a man may neither take what is another's, nor be deprived of what is his own?

Yes; that is their principle.

Which is a just principle?

Yes.

Then on this view also justice will be admitted to be the having and doing what is a man's own, and belongs to him?

Very true.

Think, now, and say whether you agree with me or not. Suppose a carpenter to be doing the business of a cobbler, or a cobbler of a carpenter; and suppose them to exchange their implements or their duties, or the same person to be doing the work of both, or whatever be the change; do you think that any great harm would result to the State?

Not much.

But when the cobbler or any other man whom nature designed to be a trader, having his heart lifted up by wealth or strength or the number of his followers, or any like advantage, attempts to force his way into the class of warriors, or a warrior into that of legislators and guardians, for which he is unfitted, and either to take the implements or the duties of the other; or when one man is trader, legislator, and warrior all in one, then I think you will agree with me in saying that this interchange and this meddling of one with another is the ruin of the State.

Most true.

Seeing then, I said, that there are three distinct classes, any meddling of one with another, or the change of one into another, is the greatest harm to the State, and may be most justly termed evil-doing?

Precisely.

And the greatest degree of evil-doing to one's own city would be termed by you injustice?

Certainly.

This then is injustice; and on the other hand when the trader, the auxiliary, and the guardian each do their own business, that is justice, and will make the city just.

I agree with you.

- Do you agree with Plato that people are naturally suited to play different roles in society?
- What do you think of his argument that political power should be given to the intellectual elite and not distributed equally?

In Plato's version of a meritocracy, only those people who had wisdom and exceptional rational capacities were suited to be leaders. Accordingly, he said in the *Republic* that society would not be well-ordered and just unless "philosophers become kings or kings become philosophers." Plato thought that a child of a ruler would usually have the capacity to grow up to be a ruler, but he realized that this succession would not always be true. In some instances the child of a ruler might be best suited to be a merchant, whereas the child of a carpenter might have the aptitude to be a ruler. To settle this problem, Plato proposed that, throughout their early life, children be tested to determine what their abilities were and how they could best serve society. As a result of this process, all children would be given the appropriate education to best develop their talents and to prepare them to best employ their abilities in serving society.

In setting out his vision of the ideal society, Plato said that the health of the state needed to be as carefully regulated as the health of the body and thus could be left neither to happenstance nor to popular opinion. Plato therefore held a very strong view of the amount of control the government should have over its citizen's lives. For example, he believed in scientific mating to ensure that the very best specimens of humanity were produced. He also believed in arranged marriages and assigned the raising of children to the community. Furthermore, just as our society controls hallucinogenic drugs, quack medicines, and other harmful substances to protect people's bodies, so Plato believed in government censorship of the arts and all forms of communication so that its citizens' minds should be kept free of harmful ideas.

LOOKING THROUGH PLATO'S LENS

1. Think about our present-day political campaigns in which candidates are packaged and marketed in the same way that a particular brand of car is promoted to the public. What would Plato have to say about our approach to the political process?

2. Plato believed that children at an early age should be tested to discover their abilities and determine what role they should play in society. How do we use such testing in our current educational system? Are there any similarities between our system and Plato's? What are the advantages and disadvantages of Plato's proposal?

3. In Plato's society, the producers had the most freedom and personal possessions, but the least power. On the other hand, his auxiliaries and guardians had the most power, but lived disciplined, frugal lives. If you could choose (even though in Plato's society you couldn't choose for yourself), which role would you prefer to be placed into?

EXAMINING THE STRENGTHS AND WEAKNESSES OF PLATO'S THEORY OF JUSTICE

Positive Evaluation

1. Although Plato's political philosophy offends our democratic sensibilities, doesn't it also have some advantages? In our society, the family you are born into, including its influence, wealth, and social standing, plays a large role in determining the opportunities you have in life. In what ways is this determination good, and in what ways is it bad? How does Plato's system avoid some of the problems of our system?

2. By structuring his society so that wealth and political power would be separated, Plato guaranteed that the rulers would be motivated solely by their desire to serve. Isn't this structure a good idea?

3. Think back to the first leading question. Don't we base a person's opportunities in medicine, education, business, sports, and other careers solely on his or her merit and not on democratic equality? Does Plato have a point in saying that the same principle should apply to our political rulers?

Negative Evaluation

1. Although Plato tried to design the perfect society based on rational principles, critics argued that it is based on a number of questionable assumptions. For example, in determining the career track that children will be channeled into, Plato assumes that he will be able to accurately discern their abilities through testing. But is this assumption always true? Aren't some people late bloomers? For example, the great physicist Albert Einstein performed terribly in mathematics as a child. In Plato's society he might have ended up a carpenter instead of a great scientist. Furthermore, Plato assumes that those people with the best intellects will also be the wisest. But is intellectual ability necessarily the same as wisdom and leadership skills?

2. Critics charge that Plato's society is a thinly veiled tyranny in which the rulers have absolute control over the society, including the censorship of the arts and the flow of information. Wouldn't this control mean that Plato's society would never be able to change and would not accommodate new ideas that might lead it to improve?

3. Even if we accept Plato's belief that his society would be perfectly rational and efficient, are these qualities all that make up a good society? Does it make sense to say that a society is perfectly just and good if people have no autonomy and no freedom to make important decisions about their own lives? Hasn't Plato assumed that having a well-ordered society is the only element in human flourishing?

SURVEYING THE CASE FOR JUSTICE AS CONFORMITY TO THE NATURAL LAW

The advocates of the natural law theory have a number of points in common with Plato. They agree with him that justice has to do with the rational and moral ordering of society. However, they would say that the sort of ordered society he had in mind is, in many ways, not natural and would inhibit human flourishing.

The natural law theory is a conception of law and justice that has deep roots in the Western tradition and continues to inform our ways of thinking even today. It was given its initial impetus by Aristotle, found its way into the thought of the Greek Stoics around 300 B.C., helped shape the Roman conception of law, and was further developed by the medieval philosophers. The **natural law theory** claims that there is an objective moral law that transcends human conventions and decisions, governs individuals and the conduct of society, and can be known through reason and experience on the basis of the natural order of the world and the built-in tendencies of human nature.

The natural law theory applied to justice says that any civil law that human beings legislate is just (or properly called a law) only if it is in conformity to the natural law. On the other hand, if a law of a particular society violates the natural law, then it is unjust and not really a law at all. Obviously, when we are referring to the natural law in the context of ethics and political philosophy, we are not talking about scientific, physical laws (such as the law of gravity). Nevertheless, the two concepts are similar, because the natural law theorist believes that there is an objective moral order in reality that is independent of us, just as there is a physical order in nature.

Although some of the features of the natural law theory can be found in Socrates, Plato, and even some of the earlier Greeks, its origins are primarily in the thought of Plato's student Aristotle (384–322 B.C.). (See the discussion of Aristotle's virtue ethics in section 5.5.) Aristotle did not believe that the state is a human invention; in this way his theory contrasted with the social contract theory discussed in section 6.1. Aristotle claimed that

natural law theory the theory that there is an objective moral law that transcends human conventions and decisions, governs individuals and the conduct of society, and can be known through reason and experience on the basis of the natural order of the world and the built-in tendencies of human nature human beings are political animals whose very nature dictates that they are made to live in society. In this way, we are like other social creatures, such as ants or wolves, who live in colonies or packs and who have leaders and an implicit social structure. However, we are also different in that we have speech, reason, and the ability to discern good and evil. Hence, unlike the social structure of other animals, our social life is not governed by instinct but by our ability to make rational and moral decisions.

According to the natural law theorist, all morally aware people have the potential to recognize these laws, although as little children this potential needs to be developed through moral training. The moral principles that make up the natural law are not capable of being proven because they are so basic. As Immanuel Kant said (see section 5.4), to deny the moral law is to fall into a contradiction. Obviously, some people, through their behavior or in their theories, deny the existence of the natural law. However, the natural law theorist would say that this denial does not prove that the natural law is not real any more than the fact that color-blind people cannot distinguish blue from green or that tone-deaf people are not sensitive to music proves that colors or melodies are not real.

Because this moral law is called "natural," the point is being made that we can discover the basic principles of morality by using our natural human faculties. Although many natural law theorists were religious and believed that the natural law was ultimately rooted in God and the way we were created, it is not necessary to be a theist to be a natural law theorist. From Aristotle on, natural law theorists have believed that whether we are religious or not, we can discover the natural law by reasoning about experience and human nature.

The natural law theorist does not claim that we always have a complete and infallible knowledge of this natural law any more than we are always correct in discerning the objective physical laws. For example, the framers of the U.S. Constitution correctly realized that all persons are created equal and have basic rights at the same time that they held slaves. It took a century for our society to realize that the institution of slavery violated the natural law. It took another century to begin to change those laws in our society that discriminated against minorities and women. We are still in the process of trying to bring our society's practices and civil laws in conformity with the moral law.

Critics sometimes object that the natural law theory is an attempt to "legislate morality." But the natural law theorist would respond that legislating morality is precisely what a large portion of our current laws do. For example, stealing is wrong and so we make it illegal. But the converse is not true; that is, the reason that stealing is wrong is not that it is illegal. Furthermore, as the medieval natural law theorist Thomas Aquinas said, not every matter of morality should be legislated, because then, since none of us is perfectly moral, we would all deserve to be in jail. For example, it is immoral to ridicule someone because of his or her disability, even if we do it without that person knowing it. Under most circumstances, that sort of crude, tasteless, and moral insensitivity is not illegal, even though it is immoral. However, those issues of morality that are so fundamental that their violation would degrade human life, impair human flourishing, and destroy society are the features of the natural law that find their way into the civil law.

Unlike the laws against actions such as murder and stealing, some laws are only indirectly derived from the natural law. Americans drive on the right side of the street, and the British drive on the left side of the street. Obviously, neither practice is more in conformity with the natural law than the other. However, our traffic laws and other such laws are derived from the natural law that human life should be preserved.

We first encountered Thomas Aquinas (1225–1274) when we discussed his proofs for God in section 4.1. Here, we examine his argument that a government and its laws are just if they conform to the natural law.

Summa Theologica[5]

As Augustine says, *that which is not just seems to be no law at all.* Hence the force of a law depends on the extent of its justice. Now in human affairs a thing is said to be just from being right, according to the rule of reason. But the first rule of reason is the law of nature, as is clear from what has been stated above. Consequently, every human law has just so much of the nature of law as it is derived from the law of nature. But if in any point it departs from the law of nature, it is no longer a law but a perversion of law. . . .

Laws framed by man are either just or unjust. If they be just, they have the power of binding in conscience from the eternal law whence they are derived. . . . Now laws are said to be just, both from the end (when, namely, they are ordained to the common good), from their author (that is to say, when the law that is made does not exceed the power of the lawgiver), and from their form (when, namely, burdens are laid on the subjects according to an equality of proportion and with a view to the common good). For, since one man is a part of the community, each man, in all that he is and has, belongs to the community; just as a part, in all that it is, belongs to the whole. So, too, nature inflicts a loss on the part in order to save the whole; so that for this reason such laws as these, which impose proportionate burdens, are just and binding in conscience, and are legal laws.

On the other hand, laws may be unjust in two ways: first, by being contrary to human good, through being opposed to the things mentioned above:—either in respect of the end, as when an authority imposes on his subjects burdensome laws, conducive, not to the common good, but rather to his own cupidity or vainglory; or in respect of the author, as when a man makes a law that goes beyond the power committed to him; or in respect of the form, as when burdens are imposed unequally on the community, although with a view to the common good. Such are acts of violence rather than laws, because, as Augustine says, a law that is not just seems to be no law at all. Therefore, such laws do not bind in conscience, except perhaps in order to avoid scandal or disturbance, for which cause a man should even yield his right. . . .

Secondly, laws may be unjust through being opposed to the divine good. Such are the laws of tyrants inducing to idolatry, or to anything else contrary to the divine law. Laws of this kind must in no way be observed.

The most fundamental principles of the natural law, according to Aquinas, are the preservation of life, the propagation and education of offspring, and the pursuit of truth and a peaceful society. Although the natural law is built into human nature, we can violate the natural law of morality (unlike physical laws). This feature enables us to freely make good or bad choices and, hence, to have morality at all. Nevertheless, we tend to feel that the natural order of things has been violated when someone violates the law of nature. For example, we all recognize a case of suicide as deeply tragic because, Aquinas would say, the natural tendency is for a person to want to maintain his or her life. Similarly, we are appalled when we read about a wanton murder. But why are we particularly horrified when a parent murders his or her own child? Because it is a very deep feature of the natural and right order of things for parents to love and care for their children.

LOOKING THROUGH THE LENS
OF NATURAL LAW THEORY

1. If there were no natural law that stands over and above the laws made by human governments, would there be any basis for saying that a particular civil law was unjust if it had come about through a legal process?

2. The American Declaration of Independence says, "We hold these truths to be self-evident, that all men are created equal, that they are endowed by their Creator with certain unalienable Rights, that among these are Life, Liberty, and the pursuit of Happiness." What key terms in this passage indicate that the founders of the American government believed in the natural law?

3. If the natural law is available to be known by all, why is there a need to have written laws? Couldn't a society be run entirely on the basis of people's intuition of the moral law? How might a natural law theorist respond to this objection?

4. The U.S. Fugitive Slave Law of 1793 allowed slaveholders to capture and retrieve slaves who had sought freedom in other states. How would you attempt to convince the framers of this law that it was unjust? In doing so, would you have to appeal to some notion of a natural moral law that defines justice?

EXAMINING THE STRENGTHS AND
WEAKNESSES OF NATURAL LAW THEORY

Positive Evaluation

1. Supporters of this theory claim that it provides a basis for critiquing the laws of a society. As a matter of fact, this theory has been explicitly or tacitly appealed to by all great social reformers throughout history, such as the antislavery movement in the 19th century and the civil rights movement in the 1960s led by Martin Luther King Jr. Apart from the natural law theory, would there be any theoretical basis for social reform?

2. Don't good legislators continually ask themselves, "Is this proposed legislation right? Is it just? Does it promote the common good? Does it protect the fundamental rights of our citizens?" Aren't these questions rooted in the natural law? Apart from some conception of the natural law, wouldn't legislation be based on simply the will of the 51 percent majority or on whatever the current political fashion of the day might be? Wouldn't this basis be bad?

Negative Evaluation

1. Critics maintain that even if there is a natural moral law, it is too vague and too hard to discern to be much use in political theory. The natural law is supposed to be based on human nature. But aren't we often naturally inclined to do something that is bad for us or that is immoral? Given this fact, does it make sense to define justice in terms of what is "natural"? Aren't there alternative conceptions of what is natural or good?

2. Some people object that the natural law theory is based on a particular conception of reality, one that tends to be biased toward a religious view of the world. For example, critics claim that the theory assumes that there are oughts in nature and that human nature is fixed and preordained. Given the fact that our society has so many alternative conceptions of what constitutes the best life, how can the natural law theory be the basis of law in a pluralistic society such as ours?

SURVEYING THE CASE FOR JUSTICE AS SOCIAL UTILITY

JOHN STUART MILL (1806–1873)

One of the most influential political theorists in the past two centuries was John Stuart Mill. Whether or not you have read Mill, it is likely that your ideas about society show traces of his influence. We encountered Mill previously in our discussion of utilitarian ethics (see section 5.3 for the discussion of Mill's ethics and a brief account of his life). Because Mill believed that the morally right action was one that produced the greatest happiness for the greatest number, it is natural that his ethical concerns would lead to a political theory. In the realm of politics, Mill's concern was, "What sort of society will produce the greatest happiness for the greatest number?" In previous centuries Mill's native country of England had endured a turbulent civil war that led to the rise of parliamentary government, and just a few decades before Mill was born, political unrest produced the American and French Revolutions. In Mill's own lifetime, the beginning of the industrial revolution was foreshadowing major social changes and turmoil. Consequently, Mill saw the need for a political philosophy that would ensure social stability and protect individual freedom.

Mill's solution was to argue that the just society is one that attempts to minimize social harms and maximize social benefits for the greatest number of people. He called this solution the "principle of utility" or "expediency." In other words, he believed that *justice* is just an empty word unless it is tied to observable consequences such as the satisfaction of the interests of the majority of people in society. The following reading by Mill illustrates the utilitarian theory of justice.

- How does Mill define the word *right?*
- What is the basis of our rights, according to Mill?
- How does Mill's notion of rights differ from Locke's notion of natural, inalienable rights? What are some implications of this difference?
- On what basis does Mill say that a society ought to defend individual rights?

FROM JOHN STUART MILL

Utilitarianism[6]

When we call anything a person's right, we mean that he has a valid claim on society to protect him in the possession of it, either by the force of law, or by that of education and opinion. If he has what we consider a sufficient claim, on whatever account, to have something guaranteed to him by society, we say that he has a right to it. . . .

To have a right, then, is, I conceive, to have something which society ought to defend me in the possession of. If the objector goes on to ask, why it ought? I can give him no other reason than general utility. If that expression does not seem to convey a sufficient feeling of the strength of the obligation, nor to account for the peculiar energy of the feeling, it is because there goes to the composition of the sentiment, not a rational only, but also an animal element, the thirst for retaliation; and this thirst derives its intensity, as well as its moral justification, from the extraordinarily important and impressive kind of utility which is concerned. The interest involved is that of security, to every one's feelings the most vital of all interests. All other earthly benefits are needed by one person, not needed by another; and many of them can, if necessary, be cheerfully foregone, or replaced by something else; but security no human being can possibly do without; on it we depend for all our immunity from evil, and for the whole value of all and every good, beyond the passing moment; since nothing but the gratification of the instant could be of any worth to us, if we could be deprived of anything the next instant by whoever was momentarily stronger than ourselves. Now this most indispensable of all necessaries, after physical nutriment, cannot be had, unless the machinery for providing it is kept unintermittedly in active play. Our notion, therefore, of the claim we have on our fellow-creatures to join in making safe for us the very groundwork of our existence, gathers feelings around it so much more intense than those concerned in any of the more common cases of utility, that the difference in degree (as is often the case in psychology) becomes a real difference in kind. The claim assumes that character of absoluteness, that apparent infinity, and incommensurability with all other considerations, which constitute the distinction between the feeling of right and wrong and that of ordinary expediency and inexpediency. The feelings concerned are so powerful, and we count so positively on finding a responsive feeling in others (all being alike interested), that *ought* and *should* grow into *must,* and recognized indispensability becomes a moral necessity, analogous to physical, and often not inferior to it in binding force.

STOP AND THINK

If, as Mill believes, our rights are granted to us by law or social opinion and are based on general utility, could society decide to change these rights when it was socially useful to do so? What would be the implications of this position? What would Locke say about Mill's notion of rights?

- In the next passage, Mill cites critics who claim that his principle of utility is too vague and should be replaced with the concept of "justice." Why does he think that justice alone cannot be the standard for evaluating a society?
- What does Mill think about the social contract theory?

We are continually informed that Utility is an uncertain standard, which every different person interprets differently, and that there is no safety but in the immutable, ineffaceable, and unmistakable dictates of justice, which carry their evidence in themselves, and are independent of the fluctuations of opinion. One would suppose from this that on questions of justice there could be no controversy; that if we take that for our rule, its application to any given case could leave us in as little doubt as a mathematical demonstration. So far is this from being the fact, that there is as much difference of opinion, and as much discussion, about what is just, as about what is useful to society. Not only have different nations and individuals different notions of justice, but in the mind of one and the same individual, justice is not some one rule, principle, or maxim, but many, which do not always coincide in their dictates, and in choosing between which, he is guided either by some extraneous standard, or by his own personal predilections.

For instance, there are some who say, that it is unjust to punish any one for the sake of example to others; that punishment is just, only when intended for the good of the sufferer himself. Others maintain the extreme reverse, contending that to punish persons who have attained years of discretion, for their own benefit, is despotism and injustice, since if the matter at issue is solely their own good, no one has a right to control their own judgment of it; but that they may justly be punished to prevent evil to others, this being the exercise of the legitimate right of self-defense. Mr. Owen, again, affirms that it is unjust to punish at all; for the criminal did not make his own character; his education, and the circumstances which surrounded him, have made him a criminal, and for these he is not responsible. All these opinions are extremely plausible; and so long as the question is argued as one of justice simply, without going down to the principles which lie under justice and are the source of its authority, I am unable to see how any of these reasoners can be refuted. For in truth every one of the three builds upon rules of justice confessedly true. The first appeals to the acknowledged injustice of singling out an individual, and making a sacrifice, without his consent, for other people's benefit. The second relies on the acknowledged justice of self-defense, and the admitted injustice of forcing one person to conform to another's notions of what constitutes his good. The Owenite invokes the admitted principle, that it is unjust to punish any one for what he cannot help. Each is triumphant so long as he is not compelled to take into consideration any other maxims of justice than the one he has selected; but as soon as their several maxims are brought face to face, each disputant seems to have exactly as much to say for himself as the others. No one of them can carry out his own notion of justice without trampling upon another equally binding. These are difficulties; they have always been felt to be such; and many devices have been invented to turn rather than to overcome them. As a refuge from the last of the three, men imagined what they called the freedom of the will; fancying that they could not justify punishing a man whose will is in a thoroughly hateful state, unless it be supposed to have come into that state through no influence of anterior circumstances. To escape from the other difficulties, a favorite contrivance has been the fiction of a contract, whereby at some unknown period all the members of society engaged to obey the laws, and consented to be punished for any disobedience to them, thereby giving to their legislators the right, which it is assumed they would not otherwise have had, of punishing them, either for their own good or for that of society. This happy thought was considered to get rid of the whole difficulty, and to legitimate the infliction of punishment, in virtue of another received maxim of justice, *Volenti non fit injuria;* that is not unjust which is done with the consent of the person who is supposed to be hurt by it. I need hardly remark, that even if the consent were not a mere fiction, this maxim is not superior in authority to the others which it is brought in to supersede. It is, on the contrary, an instructive specimen of the loose and irregular manner in which supposed principles of justice grow up. This particular one evidently came into use as a help to the coarse exigencies of courts of law, which are sometimes obliged to be content with very uncertain presumptions, on account of the greater evils which would often arise from any attempt on their part to cut finer. But even courts of law are not able to adhere consistently to the maxim, for they allow voluntary engagements to be set aside on the ground of fraud, and sometimes on that of mere mistake or misinformation. . . .

To take another example from a subject already once referred to. In a cooperative industrial association, is it just or not that talent or skill should give a title to superior remuneration? On the negative side of the question it is argued, that whoever does the best he can, deserves equally well, and ought not in justice to be put in a position of inferiority for no fault of his own; that superior abilities have already advantages more than enough, in the admiration they excite, the personal influence they command, and the internal sources of satisfaction attending them, without adding to these a superior share of the world's goods; and that society is bound in justice rather to make compensation to the less favored, for this unmerited inequality of advantages, than to aggravate it. On the contrary side it is contended, that society receives more from the more efficient laborer; that his services being more useful, society owes him a larger return for them; that a greater share of the joint result is actually his work, and not to allow his claim to it is a kind of robbery; that if he is only to receive as much as others, he can only be justly required to produce as much, and to give a smaller amount of time and exertion, proportioned to his superior efficiency. Who shall decide between these appeals to conflicting principles of justice? Justice has in this case two sides to it, which it is impossible to bring into harmony, and the two disputants have chosen opposite sides; the one looks to what it is just that the individual should receive, the other to what it is just that the community should give. Each, from his own point of view, is unanswerable; and any choice between them, on grounds of justice, must be perfectly arbitrary. Social utility alone can decide the preference.

- In the next passage, how does Mill describe the relationship between justice and expediency (utility)?

Is, then, the difference between the just and the expedient a merely imaginary distinction? Have mankind been under a delusion in thinking that justice is a more sacred thing than policy, and that the latter ought only to be listened to after the former has been satisfied? By no means. The exposition we have given of the nature and origin of the sentiment, recognizes a real distinction; and no one of those who profess the most sublime contempt for the consequences of actions as an element in their morality, attaches more importance to the distinction than I do. While I dispute the pretensions of any theory which sets up an imaginary standard of justice not grounded on utility, I account the justice which is grounded on utility to be the chief part, and incomparably the most sacred and binding part, of all morality. Justice is a name for certain classes of moral rules, which concern the essentials of human well-being more nearly, and are therefore of more absolute obligation, than any other rules for the guidance of life; and the notion which we have found to be of the essence of the idea of justice, that of a right residing in an individual implies and testifies to this more binding obligation. . . .

The considerations which have now been adduced resolve, I conceive, the only real difficulty in the utilitarian theory of morals. It has always been evident that all cases of justice are also cases of expediency: the difference is in the peculiar sentiment which attaches to the former, as contradistinguished from the latter. If this characteristic sentiment has been sufficiently accounted for; if there is no necessity to assume for it any peculiarity of origin; if it is simply the natural feeling of resentment, moralized by being made coextensive with the demands of social good; and if this feeling not only does but ought to exist in all the classes of cases to which the idea of justice corresponds; that idea no longer presents itself as a stumbling-block to the utilitarian ethics. Justice remains the appropriate name for certain social utilities which are vastly more important, and therefore more absolute and imperative, than any others are as a class (though not more so than others may be in particular cases); and which, therefore, ought to be, as well as naturally are, guarded by a sentiment not only different in degree, but also in kind; distinguished from the milder feeling which attaches to the mere idea of promoting human pleasure or convenience, at once by the more definite nature of its commands, and by the sterner character of its sanctions.

Because Mill's political philosophy is based on his ethical theory, they rise or fall together. If you think that his ethical principles are the best way of deciding what an individual ought to do, then you probably also think that his political philosophy is the best way of deciding what a society ought to do. At the same time, the objections that were made against his ethical theory are also raised against his political philosophy.

LOOKING THROUGH MILL'S LENS

1. Does Mill's theory dictate a particular form of government, or could it be applied to many different and even incompatible governmental systems? Is this quality a strength or a weakness of the theory?

2. Think about different societies in history and in the world today. In applying his political philosophy, how would Mill evaluate each one? Which ones would he say were good (or just) societies and which ones would he consider bad (or unjust) societies? Why?

3. Think about a current political controversy (e.g., abortion, legalization of marijuana, foreign policy, welfare). Try to imagine what policy Mill would recommend for that controversy in our society.

EXAMINING THE STRENGTHS AND WEAKNESSES OF MILL'S THEORY OF JUSTICE

Positive Evaluation

1. How do we decide if an educational program is a good one? How do we decide if a medicine is safe and effective? How do we decide whether a particular brand of computer is a good buy? In all areas of life, we judge the goodness or badness of a policy or practice in terms of its consequences. Shouldn't the same be true of our social and political policies?

2. What is the purpose of government if not to satisfy of the needs of its citizens? Can't we evaluate a society on this basis without worrying about the natural law or the alleged social contract? Isn't Mill's principle of utility the most clear and efficient measure of the goodness and justice of a society?

3. Think about situations in which we decided that our society was acting unjustly and we changed the laws (e.g., slavery, discriminatory laws, the lack of women's rights). In all these situations, weren't the changes preceded by social unrest and the realization that large numbers of our citizens were not satisfied with current conditions? In other words, doesn't Mill's political theory describe how we actually go about deciding that a law is unjust?

Negative Evaluation

1. In the first paragraph of the reading, Mill suggests that individual rights are those that are recognized as such by the law or by the general opinion of the community. Is social consensus an adequate way to define an individual's rights with respect to the government? How might a natural law theorist critique this socially defined notion of "rights"?

2. Isn't it possible for the majority of society to be satisfied with the government even though the government and its policies are unjust with respect to those in the minority? Is social utility always consistent with our notion of justice? Does Mill's utilitarian theory have any way of addressing this problem?

3. Isn't it possible for a policy to result in the greatest good for society as a whole while clashing with individual interests? For example, putting a nuclear waste dump in your state (or behind your property) might serve the needs of the rest of the nation, but it might be risky or unpleasant for you. Doesn't utilitarian political philosophy give priority to the public interest over individual interests? Couldn't this priority be unjust?

SURVEYING THE CASE FOR JUSTICE AS FAIRNESS

JOHN RAWLS (1921–2002)

John Rawls was professor of philosophy at Harvard University and published many influential articles and books on moral and political philosophy. No book has been more in the forefront of current discussions about political philosophy than Rawls's 1971 book, *A Theory of Justice*. In this book, Rawls attempts to find a balance between individual liberty and rights on the one hand and society's duties and interest in maintaining an equitable distribution of goods on the other hand. In seeking this balance, Rawls sets out a blueprint of a society in which people are encouraged to succeed and better their position and yet are guaranteed that no one will be hopelessly left behind.

Rawls takes a dim view of the notion that society's goods are the reward for having the most merit. Rawls argues that people who possess merit, whether measured by intelligence, personality traits, or other natural gifts, did not earn their abilities but received them as a fortunate accident of birth or circumstances. Such people are no more deserving of a larger share of society's benefits than the winner of a lottery is more deserving of the prize than are the losers. Rawls's alternative to "justice as merit" is "justice as fairness," a system in which justice is directed toward a minimal level of equality.

Rawls directly criticizes the utilitarian theory of Mill. He agrees with utilitarianism's critics that this position opens up the possibility that the general good of the majority could be pursued at the expense of the rights and well-being of some individual or group. If we were completely impartial and did not know ahead of time whether we would be included in the prospering majority, Rawls claims, we would not agree to a social system in which our rights and our goods would be sacrificed for those of the many.

According to Rawls, an adequate theory of justice must be one that will be acceptable to everyone. But how is this general acceptance possible? Each person has different needs, interests, abilities, social circumstances, and agendas. I may think, for example, that it would be just for philosophy professors to be paid the most, but English professors probably would not agree with my notion of justice. Rawls's answer is that people will accept a theory of justice only if they think it is fair. But once again, how can different people in different circumstances agree on what is fair? To solve this problem, Rawls comes up with a clever solution based on a thought experiment. He asks us to imagine that there is as yet no society, but that we are all coming together in a state of perfect equality to create a new society and to decide what principles shall govern it. Rawls calls this initial situation the "original position."

- In what ways is Rawls's notion of the original position similar to Hobbes's and Locke's notion of the state of nature?

FROM JOHN RAWLS

A Theory of Justice[7]

The Main Idea of the Theory of Justice

My aim is to present a conception of justice which generalizes and carries to a higher level of abstraction the familiar theory of the social contract as found, say, in Locke, Rousseau, and Kant. In order to do this we are not to think of the original contract as one to enter a particular society or to set up a particular form of government. Rather, the guiding idea is that the principles of justice for the basic structure of society are the object of the original agreement. They are the principles that free and rational persons concerned to further their own interests would accept in an initial position of equality as defining the fundamental terms of their association. These principles are to regulate all further agreements; they specify the kinds of social cooperation that can be entered into and the forms of government that can be established. This way of regarding the principles of justice I shall call justice as fairness.

Thus we are to imagine that those who engage in social cooperation choose together, in one joint act, the principles which are to assign basic rights and duties and to determine the division of social benefits. Men are to decide in advance how they are to regulate their claims against one another and what is to be the foundation charter of their society. Just as each person must decide by rational reflection what constitutes his good, that is, the system of ends which it is rational for him to pursue, so a group of persons must decide once and for all what is to count among them as just and unjust. The choice which rational men would make in this hypothetical situation of equal liberty, assuming for the present that this choice problem has a solution, determines the principles of justice.

In justice as fairness the original position of equality corresponds to the state of nature in the traditional theory of the social contract. This original position is not, of course, thought of as an actual historical state of affairs, much less as a primitive condition of culture. It is understood as a purely hypothetical situation characterized so as to lead to a certain conception of justice.

Many philosophers would say (contrary to Rawls) that in our current society, those people who have the most gifts or the most superior character should have the greater advantage over the rest. In other words, the critics claim, if you are very intelligent, athletic, or good-looking on the one hand (natural gifts), or if you are persistent, highly motivated, or optimistic on the other hand (superior character), you have a right to reap society's richest rewards (such as wealth, fame, or opportunities) by making use of your gifts or character traits. But Rawls argues that this position is indefensible.

- In the following passage, how does Rawls respond to the suggestion that those people who are naturally superior have no obligations to others but deserve all the advantages their abilities bring them?

Perhaps some will think that the person with greater natural endowments deserves those assets and the superior character that made their development possible. Because he is more worthy in this sense, he deserves the greater advantages that he could achieve with them. This view, however, is surely incorrect. It seems to be one of the fixed points of our considered judgments that no one deserves his place in the distribution of native endowments, any more than one deserves one's initial starting place in society. The assertion that a man deserves the superior character that enables him to make the effort to cultivate his abilities is equally problematic; for his character depends in large part upon fortunate family and social circumstances for which he can claim no credit. The notion of desert seems not to apply to these cases. Thus the more advantaged representative man cannot say that he deserves and therefore has a right to a scheme of cooperation in which he is permitted to acquire benefits in ways that do not contribute to the welfare of others. There is no basis for his making this claim.

STOP AND THINK

You are a person of a particular gender, race, age, physical condition, personality, education, and certain social and economic circumstances. Given these facts, what would be the ideal society for you that would enable you to flourish and achieve maximum gains?

The problem that Rawls wrestles with is that everyone has different circumstances and so would want to design a society that would enhance his or her own life. Consequently, it seems impossible to figure out how everyone could ever come to agree on the principles that will govern society in a way that will be fair to all. In the next passage, Rawls solves this problem by adding one more crucial feature to his thought experiment concerning the original position.

- State in your own words what Rawls means by the "veil of ignorance."

The Veil of Ignorance

The idea of the original position is to set up a fair procedure so that any principles agreed to will be just. The aim is to use the notion of pure procedural justice as a basis of theory. Somehow we must nullify the effects of specific contingencies which put men at odds and tempt them to exploit social and natural circumstances to their own advantage. Now in order to do this I assume that the parties are situated behind a veil of ignorance. They do not know how the various alternatives will affect their own particular case and they are obliged to evaluate principles solely on the basis of general considerations.

It is assumed, then, that the parties do not know certain kinds of particular facts. First of all, no one knows his place in society, his class position or social status; nor does he know his fortune in the distribution of natural assets and abilities, his intelligence and strength, and the like. Nor, again, does anyone know his conception of the good, the particulars of his rational plan of life, or even the special features of his psychology such as his aversion to risk or liability to optimism or pessimism. More than this, I assume that the parties do not know the particular circumstances of their own society. That is, they do not know its economic or political situation, or the level of civilization and culture it has been able to achieve. The persons in the original position have no information as to which generation they belong. These broader restrictions on knowledge are appropriate in part because questions of social justice arise between generations as well as within them, for example, the question of the appropriate rate of capital saving and of the conservation of natural resources and the environment of nature. There is also, theoretically anyway, the question of a reasonable genetic policy. In these cases too, in order to carry through the idea of the original position, the parties must not know the contingencies that set them in opposition. They must choose principles the consequences of which they are prepared to live with whatever generation they turn out to belong to. . . .

Thus there follows the very important consequence that the parties have no basis for bargaining in the usual sense. No one knows his situation in society nor his natural assets, and therefore no one is in a position to tailor principles to his advantage. We might imagine that one of the contractees threatens to hold out unless the others agree to principles favorable to him. But how does he know which principles are especially in his interests? The same holds for the formation of coalitions: if a group were to decide to band together to the disadvantage of the others, they would not know how to favor themselves in the choice of principles. Even if they could get everyone to agree to their proposal, they would have no assurance that it was to their advantage, since they cannot identify themselves either by name or description. . . .

The restrictions on particular information in the original position are, then, of fundamental importance. Without them we would not be able to work out any definite theory of justice at all. We would have to be content with a vague formula stating that justice is what would be agreed to without being able to say much, if anything, about the substance of the agreement itself. The formal constraints of the concept of right, those applying to principles directly, are not sufficient for our purpose. The veil of ignorance makes possible a unanimous choice of a particular conception of justice. Without these limitations on knowledge the bargaining problem of the original position would be hopelessly complicated. Even if theoretically a solution were to exist, we would not, at present anyway, be able to determine it.

- Imagine that while you are behind the veil of ignorance you must decide what principles should govern society. How would this cloak make it possible for you and everyone else to be impartial and fair in deciding what would be the best society?
- If you were in this situation, how would you want society to be run? What principles would you choose?

In the next passage, Rawls sets out two principles of justice that he thinks all rational persons would choose if they were ideally impartial and fair—that is, if they had to choose a political philosophy from behind the veil of ignorance.

Two Principles of Justice

I shall now state in a provisional form the two principles of justice that I believe would be chosen in the original position. . . .

The first statement of the two principles reads as follows.

First: each person is to have an equal right to the most extensive basic liberty compatible with a similar liberty for others.

Second: social and economic inequalities are to be arranged so that they are both (a) reasonably expected to be to everyone's advantage, and (b) attached to positions and offices open to all. . . .

By way of general comment, these principles primarily apply, as I have said, to the basic structure of society. They are to govern the assignment of rights and duties and to regulate the distribution of social and economic advantages. As their formulation suggests, these principles presuppose that the social structure can be divided into two more or less distinct parts, the first principle applying to the one, the second to the other. They distinguish between those aspects of the social system that define and secure the equal liberties of citizenship and those that specify and establish social and economic inequalities. The basic liberties of citizens are, roughly speaking, political liberty (the right to vote and to be eligible for public office) together with freedom of speech and assembly; liberty of conscience and freedom of thought; freedom of the person along with the right to hold (personal) property; and freedom from arbitrary arrest and seizure as defined by the concept of the rule of law. These liberties are all required to be equal by the first principle, since citizens of a just society are to have the same basic rights.

The second principle applies, in the first approximation to the distribution of income and wealth and to the design of organizations that make use of differences in authority and responsibility, or chains of command. While the distribution of wealth and income need not be equal, it must be to everyone's advantage, and at the same time, positions of authority and offices of command must be accessible to all. One applies the second principle by holding positions open, and then, subject to this constraint, arranges social and economic inequalities so that everyone benefits.

Principle 1 is the *principle of equal liberty,* which applies to our political institutions. Basically, it says that everyone should have the maximum amount of political rights and freedom as long as everyone has an equal amount of these liberties. For example, to allow everyone an equal right to have their opinion heard at a public meeting, it will be necessary to restrict one group from speaking as much as they may like. Principle 2 applies to society's social and economic institutions. Unlike in the political sphere, in which absolute equality is necessary, in the social and economic spheres it is inevitable and even good that some inequalities be allowed. If a person who risked her life savings to invent a better computer received no greater reward than someone who risked nothing and produced nothing new, she would be discouraged from productivity and innovation. Rewarding people for their extraordinary achievements and hard work will motivate them to be more creative and productive, and as a result, society as a whole will benefit. If the efforts of the computer inventor are successful, more jobs will be created, the world will have better computers, and other people will strive to excel. The first half of this principle is what Rawls calls the *difference principle* because it focuses on the differences among people. This principle states that social and economic inequalities should be arranged so they result in everyone's advantage. What does this statement mean? Obviously, if people are unequal, then those who have more are already reaping an advantage. So, the difference principle implies that those who are on the short end of a situation of inequality also should gain some benefit from it in the long run. Indeed, in a later passage Rawls spells out this point by saying that such inequalities should be "to the greatest benefit of the least advantaged."[8] For example, if your physician earns more money than you do, isn't that still to your advantage if it means that you receive better medical care?

Rawls doesn't discuss specific policies in his book, but there are many ways to bring about this balance between the goal of allowing people to achieve all they can and the goal of providing for the least advantaged. One way is to provide food, shelter, medical care, education, and job opportunities for the least advantaged through such devices as corporate, income, and luxury taxes. Another way is for society to provide incentives for those who have achieved the most to compensate the less well-off through the creation of jobs and charitable contributions. Only in this way will society achieve stability, because revolutions are nurtured in situations in which extreme wealth and extreme poverty exist side by side. Rawls believes that rational persons in the original position would favor the difference principle because they might end up in the neediest group. Many corporate executives who used to rail against welfare came to appreciate unemployment benefits when they suddenly found themselves laid off and having difficulties securing a new job.

The latter half of the second principle is the *principle of fair equality of opportunity*. This principle says that the opportunities to achieve more than the basic minimum should be open to all. In other words, a caste system or an aristocracy in which people are locked into their social or economic niche would not be just, even if the least advantaged were being taken care of. There should be no intrinsic barriers to moving from the least advantaged to the most advantaged. This feature of society is certainly one that we all would want if we were behind the veil of ignorance and did not know where we would land in the social and economic hierarchy.

Whenever two or more principles govern our actions, the question always arises: What if the principles conflict? Which one has priority? Plato's society, for example, had a fairly even distribution of wealth. The society was not divided between the "haves" and the "have-nots." In fact, the common people were allowed to accumulate property and private possessions, whereas the rulers were not. However, the common people had no voice in politics and few of the political liberties we enjoy. In other words, Plato gave priority to principle 2 (economic justice) over principle 1 (political equality).

- In the following passage, how does Rawls address these issues?

These principles are to be arranged in a serial order with the first principle prior to the second. This ordering means that a departure from the institutions of equal liberty required by the first principle cannot be justified by, or compensated for, by greater social and economic advantages. The distribution of wealth and income, and the hierarchies of authority, must be consistent with both the liberties of equal citizenship and equality of opportunity.

. . . For the present, it should be observed that the two principles (and this holds for all formulations) are a special case of a more general conception of justice that can be expressed as follows.

> All social values—liberty and opportunity, income and wealth, and the bases of self-respect—are to be distributed equally unless an unequal distribution of any, or all, of these values is to everyone's advantage.

Injustice, then, is simply inequalities that are not to the benefit of all. Of course, this conception is extremely vague and requires interpretation.

As a first step, suppose that the basic structure of society distributes certain primary goods, that is, things that every rational man is presumed to want. These goods normally have a use whatever a person's rational plan of life. For simplicity, assume that the chief primary goods at the disposition of society are rights and liberties, powers and opportunities, income and wealth. . . . These are the social primary goods. Other primary goods such as health and vigor, intelligence and imagination, are natural goods; although their possession is influenced by the basic structure, they are not so directly under its control. Imagine, then, a hypothetical initial arrangement in which all the social primary goods are equally distributed: everyone has similar rights and duties, and income and wealth are evenly shared. This state of affairs provides a benchmark for judging improvements. If certain inequalities of wealth and organizational powers would make everyone better off than in this hypothetical starting situation, then they accord with the general conception.

Now it is possible, at least theoretically, that by giving up some of their fundamental liberties men are sufficiently compensated by the resulting social and economic gains. The general conception of justice imposes no restrictions on what sort of inequalities are permissible; it only requires that everyone's position be improved. We need not suppose anything so drastic as consenting to a condition of slavery. Imagine instead that men forego certain political rights when the economic returns are significant and their capacity to influence the course of policy by the exercise of these rights would be marginal in any case. It is this kind of exchange which the two principles as stated rule out; being arranged in serial order they do not permit exchanges between basic liberties and economic and social gains. The serial ordering of principles expresses an underlying preference among primary social goods. When this preference is rational so likewise is the choice of these principles in this order.

Reprinted by permission of the publisher from *A Theory of Justice* by John Rawls, pp. 11–12, 60–63, 103–104, 136–137, 139–140, Cambridge, Mass: The Belknap Press of Harvard University Press, Copyright © 1971, 1999 by The President and Fellows of Harvard College.

A Feminist Critique of Rawls

Although John Rawls is often thought to be the spokesperson for contemporary liberalism, some feminists think that his theory of justice contains important gaps and flaws. In her book *Justice, Gender, and the Family*, Stanford University professor Susan Moller Okin (1946–2004) critically analyzes Rawls's account. She begins with the general problem that even though American society is built on the principle of equality of opportunity, the implications of this principle have not been fully realized.

FROM SUSAN MOLLER OKIN

Justice, Gender, and the Family[9]

Yet substantial inequities between the sexes still exist in our society. In economic terms, full-time working women (after some very recent improvement) earn on average 71 percent of the earnings of full-time working men. One-half of poor and three-fifths of chronically poor households with dependent children are maintained by a single female parent. The poverty rate for elderly women is nearly twice that for elderly men.

Okin goes on to note the disproportionate burdens that women bear in child rearing and housework. Furthermore, she cites the fact that, in spite of great strides, women are still underrepresented in legislative bodies, judgeships, and other professional offices. As I pointed out earlier (section 5.6, "Rethinking the Western Tradition: Feminist Ethics"), feminists criticize ethical and political theorists who focus on public morality while ignoring what goes on in families and who ignore the role of gender in their account of human relationships. She takes this shortcoming of contemporary political theories as the focus of her book:

Yet, remarkably, major contemporary theorists of justice have almost without exception ignored the situation I have just described [the status of women]. They have displayed little interest in or knowledge of the findings of feminism. They have largely bypassed the fact that the society to which their theories are supposed to pertain is heavily and deeply affected by gender, and faces difficult issues of justice stemming from its gendered past and present assumptions. Since theories of justice are centrally concerned with whether, how, or why persons should be treated differently from one another, this neglect seems inexplicable. . . . [Justice, Gender, and the Family] is about this remarkable case of neglect. It is also an attempt to . . . point the way toward a more fully humanist theory of justice by confronting the question, "How just is gender?"

While acknowledging that Rawls's book is not blatantly sexist, Okin still finds it problematic, particularly in the male biases that creep into his choice of terms:

Men, mankind, he, and *his* are interspersed with gender-neutral terms of reference such as *individual* and *moral person.* Examples of intergenerational concern are worded in terms of "fathers" and "sons." . . .

Thus, there is a blindness to the sexism of the tradition in which Rawls is a participant, which tends to render his terms of reference more ambiguous than they might otherwise be. A feminist reader finds it difficult not to keep asking, Does this theory apply to women?

To Rawls's credit, he does say that our sex is one of the features of nature's lottery that we cannot know behind the veil of ignorance. But feminist critics such as Okin point out that Rawls appears to forget his comment when he describes the original position: "Among the essential features of this situation is that no one knows *his* place in society, *his* class position or social status, nor does any one know *his* fortune in the distribution of natural assets and abilities, *his* intelligence, strength, and the like" (emphasis added).[10] To this, Okin says, "One might think that whether or not they knew their sex might matter enough to be mentioned. Perhaps, Rawls meant to cover it by his phrase 'and the like,' but it is also possible that he did not consider it significant."[11] Okin goes on to observe that knowledge of a person's gender is more significant than Rawls seems to imply:

The significance of Rawls's central, brilliant idea, the original position, is that it forces one to question and consider traditions, customs, and institutions from all points of view, and ensures that the principles of justice will be acceptable to everyone, regardless of what position "he" ends up in. . . . The theory, in principle, avoids both the problem of domination that is inherent in theories of justice based on traditions or shared understandings and the partiality of libertarian theory to those who are talented or fortunate. For feminist readers, however, the problem of the theory as stated by Rawls himself is encapsulated in the ambiguous "he." . . . If, however, we read Rawls in such a way as to take seriously both the notion that those behind the veil of ignorance do not know what sex they are and the requirement that the family and gender system, as basic social institutions, are to be subject to scrutiny, constructive feminist criticism of these contemporary institutions follows. . . .

Finally . . . if those in the original position did not know whether they were to be men or women, they would surely be concerned to establish a thoroughgoing social and economic equality between the sexes that would protect either sex from the need to pander to or servilely provide for the pleasure of the other. They would emphasize the importance of girls and boys growing up with an equal sense of respect for themselves and equal expectations of self-definition and development. . . . In general, they would be unlikely to tolerate basic social institutions that asymmetrically either forced or gave strong incentives to members of one sex to serve as sex objects for the other.

. . . I reach the conclusions not only that our current gender structure is incompatible with the attainment of social justice, but also that the disappearance of gender is a prerequisite for the complete development of a nonsexist, fully human theory of justice.

Copyright © 1989 by Basic Books, Inc. Reprinted by permission of Basic Books, a member of the Perseus Books Group.

THOUGHT EXPERIMENT: *The Original Position*

- If you were in Rawls's original position but knew you would be a male, would you be satisfied with the way your current society treats males, or would you want to make some changes?
- If you knew that you would be a female, would you be satisfied with your current society, or would you want to make some changes?
- If you were able to design the society in which you would live but didn't know what gender you would be in this society, are there any changes to our current society that you would make with respect to the status of either men or women?

LOOKING THROUGH RAWLS'S LENS

1. Hobbes's and Locke's social contract theory was an attempt to explain the existence of the governments that actually exist. Rawls's social contract theory, however, is not concerned with the past but is a way of thinking about what sort of government we ought to have. Do you think that his use of the social contract theory avoids some of the criticisms of Hobbes's and Locke's versions?

2. Rawls has given us principles that apply to our political, social, and economic institutions: the principle of equal liberty, the difference principle, and the principle of fair equality of opportunity. Which one of these three do you think is given priority in our society?

3. If we adopted Rawls's theory, what changes would be made in our current society? Do you think these changes would make our society better or worse?

EXAMINING THE STRENGTHS AND WEAKNESSES OF RAWLS'S THEORY OF JUSTICE

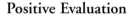

Positive Evaluation

1. Most people would agree that a just government is one that treats everyone fairly. Would you agree that Rawls's original position and veil of ignorance scenarios are an effective way of getting us to think in an objective fashion without favoritism toward anyone?

2. Most societies are faced with a dilemma. If they strive for complete economic equality by distributing wealth equally, they will stifle the incentive of the high achievers and productivity will suffer. On the other hand, because a person's abilities are mainly a gift of fortune, neglecting the disadvantaged would be unfair and the result could be vast social and economic inequalities that would make the society unstable. Rawls solves this problem by guaranteeing that any social and economic inequalities will always result in benefits to the disadvantaged. Do you think Rawls makes an effective compromise between allowing people to achieve and get all they can while not leaving the rest too far behind?

3. The French Revolution was caused (in part) by the large-scale social and economic inequalities of that society. The fall of the former U.S.S.R. was caused (in part) by the lack of political liberty and economic productivity. Hasn't Rawls avoided these problems by insisting on both economic justice and political liberty? Doesn't his theory capture our present-day Western social, economic, and political ideals that have seemed to work reasonably well?

Negative Evaluation

1. One of Rawls's strongest critics is his Harvard colleague Robert Nozick (born 1938). Nozick charges that Rawls's theory says that society should play some role in dictating how wealth and goods should be distributed among its members. But Nozick thinks that in applying its formula, a society will have to interfere with people's political liberties. If, for example, sports fans wish to buy tickets to watch a famous basketball star and the star becomes a millionaire as a result, this economic inequality is not unjust if it is based on people's free choices. Do you think this criticism is fair?

2. Consider four poker players about to start a high-stakes game. In one sense, they are behind the veil of ignorance because none of them knows who will win. Even though some of them may lose all their money, none of them would want to change the rules of the game to redistribute the winnings after it is all over. They are each willing to risk a great loss for the chance of a big win. Does this situation suggest that people behind the veil of ignorance will not always choose to diminish inequalities as Rawls suggests?

3. Critics of Rawls, such as Nozick, who give priority to individual liberty (known as "political libertarians") say that Rawls sacrifices the individual's good for the good of society. On the other hand, critics who believe that the common good is more important than individual liberty say that society is like a biological organism whose overall well-being should receive the priority. In seeking a compromise between these two concerns, has Rawls achieved the "best of both worlds," or has he actually ended up with the "worst of both worlds"? In other words, does his political philosophy try to serve two incompatible goals?

LEADING QUESTIONS: *The Individual and the State*

1. *Questions from classical liberalism:* Who potentially has the most power, the government or a single individual? Since the government obviously has the most power, shouldn't the protection of our individual liberties be the priority in any political philosophy?

2. *Questions from classical liberalism:* Who knows best what is in your own interest, you or the government? Even if you make choices that are not in your best interest, as long as those choices harm no one but yourself, does the government have the right to act as your parent by controlling your actions? Won't the best society be achieved if people are allowed to pursue their own interests as best they can, without the government intervening?

3. *Questions from the Marxist:* Who has the most political power and influence in society, the working poor or the wealthy? Who is in the majority, the working poor or the wealthy? Isn't there something unjust about a social structure in which the workers make up the bulk of society but have the least power and the wealthy are the elite minority but have the most power?

4. *Questions from the Marxist:* Suppose you lived in a society that claimed to be perfectly just and moral. Furthermore, suppose a few people managed to accumulate all the wealth in the society and were able to pass it on to their children without sharing any of it for the common good. However, those citizens who were born disadvantaged through no fault of their own were forced by desperation to work for starvation wages and had little opportunity to break out of the chains of their poverty. Suppose further that the government and its laws served the interests of the wealthy but turned a deaf ear to the needs of the disadvantaged. Would this society be able to defend its claim of being perfectly just and moral?

As the four leading questions suggest, both the protection of individual freedoms and governmental concern for the common good are important ingredients in a good society. The problem is that there is an inevitable tension between the two. Some political thinkers try to eliminate the tension by advocating one extreme or the other. On the side of individual freedom, the most extreme position is *anarchism* (discussed in section 6.1), which claims that no government ever has a right to interfere with human autonomy. At the other extreme is *absolute totalitarianism,* which claims that individual freedom and rights always should be sacrificed for the good of the society. Under absolute totalitarianism, the government controls virtually every sphere of human life. A fictional representation of life under a totalitarian government is found in George Orwell's novel *1984.* The residence of every citizen contains a television on which the figure of Big Brother (who represents the government) shouts political propaganda and leads the citizens in state-enforced calisthenics. To make sure that each citizen's every action is in compliance with the government, television cameras monitor every movement at home and outside.

These two extreme positions are untenable to most people. There are, however, more moderate positions that place priority on either individual freedom or government control without eliminating the other concern entirely. Those positions that emphasize individual freedom could be called *individualism.* One of the most important versions of this viewpoint was classical liberalism. In this section, we look at this position as it was represented by the 19th-century English philosopher John Stuart Mill. Those positions that subordinate individual liberty to the needs of society could be called *collectivism* because they believe that the collective or the common good is all-important. Representing collectivism in this section is the 19th-century German philosopher Karl Marx. Although both these thinkers were writing more than a century ago, their ideas were so important that they still influence contemporary political philosophers.

SURVEYING THE CASE FOR CLASSICAL LIBERALISM

Today, some people associate the word *liberal* with left-wing politics and the promotion of big government. However, the position we are examining here is *classical* liberalism as developed by such thinkers as the English philosophers John Locke in the 17th century and John Stuart Mill in the 19th century. (Locke's and Mill's political philosophies have been introduced in sections 6.1 and 6.2 respectively.) *Liberalism* comes from the Latin word *libertas,* which means "liberty" or "freedom." Hence, classical liberalism emphasizes the freedom of the individual. This emphasis includes individual freedom *from* inappropriate government control and the individual's freedom *to* pursue his or her legitimate individual interests. Ironically, people who are called liberals and people who are called conservatives in today's terminology, in spite of their differences, both promote this sort of freedom. One difference between them is how they work out the details. In other words, liberals and conservatives differ in their conceptions of what is "inappropriate" government control and "legitimate" individual interests. The contemporary movement known as political libertarianism most closely follows the classical liberal ideals of a very limited government. The point is that you can find the basic principles of classical liberalism woven into our whole social and political system whether you lean to the left or to the right.

JOHN STUART MILL

We first encountered John Stuart Mill in the section on utilitarian ethics (5.3), where a brief account of his life may be found. We also looked at his theory of justice in section 6.2. Previous democratic thinkers had been so concerned about defending the rights of the citizens from the tyranny of the king that they had ignored the sort of tyranny that can arise in a democracy—the tyranny of the majority. Realizing that the will of the majority, when enforced by the state, could be as oppressive as any monarch, Mill sought for principles that would limit the power of the government over individual lives. From his standpoint, censorship, intolerance, government-imposed morality, and legislated conformity are some of the greatest dangers that a society can face, because, unlike a foreign invader, they arise in the midst of a society and masquerade as defenders of the social good. However, allowing total individual freedom is not feasible either, because society needs to prevent individuals from harming one another and from undermining the general welfare. With these problems in mind, Mill published *On Liberty* in 1859 to establish the proper balance between governmental control and individual freedom. Since then, it has become a classic and is one of the most influential essays ever published on this topic.

- According to Mill, what is the "one very simple principle" that determines when society is allowed to impose its will on an individual?
- Does Mill believe it is legitimate for society to force you to act in a certain way for the sake of your own self-interest?

On Liberty [12]

The object of this Essay is to assert one very simple principle, as entitled to govern absolutely the dealings of society with the individual in the way of compulsion and control, whether the means used be physical force in the form of legal penalties, or the moral coercion of public opinion. That principle is, that the sole end for which mankind are warranted, individually or collectively in interfering with the liberty of action of any of their number, is self-protection. That the only purpose for which power can be rightfully exercised over any member of a civilized community, against his will, is to prevent harm to others. His own good, either physical or moral, is not a sufficient warrant. He cannot rightfully be compelled to do or forbear because it will be better for him to do so, because it will make him happier, because, in the opinions of others, to do so would be wise, or even right. These are good reasons for remonstrating with him, or reasoning with him, or persuading him, or entreating him, but not for compelling him, or visiting him with any evil, in case he do otherwise. To justify that, the conduct from which it is desired to deter him must be calculated to produce evil to some one else. The only part of the conduct of any one, for which he is amenable to society, is that which concerns others. In the part which merely concerns himself, his independence is, of right, absolute. Over himself, over his own body and mind, the individual is sovereign.

Obviously, Mill does not believe in governmental paternalism, the view that the government should play the role of our parent by forcing us to do what it thinks is best for us. Because individual autonomy is essential for people and societies to flourish, Mill says the state cannot intrude on the sphere of your personal life. He provides one exception to this rule, however. In the case of children or others who do not have the rational capacity to make their own decisions, it is legitimate for adults and even society to protect them from their own actions that may be harmful to themselves. As long as you are an adult and of a sound mind, however, and even if your actions are unwise, imprudent, or self-destructive, society has no authority to interfere with your freedom in order to protect you from yourself. In other words, it is your life and you have a right to live it as you please. There are only two conditions under which the government has a legitimate interest in controlling your behavior. One condition is when such interference will prevent harm to others. As the old cliché goes, your right to swing your arm ends at the tip of my nose. The second condition in which the government may compel you to act a certain way is when it is essential that you help society or another person. Examples would be serving in the army, serving on a jury, or rescuing a drowning person. In these cases, your private actions have effects on the public sphere, where the government has its proper domain of authority.

In the next passage, Mill states that his political philosophy does not rest on the notion of "individual rights" (as did John Locke's). This idea is too vague and abstract for the utilitarians. Rights are incapable of observation, which is why there is so much disagreement over what rights we have. Instead, the utilitarians want ethics and political theory to be based on empirical, scientific observations of human nature and the observable consequences of behavior. Accordingly, Mill states that his view of society is based on the principle of utility, or the principle that determines the rightness or wrongness of actions and public policies in terms of the observable good consequences they produce or the harms they prevent. Although Mill sometimes talks about "rights," he believes that these rights are not intrinsic or built into human nature but are given to us by law and social consensus and are based on the principle of utility.

- In the next paragraph, Mill concerns himself with the question of when society may force you *not to do* something or punish you for what you have done. He also speaks of when society may compel you *to perform* an action or hold you responsible for failing to act. What considerations govern each of these situations?

It is proper to state that I forego any advantage which could be derived to my argument from the idea of abstract right as a thing independent of utility. I regard utility as the ultimate appeal on all ethical questions; but it must be utility in the largest sense, grounded on the permanent interests of man as a progressive being. Those interests, I contend, authorize the subjection of individual spontaneity to external control, only in respect to those actions of each, which concern the interest of other people. If any one does an act hurtful to others, there is a prima facie case for punishing him, by law, or, where legal penalties are not safely applicable, by general disapprobation. There are also many positive acts for the benefit of others, which he may rightfully be compelled to perform; such as, to give evidence in a court of justice; to bear his fair share in the common defence, or in any other joint work necessary to the interest of the society of which he enjoys the protection; and to perform certain acts of individual beneficence, such as saving a fellow-creature's life, or interposing to protect the defenceless against ill-usage, things which whenever it is obviously a man's duty to do, he may rightfully be made responsible to society for not doing. A person may cause evil to others not only by his actions but by his inaction, and in either case he is justly accountable to them for the injury. The latter case, it is true, requires a much more cautious exercise of compulsion than the former. To make any one answerable for doing evil to others, is the rule; to make him answerable for not preventing evil, is, comparatively speaking, the exception. Yet there are many cases clear enough and grave enough to justify that exception. In all things which regard the external relations of the individual, he is de jure amenable to those whose interests are concerned, and if need be, to society as their protector. There are often good reasons for not holding him to the responsibility; but these reasons must arise from the special expediencies of the case: either because it is a kind of case in which he is on the whole likely to act better, when left to his own discretion, than when controlled in any way in which society have it in their power to control him; or because the attempt to exercise control would produce other evils, greater than those which it would prevent. When such reasons as these preclude the enforcement of responsibility, the conscience of the agent himself should step into the vacant judgment-seat, and protect those interests of others which have no external protection; judging himself all the more rigidly, because the case does not admit of his being made accountable to the judgment of his fellow-creatures.

- As you read the next passage, make a list of the various kinds of individual liberties Mill thinks the government should protect.

But there is a sphere of action in which society, as distinguished from the individual, has, if any, only an indirect interest; comprehending all that portion of a person's life and conduct which affects only himself, or, if it also affects others, only with their free, voluntary, and undeceived consent and participation. When I say only himself, I mean directly, and in the first instance: for whatever affects himself, may affect others through himself; and the objection which may be grounded on this contingency, will receive consideration in the sequel. This, then, is the appropriate region of human liberty. It comprises, first, the inward domain of consciousness; demanding liberty of conscience, in the most comprehensive sense; liberty of thought and feeling; absolute freedom of opinion and sentiment on all subjects, practical or speculative, scientific, moral, or theological. The liberty of expressing and publishing opinions may seem to fall under a different principle, since it belongs to that part of the conduct of an individual which concerns other people; but, being almost of as much importance as the liberty of thought itself, and resting in great part on the same reasons, is practically inseparable from it. Secondly, the principle requires liberty of tastes and pursuits; of framing the plan of our life to suit our own character; of doing as we like, subject to such consequences as may follow; without impediment from our fellowcreatures, so long as what we do does not harm them even though they should think our conduct foolish, perverse, or wrong. Thirdly, from this liberty of each individual, follows the liberty, within the same limits, of combination among individuals; freedom to unite, for any purpose not involving harm to others: the persons combining being supposed to be of full age, and not forced or deceived.

No society in which these liberties are not, on the whole, respected, is free, whatever may be its form of government; and none is completely free in which they do not exist absolute and unqualified. The only freedom which deserves the name, is that of pursuing our own good in our own way, so long as we do not attempt to deprive others of theirs, or impede their efforts to obtain it. Each is the proper guardian of his own health, whether bodily, or mental or spiritual. Mankind are greater gainers by suffering each other to live as seems good to themselves, than by compelling each to live as seems good to the rest.

Interpreting Mill's discussion, we could say that the sphere of individual liberty can be divided into two main sectors. The first is our inward life in which there is the absolute right to freedom of thought and expression. Mill recognizes that speaking or publishing our opinions intrudes on the public sphere, but he thinks that our personal opinions are so intimately related to the sanctity of our individual conscience that it is a natural extension of the personal sphere. The second sector of individual liberty concerns our outward life, which involves our choices and actions. Let's discuss each sphere in turn.

Mill's discussion of the first realm of freedom, the right to free expression and discussion of ideas, has been enormously influential and is the basis of much of our thinking about free speech today. Because he devotes the entire second chapter of his book to this issue, I can only summarize his main points here. Mill says that society is harmed by the suppression of free speech regardless of whether the ideas in question are true or false. First, the unpopular idea that is suppressed may, in fact, be true. In this case, it will not get a fair hearing, and society's need to correct its false beliefs will not be met. The case of Galileo showed that the majority is often wrong and the nonconformist is right. Because we are not infallible, we need to be exposed to ideas that will make us check the soundness of our beliefs. Second, even if an idea is false, we still should allow it to be heard in order to expose it to the light of free discussion so that its errors may be revealed and so that the outlines of the true opinion can be seen more clearly. Third, even when their ideas are false, dissenters from the ideological status quo make a contribution because they prevent intellectual stagnation and force us to reexamine the grounds for the prevailing convictions. Unless this scrutiny is done, a true opinion will become "a dead dogma, not a living truth." Notice that Mill defends freedom of speech not because it is an intrinsic "right" that individuals possess, but because it will produce the greatest good for society in the long run.

The only restriction on free speech Mill allowed was when it threatened to cause immediate harm. However, this situation is not really an exception to his rule, because his whole theory of personal liberty is based entirely on what will promote the social good and prevent harm. The example he provides is:

> An opinion that corn-dealers are starvers of the poor . . . ought to be unmolested when simply circulated through the press, but may justly incur punishment when delivered orally to an excited mob assembled before the house of a corn-dealer.[13]

This principle found its way into the "clear and present danger" criterion that the U.S. Supreme Court uses to determine when free speech may be limited.

With respect to the second sphere of individual liberty, that of personal choices and overt actions, Mill continues to guard the freedom of the individual from the intrusion of the government. He recognizes, however, that it is difficult to maintain the correct balance here between the individual's interests and society's interests. Let's begin with his general statement of the issue.

- Notice in the following passage that when Mill talks about "rights," he says that they are the result of "legal provision or tacit understanding." They are socially "constituted" rights, meaning they are not intrinsic to us apart from a social context. What are some implications of the view that there are no intrinsic rights apart from society?
- Mill says that some actions may harm others but not to the extent that they should be punishable by law. Does he then conclude that no punishment of any sort is appropriate? Do we have to refrain from all judgments about such actions? What would be some examples of actions that are, in some sense, harmful to others but are not serious enough to be illegal? How should society respond to such actions?

Give five people outside your class the following list. Ask them which of the following items, if any, should *not* be protected under the U.S. Constitution's guarantee of freedom of speech. Ask them to justify their answers.

1. Prayer in public schools.
2. Expressing the opinion in public that an unpopular president should be assassinated.
3. Burning the country's flag as a form of political protest.
4. Advocating the overthrow of the government.
5. Expressing hate speech in public toward a particular racial group.
6. Distributing pornography to adults.
7. Shouting "fire" in a crowded theater as a joke.
8. Publishing sensational lies about a movie star in a Hollywood gossip magazine.
9. Publicly proclaiming that all religions are fraudulent.

After gathering the answers, decide which views would conform most closely to Mill's principles on personal liberty and which forms of public expression Mill would not allow.

PHILOSOPHY
in the
MARKETPLACE

What, then, is the rightful limit to the sovereignty of the individual over himself? Where does the authority of society begin? How much of human life should be assigned to individuality, and how much to society?

Each will receive its proper share, if each has that which more particularly concerns it. To individuality should belong the part of life in which it is chiefly the individual that is interested; to society, the part which chiefly interests society.

Though society is not founded on a contract, and though no good purpose is answered by inventing a contract in order to deduce social obligations from it, every one who receives the protection of society owes a return for the benefit, and the fact of living in society renders it indispensable that each should be bound to observe a certain line of conduct towards the rest. This conduct consists, first, in not injuring the interests of one another; or rather certain interests, which, either by express legal provision or by tacit understanding, ought to be considered as rights; and secondly, in each person's bearing his share (to be fixed on some equitable principle) of the labors and sacrifices incurred for defending the society or its members from injury and molestation. These conditions society is justified in enforcing, at all costs to those who endeavor to withhold fulfilment. Nor is this all that society may do. The acts of an individual may be hurtful to others, or wanting in due consideration for their welfare, without going the length of violating any of their constituted rights. The offender may then be justly punished by opinion, though not by law. As soon as any part of a person's conduct affects prejudicially the interests of others, society has jurisdiction over it, and the question whether the general welfare will or will not be promoted by interfering with it, becomes open to discussion. But there is no room for entertaining any such question when a person's conduct affects the interests of no persons besides himself, or needs not affect them unless they like (all the persons concerned being of full age, and the ordinary amount of understanding). In all such cases there should be perfect freedom, legal and social, to do the action and stand the consequences.

THOUGHT EXPERIMENT: *Private versus Public Interests*

Mill has just expressed the principle that "to individuality should belong the part of life in which it is chiefly the individual that is interested; to society, the part which chiefly interests society." Consider the following list of actions (assume that they are all performed by an adult). Assign each action to one of the following three categories:

(a) This action is a matter of personal choice, and society should have nothing to say about it.

(b) This action affects the interests of society, and laws should govern it. (Ignore the question of whether the action currently is illegal or not.)

(c) This action should not be illegal, but the person should be criticized and persuaded not to do it and should receive social rebuke.

1. In spite of numerous reports of head injuries from motorcycle accidents, Barlow refuses to wear a safety helmet when he rides his motorcycle.
2. Cassie routinely gets high on hallucinogenic drugs in the privacy of her own home, but never takes them when she is going out somewhere.
3. Williford frequently drives while intoxicated, claiming that even then he is a better driver than most drivers who are sober.
4. Lucy is in pain from a terminal disease and requests the services of a physician to help her commit suicide.
5. Dale and Britt are a same-sex couple who are sexually intimate.
6. Brenda helps people suffering from sexual disorders by having therapeutic sex with them for a fee.
7. Harriet is a single woman who spends most of her paycheck on gambling and often does not have enough money to buy food or the medicine she herself needs.
8. Brad, a single father, spends most of his paycheck on gambling and often does not have enough money to buy food or medicine for his children.
9. Chase is married to five women who all live together with him and are fully in favor of their polygamous marriage.

- For each one of your judgments, state how you would defend it to someone who disagreed with you.
- In each case, try to figure out whether Mill would agree with you.

Mill's second area of freedom, the liberty to act as we wish, was based on his undying conviction that, on the whole, individuals are the best judges of their own interest but are not always the best judges of the interests of others. In particular cases, of course, someone's personal choices concerning his or her way of life may not actually be what is best for that individual (for people do make foolish choices), but it is best to allow people to make such choices simply because it is their own choice. Hence, personal autonomy is one of the highest values in Mill's vision of society.

The implications for legal theory are enormous if we adopt Mill's principle that society has no right to infringe on an individual's freedom except when that person's actions harm others. Some of the examples he provides of *unjustifiable* interference with personal liberty are the punishment of nonviolent drunkenness; the suppression of polygamy among the Mormons; the prohibition of recreational drugs, gambling, and sexual relations between consenting adults (such as prostitution); restrictions on Sunday amusements; and restrictions on the sale of poisons. We may personally find the sorts of behavior listed here repugnant, but the persons who engage in them do not inflict harm on others. Hence, for Mill, these examples are all what are often called victimless crimes and should be tolerated.

With the right to freely engage in such behavior, however, comes the necessity of accepting that behavior's natural consequences. For example, although Mill says we are not allowed to prevent people from drinking, he points out that the offensive drunk may find that people shun his or her company. Critics of Mill have asked if we can draw the line so cleanly between actions that affect only the person engaging in them and actions that affect society. The person who gets drunk in the privacy of his own home may seem to be harming only himself, but what if this personal vice leaves his family to starve? Mill's response was that we may justly punish him for nonsupport, the only socially harmful act he has committed. We may urge the drunk, the prostitute, and the compulsive gambler to mend their ways, but society cannot otherwise interfere in their personal lifestyle choices.

In spite of the strong tone of political freedom that permeates Mill's writings, it should be remembered that personal liberty according to him is not an intrinsic right but is always grounded in social utility. Thus, the government may always intervene in personal liberty when it serves the common good. For example, in chapter 5 of *On Liberty*, Mill says that when overpopulation threatens the economy, the state may legitimately forbid people to marry if they have insufficient means of supporting a family. Likewise, he says, justified governmental limitations on our liberty that are necessary to protect society's interests might include requiring the registration of poisons (to guard against their criminal use), enforcing sanitary conditions, or restricting the location of a casino. In his later years, Mill began to abandon the economic individualism of his earlier work and saw a greater need for state control of the distribution of wealth. It is at this point that his strong plea for individual liberty came into conflict with his concern for the public good.

Whereas classical liberals such as Mill argue for the primacy of individual liberty and minimal government interference, the advocates of collectivism claim that a concern for the big picture and more government control will guarantee the best society.

STOP AND THINK

Just six weeks after the terrorist attacks on the United States that occurred on September 11, 2001, Congress passed the U.S.A. Patriot Act. Among its many consequences, the act instantly expanded the government's authority to spy on its own citizens while reducing the traditional checks and balances on the government's power, such as judicial

(continued . . .)

(. . . continued)

oversight, public accountability, and the ability to challenge government searches in court. For example, the new law now allows the FBI to search through an individual's financial records, medical histories, Internet usage, bookstore purchases, library usage, travel patterns, or any other record pertaining to an individual's life. Persons or agencies holding these records are forced to turn them over. Previously, Americans were protected against abuse of this authority by the requirement that the government show evidence that the persons under scrutiny were agents of a foreign power. However, this restriction has now been removed. Furthermore, government agents need not demonstrate a reasonable suspicion that the records are related to criminal activity, but merely have to assert that the request for information is related to an ongoing terrorism investigation. The previous requirements for receiving a search warrant no longer apply in these investigations. Finally, the new law allows for secret searches, because the person or organization forced to turn over the records is prohibited from disclosing the search to anyone, including the individual who is affected by it.

Many Americans welcome this new arsenal of intelligence weapons in the war against terrorism. However, some claim that this law undermines the Fourth Amendment of the Bill of Rights, which requires that officers of the law have to demonstrate *probable cause* that a crime has been or is being committed before searching an individual's premises without permission. Liberals fear that the act will allow the government to infringe on a political dissident's First Amendment rights. Likewise, some conservatives see it as sacrificing individual freedom on the altar of government control.

A number of philosophical questions arise here. Granted, we all want to live in a society that is safe and secure. However, how many of the liberties you now enjoy are you willing to sacrifice to the government in order to achieve security? Which freedoms or privacy rights are you willing to allow the government to take away from you? What long-term harms to our society will result from these losses of individual freedom and protection from governmental control and intrusion? What is the likelihood that these measures can guarantee us a greater level of security? Given the fact that Thomas Hobbes believed that an absolute government was better than a state of war and insecurity, what would he say about the Patriot Act? Given the fact that John Stuart Mill emphasized individual liberty, would he nevertheless justify the Patriot Act on utilitarian grounds, or would he stand against it? What would other political philosophers say about it? Given the state of the world that we live in today, where would you draw the boundary between an individual's right to freedom and privacy on the one hand and the welfare of society on the other?

LOOKING THROUGH THE LENS OF CLASSICAL LIBERALISM

1. If John Stuart Mill were our president, what changes would he want to make in our society? In what ways would he think that our government was intruding into the sphere of individual liberty?

2. Suppose a student group wanted to bring to campus a very controversial speaker who would be offensive to many other students (e.g., a neo-Nazi, a racist, a communist, an outspoken atheist). The administration, in an attempt to avoid public controversy and to protect the sensibilities of those students who would be offended by this presentation,

decides to ban this speaker. Imagine that you are Mill. What arguments would you give to the administration as to why this speaker should be allowed to publicly express his or her opinions?

3. If governments throughout history had adopted Mill's principles and had they not censored, imprisoned, or put to death people whose ideas were controversial for their time, how would history have been different? Would it be better or worse? Would the free expression of ideas have resulted in more progress, more tolerance, and a better society? Or would allowing deviant and even dangerous ideas to be freely expressed have caused more harm and social problems than Mill imagined?

EXAMINING THE STRENGTHS AND WEAKNESSES OF CLASSICAL LIBERALISM

Positive Evaluation

1. Western societies pride themselves on the amount of personal liberty they allow. They also claim that protecting freedom of speech is one of the foundation stones of a democratic, free society. Doesn't the fact that many of our current policies concerning freedom of speech were influenced by Mill's essay or are captured in it lend credibility to his political philosophy?

2. The government can provide a number of services and benefits that will maximize the common good, but it also has a tremendous amount of power. Without strict limits on the government's power, it is hard for individuals to protect their liberties apart from radical social actions and even revolutions. Therefore, isn't Mill correct in trying to drastically limit the power of the government and giving priority to individual liberty?

3. Martin Niemoeller, a German pastor imprisoned by the Nazis, wrote this: "First the Nazis went after the Jews, but I was not a Jew, so I did not object. Then they went after the Catholics, but I was not a Catholic, so I did not object. Then they went after the Trade-Unionists, but I was not a Trade-Unionist, so I did not object. Then they came after me, and there was no one left to object." It is hard to tolerate ideas and practices that are contrary to our own. As Niemoeller suggests, it is also easy to be apathetic when groups we don't belong to are suppressed and even persecuted. But hasn't Niemoeller effectively demonstrated Mill's point that if we don't protect everyone's freedoms, even those freedoms that are distasteful or contrary to our values, then our freedoms as well are in jeopardy?

Negative Evaluation

1. Mill argues that the government can intervene only to prevent actions that harm others. But aren't there other types of "harms" besides physical harm? Can't hateful speech be harmful to those it targets or create a social climate that is harmful to society?

2. Mill claims that prostitution, the use of recreational drugs, and gambling may be bad for the individuals who freely engage in these activities but that others are not harmed. Whether or not we believe in the legalization of these activities, can we really say that they have no social consequences whatsoever? In other words, isn't it hard to draw the line between activities of individuals that harm only themselves and those that negatively affect the common good? Hasn't Mill glossed over this problem?

3. Isn't there a conflict between Mill's commitment to individual liberty and his claim that the best society is one that creates the greatest amount of happiness for the greatest number? Whereas the first concern leads to a minimal government, doesn't the second concern presuppose more involvement of the government in people's lives? Isn't it dangerous for the government to assume that it is in charge of our happiness? In fact, as we read in the text, Mill later believed in a need for state control of the distribution of wealth in order to maximize the amount of satisfaction in society. Isn't this sort of "social engineering" in tension with his emphasis on individualism?

SURVEYING THE CASE FOR MARXISM

KARL MARX (1818–1883)

Marx's Life

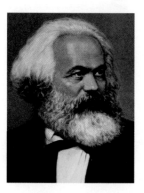

KARL MARX
(1818–1883)

Karl Marx was born in 1818 in the Rhineland of Germany. Although his family was Jewish, his father converted to Lutheranism (which was a political necessity at that time). As a teenager, Marx was very pious. He studied at the universities of Bonn and Berlin, hoping to become a lawyer like his father. At the University of Berlin, however, Marx joined a group of political radicals known as the Young Hegelians, named after the German philosopher Georg W. F. Hegel. Although Hegel had been dead for five years, the German universities were charged with his influence, and philosophical debates filled the air. Marx became caught up in the excitement and abandoned law for the study of philosophy. He ended up getting a doctorate in philosophy at the University of Jena.

Although Marx was destined to be a philosophy professor, the conservative Prussian government closed this option when they prohibited political radicals such as Marx from teaching in the universities. Consequently, he became a political journalist but was forced to continually move from city to city and country to country as his journals were banned by various governments. Marx finally settled in London in 1849, where he remained for the rest of his life. The only stable job he ever held was as a European correspondent for the *New York Tribune* from 1851 to 1862. The rest of the time he survived on family donations, loans, and subsidies from his lifelong friend and collaborator,Friedrich Engels.

Although he is thought of as a social activist, the bulk of Marx's life was spent in the library of the British Museum, where he worked every day from nine in the morning until it closed at seven at night, researching and writing his philosophical, historical, political, and economic manuscripts. When the library closed, he would go home to his wife, Jenny, and their children, where he would work at night until he was exhausted. (Although the couple had six children, only three lived to reach adulthood. In spite of Marx's poverty and single-minded dedication to his writings, however, his children recalled that he was a wonderful, playful father.) After suffering for months from a diseased lung, Marx died on March 14, 1883, while sleeping in his favorite armchair in his study. He was buried next to his wife in a cemetery near London.

Marx's Philosophy

Marx's impoverished life and his long hours of research were not fruitless. His radical, political philosophy eventually became both the rallying trumpet and the theoretical foundation of angry, impoverished, oppressed workers throughout Europe (and later the entire world). People can debate the credibility of Marx's theories, but no one can dispute their influence. No philosopher in history can claim to have had an international, organized, and activist following of such proportions. As a result of his theories, governments have been overthrown, maps have been changed, and his name became a household word. As Marx said in one of his more famous quotes, "The philosophers have only *interpreted* the world, in various ways; the point is to *change* it."

Marx's vision of history and society began when he was a young university student and first encountered Georg Hegel's ideas. Hegel's philosophy taught that human history has meaning and purpose, that it is a rational, determined, evolutionary process in which each stage encounters tensions and contradictions that cause it to change and bring forth a new form of social, cultural, and political organization. Some fans of Hegel gave him a very conservative interpretation and saw his philosophy as implying that the present stage of history was thoroughly rational and inevitable. This view helped support the status quo. Marx and his friends, however, saw Hegel's philosophy as leading in a more radical direction. They believed that the historical development of society has not yet finished its journey and that the present stage will inevitably be destroyed and give way to a better, more rational social structure. It was their goal to move history along to its final, rational stage through political action.

The main themes of Marx's philosophy can be summarized in five points. Let us examine each point.

Economics Rules Everything

Marx is noted for the claim that the fundamental driving force in human behavior and history is economics. He begins with the undeniable truth that people cannot eat ideas but must live on the material products of labor. In other words, before you can philosophize, paint, write novels, do science, or practice your religion, you first have to survive. And in order to survive, you must have the means to secure food, shelter, and clothes. Economics, Marx argued, is at the root of all human existence. Hence, the changes in society and philosophy are the result of underlying changes in technology and the economic system. In the Middle Ages, with its rural economy, one set of ideas and political system prevailed; in industrial Europe, another set of ideas and political system results. This approach was quite a slap in the face to traditional philosophers, who thought that ideas brought about the changes in history. According to Marx, however, economics is the basis of all other facets of society and culture. Marx argued that whether an idea gets a hearing in society or is suppressed is the result of whether it supports the prevailing power structure. As Marx puts it: "The ideas of the ruling class are in every epoch the ruling ideas; . . . The class which has the means of production at its disposal, has control at the same time over the means of mental production."[14] Locke's theory of government, for example, stressed individualism, the fundamental right to own property, and noninterference from the government. But these ideas are supportive of the interests of those who are powerful, own property, and are well-to-do. In other words, according to Marx, Locke's philosophy supported the aristocratic establishment of which he was a part. His economic interests were the basis of his philosophical ideas.

This tendency for social institutions to protect the interests of those in power is the reason why Marx is notorious for being so opposed to religion. He said that religion is the "opium of the people" because it tells the workers to endure their earthly suffering and to focus on their eternal destiny instead of trying to change their wretched social conditions. From Marx's perspective, religion was merely one more expression of the economic status quo that said that the current social hierarchy is God-ordained.

STOP AND THINK

A stanza from a 19th-century Christian hymn says, "The rich man in his castle,/ the poor man at his gate,/ God made them high or lowly,/ and ordered their estate." In what way do these lines support Marx's theory that religion promotes the status quo and economic injustice?

Class Struggle Is the One Constant throughout History

According to Marx, the story of history is the story of those who have power and those who do not, a struggle between the exploiters and the exploited. With the advent of private property, human affairs became a struggle between those who have property and those who do not. In the modern era, this struggle has been carried on between two classes: the bourgeoisie and the proletariat. The *bourgeoisie* are the capitalists, or the owners of the means of industrial production (such as the factories) and the employers of wage labor. They also include the middle class, who benefit from the current economic system. The other half of society is made up of the *proletariat,* or the workers, those who own no property and who must survive by selling their labor as a commodity.

STOP AND THINK

In terms of your current position in society or your family background, would you place yourself in the bourgeoisie and the middle class or in the proletariat? How do you think your economic and social background and your current circumstances affect your outlook on society? How would your social, political, and economic views have been influenced if you had been born into a different segment of society?

Capitalism Survives by Exploiting the Workers

In Marx's terminology, *capital* is anything that constitutes economic wealth in that it has exchange value, for example, money, property, or goods. The *capitalists* are people who control the economic resources of society, such as the factories. *Capitalism* is that political and economic system in which the means of production and economic wealth are privately controlled. In order to maintain an edge over the competition, Marx says, the capitalist must increase profits by paying workers as little as possible. In Marx's day, society did not have effective unions, minimum wage laws, grievance procedures, or government-imposed standards of health and safety. Furthermore, there was an abundance of labor, so the capitalists could treat their workers as they pleased. Marx said that the vision of hell in Dante's *Inferno* paled in comparison to the inhuman degradation of the industrial England of his time. To prove his comment, he quotes freely from the British government's own documents. One official report had this to say about the lace factories:

> Children of nine or ten years are dragged from their squalid beds at two, three, or four o'clock in the morning and compelled to work for a bare subsistence until ten, eleven, or twelve at night, their limbs wearing away, their frames dwindling, their faces whitening, and their humanity absolutely sinking into a stone-like torpor, utterly horrible to contemplate.[15]

Because of these sorts of horror stories, Marx believed that the type of freedom espoused by liberal philosophers such as Mill was really a sham. For the government to allow everyone

Monument to the Third International (1919, reconstructed 1967–1968) by Vladimir Tatlin. In this model of his never-completed sculpture, the Russian artist Tatlin graphically represented Marx's vision. The spiraling structure illustrates the twists and turns of the progressive dialectic of history as it moves toward its culmination.

to do as he or she wished simply meant that those people who were wealthy, owned the factories, and controlled all the political power were free to exploit the rest.

History Is a Deterministic, Dialectical Process

In developing his view of history, Marx borrowed Hegel's view that history follows a dialectical pattern. The word *dialectic* derives from the Greek word for conversation and suggests a back and forth pattern (like a conversation) in which progress is made. For both Hegel and Marx, the **dialectic** is a historical process in which different, opposing forces resolve their tension by bringing into being a new stage of history. Thus, every era in history is only a temporary stopping place as history moves to its fulfillment. For Hegel, however, this dialectical development was one of *ideas,* for he believed that it was ideas that drive history. Marx turned Hegel's philosophy upside down and made it a dialectic of

dialectic In Hegel and Marx, a historical process in which different opposing forces resolve their tension by bringing into being a new stage of history

material, economic forces. Using the terminology of Hegel's predecessor, Johann Gottlieb Fichte, Marx said that each era of history goes through three stages. The initial state of affairs (called the *thesis*) develops to a point at which it produces its own contradiction (the *antithesis*). The two remain in tension until another state of affairs supersedes them (the *synthesis*). In each round of the dialectic, the deficiencies of one stage bring forth opposing forces to balance out what is lacking. Thus, conflict and struggle are an inevitable part of history.

Like Hegel, Marx had a deterministic view of history. He refers to the laws of history as "tendencies working with iron necessity towards inevitable results."[16] Thus, the various movements and stages in history are not a matter of happenstance; instead, internal laws are at work, bringing about a certain outcome. Accordingly, in Marx's theory, the oppressed class does not need to hope for social justice as merely a tentative possibility, because the laws of history are on their side and guarantee the outcome. But where is the role of human freedom in this scenario? On this topic, Marx says:

> *History* does *nothing,* it 'possesses no immense wealth,' it 'wages *no* battles.' It is *man,* real living man, that does all that, that possesses and fights; 'history' is not a person apart, using man as a means for *its own* particular aims; history is *nothing but* the activity of man pursuing his aims.[17]

One way of looking at Marx's theory is to compare the forces of history to a boulder that someone has sent rolling down a mountain. Once set in motion, the boulder becomes an independent force with its own momentum. Obstructions may be set in its path to slow it down, or obstacles may be minimized to speed up the boulder's descent. However, because of its mass and momentum, it cannot be stopped, and when it has passed through each stage of its descent, it will finally reach its destination. Thus, history is controlled by its own internal laws as well as by human actions. The goal of social activists is to help speed up the inevitable changes of social reform and revolution.

Capitalism Will Undermine Itself and Lead to Communism

According to Marx, capitalism arises as a system in which a small class of people own and control the major forces of production as their private property, and they employ workers who have no economic resources but their own labor power. Within this system a contradiction will begin to arise. The ideology of capitalism is based on individualism and private property. However, the growth of capitalism will necessarily require a highly organized, socialized base with a continually increasing size, complexity, and interdependence. As competition for profits increases, capitalists will keep wages low and replace workers with machines. These actions will result in more unemployment and will drive wages down. The stronger companies will buy up the smaller ones, monopolies will increase, and companies will expand to an international scale. In the process, the capitalists whose companies have failed will join the growing pool of the unemployed.

Using the terms of Marx's dialectic, capitalism is the *thesis* that produces its own *antithesis,* an ever-growing, international, embittered, and impoverished, but unified, class of proletarians (or workers). For this reason, Marx says of the bourgeois (or capitalist) class: "What the bourgeoisie, therefore, produces, above all, is its own grave-diggers. Its fall and the victory of the proletariat are equally inevitable." While the capitalists strive to maintain their position, the situation of the workers becomes intolerable. Society becomes like a tire continually being pumped with air until the internal pressure becomes so great that it explodes. This explosion leads to the third stage of the final cycle of history.

Once capitalism has been discarded on the junkpile of history, the final stage of the dialectic (the *synthesis*) will emerge in three phases. The first phase will be a stage of transition called "the dictatorship of the proletariat." This transition is when the proletariat use their newly gained political power to cleanse society of the last remnants of capitalism. The next phase is the first stage of communism, the stage now known as socialism. The state takes over the means of production that were formerly in the hands of private ownership. This stage, however, will eventually give way to the final stage of ultimate communism, in which the people themselves will control not only political decisions but also the economic life of the country.

The following passage is from the *Communist Manifesto* of 1848, the most popular expression of Marxist theory, written by Marx and his friend and coauthor, Friedrich Engels. In this political tract, Marx and Engels depict history as a long, sorry parade of class conflicts. Although each historical period has different social and economic structures and although the main players go by different sets of labels, in each age there are the "haves" and the "have-nots," the exploiters and the exploited, the oppressors and the oppressed. Ironically, according to Marx's theory, the so-called freedom of modern, liberal democracies is simply the freedom of those with political and economic power to exploit those who are powerless. The word *freedom* rings hollow, Marx says, when the laws, social institutions, economic systems, and even philosophies of a society are controlled by a few to maintain the status quo and promote their own interests. True freedom for the masses of society will come about only with an economic and political revolution such that society will be run by the people for the benefit of all and will guarantee them a living wage, education, health care, and cultural enrichment. According to Marx's version of collectivism, less government means less freedom and more government means more freedom. Only if the government, ruled by the workers, takes charge of things, will true freedom and well-being result.

- What does Marx believe is the dominant theme in history?
- What is the distinctive feature of our epoch?

FROM KARL MARX AND FRIEDRICH ENGELS

Communist Manifesto[18]

Bourgeois and Proletarians

The history of all hitherto existing societies is the history of class struggles.

Freeman and slave, patrician and plebeian, lord and serf, guild-master and journeyman, in a word, oppressor and oppressed, stood in constant opposition to one another, carried on an uninterrupted, now hidden, now open fight, a fight that each time ended, either in a revolutionary re-constitution of society at large, or in the common ruin of the contending classes.

In the earlier epochs of history, we find almost everywhere a complicated arrangement of society into various orders, a manifold gradation of social rank. In ancient Rome we have patricians, knights, plebeians, slaves; in the Middle Ages, feudal lords, vassals, guild-masters, journeymen, apprentices, serfs; in almost all of these classes, again, subordinate gradations.

The modern bourgeois society that has sprouted from the ruins of feudal society has not done away with class antagonisms. It has but established new classes, new conditions of oppression, new forms of struggle in place of the old ones. Our epoch, the epoch of the bourgeoisie, possesses, however, this distinctive feature: it has simplified the class antagonisms: Society as a whole is more and more splitting up into two great hostile camps, into two great classes, directly facing each other: Bourgeoisie and Proletariat.

According to Marx's dialectical view of history, each economic system based on class conflicts produces its own contradiction, which eventually becomes its undoing. In the age of capitalism, the capitalists (or bourgeoisie) require a large body of underpaid workers to make goods at low costs that the capitalists sell to make their profits. The capitalists are driven by their own nature to increase their profits by increasingly exploiting the workers. However, Marx says, the growth and centralization of modern industry has caused large bodies of workers to collect together in their common misery, allowing them to become organized into unions and social action groups. In this way, the bourgeoisie are producing their own "grave-diggers."

Hitherto, every form of society has been based, as we have already seen, on the antagonism of oppressing and oppressed classes. But in order to oppress a class, certain conditions must be assured to it under which it can, at least, continue its slavish existence. The serf, in the period of serfdom, raised himself to membership in the commune, just as the petty bourgeois, under the yoke of feudal absolutism, managed to develop into a bourgeois. The modern labourer, on the contrary, instead of rising with the progress of industry, sinks deeper and deeper below the conditions of existence of his own class. He becomes a pauper, and pauperism develops more rapidly than population and wealth. And here it becomes evident, that the bourgeoisie is unfit any longer to be the ruling class in society, and to impose its conditions of existence upon society as an over-riding law. It is unfit to rule because it is incompetent to assure an existence to its slave within his slavery, because it cannot help letting him sink into such a state, that it has to feed him, instead of being fed by him. Society can no longer live under this bourgeoisie, in other words, its existence is no longer compatible with society.

The essential condition for the existence, and for the sway of the bourgeois class, is the formation and augmentation of capital; the condition for capital is wage-labour. Wage-labour rests exclusively on competition between the labourers. The advance of industry, whose involuntary promoter is the bourgeoisie, replaces the isolation of the labourers, due to competition, by their revolutionary combination, due to association. The development of Modern Industry, therefore, cuts from under its feet the very foundation on which the bourgeoisie produces and appropriates products. What the bourgeoisie, therefore, produces, above all, is its own grave-diggers. Its fall and the victory of the proletariat are equally inevitable.

Notice in the final sentence that Marx says that the fall of capitalism and the victory of the working-class is "inevitable," which is an expression of his deterministic view of history. In the next passage, Marx proposes the abolition of private property. He does not mean that you cannot own your own toothbrush; instead, he is talking about property that produces profits for an individual capitalist, such as a factory.

Property and Freedom

All property relations in the past have continually been subject to historical change consequent upon the change in historical conditions.

The French Revolution, for example, abolished feudal property in favour of bourgeois property.

The distinguishing feature of Communism is not the abolition of property generally, but the abolition of bourgeois property. But modern bourgeois private property is the final and most complete expression of the system of producing and appropriating products, that is based on class antagonisms, on the exploitation of the many by the few.

In this sense, the theory of the Communists may be summed up in the single sentence: Abolition of private property.

We Communists have been reproached with the desire of abolishing the right of personally acquiring property as the fruit of a man's own labour, which property is alleged to be the groundwork of all personal freedom, activity and independence.

Hard-won, self-acquired, self-earned property! Do you mean the property of the petty artisan and of the small peasant, a form of property that preceded the bourgeois form? There is no need to abolish that; the development of industry has to a great extent already destroyed it, and is still destroying it daily.

Or do you mean modern bourgeois private property?

But does wage-labour create any property for the labourer? Not a bit. It creates capital, i.e., that kind of property which exploits wage-labour, and which cannot increase except upon condition of begetting a new supply of wage-labour for fresh exploitation. Property, in its present form, is based on the antagonism of capital and wage-labour. Let us examine both sides of this antagonism.

To be a capitalist, is to have not only a purely personal, but a social status in production. Capital is a collective product, and only by the united action of many members, nay, in the last resort, only by the united action of all members of society, can it be set in motion.

Capital is, therefore, not a personal, it is a social power.

When, therefore, capital is converted into common property, into the property of all members of society, personal property is not thereby transformed into social property. It is only the social character of the property that is changed. It loses its class-character.

Let us now take wage-labour.

The average price of wage-labour is the minimum wage, i.e., that quantum of the means of subsistence, which is absolutely requisite in bare existence as a labourer. What, therefore, the wage-labourer appropriates by means of his labour, merely suffices to prolong and reproduce a bare existence. We by no means intend to abolish this personal appropriation of the products of labour, an appropriation that is made for the maintenance and reproduction of human life, and that leaves no surplus wherewith to command the labour of others. All that we want to do away with, is the miserable character of this appropriation, under which the labourer lives merely to increase capital, and is allowed to live only in so far as the interest of the ruling class requires it.

In bourgeois society, living labour is but a means to increase accumulated labour. In Communist society, accumulated labour is but a means to widen, to enrich, to promote the existence of the labourer.

In bourgeois society, therefore, the past dominates the present; in Communist society, the present dominates the past. In bourgeois society capital is independent and has individuality, while the living person is dependent and has no individuality.

And the abolition of this state of things is called by the bourgeois, abolition of individuality and freedom! And rightly so. The abolition of bourgeois individuality, bourgeois independence, and bourgeois freedom is undoubtedly aimed at.

By freedom is meant, under the present bourgeois conditions of production, free trade, free selling and buying.

But if selling and buying disappears, free selling and buying disappears also. This talk about free selling and buying, and all the other "brave words" of our bourgeoisie about freedom in general, have a meaning, if any, only in contrast with restricted selling and buying, with the fettered traders of the Middle Ages, but have no meaning when opposed to the Communistic abolition of buying and selling, of the bourgeois conditions of production, and of the bourgeoisie itself.

You are horrified at our intending to do away with private property. But in your existing society, private property is already done away with for nine-tenths of the population; its existence for the few is solely due to its non-existence in the hands of those nine-tenths. You reproach us, therefore, with intending to do away with a form of property, the necessary condition for whose existence is the non-existence of any property for the immense majority of society.

In one word, you reproach us with intending to do away with your property. Precisely so; that is just what we intend.

From the moment when labour can no longer be converted into capital, money, or rent, into a social power capable of being monopolised, i.e., from the moment when individual property can no longer be transformed into bourgeois property, into capital, from that moment, you say individuality vanishes.

You must, therefore, confess that by "individual" you mean no other person than the bourgeois, than the middle-class owner of property. This person must, indeed, be swept out of the way, and made impossible.

Communism deprives no man of the power to appropriate the products of society; all that it does is to deprive him of the power to subjugate the labour of others by means of such appropriation.

- In the next passage, what does Marx say causes the changes in our views, conceptions, and consciousness?

Culture and Ideology Controlled by Those in Power

The charges against Communism made from a religious, a philosophical, and, generally, from an ideological standpoint, are not deserving of serious examination.

Does it require deep intuition to comprehend that man's ideas, views and conceptions, in one word, man's consciousness, changes with every change in the conditions of his material existence, in his social relations and in his social life?

What else does the history of ideas prove, than that intellectual production changes its character in proportion as material production is changed? The ruling ideas of each age have ever been the ideas of its ruling class.

When people speak of ideas that revolutionise society, they do but express the fact, that within the old society, the elements of a new one have been created, and that the dissolution of the old ideas keeps even pace with the dissolution of the old conditions of existence.

When the ancient world was in its last throes, the ancient religions were overcome by Christianity. When Christian ideas succumbed in the 18th century to rationalist ideas, feudal society fought its death battle with the then revolutionary bourgeoisie. The ideas of religious liberty and freedom of conscience merely gave expression to the sway of free competition within the domain of knowledge.

"Undoubtedly," it will be said, "religious, moral, philosophical and juridical ideas have been modified in the course of historical development. But religion, morality, philosophy, political science, and law, constantly survived this change."

"There are, besides, eternal truths, such as Freedom, Justice, etc. that are common to all states of society. But Communism abolishes eternal truths, it abolishes all religion, and all morality, instead of constituting them on a new basis; it therefore acts in contradiction to all past historical experience."

What does this accusation reduce itself to? The history of all past society has consisted in the development of class antagonisms, antagonisms that assumed different forms at different epochs.

But whatever form they may have taken, one fact is common to all past ages, viz., the exploitation of one part of society by the other.

No wonder, then, that the social consciousness of past ages, despite all the multiplicity and variety it displays, moves within certain common forms, or general ideas, which cannot completely vanish except with the total disappearance of class antagonisms.

The Communist revolution is the most radical rupture with traditional property relations; no wonder that its development involves the most radical rupture with traditional ideas.

But let us have done with the bourgeois objections to Communism.

- In the next passage, how does Marx say the proletariat will use its political power?
- What does Marx say about the future of class divisions?

The Future

We have seen above, that the first step in the revolution by the working class, is to raise the proletariat to the position of ruling as to win the battle of democracy.

The proletariat will use its political supremacy to wrest, by degrees, all capital from the bourgeoisie, to centralise all instruments of production in the hands of the State, i.e., of the proletariat organised as the ruling class; and to increase the total of productive forces as rapidly as possible.

Of course, in the beginning, this cannot be effected except by means of despotic inroads on the rights of property, and on the conditions of bourgeois production; by means of measures, therefore, which appear economically insufficient and untenable, but which, in the course of the movement, outstrip themselves, necessitate further inroads upon the old social order, and are unavoidable as a means of entirely revolutionising the mode of production. These measures will of course be different in different countries.

Nevertheless in the most advanced countries, the following will be pretty generally applicable.

1. Abolition of property in land and application of all rents of land to public purposes.
2. A heavy progressive or graduated income tax.
3. Abolition of all right of inheritance.
4. Confiscation of the property of all emigrants and rebels.
5. Centralisation of credit in the hands of the State, by means of a national bank with State capital and an exclusive monopoly.
6. Centralisation of the means of communication and transport in the hands of the State.
7. Extension of factories and instruments of production owned by the State; the bringing into cultivation of waste-lands, and the improvement of the soil generally in accordance with a common plan.
8. Equal liability of all to labour. Establishment of industrial armies, especially for agriculture.
9. Combination of agriculture with manufacturing industries; gradual abolition of the distinction between town and country, by a more equable distribution of the population over the country.
10. Free education for all children in public schools. Abolition of children's factory labour in its present form. Combination of education with industrial production, &c., &c.

When, in the course of development, class distinctions have disappeared, and all production has been concentrated in the hands of a vast association of the whole nation, the public power will lose its political character. Political power, properly so called, is merely the organised power of one class for oppressing another. If the proletariat during its contest with the bourgeoisie is compelled, by the force of circumstances, to organise itself as a class, if, by means of a revolution, it makes itself the ruling class, and, as such, sweeps away by force the old conditions of production, then it will, along with these conditions, have swept away the conditions for the existence of class antagonisms and of classes generally, and will thereby have abolished its own supremacy as a class.

In place of the old bourgeois society, with its classes and class antagonisms, we shall have an association, in which the free development of each is the condition for the free development of all.

The following conclusion of the *Communist Manifesto* is Marx's famous rallying cry to the workers. If you were an impoverished, exploited laborer, what effect would it have on you?

The Communists disdain to conceal their views and aims. They openly declare that their ends can be attained only by the forcible overthrow of all existing social conditions. Let the ruling classes tremble at a Communist revolution. The proletarians have nothing to lose but their chains. They have a world to win.

WORKING MEN OF ALL COUNTRIES UNITE!

LOOKING THROUGH THE LENS OF MARXISM

1. Marx believed that economics was the basis of all other cultural institutions. Based on this point, work out a Marxist analysis of the worlds of sports, music, religion, education, and politics as they exist in our society today. Do you think the Marxist analysis has captured any of the truth about these features of our contemporary culture?

2. One hundred years after the publication of *The Communist Manifesto,* philosopher Sidney Hook listed the following features of capitalism as described by Marx:

Economic centralization and monopoly, the cycle of boom and depression, unemployment and the effects of technological change, political and economic class wars, excessive specialization and division of labor, the triumph of materialistic and money values on the rest of our culture.[19]

How many of these problems of capitalism described by Marx still exist in our society today?

3. Contrary to Marx's predictions, the plight of the worker has not gotten worse. Salaries, health and safety standards, the length of the working day, and benefits are all better than they were in Marx's day. However, contemporary Marxist Herbert Marcuse argues that capitalists will make working conditions better only if it serves to increase their profits. Furthermore, he says, by giving workers more materialistic benefits, capitalists have actually made them blind to their true alienation and lack of political power. In spite of the better conditions of the worker, do you think that the capitalist system is still as unjust as the Marxists claim?

4. Under capitalism, you have the opportunity to form your own corporation and, if it is successful, become a millionaire. Under communism, private, profit-making corporations did

not exist and personal wealth was severely restricted. However, people received a guaranteed income, free education, and free medical care, and the costs of cultural events such as the opera were available to the common person. Very few people in our society are able to become millionaires as a result of our economic freedom. However, everyone would benefit from free education and medical care. Do you think the individual freedom of capitalism is enough to justify the lack of these governmental benefits? Or would it be worth sacrificing some freedoms so that everyone in society would benefit from the government-provided benefits?

EXAMINING THE STRENGTHS AND WEAKNESSES OF MARXISM

Positive Evaluation

1. As Eastern Europe shifted to capitalism in the latter part of the 20th century, there were good and bad results. People who had lived their lives under communism suddenly were confronted with unemployment, homelessness, poverty, and an increase in crime because strong governmental control and paternalistic benefits had declined in the new capitalistic economy. Do these results suggest that communism had some positive effects on society?

2. Think of the ways in which money is able to buy power and influence in our society. To what degree are wealthy individuals and large corporations able to influence political campaigns and the flow of information as well as our nation's laws and policies? Does Marx have a point in stressing the role of economics in culture and the power of the wealthy?

3. Western capitalist societies have brought about important social reforms and cured many of the evils that existed in Marx's industrial England in the 19th century. However, would these reforms have come about if anticapitalist critics such as Marx had not raised our social conscience by drawing attention to the plight of the workers? Would corporations have become more benevolent if they did not have to respond to the pressure of unions, social protests, and critics that were inspired by Marx's critique of capitalism?

Negative Evaluation

1. Marx seemed to assume that the only alternatives were a total laissez-faire economy in which the capitalists could do whatever they pleased and a total collectivism in which the government controlled everything. But hasn't our capitalist society actually evolved into a mixed economy that balances the power of the corporations with the common good? What would have happened if Marx had been able to view our 20th-century society and had seen the power of the labor unions, the government's prosecution of monopolies, the extensive regulations governing the health and safety of workers, the affirmative action programs, the increased leisure of workers, and the numerous employee benefits? Wouldn't he have had to change many of his ideas and moderate his critique of capitalism?

2. Did Marx have a romantic view of human nature? He seemed to think that the motivation of self-interest and the lust for power and control were exclusively the results of the capitalist system and would not carry over to humanity under a socialist government. But isn't it true that, for better or worse, some features of human nature will be the same in any economic system? Furthermore, haven't capitalists and corporations

sometimes acted against their best interests for the common good of society (contrary to what Marx claimed)?

3. Although it is hard to deny that economic factors have played an important role in history and contemporary society, doesn't Marx overemphasize this point? Can all aspects of human life and culture be explained on the basis of economic motivations? Isn't there more to human behavior than this one, narrow dimension?

6.4 CIVIL DISOBEDIENCE

 LEADING QUESTIONS: *Civil Disobedience*

1. *Questions from the Opponents of Civil Disobedience:* One of the purposes of government is to maintain law and order so that its citizens can enjoy peace and security. But aren't people who break the laws (even if they believe their cause is just) undermining the stability of society? Furthermore, doesn't such behavior promote disrespect for the law?

2. *Questions from the Opponents of Civil Disobedience:* Some people claim that it is morally justified to break the law in order to draw attention to what they feel is an unjust law. But does the end justify the means? There is never going to be universal agreement about which laws are good and which ones are not. If everyone broke the laws they did not like, then lawlessness rather than order would be the norm. Even if people think that disobeying the law will cure the ills of society, isn't the cure worse than the disease?

3. *Questions from the Supporters of Civil Disobedience:* Everyone generally has an obligation to obey the law, but what about laws that are unjust and that violate people's rights? Furthermore, what if the people in power are deeply committed to the status quo and are unwilling to change? Isn't it sometimes true that the only way to draw attention to unjust laws is to disobey them?

4. *Questions from the Supporters of Civil Disobedience:* How would history have been different if everyone had believed that it was never justified to break the law? Moses and the Israelites would not have defied the Egyptian pharaoh. Socrates would have ceased to teach his philosophy in defiance of the state. Christianity might never have gotten off the ground because the early Christians were forbidden by the Jewish and Roman authorities to preach their new religion. The American Revolution would never have occurred. People would not have helped slaves escape from their masters in the 19th century. Unsafe conditions and starvation wages for workers would have continued if workers did not go on strike at a time when striking was illegal. Who knows when or if women would have been allowed to vote without the civil disobedience of the women protesters. The Civil Rights Act of 1964 might not have been enacted without the protests and acts of civil disobedience that led up to it. Doesn't history show that civil disobedience can be a necessary impetus for social improvement?

As leading questions 1 and 2 suggest, for there to be a government, there have to be laws. If you believe that government is generally a good thing (assuming you are not an anarchist), then you must believe that it is essential for the good of society to have laws. If people do not obey the laws, however, then there might as well not be any laws at all, and practically speaking, society would be an anarchy. So initially, it seems as though disobeying the laws of your government is never morally justified. But leading questions 3 and 4 throw a different light on the issue. What if the laws that a government passes are illegal (they violate its own constitution or the social contract)? Or what if the laws are legal but are deeply immoral? Adolph Hitler, for example, rose to power in Nazi Germany through a legal political process. Once in power, he began to change the laws (again through legal procedures) so that many of the horrors of that society, such as the confiscation of people's property and imprisonment of innocent "enemies of the state," were perfectly legal. In the 18th and 19th centuries it was legal to own slaves in portions of the United States, even though this practice is clearly immoral. Furthermore, up until the latter half of the 20th century, racial discrimination was protected by the law in the United States. What should a citizen do in these cases? Although most political philosophers agree that obedience to the law is an important foundation stone of any society, many have argued that there are limits to this obligation.

Before I go any further in examining the opposing sides of this issue, I should back up and define my terms. **Civil disobedience** is an illegal action performed for the purpose of making a moral protest. It isn't just an act of protest that frustrates or aggravates the authorities. It has to be a blatant violation of the law or a disobeying of an explicit order of some civil authority. This authority could be at the city, state, or federal level. An example of civil disobedience would be sitting in at some governmental office in order to disrupt its course of business and then refusing to leave when ordered to do so. But what is the difference between criminal disobedience and civil disobedience, since both categories involve illegal actions? The major difference is that civil disobedience (unlike criminal disobedience) is a form of moral protest. It is an attempt to protest some law, policy, or action of a governmental body in order to draw attention to the unjustness of the law, the problems with the policy, or the wrongness of a particular action on the part of the government. Ultimately, of course, the goal is to change the law or the government's behavior. In contrast, a simple criminal act does not have any sort of high-minded purpose. The criminal breaks the law for personal gain, by robbing a bank or driving with an illegal license, for example.

To be classified as an act of moral protest, the lawbreaking must be public. The authorities and the public must be aware that the government is being disobeyed. Furthermore, most defenders of civil disobedience would say that protesters who cannot win their case in court must be willing to accept the penalty that follows this action, such as a jail sentence or a fine. Hence, those people who engage in civil disobedience must be willing to become martyrs for their moral cause. More important, accepting the penalty shows respect for the political system and the law in general while drawing attention to its problems. On the other hand, a criminal action is done secretly with the intent of evading the law. By this criterion, bombing an abortion clinic or a governmental office and then evading capture is a criminal act. However, placing your body in front of the door until you are arrested and dragged away by the police is an act of civil disobedience. Both types of action may be motivated by a dissatisfaction with the system, but the difference is in the means used to protest it.

Also, many social activists believe that for an action to count as a moral protest, it must be nonviolent. This approach was stressed by Mahatma Gandhi and Martin Luther King Jr., who are both known for their use of civil disobedience as a technique for social change. But where do we draw the line between violence and nonviolence? Certainly an action that caused personal injury would be an example of violence. But what about destruction of property? On one occasion, environmentalists poured sludge from a polluted river into the files of a corporation that they claimed was a major polluter. Although this action falls short of bombing the building, is it still violence? Other social activists would define violence more broadly and include the violation of an individual's legal rights. Under this definition, preventing a client from entering an abortion clinic would not be a legitimate form of protest. Now that we have our terms defined, let's go on to examine the arguments against and for civil disobedience.

civil disobedience an illegal action performed for the purpose of making a moral protest

SURVEYING THE CASE AGAINST CIVIL DISOBEDIENCE

If you are living in a completely totalitarian state in which the people have no freedoms and human rights are being persistently and grossly violated, you could argue that civil disobedience (even to the point of violence) is the only remedy left. To discuss whether civil disobedience is justified in this context is to make the debate too trivial. On the other hand, what if you are living in a democratic society in which the people are able to elect their leaders and have a voice in making the laws? Furthermore, what if the laws are, for the most part, just and good laws? In this society, are there any situations in which civil disobedience can be justified?

The following four arguments are the most common ones used to defend the view that civil disobedience is never morally justified. They are expressed in the voice of an opponent of civil disobedience.

A Violation of the Social Contract. By the time that you begin considering an act of civil disobedience, you have lived for a while (typically all your life) in the society whose laws you are going to violate. In doing so, you have been continuously protected by the government and have benefited from the government's services. Hence, you have tacitly entered into a agreement with the state to be one of its citizens. Because you have reaped the benefits of being a citizen of this country, you also have an obligation to the state to obey its laws. You cannot enjoy being a citizen when it is convenient, expecting the government to hold up its end of the bargain, and then turn around and disobey it when it is convenient to do so. Hence, civil disobedience is a violation of the social contract that every citizen has tacitly approved.

Majority Rule. The government is not some alien entity that has invaded our lives. The government rules according to the will of the people through our elected representatives. However, none of us is happy with the outcome of every election or with each and every law. But whether we like the outcome or not, the government is a creation of the will of the majority. We all have an obligation to abide by the will of the majority or to seek to change it. When you dissent through civil disobedience, you are trying to accomplish through breaking the law what you were unable to accomplish through the democratic process, but in doing so, you are undermining the very principle of democracy. Therefore, civil disobedience is never justified.

Ends That Do Not Justify the Means. Let's assume, for the sake of the discussion, that you are breaking the law in the name of a good cause. But does having good motivations and trying to achieve a good end justify anything you do? The good that might be accomplished through civil disobedience has to be measured against its other results. Breaking the law, for whatever reasons, promotes a lack of respect for the law and the government. Furthermore, it leads to social chaos and other evils. The work of the government is so disrupted and officials have to spend so much time dealing with protesters that they are diverted from doing the normal and essential tasks involved in running the society. Finally, in spite of their best intentions, law-breaking protesters often provoke violence and lawlessness. The violence may erupt from the protesters' own ranks, from members who are less disciplined and cannot channel their anger. Or perhaps the protesters ignite the strong feelings of opponents who disagree with their cause. Even if these dire outcomes never occur, the negative results of civil disobedience still outweigh its positive fruits.

Other Alternatives. The issues raised in the first three arguments culminate in this last one. A democracy always offers less drastic means than civil disobedience to make your voice heard and to affect society. Without breaking the law, you can exercise your rights to free speech, peaceful assembly, petitioning support, voting, and demonstrating. True, these methods are not as dramatic and as attention getting as civil disobedience is. Nevertheless, they can work, and they avoid the problems generated by breaking the law. Furthermore, if you really believe that your society is so evil and unjust that breaking the law is justified, then you always have the option of renouncing your citizenship and moving to a society that is more to your liking. Hence, civil disobedience is an unnecessary evil and is always wrong in a free society.

STOP AND THINK

Do you find these arguments convincing? Which one do you think is the strongest? Which one is the weakest? How would a defender of civil disobedience respond to these points?

One of the classic spokespersons for opposing civil disobedience is Socrates. We have encountered the figure of Socrates throughout this book, starting with the discussion of his trial for heresy and corrupting the youth in section 1.1. In a sequel to the story of the trial, Plato tells about Socrates' discussion with one of his students while Socrates was in jail waiting for his execution. Crito, the young disciple, begs Socrates to escape from prison. In the course of the discussion, Socrates makes clear his controversial stand on civil disobedience.

- In the following reading, see how many of the four arguments against civil disobedience you can find in Socrates' discussion.

FROM PLATO

Crito[20]

SOCRATES: Why have you come at this hour, Crito? It must be quite early.

CRITO: Yes, certainly.

SOCRATES: What is the exact time?

CRITO: The dawn is breaking.

SOCRATES: I am surprised the keeper of the prison would let you in.

CRITO: He knows me because I often come, Socrates; moreover, I have done him a kindness.

SOCRATES: Did you just get here?

CRITO: No, I came some time ago.

SOCRATES: Then why did you sit and say nothing, instead of awakening me at once? . . .

CRITO: Oh, my beloved Socrates, let me entreat you once more to take my advice and escape. For if you die I shall not only lose a friend who can never be replaced, but there is another evil: people who do not know you and me will believe that I might have saved you if I had been willing to give money, but that I did not care. . . . Nor can I think that you are justified, Socrates, in betraying your own life when you might be saved; this is playing into the hands of your enemies and destroyers; and moreover I should say that you were betraying your children; for you might bring them up and educate them; instead of which you go away and leave them, and they will have to take their chance; and if they do not meet with the usual fate of orphans, there will be small thanks to you. No man should bring children into the world who is unwilling to persevere to the end in their nurture and education. . . .

SOCRATES: Dear Crito, your zeal is invaluable, if a right one; but if wrong, the greater the zeal the greater the evil; and therefore we ought to consider whether these things shall be done or not. For I am and always have been one of those natures who must be guided by reason, whatever the reason may be which upon reflection appears to me to be the best; and now that this fortune has come upon me, I cannot put away the reasons which I have before given: the principles which I have hitherto honored and revered I still honor, and unless we can find other and better principles on the instant, I am certain not to agree with you. . . .

Let us consider the matter together, and either refute me if you can, and I will be convinced; or else cease, my dear friend, from repeating to me that I ought to escape against the wishes of the Athenians: for I am extremely desirous to be persuaded by you, but not against my own better judgment. . . .

CRITO: I will do my best.

SOCRATES: Are we to say that we are never intentionally to do wrong, or that in one way we ought and in another way we ought not to do wrong, or is doing wrong always evil and dishonorable? Are all our former admissions which were made within a few days to be thrown away? And have we, at our age, been earnestly discoursing with one another all our life long only to discover that we are no better than children? Or are we to rest assured, in spite of the opinion of the many, and in spite of consequences whether better or worse, of the truth of what was then said, that injustice is always an evil and dishonor to him who acts unjustly? Shall we affirm that?

CRITO: Yes.

SOCRATES: Then we must do no wrong?

CRITO: Certainly not.

SOCRATES: When we are injured should we injure in return, as the many imagine. Or must we injure no one at all?

CRITO: Clearly not.

SOCRATES: Again, Crito, may we do evil?

CRITO: Surely not, Socrates.

SOCRATES: And what of doing evil in return for evil, which is the morality of the many—is that just or not?

CRITO: Not just.

SOCRATES: For doing evil to another is the same as injuring him?

CRITO: Very true.

SOCRATES: Then we ought not to retaliate or render evil for evil to anyone, whatever evil we may have suffered from him. But I would have you consider, Crito, whether you really mean what you are saying. For this opinion has never been held, and never will be held, by any considerable number of persons; and those who are agreed and those who are not agreed upon this point have no common ground, and can only despise one another when they see how widely they differ. Tell me, then, whether you agree with and assent to my first principle, that neither injury nor retaliation nor warding off evil by evil is ever right. And shall that be the premise of our argument? Or do you decline and dissent from this? For this has been of old and is still my opinion; but, if you are of another opinion, let me hear what you have to say. If, however, you remain of the same mind as formerly, I will proceed to the next step.

CRITO: You may proceed, for I have not changed my mind.

SOCRATES: Then I will proceed to the next step, which may be put in the form of a question: Ought a man to do what he admits to be right, or ought he to betray the right?

CRITO: He ought to do what he thinks right.

SOCRATES: But if this is true, what is the application? In leaving the prison against the will of the Athenians, do I wrong any? or rather do I not wrong those whom I ought least to wrong? Do I not desert the principles which were acknowledged by us to be just? What do you say?

CRITO: I cannot tell, Socrates, for I do not know.

SOCRATES: Then consider the matter in this way: Imagine that I am about to play truant (you may call the proceeding by any name which you like), and the laws and the government come and interrogate me: "Tell us, Socrates," they say; "what are you trying to do? Are you attempting to overturn us—the laws and the whole State, as far as you are able? Do you imagine that a State can subsist and not be overthrown, in which the decisions of law have no power, but are set aside and overthrown by individuals?" What will be our answer, Crito, to these and the like words? Anyone, and especially a clever rhetorician, will have a good deal to urge about the evil of setting aside the law which requires a sentence to be carried out; and we might reply, "Yes; but the State has injured us and given an unjust sentence." Suppose I say that?

CRITO: Very good, Socrates.

SOCRATES: "And was that our agreement with you?" the law would say; "or were you to abide by the sentence of the State?" And if I were to express astonishment at their saying this, the law would probably add: "Answer, Socrates, instead of opening your eyes: you are in the habit of asking and answering questions. Tell us what complaint you have to make against us which justifies you in attempting to destroy us and the State? In the first place did we not bring you into existence? Your father married your mother by our aid and begat you. Say whether you have any objection to urge against those of us who regulate marriage?" None, I should reply. "Or against those of us who regulate the system of nurture and education of children in which you were trained? Were not the laws, who have the charge of this, right in commanding your father to train you in music and gymnastic?" Right, I should reply. . . . What answer shall we make to this, Crito? Do the laws speak truly, or do they not?

CRITO: I think that they do.

SOCRATES: Then the laws will say: "Consider, Socrates, if this is true, that in your present attempt you are going to do us wrong. For, after having brought you into the world, and nurtured and educated you, and given you and every other citizen a share in every good that we had to give, we further proclaim and give the right to every Athenian, that if he does not like us when he has come of age and has seen the ways of the city, and made our acquaintance, he may go where he pleases and take his goods with him; and none of us laws will forbid him or interfere with him. Any of you who does not like us and the city, and who wants to go to a colony or to any other city, may go where he likes, and take his goods with him. But he who has experience of the manner in which we order justice and administer the State, and still remains, has entered into an implied contract that he will do as we command him. And he who disobeys us is, as we maintain, thrice wrong: first, because in disobeying us he is disobeying his parents; secondly, because we are the authors of his education; thirdly, because he has made an agreement with us that he will duly obey our commands; and he neither obeys them nor convinces us that our commands are wrong; and we do not rudely impose them, but give him the alternative of obeying or convincing us; that is what we offer, and he does neither.

"These are the sort of accusations to which, as we were saying, you, Socrates, will be exposed if you accomplish your intentions; you, above all other Athenians." Suppose I ask, why is this? They will justly retort upon me that I above all other men have acknowledged the agreement. "There is clear proof, Socrates," they will say, "that we and the city were not displeasing to you. Of all Athenians you have been the most constant resident in the city, which, as you never leave, you may be supposed to love. For you never went out of the city either to see the games, except once when you went to the Isthmus, or to any other place unless when you were on military service; nor did you travel as other men do. Nor had you any curiosity to know other States or their laws: your affections did not go beyond us and our State; we were your special favorites, and you acquiesced in our government of you; and this is the State in which you begat your children, which is a proof of your satisfaction.

"Moreover, you might, if you had liked, have fixed the penalty at banishment in the course of the trial—the State which refuses to let you go now would have let you go then. But you pretended that you preferred death to exile, and that you were not grieved at death. And now you have forgotten these fine sentiments, and pay no respect to us, the laws, of whom you are the destroyer; and are doing what only a miserable slave would do, running away and turning your back upon the compacts and agreements which you made as a citizen. And first of all answer this very question: Are we right in saying that you agreed to be governed according to us in deed, and not in word only? Is that true or not?"

How shall we answer that, Crito? Must we not agree?

CRITO: There is no help, Socrates.

SOCRATES: Then will they not say: "You, Socrates, are breaking the covenants and agreements which you made with us at your leisure, not in any haste or under any compulsion or deception, but having had seventy years to think of them, during which time you were at liberty to leave the city, if we were not to your mind, or if our covenants appeared to you to be unfair. You had your choice, and might have gone either to Lacedaemon or Crete, which you often praise for their good government, or to some other Hellenic or foreign State. Whereas you, above all other Athenians, seemed to be so fond of the State, or, in other words, of us her laws (for who would like a State that has no laws), that you never stirred out of her. . . . And now you run away and forsake your agreements. Not so, Socrates, if you will take our advice; do not make yourself ridiculous by escaping out of the city. . . .

"Listen, then, Socrates, to us who have brought you up. Think not of life and children first, and of justice afterwards, but of justice first, that you may be justified before the princes of the world below. For neither will you nor any that belong to you be happier or holier or more just in this life, or happier in another, if you do as Crito bids. Now you depart in innocence, a sufferer and not a doer of evil; a victim, not of the laws, but of men. . . . Listen, then, to us and not to Crito."

This is the voice which I seem to hear murmuring in my ears, like the sound of the flute in the ears of the mystic; that voice, I say, is humming in my ears, and prevents me from hearing any other. And I know that anything more which you may say will be in vain. Yet speak, if you have anything to say.

CRITO: I have nothing to say, Socrates.

SOCRATES: Then let me follow the intimations of the will of God.

STOP AND THINK

What do you think of Socrates' arguments? Assuming that the decision of the court was wrong, did Socrates do the right thing in refusing to escape from prison? If you were Crito, how would you convince Socrates not to stay and die?

LOOKING THROUGH THE LENS OF THE OPPONENTS OF CIVIL DISOBEDIENCE

1. What advice would Socrates give to a German living during the time of the Nazi regime concerning his or her response to the government?

2. At the end of their speech, the laws tell Socrates that he is "a victim, not of the laws, but of men." Is this distinction between the justice of the laws and the injustice of people's application of them a helpful one? What would be the practical application of this distinction?

3. What would be the advantages of living in a society in which everyone supported Socrates' political ideas? What would be the disadvantages?

EXAMINING THE STRENGTHS AND WEAKNESSES OF THE OPPOSITION TO CIVIL DISOBEDIENCE

Positive Evaluation

1. Doesn't the opposition to civil disobedience encourage people to find creative and legal ways to make their voices heard and to change society? On the other hand, doesn't civil disobedience run the risk of opening the floodgates of social disorder?

2. The laws said to Socrates that if he disagreed with them, he always had the option either of trying to convince them of his position or of settling in another country in which he found the laws more agreeable. Aren't these alternatives reasonable? Aren't there always ways in a democracy of dealing with a problem other than breaking the law?

3. Could we apply Kant's notion of universalizability here? (See section 5.4 on Kant's moral philosophy.) If we all followed the rule, "Always obey the law unless you think you shouldn't," wouldn't we negate the very notion of law? Because different people have different notions of what is just and unjust, wouldn't obedience to the law be a rather individualistic and subjective matter? Can we pick and choose which laws we want to obey?

Negative Evaluation

1. If we believe with Socrates that we have an agreement with our government, does it follow that we have agreed to obey any and all laws no matter what? Or is our agreement that we will obey laws that are justly written and justly applied? Doesn't this qualification allow for respect for the social contract as well as for the possibility of disobeying unjust laws and governmental actions?

2. Isn't Socrates' position rather extreme? Doesn't it support glib slogans like "My country, right or wrong!" or "Either obey your government unconditionally or leave"? Isn't there some middle ground between passively accepting everything your government does

and moving? Doesn't Socrates' death sentence at the hands of his government show that the government is not always justified in what it does?

3. Certainly the opponents of civil disobedience have a point in drawing attention to the dangers and possible abuses of this form of protest. But aren't they attacking a straw man in suggesting that this approach would lead to a total disregard for the law? (See the discussion of the straw man fallacy in the appendix at the end of the text.) If people who engage in civil disobedience don't resist arrest and are willing to accept punishment for their dissent, aren't they exhibiting respect for the law?

SURVEYING THE CASE FOR CIVIL DISOBEDIENCE

Although the position we just examined, represented by Socrates, maintained that it is *never* right to break the law, the opposing position does not contend that it is *always* right to break the law. Instead, the position we now discuss argues that it is *sometimes* justified to commit acts of civil disobedience. Whether breaking the law in this way is morally justified is said to depend on the circumstances. Hence, because the position contains this qualification, different people could agree on the principle of using civil disobedience as a form of moral action while disagreeing on the circumstances in which it should be used. Nevertheless, although they disagree on the details, all defenders of this position use the same basic set of arguments. In his book *Morals and Ethics,* philosopher Carl Wellman lists five arguments typically used to justify civil disobedience.[21]

Preservation of Moral Integrity. Although we normally may have a duty to obey the law, if the law is unjust, then such obedience would force a conscientious citizen to commit a moral evil. It is impossible for any one individual to eradicate all evil, but each of us does have an obligation to refuse to cooperate with evil and to preserve our moral integrity. As Wellman puts it, "Since one ought never to participate in moral wrong and since civil disobedience is sometimes the only way to refrain from being a party to moral evil, civil disobedience is sometimes right."

The Duty to Combat Immorality. Even if you refrain from participating in moral evil yourself, nonaction can facilitate the perpetuation of injustice. Hence, you have a moral duty to actively combat the evils in society by whatever means are effective. Sometimes the only effective way to fight the evils in society is through civil disobedience. Therefore, civil disobedience is sometimes a morally right action.

A Means of Social Progress. It is morally good to seek to improve your society, and you have many ways to do so. Sometimes, however, the normal methods of the political process are ineffective or thwarted; therefore, more direct action is necessary. An act of civil disobedience typically receives media coverage and draws attention to an unjust law. The challenge to the law and the courage of the dissenters can prick the conscience of a nation's citizens and lead them to reexamine society's policies. Americans in the 1960s who were isolated from the injustices of their society or who were not present at the sites of the civil rights clashes in the 1960s were forced to come to terms with their society's problems on the evening news. In this way, civil disobedience is a form of communication and an effective political technique for moving society in the right direction.

No Practical Alternative. The machinery of democracy may move too slowly to keep pace with escalation of social problems. Furthermore, even in a democratic society, the ballot box, the courts, and the press may be controlled by people who want to protect the unjust status quo. Hence, if all other alternatives are ruled out, civil disobedience may be the only means available to influence public opinion and bring about social and political change.

Government May Exceed Its Authority. Sometimes a government may violate its own constitution or may infringe on the rights of its citizens. In such cases, the laws it makes or the demands it makes on its citizens are no longer morally binding. In section 6.2, we read that Aquinas said, "The force of a law depends on the extent of its justice." As Aquinas illustrates, people who justify civil disobedience frequently assume some version of the natural law theory. If the government decides what shall constitute justice, as Hobbes claimed in his version of the social contract theory, then by definition, the government cannot be unjust and civil disobedience cannot be justified.

STOP AND THINK

Do you find these arguments convincing? Which one do you think is the strongest? Which one is the weakest? How would an opponent of civil disobedience respond to these points?

Although these five defenses of civil disobedience overlap somewhat, they each emphasize a slightly different point. In the remainder of this section, we examine the thoughts of two well-known political activists, Mohandas Gandhi and Martin Luther King Jr., and we look for these five defenses in their writings.

MOHANDAS K. GANDHI (1869–1948)

Gandhi's Life

Mohandas Gandhi, the great Indian political and spiritual leader, is best known by the Indian title *Mahatma,* which means "great soul." He was born in Porbandar, India, where he spent his childhood. As a young man, he studied law in London and in 1893 went to South Africa to do legal work. Although South Africa was controlled by the British at that time, and Gandhi was a British subject, he found that he and his fellow Indians were victims of discriminatory laws. He stayed there for 21 years, working to secure rights for the Indian people. But in 1914 he returned to India, the land he loved, and spent the rest of his life working to win India's independence from the British government by applying the method and philosophy of nonviolent civil disobedience he had developed. Gandhi was frequently jailed and beaten by the British government for his civil disobedience, and he spent a total of seven years in prison for his political activities. However, he taught that it was honorable to go to jail for a just cause.

Gandhi was so effective at organizing massive nonviolent resistance to the government that he broke Britain's will to continue its hold over India. His goal of India's independence was achieved in 1947. In January of the following year, however, he was assassinated by a Hindu fanatic who opposed Gandhi's efforts to promote tolerance of all creeds and religions.

Gandhi's Philosophy

Although he is known for his opposition to violence, Gandhi acknowledged that sometimes violence is the only thing that will stop major evils; he himself took part in several wars. Nevertheless, he believed that most of the time violence only breeds worse evils. The preferred method of bringing injustice in a society to an end, Gandhi thought, is a massive movement of morally committed citizens resisting the government by refusing to cooperate with the machinery of injustice. He used such tactics as sit-ins on government property, which forced the government to haul away dozens of people who neither resisted it nor submitted to its demands. On one occasion, Gandhi led a 200-mile march to the sea to collect salt in defiance of the government monopoly on the product. He called his method *satyagraha,* a word coined from the Hindu words *satya* (truth) and *agraha* (force). His political theory grew out of his spirituality, which reflected the Hindu philosophy discussed in section 4.6. He was also influenced by the 19th-century American author Henry David Thoreau, who advocated resistance to unjust laws.

PHILOSOPHY
in the
MARKETPLACE

Ask five to ten people the following questions.

1. Is breaking the law ever *morally* justified? Why?
2. If so, under what conditions would breaking the law be morally justified?
3. Can you think of any examples from history in which people were justified in disobeying the law? Why do you think these cases of lawbreaking were justified?
4. Can you think of any examples from history or the news in which people sincerely believed they were justified in breaking the law, but you believe they were mistaken? Why do you think they were wrong?

After collecting the answers, compare them to Socrates' arguments for not breaking the law and to the five justifications for civil disobedience. Do you see any similarities? Did any of your friends come up with new arguments for either side? Which response do you think was the best? Why? Which response did you disagree with most? Why?

Gandhi's philosophy of nonviolent resistance sounds naive to some people, but he used it to win political victories in South Africa, and he and his followers showed its effectiveness by bringing the British government to its knees. His method has been a model for political action ever since. Martin Luther King Jr. and the civil rights leaders in the 1960s brought dramatic changes to American society by employing Gandhi's techniques. Furthermore, Gandhi's ideas have inspired both antiabortion and proabortion protesters, antiwar activists, environmentalists, animal rights advocates, and other groups lobbying for social change. The spirit of Gandhi's philosophy of nonviolent civil disobedience is illustrated in this passage from one of his books.

- In the following reading, see how many of the five justifications for civil disobedience you can find.

 FROM MOHANDAS GANDHI

Young India[22]

The Law of Suffering

No country has ever risen without being purified through the force of suffering. The mother suffers so that her child may live. The condition of wheat growing is that the seed grain should perish. Life comes out of Death. Will India rise out of her slavery without fulfilling this eternal law of purification through suffering? . . .

. . . What then is the meaning of Non-co-operation in terms of the Law of Suffering? We must voluntarily put up with the losses and inconveniences that arise from having to withdraw our support from a Government that is ruling against our will. Possession of power and riches is a crime under an unjust government; poverty in that case is a virtue, says Thoreau. It may be that, in the transition state, we may make mistakes; there may be avoidable suffering. These things are preferable to national emasculation.

We must refuse to wait for the wrong to be righted till the wrongdoer has been roused to a sense of his iniquity. We must not, for fear of ourselves or others having to suffer, remain participators in it. But we must combat the wrong by ceasing to assist the wrong-doer directly or indirectly.

If a father does an injustice, it is the duty of his children to leave the parental roof. If the head-master of a school conducts his institution on an immoral basis, the pupils must leave the school. If the chairman of a corporation is corrupt, the members thereof must wash their hands clean of his corruption by withdrawing from it; even so, if a government does a grave injustice, the subject must withdraw co-operation wholly or partially, sufficiently to wean the ruler from his wickedness. In each of the cases conceived by me, there is an element of suffering whether mental or physical. Without such suffering, it is not possible to attain freedom. . . .

The Momentous Issue

The next few weeks should see Civil Disobedience in full working order in some part of India. With illustrations of partial and individual Civil Disobedience the country has become familiar. Complete Civil Disobedience is rebellion without the element of violence in it. An out and out civil resister simply ignores the authority of the state. He becomes an outlaw claiming to disregard every unmoral state law. Thus, for instance, he may refuse to pay taxes, he may refuse to recognise the authority of the state in his daily intercourse. He may refuse to obey the law of trespass and claim to enter military barracks in order to speak to the soldiers, he may refuse to submit to limitations upon the manner of picketing and may picket within the prescribed area. In doing all this, he never uses force and never resists force when it is used against him. In fact, he invites imprisonment and other uses of force against himself. This he does because, and when, he finds the bodily freedom he seemingly enjoys to be an intolerable burden. He argues to himself that a state allows personal freedom only in so far as the citizen submits to its regulations. Submission to the state law is the price a citizen pays for his personal liberty. Submission, therefore, to a state wholly or largely unjust is an immoral barter for liberty. A citizen who thus realises the evil nature of a state is not satisfied to live on its sufferance, and therefore appears to the others who do not share his belief to be a nuisance to society, whilst he is endeavouring to compel the state without committing a moral breach to arrest him. Thus considered, civil resistance is a most powerful expression of a soul's anguish and an eloquent protest against the continuance of an evil state. Is not this the history of all reform? Have not reformers, much to the disgust of their fellows, discarded even innocent symbols associated with an evil practice?

Civil versus Criminal

. . . What legal remedy has the afflicted individual against the Government? There is certainly no sanction provided against the Government in law when it prostitutes the law itself to its own base ends. When therefore a Government thus becomes lawless in an organised manner, Civil Disobedience becomes a sacred duty and is the only remedy open specially to those who had no hand in the making of the Government or its laws. Another remedy there certainly is, and that is armed revolt. Civil Disobedience is a complete, effective and bloodless substitute. And it is well that by exemplary restraint and discipline in the way of submission to unjust and even illegal orders we have created the necessary atmosphere for Civil Disobedience. For thereby on the one hand the tyrannical nature of the Government has been made more manifest, and on the other by willing obedience we have fitted ourselves for Civil Disobedience.

It is equally as well that Civil Disobedience is being confined even now to the smallest area possible. It must be admitted that it is an abnormal state, even as a corrupt and unpopular Government should be in civilised society, like disease, an abnormal state. Therefore, only when a citizen has disciplined himself in the art of voluntary obedience to the state laws is he justified on rare occasions deliberately but non-violently to disobey them, and expose himself to the penalty of the breach. If then we are to achieve the maximum result in the minimum of time, whilst fiercest disobedience is going on in a limited area, perfect submission to the laws must be yielded in all the other parts so as to test the nation's capacity for voluntary obedience and for understanding the virtue of Civil Disobedience. Any unauthorised outbreak of disobedience, therefore, in any part of India will most certainly damage the cause and will betray an unpardonable ignorance of the principles of Civil Disobedience.

We must expect the Government to take the strictest measures to suppress this impending defiance of authority, for on it depends its very existence. Its instinct of self-preservation alone will actuate measures of repression adequate for suppression. And if it fails, the Government of necessity disappears. That is, it either bends to the national will or it is dissolved. The greatest danger lies in violence breaking out anywhere by reason of provocation. But it would be wrong and unmanly to invite the sternest measures and then to be incensed against them, apart from the fact that it will be a breach of our solemn pledge of non-violence. I may be arrested, thousands who take part in the peaceful revolt may also be arrested, imprisoned, even tortured. The rest of India must not lose its head. When the proper time comes, the rest of India may respond by undertaking Civil Disobedience and inviting arrests, imprisonments and tortures. It is the sacrifice of the innocent we want to make. That alone will appear pleasing to God. And therefore, on the eve of the great battle the nation is embarking upon, my earnest exhortation to every Non-co-operator is to fit himself for Civil Disobedience by fulfilling to the letter and in the spirit the conditions of Civil Disobedience laid down at Delhi, and to ensure non-violence everywhere. Let us not be satisfied that we remain non-violent individually. We boast that Non-co-operation has become universal in India. We boast that we have acquired sufficient influence even over the unruly masses to restrain them from violence. Let us prove true to our claim. . . .

The Immediate Issue

I wish I could persuade everybody that Civil Disobedience is the inherent right of a citizen. He dare not give it up without ceasing to be a man. Civil Disobedience is never followed by anarchy. Criminal Disobedience can lead to it. Every state puts down Criminal Disobedience by force. It perishes, if it does not. But to put down Civil Disobedience is to attempt to imprison conscience. Civil Disobedience can only lead to strength and purity. A civil resister never uses arms and, hence, he is harmless to a state that is at all willing to listen to the voice of public opinion. He is dangerous for an autocratic state, for he brings about its fall by engaging public opinion upon the matter for which he resists the state. Civil Disobedience, therefore, becomes a sacred duty when the state has become lawless, or which is the same thing, corrupt. And a citizen that barters with such a state shares its corruption or lawlessness.

It is, therefore, possible to question the wisdom of applying Civil Disobedience in respect of a particular act or law; it is possible to advise delay and caution. But the right itself cannot be allowed to be questioned. It is a birthright that cannot be surrendered without surrender of one's self-respect.

At the same time that the right of Civil Disobedience is insisted upon, its use must be guarded by all conceivable restrictions. Every possible provision should be made against an outbreak of violence or general lawlessness. Its area as well as its scope should also be limited to the barest necessity of the case. In the present case, therefore, aggressive Civil Disobedience should be confined to a vindication of the right of free speech and free association. In other words, Non-co-operation, so long as it remains non-violent, must be allowed to continue without let or hindrance.

MARTIN LUTHER KING JR. (1929–1968)

King's Life

MARTIN LUTHER KING JR.
(1929–1968)

Like Gandhi before him, Martin Luther King Jr. is noted not only for being an effective political leader and agent of social change but also for developing a philosophy of political action to guide his activism. King was born in Atlanta, Georgia, the son and grandson of Baptist ministers. As the result of skipping two grades, he was able to enter Morehouse College at age 15. While in college he felt called to follow his father's and grandfather's example and decided to become a minister. He went on to obtain a degree from Crozer Theological Seminary in Pennsylvania and then earned a doctorate in systematic theology from Boston University. While in Boston, he met and married Coretta Scott, who would become a great civil rights leader herself. Although he had offers for academic positions, Martin and Coretta returned to the South, where King became the pastor of a prominent Baptist church in Montgomery, Alabama.

In 1955, a pivotal event in American social history set the course of King's life. An African-American seamstress named Rosa Parks climbed onto a Montgomery bus after a long day of work. Because all the seats in the back of the bus were taken, she sat down on a seat in the "whites only" section. Consequently, she was forcibly removed and arrested for violating the city's segregationist laws. As a popular minister and community leader, Dr. King was elected president of an organization formed to protest the racist laws of the city. King put into effect the philosophy of nonviolent resistance that he had been developing since college. The bus boycott that he and his followers started would last a year. As a result, King's house was bombed, his life was continually threatened, and he and his associates were convicted of conspiracy. Finally, the U.S. Supreme Court ruled that Montgomery had to provide equal treatment to all people on public buses.

Building on this success, King and other African-American ministers founded the Southern Christian Leadership Conference, and King's life became a succession of protest marches, speeches, books, and other forms of political action. Seeking to refuel his spirit, he took some time off to tour India in order to deepen his understanding of Gandhi's nonviolent strategies. In August 1963, King attracted more than a quarter of a million people to Washington, D.C., for a civil rights rally. There, on the steps of the Lincoln Memorial, he delivered his famous "I Have a Dream" speech. Finally, after years of social unrest in America, Congress passed the Civil Rights Act of 1964. That year, King received the Nobel Prize and the following year he became *Time Magazine*'s Man of the Year. In spite of these honors, King continued to be the center of controversy. In former years he had been the target of racists as well as well-meaning critics who thought he was going too far and too fast with his calls for change. Now, he was criticized by radical leaders within his own cause who argued for more aggressive techniques under the label of Black Power. King, however, continued to hold high the banner of nonviolence.

In 1967, King began to turn his struggle for political equality into one that emphasized economic rights. He had became convinced that economic poverty was just as great an evil as political discrimination. On April 4, 1968, while lending support to a garbage workers' strike in Memphis, Tennessee, King was assassinated.

The following selection is taken from Dr. King's famous "Letter from Birmingham Jail." In 1963, one year before he won the Nobel Prize, he was jailed for participating in a civil rights demonstration. Eight prominent Alabama clergy wrote an open letter critical of King's methods. In his own letter, King responded to their criticisms and provided an eloquent justification of civil disobedience.

- As you did with the Gandhi selection, try to find examples of the five justifications of civil disobedience discussed previously.
- What similarities or differences are there between King's justification of civil disobedience and Gandhi's?
- How does King respond to the criticism that he should have used negotiation instead of direct action to address the issues?

FROM MARTIN LUTHER KING JR.

Letter from Birmingham Jail[23]

April 16, 1963

My Dear Fellow Clergymen:

While confined here in the Birmingham city jail, I came across your recent statement calling my present activities "unwise and untimely." Seldom do I pause to answer criticism of my work and ideas. If I sought to answer all the criticisms that cross my desk, my secretaries would have little time for anything other than such correspondence in the course of the day, and I would have no time for constructive work. But since I feel that you are men of genuine good will and that your criticisms are sincerely set forth, I want to try to answer your statement in what I hope will be patient and reasonable terms. . . .

You deplore the demonstrations taking place in Birmingham. But your statement, I am sorry to say, fails to express a similar concern for the conditions that brought about the demonstrations. I am sure that none of you would want to rest content with the superficial kind of social analysis that deals merely with effects and does not grapple with underlying causes. It is unfortunate that demonstrations are taking place in Birmingham, but it is even more unfortunate that the city's white power structure left the Negro community with no alternative.

In any nonviolent campaign there are four basic steps: collection of the facts to determine whether injustices exist; negotiation; self-purification; and direct action. We have gone through all these steps in Birmingham. There can be no gainsaying the fact that racial injustice engulfs this community. . . .

You may well ask: "Why direct action? Why sit-ins, marches and so forth? Isn't negotiation a better path?" You are quite right in calling for negotiation. Indeed, this is the very purpose of direct action. Nonviolent direct action seeks to create such a crisis and foster such a tension that a community which has constantly refused to negotiate is forced to confront the issue. It seeks so to dramatize the issue that it can no longer be ignored. My citing the creation of tension as part of the work of the nonviolent-resister may sound rather shocking. But I must confess that I am not afraid of the word "tension." I have earnestly opposed violent tension, but there is a type of constructive, nonviolent tension which is necessary for growth. Just as Socrates felt that it was necessary to create a tension in the mind so that individuals could rise from the bondage of myths and half-truths to the unfettered realm of creative analysis and objective appraisal, so must we see the need for nonviolent gadflies to create the kind of tension in society that will help men rise from the dark depths of prejudice and racism to the majestic heights of understanding and brotherhood.

The purpose of our direct-action program is to create a situation so crisis-packed that it will inevitably open the door to negotiation. I therefore concur with you in your call for negotiation. Too long has our beloved Southland been bogged down in a tragic effort to live in monologue rather than dialogue. . . .

- In the next passage, how does King distinguish between just laws and unjust laws? Does he present a useful distinction?
- According to King, under what conditions is it permissible to break the law?

You express a great deal of anxiety over our willingness to break laws. This is certainly a legitimate concern. Since we so diligently urge people to obey the Supreme Court's decision of 1954 outlawing segregation in the public schools, at first glance it may seem rather paradoxical for us consciously to break laws. One may well ask: "How can you advocate breaking some laws and obeying others?" The answer lies in the fact that there are two types of laws: just and unjust. I would be the first to advocate obeying just laws. One has not only a legal but a moral responsibility to obey just laws. Conversely, one has a moral responsibility to disobey unjust laws. I would agree with St. Augustine that "an unjust law is no law at all."

Now, what is the difference between the two? How does one determine whether a law is just or unjust? A just law is a man-made code that squares with the moral law or the law of God. An unjust law is a code that is out of harmony with the moral law. To put it in the terms of St. Thomas Aquinas: An unjust law is a human law that is not rooted in eternal law and natural law. Any law that uplifts human personality is just. Any law that degrades human personality is unjust. All segregation statutes are unjust because segregation distorts the soul and damages the personality. It gives the segregator a false sense of superiority and the segregated a false sense of inferiority. Segregation, to use the terminology of the Jewish philosopher Martin Buber, substitutes an "I-it" relationship for an "I-thou" relationship and ends up relegating persons to the status of things. Hence segregation is not only politically, economically and sociologically unsound, it is morally wrong and sinful. Paul Tillich has said that sin is separation. Is not segregation an existential expression of man's tragic separation, his awful estrangement, his terrible sinfulness? Thus it is that I can urge men to obey the 1954 decision of the Supreme Court, for it is morally right; and I can urge them to disobey segregation ordinances, for they are morally wrong.

Let us consider a more concrete example of just and unjust laws. An unjust law is a code that a numerical or power majority group compels a minority group to obey but does not make binding on itself. This is *difference* made legal. By the same token, a just law is a code that a majority compels a minority to follow and that it is willing to follow itself. This is *sameness* made legal.

Let me give another explanation. A law is unjust if it is inflicted on a minority that, as a result of being denied the right to vote, had no part in enacting or devising the law. Who can say that the legislature of Alabama which set up that state's segregation laws was democratically elected? Throughout Alabama all sorts of devious methods are used to prevent Negroes from becoming registered voters, and there are some counties in which, even though Negroes constitute a majority of the population, not a single Negro is registered. Can any law enacted under such circumstances be considered democratically structured?

Sometimes a law is just on its face and unjust in its application. For instance, I have been arrested on a charge of parading without a permit. Now, there is nothing wrong in having an ordinance which requires a permit for a parade. But such an ordinance becomes unjust when it is used to maintain segregation and to deny citizens the First-Amendment privilege of peaceful assembly and protest.

I hope you are able to see the distinction I am trying to point out. In no sense do I advocate evading or defying the law, as would the rabid segregationist. That would lead to anarchy. One who breaks an unjust law must do so openly, lovingly, and with a willingness to accept the penalty. I submit that an individual who breaks a law that conscience tells him is unjust, and who willingly accepts the penalty of imprisonment in order to arouse the conscience of the community over its injustice, is in reality expressing the highest respect for law.

Of course, there is nothing new about this kind of civil disobedience. It was evidenced sublimely in the refusal of Shadrach, Meshach and Abednego to obey the laws of Nebuchadnezzar, on the ground that a higher moral law was at stake. It was practiced superbly by the early Christians, who were willing to face hungry lions and the excruciating pain of chopping blocks rather than submit to certain unjust laws of the Roman Empire. To a degree, academic freedom is a reality today because Socrates practiced civil disobedience. In our own nation, the Boston Tea Party represented a massive act of civil disobedience.

We should never forget that everything Adolf Hitler did in Germany was "legal" and everything the Hungarian freedom fighters did in Hungary was "illegal." It was "illegal" to aid and comfort a Jew in Hitler's Germany. Even so, I am sure that, had I lived in Germany at the time, I would have aided and comforted my Jewish brothers. If today I lived in a Communist country where certain principles dear to the Christian faith are suppressed, I would openly advocate disobeying that country's antireligious laws. . . .

Let us all hope that the dark clouds of racial prejudice will soon pass away and the deep fog of misunderstanding will be lifted from our fear-drenched communities, and in some not too distant tomorrow the radiant stars of love and brotherhood will shine over our great nation with all their scintillating beauty.

Yours for the cause of Peace and Brotherhood,

Martin Luther King, Jr.

THOUGHT EXPERIMENT: *The Pros and Cons of Civil Disobedience*

Write a letter to the person with whom you *disagree* the most (Socrates, Gandhi, or King). Explain to him why he is wrong by refuting his arguments and providing a defense of the opposing point of view. Don't just disagree with him but try to be as convincing as possible, providing strong reasons for your position. How do you think he might reply?

LOOKING THROUGH THE LENS OF THE SUPPORTERS OF CIVIL DISOBEDIENCE

1. If you were a supporter of civil disobedience, how would you respond to critics who say that there are always less radical means for achieving social change?

2. Taking the point of view of the civil disobedience defender once again, how would you determine when a minor wrong should be tolerated or addressed through legal means for the sake of social stability and when the injustice is severe enough to warrant breaking the law? Think of some examples of minor injustices in which civil disobedience would not be justified and more serious infractions of justice in which civil disobedience would be justified.

3. Why do most defenders of civil disobedience believe it is important that the breaking of the law be a public event and that the protester not use further illegal means to evade the law?

EXAMINING THE STRENGTHS AND WEAKNESSES OF THE CIVIL DISOBEDIENCE POSITION

Positive Evaluation

1. You don't go in for stomach surgery whenever you have indigestion from eating too much pizza. Radical surgery is used only in severe situations in which other remedies are not effective. Similarly, even though civil disobedience is an extreme measure that should not be used if it can be avoided, can't it be justified in extreme cases in which there are no other effective alternatives?

2. Isn't civil disobedience consistent with a love for your country, a respect for its institutions, and a general acceptance of the political system as a whole? Aren't the dangers of not doing everything possible to correct injustices just as grave and likely to lead to social unrest as are the alleged dangers of civil disobedience?

3. Hasn't history shown that significant social progress often results when people refuse to participate in an unjust system and rebuke the system by acts of civil disobedience? Wouldn't society become set in its ways and refuse to improve if there weren't dissenters, protesters, and social reformers who were willing to risk imprisonment and even death to stop the machinery of injustice?

Negative Evaluation

1. The advocate of civil disobedience claims that this method of moral protest will bring political injustice to the attention of the nation's moral conscience. But this argument implies that civil disobedience will work only if the people in a society are open and responsive to moral appeals. If so, then the citizen's moral conscience can be informed and appealed to through legal means. On the other hand, if a society has no compassion and no sense of justice or fair play, then civil disobedience will not work and will only bring more oppression. In other words, if civil disobedience will be effective, it is unnecessary, but if it is necessary, it is likely to be ineffective. Aren't the advocates of civil disobedience left in a dilemma that undermines their position?

2. Isn't civil disobedience an example of using an immoral means to achieve a supposedly moral end? Furthermore, won't the good results sought for always be an uncertain possibility? Can we ever know ahead of time if civil disobedience will be worth the price? On the other hand, aren't the social harms produced by breaking the law almost always inevitable?

3. Is it inconsistent for people engaging in civil disobedience to expect protection from the law at the same time they are breaking the law? For example, they expect the police to protect them from physical harm that their opponents might wish to inflict on them. Furthermore, isn't an individual law part of the total system of laws created and enforced by the legal institutions of the land? Is it possible to violate one law without harming the system as a whole? Doesn't every law, simply because it is part of the total system of laws, impose an obligation of obedience on us until we can get it changed?

REVIEW FOR CHAPTER 6
Philosophers

6.1 The Justification of Government
   Robert Paul Wolff
   John Locke
6.2 The Question of Justice
   Plato
   Thomas Aquinas
   John Stuart Mill
   John Rawls
   Susan Moller Okin
6.3 The Individual and the State
   John Stuart Mill
   Karl Marx
6.4 Civil Disobedience
   Socrates
   Mohandas Gandhi
   Martin Luther King Jr.

Concepts

6.1 The Justification of Government
   authority vs. power
   divine right theory
   justice theory
   naive anarchism
   militant anarchism
   theoretical anarchism
   social contract theory
   John Locke's view of rights
   Locke's notion of the state of nature
   Locke's notion of the social contract
6.2 The Question of Justice
   meritocracy
   the three kinds of people according to Plato
   Plato's theory of justice
   natural law theory
   Thomas Aquinas's theory of justice
   John Stuart Mill's theory of justice
   the principle of utility

John Rawls's theory of justice
   the original position
   the veil of ignorance
   the principle of equal liberty
   the difference principle
   the principle of fair equality of opportunity
   Susan Moller Okin's critique of Rawls
6.3 The Individual and the State
   individualism
   collectivism
   John Stuart Mill's view of individual liberty
   Mill's view of justified government restrictions on liberty
   five main themes of Karl Marx's philosophy
   dialectic
   capitalism
6.4 Civil Disobedience
   civil disobedience vs. criminal disobedience
   four arguments against civil disobedience
   Socrates' arguments against civil disobedience
   five justifications of civil disobedience
   Mohandas Gandhi's philosophy of civil disobedience
   Martin Luther King Jr.'s defense of civil disobedience
   King's criteria for distinguishing just and unjust laws

SUGGESTIONS FOR FURTHER READING

General Works on Political Philosophy

Hampton, Jean. *Political Philosophy.* Boulder, Colo.: Westview, 1996. An engaging introduction to both the classical and contemporary issues.

Kymlicka, Will. *Contemporary Political Theory:* An Introduction. New York: Oxford University Press, 1990. A very good introduction to the topic.

Luper, Steven, ed. *Social Ideals and Policies: An Introduction to Social and Political Philosophy.* Mountain View,

Calif.: Mayfield, 1999. A topically organized anthology containing classical and contemporary readings.

Sterba, James. *Contemporary Social and Political Philosophy.* Belmont, Calif.: Wadsworth, 1995. A discussion of current issues in social and political philosophy.

The Justification of Government

Barker, Ernest, ed. *Social Contract: Essays by Locke, Hume, and Rousseau.* Oxford: Oxford University Press, 1962. A collection of the classic essays on the topic, with an introduction by the editor.

Forman, James. *Anarchism: Political Innocence or Social Violence?* New York: Dell, 1977. A useful discussion of the topic.

Hampton, Jean. *Hobbes and the Social Contract Tradition.* Cambridge, England: Cambridge University Press, 1988. This work analyzes Hobbes's theory in the light of contemporary perspectives.

Woodcock, George. *Anarchism: A History of Libertarian Ideas and Movements.* Cleveland: Meridian Books, 1962. This author is one of the leading writers on anarchism.

The Nature of Justice

Anna, Julia. *An Introduction to Plato's "Republic."* Oxford: Clarendon Press, 1981. A systematic introduction to Plato's most important work.

Aquinas, Thomas. *On Law, Morality, and Politics.* Ed. William Baumgarth and Richard Regan. Indianapolis: Hackett, 1988. Aquinas's central writings on law, morality, and politics.

Finnis, John. *Natural Law and Natural Rights.* Oxford: Oxford University Press, 1980. A contemporary defense of natural law theory.

Kukathas, Chandran, and Philip Pettit. *Rawls: "A Theory of Justice" and Its Critics.* Stanford, Calif.: Stanford University Press, 1990. A discussion of Rawls's work, including the arguments of his critics.

Manning, Rita, and René Trujillo, eds. *Social Justice in a Diverse Society.* Mountain View, Calif.: Mayfield, 1996. A collection of essays on current issues related to justice.

Popper, Karl. *The Open Society and Its Enemies. Vol. 1, The Spell of Plato.* 5th ed., rev. Princeton, N.J.: Princeton University Press, 1966. This controversial book provides a passionate defense of democracy and an equally passionate critique of Plato's utopian vision.

Rawls, John. *Political Liberalism.* New York: Columbia University Press, 1994. In this work Rawls refines and develops his earlier theory.

Rawls, John. *A Theory of Justice.* Cambridge, Mass.: Harvard University Press, 1971. Many consider this work to be the most significant one in political philosophy in this century.

Sandel, Michael. *Liberalism and the Limits of Justice.* Cambridge: Cambridge University Press, 1982. A critique of Rawls's work.

Sterba, James, ed. *Justice: Alternative Political Perspectives.* 2d ed. Belmont, Calif.: Wadsworth, 1992. A wide range of readings on the topic.

The Individual and the State

Gray, John, and G. W. Smith, eds. *J. S. Mill's "On Liberty" in Focus.* London and New York: Routledge, 1991. A collection of important essays discussing Mill's famous work.

Marcuse, Herbert. *One-Dimensional Man.* Boston: Beacon Press, 1964. A very readable analysis of our technological society that brings Marx's critique of capitalism into the 20th century.

Marx, Karl. *The Marx-Engels Reader.* 2d ed. Ed. Robert C. Tucker. New York: W. W. Norton, 1978. Contains selections from the full range of Marx's works.

Mill, J. S. *On Liberty.* Ed. E. Rapaport. Indianapolis: Hackett, 1978. Mill's argument for classical liberalism.

Nozick, Robert. *Anarchy, State, and Utopia.* New York: Basic Books, 1974. Nozick is famous for his political libertarianism (a position that advocates maximum individual liberty). His book is notable for its critique of Rawls's theory.

Popper, Karl. *The Open Society and Its Enemies. Vol. 2, The High Tide of Prophecy: Hegel, Marx, and the Aftermath.* 5th ed., rev. Princeton, N.J.: Princeton University Press, 1966. Contains a passionate critique of Marxist political philosophy.

Schmitt, Richard. *Introduction to Marx and Engels: A Critical Reconstruction.* 2d ed. Boulder, Colo.: Westview, 1997. One of the best introductions to Marxism.

Civil Disobedience

Bedau, Hugo Adam, ed. *Civil Disobedience in Focus.* London and New York: Routledge, 1991. A collection of the most significant essays on the topic, ranging from Socrates to contemporary thinkers.

Thoreau, Henry David. *Civil Disobedience and Other Essays.* New York: Dover, 1993. An important defense of civil disobedience by the famous 19th-century American writer.

NOTES

1. Robert Paul Wolff, *In Defense of Anarchism* (Berkeley: University of California Press, 1998), pp. 3–6, 12–14, 18–19. Copyright 1970 by Robert Paul Wolff. Reproduced with permission of the University of California Press.
2. John Locke, *An Essay Concerning the True Original, Extent and End of Civil Government,* the second essay in *Two Treatises of Government* (1680). Many versions of this essay are available in the public domain. The section headings have been added.
3. Ibid., Sec. 131.
4. Plato, *Republic,* 433a–434c, trans. Benjamin Jowett (1894).
5. Thomas Aquinas, *Summa Theologica,* I–II, ques. 95, art. 2, and ques. 96, art. 4, in *Basic Writings of Saint Thomas Aquinas,* vol. 2, ed. Anton C. Pegis (New York: Random House, 1945).
6. John Stuart Mill, *Utilitarianism,* chapter 5. Many editions of this work are available in the public domain.
7. John Rawls, *A Theory of Justice* (Cambridge, Mass.: Harvard University Press, 1971), pp. 11–12, 60–63, 103–4, 136–37, 139–40. Reprinted by permission of the publisher from A Theory of Justice by John Rawls, pp. 11-12, 60-63, 103-104, 136-137, 139-140, Cambridge, Mass: The Belknap Press of Harvard University Press, Copyright © 1971, 1999 by The President and Fellows of Harvard College.
8. Ibid., p. 83.
9. Susan Moller Okin, *Justice, Gender, and the Family* (New York: Basic Books, 1989), pp. 3, 8, 90, 91, 101, 104–5. Copyright © 1989 by Basic Books, Inc. Reprinted by permission of Basic Books, a member of the Perseus Books Group.
10. Rawls, *A Theory of Justice,* p. 12.
11. Okin, *Justice, Gender, and the Family,* p. 91.
12. John Stuart Mill, *On Liberty.* Many editions are available in the public domain. The selections are taken from chapters 1 and 4.
13. Ibid., chap. 3.
14. Karl Marx, *The German Ideology,* in *The Marx-Engels Reader,* 2d ed., ed. Robert C. Tucker (New York: Norton, 1978), p. 172.
15. Karl Marx, *Capital,* in *The Marx-Engels Reader,* p. 367.
16. Ibid., p. 296.
17. Karl Marx, *The Holy Family,* quoted in *Essential Writings of Karl Marx,* ed. David Caute (New York: Collier Books, 1967), p. 50.
18. Karl Marx and Friedrich Engels, *Communist Manifesto,* trans. Samuel Moore in 1888 from the original German text of 1848. Many versions from this edition are available in the public domain. The selections are from chapters 1 and 2. The section titles have been added.
19. Sidney Hook, "*The Communist Manifesto* 100 Years After," *New York Times Magazine,* February 1, 1948, in *Molders of Modern Thought,* ed. Ben B. Seligman (Chicago: Quadrangle Books, 1970), p. 80.
20. Plato, *Crito,* trans. Benjamin Jowett (1898). I have edited the translation.
21. Carl Wellman, *Morals and Ethics* (Glenview, Ill.: Scott, Foresman & Co., 1975), pp. 10–13.
22. Mahatma Gandhi, *Young India 1919–1922* (Madras, India: S. Ganesan, 1922), pp. 230, 233–34, 933–34, 937–39, 943–44.
23. Martin Luther King Jr., "Letter from Birmingham Jail," in *Why We Can't Wait* (New York: Harper & Row, 1964), pp. 77, 79, 81–82, 84–87, 100.

Auguste Rodin, *The Thinker*, 1880

CHAPTER 7

PHILOSOPHY AND THE MEANING OF LIFE

 CHAPTER OBJECTIVES

Upon completion of this chapter you should be able to

1. Explain the questioning the question view.
2. Discuss the view of pessimism and Arthur Schopenhauer's analysis of the human condition.
3. Discuss the religious view of the meaning of life and Leo Tolstoy's struggle to find meaning.
4. Discuss the secular-humanist view and Hazel E. Barnes's version of it.
5. State several common themes of existentialist philosophy.
6. List five general insights of existentialism that might be useful for developing your own personal philosophical perspective.
7. Explain how Søren Kierkegaard and Jean-Paul Sartre illustrate the five insights.

SCOUTING THE TERRITORY:
Questions about the Meaning of Life

To both ask and answer the question What is the meaning of life? requires you to first answer several preliminary questions. In order to "scout the territory" and to prepare you for the discussion that follows, consider the following questions concerning the topic of the meaning of life.

1. Leo Tolstoy, the famous Russian novelist, found himself in midlife blessed with literary fame, wealth, and a good family. Yet he confessed that "I felt that what I was standing on had given way, that I had no foundation to stand on, . . . that I had nothing to live by." He tells us that this deep despair came from his inability to answer these questions: "What is the meaning of my life? What will come of my life?" On the other hand, the psychiatrist Sigmund Freud stated, "The moment a man questions the meaning and value of life, he is sick." Whose attitude do you agree with the most? Do you think with Tolstoy that all your accomplishments are empty if you do not answer the question of the meaning of your life? Or do you agree with Freud that this question is a distracting, unhealthy concern that ought to be ignored?

2. How would you know that you had found the meaning of life? If you feel as though life is meaningless, you are likely to experience emotional dissatisfaction with your life. On the other hand, if you feel as though your life is meaningful and purposeful, you have a sense of emotional satisfaction. But is emotional satisfaction enough? Do you want to be emotionally satisfied by an illusion? Isn't it important that your sense of meaning and purpose be based on what is true and real? Do questions about the meaning of life also involve questions about epistemology and metaphysics, or are the answers to such questions simply a matter of pleasant and unpleasant psychological states?

3. Do we share enough of a common human nature that it is likely that the meaning of life will be more or less the same for everyone? Or do you think there is no *one* answer to the meaning of life that will be the same for everyone?

4. The German writer Gotthold Lessing (1729–1781) said, "If God set forth before me the Eternal, unchangeable Truth in his right hand and the eternal quest for Truth in his left hand and said, 'Choose,' I would point to the left hand and say, 'Father, give me this, for the Eternal unchangeable Truth belongs to you alone.'" If faced with this choice, would you choose as Lessing would or would you want to be given the truth, without any effort on your part? Generalizing from this choice, do you think the meaning of life is found in some final trophy you obtain at the end of your searching, or is it the ongoing journey of your life itself and simply the joy of living it that makes it worthwhile?

CHARTING THE TERRAIN OF QUESTIONS ABOUT THE MEANING OF LIFE: *What Are the Issues?*

Does life have meaning? If so, what is it? Almost everybody has tried their hand at a jigsaw puzzle at one time or another. Typically, the finished picture is represented on the cover of the box. This picture is helpful in solving the puzzle, for without a clue as to what you are working toward, the individual pieces are a chaotic and meaningless jumble of colors and shapes. Here is a piece that is blue. Is this the blue of a sky? Of the ocean? Is it part of a cluster of blueberries? Without the big picture, the individual pieces could represent almost anything. Is the same thing true with our lives? Our lives are made up of fragments of experiences and events—some of them are joyous, some are tragic, but most are the mundane details of our daily routine. But do these pieces of our lives contribute to some overall meaning? Do they somehow fit into a bigger picture? What is the meaning of it all?

Notice the assumption entailed in the jigsaw metaphor. It suggests that there is one, final picture into which we fit the pieces of our lives, and it assumes that this picture will be the same for each person. In contrast to the jigsaw metaphor, some philosophers would prefer the metaphor of a mosaic. The mosaic is created out of many differently colored pieces of tile, but they can be arranged in a number of ways. We are each taking the individual pieces of our lives and composing a picture that is meaningful and satisfying to us. However, the meaning of life to me may not be what is meaningful to you. As we will see, the search for the "big picture" approach of the jigsaw metaphor and the "many meaningful patterns" approach of the mosaic metaphor will constitute a major division in the way different philosophers struggle with the question of meaning.

STOP AND THINK

Which metaphor do you think best describes the search for the meaning of life?

- The jigsaw metaphor: There is only one correct answer that describes the meaning of human life. If we can't find the one big picture, our lives will be meaningless.
- The mosaic metaphor: There are many possible ways to pattern the experiences in our lives to make a meaningful picture. What matters is if you are satisfied with the pattern of your life.

What are the implications of choosing one metaphor over the other? Are both metaphors equally compatible with a religious view of the world? Are both metaphors compatible with a nonreligious view of the world? Why?

In many activities, an understanding of the purpose or the goal of the activity is important to understand what you are doing. For example, the purpose of football is to get a higher score than your opponent. In contrast, the purpose of golf is to get the lowest score possible. If you were playing an unfamiliar game in which you moved pieces about a game board but hadn't a clue as to what the purpose of the game was, you would be in the dark as to whether you were playing well or badly. This comparison illustrates why most philosophers as well as most ordinary people believe that worrying about the meaning of life is so important. Socrates, for one, pointed out that we are all engaged in particular pursuits. Some people are artists, some are businesspeople, others are physicians, politicians, athletes, or shoemakers. Each particular craft or activity has its own goal and purpose. But Socrates believed that being a human being is *itself* an activity in which we are engaged. As with any of the other activities we engage in, we can either be excellent or do poorly in the job of being a human being. With respect to our lives, as with any activity, Socrates thought we need to have a clear conception of what *human existence* is all about. However, some philosophers would say that Socrates is asking for too much. Perhaps all we need to know is the answer to the question "What is *my* life all about?" Once again, we are faced with the question of whether the meaning of life will be found in some sort of universal answer or in a number of individual answers.

If you read between the lines of each philosophy and topic discussed in this book, you will find that they indirectly shed some light on the question of the meaning of life. Each chapter has provided you with attempts at filling out one portion of the picture, whether in terms of the nature of knowledge, the nature of reality, religious issues, ethics, or political thought.

STOP AND THINK

Think over each of the chapters you have read. How might the issues raised in each chapter—knowledge, the mind and body, freedom and determinism, philosophy of religion, ethics, and political philosophy—relate to the issue of the meaning of life?

CHOOSING A PATH: *What Are My Options Concerning the Meaning of Life?*

Although there are many varieties of answers to the question "What is the meaning of life?" it may be helpful to set out a general classification of those answers.[1] The range of answers can be organized under four main headings. (1) Some people find the question to be too obscure or ill-formed to lead to a satisfactory answer. I call this position the *questioning the question view.* (2) Some people claim that human life is meaningless. This position is *pessimism.* (3) Some people seek the answer in religious or metaphysical accounts of human life and its relationship to the grand scheme of things. This position is the *religious view.* (4) Some people believe that they can find personal meaning in their individual lives even without some grand, pre-given meaning to human life in general. This position is often referred to as *secular-humanism.* After a brief questionnaire, we will examine each of these positions in turn.

WHAT DO I THINK? *Questionnaire on the Meaning of Life*

	Agree	Disagree
1. When someone asks "What is the meaning of life?" I have no idea what they are asking.		
2. The search for the meaning of life is a natural human quest, but it is like searching for the fountain of youth. In both cases, the object of the search will never be found.		
3. Everything that happens in my life was meant to happen to fulfill some larger purpose. The most important goal in life is to discover what that purpose is.		
4. If I can say at the end of my life, "I've had my ups and downs, my moments of happiness and moments of sadness, but, overall, life is good," then I have found "the meaning of life."		
5. People are born, they sustain themselves for 70 years by eating, working, and sleeping, and then they die. That is all that can be said about the meaning of life.		
6. People may feel as though they have found the purpose of life, but it is possible that they are mistaken about this feeling, because human existence has an objective purpose that is independent of human opinions about it.		

	Agree	Disagree
7. There is no single answer to the question of the meaning of life that applies to everyone, because each individual has to seek his or her own personal meaning.		
8. If people don't obtain what they want in life, they will be frustrated. However, if they do get what they want, they either will be bored or will develop new desires and, hence, new occasions for frustration. It seems clear that in the final analysis, frustration or boredom and meaningless suffering is people's lot in life.		
9. Unless they are completely numb to their own existence, most people experience a vague emptiness and yearning throughout their life, because they are trying to fill that void with that which is transitory and finite when only an eternal and infinite meaning will satisfy them.		
10. It is incorrect to speak of "seeking the meaning of life," because this statement implies that it is out there, like an Easter egg, waiting for people to find it. Instead, each person should speak of "creating meaning for my life." People are like artists facing blank canvases, considering what work of personal creation they will find satisfying.		

KEY TO THE QUESTIONNAIRE ON THE MEANING OF LIFE

Statement 1 represents the questioning the question view. It conflicts with all the other statements.

Statements 2, 5, and *8* represent the pessimistic view. They conflict with all the other statements.

Statements 3, 6, and *9* represent the religious view. They conflict with all the other statements.

Statements 4, 7, and *10* represent the secular-humanist view. They conflict with all the other statements.

SURVEYING THE CASE FOR THE QUESTIONING THE QUESTION VIEW

First are the people who claim that the whole issue discussed in this chapter is a meaningless one. In terms of our jigsaw metaphor, these philosophers would say that it is a mistake to suppose that the collection of experiences that compose our lives are like pieces of a puzzle that we were meant to piece together. Hence, the metaphor of a puzzle has no application to our lives. Why do these philosophers think that questions about the meaning of life make no sense? Think about the difference between meaningful questions and nonsensical questions. For example, we can ask "What time is it in Chicago?" However, it makes no sense to ask "What time is it on the sun?" because we tell time on earth with respect to our relationship to the sun. Similarly, we can ask about the meaning of the French word *coeur* or we can ask about the meaning of a painting or a novel. But some philosophers think that we fall into a linguistic muddle when we ask the same question about human existence. Philosopher Ronald Hepburn observes that many philosophers today contend that "questions about the meaning of life are, very often, conceptually obscure and confused. They are amalgams of logically diverse questions, some coherent and answerable, some neither." For example, in response to questions about the meaning of human existence, American philosopher Sidney Hook writes, "It would be easy to show . . . that it is these questions themselves, and the answers to them, that are meaningless." When the 20th-century philosopher Bertrand Russell was challenged to explain what meaning life can have to an agnostic, he replied, "I feel inclined to answer by another question: What is the meaning of 'the meaning of life'?" Nevertheless, most philosophers insist that though the question of the meaning of life is complicated, it is too important to easily dismiss in this way. In fact, all the philosophers I just quoted would say that the question is meaningless only if we are looking for some single, ultimate purpose to human existence; they acknowledge that the question may be meaningful in some more qualified sense. Because the questioning the question position is mainly an attack on the religious view that human existence must have one ultimate meaning, this position essentially collapses into the secular-humanist perspective. Consequently, we won't consider it any further at this point.

SURVEYING THE CASE FOR PESSIMISM

The second approach is that of the pessimist. To put it simply, the pessimist claims that there is no meaning to life. This position is sometimes referred to as *nihilism,* which literally means "nothing is ultimate." In other words, nihilism is the claim that there are no values worth pursuing. This pessimistic view is expressed in Shakespeare's *Macbeth,* in which life is described as "a tale told by an idiot—full of sound and fury, signifying nothing."

Ironically, the pessimist agrees with the religious view that if life is to be meaningful, it must have some ultimate, transcendent, enduring value and humans must be given some ultimate purpose. However, the pessimist believes that there are no such ultimate values and purpose and so concludes that, in the final analysis, life can have no meaning. Hence, in terms of our jigsaw metaphor, the pessimist seems to think that we have a pathological need to make the pieces fit into some meaningful picture. However, in the end, all we will find is a transitory, meaningless jumble of unrelated pieces. The 19th-century German philosopher Arthur Schopenhauer gives this grim analysis of the human condition:

> . . . what a difference there is between our beginning and our end! We begin in the madness of carnal desire and the transport of voluptuousness, we end in the dissolution of all our parts and the musty stench of corpses. And the road from the one to the other too goes, in regard to our well-being and enjoyment of life, steadily downhill: happily dreaming childhood, exultant youth, toil-filled years of manhood, infirm and often wretched old age, the torment of the last illness and finally the throes of death—does it not look as if existence were an error the consequences of which gradually grow more and more manifest?
>
> We shall do best to think of life as . . . a process of disillusionment: since this is clearly enough, what everything that happens to us is calculated to produce.[2]

A critic could respond that insofar as a pessimist such as Schopenhauer chooses to go on living instead of committing suicide, the pessimist must believe that living has more

Nighthawks (1942) by Edward Hopper. One of the most recognizable images in 20th-century art, this painting depicts an all-night diner in which three people sit isolated and alienated from one another in spite of their physical proximity. We wonder why they don't seek relief from their loneliness by engaging in conversation with each other. Instead, they seem to be resigned to the meaninglessness and despair of their lives. Perhaps they agree with Schopenhauer that to seek meaning will only lead to frustation and disillusionment, for every moment in life and everything we value is transitory and, like a soap bubble, vanishes as soon as we grasp it.

meaning than death. Hence, many philosophers think that the pessimist position represents more of a psychological malaise than a defensible philosophical stance. Like the religious person, the pessimist thinks that life ought to have some higher, ultimate purpose. Like the secular-humanist, the pessimist thinks that there is no ultimate purpose to human existence. Thus, the pessimist seems to be inconsistently caught halfway in between the religious view and the secular-humanist view. On the one hand, if I don't believe in God, why should I think that life ought to have some ultimate purpose? On the other hand, if I choose to go on living, then practically speaking, I have adopted the secular-humanist answer. Consequently, I conclude my discussion of pessimism at this point and go on to give a more extensive treatment of the remaining two views, because they are the most common ways that people address the issue of the meaning of life.

SURVEYING THE CASE FOR THE RELIGIOUS VIEW

The third major approach to the question of the meaning of life is taken by philosophers who seek the answer in some sort of religious or metaphysical account. These philosophers think that there is one grand picture into which the individual pieces of our lives can be fitted. (Think of the jigsaw metaphor.) They look for an all-encompassing perspective that transcends the human situation and that gives meaning to human life. In other words, they seek the MEANING of life (in capital letters). Typically, this approach is used by most religious thinkers who believe that humans were brought into the world to serve some divine purpose. After all, if you observed an arrangement of colors on a canvas, you would ask "What does it mean?" only if you thought that some artist had purposely created it rather than it being the product of a random explosion of paint pigments.

However, the search for some ultimate meaning is not confined exclusively to religious philosophers. Some philosophers, such as Plato and Aristotle, seek the ultimate purpose of human life in the rational nature of the cosmos or in the structure of human nature without referring to any divine purposes. Hence, although philosophers like Plato and Aristotle might not believe in a personal God who provides us with meaning, they do agree with religious philosophers that there is some nonhuman, objective metaphysical order with which we must be properly aligned if our lives are to have meaning. For the remainder of this discussion, however, I focus on the religious version of this position.

According to theists, the world is a purposeful creation of a loving, intelligent God. Likewise, they say, we have been created to fulfill a divine purpose, which is to live in relationship with our creator and to follow the path that is laid out for us. A popular quote, often attributed to the 17th-century mathematician and philosopher Pascal, says "There is a God-shaped vacuum in every man's heart that only God can fill." Similarly, the Hindu teacher Kabīr wrote "Until you have found God in your own soul, the world will seem meaningless to you." In contrast to the cynicism of American writer Elbert Hubbard, who said, "Life is just one damned thing after another," the religious view claims that life has meaning because rooted in the nature of God is an objective order of values. For this reason the American philosopher William James said "The smallest details of this world derive infinite significance from their relation to an unseen divine order." Finally, death is not the final chapter of our lives, according to theists, because we were made for eternity. Our lives are not like a beautiful soap bubble that lasts for awhile and then is gone. The American author Nathaniel Hawthorne said that "Our Creator would never have made such lovely days, and have given us the deep hearts to enjoy them, unless we were meant to be immortal." The religious approach to the meaning of life is expressed in the autobiography of Leo Tolstoy.

Count Leo Tolstoy (1828–1910) was an acclaimed Russian writer. His epic novels, especially *War and Peace* and *Anna Karenina,* as well as his short stories and essays, have earned him the title of one of Russia's best-known and beloved authors.

At age 50, Tolstoy experienced a spiritual crisis that led to a search for the meaning of life. His search culminated in his embracing the simple Christianity of the Gospels, which he believed was exemplified in the lives of the Russian peasants. The following selection is from his *Confession,* written in the years from 1879 to 1882, which details Tolstoy's spiritual journey and represents his theistic answer about the meaning of life. In telling the story of his life, Tolstoy says that (initially) his success as an author enabled him to throw himself into his work as a way of "stifling any questions in my soul concerning the meaning of my life and of life in general." But as Tolstoy's account makes clear, this evasive tactic eventually began to fail him.

- What questions caused Tolstoy, in the midst of a successful writing career, to experience a sense of bewilderment?
- Why was he dissatisfied with the answers provided by the sciences and rational knowledge concerning the meaning of life?
- After finding no satisfying answers among the intellectuals, why does Tolstoy turn to the working class in his search for meaning?
- What is the solution to the meaning of life that Tolstoy eventually embraces? Why does he think that it is the correct answer?

My Confession [3]

At first I began having moments of bewilderment, when my life would come to a halt, as if I did not know how to live or what to do; I would lose my presence of mind and fall into a state of depression. But this passed, and I continued to live as before. Then the moments of bewilderment recurred more frequently, and they always took the same form. Whenever my life came to a halt, the questions would arise: Why? And what next? . . .

And this was happening to me at a time when, from all indications, I should have been considered a completely happy man; this was when I was not yet fifty years old. I had a good, loving, and beloved wife, fine children, and a large estate that was growing and expanding without any effort on my part. More than ever before I was respected by friends and acquaintances, praised by strangers, and I could claim a certain renown without really deluding myself. Moreover, I was not physically and mentally unhealthy; on the contrary, I enjoyed a physical and mental vigor such as I had rarely encountered among others my age. . . . And in such a state of affairs I came to a point where I could not live; and even though I feared death, I had to employ ruses against myself to keep from committing suicide. . . .

Had I simply understood that life has no meaning, I might have been able to calmly accept it; I might have recognized that such was my lot. But I could not rest content at this. Had I been like a man who lives in a forest from which he knows there is no way out, I might have been able to go on living; but I was like a man lost in the forest who was terrified by the fact that he was lost, like a man who was rushing about, longing to find his way and knowing that every step was leading him into deeper confusion, and yet who could not help rushing about. . . .

In my search for answers to the question of life I felt exactly as a man who is lost in a forest.

I came to a clearing, climbed a tree, and had a clear view of the endless space around me. But I could see that there was no house and that there could be no house; I went into the thick of the forest, into the darkness, but again I could see no house—only darkness.

Thus I wandered about in the forest of human knowledge. On one side of me were the clearings of mathematical and experimental sciences, revealing to me sharp horizons; but in no direction could I see a house. On the other side of me was the darkness of the speculative sciences, where every step I took plunged me deeper into darkness, and I was finally convinced that there could be no way out.

When I gave myself over to the bright light of knowledge, I was only diverting my eyes from the question. However clear and tempting the horizons that opened up to me might have been, however tempting it was to sink into the infinity of this knowledge, I soon realized that the clearer this knowledge was, the less I needed it, the less it answered my question.

"Well," I said to myself, "I know everything that science wants so much to know, but this path will not lead me to an answer to the question of the meaning of my life." In the realm of speculative science I saw that in spite of—or rather precisely because of—the fact that this knowledge was designed to answer my question, there could be no answer other than the one I had given myself: What is the meaning of my life? It has none. Or: What will come of my life? Nothing. Or: Why does everything that is exist, and why do I exist? Because it exists.

Tolstoy says that at this point in his life, he was living in a state of madness, with continual thoughts of suicide. He sought out people who seemed to have a sense of the meaning of life, but did not find any among the company of his fellow intellectuals. However, when he looked to the working people, he found a peace and contentment that was based on their religious faith. This discovery provoked a new crisis. Up until now, he had placed his confidence in rational knowledge, which, he believed, excluded faith. But reason provided no answers to his questions about the meaning of life. On the other hand, people of faith seemed to have found the answer, but their answer required embracing a form of life that Tolstoy held in contempt because he thought it was irrational. Finally, he was forced to reevaluate all his former assumptions. As Tolstoy says:

> I ran into a contradiction from which there were only two ways out: either the thing that I had referred to as reason was not as rational as I had thought, or the thing that I took to be irrational was not as irrational as I had thought. And I began to examine the course of the arguments that had come of my rational knowledge.

However, he finally concluded that neither science nor philosophy could give him what he sought. Thus, a new approach to the problem was required.

> . . . I realized that I could not search for an answer to my question in rational knowledge. The answer given by rational knowledge is merely an indication that an answer can be obtained only by formulating the question differently, that is, only when the relationship between the finite and the infinite is introduced into the question. I also realized that no matter how irrational and unattractive the answers given by faith, they have the advantage of bringing to every reply a relationship between the finite and the infinite, without which there can be no reply. However I may put the question of how I am to live, the answer is: according to the law of God. Is there anything real that will come of my life? Eternal torment or eternal happiness. What meaning is there which is not destroyed by death? Union with the infinite God, paradise. . . .
>
> Rational knowledge led me to the conclusion that life is meaningless; my life came to a halt, and I wanted to do away with myself. As I looked around at people, I saw that they were living, and I was convinced that they knew the meaning of life. Then I turned and looked at myself; as long as I knew the meaning of life, I lived. As it was with others, so it was with me: faith provided me with the meaning of life and the possibility of living.
>
> Upon a further examination of the people in other countries, of my contemporaries, and of those who have passed away, I saw the same thing. Wherever there is life, there is faith; since the origin of mankind faith has made it possible for us to live, and the main characteristics of faith are everywhere and always the same.
>
> No matter what answers a given faith might provide for us, every answer of faith gives infinite meaning to the finite existence of man, meaning that is not destroyed by suffering, deprivation, and death. Therefore, the meaning of life and the possibility of living may be found in faith alone. . . . Faith is the knowledge of the meaning of human life, whereby the individual does not destroy himself but lives. Faith is the force of life. If a man lives, then he must have faith in something. If he did not believe that he had something he must live for, then he would not live. If he fails to see and understand the illusory nature of the finite, then he believes in the finite; if he understands the illusory nature of the finite, then he must believe in the infinite. Without faith it is impossible to live.

Convinced that faith was the key to the meaning of life, Tolstoy began to study more closely the lives of believers among "the poor, the simple, and uneducated folk," people who had been slighted by his more learned but spiritually empty peers.

So I began to examine the life and the teachings of these people, and the closer I looked, the more I was convinced that theirs was the true faith, that their faith was indispensable to them and that this faith alone provided them with the meaning and possibility of life. Contrary to what I saw among the people of our class, where life was possible without faith and scarcely one in a thousand was a believer, among these people there was scarcely one in a thousand who was not a believer. Contrary to what I saw among the people of our class, where a lifetime is passed in idleness, amusement, and dissatisfaction with life, these people spent their lives at hard labor and were less dissatisfied with life than the wealthy. Contrary to the people of our class who resist and are unhappy with the hardship and suffering of their lot, these people endure sickness and tribulation without question or resistance—peacefully, and in the firm conviction that this is as it should be, cannot be otherwise, and is good. Contrary to the fact that the greater our intellect, the less we understand the meaning of life and the more we see some kind of evil joke in our suffering and death, these people live, suffer, and draw near to death peacefully and, more often than not, joyfully. Contrary to peaceful death—death without horror and despair, which is the rarest exception in our class—it is the tormenting, unyielding, and sorrowful death that is the rarest exception among the people. And these people, who are deprived of everything that for Solomon and me constituted the only good in life, yet who nonetheless enjoy the greatest happiness, form the overwhelming majority of mankind. I looked further still around myself. I examined the lives of the great masses of people who have lived in the past and live today. Among those who have understood the meaning of life, who know how to live and die, I saw not two or three or ten but hundreds, thousands, millions. And all of them, infinitely varied in their customs, intellects, educations, and positions and in complete contrast to my ignorance, knew the meaning of life and death, labored in peace, endured suffering and hardship, lived and died, and saw in this not vanity but good.

I grew to love these people. The more I learned about the lives of those living and dead about whom I had read and heard, the more I loved them and the easier it became for me to live. I lived this way for about two years, and a profound transformation came over me, one that had been brewing in me for a long time and whose elements had always been a part of me. The life of our class, of the wealthy and the learned, was not only repulsive to me but had lost all meaning. The sum of our action and thinking, of our science and art, all of it struck me as the overindulgences of a spoiled child. I realized that meaning was not to be sought here. The actions of the laboring people, of those who create life, began to appear to me as the one true way. I realized that the meaning provided by this life was truth, and I embraced it.

In reflecting on his period of stumbling toward faith in God, Tolstoy says that he wavered between faith and unbelief, between life and psychological death. However, he finally terminated his struggle with a firm resolution of faith.

But at that point I took a closer look at myself and at what had been happening within me; and I remembered the hundreds of times I had gone through these deaths and revivals. I remembered that I had lived only when I believed in God. Then, as now, I said to myself, "As long as I know God, I live; when I forget, when I do not believe in him, I die." What are these deaths and revivals? It is clear that I do not live whenever I lose my faith in the existence of God, and I would have killed myself long ago if I did not have some vague hope of finding God. I truly live only whenever I am conscious of him and seek him. "What, then, do I seek?" a voice cried out within me. "He is there, the one without whom there could be no life." To know God and to live come to one and the same thing. God is life.

"Live, seeking God, for there can be no life without God." And more powerfully than ever a light shone within me and all around me, and this light has not abandoned me since.

Translated by David Patterson. Copyright © 1983 by David Patterson. Used by permission of W. W. Norton & Company, Inc. This selection may not be reproduced, stored in a retrieval system, or transmitted in any form or by any means without the prior written permission of the publisher.

LOOKING THROUGH THE LENS OF THE RELIGIOUS VIEW

1. Singer Peggy Lee was famous for the song "Is That All There Is?" in which she asks that question at each stage of her life. Like her, we all engage in purposeful activities, such as going to school, pursuing a career, forming friendships. However, when we step back from all our busy activities and reflect on our lives, aren't we likewise faced with the question "Is that all there is?" If we have the courage to face that question, why are we often left with an empty, yearning feeling, as though there should be something more? What is the answer provided by the religious view?

2. Modern secular and moral philosophies often assume that all persons are of equal worth and dignity. But because people seem to be unequal in terms of their abilities, what is the basis for this assumption? If we are all made in the image of God and were placed here to serve a purpose, however, don't we now have a foundation for treating one another equally, as children of God and members of the same human family? In what ways does the religious view make sense of the notion of the equal dignity and worth of all persons?

EXAMINING THE STRENGTHS AND WEAKNESSES OF THE RELIGIOUS VIEW

Positive Evaluation

1. Given human nature, we all have a number of basic needs, such as the need for water, food, and friendship. In each case, life provides us with the possibility of satisfying those needs. Likewise, we seem to have a universal need to find some ultimate meaning and purpose in life. Wouldn't it be strange if we all appear to have this need, but there is no way to satisfy it? Doesn't this suggest that we were made to fulfill some purpose?

2. The agnostic philosopher Bertrand Russell concluded his famous essay "A Free Man's Worship" with the pessimistic proclamation that "all the labors of the ages, all the devotion, all the inspiration, all the noonday brightness of human genius, are destined to extinction in the vast death of the solar system, and the whole temple of man's achievement must inevitably be buried beneath the debris of a universe in ruins." Isn't Russell voicing the honest conclusion we would have to draw if we reject the religious view of the purpose of human life?

Negative Evaluation

1. Some people would respond to Tolstoy by saying "It's fine that you found meaning through religious faith. But doesn't your conclusion merely indicate that religion met your

own, personal psychological needs? Why do you suppose a religious meaning is necessary for everyone?" Isn't the extremely personal nature of Tolstoy's narrative an indication that religion was his answer but that it will not be everyone's answer?

2. Aren't many nonreligious people living meaningful, joyous lives by serving others or by pursuing satisfying careers and relationships? Don't these people prove that religion is not a necessary ingredient in life?

SURVEYING THE CASE FOR SECULAR-HUMANISM

The fourth approach is called secular-humanism. Advocates of this view think that there is no ultimate meaning to either the universe or human life. Secular-humanists see the pieces of our lives as fitting together in various ways to make many interesting and satisfying combinations but without supposing that there is one, pre-given picture that we were all intended to complete. These philosophers contend that life can be worth living in terms of the little *meanings* (small letters) that we find or create during our journey in life. Whereas the religious approach says that our lives will be meaningful only if we discover the purpose *of* life, the secular-humanist says we can live meaningful lives if we individually find purpose *in* our respective lives.

In contrast to the jigsaw metaphor, which offers one, final picture into which we fit the pieces of our lives, the secular-humanist would use the metaphor of a mosaic. Our lives are made up of many moments and experiences that are like the colored tiles that go into the mosaic. The general experiences of birth, friendship, love, suffering, a career, and finally death are common to all. Other experiences are unique to each individual. From these pieces, each of us is trying to compose a meaningful pattern. Hence, each of us is engaged in the project of making our life into an original work of art, not one that we are merely duplicating. Although there may be some general similarities between different lives, each of us is composing our own, unique picture. As contemporary philosopher Richard Taylor puts it, "The meaning of life is from within us, it is not bestowed from without, and it far exceeds in both its beauty and permanence any heaven of which men have ever dreamed or yearned for."

The reading selection on the secular-humanist viewpoint is by existentialist philosopher Hazel E. Barnes (b. 1915). Barnes is retired from the University of Colorado, where she taught both classics and philosophy. She is best known as a spokesperson for atheistic existentialism (in contrast to the religious existentialism of Søren Kierkegaard). Throughout her work she sought to follow up and apply the ideas of Jean-Paul Sartre. Barnes authored *Humanistic Existentialism* and *An Existentialist Ethics* and translated Sartre's *Being and Nothingness*. Not every advocate of secular-humanism accepts all the tenets of existentialism, but the following selection provides a good statement of the key points of the secular-humanist solution to questions about the meaning of life.

- According to Barnes, what are the two alternatives presented by religion on the one hand and nihilism (pessimism) on the other?
- What is the third alternative of Barnes's existentialism? In what way does it offer us a satisfying life?
- How does she respond to the need that people have for an eternal "measuring stick"?
- Why does Barnes welcome the apparent chaos of divergent value systems that results from her philosophy?
- Barnes is an atheist, so why does she reject the notion that "we exist in an impersonal Universe"?

Black Lines (1913) by Vasily Kandinsky. In looking at a modern, abstract painting such as this one, we are tempted to ask, "What does it mean?" The answer is that there isn't one, definitive meaning that we should seek in this painting. It is simply a series of energized black lines dancing over vibrantly colored patches that seem to float on the canvas. Kandinsky is expressing his inner being through these shapes and enjoying the play of colors. If our senses are similarly enriched by this display, then so much the better. What more should we expect from the artist's work? Similarly, the secular-humanist explains that we should not seek some pre-given, ultimate MEANING in human existence. Instead, our lives are like works of art that we are creating. If we find value and enjoyment in the patterns we produce, we can be satisfied. Furthermore, if the patterns of our lives enrich others and help them in creating their own satisfying life patterns, then we are doubly enriched.

FROM HAZEL E. BARNES
An Existentialist Ethics [4]

In contrasting traditional and existentialist attitudes toward the question of the meaning of life, I should like to use a homely example as an illustration. Let us imagine reality to have the shape of a gigantic Chinese checkerboard—without even the logically arranged spacing of the regularly shaped holes as in the usual game board, and with various-sized marbles, only some of which will fit into the spaces provided. The traditional attitude of religion and philosophy has been that we faced two alternatives. Theological and rational positions have assumed that there exists some correct pattern, impressed into the board itself, which can be discovered and which will then show us how we may satisfactorily and correctly arrange the piles of marbles near us. They have assumed—and so have the Nihilists—that if there is no such pattern, then there is no reason to play at all. If there is no motive for making a particular pattern, they have concluded that one might as well destroy the patterns set up by others or commit suicide. Existentialism holds that there is a third possibility. There is no pre-existing pattern. No amount of delving into the structure of the board will reveal one inscribed there in matter. Nor is it sensible to hope for some nonmaterial force which might magnetically draw the marbles into their correct position if we put ourselves in touch with such a power by prayer or drugs or any other device which man might think of. But while this lack deprives man of guide and certain goal, it leaves him free to create his own pattern. It is true that there is no external model according to which one may pronounce the new pattern good or bad, better or worse. There are only the individual judgments by him who makes it and by those who behold it, and these need not agree. If the maker finds value in his own creation, if the process of making is satisfying, if the end result compares sufficiently favorably with the intention, then the pattern *has* value and the individual life has been worthwhile. I must quickly add that no such pattern exists alone. Although its unique form and color remain distinctly perceptible, it is intermeshed with the edges of the patterns of others—like the design of a paisley print. The satisfaction in a life may well result in large part from the sense that these intermeshings have positive significance for the individual pattern. There is another kind of satisfaction—that which comes from the knowledge that other persons have declared one's pattern good. Still a third derives from the realization that what one has done has helped make it easier for others to live patterns intrinsically satisfying to them.

That a positive value is present in experiencing a delight in what one has created and in the approval of others cannot be denied. For many people this is not enough. The sense that there is something missing is sufficient to undermine any quiet content with what one has. . . . First, there is the feeling that we need some sort of eternal archetype or measuring stick. Existentialism admits that there is nothing of the sort and that life is harder without it. Yet we may well ask whether the privilege of having such an authority would not come at too high a price, and cost more than it is worth. Pragmatically, the over-all destiny and purpose of the Universe play a small part in the daily projects of Western man—with the possible exception of those remaining fundamentalists who still take the promise of Heaven and Hell quite literally. Mostly it is there as a kind of consolation at moments of failure, cheering our discouragement with the idea that things may be better sometime in a way that we cannot begin to comprehend. I do not deny the psychic refreshment of such comfort. But if the belief in any such authority and plan is sufficiently specific to be more than a proud hope, it must be restrictive as well. If man can be sure that he is right by any nonhuman standard, then his humanity is strictly confined by the nonhuman. He is not free to bring anything new into the world. His possibilities are those of the slave or the well-bred child. Higher meaning is itself a limitation for a being-who-is-a-process. Such a future is not open but prescribed. Man as a tiny being in an impersonal world may be without importance from the theoretical but nonexistent point of view of an omniscient objective observer. Man in the theological framework of the medieval man-centered Universe has only the dignity of the child, who must regulate his life by the rules laid down by adults. The human adventure becomes a conducted tour. . . . The time has come for man to leave his parents and to live in his own right by his own judgments.

The second disturbing aspect of a life of self-created patterns emerges when we compare ourselves with our fellow man. Obviously some people are satisfied with patterns which others regard as deplorable. Can we allow this chaos of judgments and still cling to the belief in the positive value of whatever patterns we ourselves have made? Is the result not such an anarchy of the arbitrary that to speak of pattern at all is nonsense? Here existentialism begins by saying that up to a point, arbitrariness, inconsistency, and the simultaneous existence of divergent value systems are not to be lamented but welcomed. The creative freedom to choose and structure one's own pattern would be worthless if we were to agree that we would all work in the same way toward the same end. Just as we expect persons to differ in their specific projects, so we should allow for those individual overall orientations which bestow upon the project its significance and which are, in turn, colored by it. Sartre has declared that the creation of a value system by which one is willing to live and to judge one's life is man's most important creative enterprise. This means more than the working out of standards of right and wrong and the regulation of one's own demands in the light of our relations with others. It involves the whole context of what we might call "the style" of a life—not just the moral but the aesthetic, the temperamental—everything which goes to make up the personality which continues, with varying degrees of modification, until death and which even then will leave behind it an objectified "Self for Others." Every such life is unique, no matter how hard the one who lives it may have tried to mold himself after the pattern of his contemporaries. Existentialism prizes this uniqueness and resists all attempts to reduce it to the lowest possible minimum. Existentialism recognizes and exults in the fact that since everyone *is* a point of view, there is no more possibility of all persons becoming the same than there is of reducing to one perspective the views of two people looking at a landscape from different spots. . . .

It is illogical to conclude that human values and meanings are unreal and of no importance simply because they do not originate in the structure of the nonhuman Universe. It is enough that the world serves to support these subjective structures for the consciousness which lives them. At the same time it is only natural that an individual man, whose being is a self-projection, should rebel at the prospect of seeing his projects suddenly brought to a stop. If the patterns and meanings which a consciousness creates were restricted to those experiences which we can live directly, then despair would in truth seem to be our only proper response. But man's being is that of a creature who is always about-to-be. In a peculiar sense also, he is, in his being, always outside or beyond himself, out there in the objects of his intentions or—more accurately—in his projects in the world. An impersonal Universe cannot sustain these subjective structures. But we do not exist in an impersonal Universe. We live in a human world where multitudes of other consciousnesses are ceaselessly imposing their meanings upon Being-in-itself and confronting the projects which I have introduced. It is in the future of these intermeshed human activities that I most fully transcend myself. In so far as "I" have carved out my being in this human world, "I" go on existing in its future.

LOOKING THROUGH THE LENS OF SECULAR-HUMANISM

1. When we were children (and particularly when we were teenagers), we couldn't wait to grow up and become adults. But too often, people can be adults in terms of their physical age but are still like children in terms of their emotional needs. However, we tend to look on such people with disdain or pity. Doesn't the secular-humanist view encourage us to become adults in our outlook on life by calling us to take charge of our lives, to

become autonomous and independent, and to make our own decisions and choose our own purpose?

2. To both the religious person and the pessimist, the ravages of time and death destroy any value we have created unless we have an eternal destiny. But to this objection Ronald Hepburn replies:

> Consider the familiar claim that life is meaningless if death ends all, that a necessary condition of life being meaningful is immortality or resurrection. Against this it is argued that there is no entailment between temporal finiteness and disvalue, futility. We can and do love flowers that fade; and the knowledge that they will fade may even enhance their preciousness. To be everlasting, that is, is no necessary or sufficient condition of value or worthwhileness, nor therefore of meaningfulness.[5]

Does Hepburn provide a satisfactory answer to the objection that secular-humanism does not provide any eternal meaning to our lives?

EXAMINING THE STRENGTHS AND WEAKNESSES OF SECULAR-HUMANISM

Positive Evaluation

1. Think about the activities you did this week (big or small) that helped give your life meaning. Maybe you conversed with a friend, listened to music you enjoy, wrote a poem, tutored a child, or even played an invigorating game of tennis. If your life can be made up of an abundance of such small, meaningful moments, is it necessary that there be one, big purpose to your life?

2. No proposal about the purpose of human existence will do me any good unless I can make it *my* purpose. So in the final analysis, isn't the main goal of life to answer the question "What gives *my* life meaning?" Isn't the highly individual nature of this question exactly what we would expect if secular-humanism is correct?

Negative Evaluation

1. Hazel E. Barnes suggests that the meaning of life is found in creatively pursuing projects of our own choosing. But doesn't this solution leave some important questions unanswered? Suppose two people are equally satisfied with their lives, and each one finds life meaningful. However, one person's life is devoted to building affordable homes for hard-working poor families, and the other person's life is devoted to trying to get a perfect score in some trivial video game. Wouldn't we say that the first person's life was more meaningful, purposeful, and worthy of being lived? Doesn't this example suggest (contrary to Barnes) that there is some sort of "measuring stick" against which our lives should be gauged? Is personal, psychological satisfaction the only criterion for living a meaningful life?

2. Leo Tolstoy would say that the secular-humanist notion that we can find meaning in our individual pursuits is an illusion. Whatever we stake our life on, whether it is our career, health, fortune, or friends, can be taken away from us, leaving us empty. Likewise, the pessimist Arthur Schopenhauer said that if we get everything we want we will be bored, but if we fail to get everything we want we will be frustrated. But is the haunting threat of

emptiness, boredom, or frustration all that we should expect? Don't Tolstoy's and Schopenhauer's reflections suggest that the meaning of our lives cannot be built on anything that is finite, temporary, or capable of being destroyed? The religious person might ask "Are we too easily satisfied with crumbs, when the banquet table of a transcendent, eternal source of meaning is the only thing that will fill our hunger?"

HOW DO I APPLY PHILOSOPHY TO MY LIFE? —THE PERSPECTIVE OF EXISTENTIALISM

Probably few philosophical movements in the modern era have been as concerned with the meaning of human existence (and the terrifying threat of meaninglessness) as that of existentialism. For this reason, it is appropriate to end this chapter (and this book) with a brief examination of the insights that the existentialists have to offer on this topic.

existentialism a philosophical movement that believes in subjective choosing over objective reasoning, concrete experience over intellectual abstractions, individuality over mass culture, human freedom over determinism, and authentic living over inauthenticity

Existentialism is a philosophical movement that arose in the 19th century in the writings of two disparate philosophers: Søren Kierkegaard, a passionate Christian, and Friedrich Nietzsche, an equally intense atheist. Their writings were not appreciated in their own time, but like intellectual time bombs, their ideas exploded in the 20th century and existentialism became one of the most popular movements in the contemporary age. Some of the leading existential philosophers in the 20th century were Jean-Paul Sartre, Maurice Merleau-Ponty, Gabriel Marcel, Karl Jaspers, and Martin Heidegger. From its very beginnings in the writings of Kierkegaard and Nietzsche, existentialism attracted both religious and nonreligious thinkers. Sartre was an outspoken atheist, Merleau-Ponty was nonreligious, Marcel was a Catholic, and Jaspers and Heidegger, while not explicitly religious, incorporated a number of religious themes in their writings that influenced theologians. The influence of existentialism spread far beyond the confines of philosophy and had an impact on literature, art, drama, psychology, and theology.

Because individualism is one of the major themes of existentialism, there is no common list of doctrines to which all the existentialists subscribe. They are a diverse group of thinkers whose personalities differ as much as their writings. However, a number of themes persist throughout all existentialist thought. Some of the hallmarks of existentialism are the priority of subjective choosing over objective reasoning, concrete experience over intellectual abstractions, individuality over mass culture, human freedom over determinism, and authentic living over inauthenticity.

Even though obviously vast differences exist between religious existentialists and secular or atheistic existentialists, they both share a number of insights in common concerning how to approach the issue of the meaning of life. I list here five of these insights, for which I draw on both the Christian existentialist Søren Kierkegaard and the atheistic existentialist Jean-Paul Sartre.*

Five Insights of Existentialism

1. **In answering the questions of philosophy, make sure the answers are *your* answers.**

In one of his journals Søren Kierkegaard said, "There are many people who reach their conclusions about life like schoolboys: they cheat their master by copying the answer out of a book without having worked the sum out themselves." In philosophy as in arithmetic,

---

*Søren Kierkegaard opened this book in section 1.0 and was also discussed in section 4.4 on pragmatic and subjective justifications of religious belief. Jean-Paul Sartre was discussed in section 3.7 on libertarianism. For a brief account of their lives, refer back to those sections.

using someone else's answers may work in the short run, but it doesn't help you get through life in the long haul. You can model yourself after the great minds in philosophy, but in the end, you have to work out the "sum" for yourself.

Kierkegaard said there is a difference between *knowing the truth* and *being in the truth*. Similarly, he once noted that there were two kinds of people, those who suffer and those who become professors of suffering. His comment explains the difference between knowledge that can be gained only by participating in life and knowledge that is approached in a detached, academic sort of way. For Kierkegaard "the professor" is not just an occupation, it is an attitude toward life. His point was reflected in the words of a little-known author, Friedrich Hebbel, who once said:

> The hell-fire of life consumes only the select among men.
> The rest stand in front of it, warming their hands.[6]

This Kierkegaardian theme can be illustrated with several analogies. For example, here is how to ride a bike: adjust the curvature of your bicycle's path in proportion to the ratio of your unbalance over the square of your speed.[7] Obviously, knowing that physics formula will not enable you to ride a bicycle (even though it is objectively true). You learn to ride a bicycle through participating in that reality and having the subjective experience of feeling the point of balance and not through an intellectual understanding of a physics formula.

The distinction between objectively knowing the truth and subjectively being in the truth is related to another distinction Kierkegaard makes between the result and the process. In some cases the result and the process can be separated. For example, you can look up the distance from the earth to the moon in a book. You can get the results without having to go through the process of calculating it yourself. On the other hand, you cannot become physically fit in a secondhand way. The only way to get the result is to go through a certain process yourself. For Kierkegaard, the kinds of truths that really matter (self-knowledge, the way one should live, or religious understanding) are more similiar to physical fitness than to mathematical information. *What* you know is bound up with *how* you know it. The journey to self-understanding is a tortuous one that only you can take.

One last example will help make Kierkegaard's point clear. During a graduate philosophy seminar I was in, a philosopher who was famous for his defense of the ontological argument for God had reduced the argument to logical symbols that were spread all over the blackboard.* At the end of this clutter of mathematical symbols was the conclusion: "God, the greatest possible being, necessarily exists." One of my friends exclaimed to me, "Damn! The argument is sound. I can find no logical errors in it." Then a look of horror came over his face because he was a doctoral student in philosophy who was committed to living his life on the basis of reason, and he had just been presented with an argument for God's existence that he thought was sound. Yet he realized that he would leave the room and his life would be no different. Kierkegaard would have understood what this young man was feeling, because he believed that objective truth was sterile, dry, cold, and useless if it did not make a subjective impact on a person's life.

Jean-Paul Sartre makes a similar point when he tells of a student of his during World War II who was wrestling with the decision of either staying with his aged mother or going to fight the Nazis. As Sartre says:

> What could help him choose? Could the Christian doctrine? No. Christian doctrine
> says: Act with charity, love your neighbour, deny yourself for others, choose the way

---

*See the discussion of the ontological argument in section 4.3.

The Intellectual versus the Existential Meaning of Death

Leo Tolstoy's story "The Death of Ivan Illych" concretely illustrates the difference between knowing the truth intellectually and knowing it subjectively and existentially. Ivan Illych had always known the truth of the statement "All men are mortal." But "men" in that statement was abstract. Ivan could not envision it as including him. One day at his doctor's office, however, Ivan discovered that *he* was dying. Suddenly, the objective truth he had always known took on a new meaning. The inevitability of death was easy to contemplate when it referred to humanity in general. But when Ivan realized that "I, Ivan Illych, am dying," the concept of mortality suddenly changed for him.

which is hardest, and so forth. But which is the harder road? To whom does one owe the more brotherly love, the patriot or the mother? Which is the more useful aim, the general one of fighting in and for the whole community, or the precise aim of helping one particular person to live?"[8]

STOP AND THINK

Was there a time when you knew something was true with your intellect, but it made no impact on your life (as in the case of the philosophy student contemplating a proof of God's existence)? Did you ever have the sort of experience that occurred to Ivan Illych, that something you had known abstractly became concretely and personally real? Is it possible to know something intellectually but not know it subjectively?

Sartre's point is that even if the student chose to follow Christian principles, they would not give him ready-made answers for his specific situation. He would still have to figure out how they apply to his life. Furthermore, Sartre points out that if the young man were to consult a priest, this approach wouldn't relieve the young man of the burden of deciding for himself either. Some priests were part of the resistance to Nazism and others waited passively for the tide to turn. Whichever priest the student consulted, the young man would be deciding beforehand which advice he would receive. Hence, even if we look to resources outside ourselves to choose our path, we have to decide whom to consult, how to interpret their advice, and whether or not we will follow their advice. Ultimately, we cannot escape the burden of taking responsibility and realizing that the decision is up to us and our own judgment. That is why Sartre told the student, "You are free, therefore choose."

I have stressed that philosophy is personal and subjective. However, it is not subjective in the sense that my hatred of raw oysters and my love of bluegrass music are a matter of my personal preferences. Instead, philosophy is both personal and objective in the same way that death is personal and objective. Death is personal because it matters to me. Yet, at the same time, death is an objective fact about the human condition. Hence, in philosophy the personal and the objective are intertwined. *Underlying every objective claim is a personal judgment.* You can follow the standards of divine commands, impersonal reason, or the findings of science (to name just a few possibilities). Yet, in each case, you are making a personal judgment that this resource is a trustworthy guide and that you are well-served in following it. The converse is also true. *Underlying every personal judgment is an objective claim.* You can make personal judgments in philosophy concerning what is true, or good, or what you should do. However, as Sartre points out, you are thereby tacitly making an objective claim that this judgment is the best way to look at things and that it would be so for anyone in your situation. So, in the final analysis, philosophy could be understood as *the attempt to subjectively appropriate what you have found to be objectively true*.

2. Take the standpoint of one who is down on the field engaged with the game and not that of a spectator.

One of the worst classes I ever taught was a course on business ethics to undergraduate accounting majors. Besides the problems caused by my failures as a teacher, the students did not understand how discussing all these ethical issues would be practically useful to them in their corporate careers. But then I taught a workshop to professional accountants in industry and the difference in the response was astonishing. Those practicing accountants were "down on the field," experiencing the ethical pressures to compromise their professional integrity so that the financial figures would be favorable to their employer. Consequently, they were enthusiastic about what I had to say and eagerly shared their own "ethics horror stories" to illustrate the points I was making. In contrast, the college students could not appreciate the relevance of the class because they were still viewing the profession as spectators or from a detached, theoretical standpoint.

In stressing the importance of being a participant and not a spectator, Sartre says "Man is nothing else but what he purposes, he exists only in so far as he realizes himself, he is therefore nothing else but the sum of his actions, nothing else but what his life is."[9] Sartre goes on to criticize the person who says "Circumstances have been against me, I was worthy to be something much better than I have been." Instead, Sartre says, "There is no love apart from the deeds of love; no potentiality of love other than that which is manifested in the loving; there is no genius other than that which is expressed in works of art."

To underscore the importance of engagement, consider this analogy. A book like the one you are reading right now can provide you with a delightful cafeteria of philosophical ideas. In a cafeteria line you get to compose your own meal by picking and choosing what you want. Similarly, as you read each chapter of this book you undoubtedly found some options to be appealing and rejected others. However, a collection of delicious and nutritious foods sitting on your tray will not do you much good unless you consume them. So what will you do now with the philosophical alternatives you have studied? Will you simply leave them on your tray? As Kierkegaard asked himself (and each of us have to ask ourselves), "What would be the use of… working through all the systems of philosophy and of being able, if required, to review them all and show up the inconsistencies within each system… if [they] had *no* deeper significance *for me and for my life*… ?" Of course, working through all the ideas in this book may get you a good grade in a course (and that is important). But it is equally obvious that there is more to your life and to you as a person than a collection of grades and transcripts. It would be interesting and, perhaps, not that hard to answer the question "What have I learned from reading this book on philosophy?" However, it might be more difficult and certainly more self-revealing to ask yourself the question "How have I changed after thinking about philosophy?"

3. Recognize that choice, commitment, responsibility, and risk are inescapable.

For every option there are three responses: "Yes," "No," and "I'll decide later." For some questions we can choose the third response. If you asked me, "Is there life in outer space?" I would respond, "I don't know, I'll wait and decide when we get more information." This alternative is acceptable, because nothing in my life hinges on the answer to that question. But with respect to the options we face concerning the meaning of life, we don't have this luxury. We are like someone at sea, trying to decide which way to steer our ship. If we put off the decision, we will drift aimlessly until death overtakes us. With our philosophy of

Wanderer Above a Sea of Fog (1818) by Caspar David Friedrich. Like the solitary figure in this painting, each individual stands alone, facing the question of the meaning of life. Even if you find that meaning in something larger than yourself, whether it be God or your bond with your fellow human beings, you still have to decide what your stance in life shall be. Both the religious existentialist Søren Kierkegaard and the atheistic existentialist Jean-Paul Sartre argue that each person alone has to bear the weight of responsibility and the risk of choosing ultimate commitments.

life as with marine navigation, we have to make the best decision we can, using all the information we have. In this case, not making a decision is really making a decision, but making it passively and irresponsibly.

In describing the situation in Nazi-occupied France during World War II, Sartre says,

We were never more free than under the German Occupation. We had lost all our rights, above all the right to speak; we were insulted daily and had to remain silent, we were deported, because we were workers, because we were Jews, because we were political prisoners. All around us on the walls, in the newspapers, on the screen, we met that foul and insipid image that our oppressors wanted us to accept as ourselves. Because of all this we were free.[10]

Under these oppressive conditions, why does Sartre say that the French people were never more free? The reason is that they were forced to make choices; they could not avoid the weight of responsibility for having to choose what they would do. In every word and every action they would either choose to be collaborators with the Nazis or align themselves with the resistance. Making authentic choices was the only option, because avoiding commitment was not possible.

Kierkegaard ridicules the strategy of not making a decision until you achieve absolute, objective certainty as that of following an "approximation-process." When considering an option you can pile up the evidence and reasons until they approximate some decision. The evidence convinces you that the position you are considering is probably true or even extremely probable. Still, there is always the possibility that the next argument you hear or the next book you read will affect your estimate of these probabilities. However, for some issues you cannot wait forever, because putting off a decision indefinitely may be making a decision by default. Examples of such issues might be "Shall I wait to be rescued or should I try to find my way back to a safe port?" or "Shall I marry this person?" or "Shall I embrace this philosophy?" In these cases the evidence can be a matter of approximation but the decision eventually has to be a flat yes or no. At a carnival you can plunk down a quarter in some petty game of chance in hopes of winning some cheap trinket. You won't gain much, but you haven't risked much either. However, the really worthwhile goals in life require a greater amount of risk and a greater amount of commitment.

4. **Make use of all the rational, objective considerations possible, but realize that, in the end, philosophy does not make the decisions for you.**

One of the major decisions in Kierkegaard's life was whether to marry the love of his life, Regina Olsen. Even though Kierkegaard had an advanced degree in philosophy, he knew that all the logic in the world could not make the decision for him. He, and he alone, had to make the decision in a passionate and personal way. It was not only a decision as to what to do, or what kind of life he would live, but even more profoundly it was a decision as to *what person he would be.* (In the end he decided not to marry her.)

In contrast to Kierkegaard, I once had a friend who devised his own rational calculus for making life's decisions. He would list all the pros and cons concerning an option and assign weights to each one. For example, on the question, "Should I get married?" he would list

Companionship = + 10
The joys of children = + 6
Affection = + 9

but

Responsibility = − 7
Lack of freedom = − 10

and so on. He would then add up the results and make his decision, secure that the objectivity of mathematics had led him to the rational choice. Of course, the items he thought significant and the numbers he assigned to them were the result of his own subjective choices.

Similarly, in the earlier situation in which Sartre was advising the young man who was deciding whether to join the war effort, Sartre said that Christian doctrine or Kantian ethics can give the student general principles to shape his decision. In the final analysis, however, the student himself has to decide which principles he will follow and how they should be interpreted in his situation.

Philosophy and rational considerations make the issues and the options clear for you and can inform your decisions, but in the end you have to decide which arguments are the most compelling, which philosophies the most coherent, and what choices you will make. Socrates, Aristotle, Descartes, Hume, Kant, Rand, Mill, and all the other philosophers have drawn maps for you that were made on *their* intellectual journeys. However, you have to make your own journey and decide from all these considerations which is the best direction to go.

5. Live out your choices authentically.

Sartre ridiculed people who think that everyone is born with a certain nature or a certain label attached to them, as though character traits are as fixed as a person's eye color. Such people are prone to make comments like "this man is a coward and this man is a hero." Such an outlook is too convenient, Sartre says, because it follows from this idea that "If you are born cowards, you can be quite content, you can do nothing about it and you will be cowards all your lives whatever you do; and if you are born heroes you can again be quite content; you will be heros all your lives, eating and drinking heroically."[11] But in contrast to this simplistic picture, Sartre replies, "The coward makes himself cowardly, the hero makes himself heroic; and there is always the possibility for the coward to give up cowardice and the hero to stop being a hero. What counts is the total commitment." In other words, realize that you are not a label but a chooser and that you must take responsibility for your choices.

Kierkegaard once described the sort of person who has made all the socially acceptable choices and who (from external appearances) is an ideal person.

> Outwardly he is completely "a real man." He is a university man, husband and father, an uncommonly competent civil functionary even, a respectable father, very gentle to his wife and carefulness itself with respect to his children. And a Christian? Well, yes, he is that too after a sort.[12]

The problem is that this person (as Kierkegaard describes him) lacks a self. He is nothing but a collection of social roles: husband, father, civil servant. The preceding description could fit any number of people. The question is, Where is the unique, authentic self behind all these descriptions? In another passage Kierkegaard describes a similar kind of person:

> By seeing the multitude of men about [him], by getting engaged in all sorts of worldly affairs, by becoming wise about how things go in this world, such a man forgets himself, … does not dare to believe in himself, finds it too venturesome a thing to be himself, far easier and safer to be like the others, to become an imitation, a number, a cipher in the crowd.[13]

In some tasks in life, you can be cautious and experimental—trying things in small doses. If you are not sure whether you will like a spicy sauce, try a little bit of it on your meat before pouring it all over your food. But with philosophy it is different. You can't try out the religious stance toward life on Sundays, Tuesdays, and Thursdays, then experiment with being an atheist on Mondays, Wednesdays, and Fridays, and then remain an agnostic on Saturdays. Similarly, in terms of ethics, you can't be one-fourth an ethical relativist, one-fourth an egoist, one-fourth a Kantian, and one-fourth a utilitarian. The "try a little bit of this and a little bit of that" approach doesn't work very well for a basic stance toward life.

In stressing the importance of commitment and making decisions, I haven't meant to imply that you should never change your mind. Many of the great philosophers made radical shifts in their point of view throughout their careers. However, these shifts were not impulsive or capricious. The philosophers changed their minds only because they passionately embraced a philosophy and were continually putting it to the test, both within their lives and in the arena of ideas. Although a commitment to your own philosophical stance is important, it should always be trumped by your commitment to the truth. In writing this current sentence, which is the last sentence of the last chapter of this book, I have finished my task—and now the rest is up to you.

REVIEW FOR CHAPTER 7

Philosophers

Arthur Schopenhauer
Leo Tolstoy
Hazel E. Barnes
Søren Kierkegaard
Jean-Paul Sartre

Concepts

the questioning the question view
pessimism (or nihilism)
how pessimism is both similar to and different from the
    religious view
how pessimism is both similar to and different from
    secular-humanism
the religious view
the secular-humanist view
existentialism
the five insights of existentialism

SUGGESTIONS FOR FURTHER READING

Frankl, Viktor. *Man's Search for Meaning.* New York: Pocket Books, 1997. A best-selling classic in psychiatric literature. Frankl is a psychotherapist who endured a Nazi concentration camp and from this experience developed his theory about the role of meaning and purpose in human life.

Klemke, E. D., ed. *The Meaning of Life.* 2d ed. Oxford: Oxford University Press, 1999. A collection of readings on the meaning of life that cover the four positions discussed in this chapter.

Nicholi, Armand, Jr. *The Question of God: C. S. Lewis and Sigmund Freud Debate God, Love, Sex, and the Meaning of Life.* New York: Free Press, 2002. In this book, written by a Harvard psychiatrist and Christian, the views of a secular-humanist (Freud) and a Christian (Lewis) are juxtaposed on the great questions of life. This book was the basis of a two-part PBS special.

Runzo, Joseph, and Nancy M. Martin, eds. *The Meaning of Life in the World Religions.* Oxford: Oneworld Publications, 2000. Readings on the meaning of life by representatives of major religious traditions throughout the world.

Thomson, Garrett. *On the Meaning of Life.* Belmont, Calif.: Wadsworth, 2002. An accessible survey of issues relating to the meaning of life.

NOTES

1. For this general classificatory scheme I am indebted to the introductory discussion in Steven Sanders and David R. Cheney, *The Meaning of Life: Questions, Answers, and Analysis* (Englewood Cliffs, N.J.: Prentice Hall, 1980).

2. Arthur Schopenhauer, *Essays and Aphorisms,* trans. R. J. Hollingdale, quoted in Sanders and Cheney, *The Meaning of Life,* p. 36.

3. Leo Tolstoy, *Confession,* trans. David Patterson (New York: W. W. Norton, 1983), pp. 26, 29, 32–33, 40–41, 58, 60–61, 66–68, 74–75. Translated by David Patterson. Copyright

4. Hazel E. Barnes, *An Existentialist Ethics* (New York: Alfred A. Knopf, 1967), pp. 106–109, 114–115.

5. Ronald W. Hepburn, "Questions about the Meaning of Life," *Religious Studies* 1 (April 1966), pp. 125–40.

6. Quoted in Dallas M. High, *Language, Persons, and Belief* (New York: Oxford University Press, 1967), p. 11.

7. This example was taken from Michael Polanyi, *Personal Knowledge* (Chicago: The University of Chicago Press, 1962), p. 50.

8. Jean-Paul Sartre, "Existentialism and Humanism," trans. Philip Mairet, in Steven Luper, *Existing: An Introduction to Existential Thought* (Mountain View, Calif.: Mayfield, 2000), p. 269.

9. Ibid., pp. 270–71.

10. Jean-Paul Sartre, "The Republic of Silence," in *Situations III,* quoted in *The Philosophy of Jean-Paul Sartre,* ed. Robert Denoon Cumming (New York: Vintage Books, 1965), p. 233.

11. Sartre, *"Existentialism and Humanism,"* p. 271.

12. Søren Kierkegaard, *Sickness unto Death,* in *Fear and Trembling and The Sickness unto Death,* trans. Walter Lowrie (Princeton: Princeton University Press, 1968), p. 197.

13. Ibid., pp. 166–67.

REASONING EFFECTIVELY

What to Do and What Not to Do

In section 1.3 I discussed the nature of arguments and the distinction between deductive and inductive reasoning. In this appendix I will go into more detail by examining good and bad argument forms that are commonly found both in everyday discourse and in philosophical writings. Typically, when I introduce each argument form, I do so by means of a simple, everyday example for clarity. Then I will provide examples of philosophical arguments that are based on the form in question. In ordinary life and in philosophical works, these argument forms are often not set out as neatly as they are in this discussion. When you are reading philosophy (or some other argumentative passage) you will usually have to search for the argumentative structure that lies beneath the surface in order to find the sorts of forms covered here.

DEDUCTIVE ARGUMENTS

In this appendix, I will examine a number of valid argument forms that are very common (and a few that are invalid). As we go through these examples, keep the following complementary definitions of validity in mind: In a valid argument, it is impossible for the premises to be true and the conclusion false; and in a valid argument, *if* the premises are true, then the conclusion *must* be true. The argument forms that I discuss are so frequently employed that they have been given names, sometimes in Latin. In each case, I represent the skeletal structure of the argument in terms of various letters, such as P and Q. The letters are variables that stand for propositions. To the right of each argument form, I add flesh to the skeleton by replacing the letter variables with actual propositions. To make this discussion of logic relevant to our philosophical journey, I then provide a simple philosophical argument that makes use of the form in question. While examining these examples of valid or invalid arguments for a philosophical conclusion, do not suppose that the example is the last word on the particular issue or that the arguments are the best ones available for the conclusion. In each case, if the argument is valid and you disagree with the conclusion (e.g., "There is a God" or "There is not a God"), then try to figure out a basis for questioning one or more of the premises.

Before discussing the first set of argument forms, we need to examine the nature of conditional statements (also known as hypothetical statements). A **conditional statement** contains two simpler statements that are connected with the words *if-then*. For example:

If it is raining, then the ground is wet.
If you study, then you will get good grades.
If Jones is pregnant, then Jones is a female.

The first part of a conditional statement (which follows the "if") is called the **antecedent.** The second part (which follows the "then") is called the **consequent.** In the examples the antecedents are "it is raining," "you study," and "Jones is pregnant." The consequents are "the ground is wet," "you will get good grades," and "Jones is a female."

A conditional statement claims that the truth of the antecedent is a **sufficient condition** for the truth of the consequent. To say that A is a sufficient condition for B means that if A is true, then B is true. Sometimes the conditions that would make the antecedent true would *cause* conditions that would make the consequent true (as in the first two of the previous examples). However, Jones being pregnant does not *cause* Jones to be a female. So the notion of a sufficient condition has to do with the relationship between the truth of each statement and does not always express a causal relationship. A conditional statement also claims that the consequent is a **necessary condition** for the antecedent to be true. To say that A is a necessary condition for B means that for B to be true, A must be true. For

conditional statement two simpler statements that are connected with the words *if* and *then*

antecedent the first part of a conditional statement (the *if* clause)

consequent the second part of a conditional statement (the *then* clause)

sufficient condition statement A is a sufficient condition for statement B if the truth of A guarantees the truth of B

necessary condition statement A is a necessary condition for statement B if the truth of B requires the truth of A

example, being a female is a necessary condition for being pregnant. However, being a female is not a sufficient condition for being pregnant. These remarks about conditional statements are illustrated by the first five argument forms, which all contain conditional statements.

Modus Ponens

1. If P, then Q.   1. If Spot is a dog, then Spot is a mammal.
2. P.   2. Spot is a dog.
3. Therefore, Q.   3. Therefore, Spot is a mammal.

Philosophical Example of Modus Ponens

1. If the universe shows evidence of design, then there is a God.
2. The universe shows evidence of design.
3. Therefore, there is a God.

Modus ponens is also known as *affirming the antecedent.*

modus ponens a valid argument form that has this pattern: If P, then Q; P, therefore, Q

Modus Tollens

1. If P, then Q.   1. If John is eligible for the award, then he is a junior.
2. Not-Q.   2. John is not a junior.
3. Therefore, not-P.   3. Therefore, John is not eligible for the award.

Philosophical Examples of Modus Tollens

1. If we are morally responsible for our actions, then we have freedom of the will.
2. We do not have freedom of the will.
3. Therefore, we are not morally responsible for our actions.

1. If God exists, there would be no unnecessary evil in the world.
2. There is unnecessary evil in the world.
3. Therefore, God does not exist.

modus tollens a valid argument form that has this pattern: If P, then Q; not-Q, therefore, not-P

Since modus tollens (also known as *denying the consequent*) is a valid argument form, it is clear that this argument about God's existence is valid; that is, if the premises are true, then the conclusion logically follows. Consequently, a theist who rejects the conclusion would have to find reasons for rejecting at least one of the premises. The first premise seems consistent with the traditional concept of God. So a theist would probably want to question the truth of the second premise by asking, Do we really know that there is unnecessary evil in the world? and Isn't it possible that all apparent evil is justified in terms of some greater good that the evil achieves? I explored these issues in the section on the problem of evil in chapter 4 (section 4.5).

Fallacy of Denying the Antecedent

A **fallacy** is an argument form that is logically defective because the premises provide little or no support for the conclusion. Two invalid arguments (deductive fallacies) can be confused with either modus ponens or modus tollens. The first is the fallacy of denying the antecedent, which has this form:

fallacy an argument form that is logically defective because the premises provide little or no support for the conclusion

1. If P, then Q.	1. If Jones is a mother, then Jones is a parent.
2. Not-P.	2. Jones is not a mother.
3. Therefore, not-Q.	3. Therefore, Jones is not a parent.

As the example illustrates, this argument form is invalid because we can imagine a situation in which the premises are true and the conclusion false. If Jones is a father, then it is true that Jones is not a mother but false that Jones is not a parent.

Philosophical Example of the Fallacy of Denying the Antecedent

1. If Thomas Aquinas's arguments for God are valid, then there is a God.
2. Thomas Aquinas's arguments for God are not valid.
3. Therefore, there is not a God.

This example is an argument about arguments, and it illustrates an important point. If you refute a philosopher's argument, you have not shown that his or her conclusion is false; you have merely shown that this particular proof for the conclusion fails. A theist could agree with both premises of the previous argument but still not accept the conclusion, because other arguments besides those of Aquinas could prove God's existence. Furthermore, some theists, such as Blaise Pascal (see section 4.4), would claim that from a lack of rational arguments for God's existence it does not follow that God does not exist, but merely that reason is not the correct means to find God.

Fallacy of Affirming the Consequent

The fallacy of affirming the consequent is another invalid argument form that is also a counterfeit version of the valid forms of modus ponens and modus tollens.

1. If P, then Q.	1. If George Washington was assassinated, then he is dead.
2. Q.	2. George Washington is dead.
3. Therefore, P.	3. Therefore, George Washington was assassinated.

Philosophical Example of the Fallacy of Affirming the Consequent

1. If morality is completely subjective, then people will differ in their moral beliefs.
2. People do differ in their moral beliefs.
3. Therefore, morality is completely subjective. (There are no objective truths about what is morally right or wrong.)

One way to show that an argument is invalid is to construct another argument that has the same form as the original but goes from true premises to a false conclusion. This argument would be an invalid argument because a valid argument will always carry us from true information to a true conclusion. However, if the form of reasoning is the same as the original argument, the counterexample will show that the original argument is invalid also. Because the following argument is the same as the argument about morality except for the subject matter, it shows that the previous argument is invalid.

1. If medical science is completely subjective, then people will differ in their medical beliefs.
2. People do differ in their medical beliefs. (Some people believe that sacrificing twin babies will cure the community of a plague; on the other hand, our society doesn't believe this.)

3. Therefore, medical science is completely subjective. (There are no objective truths about what will or won't cure disease—a false conclusion.)

Hypothetical Syllogism

A **syllogism** is a deductive argument with two premises and a conclusion. Some logic books call the following type of syllogism a *pure* hypothetical syllogism to distinguish it from arguments such as modus ponens and modus tollens, which are partially hypothetical in that they contain one hypothetical (or conditional) premise.

<table>
<tr><td>1. If P, then Q.</td><td>1. If I learn logic, then I will write better essays.</td></tr>
<tr><td>2. If Q, then R.</td><td>2. If I write better essays, then I will get better grades.</td></tr>
<tr><td>3. Therefore, if P, then R.</td><td>3. Therefore, if I learn logic, then I will get better grades.</td></tr>
</table>

Philosophical Example of a Valid Hypothetical Syllogism

1. If the methods of science give us only information about physical reality, then science cannot tell us whether a nonphysical reality exists.
2. If science cannot tell us whether a nonphysical reality exists, then science cannot tell us whether we have a soul.
3. Therefore, if the methods of science give us only information about physical reality, then science cannot tell us whether we have a soul.

Notice that the key to a hypothetical syllogism is that the consequent (Q) of one premise is the antecedent (Q) of the other premise such that the premises could be linked up like a chain if they were laid end to end. This connection would be true even if the order of the premises were reversed. Furthermore, the antecedent of the conclusion (P) is the beginning of the chain formed by the premises, and the consequent of the conclusion (R) is the end of the chain. Any other arrangement will be invalid, as in the following examples.

Counterfeit (Invalid) Hypothetical Syllogisms

<table>
<tr><td>1. If P, then Q.</td><td>1. If P, then Q.</td></tr>
<tr><td>2. If R, then Q.</td><td>2. If Q, then R.</td></tr>
<tr><td>3. Therefore, if P, then R.</td><td>3. Therefore, if R, then P.</td></tr>
</table>

STOP AND THINK

See if you can substitute statements for the letter variables in the previous invalid hypothetical syllogisms. Try to construct arguments that follow the given forms but in which true premises lead to a false conclusion, thereby showing that something is wrong with these types of arguments.

Disjunctive Syllogism

A disjunctive argument contains a disjunctive statement in a premise. A **disjunctive statement** asserts that at least one of two alternatives is true. It typically is expressed as an *either-or* statement. Normally a disjunctive statement asserts that at least one alternative is true

syllogism a deductive argument with two premises and a conclusion

disjunctive statement a statement that asserts that at least one of two alternatives is true and possibly both. For example, if Sherlock Holmes determines that the murder was an inside job, he might state, "Either the butler is guilty or the maid is guilty." Obviously, the fact that one of them must be guilty also includes the possibility that both of them are guilty. Here is what a disjunctive syllogism looks like:

1. Either P or Q.   1. Either the bulb is burnt out or it is not receiving electricity.
2. Not-P.   2. The bulb is not burnt out.
3. Therefore, Q.   3. Therefore, the bulb is not receiving electricity.

Philosophical Example of a Disjunctive Syllogism

1. Either the universe contains in itself a sufficient reason for its existence or it was caused to exist.
2. The universe does not contain in itself a sufficient reason for its existence.
3. Therefore, the universe was caused to exist.

Fallacy of Affirming the Disjunct

1. Either P or Q.   1. Either the bulb is burnt out or it is not receiving electricity.
2. P.   2. The bulb is burnt out.
3. Therefore, not-Q.   3. Therefore, the bulb is receiving electricity.

The fallacy of affirming the disjunct is an invalid argument form that is a counterfeit of the disjunctive syllogism. In the example just given, the fact that the bulb is burnt out does not exclude the possibility that there are problems with the electricity as well. Because both alternatives could be true in a normal disjunction, simply affirming one alternative does not prove that the other is false. However, if the disjunction contained two contradictories (two opposite claims), then this type of argument would be valid. For example, if the first premise was "Either Howard is married or he is single," then the truth of one statement would imply the falsity of the other.

Philosophical Example of the Fallacy of Affirming the Disjunct

1. Either reason is the source of moral principles or divine revelation is.
2. Reason is the source of moral principles.
3. Therefore, divine revelation is not the source of moral principles.

In this case, the conclusion does not follow because the two statements in the disjunction could both be true. (Some philosophers, such as Thomas Aquinas, believed that both reason and revelation could provide us with moral principles.)

Reductio ad Absurdum Arguments

reductio ad absurdum argument argument form that begins with an assumption that the opponent's position is true and then proceeds to show that that position logically implies an absurd conclusion, a conclusion that contradicts itself, or a conclusion that contradicts other conclusions held by the opponent

The label of the **reductio ad absurdum argument,** a valid argument form, means "reducing to an absurdity." To use this technique, you begin by assuming that your opponent's position is true and then you show that it logically implies either an absurd conclusion or one that contradicts itself or that it contradicts other conclusions held by your opponent. Deducing a clearly false statement from a proposition is definitive proof that the original assumption was false and is a way of exposing an inconsistency that is lurking in an opponent's position. When the reductio ad absurdum argument is done well, it is an effective way to refute a position. Typically, the argument follows this form:

1. Suppose the truth of A (the position that you wish to refute).
2. If A, then B.
3. If B, then C.
4. If C, then not-A.
5. Therefore, both A and not-A.
6. But 5 is a contradiction, so the original assumption must be false and not-A must be true.

Philosophical Example of a Reductio Ad Absurdum Argument

As I mentioned in section 1.1, Socrates' philosophical opponents, the Sophists, believed that all truth was subjective and relative. Protagoras, one of the most famous Sophists, argued that one opinion is just as true as another opinion. The following is a summary of the argument that Socrates used to refute this position.[1]

1. One opinion is just as true as another opinion. (Socrates assumes the truth of Protagoras's position.)
2. Protagoras's critics have the following opinion: "Protagoras's opinion is false and that of his critics is true."
3. Since Protagoras believes premise 1, he believes that the opinion of his critics in premise 2 is true.
4. Hence, Protagoras also believes it is true that: "Protagoras's opinion is false and that of his critics is true."
5. Since individual opinion determines what is true and everyone (both Protagoras and his critics) believes the statement "Protagoras's opinion is false," it follows that
6. Protagoras's opinion is false.

INDUCTIVE ARGUMENTS

Unlike deductive arguments, inductive arguments do not show that the conclusion necessarily follows from the premises. Instead, these arguments try to demonstrate that if the premises are true, then it is highly probable that the conclusion is true. One common form of inductive argument starts from the observation that a number of similar cases have a certain property in common and concludes that all other cases of this type will also have that property. For example, a medical researcher finds that everyone who has a rare form of cancer was exposed to a certain toxic chemical; when she encounters a new patient with this disease, she will suspect that this person has been exposed to the same chemical. Here are two examples of philosophical arguments based on inductive reasoning. Because different philosophers will evaluate these arguments differently, I leave it up to you to decide how strong you think these arguments are.

1. Every event that we have observed has had a cause.
2. Therefore, it is rational to presume that all events have a cause.

1. In the past, when something seemed mysterious and unexplainable (such as solar eclipses), eventually it was found that it could be scientifically explained as the result of physical causes.
2. Consciousness seems mysterious and unexplainable.
3. Therefore it is probable that someday consciousness will be scientifically explained as the result of physical causes.

Although a large part of our everyday lives and the scientific method is based on inductive reasoning, inductive arguments do not have the simple techniques that deductive arguments do for deciding whether the arguments are strong or weak. There are, however, a few rules to keep in mind when watching out for fallacious inductive arguments. I discuss three such fallacious inductive arguments here.

Hasty Generalization Fallacy

When generalizing from facts about some cases of a certain type to a conclusion about all cases of that type, you must be sure that the premises are based on a sufficient number of observations and that the sample is representative. Failure to do so is to commit the fallacy of **hasty generalization.**

Philosophical Examples of the Hasty Generalization Fallacy

hasty generalization fallacy in which a general conclusion is drawn from premises that are not based on a sufficient number of observations or from premises in which the sample is not representative

The physician and psychologist Sigmund Freud was the founder of the 20th-century theory of psychoanalysis. In developing his theory he formed conclusions about the nature of religious belief. He speculated that religion was embraced by people who were emotionally weak and who projected the image of their own father onto the cosmos to create a heavenly father who would always be there for them. The problem was that as a therapist, Freud was exposed to multitudes of patients who were emotionally disturbed. Given the times and the culture, most of them were also religious. So, Freud studied numerous cases of emotionally disturbed religious people and concluded that religion was psychologically dysfunctional. Given the biased sample of religious people he studied, it is likely that he committed the fallacy of hasty generalization. Since then, psychologists of religion have also studied emotionally mature religious people and developed a more balanced view of religious belief.

The citizens of a small, rural town were shocked when a local teenager took a gun to school and massacred many of his classmates. It was discovered that he belonged to a cult of like-minded youths who engaged in satanic practices and read the philosopher Nietzsche. Some ministers used this incident as evidence that people who read "weird stuff" like philosophy are dangerous to society. But this hasty generalization ignores the millions of people who have read and enjoyed Nietzsche but who did not kill their colleagues. It also assumes that reading Nietzsche was the cause of the student's violence. The student may have been psychologically compelled to violence even if he had not read Nietzsche (see the false cause fallacy, discussed next).

"There have been a number of financial and sexual scandals involving television evangelists in recent years. Therefore, it is likely that all religious people are frauds." This argument is a hasty generalization because the conclusion is about all religious people, but it is based on a small and unrepresentative sample of this group.

False Cause Fallacy

false cause fallacy the assumption that because event X occurred before event Y, X caused Y

Another form of induction reasons to the causes of a given event. The **false cause fallacy** is committed when we assume that simply because event X occurred before event Y, we may conclude that X caused Y. Causal connections are very difficult to establish; simple priority in time all by itself is usually insufficient to draw these connections.

Philosophical Examples of the False Cause Fallacy

"Nietzsche spent a lifetime publishing his atheistic philosophy. He died totally insane. Therefore, his own, dismal philosophy drove him mad." This causal reasoning overlooks the fact that some religiously pious people have gone insane and ignores the evidence that Nietzsche had a neurological disease.

"As sexually explicit movies have increased in number over the years, so has the number of sex crimes. Therefore, the movies have caused the crimes." These data are insufficient to establish a causal connection. It is also a fact that church attendance has increased over the years. Could we then conclude that the movies have caused church attendance to rise or that the increase in church attendance has caused the increase in crime?

False Analogy Fallacy

Some inductive arguments are based on an analogy. An argument from analogy is one in which the premises state that two cases share one or more properties in common. It is then concluded that a further property of the first case will also be a property of the second case. Some analogies can be useful, such as when we learn about human physiology by studying that of primates. However, the **false analogy fallacy** is committed when there are more differences between the two situations than there are similarities. For example, if I have a 1980 gas-guzzling car that is blue and my friend has a brand new compact car that is blue, the similarity in color is not sufficient to conclude that her car will get the same gas mileage as mine.

false analogy fallacy fallacy in which the premises are based on two or more cases that contain more differences than similarities

Philosophical Examples of the False Analogy Fallacy

"No body can be healthful without exercise, neither natural body or politic; and certainly to a kingdom or estate, a just and honourable war is the true exercise. A civil war indeed is like the heat of a fever; but a foreign war is like the heat of exercise, and serveth to keep the body in health."[2] This defense of war by Francis Bacon fails to note that there are significant differences between individuals and nations and that individual exercise, unlike war, does not kill people.

It was common in the 18th century to argue for God's existence from the evidence of design in the world. It was said, for example, that the regular movements of the planets were like those of a clock. Because a clock had a designer, so the universe must have had a divine designer. The skeptic David Hume countered by saying, in effect, that this argument committed the fallacy of false analogy. It picked out one analogy in preference to many other possible ones. By way of counterexample, he suggested that the universe could more likely be compared to a vegetable than a clock. The particles given off by comets, for example, might function like the seeds given off by trees. After the comet passes through our galaxy, it sprouts new planetary systems in the outer darkness. Hume's point was that the clock analogy of the theists is no more likely than this analogy.[3]

INFORMAL FALLACIES

In this section, I survey several types of defective arguments known as informal fallacies. **Informal fallacies** are types of bad reasoning that can be detected only by examining the content of the argument. In most cases, if you set out the formal structure of the arguments using the letters P and Q as we did previously, the problem with the reasoning would not be evident. On the surface, the following invalid argument has the valid form of a modus ponens argument: "If something is a ruler, then it is 12 inches long, and the Queen is a ruler, so the Queen is twelve inches long." Actually, it only superficially has the form of a modus ponens argument because the term *ruler* shifts its meaning from one premise to the next. The following selection of informal fallacies is not an exhaustive list, but it contains

informal fallacy a type of bad reasoning that can be detected only by examining the content of the argument

many of the typical kinds of bad reasoning that you are likely to encounter in philosophical discussions.

Ad Hominem (Abusive)

Ad hominem means "against the person." The abusive ad hominem fallacy consists of an attempt to reject someone's conclusion by attacking the person making the claim. The problem is that simply providing negative information about a person does not prove that his or her claims are false.

Philosophical Examples of the Abusive Ad Hominem Fallacy

"After a lifetime of proclaiming the death of God, Friedrich Nietzsche died completely insane. Therefore, his arguments for atheism must be worthless."

"Immanuel Kant was a rigid neurotic who never traveled more than 60 miles from the place of his birth. How could anyone who was so limited and inexperienced have anything worthwhile to say about morality? Therefore, we do not need to bother looking at Kant's arguments for an objective morality."

Ad Hominem (Circumstantial)

Someone using the circumstantial ad hominem argument does not verbally abuse the opponent but dismisses his or her arguments by suggesting that the opponent's circumstances are the sole reason why he or she embraces the conclusion. In other words, this argument is a way of ignoring the opponent's arguments and of refusing to evaluate them on their own terms.

Philosophical Examples of the Circumstantial Ad Hominem Fallacy

"We do not need to consider Thomas Aquinas's arguments for the existence of God, because he was a Christian monk. Of course he thought belief in God was reasonable. In putting forth his proofs he was simply trying to rationalize a faith he already held."

"We do not need to consider philosopher Bertrand Russell's arguments against the existence of God. He was raised in a very strict religious home, which turned him against religion. That upbringing is the real reason he was an atheist."

Appeal to Ignorance

The "appeal to ignorance" fallacy occurs when lack of evidence against a conclusion is used to prove the conclusion true or when lack of evidence for a conclusion is used to prove a conclusion false. For example, "The president of this university is a spy for a foreign power, because you cannot prove that he isn't." Generally, the person making an extraordinary claim has the burden of proof to provide positive arguments for the conclusion. Lack of evidence against the conclusion is not sufficient. When a person's character is being maligned (as in this example), the principle of law that states "innocent until proven guilty" should prevail.

Philosophical Examples of the Appeal to Ignorance

"There must be a God, because no one has ever proven there isn't."

"Atheism is true, because no one has ever proven there is a God."

With respect to philosophical issues such as the existence of God, if we really believe there is a lack of compelling evidence either way, then we should suspend judgment.

Begging the Question

Begging the question also goes by the name of *circular reasoning* for reasons that will soon be evident. This fallacy is committed when the premises assume the truth of the conclusion instead of providing independent evidence for it. In the simplest version begging the question has the form, "P is true, therefore P is true." For example, "The dean is a liar because he never tells the truth." If you did not believe the conclusion, you would not believe the premise either, for they make identical claims.

Philosophical Examples of Begging the Question

"God exists because the Bible says he does, and we can trust the Bible because the Bible is the inspired word of God, and we know the Bible is the word of God because God has told us in II Timothy 3:16 that 'All scripture is inspired by God.'" This argument contains two pieces of circular reasoning. It assumes the words in the Bible are the words of God and uses this assumption as evidence for the claim that the words in the Bible are the words of God. Furthermore, it assumes that there is a God who inspired the words in the Bible and uses the claims in the Bible as evidence that there is a God.

In one of his arguments against belief in divine miracles, the 18th-century philosopher David Hume said that the laws of nature have been established not simply by the majority of human experiences but by their unanimous testimony that collectively forms "a firm and unalterable experience." Furthermore, he claimed that there is "a uniform experience against every miraculous event."[4] But Hume could know this statement is true only if he knew that all the reports of miracles were false. And he could know this claim only if he knew that miracles never happened. At this point in his essay, it appears he is arguing in this fashion:

1. No miracle has ever happened.
2. So, all reports of miracles are false.
3. Human experience universally counts against miracles.
4. Therefore, no miracle has ever happened.

Composition

In the fallacy of composition a person argues from a property of each part of a whole (or member of a group) taken individually and concludes that this property also may be attributed to the whole (or group). A silly example: "Every member of this 100-student class weighs less than 500 pounds. Therefore, the class as a whole weighs less than 500 pounds." A more subtle but equally fallacious example: "This essay is well written because every sentence in it is well written." Taken individually, each sentence may be well written, but the essay as a whole may be poorly written because it rambles, is disorganized, and lacks a central theme. Another example: "Because every member of this organization is a veteran, this organization must be a veteran's organization."

Philosophical Examples of the Fallacy of Composition

In a famous debate with Father Frederick Copleston on the existence of God, Bertrand Russell accused Copleston of committing the fallacy of composition. Copleston had argued that because everything in the universe has a cause, the universe as a whole must have had a cause. Russell responded with this counterexample: "Every man who exists has a mother, and it seems to me that your argument is that therefore the human race must have a mother, but obviously the human race hasn't a mother—that's a different logical sphere."[5] (Copleston responded by arguing that the notion of *cause* in his argument differed from that in Russell's counterexample.)

Early in the 20th century, physicists discovered that the behavior of subatomic particles was random and not perfectly predictable. This discovery is called Heisenberg's principle of indeterminacy and is part of quantum mechanics. Some philosophers have used this principle as a premise in the following argument: "Because the behavior of subatomic particles is not determined but is unpredictable, and because we are made up of such particles, it follows that our behavior is unpredictable, not determined, and that we have freedom." But, critics respond, this argument is the fallacy of composition. For example, the particles making up my desk may be moving in random ways, but the statistical average of their behavior as exhibited in the desk as a whole is very predictable and determined. The same could be true of our behavior.

Division

The fallacy of division is the exact reverse of composition. Here the premise asserts that a whole or a group has some property and the argument concludes that this property applies to each one of the parts or members of the group as well. Example: "Because every third child born in New York is Roman Catholic, Protestant families there should not have more than two children." Even though the population as a whole may be one-third Catholic, it does not follow that a particular, individual family will be one-third Catholic.

Philosophical Example of the Fallacy of Division

"If there is no God, then the universe has no purpose. It follows that our individual lives have no purpose." But if the universe as a whole has no purpose, that does not mean that some parts of the universe (such as you and I) cannot find purpose in our own lives.

Equivocation

The fallacy of equivocation occurs when a word or phrase changes its meaning in the course of the argument. Consider this obvious example of equivocation: "My client, your honor, should not be sent to jail, for by your own admission he is a good burglar. Surely someone who is good does not belong in jail." (In the first statement *good* means "competent"or "skilled." A "good burglar" is a competent burglar. In the second statement *good* means "morally good.")

Philosophical Examples of Equivocation

"I had a legal *right* to foreclose on this widow's property without giving her a chance to negotiate, so how can you say that what I did is not *right?*" Here the speaker confuses a *legal* right with doing what is *morally* right. Obviously, the two are different.

The famous 19th-century British philosopher John Stuart Mill (see chapter 5, section 5.3) seems to be guilty of equivocation in one of his arguments for hedonistic utilitarian ethics. He claims that happiness (which he defines as the experience of pleasure and the absence of pain) is the only thing desirable in itself. His argument is that the only proof capable of being given that an object is visible is that people actually see it. The only proof that a sound is audible is that people hear it: and so of the other sources of our experience. In like manner, I apprehend, the sole evidence it is possible to produce that anything is desirable is that people actually desire it.[6]

Now it is true that *visible* means "capable of being seen." But does the same sort of definition apply to *desirable*? Two meanings of the word *desirable* seem to be lurking in this passage: (1) It is trivially true that if someone desires something, we can say that for that person the thing is desirable, (2) but in ethics, *desirable* does not mean simply "desired," it means "worthy of being desired" or "something that *ought* to be desired." The two meanings of the word that Mill confuses are illustrated by this sentence: "Trixie finds drugs desirable (meaning 1), but compulsive drug addiction is not a very desirable (meaning 2) lifestyle for anyone to pursue."

"Doctors are saying the new pill that cures baldness is nothing short of miraculous. Therefore, religious people are correct in saying that miracle healings can occur." In the premise, saying the new pill is "miraculous" is a metaphorical exaggeration, but in the conclusion, the word is being used literally.

False Dichotomy

The false dichotomy fallacy is also known as *false dilemma,* the *either-or fallacy, bifurcation,* or the *black-or-white fallacy.* It is called the black-or-white fallacy because one of the premises assumes that the only alternatives are the extremes of black or white (figuratively speaking), and it ignores the fine shades of gray in between. A false dichotomy argument begins with a disjunction (P or Q). However, the fallacy is committed when one or more other alternatives, such as R, are not being acknowledged. If there are other possibilities, then both P and Q could be false. Thus, by eliminating P, you have not proven that Q is true. A simple example: "Son, you will either graduate from college and make something of yourself or you will be a bum all your life." Are there other possibilities? Bill Gates, the chairman and CEO of the Microsoft Corporation and one of the richest persons in the world, dropped out of Harvard University.

On the surface, an argument based on a false dichotomy has the valid form of a disjunctive syllogism, which is the argument on the left in the following example, whereas the real situation, represented in the argument on the right, makes clear the fallacious reasoning.

(Apparent Form)	*(Real Situation)*
1. P or Q.	1. P or Q or R
2. Not-P.	2. Not-P.
3. Therefore, Q.	3. Therefore, Q.

Philosophical Example of a False Dichotomy

The 17th-century mathematician, scientist, theologian, and philosopher Blaise Pascal proposed his famous wager in which he suggested that considering religious belief is like making a bet as to which option had the best possible payoff and the least risk (see section 4.4). Pascal's argument went like this:

1. We are faced with two choices in life: either to believe in atheism or to believe in the biblical God.

2. It is not prudent to believe in atheism. (For if we are wrong, then we will lose eternal life.)
3. Therefore, it is prudent to believe in the biblical God.

As with all cases of a false dichotomy, the problem is with the disjunction. The only alternatives are not limited to atheism or belief in the biblical God. There are many other religions, some of which have quite different ideas about the afterlife and some in which there is no notion of the afterlife. There is also **agnosticism,** the decision to believe in neither atheism nor religion until more convincing evidence is found for one view or the other. So, even a rejection of atheism does not automatically prove the wisdom of belief in Pascal's version of the biblical God.

Straw Man

The straw man fallacy occurs when someone attacks a weak version of an opponent's position or attacks a conclusion that the opponent does not support. This fallacy is like knocking over a straw man and claiming that in doing so you have defeated the world heavyweight boxing champion.

Philosophical Examples of the Straw Man Fallacy

"Thomas Aquinas argues that we should believe in God, but having religious faith requires that we throw our reason out the window. So, Aquinas thinks we should commit intellectual suicide." Because Aquinas thought that reason can show that belief in God is rational, he did not hold that we should "commit intellectual suicide" (see section 4.1).

"My opponent claims that we evolved from the lower animals. Therefore, because he believes we are just animals, he must believe that we should live without any civil laws, without any moral rules, and that we should mate in the streets just like dogs." But supporting the theory of evolution obviously does not entail any of the conclusions the speaker attributes to his opponent.

Wishful Thinking

Sometimes we may be tempted to believe a claim because we find the opposite conclusion to be so unpleasant. But whether we find a claim to be subjectively pleasant or not tells us nothing about its truth or falsity. Sometimes the truth about reality may be unpleasant and we simply have to face it. The problem with wishful thinking is illustrated by this example: "If I thought there was no money in my checking account, I could not sleep at night. Therefore, there must be money in my account." Here is another example of the wishful thinking fallacy: "If there was no God, I could not bear to live my life. Therefore, there is a God." A similar example: "If there is a God, then we could not live our lives any way we please. Because human beings must have moral freedom to have dignity, there cannot be a God."

LEARNING MORE ABOUT ARGUMENTS AND EVIDENCE

Much more could be said about evaluating arguments and claims. If you want to learn more about this skill, pick up a book on logic or critical reasoning in the library or bookstore. Better yet, take a course in the subject.

REVIEW FOR APPENDIX

conditional statement
antecedent and consequent
sufficient condition and necessary condition
modus ponens
modus tollens
fallacy
fallacy of denying the antecedent
fallacy of affirming the consequent
syllogism
hypothetical syllogism
disjunctive syllogism
disjunctive statement
fallacy of affirming the disjunct
reductio ad absurdum argument
fallacy of hasty generalization
false cause fallacy
false analogy fallacy
informal fallacies
ad hominem (abusive) fallacy
ad hominem (circumstantial) fallacy
appeal to ignorance
begging the question
composition fallacy
division fallacy

equivocation
false dichotomy
agnosticism
straw man fallacy
fallacy of wishful thinking

NOTES

1. Plato, *Theaetetus* 171a, b, in *The Dialogues of Plato,* 3d ed., rev., 5 vols., trans. Benjamin Jowett (New York: Oxford University Press, 1892).
2. Francis Bacon, "Of the True Greatness of Kingdoms and Estates," in *The Complete Essays of Francis Bacon* (New York: Washington Square Press, 1963), p. 83.
3. David Hume, *Dialogues Concerning Natural Religion,* ed. Norman Kemp Smith (London: Oxford University Press, 1935), pt. 7.
4. David Hume, "Of Miracles," in *An Enquiry Concerning Human Understanding,* ed. L. A. Selby-Bigge (Oxford: Clarendon Press, 1894), sec. 10, pt. 1.
5. Bertrand Russell and F. C. Copleston, "A Debate on the Existence of God," in *Bertrand Russell on God and Religion,* ed. Al Seckel (Buffalo: Prometheus Books, 1986), p. 131.
6. John Stuart Mill, *Utilitarianism* (1863), chap. 4.

Credits

Text Credits

p. 4. Søren Kierkegaard, *Concluding Unscientific Postscript*, translated by David Swenson and Walter Lowrie. © 1941 Princeton University Press, copyright renewed 1968. Reprinted by permission of Princeton University Press.

pp. 65–68, 69, 82, 83–85. René Descartes, *Meditations on First Philosophy*, revised edition, edited and translated by John Cottingham. © Cambridge University Press 1996. Reprinted with the permission of Cambridge University Press.

pp. 123, 129. Immanuel Kant, *Critique of Pure Reason*, translated by Norman Kemp Smith. © The estate of Norman Kemp Smith 1929, 1933, 2003. Published 1991, Palgrave Macmillan. Reproduced with permission of Palgrave Macmillan.

p. 139. True/False graphic from Scott Kim, *Inversions* (Berkeley, CA: Key Curriculum Press, 1996), p. 21. Copyright © 1981 by Scott Kim. All rights reserved. Reprinted by permission of Scott Kim.

pp. 141, 146–48. From *Beyond Good and Evil* by Friedrich Nietzsche, translated by Walter Kaufmann, copyright © 1966 by Random House, Inc. Used by permission of Random House, Inc.

pp. 172–74. From the Introduction to *Women, Knowledge, and Reality: Explorations in Feminist Philosophy*, 1st edition, edited by Ann Garry and Marilyn Pearsall, pp. xi–xiv. Copyright © 1989 by Unwin Hyman, Inc. Reproduced by permission of Taylor & Francis Books UK.

pp. 223, 225. René Descartes, *Meditations on First Philosophy*, revised edition, edited and translated by John Cottingham. © Cambridge University Press 1996. Reprinted with the permission of Cambridge University Press.

p. 233. Text from *Nine Chains To the Moon* by R. Buckminster Fuller © 1938, 2010 The Estate of R. Buckminster Fuller. All rights reserved.

pp. 237–40. From Jeffrey Olen, *Persons and Their World* (New York: Random House/McGraw-Hill, 1983), pp. 213–214, 220–224. Reprinted by permission of Jeffrey Olen.

pp. 247, 248–49. From Jerry A. Fodor, "The Mind-Body Problem," *Scientific American*, January 1981. Reprinted with permission. Copyright © 1981 *Scientific American*, a division of Nature America, Inc. All rights reserved.

pp. 254–55. Marvin Minsky, excerpt from "Why People Think Computers Can't," from *The Computer Culture*, edited by Denis P. Donnelly (Rutherford, NJ: Fairleigh Dickinson University Press, 1985). Copyright © 1985 by Associated University Presses, Inc. Reprinted with the permission of Associated University Presses, Inc.

p. 274. B. F. Skinner, *Walden Two*, pp. 241–243. Copyright © 1948, 1976 by B. F. Skinner. Reprinted 2005, Hackett Publishing Company, Inc. Reprinted by permission of Hackett Publishing Company, Inc. All rights reserved.

pp. 294–95. Richard Taylor, *Metaphysics*, 4th ed., © 1992. Reproduced in print and electronically by permission of Pearson Education, Inc., Upper Saddle River, New Jersey.

pp. 299–300. From Jean-Paul Sartre, *Being and Nothingness*, translated by Hazel E. Barnes. Copyright © 1956 by Philosophical Library, Inc. Copyright renewed 1984 by Philosophical Library, Inc. Reprinted by permission of Philosophical Library, Inc., New York.

pp. 306–10. "Is Determinism Inconsistent with Free Will?" pp. 249–258 from *Religion and the Modern Mind* by W. T. Stace. Copyright 1952 by W. T. Stace, renewed © 1980 by Blanche Stace. Reprinted by permission of HarperCollins Publishers.

p. 320. Peter Kreeft, excerpt from "Introduction" from J. P. Moreland and Kai Nielsen, *Does God Exist? The Great Debate* (Nashville, TN: Thomas Nelson, 1990). Copyright © 1990 by Peter Kreeft. Reprinted by permission of the author.

pp. 327–28. Thomas Aquinas, "Summa Theologica" from *Basic Writings of Saint Thomas Aquinas*, vol. I, edited by Anton C. Pegis, p. 22. Copyright © 1945 by Random House, Inc. Copyright renewed 1973 by Random House, Inc. Reprinted 1997 by Hackett Publishing Company, Inc. Reprinted by permission of Hackett Publishing Company, Inc. All rights reserved.

pp. 331–34. Richard Taylor, *Metaphysics*, 4th ed., © 1992. Reproduced in print and electronically by permission of Pearson Education, Inc., Upper Saddle River, New Jersey.

pp. 359, 360, 360–61. Søren Kierkegaard, *Concluding Unscientific Postscript*, translated by David Swenson and Walter Lowrie. © 1941 Princeton University Press, copyright renewed 1968. Reprinted by permission of Princeton University Press.

pp. 365–66. From *The Plague* by Albert Camus, translated from the French by Stuart Gilbert, copyright 1948 by Stuart Gilbert, copyright renewed 1975 by Stuart Gilbert. Used by permission of Alfred A. Knopf, a division of Random House, Inc., and Penguin Books Ltd. Originally published in France as *La Peste* by Librairie Gallimard. Copyright 1947 by Èditions Gallimard. Copyright renewed 1974 by Madame Albert Camus. Used by permission of Èditions Gallimard. www.gallimard.fr.

pp. 372–74. John Hick, *Evil and the God of Love*. Copyright © 1966, 1977 by John Hick. Reissued in 2007 by Palgrave Macmillan. Reproduced with permission of Palgrave Macmillan.

pp. 377–78. *The Problem of Pain* by C.S. Lewis copyright © C.S. Lewis Pte. Ltd. 1962. Extract reprinted by permission.

p. 383. From *The Upanishads*, vol. 2, trans. Swami Nikhilananda. Copyright 1952 by Swami Nikhilananda. Reprinted by permission of the Ramakrishna-Vivekananda Center of New York.

p. 384. From *The Upanishads*, vol. 1, trans. Swami Nikhilananda. Copyright 1949 by Swami Nikhilananda. Reprinted by permission of the Ramakrishna-Vivekananda Center of New York.

pp. 386, 388–89. From *The Upanishads*, vol. 3, trans. Swami Nikhilananda. Copyright 1956 by Swami Nikhilananda. Reprinted by permission of the Ramakrishna-Vivekananda Center of New York.

pp. 391, 392, 393. From *Teachings of the Buddha*, edited by Jack Kornfield, © 1993, 1996 by Jack Kornfield. Reprinted by arrangement with Shambhala Publications Inc., Boston, MA. www.shambhala.com

pp. 398–99. From *Siddhartha* by Herman Hesse, copyright © 1951 by New Directions Publishing Corp. Reprinted by permission of New Directions Publishing Corp.

p. 400. Paul Simon, "I Am a Rock." © 1965 Paul Simon (BMI).

pp. 437–39. From Ruth Benedict, "Anthropology and the Abnormal," *The Journal of General Psychology*, vol. 10, no. 2 (1934), pp. 59–82. Reprinted by permission of the publisher (Taylor & Francis Ltd, http://www.informaworld .com).

pp. 446–52. James Rachels, "The Challenge of Cultural Relativism" from *The Elements of Moral Philosophy*. Copyright © 1986 by The McGraw-Hill Companies, Inc. Reprinted with permission.

p. 458. From *Beyond Good and Evil* by Friedrich Nietzsche, translated by Walter Kaufmann, copyright © 1966 by Random House, Inc. Used by permission of Random House, Inc.

p. 470. James Rachels, *The Elements of Moral Philosophy*. Copyright © 1986 by The McGraw-Hill Companies, Inc. Reprinted with permission.

pp. 482–85. Alastair Norcross, from "Comparing Harms: Headaches and Human Lives," *Philosophy and Public Affairs* 26, no. 2 (Spring 1997). Reprinted by permission of John Wiley & Sons, Inc. http://onlinelibrary.wiley .com/journal/10.1111/(ISSN)1088-4963.

pp. 491–96, 498, 500–01. Immanuel Kant, *Foundations of the Metaphysics of Morals*, trans. Lewis White Beck, 2nd ed., © 1990. Reproduced in print and electronically by permission of Pearson Education, Inc., Upper Saddle River, New Jersey.

p. 522. Janet Smith, originally published as "Moral Character and Abortion," *Abortion: A New Generation of Catholic Responses* (Braintree, Massachusetts: The Pope John XXIII Medical-Moral Research and Education Center, 1996), 189–208. © 1996 The National Catholic Bioethics Center. All rights reserved. Reprinted by permission.

pp. 538–41. Reprinted from Marilyn Friedman, "Liberating Care" from *What Are Friends For? Feminist Perspectives on Personal Relationships and Moral Theory*, pp. 142–183. Copyright © 1993 Cornell University. Used by permission of the publisher, Cornell University Press.

pp. 560–63. From *In Defense of Anarchism* by Robert Paul Wolff. Copyright 1970 by Robert Paul Wolff. Reproduced with permission of the University of California Press in the format Textbook via Copyright Clearance Center.

p. 578. Thomas Aquinas, "Summa Theologica" from *Basic Writings of Saint Thomas Aquinas*, vol. II, edited by Anton C. Pegis, pp. 784, 794–795. Copyright © 1945 by Random House, Inc. Copyright renewed 1973 by Random House, Inc. Reprinted 1997 by Hackett Publishing Company, Inc. Reprinted by permission of Hackett Publishing Company, Inc. All rights reserved.

pp. 585–90. Reprinted by permission of the publisher from *A Theory of Justice* by John Rawls, pp. 11–12, 60–63, 103–104, 136–137, 139–140, Cambridge, Mass: The Belknap Press of Harvard University Press, Copyright © 1971, 1999 by The President and Fellows of Harvard College.

pp. 590–92. From Susan Moller Okin, *Justice, Gender, and the Family*. Copyright © 1989 by Basic Books, Inc. Reprinted by permission of Basic Books, a member of the Perseus Books Group.

pp. 630–32. Martin Luther King Jr., "Letter from Birmingham Jail" from *Why We Can't Wait*. Reprinted by arrangement with The Heirs to the Estate of Martin Luther King Jr., c/o Writers House as agent for the proprietor New York, NY. Copyright 1963 Dr. Martin Luther King Jr.; copyright renewed 1991 Coretta Scott King.

pp. 647–50. From *Confession* by Leo Tolstoy, translated by David Patterson. Copyright © 1983 by David Patterson. Used by permission of W. W. Norton & Company, Inc. This selection may not be reproduced, stored in a retrieval system, or transmitted in any form or by any means without the prior written permission of the publisher.

pp. 652–54. Hazel E. Barnes, *An Existentialist Ethics* (New York: Alfred A. Knopf, 1967). Copyright © 1967 by Hazel E. Barnes. Reprinted by permission of Betty Cannon, Hazel E. Barnes Literary Executor. www.boulderpsych.com.

Photo Credits

CHAPTER 1

Page 2: Winslow Homer, *Adirondack Guide*, 1894. Watercolor over graphite pencil on paper, Sheet: 38.5 × 54.6 cm (15 3/16 × 21 1/2″), Museum of Fine Arts, Boston: Bequest of Mrs. Alma H. Wadleigh 47.268. © Burstein Collection/Corbis; p. 15: © Image Source/PunchStock; p. 16: Jacques Louis David *The Death of Socrates*, 1787. Oil on canvas, 51 × 77 1/4 in. (129.5 × 196.2cm) © The Metropolitan Museum of Art / Art Resource, NY; p. 39: © Topham / The Image Works

CHAPTER 2

Page 48: © Michael Pole/Corbis; p. 63: Réunion des Musées Nationaux / Art Resource, NY; p. 68: Rene Magritte (1898–1967), *La Condition Humaine*, 1934. © 2010 C. Herscovici, London / Artists Rights Society (ARS), New York, © Herscovici / Art Resource, NY; p. 76: © Gianni Dagli Orti/Corbis; p. 93: © Bettmann/Corbis; p. 99: National Portrait Gallery, Smithsonian Institution / Art Resource, NY; p. 106: *David Hume* (1711–76) 1766 (oil on canvas), Ramsay, Allan (1713–84) / Scottish National Portrait Gallery, Edinburgh, Scotland / The Bridgeman Art Library; p. 121: *Portrait of Emmanuel Kant* (1724–1804) (oil on canvas), German School, (18th century) / Private Collection / The Bridgeman Art Library; p. 131: Paul Signac (1863–1935) *The Port of St. Tropez* (Le Quai, St. Tropez), 1899. Oil on canvas, 65 × 81 cm. Inv.1942 1.1. Location: Musée de l'Annonciade, St. Tropez, France. © Erich Lessing / Art Resource, NY; p. 143: © Stefano Bianchetti/Corbis; p. 156 (top to bottom): © The Granger Collection; p. 172: Courtesy of Ann Garry; p. 175: Courtesy of Lorraine Code

CHAPTER 3

Page 200: Vincent van Gogh (1853–1890), *The Starry Night*, 1889. Oil on canvas, 29 × 36 1/4″. Acquired through the Lillie P. Bliss Bequest. (472.1941), The Museum of Modern Art, New York, NY, U.S.A., Digital Image © The Museum of Modern Art/Licensed by Scala / Art Resource, NY; p. 204: Rene Magritte (1898–1967), *La Trahison des images* (Ceci n'est pas une pipe), 1929. Oil on canvas, 60 × 81 cm. © 2010 C. Herscovici, London, Artists Rights Society (ARS), New York. © Banque d'Images, ADAGP/ Art Resource, NY; p. 226: © The Granger Collection; p. 236: Courtesy of the National Library of Medicine; p. 245: Bebeto Matthews/AP Photo; p. 247: © Duncan Smith/Getty Images; p. 248: © Hulton-Deutsch Collection/Corbis; p. 252: Picture Library, National Portrait Gallery, London; p. 254: © Rick Friedman/Corbis; p. 255: Courtesy of John Searle; p. 268: © Images.com/Corbis; p. 296: © Bettmann/Corbis

CHAPTER 4

Page 318: Frontispiece from *Europe. A Prophecy*, 1794 (relief etching printed in dark brown ink with watercolour on paper), Blake, William (1757–1827) / Yale Center for British Art, Paul Mellon Collection, USA / The Bridgeman Art Library; p. 327: © NTPL / John Hammond / The Image Works; p. 330: Scala / Art Resource, NY; p. 338: © The Granger Collection; p. 339: Joseph Wright of Derby (1734–1797), A Philosopher's Lesson, 1766. Oil on canvas, 147.3 × 203.2 cm., Derby Museum and Art Gallery, Derby, Great Britain, © Erich Lessing / Art Resource, NY; p. 346 © The Granger Collection; p. 352: © The Granger Collection; p. 357: Akg-images; p. 367: Georges de La Tour (1593–1652), *Job and His Wife* (early 1630s). Musee Departemental des Vosges, Epinal, France, © Erich Lessing / Art Resource, NY; p. 381: © Bettmann/Corbis; p. 390: Royalty-Free/Corbis

CHAPTER 5

Page 414: Auguste Rodin (1840–1917), *Burghers of Calais*, 1889. Musée Rodin, Paris, France. © Alexis Wallerstein / Impact / HIP / The Image Works; p. 435: Paul Gauguin (1848–1903), *Where Do We Come From? What Are We? Where Are We Going?* 1897–1898. Oil on canvas, Image: 139.1 × 374.6 cm (54 3/4 × 147 1/2 in.), Museum of Fine Arts, Boston: Tompkins Collection 36.270; p. 436: Library of Congress, Prints and Photographs Division [LC-USZ62-114649 (b&w film copy neg.)]; p. 446: Courtesy of the University of Alabama at Birmingham; p. 465: © Bettmann/Corbis; p. 474: © Mary Evans Picture Library; p. 477: © The Granger Collection;

p. 499: Norman Rockwell, *Golden Rule*, 1961. Oil on canvas, 44.5 × 39.5″. Norman Rockwell Art Collection Trust, The Normal Rockwell Museum. Printed by permission of the Normal Rockwell Family Agency. Copyright 1961, The Norman Rockwell Family Entities; p. 515: Réunion des Musées Nationaux / Art Resource, NY; p. 520: Photographer's Choice/Getty Images; p. 522: Courtesy of Janet Smith; p. 530: Courtesy of Carol Gilligan; p. 534: Mary Cassatt (1844–1926), *Mother and Child*, 1893. Pushkin Museum of Fine Arts, Moscow, Russia, © Art Resource, NY; p. 537: Courtesy of Marilyn Friedman

CHAPTER 6

Page 550: The Code of Hammurabi (1792–1750 BCE), 282 laws. Hammurabi standing before the sun-god Shamash. Louvre, Paris, France, © Erich Lessing/Art Resource, NY; p. 553: George Tooker (1920–), *Government Bureau*, 1956. Egg tempera on wood; 19 5/8 × 29 5/8 in. (49.8 × 75.2 cm). The Metropolitan Museum of Art, George A. Hearn Fund, 1956. (56.78) Photograph © 1984 The Metropolitan Museum of Art; p. 604: Portrait of Karl Marx (1818–93) c.1970 (chromolitho), Chinese School, (20th century) / Private Collection / Archives Charmet / The Bridgeman Art Library; p. 607: Courtesy of Kathleen Cohen, School of Art and Design, San Jose State University, WorldArt Image Database; p. 629: © Flip Schulke/Corbis

CHAPTER 7

Page 638: © Philadelphia Museum of Art/Corbis; p. 645: Edward Hopper (1882–1967), *Nighthawks*, 1942. Oil on canvas, 1942; 84.1 × 152.4 cm. Friends of American Art Collection, 1942.51. © Art Institute of Chicago, Illinois/ A.K.G., Berlin/SuperStock; p. 652: Wassily Kandinsky (1866–1944), *Black Lines*, 1913. Oil on canvas, 129.4 × 131.1 cm. Guggenheim Museum, New York, NY, U.S.A. 2010 Artists Rights Society (ARS), New York/ ADAGP, Paris. © Erich Lessing/Art Resource, NY; p. 660: Caspar David Friedrich (1774–1840) *Wanderer Above a Sea of Fog*, 1817. Oil on canvas, 94.8 × 74.8 cm. Inv.: 5161. On permanent loan from the Foundation for the Promotion of the Hamburg Art Collections. Photo: Elke Walford. Hamburger Kunsthalle, Hamburg, Germany. © Bildarchiv Preussischer Kulturbesitz/ Art Resource, NY

Index

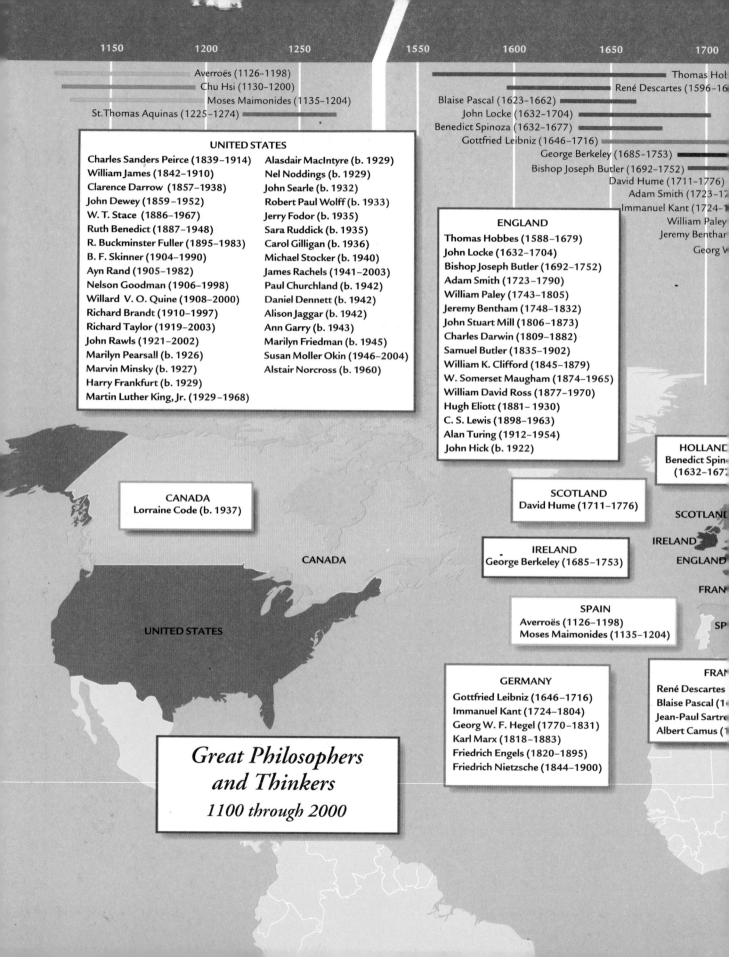

Great Philosophers and Thinkers
1100 through 2000

Timeline markers: 1150   1200   1250   1550   1600   1650   1700

Averroës (1126–1198)
Chu Hsi (1130–1200)
Moses Maimonides (1135–1204)
St. Thomas Aquinas (1225–1274)

Thomas Hob...
René Descartes (1596–16...
Blaise Pascal (1623–1662)
John Locke (1632–1704)
Benedict Spinoza (1632–1677)
Gottfried Leibniz (1646–1716)
George Berkeley (1685–1753)
Bishop Joseph Butler (1692–1752)
David Hume (1711–1776)
Adam Smith (1723–17...
Immanuel Kant (1724–...
William Paley
Jeremy Benthar...
Georg V...

UNITED STATES

Charles Sanders Peirce (1839–1914)	Alasdair MacIntyre (b. 1929)
William James (1842–1910)	Nel Noddings (b. 1929)
Clarence Darrow (1857–1938)	John Searle (b. 1932)
John Dewey (1859–1952)	Robert Paul Wolff (b. 1933)
W. T. Stace (1886–1967)	Jerry Fodor (b. 1935)
Ruth Benedict (1887–1948)	Sara Ruddick (b. 1935)
R. Buckminster Fuller (1895–1983)	Carol Gilligan (b. 1936)
B. F. Skinner (1904–1990)	Michael Stocker (b. 1940)
Ayn Rand (1905–1982)	James Rachels (1941–2003)
Nelson Goodman (1906–1998)	Paul Churchland (b. 1942)
Willard V. O. Quine (1908–2000)	Daniel Dennett (b. 1942)
Richard Brandt (1910–1997)	Alison Jaggar (b. 1942)
Richard Taylor (1919–2003)	Ann Garry (b. 1943)
John Rawls (1921–2002)	Marilyn Friedman (b. 1945)
Marilyn Pearsall (b. 1926)	Susan Moller Okin (1946–2004)
Marvin Minsky (b. 1927)	Alstair Norcross (b. 1960)
Harry Frankfurt (b. 1929)	
Martin Luther King, Jr. (1929–1968)	

ENGLAND

Thomas Hobbes (1588–1679)
John Locke (1632–1704)
Bishop Joseph Butler (1692–1752)
Adam Smith (1723–1790)
William Paley (1743–1805)
Jeremy Bentham (1748–1832)
John Stuart Mill (1806–1873)
Charles Darwin (1809–1882)
Samuel Butler (1835–1902)
William K. Clifford (1845–1879)
W. Somerset Maugham (1874–1965)
William David Ross (1877–1970)
Hugh Eliott (1881–1930)
C. S. Lewis (1898–1963)
Alan Turing (1912–1954)
John Hick (b. 1922)

HOLLAND
Benedict Spino...
(1632–167...

CANADA
Lorraine Code (b. 1937)

SCOTLAND
David Hume (1711–1776)

SCOTLAND
IRELAND
ENGLAND
FRAN...

IRELAND
George Berkeley (1685–1753)

SPAIN
Averroës (1126–1198)
Moses Maimonides (1135–1204)

SP...

FRAN...
René Descartes
Blaise Pascal (1...
Jean-Paul Sartre...
Albert Camus (1...

GERMANY
Gottfried Leibniz (1646–1716)
Immanuel Kant (1724–1804)
Georg W. F. Hegel (1770–1831)
Karl Marx (1818–1883)
Friedrich Engels (1820–1895)
Friedrich Nietzsche (1844–1900)

CANADA

UNITED STATES